# AMERICAN DECADES
## PRIMARY SOURCES

### 1910–1919

# AMERICAN DECADES

## PRIMARY SOURCES

## 1910-1919

CYNTHIA ROSE, PROJECT EDITOR

GALE®

THOMSON

™

GALE

Detroit • New York • San Diego • San Francisco • Cleveland • New Haven, Conn. • Waterville, Maine • London • Munich

## THOMSON

### GALE

American Decades Primary Sources, 1910–1919

**Project Editor**
Cynthia Rose

**Editorial**
Jason M. Everett, Rachel J. Kain, Pamela A. Dear, Andrew C. Claps, Thomas Carson, Kathleen Droste, Christy Justice, Lynn U. Koch, Michael D. Lesniak, Nancy Matuszak, John F. McCoy, Michael Reade, Rebecca Parks, Mark Mikula, Polly A. Rapp, Mark Springer

**Data Capture**
Civie A. Green, Beverly Jendrowski, Gwendolyn S. Tucker

**Permissions**
Margaret Abendroth, Margaret A. Chamberlain, Lori Hines, Jacqueline Key, Mari Masalin-Cooper, William Sampson, Shalice Shah-Caldwell, Kim Smilay, Sheila Spencer, Ann Taylor

**Indexing Services**
Jennifer Dye

**Imaging and Multimedia**
Randy Bassett, Dean Dauphinais, Leitha Etheridge-Sims, Mary K. Grimes, Lezlie Light, Daniel W. Newell, David G. Oblender, Christine O'Bryan, Kelly A. Quin, Luke A. Rademacher, Denay Wilding, Robyn V. Young

**Product Design**
Michelle DiMercurio

**Composition and Electronic Prepress**
Evi Seoud

**Manufacturing**
Rita Wimberley

**LIBRARY OF CONGRESS CATALOGING-IN-PUBLICATION DATA**

American decades primary sources / edited by Cynthia Rose.
    v. cm.
Includes bibliographical references and index.
Contents: [1] 1900-1909 — [2] 1910-1919 — [3] 1920-1929 — [4] 1930-1939 — [5] 1940-1949 — [6] 1950-1959 — [7] 1960-1969 — [8] 1970-1979 — [9] 1980-1989 — [10] 1990-1999.
    ISBN 0-7876-6587-8 (set : hardcover : alk. paper) — ISBN 0-7876-6588-6 (v. 1 : hardcover : alk. paper) — ISBN 0-7876-6589-4 (v. 2 : hardcover : alk. paper) — ISBN 0-7876-6590-8 (v. 3 : hardcover : alk. paper) — ISBN 0-7876-6591-6 (v. 4 : hardcover : alk. paper) — ISBN 0-7876-6592-4 (v. 5 : hardcover : alk. paper) — ISBN 0-7876-6593-2 (v. 6 : hardcover : alk. paper) — ISBN 0-7876-6594-0 (v. 7 : hardcover : alk. paper) — ISBN 0-7876-6595-9 (v. 8 : hardcover : alk. paper) — ISBN 0-7876-6596-7 (v. 9 : hardcover : alk. paper) — ISBN 0-7876-6597-5 (v. 10 : hardcover : alk. paper)
    1. United States—Civilization—20th century—Sources. I. Rose, Cynthia.
E169.1.A471977 2004
973.91—dc21
                        2002008155

# CONTENTS

*Entries are arranged in chronological order by date of primary source. For entries with one primary source, the entry title is the primary source title. Entries with more than one primary source have an overall entry title, followed by the titles of the primary sources.*

Advisors and Contributors . . . . . . . . . . . . . . . . xiii

Acknowledgments . . . . . . . . . . . . . . . . . . . . . . xvii

About the Set . . . . . . . . . . . . . . . . . . . . . . . . . . xix

About the Volume . . . . . . . . . . . . . . . . . . . . . . . xxi

About the Entry . . . . . . . . . . . . . . . . . . . . . . . . xxiii

Using Primary Sources . . . . . . . . . . . . . . . . . xxvii

Selected World Events Outside the United
   States, 1910–1919 . . . . . . . . . . . . . . . . . . . xxxiii

## The Arts

CHAPTER CONTENTS . . . . . . . . . . . . . . . . . . . . . . 1

CHRONOLOGY

Important Events in the Arts, 1910–1919 . . . . . . . . 2

PRIMARY SOURCES

*The Masquerade Dress*
   Robert Henri, 1911 . . . . . . . . . . . . . . . . . . . . 9

*O Pioneers!*
   Willa Cather, 1913 . . . . . . . . . . . . . . . . . . . . 11

*Ethiopia Awakening*
   Meta Vaux Warrick Fuller, 1914 . . . . . . . . . . 14

*Modern Dancing*
   Vernon and Irene Castle, 1914 . . . . . . . . . . . 16

"St. Louis Blues"
   W.C. Handy, 1914 . . . . . . . . . . . . . . . . . . . . 18

Debate Over *The Birth of a Nation* . . . . . . . . . . . . 24
"Capitalizing Race Hatred"
   *New York Globe*, April 6, 1915
"Reply to the *New York Globe*"
   D.W. Griffith, April 10, 1915

"The Imagining Ear"
   Robert Frost, 1915 . . . . . . . . . . . . . . . . . . . . 30

Charlie Chaplin as the "Little Tramp"
   Charlie Chaplin, 1915 . . . . . . . . . . . . . . . . . 32

*Boy With Baby Carriage*
   Norman Rockwell, 1916 . . . . . . . . . . . . . . . . 35

"Chicago"
   Carl Sandburg, 1916 . . . . . . . . . . . . . . . . . . 37

*Evening Star, III* . . . . . . . . . . . . . . . . . . . . . . . . 39
   Georgia O'Keeffe, 1917

"Over There"
   George M. Cohan, 1917 . . . . . . . . . . . . . . . . 41

"Mandy"
   Irving Berlin, 1919 . . . . . . . . . . . . . . . . . . . 45

"September, 1918"
   Amy Lowell, 1919 . . . . . . . . . . . . . . . . . . . . 51

"Paper Pills"
   Sherwood Anderson, 1919 . . . . . . . . . . . . . . 52

*A Poet's Life: Seventy Years in a Changing
World*
   Harriet Monroe, 1938 . . . . . . . . . . . . . . . . . 55

## Business and the Economy

CHAPTER CONTENTS . . . . . . . . . . . . . . . . . . . . . . 59

CHRONOLOGY

Important Events in Business and the
Economy, 1910–1919 . . . . . . . . . . . . . . . . . . 60

PRIMARY SOURCES

Triangle Shirtwaist Factory Fire . . . . . . . . . . . . . 63
"Eyewitness at the Triangle"
    William Gunn Shepherd, March 27, 1911
*Preliminary Report of the Factory
    Investigating Commission*
    New York (State) Factory Investigating
        Commission, 1912

Scientific Management. . . . . . . . . . . . . . . . . . . . . 68
*The Principles of Scientific Management*
    Frederick W. Taylor, 1911
Letter to Lindley Garrison
    Maurice W. Bowen, June 17, 1913

Dollar Diplomacy and Its Repudiation. . . . . . . . . . 71
Speech Advocating "Dollar Diplomacy"
    William Howard Taft, December 3, 1912
Speech Repudiating "Dollar Diplomacy"
    Woodrow Wilson, March 19, 1913

*Money Trust Investigation*
    U.S. House of Representatives, December
        19, 1912. . . . . . . . . . . . . . . . . . . . . . . . . . . 75

New Parties Challenge the Economic System . . . . . . 83
Progressive Party Platform of 1912
Socialist Party Platform of 1912

*Drift and Mastery: An Attempt to Diagnose
    the Current Unrest*
    Walter Lippmann, 1914 . . . . . . . . . . . . . . . . . 88

*National Old Trails Road: Ocean to Ocean
    Highway*
    Charles Henry Davis, 1914 . . . . . . . . . . . . . . 94

Henry Ford's Business Philosophy . . . . . . . . . . . . 98
*John F. and Horace E. Dodge v. Ford
    Motor Co., Henry Ford, et. al.*
    Henry Ford, 1916
Interview with Henry Ford
    Henry Ford, 1916

J. Walter Thompson House Ads
    "A New Profession"; "Packages That
        Speak Out"; "Women in Advertising" . . . . . . 102
    J. Walter Thompson Company,
        1917–1919

*Women Wanted*
    Mabel Potter Daggett, 1918 . . . . . . . . . . . . . . 106

*American Industry in the War*
    Bernard Baruch, 1921 . . . . . . . . . . . . . . . . . . 108

*All God's Dangers: The Life of Nate Shaw*
    Nate Shaw, 1974. . . . . . . . . . . . . . . . . . . . . . 114

"Last of the Vigilantes"
    Miriam E. Tefft, February 2, 1982 . . . . . . . . . . 117

## Education

CHAPTER CONTENTS . . . . . . . . . . . . . . . . . . . . . . 123

CHRONOLOGY

Important Events in Education, 1910–1919 . . . . . . 124

PRIMARY SOURCES

"The College-bred Community"
    W.E.B. Du Bois, 1910. . . . . . . . . . . . . . . . . . . 127

*The Indian and His Problem*
    Francis E. Leupp, 1910 . . . . . . . . . . . . . . . . . 131

Equal Pay for Women Teachers . . . . . . . . . . . . . . 134
*Equal Pay for Equal Work*
    Grace C. Strachan, 1910
"The Ideal Candidates"
    Alice Duer Miller, 1915
"An Unequal Footing!"
    Anonymous, 1911

"The Contribution of Psychology to
    Education"
    Edward L. Thorndike, 1910 . . . . . . . . . . . . . . 139

*Medical Education in the United States and
    Canada*
    Henry S. Pritchett, 1910. . . . . . . . . . . . . . . . . 143

"An Address Delivered Before the National
    Colored Teachers' Association"
    Booker T. Washington, 1911 . . . . . . . . . . . . . . 148

*A New Conscience and an Ancient Evil*
    Jane Addams, 1912 . . . . . . . . . . . . . . . . . . . . 152

*The Montessori Method*
    Maria Montessori, 1912 . . . . . . . . . . . . . . . . . 154

"Why Should the Kindergarten Be
    Incorporated as an Integral Part of the
    Public School System?"
    Philander P. Claxton, 1913. . . . . . . . . . . . . . . 159

*Smith-Lever Act of 1914*
    Hoke Smith and Asbury Francis Lever,
        May 8, 1914 . . . . . . . . . . . . . . . . . . . . . . . . 161

*Report of the Committee on Academic
    Freedom and Tenure*
    American Association of University
        Professors, 1915 . . . . . . . . . . . . . . . . . . . . . 164

*Democracy and Education*
    John Dewey, 1916. . . . . . . . . . . . . . . . . . . . . 169

*The Measurement of Intelligence*
    Lewis M. Terman, 1916. . . . . . . . . . . . . . . . 172

*Smith-Hughes Act of 1917*
    Hoke Smith and Dudley M. Hughes,
        February 23, 1917 . . . . . . . . . . . . . . . . . . . 175

*Cardinal Principles of Secondary Education*
    Commission on the Reorganization of
        Secondary Education, 1918 . . . . . . . . . . . . 179

"The Project Method"
    William Heard Kilpatrick, 1918 . . . . . . . . . . 183


## Fashion and Design

**CHAPTER CONTENTS** . . . . . . . . . . . . . . . . . . . . . . 187

**CHRONOLOGY**

Important Events in Fashion and Design,
    1910–1919 . . . . . . . . . . . . . . . . . . . . . . . . . . . 188

**PRIMARY SOURCES**

Ford's Highland Park Plant
    Albert Kahn, 1910. . . . . . . . . . . . . . . . . . . . . 190

"Craftsman Furniture Made by Gustav
    Stickley"
    Gustav Stickley, 1910 . . . . . . . . . . . . . . . . . . 191

"Five Pretty Ways to Do the Hair"
    *Ladies' Home Journal*, October 1911 . . . . . . . 193

"Flower Dresses for Lawn Fêtes"
    *Ladies' Home Journal*, 1911 . . . . . . . . . . . . . 195

"What Is a Bungalow?"
    Phil M. Riley, 1912 . . . . . . . . . . . . . . . . . . . . 197

"Audacious Hats for Spineless Attitudes"
    *Dress & Vanity Fair*, September 1913. . . . . . . 199

Woolworth Building . . . . . . . . . . . . . . . . . . . . . . 202
"The Woolworth Building"
    Cass Gilbert, ca. 1913
*The Cathedral of Commerce*
    Edwin A. Cochran, 1916

"Proper Dancing-Costumes for Women"
    Vernon and Irene Foote Castle, 1914 . . . . . . . 207

"Whether at Home or Away, Your Summer
    Equipment Should Include a Bottle of
    Listerine"
    Lambert Pharmacal Company, 1915 . . . . . . . . 210

"Shopping for the Well-Dressed Man"
    *Vanity Fair*, July 1916. . . . . . . . . . . . . . . . . . 212

"A Woman Can Always Look Younger
    Than She Really Is"
    Elizabeth Arden, July 1916 . . . . . . . . . . . . . . 214

"Wealthiest Negro Woman's Suburban
    Mansion"
    *The New York Times Magazine*,
        November 4, 1917. . . . . . . . . . . . . . . . . . . . 216

"YWCA Overseas Uniform, 1918"
    House of Worth, 1918 . . . . . . . . . . . . . . . . . . 217

"Is There News in Shaving Soap?"
    J. Walter Thompson Company, May 29,
        1919. . . . . . . . . . . . . . . . . . . . . . . . . . . . . . . 219

"Henry Ford in a Model T" . . . . . . . . . . . . . . . 221


## Government and Politics

**CHAPTER CONTENTS** . . . . . . . . . . . . . . . . . . . . . . 225

**CHRONOLOGY**

Important Events in Government and Politics,
    1910–1919 . . . . . . . . . . . . . . . . . . . . . . . . . . . 226

**PRIMARY SOURCES**

"The New Nationalism"
    Theodore Roosevelt, August 31, 1910. . . . . . . 232

"Henry Cabot Lodge: Corollary to the
    Monroe Doctrine"
    Henry Cabot Lodge Sr., August 2, 1912 . . . . . 236

"Votes for Women"
    W.E.B. Du Bois, September 1912. . . . . . . . . . 239

*The Yosemite*
    John Muir, 1912 . . . . . . . . . . . . . . . . . . . . . . 241

"Composition and Characteristics of the
    Population for Wards of Cities of 50,000
    or More: Lawrence"
    Federal Bureau of the Census, 1913–1914. . . . 246

"Woodrow Wilson: *The Tampico Affair*"
    Woodrow Wilson, April 20, 1914. . . . . . . . . . 249

*Family Limitation*
    Margaret Sanger, 1914. . . . . . . . . . . . . . . . . . 252

The Zimmermann Telegram . . . . . . . . . . . . . . . 254
Telegram from Arthur Zimmermann to
    Heinrich J.F. von Eckhardt
    Arthur Zimmermann, January 16, 1917

Telegram from U.S. Ambassador Walter
Page to President Woodrow Wilson
Walter Page, February 24, 1917

Woodrow Wilson's Declaration of War
Message
Woodrow Wilson, April 2, 1917. . . . . . . . . . . 258

"Opposition to Wilson's War Message"
George W. Norris, April 4, 1917 . . . . . . . . . . 261

*"Over the Top": By an American Soldier
Who Went*
Arthur Guy Empey, 1917. . . . . . . . . . . . . . . 265

"Henry Cabot Lodge Speaks Out Against
the League of Nations, Washington, D.C.,
August 12, 1919"
Henry Cabot Lodge Sr., August 12, 1919 . . . . . 267

"Statement by Emma Goldman at the Federal
Hearing in Re Deportation"
Emma Goldman, October 27, 1919. . . . . . . . . 270

*Volstead Act of 1919*
Andrew Volstead, October 28, 1919 . . . . . . . . 273

## Law and Justice

**CHAPTER CONTENTS** . . . . . . . . . . . . . . . . . . . . . 277

**CHRONOLOGY**

Important Events in Law and Justice,
1910–1919. . . . . . . . . . . . . . . . . . . . . . . . . . 278

**PRIMARY SOURCES**

*New York Worker's Compensation Act*
New York State Legislature, 1910 . . . . . . . . . 281

*Standard Oil Co. of New Jersey v. U.S.*
Edward D. White and John Marshall
Harlan, 1911. . . . . . . . . . . . . . . . . . . . . . 283

*Hoke v. U.S.*
Joseph McKenna, February 24, 1913. . . . . . . . 287

*Weeks v. U.S.*
William R. Day, February 24, 1914 . . . . . . . . 292

*Houston, East & West Texas Railway Co. v.
U.S.*
Charles Evans Hughes, June 8, 1914. . . . . . . . 294

*Bunting v. Oregon*
Joseph McKenna, April 9, 1917 . . . . . . . . . . 298

*Buchanan v. Warley*
William R. Day, November 5, 1917 . . . . . . . . 301

*"Dissent During World War I: The Kate
O'Hare Trial: 1919"*
Kate Richards O'Hare and Martin J. Wade,
December 1917. . . . . . . . . . . . . . . . . . . . . 304

*Selective Draft Law Cases*
Edward D. White, January 7, 1918 . . . . . . . . . 310

The Lynching of Robert P. Prager
"German Is Lynched by an Illinois Mob";
"Cabinet Discusses Prager's Lynching";
"Prager Asked Mob to Wrap Body in
Flag"; "Tried for Prager Murder"; "The
Prager Case"
*The New York Times,* April 5–June 3, 1918. . . . 313

*Schenck v. U.S.*
Oliver Wendell Holmes Jr., March 3,
1919. . . . . . . . . . . . . . . . . . . . . . . . . . . . 316

*Debs v. U.S.*
Oliver Wendell Holmes Jr., March 10,
1919. . . . . . . . . . . . . . . . . . . . . . . . . . . . 319

*Abrams v. U.S.*
Oliver Wendell Holmes Jr., November
10, 1919. . . . . . . . . . . . . . . . . . . . . . . . . 322

## Lifestyles and Social Trends

**CHAPTER CONTENTS** . . . . . . . . . . . . . . . . . . . . . 327

**CHRONOLOGY**

Important Events in Lifestyles and Social
Trends, 1910–1919 . . . . . . . . . . . . . . . . . . . 328

**PRIMARY SOURCES**

*The Conflict of Colour*
B. L. Putnam Weale, 1910. . . . . . . . . . . . . . 333

"The Woman Shopper: How to Make Her
Buy"
Isaac F. Marcosson, 1910. . . . . . . . . . . . . . . 335

*The Social Evil in Chicago*
The Vice Commission of Chicago, 1911 . . . . . . 340

*The Immigration Problem*
Jeremiah W. Jenks and W. Jett Lauck,
1912. . . . . . . . . . . . . . . . . . . . . . . . . . . . 342

"On the Imitation of Man"
Ida M. Tarbell, 1913 . . . . . . . . . . . . . . . . . 345

America's Sex Hysteria . . . . . . . . . . . . . . . . . . . 347
"Sex O'Clock in America"
*Current Opinion,* 1913

"Popular Gullibility as Exhibited in the New
White Slavery Hysteria"
*Current Opinion*, 1914

"Making Men of Them"
Thornton W. Burgess, 1914 . . . . . . . . . . . . . . 351

"The Next and Final Step"
P.A. Baker, 1914 . . . . . . . . . . . . . . . . . . . . . 354

"The Flapper"
Henry L. Mencken, 1915 . . . . . . . . . . . . . . . 357

"How We Manage"
E.S.E., 1915 . . . . . . . . . . . . . . . . . . . . . . . . 359

*The Passing of the Great Race*
Madison Grant, 1916 . . . . . . . . . . . . . . . . . 362

"Are the Movies a Menace to the Drama?"
Brander Matthews, 1917 . . . . . . . . . . . . . . . 364

"Influence of Pictures"
William Healy, 1918 . . . . . . . . . . . . . . . . . . 367

Dark Side of Wartime Patriotism . . . . . . . . . . . 370
Woodrow Wilson's Memorandum to His
Secretary, Joseph Tumulty
Woodrow Wilson, 1918
"Chicagoans Cheer Tar Who Shot Man"
1919

"The Negro Should Be a Party to the
Commercial Conquest of the World"
Marcus Garvey, 1919 . . . . . . . . . . . . . . . . . 372

## The Media

**CHAPTER CONTENTS** . . . . . . . . . . . . . . . . . . . . 375

**CHRONOLOGY**
Important Events in the Media, 1910–1919 . . . . . 376

**PRIMARY SOURCES**
Photographs by Lewis Hine
Lewis Hine, 1908–1912 . . . . . . . . . . . . . . . . 379

National American Woman Suffrage
Association Broadsides . . . . . . . . . . . . . . . . 383
"Votes for Women"; "Why Women Want
to Vote"; "Women in the Home"
National American Woman Suffrage
Association, 1910, 1912

Early Baseball Cards . . . . . . . . . . . . . . . . . . . 387
"Chicago Cubs Baseball Card"; "Tris
Speaker Baseball Card"; "Cy Young
Baseball Card"
Liggett & Myers, Co.; American Tobacco
Company, 1913; 1911; 1911

"Fun's Word Cross Puzzle"
Arthur Wynne, December 21, 1913 . . . . . . . . 390

*The Woman Rebel*
Margaret Sanger, March 1914 . . . . . . . . . . . 392

The First Pulitzer Prizes . . . . . . . . . . . . . . . . . . 395
"The Anniversary"
*New York Tribune*, May 7, 1916
"Germany Keen for Peace, but Expects and
is Ready to Battle for Years"
Herbert Bayard Swope, 1917

"Warning: The Deadly Parallel"
Industrial Workers of the World, 1916 . . . . . . 400

Letters to the Chicago *Defender*
Chicago *Defender*, 1916–1918 . . . . . . . . . . . 403

"For Freedom and Democracy"
*North American Review*, March 30, 1917 . . . . . 407

*Sedition Act, 1918*
Woodrow Wilson, May 16, 1918 . . . . . . . . . . 410

Chicago Race Riots . . . . . . . . . . . . . . . . . . . . . 413
"A Crowd of Howling Negroes"
*Chicago Tribune*, July 28, 1919
"Ghastly Deeds of Race Rioters Told"
Chicago *Defender*, August 2, 1919

*The Brass Check*
Upton Sinclair, 1919 . . . . . . . . . . . . . . . . . . 419

## Medicine and Health

**CHAPTER CONTENTS** . . . . . . . . . . . . . . . . . . . . 425

**CHRONOLOGY**
Important Events in Medicine and Health,
1910–1919; . . . . . . . . . . . . . . . . . . . . . . . . . 426

**PRIMARY SOURCES**
"Nursing as a Profession for College Women"
Edna L. Foley, May 1910 . . . . . . . . . . . . . . . 429

"How Physical Training Affects the Welfare
of the Nation"
Baroness Rose Posse, October 1910 . . . . . . . . 432

*Changes in Bodily Form of Descendants of
Immigrants*
Immigration Commission; Franz Boas, 1910 . . . 434

"Tobacco: A Race Poison"
Daniel Lichty, January 1914 . . . . . . . . . . . . . 437

*Painless Childbirth*
Henry Smith Williams, 1914 . . . . . . . . . . . . . 439

"The Endowment of Motherhood"
John F. Moran, January 9, 1915 . . . . . . . . . . 441

"How the Drug Dopers Fight"
George Creel, January 30, 1915 . . . . . . . . . . 443

"The Heart of the People"
Randolph Bourne, July 3, 1915. . . . . . . . . . . 447

"Progress in Pediatrics"
Philip Van Ingen, September 1915 . . . . . . . . . 449

"Orthopedic Surgery in War Time"
Robert B. Osgood, 1916. . . . . . . . . . . . . . . 452

"War and Mental Diseases"
Pearce Bailey, October 19, 1917. . . . . . . . . . 454

"Some Considerations Affecting the
Replacement of Men by Women Workers"
Josephine Goldmark, October 19, 1917 . . . . . . 457

Influenza Epidemic . . . . . . . . . . . . . . . . . . 460
"100 Sailors at Great Lakes Die of Influenza"
*Chicago Tribune*, September 23, 1918
"Find Influenza Germ"
*Washington Post*, September 21, 1918

"The Fight Against Venereal Disease"
Raymond B. Fosdick, November 30, 1918. . . . . 463

"The Next War"
Harvey Washington Wiley, January 1919 . . . . . 465

## Religion

**CHAPTER CONTENTS** . . . . . . . . . . . . . . . . . . . 469

**CHRONOLOGY**
Important Events in Religion, 1910–1919 . . . . . . 470

**PRIMARY SOURCES**
*A Living Wage: Its Ethical and Economic
Aspects*
John A. Ryan, 1906. . . . . . . . . . . . . . . . . . 474

"The Church and the Labor Question"
Washington Gladden, May 6, 1911 . . . . . . . . . 476

"Cardinal's Golden Jubilee"
James Cardinal Gibbons, October 1, 1911 . . . . . 478

*America in the Making*
Lyman Abbott, 1911 . . . . . . . . . . . . . . . . . 481

*Acres of Diamonds*
Russell H. Conwell, 1915. . . . . . . . . . . . . . 484

*Prisoners of Hope and Other Sermons*
Rev. Charles H. Brent, 1915. . . . . . . . . . . . 486

"What the Bible Contains for the Believer"
Rev. George F. Pentecost, 1915 . . . . . . . . . . 489

*A Theology for the Social Gospel*
Walter Rauschenbusch, 1917 . . . . . . . . . . . . 492

*The Churches of Christ in Time of War*
Federal Council of the Churches of
Christ in America, 1917. . . . . . . . . . . . . . . 494

Cardinal Gibbons' Letter to the U.S.
Archbishops
James Cardinal Gibbons, May 1, 1919 . . . . . . . 498

"A Program for the Reconstruction of Judaism"
Mordecai M. Kaplan, August 1920 . . . . . . . . . 500

"Interchurch World Movement Report"
Interchurch World Movement, 1920 . . . . . . . . 502

*Leaves From the Notebook of a Tamed
Cynic*
Reinhold Niebuhr, 1929. . . . . . . . . . . . . . . 505

## Science and Technology

**CHAPTER CONTENTS** . . . . . . . . . . . . . . . . . . . 509

**CHRONOLOGY**
Important Events in Science and Technology,
1910–1919 . . . . . . . . . . . . . . . . . . . . . . . 510

**PRIMARY SOURCES**
*The Future of Electricity*
Charles Proteus Steinmetz, 1910. . . . . . . . . . 513

*The Mind of Primitive Man*
Franz Boas, 1911. . . . . . . . . . . . . . . . . . . 516

"Manufacture of Gasolene"
William Burton, January 7, 1913 . . . . . . . . . . 520

"On the Constitution of Atoms and
Molecules"
Niels Bohr, 1913. . . . . . . . . . . . . . . . . . . 525

"Psychology as the Behaviorist Views It"
John B. Watson, 1913 . . . . . . . . . . . . . . . . 527

"A Direct Photoelectric Determination of
Planck's '$h$'"
Robert A. Millikan, March 1916. . . . . . . . . . . 530

*Psychology of the Unconscious*
Carl Jung, 1916. . . . . . . . . . . . . . . . . . . . 534

"The Atom and the Molecule"
Gilbert N. Lewis, 1916 . . . . . . . . . . . . . . . 537

"Globular Clusters and the Structure of the
Galactic System"
Harlow Shapley, February 1918 . . . . . . . . . . 541

*Report on the Relativity Theory of Gravitation*
Arthur Eddington, 1918 . . . . . . . . . . . . . . . . 546

*The Physical Basis of Heredity*
Thomas Hunt Morgan, 1919 . . . . . . . . . . . . . 550

A General Introduction to Psycho-Analysis
Sigmund Freud, 1920 . . . . . . . . . . . . . . . . . 553

## Sports

**CHAPTER CONTENTS** . . . . . . . . . . . . . . . . . . . . 561

**CHRONOLOGY**
Important Events in Sports, 1910–1919 . . . . . . . . 562

**PRIMARY SOURCES**
"University Athletics"
Simon Newcomb, 1907 . . . . . . . . . . . . . . . . 566

"Johnson Wins in 15 Rounds; Jeffries Weak"
John L. Sullivan, July 5, 1910 . . . . . . . . . . . . 570

"Burman Lowers Speedway Records"
*The New York Times*, May 30, 1911 . . . . . . . . 574

"Are Athletics Making Girls Masculine?"
Dudley A. Sargent, March 1912 . . . . . . . . . . . 577

"The Amateur"
Lyman Abbott, Hamilton W. Mabie, and
Theodore Roosevelt, February 8, 1913 . . . . . . 581

"Baseball and the National Life"
Henry Addington Bruce, May 17, 1913 . . . . . . 585

"Ouimet World's Golf Champion"
*The New York Times*, September 21, 1913 . . . . 591

Page from George Weiss's scrapbook
George Weiss, 1916 . . . . . . . . . . . . . . . . . . . 595

*You Know Me Al: A Busher's Letters*
Ring Lardner, 1916 . . . . . . . . . . . . . . . . . . . 597

*Girls and Athletics*
Mary C. Morgan, 1917 . . . . . . . . . . . . . . . . . 600

Memorandum to Colonel Bruce Palmer,
Elwood S. Brown, October 15, 1918 . . . . . . . . 603

*Basket Ball: for Coach, Player and
Spectator*
E.D. Angell, 1918 . . . . . . . . . . . . . . . . . . . . 607

"Boxers Spend Last Night Under Guard"
George R. Pulford, July 4, 1919 . . . . . . . . . . . 611

*Pioneer in Pro Football*
Jack Cusack, 1963 . . . . . . . . . . . . . . . . . . . . 614

Interview with Edd Roush
Edd Roush, 1966 . . . . . . . . . . . . . . . . . . . . . 619

**General Resources** . . . . . . . . . . . . . . . . . . 623

**Primary Source Type Index** . . . . . . . . . . . . . 635

**General Index** . . . . . . . . . . . . . . . . . . . . . . 639

# Advisors and Contributors

## Advisors

**CARL A. ANTONUCCI JR.** has spent the past ten years as a reference librarian at various colleges and universities. Currently director of library services at Capital Community College, he holds two master's degrees and is a doctoral candidate at Providence College. He particularly enjoys researching Rhode Island political history during the 1960s and 1970s.

**KATHY ARSENAULT** is the dean of library at the University of South Florida, St. Petersburg's Poynter Library. She holds a master's degree in Library Science. She has written numerous book reviews for *Library Journal*, and has published articles in such publications as the *Journal of the Florida Medical Association* and *Collection Management*.

**JAMES RETTIG** holds two master's degrees. He has written numerous articles and has edited *Distinguished Classics of Reference Publishing* (1992). University librarian at the University of Richmond, he is the recipient of three American Library Association awards: the Isadore Gibert Mudge Citation (1988), the G.K. Hall Award for Library Literature (1993), and the Louis Shores-Oryx Press Award (1995).

**HILDA K. WEISBURG** is the head library media specialist at Morristown High School Library and specializes in building school library media programs. She has several publications to her credit, including *The School Librarians Workshop*, *Puzzles, Patterns, and Problem Solving: Creative Connections to Critical Thinking*, and *Learning, Linking & Critical Thinking: Information Strategies for the K-12 Library Media Curriculum*

## Contributors

**DENNIS A. CASTILLO** received his doctorate in the History of Christianity from the University of Chicago. Currently an associate professor of Church History at Christ the King Seminary in East Aurora, New York, he is at work on his first book, *The Maltese Cross: A Military History of Malta*. A Detroit native, he now lives in Buffalo, New York.
*Chapter:* Religion.

**PAUL G. CONNORS** earned a doctorate in American History from Loyola University in Chicago. He has a strong interest in Great Lakes maritime history, and has contributed the article "Beaver Island Ice Walkers" to *Michigan History*. He has worked for the Michigan Legislative Service Bureau as a research analyst since 1996.
*Essay:* Using Primary Sources. *Chapter:* Government and Politics. *Chronologies:* Selected Events Outside the United States; Government and Politics, Sports chapters. *General Resources:* General, Government and Politics, Sports.

**CHRISTOPHER CUMO** is a staff writer for *The Adjunct Advocate Magazine*. Formerly an adjunct professor of history at Walsh University, he has written two books, *A History of the Ohio Agricultural Experiment Station, 1882–1997* and *Seeds of Change*, and has contributed to numerous scholarly journals. He holds a doctorate in History from the University of Akron.

*Chapter Chronology, General Resources:* Business and the Economy, Education, Medicine and Health, Science and Technology.

**MICHAEL R. FEIN** is an adjunct faculty member at Lesley University in Cambridge, Massachusetts. He is presently at work on a doctoral dissertation on twentieth century highway politics in New York. He has also contributed articles to *The Encyclopedia of New York State* and written book reviews for the *Business History Review*.

*Chapter:* Business and the Economy.

**JENNIFER HELLER** holds bachelor's degrees in Religious Studies and English Education, as well as a master's in Curriculum and Instruction, all from the University of Kansas. She has been an adjunct associate professor at Johnson County Community College in Kansas since 1998. She is currently at work on a dissertation on contemporary women's religious literature.

*Chapter Chronology, General Resources:* Religion.

**DAVID M. HOLFORD** has worked as an adjunct instructor at Ohio University, Park College, and Columbus State Community College; education curator for the Ohio Historical Society; and held editorial positions at Glencoe/McGraw Hill and Holt, Rinehard, and Winston. He also holds a doctorate History from Ohio State University. A freelance writer/editor since 1996, he has published *Herbert Hoover* (1999) and *Abraham Lincoln and the Emancipation Proclamation* (2002).

*Chapter Chronologies, General Resources:* Lifestyles and Social Trends, The Media.

**MILLIE JACKSON** is an associate librarian at Grand Valley State University in Allendale, Michigan. She has previously worked as an English teacher and as the special collections librarian at Oklahoma State University. Dr. Jackson's dissertation on ladies's library associations in Michigan won the American Library Association's Phyllis Dain Library History Dissertation Award in 2001.

*Chapters:* The Arts, Fashion and Design.

**JONATHAN KOLKEY** is the author of *The New Right, 1960–1968,* and *Germany on the March: A Reinterpretation of War and Domestic Politics Over the Past Two Centuries*. He earned a Ph.D. in history from

UCLA. Currently an instructor at West Los Angeles College, he is at work on *The Decision for War*, a comprehensive historical study of the politics and decision-making process behind war. Dr. Kolkey lives in Playa Del Rey, California.

*Chapters:* Lifestyles and Social Trends, Medicine and Health.

**JACQUELINE LESHKEVICH** joined the Michigan Legislative Service Bureau as a science research analyst in 2000. She earned her B.S. in Biochemistry from Northern Michigan University and a master's degree, also in Biochemistry, from Michigan Technological University. A contributor to such publications as *Nature Biotechnology* and *Plant Cell*, she is also an amateur astronomer.

*Chapter:* Science and Technology.

**SCOTT A. MERRIMAN** currently works as a part-time instructor at the University of Kentucky and is finishing his doctoral dissertation on Espionage and Sedition Acts in the Sixth Court of Appeals. He has contributed to *The History Highway* and *History.edu*, among others. Scott is a resident of Lexington, Kentucky.

*Chapter:* Law and Justice.

**KRISTINA PETERSON** earned her bachelor's degree in Psychology from Northland College. She also holds an M.A. in Education from the College of William and Mary, as well as a Ph.D. in History and Philosophy of Education from the University of Minnesota.

*Chapter:* Education.

**DAN PROSTERMAN** is an adjunct professor of history at St. Francis College, as well as an adjunct lecturer at Pace University. He holds an M.A. in History at New York University and is working on his doctoral dissertation on the subject of anti-Communism in New York City during the Great Depression and World War II.

*Chapter:* The Media.

**LORNA BIDDLE RINEAR** is the editor and coauthor of *The Complete Idiot's Guide to Women's History*. A Ph.D. candidate at Rutger's University, she holds a B.A. from Wellesley College and a master's degree from Boston College. She resides in Bellingham, Massachusetts.

*Chapter Chronologies, General Resources:* The Arts, Fashion and Design.

**MARY HERTZ SCARBROUGH** earned both her B.A. in English and German and her J.D. from the Univeristy of South Dakota. Prior to becoming a freelance writer in 1996, she worked as a law clerk in the Federal District Court for the District of South Dakota and as legal counsel for the Immigration and Naturalization Service. She lives in Storm Lake, Iowa, with her husband and three daughters.

*Chapter Chronology, General Resources:* Law and Justice.

**COREY SEEMAN** is the assistant dean for library systems at the University of Toledo, University Libraries.

The author of numerous articles, book reviews, and encyclopedia entries, he is currently at work on a history of the Midwest League (a baseball minor league) and a history of autism.

*Chapter:* Sports.

# ACKNOWLEDGMENTS

*Following is a list of the copyright holders who have granted us permission to reproduce material in this volume of* American Decades Primary Sources. *Every effort has been made to trace copyright, but if omissions have been made, please let us know.*

Copyrighted material in *American Decades Primary Sources, 1910–1919* was reproduced from the following books: Boas, Franz. From *The Mind of Primitive Man.* Revised edition. Macmillan Company, 1938. Copyright, 1938, by The Macmillan Company. Copyright renewed (c) 1966 by Franziska Boas Nichelson. Reproduced by permission. —Brandeis, Louis D. From *Other People's Money and How the Bankers Use It.* Frederick A. Stokes Company, 1932. Reproduced by permission. Cusack, Jack. From *Pioneer in Pro Football.* —Frost, Robert. *From Collected Poems, Prose & Plays.* The Library of America, 1995. Volume compilation (c) 1995 by Literary Classics of the United States, Inc. Essay (c) by Peter A. Gilbert. Reproduced by permission of The Estate of Robert Frost. —Moynihan, Ruth Barnes, Cynthia Russet, Laurie Crumpacker. From *Second to None: A Documentary History of American Women, Vol: II, From 1865 to the Present.* University of Nebraska Press, 1993. Copyright (c) 1993 by University of Nebraska Press. Reproduced by permission. —Niebuhr, Reinhold. From *Leaves from the Notebook of a Tamed Cynic.* Harper & Row Publishers, 1980. Copyright (c) 1929, renewed 1956 by Reinhold Niebuhr. Reproduced by permission of the Estate of Reinhold Niebuhr. —Rosengarten, Theodore. From *All God's Dangers: The Life of Nate Shaw.* Edited by Theodore Rosengarten. Alfred A. Knopf, 1974. Copyright (c) 1974 by Theodore Rosengarten. Reproduced by permission of Alfred A. Knopf, a division of Random House, Inc. —Roush, Edd. From "Edd Roush," in *The Glory of Their Times: The Story of the Early Days of Baseball Told by the Men Who Played It.* Enlarged edition. Edited by Lawrence S. Ritter, Vintage Books, 1985. Copyright (c) 1966 by Lawrence S. Ritter. Reproduced in the U.K. and British Commonwealth by permission of the author, in the rest of the world by permission of HarperCollins Publishers.

Copyrighted material in *American Decades Primary Sources, 1910–1919,* was reproduced from the following web sites: Alexander Shulgin, "Appendix 4: Bibliography: Chemistry," 1994, E Is for Ecstasy by Nicholas Saunders. Online at: http://www.ecstasy.org/books/e4x /e4x.ap.04/e4x.ap.04.10.html (June 9, 2002). Copyright Nicholas Saunders and Alexander Shulgin 1994. Reproduced by permission of Alexander Shulgin and the Literary Estate of Nicholas Saunders. —Alexander Shulgin, "Appendix 4: Bibliography: Chemistry," 1994, E Is for Ecstasy by Nicholas Saunders. Online at: http://www .ecstasy.org/books/e4x/e4x.ap.04/e4x.ap.04.10.html (June 9, 2002). Copyright Nicholas Saunders and Alexander Shulgin 1994. Reproduced by permission of Alexander Shulgin and the Literary Estate of Nicholas Saunders. — Miriam E. Teft, "Last of the Vigilantes," February 2, 1982. Online at: http://www.digital.library.arizona.edu /bisbee/docs2/rec_teft.htm (April 17, 2002). Arizona Historical Society. Reproduced by permission.

# ABOUT THE SET

*American Decades Primary Sources* is a ten-volume collection of more than two thousand primary sources on twentieth-century American history and culture. Each volume comprises about two hundred primary sources in 160 170 entries. Primary sources are enhanced by informative context, with illustrative images and sidebars—many of which are primary sources in their own right—adding perspective and a deeper understanding of both the primary sources and the milieu from which they originated.

Designed for students and teachers at the high school and undergraduate levels, as well as researchers and history buffs, *American Decades Primary Sources* meets the growing demand for primary source material.

Conceived as both a stand-alone reference and a companion to the popular *American Decades* set, *American Decades Primary Sources* is organized in the same subject-specific chapters for compatibility and ease of use.

## Primary Sources

To provide fresh insights into the key events and figures of the century, thirty historians and four advisors selected unique primary sources far beyond the typical speeches, government documents, and literary works. Screenplays, scrapbooks, sports box scores, patent applications, college course outlines, military codes of conduct, environmental sculptures, and CD liner notes are but a sampling of the more than seventy-five types of primary sources included.

Diversity is shown not only in the wide range of primary source types, but in the range of subjects and opin-

ions, and the frequent combination of primary sources in entries. Multiple perspectives in religious, political, artistic, and scientific thought demonstrate the commitment of *American Decades Primary Sources* to diversity, in addition to the inclusion of considerable content displaying ethnic, racial, and gender diversity. *American Decades Primary Sources* presents a variety of perspectives on issues and events, encouraging the reader to consider subjects more fully and critically.

*American Decades Primary Sources'* innovative approach often presents related primary sources in an entry. The primary sources act as contextual material for each other—creating a unique opportunity to understand each and its place in history, as well as their relation to one another. These may be point-counterpoint arguments, a variety of diverse opinions, or direct responses to another primary source. One example is President Franklin Delano Roosevelt's letter to clergy at the height of the Great Depression, with responses by a diverse group of religious leaders from across the country.

Multiple primary sources created by particularly significant individuals—Dr. Martin Luther King, Jr., for example—reside in *American Decades Primary Sources*. Multiple primary sources on particularly significant subjects are often presented in more than one chapter of a volume, or in more than one decade, providing opportunities to see the significance and impact of an event or figure from many angles and historical perspectives. For example, seven primary sources on the controversial Scopes "monkey" trial are found in five chapters of the

1920s volume. Primary sources on evolutionary theory may be found in earlier and later volumes, allowing the reader to see and analyze the development of thought across time.

## Entry Organization

Contextual material uses standardized rubrics that will soon become familiar to the reader, making the entries more accessible and allowing for easy comparison. Introduction and Significance essays—brief and focused—cover the historical background, contributing factors, importance, and impact of the primary source, encouraging the reader to think critically—not only about the primary source, but also about the way history is constructed. Key Facts and a Synopsis provide quick access and recognition of the primary sources, and the Further Resources are a stepping-stone to additional study.

## Additional Features

Subject chronologies and thorough tables of contents (listing titles, authors, and dates) begin each chapter. The main table of contents assembles this information conveniently at the front of the book. An essay on using primary sources, a chronology of selected events outside the United States during the twentieth century, substantial general and subject resources, and primary source-type and general indexes enrich *American Decades Primary Sources*.

The ten volumes of *American Decades Primary Sources* provide a vast array of primary sources integrated with supporting content and user-friendly features.

This value-laden set gives the reader an unparalleled opportunity to travel into the past, to relive important events, to encounter key figures, and to gain a deep and full understanding of America in the twentieth century.

## Acknowledgments

A number of people contributed to the successful completion of this project. The editor wishes to acknowledge them with thanks: Eugenia Bradley, Luann Brennan, Neva Carter, Katrina Coach, Pamela S. Dear, Nikita L. Greene, Madeline Harris, Alesia James, Cynthia Jones, Pamela M. Kalte, Arlene Ann Kevonian, Frances L. Monroe, Charles B. Montney, Katherine H. Nemeh, James E. Person, Tyra Y. Phillips, Elizabeth Pilette, Noah Schusterbauer, Andrew Specht, Susan Strickland, Karissa Walker, Tracey Watson, and Jennifer M. York.

## Contact Us

The editors of *American Decades Primary Sources* welcome your comments, suggestions, and questions. Please direct all correspondence to:

Editor, *American Decades Primary Sources*
The Gale Group, Inc.
27500 Drake Road
Farmington Hills, MI 48331–3535
(800) 877–4253

For email inquiries, please visit the Gale website at www.gale.com, and click on the Contact Us tab.

# ABOUT THE VOLUME

The United States in the 1910s grappled with war "over there," women's suffrage, and the Great Migration of African Americans. The first world war, called "the war to end all wars," ushered the United States onto the international stage and made the country a reluctant leader. Domestically, African Americans left the strongly segregated and racially divided South in search of more opportunities in the North, though not necessarily more acceptance. While industry was booming in the North, working conditions were unregulated and unsafe, a point brought home by the Triangle Shirtwaist Factory fire in New York. By the decade's end, the Girl Scouts of America were formed, women had achieved the right to vote, and the temperance movement had succeeded in putting a proposal to prohibit the sale and consumption of alcohol before Congress. The following documents are just a sampling of the offerings available in this volume.

## Highlights of Primary Sources, 1910–1919

- Norman Rockwell's first Saturday Evening Post cover
- President Woodrow Wilson's Declaration of War message, April 2, 1917
- The Zimmerman Telegram
- Letters to the Chicago Defender by African Americans during the Great Migration from the South to the North
- *The Mind of the Primitive Man*, by Franz Boaz, groundbreaking work in cultural anthropology

- Letter to U.S. Archbishops from Cardinal James Gibbons regarding the Catholic Welfare Conference, May 1, 1919
- Excerpt from *Painless Childbirth* describing the new method of "twilight sleep," or use of anesthesia, during labor and delivery
- "Five Pretty Ways to Do the Hair," article from October 1911 issue of *Ladies' Home Journal*
- "Flexner Report" on the state of medical education in the U.S.
- First newspaper crossword puzzle, December 21, 1913.
- Speeches on "Dollar Diplomacy" by President Taft (for) and President Wilson (against)
- Editorial by Marcus Garvey in Garvey's own newspaper, *The Negro World*
- Photographs of child laborers by Lewis Hine

## Volume Structure and Content

### Front matter

- Table of Contents—lists primary sources, authors, and dates of origin, by chapter and chronologically within chapters.
- About the Set, About the Volume, About the Entry essays—guide the reader through the set and promote ease of use.

- Highlights of Primary Sources—a quick look at a dozen or so primary sources gives the reader a feel for the decade and the volume's contents.
- How to Use Primary Sources—provides a crash course in reading and interpreting primary sources.
- Selected Events Outside the United States—lends additional context in which to place the decade's primary sources.

**Chapters:**

- The Arts
- Business and the Economy
- Education
- Fashion and Design
- Government and Politics
- Law and Justice
- Lifestyles and Social Trends
- The Media
- Medicine and Health
- Religion
- Science and Technology
- Sports

**Chapter structure**

- Chapter table of contents—lists primary sources, authors, and dates of origin chronologically, showing each source's place in the decade.
- Chapter chronology—highlights the decade's important events in the chapter's subject.
- Primary sources—displays sources surrounded by contextual material.

**Back matter**

- General Resources—promotes further inquiry with books, periodicals, websites, and audio and visual media, all organized into general and subject-specific sections.
- General Index—provides comprehensive access to primary sources, people, events, and subjects, and cross-referencing to enhance comparison and analysis.
- Primary Source Type Index—locates primary sources by category, giving readers an opportunity to easily analyze sources across genres.

# ABOUT THE ENTRY

The primary source is the centerpiece and main focus of each entry in *American Decades Primary Sources*. In keeping with the philosophy that much of the benefit from using primary sources derives from the reader's own process of inquiry, the contextual material surrounding each entry provides access and ease of use, as well as giving the reader a springboard for delving into the primary source. Rubrics identify each section and enable the reader to navigate entries with ease.

## Entry structure

- Key Facts—essential information pertaining to the primary source, including full title, author, source type, source citation, and notes about the author.

- Introduction—historical background and contributing factors for the primary source.

- Significance—importance and impact of the primary source, at the time and since.

- Primary Source—in text, text facsimile, or image format; full or excerpted.

- Synopsis—encapsulated introduction to the primary source.

- Further Resources—books, periodicals, websites, and audio and visual material.

## Navigating an Entry

Entry elements are numbered and reproduced here, with an explanation of the data contained in these elements explained immediately thereafter according to the corresponding numeral.

### Primary Source/Entry Title, Primary Source Type

•1• | ## "Ego"
•2• | Magazine article

•1• **PRIMARY SOURCE/ENTRY TITLE** The entry title is the primary source title for entries with one primary source. Entry titles appear as catchwords at the top outer margin of each page.

•2• **PRIMARY SOURCE TYPE** The type of primary source is listed just below the title. When assigning source types, great weight was given to how the author of the primary source categorized it. If a primary source comprised more than one type—for example, an article about art in the United States that included paintings, or a scientific essay that included graphs and photographs—each primary source type included in the entry appears below the title.

### Composite Entry Title

•3• | # Debate Over *The Birth of a Nation*

•1• ## "Capitalizing Race Hatred"
•2• **Editorial**

## •1• "Reply to the *New York Globe*"

•2• Letter

•3• **COMPOSITE ENTRY TITLE** An overarching entry title is used for entries with more than one primary source, with the primary source titles and types below.

### Key Facts

•4• **By:** Norman Mailer

•5• **Date:** March 19, 1971

•6• **Source:** Mailer, Norman. "Ego." *Life* 70, March 19, 1971, 30, 32–36.

•7• **About the Author:** Norman Mailer (1923– ) was born in Long Branch, New Jersey. After graduating from Harvard and military service in World War II (1939–1945), Mailer began writing, publishing his first book, the best-selling novel *The Naked and the Dead,* in 1948. Mailer has written over thirty books, including novels, plays, political commentary, and essay collections, as well as numerous magazine articles. He won the Pulitzer Prize in 1969 and 1979. ■

•4• **AUTHOR OR ORIGINATOR** The name of the author or originator of the primary source begins the Key Facts section.

•5• **DATE OF ORIGIN** The date of origin of the primary source appears in this field, and may differ from the date of publication in the source citation below it; for example, speeches are often given before they are published.

•6• **SOURCE CITATION** The source citation is a full bibliographic citation, giving original publication data as well as reprint and/or online availability (usually both the deep-link and home-page URLs).

•7• **ABOUT THE AUTHOR** A brief bio of the author or originator of the primary source gives birth and death dates and a quick overview of the person's life. This rubric has been customized in some cases. If the primary source is the autobiography of an artist, the term "author" appears; however, if the primary source is a work of art, the term "artist" is used, showing the person's direct relationship to the primary source. Terms like "inventor" and "designer" are used similarly. For primary sources created by a group, "organization" may have been used instead of "author." If an author is anonymous or unknown, a brief "About the Publication" sketch may appear.

### Introduction and Significance Essays

### •8• Introduction

. . . As images from the Vietnam War (1964–1975) flashed onto television screens across the United States in the late 1960s, however, some reporters took a more active role in questioning the pronouncements of public officials. The broad cul-

tural changes of the 1960s, including a sweeping suspicion of authority figures by younger people, also encouraged a more restive spirit in the reporting corps. By the end of the decade, the phrase "Gonzo Journalism" was coined to describe the new breed of reporter: young, rebellious, and unafraid to get personally involved in the story at hand. . . .

•8• **INTRODUCTION** The introduction is a brief essay on the contributing factors and historical context of the primary source. Intended to promote understanding and jump-start the reader's curiosity, this section may also describe an artist's approach, the nature of a scientific problem, or the struggles of a sports figure. If more than one primary source is included in the entry, the introduction and significance address each one, and often the relationship between them.

### •9• Significance

Critics of the new style of journalism maintained that the emphasis on personalities and celebrity did not necessarily lead to better reporting. As political reporting seemed to focus more on personalities and images and less on substantive issues, some observers feared that the American public was ill-served by the new style of journalism. Others argued that the media had also encouraged political apathy among the public by superficial reporting. . . .

•9• **SIGNIFICANCE** The significance discusses the importance and impact of the primary source. This section may touch on how it was regarded at the time and since, its place in history, any awards given, related developments, and so on.

### Primary Source Header, Synopsis, Primary Source

### •10• Primary Source

*The Boys on the Bus* [excerpt]

•11• **SYNOPSIS:** A boisterous account of Senator George McGovern's ultimately unsuccessful 1972 presidential bid, Crouse's work popularized the term "pack journalism," describing the herd mentality that gripped reporters focusing endlessly on the same topic. In later years, political advisors would become more adept at "spinning" news stories to their candidates' advantage, but the essential dynamics of pack journalism remain in place.

•12• The feverish atmosphere was halfway between a high school bus trip to Washington and a gambler's jet junket to Las Vegas, where small-time Mafiosi were lured into betting away their restaurants. There was giddy camaraderie mixed with fear and low-grade hysteria. To file a story late, or to make one glaring factual error, was to chance losing everything—one's job, one's expense account, one's drinking buddies, one's mad-dash existence, and the methedrine buzz that comes from knowing stories that the public would not know for hours and secrets that the public would never know. Therefore reporters channeled their gambling instincts into late-night poker games and private bets on the outcome of the elections. When it came to writing a story, they were as cautious as diamond-cutters. . . .

**•10• PRIMARY SOURCE HEADER** The primary source header signals the beginning of the primary source, and "[excerpt]" is attached if the source does not appear in full.

**•11• SYNOPSIS** The synopsis gives a brief overview of the primary source.

**•12• PRIMARY SOURCE** The primary source may appear excerpted or in full, and may appear as text, text facsimile (photographic reproduction of the original text), image, or graphic display (such as a table, chart, or graph).

### Text Primary Sources

The majority of primary sources are reproduced as plain text. The font and leading of the primary sources are distinct from that of the context—to provide a visual clue to the change, as well as to facilitate ease of reading. Often, the original formatting of the text was preserved in order to more accurately represent the original (screenplays, for example). In order to respect the integrity of the primary sources, content some readers may consider sensitive was retained where it was deemed to be integral to the source. Text facsimile formatting was used sparingly and where the original provided additional value (for example, Aaron Copland's typing and handwritten notes on "Notes for a Cowboy Ballet").

### Narrative Break

**•13•** I told him I'd rest and then fix him something to eat when he got home. I could hear someone enter his office then, and Medgar laughed at something that was said. "I've got to go, honey. See you tonight. I love you." "All right," I said. "Take care." Those were our last words to each other.

■ ■ ■

Medgar had told me that President Kennedy was speaking on civil rights that night, and I made a mental note of the time. We ate alone, the children and I. It had become a habit now to set only four places for supper. Medgar's chair stared at us, and the children, who had heard

about the President's address to the nation, planned to watch it with me. There was something on later that they all wanted to see, and they begged to be allowed to wait up for Medgar to return home. School was out, and I knew that Van would fall asleep anyway, so I agreed.

**•13• NARRATIVE BREAK** A narrative break appears where there is a significant amount of elided material, beyond what ellipses would indicate (for example, excerpts from a nonfiction work's introduction and second chapter, or sections of dialogue from two acts of a play).

### Image Primary Sources

Primary source images (whether photographs, text facsimiles, or graphic displays) are bordered with a distinctive double rule. The Primary Source header and Synopsis appear under the image, with the image reduced in size to accommodate the synopsis. For multipart images, the synopsis appears only under the first part of the image; subsequent parts have brief captions.

**•14•** "Art: U.S. Scene": *The Tornado* by John Steuart Curry (2 OF 4)

**•14• PRIMARY SOURCE IMAGE HEADER** The primary source image header assists the reader in tracking the images in a series. Also, the primary source header listed here indicates a primary source with both text and image components. The text of the *Time* magazine article "Art: U.S. Scene," appears with four of the paintings from the article. Under each painting, the title of the article appears first, followed by a colon, then the title of the painting. The header for the text component has a similar structure, with the term "magazine article" after the colon. Inclusion of images or graphic elements from primary sources, and their designation in the entry as main primary sources, is discretionary.

### Further Resources

**•15• Further Resources**

**BOOKS**
Dixon, Phil. *The Negro Baseball Leagues, 1867–1955: A Photographic History.* Mattituck, N.Y.: Amereon House, 1992.

**PERIODICALS**
"Steven Spielberg: The Director Says It's Good-Bye to Spaceships and Hello to Relationships." *American Film* 13, no. 8, June 1988, 12–16.

**WEBSITES**
*Architecture and Interior Design for 20th Century America, 1935–1955.* American Memory digital primary source collection, Library of Congress. Available online at http://memory.loc.gov/ammem/gschtml/gotthome

.html; website home page: http://memory.loc.gov /ammem/ammemhome.html (accessed March 27, 2003).

**AUDIO AND VISUAL MEDIA**

*E.T.: The Extra-Terrestrial.* Original release, 1982, Universal. Directed by Steven Spielberg. Widescreen Collector's Edition DVD, 2002, Universal Studios.

•**15**• **FURTHER RESOURCES** A brief list of resources provides a stepping stone to further study. If it's known that a resource contains additional primary source material specifically related to the entry, a brief note in italics appears at the end of the citation. For websites, both the deep link and home page usually appear.

# USING PRIMARY SOURCES

The philosopher R.G. Collingwood once said, "Every new generation must rewrite history in its own way." What Collingwood meant is that new events alter our perceptions of the past and necessitate that each generation interpret the past in a different light. For example, since September 11, 2001, and the "War on Terrorism," the collapse of the Soviet Union seemingly is no longer as historically important as the rise of Islamic fundamentalism, which was once only a minor concern. Seen from this viewpoint, history is not a rigid set of boring facts, but a fascinating, ever-changing field of study. Much of this fascination rests on the fact that historical interpretation is based on the reading of primary sources. To historians and students alike, primary sources are ambiguous objects because their underlying meanings are often not crystal clear. To learn a primary document's meaning(s), students must identify its main subject and recreate the historical context in which the document was created. In addition, students must compare the document with other primary sources from the same historical time and place. Further, students must cross-examine the primary source by asking of it a series of probing investigative questions.

To properly analyze a primary source, it is important that students become "active" rather than "casual" readers. As in reading a chemistry or algebra textbook, historical documents require students to analyze them carefully and extract specific information. In other words, history requires students to read "beyond the text" and focus on what the primary source tells us about the person or group and the era in which they lived. Unlike chemistry and algebra, however, historical primary sources have the additional benefit of being part of a larger, interesting story full of drama, suspense, and hidden agendas. In order to detect and identify key historical themes, students need to keep in mind a set of questions. For example, Who created the primary source? Why did the person create it? What is the subject? What problem is being addressed? Who was the intended audience? How was the primary source received and how was it used? What are the most important characteristics of this person or group for understanding the primary source? For example, what were the authors' biases? What was their social class? Their race? Their gender? Their occupation? Once these questions have been answered reasonably, the primary source can be used as a piece of historical evidence to interpret history.

In each *American Decades Primary Sources* volume, students will study examples of the following categories of primary sources:

- Firsthand accounts of historic events by witnesses and participants. This category includes diary entries, letters, newspaper articles, oral-history interviews, memoirs, and legal testimony.

- Documents representing the official views of the nation's leaders or of their political opponents. These include court decisions, policy statements, political speeches, party platforms, petitions, legislative debates, press releases, and federal and state laws.

- Government statistics and reports on such topics as birth, employment, marriage, death, and taxation.

- Advertisers' images and jingles. Although designed to persuade consumers to purchase commodities or to adopt specific attitudes, advertisements can also be valuable sources of information about popular beliefs and concerns.

- Works of art, including paintings, symphonies, play scripts, photographs, murals, novels, and poems.

- The products of mass culture: cartoons, comic books, movies, radio scripts, and popular songs.

- Material artifacts. These are everyday objects that survived from the period in question. Examples include household appliances and furnishings, recipes, and clothing.

- Secondary sources. In some cases, secondary sources may be treated as primary sources. For example, from 1836 to 1920, public schools across America purchased 122 million copies of a series of textbooks called the McGuffey Reader. Although current textbooks have more instructional value, the Reader is an invaluable primary source. It provides important insights into the unifying morals and cultural values that shaped the worldview of several generations of Americans, who differed in ethnicity, race, class, and religion.

Each of the above-mentioned categories of primary sources reveals different types of historical information. A politician's diary, memoirs, or collection of letters, for example, often provide students with the politicians' unguarded, private thoughts and emotions concerning daily life and public events. Though these documents may be a truer reflection of the person's character and aspirations, students must keep in mind that when people write about themselves, they tend to put themselves at the center of the historical event or cast themselves in the best possible light. On the other hand, the politician's public speeches may be more cautious, less controversial, and limited to advancing his or her political party's goals or platform.

Like personal diaries, advertisements reveal other types of historical information. What information does the WAVES poster on this page reveal?

John Phillip Faller, a prolific commercial artist known for his *Saturday Evening Post* covers, designed this recruitment poster in 1944. It was one of over three hundred posters he produced for the U.S. Navy while enrolled in that service during World War II. The purpose of the poster was to encourage women to enlist in the WAVES (Women Accepted for Volunteer Emergency Service), a women's auxiliary to the Navy established in

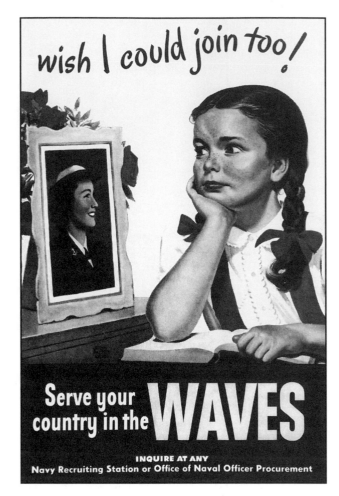

COURTESY OF THE NAVAL HISTORICAL FOUNDATION.
REPRODUCED BY PERMISSION.

1942. It depicts a schoolgirl gazing admiringly at a photograph of a proud, happy WAVE (perhaps an older sister), thus portraying the military service as an appropriate and admirable aspiration for women during wartime. However, what type of military service? Does the poster encourage women to enlist in military combat like World War II male recruitment posters? Does it reflect gender bias? What does this poster reveal about how the military and society in general feel about women in the military? Does the poster reflect current military and societal attitudes toward women in the military? How many women joined the WAVES? What type of duties did they perform?

Like personal diaries, photographs reveal other types of historical information. What information does the next photograph reveal?

Today, we take electricity for granted. However, in 1935, although 90 percent of city dwellers in America had electricity, only 10 percent of rural Americans did. Private utility companies refused to string electric lines

THE LIBRARY OF CONGRESS.

to isolated farms, arguing that the endeavor was too expensive and that most farmers were too poor to afford it anyway. As part of the Second New Deal, President Franklin Delano Roosevelt issued an executive order creating the Rural Electrification Administration (REA). The REA lent money at low interest rates to utility companies to bring electricity to rural America. By 1950, 90 percent of rural America had electricity. This photograph depicts a 1930s tenant farmer's house in Greene County, Georgia. Specifically, it shows a brand-new electric meter on the wall. The picture presents a host of questions: What was rural life like without electricity? How did electricity impact the lives of rural Americans, particularly rural Georgians? How many rural Georgians did not have electricity in the 1930s? Did Georgia have more electricity-connected farms than other Southern states? What was the poverty rate in rural Georgia, particularly among rural African Americans? Did rural electricity help lift farmers out of poverty?

Like personal diaries, official documents reveal other types of historical information. What information does the next document, a memo, reveal?

From the perspective of the early twenty-first century, in a democratic society, integration of the armed services seems to have been inevitable. For much of American history, however, African Americans were prevented from joining the military, and when they did enlist they were segregated into black units. In 1940, of the nearly 170,000-man Navy, only 4,007, or 2.3 percent, were African American personnel. The vast majority of these men worked in the mess halls as stewards—or, as labeled by the black press, "seagoing bellhops." In this official document, the chairman of the General Board refers to compliance with a directive that would enlist African Americans into positions of "unlimited general service." Who issued the directive? What was the motivation behind the new directive? Who were the members of the General Board? How much authority did they wield? Why did the Navy restrict African Americans to the "messman branch"? Notice the use of the term "colored race." Why was this term used and what did it imply? What did the board conclude? When did the Navy become integrated? Who was primarily responsible for integrating the Navy?

CONFIDENTIAL

DOD Dir. 5200.10, June 29, 1960
NND by *RB* date Oct 5, 1961

DOWNGRADED AT 3 YEAR INTERVALS;
DECLASSIFIED AFTER 12 YEARS
DOD DIR 5200.10 NARS-NT

G.B. No. 421
(Serial No. 201)
SECRET

SECRET

Feb 3, 1942

From:        Chairman General Board.
To:           Secretary of the Navy.

Subject:      Enlistment of men of colored race to other than
                  Messman branch.

Ref:          (a) SecNav let. (SC)P14-4/MM (03200A)/Gen of
                  Jan 16, 1942.

       1.      The General Board, complying with the directive
contained in reference (a), has given careful attention to the
problem of enlisting in the Navy, men of the colored race
in other than the messman branch.

       2.      The General Board has endeavored to examine the
problem placed before it in a realistic manner.

A.      Should negroes be enlisted for **unlimited** general service?

          (a) Enlistment for general service implies that the
individual may be sent anywhere, - to any ship or station where
he is needed. Men on board ship live in particularly close
association; in their messes, one man sits beside another; their
hammocks or bunks are close together; in their common tasks they
work side by side; and in particular tasks such as those of a
gun's crew, they form a closely knit, highly coordinated team.
How many white men would choose, of their own accord, that their
closest associates in sleeping quarters, at mess, and in a gun's
crew should be of another race? How many would accept such
conditions, if required to do so, without resentment and just
as a matter of course? The General Board believes that the
answer is "Few, if any," and further believes that if the issue were
forced, there would be a lowering of contentment, teamwork
and discipline in the service.

          (b) One of the tennets of the recruiting service
is that each recruit for general service is potentially a leading
petty officer. It is true that some men never do become petty
officers, and that when recruiting white men, it is not possible
to establish which will be found worthy of and secure promotion
and which will not. If negroes are recruited for general service,
it can be said at once that few will obtain advancement to petty
officers. With every desire to be fair, officers and leading
petty officers in general will not recommend negroes for promotion
to positions of authority over white men.

- 1 -

CONFIDENTIAL

The General Board is convinced that the enlistment of negroes for unlimited general service is unadvisable.

B.    Should negroes be enlisted in general service but detailed in special ratings or for special ships or units?

(a) The ratings now in use in the naval service cover every phase of naval activity, and no new ratings are deemed necessary merely to promote the enlistment of negroes.

(b) At first thought, it might appear that assignment of negroes to certain vessels, and in particular to small vessels of the patrol type, would be feasible.  In this connection, the following table is of interest:

| Type of Ship | Total Crew | Men in Pay Grades 1 to 4 | Men in Pay Grades 5 to 7 (Non-rated) |
|---|---|---|---|
| Battleship | 1892 | 666 | 1226 |
| Light Cruiser (10,000 ton) | 988 | 365 | 623 |
| Destroyer (1630 ton) | 206 | 109 | 97 |
| Submarine | 54 | 47 | 7 |
| Patrol Boat (180 foot) | 55 | 36 | 19 |
| Patrol Boat (110 foot) | 20 | 15 | 5 |

NOTE:    Pay grades 1 to 4 include Chief Petty Officers and Petty Officers, 1st, 2nd and 3rd Class; also Firemen, 1st Class and a few other ratings requiring length of service and experience equal to that required for qualification of Petty Officers, 3rd class.  Pay grades 5 to 7 include all other non-rated men and recruits.

There are no negro officers and so few negro petty officers in the Navy at present that any vessels to which negroes might be assigned must have white officers and white petty officers.  Examination of the table shows the small number of men in other than petty officer ratings that might be assigned to patrol vessels and indicates to the General Board that such assignments would not be happy ones.  The assignment of negroes to the larger ships, where well over one-half of the crews are non-rated men, with mixture of whites and negroes, would inevitably lead to discontent on the part of one or the other, resulting in clashes and lowering of the efficiency of the vessels and of the Navy.

- 2 -

CONFIDENTIAL

The material collected in these volumes of *American Decades Primary Sources* are significant because they will introduce students to a wide variety of historical sources that were created by those who participated in or witnessed the historical event. These primary sources not only vividly describe historical events, but also reveal the subjective perceptions and biases of their authors. Students should read these documents "actively," and with the contextual assistance of the introductory material, history will become relevant and entertaining.

—*Paul G. Connors*

# Chronology of Selected World Events Outside the United States, 1910–1919

## 1910

- British mathematicians and philosophers Bertrand Russell and Alfred North Whitehead publish the first volume of their *Principia Mathematica* (1910–1913), an attempt to prove that all mathematics are the logical extension of a small number of axioms.

- Spanish architect Antonio Gaudi completes one of his best-known buildings, Casa Milá, in Barcelona.

- Lord Robert Stephenson Smyth Baden-Powell, who started the Boy Scouts in 1908, founds the Girl Guides.

- On January 15, France merges its colonies Chad, Gabon, Middle Congo, and Ubangi-Shari into French Equatorial Africa, a single administrative unit.

- On April 28, the British Parliament adopts the so-called People's Budget, a major step in the creation of a welfare state in Great Britain.

- On May 18, Halley's Comet, which is visible from Earth every seventy-six years, blazes in the night sky.

- On May 31, the British Parliament merges the Cape Colony, the Orange Free State, Natal, and the Transvaal into the Union of South Africa as a dominion of the British Empire.

- On August 10, a typhoon kills some five hundred people in Japan and leaves four hundred thousand homeless.

- On August 22, Korea signs a treaty recognizing Japanese authority over the peninsula.

- On September 15, the Nationalist Party, led by Louis Botha, a Dutch settler, defeats the Union Party, which runs on a platform advocating close ties to the British Empire, in the first elections in the Union of South Africa.

- On October 4, Manuel II of Portugal flees to England amid a revolt by the army.

## 1911

- In October, American archaeologist Harem Bingham discovers Machu Picchu, a lost city of the Incan Empire, high in the Peruvian Andes.

- Japan, the United States, Great Britain, and Russia empower Canada to limit the hunting of fur seals in the North Pacific and the Bering Sea.

- Joseph Schumpeter, a Moravian economist at the University of Graz, publishes his *Theory of Economic Development*, a work that influences economists.

- Traveling by rail and ship, André Jaeger-Schmidt sets a new around-the-world record of thirty-nine days, nineteen hours.

- German novelist Thomas Mann publishes *Death in Venice*.

- French artist Georges Braque, one of the founders of Cubism, paints *Man With a Guitar*.

- In April, the Chinese Revolution begins in Szechwan province, sparked by the belief that foreigners dominate the Manchu (Ch'ing) dynasty.

- On May 15, the British House of Commons adopts the Parliament Act, which strips the House of Lords of its ability to veto legislation.

- In June, British physicist Ernest Rutherford announces that the atom has a positively charged nucleus surrounded by negatively charged electrons.

- On June 21, the SS *Olympic* of the British White Star Line arrives in New York City on its maiden voyage.

- On August 22, Leonardo da Vinci's masterpiece the *Mona Lisa* is stolen from the Louvre in Paris.

- In September, a Yangtze River flood kills one hundred thousand people in China.

- On September 9, Italy declares war on the Ottoman Empire.

- On September 14, Mordkha Bogrov, a revolutionary assassin, shoots Russian prime minister Pëtr Arkadevich Stolypin, who dies four days later.

- On October 5, Italian forces capture Tripoli (in modern Libya) after shelling the North African city.

- On October 10, Chinese imperial troops mutiny at Wuch'ang, the capital of Hukwang province.

- On October 26, China becomes a republic, ending nearly three centuries of rule by the Manchu dynasty.

- On November 1, Italian planes bomb an oasis on Tripoli's coast in the first use of the airplane to drop bombs.

- On November 5, Italy annexes Cyrenaica and Tripolitania, an action Istanbul, capital of the Ottoman Empire, refuses to recognize.

- In December, Parliament passes the National Insurance Bill, which provides unemployment compensation and health insurance to British workers.

- On December 4, an armistice ends fighting in China.

- On December 6, Russia declares Mongolia a protectorate after Mongolia had declared independence from China on November 18.

- On December 11, French chemist Marie Curie receives the Nobel Prize in chemistry for her discovery of the elements radium and polonium and for her discovery that radium spontaneously decays.

- On December 14, an expedition led by Norwegian explorer Roald Amundsen reaches the South Pole.

## 1912

- Dutch aircraft designer Anthony Herman Gerard Fokker founds Fokker Aircraft.

- German scientist Alfred L. Wegener publishes *The Origins of Continents and Oceans,* which asserts that continents ride on top of plates that move at the rate of only a few centimeters a century.

- Rowenta, a German firm, introduces the first electric iron.

- French painter Marcel Duchamp completes one of his best-known and most controversial works, *Nude Descending a Staircase.*

- An International Radio-Telegraph Conference adopts the Morse code signal SOS—three dots, three dashes, three dots—as a universal signal of distress.

- On January 1, Sun Yat-sen becomes provisional president of the Republic of China.

- On February 12, Hsüan t'ung, the boy emperor of China, abdicates.

- On February 14, Sun Yat-sen resigns as president of China.

- On March 7, Henri Semiet completes the first nonstop flight from Paris to London.

- On March 10, Yüan Shih-k'ai becomes president of China.

- On March 13, Bulgaria and Serbia form an alliance against the Ottoman Empire, weakened by its war with Italy.

- On March 30, the Treaty of Fez makes most of Morocco a French protectorate with Rabat as its capital.

- In April, British lawyer and amateur archeologist Charles Dawson announces the discover of an ancient skull in Piltdown, England.

- On April 13, the Royal Flying Corps, predecessor of the Royal Air Force, is established in Great Britain.

- From April 14 to April 15, the British White Star liner *Titanic,* on its maiden voyage from Southampton to New York, strikes an iceberg in the North Atlantic and sinks within hours, despite belief that the ship is unsinkable.

- On May 1, *L'Après-Midi d'un Faune* (Afternoon of the Faun), a ballet by Russian dancer Vaslav Nijinsky, premieres in Paris.

- On May 5, the first issue of the revolutionary journal *Pravda* (Truth) is published in Saint Petersburg, Russia.

- From May 5 to July 22, more than twenty-five hundred athletes from twenty-eight countries participate in the fifth summer games of the modern Olympiad in Stockholm, Sweden.

- On July 22, the British admiralty transfers its warships from the Mediterranean to the North Sea in response to Germany's naval presence there.

- In August, several factions unite in China to form the National People's Party, or Kuomintang, under the leadership of Sun Yat-sen.

- On August 1, airmail service begins between London and Paris.

- On August 7, Japan and Russia agree on their spheres of influence in Manchuria and Mongolia.

- On September 28, conservative Irish and British political parties sign the Ulster Covenant of Resistance in Belfast.

- On October 8, Montenegro declares war on the Ottoman Empire.

- On October 14, the Ottoman Turks invade Serbia but retreat by month's end.

- On October 18, Italy and the Ottoman Empire sign a treaty at Ouchy, Switzerland, recognizing Italian control of Tripoli and Cyrenaica.

- On November 28, Albania declares independence from the Ottoman Empire.

- On December 4, the Turks agree to an armistice with Bulgaria and Serbia, but Greece refuses to participate.

## 1913

- British novelist D.H. Lawrence publishes *Sons and Lovers,* a novel whose open treatment of sex shocks conservatives.

- John Henry Mears, a reporter for the *New York Evening Sun,* sets a new round-the-world record of thirty-five days, twenty-one hours.

- On January 23, a coup by the nationalist Young Turks replaces Kiamil Pasha with Mahmud Shevket Pasha as grand vizier of the Ottoman Empire.

- On February 23, Francisco Madero is executed, presumably at the behest of Huerta. Madero had been deposed as president of Mexico the week before in a coup led by Victoriano Huerta.

- In March, British scientist Henry Gwyn-Jeffreys discovers that the number of electrons in an element is the same as its atomic number.

- On March 6, war again embroils the Balkans when Greek forces capture Janina and take thirty-two thousand Turks prisoner.

- On April 3, a jury sentences British suffragist Emmeline Pankhurst to three years in prison for inciting arson.

- On April 8, the first parliament in Chinese history opens in Beijing.

- On April 26, the International Women's Peace Conference opens at The Hague, drawing women from around the world who fear militarism and international tensions in the Balkans and elsewhere.

- On May 29, Igor Stravinsky's ballet *The Rites of Spring* premieres in Paris.

- On May 30, the Treaty of London ends the Balkan conflict.

- In June French physicist Charles Fabry discovers the ozone layer in the earth's stratosphere.

- On June 6, the Reichstag passes a measure increasing the size of the German army in anticipation of war.

- On June 20, whites, under the terms of the Native Land Act, seize more than 80 percent of the land in South Africa despite the fact that blacks outnumber whites four to one.

- On June 24, Greece and Serbia end their alliance with Bulgaria because of a border controversy they are unable to resolve.

- On June 29, Norway becomes the first European nation to enact permanent universal suffrage for women.

- On June 30, Bulgaria attacks Serbia and Greece.

- On July 8, China, under pressure from western powers, recognizes Mongolia's independence.

- On July 11, Romania declares war on Bulgaria and launches an invasion.

- On July 15, the British House of Lords rejects a proposal to grant Ireland home rule.

- On August 10, the latest Balkan war ends with the Treaty of Bucharest.

- On September 1, Kuomintang forces in China stage an unsuccessful uprising against the repressive measures of Yüan Shih-k'ai's government.

- On September 23, French aviator Roland Garros lands in Tunis, completing the first flight across the Mediterranean Sea.

- On October 10, the Panama Canal opens, allowing ships to cross between the Pacific and Atlantic oceans through the isthmus of Panama.

- On October 11, Victoriano Huerta, president of Mexico, declares himself dictator.

- On November 15, forces led by Mexican rebel Pancho Villa capture Ciudad Juarez, near the U.S.-Mexico border.

## 1914

- Irish novelist and short-story writer James Joyce publishes *Dubliners* and *A Portrait of the Artist as a Young Man*.

- On April 13, British playwright Bernard Shaw premieres *Pygmalion* in London.

- On April 21, U.S. Marines occupy the Mexican port city of Veracruz after officials there refused to order a twenty-one-gun salute to the American flag.

- In May, Yüan Shih-k'ai establishes himself as dictator of China.

- On May 25, the British Parliament passes a bill granting home rule to Ireland (with a six-year exemption granted for the mostly Protestant province of Ulster).

- On May 29, a Canadian steamship sinks in the Saint Lawrence River after hitting another vessel. More than one thousand passengers and crew die.

- On June 28, Serbian nationalist Gavrilo Princip assassinates Archduke Franz Ferdinand, heir to the throne of the Austro-Hungarian Empire, and his wife in Sarajevo.

- On July 28, Austria-Hungary declares war against Serbia.

- On July 30, Russia mobilizes its army to support Serbia against Austria-Hungary.

- On August 1, Russia refuses German demand to stop mobilization.

- On August 2, Germany, having occupied tiny Luxembourg, demands that Belgium allow German troops to sweep through Belgium in order to attack France from the north despite a Belgian declaration of neutrality.

- On August 3, Germany declares war on France and launches an offensive through Belgium the following day.

- On August 4, Great Britain declares war on Germany for violating Belgian neutrality.

- On August 5, Montenegro declares war on Austria-Hungary.

- On August 6, Austria-Hungary declares war on Russia.

- On August 8, French and British troops attack the German army in Lorraine.

- On August 12, France and Great Britain declare war on Austria-Hungary.

- On August 18, Russian forces attack Galicia (in present-day Poland).

- On August 20, the Anglo-French offensive in Lorraine and along the Franco-Belgian border stalls.

- On August 23, Japan declares war on Germany, intent on capturing German colonies in Asia, and attacks Tsingtao, a German-controlled city in the Chinese province of Chiao Hsien.

- From August 26 to August 29, Russian forces led by Grand Duke Nicholas lose the Battle of Tannenberg.

- On August 28, the war at sea begins when the Royal Navy sinks three German cruisers and two destroyers off Helgoland Bight in the North Sea.

- On August 29, an expeditionary force from New Zealand, fighting alongside Britain, captures German Samoa and three weeks later takes German New Guinea.

- On September 5, Russia, Great Britain, and France ally against Germany and Austria-Hungary.
- From September 6 to September 9, British and French troops halt a Germany offensive in the first Battle of the Marne, north of Paris.
- From September 7 to September 14, Germany defeats Russia in the first Battle of Masurian Lakes, in what is now northeastern Poland.
- On September 12, Russian forces capture Lemberg, the provincial capital of Galicia.
- On September 18, the German army retreats after intense fighting along the Aisne River in northern France.
- On October 1, thirty thousand Canadian troops sail for Europe to join the British.
- On October 10, German troops capture the Belgian coastal town of Antwerp, raising fears in Great Britain that German might invade Britain by crossing the English Channel.
- On October 21, British, French, and German forces fight at Ypres, a month long battle that ends in stalemate with 250,000 casualties.
- On October 30, the Ottoman Empire declares war on Russia and Great Britain.
- On November 3, Russia declares war on Turkey after the Ottomans, who are allied with Germany, allow German ships to enter the Black Sea.
- On November 5, Great Britain declares war on Turkey.
- On November 12, Louis Botha puts down a Boer revolt in South Africa that stemmed from the Boers' opposition to an attack on German troops in neighboring southwest Africa.
- On December 2, the Austrians capture the Serbian capital, Belgrade, but the Serbs retake it a month later.
- On December 11, the Royal Navy sinks four German cruisers off the Falkland Islands in the South Atlantic without suffering any losses.
- On December 16, Great Britain establishes a protectorate over Egypt, sending troops there to attack the Ottoman Empire.

## 1915

- British novelist W. Somerset Maugham publishes *Of Human Bondage.*
- Austrian novelist Franz Kafka publishes *The Metamorphosis.*
- Japanese writer Ryunosuke Akutagawa publishes *Rashomon.*
- On January 13, twenty-nine thousand people die in an earthquake in central Italy.
- On January 24, the British navy defeats a German squadron in the Battle of Dogger Bank.
- On February 18, Germany fulfills its February 2 pledge to use submarines (U-boats) to blockade France and the British Isles.
- From February to November, German and Austrian forces push Russian troops east through Poland.

- On March 1, Great Britain announces a blockade of Germany, which includes seizure of neutral ships carrying food to German ports, in retaliation for Germany's inclusion of food in its naval blockade of Britain and France.
- On March 22, German troops stop a Russian advance in the Battle of Przemysl.
- From April 22 to May 25, German troops fire mortar shells filled with chlorine gas into the French lines in the first chemical attack in World War I.
- On April 25, in an attempt to capture the strategic Dardanelles Straits from Turkey, Allied troops (including French, British, Australian, and New Zealand forces) land at Gallipoli.
- On April 26, Russia, Great Britain, and France conclude a series of secret treaties in London that establish a plan for dividing the postwar spoils.
- On May 7, a German submarine torpedoes and sinks without warning the British passenger liner *Lusitania,* en route from New York to Liverpool, eight miles off the coast of Ireland.
- On May 23, in accordance with a treaty signed with the Allies the previous month, Italy declares war on Austria in return for an Allied promise that Italy will gain land in the South Tirol, as well as the city of Trieste, at the end of the war.
- On May 25, Chinese president Yüan Shih-k'ai accepts the conditions in Japan's Twenty-One Demands of January 18 in order to prevent a Japanese invasion.
- The British Liberal and Conservative Parties form a coalition government for the duration of the war.
- On June 1, Germany launches the first of its zeppelin airship raids over London and eastern England.
- On June 23, Italy launches an offensive in hopes of capturing Trieste from the Austrians, but fails in four battles along the Isonzo River, suffering 250,000 casualties.
- In July, Albert Einstein publishes his general theory of relativity.
- On August 5, Austrian and German troops capture Warsaw, Poland.
- On August 30, German troops capture the Russian fortress at Brest Litovsk.
- On September 5, Czar Nicholas II, after watching his army suffer a series of defeats, takes personal command of the Russian army.
- On September 22, Allied troops begin an offensive in Artois and Champagne, in northern France.
- On October 6, Germany and Austria invade Serbia, driving the Serbian army across Albania and onto the island of Corfu.
- On October 14, Bulgaria joins the Central Powers, declaring war on Serbia.
- On October 21, Arlington, Virginia, and Paris exchange the first transatlantic radiotelephone call.
- On October 29, socialist Aristide Briand becomes prime minister of France following the resignation of René Viviani.

- On November 14, Czech nationalist Tomás Masaryk calls for the establishment of a Czech national council as a first step toward independence.

- On November 21, the Ottoman Empire halts a British invasion from India at the Battle of Ctesiphon, near Baghdad.

- On December 10, French novelist and poet Romain Rolland receives the Nobel Prize in literature.

---

## 1916

- On January 24, Great Britain adopts compulsory military service, with exceptions for conscientious objectors.

- On February 21, German troops attack Verdun, the French fortress on the Meuse River in northern France.

- On March 5, the Allies invade German East Africa.

- On March 8, Mexican rebel Pancho Villa raids Columbus, New Mexico.

- On March 9, Germany declares war on Portugal.

- Great Britain and France sign the Sykes-Picot Agreement, dividing Turkey between them.

- On March 24, a German U-boat sinks the French ship *Sussex*.

- On April 14, Allied forces shell the ancient city of Istanbul in Turkey.

- On April 25, the Easter Uprising begins in Dublin, Ireland.

- On April 29, British troops at Kut-al-Imara, in present-day Iraq, surrender to the Turks after a 143-day siege.

- In May, Germany acquiesces to U.S. pressure, temporarily revoking its order to fire on any ship attempting to break the German naval blockade of Great Britain and France.

- On May 12, the British execute James Connolly, the last of the seven leaders of the Easter Uprising in Dublin.

- On May 15, Austria attacks Italian troops in the Trentino, along the Italo-Austrian border.

- On May 31, both Great Britain and Germany claim victory in a sea battles off Jutland (Denmark).

- On June 23, the Russians begin an offensive that reconquers most of Galicia.

- On June 24, the German army again attacks Verdun, scene of some of the war's bloodiest fighting.

- On July 1, the Allies launch an offensive along the Somme River in northeastern France.

- On August 9, Italian troops capture Gorizia (in present-day northeastern Italy).

- On August 24, German socialist leader Karl Liebknecht is jailed for his role in organizing anti-war protests.

- On August 27, Italy declares war on Germany, Romania declares war on Austria, and Germany declares war on Romania.

- Paul von Hindenburg, hero of the Battle of Tannenberg, becomes chief of the German general staff.

- In September, the Allies deploy tanks for the first time in war against German positions in the Battle of the Somme.

- On September 10, the Allies begin an offensive in Salonika, Greece, part of Britain's plan to consolidate its gains in the eastern Mediterranean.

- On September 16, German reinforcements of the Austrian army prevent Russia from retaking Lemberg, the provincial capital of Galicia.

- On September 27, Greece declares war on Bulgaria, which had declared war on Romania.

- In October, German astronomer Karl Schwarzchild, working from Albert Einstein's theory of relativity, posits the existence of "black holes."

- On October 17, the Allies occupy Athens and recognize the rebel provisional government of Eleuthérios Venizélos.

- On October 24, French soldiers break through the German lines along a four-mile front in fighting at Verdun.

- On November 5, Germany and Austria recognize the independence of Poland, which had been under Russian rule, in an attempt to establish a buffer between their territory and Russia.

- On December 7, Liberal Party leader David Lloyd George becomes prime minister of Great Britain.

- On December 30, Russian troops murder mystic Rasputin, confidant of Czarina Alexandra of Russia.

---

## 1917

- Guillaume Apollinaire invents the term "Surrealism" *to describe art that questions traditional concepts of form, composition, and taste.*

- Dutch painter Piet Mondrian founds the art journal *De Stijl.*

- On January 27, the army deposes the president of Costa Rica.

- On February 1, Germany announces its resumption of unrestricted submarine warfare.

- On February 3, the United States breaks off diplomatic relations with Germany in response to Germany's resumption of unrestricted submarine warfare.

- On February 5, the Mexican government of President Venustiano Carranza adopts a reformist constitution, promising to end centuries of feudalism in which powerful landowners exploited peasants.

- On March 8, the Russian Revolution of 1917 begins.

- On March 11, British troops capture Baghdad, capital of present-day Iraq.

- On March 12, the Russian Duma (parliament) establishes a provisional government despite Czar Nicholas II's decree disbanding the Duma.

- On March 16, Czar Nicholas II abdicates the Russian throne, ending three centuries of Romanov rule.

- On March 27, British troops defeat Turkish forces near Gaza.

- On April 6, President Woodrow Wilson signs Congress's declaration of war against Germany, bringing the United States into World War I in support of the Allies and against the Central Powers.

- On April 16, Allied forces attack German units defending the Hindenburg line along the Aisne River.
- On April 17, Bolshevik leader Vladimir Lenin returns to Russia from a three-year exile in Switzerland and calls for the transfer of state power from the provisional government to workers' soviets.
- On May 3, Canadian troops capture the Vimy Ridge, ending the third Battle of Arras.
- On June 4, Brazil declares war on Germany and seizes German ships in Brazilian ports.
- On June 8, British forces take the Messines Ridge, south of Ypres.
- On June 12, King Constantine of Greece, who allied with the Central Powers and dismissed the pro-Allied government of Venizélos, abdicates the throne under pressure from the Allies.
- On June 16, the Congress of Soviets brings together Bolshevik leaders throughout Russia.
- On June 17, the British royal family, the House of Saxe-Coburg, renounces ties to its German relatives and becomes the House of Windsor.
- On June 26, the first contingent of the American Expeditionary Force lands in France, commanded by Gen. John J. "Black Jack" Pershing.
- On June 29, the Ukraine declares independence from Russia.
- On July 6, British commander Thomas Edward Lawrence (Lawrence of Arabia) leads a daring and successful attack on Aqaba, capturing the city from the Turks.
- Finland declares independence from Russia.
- On July 16, a Russian provisional government crushes a Bolshevik rebellion, forcing Vladimir Lenin to flee to Finland to avoid arrest.
- On July 17, Catholic pilgrims flock to Fátima in Portugal following reports that the Virgin Mary has appeared to several children there.
- On July 20, Aleksandr Kerensky becomes pime minister of the Russian provisional government.
- On July 25, a French court convicts Mata Hari, an enchanting Dutch dancer, of spying and sentences her to death in Paris.
- On August 20, French troops break through German lines along an eleven-mile front at Verdun.
- On September 15, Aleksandr Kerensky proclaims Russia a republic.
- On September 17, the German army expels Russian troops from Riga, Latvia, on the Baltic Sea, unsettling Kerensky's provisional government.
- In October, Dutch astronomer Willem de Sitter announces that Albert Einstein's general theory of relativity implies that the universe is expanding.
- On October 24, German and Austrian troops attack Italy in the Battle of Caporetto, driving the Italian army back to the Piave River.

- On November 6, the third Battle of Ypres, in Flanders, ends when Canadian forces capture the town of Passchendaele.
- On November 7, Bolsheviks under Vladimir Lenin, ousts Kerensky's provisional government in Russia.
- On November 9, British foreign secretary Arthur Balfour announces plans for a postwar Jewish homeland in Palestine.
- On November 16, Moscow falls to Bolshevik troops.
- On November 17, British troops take Jaffa, a port in Palestine.
- On December 5, Germany and Russia sign an armistice at Brest Litovsk.
- On December 6, a collision between a French munitions vessel and a Belgian relief ship in the harbor at Halifax, Nova Scotia, causes an explosion that kills more than sixteen hundred people and levels much of the city.
- On December 7, the United States declares war on Austria.
- On December 9, British troops capture Jerusalem, a city sacred to Jews, Christians and Muslims.
- On December 22, the Bolshevik government in Russia opens peace talks with Austria and Germany.

---

## 1918

- In the worst pandemic since the fourteenth century Black Death, Spanish influenza sweeps the globe, killing more than twenty-one million people.
- On January 18, Vladimir Lenin dissolves the Russian Constituent Assembly and proclaims a dictatorship of the proletariat.
- On February 6, the British Parliament extends suffrage to married women over thirty and removes ownership of property as a qualification for suffrage.
- On February 24, Estonia declares independence from Russia.
- On March 3, the Soviet Union and the Central Powers sign the Treaty of Brest Litovsk.
- Allied troops land in Murmansk, in northwestern Russia, claiming that they are there to prevent war materiel from falling into German hands.
- On March 5, the capital of the Soviet Union moves from Petrograd to Moscow.
- On March 21, German troops attack the French and British in the second Battle of the Somme.
- On March 26, Ferdinand Foch becomes supreme commander of the Allied forces in Europe.
- On April 1, the Royal Air Force becomes a branch of the British military.
- On April 22, the Soviet government institutes state control over all foreign trade with Russia.
- On May 7, Romania signs the Treaty of Bucharest with the Central Powers, acknowledging its defeat to the Germans.
- On May 19, Britain imprisons five hundred members of Sinn Fein.

- On May 27, German troops push back Allied forces to capture bridges near Chemin des Dames in the third battle of the Aisne River.

- On July 16, Bolsheviks execute Czar Nicholas II and his family in the provincial town of Ekaterinburg, in the Ural Mountains.

- On August 3, Allied troops occupy Archangel, Russia.

- On August 8, the Allies attack German troops holding the Paris-Amiens railway near Amiens, in northern France.

- On August 15, the United States ends diplomatic relations with the Soviet Union.

- On September 12, American troops take the German salient at Saint-Mihiel.

- On September 18, Great Britain launches its last offensive of the war against the Turks, capturing Beirut and Damascus in October.

- On September 30, Bulgaria surrenders to the Allies, who sense that the Central Powers are near collapse.

- On October 4, the Austrian foreign minister seeks peace under the terms of President Woodrow Wilson's "Fourteen Points."

- On October 6, Poland becomes an independent republic, but Russian troops reconquer Poland as the German army retreats.

- On October 15, Czechoslovakia declares independence from Austria Hungary.

- On October 17, Hungary declares independence from Austria-Hungary.

- On October 24, Italian and British troops drive Austrian forces from Italy in the Battle of Vittorio Veneto.

- On October 31, the Ottoman Empire surrenders, and the Dardenelles reopen to Allied ships.

- On November 9, Kaiser William II abdicates at the insistence of German chancellor Prince Max of Baden, who resigns on the same day.

- On November 11, at 11 A.M., an armistice ends World War I.

- On November 12, the last Hapsburg emperor, Charles I, renounces his throne as ruler of Austria and Hungary.

- On November 14, Tomás Masaryk is elected first president of the Czech republic.

- On November 16, Hungary becomes a republic, led by Mihály Károlyi.

- On November 18, Latvia becomes a republic.

- On November 24, Bosnia, Dalmatia, Croatia, Macedonia, Montenegro, Serbia, and Slovenia proclaim themselves one nation.

- On December 1, Denmark grants Iceland independence, though Denmark maintains the fiction of control of Iceland.

## 1919

- British economist John Maynard Keynes publishes *The Economic Consequences of the Peace.*

- German architect Walter Gropius founds the Bauhaus school in Weimar, Germany, to promote modern ideas of home construction, furnishings, and design.

- On January 5, Soviet troops occupy Vilnius, Lithuania, and two weeks later capture the city of Kaunas.

- On January 16, German soldiers murder Rosa Luxemburg and Karl Liebknecht, who led a Sparticist (communist) uprising against the German government on January 5 in Berlin.

- On January 18, the Paris Peace Conference begins as representatives of the Big Four—Vittorio Emanuele Orlando of Italy, Woodrow Wilson of the United States, David Lloyd George of Great Britain, and Georges Clemenceau of France—gather at Versailles.

- On January 21, an unofficial Irish Parliament convenes when twenty-five Sinn Fein members of the British Parliament boycott the House of Commons and meet separately in Dublin.

- On February 3, White Russian armies, fighting to restore czarist government, defeat the Red Army in a series of clashes in the Caucasus.

- On February 6, a German National Assembly meeting in Weimar creates the framework for a republic.

- On March 1, nationalists declare Korean independence from Japan, but Japanese troops crush them.

- On March 3, Bolshevik leaders and representatives from other European communist parties form the Comintern, or Third International, as a means of coordinating international communist activity.

- On March 11, the Allies agree to deliver food to famished Germans.

- On March 21, Hungarian communist leader Béla Kun seizes power in a coup.

- On March 23, Benito Mussolini founds a new political party in Italy, the Fasci di Combattimento, to counter both communism and liberalism.

- On March 30, Indian nationalist Mohandas K. Gandhi leads a peaceful protest against British rule.

- On April 10, Mexican troops kill revolutionary leader Emiliano Zapata, who had advocated the return of land to the peasants.

- On April 13, troops led by Reginald Dyer kill four hundred and wound twelve hundred peaceful protesters in the northern Indian city of Amritsar.

- On April 20, a Polish army led by Józef Pilsudski captures Vilnius and Kaunas. Poland and Russia clash over control of Lithuania until November 1920.

- On May 4, students in China initiate the May Fourth Movement, protesting the decision of the Paris Peace Conference to cede control of China's Shantung province to Japan.

- On May 29, astronomers confirm Albert Einstein's general theory of relativity.

- On June 21, German sailors manning what remains of Germany's once-powerful navy scuttle the fleet at Scapa Flow, off northern Scotland, to prevent it from falling into Allied hands.

• On June 28, the Allies sign the Treaty of Versailles in the Hall of Mirrors, ending World War I.

• On July 13, British airship, the *R-34* completes the first two-way crossing of the Atlantic.

• On August 4, Romanian troops oust Hungarian leader Béla Kun, ending his 133-day communist rule.

• On August 25, the first international daily air service begins between Paris and London.

• On September 3, following the death of Louis Botha, Jan Smuts becomes prime minister of South Africa.

• On September 10, Austria and the Allies sign the Treaty of Saint-Germain, which sets Austria's borders, prohibits its union with Germany, and forces Austria to recognize the independence of Yugoslavia, Czechoslovakia, Hungary, and Poland.

• On September 23, Italian poet, aviator, and war hero Gabriele D'Annunzio leads a band of Italian nationalists into land claimed by both Italy and Yugoslavia, seizing the port city of Fiume.

• On November 28, voters elect Nancy, Lady Astor, to the British House of Commons. She is the first woman in British history to hold a seat in Parliament.

• On December 8, Polish leader Józef Pilsudski leads an army into Ukraine and Belarus in an attempt to end Poland's 150-year-old border dispute with Russia.

# 1

# THE ARTS

MILLIE JACKSON

*Entries are arranged in chronological order by date of primary source. For entries with one primary source, the entry title is the same as the primary source title. Entries with more than one primary source have an overall entry title, followed by the titles of the primary sources.*

**CHRONOLOGY**

Important Events in the Arts, 1910–1919 . . . . . . . . 2

**PRIMARY SOURCES**

*The Masquerade Dress*
    Robert Henri, 1911 . . . . . . . . . . . . . . . . . . . 9

*O Pioneers!*
    Willa Cather, 1913 . . . . . . . . . . . . . . . . . . . 11

*Ethiopia Awakening*
    Meta Vaux Warrick Fuller, 1914 . . . . . . . . . . . 14

*Modern Dancing*
    Vernon and Irene Castle, 1914 . . . . . . . . . . . . 16

"St. Louis Blues"
    W.C. Handy, 1914. . . . . . . . . . . . . . . . . . . . 18

Debate Over *The Birth of a Nation* . . . . . . . . . . . 24
"Capitalizing Race Hatred"
    *New York Globe*, April 6, 1915
"Reply to the *New York Globe*"
    D.W. Griffith, April 10, 1915

"The Imagining Ear"
    Robert Frost, 1915. . . . . . . . . . . . . . . . . . . 30

Charlie Chaplin as the "Little Tramp"
    Charlie Chaplin, 1915 . . . . . . . . . . . . . . . . . 32

*Boy With Baby Carriage*
    Norman Rockwell, 1916 . . . . . . . . . . . . . . . . 35

"Chicago"
    Carl Sandburg, 1916 . . . . . . . . . . . . . . . . . . 37

*Evening Star, III* . . . . . . . . . . . . . . . . . . . . . 39
    Georgia O'Keeffe, 1917

"Over There"
    George M. Cohan, 1917. . . . . . . . . . . . . . . . . 41

"Mandy"
    Irving Berlin, 1919 . . . . . . . . . . . . . . . . . . . 45

"September, 1918"
    Amy Lowell, 1919 . . . . . . . . . . . . . . . . . . . . 51

"Paper Pills"
    Sherwood Anderson, 1919 . . . . . . . . . . . . . . . 52

*A Poet's Life: Seventy Years in a Changing
    World*
    Harriet Monroe, 1938 . . . . . . . . . . . . . . . . . 55

## Important Events in The Arts, 1910–1919

### 1910

- The Christian Endeavor Group and other organizations seek censorship of all motion pictures that portray kissing.

- The Poetry Society of America is founded at the National Arts Club in New York City.

- On February 28, Russian ballerina Anna Pavlova makes her American debut at the Metropolitan Opera House in New York City.

- On March 18, the Metropolitan Opera presents its first production of an opera by an American composer, Frederick Shepherd Converse's *The Pipe of Desire.*

- On March 21, Gustav Mahler conducts for the last time at the Metropolitan Opera.

- On March 28, Pablo Picasso's first one-man show opens at Alfred Stieglitz's 291 gallery in New York City.

- On April 1, some two thousand people attend the opening of the Exhibition of Independent Artists in New York City. The show continues through April 28.

- On June 20, Fanny Brice makes her debut in the *Ziegfeld Follies.*

- On November 3, the Chicago Grand Opera opens with a production of Giuseppe Verdi's *Aida.*

- On November 7, Victor Herbert's operetta *Naughty Marietta* premieres at the New York Theatre.

- On December 10, in New York City Ruth St. Denis opens in *Egypta,* a play that features the modern dances she has based on traditional Eastern dance forms.

- Giacomo Puccini's *La Fanciulla del West* (The Girl of the Golden West), based on David Belasco's play of the same name, becomes the first opera to have its world premiere at the Metropolitan Opera House in New York City.

**MOVIES:** *As It Is in Life,* directed by D. W. Griffith, starring Mary Pickford; *Dr. Lafleur's Theory,* starring Maurice Costello and Clara Kimball Young; *The Fire Chief's Daughter,* starring Kathlyn Williams; *His Trust/His Trust Fulfilled,* directed by D. W. Griffith; *In the Days of the Thundering Herd,* starring Tom Mix; *A Romance of the Western Hills,* directed by D. W. Griffith, starring Mary Pickford; *The Saloon Next Door, Ye Vengeful Vagabonds.*

**FICTION:** Mary Austin, *The Basket Woman;* Finley Peter Dunne, *Mr. Dooley Says;* Hamlin Garland, *Other Main-*

*Travelled Roads;* Joel Chandler Harris, *Uncle Remus and the Little Boy;* O. Henry, *Strictly Business;* Robert Herrick, *A Life for a Life;* Henry James, *The Finer Grain;* Owen Johnson, *The Varmint;* Jack London, *Burning Daylight;* Clarence Mulford, *Hopalong Cassidy;* David Graham Phillips, *The Husband's Story;* Anne Douglas Sedgwick, *Franklin Winslow Kane;* Edith Wharton, *Tales of Men and Ghosts.*

**POETRY:** Robert Underwood Johnson, *Saint-Gaudens, an Ode;* Edwin Arlington Robinson, *The Town Down the River.*

**POPULAR SONGS:** "Ah, Sweet Mystery of Life," by Victor Herbert; "Any Little Girl That's a Nice Little Girl Is the Right Little Girl for Me," by Fred Fisher and Thomas Gray; "Call Me Up Some Rainy Afternoon," by Irving Berlin; "Come, Josephine, in My Flying Machine," by Fred Fisher and Alfred Bryan; "Down by the Old Mill Stream," by Tell Taylor; "Dynamite Rag," by Russel Robinson; "Every Girl Loves Me but the Girl I Love," by Herbert Ingraham and Beth Slater Whitson; "Grizzly Bear," by Irving Berlin; "Heaven Will Protect the Working Girl," by A. Baldwin Sloane; "Hilarity Rag," by James Scott; "I'm Falling in Love with Someone," by Victor Herbert and Rida Johnson Young; "Let Me Call You Sweetheart," by Leo Friedman and Beth Slater Whitson; "Lovey Joe," by Joe Jordan; "Play that Barber Shop Chord," by Lewis F. Muir and William Tracey; "Put Your Arms Around Me, Honey," by Albert Von Tilzer and Junie McCree; "Stoptime Rag," by Scott Joplin; "Under the Yum Yum Tree," by Harry Von Tilzer and Andrew B. Sterling.

### 1911

- *Mother* by Kathleen Norris, *The Harvester* by Gene Stratton Porter, and *The Winning of Barbara Worth* by Harold Bell Wright are the best-sellers of 1911.

- The Irish Players from the Abbey Theatre in Dublin tour the United States. Their repertoire includes John Millington Synge's *The Playboy of the Western World.*

- Pennsylvania becomes the first state to create a board of motion-picture censors.

- On March 21, the Winter Garden Theatre opens at Broadway and 51st Street in New York City.

- On April 22, *Variety* reports that vaudeville-theater owner Marcus Loew has secured backing, largely from the Shubert organization, to expand his chain of theaters and equip them for showing movies.

- On May 23, President William Howard Taft dedicates the New York Public Library.

- On August 8, *Pathé's Weekly,* the first newsreel made in America (produced in New Jersey by the French-owned Pathé company), is released and shown in movie theaters.

- On December 9, John Philip Sousa and his band conclude their year-long world tour with a concert at the five-thousand-seat Hippodrome in New York City. The tour has popularized American marching music.

- On December 19, the Association of American Painters and Sculptors is founded.

**MOVIES:** *Artful Kate,* directed by Thomas Ince, starring Mary Pickford; *Bronco Billy's Adventure* and *Enoch Arden,* directed by D. W. Griffith; *The Fisher-Maid,* directed by Thomas Ince, starring Mary Pickford; *From the Manger to the Cross; A Girlish Impulse,* starring Florence Lawrence; *In the Sultan's Garden,* directed by Thomas Ince, starring Mary Pickford; *A Knight of the Road,* directed by D. W. Griffith; *The Last Drop of Water,* directed by D. W. Griffith; *The Lonedale Operator,* directed by D. W. Griffith, starring Blanche Sweet; *A Tale of Two Cities.*

**FICTION:** Frances Hodgson Burnett, *The Secret Garden;* Margaret Deland, *The Iron Woman;* Theodore Dreiser, *Jennie Gerhardt;* Edna Ferber, *Dawn O'Hara;* Zona Gale, *Mothers to Men;* Hamlin Garland, *Victor Ollnee's Discipline;* Ellen Glasgow, *The Miller of Old Church;* O. Henry, *Sixes and Sevens;* Robert Herrick, *The Healer;* Owen Johnson, *Stover at Yale;* Mary Johnston, *The Long Roll;* Jack London, *South Sea Tales;* Kathleen Norris, *Mother;* David Graham Phillips, *The Conflict;* Gene Stratton-Porter, *The Harvester;* Edith Wharton, *Ethan Frome;* Harold Bell Wright, *The Winning of Barbara Worth.*

**POETRY:** Ezra Pound, *Canzoni;* George Sterling, *The House of Orchids;* Sara Teasdale, *Helen of Troy.*

**POPULAR SONGS:** "Alexander's Ragtime Band," by Irving Berlin; "All Alone," by Harry Von Tilzer and Will Dillon; "Everybody's Doin' It Now," by Irving Berlin; "Felicity Rag," by Scott Hayden; "Hello, Central, Give Me 603," by Harry Von Tilzer; "I Want a Girl Just Like the Girl that Married Dear Old Dad," by Harry Von Tilzer and Will Dillon; "If You Talk in Your Sleep, Don't Mention My Name," by Nat D. Ayer and A. Seymour Brown; "The Little Millionaire," by George M. Cohan; "Moontime Is Spoontime," by Paul Pratt; "Novelty Rag," by May Aufderheide; "Oh, You Beautiful Doll," by Nat D. Ayer and A. Seymour Brown; "The Rag-time Violin," by Irving Berlin; "Red Rose Rag," by Percy Wenrich; "A Ring on the Finger Is Worth Two on the Phone," by George W. Meyer and Jack Mahoney; "Whirlwind Rag," by Russel Robinson.

## 1912

- Zane Grey's *Riders of the Purple Sage* is the year's best-seller.

- The Little Theater in Chicago and the Toy Theater in Boston, the first influential little theaters in America, are founded.

- A revival of George M. Cohan's 1906 hit musical, *Forty-Five Minutes from Broadway,* opens in New York City.

- The Dramatists Guild is founded in New York City.

- On March 14, Horatio Parker's opera *Mona,* winner of the Metropolitan Opera's ten thousand dollar prize for the best new American opera, premieres in New York City.

- On July 22, the first of the Shuberts' annual *Passing Show* musical revues opens at the Winter Garden Theater in New York City.

- In August, Alfred Stieglitz devotes an issue of his periodical *Camera Work* to modern art, including Gertrude Stein's word portraits of artists Henri Matisse and Pablo Picasso.

- On September 1, in Los Angeles the one-thousand-seat Walker Theatre opens—a theater devoted exclusively to showing movies (admission prices range from ten to twenty-five cents).

- On September 5, *Queen Elizabeth,* a French feature film starring Sarah Bernhardt, opens in Marcus Loew's New York City movie theaters—after Loew pays twenty five thousand dollars for the American rights to the movie. It is the first 4-reel movie, running one hour.

- On September 23, the first Keystone Comedy movie, the split-reel *Cohen Collects a Debt* and *The Water Nymph,* directed by Mack Sennett, is released.

- The first issue of *Poetry: A Magazine of Verse,* edited by Harriet Monroe, is published in Chicago, with expatriate Ezra Pound as overseas editor. The magazine is dedicated to publishing the work of American poets.

**MOVIES:** *The Bearded Bandit; Custer's Last Raid,* directed by Thomas Ince; *Father's Flirtation; A Feud in the Kentucky Hills,* directed by D. W. Griffith; *A Girl and Her Trust,* directed by D. W. Griffith, starring Mary Pickford; *The Indian Massacre,* directed by Thomas Ince; *Lena and the Geese,* directed by D. W. Griffith, starring Mary Pickford; *The Musketeers of Pig Alley,* directed by D. W. Griffith; *The Old Actor,* directed by D. W. Griffith; *An Unseen Enemy,* directed by D. W. Griffith, starring Lillian Gish; *War on the Plains,* directed by Thomas Ince.

**FICTION:** Mary Austin, *A Woman of Genius;* Willa Cather, *Alexander's Bridge;* Theodore Dreiser, *The Financier;* Sui Sin Far, *Mrs. Spring Fragrance;* Dorothy Canfield Fisher, *The Squirrel Cage;* Zane Grey, *Riders of the Purple Sage;* James Weldon Johnson, *The Autobiography of an Ex-Colored Man;* Mary Johnston, *Cease Firing;* Jack London, *Smoke Bellew;* David Graham Phillips, *The Price She Paid;* Edith Wharton, *The Reef.*

**POETRY:** Robinson Jeffers, *Flagons and Apples;* William Ellery Leonard, *The Vaunt of Man;* Vachel Lindsay, *Rhymes to be Traded for Bread;* Amy Lowell, *A Dome of Many-Coloured Glass;* Ezra Pound, *Ripostes;* Elinor Wylie, *Incidental Numbers.*

**POPULAR SONGS:** "And the Green Grass Grew All Around," by Harry Von Tilzer and William Jerome; "Be My Little Baby Bumble Bee," by Henry I. Marshall and Stanley Murphy; "The Bunny Hug," by Harry Von Tilzer; "Clover Blossoms Rag," by E. J. Stark Jr.; "Everybody Two-Step," by Wallie Herzer and Earl C. Jones; "Hitchy Koo," by Lewis F. Muir, Maurice Abrahams, and L. Wolfe Gilbert; "It's a Long, Long Way to Tipperary," by Jack Judge and Harry H. Williams; "Melancholy (My Melancholy Baby)," by Ernie Burnett and George A. Norton; "On the Eight O'Clock Train," by Russel Robinson; "Scott Joplin's New Rag," by Scott Joplin; "The Sweetheart of Sigma Chi," by Dudleigh Vernor and Byron D. Stokes; "That Demon Rag," by Russell Smith; "That Mysterious Rag," by Irving Berlin; "The Turkey Trot," by Ribe Danmark (J. Bodewalt Lampe); "Waiting for the Robert E. Lee," by Lewis F. Muir and L. Wolfe Gilbert; "When Irish Eyes Are Smiling," by Ernest R. Ball, Chauncey Olcott, and George Graff Jr.; "Wise Old Moon," by Artie Matthews.

## 1913

- Eleanor Hodgman Porter's *Pollyanna* and Gene Stratton Porter's *Laddie* are the best-sellers of 1913.

- The Jesse L. Lasky Feature Play Company (later Paramount Pictures) is founded in Hollywood, California.

- The New York Motion Picture Company sends director-producer Thomas Ince to California to make Westerns.

- On February 17, the International Exhibition of Modern Art, commonly called the Armory Show, opens in New York City, with more than thirteen hundred paintings and sculptures. For many Americans the show is their first opportunity to see works of avant-garde modern art.

- On March 24, the million-dollar, eighteen-hundred-seat Palace Theatre opens on Seventh Avenue between 46th and 47th Streets in New York City, charging a top ticket price of two dollars, twice that of other vaudeville theaters.

- On April 1, with admission costing as much as one dollar a ticket, *Quo Vadis,* an eight-reel movie made in Italy, opens at the Astor Theatre in New York City, beginning a twenty-two-week run and fueling Americans' desires for longer movies.

- On April 13, Arturo Toscanini conducts his first concert in America, Beethoven's *Ninth Symphony* at the Metropolitan Opera House in New York City.

- On May 26, the Actors Equity Association is founded.

- On June 7, in New York City more than one thousand striking silk-mill workers from Paterson, New Jersey, march up Fifth Avenue to Madison Square Garden, where they stage a political pageant intended to dramatize the plight of industrial workers, with sets by theatrical designer Robert Edmond Jones and painted under the direction of artist John Sloan.

- On June 20, *Variety* reports that "the feature-length movie is now an establishment. . . . The future will see little else."

- On October 1, Director D. W. Griffith leaves Biograph, the company for which he has made more than four hundred movies in five and a half years.

**MOVIES:** *The Adventures of Kathlyn* (serial), starring Kathlyn Williams; *The Battle of Gettysburg,* directed by Thomas Ince; *Caprice,* starring Mary Pickford; *In the Bishop's Carriage,* starring Mary Pickford; *The New York Hat,* directed by D. W. Griffith, starring Mary Pickford; *The Prisoner of Zenda,* starring James K. Hackett; *Tess of the D'Urbervilles,* starring Minnie Maddern Fiske; *A Versatile Villain.*

**FICTION:** Willa Cather, *O Pioneers!;* Ellen Glasgow, *Virginia;* O. Henry, *Rolling Stones;* Robert Herrick, *One Woman's Life;* Eleanor H. Porter, *Pollyanna;* Gene Stratton Porter, *Laddie;* Edith Wharton, *The Custom of the Country.*

**POETRY:** Witter Bynner, *Tiger;* Paul Laurence Dunbar, *Complete Poems;* John Gould Fletcher, *Fire and Wine;* Robert Frost, *A Boy's Will;* Vachel Lindsay, *General William Booth Enters into Heaven and Other Poems;* William Carlos Williams, *The Tempers.*

**POPULAR SONGS:** "American Beauty Rag," by Joseph Lamb; "Danny Boy," by Fred E. Weatherly; "The Dogin' Rag," by Rob Hampton; "Don't Blame It All on Broadway," by Bert Grant, Harry Williams, and Joe Young; "The International Rag," by Irving Berlin; "Junk Man Rag," by Luckey Roberts; "Kismet Rag," by Scott Hayden; "Memphis Blues," by W. C. Handy; "On the Old Fall River Line," by Harry Von Tilzer, William Jerome, and Andrew B. Sterling; "Peg o' My Heart," by Fred Fisher and Alfred Bryan; "Sailing Down the Chesapeake Bay," by George Botsford and Jean C. Havez; "Snookey Ookums," by Irving Berlin; "The Trail of the Lonesome Pine," by Harry Carroll and Ballard Macdonald; "When I Lost You," by Irving Berlin; "You Made Me Love You (I Didn't Want to Do It)," by James V. Monaco and Joseph McCarthy; "You've Got Your Mother's Big Blue Eyes," by Irving Berlin.

## 1914

- Edgar Rice Burroughs's *Tarzan of the Apes,* Booth Tarkington's *Penrod,* and Harold Bell Wright's *The Eyes of the World* are the best-sellers of 1914.

- Heiress and sculptor Gertrude Vanderbilt Whitney founds the Whitney Studio Club (later the Whitney Museum) in New York City.

- On February, actor Charlie Chaplin's first movie *Making a Living* premieres.

- Marie Dressler and Charlie Chaplin star in the first six-reel movie (90 minutes) *Tillie's Punctured Romance.*

- On February 13, the American Society of Composers, Authors, and Publishers (ASCAP) is founded in New York City.

- In March, *Mabel's Strange Predicament,* the Keystone comedy that introduces Charlie Chaplin's Little Tramp character, is released.

- On April 1, the Strand Theater opens in New York, designed as a vaudeville and movie house for upscale audiences.

- On April 27, Vernon and Irene Castle begin their twenty-eight-day tour of thirty-two cities, which culminates in a national dance competition held in Madison Square Garden, New York City.

- On June 4, Finnish composer Jean Sibelius makes his first American appearance, conducting the world premiere of his symphonic poem *Oceanides* at a music festival in Norwalk, Connecticut.

- On November 3, the first American show of African sculpture opens at Stieglitz's 291 gallery in New York City.

- On December 3, the Isadorables, six young European dancers trained by Isadora Duncan, appear at Carnegie Hall in New York City, after escaping with her from war-torn Paris.

- On December 8, Irving Berlin's first musical, *Watch Your Step,* starring Vernon and Irene Castle, opens on Broadway.

**MOVIES:** *The Avenging Conscience,* directed by D. W. Griffith; *The Bargain,* directed by Thomas Ince, starring William S. Hart; *The Battle of the Sexes,* directed by D. W. Griffith, starring Lillian Gish; *Between Showers,* starring Charlie Chaplin; *The Call of the North,* directed by Oscar Apfel and Cecil B. DeMille; *Cinderella,* starring Mary Pickford and Owen Moore; *Dough and Dynamite,* starring

Charlie Chaplin; *The Eagle's Mate,* starring Mary Pickford; *The Escape,* directed by D. W. Griffith, starring Donald Crisp, Blanche Sweet, Mae Marsh, and Robert Harron; *The Exploits of Elaine* (serial), starring Pearl White; *Hearts Adrift,* starring Mary Pickford; *Home, Sweet Home,* directed by D. W. Griffith, starring Lillian and Dorothy Gish; *The Horrors of War, In the Latin Quarter,* starring Constance Talmadge; *Judith of Bethulia,* directed by D. W. Griffith; *Kid Auto Races at Venice, California,* starring Charlie Chaplin; *Mabel's Strange Predicament,* starring Charlie Chaplin and Mabel Normand; *The Man from Home,* directed by Cecil B. DeMille; *The Perils of Pauline* (serial), starring Pearl White; *Pool Sharks,* starring W. C. Fields; *The Squaw Man,* directed by Cecil B. DeMille; *Tess of the Storm Country,* starring Mary Pickford; *Tillie's Punctured Romance,* directed by Mack Sennett, starring Marie Dressler, Charlie Chaplin, and Mabel Normand; *The Virginian,* directed by Cecil B. DeMille; *War Is Hell; Wildflower,* starring Marguerite Clark; *The Wrath of the Gods,* directed by Thomas Ince.

**FICTION:** Edgar Rice Burroughs, *Tarzan of the Apes;* George Washington Cable, *Gideon's Band;* Theodore Dreiser, *The Titan;* Hamlin Garland, *The Forester's Daughter;* Robert Herrick, *Clark's Field;* Jack London, *The Mutiny on the Elsinore;* Frank Norris, *Vandover and the Brute;* Booth Tarkington, *Penrod;* Harold Bell Wright, *The Eyes of the World.*

**POETRY:** Conrad Aiken, *Earth Triumphant;* Emily Dickinson, *The Single Hound;* Robert Frost, *North of Boston;* Joyce Kilmer, *Trees and Other Poems;* Vachel Lindsay, *The Congo and Other Poems;* Amy Lowell, *Sword-Blades and Poppy Seed;* James Oppenheim, *Songs for the New Age;* Gertrude Stein, *Tender Buttons.*

**POPULAR SONGS:** "Aba Daba Honeymoon," by Arthur Fields and Walter Donovan; "The Boston Stop—Hesitation Waltz," by Henry Lodge; "By the Beautiful Sea," by Harry Carroll and Harold R. Atteridge; "Chevy Chase (A Rag)," by Eubie Blake; "Chicken Tango," by E.J. Stark Jr.; "Fascination Waltz," by Henry Lodge; "Fizz Water (A Rag)," by Eubie Blake; "Hot House Rag," by Paul Pratt; "The Land of My Best Girl," by Harry Carroll and Ballard Macdonald; "The Lily Rag," by Charles Thompson; "Missouri Waltz," by Frederick Knight Logan and J.R. Shannon; "Oh! You Turkey—a Rag Trot," by Henry Lodge; "Play a Simple Melody," by Irving Berlin; "St. Louis Blues," by W. C. Handy; "The Syncopated Walk," by Irving Berlin; "They Didn't Believe Me," by Jerome Kern and Herbert Reynolds; "When You Wore a Tulip and I Wore a Big Red Rose," by Percy Wenrich and Jack Mahoney; "Yellow Dog Blues," by W.C. Handy.

# 1915

• *Michael O'Halloran* by Gene Stratton Porter is the best-seller of 1915.

• The year's most popular song spells out "Mother."

• Americans use the term "Victrola" to describe all record players after the Victor Talking Machine Company refines Edison's phonograph into its Victrola with a built-in horn speaker.

• Modern dancers Ruth St. Denis and Ted Shawn, who were married on August 13, 1914, found the Denishawn School of Dancing in Los Angeles.

• On February 8, despite protests by the National Association for the Advancement of Colored People (NAACP), D.W. Griffith's twelve-reel movie *The Birth of a Nation,* about the Ku Klux Klan in the post-Reconstruction South, has its world premiere at Clune's Theater in Los Angeles.

• On March 20, the Russian Symphony Orchestra plays the premiere performance of Aleksandr Scriabin's symphony *Prometheus* at Carnegie Hall in New York City. The performance includes the projection of color images onto a screen.

• On May 21, *Variety* notes that "the bottom has apparently fallen out" of the market for one-reel movies.

• In summer, Thomas Ince's Kay Bee studio, Mack Sennett's Keystone studio, and D.W. Griffith's Reliance-Majestic studio are combined to form the Triangle Film Corporation.

• On July 15, the Provincetown Players give their first performance: a double-bill production of *Constancy* by Neith Boyce and *Suppressed Desires* by Susan Glaspell and George Cram Cook, in Provincetown, Massachusetts.

**MOVIES:** *The Arab,* directed by Cecil B. DeMille; *The Bank,* directed by and starring Charlie Chaplin; *The Battle Cry of Peace,* starring Norma Talmadge; *The Birth of a Nation,* directed by D.W. Griffith, starring Lillian Gish, Mae Marsh, and Miriam Cooper; *The Captive,* directed by Cecil B. DeMille, starring Blanche Sweet; *Carmen,* directed by Cecil B. DeMille, starring Geraldine Farrar and Wallace Reid; *The Champion,* starring and directed by Charlie Chaplin; *Chimmie Fadden,* directed by Cecil B. DeMille, starring Victor Moore; *The Coward,* directed by Thomas Ince; *Esmeralda,* starring Mary Pickford; *The Fairy and the Waif,* starring Mary Miles Minter; *A Fool There Was,* starring Theda Bara; *The Girl of the Golden West,* directed by Cecil B. DeMille; *The Goose Girl,* starring Marguerite Clark; *Graustark,* starring Francis X. Bushman; *Hell's Hinges,* directed by Thomas Ince, starring William S. Hart; *His New Job,* starring and directed by Charlie Chaplin; *The Iron Strain; The Lamb,* starring Douglas Fairbanks; *Mistress Nell,* starring Mary Pickford; *My Valet,* directed by Mack Sennett; *The New Exploits of Elaine* (serial), starring Pearl White; *A Night Out,* directed by and starring Charlie Chaplin; *Rags,* starring Mary Pickford; *The Romance of Elaine* (serial), starring Pearl White; *The Tramp,* directed by and starring Charlie Chaplin; *The Warrens of Virginia,* directed by Cecil B. DeMille, starring Blanche Sweet; *The Whirl of Life,* starring Vernon and Irene Castle; *The Wild Goose Chase,* directed by Cecil B. DeMille, starring Ina Claire; *Work,* directed by and starring Charlie Chaplin.

**FICTION:** Willa Cather, *The Song of the Lark;* Irvin S. Cobb, *Old Judge Priest;* Theodore Dreiser, *The "Genius";* Dorothy Canfield Fisher, *The Bent Twig;* Jack London, *The Scarlet Plague;* Ernest Poole, *The Harbor;* Booth Tarkington, *The Turmoil;* Harry Leon Wilson, *Ruggles of Red Gap.*

**POETRY:** Stephen Vincent Benét, *Five Men and Pompey;* John Gould Fletcher, *Irradiations: Sand and Spray;* Ring W. Lardner, *Bib Ballads;* Archibald MacLeish, *Songs for a Summer's Day;* Edgar Lee Masters, *Spoon River Anthology;*

John G. Neihardt, *The Song of Hugh Glass;* Ezra Pound, *Cathay;* Sara Teasdale, *Rivers to the Sea.*

**POPULAR SONGS:** "Agitation Rag," by Shelton Brooks; "Babes in the Wood," by Jerome Kern; "Down Among the Sheltering Palms," by Abe Olman and James Brockman; "The Girl on the Magazine Cover," by Irving Berlin; "Hesitating Blues," by W.C. Handy; "I Didn't Raise My Boy to Be a Soldier," by Al Piantadosi and Alfred Bryan; "I Love a Piano," by Irving Berlin; "The Jelly Roll Blues," by Jelly Roll Morton; "Joe Turner Blues," by W.C. Handy; "The Little House Upon the Hill," by Harry Puck, Ballard Macdonald, and Joe Goodwin; "Memories," by Gus Kahn and Egbert Van Alstyne; "Pack Up Your Troubles in Your Old Kitbag and Smile, Smile, Smile" [British], by Felix Powell and George Asaf; "There's a Broken Heart for Every Light on Broadway," by Fred Fisher and Howard Johnson; "Weary Blues," by Artie Matthews; "When I Leave the World Behind," by Irving Berlin; "You'll Always Be the Same Sweet Girl," by Harry Von Tilzer and Andrew B. Sterling.

## 1916

- Edgar A. Guest's *A Heap o' Livin',* and Harold Bell Wright's *When a Man's a Man* are the best-sellers of 1916.

- Victor Records enjoys success recording skits by vaudeville comedians.

- From January to May, Sergei Diaghilev's Ballets Russes performs at the Metropolitan Opera House in New York City.

- In spring, Charlie Chaplin signs with Mutual for $10,000 a week, plus a $150,000 signing bonus.

- On April 12, Russian ballet dancer Vaslav Nijinsky makes his American debut.

- On June 24, Mary Pickford negotiates a new contract with Adolph Zukor's Famous Players Company for more than $1 million over the next two years.

- On July 28, at the Wharf Theater in Provincetown, Massachusetts, the Provincetown Players stage *Bound East for Cardiff,* the first production of a Eugene O'Neill play.

- On December 5, the Society of Independent Artists is established.

**MOVIES:** *The Apostle of Vengeance,* starring William S. Hart; *Behind the Screen,* directed by and starring Charlie Chaplin; *Civilization,* directed by Thomas Ince; *The Dream Girl,* directed by Cecil B. DeMille; *The Eternal Grind,* starring Mary Pickford; *The Fall of a Nation; Fatty and Mabel Adrift,* directed by Mack Sennett, starring Fatty Arbuckle and Mabel Normand; *The Floorwalker,* directed by and starring Charlie Chaplin; *The Good Bad Man,* starring Douglas Fairbanks; *The Heart of Nora Flynn,* directed by Cecil B. DeMille; *Hulda from Holland,* starring Mary Pickford; *Intolerance,* directed by D.W. Griffith, starring Lillian Gish and Mae Marsh; *Less Than the Dust,* starring Mary Pickford; *Maria Rosa,* directed by Cecil B. DeMille, starring Geraldine Farrar and Wallace Reid; *One A.M.,* directed by and starring Charlie Chaplin; *Patria,* starring Irene Castle; *The Pawnshop,* directed by and starring Charlie Chaplin; *Pearl of the Army,* starring Pearl White; *Poor Little Pep-*

*pina,* starring Mary Pickford; *The Rink,* directed by and starring Charlie Chaplin; *Temptation,* directed by Cecil B. DeMille, starring Geraldine Farrar; *The Trail of the Lonesome Pine,* directed by Cecil B. DeMille; *The Vagabond,* directed by and starring Charlie Chaplin; *The Vixen,* starring Theda Bara; *War Brides,* starring Alla Nazimova and Richard Barthelmess; *The Wharf Rat,* starring Mae Marsh.

**FICTION:** Sherwood Anderson, *Windy McPherson's Son;* James Branch Cabell, *The Certain Hour;* Margaret Deland, *The Rising Tide;* Hamlin Garland, *They of the High Trails;* Ellen Glasgow, *Life and Gabriella;* William Dean Howells, *The Leather-wood God;* Ring W. Lardner, *You Know Me Al;* Booth Tarkington, *Seventeen;* Mark Twain, *The Mysterious Stranger;* Edith Wharton, *Xingu and Other Stories;* Harold Bell Wright, *When a Man's a Man.*

**POETRY:** Conrad Aiken, *Turns and Movies;* John Gould Fletcher, *Goblins and Pagodas;* H.D., *Sea Garden;* Robert Frost, *Mountain Interval;* Edgar A. Guest, *A Heap o' Livin';* Robinson Jeffers, *Californians;* Sarah Orne Jewett, *Verses;* Alfred Kreymborg, *Mushrooms;* Amy Lowell, *Men, Women, and Ghosts;* Edgar Lee Masters, *Songs and Satires;* James Oppenheim, *War and Laughter;* Ezra Pound, *Lustra;* Edwin Arlington Robinson, *The Man Against the Sky;* Carl Sandburg, *Chicago Poems;* Alan Seeger, *Poems.*

**POPULAR SONGS:** "Beale Street Blues," by W.C. Handy; "Bugle Call Rag," by Eubie Blake; "Chromatic Rag," by Will Held; "Everybody Rag with Me," by Gus Kahn and Grace LeBoy; "Have a Heart," by Jerome Kern and P.G. Wodehouse; "Home-sickness Blues," by Cliff Hess; "Mama and Papa Blues," by James P. Johnson; "Mother (Her Soldier Boy)," by Sigmund Romberg and Rida Johnson Young; "Nola," by Felix Arndt; "Oh! How She Could Yacki, Hacki, Wicki, Wacki, Woo," by Albert Von Tilzer, Stanley Murphy, and Charles McCarron; "Poor Butterfly," by Raymond Hubbell and John L. Golden; "Pretty Baby," by Gus Kahn, Tony Jackson, and Egbert Van Alstyne; "Prosperity Rag," by James Scott; "Springtime Rag," by Paul Pratt; "There's a Little Bit of Bad in Every Good Little Girl," by Fred Fisher and Grant Clarke; "Twelfth Street Rag," by Euday L. Bowman; "You Belong to Me," by Victor Herbert and Harry B. Smith.

## 1917

- The Supreme Court rules in favor of ASCAP in a test case concerning the payment of royalties to songwriters for public performances of their works.

- Eddie Cantor and Will Rogers make their debuts in the *Ziegfeld Follies.*

- The New York Philharmonic Orchestra celebrates its seventy-fifth anniversary.

- Seventy-two-year-old French actress Sarah Bernhardt makes her last tour of the United States, playing (among other roles) Portia in *The Merchant of Venice.*

- On April 1, Victor becomes the first record company to release a recording of jazz, by the (all-white) Original Dixieland Jazz Band.

- On April 9, the opening day of its first exhibition, the Society of Independent Artists rejects Marcel Duchamp's *Foun-*

*tain,* a urinal that he entered as sculpture under the name of Richard Mutt.

- On April 11, Isadora Duncan, draped in an American flag, performs a modern-dance work called *Star-Spangled Banner* at the Metropolitan Opera House in New York City.
- On April 14, President Woodrow Wilson appoints a Committee on Public Information (also known as the Creel Committee, after its head, George Creel) to design a code for voluntary censorship of media and arts during the war.
- On October 27, sixteen-year-old Russian prodigy Jascha Heifetz makes his American debut at Carnegie Hall in New York City.
- On November 10, the Philadelphia Orchestra announces that it will play no works by German composers for the duration of the war.
- On November 14, acting on orders originating with Secretary of War Newton D. Baker, the mayor of New Orleans closes Storyville—the city's red-light district, where many African American musicians are employed—prompting an exodus of blues and jazz artists to northern cities.
- On December 25, the Jesse Lynch Williams comedy *Why Marry?* opens at the Astor Theatre in New York City.

**MOVIES:** *The Adopted Son,* starring Francis X. Bushman; *Cleopatra,* starring Theda Bara; *The Clodhopper; The Cure,* directed by and starring Charlie Chaplin; *The Fall of the Romanoffs; The Gun Fighter,* directed by and starring William S. Hart; *The Immigrant,* directed by and starring Charlie Chaplin; *Joan, The Woman,* directed by Cecil B. DeMille, starring Geraldine Farrar; *Just Nuts,* starring Harold Lloyd and Bebe Daniels; *The Little American,* directed by Cecil B. DeMille, starring Mary Pickford; *A Modern Musketeer,* starring Douglas Fairbanks; *The Poor Little Rich Girl,* starring Mary Pickford; *Rebecca of Sunnybrook Farm,* starring Mary Pickford; *A Romance of the Redwoods,* directed by Cecil B. DeMille, starring Mary Pickford; *The Spirit of '76; Thais,* starring Mary Garden; *The Woman God Forgot,* directed by Cecil B. DeMille, starring Geraldine Farrar.

**FICTION:** Sherwood Anderson, *Marching Men;* Mary Austin, *The Ford;* James Branch Cabell, *The Cream of the Jest;* Abraham Cahan, *The Rise of David Levinsky;* John Dos Passos, *One Man's Initiation;* Edna Ferber, *Fanny Herself;* Henry James, *The Ivory Tower;* Ring W. Lardner, *Gullible's Travels;* Jack London, *Jerry of the Islands;* David Graham Phillips, *Susan Lenox: Her Fall and Rise;* Ernest Poole, *His Family;* Upton Sinclair, *King Coal;* Edith Wharton, *Summer.*

**POETRY:** Conrad Aiken, *Nocturne of a Remembered Spring;* Witter Bynner, *Grenstone Poems;* T.S. Eliot, *Prufrock and Other Observations;* Edgar A. Guest, *Just Folks;* James Weldon Johnson, *Fifty Years and Other Poems;* Vachel Lindsay, *The Chinese Nightingale and Other Poems;* Archibald MacLeish, *Tower of Ivory;* Edna St. Vincent Millay, *Renascence and Other Poems;* Edwin Arlington Robinson, *Merlin;* Sara Teasdale, *Love Songs;* William Carlos Williams, *Al Que Quiere!*

**POPULAR SONGS:** "Au Revoir, But Not Goodbye, Soldier Boy," by Albert Von Tilzer and Lew Brown; "The Bells of St. Mary's," by A. Emmett Adams and Douglas Furber; "Dance and Grow Thin," by Irving Berlin; "The Darktown Strutter's Ball," by Shelton Brooks; "Efficiency Rag," by James Scott; "For Me and My Gal," by George W. Meyer, Edgar Leslie, and E. Ray Goetz; "Gum Shoe Fox Trot," by E. J. Stark Jr.; "Hail, Hail, The Gang's All Here," by Theodore Morse, Arthur Sullivan, and D.A. Morse; "Harlem Strut," by James P. Johnson; "Magnetic Rag," by Scott Joplin; "Oh, Johnny! Oh!," by Abe Oleman and Ed Rose; "Over There," by George M. Cohan; "The Ragtime Volunteers Are Off to War," by James F. Hanley and Ballard Macdonald; "Smiles," by Lee S. Roberts and J. Will Callahan; "Tiger Rag," by the Original Dixieland Jass Band; "'Till the Clouds Roll By," by Jerome Kern and P. G. Wodehouse; "Till We Meet Again," by Richard A. Whiting and Ray Egan; "When the Boys Come Home," by Oley Speaks and John Hay; "Where Do We Go from Here?," by Percy Wenrich; "Where the Morning Glories Grow," by Richard A. Whiting, Gus Kahn, and Ray Egan; "Whose Little Heart Are You Breaking Now?," by Irving Berlin; "Why Keep Me Waiting So Long?," by Tony Jackson.

## 1918

- Edward Streeter's *Dere Mable,* Henry Adams' *The Education of Henry Adams,* and Zane Grey's *The U.P. Trail* are the best-sellers of 1918.
- Italian operatic tenor Enrico Caruso, who is extremely popular in America, records George M. Cohan's wartime hit "Over There."
- The annual O. Henry Awards are created to honor the short-story writer, who died in 1910.
- Edison Records releases some novelty recordings that include the sounds of a saw mill and chickens.
- The first Pulitzer Prizes are awarded for drama (Jesse Lynch Williams's *Why Marry?*) and fiction (Ernest Poole's *His Family*).
- From February through April, Broadway theaters are closed due to a shortage of coal.
- On February 15, serving as a pilot in the war, dancer Vernon Castle is killed during a training exercise.
- In March, *The Little Review* begins serializing James Joyce's *Ulysses.*
- On March 25, German-born Boston Symphony Orchestra conductor Carl Muck is arrested and imprisoned as an enemy alien.
- On October 16, Congress passes the Alien Act, which allows for the deportation of immigrants and aliens with radical political views. The act is later used to justify the deportation of Muck and the harassment of other German- and Austrian-born artists working in America.
- In December, the Theatre Guild is founded in New York City.
- On December 14, Giacomo Puccini's *Il trittico,* a trilogy of one-act operas—*Il Tabarro, Suor Angelica,* and *Gianni Schicchi*—is given its world premiere at the Metropolitan Opera House in New York City.

**MOVIES:** *Amarilly of Clothes-Line Alley,* starring Mary Pickford; *Beware of Boarders,* directed by Mack Sennett; *A Dog's Life,* directed by and starring Charlie Chaplin; *Fatty in Coney Island,* directed by Mack Sennett, starring Fatty Arbuckle and Buster Keaton; *The Ghost of Rosy Taylor,* starring Mary Miles Minter; *The Great Love,* directed by D. W. Griffith, starring Lillian Gish; *Hearts of the World,* directed by D.W. Griffith, starring Lillian Gish; *Huns Within Our Gates; Johanna Enlists,* starring Mary Pickford; *Mickey,* directed by Mack Sennett, starring Mabel Normand; *Old Wives for New,* directed by Cecil B. DeMille; *One Hundred Percent American,* starring Mary Pickford; *Prunella,* starring Marguerite Clark; *Shoulder Arms,* directed by and starring Charlie Chaplin; *Stella Maris,* starring Mary Pickford; *Tarzan of the Apes,* starring Elmo Lincoln; *Till I Come Back to You,* directed by Cecil B. DeMille; *The Venus Model,* starring Mabel Normand.

**FICTION:** Willa Cather, *My Ántonia;* Theodore Dreiser, *Free and Other Stories;* Mary E. Wilkins Freeman, *Edgewater People;* Zona Gale, *Birth;* Zane Grey, *The U.P. Trail;* Joel Chandler Harris, *Uncle Remus Returns;* Ring W. Lardner, *Treat 'Em Rough;* Jack London, *The Red One;* Ernest Poole, *His Second Wife;* Thorne Smith, *Biltmore Oswald;* Wilbur Daniel Steele, *Land's End;* Edward Streeter, *Dere Mable: Love Letters of a Rookie;* Booth Tarkington, *The Magnificent Ambersons;* Edith Wharton, *The Marne.*

**POETRY:** Sherwood Anderson, *Mid-American Chants;* Stephen Vincent Benét, *Young Adventure;* John Gould Fletcher, *The Tree of Life;* Amy Lowell, *Can Grandes Castle;* Edgar Lee Masters, *Toward the Gulf;* Carl Sandburg, *Cornhuskers;* Margaret Widdemer, *Old Road to Paradise.*

**POPULAR SONGS:** "Beautiful Ohio," by Mary Earl (Robert A. King) and Ballard Macdonald; "The Daughter of Rosie O'Grady," by Walter Donaldson and Monty C. Brice; "Dream On, Little Soldier Boy," by Irving Berlin; "Everybody Knows I Love Him," by Russell Smith; "A Good Man Is Hard to Find," by Eddie Green; "Hinky-Dinky Parlezvous," anonymous; "I'll Say She Does," by Gus Kahn; "I'm Always Chasing Rainbows," by Harry Carroll and Joseph McCarthy; "I'm Gonna Pin a Medal on the Girl I Left Behind," by Irving Berlin; "The Kaiser's Got the Blues," by W.C. Handy; "K-K-K-Katy," by Geoffrey O'Hara; "Oh, How I Hate to Get Up in the Morning," by Irving Berlin; "Rock-a-Bye Your Baby with a Dixie Melody," by Joe Young and Sam M. Lewis; "Snookums Rag," by Charles L. Johnson; "The U.S. Field Artillery March," by John Philip Sousa; "When Alexander Takes His Ragtime Band to France," by Alfred Bryan, Cliff Hess, and Edgar Leslie.

## 1919

- Irving Berlin's song "Oh, How I Hate to Get Up in the Morning" is popular now that the war is over.

- *Maid of Harlem,* an all-African American musical starring Fats Waller, Mamie Smith, Johnny Dunn, and Perry Bradford, is a hit at Lincoln Theater in New York City.

- The U.S. Post Office seizes magazines carrying excerpts from James Joyce's novel *Ulysses* on grounds of obscenity.

- On February 5, United Artists is founded in Hollywood by Charlie Chaplin, Mary Pickford, Douglas Fairbanks, D.W. Griffith, and other investors.

- On April 19, the Theatre Guild opens its first production, Jacinto Benavente's *The Bonds of Interest,* in New York City.

- On August 7, the Actors Equity strike begins, soon including more than two thousand actors, stagehands, and musicians.

- On September 6, the Actors Equity strike is settled, with theatrical management meeting the actors' demands on pay, job security, and control over contracts.

- On October 24, during the opening performance at Capitol Theatre on Broadway, sixty chorus girls dance to George Gershwin's new hit song "Swanee," which Al Jolson also sings in his Winter Garden show a few weeks later.

- On October 31, the Provincetown Players stage Eugene O'Neill's play *The Dreamy Kid* with an all-African American cast.

**MOVIES:** *Broken Blossoms,* directed by D.W. Griffith, starring Lillian Gish and Richard Barthelmess; *Captain Kidd, Jr.,* starring Mary Pickford; *Daddy Long Legs,* starring Mary Pickford; *A Day's Pleasure,* directed by and starring Charlie Chaplin; *Don't Change Your Husband,* directed by Cecil B. DeMille, starring Gloria Swanson; *The Girl Who Stayed at Home,* directed by D.W. Griffith, starring Carol Dempster; *Girls,* starring Marguerite Clark; *Heart o' the Hills,* starring Mary Pickford; *Kathleen Mavourneen,* starring Theda Bara; *Male and Female,* directed by Cecil B. DeMille, starring Gloria Swanson; *The Miracle Man,* starring Lon Chaney; *Sunnyside,* directed by and starring Charlie Chaplin; *True Heart Susie,* directed by D.W. Griffith, starring Lillian Gish.

**FICTION:** Sherwood Anderson, *Winesburg, Ohio;* James Branch Cabell, *Jurgen;* Finley Peter Dunne, *Mr. Dooley on Making a Will;* Ellen Glasgow, *The Builders;* Fannie Hurst, *Humoresque;* Ring W. Lardner, *Own Your Own Home;* Jack London, *On the Makaloa Mat;* Upton Sinclair, *Jimmie Higgins;* Albert Payson Terhune, *Lad: A Dog.*

**POETRY:** T.S. Eliot, *Poems;* Amy Lowell, *Pictures of a Floating World;* Edgar Lee Masters, *Starved Rock;* Ezra Pound, *Quia Pauper Amavi;* John Crowe Ransom, *Poems about God.*

**POPULAR SONGS:** "Alice Blue Gown," by Harry Tierney and Joseph McCarthy; "Bohemia Rag," by Joseph Lamb; "Castle of Dreams," by Harry Tierney and Joseph McCarthy; "Daddy Long Legs," by Harry Ruby, Sam M. Lewis, and Joe Young; "Dardanella," by Fred Fisher; "How You Gonna Keep 'em Down on the Farm," by Walter Donaldson, Sam M. Lewis, and Joe Young; "Indian Summer," by Victor Herbert; "Liberty Loan March," by John Philip Sousa; "The Little Church Around the Corner," by Sigmund Romberg and Alexander Gerber; "Mandy," by Irving Berlin; "Peace and Plenty Rag," by James Scott; "Peggy," by Neil Moret and Harry Williams; "A Pretty Girl Is Like a Melody," by Irving Berlin; "Rose Room," by Art Hickman; "Swanee," by George Gershwin and Irving Caesar; "You Ain't Heard Nothing Yet," by Al Jolson, Gus Kahn, and B. G. De Sylva.

# The Masquerade Dress
Painting

**By:** Robert Henri

**Date:** 1911

**Source:** Henri, Robert. *The Masquerade Dress.* 1911. Available online at http://www.metmuseum.org/collections/view1 .asp?dep=21&full;=0&item;=58%2E157; website home page: http://www.metmuseum.org (accessed November 12, 2002).

**About the Artist:** Robert Henri (1865–1929) was born Robert Cozad in Cincinnati, Ohio. Robert's family moved frequently, living in Nebraska and New Jersey before he was eighteen. A legal dispute between his father and a neighbor ended in the death of the neighbor, forcing Robert's father to flee town. Following this event, Robert changed his last name from Cozad to Henri, so he would not be connected to his father. After attending the Pennsylvania Academy of the Fine Arts in Philadelphia and the Académie Julian in Paris, Henri steadily developed a reputation as a highly respected artist and teacher. His New York studio served as a meeting place for many of the most notable artists of the day. ∎

## Introduction

In the late nineteenth and early twentieth centuries, many American artists retreated to Europe to study painting. Paris, in particular, was considered the artistic and cultural capital of the world, and was home to a host of museums and schools. Artists accustomed to working in one specific style found freedom in the experimental atmosphere of Europe. The colors and techniques of the Impressionists, in particular, changed the way artists worked. Prior to this artistic period, painters focused on the realism of their subjects and sought to create works of art that represented their subjects very realistically, down to the smallest detail.

Impressionists, on the other hand, tried to capture images on canvas in a way that appeared accidental but was actually planned. In other words, they wanted to portray the visual impression of a moment rather than an object. Europe turned out to be a welcoming home for artists interested in expanding their horizons, and many remained there, while those who returned to the United States—Henri included—faced new challenges.

Painter Robert Henri was founder of the Ashcan School, which advocated realism in art. **DOVER PUBLICATIONS, INC. REPRODUCED BY PERMISSION.**

Henri fought for and supported artists who were struggling for independence against the New York art scene in the early twentieth century. He believed that American art should depict American subjects and not merely copy European styles. Henri was an engaging teacher, and in 1908, he opened his own school. In the same year, he became part of a group known as The Eight, a group of urban realists who exhibited their work together as a revolt against the art establishment. These artists were mainly newspaper illustrators, many of whom Henri had encouraged to become painters. Although familiar with both current trends in art and the older styles, members of The Eight sought to depict the ordinary objects of life in a vivid and refreshing way. A smaller core group later became known as the Ashcan School. Recognized for their bold work and spontaneity, these artists portrayed various subjects, including mundane scenes from daily urban life, street scenes, and the grittier aspects of life in the city. This was not all they painted, however. Their work encompassed portraits of themselves and others, as well.

*The Masquerade Dress,* also known as *The Ancient Dress,* was painted in 1911. A portrait of his second wife, Marjorie, the painting is typical of Henri's portrait work. There is nothing unusual about the portrait; it is a

## Primary Source

### The Masquerade Dress

**SYNOPSIS:** *The Masquerade Dress* by Robert Henri, 1911. Many of the influences of Henri's training and reading are evident in *The Masquerade Dress*. It is a blending of the European styles of art with his own belief that art was a noble activity. The use of the entire canvas, the creation of a unified composition, and quick brushstrokes combine to make this painting a symbol of a general philosophy about the nature of art and life. THE METROPOLITAN MUSEUM OF ART, ARTHUR H. HEARN FUND, 1958. (58.157) REPRODUCED BY PERMISSION.

simple painting, painted simply. The model gazes out at the viewer with one foot forward and her arm extended. There are no distracting background pieces; however, there is a noticeable contrast in the dark and light colors used, and Henri infuses his painting with a hint of Oriental influence in the design of the dress.

## Significance

Henri was mainly a portrait and landscape painter. *The Masquerade Dress* is one of his more conventional paintings in terms of subject and style, for there is no evidence of the experimentation typical of The Eight. What is evident is that Henri's studies of Manet, Hals, and Velazquez influenced his work, as did Impressionism, and all are evident in this painting. Henri liked vitality in his work, and used bold strokes, strong chiaroscuro (representation of light and shading), and experimentation. His technique included painting quickly, which gave his brushstrokes and work a sense of life and animation. This was unusual at the beginning of the twentieth century, when most paintings were finely detailed and rigid in their composition. Contrast Henri's paintings with those of an artist such as John Singer Sargent to see the differences in portrait-painting techniques of the era. Sargent's subjects have very well-defined facial features, while Henri's have softer features, making them seem more alive and natural. This naturalness and warmth reflects the influence of Rembrandt and Goya, whose portraits tended to depict real human beings—flaws and all—rather than just the physically appealing people often found in art.

Henri's philosophy of painting differentiated him from his fellow artists. He believed that painters should express their own individual styles rather than mimic those of other artists. He also believed that there was beauty in ordinary life, which makes the *The Masquerade Dress* a significant representation of his overall artistic philosophy. In an article entitled "The New York Exhibition of Independent Artists," Henri wrote that "artists must be philosophers; they must be creators; they must be experimenters." He also believed that art was not separate from life, which was why an artist must observe and paint what was around him. In keeping with this philosophy, many of his paintings depict street scenes of New York. His favorite subject, however, was his wife Marjorie. Henri used her as a model for many years, beginning at the time of their engagement.

## Further Resources

### BOOKS

Henri, Robert. *The Art Spirit.* Philadelphia: J.B. Lippincott, 1960.

Perlman, Bernard B. *Robert Henri: His Life and Art.* New York: Dover, 1991.

### WEBSITES

The Metropolitan Museum of Art. Available online at http://www.metmuseum.org (accessed November 12, 2002).

"Robert Henri (1865–1929)." New Hampshire Public Television. Available online at http://www.nhptv.org/kn/vs/artlabhenri.htm; website home page: http://www.nhptv.org (accessed November 12, 2002).

---

# *O Pioneers!*
Novel

**By:** Willa Cather

**Date:** 1913

**Source:** Cather, Willa. Chapter 1 of *O Pioneers!* Boston: Houghton Mifflin Co., 1913. Reprinted, with historical essay and explanatory notes, by David Stouck. Lincoln, Nebr.: University of Nebraska Press, 1992. Available online at http://www.pagebypagebooks.com/Willa_Cather/O_Pioneers/Part_I_The_Wild_Land_Chapter_I_p1.html; website home page: http://www.pagebypagebooks.com (accessed November 14, 2002).

**About the Author:** Willa Cather (1873–1947) was born in Virginia. When she was ten, her family moved to Nebraska, which became the setting for many of her works of fiction. After graduating from the University of Nebraska in 1895, Cather moved to Pittsburgh and worked as a journalist. From 1906 to 1912, she was the editor of *McClure's Magazine* in New York. Her poetry, short stories, novels, and essays won many awards, including a Pulitzer Prize for *One of Ours* (1922). ∎

## Introduction

In her essay "My First Novels (There Were Two)," Willa Cather writes, "My first novel, *Alexander's Bridge,* was very like what painters call a studio picture." To Cather, *Alexander's Bridge* was largely imitative, clearly patterned after the work of Edith Wharton and Henry James. *O Pioneers!,* her second "first" novel, was the novel she was meant to write. The book grew out of two short stories, "Alexandra" (1911) and "The White Mulberry Tree" (1913). Cather wrote that *O Pioneers!* was about "the kind of country I loved, because it was about old neighbours, once very dear, whom I had almost forgotten in the hurry and excitement of growing up."

*O Pioneers!* explores the journey of Alexandra Bergenson, a typically strong Cather heroine fighting to save the land she respects. A child of Swedish immigrants, Alexandra takes over the farm when her father dies and tries to save both the farm and the family. Old-world values collide with new ways of American life as Alexandra struggles with her newfound responsibilities. The vitality of the land, the sacred space of the prairies, and the endurance of the pioneer immigrants are all important themes.

Willa Cather wrote numerous well-received novels and stories that were set in the American Southwest or Great Plains. © BETTMANN/CORBIS. REPRODUCED BY PERMISSION.

## Significance

*O Pioneers!* was generally well received when it was published in 1913. Although one New York critic wondered why he should care about Nebraska, most reviewers recognized Cather's talent for writing about and observing the land and its people, noting that her work had "great dramatic power" and was "American in the best sense." The book broke new ground in fiction by exposing the East Coast literary establishment to stories of the Nebraska prairie. Cather effectively captured on paper the voices of the Norwegian and Czech immigrants who were her childhood neighbors. She understood life on the prairie because she had lived it, and her ability to create that reality on the printed page made for a riveting tale. The book also rewrote the pioneer myth by putting a female in a role that traditionally belonged to men. Beyond this, *O Pioneers!* is important because it laid the foundation for Cather's subsequent novels, *Song of the Lark* (1915) and *My Ántonia* (1918), which continued the theme of immigrant life in Nebraska.

Cather experiments with form, subject, and setting in *O Pioneers!* and finds her own style. She explores the gender roles of her characters, especially Alexandra. The work is not satiric, as her earlier stories about Nebraska had been. When her friend Elizabeth Sergeant told her that the book lacked a sharp skeleton, Cather replied that the prairie had no skeleton. The land became a metaphor in her writing, showing the relationship between the people, the culture, and the soil. She also shows her knowledge of, and interest in, history through cultural references to other countries. These references expand her novel from being merely a story about a small town to one about the larger world.

Readers continue to appreciate *O Pioneers!'* "unique and poetic blending of New World experience and Old World cultural and literary traditions, as a myth-making text." Though some of Cather's other novels may be more popular, *O Pioneers!* remains the novel in which she discovered her true muse.

## Primary Source

*O Pioneers!* [excerpt]

> **SYNOPSIS:** Chapter 1 of *O Pioneers!* vividly creates the scene and sets the tone of urban life in nineteenth-century Nebraska. The town of Hanover is a harsh place in January 1882. Cather captures both the climate of the culture and the despair of Emil, the little Swedish boy whose kitten cannot get down from her high perch on a pole. His sister, Alexandra, provides his only "ray of hope," a role she plays throughout the novel.

One January day, thirty years ago, the little town of Hanover, anchored on a windy Nebraska tableland, was trying not to be blown away. A mist of fine snowflakes was curling and eddying about the cluster of low drab buildings huddled on the gray prairie, under a gray sky. The dwelling-houses were set about haphazard on the tough prairie sod; some of them looked as if they had been moved in overnight, and others as if they were straying off by themselves, headed straight for the open plain. None of them had any appearance of permanence, and the howling wind blew under them as well as over them. The main street was a deeply rutted road, now frozen hard, which ran from the squat red railway station and the grain "elevator" at the north end of the town to the lumber yard and the horse pond at the south end. On either side of this road straggled two uneven rows of wooden buildings; the general merchandise stores, the two banks, the drug store, the feed store, the saloon, the post-office. The board sidewalks were gray with trampled snow, but at two o'clock in the afternoon the shopkeepers, having come back from dinner, were keeping well behind their frosty windows. The children were all in school, and there was nobody abroad in the streets but a few rough-looking countrymen in coarse overcoats, with their long caps pulled down to their noses. Some of them had brought their wives to town, and now and then a red or a plaid shawl flashed out of one store into the shelter of another. At the hitch-bars along the street a few heavy work-horses, harnessed to farm wagons, shivered under their blankets. About the station everything was quiet, for there would not be another train in until night.

On the sidewalk in front of one of the stores sat a little Swede boy, crying bitterly. He was about five years old. His black cloth coat was much too big for him and made him look like a little old man. His shrunken brown flannel dress had been washed many times and left a long stretch of stocking between the hem of his skirt and the tops of his clumsy, copper-toed shoes. His cap was pulled down over his ears; his nose and his chubby cheeks were chapped and red with cold. He cried quietly, and the few people who hurried by did not notice him. He was afraid to stop any one, afraid to go into the store and ask for help, so he sat wringing his long sleeves and looking up a telegraph pole beside him, whimpering, "My kitten, oh, my kitten! Her will fweeze!" At the top of the pole crouched a shivering gray kitten, mewing faintly and clinging desperately to the wood with her claws. The boy had been left at the store while his sister went to the doctor's office, and in her absence a dog had chased his kitten up the pole. The little creature had never been so high before, and she was too frightened to move. Her master was sunk in despair. He was a little country boy, and this village was to him a very strange and perplexing place, where people wore fine clothes and had hard hearts. He always felt shy and awkward here, and wanted to hide behind things for fear some one might laugh at him. Just now, he was too unhappy to care who laughed. At last he seemed to see a ray of hope: his sister was coming, and he got up and ran toward her in his heavy shoes.

His sister was a tall, strong girl, and she walked rapidly and resolutely, as if she knew exactly where she was going and what she was going to do next. She wore a man's long ulster (not as if it were an affliction, but as if it were very comfortable and belonged to her; carried it like a young soldier), and a round plush cap, tied down with a thick veil. She had a serious, thoughtful face, and her clear, deep blue eyes were fixed intently on the distance, without seeming to see anything, as if she were in trouble. She did not notice the little boy until he pulled her by the coat. Then she stopped short and stooped down to wipe his wet face. . . .

Illustration of Alexandra from Willa Cather's *O Pioneers!*
THE LIBRARY OF CONGRESS.

## Further Resources

### BOOKS

O'Brien, Sharon. *Willa Cather: The Emerging Voice.* New York: Oxford University Press, 1987.

Woodress, James. *Willa Cather: A Literary Life.* Lincoln, Nebr.: University of Nebraska Press, 1987.

### WEBSITES

The Willa Cather Electronic Archive. University of Nebraska. Available online at http://www.unl.edu/Cather; website home page: http://www.unl.edu (accessed November 15, 2002).

Willa Cather Home Page. Instructional Computing Group, Harvard University. Available online at http://icg.harvard.edu/~cather/home.html; website home page: http://icg.harvard.edu (accessed June 25, 2002).

### AUDIO AND VISUAL MEDIA

*O Pioneers!* Hallmark Hall of Fame Production. Republic Pictures Home Video. Videocassette, 1992.

# *Ethiopia Awakening*
## Sculpture

**By:** Meta Vaux Warrick Fuller

**Date:** 1914

**Source:** Fuller, Meta Vaux Warrick. *Ethiopia Awakening*, 1914. Available online at http://wiscinfo.doit.wisc.edu /fhigh/Ethiopia_Awakening_1.htm; website home page: http://www.wisc.edu (accessed November 13, 2002).

**About the Artist:** Meta Vaux Warrick Fuller (1877–1968) was born in Philadelphia. The youngest of three children, Fuller attended a segregated school in Philadelphia until she was awarded a scholarship to the Philadelphia Museum School for the Industrial Arts. She also studied in Paris. Fuller's early work was influenced by her brother's and grandfather's horror stories, earning her the title "the sculptor of horror." ∎

## Introduction

Meta Vaux Warrick Fuller was not deterred by the social expectations for women at the beginning of the twentieth century. Nor did she allow racism to keep her from her artistic endeavors. Fuller's awareness of racial differences was developed as a child and young woman. She first experienced prejudice when she vacationed with her family in Atlantic City, New Jersey, and was not allowed to play with the white children. Later, when she tried to rent an apartment in Paris, the landlady refused to rent to her because of her race. When she married Solomon Carter Fuller, a Liberian physician, their neighbors feared that the young couple would lower property values in the neighborhood.

Fuller's sense of racial prejudice and unfair treatment was heightened as she learned about the philosophies of W.E.B. Du Bois, one of the earliest advocates of black nationalism. This racial awareness clearly informs her signature piece, *Ethiopia Awakening*. Crafted in 1914, the sculpture challenges the stereotypes of black America in the early twentieth century. Using an Egyptian motif and the image of a strong woman swathed in unwrapped bandages, it represents a discarding of past trials and an optimism for the future.

## Significance

Much of Fuller's work was done prior to the Harlem Renaissance, a period of intense artistic creativity in the African American community. According to David C. Driskell, "Fuller's art bridged the gap between a well established Black presence in European art circles and the gradual acceptance of the Black artists' work at home."

There is disagreement about what or who influenced *Ethiopia Awakening*. Some theories credit the influence of W.E.B. Du Bois, who encouraged artists to use African American subjects for their work in an effort to dispel negative stereotypes. Others cite J.E. Casely Hayford's novel *Ethiopia Awakening* as a source. It is also possible that Fuller may have known about the Pan-African movement of Ethiopianism, which prophesied that "Ethiopia shall soon stretch forth her hands to God" (Ps. 68:31). This nationalist movement resulted from the 1885 conference that partitioned Africa and from an 1896 uprising by Ethiopians against Italians. "Ethiopian" was also a term used for African Americans and Africans at the time.

Stacey Williams suggests that it was Fuller's own views and beliefs that provided inspiration for her sculpture. Williams says that *Ethiopia Awakening* represents the process of "awakening, gradually unwinding the bandages of [her] past and looking out on life again, expectant but unafraid." She also identifies three "spatial tropes," or regions, in the sculpture. The first trope includes the feet and legs, which are restricted by wrappings. The clothed torso is the second trope, and the third is the crown. This third trope is interesting in that it appears to have been influenced by Cubism, evidence that Fuller was exploring artistic methods even as she was making political statements. The figure is vertical, with an upraised hand, and the head is turned outward. Unlike other sculptures of the same period, Fuller's piece suggests awakening rather than retreating, and an emergence from slavery. The sculpture is especially important for its vision of a woman emerging from bondage, particularly a black female in the early twentieth century.

## Further Resources

### BOOKS

Driskell, David. "The Flowering of the Harlem Renaissance: The Art of Aaron Douglas, Meta Warrick Fuller, Palmer Hayden, and William H. Johnson." In *Harlem Renaissance: Art of Black America.* New York: Abrams, 1987, 105–154.

Kerr, Judith N. "Meta Vaux Warrick Fuller." In *Black Women in America: An Historical Encyclopedia.* Darlene Clark Hine, ed. Brooklyn, N.Y.: Carlson, 1993, 470–473.

Meta Warrick Fuller Papers, 1864–1990. Schomburg Center for Research in Black Culture, New York Public Library.

Patton, Sharon F. *African-American Art.* New York: Oxford University Press, 1998.

### PERIODICALS

Hoover, Velma J. "Meta Vaux Warrick Fuller: Her Life and Art." *Negro History Bulletin* 40, 1977, 678–681.

### WEBSITES

"Meta Vaux Warrick Fuller." Hall of Black Achievement, Bridgeater State College. Available online at http://www .bridgew.edu/HOBA/fuller.htm; website home page: http:// www.bridgew.edu (accessed November 13, 2002).

Williams, Stacey. "Meta Vaux Warrick Fuller and Pan-Africanist Feminism in *Ethiopia Awakening.*" Doctoral Students Council, City University of New York. Available online at http:// dsc.gc.cuny.edu/part/articles/swilli.html; website home page: http://dsc.gc.cuny.edu (accessed November 13, 2002).

## Primary Source

*Ethiopia Awakening*

**SYNOPSIS:** This is a photograph of *Ethiopia Awakening*. The sculpture is cast in stone and plaster. In 1921, Fuller sculpted another version of this figure in bronze. In keeping with the atmosphere of the Harlem Renaissance, Fuller's work challenged racist attitudes by reflecting the awakening defiance of her people. ART & ARTIFACTS DIVISION, SCHOMBURG CENTER FOR RESEARCH IN BLACK CULTURE, THE NEW YORK PUBLIC LIBRARY, ASTOR, LENOX AND TILDEN FOUNDATIONS. META WARRICK FULLER. *THE AWAKENING OF ETHIOPIA*, CIRCA 1910. [SCULPTURE]

# *Modern Dancing*

Reference work

**By:** Vernon and Irene Castle

**Date:** 1914

**Source:** Castle, Vernon and Irene. *Modern Dancing.* Special Edition. New York: The World Syndicate Co., 1914.

**About the Authors:** Vernon and Irene Castle danced together from 1912 to 1916. Vernon Castle (1887–1918) was born in England. He was the youngest child in his family. Castle attended Birmingham University and graduated with a degree in engineering, but his career took a different direction when he moved to New York. He appeared in musicals and stage productions between 1907 and 1911, using the stage name Castle rather than his birth name of Blythe so he would not be confused with his sister, actress Coralie Blythe. Castle was known as an eccentric. Irene Foote Castle (1893–1969) was born in New Rochelle, New York. She studied dance as a child. Her parents sent her to Saint Mary's Episcopal Convent and to the National Park Seminary, but Irene had other ambitions. At the age of sixteen she appeared in theatricals, where she learned dance techniques that would become part of the Castle style. Irene and Vernon met in 1910 and married in 1911. Vernon Castle died in a plane crash during World War I. Irene continued to perform after his death and married three more times. ■

## Introduction

Mrs. and Mrs. Vernon Castle became dance sensations at the beginning of the twentieth century. They were both dancers and teachers. As a married couple they could dance in more suggestive ways than unmarried couples could. Their first public performance was in 1912 in Paris, where they danced to the Irving Berlin tune, "Alexander's Ragtime Band." The Castles were extremely popular when they returned from Europe. They brought back with them dances such as the Turkey Trot, the Castlewalk, the Maxixe, and the Toddle. Their agent, Elisabeth Marbury, made them a success when she realized that the popular couple had potential to draw audiences and make money. They gained a large following from the upper and middle classes.

*Modern Dancing* was published in 1914 as a manual to teach the newest dances. It features photographs of the Castles in various dance positions and provides instruction in dance moves and dress. The first chapter describes dance as an art form and discusses the history of dance. The Castles also include a section on morality and health as they relate to dance. They counter the objections that dance is immoral by telling the reader that when done properly, dance is not "vulgar" or "against any religious creed." Further, dance is promoted as a way to maintain health, which also contributes to its morality.

## Significance

Vernon and Irene Castle popularized ballroom dance. Dance had been around for centuries, but the Castles made it their career. The Castles danced at supper clubs and in rooftop dances, which were very popular at the time, since air-conditioning had yet to be invented. The Castles were considered a wholesome couple, and were deemed "The Aristocrats of Dance" by the press. Vernon was tall and thin, while Irene attracted attention with her stylish clothes and bobbed hair. Soon, women across the country were following her trends. The couple rehearsed each act over and over until it was perfect. They included little kicks, flips, dips, and steps that brought attention to their elegance and grace. The Castles made the Castlewalk, a one-step dance, their signature dance. In this dance, the man propels the lady backwards, and steers her in smaller and smaller circles until they stop. Then they unwind and start over again. The Castles also adapted dances from earlier time periods.

*Modern Dancing* is one example of the way the Castles capitalized on their fame. The book promoted them through its explanation of why people should dance, how they should dance, and how they should dress. They also commercialized dance through their studio, Castle House, where the couple taught dance. In addition, they performed in numerous Broadway plays, and even made a movie with the legendary Fred Astaire.

## Primary Source

*Modern Dancing* [excerpt]

**SYNOPSIS:** The Castles promote dance as a healthy way to look younger and feel good. They claim that dancers drink less alcohol because they are not just sitting around. Dancing, according to the Castles' claims, is especially good for women. The chapter also outlines the history of dance and the benefits of performing dance properly and morally.

### Dancing as an Art

We all know that the art of dancing is very old. We read of it in ancient history, and it is often mentioned in the Bible, while "dancing-girls" have been known in the East for many centuries.

Times and dances have changed. In early times dancing was limited to the few; now almost any girl who does not dance is either an invalid or the piano-player! We have nearly all come to realize that dancing is part of our education, and the more proficient we become the better we like it.

Modern dancing has come to stay, whatever may be the current opinion. Of course, individual dances are bound to change; undoubtedly we shall have a revival of the older dances. Some of these were very pretty, but some were appalling. Personally, my wife and I have never been able to see why people danced the old "square dances." For the benefit of those who do not know what is meant by square dances I will try to explain.

Years ago dances were divided into two groups, the "Round" and the "Square." The latter were usually danced by a number of couples arranged in the form of a square, and the various movements were "called out" by the leader of the orchestra. The Quadrille, the Lancers, and the Caledonia were among the most familiar examples, while the German, or Cotillion, constitutes a dance by itself.

"Round" dances comprised the Waltz, the Polka, the Yorke, and the Schottische, the Varsuvienne, and the Gallop. Practically none of these dances is seen nowadays. For this we are duly thankful; even though Gavottes, Mazurkas, and Minuets could be modified and made quite charming. As they exist now they are pleasant to watch, but our tired business men would probably fall fast asleep while dancing the Minuet.

Objections to dancing have been made on the ground that it is wrong, immoral, and vulgar. This it certainly is not—when the dancers regard propriety. It is possible to make anything immoral and vulgar; all depends on how it is done.

A vulgar man or woman betrays lack of breeding even in walking across the room; sitting down may be performed in a vulgar manner, or any other smallest act. The modern dances properly danced are *not* vulgar; on the contrary, they embody grace and refinement; and impartial critics who have been called upon to pronounce judgment upon them have ended by saying that there is nothing objectionable in any of them. They are, then, not immoral, not against any religious creed.

From the standpoint of health, dancing is fine exercise and keeps one absolutely fit. We ourselves can vouch for that, and we know of many people who looked fifty years of age three years ago and look less than forty to-day. They owe it all to dancing. These facts are significant. Other facts are equally so. There was less champagne sold last year than in any one of the ten previous years. People who dance drink less, and when they drink at all they exercise, instead of becoming torpid around a card-table. There are so many arguments in favor of dancing that reasonable minds must be convinced that the present popularity of dancing among people of

Irene and Vernon Castle were known as the "Aristocrats of Dance."

all ages and classes is one of the best things that has happened in a long time.

Expert medical testimony as to the value of dancing is in its favor. Our modern physicians unite in thinking it a valuable health and youth preserver. Dr. Charles L. Dana, for instance, in his *Text Book of Nervous Diseases and Psychiatry* (8th ed.) says:

> Dancing, including gymnastic dancing and folk dancing, under proper conditions and limitations, is one of the best exercises for persons of all ages. It is especially adapted to the temperament, physique, and dress of women.

## Further Resources

### BOOKS

Castle, Irene. *Castles in the Air.* Garden City, N.Y.: Double-day, 1953.

Kendall, Elizabeth. *Where She Danced.* New York: Alfred A. Knopf, 1979.

Malnig, Julie. *Dancing Till Dawn: A Century of Exhibition Ballroom Dance.* New York: Greenwood Press, 1992.

### PERIODICALS

Erenberg, Lewis A. "Everybody's Doin' It: The Pre-World War I Dance Craze, The Castles, and the Modern American Girl." *Feminist Studies* 3, 1975, 155-170.

### AUDIO AND VISUAL MEDIA

*The Story of Vernon and Irene Castle.* Turner Home Entertainment, 2000.

---

# "St. Louis Blues"
Song

**By:** W.C. Handy

**Date:** 1914

**Source:** Handy, W.C. "St. Louis Blues." Handy Bros. Music Co., 1914. *Historic American Sheet Music, 1850–1920.* Sheet Music Collection, The John Hay Library, Brown University.

**About the Artist:** William Christopher Handy (1871–1958) was born in Florence, Alabama, the son and grandson of ministers. Although his family didn't approve of his interest in music, Handy played in a minstrel show, sang in the church choir, and played in a brass band when he was growing up. Trained as a teacher, as a young man he taught, worked in a factory, and was a faculty member at the Agricultural and Mechanical College in Normal, Alabama. During that time he also played in several bands, lived in a handful of cities, and performed throughout the United States. In 1909, he moved to Memphis, Tennessee, where he began writing his own version of Mississippi Delta blues music. His songs are credited with popularizing the genre. Known as the "Father of the Blues," Handy also compiled traditional blues tunes and published them in *Blues: An Anthology* in 1926. He also wrote an autobiography and two books about the history of African American music. ■

## Introduction

In 1912, W.C. Handy's "Memphis Blues" became the first blues composition to be published commercially. "St. Louis Blues" followed two years later. Handy had been trained in traditional music and knew European styles. When he was on the road with his bands, however, he rediscovered a kind of music that he had heard his whole life, the music of small southern towns. While playing in Cleveland, Mississippi, his band was asked to step aside for a local band that knew the folk songs and the blues tunes that the people wanted to hear. They did,

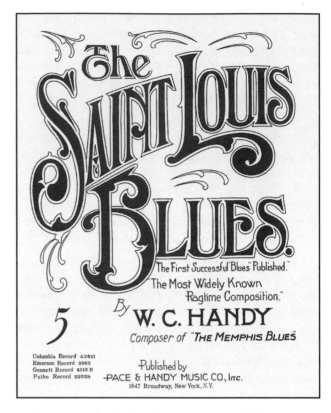

An alternate cover for the "St. Louis Blues" sheet music. The song was the first blues composition to be published commercially. **THE LIBRARY OF CONGRESS.**

and Handy was inspired to write a different style of music, a style that would make him famous.

Blues music has a twelve-bar structure; in classic blues lyrics the first line repeats and is then followed by a rhyming line. The Mississippi Delta, home of the blues, was where Handy honed his craft. He composed his songs at Pee Wee's bar on Beale Street, a gathering place for many of Memphis's African American musicians.

The "St. Louis Blues" can be performed as either an instrumental or vocal piece. The lyrics tell the story of a woman down on her luck. She lost her man and is still lovesick for him. The song is rooted in Handy's memories of his own hard times. It uses dialect and phrasing that was familiar to African Americans of the time.

## Significance

W.C. Handy's most famous tune, "St. Louis Blues" ranks among the most popular songs of the twentieth century. The song, according to Handy, was a combination of ideas, none of them really original. But that may be the source of its popularity. Handy was attempting to reach a wide audience with this composition. He wanted to appeal to those who liked the traditional blues, but he also wanted to attract the white audience who frequented the dance halls. The song succeeded on both counts.

## Primary Source

**"St. Louis Blues"** (1 OF 5)

**SYNOPSIS:** The mournful tale of a woman's lost love is the story told by the "St. Louis Blues." Some experts say that W.C. Handy adapted the blues to his audience and that his tunes were not pure blues, but a combination of styles. In fact, they were just that. But the "Father of the Blues" knew what the people liked, and the "St. Louis Blues" became one of his most popular compositions. JUSTIN HERMAN COLLECTION; MUSIC A-1311, DUKE UNIVERSITY RARE BOOK, MANUSCRIPT, AND SPECIAL COLLECTIONS LIBRARY.

**Primary Source**

"St. Louis Blues" (2 OF 5)

Sheet music to "St. Louis Blues," page 2. "ST. LOUIS BLUES." WORDS AND MUSIC BY W.C. HANDY. COPYRIGHT HANDY BROTHERS MUSIC COMPANY, INC. REPRODUCED BY PERMISSION.

**Primary Source**

"St. Louis Blues" (3 OF 5)

Sheet music to "St. Louis Blues," page 3. "ST. LOUIS BLUES." WORDS AND MUSIC BY W.C. HANDY. COPYRIGHT HANDY BROTHERS MUSIC COMPANY, INC. REPRODUCED BY PERMISSION.

**Primary Source**

"St. Louis Blues" (4 OF 5)

Sheet music to "St. Louis Blues," page 4. "ST. LOUIS BLUES." WORDS AND MUSIC BY W.C. HANDY. COPYRIGHT HANDY BROTHERS MUSIC COMPANY, INC. REPRODUCED BY PERMISSION.

**Primary Source**

"St. Louis Blues" (5 OF 5)
Sheet music to "St. Louis Blues," page 5. "ST. LOUIS BLUES." WORDS AND MUSIC BY W.C. HANDY. COPYRIGHT HANDY BROTHERS MUSIC COMPANY, INC. REPRODUCED BY PERMISSION.

Dancing was all the rage at this time, and Handy exploited the trend by beginning the "St. Louis Blues" with a tango. The song then reverts to the blues, with its traditional twelve-bar structure.

Handy's songs popularized blues music. The term "blues" became more specialized, not just a catchall word for all southern music. Ironically, some people say that Handy didn't really write the blues, that his works were too formal.

"St. Louis Blues" is one of the most recorded songs of the twentieth century. Singers such as Rudy Vallee, Bessie Smith, and Louis Armstrong all recorded it. The recording by Sophie Tucker in 1917 was the first blues record to sell a million copies. The song was popular internationally. It has been featured in films, including one called *St. Louis Blues*. The tune remains popular almost ninety years after it was composed.

## Further Resources

### BOOKS

Davis, Francis. *The History of the Blues.* New York: Hyperion, 1995.

Handy, W.C. *Father of the Blues: An Autobiography.* New York: The Macmillan Co., 1941.

Oakley, Giles. *The Devil's Music: A History of the Blues.* 2nd ed. New York: De Capo Press, 1997.

### PERIODICALS

Gussow, Adam. "Make My Getaway: The Blues Lives of Black Minstrels in W.C. Handy's *Father of the Blues.*" *African American Review,* Spring 2001, 5–28.

### WEBSITES

W.C. Handy "Father of the Blues." University of North Alabama Libraries. Available online at http://www2.una.edu /library/handy/index.html; website home page: http://www2 .una.edu/library/ (accessed July 31, 2002).

### AUDIO AND VISUAL MEDIA

Armstrong, Louis. *Louis Armstrong plays W.C. Handy.* Columbia. LP, 1954.

# Debate Over *The Birth of a Nation*

## "Capitalizing Race Hatred"
Editorial

**By:** *New York Globe*
**Date:** April 6, 1915
**Source:** "Capitalizing Race Hatred." *New York Globe,* April 6, 1915. Reprinted in *"The Birth of a Nation": D.W. Griffith, Director.* Robert Lang, ed. New Brunswick, N.J.: Rutgers University Press, 1994.

## "Reply to the *New York Globe*"
Letter

**By:** D.W. Griffith
**Date:** April 10, 1915
**Source:** Griffith, D.W. "Reply to the *New York Globe.*" *New York Globe,* April 10, 1915. Reprinted in *"The Birth of a Nation": D.W. Griffith, Director.* Robert Lang, ed. New Brunswick, N.J.: Rutgers University Press, 1994.
**About the Author:** David Lewelyn Wark Griffith (1875–1948) was born into an impoverished family in Crestwood, Kentucky. The son of a former Confederate soldier, Griffith wanted to be a playwright, but instead became an actor and director, working for Edison Studios and Biograph Company. As director at Biograph from 1908 to 1913, Griffith made over 400 films, introducing actors such as Mary Pickford and Lillian Gish and pioneering a style of filmmaking now standard in the movie industry. ■

## Introduction

D.W. Griffith's 1915 film, *The Birth of a Nation*, was both controversial and innovative. Griffith based his film in part on Thomas Dixon's book *The Clansman: An Historical Romance of the Ku Klux Klan*. Both Dixon and Griffith were Southerners, though Dixon was far more adamant in his racial beliefs. Through his book, Dixon sought to "create a feeling of abhorrence in white people, especially white women against colored men." Griffith, meanwhile, wanted to "offer a 'picturisation' of the Civil War and Reconstruction that [would] honor the Southern Legend." Critics argued that Griffith cared more for the narrative story line than for historical facts, but he maintained that the film was accurate. The result was a melodrama that, to many viewers, seemed to portray whites as absolute good and blacks as absolute evil. Griffith often explained that his life as a son of a Confederate soldier influenced the story of *The Birth of a Nation*. He said, "You can't hear your father tell of fighting day after day, night after night with nothing to eat but parched corn . . . and your mother staying up night after night sewing robes for the Klan and not feel it is true."

During the early 1900s, African Americans were struggling for equality. Segregation was rampant, most African Americans did not have the right to vote, and Jim Crow laws (state laws passed after the end of slavery to keep African Americans segregated from whites) were the norm. Reform groups such as the Urban League and the National Association for the Advancement of Colored People (NAACP) were created to help make life better for African Americans. The NAACP protested *The Birth of a Nation* and succeeded in having some scenes removed from the final version, including a love scene between a white Reconstructionist senator and his mulatto (of mixed white and black ancestry) mistress. Still, the NAACP had to decide how to counteract a three-hour film that perpetuated negative stereotypes

## New York Post, Review of "The Birth of a Nation"

An appeal to race prejudice as subtle and malicious as any that has been made in New York, a thrilling historic spectacle of the battles and life of the days of the Civil War, and an explanation of Southern feeling in the reconstruction days in defence of the Ku Klux Klan which terrorized negroes during that period—these were the things presented to the spectators who filled the Liberty Theatre last evening for the first presentation of the motion-picture drama, "The Birth of a Nation." As an achievement in motion-picture photography upon a tremendous scale, surprisingly effective in artistic realization, the film is as remarkable as it is audacious in its characterization of the negro as a primitive brute, either vicious or childlike, only to be controlled by violence.

People were moved to cheers, hisses, laughter, and tears, apparently unconscious, and subdued, by tense interest in the play; they clapped when the masked riders took vengeance on negroes, and they clapped when the hero refused to shake the hand of a mulatto who has risen by political intrigue to become lieutenant-governor. This remark, made by a typical New Yorker leaving the theatre, characterizes the sentiment which was expressed in much of the comment: "That show certainly does make you hate those blacks. And if it gets that effect on me, when I don't care anything about it imagine what it would be in the South with a man whose family was mixed up in it. It makes you feel as if you'd do the same thing."

That is the element which mars one of the most ambitious and successful picture dramas which has yet been attempted; and it is an element which does not seem necessary to the effectiveness of the film. To show the fact that there were individual outrages which roused the Southern whites of the 60's to organized violence, it does not appear necessary to characterize a race as either so vicious or so simple-minded that extermination or feudal control were the only methods of managing them; and this is the conclusion of "The Birth of a Nation." The blame for much of the trouble is shown to have lain upon the unscrupulous or misguided white political leaders of the North, who went to excess in their power to institute radical measures for negro freedom and equality of right. Stoneman, known really under another name, the Congressional leader, who held the reins of influence after the assassination of Lincoln, is represented as the cause of reconstruction turbulence.

The war scenes in the first half of the play have been photographed with striking realism. Troops charging, artillery trains galloping, flags waving, shells bursting over barricades, the flow of battle over a field miles in length, are shown in full detail; and immediately after the excitement of the charge there is the sight of trenches full of torn and tangled bodies. The truth of the horror of war is not forgotten in presenting its fascination.

The assassination of Lincoln has also been well reproduced. The scene in the theatre, with the play, "Our American Cousin," going forward on the stage, is shown in careful accordance with the historical accounts of it. How Lincoln's guard left his post to get a view of the play; how Booth, waiting in the rear of another box, slipped through the door in the interval and fired at the President as he watched the play, are all seen. Booth's leap to the stage and his escape in the sudden excitement are faithfully portrayed, amid an equal excitement on the part of the spectators of to-day reviewing the scene.

The second part of the play, in which attempted outrages by a renegade negro and the mulatto protégé of Stoneman upon white girls, and the election injustices in which whites were refused the vote and in which negroes gained control of legislative power, with the resulting intense hatred and friction between the races, are shown, is the part which roused the emotion of the audience. A long chase of a white girl by a negro, ending with the girl's suicide by throwing herself over a cliff, called forth many excited whispered comments; and from then on to the end of the film there was ready applause for anything derogatory to negroes and for the activity of the Ku Klux Klan.

Thomas Dixon, author of "The Clansman," upon which the picture-drama is based, was called before the curtain last evening and made a short speech. In introducing D. W. Griffith, the producer of the pictures, he declared that none but the son of a Confederate soldier could have reproduced the spirit of his book.

**SOURCE:** "The Birth of a Nation." *New York Post*, March 4, 1915, 8–9.

of African Americans and glorified the Ku Klux Klan. Part of the answer was to voice its objections in the media.

### Significance

Some early reviewers criticized *The Birth of a Nation* for containing racist content, but it wasn't until criticism of the film began to appear in editorials and magazine articles that a firestorm of controversy was ignited. An editorial in the April 6, 1915, edition of the *New York Globe* entitled "Capitalizing Race Hatred" took on the issues that many reviewers either skirted or ignored. The author wrote, "It is insulting to every man of Southern birth to assume that he is pleased by misrepresentation so colossal." He also stated that the title of the film was an insult, because America was not born during the Civil War. Griffith frequently responded to his critics in letters, articles, and interviews, and his reply to this editorial was typical of his responses. He defended

Actresses Dorothy Gish (left) and Lillian Gish with director D.W. Griffith. Griffith's *Birth of a Nation* made many advances in American filmmaking but is also remembered for its racist storyline. © CORBIS. REPRODUCED BY PERMISSION.

the story and stated that the film "does show historic events." In later years, Griffith acknowledged that *The Birth of a Nation* was not a film for the general public. In 1941, he said, "Although the picture was made with no intention of embarrassing the Negro, as it stands to-day, it should not be shown to general audiences."

Though it is often dismissed as a cultural embarrassment, many film historians regard *The Birth of a Nation* as a landmark film in the development of American cinema. It employed many innovative techniques that are now standard in the motion-picture industry, including orchestral scoring, night photography, and outdoor scenes. For the first time on-screen, history was dramatized in epic fashion, featuring expert storytelling, impressive battle scenes, and hundreds of extras. For better or worse, filmmaking would never be the same again.

## Primary Source

### "Capitalizing Race Hatred"

**SYNOPSIS:** This April 6, 1915, editorial printed in the *New York Globe* complains that D.W. Griffith's film, *The Birth of a Nation*, was historically inaccurate and contained racist overtones. It sparked a heated editorial reply by Griffith defending his film.

In view of the splendors of national reunion what should be the attitude of every right-minded person toward attempts to revive the passions of the Civil War period, relight the fires of sectionalism, and intensify race prejudices that are unhappily still much alive? The questions sufficiently answer themselves, and when they are answered there is no reason to ask the further question of whether it is desirable, for purely sordid reasons, to exhibit such a moving-picture film as the so-called *The Birth of a Nation*.

Few of us are competent to pass judgment with respect to the tangled facts of the Reconstruction period. A fair and impartial narrative has never been written and probably never will be. But certain big facts shine out in the confusion. One is that never in human history did a victor show more consideration for the defeated. Men but lately in arms were restored to full citizenship, states in rebellion were received back in the sisterhood of the states. Let us rejoice that the Stonemans of Washington were magnanimous, but let us not dishonor ourselves by calling in question their great merit by presenting them as the paramours of quadroon mistresses, moved by petty spite. It is insulting to every man of

Southern birth to assume that he is pleased by misrepresentation so colossal.

Another big fact of the Reconstruction period is that the 4,000,000 former slaves, suddenly emancipated but with no way of earning their livelihood except by working at small wages for their former masters, displayed, all things considered, the most exemplary patience. They had protected the women and children on the plantations while the struggle went on which was to decide whether they were to become men or to remain as chattels, and the great body of them continued to exhibit, under the most trying circumstances, docility and kindliness. To present the members of the race as women-chasers and foul fiends is a cruel distortion of history. Bad things occurred, but what man will say that the outrages of black on white equalled in number the outrages of white on black? Which race even to the present day has the better right to complain of the unfairness and brutality of the other?

The very name of *The Birth of a Nation* is an insult to Washington, who believed that a nation, not merely a congeries of independent states, was born during the common struggles of the Revolutionary War, and devoted himself to cementing the union. It is an insult to Lincoln and the great motives inspiring him when he was called on to resist the attempt to denationalize a nation. This nation of ours was not born between 1861 and 1865, and no one will profit from trying to pervert history.

White men in this country have never been just to black men. We tore them from Africa and brought them over as slaves. For generations they toiled without recompense that their white owners might have unearned wealth and ape the ways of aristocracy. The nation finally freed them, but has but slightly protected them in the enjoyment of the legitimate fruits of their freedom. We nominally gave them the vote, but looked on inactive when the right was invaded. We do not, in any state of the Union, grant to the Negro economic and political equality. No white man of proper feeling can be proud of the record. The wonder is that the Negro is as good as he is. Then to the injury is added slander. To make a few dirty dollars men are willing to pander to depraved tastes and to foment a race antipathy that is the most sinister and dangerous feature of American life.

## Primary Source

"Reply to the *New York Globe*"

**SYNOPSIS:** The following document is D.W. Griffith's response to an April 1915 editorial printed in the

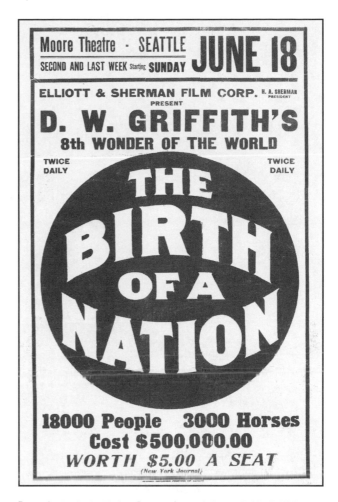

Poster for *Birth of a Nation*. Screenwriter and director D.W. Griffith vigorously defended the film from accusations of racist content. THE LIBRARY OF CONGRESS.

*New York Globe.* The writer of that editorial complained that *The Birth of a Nation* contained numerous historical inaccuracies as well as racist overtones. Here, Griffith responds to his critics without apology, defending the film as accurate and unbiased.

Editor of the Globe, Sir—In an editorial in your issue of April 6, 1915, under the heading: "Capitalizing Race Hatred," you undertake to label our picture *The Birth of a Nation* with alleged feelings of sectional difference between the North and South. You ask yourself questions and proceed to answer them in the same old way that the same things have been gone over and over again. Where I must take issue with you is that you intimate that these old differences have been raised and exhibited "for purely sordid reasons," to quote your own words.

In presenting this motion-picture story before the intelligent theater-goers of New York City, in a regu-

*Birth of a Nation* portrayed African Americans as lustful criminals running wild in the South after the end of the Civil War (1861–1865). In a particularly powerful sequence, actress Lillian Gish flees from an African American man's unwanted advances, finally committing suicide to escape him. **AP/WIDE WORLD PHOTOS. REPRODUCED BY PERMISSION.**

lar theater, which has been well advertised, I thought the moving drama told its own story. My associates have maintained a dignified silence in the face of an organized attack of letter writers, publicity seekers, and fanatics against our work. We have traced this attack to its source, and know the reasons for it. Without wishing to tell any newspaper its business, permit me to suggest that a cub reporter in one hour could find out that this attack is an organized effort to suppress a production which was brought forth to reveal the beautiful possibilities of the art of motion pictures and to tell a story which is based upon truth in every vital detail. Our story states, as plainly as the English language can express a fact, the reasons for this presentation. In our captions we reiterate that the events depicted upon the screen are not meant as a reflection upon any race or people of today.

I demand to know the authority upon which you base your intimation that this work of art has been exhibited "for purely sordid reasons." I further demand that failing to establish this authority you retract your statement in as prominent and direct a manner as you have given publicity to the opinions of the writer of your editorial.

Our picture tells its own story and we are willing to stand upon the verdict of the New York public as to the fitness of this work of art to be judged as a drama of action based upon the authenticated history of the period covering the action of our plot.

The succeeding paragraphs of your editorial are political generalities which have nothing in common with the truths and purposes of the motion picture *The Birth of a Nation*. Our picture does show historic events which you undertake to use for an entirely different argument. We have contrasted the bad with the good and following the formula of the best dramas of the world we establish our ideals by revealing the victory of right over wrong.

I do not agree with your statements regarding the history of slavery and the Reconstruction period of this nation, but that is not a matter of importance in this connection. Most well-informed men know now that slavery was an economic mistake. The treatment of the Negroes during the days of Reconstruction is shown effectually and graphically in our picture. We show many phases of the question and we do pay particular attention to those faithful Negroes who stayed with their former masters and were ready to give up their lives to protect their white friends. No characters in the story are applauded with greater fervor than the good Negroes whose devotion is so clearly shown. If prejudiced witnesses do not see the message in this portion of the entire drama we are not to blame.

Your editorial is an insult to the intelligence and the human kindness of nearly 100,000 of the best people in New York City, who have viewed this picture from artistic interests and not through any depraved taste such as you try to indicate. Among those you have insulted are your contemporaries on the newspapers of New York, whose expert reviewers were unanimous in their praise of this work as an artistic achievement. Included in this list is your own able critic, Mr. Louis Sherwin, of the *Globe.*

We have received letters of the heartiest commendation from statesmen, writers, clergymen, artists, educators, and laymen. I have in my possession applications for reservations from the principals of ten schools, who having seen the picture, are desirous of bringing their pupils to view it for its historic truths.

The Rev. Dr. Charles H. Parkhurst, the Rev. Father John Talbot Smith, and the Rev. Thomas B. Gregory are among the clergy who have given us permission to use their names in approval of this picture in its entirety. Parents have asked us to make reservation for them that they may bring their children to see it. In every walk of life there are men and women of this city who have expressed their appreciation of this picture. Do you dare to intimate that these voluntary expressions of approval were voiced "for purely sordid reasons"?

The attack of the organized opponents to this picture is centered upon that feature of it which they deem might become an influence against the inter-marriage of blacks and whites. The organizing opponents are white leaders of the National Association for the Advancement of the Colored People, including Oswald Garrison Villard and J. E. Spingarn, who hold official positions in this prointermarriage organization.

May I inquire if you desire to espouse the cause of a society which openly boasts in its official organ, *The Crisis,* that it has been able to throttle "anti-intermarriage legislation" in over ten states? Do you know what this society means by "anti-intermarriage legislation"? It means that they successfully opposed bills which were framed to prohibit the marriage of Negroes to whites.

Do you know that in their official organ, *The Crisis,* for March 1915, they brand 238 members of the Sixty-third Congress as "Negro baiters" because these Representatives voted to prohibit the marriage of Negroes to whites in the District of Columbia?

You close your editorial, in which by innuendo you link our picture to your own assertions, with this sentence:

"To make a few dirty dollars, men are willing to pander to depraved tastes and to foment a race antipathy that is the most sinister and dangerous feature of American life."

That statement is obviously a generality, but it is printed at the end of an editorial which is a covert attack upon our picture, *The Birth of a Nation.* As the producer of that picture, I wish to say if the man who wrote it meant one iota of the sentence just quoted to apply to our picture he is a liar and a coward.

Whether this was the intent of the sentence quoted it could not fail to create an impression in the minds of your readers, damaging my reputation as a producer. Therefore, as a matter of justice, I ask that you publish my statement of the facts.

## Further Resources

### BOOKS

Henderson, Robert. *D.W. Griffith: His Life and Work.* New York: Oxford University Press, 1972.

Silva, Fred, ed. *Focus on "The Birth of a Nation."* Englewood Cliffs, N.J.: Prentice Hall, 1971.

Wagenknecht, Edward, and Anthony Slide. *The Films of D.W. Griffith.* New York: Crown, 1975.

### PERIODICALS

Franklin, John Hope. "*Birth of a Nation*: Propaganda as History." *Massachusetts Review* 20, no. 3, 1979, 417–434.

Tyler, Bruce M. "Racist Art and Politics at the Turn of the Century." *Journal of Ethnic Studies* 15, no. 4, 1988, 85–103.

**WEBSITES**

*The Birth of a Nation.* The Internet Movie Database. Available online at http://www.imdb.com/Title?0004972; website home page: http://www.imdb.com (accessed November 21, 2002).

**AUDIO AND VISUAL MEDIA**

*The Birth of a Nation.* Special Edition. Directed by D.W. Griffith. Kino Video. Videocassette, 1993.

---

# "The Imagining Ear"

Lecture

**By:** Robert Frost

**Date:** 1915

**Source:** Frost, Robert. "The Imagining Ear." *Collected Poems, Prose & Poetry.* New York: Library of America, 1995.

**About the Author:** Robert Frost (1874–1963) was born in San Francisco, California. His father, William Prescott Frost, was a New Englander, and his mother, Isabel Moodie Frost, was Scottish. William, a journalist and local politician, died when Frost was 11, and the family returned to the East coast to live with family members. Though not an ambitious student, young Robert found that he loved literature during high school. He eventually attended both Dartmouth College and Harvard, but did not earn a degree from either school. Frost supported himself by teaching, farming, and working in a textile mill before he began publishing poetry. In 1895, he married Elinor White. His first poem had been published in 1894 and he continued to try to write poetry. In 1912, the Frosts went to live in England, where they remained for three years. During this time, Robert Frost published his first book of poetry, *A Boy's Will* (1914). His second book, *North of Boston,* was published the following year and is generally considered his best work. These volumes established Frost as a poet. Throughout his career, he received many awards, including four Pulitzer Prizes and the Bollingen Prize for Poetry. He served as a poet in residence at several universities and published many more volumes of poetry. Frost died in 1963. ∎

## Introduction

Robert Frost delivered a lecture to the Browne and Nichols School on May 10, 1915. In the lecture he differentiated between sound and visual cues of the poet. Visual cues (colors, sights, and so on) are often discussed, but according to Frost the "imaginary ear" is just as important. He describes the difficulty of capturing tones, or real speech, on paper. Frost objects to "mechanical repetition" or repeating sounds just for the sake of repetition. Frost encourages his audience to "Get the stuff of life into the technique of your writing." He uses two of his well-known poems, "The Pasture" and "Mending Wall" to make his points.

Frost relied on the Romantic traditions for his poetry. Victorian poetry had moved away from the Romantic tradition, using flowery and highly rhetorical speech and language instead of language of everyday. Frost liked to think that he was original in his use of sound. But he wasn't. Poets had worked on capturing the sounds of spoken language for centuries. What Frost did was capture the language of the New England region.

Frost's poetry is sometimes seen as deceptively simple. It is easy to read and, therefore, people think it is easy to understand. He did not receive as much attention as his contemporaries because of the seemingly simple style but he never betrayed his style to try to imitate others. Frost often adds an ironic twist in his poetry. For example, in "Mending Wall" he uses the lines "Good fences make good neighbors" twice to make a point about the neighbor's attitude. He relied on techniques, on discovering the sounds and the meters that would get his message across and left the interpretation to the reader. His emphasis on the pastoral, or rural, setting may have added to the thought that he was easy to understand. In both "The Pasture" and "Mending Wall," the topics are familiar: Going to clean the spring and fetch a calf in the first poem and fixing the traditional New England stone wall in the second.

## Significance

By emphasizing sound and speech, Frost was returning to the Romantic tradition in poetry. William Wordsworth believed that poets were "men speaking to men." Frost relied on the speech of those around him, the New England farmer, and his neighbors in New Hampshire, to provide him with idiomatic and dialectic speech for his poetry.

Frost's poetry differed from his contemporaries who were experimenting with free verse, Imagism, and Vortexism. His poetry seemed more traditional. In fact, he was experimenting not only with sound but also with meter and blank verse. Frost's poems did confront the modernist feeling of alienation.

Frost's essay is important because it shows his awareness of his craft. He realized what he was doing in the poetry and how he was crafting lines and selecting words to influence the reader's interpretation. Beyond that, the poems that he chose as illustrations are ones that have gained prominence in the Frost canon. Both poems were published in *North of Boston.* "The Pasture" was used as a preface in that volume and in other later volumes. "Mending Wall" was the first poem in the collection. "The Pasture" has one speaker. It was originally written as an apology to his wife Elinor, attempting to demonstrate his devotion to her. The speaker would not spend long on the mundane things. The poem is in the pastoral tradition. Nature plays a central role in the poem, with the water, the leaves, and the calf each playing a part. In his lecture, Frost emphasizes capturing the thing you are writing about. He does this here in simple description and an invitation for a companion to experience the natural world by his side.

"Mending Wall" is mentioned as the second example but the text is not included. It is worth some examination to show how Frost's ideas are also depicted in this poem. Again, Frost captures the language of the people. The narrator and his neighbor set out to fix the wall one more year. In a dramatic monologue the narrator challenges his neighbor's ideas about fences with questions about their use. In this poem Frost uses repetition twice. The line "Something there is that doesn't love a wall" and "Good fences make good neighbors" are both repeated. There are good reasons for this. The fence or wall works as a metaphor to explore boundaries, individualism, and neighborliness. There are questions about tradition woven into the poem. Fences are mended each year because they always have been, but do they need to be? The fence not only separates crops, but it also separates people. The poem is sometimes interpreted as pitting pragmatic reasons for walls or boundaries against limitless imagination. Others interpret the speaker as not taking sides and leaving it to the reader. No matter the interpretation of either poem, both demonstrate Frost's craft and his philosophy of composing poetry.

## Primary Source

### "The Imagining Ear"

**SYNOPSIS:** Robert Frost's lecture on the Imagining Ear is summarized from notes by George Browne. The entire lecture is not included. The examples that Frost provided for "The Pasture" provide insight into Frost's mind and how he saw his poetry.

Mr. Browne has alluded to the seeing eye. I want to call your attention to the function of the imagining ear. Your attention is too often called to the poet with extrordinarily vivid sight, and with the faculty of choosing exceptionally telling words for the sight. But equally valuable, even for school-boy themes, is the use of the ear for material for compositions. When you listen to a speaker, you hear words, to be sure,—but you also hear tones. The problem is to note them, to imagine them again, and to get them down in writing. But few of you probably ever thought of the possibility or of the necessity of doing this. You are generally told to distinguish simple, compound, and complex sentences,—long and short,—

Though extraordinarily popular with the American public, Robert Frost's poems have been generally overlooked for their technical achievements. **THE LIBRARY OF CONGRESS.**

periodic and loose,—to varying sentence structure, etc. "Not all sentences are short, like those of Emerson, the writer of the best American prose. You must vary your sentences, like Stevenson, etc." All this is missing the vital element. I always had a dream of getting away from it, when I was teaching school,—and, in my own writing and teaching, of bringing in the *living* sounds of speech. For it is a fundamental fact that certain forms depend on the sound;—e.g., note the various tones of irony, acquiescence, doubt, etc. in the farmer's "I guess so." And the great problem is, can you get these tones down on paper? How *do* you tell the tone? By the context, by the animating spirit of the living voice. And how many tones do you think there are flying around? Hundreds of them—hundreds never brought to book. Compare T. E. Brown's *To a Blackbird* : "O blackbird, what a boy you are" Compare W. B. Yeats's "Who dreamed that beauty passes like a dream"

I went to church, once (loud laughter)—this will sound funnier when I tell you that the only thing I remember is the long line of "Nows" that I counted. The repetition grew tiresome. I knew just when to expect a 'Now', and I knew beforehand just what the tone was going to be. There is no objection to repetition of the right kind,—only to the mechanical repetition of the tone. It is all right to repeat, if there is something for the voice to do. The vital thing, then, to consider in all composition, in prose or verse, is the ACTION of the voice,—sound-posturing, gesture. Get the *stuff* of life into the technique of your writing. That's the only escape from dry rhetoric.

When I began to teach, and long after I began to write, I didn't know what the matter was with me and my writing and with other people's writing. I recall distinctly the joy with which I had the first satisfaction of getting an expression adequate for my thought. I was so delighted that I had to cry. It was the second stanza of the little poem on the Butterfly, written in my eighteenth year. And the Sound in the mouths of men I found to be the basis of all effective expression,—not merely words or phrases, but sentences,—living things flying round,—the vital parts of speech. And my poems are to be read in the appreciative tones of this live speech. For example, there are five tones in this first stanza,

### "The Pasture"

I'm going out to clean the pasture spring; *(light, informing tone)*
I'll only stop to rake the leaves away *("only" tone—reservation)*
(And wait to watch the water clear, I may): *(supplementary, possibility)*
I shan't be gone long.—You come too. *(free tone, assuring) (after thought, inviting) "Rather well for me"—*

I'm going out to fetch the little calf
That's standing by the mother. It's so young,
It totters when she licks it with her tongue.
I shan't be gone long.—You come too. *Similar, free, persuasive, assuring, and inviting tones in second stanza)*

### Further Resources

**BOOKS**

Faggen, Robert, ed. *The Cambridge Companion to Robert Frost.* Cambridge, Mass.: Cambridge University Press, 2001.

Frost, Robert. *Collected Poems, Prose, & Plays.* New York: Library of America, 1995.

Parini, Jay. *Robert Frost: A Life.* New York: Henry Holt, 1999.

**PERIODICALS**

*The Robert Frost Review.* Rock Hill, S.C.: Robert Frost Society, 1991–present

**WEBSITES**

The Robert Frost Web Page. Available online at http://www.robertfrost.org/indexgood.html (accessed March 4, 2003).

"Robert Frost." The Academy of American Poets. Available

online at http://www.poets.org/poets/poets.cfm?prmID=196 (accessed March 4, 2003).

**AUDIO AND VISUAL MEDIA**

Frost, Robert. *Robert Frost Reads.* New York: Cademon, 1992.

---

# Charlie Chaplin as the "Little Tramp"

Movie still

**By: Charlie Chaplin**

**Date:** 1915

**Source:** The Kobal Collection. Reproduced by permission.

**About the Artist:** Charlie Chaplin (1889–1977) was born in London, England. His parents were both performers, and he began performing at an early age. Chaplin's father died when he was twelve years old, and his mother suffered from mental illness, so Charlie and his brother eventually were placed in a charity home. By age 17, Chaplin had joined a vaudeville troupe and was touring the United States. Mack Sennett, a director for Keystone Pictures, saw him perform and signed him to a movie contract in 1913. His first film, *Making a Living,* was released in 1914. Chaplin would eventually star in more than eighty films. He was also a director, film writer, and one of the founding members of the United Artists film company. He was married four times. Plagued by questions about his politics and his personal life, Chaplin moved to Switzerland in 1952. He returned to the United States only once, to accept an Oscar for lifetime achievement in 1972, five years before he died. ∎

## Introduction

The Little Tramp first appeared in 1915 in the film *Kid Auto Races at Venice.* The character was born when Chaplin, told to find a funny costume, threw together a few articles of clothing and some props he found around the studio. Chaplin continued using the same costume, with slight refinements, for the next twenty-five years. As Theodore Huff has observed, the "costume personifies shabby gentility—the fallen aristocrat at grips with poverty."

The Little Tramp quickly became a well-known character, and Charlie Chaplin was soon famous—and rich. When Chaplin signed his contract with Keystone Pictures it was for $150 a week. In 1915, he switched to Essanay, another film company, demanding a $10,000 signing bonus and $1,250 per week. The deal made Chaplin the highest-paid actor in the United States, but he proved his worth when the Little Tramp became a nationwide craze. The character was featured in most of Chaplin's movies, including such silent film classics as *The Tramp* (1915), *Work* (1915), *The Floorwalker*

## Primary Source

### Charlie Chaplin as the "Little Tramp"

**SYNOPSIS:** Charlie Chaplin in a scene from *The Tramp.* The "Little Tramp," one of the most beloved characters of the silent film era, was created on the spur of the moment. Charlie Chaplin threw together oversize pants that belonged to actor Fatty Arbuckle; size 14 shoes from another actor, Ford Sterling; a tight-fitting coat; and a small derby. A toothbrush mustache completed the costume—and a cultural icon was born. THE KOBAL COLLECTION. REPRODUCED BY PERMISSION.

(1916), *A Dog's Life* (1918), *City Lights* (1931), and *Modern Times* (1936).

## Significance

The Little Tramp is perhaps the best-known character of the silent screen. Charlie Chaplin's image of the lost innocent spoke to his war-battered generation. He was carefree and funny, providing a welcome relief from the cares of hard times. Chaplin often mixed the vulgar with the genteel when he was portraying his character; The Little Tramp could be abrasive and crude in his early films. But within a few years, Chaplin had softened his character to attract larger audiences. Even when the character was vulgar, however, Chaplin's humor was obvious, and people lined up to see his films.

Imitators abounded. In the Ziegfeld Follies, the dancing girls donned bowlers, baggy pants, and mustaches. Magazines ran Charlie Chaplin caricatures and popularity contests. Songs appeared with Chaplin's name in the title. Chaplin's image was used to sell a variety of products—an example of early commercial tie-ins with movie stars. Dolls, hats, squirt rings, and other merchandise were created to take advantage of his star power.

Chaplin's skills, which he honed on vaudeville stages, were perfectly suited to silent films. His talent for pantomime was what made the exaggerated walk and other characteristics of the Little Tramp so humorous. Chaplin despaired when the "talkies" appeared. He said, "Talkies are spoiling the oldest art in the world—the art of pantomime. They are ruining the great beauty of silence. They are defeating the meaning of the screen."

Chaplin believed in shooting great amounts of film and in saving the film that had been cut. These habits, seen as wasteful at the time, have helped preserve his legacy. Today Chaplin's films, which are among the best of the period, are more widely available than those of any other silent movie star. This has allowed film historians and others to examine his techniques and to learn more about the silent film era.

## Further Resources

### BOOKS

Huff, Theodore. *Charlie Chaplin.* New York: Arno Press and *The New York Times,* 1972.

Maland, Charles J. *Chaplin and American Culture: The Evolution of a Star Image.* Princeton: Princeton University Press, 1989.

McDonald, Gerald D., Michael Conway, and Mark Ricci. *The Films of Charlie Chaplin.* New York: Bonanza Books, 1965.

### PERIODICALS

Benjamin, Walter, and Rudolph Arnheim. "On Charlie Chaplin." Translated by John Mackay. *Yale Journal of Criticism* 9, 1996, 309–314.

A poster for one of the dozens of films in which Chaplin played his "Little Tramp" role. **THE LIBRARY OF CONGRESS.**

Kuriyama, Constance Brown. "Chaplin's Impure Comedy: The Art of Survival." *Film Quarterly* 45.3, 1992, 26–38.

Lyons, Timothy. "An Introduction to the Literature on Chaplin." *Journal of the University Film Association,* Winter 1979, 3–10.

### WEBSITES

Talkie and the Tramp: Charlie Chaplin Stays Silent in the Machine Age. Available online at http://xroads.virginia.edu/g /1930s/FILM/chaplin/frames.html (accessed October 26, 2002).

### AUDIO AND VISUAL MEDIA

*The Artist in His Prime: Starring Charlie Chaplin.* Koch Vision. DVD.

*Chaplin: The Collection.* Madacy Entertainment. Videocassette.

*Charlie Chaplin: The Eternal Tramp.* Twentieth Century Fox. Videocassette, 1992.

*Charlie Chaplin Marathon.* Laserlight Video. Videocassette.

*Early Masterpieces Starring Charlie Chaplin.* Koch Vision. DVD.

*The Unknown Chaplin.* Documentary. Written, directed, and produced by Kevin Brownlow and David Gill. HBO Video. Videocassette, 1983.

# *Boy With Baby Carriage*

Magazine cover

**By:** Norman Rockwell

**Date:** 1916

**Source:** *Saturday Evening Post*

**About the Author:** Norman Rockwell (1894–1978) was born in Manhattan, New York. His father, a textile company executive, liked to draw for amusement, so young Norman grew up in a home where art was a part of everyday life. Rockwell began art classes at age 14 at the New York School of Art. He left high school to pursue art studies full time, and went on to study at the Art Students League with Thomas Fogarty and George Bridgman. Here he learned the techniques that would make him a success. By sixteen, Rockwell was painting Christmas cards on commission. He worked for *Boys' Life* as a teenager as well. When he was twenty-one, Rockwell moved from Manhattan to New Rochelle, N.Y. He continued to paint for magazines such as *Life, Literary Digest,* and *Country Gentleman.* In 1916, he sold his first cover to *Saturday Evening Post,* thereby beginning a relationship that would continue for 47 years. His most famous series of paintings may be the *Four Freedoms,* completed in 1943. In 1977, Rockwell received the Presidential Medal of Freedom for his "vivid and affectionate portraits of our country." Rockwell was married three times and had three sons with his second wife, Mary. ■

## Introduction

Norman Rockwell was considered the Painter of the People. His art, through magazine covers and paintings, became icons for American life in the twentieth century. Rockwell painted 322 covers for *The Saturday Evening Post* during a 47-year period. His subjects included small-town folk—in other words, ordinary Americans. While some have criticized Rockwell's work as overly sentimental, generations have embraced the themes that he portrayed because they were sentimental. Rockwell painted anecdotes and stories that were valuable because they represented experiences any person could identify with. His paintings, such as the *Four Freedoms,* symbolized what America stood for during World War II.

Rockwell painted his first *Saturday Evening Post* cover in 1916 when he was twenty-two. He had a secret ambition to paint for the *Post* because the circulation was high and the magazine was respected. But like many artists, he feared rejection. Rockwell first tried to paint covers like the ones that had been appearing on the *Post.* The figures of Gibson girls and High Society characters did not suit his style, however. Clyde, Rockwell's studio partner, encouraged him to do what he was good at: children. Rockwell called on Billy Paine, a neighbor, and began creating prototypes for covers. What he finally came up with was *Boy With Baby Carriage.* In the painting, two boys are teasing another one. The boy who is being teased

is dressed formally, like an adult, and wheeling a baby carriage. The boys who are doing the teasing are dressed for play. Rockwell sold two covers to the *Post* on the first try and was given a contract for three more. Little did he know he was destined to create more than 300 covers for the *Post.* Rockwell recalls that "I still have a warm spot in my heart for [my first cover], as it initiated my long and enjoyable association with the *Post.* . . . The best part of the gag was the baby's bottle in the boy's pocket; I received lots of letters about his humiliation. My model was Billy Paine, who posed for many of my early covers."

## Significance

Rockwell understood what would reach an audience. Over a seven-decade period, he produced thousands of images. He painted every day, no matter what the day. "The commonplace Americans are to me the richest subjects in art," Rockwell wrote in 1936. "Boys batting flies on vacant lots; little girls playing jacks on the front steps; old men plodding home at twilight, umbrellas in hand— all of these things arouse feeling in me. Commonplaces never become tiresome. It is we who become tired when we cease to be curious and appreciative" (Hennessey, 24).

*Boy With Baby Carriage* began Rockwell's long career with the *Saturday Evening Post.* The circulation of

Illustrator Norman Rockwell was well-known for his gentle and humorous depictions of small-town American life. **GETTY IMAGES. REPRODUCED BY PERMISSION.**

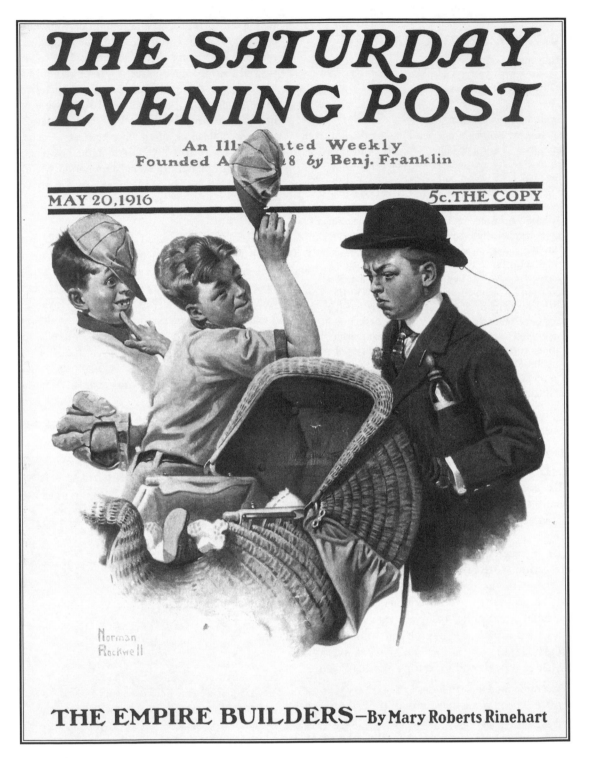

THE SATURDAY EVENING POST

An Illustrated Weekly
Founded A.     18 *by* Benj. Franklin

MAY 20, 1916                                   5c. THE COPY

Norman
Rockwell

THE EMPIRE BUILDERS—By Mary Roberts Rinehart

## Primary Source

*Boy With Baby Carriage*

**SYNOPSIS:** Three boys and a baby appear in the first cover Norman Rockwell produced for the *Saturday Evening Post*. The cover tells the story of an obviously miserable older brother given the duty of strolling with a younger sibling. The boys cannot resist making fun of the "little man" who looks so formal and so unhappy. COLLECTION OF THE NORMAN ROCKWELL MUSEUM AT STOCKBRIDGE, NORMAN ROCKWELL ART COLLECTION TRUST.

the *Post* had reached one million by 1908 and doubled that by 1929. Rockwell's paintings reached this audience through this first—and all subsequent—covers. Readers were introduced to fine art through familiar subjects and in the comfort of their homes. Even though Rockwell's paintings did not look like formal museum pieces, they were still examples of fine art, and now they were readily available to the average citizen. The readers of the *Post* could feel like they were looking at themselves and their neighbors as they gazed at a Rockwell cover. These were the boys next door or down the street. People could attach a narrative to the cover immediately and know the story behind the painting. This was part of the *Post* philosophy espoused by George Lorimer, editor until 1936. Rockwell's paintings epitomized the ideology of the *Saturday Evening Post.* Lorimer set out to "create America" through the pages of the *Post* by presenting readers with current information, fiction, articles, and illustrations. Lorimer said that Rockwell's covers, or any other artists' covers, had to hit him right away. If they didn't, he didn't want them. Rockwell knew that formula that would "hit" Lorimer and the readers. His covers were always best sellers because he painted the ordinary person and told a story whose ending was already known.

## Further Resources

### BOOKS

Hennessey, Maureen Hart, and Anne Knutson. *Norman Rockwell: Pictures for the American People.* Atlanta: High Art Museum, 2000.

### WEBSITES

The Norman Rockwell Museum at Stockbridge. Available online at http://www.nrm.org (accessed March 4, 2003).

# "Chicago"
Poem

**By:** Carl Sandburg

**Date:** 1916

**Source:** Sandburg, Carl. "Chicago." *Chicago Poems.* New York: Holt, 1916. Reprinted in *The Complete Poems of Carl Sandburg,* rev. and exp. New York: Harcourt Brace Jovanovich, 1970, 3–4.

**About the Author:** Carl Sandburg (1878–1967) was a poet, biographer, journalist, novelist, children's author, and folk musician. He was born in Galesburg, Illinois, to Swedish immigrants. Sandburg left school in the eighth grade, worked odd jobs, traveled by rail, and fought in the Spanish-American War (1898). He eventually returned to Galesburg and enrolled in Lombard College. He never graduated, but he did meet Professor Philip Green Wright, who encouraged him

to write poetry. Sandburg held a number of jobs after he left college, including working for the Social Democratic Party and as a journalist for the *Chicago Daily News* and other papers. In addition to poetry, he is remembered for his biographical works on Abraham Lincoln. He was awarded Pulitzer Prizes in both history and literature. ∎

## Introduction

Carl Sandburg was working as a journalist and editor when he wrote the poems that would be published in his first volume of poetry, *Chicago Poems.* In 1914, he sent some of his work to Harriet Monroe, editor of *Poetry: A Magazine of Verse.* Reportedly, the opening lines of the poem "Chicago" shocked Monroe, but she realized that Sandburg was a promising poet. Monroe published nine of Sandburg's poems in the March 1914 issue of *Poetry.* For his efforts, the poet received a check for $100 and the $200 Helen Haire Levinson Prize for the best poems of the year.

During this period, Sandburg became acquainted with many of the other poets and writers living in Chicago. Among his friends and colleagues were Edgar Lee Masters, Sherwood Anderson, Vachel Lindsay, and Amy Lowell.

*Chicago Poems* was published in 1916. Reviews either praised the volume or dismissed it. *The Dial* called Sandburg's work "gross, simple-minded, sentimental, sensual." A reviewer for the *Boston Transcript,* on the other hand, saw the poems' "visual strength." Amy Lowell criticized Sandburg for the political slant of the poems, labeling them "propaganda."

## Significance

*Chicago Poems* is considered one of Sandburg's best volumes of poetry. It established his reputation as the literary voice of Chicago and as a "poet of the people." "Chicago," the opening poem of the volume and one of Sandburg's best-known poems, is significant both for its style and its subject matter.

Sandburg was inspired by Walt Whitman's style and adopted a free verse structure in his work. Unlike the poetry of the previous century, or of some of his contemporaries, Sandburg's poetry had no rhyme. The lines varied in length, and the construction of the poem on the page communicated some of the meaning.

The harsh images and working-class subjects of Sandburg's poems were also unusual at the time. "Chicago" seemed rough to many, but it expressed the individual voices of Sandburg and of the Midwestern city he called home. Sandburg selected unconventional subjects and images to depict the Chicago that he knew. In "Chicago," writes his biographer, Richard Crowder, Sandburg "unlocked language, form and subject matter some found distasteful, some puzzling, some invigorating."

Acclaimed poet and author Carl Sandburg in 1919. Sandburg first gained public notice with his 1914 poem *Chicago.* © BETTMANN/CORBIS. REPRODUCED BY PERMISSION.

Sandburg was part of the immigrant working class that lived in the Midwest and migrated to Chicago in hopes of finding a better life. Sandburg often described the immigrant experience in his poetry, and he was a strong supporter of the laboring classes. He experimented with images that showed readers he was a voice of (in his words) the "people—the mob—the crowd—the mass." These traits are evident in "Chicago," and for this reason, the poem has been viewed as propaganda. But Sandburg's themes demonstrate not only his Socialist background, but also his understanding of the common man. In the poem's opening lines and in the last stanza, he describes the city through the industrial roles its people play. He presents a city and a people who are both tragic and full of life.

In *Chicago Poems,* Sandburg demonstrates his versatility as a poet and stylist. While some of the works are overtly political, the volume also includes lyrical and imagist poetry. Sandburg was a newspaper writer, so it may be not surprising that some of his images are spare. But he always manages to select the right word to convey his perceptions of the city. In "Chicago," for instance, he describes the city as "bareheaded," in a single word evoking the image of an unpretentious, hardworking man.

## Primary Source

### "Chicago"

**SYNOPSIS:** The harsh images that Sandburg uses in "Chicago" surprised many readers. But he wrote about a reality that many Midwesterners knew. In the poem, Chicago, like all large cities, has two faces: a pleasant face presented to the public, and an ugly face seen only by those living in certain neighborhoods or working in industrial jobs. Sandburg presents the city's evil characteristics—prostitutes, thieves, poverty—but he contrasts them with its strengths. His vivid words depict a vital city emerging into greatness.

### Chicago

Hog Butcher for the World,
Tool Maker, Stacker of Wheat,
Player with Railroads and the Nation's
 Freight Handler;
Stormy, husky, brawling,
City of the Big Shoulders:

They tell me you are wicked and I believe them, for I
 have seen your painted women under the gas
 lamps luring the farm boys.
And they tell me you are crooked and I answer: Yes,
 it is true I have seen the gunman kill and go free to
 kill again.
And they tell me you are brutal and my reply is: On
 the faces of women and children I have seen the
 marks of wanton hunger.
And having answered so I turn once more to those
 who sneer at this my city, and I give them back the
 sneer and say to them:
Come and show me another city with lifted head
 singing so proud to be alive and coarse and strong
 and cunning.
Flinging magnetic curses amid the toil of piling job on
 job, here is a tall bold slugger set vivid against the
 little soft cities;
Fierce as a dog with tongue lapping for action,
 cunning as a savage pitted against the wilderness,
  Bareheaded,
  Shoveling,
  Wrecking,
  Planning,
  Building, breaking, rebuilding,
Under the smoke, dust all over his mouth, laughing
 with white teeth,
Under the terrible burden of destiny laughing as a
 young man laughs,
Laughing even as an ignorant fighter laughs who
 has never lost a battle,
Bragging and laughing that under his wrist is
 the pulse, and under his ribs the heart of the
 people,
    Laughing!
Laughing the stormy, husky, brawling laughter of
 Youth, half-naked, sweating, proud to be Hog
 Butcher, Tool Maker, Stacker of Wheat, Player with
 Railroads and Freight Handler to the Nation.

## Further Resources

### BOOKS

Crowder, Richard. *Carl Sandburg.* New York: Twayne, 1964.

Niven, Penelope. *Carl Sandburg: A Biography.* New York: Charles Scribner's Sons, 1991.

### PERIODICALS

Alexander, William. "The Limited American, the Great Loneliness, and the Singing Fire: Carl Sandburg's 'Chicago Poems.'" *American Literature: A Journal of Literary History, Criticism and Bibliography* 45, 1973, 67–83.

Van Wienen, Mark. "Taming the Socialist: Carl Sandburg's Chicago Poems and Its Critics." *American Literature: A Journal of Literary History, Criticism and Bibliography* 63.1, 1991, 89–103.

### WEBSITES

"Carl Sandburg (1878–1967)." University of Illinois at Urbana-Champaign Department of English. Available online at http://www.english.uiuc.edu/maps/poets/s_z/sandburg/sandburg.htm; website home page: http://www.english.uiuc.edu (accessed July 31, 2002).

Carl Sandburg: Chicago Poems. Available online at http://carl-sandburg.com (accessed March 4, 2003).

"Carl Sandburg Web." University of Illinois at Urbana-Champaign Graduate School of Library and Information Science. Available online at http://alexia.lis.uiuc.edu/~rmrober/sandburg/index.html; website home page: http://www.lis.uiuc.edu (accessed July 31, 2002).

### AUDIO AND VISUAL MEDIA

Sandburg, Carl. *Carl Sandburg Reads: A Poetry Collection.* Harper Audio. Audiocassette, 2001.

# Evening Star, III

Painting

**By:** Georgia O'Keeffe

**Date:** 1917

**Source:** O'Keeffe, Georgia. *Evening Star, III.* The Museum of Modern Art. Available online at http://www.moma.org (accessed May 7, 2003).

**About the Author:** Georgia O'Keeffe (1887–1986) was born in Sun Prairie, Wisconsin. At the age of 12, she decided to

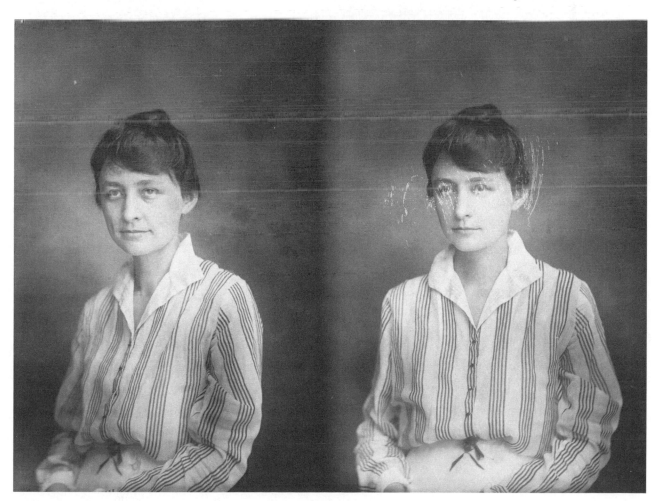

Studio portraits of artist Georgia O'Keeffe, taken July 19, 1915. THE HOLSINGER STUDIO COLLECTION, X3371A, SPECIAL COLLECTIONS DEPARTMENT, UNIVERSITY OF VIRGINIA LIBRARY (HTTP://WWW.LIB.VIRGINIA.EDU/SPECCOL/HOLSINGER/).

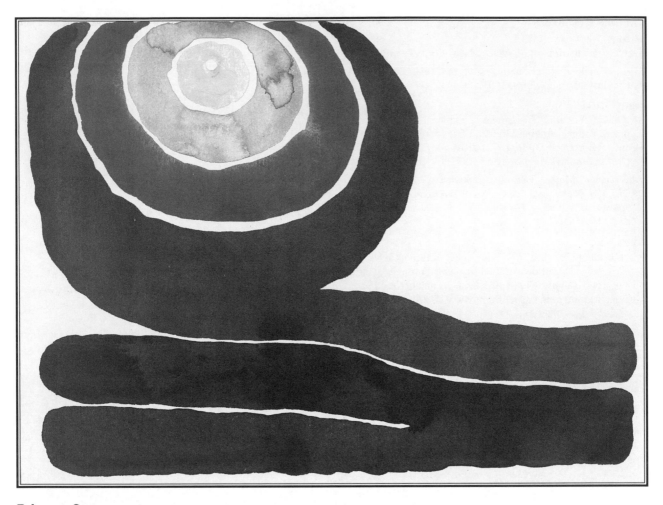

## Primary Source

*Evening Star, III*

**SYNOPSIS:** *Evening Star, III.* 1917. Watercolor on paper, 8 7/8" x 11 7/8." Mr. And Mrs. Donald B. Straus Fund (91.1958).

DIGITAL IMAGE © THE MUSEUM OF MODERN ART/LICENSED BY SCALA/ART RESOURCE NY. © 2003 THE GEORGIA O'KEEFFE FOUNDATION/ARTISTS RIGHTS SOCIETY (ARS), NEW YORK.

become an artist. She studied at the Art Institute of Chicago, at the Art Students League of New York, and with several well-known artists including William Merritt Chase and Arthur Wesley Dow. As a young woman O'Keeffe taught art in Virginia, Texas, and South Carolina. Her first exhibition was in 1916 at the 291 gallery in New York City, run by photographer Alfred Stieglitz, whom she married in 1924. O'Keeffe became one of the most important American painters of the twentieth century, known for large-scale, close-up abstract paintings of flowers, and landscapes, particularly of the American Southwest. She spent the later part of her life in New Mexico. ∎

### Introduction

Georgia O'Keeffe received an excellent formal education in art. After finishing her studies in Chicago and New York, she continued to study during summers at the University of Virginia. But although she learned her craft, she did not feel that she expressed herself through her art. At Virginia she developed an interest in anti-academic art movements and in Symbolist notions of art. She taught these concepts to her students in Virginia, Texas, and South Carolina. By 1914, O'Keeffe had become interested in the Modernist movement in Europe.

While teaching at a women's college in South Carolina in 1915–1916, O'Keeffe began to define her own theories about her art. The isolation of being at a small school where she knew no one allowed O'Keeffe to discover her own approach. She took time to paint and draw and to discover her strengths as an artist. She questioned the purpose of her art and whom she painted for, eventually deciding that she needed to incorporate her own vision in her work. She crawled around on the floor drawing with charcoal, using her whole body to express what her mind envisioned.

O'Keeffe was not comfortable exhibiting her work at this time; she felt it was too personal. But she did send some of her charcoal drawings to a friend, Anita Pollitzer, in New York. Against O'Keeffe's instructions, Pollitzer showed the drawings to Alfred Stieglitz. He would exhibit them at his gallery, 291, later that year.

The following year, Stieglitz mounted a one-person exhibit of O'Keeffe's work, then convinced her to move to New York and paint, with his financial support. This was the beginning of the couple's lifelong personal and professional collaboration.

## Significance

The year that she spent in South Carolina was one of revelation for Georgia O'Keeffe. During that time she uncovered the emotions and the self-expression she had been holding back from her art. In her autobiography, O'Keeffe describes this critical period in the development of her art and explains the process that led to her artistic breakthrough.

O'Keeffe viewed her own work and studied what she liked and disliked. At one point she wrote in her autobiography, "This thing that is our own is so close to you, often you never realize it's there." She envisioned abstract images and shapes and eventually decided to paint them. Through this process she uncovered the abstraction that would be the basis of her future work.

The series of charcoal drawings that O'Keeffe produced from 1915–1916 opened up new possibilities for her art—and led to her personal and professional relationship with her mentor and husband. Stieglitz responded to the freedom of expression in O'Keeffe's drawings, which corresponded to his own ideas about art.

O'Keeffe's newly found artistic vision and passion, combined with Stieglitz's recognition of her talent and willingness to show her art, launched her career. The first exhibition of O'Keeffe's drawings at the 291 gallery was well received by the critics. The works were viewed as sexual, psychological, and biographical renderings. O'Keeffe went on to become one of the century's best known and important American artists.

## Further Resources

**BOOKS**

Eldredge, Charles C. *Georgia O'Keeffe.* New York: Harry N. Abrams Publishers, 1991.

Lisle, Laurie. *Portrait of an Artist: A Biography of Georgia O'Keeffe.* New York: Seaview Books, 1980.

O'Keeffe, Georgia. *Georgia O'Keeffe.* New York: Viking Press, 1976.

Peters, Sarah Whitaker. *Becoming O'Keeffe: The Early Years.* New York: Abbeville Press Publishers, 1991.

**WEBSITES**

Georgia O'Keeffe Museum. Available online at http://www.okeeffemuseum.org/indexflash.html (accessed July 31, 2002).

# "Over There"
Song

**By:** George M. Cohan

**Date:** 1917

**Source:** Cohan, George M. "Over There." New York: Leo Feist, 1917. Historic American Sheet Music: 1910–1920, music no. 1170. Rare Book, Manuscript, and Special Collections Library, Duke University. Available online at http://scriptorium.lib.duke.edu/cgi-bin/nph-dweb/dynaweb/sheetmusic/1910-1920/@Generic__BookTextView/35813; website home page: http://scriptorium.lib.duke.edu (accessed November 26, 2002).

**About the Artist:** George Michael Cohan (1878–1942) was born on either the third or fourth of July in Providence, Rhode Island. As a child, he performed with his family in a vaudeville act called "The Four Cohans." He began composing music at age ten and sold his first song at sixteen. His big break came with the 1904 Broadway musical *Little Johnny Jones.* Cohan was involved in eighty-seven Broadway shows, including twenty-three musicals, and wrote more than five hundred songs. ■

In addition to composing music and lyrics, George Cohan also acted, directed, and wrote plays and movies. GETTY IMAGES. REPRODUCED BY PERMISSION.

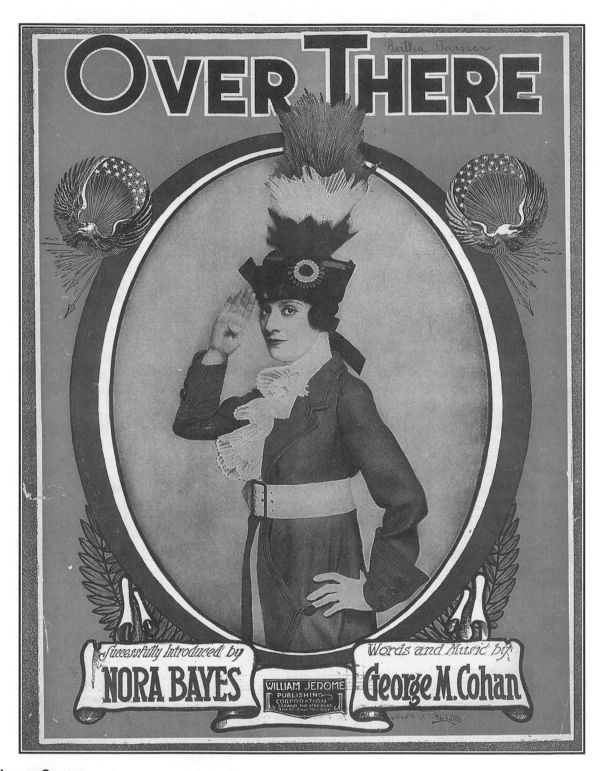

## Primary Source

**"Over There"** (1 OF 3)

**SYNOPSIS:** With very little formal training, George Cohan managed to write what is considered by most historians to be the most popular morale song of World Wars I and II—"Over There." Originally published in English, the lyrics were also translated into French. There were a variety of sheet-music releases, with three different covers in all. MUSIC 1186, DUKE UNIVERSITY RARE BOOK, MANUSCRIPT, AND SPECIAL COLLECTIONS LIBRARY.

**Primary Source**

"Over There" (2 OF 3)

Sheet music for George Cohan's "Over There," page 1. "OVER THERE." WORDS AND MUSIC BY GEORGE M. COHAN. REPRODUCED BY PERMISSION.

**Primary Source**

**"Over There" (3 OF 3)**

Sheet music for George Cohan's "Over There," page 2. "OVER THERE." WORDS AND MUSIC BY GEORGE M. COHAN. REPRODUCED BY PERMISSION.

## Introduction

The United States officially entered World War I on April 6, 1917. Although the war had begun in 1914, the United States remained neutral until May 1915, when a German U-boat sank the British passenger liner *Lusitania,* killing 128 Americans, most of them civilians. After an unsuccessful attempt to give Germany a chance to enter into negotiations, the United States sided with the Allies and prepared for war. The scope of World War I was different from that of any other war America had fought. This was no revolution, no civil war, but a global conflict involving thirty-two nations. Families feared for their sons as they sent them off to a foreign land they knew virtually nothing about, to fight an enemy they knew only from radio reports and wartime propaganda. Building patriotism and keeping hope alive was important on the home front.

1917 was still a time of innocence in America, and Cohan's timing couldn't have been better. The actor and playwright composed the song "Over There" at a critical moment, just as American soldiers were beginning to enter the war. The "doughboys," as these soldiers were called, were eager to fight the good fight, not yet ever having experienced the atrocities of wartime, and "Over There" generated an enthusiasm that helped whip Americans into a patriotic fervor. By stressing pride, bravery, and liberty, the song brilliantly conveyed America's strength and integrity and proved invaluable in organizing the U.S. Army's recruitment drive.

## Significance

Although Cohan's family claims he wrote "Over There" at home, many accounts report that he created the tune and lyrics while riding on a train. Inspired by the patriotic headlines of the newspapers being read by fellow passengers, Cohan reportedly had the song completely figured out by the time he reached his destination. Regardless of where it came about, "Over There" was written on the eve of April 6, 1917, as the United States entered World War I. Having enjoyed great success with songs such as "Yankee Doodle Boy" and "Give My Regards to Broadway," Cohan was already well known, which put him in a perfect position to stir the patriotism and "war fever" simmering in the hearts of many Americans. Cohan achieved this by imitating a bugle call in the song, dramatizing the notes and words he felt would inspire listeners. Americans needed to feel confident and morally justified in marching into a battle many were not prepared to fight.

"Over There" was first performed publicly by singer Charles King at a Red Cross benefit concert. In 1918, it was recorded by Nora Bayes and became a smash hit, selling more than a million copies and two million copies of sheet music. Opera star Enrico Caruso even recorded a version partially sung in French. Through the years, the song was recorded dozens of times, becoming one of Cohan's most enduring hits. In 1936, Cohan was awarded the Congressional Medal of Honor for "Over There" and "You're a Grand Old Flag." Several years later, "Over There" would be revived as a patriotic rallying call during World War II (1939–1945).

## Further Resources

### BOOKS

Cohan, George. *Twenty Years on Broadway, and the Years It Took to Get There: The True Story of a Trouper's Life From the Cradle to the "Closed Shop."* Westport, Conn.: Greenwood, 1971.

McCabe, John. *George M. Cohan: The Man Who Owned Broadway.* New York: Doubleday, 1973.

Morehouse, Ward. *George M. Cohan: Prince of the American Theater.* Philadelphia, Pa.: J.B. Lippincott, 1943. Reprint, Westport, Conn.: Greenwood, 1972.

### PERIODICALS

Cerf, Bennett. "Sweet Notes for Music Week: How 'Over There' was Written." *Saturday Review of Literature* 27, January 22, 1944, 14.

Rose, K.D. "Patriotic Music: 'Over There.'" *Hobbies* 49, August 1994, 113.

### WEBSITES

George M. Cohan Landmark. Available online at http://www.cohanlandmark.com (accessed November 26, 2002).

"George M. Cohan's Theatre." Internet Broadway Database. Available online at http://www.ibdb.com/venue.asp?ID=1171; website home page: http://www.ibdb.com (accessed November 26, 2002).

Kenrick, John, comp. "George M. Cohan 101." Musicals101.com. Available online at http://www.musicals101.com/cohan.htm; website home page: http://www.musicals101.com (accessed November 26, 2002).

"Meet George M. Cohan." Institute for Elementary and Secondary Education, Brown University. Available online at http://www.brown.edu/Departments/IESE/attlas/gregorian/cohan; website home page: www://www.brown.edu (accessed November 26, 2002).

### AUDIO AND VISUAL MEDIA

Feinstein, Michael. *Over There: Songs of War and Peace, 1900–1920.* EMI Angel CDC-7-49768-2. CD, 1989.

# "Mandy"

Song

**By:** Irving Berlin

**Date:** 1919

**Source:** Berlin, Irving. "Mandy: Ziegfeld Follies of 1919." Irving Berlin, Inc. *Historic American Sheet Music: 1910–1920.* Duke University Rare Book, Manuscript, and Special Collections Library.

**Primary Source**

Mandy, *Ziegfeld Follies of 1919* (1 OF 4)

**SYNOPSIS:** "Mandy" ended Act One of the Ziegfeld Follies of 1919. It was a minstrel-style number: A soft-shoe dance preceded it, and a tambourine routine was performed during the song. The refrain was sung first by a singer dressed as a black child, with a chorus of African American children. Then three other performers entered and sang the entire song. It is a typical Irving Berlin tune, one that made the listener feel good and one that reached several generations. COURTESY OF THE ESTATE OF IRVING BERLIN. REPRODUCED BY PERMISSION.

## Primary Source

**Mandy, *Ziegfeld Follies of 1919* (2 OF 4)**
Sheet music of "Mandy" from *Ziegfeld Follies of 1919,* page 3. "MANDY." WORDS AND MUSIC BY IRVING BERLIN. © COPYRIGHT 1919
BY IRVING BERLIN. COPYRIGHT RENEWED. COPYRIGHT ASSIGNED TO THE TRUSTEES OF THE GOD BLESS AMERICA FUND. INTERNATIONAL COPY-
RIGHT SECURED. ALL RIGHTS RESERVED.

**Primary Source**

Mandy, *Ziegfeld Follies of 1919* (3 OF 4)

Sheet music of "Mandy" from *Ziegfeld Follies of 1919,* page 4. "MANDY." WORDS AND MUSIC BY IRVING BERLIN. © COPYRIGHT 1919 BY IRVING BERLIN. COPYRIGHT RENEWED. COPYRIGHT ASSIGNED TO THE TRUSTEES OF THE GOD BLESS AMERICA FUND. INTERNATIONAL COPYRIGHT SECURED. ALL RIGHTS RESERVED.

## Primary Source

**Mandy,** *Ziegfeld Follies of 1919* **(4 OF 4)**

Sheet music of "Mandy" from *Ziegfeld Follies of 1919*, page 5. "MANDY." WORDS AND MUSIC BY IRVING BERLIN. © COPYRIGHT 1919 BY IRVING BERLIN. COPYRIGHT RENEWED. COPYRIGHT ASSIGNED TO THE TRUSTEES OF THE GOD BLESS AMERICA FUND. INTERNATIONAL COPYRIGHT SECURED. ALL RIGHTS RESERVED.

Prolific and popular songwriter Irving Berlin in 1914. © BETTMANN/CORBIS. REPRODUCED BY PERMISSION.

**About the Artist:** Irving Berlin (1888–1989) was born in Mohilev, Russia. His birth name was Israel Baline. He moved to the United States with his parents and five older siblings in 1893. Young Israel dropped out of school at age 13, and even though he had no musical training, he became a successful street entertainer. In 1907, he was asked to collaborate with a café pianist and published his first song, "Marie from Sunny Italy." At the same time he adopted a new name, Irving Berlin. Although he did not read or write music, Berlin became a sought-after composer for Tin Pan Alley (as the sheet music publishing business was then called). He married Dorothy Goetz in 1912, but she died soon afterward. In 1917, Berlin joined the Army; he was stationed at Camp Upton on Long Island. In 1926, he married Ellin MacKay. Berlin continued writing songs for Tin Pan Alley, Broadway, and eventually Hollywood. He founded his own music publishing company and ran his own New York City theater. One of the most successful composers of the twentieth century, he wrote the music and lyrics for more than 1,500 songs. Berlin lived to the age of 101. ■

## Introduction

Popular entertainment in the 1910s included vaudeville, minstrel shows, and musicals. Popular music was light and comic, even through the war period. Composers such as Jerome Kern, George M. Cohan, and Irving Berlin wrote tunes that America sang and danced to. At this time, a song's popularity was determined by the number of copies of sheet music it sold, rather than by the number of recordings.

Irving Berlin was an up-and-coming young composer in the 1910s. He had established his reputation with tunes like "Alexander's Ragtime Band" (1911–12), which became a wildly popular phenomena across the country. Early in his career, Berlin wrote mostly comedic parodies. After the death of his first wife, he turned to writing ballads. These would become some of his trademark songs.

Berlin first became associated with the Ziegfeld Follies in 1911. Florenz Ziegfeld had begun the Follies—musical revues that featured chorus girls, singing, and dancing—in 1907. The Ziegfeld Follies were updated yearly and remained popular through the Depression years. "Mandy" was one of the hits of the Ziegfeld Follies of 1919.

## Significance

Although not his best-known work, "Mandy" is a typical, feel-good Irving Berlin tune. It serves as an interesting example of the way Berlin recycled his own material. It is also noteworthy because, in its three incarnations, it has been popular with several generations of Americans.

"Mandy" began as a song written for the Army show *Yip! Yip! Yaphank.* Berlin was the producer of the show, a fundraiser for a service club at Camp Upton, where he was stationed. The tune was titled "The Sterling Silver Moon" in this production.

While "The Sterling Silver Moon" was one of the hits of *Yip! Yip! Yaphank,* along with "Oh, How I Hate to Get Up in the Morning," it did not receive major attention until it appeared in the Ziegfeld Follies of 1919. The 1919 Follies were an extravaganza. War had ended the year before, and Ziegfeld spared no expense in getting the best stars and composers for his show. Berlin's contributions included "A Pretty Girl is Like a Melody," a song that would become a trademark of the Follies, and a rewrite of "The Sterling Silver Moon" called "Mandy."

Berlin often imitated himself or rewrote songs that didn't quite make it the first time. The rewritten refrain for "Mandy" was more direct and upbeat. The ring, minister, and wedding chimes predict a happy life for Mandy and her beau. Gus Van, Joe Schenck, and Marilyn Miller performed the song, which was a hit. A million copies of sheet music were sold.

But Berlin was not yet finished with "Mandy." In the 1950s, he recycled it and other songs from the Ziegfeld Follies for *White Christmas,* a film starring Bing Crosby and Danny Kaye. Once again Americans across the country were humming the song. "Mandy" continues to reach an audience of film buffs, as *White Christmas* is now considered a movie classic.

## Further Resources

**BOOKS**

Barrett, Mary Ellin. *Irving Berlin: A Daughter's Memoir.* New York: Simon & Schuster, 1994.

Jablonski, Edward. *Irving Berlin: American Troubador.* New York: Henry Holt, 1997.

**WEBSITES**

"Irving Berlin on Film." Bright Lights Film Journal. Available online at http://www.brightlightsfilm.com/30/irvingberlin1 .html; website home page http://www.brightlightsfilm.com (accessed July 30, 2002).

**AUDIO AND VISUAL MEDIA**

*Irving Berlin's White Christmas.* Paramount Home Video. Videocassette, 1985.

*Ziegfeld Follies of 1919.* CBS Records. LP, 1977.

# "September, 1918"

Poem

**By:** Amy Lowell

**Date:** 1919

**Source:** Lowell, Amy. "September, 1918." In *Pictures of the Floating World.* New York: Macmillan, 1919. Reprinted in

*The Complete Poetical Works of Amy Lowell.* Boston: Houghton Mifflin, 1955.

**About the Author:** Amy Lowell (1874–1925) was born in Brookline, Massachusetts, into a wealthy, old New England family. Her predecessors founded two Massachusetts cities, Lowell and Lawrence. Her famous brother, Abbott Lawrence Lowell, was the president of Harvard, and the poet Robert Lowell was a distant cousin. Amy Lowell lived her entire life on a ten-acre estate called Sevenels. She was encouraged to write from a young age and was tutored by governesses and sent to private schools. As an adult, Lowell was known for her outspokeness and her unconventional lifestyle. A leading member of the Imagist school of poetry, she published nine volumes of verse. She was also a noted critic, biographer (of John Keats), reviewer, and spokeswoman for modern poetry. Her volume *What O'Clock* was awarded the Pulitzer Prize for poetry in 1926, the year after she died. ∎

## Introduction

Often controversial, Amy Lowell considered herself a "self-appointed prophet for American poetry." She felt it was her job to inform the American public about poetic verse and to improve its taste in poetry. After reading a poem by H.D. (the pen name of Hilda Doolittle) in a 1913 issue of *Poetry* magazine, Lowell became interested in the Imagist movement. She traveled to London to meet Ezra Pound, H.D., Richard Aldington, and others in the Imagist school. Lowell embraced the Imagist approach in her own poetry and promoted the movement in America.

Imagism relied on succinct verse and precise visual images. Lowell called it "poetry that is hard and clear, never blurred or indefinite." In her introduction to an anthology of Imagist poetry, Lowell exhorted poets to "use the language of common speech, but to employ the exact word, not the nearly exact, nor the merely decorative word."

Lowell is not remembered as a great poet, but she did experiment with innovative forms. She frequently wrote in *vers libre,* or free verse, which is poetry that does not follow a strict metrical pattern. And she was the first English-speaking poet to employ polyphonic prose in her poetry. This is rhythmical prose that employs poetic devices, but not the strict meter of poetry.

## Significance

Amy Lowell was established as an Imagist by the time she published *Pictures of the Floating World* in 1919. Critic Louis Untermeyer has described the volume as Lowell's "most personal revelation." The poem "September, 1918" appears in a section of *Pictures of the Floating World* titled "Dreams in War Time."

"September, 1918" is a good example of an Imagist poem. It uses common language, and it presents a clear image that lets the reader experience the scene. What can

American poet Amy Lowell. **HISTORICAL PICTURES SERVICES. REPRODUCED BY PERMISSION.**

This afternoon was the colour of water falling through
sunlight;
The trees glittered with the tumbling of leaves;
The sidewalks shone like alleys of dropped maple
leaves,
And the houses ran along them laughing out of
square, open windows.
Under a tree in the park,
Two little boys, lying flat on their faces,
Were carefully gathering red berries
To put in a pasteboard box.

Some day there will be no war,
Then I shall take out this afternoon
And turn it in my fingers,
And remark the sweet taste of it upon my palate,
And note the crisp variety of its flights of leaves.
To-day I can only gather it
And put it into my lunch-box,
For I have time for nothing
But the endeavour to balance myself
Upon a broken world.

## Further Resources

**BOOKS**

Benvenuto, Richard. *Amy Lowell.* Boston: Twayne Publishers, 1985.

Flint, F. Cudworth. *Amy Lowell.* Minneapolis: University of Minnesota Press, 1969.

Gould, Jean. *Amy: The World of Amy Lowell and the Imagist Movement.* New York: Dodd, Mead, 1975.

**PERIODICALS**

Francis, Lesley Lee. "A Decade of 'Stirring Times': Robert Frost and Amy Lowell." *The New England Quarterly* 59, no. 4, 1986, 508–522.

**WEBSITES**

"Amy Lowell." Modern American Poetry. Department of English, University of Illinois at Urbana-Champaign. Available online at http://www.english.uiuc.edu/maps/poets/g_l /amylowell/lowell.htm; website home page http://www .english.uiuc.edu (accessed July 26, 2002).

be perceived through the senses is important in this and other poems in *Pictures of the Floating World.* The first line of "September, 1918" helps the reader visualize the colors in the air and water. Sound also becomes important: The houses laugh. Taste—the sweetness of memory—enters in the second stanza. This aesthetic quality is one of the strengths of Lowell's poetry.

World War I also had a major impact on Lowell's work. Many of her poems explore how the war affected everyone. In "September, 1918," she reflects on the simplicity and beauty of life that is overwhelmed by the destructive presence of war.

## Primary Source

### "September, 1918"

**SYNOPSIS:** An example of Amy Lowell's Imagist poetry, "September, 1918" is also significant because it explores the effects of World War I. The first stanza of the poem concentrates on the images of a fall day and of innocent children as they gather berries, oblivious to the ravages of war. In stanza two, the unidentified speaker gathers up this image to be savored on a later day, when war and the fears that accompany it do not so dominate life.

## "Paper Pills"

Short story

**By:** Sherwood Anderson

**Date:** 1919

**Source:** Anderson, Sherwood. *"The Philosopher."* Little Review, *June–July, 1916. Reprinted as "Paper Pills," in Winesburg, Ohio: A Group of Tales of Ohio Small-Town Life.* New York: The Modern Library, 1919, 18–23.

**About the Author:** Sherwood Anderson (1875–1941) was born in Ohio. His family was poor and broke apart after his mother's death in 1895. He fought in Cuba in the Spanish-American War, moved several times, and worked at many jobs before he began his writing career. Among other things he was an advertising copywriter, the president of a manufacturing company, and a newspaper publisher and editor. In 1913 he moved to Chicago, where he began writing fiction. His fourth book, a collection of short stories called *Winesburg, Ohio,* was published in 1919, and established his literary reputation. A novelist, poet, playwright, and journalist as well as a short-story writer, he eventually produced twenty-seven books, including seven novels. A lifelong traveler, he died in Panama. ■

## Introduction

The literary atmosphere in Chicago was vibrant and exciting during the 1910s. Sherwood Anderson was acquainted with many of the prominent and up-and-coming writers who collectively formed the Chicago Renaissance. He was in a city with Carl Sandburg, Vachel Lindsay, and Edgar Lee Masters, whose *Spoon River Anthology* may have paved the way for his own *Winesburg, Ohio.* He knew Harriet Monroe, editor of *Poetry: A Magazine of Verse,* and Margaret Anderson, editor of the *Little Review.* His rooming house was full of artists and writers.

The publication of *Winesburg, Ohio* was a turning point in Anderson's career. He was in his forties and had previously published two novels and a book of poetry, but they were not terribly successful. Nine of the *Winesburg, Ohio* stories were published individually before Anderson collected them in a volume. The short story "Paper Pills" was first published as "The Philosopher" in the 1916 June–July issue of the *Little Review.*

Based on Anderson's boyhood home of Clyde, Ohio, and other Ohio towns that he had lived in, *Winesburg, Ohio* is a collection of twenty-one short stories, each one about a resident of the fictional town. It presents stories of real life and of ordinary people—their heartaches and hopes, dreams, and disappointments.

## Significance

Sherwood Anderson rebelled against middle-class politeness and the literary establishment. His stories in *Winesburg, Ohio* are dark and contain more dangerous characters than readers of the time were used to. Life was difficult and messy in Anderson's world, and he thought literature should reflect that reality. He resented writers like O. Henry and W.D. Howells, who he felt stifled the voices of true life. He did not like short stories that could be neatly wrapped up with an easy solution. Subjects and plots did not have to be pleasant, he believed. "With the publication of Winesburg," he wrote, "I felt I had really begun to write out of the repressed, muddled life about me."

Anderson's realistic depictions of small-town American life and his psychological analysis of his characters make *Winesburg, Ohio* his masterpiece and most influen-

tial work. The format of the collection, with its intertwined stories, was unusual for the time. So was its subject matter. Anderson's characters, whom he called "grotesques," are people who live in isolation, their longings for community somehow thwarted. The lives of his alienated characters—such as Dr. Reefy in "Paper Pills"—are often no better at the end of the story than at the beginning.

Anderson's book received mixed reviews. Some thought the plots were too ugly and the stories too sad. The book was referred to as "nasty" and "dirty" by some critics. But others believed the collection revealed a true and unvarnished picture of small-town American life. "Nothing quite like it has ever been done in America," wrote H.L. Mencken. "It is so vivid, so full of insight, so shiningly life-like and glowing, that the book is lifted into a category all its own." Some reviewers praised Anderson's ability to psychoanalyze his characters and their motives. J.V.A. Weaver wrote that Anderson presented "a panorama, with souls instead of trees, with minds in place of houses."

Although Anderson is not considered a major literary figure, his innovative approach to the short story served as a model for writers who would follow him. Critic Malcolm Cowley has called Anderson "the only storyteller of his generation who left his mark on the style and vision of the generation that followed. Hemingway, Faulkner, Wolfe, Steinbeck, Caldwell, Saroyan, Henry Miller . . . each of these owes an unmistakable debt to Anderson."

## Primary Source

"Paper Pills"

> **SYNOPSIS:** The protaganist of "Paper Pills" is one of Sherwood Anderson's "grotesques." Physically mishapen, socially stunted, yet also thoughtful and kind, Dr. Reefy befriends a young woman who is pregnant by a suitor who only sought her money. They fall in love and marry, but she soon dies of a mysterious disease. Dr. Reefy is left to sit in his musty office, wearing the same clothes each day and reading the scraps of paper on which he collects his thoughts. The story, with its dark realism and psychoanalytic underpinnings, is an example of Anderson's rebellion against the literary conventions of the day.

He was an old man with a white beard and huge nose and hands. Long before the time during which we will know him, he was a doctor and drove a jaded white horse from house to house through the streets of Winesburg. Later he married a girl who had money. She had been left a large fertile farm when her father died. The girl was quiet, tall, and dark, and to

Author Sherwood Anderson, best known for his collection of short stories *Winseburg, Ohio,* which explored the dark realities of small-town America. **REPRODUCED BY PERMISSION OF HAROLD OBER ASSOCIATES INC.**

many people she seemed very beautiful. Everyone in Winesburg wondered why she married the doctor. Within a year after the marriage she died.

The knuckles of the doctor's hands were extraordinarily large. When the hands were closed they looked like clusters of unpainted wooden balls as large as walnuts fastened together by steel rods. He smoked a cob pipe and after his wife's death sat all day in his empty office close by a window that was covered with cobwebs. He never opened the window. Once on a hot day in August he tried but found it stuck fast and after that he forgot all about it.

Winesburg had forgotten the old man, but in Doctor Reefy there were the seeds of something very fine. Alone in his musty office in the Heffner Block above the Paris Dry Goods Company's store, he worked ceaselessly, building up something that he himself destroyed. Little pyramids of truth he erected and after erecting knocked them down again that he might have the truths to erect other pyramids.

Doctor Reefy was a tall man who had worn one suit of clothes for ten years. It was frayed at the sleeves and little holes had appeared at the knees

and elbows. In the office he wore also a linen duster with huge pockets into which he continually stuffed scraps of paper. After some weeks the scraps of paper became little hard round balls, and when the pockets were filled he dumped them out upon the floor. For ten years he had but one friend, another old man named John Spaniard who owned a tree nursery. Sometimes, in a playful mood, old Doctor Reefy took from his pockets a handful of the paper balls and threw them at the nursery man. "That is to confound you, you blathering old sentimentalist," he cried, shaking with laughter.

The story of Doctor Reefy and his courtship of the tall dark girl who became his wife and left her money to him is a very curious story. It is delicious, like the twisted little apples that grow in the orchards of Winesburg. In the fall one walks in the orchards and the ground is hard with frost underfoot. The apples have been taken from the trees by the pickers. They have been put in barrels and shipped to the cities where they will be eaten in apartments that are filled with books, magazines, furniture, and people. On the trees are only a few gnarled apples that the pickers have rejected. They look like the knuckles of Doctor Reefy's hands. One nibbles at them and they are delicious. Into a little round place at the side of the apple has been gathered all of its sweetness. One runs from tree to tree over the frosted ground picking the gnarled, twisted apples and filling his pockets with them. Only the few know the sweetness of the twisted apples.

The girl and Doctor Reefy began their courtship on a summer afternoon. He was forty-five then and already he had begun the practice of filling his pockets with the scraps of paper that became hard balls and were thrown away. The habit had been formed as he sat in his buggy behind the jaded white horse and went slowly along country roads. On the papers were written thoughts, ends of thoughts, beginnings of thoughts.

One by one the mind of Doctor Reefy had made the thoughts. Out of many of them he formed a truth that arose gigantic in his mind. The truth clouded the world. It became terrible and then faded away and the little thoughts began again.

The tall dark girl came to see Doctor Reefy because she was in the family way and had become frightened. She was in that condition because of a series of circumstances also curious.

The death of her father and mother and the rich acres of land that had come down to her had set a train of suitors on her heels. For two years she saw suitors almost every evening. Except two they were all alike. They talked to her of passion and there was a strained eager quality in their voices and in their eyes when they looked at her. The two who were different were much unlike each other. One of them, a slender young man with white hands, the son of a jeweler in Winesburg, talked continually of virginity. When he was with her he was never off the subject. The other, a black-haired boy with large ears, said nothing at all but always managed to get her into the darkness, where he began to kiss her.

For a time the tall dark girl thought she would marry the jeweler's son. For hours she sat in silence listening as he talked to her and then she began to be afraid of something. Beneath his talk of virginity she began to think there was a lust greater than in all the others. At times it seemed to her that as he talked he was holding her body in his hands. She imagined him turning it slowly about in the white hands and staring at it. At night she dreamed that he had bitten into her body and that his jaws were dripping. She had the dream three times, then she became in the family way to the one who said nothing at all but who in the moment of his passion actually did bite her shoulder so that for days the marks of his teeth showed.

After the tall dark girl came to know Doctor Reefy it seemed to her that she never wanted to leave him again. She went into his office one morning and without her saying anything he seemed to know what had happened to her.

In the office of the doctor there was a woman, the wife of the man who kept the bookstore in Winesburg. Like all old-fashioned country practitioners, Doctor Reefy pulled teeth, and the woman who waited held a handkerchief to her teeth and groaned. Her husband was with her and when the tooth was taken out they both screamed and blood ran down on the woman's white dress. The tall dark girl did not pay any attention. When the woman and the man had gone the doctor smiled. "I will take you driving into the country with me," he said.

For several weeks the tall dark girl and the doctor were together almost every day. The condition that had brought her to him passed in an illness, but she was like one who has discovered the sweetness of the twisted apples, she could not get her mind fixed again upon the round perfect fruit that is eaten in the city apartments. In the fall after the beginning of her acquaintanceship with him she married Doctor Reefy and in the following spring she

died. During the winter he read to her all of the odds and ends of thoughts he had scribbled on the bits of paper. After he had read them he laughed and stuffed them away in his pockets to become round hard balls.

## Further Resources

### BOOKS
Townsend, Kim. *Sherwood Anderson.* Boston: Houghton Mifflin, 1987.

White, Ray Lewis, ed. *Sherwood Anderson's "Winesburg, Ohio" with Variant Readings and Annotations.* Athens: Ohio University Press, 1997.

———. *"Winesburg, Ohio": An Exploration.* Boston: Twayne, 1990.

### PERIODICALS
Dunne, Robert. "Beyond Grotesqueness in *Winesburg, Ohio.*" *The Midwest Quarterly* 31, no. 2, 1990, 180–191.

### WEBSITES
The Sherwood Anderson Literary Center. Available online at http://andersonproject.winesburg.com/ (accessed March 4, 2003).

*Winesburg, Ohio.* American Literary Classics Library Available online at http://www.americanliterature.com/WO/WOINDX .HTML; website home page http://www.americanliterature .com (accessed June 27, 2002).

### AUDIO AND VISUAL MEDIA
Anderson, Sherwood. *Winesburg, Ohio.* Cademon Audio. Audiocassette, 2002.

# A Poet's Life: Seventy Years in a Changing World
Autobiography

**By:** Harriet Monroe

**Date:** 1938

**Source:** Monroe, Harriet. *A Poet's Life: Seventy Years in a Changing World.* New York: Macmillan, 1938, 251–254.

**About the Author:** Harriet Monroe (1860–1936) was born in Chicago, the second daughter of Henry Stanton Monroe, a lawyer, and Martha Mitchell Monroe. A poet and an art critic for the *Chicago Tribune,* she also taught school and helped establish the Chicago Institute of Arts. But she is best known as the editor of *Poetry: A Magazine of Verse,* which she founded in 1912. Monroe died in 1936 while on a trip to Peru. Her autobiography, *A Poet's Life: Seventy Years in a Changing World,* was published two years later, in 1938. ∎

## Introduction

The beginning of the twentieth century was a transitional time for poetry, and for literature in general. Walt

Whitman had forged new ground for poets when he began writing in free verse at the close of the nineteenth century. In the early 1900s, the modernist movement was just emerging, and poets such as T.S. Eliot, Robert Frost, Carl Sandburg, and Amy Lowell were at or near the beginning of their careers. Poetic forms were moving from predictable rhyme schemes to more experimental approaches. Dadaism, surrealism, jazz, spirituality, and urban life were all influencing poetry. The first volumes of several noted poets were published between 1910 and 1919, including Robert Frost's *A Boy's Will* (1913) and *North of Boston* (1914), Vachel Lindsay's *The Congo and Other Poems* (1914), Carl Sandburg's *Chicago Poems* (1916), and Edgar Lee Masters' *Spoon River Anthology* (1915). Several philosophies of poetry existed during this period. Ezra Pound exhorted colleagues to "make it new" and encouraged poets to describe the "direct treatment of a thing." T.S. Eliot wanted to fix the world through his poetry, which sometimes seemed disjointed and dismal. Poets such as William Carlos Williams espoused "no ideas but in things" and sought to convey themes through concrete images rather than abstract terms.

Despite this evolution in poetic technique, poetry was still viewed as a "page filler" by many magazines. Harriet Monroe, herself a minor poet, was distressed with the place of poetry in the arts. While the visual arts, music, drama, and literature all were respected, poetry seemed to be an afterthought. In her autobiography, *A Poet's Life: Seventy Years in a Changing World,* she describes her role in promoting and publicizing the exciting developments that took place in the world of poetry in the decade following 1910. Monroe was well connected in Chicago circles, and she used her connections to raise funds for a poetry journal that would feature the best poems of the day. She also sought out contributors for her magazine, spending hours researching contemporary poets and their work. Monroe insisted on paying for submissions, an important step that would help put poetry on equal footing with other art forms. *Poetry: A Magazine of Verse* was launched in October 1912.

**Significance**

*Poetry: A Magazine of Verse* is the oldest monthly poetry magazine in the English-speaking world. Its mission is the same today as when it was founded in 1912: to publish the best poetry available. Harriet Monroe borrowed *Poetry*'s motto from Walt Whitman: "To have great poets, a nation must have a great audience." Her goal in beginning *Poetry* was to provide a place for poets to publish and be read. This was her first attempt at editorship, and she decided that she would publish poetry of any length, but not poetry with a clearly political agenda or poetry from poets who were "writing the same old thing." Monroe sought out poets whose work she found in literary magazines and who she thought had promise. She also solicited the advice of other poets, such as Ezra Pound, to help her find poetry suitable for publication. Monroe realized that what might appear to be a minor poem could in fact make a poet's career. She published the works of lesser-known poets as well as poems by those who had already made a name for themselves.

*Poetry* quickly established itself as a leading journal. The founding of the magazine came at the same time as the Chicago Renaissance, and it became a vehicle for the poets in that movement. Pound provided poems from the then-unknown T.S. Eliot, whose "The Love Song of J. Alfred Prufrock" appeared in *Poetry* in 1915. Works by Wallace Stevens, Marianne Moore, and many other noted poets have also appeared in its pages. In fact, almost every important American poet of the twentieth century has been published in *Poetry*. The monthly magazine remains fiercely independent—it is not tied to any institution, movement, or tradition. It continues to feature poems by both major American poets and those who are unknown. Monroe's philosophy of publishing the best poetry available and of being open to poetry that is new and different continues to be the credo of the publication.

In November 2002, *Poetry*'s future was secured indefinitely when pharmaceutics heiress Ruth Lilly made a staggering $100 million bequest to the magazine, overnight transforming *Poetry* from a struggling literary journal to one of the world's richest publications. "Poetry has always had the reputation as being the poor little match girl of the arts," said U.S. poet laureate Billy Collins. "Well, the poor little match girl just hit the lottery."

## Primary Source

*A Poet's Life: Seventy Years in a Changing World*
[excerpt]

> **SYNOPSIS:** In this excerpt from her autobiography, *A Poet's Life: Seventy Years in a Changing World,* Harriet Monroe describes how she founded and solicited poems for the first issue of *Poetry*. Through research and her many contacts, Monroe managed to gather works by some of the best poets of the day. She eventually came to know most of the important poets of the early twentieth century.

### Poetry: A Magazine of Verse

Through June and July of that summer of 1912 I spent many hours at the public library reading not only recent books by the better poets, but also all the verse in American and English magazines of the previous five years. To the poets I thought interesting was sent, in August and early September, a "poets' circular," which, after explaining the financial basis on which the new magazine was founded, continued as follows:

The success of this first American effort to encourage the production and appreciation of poetry, as the other arts are encouraged, by endowment, now depends on the poets. We offer them:

*First,* a chance to be heard in their own place, without the limitations imposed by the popular magazine. In other words, while the ordinary magazines must minister to a large public little interested in poetry, this magazine will appeal to, and it may be hoped will develop, a public primarily interested in poetry as an art, as the highest, most complete human expression of truth and beauty.

*Second,* within space limitations imposed at present by the small size of our monthly sheaf—from sixteen to twenty-four pages the size of this—we hope to print poems of greater length and of more intimate and serious character than the other magazines can afford to use. All kinds of verse will be considered—narrative, dramatic, lyric—quality alone being the test of acceptance. Certain numbers may be devoted entirely to a single poem, or a group of poems by one person; except for a few editorial pages of comment and review.

*Third,* besides the prize or prizes above mentioned, we shall pay contributors. The rate will depend on the subscription list, and will increase as the receipts increase, for this magazine is not intended as a money maker but as a public-spirited effort to gather together and enlarge the poet's public and to increase his earnings. If we can raise the rate paid for verse until it equals that paid for paintings, etchings, statuary, representing as much ability, time and reputation, we shall feel that we have done something to make it possible for poets to practice their art and be heard. In addition, we should like to secure as many prizes, and as large, as are offered to painters and sculptors at the annual exhibitions in our various cities.

In order that this effort may be recognized as just and necessary, and may develop for this art a responsive public, we ask the poets to send us their best verse. We promise to refuse nothing because it is too good, whatever be the nature of its excellence. We shall read with special interest poems of modern significance, but the most classic subject will not be declined if it reaches a high standard of quality.

We wish to show to an ever-increasing public the best that can be done today in English verse. We hope to begin monthly publication in November or December, 1912, at the low subscription rate of $1.50 a year. We ask that writers of verse will be interested enough to contribute their best work, and that all who love the art will subscribe.

A personal letter was sent with most of these circulars, referring individually to the poet's work or to something I had heard or felt about it. The carbons in our files, usually dated August 7th or 8th, when I hired a typist to tick the letters off, follow this general pattern: "Some of your recent verse makes me hope that you will be interested in this rather adventurous attempt to give the art of poetry a voice in the land, and that you will submit some poems for early publication."

Looking over this early correspondence, I am astonished at the amount of it, its adequacy in covering the field which existed at that time. Individual letters were sent to more than fifty poets, American and British; and this was not the whole story, for circulars sometimes went without the personal word. Among the poets who received such letters were: (American) Madison Cawein, Fannie Stearns Davis, Floyd Dell, Arthur Ficke, Hermann Hagedorn, Agnes Lee, Vachel Lindsay, John A. Lomax, Amy Lowell, Percy MacKaye, Edwin Markham, Josephine Peabody Marks, Grace Fallow Norton, James Oppenheim, Shaemus O'Sheel, Ezra Pound, Edwin Arlington Robinson, Charles Edward Russell, Louis Untermeyer, George Sylvester Viereck, Edith Wharton, Hervey White, Helen Hay Whitney, John Hall Wheelock, and George Edward Woodberry; (British) Lascelles Abercrombie, Joseph Campbell, Wilfrid Wilson Gibson, Frederic Manning, John Masefield, Alice Meynell, Harold Monro, Henry John Newbolt, Alfred Noyes, Stephen Phillips, Ernest Rhys, James Stephens, Herbert Trench, Allen Upward, and William Butler Yeats.

Answers expressing sympathetic interest and inclosing or promising poems came promptly from all these poets except Edith Wharton and Mrs. Whitney, Messrs. Yeats and Noyes via their agents. Some of these answers seemed as intimate and as expressive of personality as a handshake—from the warmth of Arthur Ficke's, who wrote on August 8th: "Your letter of yesterday has deeply interested me, and I shall be very glad to do anything I can to assist you. The project has a fine ring to it—I rejoice to see that the Bull Moose movement is not confined to politics"; from this to Mr. Woodberry's polite kindness, in a note sent from Beverly, September 1st: "I beg to thank you for your note of Aug. 7th, and to assure you of my warm interest in the success of your new magazine."

Madison Cawein, who was then near the head of the American procession, was very cordial—"This country has long been in crying need of such a magazine." Hermann Hagedorn promised to contribute "as soon as I find time to iron out the wrinkles in a couple of poems." Amy Lowell, whose recent appearance with the sonnet in *The Atlantic* had interested me, called the proposed magazine "a most excellent undertaking—it ought to do much to foster poetry which has a hard time now to get itself published." And for further testimony she inclosed a check for twenty-five dollars, "knowing that every little helps"—evidently there was at least one poet with a bank account. Floyd Dell, then still a Chicagoan, called the magazine "an exciting event— my interest grows by leaps and bounds."

## Further Resources

### BOOKS

Cahill, Daniel J. *Harriet Monroe.* New York: Twayne, 1973.

Parisi, Joseph, and Stephen Young, eds. *Dear Editor: A History of "Poetry" in Letters.* New York: W.W. Norton, 2002.

———. *The Poetry Anthology 1912–2002.* Chicago: Ivan R. Dee, 2002.

Williams, Ellen. *Harriet Monroe and the Poetry Renaissance: The First Ten Years of "Poetry," 1912–22.* Urbana, Ill.: University of Illinois Press, 1977.

### PERIODICALS

Atlas, Marilyn. "Harriet Monroe, Margaret Anderson, and the Spirit of the Chicago Renaissance." *Midwestern Miscellany* 9, 1981, 43–53.

Francis, Lesley Lee. "Between Poets: Robert Frost and Harriet Monroe." *South Carolina Review* 19, Summer 1987, 2–15.

Kinzer, Stephen. "Lilly Heir Makes $100 Million Bequest to Poetry Magazine." *The New York Times,* November 18, 2002. Available online at http://www.nytimes.com/2002 /11/19/books/19GIFT.html?ex=1038732390&ei=1&en =b94b3183f34033aa; website home page: http://www .nytimes.com (accessed November 20, 2002).

Marek, Jayne. "Alice Corbin Henderson, Harriet Monroe, and *Poetry*'s Early Years." *Illinois Writers Review* 7, no. 2, Winter 1988, 16–21.

Massa, Ann. "'The Columbian Ode' and *Poetry: A Magazine of Verse*: Harriet Monroe's Entrepreneurial Triumphs." *Journal of American Studies* 20, no. 1, April 1986, 51–69.

### WEBSITES

*Poetry: A Magazine of Verse.* Available online at http://www .poetrymagazine.org (accessed October 22, 2002).

### MEDIA OR LIT ERARY REFLECTIONS

Records of *Poetry: A Magazine of Verse,* 1912–1936 (inclusive). Department of Special Collections, University of Chicago Library.

# 2

# BUSINESS AND THE ECONOMY

JAMES N. CRAFT

*Entries are arranged in chronological order by date of primary source. For entries with one primary source, the entry title is the same as the primary source title. Entries with more than one primary source have an overall entry title, followed by the titles of the primary sources.*

**CHRONOLOGY**

Important Events in Business and the
   Economy, 1910–1919 . . . . . . . . . . . . . . . . . . 60

**PRIMARY SOURCES**

Triangle Shirtwaist Factory Fire . . . . . . . . . . . . . . 63
"Eyewitness at the Triangle"
   William Gunn Shepherd, March 27, 1911
*Preliminary Report of the Factory
   Investigating Commission*
   New York (State) Factory Investigating
   Commission, 1912

Scientific Management . . . . . . . . . . . . . . . . . . . . . . 68
*The Principles of Scientific Management*
   Frederick W. Taylor, 1911
Letter to Lindley Garrison
   Maurice W. Bowen, June 17, 1913

Dollar Diplomacy and Its Repudiation . . . . . . . . . . 71
Speech Advocating "Dollar Diplomacy"
   William Howard Taft, December 3, 1912
Speech Repudiating "Dollar Diplomacy"
   Woodrow Wilson, March 19, 1913

*Money Trust Investigation*
   U.S. House of Representatives, December
   19, 1912 . . . . . . . . . . . . . . . . . . . . . . . . . . . . 75

New Parties Challenge the Economic System . . . . . . 83
Progressive Party Platform of 1912
Socialist Party Platform of 1912

*Drift and Mastery: An Attempt to Diagnose
   the Current Unrest*
   Walter Lippmann, 1914 . . . . . . . . . . . . . . . . . . 88

*National Old Trails Road: Ocean to Ocean
   Highway*
   Charles Henry Davis, 1914 . . . . . . . . . . . . . . . 94

Henry Ford's Business Philosophy . . . . . . . . . . . . . 98
*John F. and Horace E. Dodge v. Ford
   Motor Co., Henry Ford, et. al.*
   Henry Ford, 1916
Interview with Henry Ford
   Henry Ford, 1916

J. Walter Thompson House Ads . . . . . . . . . . . . . . 102
   "A New Profession"; "Packages That
   Speak Out"; "Women in Advertising"
   J. Walter Thompson Company,
   1917–1919

*Women Wanted*
   Mabel Potter Daggett, 1918 . . . . . . . . . . . . . . 106

*American Industry in the War*
   Bernard Baruch, 1921 . . . . . . . . . . . . . . . . . . 108

*All God's Dangers: The Life of Nate Shaw*
   Nate Shaw, 1974 . . . . . . . . . . . . . . . . . . . . . . 114

"Last of the Vigilantes"
   Miriam E. Tefft, February 2, 1982 . . . . . . . . . . 117

# Important Events in Business and the Economy, 1910–1919

## 1910

- Nearly one-third of the nation's coal miners are unionized, compared to 10 percent of workers in other industries.

- On January 1, more than 2.5 million women (more than one-third of the U.S. female workforce) work as housekeepers. African American and immigrant women hold the majority of these jobs.

- On June 18, Congress passes the Mann-Elkins Act, which empowers the Interstate Commerce Commission (ICC) to regulate railroad, cable, wireless, telephone, and telegraph companies.

- In July, a survey reports that an unskilled laborer who worked twelve-hour days, seven days a week, could not support a family of five. Poverty forced wives and children to work.

- On September 7, the U.S. and Great Britain settle their dispute over fishing rights in the Atlantic Ocean.

- On October 1, twenty people are killed and seventeen injured when John J. and James McNamara blow up the *Los Angeles Times* building because the newspaper favors the right of workers to choose whether to join a union.

## 1911

- Air conditioning is invented.

- The first motor-driven hook-and-ladder truck, the "Mack," is introduced.

- On February 21, the United States and Japan sign a navigation and commerce treaty that strengthens trade between both nations.

- On March 25, fire in a New York City garment sweatshop kills 146 people, most of them Italian and Jewish women. The Triangle Shirtwaist Company owned the sweatshop and had locked the doors to prevent workers from leaving until the workday ended.

- On April 8, an explosion at a Birmingham, Alabama coalmine kills 128 miners, most of them African American men.

- On May 15, the U.S. Supreme Court rules that the Standard Oil Company of New Jersey monopolized the production and distribution of petroleum in violation of the Sherman Antitrust Act of 1890. The court orders Standard Oil to dis-

solve into several smaller companies in hopes of restoring competition and innovation to the industry.

- On May 29, the U.S. Supreme Court declares the American Tobacco Company a monopoly and orders it to dissolve into several smaller companies.

- In July, Charles Franklin Kettering invents an electric starter for automobiles. The electric starter allows a driver to start a car with a switch or key instead of turning a crank in front of the car.

- On July 7, the United States, Great Britain, Russia, and Japan sign a treaty establishing the right of each to hunt seals in the North Pacific.

- On October 26, the U.S. Justice Department charges the United States Steel Company, the world's largest producer of steel, with violating the Sherman Antitrust Act.

## 1912

- Thirty-eight states ban child labor.

- In January, thirty thousand textile workers, most of them women between ages fourteen and eighteen, strike in Lawrence, Massachusetts after discovering, by examining their paychecks, that management had lowered their wages.

- On January 9, U.S. Marines land in Honduras to protect American companies and property.

## 1913

- Henry Ford introduces the assembly line for the manufacture of automobiles, one of the most significant applications of technology in the twentieth century. Work on the assembly line is so monotonous that Ford must hire 52,000 workers that year to maintain a workforce of 13,600.

- On January 1, a new parcel post service begins, giving farmers closer contact with their fellow citizens and improving the rural post system.

- From January to February, garment workers, led by the International Ladies' Garment Workers' Union (ILGWU), strike in New York and are followed in March by workers in Boston. They demand higher wages, shorter hours, and recognition of their union.

- On February 25, the states ratify the Sixteenth Amendment to the Constitution, authorizing Congress to tax personal and corporate incomes.

- On February 28, a Congressional subcommittee, headed by Rep. Arsene Pujo of Louisiana, reports a "growing concentration of control of money and credit." That is, a small number of large banks hold most of the nation's money.

- On March 1, the Physical Valuation Act empowers the ICC to determine the value of railroad property in order to establish rates.

- From March to April, garment workers win higher wages in New York City and Boston.

- On April 8, President Woodrow Wilson asks Congress to lower tariffs in hopes other countries will reciprocate. A low tariff at home would allow the U.S. to import cheap goods, a plus for consumers; a low tariff in other countries would open them to U.S. goods, a plus for U.S. exporters.

- In May, Grand Central Terminal opens in New York City.

- On June 19, the U.S. Supreme Court allows a state to establish railroad rates within its own borders so long as its rates do not exceed rates set by the ICC.

- In July, the Woolworth Building opens in New York City. At a height of 792 feet, it symbolizes U.S. wealth and technology.

- On August 26, the Keokuk Dam opens. It is the world's largest hydroelectric dam and spans the Mississippi River from Keokuk, Iowa, to Hamilton, Illinois.

- In September, ten thousand coal miners strike in Colorado in response to an open-shop drive led by John D. Rockefeller's Colorado Fuel and Iron Company.

- On October 3, Congress passes the Underwood Tariff Act, as President Woodrow Wilson had urged, reducing tariffs to an average of 26 percent of the value of the good. The act also expands the number of goods free from tariff.

- On December 23, Congress creates the Federal Reserve System.

## 1914

- Henry Ford introduces the five-dollar day for workers on his assembly lines, in the hope that a high wage will keep workers from unionizing and lower a turnover rate that costs Ford millions of dollars in inefficiency and lost productivity.

- On January 20, President Woodrow Wilson, in an address to Congress, asks for tough enforcement of antitrust laws.

- In April, police kill fourteen demonstrators, eleven of them children, who wanted a pay raise in the mines of Ludlow, Colorado.

- On August 15, the Panama Canal opens the isthmus of Panama to merchant ships.

- On August 20, Great Britain orders a naval blockade of Germany, one of its enemies during World War I. The United States protests the blockade as an interference of its right to export goods to any country.

- On September 26, Congress establishes the Federal Trade Commission, empowering it to investigate unfair competition in interstate trade.

- On October 15, Congress passes the Clayton Antitrust Act. The Act strengthens federal power to prosecute monopolies.

## 1915

- The taxicab first appears in American cities. Service costs a nickel, and the popularity of the cabs leads to the development of intercity bus lines.

- On January 15, the first transcontinental telephone line opens for service from New York City to San Francisco.

- On February 10, the United States protests a German declaration of a war zone around the British Isles in fear that U.S. exports to Britain might decline.

- In July, a commission appointed by President Woodrow Wilson recommends that Congress pass an inheritance tax, to prevent fortunes from concentrating in a small number of families, and that businesses and government pay the same wage for the same work, irrespective of gender.

- On October 15, U.S. banks loan $500 million to France and Great Britain. U.S. banks thus have a financial stake in an Allied victory in World War I.

- On December 10, the one millionth Model T rolls off the Ford Motor Company's assembly line in Detroit, Michigan.

## 1916

- Boeing Aircraft Company designs and produces its first model, the biplane.

- On July 17, Congress passes the Federal Farm Loan Act, which sets up twelve Farm Loan Banks to extend long-term loans to farmers.

- On July 30, German saboteurs blow up a munitions dump on Black Tom Island, New Jersey, causing $22 million in damages.

- On August 11, the Warehouse Act enables farmers to secure loans by presenting warehouse receipts to banks as evidence of their ability to repay loans. The measure adopts a central feature of the Populist Party platform of the 1890s known as the "subtreasury" plan.

## 1917

- On February 20, more than one thousand women march to New York City Hall to demand government assistance to buy food. U.S. farmers were exporting food to Britain and France during World War I, leading to shortages and higher prices at home.

- On March 31, the Council of National Defense establishes the General Munitions Board to oversee the production of weapons by U.S. factories.

- On April 24, Congress passes the Liberty Loan Act, empowering the U.S. Treasury to sell bonds to the public, an idea Alexander Hamilton had advocated in the 1780s, and to loan money to the Allies.

- On July 28, the War Industries Board replaced the General Munitions Board, retaining the goal of managing the economy to ensure victory in World War I.

- On August 10, Congress passes the Lever Food and Fuel Control Act to increase the production of food and fuel for U.S. and Allied forces. Herbert Hoover runs the program, winning acclaim for his efficiency.

- On October 3, the War Revenue Act increases taxes on individuals and corporations to finance the war.

- On October 6, the Trading with the Enemy Act forbids U.S. businesses from exporting goods, even food, to the Central Powers.

- On December 18, Congress passes the Eighteenth Amendment, prohibiting the manufacture, sale, or transportation of intoxicating liquors. The amendment goes to the states for ratification.

- On December 26, the U.S. Railroad Administration, under the direction of William Gibbs McAdoo, takes charge of the nation's railroads. They remain under government control until 1920.

## 1918

- In March, a federal arbitrator set an eight-hour workday in Chicago's meatpacking industry.

- On March 21, the Railroad Control Act empowers the U.S. Railroad Administration to set railroad rates.

- On April 5, Congress creates the War Finance Corporation to loan banks money to finance the operation of war industries.

- On April 8, Congress creates the National War Labor Board to settle labor disputes and thus avoid strikes that would interrupt war production.

- On April 10, Congress passes the Webb-Pomerene Act, allowing exporters to combine in export trade associations without fear of antitrust prosecution. The act intends U.S. businesses and farms to increase exports to the Allies.

- On May 13, the Post Office Department issues the first airmail stamps in denominations of six cents, sixteen cents, and twenty-four cents.

- On July 16, the federal government takes control of the nation's telephone and telegraph systems, another instance of what labor historian Ellis Hawley called wartime communism.

## 1919

- In January, more than sixty thousand shipyard workers in Seattle, Washington, strike to protest poor pay and harsh conditions.

- On January 29, the states ratify the Eighteenth Amendment to the Constitution, prohibiting the manufacture, sale, and transportation of intoxicating liquors. As is the case with illegal drugs today, Americans find ways to manufacture or buy alcohol despite the law.

- On September 9, Boston police go on strike, leaving the city without protection. Massachusetts Governor Calvin Coolidge comes to national prominence by crushing the strike in the name of public safety. Republicans embraced him as an antiunion man.

- On September 22, more than three hundred thousand steel workers strike to protest long hours and low pay. Company owners use strikebreakers and thugs to stop the strike.

- On November 20, the nation's first municipal airport opens in Tucson, Arizona.

# Triangle Shirtwaist Factory Fire

## "Eyewitness at the Triangle"

Eyewitness account

**By:** William Gunn Shepherd

**Date:** March 27, 1911

**Source:** Shepherd, William Gunn. "Eyewitness at the Triangle." *Milwaukee Journal,* March 27, 1911. Available online at http://www.ilr.cornell.edu/trianglefire/texts/stein_ootss/ootss_wgs.html; website home page: http://www.ilr.cornell.edu (accessed October 11, 2002).

**About the Author:** William Gunn Shepherd, a reporter for the United Press, was in Manhattan's Washington Square on March 25, 1911, when a devastating fire ripped through the Triangle Shirtwaist Company. Shepherd found a nearby telephone and dictated the details of the tragedy to his editor, who telegraphed the story to the nation's newspapers.

## *Preliminary Report of the Factory Investigating Commission*

Report, Floor plan

**By:** New York (State) Factory Investigating Commission

**Date:** 1912

**Source:** New York (State) Factory Investigating Commission. *Preliminary Report of the Factory Investigating Commission.* Albany, N.Y.: The Argus Company Printers, 1912. Available online at http://www.ilr.cornell.edu/trianglefire/texts/reports/nyfic_1912_p128.html#NEGLECT (accessed October 11, 2002).

**About the Authors:** The New York State Legislature created a special commission to investigate the Triangle Shirtwaist disaster and recommend factory safety legislation. State Senator Robert F. Wagner (later U.S. Senator) and Assemblyman Alfred E. Smith (later governor of New York) served on the commission, as did Samuel Gompers (president of the American Federation of Labor) and Mary E. Dreier (president of the Women's Trade Union League). ∎

## Introduction

The garment workers at the Triangle Shirtwaist Company, mostly young Jewish and Italian immigrant women,

spent their days crammed into stuffy, overcrowded lofts piecing together the blousy women's bodices popular at the time. Working long hours for low wages in these unsafe and unsanitary factories, the shirtwaist workers organized in 1909 and demanded better working conditions. The workers enlisted the support of the International Ladies Garment Workers Union (ILGWU) and the Women's Trade Union League (a cross-class alliance of working-class and wealthy women). In a union meeting following the Triangle walkout, thousands of garment workers rallied in support by joining a general strike.

The strike lasted several months, and during its course, the ILGWU increased in strength. Though workers won some gains in some companies (shorter working hours, higher wages), the Triangle Shirtwaist Company still refused to recognize the union. The factory managers also ignored the workers' pleas for increased workplace safety, such as better ventilation, adequate fire escapes, and open doors (which had been kept locked on each floor to better monitor workers).

The young men and women of the Triangle Shirtwaist Company worked on the top three floors of the Asch building, a ten-story building near Washington Square Park in Lower Manhattan. When a fire broke out on March 25, 1911, the locked doors and lack of effective fire escapes trapped most of the garment workers inside. William Gunn Shepherd, a reporter on the scene, recorded the harrowing moments as the workers—with an inferno raging behind them—jumped to their deaths. One hundred forty-six were killed.

The image of women leaping from eighth- and ninth-story windows with billowing, flaming skirts left an indelible imprint on the nation, state, and city. The New York State Legislature quickly created a commission charged with investigating working conditions and recommending new worker safety legislation. Senator Robert F. Wagner and Assemblyman Alfred E. Smith personally headed the investigation, along with labor leaders Samuel Gompers and Mary Dreier, who had been involved in the garment strike two years earlier.

The investigation found that the Asch building—only ten years old at the time of the fire—had met the city's loose building regulations. Considerable discretion was placed in the hands of the city's building inspectors, who were often willing to side with building owners when they complained that certain safety features were neither practical nor necessary. This allowed the Asch building to remain in compliance with city code, despite the fact that its locked doors, narrow stairwells, and wooden structures (not to mention heaps of flammable cloth) made it a fire trap.

## Significance

The investigation revealed that American industry had made impressive strides in modern manufacturing, but few businesses had shown similar zeal in providing for the well-being of their employees. Worker safety had been neglected in industries across the board. As it became clear that the Triangle Shirtwaist Factory was not a special case, the state legislature acted to prevent further disasters by passing some of the nation's earliest factory safety laws.

The exposure of New York City's hazardous working conditions fed a general atmosphere of criticism of business interests, legitimated the goals of labor unions, and intensified the call of Progressive reformers for increased attention to social welfare. The focus of the Factory Investigating Commission eventually grew to encompass not just workplace safety but minimum wage standards and women's protective legislation. The fire touched off a debate that continued in the twenty-first century about sweatshops, workers' rights, and employers' responsibilities for workplace safety.

## Primary Source

"Eyewitness at the Triangle"

**SYNOPSIS:** In this excerpt, William G. Shepherd recounts how he came across the fire at the Triangle Shirtwaist Company. Struck by the sights and sounds of workers leaping from the burning building, Shepherd captures glimpses of humanity in the last moments of their lives. Reminded of the strike that had taken place in 1909, he laments its failure to bring about a safer work environment.

I was walking through Washington Square when a puff of smoke issuing from the factory building caught my eye. I reached the building before the alarm was turned in. I saw every feature of the tragedy visible from outside the building. I learned a new sound—a more horrible sound than description can picture. It was the thud of a speeding, living body on a stone sidewalk.

Thud—dead, thud—dead, thud—dead, thud—dead. Sixty-two thud—deads. I call them that, because the sound and the thought of death came to me each time, at the same instant. There was plenty of chance to watch them as they came down. The height was eighty feet.

The first ten thud—deads shocked me. I looked up—saw that there were scores of girls at the windows. The flames from the floor below were beating in their faces. Somehow I knew that they, too, must come down, and something within me—something that I didn't know was there—steeled me.

I even watched one girl falling. Waving her arms, trying to keep her body upright until the very instant

Firefighters work to extinguish the fire at the Triangle Shirtwaist Factory in New York City. © UNDERWOOD AND UNDERWOOD/CORBIS. REPRODUCED BY PERMISSION.

she struck the sidewalk, she was trying to balance herself. Then came the thud—then a silent, unmoving pile of clothing and twisted, broken limbs.

As I reached the scene of the fire, a cloud of smoke hung over the building. . . . I looked up to the seventh floor. There was a living picture in each window—four screaming heads of girls waving their arms.

"Call the firemen," they screamed—scores of them. "Get a ladder," cried others. They were all as alive and whole and sound as were we who stood on the sidewalk. I couldn't help thinking of that. We cried to them not to jump. We heard the siren of a fire engine in the distance. The other sirens sounded from several directions.

"Here they come," we yelled. "Don't jump; stay there."

One girl climbed onto the window sash. Those behind her tried to hold her back. Then she dropped into space. I didn't notice whether those above watched her drop because I had turned away. Then came that first thud. I looked up, another girl was climbing onto the window sill; others were crowding behind her. She dropped. I watched her fall, and again the dreadful sound. Two windows away two girls were climbing onto the sill; they were fighting each other and crowding for air. Behind them I saw many screaming heads. They fell almost together, but I heard two distinct thuds. Then the flames burst out through the windows on the floor below them, and curled up into their faces.

The firemen began to raise a ladder. Others took out a life net and, while they were rushing to the sidewalk with it, two more girls shot down. The firemen held it under them; the bodies broke it; the grotesque simile of a dog jumping through a hoop struck me. Before they could move the net another girl's body flashed through it. The thuds were just as loud, it seemed, as if there had been no net there. It seemed to me that the thuds were so loud that they might have been heard all over the city.

I had counted ten. Then my dulled senses began to work automatically. I noticed things that it had not occurred to me before to notice. Little details that the first shock had blinded me to. I looked up to see whether those above watched those who fell. I noticed that they did; they watched them every inch of the way down and probably heard the roaring thuds that we heard.

As I looked up I saw a love affair in the midst of all the horror. A young man helped a girl to the window sill. Then he held her out, deliberately away from the building and let her drop. He seemed cool and calculating. He held out a second girl the same way and let her drop. Then he held out a third girl who did not resist. I noticed that. They were as unresisting as if her were helping them onto a streetcar instead of into eternity. Undoubtedly he saw that a terrible death awaited them in the flames, and his was only a terrible chivalry.

Then came the love amid the flames. He brought another girl to the window. Those of us who were looking saw her put her arms about him and kiss him. Then he held her out into space and dropped her. But quick as a flash he was on the window sill himself. His coat fluttered upward—the air filled his trouser legs. I could see that he wore tan shoes and hose. His hat remained on his head.

Thud—dead, thud—dead—together they went into eternity. I saw his face before they covered it. You could see in it that he was a real man. He had done his best.

We found out later that, in the room in which he stood, many girls were being burned to death by the flames and were screaming in an inferno of flame and heat. He chose the easiest way and was brave enough to even help the girl he loved to a quicker death, after she had given him a goodbye kiss. He leaped with an energy as if to arrive first in that mysterious land of eternity, but her thud—dead came first.

The firemen raised the longest ladder. It reached only to the sixth floor. I saw the last girl jump at it and miss it. And then the faces disappeared from the window. But now the crowd was enormous, though all this had occurred in less than seven minutes, the start of the fire and the thuds and deaths.

I heard screams around the corner and hurried there. What I had seen before was not so terrible as what had followed. Up in the [ninth] floor girls were burning to death before our very eyes. They were jammed in the windows. No one was lucky enough to be able to jump, it seemed. But, one by one, the jams broke. Down came the bodies in a shower, burning, smoking—flaming bodies, with disheveled hair trailing upward. They had fought each other to die by jumping instead of by fire.

The whole, sound, unharmed girls who had jumped on the other side of the building had tried to fall feet down. But these fire torches, suffering ones, fell inertly, only intent that death should come to them on the sidewalk instead of in the furnace behind them.

On the sidewalk lay heaps of broken bodies. A policeman later went about with tags, which he fastened with wires to the wrists of the dead girls, numbering each with a lead pencil, and I saw him fasten tag no. 54 to the wrist of a girl who wore an engagement ring. A fireman who came downstairs from the building told me that there were at least fifty bodies in the big room on the seventh floor. Another fireman told me that more girls had jumped down an air shaft in the rear of the building. I went back there, into the narrow court, and saw a heap of dead girls. . . .

The floods of water from the firemen's hose that ran into the gutter were actually stained red with

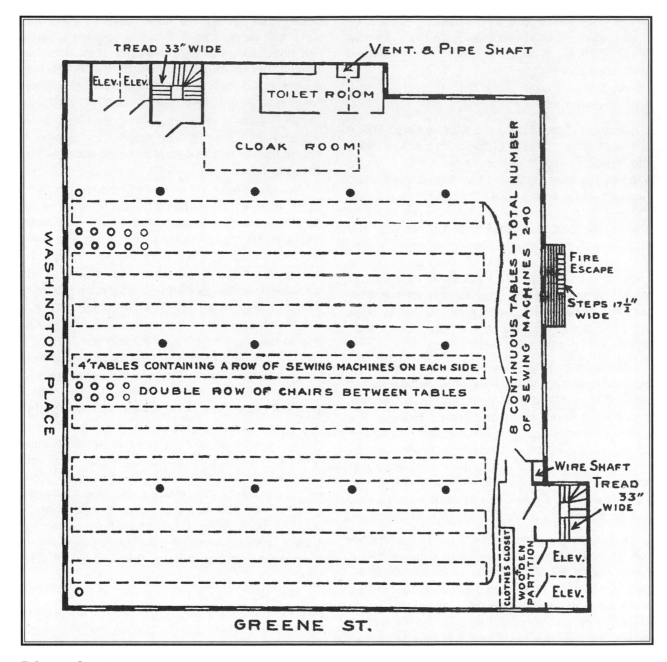

TREAD 33" WIDE

VENT. & PIPE SHAFT

ELEV. ELEV.

TOILET ROOM

CLOAK ROOM

WASHINGTON PLACE

8 CONTINUOUS TABLES – TOTAL NUMBER OF SEWING MACHINES 240

FIRE ESCAPE

STEPS 17½" WIDE

4' TABLES CONTAINING A ROW OF SEWING MACHINES ON EACH SIDE

DOUBLE ROW OF CHAIRS BETWEEN TABLES

WIRE SHAFT

TREAD 33" WIDE

CLOTHES CLOSET

WOODEN PARTITION

ELEV.

ELEV.

GREENE ST.

## Primary Source

*Preliminary Report of the Factory Investigating Commission*: Floor plan

**SYNOPSIS:** The plan of the ninth floor of the Asch building from the *Preliminary Report of the Factory Investigating Commission* illustrates the 75-foot-long tables in relation to the windows, elevators, and stairs. The 240 people working in the relatively small work floor space were trapped by chairs and work baskets. The limited space also meant that workers had to scramble over work tables to reach the exits. UNITE ARCHIVES, KHEEL CENTER, CORNELL UNIVERSITY, ITHACA, NY 14853-3901.

blood. I looked upon the heap of dead bodies and I remembered these girls were the shirtwaist makers. I remembered their great strike of last year in which these same girls had demanded more sanitary conditions and more safety precautions in the shops. These dead bodies were the answer.

## Primary Source

*Preliminary Report of the Factory Investigating Commission*: Report

**SYNOPSIS:** In this excerpt, the New York State Factory Investigating Commission, which was charged with exploring the Triangle disaster and making recommendations about such issues as workplace safety and wage standards, comments on the abysmal working conditions found in many factories of the era. Among other things, it noted that "the human factor is practically neglected in our system."

## Results of the Data Obtained by the Investigation

### Neglect of the Human Factor

Brief as was the period devoted to the investigation, limited as was the number of industries and establishments inspected, and incomplete as was necessarily all our data, the conclusion that forcibly impressed itself, after the completion of the preliminary investigation, was that the human factor is practically neglected in our industrial system.

Many of our industries were found housed in palatial loft buildings, and employing the most improved machinery and mechanical processes, but at the same time greatly neglecting the care, health and safety of their employees. Our system of industrial production has taken gigantic strides in the progressive utilization of natural resources and the exploitation of the inventive genius of the human mind, but has at the same time shown a terrible waste of human resources, of human health and life.

It is because of this neglect of the human factor that we have found so many preventable defects in industrial establishments, such a large number of workshops with inadequate light and illumination, with no provision for ventilation, without proper care for cleanliness, and without ordinary indispensable comforts such as washing facilities, water supply, toilet accommodations, dressing-rooms, etc. It is because of utter neglect on the part of many employers that so many dangerous elements are found in certain trades. These elements are not always necessary for the successful pursuit of the trade, and their elimination would mean a great improvement in the health of the workers, and would stop much of the misery caused by the occupational diseases incident to certain industries.

It is true that many enlightened employers, especially those who control large establishments, show a commendable zeal for the health of their operatives, but such care not being supervised or organized under scientific direction, leaves much to be desired.

In the matter of industrial production, we are still under the sway of the old "laissez faire" policy, and there is still very inadequate supervision of industries with a view to lessening dangers to the health and life of the working class.

There is still no regulation whatever of factory construction, outside of the rules adopted by municipal building codes which regulate only the width of walls, the strength of foundations, etc. all matters of sanitation are without control during the times when such control could best serve the purpose of the buildings and the interests of those destined to inhabit them.

The construction of tenement houses in New York City is under the strict supervision of the Tenement House Department. There is no reason why the interests of the greater number of persons inhabiting factory buildings should not be conserved as much as the interests of the tenement house dwellers. . . .

### Lack of Standards

The worker spends the greater part of his waking hours in the workshop and factory. The proper sanitation of the workplace is therefore of paramount importance to the worker, both to his health and to the security of his life.

It is only lately that intelligent employers have awakened to the fact that factory sanitation is very closely related to industrial efficiency, and that neglect of this subject by factory owners is detrimental to their own interests as well as extremely injurious to their workers.

It is also but lately that the workers themselves have realized the value of proper sanitation of factories, and have added this to the economic demands of their labor organizations.

Unfortunately, there is hardly a field of science where there is such a complete lack of standards as in industrial hygiene.

It is on account of this deplorable lack of standardization that many provisions of the labor laws are so vague and indefinite, and that large employers, willing to introduce modern safety devices and sanitary conveniences in their factories, are unable to do so with complete success. It is also this lack of standards that makes the enforcement of the sanitary clauses of the labor laws so unsatisfactory, for it is a most difficult matter for the inspector to exactly determine what is meant by "sufficient" fire protection, "proper" light, "adequate" ventilation, "fit" toilet accommodations, etc.

## Further Resources

### BOOKS

Handlin, Oscar. *Al Smith and His America.* Boston: Northeastern University Press, 1987.

Moss, David A. *Socializing Security: Progressive-Era Economists and the Origins of American Social Policy.* Cambridge, Mass.: Harvard University Press, 1996.

Stein, Leon. *The Triangle Fire.* Ithaca, N.Y.: Cornell University Press, 2001.

**PERIODICALS**

Martin, Douglas. "Rose Freedman, Last Survivor of Triangle Fire, Dies at 107." *The New York Times,* February 17, 2001.

**WEBSITES**

"The Triangle Factory Fire." Kheel Center for Labor-Management Documentation and Archives, Cornell University School of Industrial and Labor Relations. Available online at http://www.ilr.cornell.edu/trianglefire/ (accessed October 11, 2002).

# Scientific Management

## The Principles of Scientific Management

Reference work

**By:** Frederick W. Taylor

**Date:** 1911

**Source:** Taylor, Frederick W. *The Principles of Scientific Management.* New York: Harper Brothers, 1911. Reprinted in the Internet Modern History Sourcebook. Available online at http://www.fordham.edu/halsall/mod/1911taylor.html; website home page: http://www.fordham.edu (accessed October 11, 2002).

**About the Author:** Frederick Winslow Taylor (1856–1915) developed the concept of scientific management, a system of managerial control that stressed the rationalization of production processes. Taylor's work as a foreman in the steel industry in the 1880s led him to study how the precise management of workers' actions could improve industrial productivity. By the early twentieth century, his widely publicized methods were adopted in a broad range of industries.

## Letter to Lindley Garrison

Letter

**By:** Maurice W. Bowen

**Date:** June 17, 1913

**Source:** Bowen to Garrison, Auburndale, June 17, 1913. "The Taylor System of Shop Management at the Watertown Arsenal." The Frederick Winslow Taylor Collection. Available online at http://taylor.lib.stevens-tech.edu., pp. 5–7 of 66 (accessed October 11, 2002).

**About the Author:** Maurice W. Bowen worked at the Watertown Arsenal in Massachusetts, a facility that followed the Taylor System of management. He and his coworkers objected to the system, which they felt was ineffective and demeaning. Their feelings are representative of the many laborers who, threatened with the loss of their independence on the shop floor, resisted the adoption of Taylor's principles and organized to oppose them. ■

## Introduction

One key to early-twentieth-century American economic growth was a great advance in industrial organization. Railroad corporations and other large industries developed complex organizational structures to manage their businesses. Frederick W. Taylor sought to rationalize production through scientific management of the workers themselves. This meant making detailed analyses of each worker's actions, measuring the time and energy they spent on each task, and using that information to set standards for productivity. Taylor's principles of standardization were praised by manufacturers, who wanted to improve efficiency and increase industrial output while, at the same time, limiting the power of individual workers. Taylor himself felt that scientific management, which could be applied to "all kinds of human activities, from our simplest individual acts to the work of our great corporations," would lead ultimately to "greater national efficiency."

The time studies that were part of Taylor's style of management were particularly despised by American workers. In elevating the system of production over the laborers themselves, Taylor's methods devalued their skills, undercut their authority on the shop floor, and challenged traditional workplace cultures. For decades, the increased use of machinery diminished the power of craftsmen. The spread of Taylorism threatened to further weaken workers' power.

## Significance

When the United States government instituted the Taylor System at its arsenal in Watertown, Massachusetts, employees petitioned that it be discontinued. Arsenal management had tried to increase production by issuing "speed ups"—the use of stopwatch observation and pay incentives to increase the pace of piece work. Workers argued that the stopwatch system was not only humiliating, but resulted in a decrease in the quality of work, an increase in workplace accidents, and an overall decline in productivity.

When the employees' petitions failed to bring an end to the Taylor System, they went on strike. The controversy sparked a congressional investigation to debate the use of time studies in army contracts. Though much of the Taylor System remained, the use of the stopwatch to set tasks was ultimately prohibited.

At the heart of the Arsenal controversy was the question of workplace control. Arsenal employees felt that the Taylor System robbed them of power over their work environment and forced them to work according to managerial standards rather than their own sense of judgment.

Frederick Taylor's scientific management practices, such as measuring an employee's output in a given time, are still applied in workplaces today. BETTMANN/CORBIS. REPRODUCED BY PERMISSION.

Government managers, in contrast, argued that the application of Taylor's principles streamlined production and reduced inefficiency. The stopwatch controversy precipitated the clash of these two worldviews. While workers scored a victory in removing the stopwatch from the workplace, Taylor's broader principles—that management could be systematically analyzed and improved through advanced organizational structures—remained intact.

## Primary Source

*The Principles of Scientific Management* [excerpt]

> **SYNOPSIS:** In this primary source, Frederick W. Taylor relates the significant gains that can be achieved through scientific management of production.

President Roosevelt, in his address to the Governors at the White House, prophetically remarked that "The conservation of our national resources is only preliminary to the larger question of national efficiency."

The whole country at once recognized the importance of conserving our material resources and a large movement has been started which will be ef-fective in accomplishing this object. As yet, however, we have but vaguely appreciated the importance of "the larger question of increasing our national efficiency."

We can see our forests vanishing, our water-powers going to waste, our soil being carried by floods into the sea; and the end of our coal and our iron is in sight. But our larger wastes of human effort, which go on every day through such of our acts as are blundering, ill-directed, or inefficient, and which Mr. Roosevelt refers to as a lack of" national efficiency," are less visible) less tangible, and are but vaguely appreciated.

We can see and feel the waste of material things. Awkward, inefficient, or ill-directed movements of men, however, leave nothing visible or tangible behind them. Their appreciation calls for an act of memory, an effort of the imagination. And for this reason, even though our daily loss from this source is greater than from our waste of material things, the one has stirred us deeply, while the other has moved us but little.

As yet there has been no public agitation for "greater national efficiency," no meetings have been called to consider how this is to be brought about. And still there are signs that the need for greater efficiency is widely felt.

The search for better, for more competent men, from the presidents of our great companies down to our household servants, was never more vigorous than it is now. And more than ever before is the demand for competent men in excess of the supply.

What we are all looking for, however, is the ready made, competent man; the man whom some one else has trained. It is only when we fully realize that our duty, as well as our opportunity, lies in systematically cooperating to train and to make this competent man, instead of in hunting for a man whom some one else has trained, that we shall be on the road to national efficiency.

In the past the prevailing idea has been well expressed in the saying that "Captains of industry are born, not made"; and the theory has been that if one could get the right man, methods could be safely left to him. In the future it will be, appreciated that our leaders must be trained right as well as born right, and that no great man can (with the old system of personal management) hope to compete with a number of ordinary men who have been properly organized so as efficiently to cooperate.

In the past the man has been first; in the future the system must be first. This in no sense, however,

Men work in a busy factory. The application of Frederick Taylor's scientific management often increased productivity, but it also increased workplace accidents and worker dissatisfaction. **GETTY IMAGES. REPRODUCED BY PERMISSION.**

implies that great men are not needed. On the contrary, the first object of any good system must be that of developing first-class men; and under systematic management the best man rises to the top more certainly and more rapidly than ever before.

## Primary Source

Letter to Lindley Garrison

> **SYNOPSIS:** In this primary source, employees at the U.S. Government's Watertown Arsenal petition for the removal of the Taylor System, which, they argue, decreases overall productivity and "savors too much of the slave driver."

Watertown Arsenal
Hon. Lindley M. Garrison,
Secretary of War, Washington, D.C.

Dear Sir,

We, the undersigned, employees of the Government, representing 349 of a total of 373 hands employed in the various departments as indicated hereon, respectfully petition that the Taylor System, now in operation at this Arsenal, be immediately discontinued for the reasons as hereinafter set forth.

We object to the use of the Stop Watch, as it is used a means of speeding men up to a point beyond their normal capacity. It is humiliating and savors too much of the slave driver.

A comparison of the record of serious accidents occurring in the works since the introduction of the Stop Watch Premium System will convince the most skeptical that it is dangerous to limb and life, and we claim that a large percentage of these accidents are the direct result of the driving system in vogue at this Plant.

We believe that this System, instead of producing what was claimed it would produce—high wages to employees, with a low cost of production has worked exactly opposite inasmuch as the investigation into the wages paid (outside of premium) will show that there has been no material increase in wages, while the cost of production has been increased to such an extent that large deficits are being reported on nearly every job of any consequence that is done at this Arsenal.

The number of non-productive employees in proportion to the productive employees who are necessary to carry out the details of the System, has been largely responsible in the great increase in overhead expense, which in many cases, has resulted in the Government being unable to compete with outside concerns and has resulted in contracts being placed with outside parties to do work which the Arsenal is equipped to do and which, under normal conditions, could be done at a cost considerably under that charged by the Contractor securing the work. For instance, it has become the practice to let large contracts for manufacturing patterns, which the Arsenal is equipped to manufacture and could manufacture at a figure considerably below that charged by outside concerns; the quality of work being considered were it not burdened by an excessive overhead charge which must be carried to pay an abnormal non-productive force of employees.

We cite the above case to show that there is ground for our belief that the continuance of this System would finally eventuate in closing this Arsenal as a manufacturing Plant.

A large corps of inspectors are kept busy examining and rejecting material, and the number of pieces rejected since the Premium System was inaugurated has increased by a large percentage. The number of parts rejected since the System was installed will run well into the thousands.

The effect of this System here has been to create a feeling of distrust between the employees and the management; it has destroyed every vestige of coöperation between the workmen and the foremen collectively, and has produced a condition of unhappiness throughout the whole works.

For the reasons as stated above as well as many others which we will not trouble with at this time, we respectfully pray that you, as head of the War Department, take such immediate steps as will effectually remove this System from Watertown Arsenal and restore the workmen to a condition similar to that enjoyed by other artisans and laborers in the public service as well as in most private manufacturing plants.

We also respectfully petition that the records as obtained by means of stop watch observation be removed from this Arsenal or destroyed altogether as they do not represent the normal time in which given work should be accomplished, but rather they are the product of the "speed up" System which has resulted in accidents, inferior work and numerous abuses such as no American Citizen should be called upon to endure.

In conclusion let it be understood that the signatures to this petition were not obtained by coercion or unfair means and each individual signing this petition, does so of his own free will and accord.

*Respectfully submitted,*
*Maurice W. Bowen*
*Chairman Representative Committee*
*23 Charles St., Auburndale, Mass.*

Signed by 51 molders and helpers; 25 pattern makers, carpenters, and painters; 17 blacksmiths and helpers; 53 yard laboring men; 88 machinists and helpers, assembling department; 88 machinists and helpers.

## Further Resources

### BOOKS

Aitken, Hugh G.J. *Scientific Management in Action: Taylorism at Watertown Arsenal, 1908–1915.* Princeton, N.J.: Princeton University Press, 1985.

Spender, J.C., and Hugo Kijne, eds. *Scientific Management: Frederick Winslow Taylor's Gift to the World?* Boston: Kluwer Academic Publishers, 1996.

### WEBSITES

The Frederick Winslow Taylor Collection. Available online at http://taylor.lib.stevens-tech.edu (accessed October 11, 2002). *This website contains additional primary sources relating to Frederick Winslow Taylor.*

# Dollar Diplomacy and Its Repudiation

## Speech Advocating "Dollar Diplomacy"

Speech

**By:** William Howard Taft

**Date:** December 3, 1912

**Source:** Taft, William Howard. Speech Advocating "Dollar Diplomacy." Excerpt from the Fourth Annual Message of President Taft to Congress, December 3, 1912. Reprinted in Gambone, Michael D., comp. *Documents of American Diplomacy: From the American Revolution to the Present.* Westport, Conn.: Greenwood Press, 2002, 140–142.

**About the Author:** William Howard Taft (1857–1930) began his career as an Ohio lawyer and judge. In 1898, he was appointed head of the Philippine Commission, and then Governor General of those islands, which the United States had acquired in the Spanish-American War (1898). In 1904, Taft became Secretary of War to President Theodore Roosevelt. He was elected to the presidency in 1908, and served until 1913. Taft supported the expansion of American power abroad and pursued a domestic reform program intended to conserve natural resources and reduce the power of big business. However, he was not nearly as bold in his actions as

Roosevelt, who ran against him in 1912 and contributed to his reelection defeat. In 1921, Taft was appointed chief justice of the Supreme Court, where he served until shortly before his death.

# Speech Repudiating "Dollar Diplomacy"

**Speech**

**By:** Woodrow Wilson

**Date:** March 19, 1913

**Source:** Wilson, Woodrow. Speech Repudiating "Dollar Diplomacy." Speech given to American bankers of the Four-Power Consortium, March 19, 1913. Originally appeared in *American Journal of International Law* 7, 1913, 338–339. Reprinted in *Documents of American Diplomacy: From the American Revolution to the Present.* Michael D. Gambone, comp. Westport, Conn.: Greenwood Press, 2002, 142–143.

**About the Author:** Woodrow Wilson (1856–1924) was a professor of political science and then president at Princeton University, before becoming governor of New Jersey in 1910. In 1912 he won the presidency. A progressive reformer, Wilson worked to give government greater control over business and protect the public interest through lawsuits and the creation of the Federal Trade Commission and the Federal Reserve. He supported the establishment of an income tax, and the granting of the vote to women in 1918. In foreign policy Wilson was an idealist and moralist who sought the peaceful expansion of democracy. However, he often felt compelled to use military force, first in Latin America, and then, in 1917, joining the Allied powers in World War I (1914–18). During and after the War Wilson continued to push for his ideals, leading to the formation of the League of Nations. ■

## Introduction

Through much of the nineteenth century, American foreign policy had been characterized by isolationism and noninterference in world affairs. By the beginning of the twentieth century, however, these policies had been abandoned in Europe, Latin America, and Asia. War with Spain over Cuba in 1898 left no doubt that the United States was a bona fide imperial power. The United States had annexed Hawaii earlier that year, and its pursuit of its "manifest destiny" of westward expansion had led to the capture of California and much of the American southwest from Mexico in the Mexican-American War (1846–1848).

As American economic power increased, American financiers and industrialists supported an activist foreign policy designed to promote political stability—and thus a hospitable commercial environment in which their investments could flourish. Similarly, American political leaders began to use access to the nation's commercial power for leverage in advancing their diplomatic goals.

Always of special concern because of their close geographic locations, relations between the United States

President Wilson (left) and former President Taft at the White House in 1913. © BETTMANN/CORBIS. REPRODUCED BY PERMISSION.

and Latin America assumed even greater importance during the turn of the twentieth century. The construction of the Panama Canal further solidified American interest in Central America, and President William Howard Taft sought to use American economic and military power to sustain political regimes friendly to American commercial interests.

The Spanish-American War and the resultant colonization of the Philippines drew America deeper into Asian affairs, as well. Concern over security and economic access to Asian markets led America to strengthen its commitment to naval expansion and to increase its presence in China. As in Latin America, Taft saw American commercial investment and the maintenance of diplomatic ties in the Far East as mutually supportive.

## Significance

The Taft administration brought American commercial and diplomatic interests closer than they had ever been before. Taft's secretary of state, Philander C. Knox, encouraged private American banking interests to extend credit to pro-American regimes in Honduras, Nicaragua, and Haiti. The Taft administration called this foreign policy "dollar diplomacy," since it used American capital as a bargaining tool in the support or opposition of national political regimes. In the case of Nicaragua, where economic incentives were unsuccessful in bringing about U.S. foreign policy aims, Taft sent 2,700 marines to crush an internal revolt against pro-American president Aldolfo Díaz.

Taft and Knox sought to apply dollar diplomacy to the Far East, as well. Commercial relations between Asia and America had grown closer in the early twentieth century. But the construction of European-financed railroads threatened to limit this new economic access. Backed by American railroad and banking interests, Taft insisted that America preserve its influence in Asia by loaning China money for railroad construction. This blatant effort to secure an economic foothold in Asia angered China's neighbors, prompting anti-American sentiment in Russia and Japan.

The explicit use of American economic power to influence other nations' political goals ran counter to President Woodrow Wilson's commitment to national self-determination. Upon taking office, Wilson immediately denounced the Taft administration's foreign policy. He withdrew American support for investments in China and backed Latin American nations' pursuit of self-governance devoid of American intervention. Nonetheless, Wilson's diplomatic initiatives were moderated by a continuing concern for the protection of foreign markets. When revolution swept through the Caribbean, Wilson sanctioned military intervention in Haiti and the Dominican Republic. He also kept in place the troops Taft had stationed in Nicaragua, unwilling to diminish America's presence near the Panama Canal.

## Primary Source

Speech Advocating "Dollar Diplomacy"

**SYNOPSIS:** In this speech from December 3, 1912, President William Howard Taft explains how American investments—in railroads, mining, cattle, and export agriculture—can help secure American influence in the Far East and Latin America.

### China

In China the policy of encouraging financial investment to enable that country to help itself has had the result of giving new life and practical application to the open-door policy. The consistent purpose of the present administration has been to encourage the use of American capital in the development of China by the promotion of those essential reforms to which China is pledged by treaties with the United States and other powers. The hypothecation to foreign bankers in connection with certain industrial enterprises, such as the Hukuang railways, of the national revenues upon which these reforms depended, led the Department of State early in the administration to demand for American citizens participation in such enterprises, in order that the United States might have equal rights and an equal voice in all questions pertaining to the disposition of the public revenues concerned. The same policy of promoting international accord among the powers having similar treaty rights as ourselves in the matters of reform, which could not be put into practical effect without the common consent of all, was likewise adopted in the case of the loan desired by China for the reform of its currency. The principle of international cooperation in matters of common interest upon which our policy had already been based in all of the above instances has admittedly been a great factor in that concert of the powers which has been so happily conspicuous during the perilous period of transition through which the great Chinese nation has been passing.

### Central America Needs our Help in Debt Adjustment

In Central America the aim has been to help such countries as Nicaragua and Honduras to help themselves. They are the immediate beneficiaries. The national benefit to the United States is twofold. First, it is obvious that the Monroe doctrine is more vital in the neighborhood of the Panama Canal and the zone of the Caribbean than anywhere else. There, too, the maintenance of that doctrine falls most heavily upon the United States. It is therefore essential that the countries within that sphere shall be removed from the jeopardy involved by heavy foreign debt and chaotic national finances and from the ever-present danger of international complications due to disorder at home. Hence the United States has been glad to encourage and support American bankers who were willing to lend a helping hand to the financial rehabilitation of such countries because this financial rehabilitation and the protection of their customhouses from being the prey of would-be dictators would remove at one stroke the menace of foreign creditors and the menace of revolutionary disorder.

The second advantage of the United States is one affecting chiefly all the southern and Gulf ports and the business and industry of the South. The Republics of Central America and the Caribbean possess great natural wealth. They need only a measure of stability and the means of financial regeneration to enter upon an era of peace and prosperity, bringing profit and happiness to themselves and at the same time creating conditions sure to lead to a flourishing interchange of trade with this country.

I wish to call your especial attention to the recent occurrences in Nicaragua, for I believe the terrible events recorded there during the revolution of the past summer—the useless loss of life, the devastation of property, the bombardment of defenseless cities, the killing and wounding of women and children, the torturing of noncombatants to exact contributions, and the suffering of thousands of human beings—might have been averted had the Department of State, through approval of the loan convention by the Senate, been permitted to carry out its now well-developed policy of encouraging the extending of financial aid to weak Central American States with the primary objects of avoiding just such revolutions by assisting those Republics to rehabilitate their finances, to establish their currency on a stable basis, to remove the customhouses from the danger of revolutions by arranging for their secure administration, and to establish reliable banks.

## Primary Source

Speech Repudiating "Dollar Diplomacy"

**SYNOPSIS:** In this speech given March 19, 1913, President Woodrow Wilson repudiates Taft's "dollar diplomacy," arguing that the conditions of American investments in China "touch very nearly the administrative independence of China itself."

We are informed that at the request of the last administration a certain group of American bankers undertook to participate in the loan now desired by the Government of China (approximately $125,000,000). Our government wished American bankers to participate along with the bankers of other nations, because it desired that the good will of the United States towards China should be exhibited in this practical way, that American capital should have access to that great country, and that the United States should be in a position to share with the other Powers any political responsibilities that might be associated with the development of the foreign relations of China in connection with her industrial and commercial enterprises. The present administration has been asked by this group of bankers whether it would also request them to participate in the loan. The representatives of the bankers through whom the administration was approached declared that they would continue to seek their share of the loan under the proposed agreements only if expressly requested to do so by the government. The administration has declined to make such request because it did not approve the conditions of the loan or the implications of responsibility on its own part which it was plainly told would be involved in the request.

The conditions of the loan seem to us to touch very nearly the administrative independence of China itself; and this administration does not feel that it ought, even by implication, to be a party to those conditions. The responsibility on its part which would be implied in requesting the bankers to undertake the loan might conceivably go to the length in some unhappy contingency of forcible interference in the financial, and even the political, affairs of that great oriental state, just now awakening to a consciousness of its power and its obligations to its people. The conditions include not only the pledging of particular taxes, some of them antiquated and burdensome, to secure the loan, but also the administration of those taxes by foreign agents. The responsibility on the part of our government implied in the encouragement of a loan thus secured and administered is plain enough and is obnoxious to the principles upon which the government of our people rests.

The Government of the United States is not only willing, but earnestly desirous, of aiding the great Chinese people in every way that is consistent with their untrammeled development and its own immemorial principles. The awakening of the people of China to a consciousness of their possibilities under free government is the most significant, if not the most momentous event of our generation. With this movement and aspiration the American people are in profound sympathy. They certainly wish to participate, and participate very generously, in opening to the Chinese and to the use of the world the almost untouched and perhaps unrivaled resources of China.

The Government of the United States is earnestly desirous of promoting the most extended and intimate trade relationships between this country and the Chinese Republic. . . . This is the main material interest of its citizens in the development of China. Our interests are those of the open door—a door of friendship and mutual advantage. This is the only door we care to enter.

## Further Resources

### BOOKS

Gilderhaus, Mark T. *The Second Century: U.S.-Latin Relations Since 1889*. Wilmington, Del.: Scholarly Resources, 2000.

Hunt, Michael H. *The Making of a Special Relationship: The United States and China to 1914*. New York: Columbia University Press, 1983.

Iriye, Akira. *Across the Pacific: An Inner History of American-East Asian Relations*. Rev. ed. Chicago: Imprint Publications, 1992.

Munro, Dana G. *Intervention and Dollar Diplomacy in the Caribbean, 1900–1921.* Princeton, N.J.: Princeton University Press, 1964.

Schoultz, Lars. *Beneath the United States: A History of U.S. Policy Toward Latin America.* Cambridge, Mass.: Harvard University Press, 1998.

**WEBSITES**

"1866–1913: Diplomacy and the Rise to Global Power." U.S. Department of State. Available online at http://www.state .gov/www/about_state/history/time6.html; website home page: http://www.state.gov (accessed October 12, 2002).

"Documents Relating to American Foreign Policy, 1898–1914." Mount Holyoke Department of International Relations. Available online at http://www.mtholyoke.edu/acad/intrel /to1914.htm; website home page: http://www.mtholyoke .edu (accessed October 12, 2002).

Zwick, Jim, ed. "Anti-Imperialism in the United States, 1898–1935." BoondocksNet.com. Available online at http://www.boondocksnet.com/ai/index.html; website home page: http://www.boondocksnet.com (accessed October 12, 2002).

# *Money Trust Investigation*

Testimony

**By:** U.S. House of Representatives

**Date:** December 19, 1912

**Source:** U.S. House Committee on Banking and Currency. *Money Trust Investigation: Investigation of Financial and Monetary Conditions in the United States, Under House Resolutions Nos. 429 and 504, Before a Subcommittee of the Committee on Banking and Currency.* 62nd Cong., 3rd sess., 1912–13, vol. 15, pp. 1019–1024; 1049–1052.

**About the Author:** J. Pierpont Morgan (1837–1913) headed the banking firm J.P. Morgan and Company from 1890 until his death. The most powerful figure in American finance in the early twentieth century, Morgan employed his dominating personality and exceptional business acumen to bring financial order to a rapidly expanding economy. Morgan stood at the very center of that order, gaining a degree of personal control over the American economy that many found unsettling. ∎

## Introduction

The American economy surged in the late nineteenth century, securing the nation's status as one of the world's foremost industrial powers. Much of this economic expansion rested on the capital amassed by J.P. Morgan and his Wall Street associates and channeled into national railroad corporations and other industrial giants such as U.S. Steel, International Harvester, and General Electric. Morgan not only had a hand in creating these potent industrial combinations, but he also exercised great power over international banking. The central figure in New York's financial community, he rallied fellow bankers to head off the financial panic of 1907.

At first, Morgan was celebrated for averting economic catastrophe. But charges that he had profited from his role in preventing the panic led many to question Morgan's stewardship of the American economy. Fear that too much control lay in the hands of a "money trust" led to a congressional investigation.

Chairman Arsene Pujo of the House Banking and Currency Committee presided over the lengthy congressional investigation in 1912 and 1913. Morgan was one of the investigatory committee's primary targets, and lead counsel Samuel Untermyer sought to demonstrate that Morgan and his banking cohorts exerted a stranglehold over American credit. Morgan staunchly defended the wisdom and appropriateness of his conduct as the nation's premier banker. But revelations of the enormity of concentrated wealth and control over credit by a small group of financiers—the Money Trust—struck many as an undemocratic exercise of private power.

## Significance

Morgan's testimony illustrates the degree to which he believed that personal traits, such as high character and sound moral judgment, justified the great power he had over concentrated capital. For all of his life, the national government had resisted efforts to place central controls on American banking. His personal success, and the success of the industrial combinations he helped organize, rested on his ability to direct the flow of international capital, reduce economic competition, and generate stable market conditions. From his perspective, his personal business interests and the national interest in economic growth were in perfect alignment.

By contrast, Untermyer was less confident that members of the Money Trust could effectively distinguish what was good for them from what was good for the nation. As he pressed Morgan to describe the details of his banking operations, a picture emerged in which a small group of bankers, sitting on the boards of directors of large industrial corporations, squelched open competition, monopolized the control of credit, and limited economic freedom and entrepreneurial opportunity. Though many accepted Morgan's justification as sincere, few were comfortable with allowing such power to reside unchecked in one man. In 1913, the year of Morgan's death, the Federal Reserve System was created to give the government greater control of money and credit.

## Primary Source

*Money Trust Investigation* [excerpt]

**SYNOPSIS:** In this excerpt from the proceedings of the Money Trust investigation, lead counsel Samuel

Untermyer questions J.P. Morgan about the concentration and control of money and credit by New York banking firms. He inquires about their control over railroads' boards of directors, the lack of competition among banks for railroad securities, and the potential for abuse of power in limiting competitors' access to bank credit. Morgan insists that in spite of vast wealth and cooperative arrangements, no one can monopolize the control of credit.

Mr. Untermyer: Don't you think it would be better for these great interstate railroad corporations if they were entirely free to sell their securities in open competition than that they should be tied to any banking house, however just might be its methods in the issue of such securities?

Mr. Morgan: I should not think so.

Mr. Untermyer: Take the case of the Southern Railway. During all the years it has been and is still under this voting trust. The fact is, is it not, that Mr. Baker and you, as a majority of the voting trustees, designate the directors of that company?

Mr. Morgan: Yes, sir.

Mr. Untermyer: Don't you feel that in a sense when it comes to issuing the securities of that company and fixing the prices on which they are to be issued, that you are in a sense dealing with yourselves?

Mr. Morgan: I do not think so. We do not deal with ourselves.

Mr. Untermyer: Let us see if you do not.

Mr. Morgan: The voting trusts—

Mr. Untermyer: The voting trustees name the board, do they not?

Mr. Morgan: But when you have elected the board, then the board is independent of the voting trustees.

Mr. Untermyer: That is only until the next election?

Mr. Morgan: It is during that time they act independently.

Mr. Untermyer: You think, therefore, that where you name a board of directors that is to remain in existence only a year and you have the power to name another board the next year, that his board so named is in an independent position to deal with your banking house as would be a board named by the stockholders themselves?

Representative Arsene Pujo launched the investigation into the House of Morgan and its relationship to the "Money Trust" and Wall Street. **THE LIBRARY OF CONGRESS.**

Mr. Morgan: I think it would be better.

Mr. Untermyer: You think it is a great deal better?

Mr. Morgan: Yes, sir.

Mr. Untermyer: More independent?

Mr. Morgan: Better.

Mr. Untermyer: Will you tell us why?

Mr. Morgan: Simply because we select the best people that we can find for the positions.

Mr. Untermyer: Yes; but do you not see, taking the subject in a general aspect, rather than with respect to your particular banking house—

Mr. Morgan: I am not doing that, Mr. Counsel. I am speaking from a broad point of view.

Mr. Untermyer: Yes. Well, speaking from a broad point of view, do you not realize that a board thus selected is under the domination of the people who name it?

Mr. Morgan: My experience is quite otherwise, sir.

Mr. Untermyer: It is?

Mr. Morgan: Yes, sir.

Mr. Untermyer: Is it your experience, then, that the people who name a board of directors and have the right to rename them, or to drop them, have less power with them than people who have no concern in naming them?

Mr. Morgan: Very much so, sir.

Mr. Untermyer: And it is on that theory, is it—

Mr. Morgan: That is my experience.

Mr. Untermyer: And it is on that theory, is it, that you see no objection to fiscal agency agreements between directors selected by a voting trust of which you and your firm are members?

Mr. Morgan: Yes, sir.

Mr. Untermyer: These issues of securities of interstate railway companies are in vast sums, are they not, running into the hundreds of millions of dollars a year—many hundreds of millions of dollars?

Mr. Morgan: The securities?

Mr. Untermyer: Yes.

Mr. Morgan: Yes, sir.

Mr. Untermyer: I mean, you issue many hundreds of millions a year?

Mr. Morgan: Not many hundreds—not for the same company.

Mr. Untermyer: No, no; but I mean, for the different companies you issue many, many hundred millions a year, do you not?

Mr. Morgan: Yes, sir.

Mr. Untermyer: Do you not think it would be entirely feasible that securities of such corporations should be openly marketed and should be sold by competition, just as securities of the United States Government and State governments and city administrations and municipal bonds of different kinds are sold?

Mr. Morgan: I do not.

Mr. Untermyer: Do you not think there ought to be some kind of competition for them?

Mr. Morgan: There always is a competition in the end.

Mr. Untermyer: No; but I mean, do you not think there should be some competition for them between the banking houses or between the original purchaser and the company?

Mr. Morgan: No; I should think not.

Mr. Untermyer: You think not? There is not, in fact, any competition, is there, between the New York Central and J. P. Morgan & Co. in the purchase and sale of an issue of securities?

Mr. Morgan: There is very apt to be.

Mr. Untermyer: When was there ever such a thing?

Mr. Morgan (continuing): Because the company may think their securities are worth so much, and we may say that they would not sell for that; that they would sell for less.

Mr. Untermyer: Then you settle that between you, do you not?

Mr. Morgan: Yes.

Mr. Untermyer: That is not what I mean by competition. What I mean by competition is this: Do you not think the company should be in a position to have other banking houses compete for these securities and perhaps get a higher price than you might think they were worth?

Mr. Morgan: I have no doubt that could be done occasionally, but it would not be often.

Mr. Untermyer: Do you not think it ought to be done—that they ought to be open to that field?

Mr. Morgan: I do not; not for the interests of the company.

Mr. Untermyer: You do not?

Mr. Morgan: No.

Mr. Untermyer: You think it is best for the interests of the company that it should only have one purchaser available?

Mr. Morgan: There is another point—

Mr. Untermyer: Do you think so? Is that your idea, Mr. Morgan?

Mr. Morgan: There is another point that I—

Mr. Untermyer: Will you not first answer my question?

Mr. Morgan: Yes; I will answer it. What is it? [The stenographer read the pending question.] I think so.

Mr. Untermyer: Now, if you like, you may explain why that is so.

Mr. Morgan: What I was going to say has gone out of my head. Wait a moment.

Mr. Untermyer: If it occurs to you later, you may state it.

J.P. Morgan, depicted here on the cover of *Puck Magazine,* was accused of exerting a stranglehold over American credit during the early 1900s. **THE LIBRARY OF CONGRESS.**

## Bankers and the "Curse of Bigness"

[Louis D. Brandeis, a lawyer, reformer, and Supreme Court justice, campaigned widely in the 1910s against the concentration of economic power. *Other People's Money and How the Bankers Use It,* his classic work of muckraking journalism, accuses Morgan and his fellow bankers of contributing to the "curse of bigness." For Brandeis, excessive corporate size meant a corresponding diminution of economic freedom for the small entrepreneur. His long-standing emphasis on the need for open competition among small economic participants—well evidenced in the excerpt below—was a cornerstone of President Woodrow Wilson's "New Freedom" program.]

The dominant element in our financial oligarchy is the investment banker. Associated banks, trust companies and life insurance companies are his tools. Controlled railroads, public service and industrial corporations are his subjects. Though properly but middlemen, these bankers bestride as masters America's business world, so that practically no large enterprise can be undertaken successfully without their participation or approval. These bankers are, of course, able men possessed of large fortunes; but the most potent factor in their control of business is not the possession of extraordinary ability or huge wealth. The key to their power is Combination—concentration intensive and comprehensive. . . .

**SOURCE:** Brandeis, Louis D. *Other People's Money and How the Bankers Use It.* New York: Frederick A. Stokes, 1913. Reprint, with a foreword by Norman Hapgood, 1932, p. 4.

---

Mr. Morgan: I was simply going to say that there is another point about it, and that is this: You must remember that securities that are issued and sold do not always prove good. I do not say that that often happens, but it sometimes does.

Mr. Untermyer: That would not apply to bonds of the New York Central, would it?

Mr. Morgan: Not to that particular road; but it has applied to other roads in New England and to other roads in New York State, when there is no fiscal agent or person responsible for them who will put their name on them. That is a thing which is sometimes overlooked.

Mr. Untermyer: But the name does not help after the bond is proved bad, does it?

Mr. Morgan: It does in this way: The house is called upon to protect those bonds, to assist in the reorganization of the road, to make them good in case of a disaster.

Mr. Untermyer: But what I mean is that the banking house assumes no legal responsibility for the value of the bonds, does it?

Mr. Morgan: No, sir; but it assumes something else that is still more important, and that is the moral responsibility which has to be defended as long as you live.

Mr. Untermyer: Yes; but when a bond turns out to be bad, the moral responsibility never materializes into money for the bondholder, does it?

Mr. Morgan: It does, very often.

Mr. Untermyer: In what way?

Mr. Morgan: Because the company is reorganized, and bonds are issued, and the people get their money and interest.

Mr. Untermyer: Let us see about that. When the bond that you have sold defaults on its interest, and the property is reorganized, it is reorganized at the expense of the property, is it not? That is, the property pays the expense of the reorganization?

Mr. Morgan: Yes; but there is a good deal done before that.

Mr. Untermyer: But it does pay the expense?

Mr. Morgan: Yes.

Mr. Untermyer: Then, whatever the property can afford is given in new securities, is it not?

Mr. Morgan: Yes.

Mr. Untermyer: All this time the banking house is not losing any money through its error of judgment, is it?

Mr. Morgan: It is not necessarily the error of judgment of the banking house. There are a great many reasons—

Mr. Untermyer: Perhaps I ought not to have said it was an error of judgment of the banking house. Sometimes it is and sometimes it is not.

Mr. Morgan: Yes, sir.

Mr. Untermyer: Whatever the cause, if the bond turns out to be bad, the banking house does not suffer any monetary loss after it has distributed the bonds, does it?

Mr. Morgan: Why, certainly; at least, they may, very seriously.

Mr. Untermyer: How?

Mr. Morgan: Because they are obliged to do any number of things for the bondholders.

Mr. Untermyer: And they do those things out of the treasury of the company, do they not?

Mr. Morgan: They do after the company has got a treasury or money to pay them from.

Mr. Untermyer: Yes, but they get their money back, do they not?

Mr. Morgan: Not always.

Mr. Untermyer: In a reorganization, that is the first thing that is provided for, is it not?

Mr. Morgan: Yes, but it does not always go through.

Mr. Untermyer: Will you name any instance of a railroad bond issued by your firm that proved bad, where the property was reorganized and your company personally put up any money to make the bond good, that it did not get back?

Mr. Morgan: I can not recall any now, but there are cases of that kind.

Mr. Untermyer: Will you try to remember one such case, so that we may have the benefit of it?

Mr. Morgan: I will send it to you. I can not do it now.

Mr. Untermyer: You do not remember any case of that kind, do you?

Mr. Morgan: Not at the moment, no.

Mr. Untermyer: But the rule is—

Mr. Morgan: There have been such cases though.

Mr. Untermyer: The rule is, is it not, that where there is a mistake of judgment, anywhere, and the bond is proven bad, and the road has to be reorganized, the reorganization comes out of the security holders?

Mr. Morgan: Not always. It comes out of the property.

Mr. Untermyer: Yes, but that is out of the security holders, is it not?

Mr. Morgan: Yes?

Mr. Untermyer: It always comes out of them?

Mr. Morgan: I will refer you to that report of the Reading, which will show you all that.

Mr. Untermyer: We will get to that in a minute. But the fact is, at the moment, that the expense of reorganization, and whatever loss there is in the property has to be borne by the security holders in the end?

Mr. Morgan: No, sir; by the securities which are issued in the reorganization.

Mr. Untermyer: Yes; and those securities are issued to the underwriters in the reorganization?

Mr. Morgan: That depends upon whose hands the reorganization is in.

Mr. Untermyer: Assuming that it is in the best possible hands—your own?

Mr. Morgan: Thank you, sir.

Mr. Untermyer: The question then is, does not the expense and all the money necessary to reorganize the property come out of the security holders?

Mr. Morgan: I should hardly say that. It comes out of the property.

Mr. Untermyer: Yes. It comes out of the property. It does not come out of the bankers, does it?

Mr. Morgan: It comes out of the property, provided the property will pay it.

Mr. Untermyer: If the property will not pay it, the security holder has to take less, has he not?

Mr. Morgan: He will have to take the property.

Mr. Untermyer: Yes; but all this time the banker does not suffer, does he?

Mr. Morgan: He does, because very often he has to pay the money.

Mr. Untermyer: Pay the money to whom?

Mr. Morgan: To the parties who get their interest.

Mr. Untermyer: But he pays it out of the property, does he not?

Mr. Morgan: He does, if he gets it.

Mr. Untermyer: He does not pay anything until he does get it, does he?

Mr. Morgan: Yes; he does, very often.

Mr. Untermyer: Give us one instance in which a banker has done anything more than occasionally advance the interest on the securities, and then get it back out of the property.

Mr. Morgan: I think there are a great many cases of that kind. I can not recall—

Mr. Untermyer: Can you not give us one?

Mr. Morgan: I can not recall it at the moment.

Mr. Untermyer: In the whole history of railroading and railroad reorganization?

Mr. Morgan: I have had a good deal of it.

Mr. Untermyer: I know it; and that is the reason I am asking you to scan the whole history of it and give us a single instance in which the banker who advanced the interest on a defaulted security, or advanced any other money on a defaulted security, failed to get back his money in the reorganization.

Mr. Morgan: I can not recall it now, sir, but I am sure there are cases.

Mr. Untermyer: If you find any of that sort—

Mr. Morgan: I will give you the details of it.

Mr. Untermyer: It would be quite a find, would it not?

Mr. Morgan: Yes. . . .

Mr. Untermyer: Now let us take it up. Do you not know that in these banks the representatives of your firm are not only on the board, but on the executive committee?

Mr. Morgan: Even on the executive committee.

Mr. Untermyer: The executive committee runs the bank, does it not?

Mr. Morgan: You say the directors run the bank.

Mr. Untermyer: No, I do not. I say they ought to, but you say they do not. Now, who does run the bank, in your judgment?

Mr. Morgan: The officers run the bank.

Mr. Untermyer: What are the directors there for?

Mr. Morgan: They are there to pass upon what the officers do every week.

Mr. Untermyer: Then they are supposed to pass upon what the officers do?

Mr. Morgan: Yes.

Mr. Untermyer: So that each director is supposed to know what is going on in his bank?

Mr. Morgan: Yes.

Mr. Untermyer: And as he is a director in a number of competitive banks he gets the information, does he not, of what is going on among his competitor banks?

Mr. Morgan: He would do that in any bank.

Mr. Untermyer: If he was in any one bank, he would only know the business of that bank, would he not?

Mr. Morgan: If he was in another one, he would know the business of two banks.

Mr. Untermyer: If he was a member of the executive committee of all of them, he would know the business of every competitor, would he not?

Mr. Morgan: Not necessarily, but assuming that he did—

Mr. Untermyer: Do you think it is a good thing?

Mr. Morgan: I do not see any objection to it.

Mr. Untermyer: Do you think that promotes competition?

Mr. Morgan: It does not prevent it.

Mr. Untermyer: You are opposed to competition, are you not?

Mr. Morgan: No; I do not mind competition.

Mr. Untermyer: You would rather have combination, would you not?

Mr. Morgan: I would rather have combination.

Mr. Untermyer: You would rather have combination than competition?

Mr. Morgan: Yes.

Mr. Untermyer: You are an advocate of combination and cooperation, as against competition, are you not?

Mr. Morgan: Yes; cooperation I should favor.

Mr. Untermyer: Combination as against competition?

Mr. Morgan: I do not object to competition, either. I like a little competition.

Mr. Untermyer: You like a little if it does not hurt you? Competition that hurts you, you do not believe in?

Mr. Morgan: I do not mind it. What I mean to say is this—now, another point—may I go on for a moment?

Mr. Untermyer: Certainly.

Mr. Morgan: This may be a sensitive subject. I do not want to talk of it. This is probably the only chance I will have to speak of it.

Mr. Untermyer: You mean the subject of combination and concentration?

Mr. Morgan: Yes; the question of control. Without you have control, you can not do anything.

Mr. Untermyer: Unless you have got control, you can not do what?

Mr. Morgan: Unless you have got actual control, you can not control anything.

Mr. Untermyer: Well, I guess that is right. Is that the reason you want to control everything?

Mr. Morgan: I want to control nothing?

Mr. Untermyer: Then what sort of control is it that you want? You say, in order to have complete control—

Mr. Morgan: I do not want either—I do not want any control.

Mr. Untermyer: What is the point, Mr. Morgan, you want to make, because I do not quite gather it?

Mr. Morgan: What I say is this, that control is a thing, particularly in money, and you are talking about a money control—now, there is nothing in the world that you can make a trust on money.

Mr. Untermyer: What you mean is that there is no way one man can get it all?

Mr. Morgan: Or any of it, except—

Mr. Untermyer: Or control of it?

Mr. Morgan: Or control of it.

Mr. Untermyer: There is no way one man can get a monopoly of money?

Mr. Morgan: Or control of it.

Mr. Untermyer: He can make a try at it?

Mr. Morgan: No, sir; he can not. He may have all the money in Christendom, but he can not do it.

Mr. Untermyer: Let us go on. If you owned all the banks of New York, with all their resources, would you not come pretty near having a control of credit?

Mr. Morgan: No, sir; not at all.

Mr. Untermyer: Now, suppose you owned all the banks and trust companies, or controlled them.

Mr. Morgan: Yes.

Mr. Untermyer: And somebody wanted to start up in the steel business, you understand, against the United States Steel Corporation.

Mr. Morgan: Yes.

Mr. Untermyer: And wanted a vast amount of capital, and it was a good business.

Mr. Morgan: Yes.

Mr. Untermyer: New York would be the natural market for money, would it not?

Mr. Morgan: Yes.

Mr. Untermyer: If you owned all the banks and trust companies, or controlled them, you would be under a duty, would you not, to the United States Steel Corporation, to see that it was not subjected to ruinous competition?

Mr. Morgan: No, sir; it has nothing to do with it.

Mr. Untermyer: You would not be under any such obligation?

Mr. Morgan: No, sir.

Mr. Untermyer: You would welcome competition?

Mr. Morgan: I would welcome competition.

Mr. Untermyer: The more of it the better?

Mr. Morgan: Yes.

Mr. Untermyer: And the more new steel plants started up, and the bigger they were, and the more money they had—

Mr. Morgan: I would be perfectly willing for them to do it.

Mr. Untermyer (continuing): The better you would like it?

Mr. Morgan: I would not object to that. But I am not discussing the question of trade; I am talking about money.

Mr. Untermyer: Now, we are getting there. I am talking about credit rather than about money.

Mr. Morgan: Yes.

Mr. Untermyer: The concentration and control of credit. I want to know, if you controlled all those banks, and a competitor came along, or a potential competitor, who wanted to compete, whether he would get the money from those banks you control?

Mr. Morgan: Yes; he would.

Mr. Untermyer: That is what you would be there for?

Mr. Morgan: Yes.

Mr. Untermyer: Some other man who might control might not take the view you have?

Mr. Morgan: He would not have the control.

Mr. Untermyer: That is your idea, is it? Your idea is that when a man has got a vast power, such as you have—you admit you have, do you not?

Mr. Morgan: I do not know it; sir.

Mr. Untermyer: You admit you have, do you not?

Mr. Morgan: I do not think I have.

Mr. Untermyer: You do not feel it at all?

Mr. Morgan: No; I do not feel it at all.

Mr. Untermyer: Well, assuming that you had it, your idea is that when a man abuses it, he loses it?

Mr. Morgan: Yes; and he never gets it back again, either.

Mr. Untermyer: Yes, I understand. Now, have you any instance in your mind of any such man who has had any such power and control in order to experiment with it?

Mr. Morgan: No; but I know from experience.

Mr. Untermyer: Experience of your own?

Mr. Morgan: No; I am talking about the experience of having things. What I mean to say is this. Allow me. The question of control, in this country at least, is personal; that is, in money.

Mr. Untermyer: How about credit?

Mr. Morgan: In credit, also.

Mr. Untermyer: Personal to whom? To the man who controls?

Mr. Morgan: No, no; he never has it. He can not buy it.

Mr. Untermyer: No, but he gets—

Mr. Morgan: All the money in Christendom and all the banks in Christendom can not control it.

Mr. Untermyer: That is what you wanted to say, is it not?

Mr. Morgan: Yes, sir.

Mr. Untermyer: Now, having acquired that control, Mr. Morgan, you think that if he abuses it he loses it?

Mr. Morgan: Of course.

Mr. Untermyer: You think he does?

Mr. Morgan: Yes.

Mr. Untermyer: But have you not seen many instances in the history of this country of financial men getting vast control—

Mr. Morgan: General control—

Mr. Untermyer: One moment—and abusing it through a long period of years before they lost it?

Mr. Morgan: No.

Mr. Untermyer: I do not want to be invidious by stating illustrations.

Mr. Morgan: In one particular line; but nobody has what you call a money trust, or anything of that kind.

Mr. Untermyer: You have known of men in some particular department, such as the railroads, getting control and abusing that control for a series of years before they lost it?

Mr. Morgan: I want to state—

Mr. Untermyer: Will you answer that question?

Mr. Morgan: I have; and I say that I am not discussing the question of railroads or merchandise or anything else. I am talking about money and credit.

Mr. Untermyer: You admit, do you not, that men may get control of railroads or business enterprises and monopolize them and so abuse their privilege?

Mr. Morgan: Yes; anybody—

Mr. Untermyer: And retain that control?

Mr. Morgan: Yes.

Mr. Untermyer: By the force of their power?

Mr. Morgan: Yes.

Mr. Untermyer: And you say that so far as the control for the credit is concerned, they can not do the same thing?

Mr. Morgan: On money, no; they can not control it.

## Further Resources

### BOOKS

McCraw, Thomas K. *Prophets of Regulation: Charles Francis Adams, Louis D. Brandeis, James M. Landis, Alfred E. Kahn.* Cambridge, Mass.: Harvard University Press, 1984.

Strouse, Jean. *Morgan: American Financier.* New York: Random House, 1999.

Strumm, Philippa. *Brandeis: Beyond Progressivism* Lawrence, Kans.: University of Kansas Press, 1993.

### PERIODICALS

Klebaner, Benjamin J. "The Money Trust Investigation in Retrospect." *National Banking Review* 3, 1966, 393–403.

### WEBSITES

"An Inventory to the Samuel Untermyer Papers." American Jewish Archives. Available online at http://www.huc.edu /aja/Untermyer.htm; website home page: http://www.huc .edu/aja (accessed October 12, 2002).

# New Parties Challenge the Economic System

## Progressive Party Platform of 1912

Political platform

**By:** Progressive Party

**Date:** 1912

**Source:** Platform of the Progressive Party, August 7, 1912: Declaration of Principles of the Progressive Party. Available online at http://www.ssa.gov/history/trplatform.html; website home page: http://www.ssa.gov (accessed November 15, 2002).

**About the Organization:** The Progressive Party (nicknamed the Bull Moose Party) was organized in 1912 as a vehicle for reelecting Theodore Roosevelt. It took its name from the Progressive reform movement that Roosevelt had supported while serving as president between 1901 and 1909. Frustrated by the way his handpicked successor as president, William Howard Taft (served 1909–1913), handled a number of policy issues, Roosevelt caused a split in the Republican Party by challenging Taft in 1912.

# Socialist Party Platform of 1912

**Political platform**

**By:** Socialist Party

**Date:** 1912

**Source:** Platform of the Socialist Party, May 12, 1912. Available online at
http://www.nv.cc.va.us/home/nvsageh/Hist122/Part2
/SOCP1912.HTM; website home page: http://www.nv.cc
.va.us (accessed November 15, 2002).

**About the Organization:** The traditional parties (the Republicans and the Democrats) faced a challenge from both the Progressive Party and the Socialists in 1912. Many parties had formed during the nineteenth century to push for socialist and labor reforms in the United States, but the most successful was the Socialist Party founded in 1901 and led by Eugene V. Debs. Drawing on broad and diverse support from social reformers and radicals, factory workers, miners and agrarians, urban immigrants, and noted intellectuals, the party offered a pro-worker, socialist alternative to the American capitalist system. ■

# Introduction

Two issues—the regulation of industry and the conditions of labor—held a central place in the presidential campaign of 1912. The economy had been vastly transformed during the decades since the 1880s, as corporations grew in size and power. At the same time, increasing numbers of Americans, swelled by rising immigration, relied on wage-work for their livelihood. Debate centered around what sort of controls should be placed on "big business" and what sort of protections would be afforded to laborers.

For two decades, American antitrust law had sought to check corporate growth by prohibiting business combinations that restrained competitive trade. But what "restrained competitive trade" meant was unclear. Did antitrust law exist simply to stop the worst excesses of industrial monopolists? Or did its authors intend a broad assault on "bigness" in all its forms? President Roosevelt's "good trust"/"bad trust" distinction, which rested on vague notions of industrial statesmanship, did not survive in his successor's administration. Taft initiated antitrust proceedings against U.S. Steel over a merger that Roosevelt had previously sanctioned, straining relations between the former friends.

When Roosevelt formulated his Progressive Party platform in 1912, he veered away from the open-ended, legalistic, enforced competition that Taft advocated. Instead, Roosevelt sought strong federal regulation of interstate business activity. Regarding economic concentration as both inevitable and efficient, he sought to place regulatory controls over national firms while still allowing for their expansion. This stood in marked contrast to the "New Freedom" program advocated by the Democrat's candidate, Woodrow Wilson. Wilson, who claimed to stand for the "men who are on the make rather than the men who are already made," hoped to use public power to protect the economic freedom of the middle class and the small entrepreneurs from the overwhelming powers of big business.

Rejecting both the Democrats and Republicans as parties of the "capitalist class," Eugene Debs' Socialist Party endorsed social ownership of businesses and the end of "economic individualism." The platform declared that antitrust laws and other federal regulations "proved to be utterly futile and ridiculous," offering no protection to the working class. Urging citizens to vote their class, Debs hoped to offer a political alternative that would allow for serious debate over working-class issues, such as public ownership of industry, public unemployment relief, and government inspections of factories.

Indeed, industrial justice stood at the center of the Socialist platform. Ultimately, this meant the dismantling of the capitalist system, which they saw as having been built by a greedy upper class through the oppression of wage-workers. In their view, collective ownership would end the unequal distribution of wealth between workers and owners and diminish the consumption of the nation's natural resources. The Socialist platform endorsed a program geared toward achieving this new form of political economy, emphasizing, among other things, the regulation of working conditions and wages, and the abolition of child labor.

Some of these themes, such as the conservation of resources and the need for better working conditions, were echoed in the Progressive platform. Roosevelt included human resources in his conservation plan, and called for an end to child labor; the regulation of wages, hours, and conditions of labor; and the protection of unions as a countervailing force against organized businesses.

## Significance

Both the Bull Moose Progressives and the Socialists aimed to alter the American economic system to better address the issues of corporate bigness and industrial democracy for laborers. Roosevelt saw industrial expansion as both inevitable and key to American prosperity.

His solution to corporate excesses was the corresponding expansion of the federal government. A powerful national government could oversee an increasingly national economy, ensuring healthy economic growth and economic justice for American working men and women. By contrast, the Socialists argued that the American capitalist system was beyond reform. Even Roosevelt's enlarged state would still be in the hands of the capitalist class, and thus economic reform would continue to serve their interests. A party dedicated to workers' interests, however, could institute practical reform while pursuing a more just economic system.

With the Republican Party split, Wilson and his New Freedom program carried the election of 1912. But the Socialist and Progressive challenges remained significant. With more than four million votes, Roosevelt easily outran Taft's more conservative Republican campaign. And Debs received about 900,000 ballots (about 6 percent of the popular vote), indicating significant support for a genuine alternative to established parties. Much of both Debs' and Roosevelt's programs were resuscitated in the New Deal of the 1930s, when the nation again faced serious questions about the nature of the capitalist system.

## Primary Source

### The Progressive Platform of 1912 [excerpt]

**SYNOPSIS:** The Progressive Party advocated the expansion of public power to nurture big business and protect the worker, as illustrated by this excerpt from their official party platform.

The conscience of the people, in a time of grave national problems, has called into being a new party, born of the Nation's awakened sense of justice. We of the Progressive Party here dedicate ourselves to the fulfillment of the duty laid upon us by our fathers to maintain that government of the people, by the people and for the people whose foundation they laid. . . .

### The Old Parties

Political parties exist to secure responsible government and to execute the will of the people.

From these great tasks both of the old parties have turned aside. Instead of instruments to promote the general welfare, they have become the tools of corrupt interests which use them impartially to serve their selfish purposes. Behind the ostensible government sits enthroned an invisible government, owing no allegiance and acknowledging no responsibility to the people.

A banner for Theodore Roosevelt's Bull Moose Progressive Party, used during the 1912 campaign. © BETTMANN/CORBIS. REPRODUCED BY PERMISSION.

To destroy this invisible government, to dissolve the unholy alliance between corrupt business and corrupt politics is the first task of the statesmanship of the day.

The deliberate betrayal of its trust by the Republican Party, and the fatal incapacity of the Democratic Party to deal with the new issues of the new time, have compelled the people to forge a new instrument of government through which to give effect to their will in laws and institutions.

Unhampered by tradition, uncorrupted by power, undismayed by the magnitude of the task, the new party offers itself as the instrument of the people to sweep away old abuses, to build a new and nobler commonwealth. . . .

### Social and Industrial Strength

The supreme duty of the Nation is the conservation of human resources through an enlightened measure of social and industrial justice. We pledge ourselves to work unceasingly in State and Nation for:—

Effective legislation looking to the prevention of industrial accidents, occupational diseases, overwork, involuntary unemployment, and other injurious effects incident to modern industry;

The fixing of minimum safety and health standards for the various occupations, and the exercise of the public authority of State and Nation, including the Federal control over inter-State commerce and the taxing power, to maintain such standards;

The prohibition of child labor;

Minimum wage standards for working women, to provide a living scale in all industrial occupations;

The prohibition of night work for women and the establishment of an eight hour day for women and young persons;

One day's rest in seven for all wage-workers. . . .

The establishment of industrial research laboratories to put the methods and discoveries of science at the service of American producers.

We favor the organization of the workers, men and women as a means of protecting their interests and of promoting their progress.

### Business

We believe that true popular government, justice and prosperity go hand in hand, and so believing, it is our purpose to secure that large measure of general prosperity which is the fruit of legitimate and honest business, fostered by equal justice and by sound progressive laws.

We demand that the test of true prosperity shall be the benefits conferred thereby on all the citizens not confined to individuals or classes and that the test of corporate efficiency shall be the ability better to serve the public; that those who profit by control of business affairs shall justify that profit and that control by sharing with the public the fruits thereof.

We therefore demand a strong National regulation of inter-State corporations. The corporation is an essential part of modern business. The concentration of modern business, in some degree, is both inevitable and necessary for National and international business efficiency. But the existing concentration of vast wealth under a corporate system, unguarded and uncontrolled by the Nation, has placed in the hands of a few men enormous, secret, irresponsible power over the daily life of the citizen—a power insufferable in a free government and certain of abuse.

### Primary Source

The Socialist Platform of 1912 [excerpt]

**SYNOPSIS:** The Socialist Party's official platform argues that political reform is insufficient to control America's capitalist economy. At the core of the Socialist philosophy is a belief that nothing short of a complete dismantling of that system will resolve the country's economic and social woes.

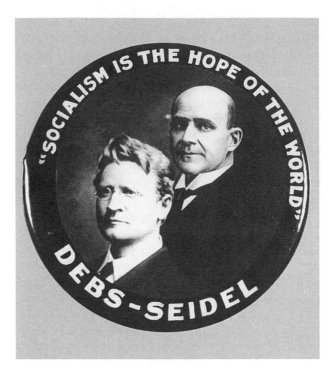

A campaign button illustrates the Socialist Party's nominees for vice president and president—Emil Seidel and Eugene Debs—during the 1912 campaign. © DAVID J. & JANICE L. FRENT COLLECTION/ CORBIS. REPRODUCED BY PERMISSION.

The Socialist party declares that the capitalist system has outgrown its historical function, and has become utterly incapable of meeting the problems now confronting society. We denounce this outgrown system as incompetent and corrupt and the source of unspeakable misery and suffering to the whole working class.

Under this system the industrial equipment of the nation has passed into the absolute control of a plutocracy which exacts an annual tribute of hundreds of millions of dollars from the producers. Unafraid of any organized resistance, it stretches out its greedy hands over the still undeveloped resources of the nation-the land, the mines, the forests and the water powers of every State of the Union.

In spite of the multiplication of laborsaving machines and improved methods in industry which cheapen the cost of production, the share of the producers grows ever less, and the prices of all the necessities of life steadily increase. The boasted prosperity of this nation is for the owning class alone. To the rest it means only greater hardship and misery. The high cost of living is felt in every home. Millions of wage-workers have seen the purchasing power of their wages decrease until life has become a desperate battle for mere existence. . . .

In the face of these evils, so manifest that all thoughtful observers are appalled at them, the legislative representatives of the Republican and Democratic parties remain the faithful servants of the oppressors. Measures designed to secure to the wage-earners of this Nation as humane and just treatment as is already enjoyed by the wage-earners of all other civilized nations have been smothered in committee without debate, the laws ostensibly designed to bring relief to the farmers and general consumers are juggled and transformed into instruments for the exaction of further tribute. The growing unrest under oppression has driven these two old parties to the enactment of a variety of regulative measures, none of which has limited in any appreciable degree the power of the plutocracy, and some of which have been perverted into means of increasing that power. Anti-trust laws, railroad restrictions and regulations, with the prosecutions, indictments and investigations based upon such legislation, have proved to be utterly futile and ridiculous. . . .

Society is divided into warring groups and classes, based upon material interests. Fundamentally, this struggle is a conflict between the two main classes, one of which, the capitalist class, owns the means of production, and the other, the working class, must use these means of production, on terms dictated by the owners.

The capitalist class, though few in numbers, absolutely controls the government, legislative, executive and judicial. This class owns the machinery of gathering and disseminating news through its organized press. It subsidizes seats of learning—the colleges and schools—and even religious and moral agencies. It has also the added prestige which established customs give to any order of society, right or wrong.

The working class, which includes all those who are forced to work for a living whether by hand or brain, in shop, mine or on the soil, vastly outnumbers the capitalist class. Lacking effective organization and class solidarity, this class is unable to enforce its will. Given such a class solidarity and effective organization, the workers will have the power to make all laws and control all industry in their own interest. All political parties are the expression of economic class interests. All other parties than the Socialist party represent one or another group of the ruling capitalist class. Their political conflicts reflect merely superficial rivalries between competing capitalist groups. However they result, these conflicts have no issue of real value

to the workers. Whether the Democrats or Republicans win politically, it is the capitalist class that is victorious economically.

The Socialist party is the political expression of the economic interests of the workers. Its defeats have been their defeats and its victories their victories. It is a party founded on the science and laws of social development. It proposes that, since all social necessities to-day are socially produced, the means of their production and distribution shall be socially owned and democratically controlled.

In the face of the economic and political aggressions of the capitalist class the only reliance left the workers is that of their economic organizations and their political power. By the intelligent and class conscious use of these, they may resist successfully the capitalist class, break the fetters of wage slavery, and fit themselves for the future society, which is to displace the capitalist system. The Socialist party appreciates the full significance of class organization and urges the wage-earners, the working farmers and all other useful workers to organize for economic and political action, and we pledge ourselves to support the toilers of the fields as well as those in the shops, factories and mines of the nation in their struggles for economic justice.

In the defeat or victory of the working class party in this new struggle for freedom lies the defeat or triumph of the common people of all economic groups, as well as the failure or triumph of popular government. Thus the Socialist party is the party of the present day revolution which makes the transition from economic individualism to socialism, from wage slavery to free co-operation, from capitalist oligarchy to industrial democracy.

## Further Resources

**BOOKS**

Bell, Daniel. *Marxian Socialism in the United States.* Ithaca, N.Y.: Cornell University Press, 1996.

Schelsinger, Arthur M., ed. *History of U.S. Political Parties,* vol. 3. 1973. Reprint, New York: Chelsea House, 2002.

**PERIODICALS**

Milkis, Sidney, and Daniel Tichenor. "'Direct Democracy' and Social Justice: The Progressive Party Campaign of 1912." *Studies in American Political Development* 8, Fall 1994, 282–340.

**WEBSITES**

1912: Competing Visions for America. Available online at http://1912.history.ohio-state.edu (accessed October 13, 2002).

"Presidential History Resources." The American President. Available online at http://www.americanpresident.org

/presidentialresources.htm; website home page: http://www
.americanpresident.org (accessed October 12, 2002).

"The Progressive Era." American Political Development. Available online at http://www.americanpoliticaldevelopment.org
/classroom/primary_resources/progressive_era.html; website
home page: http://www.americanpoliticaldevelopment.org
(accessed July 23, 2003).

"Theodore Roosevelt Papers at the Library of Congress." American Memory Historical Collections, Library of Congress.
Available online at http://lcweb2.loc.gov/ammem/trhtml;
website home page: http://lcweb2.loc.gov (accessed October
13, 2002). *Additional primary sources concerning Theodore
Roosevelt and the Progressive Party are available here.*

# Drift and Mastery: An Attempt to Diagnose the Current Unrest

Nonfiction work

**By:** Walter Lippmann

**Date:** 1914

**Source:** Lippmann, Walter. *Drift and Mastery: An Attempt to
Diagnose the Current Unrest.* New York: Mitchell Kennerly,
1914, 121–148. Reprinted in Shannon, David A., ed. *Progressivism and Postwar Disillusionment: 1898–1928.* New
York: McGraw-Hill, 1966, 104–112.

**About the Author:** Walter Lippmann (1889–1974) was just
twenty-five when he published *Drift and Mastery,* an inspired
and wide-ranging critique of the American political tradition. A
Harvard graduate whose major influences ranged from the
philosophers William James and George Santayana to the socialist Graham Wallas and the muckraking journalist Lincoln
Steffens, Lippmann soon emerged as one of the nation's preeminent public intellectuals. *Drift and Mastery* captures the young
philosopher-journalist at his most earnest, revealing the sort of
incisive social and political commentary that would become his
hallmark in writing for such publications as *The New Republic,
The New York Herald Tribune,* and *The Washington Post.* ■

## Introduction

Since the late nineteenth century, Americans had
worried about the growing concentration of economic
control by large corporations. This fear focused especially on "trusts"—groups of businesses linked by interlocking corporate boards of directors that sought to
consolidate, or strengthen, control over a particular industry. Newspaper stories and books that exposed the
workings of organizations such as the steel trust and
money trust led to a public outcry over the means by
which powerful financiers and managers squashed competition and controlled prices. This perceived threat to

American economic freedom prompted Congress to pass
the Sherman Antitrust Act in 1890.

The Sherman Act reflected the sense of moral outrage over the behavior of large corporate entities. But the
text of the law was vague and served as a poor guide for
enforcement. President Theodore Roosevelt (served
1901–1909) sought to distinguish between "good" trusts
and "bad" trusts based on whether they acted for the good
of, or against, the public welfare. Court challenges to the
law produced conflicting decisions and revealed the
weakness of the Sherman Act's rhetoric.

In 1914, President Woodrow Wilson (served
1913–1921) hoped to tighten the language and loopholes
in the Sherman Act. The passage of the Federal Trade
Commission Act and the Clayton Antitrust Act gave Congress the power to regulate business practices that restrained trade, and blocked corporate conglomeration by
prohibiting interlocking boards of directors and the purchase of competitors' stock. Nonetheless, antitrust legislation remained difficult to enforce, since it could be
interpreted in a variety of ways.

## Significance

One of many subjects discussed in *Drift and Mastery* was America's antipathy toward trusts. Lippmann
felt that the public had reacted too harshly against the
trusts and had been too quick to assume that the competitive capitalism of the nineteenth century was a golden
age of benevolence and fair dealing. From his perspective, the trusts represented an innovative response to the
destructive competition of the past, a new organizational
order designed to bring stability and prosperity to America. This was the "Mastery" to which he referred in his
title. In contrast to thoughtless and reactionary "Drift,"
"Mastery" implied the rational reordering of American
political, economic, and social institutions.

Lippmann was not always clear on exactly what this
reordering would entail, but it was certainly not to be
achieved by Woodrow Wilson's New Freedom program.
Elevating the small businessman at the expense of the
trusts, as Wilson advocated, reflected a "village" mentality. What was needed, in Lippmann's estimation, was
an honest reckoning of current economic forces and a sincere effort to master them through the scientific spirit of
management and administration. Attacking the trusts,
rather than humanizing them and tailoring them toward
a public purpose, would only perpetuate drift. Ultimately,
Lippmann was on target in criticizing progressive reformers for their failure to propose a uniform and effective means of controlling excessive combinations of
economic power. Nonetheless, the American antitrust
tradition has served over the last century to set the outer
limits of excessive corporate conduct.

In his book, *Drift and Mastery,* Walter Lippmann called on America to reject a blanket backlash against big business. **THE LIBRARY OF CONGRESS.**

## Primary Source

*Drift and Mastery: An Attempt to Diagnose the Current Unrest* [excerpt]

**SYNOPSIS:** In this chapter of *Drift and Mastery,* Walter Lippmann describes the public sentiment toward antitrust regulation. Calling on America to reject a blanket backlash against big business, Lippmann advocates a comprehensive restructuring of economic life. Only then, he argues, can the nation gain mastery over its growing centers of corporate power.

[The ellipses in the document were in the original publication and in this case do not represent missing sections.]

It has been said that no trust could have been created without breaking the law. Neither could astronomy in the time of Galileo. If you build up foolish laws and insist that invention is a crime, well—then it is a crime. That is undeniably true, but not very interesting. Of course, you can't possibly treat the trusts as crimes. First of all, nobody knows what the trust laws mean. The spectacle of an enlightened people trying in vain for twenty-five years to find out the intention of a statute that it has en-

acted—that is one of those episodes that only madmen can appreciate. You see, it is possible to sympathize with the difficulties of a scholar trying to decipher the hieroglyphics of some ancient people, but when statesmen can't read the things they've written themselves, it begins to look as if some imp had been playing pranks. The men who rule this country to-day were all alive, and presumably sane, when the Sherman Act was passed. They all say in public that it is a great piece of legislation—an "exquisite instrument" someone called it the other day. The highest paid legal intelligence has concentrated on the Act. The Supreme Court has interpreted it many times, ending with the enormous assumption that reason had something to do with the law. The Supreme Court was denounced for this: the reformers said that if there was any reason in the law, the devil himself had got hold of it. As I write, Congress is engaged in trying to define what it thinks it means by the Act. . . .

That uncertainty hasn't prevented a mass of indictments, injunctions, lawsuits. It has, if anything, invited them. But of course, you can't enforce the criminal law against every "unfair" business practice. Just try to imagine the standing army of inspectors, detectives, prosecutors, and judges, the city of courthouses and jails, the enormous costs, and the unremitting zeal—if you cannot see the folly, at least see the impossibility of the method. To work with it seriously would not only bring business to a standstill, it would drain the energy of America more thoroughly than the bitterest foreign war. Visualize life in America, if you can, when the government at Washington and forty-eight state governments really undertook not our present desultory pecking, but a systematic enforcement of the criminal law. The newspapers would enjoy it for a week, and everybody would be excited; in two weeks it would be a bore; in six, there would be such a revolt that everyone, radical and conservative, would be ready to wreck the government and hang the attorney-general. For these "criminal" practices are so deep in the texture of our lives; they affect so many, their results are so intimate that anything like a "surgical" cutting at evil would come close to killing the patient.

If the anti-trust people really grasped the full meaning of what they said, and if they really had the power or the courage to do what they propose, they would be engaged in one of the most destructive agitations that America has known. They would be breaking up the beginning of a collective organization, thwarting the possibility of coöperation, and insisting upon submitting industry to the wasteful, the planless scramble of little profiteers. They would make impossible any deliberate and constructive use of our natural resources, they would thwart any effort to form the great industries into coordinated services, they would preserve commercialism as the undisputed master of our lives, they would lay a premium on the strategy of industrial war—they would, if they could. For these anti-trust people have never seen the possibilities of organized industries. They have seen only the obvious evils, the birth-pains, the undisciplined strut of youth, the bad manners, the greed, and the trickery. The trusts have been ruthless, of course. No one tried to guide them; they have broken the law in a thousand ways, largely because the law was such that they had to.

At any rate, I should not like to answer before a just tribunal for the harm done this country in the last twenty-five years by the stupid hostility of anti-trust laws. How much they have perverted the constructive genius of this country it is impossible to estimate. They have blocked any policy of welcome and use, they have concentrated a nation's thinking on inessentials, they have driven creative business men to underhand methods, and put a high money value on intrigue and legal cunning, demagoguery and waste. The trusts have survived it all, but in mutilated form, the battered makeshifts of a trampled promise. They have learned every art of evasion—the only art reformers allowed them to learn.

It is said that the economy of trusts is unreal. Yet no one has ever tried the economies of the trust in any open, deliberate fashion. The amount of energy that has had to go into repelling stupid attack, the adjustments that had to be made underground—it is a wonder the trusts achieved what they did to bring order out of chaos, and forge an instrument for a nation's business. You have no more right to judge the trusts by what they are than to judge the labor movement by what it is. Both of them are in that preliminary state where they are fighting for existence, and any real outburst of constructive effort has been impossible for them.

But revolutions are not stopped by blind resistance. They are only perverted. And as an exhibition of blind resistance to a great promise, the trust campaign of the American democracy is surely unequalled. Think of contriving correctives for a revolution, such as ordering business men to compete with each other. It is as if we said: "Let not thy right hand know what they left hand doeth; let thy

right hand fight thy left hand, and in the name of God let neither win." Bernard Shaw remarked several years ago that "after all, America is not submitting to the Trusts without a struggle. The first steps have already been taken by the village constable. He is no doubt preparing a new question for immigrants" . . . after asking them whether they are anarchists or polygamists, he is to add "'Do you approve of Trusts?' but pending this supreme measure of national defense he has declared in several states that trusts will certainly be put in the stocks and whipped."

There has been no American policy on the trust question: there has been merely a widespread resentment. The small local competitors who were wiped out became little centers of bad feeling: these nationally organized industries were looked upon as foreign invaders. They were arrogant, as the English in Ireland or the Germans in Alsace, and much of the feeling for local democracy attached itself to the revolt against these national despotisms. The trusts made enemies right and left: they squeezed the profits of the farmer, they made life difficult for the shopkeeper, they abolished jobbers and travelling salesmen, they closed down factories, they exercised an enormous control over credit through their size and through their eastern connections. Labor was no match for them, state legislatures were impotent before them. They came into the life of the simple American community as a tremendous revolutionary force, upsetting custom, changing men's status, demanding a readjustment for which people were unready. Of course, there was anti-trust feeling; of course, there was a blind desire to smash them. Men had been ruined and they were too angry to think, too hard pressed to care much about the larger life which the trusts suggested.

This feeling came to a head in Bryan's famous "cross of gold" speech in 1896. "When you come before us and tell us that we shall disturb your business interests, we reply that you have disturbed our business interests by your action. . . . The man who is employed for wages is as much a business man as his employers. The attorney in a country town is as much a business man as the corporation counsel in a great metropolis. The merchant at the crossroads store is as much a business man as the merchant of New York. The farmer . . . is as much a business man as the man who goes upon the Board of Trade and bets upon the price of grain. The miners . . . It is for these that we speak . . . we are fighting in the defense of our homes, our families, and posterity." What Bryan was really defending was the old and simple life of America, life that was doomed by the great organization that had come into the world. He thought he was fighting the plutocracy: as a matter of fact he was fighting something much deeper than that; he was fighting the larger scale of human life. The Eastern money power controlled the new industrial system, and Bryan fought it. But what he and his people hated from the bottom of their souls were the economic conditions which had upset the old life of the prairies, made new demands upon democracy, introduced specialization and science, had destroyed village loyalties, frustrated private ambitions, and created the impersonal relationships of the modern world.

Bryan has never been able to adjust himself to the new world in which he lives. That is why he is so irresistibly funny to sophisticated newspaper men. His virtues, his habits, his ideas, are the simple, direct, shrewd qualities of early America. He is the true Don Quixote of our politics, for he moves in a world that has ceased to exist.

He is a more genuine conservative than some propertied bigot. Bryan stands for the popular tradition of America, whereas most of his enemies stand merely for the power that is destroying that tradition. Bryan is what America was; his critics are generally defenders of what America has become. And neither seems to have any vision of what America is to be.

Yet there has always been great power behind Bryan, the power of those who in one way or another were hurt by the greater organization that America was developing. The Populists were part of that power. La Follette and the insurgent Republicans expressed it. It was easily a political majority of the American people. The Republican Party disintegrated under the pressure of the revolt. The Bull Moose gathered much of its strength from it. The Socialists have got some of it. But in 1912 it swept the Democratic Party, and by a combination of circumstances, carried the country. The plutocracy was beaten in politics, and the power that Bryan spoke for in 1896, the forces that had made muckraking popular, captured the government. They were led by a man who was no part of the power that he represented.

Woodrow Wilson is an outsider capable of skilled interpretation. He is an historian, and that has helped him to know the older tradition of America. He is a student of theory, and like most theorists of his generation he is deeply attached to the doctrines that swayed the world when America was founded.

But Woodrow Wilson at least knows that there is a new world. "There is one great basic fact which underlies all the questions that are discussed on the political platform at the present moment. That singular fact is that nothing is done in this country as it was done twenty years ago. We are in the presence of a new organization of society. . . . We have changed our economic conditions, absolutely, from top to bottom; and, with our economic society, the organization of our life." You could not make a more sweeping statement of the case. The President is perfectly aware of what has happened, and he says at the very outset that "our laws still deal with us on the basis of the old system . . . the old positive formulas do not fit the present problems."

You wait eagerly for some new formula. The new formula is this: "I believe the time has come when the governments of this country, both state and national, have to set the stage, and set it very minutely and carefully, for the doing of justice to men in every relationship of life." Now that is a new formula, because it means a willingness to use the power of government much more extensively.

But for what purpose is this power to be used? There, of course, is the rub. It is to be used to "*restore* our politics to their full spiritual vigor *again,* and our national life, whether in trade, in industry, or in what concerns us only as families and individuals, to its purity, its self-respect, and its *pristine* strength and freedom." The ideal is the old ideal, the ideal of Bryan, the method is the new one of government interference.

That, I believe, is the inner contradiction of Woodrow Wilson. He knows that there is a new world demanding new methods, but he dreams of an older world. He is torn between the two. It is a very deep conflict in him between what he knows and what he feels.

His feeling is, as he says, for "the man on the make." "For my part, I want the pigmy to have a chance to come out" . . ."Just let some of the youngsters I know have a chance and they'll give these gentlemen points. Lend them a little money. They can't get any now. See to it that when they have got a local market they can't be squeezed out of it." Nowhere in his speeches will you find any sense that it may be possible to organize the fundamental industries on some deliberate plan for national service. He is thinking always about somebody's chance to build up a profitable business; he likes the idea that somebody can beat somebody else, and the small business man takes on the virtues of David in a battle with Goliath.

"Have you found trusts that thought as much of their men as they did of their machinery?" he asks, forgetting that few people have ever found competitive textile mills or clothing factories that did. There isn't an evil of commercialism that Wilson isn't ready to lay at the door of the trusts. He becomes quite reckless in his denunciation of the New Devil—Monopoly—and of course, by contrast the competitive business takes on a halo of light. It is amazing how clearly he sees the evils that trusts do, how blind he is to the evils that his supporters do. You would think that the trusts were the first oppressors of labor; you would think they were the first business organization that failed to achieve the highest possible efficiency. The pretty record of competition throughout the Nineteenth Century is forgotten. Suddenly all that is a glorious past which we have lost. You would think that competitive commercialism was really a generous, chivalrous, high-minded stage of human culture.

"We design that the limitations on private enterprise shall be removed, so that the next generation of youngsters, as they come along, will not have to become protégés of benevolent trusts, but will be free to go about making their own lives what they will; so that we shall taste again the full cup, not of charity, but of liberty,—the only wine that ever refreshed and renewed the spirit of a people." That cup of liberty—we may well ask him to go back to Manchester, to Paterson to-day, to the garment trades of New York, and taste it for himself.

The New Freedom means the effort of small business men and farmers to use the government against the larger collective organization of industry. Wilson's power comes from them; his feeling is with them; his thinking is for them. Never a word of understanding for the new type of administrator, the specialist, the professionally trained business man; practically no mention of the consumer—even the tariff is for the business man; no understanding of the new demands of labor, its solidarity, its aspiration for some control over the management of business; no hint that it may be necessary to organize the fundamental industries of the country on some definite plan so that our resources may be developed by scientific method instead of by men "on the make"; no friendliness for the larger, collective life upon which the world is entering, only a constant return to the commercial chances of young men trying to set up in business. That is the push and force of this New Freedom, a freedom for the little profiteer, but no freedom for the nation from the narrowness, the poor incentives, the limited vision of small competitors,—no freedom from clamorous advertisement, from wasteful selling, from duplication of plants, from unnecessary enterprise, from the chaos, the welter, the strategy of industrial war.

There is no doubt, I think, that President Wilson and his party represent primarily small business in a war against the great interests. Socialists speak of his administration as a revolution within the bounds of capitalism. Wilson doesn't really fight the oppressions of property. He fights the evil done by large property-holders to small ones. The temper of his administration was revealed very clearly when the proposal was made to establish a Federal Trade Commission. It was suggested at once by leading spokesmen of the Democratic Party that corporations with a capital of less than a million dollars should be exempted from supervision. Is that because little corporations exploit labor or the consumer less? Not a bit of it. It is because little corporations are in control of the political situation.

But there are certain obstacles to the working out of the New Freedom. First of all, there was a suspicion in Wilson's mind, even during the campaign, that the tendency to large organization was too powerful to be stopped by legislation. So he left open a way of escape from the literal achievement of what the New Freedom seemed to threaten. *"I am for big business,"* he said, *"and I am against the trusts."* That is a very subtle distinction, so subtle, I suspect, that no human legislation will ever be able to make it. The distinction is this: big business is a business that has survived competition; a trust is an arrangement to do away with competition. But when competition is done away with, who is the Solomon wise enough to know whether the result was accomplished by superior efficiency or by agreement among the competitors or by both?

The big trusts have undoubtedly been built up in part by superior business ability, and by successful competition, but also by ruthless competition, by underground arrangements, by an intricate series of facts which no earthly tribunal will ever be able to disentangle. And why should it try? These great combinations are here. What interests us is not their history but their future. The point is whether you are going to split them up, and if so into how many parts. Once split, are they to be kept from coming together again? Are you determined to prevent men who could coöperate from cooperating? Wilson seems to imply that a big business which has survived competition is to be let alone, and the trusts attacked. But as there is no real way of distinguishing between them, he leaves the question just where he found it: he must choose between the large organization of business and the small.

It's here that his temperament and his prejudices clash with fact and necessity. He really would like to disintegrate large business. "Are you not eager for the time," he asks, "when your sons shall be able to look forward to becoming not employees, but heads of some small, it may be, but hopeful business . . . ?" But to what percentage of the population can he hold out that hope? How many small but hopeful steel mills, coal mines, telegraph systems, oil refineries, copper mines, can this country support? A few hundred at the outside. And for these few hundred sons whose "best energies . . . are inspired by the knowledge that they are their own masters with the paths of the world before them," we are asked to give up the hope of a sane, deliberate organization of national industry brought under democratic control.

I submit that it is an unworthy dream. I submit that the intelligent men of my generation can find a better outlet for their energies than in making themselves masters of little businesses. They have the vast opportunity of introducing order and purpose into the business world, of devising administrative methods by which the great resources of the country can be operated on some thought-out plan. They have the whole new field of industrial statesmanship before them, and those who prefer the egotism of some little business are not the ones whose ambitions we need most to cultivate.

But the disintegration which Wilson promised in the New Freedom is not likely to be carried out. One year of public office has toned down the audacity of the campaign speeches so much that Mr. Dooley says you can play the President's messages on a harp. Instead of a "radical reconstruction" we are engaged in signing a "constitution of peace." These big business men who a few months ago showed not the "least promise of disinterestedness" are to-day inspired by "a spirit of accommodation." The President's own Secretary of Commerce, Mr. Redfield, has said to the National Chamber of Commerce that the number of trusts still operating "is conspicuously small." Was ever wish the father to a pleasanter thought? Was ever greater magic wrought with less effort? Or is it that politicians in office have to pretend that what they can't do has happened anyway?

Wilson is against the trusts for many reasons: the political economy of his generation was based on competition and free trade; the Democratic Party is by tradition opposed to a strong central government, and that opposition applies equally well to strong national business,—it is a party attached to local rights, to village patriotism, to humble but ambitious enterprise; its temper has always been hostile to specialization and expert knowledge, because it admires a very primitive man-to-man democracy. Wilson's thought is inspired by that outlook. It has been tempered some-what by contact with men who have outgrown the village culture, so that Wilson is less hostile to experts, less oblivious to administrative problems than is Bryan. But at the same time his speeches are marked with contempt for the specialist: they play up quite obviously to the old democratic notion that any man can do almost any job. You have always to except the negro, of course, about whom the Democrats have a totally different tradition. But among white men, special training and expert knowledge are somewhat under suspicion in Democratic circles.

Hostility to large organization is a natural quality in village life. Wilson is always repeating that the old personal relationships of employer and employee have disappeared. He deplores the impersonal nature of the modern world. Now that is a fact not to be passed over lightly. It does change the nature of our problems enormously. Indeed, it is just this breakdown of the old relationships which constitutes the modern problem. So the earlier chapters of this book were devoted to showing how in response to new organization the psychology of business men had changed; how the very nature of property had been altered; how the consumer has had to develop new instruments for controlling the market, and how labor is compelled to organize its power in order not to be trodden by gigantic economic forces.

Nobody likes the present situation very much. But where dispute arises is over whether we can by legislation return to a simpler and more direct stage of civilization. Bryan really hopes to do that, Wilson does too, but his mind is too critical not to have some doubts, and that is why he is against trusts but not against big business. But there is a growing body of opinion which says that communication is blotting out village culture, and opening up national and international thought. It says that bad as big business is to-day, it has a wide promise within it, and that the real task of our generation is to realize it. It looks to the infusion of scientific method, the careful application of administrative technique, the organization and education of the consumer for control, the discipline of labor for an increasing share of the management. Those of us who hold such a belief are pushed from behind by what we think is an irresistible economic development, and lured by a future which we think is possible.

We don't imagine that the trusts are going to drift naturally into the service of human life. We think they can be made to serve it if the American people compel them. We think that the American people may be able to do that if they can adjust their thinking to a new world situation, if they apply the scientific spirit to daily life, and if they can learn to coöperate on a large scale. Those, to be sure, are staggering *ifs*. The conditions may never be fulfilled entirely. But in so far as they are not fulfilled we shall drift along at the mercy of economic forces that we are unable to master. Those who cling to the village view of life may deflect the drift, may batter the trusts about a bit, but they will never dominate business, never humanize its machinery, and they will continue to be the playthings of industrial change.

At bottom the issue is between those who are willing to enter upon an effort for which there is no precedent, and those who aren't. In a real sense it is an adventure. We have still to explore the new scale of human life which machinery has thrust upon us. We have still to invent ways of dealing with it. We have still to adapt our abilities to immense tasks. Of course, men shudder and beg to be let off in order to go back to the simpler life for which they were trained. Of course, they hope that competition will automatically produce the social results they desire. Of course, they see all the evils of the trust and none of its promise. They can point to the failure of empires and the success of little cities. They can say that we are obliterating men in the vast organizations we are permitting.

But they are not the only people who realize that man as he is to-day is not big enough to master the modern world. It is this realization which has made men speculate on the development of what they call a "collective mind." They hope that somehow we shall develop an intelligence larger than the individual.

I see no evidence for that. There are no minds but human minds so far as our problems go. It seems to me that this notion of a collective mind over and above men and women is simply a myth created to meet difficulties greater than men and women are as yet capable of handling. It is a *deus ex machina* invented to cover an enormous need— a hope that something outside ourselves will do our

work for us. It would be infinitely easier if such a power existed. But I can't see any ground for relying upon it. We shall have, it seems to me, to develop within men and women themselves the power they need. It is an immense ambition, and each man who approaches it must appear presumptuous. But it is the problem of our generation: to analyze the weakness, to attack the obstacles, to search for some of the possibilities, to realize if we can the kind of effort by which we can face the puzzling world in which we live.

## Further Resources

### BOOKS

Bringhurst, Bruce. *Antitrust and the Oil Monopoly: The Standard Oil Cases, 1890–1911*. Westport, Conn.: Greenwood Press, 1979.

Forcey, Charles. *The Crossroads of Liberalism: Croly, Weyl, Lippmann and the Progressive Era, 1900–1925*. New York: Oxford University Press, 1961.

McCraw, Thomas K. *Prophets of Regulation: Charles Francis Adams, Louis D. Brandeis, James M. Landis, Alfred E. Kahn*. Cambridge, Mass.: Harvard University Press, 1984.

### PERIODICALS

Diggins, John Patrick. "From Pragmatism to Natural Law: Walter Lippmann's Quest for the Foundations of Legitimacy." *Political Theory* 19, November 1991, 519–538.

# *National Old Trails Road: Ocean to Ocean Highway*
## Pamphlet, Maps

**By:** Charles Henry Davis

**Date:** 1914

**Source:** Davis, Charles Henry. *National Old Trails Road: Ocean to Ocean Highway*. Washington, D.C.: National Highways Association, 1914.

**About the Author:** Charles Henry Davis (1865–1951), a civil engineer and manufacturer of road machinery, founded the National Highways Association in 1912. A prominent campaigner for improved roads, Davis advocated a federally coordinated system of national highways at a time when most roads were still locally financed, maintained, and administered. ∎

## Introduction

Even as a nationally coordinated railroad network appeared in the late nineteenth century, American public roads remained under the control of the most local of governmental units. Towns were subdivided into countless road districts, with locally appointed "pathmasters" responsible for the maintenance of short stretches of dirt

# 50,000 Miles of National Highways Will:—

Serve directly 60,000,000 people, or 66% of the total population.

Serve in adjoining counties 24,000,000 people, or 26% of the total population.

A total of 84,000,000 people, or 92% of the total population.

Traverse 393 congressional districts, or 95% of the total.

Serve direct or adjoining 2,471 counties, or 84% of the total.

Reach and connect every large and important city.

Connect every capital of every State with the National Capital.

Form only 2½% of our total road mileage, but include all main routes.

Carry 50% of our total road tonnage, estimated at 5,000,000,000 tons, at a saving of more than $300,000,000 per annum in carrying-charges.

Cost less than $1,000,000,000 to build; this cost will be saved several times per annum. Can be completed in ten (10) years.

Accentuate road building and improvement by States, Counties, and Towns.

Raise the standard of road building and maintenance by all communities.

Provide steady employment for all idle and unemployed.

Provide remunerative employment for delinquents and materially improve their condition, besides aiding them towards re-establishment in the community as desirable citizens.

Add to the annual increase of our National wealth not less than $300,000,000.

Save annually in wear and tear of vehicles not less than $500,000,000.

Increase land values adjacent to such highways over $600,000,000.

Increase the prosperity of the farmer more than any other improvement.

Reduce the cost of living more than most any other factor.

Provide better social conditions in the rural communities and thus elevate their intelligence and their moral well-being.

Make rural life more attractive, facilitate intercommunication, and thus reduce migration to cities and encourage the movement " back to the farms."

Enable the building of rural schools and thus reduce illiteracy.

Increase travel throughout the country, inducing people to " See America First," thus keeping home annually more than $250,000,000.

In other words,

Favor, foster, and further the development of Our Country

In the length and breadth of these United States of America

By securing the benefits,

Social, moral, commercial, industrial, material, educational, and personal,

In the progress and uplift of the American people

Which follow in the train of easy intercommunication and transit

Between the great centers of population and distribution

And the great rural productive areas of the Nation,

And thus " bind the States together in a common brotherhood,

And thus perpetuate and preserve the Union."

## Primary Source

*National Old Trails Road: Ocean to Ocean Highway* (1 OF 2)

**SYNOPSIS:** In this excerpt from a National Highways Association pamphlet, Charles Henry Davis lists the benefits that would come from the construction of fifty thousand miles of national roads. Davis's plan, which resembled the system of federal interstate highways created decades later, was rejected as overly ambitious. Instead, a compromise plan was adopted, which allowed for a state-implemented, federally coordinated system of highways. But Davis's proposal, along with the maps of Wyoming highways, illustrates well the engineering mindset of early-twentieth-century systems builders. This page from Charles Henry Davis' *National Old Trails Road* pamphlet gives reasons for supporting a national highway system. Most of these reasons focused on the economic development that would occur with national highway construction. *NATIONAL OLD TRAILS ROAD: OCEAN TO OCEAN HIGHWAY,* WASHINGTON, D.C.: NATIONAL HIGHWAYS ASSOCIATION, 1914. COURTESY OF THE UNIVERSITY OF MICHIGAN SPECIAL COLLECTIONS LIBRARY.

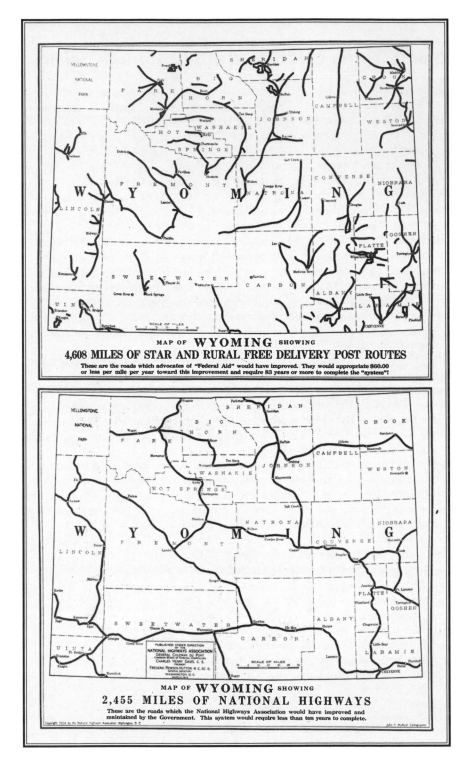

MAP OF **WYOMING** SHOWING
**4,608 MILES OF STAR AND RURAL FREE DELIVERY POST ROUTES**
These are the roads which advocates of "Federal Aid" would have improved. They would appropriate $60.00 or less per mile per year toward this improvement and require 83 years or more to complete the "system"!

MAP OF **WYOMING** SHOWING
**2,455 MILES OF NATIONAL HIGHWAYS**
These are the roads which the National Highways Association would have improved and maintained by the Government. This system would require less than ten years to complete.

## Primary Source

*National Old Trails Road: Ocean to Ocean Highway* (2 OF 2)

Maps of Wyoming show the effects of "decentralized" (top map) and "centralized" (bottom map) construction of roads. Advocates of a federally planned and funded or "centralized" national highway system maintained that the highways would lower transportation costs, resulting in a social savings that offset the cost of new roads. NATIONAL OLD TRAILS ROAD: OCEAN TO OCEAN HIGHWAY, WASHINGTON, D.C.: NATIONAL HIGHWAYS ASSOCIATION, 1914. COURTESY OF THE UNIVERSITY OF MICHIGAN SPECIAL COLLECTIONS LIBRARY.

roadways. Such a system left America's public ways in sorry shape. Depending on the season, they were rough and muddy, pitted and overgrown, cracked and dusty, or covered in snow.

By the turn of the century, "good roads" advocates—including bicyclists, motorists, academics, and engineers—lobbied intensively for systematic improvements to the nation's highways. Theirs was a progressive crusade: They preached the "gospel of good roads," describing the numerous social benefits of better roads. They also put forward an economic argument, claiming that hard-surfaced highways would lower transportation costs, resulting in a social savings that would offset the cost of new roads.

Their campaign was largely successful, and by the 1910s, most states had created some form of centralized state highway department responsible for coordinating and funding state road-building programs. Congress authorized federal grants-in-aid to the states in 1916, bringing still greater coordination to the nation's highway infrastructure. With the increase in both general economic prosperity and motor vehicle use during the 1920s, several states, in cooperation with the federal government, launched a golden age of road building.

### Significance

Though a broad consensus in support of road building had emerged by the 1910s, there remained significant disagreements. It was not at all clear which roads should be improved, or who would be responsible for implementing a new road program. Farmers wanted farm-to-market roads improved, motorists favored thoroughfares and parkways, railroad corporations preferred roads that led to rail junctions, politicians pushed for roads in their own constituencies, and engineers lobbied for the construction of a broad national system. Each group had its own ideas about the relative authority of local, state, and federal administrative bodies necessary to bring about its brand of road improvement.

The construction of public highways in the early twentieth century thus represented a profound public policy challenge. Improving the country's sprawling highway system was a challenge that was national in scope, yet state and local in implementation. The highway program that emerged by 1920 drew on the powers of federal, state, and local governments, rejecting the localism of the pathmaster system in favor of a complex and layered federalism.

Engineers were central players in this reconfiguration of public road-building authority. As states and localities turned away from politically motivated road building ("more miles, more votes," as the saying went), they increasingly relied on the expertise of engineers to help guide their work. Yet route selection was complex and sensitive, requiring engineers to make essentially political decisions about which groups—farmers, motorists, railroad corporations, truckers—would be favored with new construction.

World War I (1914–1918) and postwar inflation slowed highway building to a virtual halt during the late 1910s. But by the 1920s, much of the conflict surrounding an American road program had been resolved in favor of promoting the state construction of primary, interstate highways. These roads were designed to serve the needs of growing numbers of automobile and truck drivers. The railroad industry complained bitterly that state and federal governments unfairly granted subsidies to a competing mode of transportation. But good-roads advocates argued that private railroads had earned a reputation for corruption and inefficiency not associated with the management of public highways.

Growing public support for road construction in the 1910s had vast social and economic ramifications. The long-term consequences of this commitment to automobility—including environmental damage, urban degeneration, and highway deaths—were hard to predict. At the time, America's devotion to the road and car reflected the appeal of new patterns of suburban living, as well as a new style of commerce geared to the motor vehicle and the freedom it promised.

### Further Resources

**BOOKS**

Barron, Hal S. "And the Crooked Shall Be Made Straight: Rural Road Reform and the Politics of Localism." In *Mixed Harvest: The Second Great Transformation in the Rural North, 1870–1930.* Chapel Hill: University of North Carolina Press, 1997.

Goddard, Stephen B. *Getting There: The Epic Struggle Between Road and Rail in the American Century.* New York: Basic, 1994.

Mason, Philip Parker. "The League of American Wheelmen and the Good Roads Movement, 1880–1905." Ph.D. diss., University of Michigan, 1957.

Seely, Bruce. *Building the American Highway System: Engineers as Policy Makers.* Philadelphia: Temple University Press, 1987.

**PERIODICALS**

Seely, Bruce. "Railroads, Good Roads, and Motor Vehicles: Managing Technological Change." *Railroad History Bulletin* 155, Autumn 1986, 35–63.

**WEBSITES**

*Public Roads Online* 60, no. 1, Summer 1996. Turner-Fairbank Highway Research Center. Available online at http://www.tfhrc.gov/pubrds/summer96/p96su.htm; website home page: http://www.tfhrc.gov (accessed July 17, 2002).

# Henry Ford's Business Philosophy

## John F. and Horace E. Dodge v. Ford Motor Co., Henry Ford, et. al.

Testimony

**By:** Henry Ford

**Date:** 1916

**Source:** State of Michigan. Circuit Court of Wayne County. Transcript of the testimony of Henry Ford. *John F. and Horace E. Dodge v. Ford Motor Co., Henry Ford, et. al.* No. 56660, (1916). Reprinted in John B. Rae, ed. *Henry Ford.* Englewood Cliffs, N.J.: Prentice-Hall, Inc., 1969, 22–24.

## Interview with Henry Ford

Interview

**By:** Henry Ford

**Date:** 1916

**Source:** Interview with Henry Ford. *Detroit News,* November 4, 1916. Reprinted in John B. Rae, ed. *Henry Ford.* Englewood Cliffs, New Jersey: Prentice-Hall, Inc., 1969.

**About the Author:** Henry Ford (1863–1947) is best known as the founder of the Ford Motor Company. Beginning in 1908, Ford produced the fabulously popular Model T, an inexpensive, mass-produced motor vehicle. Millions of Americans purchased this automobile, sparking a trend that would leave life in the United States irrevocably geared to a "car culture." Ford's business philosophy, which rested on standardized, high-volume production, a vast army of well-paid labor, and low prices, became a model for the industrial economy of twentieth-century America. ■

## Introduction

The American automobile emerged in the 1890s as an experimental curiosity, a machine-powered advance over the foot-pedaled bicycle. Only a few thousand automobiles existed by the turn of the century, constructed by various firms and powered by electricity, steam, and gasoline. In this diverse and increasingly competitive environment, Henry Ford founded the Ford Motor Company in 1903 in Detroit, Michigan. At this point, most automobiles cost over $1,000 and were widely seen as playthings of the wealthy. With the production of the Model T in 1908, Ford pioneered the construction of a simple and affordable automobile for the masses.

Ford designed the Model T to be rugged enough to withstand rough country roads and straightforward enough to be repaired by anyone with rudimentary mechanical knowledge. In a quest to construct it cheaply and in great quantities, Ford developed the assembly line—a conveyor system that drew the chassis through the factory and drastically reduced production time. Savings in production allowed Ford to lower the price of the Model T, thus making it available to a wider market.

Having worked out a design for a car with mass appeal, and having devised a mass production system that could turn it out in high quantities, Ford dedicated his company solely to the manufacture of the Model T. As Ford's engineers refined the assembly line, Ford continued to cut the price of the car. In this way, he continuously increased the demand for the popular "tin lizzie." His company sold four million by 1920. That year, the Model T cost just $440.

Ford predicted he could continue to profit from the sale of the Model T, even at lower prices, by increasing the volume of his sales. But this presented a challenge to prevailing business practices. Stockholders, like the Dodge brothers, resisted the immediate loss in shareholder dividends occasioned by the reduction in price. They brought (and won) a suit against Ford, arguing that he ought to have distributed more profits to investors. In fact, the Dodge brothers, one of Ford's many rivals, hoped to use this revenue to produce a competitor to the Model T. Frustrated by their tactics and with the outcome of the trial, Ford purchased all of Ford Motor Company's stock by 1919. He ran the company as a family business, and stuck to his low-price, high-volume business philosophy.

## Significance

Despite their victory in court, the Dodge brothers failed to prevent the Model T's success. John and Horace Dodge died in the influenza epidemic of 1918–1919, and the Dodge Brothers Manufacturing Company was absorbed by Chrysler in 1928. By the late 1920s, the Big Three—Ford, General Motors, and Chrysler—dominated the automobile industry, whereas hundreds of companies had thrived just two decades earlier. But Ford Motor Company was exceptional in its unwavering reliance on Henry Ford's personal business philosophy, a way of conducting business that had a lasting impact on American corporate organization.

Ford's business philosophy rested on three fundamentals: low prices for the consumer, increased productivity (and in the long run, higher profits for the investors), and better working conditions for the laborer. Each aspect of Ford's philosophy was contingent upon the other two. A stable and accommodating labor force supported the assembly-line system and was essential to its success. Mass production allowed for an increase in the volume of sales and a decrease in the cost of production, while lower prices—along with employees' higher wages—further broadened the available market.

Workers assemble a Model 'T' automobile at the Ford Motor Company plant in Highland Park, Michigan, circa 1913. Savings in production allowed Henry Ford to lower the price of the Model T, and thus make it available to a wider market. © BETTMANN/CORBIS. REPRODUCED BY PERMISSION.

In order to maintain the high rate of productivity necessary to roll out Model Ts in high volume, Ford required a stable workforce. Assembly-line production required laborers who were familiar with the assembly process and could carry out repetitive tasks over long hours without variation. To entice workers to persist in such mind–numbing work, Ford initiated the $5 day. This incentive—about twice the average daily wage in Detroit at that time—had potential employees lining up at his factory gates. But the higher wages came at a cost. Ford required his workers to meet strict standards, not just through scientific control over the workplace, but also at home. Ford established a Sociological Department to investigate workers' domestic lives and dock their pay for infractions such as drinking.

Ford's ambitious $5 day program could not survive wartime inflation, and it collapsed by 1919. But the Fordist model of production remained. His commitment to higher profits through the sale of low-priced, mass-produced goods continued to influence corporate strategy in the 1920s and beyond.

## Primary Source

### John F. and Horace E. Dodge v. Ford Motor Co., Henry Ford, et. al. [excerpt]

**SYNOPSIS:** In this excerpt, Ford responds to questions from the Dodge brothers' attorney Elliott G. Stevenson. He is explaining and defending his business plan. The Dodge brothers had brought suit against Ford as minority shareholders seeking to compel him to distribute a greater share of corporate profits rather than reinvest the profits into the company's expansion. (The lawsuit was complicated by the fact that the Dodge brothers wanted to use their share of the profits to produce a competitor to the Model T.)

**Ford Testimony**

Stevenson: To what extent have you considered the necessity for increased facilities for production of cars?

Ford: We expect to increase it double.

Stevenson: To double; that is, you produced 500,000 cars, with the old plant, as we speak of it, as up to July 31st, 1916?

Ford: Yes, sir.

Stevenson: And you are duplicating that plant, or more than duplicating it?

Ford: About duplicating it.

Stevenson: Your policy is to increase the production to a million cars per annum?

Ford: Yes, sir.

Stevenson: Yes. You are not satisfied with producing five hundred thousand cars per annum?

Ford: The demand was not satisfied.

Stevenson: The demand was not satisfied?

Ford: No.

Stevenson: Do you mean that the Ford Motor Company during the year 1915 and '16, when it produced and sold 500,000 cars, could not meet the demand?

Ford: *Could not* quite meet the demand; and, besides, we left the price—

Stevenson: What is that?

Ford: We left the price as it was the preceding car [*sic*].

Stevenson: That is, you left the price in 1915 and '16 the same as the year 1913 and '14?

Ford: Left the price the same in 1916.

Stevenson: What?

Ford: We left the price the same in 1916 as we did in 1915.

Stevenson: Your fiscal year ends July 31st, 1916?

Ford: Yes, sir.

Stevenson: So that year would include from July 31st, 1915, to July 31st, 1916?

Ford: Yes, sir.

Stevenson: And you left the price of the car—

Ford: Yes, sir.

Stevenson: The same for 1915–16 as for 1914–15?

Ford: *Yes; for the purpose of accumulating money* to make these extensions.

Stevenson: You *found* that even with the old price, and the increased production to 500,000 cars a year, you were unable to keep up with the demand for the car?

Ford: *Just about.*

Stevenson: *Just about?*

Ford: *Yes.*

*Stevenson:* So far as your experience of 1915 and '16 was concerned, you had good reason to believe that you could duplicate that production and sell it at the same price during the next year, didn't you?

Ford: *Yes, but that isn't our policy.*

Stevenson: Well, that is, you are satisfied you could do that?

Ford: No, we couldn't do it.

Stevenson: What is that?

Ford: No, we couldn't do it; not keep the same price.

Stevenson: Not, and produce the same number of cars?

Ford: Not and keep the same price.

Stevenson: Why not?

Ford: Because the price was too high.

Stevenson: Well, you could not meet the demand the year before, you say?

Ford: That has been always our policy, to reduce the price.

Stevenson: You said, in answer to my question, that you produced 500,000 cars, and that they did not meet the demand; was that true, or wasn't it?

Ford: When?

Stevenson: For the year 1915 and '16?

Ford: I don't know as to '15 and 16; I don't know anything about it.

Stevenson: The year ending the 31st of July, 1916; that is the end of your fiscal year, is it?

Ford: Yes, sir.

Stevenson: I mean the year preceding that?

Ford: The year preceding that?

Stevenson: Yes, the year that this financial statement that we have referred to, covered and represented.

Ford: 1916 was the financial statement.

Stevenson: Do you call that the 1916 business?

Ford: Yes.

Stevenson: We will call it the 1916 business; then, for the year of 1916, you produced 500,000 cars, and you sold them?

Ford: Yes, sir.

Stevenson: And you said that didn't meet the demand, those 500,000 cars?

Ford: Not quite.

Stevenson: Not quite; so that you had no reason to believe, from the experience of 1916, that you could not sell 500,000 more cars in 1917?

Ford: No.

Stevenson: At the same price, had you?

Ford: Yes, sir, we did.

Stevenson: What reason did you have?

Ford: The price was too high.

Stevenson: Why was the price too high, if you were able to sell them?

Ford: Because we looked ahead to know what we could sell the next year.

Stevenson: How could you know what you could sell the next year?

Ford: Just from the way we run our business.

Stevenson: Tell us that secret, how you judge, when you were able to do it in 1916, you were not able to meet the demand, that you could not do it the next year?

Ford: The only thing that makes anything not sell is because the price is too high.

Stevenson: You say you do not think it is right to make so much profits? What is this business being continued for, and why is it being enlarged?

Ford: To do as much as possible for everybody concerned.

Stevenson: What do you mean by "doing as much good as possible"?

Ford: To make money and use it, give employment, and send out the car where the people can use it.

Stevenson: Is that all? Haven't you said that you had money enough yourself, and you were going to run the Ford Motor Company thereafter to employ just as many people as you could, to give them the benefits of the high wages that you paid, and to give the public the benefit of a low priced car?

Ford: I suppose I have, and incidentally make money.

Stevenson: Incidentally make money?

Ford: Yes, sir.

Stevenson: But your controlling feature, so far as your policy, since you have got all the money you want, is to employ a great army of men at high wages, to reduce the selling price of your car, so that a lot of people can buy it at a cheap price, and give everybody a car that wants one?

Ford: If you give all that, the money will fall into your hands; you can't get out of it.

## Primary Source

Interview with Henry Ford [excerpt]

**SYNOPSIS:** In this interview Ford explains why lowering the price of the Model T, Ford Motor's major product, is actually good for the company. He also questions the motives of those who want him to keep prices high.

### "A Reasonable Profit—But Not Too Much"

Bear in mind; every time you reduce the price of the car without reducing the quality, you increase the possible number of purchasers. There are many men who will pay $360 for a car who would not pay $440. We had in round numbers 500,000 buyers of cars on the $440 basis, and I figure that on the $360 basis we can increase the sales to possibly 800,000 cars for the year—less profit on each car, but more cars, more employment of labor, and in the end we get all the total profit we ought to make.

And let me say right here, that I do not believe that we should make such an awful profit on our cars. A reasonable profit is right, but not too much. So it has been my policy to force the price of the car down as fast as production would permit, and give the benefits to users and laborers, with resulting surprisingly enormous benefits to ourselves.

The men associated with me haven't always agreed with this policy—

Dodge Brothers say I ought to continue to ask $440 for a car. I don't believe in such awful profits. I don't believe it is right.

So, would I be serving the interests of our firm best by holding up the price because the manufacturer of another automobile wants us to, or by reducing the price in the interest of our own customers, our own employes, and our own business standing, and profit? I think I am right in my policy.

## Further Resources

### BOOKS

McCraw, Thomas K., and Richard S. Tedlow. "Henry Ford, Alfred Sloan, and the Three Phases of Marketing." In *Creating Modern Capitalism: How Entrepreneurs, Companies, and Countries Triumphed in Three Industrial Revolutions,* ed. Thomas K. McCraw, 264–300. Cambridge: Harvard University Press, 1997.

Meyer, Steven III. *The Five Dollar Day: Labor Management and Social Control in the Ford Motor Company, 1908–1921.* Albany: State University of New York Press, 1981.

Rae, John B. *The American Automobile: A Brief History.* Chicago: University of Chicago Press, 1965.

# J. Walter Thompson House Ads

## "A New Profession"; "Packages That Speak Out"; "Women in Advertising"
**Advertisements**

**By:** J. Walter Thompson Company

**Date:** 1917–1919

**Source:** J. Walter Thompson House Ads. "Emergence of Advertising in America: 1850–1920." John W. Hartman Center for Sales, Advertising, and Marketing History. Duke University Rare Book, Manuscript, and Special Collections Library. Available online at http://scriptorium.lib.duke.edu.eaa; website home page: http://www.scriptrorium.lib.duke.edu (accessed June 5, 2002).

**About the Author:** James Walter Thompson (1847–1928) entered the advertising business in 1868. Ten years later he was operating his own firm, the J. Walter Thompson Company, and soon had offices in New York, Chicago, Boston, Cincinnati, and London. Thompson's career spans the emergence of American advertising, from its early days when ad men simply brokered space with local newspapers, to the development of an elaborate industry devoted to the creation and national dissemination of complex marketing campaigns. ■

## Introduction

The development of a national market for consumer goods toward the end of the nineteenth century rested on a number of interrelated developments ranging from improvements in manufacturing and standardization to better systems of transportation and distribution. But to sell their products on a national scale, firms also needed a way of introducing far-flung consumers to their goods. The emergence of inexpensive, nationally distributed magazines provided just such a resource. This was an opportunity to bring marketing messages into readers' homes, encouraging potential consumers to re-evaluate their needs for various commodities while building brand recognition and loyalty.

By the 1890s, the J. Walter Thompson Company was pouring its energy into the creation of national magazine ad campaigns designed to introduce consumers to the benefits of myriad products, from nationally branded soaps and shavers to coffee and pancake batter. Ad firms like the Thompson Company made careful studies of consumer behavior, and developed images designed to appeal to certain cross-sections of the buying public. Through the frequent placement of these icons, slogans, and trademarks, the advertising industry shaped habits of consumption while entrenching readers in an emerging mass culture.

Success in the advertising industry required ad firms like Thompson's to convince other corporations of the need for their services. This meant establishing advertising as a "profession," an occupation based on specialized knowledge and expertise. To this end, the Thompson Company increasingly advertised its own services—called house ads—designed to draw in new business. In these ads, the company argued that large-scale manufacturing called for a new means of large-scale selling. National advertising, in combination with mass production, would create the demand sufficient to meet the increasing supply of goods.

## Significance

The expanding ranks of middle-class professionals were an appealing target for modern advertising. They also formed a growing part of the advertising industry itself. The Thompson Company sought college-educated men and women to study consumer behavior and analyze American's buying habits. Well-trained advertising agents helped cement the image of advertising as a respectable profession. They also played a large role in shaping advertising content, transmitting and reinforcing through repetition their own perceptions of racial, gendered, and class identities.

Some ads used text and images to portray the modernity of products, relying on a scientific appearance to sell items like Senreco brand toothpaste. But other advertisements hoped to capture consumers' trust by relying on traditional assumptions about gender and race. The Cutex manicure set, for instance, is packaged in a feminine pink.

# A New Profession

## Large-scale production opens new field for university men in advertising agencies

IN 1869 the volume of business in watches was $2,800,000; in 1914 it was five times as great—over $14,000,000. But in this period, the number of firms making watches decreased from 37 to 15.

And to-day 11 makers of watches are advertising in the national magazines.

Tremendous growth in volume—sharp decrease in the number of manufacturers—and the increasing use of advertising; this is the history not only of watches but of practically all our big industries in the last fifty years.

Large-scale manufacture with its many economies has created a vital need—large-scale selling.

We can all picture the early days in this country when shoes were made by the cobbler at his last. If his shoes were good, satisfied customers told their friends about him and his trade grew. Perhaps his reputation even spread to the neighboring village.

But how far could this word-of-mouth method expand his business? Could our New England shoe factories send their foot-wear to all corners of the United States if they had to rely on what neighbors and acquaintances told each other about shoes?

To-day the shoe manufacturer has a market of 103,000,000 people. How can he teach these Americans to know his product by name and to ask for it?

The chief problem of industry to-day is not how to *make* a product—but how to *sell* it.

This problem has been solved by *large-scale* selling. To carry the producer's message to the buying public, industry has turned to advertising and to the advertising agency.

### Carrying the manufacturer's story to the public.

Ten years ago a manufacturer in the Middle West perfected a remarkable new window shade. It was far superior to other window shades—it was made by a new process and did not crack or fade.

He placed this new shade in retail stores throughout the country. But it did not sell. Retailers refused to order it again. Their customers did not realize that it was different from other shades.

Then this manufacturer brought his problem to an advertising agency.

A name was coined for the shade—Brenlin—and this name was marked on the edge of every shade.

Advertisements were prepared by the agency, telling interestingly and clearly how the new product gave longer wear, looked better and saved money. Through carefully selected magazines and newspapers, the manufacturer's story was taken direct to the American people.

In the first year, sales of the new shade increased rapidly. American families everywhere profited by the improved shade material, because they learned to know it by name and to ask for it.

To-day this manufacturer is the largest independent maker of window-shades in the country and 70% of his business is on Brenlin.

Old-fashioned, word-of-mouth selling failed to put this product on the market. It was only when the manufacturer turned to large-scale selling—to advertising—that he made this improved shade an asset to the American home and built up a large-scale, national business.

The advertising agency is the vital link between the manufacturer and the buying public.

### What is advertising?

Thomas Henry Buckle, the historian, tells us that the percentage of letters mailed without addresses in Paris and London is the same year after year. The same proportion of people in these two cities make this same absent-minded error every year.

Buckle shows that men and women in large groups make even their most personal decisions according to fixed laws. He found that these laws applied to suicide—to all crimes—even to the percentages of individuals of different ages and to the weapons used.

Out of a thousand people, a definite percentage will always make the same decision and act in the same way under a given set of circumstances.

To study the laws of human action and to create advertisements that will guide the decisions of millions of people, is one function of the advertising agency.

It is not enough to present the manufacturer's name and product to the public. The story of the product itself must be told by word and picture, in a manner that will produce a definite response from a definite number of people.

In the J. Walter Thompson Company, a large staff of college-trained men have made it their profession to study the laws of decision.

But this study and the actual building of advertisements, is only one phase of the profession of large-scale selling, as it is practiced by the J. Walter Thompson Company.

### Solving the problems of large-scale selling.

Which of our 103,000,000 Americans are the logical consumers of a given product? Are they among the 20 million who live in towns of 200,000 or over? Or are they among the 17 million who live in towns of 15,000 and under? Are they young, middle-aged or old? What are their habits? In what are they most interested?

Which of the 19,000 newspapers in the country—which of the 5,000 other publications—will best reach these consumers?

To answer questions like these, the J. Walter Thompson Company maintains large departments to study our population and its standards of living—to analyze the circulation of newspapers and magazines.

Experienced men are sent on long trips through all parts of the country—visiting consumers in their homes—interviewing retailers and jobbers.

In the J. Walter Thompson Company, every phase of large-scale selling rests upon intensive study and close analysis. The work of this advertising agency draws upon many branches of human knowledge and culture—upon Economics, History, Social Conditions, English Composition and Literature.

Graduates of Yale and other universities have found in the J. Walter Thompson Company, a profession in which undergraduate training is a definite asset—in which full opportunity is given for original, creative achievement.

A complete course of training is conducted by the J. Walter Thompson Company for men who have had little or no advertising experience and who wish to fit themselves for responsible positions.

**J. WALTER THOMPSON COMPANY**
244 MADISON AVE., NEW YORK
CHICAGO    BOSTON    DETROIT    CINCINNATI

STANLEY RESOR, YALE '01, President
WALTER G. RESOR, YALE '97, Vice-President
GILBERT KINNEY, YALE '05, Vice-President

Other Yale men on the staff are:
HOWARD K. HOLLISTER, Ex-1910
EWING T. WEBB, 1913
RICHARD C. ROTHSCHILD, 1916
ELIOT L. WIGHT, 1918

The Yale Daily News, Monday May 26, 1919.

---

## Primary Source

### "A New Profession" (1 OF 3)

**SYNOPSIS:** These advertisements reveal one prominent advertising firm's efforts to convince manufacturers of the importance of national advertising campaigns and to draw educated men and women into the advertising profession. "A New Profession" asks Yale graduates to study the American consumer and help carry manufacturers' messages to the public. "Packages that Speak Out" shows the power of a carefully constructed image to communicate to a national audience. "Women in Advertising" notes the broadened role for women, both as primary consumers and as new advertising professionals. COURTESY OF J. WALTER THOMPSON COMPANY. AD*ACCESS ON-LINE PROJECT - AD #J0072 JOHN W. HARTMAN CENTER FOR SALES, ADVERTISING & MARKETING HISTORY DUKE UNIVERSITY RARE BOOK, MANUSCRIPT, AND SPECIAL COLLECTIONS LIBRARY HTTP://SCRIPTORIUM.LIB.DUKE.EDU/ADACCESS/

**Packages**
*that speak out*
By
J. WALTER THOMPSON COMPANY

When the consumer's eye sweeps shelf or show case does your package flash out like the one lighted house in a row of dark ones?

Still more important, does it define your product to the *mind* of the consumer after it has caught the eye?

Here are six packages that do.

The severe, black and ivory Senreco design speaks clearly of medicinal qualities.

With equal clearness the cool green of the Woodbury carton forecasts a soothing shave; and the orange and black of the Veedol package calls to mind the heat this oil resists.

In the homely face of Aunt Jemima is a promise of real southern pancakes; in the rich coffee brown of the Yuban package a similar richness of flavor, and in the pink of the Cutex label the perfection of my lady's nails.

All said, moreover, with a simplicity that can hardly be imitated without being duplicated.

Shelf value—definition—protection.

At any of our offices in New York, Boston, Chicago, Detroit or Cincinnati we shall be glad to show you these and other packages we have created, and to tell you more about the work we have done to individualize these and other products.

*From PRINTERS' INK, Issue of April 19, 1917.*

## Primary Source

### "Packages That Speak Out" (2 OF 3)

"Packages that Speak Out" advertisement by J. Walter Thompson Company, 1917. Advertising firms like the Thompson Company made careful studies of consumer behavior, developing images designed to appeal to certain cross-sections of the buying public. COURTESY OF J. WALTER THOMPSON COMPANY. AD*ACCESS ON-LINE PROJECT - AD #J0040 JOHN W. HARTMAN CENTER FOR SALES, ADVERTISING & MARKETING HISTORY DUKE UNIVERSITY RARE BOOK, MANUSCRIPT, AND SPECIAL COLLECTIONS LIBRARY HTTP://SCRIPTORIUM.LIB.DUKE.EDU/ADACCESS/

The "homely face of Aunt Jemima" uses a retrograde and condescending caricature of a plantation-era African American woman to signify quality baking products. Such sanitized depictions directed at white consumers helped to soften any sense of the nation's racial crisis. Indeed, the cumulative effect of mass advertising campaigns was to create a racialized public discourse that portrayed African Americans as innocuous and inferior.

Advertising firms directed much of their promotions toward women. In the statistically ideal middle-class professional family that the J. Walter Thompson targeted, the woman was responsible for most retail purchases. To capture this important market, ad agencies aimed to better understand the nature of women's buying habits. The Thompson Company employed many college-educated women, believing they had a special ability to communicate with a female audience. The advertising industry opened the way for women to enter what had been a male-dominated profession. At the same time, however, these ads played an important role in shaping a mass culture that tended to reinforce traditional gender roles.

*Articles sold to women through Grocery, Drug and Department Stores*

*Advertisements in the success of which the work of women has been a factor*

# Women in Advertising

## * 85% of all retail purchases are made by women

IN selling goods to women, you hear much of the "woman's point of view." It is spoken of as if there were some mystery about women, which perhaps some woman, properly gifted, could divulge.

There is far from being any mystery, but there are *facts* of the utmost importance.

It is a question of establishing *these facts*—facts in the life of the housewife, the mother, the young girl. It is a question of *knowing* their needs, their desires, their tastes, their prejudices.

To establish these facts and to base the work of presenting articles to be sold to women on *complete facts*, the J. Walter Thompson Company has developed a staff of women.

Over a period of years, this staff has illustrated that women, thoroughly trained in advertising, working with men, can establish facts which cannot be even approximated by men working alone. This staff has proved its ability to make contributions in the presentation of facts, which, without its knowledge, would lack much of their appeal.

Among the members of its creative staff, the J. Walter Thompson Company includes women holding degrees from Barnard, Smith, Vassar, University of Chicago, Wellesley and Columbia—women who have also gone through the regular course of training in advertising which the company gives.

The advertisements shown above are taken from a few of many campaigns in the success of which the work of women has been a factor.

If you are selling an article to women, you will be interested in discussing it with the organization in which such a staff has been developed.

☐ ☐ ☐

## J. WALTER THOMPSON CO.

New York

Chicago        Boston        Detroit        Cincinnati

*The most reliable figures available show that sales made to women are as follows: Department stores, 80%; Drug stores, 68.3%; Grocery stores, 89.1%; Automobile accessories...*

*From Printers' Ink of August 30, 1917.*

## Primary Source

**"Women in Advertising" (3 OF 3)**
"Women in Advertising" advertisement by J. Walter Thompson Company, 1918. Advertising firms directed much of their advertising toward women. COURTESY OF J. WALTER THOMPSON COMPANY. AD*ACCESS ON-LINE PROJECT - AD #J0066 JOHN W. HARTMAN CENTER FOR SALES, ADVERTISING & MARKETING HISTORY DUKE UNIVERSITY RARE BOOK, MANUSCRIPT, AND SPECIAL COLLECTIONS LIBRARY HTTP://SCRIPTORIUM.LIB.DUKE.EDU/ADACCESS/

## Further Resources

**BOOKS**
Laird, Pamela Walker. *Advertising Progress: American Business and the Rise of Consumer Marketing.* Baltimore: Johns Hopkins University Press, 1998.

Marchand, Roland. *Advertising the American Dream: Making Way for Modernity, 1920–1940.* Berkeley: University of California Press, 1985.

Ohmann, Richard. *Selling Culture: Magazines, Markets, and Class at the Turn of the Century.* London: Verso, 1996.

**PERIODICALS**
"J. Walter Thompson Company." *Fortune,* November 1947, 95–101ff.

**WEBSITES**
"Emergence of Advertising in America: 1850–1920." John W. Hartman Center for Sales, Advertising, and Marketing History. Duke University Rare Book, Manuscript, and Special Collections Library. Available online at http://scriptorium.lib .duke.edu/eaa/; website home page: http://www.scriptorium .lib.duke.edu (accessed June 5, 2002).

# *Women Wanted*

Nonfiction work

**By:** Mabel Potter Daggett

**Date:** 1918

**Source:** Daggett, Mabel Potter. *Women Wanted: The Story Written In Blood Red Letters on the Horizon of the Great World War.* New York: George H. Doran, 1918, 82, 84–87, 92–93.

**About the Author:** Mabel Potter Daggett (1871–1927) was a journalist who used her role to reach the public about issues she considered important. Her articles were widely published in women's magazines such as *Good Housekeeping,* and though her writing focused on issues that affected women in particular, she also wrote about broad social topics, including prohibition, and the orphan trains. Daggett made a name for herself as a journalist who didn't separate her personal convictions from her career. ■

## Introduction

America's entrance into World War I (1914–1918) had a dramatic effect on the nation's workforce. Over four million American men served in the armed forces from 1917 through 1918. During that same time, American industrial capacity increased tremendously due to wartime demands. Under these circumstances, women found new opportunities to enter fields of the workforce that had traditionally been reserved for men. They made significant gains in the railroading, metal working, and munitions industries. While many of these new hires were entering the workforce for the first time, most of these employees had switched from lower-paying, female-dominated jobs to more remunerative industrial and clerical positions.

Though increased wartime production brought new opportunities for women, the war did little to alter broad trends in American industry. For decades, managers of large manufacturing firms had sought to reduce skill levels necessary to perform industrial tasks. This process of simplification, called skill dilution, helped standardize production, enlarged the pool of available labor, and weakened the organized labor movement. The mass entrance of women into new industrial occupations was contingent upon this managerial strategy. Organized labor had a mixed response to the growing numbers of women workers. In some industries, male trade unionists actively supported women's struggles to organize for better working conditions and equal pay. But in others— where it appeared that women might undercut their male co-workers' pay—they stymied their efforts.

Daggett's travels in wartime Europe opened her eyes to the possibilities that await women in America. With great enthusiasm she wrote *Women Wanted,* and in it, she provided evidence that women could take charge without

During 1917 and 1918, women found new opportunities to enter parts of the workforce that had traditionally been reserved for men, such as delivering ice. **NATIONAL ARCHIVES AND RECORDS ADMINISTRATION.**

missing a beat, if only given the chance. She pointed out that, though men were fighting the battles, women were to be credited with not only making the munitions that allowed the men to fight, but also with keeping the home fires burning. Women stepped up to the challenge while retaining all the responsibilities they had in peacetime.

## Significance

Mabel Potter Daggett hoped that women's war work itself would constitute a significant step toward women's emancipation; her predictions did not come true. After the Armistice, women were expected to sacrifice the professional gains they made during the war. Some had taken on new work only through the pull of patriotism; they believed it was equally patriotic to vacate their position for a returning soldier. But for others, the war had presented a rare opportunity to demonstrate their capacity for work beyond the bounds of domestic drudgery. Many of these women were forced out of their positions by firms for whom the hiring of women was just a temporary expediency, or by unionists who viewed women's employment as a threat to their own job security.

Thus, the war only briefly challenged the gendered division of labor. For a short-lived moment, new work opportunities opened for women. But ultimately it was economic expansion, not the war, that had the greatest impact on women's employment. Corporate growth, especially in the communications sector and in retail sales, generated new positions for women as telephone operators, bookkeepers, sales clerks, and office staff members—the sort of non-industrial positions women were far more likely to hold in the 1920s.

Nonetheless, the experience of wartime labor proved to have far-reaching effects within the women's workforce and on social attitudes toward women in general. The war years accelerated women's mobilization for expanded rights, providing increased support for woman suffrage. Feminist activists linked poor working conditions, limited job security, and unequal pay to the lack of voting rights. For many suffragists, women's right to vote was essential to gaining the political clout necessary to challenge these economic disparities.

## Primary Source

*Women Wanted* [excerpt]

**SYNOPSIS:** In this excerpt, author Mabel Potter Daggett describes the impact of World War I on women's employment. Observing how the war in Europe drew women into new occupations, she predicted that American entrance into the war would similarly expand the range of women's professional opportunities on a permanent basis.

One Thousand Women Wanted! You may read it on a great canvas sign that stretches across an industrial establishment in lower Manhattan. The owner of this factory who put it there, only knows that it is an advertisement for labour of which he finds himself suddenly in need. But he has all unwittingly really written a proclamation that is a sign of the times.

Across the Atlantic I studied that proclamation in Old World cities. Women Wanted! Women Wanted! The capitals of Europe have been for four years placarded with the sign. And now we in America are writing it on our sky line. All over the world see it on the street car barns as on the colleges. It is hung above the factories and the coal mines, the halls of government and the farmyards and the arsenals and even the War Office. Everywhere from the fireside to the firing line, country after country has taken up the call. Now it has become the insistent chorus of civilisation: Women Wanted! Women Wanted! . . .

Listen, hear the call, Women Wanted! Women Wanted! Last Spring the Government pitched a khaki colored tent in your town on the vacant lot just beyond the post office, say. How many men have enlisted there? Perhaps there are seventy-five who have gone from the factory across the creek, and the receiving teller at the First National Bank, and the new principal of the High School where the children were getting along so well, and the doctor that everybody had because they liked him so much. . . .

Every man who enlists at that tent near the post office is going to leave a job somewhere whether it's at the factory or the doctor's office or the school teacher's desk, or whether it's your husband. That job will have to be taken by a woman. It's what happened in Europe. It's what now we may see happen here. A great many women will have a wage envelope who never had it before. That may mean affluence to a housefull of daughters. One, two, three, four wage envelopes in a family where father's used to be the only one. You even may have to go out to earn enough to support yourself and the babies. Yes, I know your husband's army pay and the income from investments carefully accumulated through the savings of your married life, will help quite a little. But with the ever rising war cost of living, it may not be enough. It hasn't been for thousands of homes in Europe. And eventually you too may go to work as other women have. It's very strange, is it not, for you of all women who have always believed that woman's place was the home. . . .

In the department store where you shopped today you noticed an elevator girl had arrived, where the operator always before has been a boy! Outside the window of my country house here as I write, off on that field on the hillside a woman is working, who never worked there before. At Lexington, Mass., I read in my morning paper, the Rev. Christopher Walter Collier has gone to the front in France and his wife has been unanimously elected by the congregation to fill the pulpit during his absence. Sometimes women by the hundred step into new vacancies. The Aeolian Company is advertising for women as piano salesmen and has established a special school for their instruction. A Chicago manufacturing plant has hung out over its employment gate the announcement, "Man's work, man's pay for all women who can qualify," and within a week two hundred women were at work. The Pennsylvania railroad, which has rigidly opposed the employment of women on its office staffs, in June, 1917, announced a change of policy and took on in its various departments five hundred women and girls. The Municipal Service Commission in New York last fall was holding its first examination to admit women to the position of junior draughtsmen in the city's employ. The Civil Service Commission at Washington, preparing to release every possible man from government positions for war service, had compiled a list of 10,000 women eligible for clerical work in government departments. . . .

Who is it that is feeding and clothing and nursing the greatest armies of history? See that soldier in the trenches? A woman raised the grain for the bread, a woman is tending the flocks that provided the meat for his rations to-day. A woman made the boots and the uniform in which he stands. A woman made the shells with which his gun is loaded. A woman will nurse him when he's wounded. A woman's ambulance may even pick him up on the battlefield. A woman surgeon may perform the operation to save his life. And somewhere back home a woman holds the job he had to leave behind. There is no task to which women have not turned to-day to carry on civilisation. For the shot that was fired in Serbia summoned men to their most ancient occupation—and women to every other.

## Further Resources

### BOOKS

American Social History Project. *Who Built America?: Working People and the Nation's Economy, Politics, Culture, and Society.* Vol. 2. New York: Pantheon, 1992.

Greenwald, Maurine Weiner. *Women, War, and Work: The Impact of World War I on Women Workers in the United States.* Westport, Conn.: Greenwood Press, 1980.

Kennedy, David. *Over Here: The First World War and American Society.* Oxford: Oxford University Press, 1980.

Kessler-Harris, Alice. *Out to Work: A History of Wage-Earning Women in the United States.* Oxford: Oxford University Press, 1982.

---

# American Industry in War: A Report of the War Industries Board

Report

**By:** Bernard Baruch

**Date:** 1921

**Source:** *American Industry in the War: A Report of the War Industries Board.* Washington, D.C.: Goverment Printing Office, 1921, 61, 63–67, 69, 98–100. Reprinted in Shannon, David A., ed. *Progressivism and Postwar Disillusionment: 1898–1928.* New York: McGraw Hill, 1966.

**About the Author:** Bernard M. Baruch (1870–1965) was born in Camden, South Carolina. At age eleven, he and his family moved to New York City, where he attended college and took a job in a Wall Street brokerage firm. Baruch's sharp financial judgment quickly made him a wealthy man. Though Baruch never abandoned his ties to the corporate world, he occasionally operated in the public sphere, supporting Woodrow Wilson's presidential campaign and advising the administration in the preparedness drive during World

War I (1914–1918). Baruch served as an economic adviser again during World War II and as the American representative to the United Nations Atomic Energy Commission. ∎

## Introduction

There was little popular support in 1914 for American entrance into the war raging in Europe, and indeed, the nation officially adopted a neutral stance. Nevertheless, America's increasing trade with the British and strong objections to the German's submarine blockade—which led to the sinking of ocean liners and the loss of American lives—made neutrality difficult to uphold. Congress passed legislation in 1915 and 1916, enlarging the army and navy and raising revenue for increased national defense. But war preparedness required the mobilization of the nation's industries as well, so Congress also authorized the creation of an agency designed to coordinate the American economy for war-making purposes.

The nature and extent of government regulation over the American economy proved to be an especially contentious topic during the Progressive era. Up to this point, national administrative powers had been relatively weak. Now, the government wanted to regulate the economy in profound ways, and the drastic change was not readily accepted. Thus, the original powers of the War Industries Board (WIB) and its predecessor agencies were quite limited. But industrial chaos followed, and by the spring of 1918, the WIB was reorganized to better direct war-related industry through the management of resources, production, and distribution. Bernard Baruch chaired the board during America's involvement in the war. Drawing on his broad knowledge of the nation's manufacturing base, he used his commanding position in the business world to streamline industry.

The WIB included a number of different divisions responsible for, among other things, prioritizing the use of raw materials, regulating prices, and conservation. The Conservation Division was charged with eliminating waste in production and distribution and achieved marked success in rationalizing industry through standardization. This required the reduction of needless variety in industrial products, setting standards of size and quality, and developing more economical modes of packaging and shipping. For instance, the WIB encouraged the automobile industry to reduce the number of styles of tires from 287 to nine, saving rubber, labor, and transportation costs. And regulations requiring the use of paper bailing rather than pasteboard boxes saved thousands of car loads of freight space each year.

## Significance

Baruch relied on trade associations to help gather information on the individual industries he supervised.

The War Industries Board, 1917. Standing from left to right: Adm. F.F. Fletcher, Hugh Frayne, Col. Palmer E. Pierce, J.P. Ingels, secretary; seated from left to right: Daniel Willard, Robert S. Brookings, Robert Lovett, and Bernard M. Baruch. **WAR INDUSTRIES BOARD, PHOTOGRAPH.**

These associations helped the WIB set standards in each sector, but they also legitimized a form of corporate self-governance. To some degree this was unavoidable: a national government with limited capacity to regulate business activity had to lean on the institutional strength of the private sector in order to quickly mobilize for war. Baruch's close connection to industry helped cement this cooperative relationship, allowing the WIB to implement its economic strategy even as it institutionalized corporate interests.

Looking back on the war years, Baruch thought that the experience of the WIB had lasting implications for the peacetime economy. The Conservation Division's work alerted the nation to the potential savings that could be gained by eliminating wasteful competition. It also suggested the possible gains that could be derived from the public promotion of corporate expansion and consolidation. Only a few years earlier, in the election of 1912 (also chronicled in this chapter), Wilson's antitrust position indicated a genuine aversion to big business. Now, one of his most eminent appointees was trumpeting the advantages of efficiency resulting from large-scale corporate enterprise. Baruch envisioned a new associationalist state, one in which large corporations and trade associations were trusted to govern themselves, albeit under a government watchdog. The industrial de-

mands of the war years, and the attendant expansion of government powers necessary to direct the American economy, shaped a new era of industrial cooperation that would last until the economic crisis of the Great Depression.

## Primary Source

### American Industry in War: A Report of the War Industries Board [excerpt]

**SYNOPSIS:** In this report of the War Industries Board, Chairman Bernard Baruch explains how the WIB's Conservation Division achieved greater economic efficiency through the rationalization of industrial practices. Baruch explores the implications of the WIB's experience for peacetime, commenting on the relative virtues of competition, cooperation, and government oversight.

The work of the Priorities Division was intimately related to that of another very important and very energetic division of the Board—the Conservation Division. The President's letter of March 4, 1918, charged the War Industries Board with the duty of promoting "the conservation of resources and facilities by means of scientific, industrial, and commercial economies." But the work was at that time already well under way, and the establishment of the Conservation Division under the Board on May 8, 1918, represented only a transfer from the council, and a reorganization of the Commercial Economy Board, which had been created as early as March 24, 1917. . . .

The plan of conservation laid down by the division for the guidance of the commodity sections and of its own agents was to undertake studies of industries, particularly those in which there were shortages of materials, facilities, or labor, with a view to formulating sets of regulations to accomplish one or more of the following purposes:

1. To secure all feasible reductions in the number of styles, varieties, sizes, colors, finishes, etc., of the several products of the industry in question. This would accomplish economies in manufacture by reducing the number of operations, and the amount of reserve stock, raw and finished, which had to be carried; it would speed up the turn-over, reduce the labor and expense of selling, and decrease the loss due to depreciation.

2. To eliminate styles and varieties of articles which violated the principle of economy in the use of constituent materials; for example, garments requiring unusual yardage could be eliminated.

3. To eliminate features of adornment which added nothing to the usefulness of articles.

4. To reduce the production and sale of such articles as were of lesser importance for the comfort and satisfaction of the population.

5. To foster the substitution of articles and materials which were plentiful for those which were scarce and difficult to produce.

6. To discourage the use for unimportant purposes of articles which were needed for more important purposes.

7. To standardize sizes, lengths, widths, thicknesses, weights, gauges, etc., in such a way as to preserve sufficient strength and durability, but to effect economies in materials and labor.

8. To reduce the waste of materials in manufacturing processes generally.

9. To secure economies in the use of samples for selling purposes.

10. To secure economy in containers by eliminating the smaller and odd sizes.

Riveters build a warship in preparation for World War I. The War Industries Board was charged with coordinating the American economy for war-making purposes. © PEMCO - WEBSTER & STEVENS COLLECTION; MUSEUM OF HISTORY & INDUSTRY, SEATTLE/CORBIS. REPRODUCED BY PERMISSION.

11. To secure economy in packing by increasing the number of units per package.

12. To secure economy in shipping space and packing materials by baling instead of boxing wherever this was practicable.

The process of drawing up tentative schedules of regulations, based on the recommendations of the trade organizations themselves, and sending them out to all parties directly interested for criticism and comment, that they might be revised before being issued as binding regulations, was designed to safeguard so far as possible against unfairness and injustice to any industry or firm. By canvassing conditions in their industries, by furnishing technical information and advice, by their loyal readiness to cooperate with the Government in carrying out the plans, often for drastic changes in trade practices, the business men in industry made these conservation projects possible. When the need was explained, they were always found ready to take the necessary steps, often at heavy sacrifices. The thoughts of the men at the helms of their own industrial enterprises were linked with the thoughts of the men at the seat of government in the common purpose of winning the war.

But there was an additional sanction for these regulations which gave confidence to each business man that all his fellows in trade would observe like practices with himself, and this last means of enforcement would have been of increasing importance had the war lasted over a long period. Whenever a schedule of conservation was issued, each manufacturer and dealer was required to give a pledge that he would observe it and do all in his power to see it observed on the part of those with whom he dealt. Most American business men will observe a pledge when once given and they need not be vigilated.

But there was a further power to encourage the good will of those who were tempted to waver. By the summer of 1918, the priorities commissioner was in a position to exercise control not only over the distribution of iron and steel, copper, and numerous other elemental constituents of manufacture, but, through the cooperation of the Fuel and Railroad Administrations, he could also withhold, for the purpose of brining recalcitrants into line, supplies of coal, coke, and oil, or the use of freight cars for transportation. With this sanction at the foundation of its efforts, the Conservation Division developed in rapid succession during the summer and fall of 1918 a series of "agreements," issued in the form of schedules of regulations to nearly a hundred different groups of producers—regulations which were already showing their effect in reducing the industrial activities of the country to a more efficient basis—when the end of the war made such undertaking no longer necessary.

Curtailment plans were carried out not by agreement among the concerns of an industry but by agreement between the industry as a group, on the one hand, and the Government, on the other. Many new trade practices were inaugurated in the same way. . . . Reference, by way of illustration, to some of these will be of general interest.

The conservation schedules for makers of men's and youths' clothing limited the length of sack coats and the length and sweep of overcoats, reduced the size of samples, and restricted each manufacturer to not more than 10 models of suits per season, resulting in a saving of 12 to 15 per cent in yardage. The number of trunks carried by traveling salesmen of dry goods houses underwent an average reduction of 44 per cent. The schedule for the women's garment industry was calculated as capable of saving 20 to 25 per cent in yardage.

The standardization of colors together with certain restrictions in styles of sweaters and analogous knitted articles released 33 per cent of the wool ordinarily used in that industry. A schedule providing that hosiery, underwear, and other knit goods, with certain small exceptions, should be packed for shipment in paper covered bales instead of pasteboard boxes resulted in a large saving in shipping space, while at the same time it released pasteboard to be used as a substitute for tin plate in the manufacture of containers for articles for which tin plate had been forbidden. It was estimated that this schedule would have effected an annual saving of 17,312 carloads of freight space, 141,000,000 cartons, and nearly a half million wooden packing cases. . . .

The manufacturers of automobile tires agreed to a reduction from 287 styles and sizes of tires to 32, with a further reduction to 9 within two years. This had a tendency to release a large amount of rubber and capital tied up in stocks everywhere. A schedule was issued also to the rubber clothing and the rubber footwear industries, the former eliminating 272 styles and types and agreeing to bale their product instead of shipping it in cartons. Even bathing caps were restricted to one style and one color for each manufacturer.

Savings in the agricultural implement industry are among the most important effected. Implement manufacturers were able to simplify manufacturing operations and reduce their stocks of raw materials; manufacturers, dealers, and jobbers found it possible to do business with smaller stocks of finished products; the steel mills saved, because every variation in size or shape had required a different set of rolls, and so on. Schedules were issued to manufacturers of portable grain elevators, plows and tillage implements, grain drills and seeders, harvesters, mowers, hay rakes, ensilage machinery, springtooth harrows, farm wagons and trucks, land rollers and pulverizers, and cream separators. The number of sizes and types of steel plows was reduced from 312 to 76; planters and drills from 784 to 29; disk harrows from 589 to 38; buggy wheels from 232 to 4; spring-wagon wheels from 32 to 4; buggy axles from over 100 to 1; buggy springs from over 120 to 1; spring wagons from over 25 to 2; buggy shafts from 36 to 1; buggy bodies from over 20 to 1 style, two widths; spring-wagon bodies from 6 to 2.

By making his line of farm wagons conform to this schedule, one manufacturer reduced his variety of front and rear gears from 1,736 to 16. Yet the farmers were as well taken care of in the growing, harvesting, and marketing of their crops with this smaller variety of agricultural implements to draw upon as they had been with the wide variety previously manufactured. The habits and prejudices of localities and individual farmers had made it necessary for manufacturers to make many more sizes and types of equipment than were essential, for all of which parts had to be carried, and the number of finished implements in the hands of manufacturers, jobbers, and retailers were unnecessarily large because of this multiplicity. . . .

The experience of the Conservation Division has clearly demonstrated that there are many practices in American industry which cost the ultimate consumers in the aggregate enormous sums without enriching the producers. These are often due to competitive demands, real or assumed. Many salesmen, in order to please the whims of particular customers, will insist upon the manufacture of new styles or new shapes of articles, requiring increased expense to the manufacturers and increased expense to both wholesalers and retailers in carrying more lines of stock; these in turn causing increased expense in maintaining salesmen and providing them with samples as well as in advertising. The consumer, the general public, is no better served by the satisfaction of these unreasonable demands, but the public ultimately pays the bill. We may well draw from this war experience a lesson to be applied to peace, by providing some simple machinery for eliminating wasteful trade practices which increase prices without in the remotest degree contributing to the well-being of the people. There is enough natural wealth in this country, and there is enough labor and technical skill for converting that wealth into objects of human satisfaction to provide abundantly for the elemental comforts of every person in the land. The problem before our Nation today is to bring about such adjustments of the industrial processes as lead toward that long-sought condition of life. . . .

The experience of the Board in exercising control over American industry leads it to make a further suggestion, which has less to do with war than with the normal practices of business.

During the past few decades, while the American business man, uniting his talents with those of the technical expert, has, through the control of great masses of capital, made such extraordinary strides in converting the natural wealth of this country into means for human comfort and satisfaction; the

processes of trade have so changed their nature that the older and simpler relations of Government to business have been gradually forced to give way before certain new principles of supervision. We have been gradually compelled to drift away from the old doctrine of Anglo-American law, that the sphere of Government should be limited to preventing breach of contract, fraud, physical injury and injury to property, and that the Government should exercise protection only over non-competent persons. The modern industrial processes have been rendering it increasingly necessary for the Government to reach out its arm to protect competent individuals against the discriminating practices of mass industrial power. We have already evolved a system of Government control of no mean significance over our railroads and over our merchant fleet, but we continue to argue, and in a measure believe, that the principles of competition can be preserved in sufficient power in respect to all other industries to protect the interests of the public and insure efficiency and wholesome growth in the development of natural wealth. With this in view, the Sherman and Clayton Acts have forbidden combinations in restraint of trade, monopolies, and many other vices attendant upon group action by individuals controlling great masses of capital. This legislation, while valuable for immediate purposes, represents little more than a moderately ambitious effort to reduce by Government interference the processes of business so as to make them conform to the simpler principles sufficient for the conditions of a bygone day.

The war has introduced a new element into this situation. The individual units of corporations which had been dissolved under the Sherman Act have, in many cases, grown during the war into corporations many fold larger than the parent organization which before the war the law construed as a menace. The conditions of war made this sort of thing necessary and in all respects desirable. The war gave rise to a kind of demand unknown in time of peace—an absolute demand, which was halted neither by prices nor difficulty of procurement. There followed an absolute shortage in some trades, and a time shortage in most of them. Group action, industry by industry, accompanied by Government control of prices and distribution, was the natural and, so far as we know, the only solution which could be devised.

In line with the principle of united action and co-operation, hundreds of trades were organized for the first time into national associations, each responsible in a real sense for its multitude of component companies, and they were organized on the suggestion and under the supervision of the Government. Practices looking to efficiency in production, price control, conservation, control in quantity of production, etc., were inaugurated everywhere. Many business men have experienced during the war, for the first time in their careers, the tremendous advantages, both to themselves and to the general public, of combination, of cooperation and common action, with their natural competitors. To drive them back through new legislation, or through the more rigid and rapid enforcement of present legislation, to the situation which immediately preceded the war will be very difficult in many cases, though in a few it is already occurring spontaneously. To leave these combinations without further supervision and attention by the Government than can be given by the Attorney General's Department, or by the Federal Trade Commission in its present form, will subject business men to such temptations as many of them will be unable to resist—temptations to conduct their businesses for private gain with little reference to general public welfare.

These associations, as they stand, are capable of carrying out purposes of greatest public benefit. They can increase the amount of wealth available for the comfort of the people by inaugurating rules designed to eliminate wasteful practices attendant upon multiplicity of styles and types of articles in the various trades; they can assist in cultivating the public taste for rational types of commodities; by exchange of trade information, extravagant methods of production and distribution can be avoided through them, and production will tend to be localized in places best suited economically for it. By acting as centers of information, furnishing lists of sources to purchasers and lists of purchasers to producers, supply and demand can be more economically balanced. From the point of vantage which competent men have at the central bureau of an association, not only can new demands be cultivated, but new sources of unexploited wealth can be indicated. In case of a national emergency, the existence of these associations at the beginning would be of incalculable aid to the supply organizations. Many of these considerations apply to large individual companies as well as to associations.

These combinations are capable also—and very easily capable—of carrying out purposes of greatest public disadvantage. They can so subtly influence production as to keep it always just short of current demand and thus keep prices ever high and going higher. They can encourage a common understanding on prices, and, without great difficulty, can hold price levels at abnormal positions. They can influence the favoring of one type of buyer over another. Nearly every business man in the country has learned by the war that a shortage in his product, if it be not too great, is distinctly to his advantage. Trade associations with real power can, in respect to most of the staples, so influence production as to keep the margin of shortage at a point most favorable to high prices and rapid turnovers.

The question, then, is what kind of Government organization can be devised to safeguard the public interest while these associations are preserved to carry on the good work of which they are capable. The country will quite properly demand the vigorous enforcement of all proper measures for the suppression of unfair competition and unreasonable restraint of trade. But this essentially negative policy of curbing vicious practices should, in the public interest, be supplemented by a positive program, and to this end the experience of the War Industries Board points to the desirability of investing some Government agency, perhaps the Department of Commerce or the Federal Trade Commission, with constructive as well as inquisitorial powers—an agency whose duty it should be to encourage, under strict Government supervision, such cooperation and coordination in industry as should tend to increase production, eliminate waste, conserve natural resources, improve the quality of products, promote efficiency in operation, and thus reduce costs to the ultimate consumer.

Such a plan should provide a way of approaching industry, or rather of inviting industry to approach the Government, in a friendly spirit, with a view to help and not to hinder. The purpose contemplated is not that the Government should undertake any such far-reaching control over industry as was practiced during the war emergency by the War Industries Board; but that the experiences of the war should be capitalized; its heritage of dangerous practices should be fully realized that they might be avoided; and its heritage of wholesome and useful practices should be accepted and studied with a view to adapting them to the problems of peace. It is recommended that such practices of cooperation and coordination in industry as have been found to be clearly of public benefit should be stimulated and encouraged by a Government agency, which at the same time would be clothed with the power and charged with the responsibility of standing watch against and preventing abuses.

### Further Resources

**BOOKS**

Eisner, Marc Allen. *From Warfare State to Welfare State: World War I, Compensatory State Building, and the Limits of the Modern Order.* University Park, Pa.: Penn State Press, 2000.

Grant, James. *Bernard M. Baruch: The Adventures of a Wall Street Legend.* New York: Simon & Schuster, 1983.

Schwarz, Jordan. *The Speculator: Bernard M. Baruch in Washington, 1917–1965.* Chapel Hill: University of North Carolina Press, 1981.

# All God's Dangers: The Life of Nate Shaw

**Autobiography**

**By:** Nate Shaw

**Date:** 1974

**Source:** Rosengarten, Theodore. *All God's Dangers: The Life of Nate Shaw.* New York: Vintage Press, 1974.

**About the Author:** Nate Shaw (1885–1973) was an African American sharecropper who struggled to earn a living under the burden of legal and economic arrangements that privileged white land owners over African American tenant farmers. Shaw joined the Alabama Sharecroppers' Union in the early 1930s, and served twelve years in prison for defying local law officers' efforts to confiscate a fellow union member's livestock. Upon release from prison in 1945, Shaw continued to farm the land not far from where he was born. ∎

## Introduction

After the Civil War (1861–1865), white and black southerners faced the challenge of redefining agrarian life that had long rested upon the institution of slavery. Struggles between southern planters and freedpeople yielded a new set of social and economic relations that offered measured autonomy to the former slaves. But white planters refused to sell them land, compelling African American farmers to live in a form of debt peonage: white planters owned the land, while African American tenant farmers were entitled to a share of the crop at the end of the season. Planters, storekeepers, cotton brokers, and fertilizer dealers all had claims on tenant farmers, however, which frequently exceeded the crop's sale price.

This is the world into which Nate Shaw was born. When Theodore Rosengarten first met Shaw—whose real name was Ned Cobb—he recognized the value of Shaw's first-hand experiences as an insightful and rare account

Alabama tenant farmer Ned Cobb (Nate Shaw) told of his experiences with trying to make a living in the face of exploitation by white landowners. REPRINTED FROM THEODORE ROSENGARTEN, *ALL GOD'S DANGERS: THE LIFE OF NATE SHAW*, NEW YORK: ALFRED A. KNOPF, 1975.

of postwar southern African American tenant farmers and the society in which they lived. Both Shaw and Rosengarten believed the preservation of Shaw's history would "prove useful to people interested in the history of his region, class, and race." Because Shaw could neither read nor write, the book was reconstructed over a period of years, based on extensive interviews conducted by Rosengarten. Through Shaw's storytelling, the reader is allowed a glimpse into a world in which the racialized economic system, which privileged the South's white rural elite, oppressed Shaw—and others like him—in countless ways: consigning him to perennial debt, denying him the opportunity to own land, and eventually landing him in prison for opposing its harsh effects.

## Significance

The system of tenant farming consistently subordinated the profits of sharecroppers' labor to the claims of white land owners, cotton brokers, fertilizer dealers, and store owners. The declining price of cotton and the destructive cotton boll weevil further limited his capacity for economic success. Despite his long hours and hard work, each year Shaw continued to come up short. Forced to buy and sell in a racially coded market, and powerless to challenge unscrupulous dealings by white merchants and land owners, Shaw and his fellow sharecroppers remained trapped in a cycle of indebtedness.

For decades, this system served to recreate the power structures that had existed in the time of slavery. And although other oral histories exist as records of this regulated oppression, Shaw's account is particularly significant because of his awareness of—and ability to depict—a complex set of social, familial, racial, and economic relations. Upon publication of the book, scholars did question Rosengarten's role in it. How did his editing of the tale impact the narrative? What effect did he have as a white, northern listener on Shaw's recollections? Still, *All God's Dangers* was widely praised for bringing to light the story of a man by turns both ordinary and extraordinary.

## Primary Source

### *All God's Dangers: The Life of Nate Shaw*

**SYNOPSIS:** In this excerpt, Nate Shaw describes his work as a cotton farmer, his dealings with the Reeve family, and his difficulty in managing his debt. Unable to challenge Mr. Tucker—a cousin of the Reeves who held his debt—Shaw is forced to pay him more than he was obligated, to deal only with merchants that Tucker approved, and to continue to accumulate debt as cotton prices fell.

I wanted to stretch out where I could get more land to work, and Miss Hattie Lu and Mr. Reeve—they had a little girl child but he weren't the father of it. Miss Hattie Lu had the chap before they married. And this girl had married and moved up there on the place with her husband. So I couldn't get more land than I had. They wanted to keep me there but on the amount of land they wanted, and it was too little for me. Then, too, me and Mrs. Reeve's son-in-law didn't agree much with each other. When he moved up on the place he wanted to take it over and boss me too. Well, you know blood's thicker than water, and Miss Hattie Lu was goin to let him have his way. I decided I'd pull out and I was pullin out in time, too.

I looked ahead and figured my best route. Moved down on Sitimachas Creek on the old Bannister place. And there, regardless to my dealins with Mr. Tucker, I begin to prosper good and heavy. I had learned a rule for my life workin with Mr. Reeve—I could make it anywhere by workin and tendin my own business. I was able to advance myself because I never made under five bales of cotton—made five bales the first year I rented from the Reeves; next year I made six; next year I made eight—with one mule and no help to speak of. Cotton picked up the second and third years to between fifteen and twenty cents, along in there. It was a big difference in the price since I started farmin for myself. I was under

the impression that the government was takin hold of the market—1912, 1913. The second year I quit workin halves and took my business in my own hands, cotton floated up to a higher level.

But things went bad the year I moved down on the creek. Cotton fell to a nickel a pound, 1914. A man couldn't pay nothin much on his old debts and nothin at all on his new ones. I disremember just exactly what I paid Mr. Reeve on the money he furnished me that year—he stuck by me, furnished me cash money the first year I dealt with Mr. Tucker—but I didn't pay him off. And I owed him a little over two hundred dollars after I sold my cotton and paid him what I could. And in addition to that, I owed Mr. Harry Black a hundred and thirty dollars for fertilize that I'd used the last year I worked on Mrs. Reeve's place. He was a guano salesman, lived out in the country above Tuskegee; and every year I lived with Mr. Reeve I bought my guano from him. 1913, I carried my guano debt over to my next crop; it weren't unusual to do that in this country and he agreed. But when cotton fell to a nickel I couldn't pay nothin hardly. And, to tell the truth, I didn't make the cotton I had been makin on the Reeve place. So I owed money for fertilize that applied to a bigger crop than I was makin now.

That was boll weevil time, the boll weevil was in circulation. He had just come in a year or two before then—these white folks down here told the colored people if you don't pick them cotton squares off the ground and destroy them boll weevils, we'll quit furnishin you. I told em that—puttin the blame on the colored man for the boll weevil comin in this country. Well, that was a shame. Couldn't nobody pay on his debts when the weevil et up his crop. The boll weevil cut in my cotton to a certain extent, but at that time it was mainly the low price that injured my chances. If I had got the price, I could have paid a heap more on my debts although I was makin less cotton.

I was runnin two plows—myself and my brother-in-law, little Waldo Ramsey, my wife's brother. But when cotton fell to the bottom both our crops combined couldn't pay what I owed. I did manage to pay Mr. Black thirty dollars; owed him a hundred and thirty dollars and I paid him thirty and that hundred runned over for five years before I could pay it.

■ ■ ■

That first year I moved on the Bannister place, Mr. Reeve died—died that fall, while I was gatherin my crop. What did Miss Hattie Lu do when he died?

She come to me and told me, "Nate, Mr. Reeve's gone now; he aint with us no more. We want to arrange to get in all of his estate, get it all together."

I agreed with her.

She said, "Now what you owed Mr. Reeve"—I couldn't pay him on account of cotton goin down, and then too that way my first year on that rocky place, my crop weren't quite what it had been; boll weevil seed to that also—"and whoever else owes him, like you do"—everybody doin business with the man owed him, you know—"we will, if it suits you, name somebody to take up your debt with Mr. Reeve."

And she named Mr. Tucker as the man to take up my debt, at ninety percent on the dollar. They knocked off ten percent to get Mr. Reeve's business closed in. Miss Hattie Lu told me, "Nate, Cousin Lemuel Tucker"—Miss Hattie Lu and Mr. Tucker was cousins someway—"he'll take up your debt, what you owe Mr. Reeve. And you only entitled to pay Cousin Lemuel ninety cents on the dollar. That ten cents, we knocked it off, that's our laws. You just pay ninety cents on the dollar to Mr. Reeve's estate; pay it to Cousin Lemuel, he taken up your debt."

I didn't know nothin against Mr. Tucker to make me contrary to the idea, so I told her, "Let him take it up." But the amount that I owed Mr. Reeve, I couldn't pay Mr. Tucker nothin on it that year. And I had that guano debt besides. Mr. Reeve transacted his business like this: he'd furnish you money to buy groceries and anything else you needed except fertilize; he wouldn't give you a penny for fertilize. You could buy fertilize from whoever you pleased but you had to arrange to pay the dealer out of your crop. I got along well under Mr. Reeve's system as long as cotton was bringin anything. But when cotton fell, that's when the trouble come.

So Miss Hattie Lu consulted with Mr. Tucker and he took my debt over. And he come down to my house on the creek one day, told me, "Nate, I took over your debt and paid Miss Hattie Lu the money you owed her dear husband's estate. I settled your account in full. Now you just pay me what you owed Mr. Reeve."

I said, "Mr. Tucker, you didn't have to pay the whole debt, you only had to pay ninety percent on the balance. The knock-off wasn't given to you."

He jumped up when I told him that. "Did she tell you that? She's mighty darn smart to tell you all that."

Right there was where I caught him. Miss Hattie Lu had put me in the light.

---

## The Face of Employment for Blacks in the 1910s

Faced with a system of oppression that trapped black southerners in a cycle of indebtedness, many sought work in northern industrial labor markets, particularly Chicago. Faced with a labor shortage during World War I (1914–1918), northern labor agents advertised jobs in black presses like the *Chicago Defender*. Most men and women migrated with the modest goals of securing stable employment and escaping the South's strict racial codes and tensions. Racism existed in the North as well, however, and blacks found that only the most menial of jobs were open to them. By the end of the 1910s, a half million African Americans had migrated to northern cities; a million more would follow in the next decade. The following document is a letter written by a Southern black worker to a potential employer, seeking employment in the North.

April 21, 1917

Houston, Texas

Dear Sir:

As I was looking over your great news paper I would like very mutch to get Some infermation from you about Comeing to your great City, I have a famile and Can give you good Referns about my Self. I am a Working man and will Prove up to what I say and would be very glad to Know from you, about a Job Allthough I am at work But, If I Could get Something to do I would be very glad to leave the South as I Read in the Chicago Defender about Some of my Race going north and makeing good.—well I would like to be on the List not with Standing my reputation is all O.K.

I thank you.

**SOURCE:** Foner, Philip S. and Ronald S. Lewis, eds. "Great Migration." In *The Black Worker from 1900 to 1919.* Philadelphia: Temple University Press, 1980.

---

He said, "The thing for you to do is pay me what you owed Mr. Reeve."

She told me to pay ninety cents on the dollar and he wanted the whole thing, what he didn't have to pay.

I said, "Mr. Tucker, she told me that ten cents weren't given to you; it's their loss, just their loss. Yes sir, she told me in a straight way; I'm entitled to pay you only ninety cents on the dollar and the dime goes loose."

He said, "The thing for you to do is pay me what you owed Mr. Reeve; that's the thing for you to do."

I said, "Do you think it's right to charge me for somethin you didn't have to pay?"

He said nothin. But I had no political pull; that was my flaw. I said, "All right, Mr. Tucker, go ahead. I'll see you later."

Well, he took up Mr. Reeve's debt and made himself ten cents on the other man's dollar. I had the brains to see how that transaction was runnin over me, but I had no voice on account of my color—and never had any with most men, only had a voice with some. . . .

I'd be askin all along for five long years and every fall I'd come up just a little deeper—1914, 1915, 1916, 1917, 1918—I'd go to Mr. Tucker for a settlement and he'd tell me, "Well, you lackin so much and so much of comin out—" For five long years I was fallin behind dealin with that man. Up until the fifth year I dropped into town to pay him: "Well, what are you holdin against me now, Mr. Tucker?"

"You owe me five hundred dollars, Nate."

Done got all of my crops for five years and I still owed him five hundred dollars. That was his tune. Five hundred dollars and one penny. I labored under that debt—I'm tellin what God's pleased with—lingered five long years and he was gettin every string I had to give.

## Further Resources

### BOOKS

Grossman, James R. *Land of Hope: Chicago, Black Southerners, and the Great Migration.* Chicago: University of Chicago Press, 1989.

Stokes, Melvyn, and Rick Halpern, eds. *Race and Class in the American South Since 1890.* Oxford: Berg Publishers, 1994.

Tindall, George B. *The Emergence of the New South, 1913–1945.* Baton Rouge: Louisiana State University Press, 1967.

### PERIODICALS

Daniel, Pete. "The Crossroads of Change: Cotton, Tobacco, and Rice Cultures in the Twentieth-Century South." *Journal of Southern History* 50, August 1984, 429–456.

Wiener, Jonathan M. "Class Structure and Economic Development in the American South." *American Historical Review* 84, October 1979, 970–992.

# "Last of the Vigilantes"

Memoir

**By:** Miriam E. Tefft (variant spelling, "Teft")

**Date:** February 2, 1982

**Source:** Tefft, Miriam E. "Last of the Vigilantes." Bisbee Deportation: Recollections. University of Arizona Library. Available online at http://digital.library.arizona.edu/bisbee/ (accessed June 29, 2002).

**About the Author:** Miriam E. Tefft was fifteen when her father, along with other armed citizens, rounded up and deported over a thousand copper miners—and other innocent citizens who were affiliated with them—from Bisbee, Arizona, to New Mexico on July 12, 1917. The Tefft family lived among Bisbee's elite and sided with the mining companies when the unionized miners went on strike. ∎

## Introduction

Mining and the American West have been intimately tied together since the discovery of California gold in the mid-nineteenth century. But unlike precious metals, copper held value only in large quantities. Mining costs were high and the price of copper, unsteady. Under these conditions, mining companies like the Phelps, Dodge and Company's Copper Queen mine (PD) and the Calumet and Arizona (C&A) struggled to maintain profitability. In extractive industries like mining, this was typically accomplished through increasing production. Most companies realized higher profits by lowering wages and standards of safety in the mines.

Mining companies exerted enormous power over the miners. In Bisbee, PD held influence over local commerce, banking, schools, and the town's only newspaper. The company-planned town of Warren, built by C&A, included a country club and a ballpark serviced by water and electricity. But the mining companies also fostered neighborhoods segregated by ethnicity and class, leaving Mexican workers, for instance, in the impoverished village of Tintown.

Unions represented a serious threat to this order. In 1907, PD imported workers from England to displace pro-union miners. Strong company opposition, decent wages, and the adoption of an eight-hour shift helped dull future union efforts. But by the time of World War I (1914–1918), the radical Industrial Workers of the World (IWW) sought another union drive. Declining copper prices, rising costs of living, and resentment over the mining companies' dominion over Bisbee brought many out in support of the strike in the summer of 1917.

When the IWW began its organizing drive in 1917, Bisbee was already a divided community. Communities were separated by ethnicity, and class distinctions were everywhere.

Over one thousand men march to box cars in Warren, Arizona on the morning of July 12, 1917. The men were deported to Columbus, New Mexico, where they remained in detention for several months. **ARIZONA HISTORICAL SOCIETY/TUSCON, AHS, PICTURES-PLACES-BISBEE-BISBEE DEPORTATION, 43181.**

## Significance

In June 1917, the copper companies rejected the IWW's list of demands, which included safer working conditions, the end of pay discrimination based on nationality, and the institution of a flat pay scale, rather than one that was tied to the price of copper. The IWW called a strike, which the companies denounced as unpatriotic, since copper was integral to the war effort. The striking miners were branded as traitors and radicals.

Many in town remained loyal to the companies. Most local merchants had a stake in the mining companies' success. And a number of the English workers, who had always received preferential treatment, joined with others in the town to form citizen's protective groups called Loyalty Leagues. Acts of violence were carried out on both sides. The lush country club was burned and miners' families were harassed. Two men died—one a Loyalty Leaguer, the other a miner—when Sheriff Wheeler's deputies began to forcibly collect the striking miners.

On the morning of July 12, 1917, Sheriff Wheeler and members of the citizens' leagues began their roundup. More than one hundred men armed with guns entered miners' homes and the homes of others deemed to be al-

lied with the union. The assemblage of over a thousand was marched two miles to the ballpark in Warren, where they were ordered into box cars piled high with manure. The detainees, most of them foreign-born, were taken 174 miles to Columbus, New Mexico. They remained in a detention camp for several months and were never allowed to return to their homes in Bisbee. Despite a federal investigation, the mining companies were not held liable for their role in this vigilante action, a form of frontier "justice" in the industrial age.

In *The Oxford History of the American West,* historian Carlos Schwantes wrote, "Next to the roundup of Japanese Americans in World War II, the Bisbee deportation is the greatest mass violation of civil liberties in the twentieth-century West." Though for a long time shrouded in mystery, the event has more recently come to light in a number of books, most of them written from a political or historical perspective. What makes Miriam Tefft's recollection unique is that she was neither a participant nor a political figure in her community. She was an ordinary, fifteen-year-old girl at the time of the deportation, and her memories reflect an innocence that comes from being a child trying to interpret an adult situation.

## Primary Source

"Last of the Vigilantes"

**SYNOPSIS:** In this memoir, Miriam E. Tefft recalls what it was like to live in Bisbee during the labor dispute of 1917. Tefft describes her reaction to union radicalism, her father's secrecy as he prepares for the deportation of the strikers, and the climactic day of the deportation itself.

I was 15. I was there when the tragic hysteria which was World War I broke out in the copper mining camp of Bisbee, Arizona where I lived, and the citizens took over the law.

Hazel Gilman and I, when we first heard of "Wobblies," wanted to know what it was all about. They were fomenting strikes in the mines, causing fear and confusion in our town. A meeting of strikers was scheduled for Finn Hall in Lowell. Though it sounded scary, that evening we took a streetcar and slipped into the back where we hoped we would be inconspicuous. We were familiar with Finn Hall; it was a church built by the Finns with volunteer help from men like our fathers.

For the first time we heard the ideology of radicals. We gathered from what speakers said that the aim was to create a revolutionary industrial union to overthrow capitalism. They maintained that once all workers combined in one big strike they could launch a national strike that would displace capitalists from power and place workers in possession. The mines would belong to the people. Men yelled and cheered the speakers, women shrieked, songs were sung. We were introduced to Joe Hill and his songs for the people. The climax of the meeting, for us, was when there was an incitement to action which reduced us to giggling fits. A skinny, rough-haired old woman whom we knew as Sally Hapgood, raced up and down the aisle yelling, "Hallelujah. Hallelujah." And denouncing capitalists at the top of her lungs.

We were a bit vague as to whom she meant. John Greenway? Dr. Bledsoe? We adored both. Walter Douglas? He was only a shadowy figure to us. Dr. Bledsoe came when we needed him, always kindly, always putting his patient first, always bringing and atmosphere of hope and calm into the sick room. Surely not he? Mr. Greenway gave us our ball park, our Vista Park with its bandstand, its trees, grass, and benches. He gave us our C and A library, and, best of all, our Greenway Junior High School. He was always courteous and pleasant. When he rode his horse he was a slender, handsome figure, and we remembered he had been one of Teddy Roosevelt's Rough Riders. He lived in the middle house of the three houses on a small rise overlooking Warren. He took interest in Children. Sometimes he would walk to the 4 room red elementary school, or to the Greenway School. If it were recess time he would watch us or ask us questions about who we were, what we were studying, or what we wanted to be when we were grown. He liked to visit classes, too. We always worked harder for a while after oen of his visits. Surely not he? I never saw Mr. Douglas, although I sometimes saw lights in his pink granite house next to Mr. Greenway's and the other side of Dr. Bledsoe's. Sometimes we saw his private pullam car on the rail road siding in Bisbee.

Finn Hall was getting noisy, and Hazel and I getting scary, so we sneaked out. We couldn't control our giggles. We giggled all the way to the street car stop and giggled on the street car all the way to Warren. When we got off at our stop we started singing, leaning on each other's shoulders:

Hallelujah, I'm a bum
Hallelujah, bum again
Hallelujah, give us a handout
To revive us again

There began to be violence in the mines. Old Mag was bombed. Miners on strike were harassed. Groups on men gathered on the streets and near mine entranced-Finns, Serbs, Welshmen, "Cousin Jacks," and Mexes, cursing, making violent gestures, shouting, having fist fights. We could see what a strike meant. We knew it was contended to be in protest over bad working conditions. Solid citizens of Bisbee saw it as unpatriotic and led by the IWW's (we called them "I Won't Work"). The IWW's had infiltrated the district. They were easy to spot; we knew the regular miners. These strangers were menacing. We'd never been afraid before. Our doors were never locked. The code we lived by was the open door and the pot of frijoles on the back of the stove.

Betty Clearly's father was the lawyer for these people, so we were not allowed to speak to her. "Whitely" was a suspect name. Milmay's father became very important. When the street car stopped at Johnson Addition Florence McKenzie wasn't there to go to school; her Mother had been assaulted by strikers because her husband remained loyal. Sadie Thomas gave us all a look that said "no compromise," her mouth was set in a straight line, and her hair was pulled back tighter than ever. Her father was an agitator.

There had been meetings in the Bisbee City Park and the Pythian Castle as well as in Finn Hall. Picnics were held in Tombstone Canyon, and planned acts of violence took place, like the fights which broke up the Fourth of July parade. That parade was the big event of the year, months of the organization-floats, bands, contests, miners drill teams. More than any single act, breaking up our parade brought the deepest anger to the people of Bisbee. This parade was particularly patriotic. Buildings were draped with flags, children carried small American flags. Every spectator sported some symbol to show patriotism.

Our beautiful country club with its wide verandas and green lawns, our touch of richness and refinement in the drab sand and stones of the surrounding countryside, was mysteriously burned one night. No more elegant dances, no more summer parties for the children, no more hiking around the greens to look for lost golf balls. Only a charred rubble remained. There were rumors and counter-rumors, all of them ugly.

You could almost smell fear. Men didn't look at each other in the face. Everyone was under suspicion. Loyalties were divided. One could sense an undercurrent of outrage seething. Our fathers were often from home. They were closed mouthed when asked questions, so one did not ask too many questions. Something was brewing in this atmosphere of wild emotions.

Posse is the legal term for vigilantes. Vigilantes left an undying mark on the forming of Arizona. I remember the men who met weekly, practiced shooting and riding. In those early days when Arizona was a territory, vigilante justice was the major force bringing law and order. The general public did not know who these men were, but these were the men who made history: bookkeepers, auditors, clerks, paymasters, teachers-mostly friendly men, hard working and just. During the Mexican Revolution these men protected the town before the U.S. troops were sent in by the government. Soft-spoken and gentle, for the main part, when called on to fight for justice they were single minded, fearless, accurate shots. "One of the most flagrant acts of vigilantism in the history of the West" was the dramatic moment in Arizona history which took place on July 12, 1917.

The street lights flickered and went out one by one. A few cars went by. The sounds of horses were muted. Voices were low, words indistinguishable. Dad got up from his bed when a low tap on the front door tattooed a signal. He hushed our questions: "Stay indoors. Keep quiet. Don't build a fire." We could hear him dressing, and speaking to his hunt-ing dog, "No, Rex. Stay here." He took his rifle down from the wall, the door opened, and he was gone. We heard Uncle Arthur's car and Mr. Bankherd's car. It seemed strange to be awake at this hour, to lie in the darkness and keep quiet.

It was so hot. The air vibrated with the shrill cicadas. We knew that Dad and the other men had been going to "meetings" every night that week, but the meetings were unexplained. We were eating a cold breakfast when the first signs of dawn appeared. We didn't leave the house. Mr. Hill and some of the miners from Black Knob View, who were not on strike, went past the house to the street car stop on the way to Lowell. Half and hour later we saw then return. This was ominous. Hortense and Carolyn White, I found out later, spent the night in their home in Jiggerville, crouching behind the piano which had been dragged across a corner of the room to form a triangle. Their father was out, they didn't know where. Jiggerville was a quiet, respectable settlement of home, not a place which would harbor a nest of troublemakers, but the sound of shooting at a near neighbor's house made them realize that they, too, were in danger. (It was learned next day that two men had been killed, an IWW agitator and one of Sheriff Wheeler's men.)

The *Bisbee Review* was delivered about 10:00 on this morning of July 12. Headline: ALL WOMEN AND CHILDREN STAY OFF THE STREETS. We were putting out the flag as Dad had told us to, when we suddenly noticed a long double line extending from the direction of Bisbee toward the ball park in Warren.

Our house was a good vantage point, only a few blocks from the park, 8 steps up to the porch on two sides. Mother brought out her favorite rocker and her crocheting. Other people began sitting on their porches and doing handwork like Mother. Children were sitting on fence railings and steps, but they didn't leave the yard.

We began to see that deputies and armed citizens were keeping the strikers in line as they were herded into the ball park behind the high board fence. The men had evidently been taken completely by surprise; some were still in their nightshirts, many in long underwear, some apparently hadn't been given time to put on their shoes. We could see snipers on the opposite hill overlooking the park. We recognized Mr. Greenway on his white horse, Dr. Bledsoe on his black, and saw that Captain Wheeler was directing maneuvers. A rather small man, he was an imposing figure on horseback.

This was too tame for me. I had to go where the action was. I slipped out the back door and joined Hazel and her brother Hoogie, and Claude and Bertha Berquist and the C and A office. They didn't know exactly where their fathers were any more than I did. We sat on the top steps where we could see what was going on. Ray Foster, whose father was detective for the Arizona Banker's Assoc., was sitting on some railroad ties near the tracks of the Southern Pacific Don Luis spur line where 25 box cars and cattle cars were standing.

A machine gun burst. Capt. Wheeler rode into the park. Through a megaphone he announced: the strikers were guilty of treason. If they wanted to go back to work there was a job for them, if not, out they would go. We could hear shouting, "Don't go. Don't go. Don't go." About half the men broke line and went out the gate. Some 1200 strikers stayed in the park. These men were driven into the cars on the siding. No guns were fired. There were oaths, some lack of cooperation, but guns are a good persuader. 25 deputies, all crack shots, mounted the tops of the cars. Every tactical movement was carried out with precision. The engine whistled, the train gathered speed. Last echoes from the train faded. Then a cheer went up from the hundreds who had been watching through this hot violent day. Justice had been done, they felt, the swift way it was always done in Arizona-no quibbling, but with authority and efficiency. Gun toting citizens straggled home. No one remembered the machine guns.

"Where are they taking them?" we wanted to know. "That you will find out in a few days," was the only answer Dad would give us. "The IWW had plans to round up our men and get rid of them. We just beat them to it." Overnight, sheriff's deputies and armed citizens had made a sweep of Bisbee, from Chihuahua Hill to Bucky O'Neill, Brewery Gulch to School Hill, taking in Tintown, Jiggerville, Bakerville, Lowell, rounding up strikers and dissidents.

The next morning, and for a few days, everything moved in slow motion. Everyone acted completely depleted. Men shuffled, women burned dinners, children drooped around. No hopscotch, no kick the can, no baseball. But it was calm. The mines were working again. The threat we had lived under was gone. We breathed quietly.

Four days later we heard the cattle cars at the train stop on the Warren siding. The weary deputies had returned. The cars were empty. The loads of strikers had been shipped to New Mexico where they were turned out into the desert near Columbus.

Greenway, Douglas, and a man named McDowell, whom we didn't know, were indicted. It was an anti-climax when President Wilson, breathing fire and brimstone, sent commission to investigate. The commission was headed by Felix Frankfurter. They found the government was helpless to punish anyone. No law could be found against kidnapping people en masse and dumping them into another state.

## Further Resources

### BOOKS

Mellinger, Philip J. *Race and Labor in Western Copper: The Fight for Equality, 1896 1918.* Tucson: University of Arizona Press, 1995.

Schwantes, Carlos, ed. *Bisbee: Urban Outpost on the Frontier.* Tucson: University of Arizona Press, 1992.

### WEBSITES

"Bisbee Deportation." University of Arizona Library. Available online at http://digital.library.arizona.edu/bisbee/index.php (accessed June 29, 2002).

# 3

# EDUCATION

KRISTINA PETERSON

*Entries are arranged in chronological order by date of primary source. For entries with one primary source, the entry title is the same as the primary source title. Entries with more than one primary source have an overall entry title, followed by the titles of the primary sources.*

**CHRONOLOGY**
Important Events in Education, 1910–1919 . . . . . . 124

**PRIMARY SOURCES**
"The College-bred Community"
  W.E.B. Du Bois, 1910 . . . . . . . . . . . . . . . . . . 127

*The Indian and His Problem*
  Francis E. Leupp, 1910 . . . . . . . . . . . . . . . . . 131

Equal Pay for Women Teachers . . . . . . . . . . . . . 134
*Equal Pay for Equal Work*
  Grace C. Strachan, 1910
"The Ideal Candidates"
  Alice Duer Miller, 1915
"An Unequal Footing!"
  Anonymous, 1911

"The Contribution of Psychology to
  Education"
  Edward L. Thorndike, 1910 . . . . . . . . . . . . . 139

*Medical Education in the United States and
  Canada*
  Henry S. Pritchett, 1910 . . . . . . . . . . . . . . . . 143

"An Address Delivered Before the National
  Colored Teachers' Association"
  Booker T. Washington, 1911 . . . . . . . . . . . . 148

*A New Conscience and an Ancient Evil*
  Jane Addams, 1912 . . . . . . . . . . . . . . . . . . . . 152

*The Montessori Method*
  Maria Montessori, 1912 . . . . . . . . . . . . . . . . . 154

"Why Should the Kindergarten Be
  Incorporated as an Integral Part of the
  Public School System?"
  Philander P. Claxton, 1913 . . . . . . . . . . . . . . . 159

*Smith-Lever Act of 1914*
  Hoke Smith and Asbury Francis Lever,
    May 8, 1914 . . . . . . . . . . . . . . . . . . . . . . . . 161

*Report of the Committee on Academic
  Freedom and Tenure*
  American Association of University
    Professors, 1915 . . . . . . . . . . . . . . . . . . . . 164

*Democracy and Education*
  John Dewey, 1916 . . . . . . . . . . . . . . . . . . . . . 169

*The Measurement of Intelligence*
  Lewis M. Terman, 1916 . . . . . . . . . . . . . . . . . 172

*Smith-Hughes Act of 1917*
  Hoke Smith and Dudley M. Hughes,
    February 23, 1917 . . . . . . . . . . . . . . . . . . . . 175

*Cardinal Principles of Secondary Education*
  Commission on the Reorganization of
    Secondary Education, 1918 . . . . . . . . . . . . . 179

"The Project Method"
  William Heard Kilpatrick, 1918 . . . . . . . . . . . 183

# Important Events in Education, 1910–1919

## 1910

- Thirty-nine percent of undergraduates in U.S. colleges and universities are women.

- Embryologist Thomas Hunt Morgan begins to attract graduate students to Columbia University not for the curriculum but for opportunities in research.

- Admissions directors at Columbia, Harvard, Yale, Princeton, Dartmouth, and Amherst begin discussions about the increasing number of Jewish male applicants.

- Only eight states have school attendance of 90 percent or higher of children ages six to fourteen. Four are in New England, and the remainder are in Iowa, Nebraska, Michigan, and New York.

- Examinations by local officials for teaching certificates are replaced in all states by examinations conducted by state boards or state departments of education.

- The U.S. Census reports that 550,000 children ages ten to fifteen are at work in factories, shops, and in other nonagricultural positions rather than at school.

- In February, the *Journal of Educational Psychology,* a forum for the research of educational psychologists, is founded.

- In May, a union of eight Boston institutions of higher education forms the Commission on University Extension Courses.

- In May, faculty in the Department of Physics at the University of Chicago vote to promote Robert Andrews Millikan to professor. Although popular with students, Millikan will seldom teach, preferring to concentrate on research. He will win the 1923 Nobel Prize in physics.

- In September, Dewey, Oklahoma, opens the nation's first nongraded school, with students in grades one to twelve working independently.

## 1911

- The average cost of books per public school student is about seventy-eight cents.

- In January, New York City public schools offer evening classes in terracotta work, gas and steam engines, boilermaking, printing, and proofreading, signaling a growing emphasis on adult and vocational education.

- In March, the Bureau of Education announces that 1,844 public and society libraries in the United States have been established; 1,005 of these are school and college libraries, and the number of volumes in their collections has increased by twenty million since 1908.

- In September, tuition at Harvard is $150 per year; at Adelphi $180; and at Colgate $60.

- In October, Rochester, New York, establishes a Bureau of Research and Efficiency to compile statistical information on public schools.

- In November, research on eighth-grade composition reveals that only 60 percent of eighth graders in Hackensack, New Jersey, schools were able to write an "acceptable" composition on "A Day of My Life" in fifteen minutes.

## 1912

- 2,569 students attend New York City evening trade schools.

- In January, the American Federation of Labor advocates that the technical and industrial education of workers in trades should be a public function and therefore part of the public school curriculum.

- In February, professors in the Psychology Department at Harvard University in Cambridge, Massachusetts, are so displeased with the academic skills of entering freshmen that they devise an experiment to teach 120 entering freshmen how to improve their study skills.

- In June, a series of conferences on English in the Public Schools of New England, in Cambridge, Massachusetts, criticizes schools for inadequate instruction in English grammar and composition.

- In June, a study of Wesleyan University graduates reveals that 33 percent had found noteworthy success, defined by their being listed in *Who's Who.* Researchers cite this study as evidence that a college degree is the ticket to success.

- In October, New Orleans, Louisiana establishes a Bureau of Research and Efficiency to compile statistics on public schools.

- On December 11, Alexis Carrol, professor at the Rockefeller Institute for Medical Research in New York City becomes the first American Nobel laureate in physiology or medicine.

## 1913

- The Bureau of Education distributes 112 issues of its *Bulletin,* more than one million copies, to school officials.

- The annual report of the Commission on Education, a public commission, includes sections on "The Junior High School," "Montessori Schools in the U.S.," "Vocational Education," "School Surveys," and "Education for Special Classes of Children."

- The average length of a term for public schools is 158.1 days.

- For the first time, the state of California provides free elementary-school books for all pupils.

- From August 16 to August 28, the annual convention of the National Education Association features keynote addresses on "The Junior College," "Military Training in the Schools," "Sex Morality and Sex Hygiene," "Education of the Negro," and "Education of the Japanese."

- In September, forty thousand people enroll in the University of Wisconsin extension departments, which includes correspondence courses.

## 1914

- The Bureau of Education estimates that total costs of U.S. public education are $750 million. This amount is less than one-third the national spending for alcoholic beverages and only three times the amount paid for admissions to movie theaters that year.

- About half the nation's 20 million schoolchildren attend rural schools.

- On May 8, Congress passes the Smith-Lever Act, establishing an extension service at each land-grant college. Through the extension service scientists would teach farmers how to apply scientific knowledge to improve the growth of crops and livestock.

- In August, Kansas enacts a law providing for the purchase of books for all elementary-school students at a cost to taxpayers of $230,000.

- In September, Eugene Gladstone O'Neill enrolls in a drama course at Harvard University. The course strengthens O'Neill's determination to become a dramatist. He will in 1936 become the first playwright to win a Nobel Prize in literature.

- In September, Harvard, Yale, Princeton, Columbia, and Cornell increase tuition. Harvard students in mechanical, electrical, and civil engineering see tuition rise from $150 to $250 a year when Harvard and the Massachusetts Institute of Technology agree to cooperate in offering certain courses.

## 1915

- Vermont adopts the junior-high-school plan, establishing one hundred school buildings to house grades seven to ten.

- Teachers in Minnesota are beneficiaries of a pension bill that allows them to retire after twenty years with a pension partially funded by a special state tax.

- On April 1, a conference in Saint Louis debates "The Problem of the Feeble-Minded in its Educational and Social Bearings."

- In July, the Boston Board of Health discontinues medical examinations of school-children after the school committee appoints its own doctors to conduct exams.

- On August 21, National Education Day is held at the Panama-Pacific Exposition in San Francisco.

- In September, the Arkansas Supreme Court declares unconstitutional an act passed by the legislature appropriating fifty thousand dollars of common school funds to build high schools.

- On September 16, Stanford University hosts a conference on War, Peace, and International Polity.

- In September, New York University offers a new two-year program leading to the degree of doctor of public health.

- In November, a court of inquiry investigates a cheating scandal at the United States Naval Academy at Annapolis, Maryland, finding that 63 percent of the first class of midshipmen (seniors) had seen prior copies of examination papers. The court files its report with the Navy Department for further review.

- On November 11, the first National Congress on University Extensions meets in Philadelphia.

- In December, in New York City the American Association of University Professors (AAUP) is chartered; John Dewey serves as the first president. One of the organization's first charges is to draft a statement on academic freedom.

## 1916

- Five states still have no compulsory-education laws.

- American colleges teach a War Aims Course to study World War I, then called the Great War.

- A study of Cleveland, Ohio schools shows that 27.6 percent of all schoolchildren are "laggards" and that every eighth child repeats at least one grade; 50 percent withdraw before the fifth grade; and 75 percent withdraw before the eighth grade.

- A study finds that two-fifths of all secondary-school teachers in Maryland are adequately trained; their salaries range from $271 per year in Saint Mary's County to $662 in Baltimore County.

- A *School and Society* study cites statistics that the U.S. is in danger because not enough college-educated women are marrying.

- On January 1, John Dewey, president of the American Association of University Professors, approves a report by the Committee on Academic Freedom and Tenure. The report supports the right of faculty to speak freely on any issue.

- On February 12, Carnegie Hall in New York City is filled to capacity for a posthumous tribute to the work of Booker T. Washington, founder in 1882 of the Tuskegee Institute (now Tuskegee University) in Tuskegee, Alabama.

- On February 18, the Emily Blackwell Ward at the New York Infirmary for Women is dedicated. Blackwell was a pioneer in medical education for women.

- In July, the Children's Bureau of the U.S. Department of Labor publishes a compilation of all child-labor laws enacted up to January 1, 1916.

- In July, Franz Boas becomes chair of the Department of Anthropology at Columbia University. He will do more than any other American in the early decades of the twentieth century to attract women to study anthropology.

- In August, New York University establishes the first full curriculum (twenty-four courses) to train teachers to work with "mental defectives."

- In November, a group of Wisconsin teachers, with guidance from John Dewey, found the American Federation of Teachers (AFT), a teacher-only labor union of the AFL. The union fights for the right to create bargaining units in school districts.

- On December 28, twenty-two papers on the subject of mental testing are read at the annual meeting of the American Psychological Association in Chicago.

## 1917

- All the former slave states except Missouri have established county training schools for African American students.

- The state school board in Minnesota requires smallpox vaccination for pupils and teachers not already immunized.

- The Pittsburgh, Pennsylvania, school board decides to pay the salaries of two women teachers who married in defiance of board policy barring women teachers from marrying.

- In response to wartime patriotic fervor and xenophobia, evening schools open nationwide for "Americanization" classes for immigrants.

- Trier Township High School in Winnetka, Illinois establishes a student council to make and enforce school regulations, try pupils for infractions, and fix punishments.

- On February 23, Congress passes the Smith-Hughes Act, providing federal grants to the states to prepare students in trade, industry, home economy, and agriculture.

- In May, final exams in civics at numerous high schools require students to bring in and analyze copies of President Wilson's April 2 address asking Congress to declare war on Germany.

- In September, Washington University Dental School upgrades its three-year course to a four-year course.

- In November, Cleveland, Ohio, residents vote to spend $2 million to erect four junior high schools that will include music rooms, print shops, wood-carving and carpentry shops, botany rooms with greenhouses, drawing rooms, domestic science and household-arts rooms, gymnasiums, and swimming pools.

## 1918

- The Division of Maps of the Library of Congress issues a several-hundred-page catalogue to schools, titled *A List of Atlases and Maps Applicable to the Present War.*

- The *Pasadena Star News* publishes "The Great War," its lesson on World War I originally prepared for the Pasadena high schools.

- *History Teacher's Magazine* establishes a public-service information bureau on World War I.

- The U.S. Commission on Education urges school superintendents to prepare for the next garden season by hiring more garden teachers to train students to prepare vegetable gardens to avert food shortages.

- In January, President Woodrow Wilson authorizes the Bureau of Education to assist state officers of education to find teachers for normal, secondary, and elementary schools because of the "national emergency" in teacher shortages.

- In January, the University of North Carolina Bureau of Extension announces a series of thirty-eight free lectures on World War I to North Carolina communities.

- In February, Indiana high-school boys and girls are urged to form Patriotic Service Leagues to coordinate war activities in the schools.

- On March 16, the Carnegie Institute of Technology hosts a conference on "How Can the Elementary, Secondary and Higher Education Schools Adapt Subject Matter and Methods So As to Help Win the War?"

- In April, the Federal Board for Vocational Education issues a bulletin on mechanical and technological training for men conscripted into the armed services.

- On April 5, the U.S. Bureau of Education issues *Guidelines on the Schools in Wartime.*

- On June 14 (Flag Day), Americanization meetings are held nationwide to emphasize the need for teaching recent immigrants English, citizenship, and ideals.

- In October, the Federal Board for Vocational Education urges disabled soldiers and sailors in hospitals to pursue an education so that they will be able to lead independent lives once World War I ends.

- On October 1, at 516 colleges and universities throughout the country, 140,000 male students become student soldiers when they are inducted into a program called the Students' Army Training Corps (SATC).

- In November, the article "The Repulsiveness of the German State" appears in *The Historical Outlook,* a journal for historians, an example of the convergence of scholarship and propaganda during the war.

## 1919

- The U.S. Bureau of Education issues a bulletin on "Opportunities at College for Returning Soldiers," a description of courses of study, tuition, and scholarships at every U.S. college and university.

- The National Education Association (NEA) Committee on History and Education for Citizenship in Schools publishes a model national curriculum for "securing higher intelligence in regard to world affairs and deeper, more fundamental appreciation of the duties and responsibilities of citizenship."

- The NEA campaign for higher teachers' salaries touts New York City's new minimum-wage policy: twenty-one thousand teachers in grades one to six have minimum salaries of $1,005; in grades seven to twelve, $1,350.

- Cleveland's Americanization Committee issues a pamphlet explaining how to nationalize aliens without making them lose their connection with their homelands. The Cleveland Museum of Art stages a Homelands Art Exhibit that features landscapes of twenty-four countries.

- In January, the Progressive Education Association is formed; members cite their dissatisfaction with the "inflexibilities" of traditional schools.

- On February 14, the Agricultural Historical Association is organized "to publish research in the history of agriculture." Its journal is *Agricultural History.*

- In March, the Women's Committee of the Council of National Defense issues a seventy-seven-page bibliography titled *Women in the War.*

- In November, John Dewey and several colleagues found the New School for Social Research in New York City in an attempt to create a truly independent university run by educators themselves.

# "The College-bred Community"

Speech

**By:** W.E.B. Du Bois

**Date:** 1910

**Source:** Du Bois, W.E.B. "The College-bred Community," 1910. In Aptheker, Herbert, ed. *The Education of Black People: Ten Critiques 1906–1960 by W.E.B. Du Bois.* Amherst: The University of Massachusetts Press, 1973, 31–40.

**About the Author:** William Edward Burghardt (W.E.B.) Du Bois (1868–1963) a prolific writer, educator, and African American activist, earned undergraduate degrees from Fisk and Harvard, and was the first African American to earn a Ph.D. from Harvard in 1895. He was a professor at Atlanta University. He founded the Niagara Movement in 1905 (which later developed into the NAACP) in opposition to the conservative position of Booker T. Washington. He was editor of *Crisis* magazine, a publication of the NAACP, from 1910 to 1934. ∎

## Introduction

The reconstruction years following the Civil War (1861–1865) raised the hope that the newly freed slaves would be accorded social equality and full civil rights under the Constitution. Disillusionment followed, as the hands-off policy of the federal government allowed the development of the Jim Crow laws establishing a system of segregation, and the rise of the Ku Klux Klan and other white supremacist groups. Basic rights of citizenship were denied African Americans, through legal means, as well as the use of fear and intimidation.

For many African American leaders near the end of the nineteenth century, education was the answer. The most prominent educational proposal was that of African American leader, Booker T. Washington. Education for African Americans, according to Washington, should focus on learning a trade and gaining economic self-sufficiency. Rather than engage in militant protest, African Americans should prove themselves to be good citizens and a valuable economic asset to the South—civil rights would naturally follow. He founded the Tuskegee Institute to provide vocational and agricultural training for African Americans.

By the early twentieth century, W.E.B. Du Bois began an outspoken campaign against Washington's plan of accommodation to white oppression, advocating instead that African Americans actively fight for their civil rights. Du Bois, once an advocate of Washington's ideas, now saw African American salvation in the higher education of the "talented tenth" of the race. This college-educated community would provide the necessary leadership for the development of all African Americans. Yet his efforts to raise funds for liberal arts education for African Americans, particularly at Atlanta University where he taught, were largely unsuccessful. Washington's position, on the other hand, was one that appealed to whites at the time; white philanthropists were happy to support Tuskegee Institute and other programs providing trades education for African Americans.

## Significance

Du Bois's speech is representative of his approach to fundraising in the North for Atlanta University. On this occasion, he was addressing "the white, rich, and well-born in Brookline, Massachusetts." Du Bois acknowledges that the need to help "the submerged classes" is one reason why philanthropists are not willing to direct their resources toward liberal college education for African Americans. While trades education is more clearly and directly associated with the struggling poor, Du Bois asserts that it is just this class of people with whom he is concerned. The development of a college-educated class is the only hope for the progress of the group as a whole. Though in other contexts Du Bois calls for an end to segregation and full access for African Americans to the social and political mainstream, he sidesteps the issue here—making "no argument for or against racial segregation." Ultimately, though Du Bois emphasizes the benefits to the "submerged mass of black people" and soft-pedals the more controversial issues, it is Booker T. Washington's educational plan that won the larger portion of support from those who held the purse-strings.

Trades education for African Americans flourished during this time period, and Washington received the backing, both political and financial, of whites in positions of power. However, Du Bois became increasingly influential among blacks and white radicals supporting civil rights. Through the NAACP, which Du Bois helped found in 1909, and his editorship of one of its publications *Crisis,* Du Bois was able to reach a wide audience. And it was W.E.B. Du Bois's activist approach to the struggle for civil rights that was reflected in the Civil Rights movement of the 1950s and 1960s.

## Primary Source

### The College-bred Community [excerpt]

**SYNOPSIS:** In this speech appealing to philanthropists for funds for Atlanta University, W.E.B. Du

Students at the National Training School for Women and Girls, Washington, D.C. W.E.B. DuBois spoke about the need for African Americans to acquire higher education in order to achieve greater social and personal success. **THE LIBRARY OF CONGRESS.**

Bois makes the case for the importance of a college-educated African American community. In the absence of contact with the majority culture due to segregation, African Americans must rely on their own leaders to overcome years of slavery and oppression.

Atlanta University is primarily a college. To be sure it has a large high school connected with it and an efficient normal school; but the students in the normal school are all of college rank, and the high school is retained because there are no public high schools in Georgia for black folk. The center, therefore, of our work in Atlanta University is the College. To the up-building of this department our chief energies are directed; by the results of this department our work must be judged; and on the basis of this

department we ask the support of the philanthropic world. Probably no other institution in the world is so entirely a Negro college as ours and certainly none in the South has as large a proportion of college students. We are, then, primarily a college. When, now, this statement is frankly made, there are a great many people who wish to help good causes in the world, who wish us well, and who with equal frankness decline to contribute to our work. They say plainly, "we are not interested in giving black boys college training. We think that the class of Negroes who have reached the plane where they can profit by such higher training have also reached the plane where they do not need outside aid. Such people, white or black, can be left to themselves to make their own way in the world." They say, "we are interested in the submerged classes of those poor people who are struggling up out of the depths. Such people we want to help, but, on the other hand, while theoretically we would be glad to help all people to a broader vision, yet on account of limited ability we are obliged to confine ourselves to cases of pressing necessity; therefore, we cannot give to Negro college work." If, now, the assumption thus stated be true, I would not only not blame philanthropists for refusing to support Atlanta University, but I would go further and change my own work; because the work which lies nearest my heart is not that of the talented few in opposition to the needs of the submerged many. But I have come here tonight purposely to set before you argument which proves to me, and I trust will prove to you, that the assumption which I mention is false, and that the first step toward lifting the submerged mass of black people in the South is through the higher training of the talented few.

There are many of us who are still surprised, not to say indignant, that it took ten years of Reconstruction even to begin the settlement of the problems raised by slavery and war. Such people strongly suspect that only the incompetence and rascality of the Reconstruction politicians can explain such an extraordinary fact. And yet, when we come to consider the matter, how few of us realize what slavery meant in the South! To kidnap a nation; to transplant it in a new land, to a new language, new climate, new economic organization, a new religion and new moral customs; to do this is a tremendous wrenching of social adjustments; and when society is wrenched and torn and revolutionized, then, whether the group be white or black, or of this race or that, the results are bound to be far reaching.

When, therefore, you say that the South had a system of slavery for 250 years, you mean that the victims of that system lost their own social heritage; gained new bonds binding them to a new community, and began to forge in that new community, new machinery for carrying on the new social life; or, in other words, religion, moral customs, family life, economic habits, literature and traditions were taken from the Africans. They became a part of a rigid caste system, out of which they could seldom legally rise, and their social organization among themselves was reduced to the barest minimum for existence.

When, after two and one-half centuries of storm and stress, the race was adjusted to these new social environments, there came abruptly a new revolution. That revolution ushered them into what was called freedom; the social heritage and the bonds which tied them to their community were again broken, and they were left with no machinery for carrying on their social life. Or again, to make the matter more explicit, the Negro was freed after he had lost much of his own native traditions and moral and economic habits and had only begun to learn other habits from his master. Moreover, as a freedman, it was made increasingly impossible for him to learn such things from his masters because he was separated more and more from the master-class. Thirdly, having forgotten or never known the methods of modern organization, it was quite impossible that he should immediately take up and guide the development of his own institutions.

What, now, was the one great pressing need? Of course this need has been variously expressed and emphasized. To some the first thing that freedom meant was work; to some it was a release from the bonds of poverty; to others it was education and the organization of religious institutions. But yet I think if we consider the matter, all of these reduce themselves to one single thing, looked at from different points of view; namely what the Negro needed was experience, that is, a knowledge of how the world accomplishes its necessary work today. And when you say that the freed Negro was ignorant of this, you mean more than mere illiteracy—for illiteracy is the cause of evils rather than the evil in itself. You mean more than shiftlessness and unmoral customs. In fact, you mean all these things together and other things added, which in the total show that the Negro did not know the accumulated wisdom and methods of the world in which he was asked to take part. Now, how was he to get this unknown experience and wisdom? . . .

The chief and great method, of course, by which a people come into the great social heritage of the modern culture-world and by which they gain close and efficient knowledge of the methods of the world's work is the training which comes primarily and essentially from human contact—a contact of those who know with those who are to learn.

Now, the great mistake which some of you and many others make, when they talk and think about the South, is to assume that there are in the South the same facilities for the transmission of culture from class to class and man to man as exist in the North. If this were so, then my argument today would be quite out of place. But I come to emphasize in your minds a thing which you all know; namely, that racial separation in the South means the voluntary and persistent isolation of those who most need to learn by race contact. People who have easily and rather lightly accepted a program of race separation in the South have, I fear, seldom thought of this. . . .

There is in the South a social separation between workman and employer, the ignorant and the learned, society and its servants, the high and low, white and black, which goes to an extent and reaches a degree quite unrealized by those who have not studied the situation.

I pause simply to remind you that white people and black people in the South do not, as a rule, live on the same streets or in the same sections; do not travel together in train or street-car; do not attend the same churches, do not listen to the same lectures, do not employ the same physicians, do not go to the same schools; do not, for the most part, work at the same kinds of work; do not read the same books and papers, are not taught the same traditions, and are not buried in the same graveyard.

Now, outside of all questions of the wisdom or necessity for such a situation, the question which interests us today is this: how far and in what way can there be any transmission of human culture and experience or knowledge of social organization and social methods or of education, in any sense, from the white group to the black? Of course, some such transmission there is and always will be—it is impossible perfectly to isolate people; but the chance of such transmission is in the South reduced to a minimum.

Mind, I make no argument for or against racial separation. But I am saying, with emphasis: state in your own mind, every argument for racial isolation at its full strength; conclude, if you will, that my child shall not be educated with yours; that it is indiscreet to eat [with me] at the same table; that you have definite matrimonial plans for your sister [which do not include me]; and that black people and white cannot righteously worship God from the same pews. Assert these beliefs, either for yourselves or in sympathy with others who passionately insist upon them, and then remember that the stronger this argument is for racial isolation, the more compelling is the righteous demand of black folk for their own racial leadership, their own fountains of knowledge, their own centers of culture; and this is not for their amusement or delectation; not to flatter their vanity, but to give them the absolute and indispensable foundation for solid and real advance in civilization and social reform, the uplifting of their masses, and rational guidance in health, work, and morals.

If, then, you propose to educate the Negro into the possibility of full citizenship in the modern world of culture, one thing you have got to admit at the very outset; and that is, he cannot, to any appreciable extent, get that education from the white people about him. . . .

What the Negro needs, therefore, of the world and civilization, he must largely teach himself; what he learns of social organization and efficiency, he must learn from his own people. His conceptions of social uplift and philanthropy must come from within his own ranks, and he must above all make and set and follow his own ideals of life and character. Now, this is putting upon a people just emerged from slavery, with neither time, traditions, nor experience, a tremendous task. In strict justice, it is asking more of this people than the American nation has any right to ask. Nevertheless, this race is not stopping to await justice in this matter; it is not asking about the righteousness of past conduct; it is not even pausing—as perhaps it ought—to discuss the advisability of present policies; but it is asking you, here and now, to place in its hands the indispensable facilities for teaching itself those things which it must know if it is going to share modern civilization.

Moreover, just as in justice you cannot ask a man to raise himself by his own boot-straps, just so you cannot logically and justly expect that a people will furnish itself, under such circumstances, with its own chief means of uplift. . . .

The *community* must be able to take hold of its individuals and give them such a social heritage, such present social teachings and such compelling social customs as will force them along the lines of progress, and not into the great forests of death. What is needed then, for any group of advancing people, is the COLLEGE-BRED COMMUNITY; for no matter how far the college may fail in individual cases, it is, after all, the center where knowledge of the past connects with the ideal of the future. Every community, therefore, must be *college-bred;* and that does not mean that every individual must be a college graduate; it may be that the proportion of college-bred men may be small, even infinitesimal; and still the community, by tradition and heritage, will hold fast to what the past has taught the world of high and ideal future accomplishment. But, given a group or community which does not know the message of the past and does not have within its own number, the men who can feel it, and is separated from contact with outside groups who can teach it—

given such a community and you have a desperate situation, which calls for immediate remedy. It is such a situation among the Negroes in the South that calls for schools like Atlanta University.

There ought to be in the South today at least five institutions with an endowment of a million dollars each, whose business it would be to furnish the teachers and professional men and thinkers and industrial leaders for the masses of the black people of the South. Such colleges would represent, not the capstone of the social organization of the South but rather its vast foundation. . . .

In the North the ordinary boy, whether he actually attends college or not, gets some college training from his surroundings. It is impossible for a boy to grow up here in Boston without getting from the air which he breathes something of that for which Harvard stands. On the other hand it is possible for a black boy to grow up in the South and be a perfect barbarian. It is for you and me to make this more and more impossible in the future by giving such support to the best of the Negro colleges as will really plant ideals of social efficiency and culture in the center of black communities and enable them to work and save and act according to the best traditions of civilized men.

To the existence of such group development and feeling among black men there can be but one objection, and that is the objection of those people who mean by "race separation" not separation but subordination; who plainly and frankly say that the Negro is to be separated from all contact with culture in order that he may never become an efficient, self-reliant, thinking race; who hope that there shall grow up in the nation, not the democracy dreamed of by the Pilgrim Fathers but a new caste ideal such as was made the cornerstone of the Confederacy. With such objections I am sure you have no sympathy and I only hope that with your willing desire to help the lowly of all races and peoples, you will use this method of approaching the problem of the submerged mass in a particular race, and through a Negro college, in a larger sense, you will be willing to help a people to help themselves.

## Further Resources

### BOOKS

Du Bois, W.E.B. *Dusk of Dawn.* New York: Harcourt, Brace, 1940.

Du Bois, W.E.B. *Souls of Black Folk.* New York: Knopf, 1993.

Harris, Thomas E. *Analysis of the Clash Over the Issues Between Booker T. Washington and W.E.B. Du Bois.* New York: Garland Publications, 1993.

Horne, Gerald, and Mary Young, eds. *W.E.B. Du Bois: An Encyclopedia.* Westport, Conn.: Greenwood Press, 2001.

Lewis, David L. *W.E.B. Du Bois: Biography of a Race, 1868–1919.* New York: Henry Holt, 1993.

Moore, Jacqueline M. *Booker T. Washington, W.E.B. Du Bois, and the Struggle for Racial Uplift.* Wilmington, Del.: Scholarly Resources, 2003.

Rudwick, Elliott M. *W.E.B. Du Bois, Voice of the Black Protest Movement.* Urbana: University of Illinois Press, 1982.

Wintz, Cary D. *African American Political Thought, 1890–1930: Washington, Du Bois, Garvey, and Randolph.* Armonk, N.Y.: M.E. Sharpe, 1996.

Wolters, Raymond. *Du Bois and His Rivals.* Columbia: University of Missouri Press, 2002.

Zamir, Shamoon. *Dark Voices: W.E.B. Du Bois and American Thought, 1888–1903.* Chicago: University of Chicago Press, 1995.

### WEBSITES

"African American Education." Available online at http://www.theatlantic.com/unbound/flashbks/blacked/aaedintr.htm; website home page http://www.theatlantic.com (accessed March 10, 2003).

"The Two Nations of Black America." Available online at http://www.pbs.org/wgbh/pages/frontline/shows/race/etc/road.html; website home page http://www.pbs.org (accessed March 10, 2003).

### AUDIO AND VISUAL MEDIA

*Black Paths of Leadership.* Directed by Pam Hughes. Churchill Films, Videocassette, 1984.

*W.E.B. Du Bois: A Biography in Four Voices.* Directed by Louis Massiah. Videocassette, 1995.

*W.E.B. Du Bois of Great Barrington.* Produced by Lillian Baulding. PBS Video, Videocassette, 1992.

---

# *The Indian and His Problem*
Nonfiction work

**By:** Francis E. Leupp

**Date:** 1910

**Source:** Leupp, Francis E. *The Indian and His Problem.* New York: C. Scribner's Sons, 1910, 125–127, 129–131.

**About the Author:** Francis E. Leupp (1849–1918), journalist and author, graduated from Williams College and Columbia University Law School. Leupp served as the Washington agent for the Indian Rights Association. He was head of the Washington Bureau of the New York Evening Post, and he served as Commissioner of Indian Affairs from 1905 to 1909. Leupp was known for his opposition to off-reservation boarding schools and his desire to preserve aspects of American Indian culture. ∎

## Introduction

In 1871, American Indians, the majority of whom were by then living on reservations, were declared by

Congress to be wards of the government. The tradition of warfare against American Indians was now to be replaced by a program of cultural assimilation. Starting in 1877, federal funds were allocated for schools for American Indians, and attendance was compulsory by 1891. By 1920, seventy percent of American Indian children were attending school.

By the early 1880s, an active reform movement focused on American Indian policy. White reformers were angered by corruption within the governmental system, run by the Office of Indian Affairs. The reformers noted the history of cruel and harsh treatment of American Indians, as well as the perceived need to educate and civilize the American Indians for their own benefit. The federal government, reformers charged, had taken the Indians' land with the promise of giving them civilization in return; yet this had not yet been accomplished.

The program of cultural assimilation was based on the assumption by white Europeans that American Indian culture was "savage" and inferior. A popular view at the time was that all cultures pass through a series of stages—from savagery to barbarism, and, finally, to civilization. It was both inevitable and desirable for American Indians, by this view, to progress toward the ideal of civilization—European Christian culture. Such a transformation would also free up American Indian land for white settlers. And it would reduce the financial burden on the federal government, converting American Indians into self-supporting farmers and laborers.

Consequently, schools for American Indian children focused on the elimination of American Indian culture, including language, clothing, hairstyles, habits, and beliefs. Children, often taken by force, were immediately given European names, clothes, and haircuts upon arrival at school. Day schools on reservations were replaced by off-reservation boarding schools. It was found that the children would return to "bad Indian habits" if allowed contact with their families.

## Significance

Former Commissioner of Indian Affairs, Francis E. Leupp, in calling for a new approach to assimilation, represents a viewpoint bridging the old reform philosophy of the 1880s with a new approach (that would begin in the 1920s). Leupp continues to stand behind a program of assimilation, but it is a "kinder and gentler" version. Consonant with the philosophy of the progressive education movement active at the time, Leupp advocates taking the knowledge and habits that children bring to school, and—slowly, gradually, and kindly—leading them in the desired direction.

The new reform movement in the 1920s went a step further. Some whites began to see American Indian culture as worth preserving. Largely as a result of the work of the American Indian Defense Association, the government commissioned a study resulting in the 1928 Meriam Report. That report recommended a "change in point of view" and advocated giving "consideration to the desires of the individual Indians" in policy making. The report suggested allowing those American Indians not wishing to assimilate to retain their traditional culture.

Despite efforts toward reform and the fact that American Indians became citizens in 1924, the education of American Indians remained under the control of the Bureau of Indian Affairs (BIA) until the mid-1970s. The 1960s saw the rise of the American Indian Movement and demands by American Indians to control their own schools. During the 1970s, the U.S. Congress enacted legislation that placed control of their schools in American Indian hands and funded the development of culturally relevant curricula. The BIA continues to exist in an advisory, rather than directive, capacity.

## Primary Source

*The Indian and His Problem* [excerpt]

> **SYNOPSIS:** In this excerpt from his book, *The Indian and His Problem*, former Commissioner of Indian Affairs, Francis Leupp, advocates ending the program of assimilation whereby American Indian children are suddenly transferred from tribe and family, and totally immersed into a foreign culture. Leupp calls for beginning with what is familiar to the child, and gradually moving to the standard academic curriculum and training in American culture.

For reasons plain to any one familiar with the disparity of local conditions, the Indian day-school in the most primitive part of the frontier differs widely from the white day-school anywhere; and, in spite of my desire to assimilate the races as far as practicable in all their activities, I have tried to accentuate this contrast in one or two respects. To me the most pathetic sight in the world is a score of little red children of nature corralled in a close room, and required to recite lessons in concert and go through the conventional daily programme of one of our graded common schools. The white child, born into a home that has a permanent building for its axis, passing most of its time within four solid walls, and breathing from its cradle days the atmosphere of wholesale discipline, is in a way prepared for the confinement and the mechanical processes of our system of juvenile instruction. The little Indian, on the other hand, is descended from a long line of ancestors who have always lived in the open and have never done anything in mass routine; and what sort of antecedents

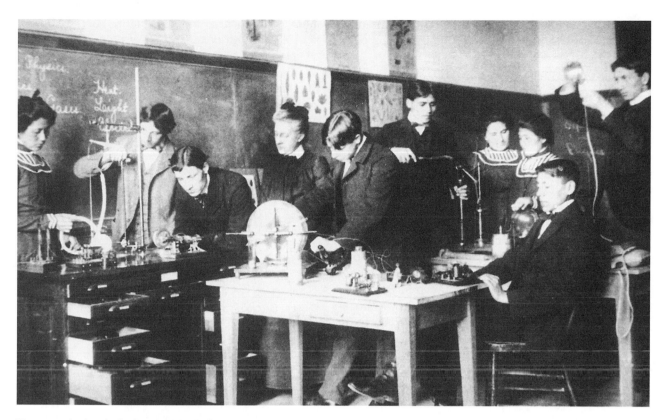

Non-reservation board schools such as the Carlisle Indian School sought to assimilate American Indian children into the predominant white culture of the country. **NATIONAL ARCHIVES AND RECORDS ADMINISTRATION.**

are these to fit him for the bodily restraints and the cut-and-dried mental exercises of his period of pupilage? Our ways are hard enough for him when he is pretty well grown; but in his comparative babyhood— usually his condition when first captured for school purposes—I can conceive of nothing more trying.

My heart warmed toward an eminent educator who once told me that if he could have the training of our Indian children he would make his teachers spend the first two years lying on the ground in the midst of the little ones, and, making a play of study, convey to them from the natural objects right at hand certain fundamental principles of all knowledge. I dare say that this plan, just as stated, would be impracticable under the auspices of a Government whose purse-strings are slow to respond to the pull of any innovation. But I should like to see the younger classes in all the schools hold their exercises in the open air whenever the weather permits. Indeed, during the last year of my administration I established a few experimental school-houses, in regions where the climate did not present too serious obstacles, which had no side-walls except fly-screen nailed to studding, with flaps to let down on the windward sides in stormy weather.

I do not mean that I regard the difference between in-door and out-door instruction as vital in the scheme of Indian schools; but this item serves as well as any other to exemplify the general principle that we shall succeed best by beginning the new life as nearly as possible where the old life left off. We should not make the separation any more violent than necessary; and it is pleasant to note that the more intelligent teachers in the Indian Service are ignoring books as far as they can in the earlier stages of their work. They are teaching elementary mathematics with feathers, or pebbles, or grains of corn; then the relations of numbers to certain symbols on the blackboard are made clear, and thus the pupils are led along almost unconsciously from point to point.

■ ■ ■

The design kept in view by the advocates of the non-reservation boarding-schools, in carrying the children hundreds of miles away from home and trying to teach them to sever all their domestic ties and forget or despise everything Indian, is to surround them with white people and institutions for the whole formative period of their lives, and thus induce them to settle down among the whites and carve out careers for themselves as the young people of other races do.

This theory has always had its attractions for a certain class of minds, but in practice it has not worked out as expected. Its most ambitious exponent is the Carlisle Indian School, set in the midst of a thrifty farming country. If any experiment in that line could hope to succeed, this one ought to have succeeded. It has been followed by more than a score of similar ventures in the West. A few of these schools were undoubtedly established, as Carlisle was, in response to what their authors believed to be a real demand of the cause of Indian civilization; but in course of time the establishment of new non-reservation schools became a mere meaningless habit. Some Senator or Representative in Congress would take a fancy to adorn his home town with a Government institution, and, if the supply of custom-houses and pension agencies and agricultural experiment stations happened for the moment to be running short, he would stir about to secure votes for an Indian school. Any educational project can count on a certain amount of legislative support on the strength of its name; and, once established, of course a school has to be kept up with goodly annual appropriations. What matter if the Indians do not care to send their children to it? Then the thing to do is to coax, urge, beg, till they give way. If opportunity to obtain an education free of cost does not offer enough attractions in itself, organize a brass band and a football eleven for the boys, and a mandolin club and a basket-ball team for the girls, circulate pictorial pamphlets showing the young players in all their brave regalia, and trust the stay-at-home children to wheedle their parents into consenting!

Nay, until a year or two ago it was the custom, when all mere material devices failed, to give one of the most wide-awake school employees a long leave of absence on full pay, in consideration of his going to this or that reservation and bringing back twenty children. Never mind how he got them—the one point was to get them, good or bad, sound or weakly, anything that would pass a very perfunctory scrutiny and add one name to the school roll. And when two or three such canvassers, representing rival schools, came into collision on the same reservation, resorted to every trick to outwit each other, and competed with bigger and bigger bids for the favor of parents of eligible children, what was the Indian to think? Is it wonderful that a certain old-fashioned Sioux asked a missionary teacher: "How much will you give me if I let my boy go to your school? That other teacher says he will give me an overcoat!"

## Further Resources

### BOOKS

Adams, David Wallace. *Education for Extinction: American Indians and the Boarding School Experience, 1875–1928.* Lawrence: University Press of Kansas, 1995.

Archuleta, Margaret L., Brenda J. Child, and K. Tsianina Lomawaima. *Away From Home: American Indian Boarding School Experiences, 1879–2000.* Phoenix: Heard Museum, 2000.

Coleman, Michael C. *American Indian Children at School, 1850–1930.* Jackson: University Press of Mississippi, 1993.

Ellis, Clyde. *To Change Them Forever: Indian Education at the Rainy Mountain Boarding School, 1893–1920.* Norman: University of Oklahoma Press, 1996.

Golden, Gertrude. *Red Moon Called Me: Memoirs of a School Teacher in the Government Indian Service.* San Antonio: Naylor, 1954.

Johnston, Basil H. *Indian School Days.* Norman: University of Oklahoma Press, 1988.

### WEBSITES

"Assimilation Through Education: Indian Boarding Schools in the Pacific Northwest." University of Washington Libraries Digital Collection. Available online at http://content.lib .washington.edu/aipnw/marr/index.html; website home page http://content.lib.washington.edu (accessed March 10, 2003).

"Carlisle Indian Industrial School (1879–1918)." Available online at http://home.epix.net/~landis/; website home page http:// home.epix.net (accessed March 10, 2003).

"The Reservation Boarding School System in the United States, 1870–1928." Available online at http://www.twofrog.com /rezsch.html; website home page http://www.twofrog.com (accessed March 10, 2003).

### AUDIO AND VISUAL MEDIA

*In the White Man's Image.* The American Experience Series. Produced by Christine Lesiak and Mathew Jones. PBS Home Video. Videocassette, 1991.

*Where the Spirit Lives.* Directed by Bruce Pittman. Studio Entertainment. Videocassette, 1989.

# Equal Pay for Women Teachers

## *Equal Pay for Equal Work*
Nonfiction work

**By:** Grace C. Strachan

**Date:** 1910

**Source:** Strachan, Grace C. *Equal Pay for Equal Work.* New York: B.F. Buck, 1910. Reprinted in Hoffman, Nancy. *Woman's "True" Profession: Voices from the History of Teaching.* New York: Feminist Press/McGraw-Hill, 1981.

**About the Author:** Grace C. Strachan (18??–1922), educator, activist, author, and school district superintendent attended the State Normal School in Buffalo, New York, and did post-graduate work at New York University. She taught in Buffalo, and then in Brooklyn, New York. She was a leader in the struggle for equal pay for women teachers, and higher salaries and pensions for all teachers in New York City. She was a popular lecturer and published articles in a number of magazines.

## "The Ideal Candidates"

**Poem**

**By:** Alice Duer Miller

**Date:** 1915

**Source:** Miller, Alice Duer. "The Ideal Candidates." *New York Tribune,* 1915. Reprinted in Altenbaugh, Richard J., ed. *The Teacher's Voice: A Social History of Teaching In Twentieth-century America.* Washington, D.C.: The Falmer Press, 1992.

**About the Author:** Alice Duer Miller (1874–1942), was an author, educator, and graduate of Barnard College in 1899. She was an active proponent of women's rights and used her writing talents to further the cause. She wrote a column for the *New York Tribune* and is very well known for her story "The White Cliffs."

## "An Unequal Footing!"

**Political cartoon**

**By:** Anonymous

**Date:** 1911

**Source:** *The Womans Journal* 42, March 4, 1911, 1. Reprinted in Altenbaugh, Richard J., ed. *The Teacher's Voice: A Social History of Teaching In Twentieth-century America.* Washington, D.C.: The Falmer Press, 1992. ∎

### Introduction

As the common school movement, led by Horace Mann, gained momentum in the first half of the nineteenth century, the opening of many new schools created a demand for more teachers. Initially, most teachers were males—generally, either regarded as unfit for other employment, or using teaching as a temporary steppingstone to other positions. While some objected to the idea of women working outside the home and doubted their ability to enforce school discipline, two factors in the increasing feminization of the profession were the shortage of teachers, and the reality that female teachers could be paid one-third the salary of men. Some common school reformers argued that women made ideal teachers. They naturally were nurturing, by virtue of their maternal instincts, as well as morally superior to men. By the Civil War (1861–1865), the majority of teachers in common schools were women.

Teaching paid far less than other professions, and it was considered a low-status position. Teachers endured constant surveillance by community members and restrictions on their social, political, and religious activities. The practice of teachers "boarding around," staying with each student's family throughout the year, was a means to monitor and control teachers. Teachers were also expected to serve as role models (by doing volunteer charity and church work) in addition to their teaching duties. Ironically, while teachers were held to a higher moral standard, higher pay and status did not follow.

After the turn of the twentieth century, teachers began to organize as a profession. At the same time, women teachers began their quest for equal pay and opportunity. While most teachers were women, there continued to be a significant gender gap in pay. By 1910, women working in urban schools were making an average of $17.38 per week, while men in the same job earned an average of $36.42. Women teachers generally were not permitted to teach after marriage; the argument that single women did not have a family to support was one justification for their lower salaries.

### Significance

Grace Strachan's efforts toward equal pay for women teachers were part of a larger movement for women's rights in the profession. The Chicago Teacher's Federation, an organization of female elementary teachers, led by Margaret Haley and Catherine Goggin, pushed for higher wages and equal pay for women. In 1900, they successfully sued local utilities for back taxes that should have gone for teacher wages. Encouraged by this success, Strachan and the Interborough Association of Women Teachers lobbied to gain equal pay for New York City's women teachers. Despite not yet having the right to vote, their efforts were successful—the New York legislature, in 1911, passed a law stating: "In the salaries of teachers hereafter appointed, there shall be no discrimination on account of the sex of the teacher." The efforts of women teachers were assisted by gains made in women's rights, including the right to vote in 1920.

Today, teachers continue to struggle with low status and low pay relative to other professions. While pay scales in public school teaching are no longer based on gender, elementary teachers, still a predominantly female group, are generally paid less than secondary teachers. In addition, women continue to be underrepresented among the higher-paid administrative positions.

### Primary Source

*Equal Pay for Equal Work* [excerpt]

**SYNOPSIS:** Grace Strachan argues against the disparity in pay between male and female teachers.

Female teachers, such as the one standing front row, center, with her students, were uniformly paid a lesser wage than their male counterparts. **THE LIBRARY OF CONGRESS.**

She takes a position against the rationale that men, because they have a family to support, should be paid more for the same work. Pay, she states, should be based only on the work performed, not on other, irrelevant criteria. She notes that single men with no family to support are paid more than single women with dependents.

### Preface

Salary—A periodical allowance made as compensation to a person for his official or professional services or for his regular work.

—Funk and Wagnalls

Notice the words, "a person." Here is no differentiation between male persons and female persons.

Yet the City of New York pays a "male" person for certain "professional services" $900, while paying a "female" person only $600 for the same "professional services." Stranger still, it pays for certain experience of a "male" person $105, while paying a "female" person only $40 for the identical experience. These are but samples of the "glaring inequalities" in the teachers' salary schedules.

Why is the male in the teaching profession differentiated from the male in every other calling, when his salary is concerned?

Why does the city differentiate the woman it hires to teach its children from the woman it hires to take stenographic notes, use a typewriter, follow up truants, inspect a tenement, or issue a license?

Why are not the appointees from the eligible lists established by the Department of Education, entitled to the same privileges and rights as appointees from Civil Service lists from other City and State Departments?

Some ask, "Shall the single woman, in teaching, be given the married woman's wage?" I do not know what they mean, But I say, "Why not the single woman in teaching just as much as the single woman in washing, in farming, in dressmaking, in nursing, in telephoning?"

Again, some ask, is there such a thing as "equal work" by two people?

Technically, no. No two people do exactly the same work in the same way. This is true of all professional and official work. Compare Mayor Gaynor's work with Mayor McClellan's. Will any one say their work as Mayor is "Equal Work"? And yet the pay is the same. Do all policemen do "Equal Work"? Yet they receive equal pay. So with firemen, school physicians, tenement house inspectors. The taxpayers, no doubt, believe that, judged by his work, Mayor Gaynor is worth a far higher salary than many of his predecessors. But a great corporation like the City of New York cannot attempt to pay each of its employees according to the work of that particular street cleaner or fireman or stenographer, and so must be content with classifying its positions, and fixing a salary for each. So should it do for its teachers. That is all we ask.

## The Family-to-Support Argument

It is rather a sad commentary on our profession that its men members are the only men who object to women members of the same profession getting the same pay for the same work. Who ever heard of a man lawyer fighting a woman lawyer in this way? A man doctor arguing that another doctor should give her services for less pay simply because she happened to be a woman? And leaving the professions, what attitude do we find the men who form our "Labor Unions" taking on this question? They form a solid phalanx on the side of "Equal Pay." The most powerful of all unions in many respects— "Big Six"— has a By-Law making it a misdemeanor to pay a woman less than a man working at the same form. All Labor Unions fight "two prices on a job."

Is it not sad to see men, American men, shoving aside, trampling down, and snatching the life preservers from their sisters? I say life preservers seriously and mean it literally. For to the woman obliged to support herself, is not her wage earning ability truly a life preserver. How can any man except one whom she is legally privileged to assist, take from a woman any part of the wages she has earned and remain worthy even in his own eyes? The excuses he makes to himself and to others in the attempt to justify his act, tend to belittle him more and more.

And yet some men whose blood sisters have by teaching provided the money to enable them, their brothers, to become teachers, oppose those very sisters in their efforts to obtain "Equal Pay for Equal Work." Can one ask for stronger proof of the insidious danger to our manhood which lurks in unjust standards of salary for service rendered? The true man, the good man, ought to put the woman who earns a respectable living, on a pedestal, as a beacon of encouragement to other women to show them one who wanted clothes to wear, and food to eat, and a place to live, and who obtained them by honorable labor.

I am firmly convinced that while teaching is a natural vocation for most women, it is rarely the true vocation of a man. And that those who enter the profession without the love for it which overshadows even the pocket returns, invariably deteriorate. Their lives are spent largely among those whom they consider their subordinates—in position or in salary, if not in intellect—the children and the women teachers. They grow to have an inordinate opinion of themselves. No matter how ridiculous or absurd or unfair may be the attitudes they take and the things they say, there is no one to say, "Nonsense!" as would one of his peers in the outer world. The novelist David Graham Phillips in the following description of one of his characters expresses my opinion better than I can myself: "Peter was not to blame for his weakness. He had not had the chance to become otherwise. He had been deprived of that hand-to-hand strife with life which alone makes a man strong. Usually, however, the dangerous truth as to his weakness was well hidden by the fictitious seeming of strength which obstinacy, selfishness and the adulation of a swarm of sycophants and dependents combine to give a man of means and position."

Recently in one of our schools, a male assistant to the principal resigned. The vacancy thus caused was filled by a woman. This woman is doing the same work as the man did, but with greater satisfaction to the principal. *But* she is being paid $800 a year less than the man was.

In another school I know there was a woman assistant to principal. As a grade teacher she had married and resigned, expecting—as most girls do when they marry—that she wouldn't have to work outside the home any more. But her husband became a victim of tuberculosis, and they went to Colorado in search of health for him. Time passed, their funds were exhausted, the invalid was unable to work, and so they came back, and the wife—after certifying, as our by-laws require, that her husband was unable to support her and had been so for two years—was reappointed. Later she secured promotion to assistant to principal. During the day she labored in a large, progressive school, composed almost wholly of children born in Russia, or of Russian parentage. At night she taught a class of foreign men. Now, although she actually had a family to support, she was receiving $800 a year less than a man in her position would receive. A married man? Oh, no, not necessarily. He might be a millionaire bachelor, or the pet of a wealthy wife— it is only necessary for him to be a "male" assistant to principal. Possibly on account of her family responsibilities, probably because she was ambitious, she strove for a principalship. During the school year, she traveled to Columbia University and took post graduate courses after school and on Saturdays; during the summer, when she should have been resting, she was studying with Professor This and Professor That. Last September she took the examination for a principal's license: in October, she died—typhoid, the doctors said. The husband she had cheerfully and lovingly supported for years survived her but a few weeks.

Why have I dwelt on this? To show the absurdity of the "family wage" argument of the male teacher. . . . Under a system of equal pay, where services should be paid for irrespective of sex, some women who now marry would remain single. But there are some men to-day who remain single because of relative economic independence, which they desire to maintain. These men are, however, relatively few. Women are as instinctive and as normal as men are, and independence, which they feared to lose, would prevent very few from marrying when they could make marriages which were attractive to them. Independence of women would improve marriage, since fewer women would marry because of necessity. By the same means divorce would be decreased, and human happiness would have a boom.

Our Association early in 1908 gathered some statistics. They showed 377 women—eleven of them married and six widows—supporting 707 others besides themselves. These teachers are all women, but the people depending wholly upon them or partly upon them are their mothers or their fathers or both or a brother or a sister or a niece or a nephew. These are actual figures collated from written answers to our questionnaire. You see, then, that here is an average of two people for every woman to support besides herself. Now, what salary is offered to these young women of twenty-one years of age, after they have spent all these years in preparing for the position of teacher? What salary is she being paid by the City of New York, the greatest city in the world, with the greatest public school system in the world? $11.53 a week. A woman in charge of one of the stations in the city gets more than that. Does the latter have to spend as much money on clothes? No. She can wear the same clothes from one end of the year to the other if she wants to, and not be criticised. But I know when I go into a classroom, among the things that I notice is the teacher's dress—whether it is neat, whether

it is appropriate. She must be a model for her class. Besides, the teacher must live in a respectable neighborhood and make a good appearance at home and abroad, and she must continue her studies in order to give satisfactory service.

## Primary Source

"The Ideal Candidates"

**SYNOPSIS:** In the early twentieth century it was widely felt that a married woman should not work, that her job was to take care of home and husband. This poem is an ironic commentary on the fact that a married woman could not get a teaching job unless she could demonstrate that her husband was gone or incapacitated.

*Characters*
Board of Education
Three women candidates

*Chorus by the Board:*
Now please don't waste your time and ours,
By pleas all based on mental powers.
She seems to us the proper stuff
who has a husband bad enough.
All other please appear to us excessively
superfluous.

*1st Teacher:* My husband's really not that bad . . .
*Board:* How very sad, how very sad!
*1st Teacher:* He's good, but hear my one excuse . . .
*Board:* Oh, what's the use, oh, what's the use?
*1st Teacher:*
Last winter in a railroad wreck,
he lost an arm and broke his neck.
He's doomed but lingers day by day.
*Board:* Her husband's doomed hurray, hurray!

*2nd Teacher:*
My husband's kind and healthy, too . . .
*Board:* Why then, of course, you will not do!
*2nd Teacher:* Just hear me out. You'll find you're wrong.
It's true his body's good and strong;
But, ah, his wits are all astray.
*Board:* Her husband's mad, hip, hip hurray!

*3rd Teacher:* My husband's wise and well—the creature!
*Board:* Then you can never be a teacher!
*3rd Teacher:* Wait. For I have lead such a life;
He could not stand me as a wife;
Last Michaelmas, he ran away.
*Board:* Her husband hates her hip hurray!

*Chorus by Board:*
Now we have found without a doubt,
By process sound and well thought out,
Each candidate is fit and truth,
to educate the mind of youth.
No teacher need apply to us,
whose married life is harmonious.

BOSTON, SATURDAY, MARCH 4, 1911

AN UNEQUAL FOOTING!

## Primary Source

### "An Unequal Footing!"

**SYNOPSIS:** "An Unequal Footing!" cartoon reprinted from *The Womans Journal*, March 4, 1911. One of the focuses of the suffrage movement during the 1910s was the inequality in pay between male and female teachers.

**THE WOMANS JOURNAL.**

## Further Resources

### BOOKS

Altenbaugh, Richard J., ed. *The Teacher's Voice: A Social History of Teaching in Twentieth Century America.* Washington, D.C.: The Falmer Press, 1992.

Butts, R. Freeman, and Lawrence Cremin. *A History of Education in American Culture.* New York: Henry Holt, 1953.

Cohen, Rosetta Marantz, and Samuel Scheer, eds. *The Work of Teachers in America: A Social History Through Stories.* Mahwah, N.J.: Lawrence Erlbaum, 1997.

Hoffman, Nancy. *Woman's "True" Profession: Voices from the History of Teaching.* Old Westbury, N.Y.: Feminist Press, New York: McGraw-Hill, 1981.

McDonnell, L.M., and A. Pascal. *Teachers Unions and Educational Reform.* Santa Monica, Calif.: Rand Corporation, 1988.

Perlmann, Joel, and Robert A. Margo. *Women's Work?: American Schoolteachers, 1650–1920.* Chicago: University of Chicago Press, 2001.

Sugg, Redding S. *Motherteacher: The Feminization of American Education.* Charlottesville: University Press of Virginia, 1978.

### WEBSITES

"Only a Teacher." PBS.org. Available online at http://www.pbs.org/onlyateacher/index.html; website home page: http://www.pbs.org (assessed March 15, 2003).

### AUDIO AND VISUAL MEDIA

*Only a Teacher.* Directed by Claudia Levin. PBS. Videocassette, 2000.

---

# "The Contribution of Psychology to Education"

Journal article

**By:** Edward L. Thorndike

**Date:** 1910

**Source:** Thorndike, Edward L. "The Contribution of Psychology to Education." *Journal of Educational Psychology* 1, 1910, 5–8.

**About the Author:** Edward L. Thorndike (1874–1949) received a B.S. from Wesleyan University, an M.A. from Harvard University, and a Ph.D. from Columbia University. He was a professor at Teachers College, Columbia University from 1899 to 1940. He published over 500 books and articles. Thorndike was well known for his work on human and animal behavior and learning, as well as psychological measurement. ■

## Introduction

With Charles Darwin's *On the Origin of Species,* (1859) came a new way of thinking about humans in relation to science. Traditionally, the study of human behavior was a matter for philosophers and theologians. After Darwin, many began to see humans as part of nature—therefore, understandable through science. They envisioned the possibility of a new "objective" science of the mind. This "New Psychology," based on the experimental methods of science, was developed by philosopher and psychologist William James and others beginning in the 1890s.

If humans evolved from lower animals, then the study of animal learning and behavior could shed light on the humans, learning process. James' student, Edward L. Thorndike, found that when animals are rewarded for a behavior, they tend to repeat that behavior. Based on his work on animal behavior, he developed his famous "Laws of Learning." The most important of these, the Law of Effect, states that behaviors become stronger when followed by a satisfying effect, and weaker when followed by an annoying effect. Learning, for Thorndike, was the process of forming neural connections, based on the linking of a stimulus and a response. Teachers could use this information in classrooms, according to Thorndike, by rewarding desired behaviors.

Edward L. Thorndike theorized that "psychology makes ideas of educational aims clearer" and helps measure the attainability of those aims. THE LIBRARY OF CONGRESS.

Thorndike is credited with defining, around the turn of the twentieth century, the new field of educational psychology. His goal was the development of an exact science of education. He believed that "whatever exists at all, exists in some amount" and can be measured. He had a great faith in mental measurement, shared by many at the time, and worked to develop intelligence tests and achievement tests in the various curricular areas. Thorndike believed that many controversies and problems involving methods, materials, curriculum, and even goals of education could be solved through science.

**Significance**

Thorndike's assertion that all areas of education can benefit from the work of educational psychology was taken seriously by educators. His work profoundly affected all aspects of schools. Various methods and materials were scientifically tested and developed. Thorndike's Laws of Learning refuted the nineteenth century view that certain studies, such as Latin, because they are difficult, will strengthen the "mental faculties." According to Thorndike's theory, there are no such faculties, only the biological potential to build neural connections—promoting some behaviors through rewards and weakening others through negative effects.

Consequently, children should learn in school the behaviors that they will need later in life. This view helped to further the process, already begun, of making the curriculum more practical and utilitarian.

Thorndike's work fit into the progressive education movement, prominent at the time. Progressives welcomed his work toward a science of education and the use of achievement and intelligence tests as tools of reform. Decisions about student placement could now be made on a "scientific" rather than a subjective basis, enabling educators to provide each student with the most suitable education possible.

Unlike "determinist" scientists working in the psychological testing field, Thorndike held that environment plays a large role in the development of intelligence—it cannot be measured outside of a cultural context. He believed that through a science of education, individuals and society can improve.

Once revolutionary, Thorndike's theories of learning are now familiar concepts. His work in intelligence tests provided the foundation for current intelligence testing. Thorndike's work in human and animal learning continue to impact profoundly the fields of psychology and education.

**Primary Source**

The Contribution of Psychology to Education [excerpt]

**SYNOPSIS:** In this excerpt, Thorndike outlines the ways that the "art of education" depends on the "science of psychology." Psychology can define, limit, clarify, and enlarge the aims of education and contribute to knowledge of the methods and means of education. Progress toward a "complete science of education" is being made including the measurement of achievement, intelligence, and the genetic basis of various characteristics. All of these studies can assist the field of education.

Psychology is the science of the intellects, characters and behavior of animals including man. Human education is concerned with certain changes in the intellects, characters and behavior of men, its problems being roughly included under these four topics: Aims, materials, means and methods.

Psychology contributes to a better understanding of the aims of education by defining them, making them clearer; by limiting them, showing us what can be done and what can not; and by suggesting new features that should be made parts of them.

Psychology makes ideas of educational aims clearer. When one says that the aim of education is culture, or discipline, or efficiency, or happiness, or utility, or knowledge, or skill, or the perfection of all one's powers, or development, one's statements and probably one's thoughts, need definition. Different people, even amongst the clearest-headed of them, do not agree concerning just what culture is, or just what is useful. Psychology helps here by requiring us to put our notions of the aims of education into terms of the exact changes that education is to make, and by describing for us the changes which do actually occur in human beings.

Psychology helps to measure the probability that an aim is attainable. For example, certain writers about education state or imply that the knowledge and skill and habits of behavior which are taught to the children of today are of service not only to this generation and to later generations through the work this generation does, but also to later generations forever through the inheritance of increased capacity for knowledge and skill and morals. But if the mental and moral changes made in one generation are not transmitted by heredity to the next generation, the improvement of the race by direct transfer of acquisitions is a foolish, because futile aim.

Psychology enlarges and refines the aim of education. Certain features of human nature may be and have been thought to be unimportant or even quite valueless because of ignorance of psychology. Thus for hundreds of years in the history of certain races even the most gifted thinkers of the race have considered it beneath the dignity of education to make physical health an important aim. Bodily welfare was even thought of as a barrier to spiritual growth, an undesirable interferer with its proper master. Education aimed to teach it its proper place, to treat it as a stupid and brutish slave. It is partly because psychology has shown the world that the mind is the servant and co-worker as well as the master of the body, that the welfare of our minds and morals is intimately bound up with the welfare of our bodies, particularly of our central nervous systems, that today we can all see the eminence of bodily health as an aim of education.

To an understanding of the material of education, psychology is the chief contributor.

Psychology shares with anatomy, physiology, sociology, anthropology, history and the other sciences that concern changes in man's bodily or mental nature the work of providing thinkers and workers in the field of education with knowledge of the material with which they work. Just as the science and art of agriculture depend upon chemistry and botany, so the art of education depends upon physiology and psychology.

A complete science of psychology would tell every fact about every one's intellect and character and behavior, would tell the cause of every change in human nature, would tell the result which every educational force—every act of every person that changed any other or the agent himself—would have. It would aid us to use human beings for the world's welfare with the same surety of the result that we now have when we use falling bodies or chemical elements. In proportion as we get such a science we shall become masters of our own souls as we now are masters of heat and light. Progress toward such a science is being made.

Psychology contributes to understanding of the means of education, first, because the intellects and characters of any one's parents, teachers and friends are very important means of educating him, and, second, because the influence of any other means, such as books, maps or apparatus, cannot be usefully studied apart from the human nature which they are to act upon.

Psychology contributes to knowledge of methods of teaching in three ways. First, methods may be deduced outright from the laws of human nature. For instance, we may infer from psychology that the difficulty pupils have in learning to divide by a fraction is due in large measure to the habit established by all the thousands of previous divisions which they have done or seen, the habit, that is, of "division—decrease" or "number divided—result smaller than the number." We may then devise or select such a method as will reduce this interference from the old habits to a minimum without weakening the old habits in their proper functioning.

Second, methods may be chosen from actual working experience, regardless of psychology, as a starting point. Thus it is believed that in the elementary school a class of fifteen pupils for one teacher gives better results than either a class of three or a class of thirty. Thus, also, it is believed that family life is better than institutional life in its effects upon character and enterprise. Thus, also, it is believed that in learning a foreign language the reading of simple discussions of simple topics is better than the translation of difficult literary masterpieces that treat subtle and complex topics. Even in such cases psychology may help by explaining why one method does succeed better and so leading the way to new insights regarding other questions not yet settled by experience.

Third, in all cases psychology, by its methods of measuring knowledge and skill, may suggest means to test and verify or refute the claims of any method. For instance, there has been a failure on the part of teachers to decide from their classroom experience whether it is better to teach the spelling of a pair of homonyms together or apart in time. But all that is required to decide the question for any given pair is for enough teachers to use both methods with enough different classes, keeping everything else except the method constant, and to measure the errors in spelling the words thereafter in the two cases. Psychology, which teaches us how to measure changes in human nature, teaches us how to decide just what the results of any method of teaching are.

So far I have outlined the contribution of psychology to education from the point of view of the latter's problems. I shall now outline very briefly the work being done by psychologists which is of special significance to the theory and practice of education and which may be expected to result in the largest and most frequent contributions.

It will, of course, be understood that directly or indirectly, soon or late, every advance in the sciences of human nature will contribute to our success in controlling human nature and changing it to the advantage of the common weal. If certain lines of work by psychologists are selected for mention here, it is only because they are the more obvious, more direct and, so far as can now be seen, greater aids to correct thinking about education.

The first line of work concerns the discovery and improvement of means of measurement of intellectual functions. (The study of means of measuring moral functions such as prudence, readiness to sacrifice an immediate for a later good, sympathy, and the like, has only barely begun.) Beginning with easy cases such as the discrimination of sensory differences, psychology has progressed to measuring memory and accuracy of movement, fatigue, improvement with practice, power of observing small details, the quantity, rapidity and usefulness of associations, and even to measuring so complex a function as general intelligence and so subtle a one as suggestibility.

The task of students of physical science in discovering the thermometer, galvanometer and spectroscope, and in defining the volt, calorie, erg, and ampère, is being attempted by psychologists in the sphere of human nature and behavior. How important such work is to education should be obvious. At least three-fourths of the problems of educational practice are problems whose solution depends upon the amount of some change in boys and girls. Of two methods, which gives the greater skill? Is the gain in general ability from a "disciplinary" study so great as to outweigh the loss in specially useful habits? Just how much more does a boy learn when thirty dollars a year is spent for his teaching than when only twenty dollars is spent? Units in which to measure the changes wrought by education are essential to an adequate science of education. And, though the students of education may establish these units by their own investigations, they can use and will need all the experience of psychologists in the search for similar units.

The second line of work concerns race, sex, age and individual differences in all the many elements of intellect and character and behavior.

How do the Igorottes, Ainus, Japanese and Esquimaux differ in their efficiency in learning to operate certain mechanical contrivances? Is the male sex more variable than the female in mental functions? What happens to keenness of sensory discrimination with age? How do individuals of the same race, sex and age differ in efficiency in perceiving small visual details or in accuracy in equaling a given length, or in the rapidity of movement? These are samples of many questions which psychologists have tried to answer by appropriate measurements. Such knowledge of the differences which exist amongst men for whatever reason is of service to the thinker about the particular differences which education aims to produce between a man and his former self.

These studies of individual differences or variability are being supplemented by studies of correlations. How far does superior vividness and fidelity in imagery from one sense go with inferiority in other sorts of imagery? To what extent is motor ability a symptom of intellectual ability? Does the quick learner soon forget? What are the mental types that result from the individual variations in mental functions and their inter-correlations? Psychology has already determined with more or less surety the answers to a number of such questions instructive in their bearing upon both scientific insight into human nature and practical arrangements for controlling it.

The extent to which the intellectual and moral differences found inhuman beings are consequences of their original nature and determined by the ancestry from which they spring, is a matter of fundamental importance for education. So also is the manner in which ancestral influence operates. Whether such qualities as leadership, the artistic temperament, originality, persistence, mathematical ability, or motor skill are represented in the germs each by one or a few unit characters so that they "Mendelize" in inheritance, or whether they are represented each by the cooperation of so many unit characters that the laws of their inheritance are those of "blending" is a question whose answer will decide in great measure the means to be employed for racial improvement. Obviously both the amount and [p. 10] the mode of operation of ancestral influence upon intellect and character are questions which psychology should and does investigate.

The results and methods of action of the many forces which operate in childhood and throughout life to change a man's original nature are subjects for study equally appropriate to the work of a psychologist, a sociologist or a student of education, but the last two will naturally avail themselves of all that the first achieves.

## Further Resources

### BOOKS

Glover, John A., and Royce R. Ronning, eds. *Historical Foundations of Educational Psychology.* New York: Plenum Press, 1987.

Sokal, Michael M. *Psychological Testing and American Society, 1890–1930.* New Brunswick, N.J.: Rutgers University Press, 1987.

Thorndike, Edward L. *Educational Psychology.* New York: Lemcke and Buechner, 1903.

———. *The Principles of Teaching Based on Psychology.* New York: A.G. Seiler, 1906.

———. *The Measurement of Intelligence.* New York: Teachers College, Columbia University, 1927.

### WEBSITES

"History of Influences in the Development of Intelligence Theory and Testing." Indiana University. Available online at http://www.indiana.edu/~intell/index.html; website home page http://www.indiana.edu (accessed February 22, 2003).

---

## Medical Education in the United States and Canada: A Report to the Carnegie Foundation for the Advancement of Teaching

Report

**By:** Henry S. Pritchett

**Date:** 1910

**Source:** Pritchett, Henry S. Introduction to *Medical Education in the United States and Canada: A Report to the Carnegie Foundation for the Advancement of Teaching.* Abraham Flexner, ed. Bulletin Number Four. New York: The Carnegie Foundation for the Advancement of Teaching, 1910, vii–viii, x–xi, xiii–xvi.

**About the Author:** Henry S. Pritchett (1857–1939) received a bachelor's degree in 1875 from the Collegiate Institute at Glasgow, Missouri. In 1895, he received a doctorate in astronomy from the University of Munich. Pritchett was a professor of astronomy at Washington University, superintendent of the United States Coast and Geodetic Survey, and president of M.I.T. He was president of the Carnegie Foundation for the Advancement of Teaching from 1905 to 1930. ■

## Introduction

Medical education in the United States prior to 1910 was woefully inadequate. Aspiring doctors might not receive any formal medical education at all, outside of an apprenticeship with a practicing physician. Of those who did receive training, many attended small, commercial medical schools lacking in equipment and quality instructors. Quacks and charlatans employing dubious methods were common. Significant advances in medical science meant that expensive equipment and facilities were necessary to conduct satisfactory medical education. Smaller schools with modest budgets were unable to meet these new standards, yet a lack of regulation allowed these "diploma mills" to continue to operate.

The American Medical Association (AMA) began preliminary efforts to study and correct some of the problems of medical education. The AMA Council on Medical Education was established in 1904. It produced a 1905 report indicating that, of the 155 medical schools in the United States and Canada, only five required students to have at least two years of college prior to admission. The Council also devised a classification ranking scheme by which medical schools could be evaluated.

In 1907, Dr. Arthur Dean Bevan, chairman of the AMA Council, asked Henry S. Pritchett, the Carnegie Foundation president, to consider the topic. Pritchett immediately saw the subjects as educational rather than medical—these were schools and should be evaluated from the standpoint of education. He was able to convince the Carnegie Foundation's executive committee and trustees of his view, and in 1908, the study was authorized. Pritchett intended the general public to be the audience for the report, rather than solely the medical profession.

Abraham Flexner was chosen to head the study. He visited every medical school in the United States and Canada and evaluated each on the following criteria: entrance requirements, faculty qualifications, size of budget, quality of facilities, and relationship with a teaching hospital. He found, in many cases, deplorable conditions,

Medical schools, like Harvard's, were the subject of a lengthy study in 1910. **THE LIBRARY OF CONGRESS.**

especially among smaller, for-profit schools. Some schools had no equipment or facilities beyond classrooms, outfitted with only blackboards and chairs. Many medical schools lacked qualified instructors and meaningful entrance requirements. The situation was ripe for change.

**Significance**

The publication of the report, and its subsequent treatment by the press, resulted in a public uproar. As awareness of the problems grew, so did the demands for change. Many schools closed, while others received complete overhauls. Schools that were small, for-profit, or that adhered to non-traditional (today referred to as "alternative") approaches were most likely to close. The result of these closures was the reduction in the number of physicians, as Flexner had recommended. There also followed an increase in admissions standards, and an overall improvement in the quality of medical education.

One significant effect of the report was the elimination of most medical schools serving female and minority students. Some critics have faulted the report for the resulting homogeneity among doctors. Critics have also questioned the qualifications of Flexner, a high-school principal with no medical training, and his high-speed approach that sometimes left only a single afternoon to visit

a school. Others have alleged undue influence by the AMA and a possible financial motivation for the recommendations—fewer doctors meant higher incomes for those already in the profession.

The general picture of medical education today reflects Flexner's recommendations. Medical schools are generally non-profit institutions, an integral part of a college or university, and associated with a teaching hospital. Medical schools adhere to accepted standards of admission and instruction.

**Primary Source**

*Medical Education in the United States and Canada: A Report to the Carnegie Foundation for the Advancement of Teaching* [excerpt]

**SYNOPSIS:** In this excerpt, from the report's preface, Henry S. Pritchett, president of the Carnegie Foundation for the Advancement of Teaching, presents the results of the study, together with his recommendations for improving medical education. Pritchett advocates for fewer, but higher quality, medical schools that operate within a university or college.

**Introduction**

Colleges and universities were discovered to have all sorts of relations to their professional schools of law, of medicine, and of theology. In some cases these relations were of the frailest texture, constituting practically only a license from the college by which a proprietary medical school or law school was enabled to live under its name. In other cases the medical school was incorporated into the college or university, but remained an *imperium in imperio,* the college assuming no responsibility for its standards or its support. In yet other cases the college or university assumed partial obligation of support, but no responsibility for the standards of the professional school, while in only a relatively small number of cases was the school of law or of medicine an integral part of the university, receiving from it university standards and adequate maintenance. For the past two decades there has been a marked tendency to set up some connection between universities and detached medical schools, but under the very loose construction just referred to.

Meanwhile the requirements of medical education have enormously increased. The fundamental sciences upon which medicine depends have been greatly extended. The laboratory has come to furnish alike to the physician and to the surgeon a new means for diagnosing and combating disease. The education of the medical practitioner under these changed conditions makes entirely different demands in respect to both preliminary and professional training. . . .

No effort has been spared to procure accurate and detailed information as to the facilities, resources, and methods of instruction of the medical schools. They have not only been separately visited, but every statement made in regard to each detail has been carefully checked with the data in possession of the American Medical Association, likewise obtained by personal inspection, and with the records of the Association of American Medical Colleges, so far as its membership extends. The details as stated go forth with the sanction of at least two, and frequently more, independent observers. . . .

The striking and significant facts which are here brought out are of enormous consequence not only to the medical practitioner, but to every citizen of the United States and Canada; for it is a singular fact that the organization of medical education in this country has hitherto been such as not only to commercialize the process of education itself, but also to obscure in the minds of the public any discrimination between the well trained physician and the physician who has had no adequate training whatsoever. As a rule, Americans, when they avail

themselves of the services of a physician, make only the slightest inquiry as to what his previous training and preparation have been. One of the problems of the future is to educate the public itself to appreciate the fact that very seldom, under existing conditions, does a patient receive the best aid which it is possible to give him in the present state of medicine, and that this is due mainly to the fact that a vast army of men is admitted to the practice of medicine who are untrained in sciences fundamental to the profession and quite without a sufficient experience with disease. A right education of public opinion is one of the problems of future medical education.

The significant facts revealed by this study are these:

(1) For twenty-five years past there has been an enormous over-production of uneducated and ill trained medical practitioners. This has been in absolute disregard of the public welfare and without any serious thought of the interests of the public. Taking the United States as a whole, physicians are four or five times as numerous in proportion to population as in older countries like Germany.

(2) Over-production of ill trained men is due in the main to the existence of a very large number of commercial schools, sustained in many cases by advertising methods through which a mass of unprepared youth is drawn out of industrial occupations into the study of medicine.

(3) Until recently the conduct of a medical school was a profitable business, for the methods of instruction were mainly didactic. As the need for laboratories has become more keenly felt, the expenses of an efficient medical school have been greatly increased. The inadequacy of many of these schools may be judged from the fact that nearly half of all our medical schools have incomes below $10,000, and these incomes determine the quality of instruction that they can and do offer.

Colleges and universities have in large measure failed in the past twenty-five years to appreciate the great advance in medical education and the increased cost of teaching it along modern lines. Many universities desirous of apparent educational completeness have annexed medical schools without making themselves responsible either for the standards of the professional schools or for their support.

(4) The existence of many of these unnecessary and inadequate medical schools has been defended by the argument that a poor medical school is justified in the interest of the poor boy. It is clear that

the poor boy has no right to go into any profession for which he is not willing to obtain adequate preparation; but the facts set forth in this report make it evident that this argument is insincere, and that the excuse which has hitherto been put forward in the name of the poor boy is in reality an argument in behalf of the poor medical school.

(5) A hospital under complete educational control is as necessary to a medical school as is a laboratory of chemistry or pathology. High grade teaching within a hospital introduces a most wholesome and beneficial influence into its routine. Trustees of hospitals, public and private, should therefore go to the limit of their authority in opening hospital wards to teaching, provided only that the universities secure sufficient funds on their side to employ as teachers men who are devoted to clinical science.

In view of these facts, progress for the future would seem to require a very much smaller number of medical schools, better equipped and better conducted than our schools now as a rule are; and the needs of the public would equally require that we have fewer physicians graduated each year, but that these should be better educated and better trained. With this idea accepted, it necessarily follows that the medical school will, if rightly conducted, articulate not only with the university, but with the general system of education. Just what form that articulation must take will vary in the immediate future in different parts of the country. Throughout the eastern and central states the movement under which the medical school articulates with the second year of the college has already gained such impetus that it can be regarded as practically accepted. In the southern states for the present it would seem that articulation with the four-year high school would be a reasonable starting-point for the future. In time the development of secondary education in the south and the growth of the colleges will make it possible for southern medical schools to accept the two-year college basis of preparation. With reasonable prophecy the time is not far distant when, with fair respect for the interests of the public and the need for physicians, the articulation of the medical school with the university may be the same throughout the entire country. For in the future the college or the university which accepts a medical school must make itself responsible for university standards in the medical school and for adequate support for medical education. The day has gone by when any university can retain the respect of educated men, or when it can fulfil its duty to education, by retain-

ing a low grade professional school for the sake of its own institutional completeness. . . .

The development which is here suggested for medical education is conditioned largely upon three factors: first, upon the creation of a public opinion which shall discriminate between the ill trained and the rightly trained physician, and which will also insist upon the enactment of such laws as will require all practitioners of medicine, whether they belong to one sect or another, to ground themselves in the fundamentals upon which medical science rests; secondly, upon the universities and their attitude towards medical standards and medical support; finally, upon the attitude of the members of the medical profession towards the standards of their own practice and upon their sense of honor with respect to their own profession.

These last two factors are moral rather than educational. They call for an educational patriotism on the part of the institutions of learning and a medical patriotism on the part of the physician.

By educational patriotism I mean this: a university has a mission greater than the formation of a large student body or the attainment of institutional completeness, namely, the duty of loyalty to the standards of common honesty, of intellectual sincerity, of scientific accuracy. A university with educational patriotism will not take up the work of medical education unless it can discharge its duty by it; or if, in the days of ignorance once winked at, a university became entangled in a medical school alliance, it will frankly and courageously deal with a situation which is no longer tenable. It will either demand of its medical school university ideals and give it university support, or else it will drop the effort to do what it can only do badly.

By professional patriotism amongst medical men I mean that sort of regard for the honor of the profession and that sense of responsibility for its efficiency which will enable a member of that profession to rise above the consideration of personal or of professional gain. As Bacon truly wrote, "Every man owes a duty to his profession," and in no profession is this obligation more clear than in that of the modern physician. Perhaps in no other of the great professions does one find greater discrepancies between the ideals of those who represent it. No members of the social order are more self-sacrificing than the true physicians and surgeons, and of this fine group none deserve so much of society as those who have taken upon their shoulders the burden of medical education. On the other hand, the profession has been diluted by the presence of a great number of men who have come from weak schools with low ideals both of education and of professional honor. If the medical education of our country is in the immediate future to go upon a plane of efficiency and of credit, those who represent the higher ideals of the medical profession must make a stand for that form of medical education which is calculated to advance the true interests of the whole people and to better the ideals of medicine itself. . . .

In the preparation of this report the Foundation has kept steadily in view the interests of two classes, which in the over-multiplication of medical schools have usually been forgotten—first, the youths who are to study medicine and to become the future practitioners, and, secondly, the general public, which is to live and die under their ministrations.

No one can become familiar with this situation without acquiring a hearty sympathy for the American youth who, too often the prey of commercial advertising methods, is steered into the practice of medicine with almost no opportunity to learn the difference between an efficient medical school and a hopelessly inadequate one. A clerk who is receiving $50 a month in the country store gets an alluring brochure which paints the life of the physician as an easy road to wealth. He has no realization of the difference between medicine as a profession and medicine as a business, nor as a rule has he any adviser at hand to show him that the first requisite for the modern practitioner of medicine is a good general education. Such a boy falls an easy victim to the commercial medical school, whether operating under the name of a university or college, or alone.

The interests of the general public have been so generally lost sight of in this matter that the public has in large measure forgot that it has any interests to protect. And yet in no other way does education more closely touch the individual than in the quality of medical training which the institutions of the country provide. Not only the personal well-being of each citizen, but national, state, and municipal sanitation rests upon the quality of the training which the medical graduate has received. The interest of the public is to have well trained practitioners in sufficient number for the needs of society. The source whence these practitioners are to come is of far less consequence. . . .

While the aim of the Foundation has throughout been constructive, its attitude towards the difficul-

ties and problems of the situation is distinctly sympathetic. The report indeed turns the light upon conditions which, instead of being fruitful and inspiring, are in many instances commonplace, in other places bad, and in still others, scandalous. It is nevertheless true that no one set of men or no one school of medicine is responsible for what still remains in the form of commercial medical education. Our hope is that this report will make plain once for all that the day of the commercial medical school has passed. It will be observed that, except for a brief historical introduction, intended to show how present conditions have come about, no account is given of the past of any institution. The situation is described as it exists today in the hope that out of it, quite regardless of the past, a new order may be speedily developed. There is no need now of recriminations over what has been, or of apologies by way of defending a régime practically obsolete. Let us address ourselves resolutely to the task of reconstructing the American medical school on the lines of the highest modern ideals of efficiency and in accordance with the finest conceptions of public service.

## Further Resources

### BOOKS

Barzansky, Barbara, and Norman Gevitz. *Beyond Flexner: Medical Education in the Twentieth Century.* New York: Press, 1992.

Bonner, Thomas Neville. *Iconoclast: Abraham Flexner and a Life in Learning.* Baltimore, Md.: Johns Hopkins University Press, 2002.

Flexner, Abraham. *Henry S. Pritchett: A Biography.* New York: Columbia University Press, 1943.

———. *I Remember: The Autobiography of Abraham Flexner.* New York: Simon and Schuster, 1940.

Vevier, Charles, ed. *Flexner: 75 Years Later: A Current Commentary on Medical Education.* Lanham, Md.: University Press of America, 1987.

Wheatley, Steven C. *The Politics of Philanthropy: Abraham Flexner and Medical Education.* Madison: University of Wisconsin Press, 1988.

### PERIODICALS

Ober, K. Patrick. "The Pre-Flexnerian Reports: Mark Twain's Criticism of Medicine in the United States." *Annals of Internal Medicine* 126, January 1997, 157–163.

### WEBSITES

"The Carnegie Foundation for the Advancement of Teaching." Available online at http://www.carnegiefoundation.org/index .htm; website home page http://www.carnegiefoundation .org (accessed March 14, 2003).

# "An Address Delivered Before the National Colored Teachers' Association"

Speech

**By:** Booker T. Washington

**Date:** 1911

**Source:** Washington, Booker T. An Address Delivered Before the National Colored Teachers' Association, 1911. Reprinted in Davidson, Washington E., ed. *Selected Speeches of Booker T. Washington.* Garden City, N.Y.: Doubleday, Doran, 1932, 200–207.

**About the Author:** Booker Taliafero Washington (1856–1915) was born into slavery and worked his way through the Hampton Institute as the school's janitor. Washington taught at the Hampton Institute, and then founded the Tuskegee Institute in Alabama in 1881, which would become one of the foremost schools for African Americans. He was a prominent African American leader, speaker, and author. His autobiography, *Up From Slavery,* was influential worldwide. ∎

## Introduction

After the Civil War (1861–1865) and the end of slavery, the period of reconstruction in the South ended in disappointment for those working toward full rights for African Americans. Jim Crow Laws and the 1896 Supreme Court decision in *Plessy v. Ferguson* created a legal basis for segregation between blacks and whites. The rise of the Ku Klux Klan and other violent, white supremacist groups used non-legal means to keep African Americans "in their place."

It was in this context, near the end of the nineteenth century, that many African American leaders looked to education to improve the circumstances of African Americans and obtain full citizenship rights. Yet education in the South had always lagged behind the rest of the nation. While education for most Southern whites was inadequate, African Americans fared much worse. The physical and economic devastation of the South, after the Civil War, also served to exacerbate the situation.

There was much consensus that among African American leaders and their advocates, quality educational opportunities for African Americans were needed; but what type of education, and leading toward which goals? Differences in philosophy emerged.

The predominant school of thought, led by Booker T. Washington, held that African Americans should temporarily accommodate themselves to the current context of discrimination and prejudice. African Americans, according to Washington, should focus on self-help—improving economically, morally, and culturally. Legal rights, and acceptance within the larger society, naturally would follow. Washington's approach to education for African Americans reflected this philosophy. He advocated that a realistic next step for the majority of African Americans was learning a manual trade, and becoming economically self-sufficient.

Other African American leaders, such as W.E.B. Du Bois, advocated that African Americans engage in an active struggle for civil rights, political power, and acceptance within the larger society. Du Bois believed that improvement for African Americans as a group lay in college education for the "talented tenth," who would then lead their people out of oppression.

## Significance

Booker T. Washington's speech illustrates the aspects of his political and educational philosophy that appealed to whites at the time. This resulted in the success of the Tuskegee Institute and his other political and social agendas. The image Washington offered—of the hard-working, thrifty, black carpenter of high moral character willing to work within the bounds of segregation and second-class citizenship—was attractive to many wealthy whites in the North and the South. They generously funded Washington's projects. On the other hand, Du Bois, who worked toward the development of a class of African American college graduates able and willing to agitate for their civil rights, often received a chilly response and little funding from white philanthropists.

The speech also illustrates points of commonality between the two men. While this contrast in their views had an enormous impact on the flow of funds and the resulting development of education for African Americans for quite some time, the differences between Washington and Du Bois can be seen as a matter of emphasis and focus. Washington, himself a college graduate and member of Du Bois's "talented tenth," points out that he is not opposed to college education for African Americans. But the emphasis, Washington insists, must be on the development of the ordinary person. Du Bois, who was not against all trades education for African Americans, believed that the development of the majority of African Americans depended on the college-educated African American leader. Both wanted a final outcome of full political, economic, and social rights for African Americans.

Great strides have been made in educational opportunities and civil rights for African Americans, within the context of continuing prejudice and discrimination. Washington is often viewed today, perhaps unfairly, as an "Uncle Tom" currying favor with whites, while advocating an inferior position for his own people. Yet many, then and now, fail to recognize that Washington had as his eventual goal complete equality of whites and African Americans.

## Primary Source

"An Address Delivered Before the National Colored Teachers' Association" [excerpt]

**SYNOPSIS:** In this speech, Washington discusses his belief that the focus of education for African Americans should be practical and useful instruction leading to the mastery of a trade and economic self-sufficiency. Teachers should instill in students the values of hard work, reliability, and thrift; a respect for the dignity of labor with the hands; a feeling of racial pride and respect for other races; and a knowledge of the opportunities available to them.

*Mr. President, Ladies and Gentlemen:*

I congratulate this association upon the progress it has made during the few years of its existence. I congratulate especially your president, Mr. W. T. B. Williams, and your secretary, Mr. J. R. E. Lee. This association is one of the most potent agencies at work for the elevation of the black citizens of America. I am glad that this association is having its annual meeting in the city of St. Louis. With perhaps one exception, St. Louis has treated the Negro race more generously in providing school accommodations, in the way of buildings, good school terms, and intelligent teachers than is true of any other city in the United States. What I say of the city of St. Louis I can add with equal emphasis of the state of Missouri. The state of Missouri has not only been generous in supporting a good school system for our people in town and country, but it has been equally as generous in supporting the Lincoln Institute at Jefferson City. In return for this generosity I am sure that the colored people of St. Louis and of the state of Missouri feel resting upon them an especial obligation to make themselves good, useful, and law-abiding citizens so that they may not become a burden upon the city or upon the state or constitute an element of danger or irritation.

As to the kinds of education, I believe in all kinds of education—college, university, and industrial education—but I am most interested in industrial, combined with public school education for the great masses of our people; that is our salvation. There is a place, an important one, in our life for the college man, the university man, as well as the man with a trade or with skill in his fingers. To indicate what I think of college education, I would add that the Tuskegee Institute employs more colored graduates of colleges than any single institution in the world.

What is the function of education in our time? In past years it used to be considered that educa-

Booker T. Washington often spoke on the importance of education for African Americans. **THE LIBRARY OF CONGRESS.**

tion was for the exceptional man, was for the classes rather than for the masses. It used to be considered that education was only to be used in connection with the extraordinary things of life rather than the ordinary things of life. All that is changing and will change in the future. The education of the future is to be that which will apply itself to the ordinary functions and activities of life, that which will link itself closely to every duty and responsibility of life. This means that education is to enter the kitchen, the dining room, the bed chamber, is to go upon the farm, into the garden, into the shop, and into every activity of life. This also means that the teacher of our race who would do his duty is to not content himself with being a mere salary-drawer but must consider it one of his highest duties to see that what is taught in the schoolroom is linked closely with the life of our people, in the home and in their work.

One of the functions of education is to help our race everywhere to become home owners, to own a little piece of soil somewhere either in town or city. This means that the colored teacher, more perhaps than any other class of teachers, should get among the people, get among the ordinary, hard-working people, study their needs, study their conditions, and enter into systematic and close cooperation with them.

Another important function of education is to see that every boy and girl, no matter what may be his or her condition in life, no matter what may be his or her ambitions, is taught the dignity of labor, is taught that all labor, either with the head or with the hand, is equally honorable. There is no hope for any race or for any group of people until they learn the fundamental lesson that labor with the hands is dignified, is something to be sought after, and something not to be shunned.

Another function of education, especially in a city like St. Louis, should be to get rid as fast as possible of that large loafing and idle element of our race who exhibit themselves on the corners of the streets, around bar-rooms and other places of disrepute. When racial outbreaks take place between white people and black people, in the majority of cases these difficulties can be traced to the idle, loafing, drinking, and gambling classes of both white and colored people. And then I sometimes fear that in many of our cities there is too large a class of our people who exist without steady, reliable employment, who float around from one community to another without any abiding place, who live upon the labor of somebody else and especially upon the labor of hardworking women. I repeat that it should be the function of education in a city like St. Louis to see to it that these loafers are reached and reformed, are gotten rid of.

For our race in its present condition, I believe in trade education as distinguished from mere manual training. Manual training is good so far as it goes in giving the principles of mechanics, but a hungry race cannot live upon "principles." Our people in their present condition need to be taught something that is definite in the way of a trade, something that will enable them to improve their economic condition. It is a dangerous thing in the case of any race of people, and it is especially dangerous in the condition of any race in the same relative stage of civilization which the masses of colored people find themselves in the United States today, to increase the wants of a race through mere book education without increasing the ability of that race to supply these increased wants along the lines in which they can find employment. There is no justification for my coming here to speak unless I am perfectly frank and straightforward in my remarks. In many parts of the country I hear complaints to the effect that Negro la-

bor is not reliable, that the employer cannot depend upon the black workman for steady, constant work; that if the laborer is paid off on Saturday night there is no certainty as to when he will return to his place of employment. If in any degree this charge has a basis of truth in the community where any of you work as teachers, you should see to it that you make your influence felt in changing the reputation of our race. Everywhere we must see to it that the black race becomes just as reliable, just as progressive, just as intelligent in all matters of labor as is true of any other race. If we do not make progress in this direction, the time will soon come when in many parts of this country black labor will be replaced by white labor from European countries.

Another function of education should be to see to it that everywhere our race not only gets a proper idea of the dignity of labor, of proper methods of labor, but equally important, even more important, that they learn to save that which they earn. But many of our young people "scatter their earnings to the wind" as fast as the money comes into their hands. As teachers we should use our influence among the masses, and especially the present generation of young men and young women, in seeing to it that they form the habit of thrift, the habit of saving. As fast as possible we should see to it that every individual in the community whom we can influence has a bank account: a bank account is a great maker of character; a bank account is a great maker of useful citizens; a bank account teaches the lesson of saving today that we may have tomorrow; teaches the lesson of doing without today that we may possess tomorrow. If our present generation of young people are taught to save, are taught to invest their money in land or houses, are taught to put their money in the bank the time will not be long before we shall be counted among the thrifty races of the earth. I have little patience with any man, white or black, with education, who goes through the country whining and crying because nobody will give him a job of work. A man with education should be able to create a job for himself, but in doing so he may have to begin at the very bottom. But we should not be ashamed to perform the most ordinary things in order that we may lay a foundation for future growth and usefulness.

Another function of education in connection with our race should be to teach pride of race; to teach the Negro boy and the Negro girl that he or she should be just as proud of being a Negro as a German, as an Irishman, and as a Frenchman are proud of being members of their races. I have no patience with the man or woman of our race who is continually seeking to get away from the race; is continually seeking to belong to another race. There are some colored people, I am sorry to say, who would rather be classed as third-rate white people than to be classed as first-rate colored people. Personally, if you will excuse the reference, I am just as proud of being a Negro as any white man can be proud of being a member of the white race.

Another function of education should be to see that it is kept in the minds of the youths of our race that there are two races in this country and that each has a duty, that each has a responsibility, to the other; that in the case of our race no boy or girl grows up with a feeling of hatred or bitterness toward any other race. In the last analysis the race that hates will grow weaker, while the race that loves will grow stronger. No one race can harm another race, can inflict injustice upon another race, can strive to keep down another race without that race itself being permanently injured in all the fundamental virtues of life.

Do not misunderstand me: I do not fail for one moment to understand our present conditions. I am not deceived; I do not overlook the wrongs that often perplex and embarrass us in this country. I do not overlook injustice. I condemn with all the strength of my nature the barbarous habit of lynching a human being, whether black or white, without legal trial. I condemn any practice in any state that results in not enforcing the law with a certainty and justice, regardless of race or color.

Another function of education should be to emphasize in the minds and hearts of our youths the fact that in the United States we have great opportunities and tremendous opportunities. The millions of unoccupied and unused lands in the South are open to the black man as freely as to any white man; while the color line may be drawn in certain directions, nature draws no color line; an acre of land in the South will yield her riches as quickly to the touch of the blackest hand as to the touch of the whitest hand in America.

As one example of the progress our race has already made within forty-eight years in one of the states, I find that according to the statistics furnished by the State Comptroller of Georgia, the Negro last year added 71,000 acres to his holdings in Georgia. He added $4,000,000 to the taxable value of his property. The Negroes of Georgia own today 1,607,000 acres of land valued at $10,000,000. Including land, furniture, tools, stock, and what not, the Negroes of Georgia are paying taxes today upon $32,000,000 worth of property.

There is but one salvation for our country, and that is obedience to law, whether this law relates to human life, to property, or to our rights as citizens. For us, however, in our present condition, I believe that our greatest hope for salvation and uplift is for us to turn our attention mainly in the direction of progressive, constructive work. Let construction be our motto in every department of our lives North and South. Pursuing this policy, we will convince the world that we are worthy of the best treatment.

We should see to it too that we not only emphasize in our work as teachers the opportunities that are before our race, but should also emphasize the fact that we ought to become a hopeful, encouraged race. There is no hope for any man or woman, whatever his color, who is pessimistic; who is continually whining and crying about his condition. There is hope for any race of people, however handicapped by difficulties, that makes up its mind that it will succeed, that it will make success the stepping stone to a life of success and usefulness.

## Further Resources

### BOOKS

Harlan, Louis R. *Booker T. Washington: The Making of a Black Leader, 1856–1901.* New York: Oxford University Press, 1972.

———. *Booker T. Washington: The Wizard of Tuskegee, 1901–1915.* New York: Oxford University Press, 1983.

———. *Booker T. Washington in Perspective: Essays of Louis R. Harlan.* Raymond W. Smock, ed. Jackson: University Press of Mississippi, 1988.

Harris, Thomas E. *Analysis of the Clash Over the Issues Between Booker T. Washington and W.E.B. Du Bois.* New York: Garland Publications, 1993.

Moore, Jacqueline M. *Booker T. Washington, W.E.B. Du Bois, and the Struggle for Racial Uplift.* Wilmington, Del.: Scholarly Resources, 2003.

Verney, Kevern. *The Art of the Possible: Booker T. Washington and Black Leadership in the United States, 1881–1925.* New York: Routledge, 2001.

Washington, Booker T. *Up From Slavery: An Autobiography.* New York: Doubleday Page, 1901.

Wintz, Cary D. *African American Political Thought, 1890–1930: Washington, Du Bois, Garvey, and Randolph.* Armonk, N.Y.: M.E. Sharpe, 1996.

### WEBSITES

"African American Education." Available online at http://www.theatlantic.com/unbound/flashbks/blacked/aaedintr.htm; website home page http://www.theatlantic.com (accessed March 10, 2003).

"Tuskegee University." Available online at http://www.tusk.edu/ (accessed March 13, 2003).

"The Two Nations of Black America." Available online at http://www.pbs.org/wgbh/pages/frontline/shows/race/etc/ro ad.html; website home page http://pbs.org (accessed March 10, 2003).

**AUDIO AND VISUAL MEDIA**

*Black Paths of Leadership.* Directed by Pam Hughes. Churchill Films. Videocassette, 1984.

*Booker T. Washington: The Life and Legacy.* Pathways to Greatness Series. Directed by William Greaves. Academic Industries Video Division. Videocassette, 1993.

# A New Conscience and an Ancient Evil

Nonfiction work

**By:** Jane Addams

**Date:** 1912

**Source:** Addams, Jane. *A New Conscience and an Ancient Evil.* New York: Macmillan, 1912. Reprinted in Elshtain, Jean Bethke, ed. *The Jane Addams Reader.* New York: Basic Books, 2002, 177–80.

**About the Author:** Jane Addams (1860–1935), the first American woman to receive the Nobel Peace Prize in 1931, was champion of social justice issues such as women's rights, the passage of child labor laws, education for immigrants, and peace. She was a speaker, author, activist, and progressive educator. In 1889, she founded the famous Hull House, a settlement house serving the urban poor in Chicago with a wide variety of programs. ∎

## Introduction

Beginning in the 1870s, and continuing through World War I (1914–1918), the progressive education movement sought to develop educational innovations in methods and curriculum. These were aimed at social reform and relieving some of the problems of the urban poor in an industrial society. Reacting against the rigidly academic, classical, and college-preparatory schooling of the nineteenth century, progressives advocated a curriculum that would be relevant and meaningful to the lives of the majority of students. The emphasis was on socialization, education of the whole child, and working from the interests of individual students. Progressives were interested in developing a science of education, and applying it to the problems of everyday schooling. This emphasis on a practical, relevant curriculum and social reform led to increasing interest in sex hygiene instruction.

In addition, changing social mores and urbanization resulted in high instances of prostitution, venereal disease, premarital sex, and children born out of wedlock.

In response to these conditions, a social hygiene movement arose in the 1900s, including such organizations as the American Federation for Sex Hygiene. The goal was promoting education for the working class on venereal diseases and sex hygiene instruction in the schools. By 1912, 138 schools and colleges taught sex hygiene.

Superintendent of the Chicago Public Schools, Ella Flagg Young, introduced the first city-wide, public school sex education program in 1913. A student of progressive educator and philosopher, John Dewey, Young was committed to a progressive approach. Students should learn about sex, reproduction, and the spread of venereal disease from the point of view of science. A student in possession of accurate facts will make better decisions. Her plan proposed a series of lectures by doctors for high school students covering anatomy, reproduction, the sex drive, and venereal disease prevention. Objections from parents and the Catholic Church led to a change in the name of the program from "sex hygiene education" to "personal purity." Opposition continued and the lectures lasted only one school year.

## Significance

Through the active promotion of sex hygiene programs by progressive educators such as Jane Addams and Ella Flagg Young, sex education gradually became a standard part of the curriculum in American public schools. Along with instruction in health, nutrition, cleanliness, and disease prevention, sex education was a part of the movement to broaden the scope of the curriculum beyond academics, and to include areas directly beneficial to the well being of students.

Jane Addams makes an argument, typical of progressive educators of the day, that schools can and should be agents of social reform. She shares with other progressive educators a faith in the possibility of social progress. In this case, "commercialized vice" (prostitution), though a "world-old evil," can be alleviated by the efforts of educators working with students, as well as their parents and communities.

The debate over whether and how sex education should be taught in the schools continues today. Parents sometimes object to schools taking on this task, feeling that it belongs to the family. As in 1913, instruction on the prevention of venereal disease is controversial. Some want "abstinence only" curricula, while others argue that disease and pregnancy prevention, especially in the age of AIDS, is the only realistic course of action. While most public schools today offer some type of sex education, an issue that is intimately connected with deeply-held values and religious beliefs—especially in the context of the high-stakes atmosphere created by the spread of AIDS— is likely to be controversial for some time.

## Primary Source

*A New Conscience and an Ancient Evil* [excerpt]

**SYNOPSIS:** In this excerpt from her book, *A New Conscience and an Ancient Evil*, Jane Addams argues that parents' and educators' unwillingness to confront the difficult topic of sex is a contributing factor to problems including prostitution and promiscuity. She advocates programs of sex hygiene instruction in the schools.

### "Moral Education and Legal Protection of Children"

No great wrong has ever arisen more clearly to the social consciousness of a generation than has that of commercialized vice in the consciousness of ours, and that we are so slow to act is simply another evidence that human nature has a curious power of callous indifference towards evils which have been so entrenched that they seem part of that which has always been. Educators of course share this attitude; at moments they seem to intensify it, although at last an educational movement in the direction of sex hygiene is beginning in the schools and colleges. Primary schools strive to satisfy the child's first questionings regarding the beginnings of human life and approach the subject through simple biological instruction which at least places this knowledge on a par with other natural acts. Such teaching is an enormous advance for the children whose curiosity would otherwise have been satisfied from poisonous sources and who would have learned of simple physiological matters from such secret undercurrents of corrupt knowledge as to have forever perverted their minds. Yet this first direct step towards an adequate educational approach to this subject has been surprisingly difficult owing to the self-consciousness of grown-up people; for while the children receive the teaching quite simply, their parents often take alarm. Doubtless cooperation with parents will be necessary before the subject can fall into its proper place in the schools. In Chicago, the largest women's club in the city has established normal courses in sex hygiene attended both by teachers and mothers, the National and State Federations of Women's Clubs are gradually preparing thousands of women throughout America for fuller co-operation with the schools in this difficult matter. In this, as in so many other educational movements, Germany has led the way. Two publications are issued monthly in Berlin, which promote not only more effective legislation but more adequate instruction in the schools on this basic subject. These journals are supported by men and women anxious for light for the sake of their children. Some of them were first stirred to ac-

Jane Addams was a strong proponent of sex education. **THE LIBRARY OF CONGRESS.**

tion by Wedekind's powerful drama "The Awakening of Spring," which, with Teutonic grimness, thrusts over the footlights the lesson that death and degradation may be the fate of a group of gifted schoolchildren, because of the cowardly reticence of their parents.

A year ago the Bishop of London gathered together a number of influential people and laid before them his convictions that the root of the social evil lay in so-called "parental modesty," and that in the quickening of the parental conscience lay the hope for the "lifting up of England's moral tone which has for so long been the despair of England's foremost men."

In America the eighth year-book of the National Society for the Scientific Study of Education treats of this important subject with great ability, massing the agencies and methods in impressive array. Many other educational journals and organized societies could be cited as expressing a new conscience in regard to this world-old evil. The expert educational opinion which they represent is practically agreed that for older children the instruction should not be confined to biology and hygiene, but may come quite naturally in history and literature, which record and portray the havoc wrought by the sexual instinct when uncontrolled, and also show that, when directed and spiritualized, it has become an inspiration to the loftiest devotions and sacrifices. The youth thus taught sees this primal instinct not only as an essential to the continuance of the race, but also, when it is transmuted to the highest ends, as a fundamental factor in social progress. The entire subject is broadened out in his mind as he learns that his own struggle is a common experience. He is able to make his own interpretations and to combat the crude inferences of his patronizing companions. After all, no young person will be able to control his impulses and to save himself from the grosser temptations, unless he has been put under the sway of nobler influences. Perhaps we have yet to learn that the inhibitions of character as well as its reinforcements come most readily through idealistic motives.

Certainly all the great religions of the world have recognized youth's need of spiritual help during the trying years of adolescence. The ceremonies of the earliest religions deal with this instinct almost to the exclusion of others, and all later religions attempt to provide the youth with shadowy weapons for the struggle which lies ahead of him, for the wise men in every age have known that only the power of the spirit can overcome the lusts of the flesh. In spite of this educational advance, courses of study in many public and private schools are still prepared exactly as if educators had never known that at fifteen or sixteen years of age, the will power being still weak, the bodily desires are keen and insistent. The head master of Eton, Mr. Lyttleton, who has given much thought to this gap in the education of youth says, "The certain result of leaving an enormous majority of boys unguided and uninstructed in a matter where their strongest passions are concerned, is that they grow up to judge of all questions connected with it, from a purely selfish point of view." He contends that this selfishness is due to the fact that any single suggestion or hint which boys receive on the subject comes from other boys or young men who are under the same potent influences of ignorance, curiosity and the claims of self. No wholesome counter-balance of knowledge is given, no attempt is made to invest the subject with dignity or to place it in relation to the welfare of others and to universal law. Mr. Lyttleton contends that this alone can explain the peculiarly brutal attitude towards "outcast" women which is a sustained cruelty to be discerned in no other relation of English life. To quote him again: "But when the victims of man's cruelty are not birds or beasts but our own country-women, doomed by

the hundred thousand to a life of unutterable shame and hopeless misery, then and then only the general average tone of young men becomes hard and brutally callous or frivolous with a kind of coarse frivolity not exhibited in relation to any other form of human suffering." At the present moment thousands of young people in our great cities possess no other knowledge of this grave social evil which may at any moment become a dangerous personal menace, save what is imparted to them in this brutal flippant spirit. It has been said that the child growing up in the midst of civilization receives from its parents and teachers something of the accumulated experience of the world on all other subjects save upon that of sex. On this one subject alone each generation learns little from its predecessors.

## Further Resources

### BOOKS

Addams, Jane. *The Spirit of Youth and the City Streets.* New York: Macmillan, 1912.

———. *Jane Addams on Education.* Ellen Condliffe Lagemann, ed. New York: Teachers College Press, 1985.

Campbell, Patricia J. *Sex Education Books for Young Adults, 1892–1979.* New York: R.R. Bowker, 1979.

Moran, Jeffrey P. *Teaching Sex: The Shaping of Adolescence in the 20th Century.* Cambridge, Mass.: Harvard University Press, 2000.

Pivar, David J. *Purity and Hygiene: Women, Prostitution, and the "American Plan," 1900–1930.* Westport, Conn.: Greenwood Press, 2002.

### PERIODICALS

Moran, Jeffrey P. "'Modernism Gone Mad:' Sex Education Comes to Chicago, 1913." *Journal of American History* 83, no. 2, September, 1996, 481–513.

### WEBSITES

"Jane Addams." Available online at http://nlu.nl.edu/ace/Resources/Addams.html; website home page http://nlu.nl.edu (accessed March 13, 2003).

# *The Montessori Method*
## Manual

**By:** Maria Montessori

**Date:** 1912

**Source:** Montessori, Maria. *The Montessori Method.* Anne E. George, trans. New York: Frederick A. Stokes, 1912, 169–175.

**About the Author:** Maria Montessori (1870–1952) was the first woman physician in Italy. She later studied psychology and philosophy and taught anthropology at the University of Rome. She was well known in Europe as a speaker, advocating for women's and children's rights, before she founded, in 1905, the Casa dei Bambini, or "Children's House." There she developed her method of education. She lectured and conducted teacher-training courses in the United States, India, Spain, England and the Netherlands. ∎

## Introduction

Maria Montessori began her career as a pediatrician and, in the course of treating patients, she noticed how children learn. In 1901, Montessori was appointed director of an asylum in Rome for children classified as "deficient and insane." Shocked by the poor treatment and lack of stimulation afforded the patients, she began a program of reform and education based on her meticulous study of the children and their behavior. The children made remarkable progress, and the results of her work received much attention. Montessori then founded, in 1905, her famous Casa dei Bambini ("Children's House"). It was originally intended as a daycare center for pre-school age children of the working class, located in one of the poorest sections of Rome.

Influenced by the work of two French physicians, Jean Itard and Edouard Séguin, Montessori took a scientific approach to education. She closely observed the behavior of the children, developed hypotheses, and tested them. She often stated, "I studied my children, and they taught me how to teach them." Her observations led her to conclude that children actually teach themselves by interacting with their environment. Education is the natural unfolding of development; the teacher's job is not to interfere with this process, but to provide an environment that facilitates natural learning.

Montessori was influenced by Friedrich Froebel, the innovator of kindergarten, in her belief that all learning begins with sense experiences. She found that the children responded enthusiastically to various perceptual training devices, taking the form of games and puzzles, and learning everyday skills such as buttoning and lacing clothing and serving food. Children worked independently for long periods of time, were highly motivated, and easily learned skills such as reading, writing, and math on their own before the age of five.

Based on her observations and the results of her experimental approach, Montessori came to believe that all children have great potential waiting to be unleashed if given the right environment. If children are allowed almost total freedom within a properly structured environment, they will learn naturally.

## Significance

Montessori belongs to the larger "Child Study" movement of the early twentieth century, that emphasized the scientific study of the child to determine the natural processes of learning. Rather than trying to fit the child

Maria Montessori is the founder of the Montessori Method of teaching. **AP/WIDE WORLD PHOTOS. REPRODUCED BY PERMISSION.**

to the school, the school should be structured to fit the child. This approach represented a radical break from the philosophy of the nineteenth century that failure was the fault of the child. Montessori, along with other advocates of child study and the child-centered school, believed that educators were to blame if the child did not succeed. It is the educator's responsibility, in this view, to find out under what conditions the child learns, and then to provide those conditions.

The work and teaching of Maria Montessori had a great impact on a number of prominent educators, psychologists, and child development experts, including Jean Piaget, Erik Erikson, and Alfred Adler. Some have noted that many of Montessori's ideas have been corroborated through modern child development research, and she has been credited with modern approaches, such as the "open classroom."

Montessori's method has been criticized as too structured, or tending to push children into early academic activity. Others counter that the method was based on

Montessori's observations of children's natural learning patterns—Montessori schools do not "push" children, rather traditional schools stand in the way of their natural development.

Today, interest in the philosophy and methods of Maria Montessori is strong. Montessori schools operate in many countries worldwide. Organizations such as Montessori Internationale, the American Montessori Society, and the American Montessori Teachers Association, conduct research, offer training, and disseminate information on the Montessori method.

## Primary Source

*The Montessori Method* [excerpt]

**SYNOPSIS:** Maria Montessori discusses the didactic ("for teaching") materials she developed: a series of puzzles and games by which children gain "sense education." She notes that for "normal" children, the materials lead to auto-education (self-education). Children have a strong desire to work with the materials, without teacher interference. And when a mistake is made, the student recognizes it and immediately takes steps to correct the mistake.

In a pedagogical method which is experimental the education of the senses must undoubtedly assume the greatest importance. Experimental psychology also takes note of movements by means of sense measurements.

Pedagogy, however, although it may profit by psychometry is not designed to *measure* the sensations, but *educate* the senses. This is a point easily understood, yet one which is often confused. While the proceedings of esthesiometry are not to any great extent applicable to little children, the *education* of the *senses* is entirely possible.

We do not start from the conclusions of experimental psychology. That is, it is not the knowledge of the average sense conditions according to the age of the child which leads us to determine the educational applications we shall make. We start essentially from a method, and it is probable that psychology will be able to draw its conclusions from pedagogy so understood, and not *vice versa*.

The method used by me is that of making a pedagogical experiment with a didactic object and awaiting the spontaneous reaction of the child. This is a method in every way analogous to that of experimental psychology.

■ ■ ■

I believe, however, that I have arrived at a selection of objects (which I do not here wish to speak of in the technical language of psychology as stimuli) representing the minimum necessary to a practical sense education.

These objects constitute the didactic system (or set of didactic materials) used by me. They are manufactured by the House of Labour of the Humanitarian Society at Milan.

A description of the objects will be given as the educational scope of each is explained. Here I shall limit myself to the setting forth of a few general considerations.

First. The difference in the reaction between deficient and normal children, in the presentation of didactic material made up of graded stimuli. This difference is plainly seen from the fact that the same didactic material used with deficients makes education possible, while with normal children it provokes auto-education.

This fact is one of the most interesting I have met with in all my experience, and it inspired and rendered possible the method of observation and liberty.

Let us suppose that we use our first object,—a block in which solid geometric forms are set. Into corresponding holes in the block are set ten little wooden cylinders, the bases diminishing gradually about ten millimetres. The game consists in taking the cylinders out of their places, putting them on the table, mixing them, and then putting each one back in its own place. The aim is to educate the eye to the differential perception of dimensions.

With the deficient child, it would be necessary to begin with exercises in which the stimuli were much more strongly contrasted, and to arrive at this exercise only after many others had preceded it.

With normal children, this is, on the other hand, the first object which we may present, and out of all the didactic material this is the game preferred by the very little children of two and a half and three years. Once we arrived at this exercise with a deficient child, it was necessary continually and actively to recall his attention, inviting him to look at the block and showing him the various pieces. And if the child once succeeded in placing all the cylinders properly, he stopped, and the game was finished. Whenever the deficient child committed an error, it was necessary to correct it, or to urge him to correct it himself, and when he was able to correct an error he was usually quite indifferent.

Now the normal child, instead, takes spontaneously a lively interest in this game. He pushes away all who would interfere, or offer to help him, and wishes to be alone before his problem.

It had already been noted that little ones of two or three years take the greatest pleasure in arranging small objects, and this experiment in the "Children's Houses" demonstrates the truth of this assertion.

Now, and here is the important point, the normal child attentively observes the relation between the size of the opening and that of the object which he is to place in the mould, and is greatly interested in the game, as is clearly shown by the expression of attention on the little face.

If he mistakes, placing one of the objects in an opening that is small for it, he takes it away, and proceeds to make various trials, seeking the proper opening. If he makes a contrary error, letting the cylinder fall into an opening that is a little too large for it, and then collects all the successive cylinders in openings just a little too large, he will find himself at the last with the big cylinder in his hand while only the smallest opening is empty. The didactic material controls every error. The child proceeds to correct himself, doing this in various ways. Most often he feels the cylinders or shakes them, in order to recognise which are the largest. Sometimes, he sees at a glance where his error lies, pulls the cylinders from the places where they should not be, and puts those left out where they belong, then replaces all the others. The normal child always repeats the exercise with growing interest.

Indeed, it is precisely in these errors that the educational importance of the didactic material lies, and when the child with evident security places each piece in its proper place, he has outgrown the exercise, and this piece of material becomes useless to him.

This self-correction leads the child to concentrate his attention upon the differences of dimensions, and to compare the various pieces. It is in just this comparison that the psycho-sensory exercise lies.

There is, therefore, no question here of teaching the child the knowledge of the dimensions, through the medium of these pieces. Neither is it our aim that the child shall know how to use, without an error, the material presented to him thus performing the exercises well.

That would place our material on the same basis as many others, for example that of Froebel, and would require again the active work of the teacher, who busies herself furnishing knowledge, and making haste to correct every error in order that the child may learn the use of the objects.

Here instead it is the work of the child, the auto-correction, the auto-education which acts, for the teacher must not interfere in the slightest way. No teacher can furnish the child with the agility which he acquires through gymnastic exercises: it is necessary that the pupil perfect himself through his own efforts. It is very much the same with the education of the senses.

It might be said that the same thing is true of every form of education; a man is not what he is because of the teachers he has had, but because of what he has done.

One of the difficulties of putting this method into practice with teachers of the old school, lies in the difficulty of preventing them from intervening when the little child remains for some time puzzled before some error, and with his eyebrows drawn together and his lips puckered, makes repeated efforts to correct himself. When they see this, the old-time teachers are seized with pity, and long, with an almost irresistible force, to help the child. When we prevent this intervention, they burst into words of compassion for the little scholar, but he soon shows in his smiling face the joy of having surmounted an obstacle.

Normal children repeat such exercises many times. This repetition varies according to the individual. Some children after having completed the exercise five or six times are tired of it. Others will remove and replace the pieces at least twenty times, with an expression of evident interest. Once, after I had watched a little one of four years repeat this exercise sixteen times, I had the other children sing in order to distract her, but she continued unmoved to take out the cylinders, mix them up and put them back in their places.

An intelligent teacher ought to be able to make most interesting individual psychological observations, and, to a certain point, should be able to measure the length of time for which the various stimuli held the attention.

In fact, when the child educates himself, and when the control and correction of errors is yielded to the didactic material, there remains for the teacher nothing but to observe. She must then be more of a psychologist than a teacher, and this shows the importance of a scientific preparation on the part of the teacher.

Indeed, with my methods, the teacher teaches little and observes much, and, above all, it is her function to direct the psychic activity of the children and their physiological development. For this reason I have changed the name of teacher into that of directress.

At first this name provoked many smiles, for everyone asked whom there was for this teacher to direct, since she had no assistants, and since she must leave her little scholars in liberty. But her direction is much more profound and important than that which is commonly understood, for this teacher directs the life and the soul.

Second. The education of the senses has, as its aim, the refinement of the differential perception of stimuli by means of repeated exercises.

There exists a sensory culture, which is not generally taken into consideration, but which is a factor in esthesiometry.

For example, in the mental tests which are used in France, or in a series of tests which De Sanctis has established for the diagnosis of the intellectual status, I have often seen used cubes of different sizes placed at varying distances. The child was to select the smallest and the largest, while the chronometer measured the time of reaction between the command and the execution of the act. Account was also taken of the errors. I repeat that in such experiments the factor of culture is forgotten and by this I mean sensory culture.

Our children have, for example, among the didactic material for the education of the senses, a series of ten cubes. The first has a base of ten centimetres, and the others decrease, successively, one centimetre as to base, the smallest cube having a base of one centimetre. The exercise consists in throwing the blocks, which are pink in colour, down upon a green carpet, and then building them up into a little tower, placing the largest cube as the base, and then placing the others in order of size until the little cube of one centimetre is placed at the top.

The little one must each time select, from the blocks scattered upon the green carpet, "the largest" block. This game is most entertaining to the little ones of two years and a half, who, as soon as they have constructed the little tower, tumble it down with little blows of the hand, admiring the pink cubes as they lie scattered upon the green carpet. Then, they begin again the construction, building and destroying a definite number of times.

If we were to place before these tests one of my children from three to four years, and one of the children from the first elementary (six or seven years old), my pupil would undoubtedly manifest a shorter period of reaction, and would not commit errors. The same may be said for the tests of the chromatic sense, etc.

This educational method should therefore prove interesting to students of experimental psychology as well as to teachers.

In conclusion, let me summarize briefly: Our didactic material renders auto-education possible, permits a methodical education of the senses. Not upon the ability of the teacher does such education rest, but upon the didactic system. This presents objects which, first, attract the spontaneous attention of the child, and, second, contain a rational gradation of stimuli.

## Further Resources

### BOOKS

Kramer, Rita. *Maria Montessori: A Biography.* Chicago: University of Chicago Press, 1983.

Montessori, Maria. *The Absorbent Mind.* Claude A. Claremont, trans. New York: Holt, Rinehart and Winston, 1967.

———. *The Discovery of the Child.* New York: Ballantine Books, 1996.

———. *Dr. Montessori's Own Handbook.* Cambridge, Mass.: Bentley, 1966.

———. *Spontaneous Activity in Education.* Florence Simmonds, trans. New York: Schocken Books, 1965.

Standing, E.M. *Maria Montessori: Her Life and Work.* New York: New American Library, 1962.

### WEBSITES

"American Montessori Society." Available online at http://www.amshq.org/ (accessed March 18, 2003.)

"Association Montessori Internationale." Available online at http://www.montessori-ami.org/ (accessed March 18, 2003).

"Montessori Online." The Montessori Foundation. Available online at http://www.montessori.org/ (accessed March 18, 2003).

### AUDIO AND VISUAL MEDIA

*Maria Montessori: Follow the Child.* Directed By Douglas Clark. Douglas Clark Associates. Videocassette, 1978.

# "Why Should the Kindergarten Be Incorporated as an Integral Part of the Public School System?"

Journal article

**By:** Philander P. Claxton

**Date:** 1913

**Source:** Claxton, Philander P. "Why Should the Kindergarten Be Incorporated as an Integral Part of the Public School System?" *Journal of Proceedings and Addresses,* National Education Association, 1913, 426–427.

**About the Author:** Philander P. Claxton (1862–1957), a graduate of the University of Tennessee and the Johns Hopkins University, was United States commissioner of education from 1911 to 1921. He had also been a teacher, superintendent, normal school instructor, and head of the Department of Education at the University of Tennessee. Claxton was president of Austin Peay Normal School from 1930 until his retirement in 1946. ∎

## Introduction

Friedrich Froebel, a German educator, was the originator of the kindergarten, and he founded the first one in 1837. Froebel was influenced by the philosophy of the Swiss educator, Johann Pestalozzi, who emphasized that the origins of all knowledge are impressions taken in by the senses and education is a natural process of unfolding abilities. For Pestalozzi, the curriculum should be adapted to children at their particular point in the developmental process. Therefore, Froebel reasoned, the education of very young children should begin with observation and activity, rather than books and intellectual tasks. Play, the "work" of children, should be the basis of their education. This philosophy is the foundation for Froebel's concept of the kindergarten or "a garden where children grow." The kindergarten concept represented a significant departure from the formal, rigid schooling practices of the time. Froebel emphasized freedom, exploration, individual expression, hands-on activities, and social development through group work.

As part of this education through play, Froebel developed a curriculum based on "gifts" and "occupations." The gifts are a numbered series of objects composed of basic shapes to be manipulated by the child. Through a directed series of activities with the gifts, the child learns about the properties of the world around them. The occupations consist of arts and crafts activities, such as painting, sewing, and clay modeling that complement the gifts. Through the gifts and occupations, academic material is later introduced.

While not widely adopted in his own time, Froebel's philosophy and methods eventually spread worldwide. Brought to the United States by German intellectuals during the 1840s, kindergarten was a common feature of American schools by 1915. The St. Louis Public Schools provided the first significant laboratory for testing the kindergarten idea, beginning in 1873. Under the leadership of superintendent, William T. Harris, and kindergarten teacher, Susan Blow, the experiment was a success. It began to attract the attention of other school districts nationwide. By 1918, just over ten percent of children in the United States between the ages of four and six attended kindergarten. By 1947, sixty percent of urban school systems had incorporated kindergartens as the first step on the educational ladder.

## Significance

A statement by a prominent educator and United States Commissioner of Education, Philander P. Claxton, endorsing kindergarten as an integral part of the public schools, signaled to teachers, administrators, and the general public that kindergarten, considered experimental fifty years before, was now to become a fixture of the educational landscape. The acceptance of kindergarten as part of the public schools prefigured a trend toward public funding for the education of young children. Claxton notes that Froebel sought to convince Germans of the importance of the early childhood period in education. Twentieth century research has supported this assertion, leading to many publicly-funded programs, including Head Start for preschool-age children.

While Froebel's general philosophy and methods continued to influence kindergartens into the twenty-first century, his complete program of gifts and occupations is rarely used. Nonetheless, interest in the gifts continues, partly due to assertions by prominent artists and architects—Frank Lloyd Wright, a famous architect, noted that the gifts had influenced greatly his development. Currently, the gifts are manufactured by a number of educational toy makers.

Since the 1910s, kindergarten has become universal in American public schools. Claxton's cautions—that kindergarten should not lose its unique qualities and that teachers should be well trained—have largely been heeded. Kindergarten retains, for the most part, an approach distinct from that of the early elementary grades. Play and hands-on activities within a nurturing environment are emphasized. And teachers desiring kindergarten positions frequently must have a special license or "endorsement."

## Primary Source

"Why Should the Kindergarten Be Incorporated as an Integral Part of the Public School System?"

Children receive snacks during kindergarten in the University settlement in New York City, 1915. © BETTMANN/CORBIS. REPRODUCED BY PERMISSION.

**SYNOPSIS:** United States Commissioner of Education, Philander P. Claxton, summarizes the growth of the kindergarten movement and offers his endorsement of kindergarten as an essential part of U.S. public schooling.

It is a well-known fact that all organized bodies are conservative, that to introduce a new feature it is necessary that the idea be completely worked thru a series of evolutions, beginning with specialists on the subject. Froebel was the great discoverer of infancy as a phase of life worth considering, as the beginning of the moral, aesthetic, and educational tasted of life. He was the pioneer specialist in kindergarten work and his life was spent in trying to convince the German nation of one fact, that early childhood is an important period in the formation of tendencies or the creation of attitudes in life. He died without seeing any tangible results, but since 1836 he has been the authority which modern thought has followed. The gradual growth of his ideas, the try out of his plans by organizing kindergartens in the slums among the poor and uneducated class, has taken over half a century.

The kindergarten, like every other new movement, has had to be fostered by individuals and as-

sociations especially interested. Organized institutions do not undertake new interests. Ideas must first be worked out and their practical worth proven before they are adopted by public institutions.

Upon the answers to three questions must depend the answer to the question whether the kindergarten should now be adopted as an integral part of the public-school systems of states and cities:

1. Is all education a function of the state?

2. Should there be formal education provided for children before the age of six?

3. Is the kindergarten program an effective one?

My answer to each of these is in the affirmative, and therefore do I believe that the kindergarten should be adopted as an integral part of our system of education.

When this is done, great care will be necessary to prevent the kindergarten work becoming over-formal and losing its most essential characteristics. To prevent this there must be no attempt to grade children on their attainments or take out definite and fixed courses of study, nor must we suppose that because the children are small, teachers do not need a high degree of education. Women of the best education and training must be selected for teachers of the kindergarten classes. Personality counts more here than anywhere else.

## Further Resources

### BOOKS

Brosterman, Norman. *Inventing Kindergarten.* New York: H.N. Abrams, 1997.

Froebel, Friedrich. *Froebel's Education by Development: The Second Part of the Pedagogics of the Kindergarten.* New York: D. Appleton and Company, 1899.

———. *Froebel's Pedagogics of the Kindergarten.* New York: D. Appleton and Company, 1895.

Ross, Elizabeth D. *The Kindergarten Crusade: The Establishment of Preschool Education in the United States.* Athens: Ohio University Press, 1976.

Shapiro, Michael S. *The Kindergarten Movement From Froebel to Dewey.* University Park: Pennsylvania State University Press, 1983.

### PERIODICALS

Brosterman, Norman. "The Case for Kindergarten: A Call for Another Look at Friedrich Froebel's Amazing Invention." *Architectural Record* 185, March 1997, 17.

### WEBSITES

"Celebrating Kindergarten." Available online at http://home .earthlink.net/~esmejake/kinder.htm; website home page http://home.earthlink.net (accessed March 3, 2003).

"The Froebel Education Center." Available online at http:// www.froebel.com/ (accessed March 3, 2003).

"The Froebel Foundation." Available online at http://www .froebelfoundation.org/ (accessed March 5, 2003).

"Froebel Web." Available online at http://members.tripod .com/~FroebelWeb/webindex.html; website home page http:// members.tripod.com (accessed March 3, 2003).

# *Smith-Lever Act of 1914*
Law

**By:** Hoke Smith and Asbury Francis Lever

**Date:** May 8, 1914

**Source:** *Smith-Lever Act (Agricultural Extension Act) of 1914.* Stat. 372, 7 USC 341 et seq., May 8, 1914. Reprinted in *The Statutes at Large of the United States of America from March 1913 to March 1915, volume 38.* Washington, D.C.: GPO, 1915, 372–374. Available online at http://www .reeusda.gov/1700/legis/s-l.htm; website homepage http:// www.reeusda.gov (accessed May 15, 2003).

**About the Authors:** Hoke Smith (1879–1931) began his career as a lawyer in private practice. He was appointed Secretary of the Interior under President Grover Cleveland (served 1885–1889 and 1893–1897) and was twice elected governor of Georgia. As governor and Democratic Georgia senator,

Smith was an advocate for rural and agricultural interests. He was chairman of the Commission on National Aid to Vocational Education in 1914.

Asbury Francis Lever (1875–1940) graduated from Newberry College in 1895 and Georgetown Law School in 1899. He represented South Carolina in the U.S. House of Representatives for ten consecutive terms from 1901 to 1919, and was chairman of that body's Committee on Agriculture from 1913 to 1919. ∎

## Introduction

After the Civil War (1861–1865), the U.S. federal government became larger and more powerful, and its influence extended to new spheres. Education, traditionally funded and controlled solely by states and localities, was one area affected by this change. Two important examples of federal participation in education in the nineteenth century are the Morrill Acts of 1862 and 1890, and the Hatch Experiment Station Act of 1887. The Morrill Act granted land to each state for the purpose of financing public colleges of "agriculture and mechanic arts." The Hatch Act allocated funds for each state to conduct agricultural experiment stations in partnership with the land-grant colleges and to distribute agricultural information.

During the late–nineteenth century and early–twentieth century, the need for more productive and efficient farms, combined with an explosion in agricultural science and the rapid development of new farming methods, resulted in a demand for accessible agricultural education for the farmer and rural youth. In addition, high schools were increasingly called upon to provide a more practical and vocationally oriented curriculum. The Hatch Act, with its provision for the distribution of information, was largely responsible for the development of special agricultural high schools, often begun as part of the experiment stations. Through the efforts of the Office of Experiment Stations, including advocacy and curriculum development, agricultural education became widespread in the public secondary schools. By 1916, over 4,000 high schools offered agricultural courses.

The Smith-Lever Act of 1914, which created the Cooperative Extension Service, is often considered an expansion of the Hatch Act. Smith-Lever provided funding for "cooperative agricultural extension" programs: The U.S. Department of Agriculture, in cooperation with the land-grant college and their experiment stations, would "extend" agricultural education to "persons not attending or resident in said colleges." The law provided funding for a wide variety of programs and activities for rural adults and youth on farming practices and home economics including classes, lectures, clubs, conferences, and demonstrations. Educational publications were also produced.

**Significance**

The Smith-Lever Act made it possible for farmers to learn about new methods developed at the experiment stations, through demonstrations and other direct instruction by county agricultural agents. Farmers had previously resisted learning about and using new techniques developed at the colleges and universities. Representative Lever pointed out that the Cooperative Extension Service could solve this problem by showing the farmer " . . . under his own vine and fig tree as it were, that you have a system better than the system which he himself has been following." The Cooperative Extension Service has been credited with the subsequent rapid diffusion of information on scientific farming methods.

The Smith-Lever Act set a precedent for large-scale federal involvement in vocational education. Three years later, the Smith-Hughes Act provided funds directly to secondary schools for vocational and agricultural education. The Smith-Lever Act was the first instance of a large-scale, federal education program requiring matching dollars from states, a method of funding subsequently used for the Smith-Hughes Act as well.

The law, having undergone a number of revisions, is still in effect today and includes land-grant universities in each of the 50 states and the District of Columbia. Programs begun under the Cooperative Extension Service, such as 4-H Clubs, continue to provide important sources of agricultural education for youth and adults.

**Primary Source**

*Smith-Lever Act of 1914*

> **SYNOPSIS:** The text of the Smith-Lever Act discusses the aims and goals of the law, the types of instruction included, and how and by whom such instruction will be carried out. Also included are the details of the amount of funding to be distributed, and the method for doing so.

Chap. 79.—AN ACT To provide for cooperative agricultural extension work between the agricultural colleges in the several States receiving the benefits of an Act of Congress approved July second, eighteen hundred and sixty-two, and of Acts supplementary thereto, and the United States Department of Agriculture.

*Be it enacted by the Senate and House of Representatives of the United States of America in Congress assembled,* That in order to aid in diffusing among the people of the United States useful and practical information on subjects relating to agriculture and home economics, and to encourage the application of the same, there may be inaugurated in connection with the college or colleges in each State now receiving, or which may here-after receive, the benefits of the Act of Congress approved July second, eighteen hundred and sixty-two, entitled "An Act donating public lands to the several States and Territories which may provide colleges for the benefit of agriculture and the mechanic arts" (Twelfth Statues at Large, page five hundred and three), and of the Act of Congress approved August thirtieth, eighteen hundred and ninety (Twenty-sixth Statutes Large, page four hundred and seventeen and chapter eight hundred and forty-one), agricultural extension work which shall be carried on in cooperation with the United States Department of Agriculture: *Provided,* That in any State in which two or more such colleges have been or hereafter may be established, the appropriations hereinafter made to such State shall be administered by such college or colleges as the legislature of such State may direct: *Provided further,* That, pending the inauguration and development of the cooperative extension work herein authorized, nothing in this Act shall be construed to discontinue either the farm management work or the farmers' cooperative demonstration work as now conducted by the Bureau of Plant Industry of the Department of Agriculture.

Sec. 2. That cooperative agricultural extension work shall consist of the giving of instruction and practical demonstrations in agriculture and home economics to persons not attending or resident in said colleges in the several communities, and imparting to such persons information on said subjects through field demonstrations, publications, and otherwise; and this work shall be carried on in such manner as may be mutually agreed upon by the Secretary of Agriculture and the State agricultural college or colleges receiving the benefits of this Act.

Sec. 3. That for the purpose of paying the expenses of said cooperative agricultural extension work and the necessary printing and distributing of information in connection with the same, there is permanently appropriated, out of any money in the Treasury not otherwise appropriated, the sum of $480,000 for each year, $10,000 of which shall be paid annually, in the manner hereinafter provided, to each State which shall by action of its legislature assent to the provisions of this Act: *Provided,* That payment of such installments of the appropriation herein before made as shall become due to any State before the adjournment of the regular session of the legislature meeting next after the passage of this Act may, in the absence of prior legislative assent, be made upon the assent of the governor

The Smith-Lever Act supported the establishment of agricultural colleges such as this one in Michigan. **THE LIBRARY OF CONGRESS**

thereof, duly certified to the Secretary of the Treasury: *Provided further,* That there is also appropriated an additional sum of $600,000 for the fiscal year following that in which the foregoing appropriation first becomes available, and for each year thereafter for seven years a sum exceeding by $500,000 the sum appropriated for each preceding year, and for each year thereafter there is permanently appropriated for each year the sum of $4,100,000 in addition to the sum of $480,000 hereinbefore provided: *Provided further,* That before the funds herein appropriated shall become available to any college for any fiscal year plans for the work to be carried on under this Act shall be submitted by the proper officials of each college and approved by the Secretary of Agriculture. Such additional sums shall be used only for the purposes hereinbefore stated, and shall be allotted annually to each State by the Secretary of Agriculture and paid in the manner hereinbefore provided, in the proportion which the rural population of each State bears to the total rural population of all the States as determined by the next preceding Federal census: *Provided further,* That no payment out of the additional appropriations herein provided shall be made in any year to any State until an equal sum has been appropriated for that year by the legislature of such State, or provided by State, county, college, local authority, or individual contributions from within the State, for the maintenance of the cooperative agricultural extension work provided for in this Act.

Sec. 4. That the sums hereby appropriated for extension work shall be paid in equal semiannual payments on the first day of January and July of each year by the Secretary of the Treasury upon the warrant of the Secretary of Agriculture, out of the Treasury of the United States, to the treasurer or other officer of the State duly authorized by the laws of the State to receive the same; and such officer shall be required to report to the Secretary of Agriculture, on or before the first day of September of each year, a detailed statement of the amount so received during the previous fiscal year, and of its disbursement, on forms prescribed by the Secretary of Agriculture.

Sec. 5. That if any portion of the moneys received by the designated officer of any State for the support and maintenance of cooperative agricultural extension work, as provided in this Act, shall by any action or contingency be diminished or lost, or be misapplied, it shall be replaced by said State to which it belongs, and until so replaced no subsequent appropriation shall be apportioned or paid to said State, and no portion of said moneys shall be applied, directly or indirectly, to the purchase, erection, preservation, or repair of any building or buildings, or the purchase or rental of land, or in college-course teaching, lectures in colleges, promoting agricultural trains, or any other purpose not specified in this Act, and not more than five per centum of each annual appropriation shall be applied to the printing and distribution of publications. Shall be the duty of each of said colleges annually, on or before the first day of January, to make to the governor of the State in which it is located a full and detailed report of its operations in the direction of extension work as defined in this Act, including a detailed statement of receipts and expenditures from all sources for this purpose, a copy of which report shall be sent to the Secretary of Agriculture and to the Secretary of the Treasury of the United States.

Sec. 6. That on or before the first day of July in each year after the passage of this Act the Secretary of Agriculture shall ascertain and certify to the Secretary of the Treasury as to each State whether it is entitled to receive its share of the annual appropriation for cooperative agricultural extension work under this Act, and the amount which it is entitled to receive. If the Secretary of Agriculture shall withhold a certificate from any State of its appropriation, the facts and reasons therefor shall be reported to the President, and the amount involved shall be kept separate in the Treasury until the expiration of the Congress next succeeding a session of the legislature of any State from which a certificate has been withheld, in order that the State may, if it should so desire, appeal to Congress from the determination of the Secretary of Agriculture. If the next Congress shall not direct such sum to be paid, it shall be covered into the Treasury.

Sec. 7. That the Secretary of Agriculture shall make an annual report to Congress of the receipts, expenditures, and results of the cooperative agricultural extension work in all of the States receiving the benefits of this Act, and also whether the appropriation of any State has been withheld; and if so, the reasons therefor.

Sec. 8. That Congress may at any time alter, amend, or repeal any or all of the provisions of this Act.

Approved, May 8, 1914.

## Further Resources

### BOOKS

Butts, R. Freeman, and Lawrence Cremin. *A History of Education in American Culture.* New York: Henry Holt, 1953.

Prawl, M., et al. *Adult and Continuing Education Through the Cooperative Extension Service.* Columbia: University of Missouri, 1984.

Seevers, Brenda. *Education Through Cooperative Extension.* Albany, N.Y.: Delmar Publishers, 1997.

True, Alfred C. *A History of Agricultural Education in the United States, 1785–1925.* U.S. Department of Agriculture, Miscellaneous Publication No. 36. Washington, D.C.: U.S. Government Printing Office, 1929.

### PERIODICALS

Camp, W.G., and J.R. Crunkilton. "History of Agricultural Education in America: The Great Individuals and Events." *The Journal of the American Association of Teacher Educators in Agriculture* 26, no. 1, 1985, 57–63.

Fuller, Wayne. "Making Better Farmers: The Study of Agriculture in Midwestern Schools, 1900–1923." *Agricultural History* 60, no. 2, 1986, 154–168.

Moore, Gary E. "The Involvement of Experiment Stations in Secondary Agricultural Education, 1887–1917." *Agricultural History* 62, no. 2, Spring 1988.

### WEBSITES

"4-H Centennial." Available online at http://www.4hcentennial.org/default.asp; website home page http://www.4hcentennial.org (accessed March 6, 2003).

"Agricultural History Society." Available online at http://www.iastate.edu/~history_info/aghissoc.htm; website home page http://www.iastate.edu (accessed March 6, 2003).

"Center for Agricultural History." Available online at http://www.iastate.edu/%7Ehistory/cenaghis.htm; website home page http://www.iastate.edu (accessed March 6, 2003).

# Report of the Committee on Academic Freedom and Tenure

Report

**By:** American Association of University Professors, Committee on Academic Freedom and Tenure

**Date:** 1915

**Source:** American Association of University Professors. *Report of the Committee on Academic Freedom and Tenure.* n.p., 1915.

**About the Organization:** At the January 1915 meeting of the American Association of University Professors (AAUP), the president of the Association was authorized to appoint a committee of fifteen members "to take up the problem of academic freedom in general." The result was the Committee on Academic Freedom and Tenure, chaired by Edwin R.A. Seligman of Columbia University. The report of the Committee included the "General Declaration of Principles," outlining the AAUP's position on academic freedom. ∎

## Introduction

From the colonial period, boards overseeing colleges and colonial governments were concerned with the adherence of college professors to the religious and moral standards of the community, and their loyalty to the government—professors could be asked to swear loyalty to England. Increasingly, after the Civil War (1861–1865), American universities took on a more secular character in their curricula and aims. By the early part of the twentieth century, the AAUP report notes, infringements on the academic freedom of professors were less likely to be the result of religious disapproval of new ideas in the disciplines of philosophy and natural science. Rather, innovations in the fields of political and social science were subject to objections from the trustees, benefactors, and parents—representing the social classes with a vested interest in maintaining current social and economic conditions. One such instance was the firing of a Stanford University professor for his political activities in 1900. His actions offended the University's benefactor, Jane Stanford. Six other professors resigned in protest.

Challenges to academic freedom increase when the country is faced with a crisis, such as war or internal turmoil. The time period from the entrance of the United States into World War I (1914–1918) through the early 1920s was characterized by intense nationalism, suspicion of anything foreign, and a fear of communism and socialism. Professors proposing social, political, or economic ideas, even off campus, that seemed radical, foreign, or strange risked censure or dismissal. At the time that the AAUP Committee was writing the report, infringements on academic freedom were on the rise. During 1915, the Committee received eleven complaints alleging violations of academic freedom in the dismissals or forced resignations of university professors or presidents.

Motivations behind attempts to censor the speech, writing, and actions of college and university professors ranged from personal interest to a genuine concern for national security. Objections were raised by those charging that such actions infringe upon the civil rights that professors held in common with other citizens. It also interfered with the ability of the college or university to pursue unbiased knowledge for the benefit of all.

**Significance**

From World War I through the 1950s, college and university professors were faced with a rise in mandatory loyalty oaths, dismissals for membership in particular organizations, and restrictions on speech, writing, and political activities on and off campus. This trend also affected teachers in the elementary and secondary schools. The AAUP continued to advocate for academic freedom as part of a larger effort that included organizations, including the American Civil Liberties Union and the American Federation of Teachers.

The report's authors left open the question of whether academic freedom extends to positions of leadership in political parties or candidacy for public office. The report states that, "it is manifestly desirable that such teachers have minds untrammeled by party loyalties." On the other hand, the authors recognized that professors could not be banned from all political activities. The issue is recommended for further study.

Thirty-five years later, another wave of dismissals and loyalty oaths came with the "Red Scare" of 1950s. Many professors who held memberships in the Communist Party or espoused Communist ideas lost their jobs. Although the AAUP continued to take a stand against loyalty oaths and the censoring of ideas, a 1953 report by the Association stated that professors could be removed from their jobs for membership in the Communist Party.

Fears relating to terrorism and national security in the aftermath of September 11, 2001 have resulted in new challenges to academic freedom. The AAUP disseminated information for professors who might find themselves or their institutions under investigation through the USA Patriot Act of 2001. The Association also appointed a special Committee on Academic Freedom and National Security in Time of Crisis.

**Primary Source**

*Report of the Committee on Academic Freedom and Tenure* [excerpt]

> **SYNOPSIS:** In this excerpt from its report, the AAUP Committee argues that the trustees of a university drawing public funds have a responsibility to the general public not to interfere with the academic freedom of professors. Professors, if they are to properly discharge their duties to the public, their students, and the government, must be assured of the right to report the outcomes of their research without fear of retribution or expectation of reward.

**General Declaration of Principles**

The term "academic freedom" has traditionally had two applications—to the freedom of the teacher and to that of the student, *Lehrfreiheit* and *Lernfreiheit*. It need scarcely be pointed out that the freedom which is the subject of this report is that of the teacher. Academic freedom in this sense comprises three elements: freedom of inquiry and research; freedom of teaching within the university or college; and freedom of extramural utterance and action. The first of these is almost everywhere so safeguarded that the dangers of its infringement are slight. It may therefore be disregarded in this report. The second and third phases of academic freedom are closely related, and are often not distinguished. The third, however, has an importance of its own, since of late it has perhaps more frequently been the occasion of difficulties and controversies than has the question of freedom of intra-academic teaching. All five of the cases which have recently been investigated by committees of this Association have involved, at least as one factor, the right of university teachers to express their opinions freely outside the university or to engage in political activities in their capacity as citizens. The general principles which have to do with freedom of teaching in both these senses seem to the committee to be in great part, though not wholly, the same. In this report, therefore, we shall consider the matter primarily with reference to freedom of teaching within the university, and shall assume that what is said thereon is also applicable to the freedom of speech of university teachers outside their institutions, subject to certain qualifications and supplementary considerations which will be pointed out in the course of the report.

An adequate discussion of academic freedom must necessarily consider three matters: (1) the scope and basis of the power exercised by those bodies having ultimate legal authority in academic affairs; (2) the nature of the academic calling; and (3) the function of the academic institution or university.

## 1. Basis of Academic Authority

American institutions of learning are usually controlled by boards of trustees as the ultimate repositories of power. Upon them finally it devolves to determine the measure of academic freedom which is to be realized in the several institutions. It therefore becomes necessary to inquire into the nature of the trust reposed in these boards, and to ascertain to whom the trustees are to be considered accountable.

The simplest case is that of a proprietary school or college designed for the propagation of specific doctrines prescribed by those who have furnished its endowment. It is evident that in such cases the trustees are bound by the deed of gift, and, whatever be their own views, are obligated to carry out the terms of the trust. If a church or religious denomination establishes a college to be governed by a board of trustees, with the express understanding that the college will be used as an instrument of propaganda in the interests of the religious faith professed by the church or denomination creating it, the trustees have a right to demand that everything be subordinated to that end. If, again, as has happened in this country, a wealthy manufacturer establishes a special school in a university in order to teach, among other things, the advantages of a protective tariff, or if, as is also the case, an institution has been endowed for the purpose of propagating the doctrines of socialism, the situation is analogous. All of these are essentially proprietary

institutions, in the moral sense. They do not, at least as regards one particular subject, accept the principles of freedom of inquiry, of opinion, and of teaching; and their purpose is not to advance knowledge by the unrestricted research and unfettered discussion of impartial investigators, but rather to subsidize the promotion of opinions held by the persons, usually not of the scholar's calling, who provide the funds for their maintenance. Concerning the desirability of the existence of such institutions, the committee does not wish to express any opinion. But it is manifestly important that they should not be permitted to sail under false colors. Genuine boldness and thoroughness of inquiry, and freedom of speech, are scarcely reconcilable with the prescribed inculcation of a particular opinion upon a controverted question.

Such institutions are rare, however, and are becoming ever more rare. We still have, indeed, colleges under denominational auspices; but very few of them impose upon their trustees responsibility for the spread of specific doctrines. They are more and more coming to occupy, with respect to the freedom enjoyed by the members of their teaching bodies, the position of untrammeled institutions of learning, and are differentiated only by the natural influence of their respective historic antecedents and traditions.

Leaving aside, then, the small number of institutions of the proprietary type, what is the nature of the trust reposed in the governing boards of the ordinary institutions of learning? Can colleges and universities that are not strictly bound by their founders to a propagandist duty ever be included in the class of institutions that we have just described as being in a moral sense proprietary? The answer is clear. If the former class of institutions constitutes a private or proprietary trust, the latter constitutes a public trust. The trustees are trustees for the public. In the case of our state universities this is self-evident. In the case of most of our privately endowed institutions, the situation is really not different. They cannot be permitted to assume the proprietary attitude and privilege, if they are appealing to the general public for support. Trustees of such universities or colleges have no moral right to bind the reason or the conscience of any professor. All claim to such right is waived by the appeal to the general public for contributions and for moral support in the maintenance, not of a propaganda, but of a non-partisan institution of learning. It follows that any university which lays restrictions upon the intellectual freedom of its professors proclaims itself a proprietary institution, and should be so described whenever it makes a general appeal for funds; and the public should be advised that the institution has no claim whatever to general support or regard.

This elementary distinction between a private and a public trust is not yet so universally accepted as it should be in our American institutions. While in many universities and colleges the situation has come to be entirely satisfactory, there are others in which the relation of trustees to professors is apparently still conceived to be analogous to that of a private employer to his employees; in which, therefore, trustees are not regarded as debarred by any moral restrictions, beyond their own sense of expediency, from imposing their personal opinions upon the teaching of the institution, or even from employing the power of dismissal to gratify their private antipathies or resentments. An eminent university president thus described the situation not many years since:

> In the institutions of higher education the board of trustees is the body on whose discretion, good feeling, and experience the securing of academic freedom now depends. There are boards which leave nothing to be desired in these respect; but there are also numerous bodies that have everything to learn with regard to academic freedom. These barbarous boards exercise an arbitrary power of dismissal. They exclude from the teachings of the university unpopular or dangerous subjects. In some states they even treat professors' positions as common political spoils; and all too frequently, in both state and endowed institutions, they fail to treat the members of the teaching staff with that high consideration to which their functions entitle them.

It is, then, a prerequisite to a realization of the proper measure of academic freedom in American institutions of learning, that all boards of trustees should understand—as many already do—the full implications of the distinction between private proprietorship and a public trust.

## 2. The Nature of the Academic Calling

The above-mentioned conception of a university as an ordinary business venture, and of academic teaching as a purely private employment, manifests also a radical failure to apprehend the nature of the social function discharged by the professional scholar. While we should be reluctant to believe that any large number of educated persons suffer from such a misapprehension, it seems desirable at this time to restate clearly the chief reasons, lying in the nature of the university teaching profession, why it is in the public interest that the professorial office should be one both of dignity and of independence.

If education is the cornerstone of the structure of society and if progress in scientific knowledge is essential to civilization, few things can be more important than to enhance the dignity of the scholar's profession, with a view to attracting into its ranks men of the highest ability, of sound learning, and of strong and independent character. This is the more essential because the pecuniary emoluments of the profession are not, and doubtless never will be, equal to those open to the more successful members of other professions. It is not, in our opinion, desirable that men should be drawn into this profession by the magnitude of the economic rewards which it offers; but it is for this reason the more needful that men of high gift and character should be drawn into it by the assurance of an honorable and secure position, and of freedom to perform honestly and according to their own consciences the distinctive and important function which the nature of the profession lays upon them.

That function is to deal at first hand, after prolonged and specialized technical training, with the sources of knowledge; and to impart the results of their own and of their fellow-specialists' investigations and reflection, both to students and to the general public, without fear or favor. The proper discharge of this function requires (among other things) that the university teacher shall be exempt from any pecuniary motive or inducement to hold, or to express, any conclusion which is not the genuine and uncolored product of his own study or that of fellow specialists. Indeed, the proper fulfillment of the work of the professoriate requires that our universities shall be so free that no fair-minded person shall find any excuse for even a suspicion that the utterances of university teachers are shaped or restricted by the judgment, not of professional scholars, but of inexpert and possibly not wholly disinterested persons outside of their ranks. The lay public is under no compulsion to accept or to act upon the opinions of the scientific experts whom, through the universities, it employs. But it is highly needful, in the interest of society at large, that what purport to be the conclusions of men trained for, and dedicated to, the quest for truth, shall in fact be the conclusions of such men, and not echoes of the opinions of the lay public, or of the individuals who endow or manage universities. To the degree that professional scholars, in the formation and promulgation of their opinions, are, or by the character of their tenure appear to be, subject to any motive other than their own scientific conscience and a desire for the respect of their fellow experts, to that degree the university teaching profession is corrupted; its proper influence upon public opinion is diminished and vitiated; and society at large fails to get from its scholars, in an unadulterated form, the peculiar and necessary service which it is the office of the professional scholar to furnish.

These considerations make still more clear the nature of the relationship between university trustees and members of university faculties. The latter are the appointees, but not in any proper sense the employees, of the former. For, once appointed, the scholar has professional functions to perform in which the appointing authorities have neither competency nor moral right to intervene. The responsibility of the university teacher is primarily to the public itself, and to the judgment of his own profession; and while with respect to certain external conditions of his vocation, he accepts a responsibility to the authorities of the institution in which he serves, in the essentials of his professional activity his duty is to the wider public to which the institution itself is morally amenable. So far as the university teacher's independence of thought and utterance is concerned—though not in other regards—the relationship of professor to trustees may be compared to that between judges of the federal courts and the executive who appoints them. University teachers should be understood to be, with respect to the conclusions reached and expressed by them, no more subject to the control of the trustees, than are judges subject to the control of the president, with respect to their decisions; while of course, for the same reason, trustees are no more to be held responsible for, or to be presumed to agree with, the opinions or utterances of professors, than the president can be assumed to approve of all the legal reasonings of the courts. A university is a great and indispensable organ of the higher life of a civilized community, in the work of which the trustees hold an essential and highly honorable place, but in which the faculties hold an independent place, with quite equal responsibilities—and in relation to purely scientific and educational questions, the primary responsibility. Misconception or obscurity in this matter has undoubtedly been a source of occasional difficulty in the past, and even in several instances during the current year, however much, in the main, a long tradition of kindly and courteous intercourse between trustees and members of university faculties has kept the question in the background.

## 3. The Function of the Academic Institution

The importance of academic freedom is most clearly perceived in the light of the purposes for which universities exist. These are three in number:

a. to promote inquiry and advance the sum of human knowledge;

b. to provide general instruction to the students; and

c. to develop experts for various branches of the public service.

Let us consider each of these. In the earlier stages of a nation's intellectual development, the chief concern of educational institutions is to train the growing generation and to diffuse the already accepted knowledge. It is only slowly that there comes to be provided in the highest institutions of learning the opportunity for the gradual wresting from nature of her intimate secrets. The modern university is becoming more and more the home of scientific research. There are three fields of human inquiry in which the race is only at the beginning: natural science, social science, and philosophy and religion, dealing with the relations of man to outer nature, to his fellow men, and to ultimate realities and values. In natural science all that we have learned but serves to make us realize more deeply how much more remains to be discovered. In social science in its largest sense, which is concerned with the relations of men in society and with the conditions of social order and well-being, we have learned only an adumbration of the laws which govern these vastly complex phenomena. Finally, in the spirit life, and in the interpretation of the general meaning and ends of human existence and its relation to the universe, we are still far from a comprehension of the final truths, and from a universal agreement among all sincere and earnest men. In all of these domains of knowledge, the first condition of progress is complete and unlimited freedom to pursue inquiry and publish its results. Such freedom is the breath in the nostrils of all scientific activity.

The second function—which for a long time was the only function—of the American college or university is to provide instruction for students. It is scarcely open to question that freedom of utterance is as important to the teacher as it is to the investigator. No man can be a successful teacher unless he enjoys the respect of his students, and their confidence in his intellectual integrity. It is clear, however, that this confidence will be impaired if there is suspicion on the part of the student that the teacher is not expressing himself fully or frankly, or that college and university teachers in general are a repressed and intimidated class who dare not speak with that candor and courage which youth always demands in those whom it is to esteem. The average student is a discerning observer, who soon takes the measure of his instructor. It is not only the character of the instruction but also the character of the instructor that counts; and if the student has reason to believe that the instructor is not true to himself, the virtue of the instruction as an educative force is incalculably diminished. There must be in the mind of the teacher no mental reservation. He must give the student the best of what he has and what he is.

The third function of the modern university is to develop experts for the use of the community. If there is one thing that distinguishes the more recent developments of democracy, it is the recognition by legislators of the inherent complexities of economic, social, and political life, and the difficulty of solving problems of technical adjustment without technical knowledge. The recognition of this fact has led to a continually greater demand for the aid of experts in these subjects, to advise both legislators and administrators. The training of such experts has, accordingly, in recent years, become an important part of the work of the universities; and in almost every one of our higher institutions of learning the professors of the economic, social, and political sciences have been drafted to an increasing extent into more or less unofficial participation in the public service. It is obvious that here again the scholar must be absolutely free not only to pursue his investigations but to declare the results of his researches, no matter where they may lead him or to what extent they may come into conflict with accepted opinion. To be of use to the legislator or the administrator, he must enjoy their complete confidence in the disinterestedness of his conclusions.

It is clear, then, that the university cannot perform its threefold function without accepting and enforcing to the fullest extent the principle of academic freedom. The responsibility of the university as a whole is to the community at large, and any restriction upon the freedom of the instructor is bound to react injuriously upon the efficiency and the *morale* of the institution, and therefore ultimately upon the interests of the community.

## Further Resources

### BOOKS

Butts, R. Freeman, and Lawrence Cremin. *A History of Education in American Culture.* New York: Henry Holt, 1953.

Lucas, Christopher J. *American Higher Education: A History.* New York: St. Martin's Press, 1994.

Metzger, Walter P. *Professors on Guard: The First AAUP Investigations.* New York: Arno Press, 1977.

### PERIODICALS

Burgan, Mary. "Academic Freedom in a World of Moral Crisis." *The Chronicle of Higher Education,* September 6, 2002, 49, no. 2, B20.

### WEBSITES

"American Association of University Professors." Available online at http://www.aaup.org/ (accessed March 14, 2003).

# *Democracy and Education*

Nonfiction work

**By:** John Dewey

**Date:** 1916

**Source:** Dewey, John. *Democracy and Education.* New York: Macmillan, 1916.

**About the Author:** John Dewey (1859–1952), a prolific and enormously influential philosopher of education, psychology, politics, and social issues, was associated with the progressive education movement. He was a professor of philosophy, psychology, and pedagogy at the University of Chicago, where he founded the Laboratory School, a progressive, experimental school associated with the University. In 1904, Dewey left Chicago for Teachers College, Columbia University. After his retirement from teaching in 1939, he continued to publish, and he was in demand as a speaker until his death. ■

## Introduction

Education, for Dewey, is growth. The teacher's job is to start with the abilities and understandings the students bring to school, and to guide the student's growth in the proper direction. He emphasized that teachers should begin this process with the child's own motivations and interests. Through the careful selection of environmental influences and individual guidance, the teacher gradually assists the student in moving toward an understanding of the major areas of human knowledge. Children should initially learn concepts through hands-on activities, and only then should teachers introduce abstract symbols such as maps and mathematical algorithms. The school, according to Dewey, should be an authentic social community, where the child will learn social skills, positive social values, and citizenship. He viewed education as a means to social progress and reform. Students should be taught how to think, rather than what to think, so that they will be able to function in a constantly changing society.

While he did not start the progressive education movement or coin the phrase, Dewey is viewed by many

Young women learn how to make mattresses at the Tuskegee Institute. John Dewey was opposed to narrow trades education. © CORBIS.
REPRODUCED BY PERMISSION.

as the primary leader and spokesperson of the movement. It began in the 1870s and continued through the 1950s. In its early phase, progressives emphasized education for social reform through a variety of measures—such as free lunches and health education—aimed at improving the lives of the urban poor. In the 1920s, the movement turned toward a concern with individual expression, freedom, and creativity. In general, progressive educators advocated an experimental approach to education, socialization, a focus on the individual child, and a concern for what is relevant and meaningful to students.

The early twentieth century saw a growing interest in vocational education, often characterized as part of the progressive education movement. Many schools began to offer courses in agricultural and industrial education. Special manual training and agricultural high schools appeared. Legislation such as the Smith-Hughes Act in 1917 allocated federal funds for the development of such programs in secondary schools. Many secondary students enrolled in vocational programs spent from a half to a full day in vocational training activities.

While some progressives hailed vocational education as creating a more relevant, hands-on curriculum, Dewey was an opponent of narrow trades education. For Dewey, occupational studies should be embedded in a curriculum that imparts an understanding of the historical, social, po-

litical, and scientific context of the vocation. Dewey asserted that schools should educate all students to be citizens in a democracy, students in possession of "a courageous intelligence"—able to adapt, learn, and make decisions.

## Significance

*Democracy and Education* is Dewey's most complete statement of his educational philosophy, covering the definition of education, goals and aims, the approach to subject matter, and method, all within the context of an education appropriate to a democracy in a rapidly changing society. This text had, and continues to have, an enormous impact on education thought and practice.

The issues surrounding vocational education in the 1910s continue to be debated today. Those viewing current vocational education from Dewey's perspective are critical of several aspects of the educational system: widespread tracking, especially of disadvantaged and minority students, that perpetuates the current class structure; a curriculum intended to produce a workforce meeting the needs of businesses, rather than students; a failure to educate vocational students about the history of labor conflict; a failure to teach students to critically examine the nature of the workplace; and a general failure to educate students with the perspective that education can be a vehicle for transforming society. Others look at vocational education from an "instrumental" perspective—how can vocational education best meet the economic needs of society and industry?

## Primary Source

*Democracy and Education* [excerpt]

**SYNOPSIS:** Dewey argues against a vocational education focusing narrowly on specific skills. Such an education will tend to make class distinctions permanent, making it, therefore, undemocratic. Without a proper understanding of the historical and social context for their work, these workers will be locked into a system they do not understand, and from which they cannot escape. Dewey notes that the controlling class chooses a liberal education for their own children. Yet, to ensure a docile workforce, they advocate a narrow education for the working class.

Any scheme for vocational education which takes its point of departure from the industrial regime that now exists, is likely to assume and to perpetuate its divisions and weaknesses, and thus to become an instrument in accomplishing the feudal dogma of social predestination. Those who are in a position to make their wishes good, will demand a liberal, a cultural occupation, and one which fits for directive power the youth in whom they are directly interested. To split the system, and give to others, less fortunately situated, an education conceived mainly as specific trade preparation, is to treat the schools as an agency for transferring the older division of labor and leisure, culture and service, mind and body, directed and directive class, into a society nominally democratic. Such a vocational education inevitably discounts the scientific and historic human connections of the materials and processes dealt with. To include such things in narrow trade education would be to waste time; concern for them would not be "practical." They are reserved for those who have leisure at command—the leisure due to superior economic resources. Such things might even be dangerous to the interests of the controlling class, arousing discontent or ambitions "beyond the station" of those working under the direction of others. But an education which acknowledges the full intellectual and social meaning of a vocation would include instruction in the historic background of present conditions; training in science to give intelligence and initiative in dealing with material and agencies of production; and study of economics, civics, and politics, to bring the future worker into touch with the problems of the day and the various methods proposed for its improvement.

Above all, it would train power of readaptation to changing conditions so that future workers would not become blindly subject to a fate imposed upon them. This ideal has to contend not only with the inertia of existing educational traditions, but also with the opposition of those who are entrenched in command of the industrial machinery, and who realize that such an educational system if made general would threaten their ability to use others for their own ends.

But this very fact is the presage of a more equitable and enlightened social order, for it gives evidence of the dependence of social reorganization upon educational reconstruction. It is accordingly an encouragement to those believing in a better order to undertake the promotion of a vocational education which does not subject youth to the demands and standards of the present system, but which utilizes its scientific and social factors to develop a courageous intelligence, and to make intelligence practical and executive.

## Further Resources

### BOOKS

Cremin, Lawrence A. *The Transformation of the School: Progressivism in American Education, 1876–1957.* New York: Alfred A. Knopf, 1961.

Dewey, John, with Martin S. Dworkin, ed. *Dewey on Education: Selections.* New York: Teachers College Press, 1959.

Dykhuizen, George. *The Life and Mind of John Dewey.* Carbondale: Southern Illinois University Press, 1973.

Gordon, Howard R. D. *The History and Growth of Vocational Education in America.* Boston: Allyn and Bacon, 1999.

Katznelson, Ira & Margaret Weir. *Schooling for All: Class, Race, and the Decline of the Democratic Ideal.* New York: Basic Books, 1985.

True, Alfred C. *A History of Agricultural Education in the United States, 1785–1925.* U.S. Department of Agriculture, Miscellaneous Publication No. 36. Washington, D.C.: U.S. Government Printing Office, 1929.

### PERIODICALS

Gregson, J. A. "The School-to-Work Movement and Youth Apprenticeship in the U.S.: Educational Reform or Democratic Renewal?" *Journal of Industrial Teacher Education* 32, no. 3, Spring 1995, 7–29.

### WEBSITES

"The Center for Dewey Studies, Southern Illinois University." Available online at http://www.siu.edu/~deweyctr; website home page http://www.siu.edu (accessed April 26, 2003).

"The John Dewey Society for the Study of Education and Culture. University of Chicago." Available online at http://cuip.uchicago.edu/jds; website home page http://cuip.uchicago.edu (accessed April 26, 2003).

### AUDIO AND VISUAL MEDIA

*John Dewey: His Life and Work.* Directed by Frances W. Davidson. Davidson Films. Videocassette, 2001.

# The Measurement of Intelligence

**Manual**

**By:** Lewis M. Terman

**Date:** 1916

**Source:** Terman, Lewis M. *The Measurement of Intelligence: An Explanation of and a Complete Guide for the Use of the Stanford Revision and Extension of the Binet-Simon Intelligence Scale.* Boston: Houghton Mifflin, 1916.

**About the Author:** Lewis M. Terman (1877–1956), well-known for his longitudinal study of gifted children, received his undergraduate and masters degree from Indiana University, and his Ph.D. from Clark University. He was a professor of education and psychology at Stanford University, and he worked with the U.S. Army during World War I (1914–1918) testing and classifying recruits. ∎

## Introduction

Beginning in the 1890s, William James and others developed what was called the "New Psychology" based on "objective" science. While the study of human behavior had once been the exclusive realm of theology and philosophy, the publication of Charles Darwin's *On the Origin of Species* in 1859 led many to view humans as part of nature and understandable through science. Human intelligence was one area of inquiry. In 1905, Alfred Binet began work on an intelligence scale to identify those of subnormal mental ability. He based the scale on the idea of "mental age," or an individual child's intellectual ability relative to a normal child of the same age.

Other psychologists, including Edward L. Thorndike and Lewis M. Terman, continued the effort to develop reliable and valid intelligence tests. It was Terman who revised Binet's test, published it as the famous and widely used *Stanford-Binet,* and popularized the term "IQ," or intelligence quotient. Terman believed that intelligence, a hereditary and unchanging characteristic, could be defined and accurately measured. Terman attributed the lower IQ scores of some non-white racial groups to genetic inferiority. He supported a program of eugenics, whereby these groups would be encouraged, for the benefit of society, not to reproduce. Environmental factors, such as schools, Terman believed, could do little to improve an individual's intelligence.

The early twentieth century was a time of incredible optimism about the possibility of fields such as psychology and sociology becoming exact sciences capable of predicting and controlling human behavior for the benefit of society. Many believed that these areas of study were on the brink of a major revolution and that, soon, complex constructs such as "moral character" and "artistic ability" would be objectively and accurately defined, measured, and predicted. For Terman and others, intelligence tests held the promise of significant educational reform. Teachers could identify the "feeble-minded" and place them in vocational or special classes. These students would no longer suffer from chronic failure, but rather find their schooling meaningful and useful. Schools would no longer waste money and time trying to educate the uneducable.

## Significance

By the 1920s, intelligence testing was commonplace, as was the practice of using the tests to sort students into various academic tracks. Testing was a significant aspect of the progressive education movement, prominent at the time. Tests were viewed by some progressives as progress toward a science of education and as a tool for reform. Decisions could be made for individual students based on "objective fact" rather than guesswork—resulting in a more appropriate curriculum for students unsuited to traditional academics. Some progressive educators, such as John Dewey, disagreed with the use of intelligence tests to sort students, calling the process "undemocratic."

Critics charged that tests only measured achievement, often based on environment and educational opportunity, rather than an inborn characteristic called "intelligence." Testing opponents also pointed out that intelligence is too complex to define, much less measure accurately. Therefore, many believed that tracking students based on tests would unfairly limit an individual's future. Public controversy was fueled in the early 1920s by a series of articles in the *New Republic* questioning the objectivity of intelligence tests.

Intelligence tests continue to be used by schools as one means of sorting students into academic and vocational tracks as well as classifying students for special education. Yet many oppose tests as racially and culturally biased and cite environment, especially in early childhood, as a major determinant of test scores. The concept of "intelligence" as a single type of ability has been challenged by Howard Gardner and his theory of multiple intelligences. Today, a more complete picture of the complexities involved in the measurement of intelligence exists.

## Primary Source

*The Measurement of Intelligence* [excerpt]

> **SYNOPSIS:** *The Measurement of Intelligence* is partly an instruction manual for the use of the *Stanford-Binet* intelligence test and partly a discourse on the nature of intelligence and its measurement. In this Excerpt, Terman discusses the usefulness of intelligence tests for determining which factors affect

mental development and which educational methods are effective. He also sets forth his view that intelligence is largely inherited and that schooling cannot help "the inferior child."

Another important use of intelligence tests is in the study of the factors which influence mental development. It is desirable that we should be able to guard the child against influences which affect mental development unfavorably; but as long as these influences have not been sifted, weighed, and measured, we have nothing but conjecture on which to base our efforts in this direction.

When we search the literature of child hygiene for reliable evidence as to the injurious effects upon mental ability of malnutrition, decayed teeth, obstructed breathing, reduced sleep, bad ventilation, insufficient exercise, etc., we are met by endless assertion painfully unsupported by demonstrated fact. We have, indeed, very little exact knowledge regarding the mental effects of any of the facts just mentioned. When standardized mental tests have come into more general use, such influences will be easy to detect wherever they are really present.

Again, the most important question of heredity is that regarding the inheritance of intelligence; but this is a problem which cannot be attacked at all without some accurate means of identifying the thing which is the object of study. Without the use of scales for measuring intelligence we can give no better answer as to the essential difference between a genius and a fool than is to be found in legend and fiction.

Applying this to school children, it means that without such tests we cannot know to what extent a child's mental performances are determined by environment and to what extent by heredity. Is the place of the so-called lower classes in the social and industrial scale the result of their inferior native endowment, or is their apparent inferiority merely a result of their inferior home and school training? Is genius more common among children of the educated classes than among the children of the ignorant and poor? Are the inferior races really inferior, or are they merely unfortunate in their lack of opportunity to learn?

Only intelligence tests can answer these questions and grade the raw material with which education works. Without them we can never distinguish the results of our educational efforts with a given child from the influence of the child's original endowment. Such tests would have told us, for example, whether the much-discussed "wonder children," such as the Sidis and Wiener boys and the Stoner girl, owe their precocious intellectual prowess to superior training (as their parents believe) or to superior native ability. The supposed effects upon mental development of new methods of mind training, which are exploited so confidently from time to time (e.g., the Montessori method and the various systems of sensory and motor training for the feeble-minded), will have to be checked up by the same kind of scientific measurement.

In all these fields intelligence tests are certain to play an ever-increasing role. With the exception of moral character, there is nothing as significant for a child's future as his grade of intelligence. Even health itself is likely to have less influence in determining success in life. Although strength and swiftness have always had great survival value among the lower animals, these characteristics have long since lost their supremacy in man's struggle for existence. For us the rule of brawn has been broken, and intelligence has become the decisive factor in success. Schools, railroads, factories, and the largest commercial concerns may be successfully managed by persons who are physically weak or even sickly. One who has intelligence constantly measures opportunities against his own strength or weakness and adjusts himself to conditions by following those leads which promise most toward the realization of his individual possibilities.

All classes of intellects, the weakest as well as the strongest, will profit by the application of their talents to tasks which are consonant with their ability. When we have learned the lessons which intelligence tests have to teach, we shall no longer blame mentally defective workmen for their industrial inefficiency, punish weak-minded children because of their inability to learn, or imprison and hang mentally defective criminals because they lacked the intelligence to appreciate the ordinary codes of social conduct. . . .

**Influence of social and educational advantages**

The criticism has often been made that the responses to many of the tests are so much subject to the influence of school and home environment as seriously to invalidate the scale as a whole. Some of the tests most often named in this connection are the following: Giving age and sex; naming common objects, colors, and coins; giving the value of stamps; giving date; naming the months of the year and the days of the week; distinguishing forenoon and afternoon; counting; making change; reading for memories; naming sixty words; giving definitions;

finding rhymes; and constructing a sentence containing three given words.

It has in fact been found wherever comparisons have been made that children of superior social status yield a higher average mental age than children of the laboring classes. The results of Decroly and Degand and of Meumann, Stern, and Binet himself may be referred to in this connection. In the case of the Stanford investigation, also, it was found that when the unselected school children were grouped in three classes according to social status (superior, average, and inferior), the average I Q for the superior social group was 107, and that of the inferior social group 93. This is equivalent to a difference of one year in mental age with 7-year-olds, and to a difference of two years with 14-year-olds.

However, the common opinion that the child from a cultured home does better in tests solely by reason of his superior home advantages is an entirely gratuitous assumption. Practically all of the investigations which have been made of the influence of nature and nurture on mental performance agree in attributing far more to original endowment than to environment. Common observation would itself suggest that the social class to which the family belongs depends less on chance than on the parents' native qualities of intellect and character.

The results of five separate and distinct lines of inquiry based on the Stanford data agree in supporting the conclusion that the children of successful and cultured parents test higher than children from wretched and ignorant homes for the simple reason that their heredity is better. The results of this investigation are set forth in full elsewhere.[See *The Stanford Revision and Extension of the Binet-Simon Measuring Scale of Intelligence.* (Warwick and York, 1916.)]

■■■

It would, of course, be going too far to deny all possibility of environmental conditions affecting the result of an intelligence test. Certainly no one would expect that a child reared in a cage and denied all intercourse with other human beings could by any system of mental measurement test up to the level of normal children. There is, however, no reason to believe that *ordinary* differences in social environment (apart from heredity), differences such as those obtaining among unselected children attending approximately the same general type of school in a civilized community, affects to any great extent the validity of the scale.

A crucial experiment would be to take a large number of very young children of the lower classes and, after placing them in the most favorable environment obtainable, to compare their later mental development with that of children born into the best homes. No extensive study of this kind has been made, but the writer has tested twenty orphanage children who, for the most part, had come from very inferior homes. They had been in a well-conducted orphanage for from two to several years, and had enjoyed during that time the advantages of an excellent village school. Nevertheless, all but three tested below average, ranging from 75 to 90 I Q.

The impotence of school instruction to neutralize individual differences in native endowment will be evident to any one who follows the school career of backward children. The children who are seriously retarded in school are not normal, and cannot be made normal by any refinement of educational method. As a rule, the longer the inferior child attends school, the more evident his inferiority becomes. It would hardly be reasonable, therefore, to expect that a little incidental instruction in the home would weigh very heavily against these same native differences in endowment.

## Further Resources

### BOOKS

Bagley, William C. *Determinism in Education.* Baltimore: Warwick and York, 1925.

Chapman, Paul Davis. *Schools as Sorters: Lewis M. Terman, Applied Psychology, and the Intelligence Testing Movement, 1890–1930.* New York: New York University Press, 1988.

Gardner, Howard. *Frames of Mind: The Theory of Multiple Intelligences.* New York: Basic Books, 1983.

Gould, Stephen Jay. *The Mismeasure of Man.* New York: Norton, 1996.

Herrnstein, Richard J., and Charles Murray. *The Bell Curve.* New York: The Free Press, 1994.

Minton, Henry L. *Lewis M. Terman: Pioneer in Psychological Testing.* New York: New York University Press, 1988.

Sokal, Michael M. *Psychological Testing and American Society, 1890–1930.* New Brunswick, N.J.: Rutgers University Press, 1987.

Terman, Lewis M. *Genius and Stupidity.* New York: Arno Press, 1975.

———. *Intelligence Tests and School Reorganization.* Yonkers-on-Hudson, N.Y.: World Book Company, 1922.

### PERIODICALS

Lippmann, Walter. "The Mental Age of Americans." *New Republic* 32, no. 412, October 25, 1922, 213–215.

———. "The Mystery of the 'A' Men." *New Republic* 32, no. 413, November 1, 1922, 246–248.

————. "The Reliability of Intelligence Tests." *New Republic* 32, no. 414, November 8, 1922, 275–277.

————. "The Abuse of the Tests." *New Republic* 32, no. 415, November 15, 1922, 297–298.

————. "Tests of Hereditary Intelligence." *New Republic* 32, no. 416, November 22, 1922, 328–330.

————. "A Future for the Tests." *New Republic* 33, no. 417, November 29, 1922, 9–11.

**WEBSITES**

"History of Influences in the Development of Intelligence Theory and Testing." Indiana University. Available online at http://www.indiana.edu/~intell/index.html; website home page http://www.indiana.edu (accessed April 26, 2003).

# Smith-Hughes Act of 1917

Law

**By:** Hoke Smith and Dudley M. Hughes

**Date:** February 23, 1917

**Source:** *Smith-Hughes Act (Vocational Education Act) of 1917.* Public Law 347. 64th Cong., 2d sess., February 23, 1917. Reprinted in *The Statutes at Large of the United States of America from December, 1915, to March, 1917.* Vol. 39, Part 1. Washington, D.C.: GPO, 1917, 929–936.

**About the Authors:** Hoke Smith (1879–1931), known as a staunch advocate for farmers and their interests, began his career as a lawyer. He served two terms as governor of Georgia, and he was appointed Secretary of the Interior under President Grover Cleveland (served 1885–1889 and 1893–1897). Smith was a Democratic senator from Georgia, and chairman of the Commission on National Aid to Vocational Education.

Dudley M. Hughes (1848–1927) attended the University of Georgia and was involved in agricultural businesses. He was a Georgia State Senator from 1882 to 1883, and he served in the U.S. House of Representatives from 1909 to 1917. He was Chairman of the House Committee on Education, and he was appointed to the Commission on National Aid to Vocational Education in 1914. He was known as a strong supporter of agricultural education. ∎

## Introduction

During the last half of the nineteenth century, the federal government expanded and became more involved in areas previously controlled and funded by state and local governments. While efforts to obtain federal funds for public schools in general were unsuccessful, legislation was passed to aid specific programs, including agricultural education. Important examples are the Morrill Act of 1862 (establishing public colleges for agricultural and mechanical education) and the Hatch Act of 1887 (creating agricultural experiment stations in conjunction with these colleges). This trend continued in the early twentieth

*Raised 'em myself in my* **U.S. School Garden**

ISSUED BY THE U. S. SCHOOL GARDEN ARMY BUREAU OF EDUCATION, DEPARTMENT OF INTERIOR, WASHINGTON, D. C.

As the United States entered World War I, attaining a better-prepared labor force and higher agricultural yields became part of the war effort. © SWIM INK/CORBIS. REPRODUCED BY PERMISSION.

century, with the 1914 Smith-Lever Act establishing the Cooperative Extension Service.

After 1900, agriculture and industry groups called for federal aid to provide more vocational education at the secondary level. These calls came in the context of a rapidly expanding industrial sector and resulting shortages of skilled workers, as well as a decline in the traditional apprenticeship system. As the United States entered World War I (1914–1918), attaining a better-prepared labor force and higher agricultural yields became a focus of the war effort. Various bills were introduced seeking federal support for industrial or vocational education in the secondary schools, but none were passed.

In 1906, the National Society for the Promotion of Industrial Education was established for the purpose of obtaining federal funds for industrial education. The group was able to bring together many, sometimes opposing, groups interested in the issue. Charles A. Prosser, as executive secretary of the Society, lobbied for the legislation that would become the Smith-Hughes Act. These efforts paid off and, in 1914, Congress appointed the Commission on National Aid to Vocational Education to study the problem of federal aid to schools for industrial and agricultural education. Prosser and other members of the Society were appointed to the Commission. The 1914 report produced by the Commission indicated a pressing need for the expansion and improvement of vocational education. It recommended that federal assistance be granted to the states for this purpose.

The Commission's report, and the precedent set by the Smith-Lever Act, led to the passage of the Smith-Hughes Act. The provisions of the Act are almost identical to the measures called for in the report, including aid for vocational teacher training and salaries, and the creation of the Federal Board for Vocational Education.

**Significance**

The Smith-Hughes Act is credited with expediting the process, already begun, toward establishing widespread, quality vocational education in the secondary schools. This resulted in the availability of meaningful, relevant, and practical curricula for non-college bound students. Many proponents view the Act as providing industry with a larger pool of skilled workers and assisting the war effort.

Critics contend that the Act resulted in the segregation of vocational curriculum and students from mainstream education. They also allege that it failed to provide adequate job training in the context of fast-paced technological change. While the progressive education movement, active at the time, generally advocated a more meaningful, hands-on curriculum, some progressive educators, such as John Dewey, described the Smith-Hughes type of vocational education as undemocratic. Dewey charged that narrow preparation for a specific trade for a particular group of students at the secondary level benefits the employers, while depriving the students of an education for meaningful citizenship in a democracy.

The Smith-Hughes Act was amended by the Vocational Education Act of 1963, which gave more freedom to the states to decide how to spend funds. It also dropped the procedure of funding by specific categories: agricultural, industrial, and home economics. Smith-Hughes was repealed in 1997, and the current federal legislation related to vocational education is the Carl Perkins Act (1984, 1990, 1998), which targets disadvantaged populations. It emphasizes accessibility to all and improving the quality of vocational education.

**Primary Source**

*Smith-Hughes Act of 1917* [excerpt]

**SYNOPSIS:** This excerpt from the text of the Smith-Hughes Act presents the objectives of the act, including cooperating with the states in paying for the training and salaries of vocational teachers, as well as the creation of the Federal Board for Vocational Education to oversee the application of the act. Specifics of the distribution of funds and the responsibilities of the board, including research in the various vocational areas, are outlined.

CHAP. 114.—An Act To provide for the promotion of vocational education; to provide for cooperation with the States in the promotion of such education in agriculture and the trades and industries; to provide for cooperation with the States in the preparation of teachers of vocational subjects; and to appropriate money and regulate its expenditure.

*Be it enacted by the Senate and House of Representatives of the United States of America in Congress assembled,* That there is hereby annually appropriated, out of any money in the Treasury not otherwise appropriated, the sums provided in sections two, three, and four of this Act, to be paid to the respective States for the purpose of cooperating with the States in paying the salaries of teachers, supervisors, and directors of agricultural subjects, and teachers of trade, home economics, and industrial subjects, and in the preparation of teachers of agricultural, trade, industrial, and home economics subjects; and the sum provided for in section seven for the use of the Federal Board for Vocational Education for the administration of this Act and for the purpose of making studies, investigations, and reports to aid in the organization and conduct of vocational education, which sums shall be expended as hereinafter provided.

Sec. 2. That for the purpose of cooperating with the States in paying the salaries of teachers, supervisors, or directors of agricultural subjects there is hereby appropriated for the use of the States, subject to the provisions of this Act, for the fiscal year ending June thirtieth, nineteen hundred and eighteen, the sum of $500,000; for the fiscal year ending June thirtieth, nineteen hundred and nineteen, the sum of $750,000; for the fiscal year ending June thirtieth, nineteen hundred and twenty, the sum of $1,000,000; for the fiscal year ending June thirtieth, nineteen hundred and twenty-one, the sum of $1,250,000; for the fiscal year ending June thirtieth, nineteen hundred and twenty-two, the sum of $1,500,000; for the fiscal year ending June thirtieth, nineteen hundred and twenty-three, the sum of $1,750,000; for the fiscal year ending June thirtieth, nineteen hundred and twenty-four, the sum of $2,000,000; for the fiscal year ending June thirtieth, nineteen hundred and twenty-five, the sum of $2,500,000; for the fiscal year ending June thirtieth, nineteen hundred and twenty-six, and annually thereafter, the sum of $3,000,000. Said sums shall be allotted to the States in the proportion which their rural population bears to the total rural population in the United States, not including outlying possessions, according to the last preceding United States census: *Provided,* That the allotment of funds to any State shall be not less than a minimum of $5,000 for any fiscal year prior to and including the fiscal year ending June thirtieth, nineteen hundred and twenty-three, nor less than $10,000 for any fiscal year thereafter, and there is hereby appropriated the following sums, or so much thereof as may be necessary, which shall be used for the purpose of providing the minimum allotment to the States provided for in this section: For the fiscal year ending June thirtieth, nineteen hundred and eighteen, the sum of $48,000; for the fiscal year ending June thirtieth, nineteen hundred and nineteen, the sum of $34,000; for the fiscal year ending June thirtieth, nineteen hundred and twenty, the sum of $24,000; for the fiscal year ending June thirtieth, nineteen hundred and twenty-one, the sum of $18,000; for the fiscal year ending June thirtieth, nineteen hundred and twenty-two, the sum of $14,000; for the fiscal year ending June thirtieth, nineteen hundred and twenty-three, the sum of $11,000; for the fiscal year ending June thirtieth, nineteen hundred and twenty-four, the sum of $9,000; for the fiscal year ending June thirtieth, nineteen hundred and twenty-five, the sum of $34,000; and annually thereafter the sum of $27,000.

Sec. 3. That for the purpose of cooperating with the States in paying the salaries of teachers of trade, home economics, and industrial subjects there is hereby appropriated for the use of the States, for the fiscal year ending June thirtieth, nineteen hundred and eighteen, the sum of $500,000; for the fiscal year ending June thirtieth, nineteen hundred and nineteen, the sum of $750,000; for the fiscal year ending June thirtieth, nineteen hundred and twenty, the sum of $1,000,000; for the fiscal year ending June thirtieth, nineteen hundred and twenty-one, the sum of $1,250,000; for the fiscal year ending June thirtieth, nineteen hundred and twenty-two, the sum of $1,500,000; for the fiscal year ending June thirtieth, nineteen hundred and twenty-three, the sum of $1,750,000; for the fiscal year ending June thirtieth, nineteen hundred and twenty-four, the sum of $2,000,000; for the fiscal year ending June thirtieth, nineteen hundred and twenty-five, the sum of $2,500,000; for the fiscal year ending June thirtieth, nineteen hundred and twenty-six, the sum of

$3,000,000; and annually thereafter the sum of $3,000,000. Said sums shall be allotted to the States in the proportion which their urban population bears to the total urban population in the United States, not including outlying possessions, according to the last preceding United States census: *Provided,* That the allotment of funds to any State shall be not less than a minimum of $5,000 for any fiscal year prior to and including the fiscal year ending June thirtieth, nineteen hundred and twenty-three, nor less than $10,000 for any fiscal year thereafter, and there is hereby appropriated the following sums, or so much thereof as may be needed, which shall be used for the purpose of providing the minimum allotment to the States provided for in this section: For the fiscal year ending June thirtieth, nineteen hundred and eighteen, the sum of $66,000; for the fiscal year ending June thirtieth, nineteen hundred and nineteen, the sum of $46,000; for the fiscal year ending June thirtieth, nineteen hundred and twenty, the sum of $34,000; for the fiscal year ending June thirtieth, nineteen hundred and twenty-one, the sum of $28,000; for the fiscal year ending June thirtieth, nineteen hundred and twenty-two, the sum of $25,000; for the fiscal year ending June thirtieth, nineteen hundred and twenty-three, the sum of $22,000; for the fiscal year ending June thirtieth, nineteen hundred and twenty-four, the sum of $19,000; for the fiscal year ending June thirtieth, nineteen hundred and twenty-five, the sum of $56,000; for the fiscal year ending June thirtieth, nineteen hundred and twenty-six, and annually thereafter, the sum of $50,000.

That not more than twenty per centum of the money appropriated under this Act for the payment of salaries of teachers of trade, home economics, and industrial subjects, for any year, shall be expended for the salaries of teachers of home economics subjects.

Sec. 4. That for the purpose of cooperating with the States in preparing teachers, supervisors, and directors of agricultural subjects and teachers of trade and industrial and home economics subjects there is hereby appropriated for the use of the States for the fiscal year ending June thirtieth, nineteen hundred and eighteen, the sum of $500,000; for the fiscal year ending June thirtieth, nineteen hundred and nineteen, the sum of $700,000; for the fiscal year ending June thirtieth, nineteen hundred and twenty, the sum of $900,000; for the fiscal year ending June thirtieth, nineteen hundred and twenty-one, and annually thereafter, the sum of $1,000,000. Said sums shall be allotted to the States in the proportion which their population bears to the total population of the United States, not including outlying possessions, according to the last preceding United States census: *Provided,* That the allotment of funds to any State shall be not less than a minimum of $5,000 for any fiscal year prior to and including the fiscal year ending June thirtieth, nineteen hundred and nineteen, nor less than $10,000 for any fiscal year thereafter. And there is hereby appropriated the following sums, or so much thereof as may be needed, which shall be used for the purpose of providing the minimum allotment provided for in this section: For the fiscal year ending June thirtieth, nineteen hundred and eighteen, the sum of $46,000; for the fiscal year ending June thirtieth, nineteen hundred and nineteen, the sum of $32,000; for the fiscal year ending June thirtieth, nineteen hundred and twenty, the sum of $24,000; for the fiscal year ending June thirtieth, nineteen hundred and twenty-one, and annually thereafter, the sum of $90,000.

Sec. 5. That in order to secure the benefits of the appropriations provided for in sections two, three, and four of this Act, any State shall, through the legislative authority thereof, accept the provisions of this Act and designate or create a State board, consisting of not less than three members, and having all necessary power to cooperate, as herein provided, with the Federal Board for Vocational Education in the administration of the provisions of this Act. The State board of education, or other board having charge of the administration of public education in the State, or any State board having charge of the administration of any kind of vocational education in the State may, if the State so elect, be designated as the State board, for the purposes of this Act.

In any State the legislature of which does not meet in nineteen hundred and seventeen, if the governor of that State, so far as he is authorized to do so, shall accept the provisions of this Act and designate or create a State board of not less than three members to act in cooperation with the Federal Board for Vocational Education, the Federal board shall recognize such local board for the purposes of this Act until the legislature of such State meets in due course and has been in session sixty days.

Any State may accept the benefits of any one or more of the respective funds herein appropriated, and it may defer the acceptance of the benefits of any one or more of such funds, and shall be required to meet only the conditions relative to the fund or

funds the benefits of which it has accepted: *Provided,* That after June thirtieth, nineteen hundred and twenty, no State shall receive any appropriation for salaries of teachers, supervisors, or directors of agricultural subjects, until it shall have taken advantage of at least the minimum amount appropriated for the training of teachers, supervisors, or directors of agricultural subjects, as provided for in this Act, and that after said date no State shall receive any appropriation for the salaries of teachers of trade, home economics, and industrial subjects until it shall have taken advantage of at least the minimum amount appropriated for the training of teachers of trade, home economics, and industrial subjects, as provided for in this Act.

Sec. 6. That a Federal Board for Vocational Education is hereby created, to consist of the Secretary of Agriculture, the Secretary of Commerce, the Secretary of Labor, the United States Commissioner of Education, and three citizens of the United States to be appointed by the President, by and with the advice and consent of the Senate. One of said three citizens shall be a representative of the manufacturing and commercial interests, one a representative of the agricultural interests, and one a representative of labor. The board shall elect annually one of its members as chairman. In the first instance, one of the citizen members shall be appointed for one year, one for two years, and one for three years, and thereafter for three years each. The members of the board other than the members of the Cabinet and the United States Commissioner of Education shall receive a salary of $5,000 per annum.

The board shall have power to cooperate with State boards in carrying out the provisions of this Act. It shall be the duty of the Federal Board for Vocational Education to make, or cause to have made studies, investigations, and reports, with particular reference to their use in aiding the States in the establishment of vocational schools and classes and in giving instruction in agriculture, trades and industries, commerce and commercial pursuits, and home economics. Such studies, investigations, and reports shall include agriculture and agricultural processes and requirements upon agricultural workers; trades, industries, and apprenticeships, trade and industrial requirements upon industrial workers, and classification of industrial processes and pursuits; commerce and commercial pursuits and requirements upon commercial workers; home management, domestic science, and the study of related facts and principles; and problems of administration of vocational schools and of courses of study and instruction in vocational subjects.

When the board deems it advisable such studies, investigations, and reports concerning agriculture, for the purposes of agricultural education, may be made in cooperation with or through the Department of Agriculture; such studies, investigations, and reports concerning trades and industries, for the purposes of trade and industrial education, may be made in cooperation with or through the Department of Labor; such studies, investigations, and reports concerning commerce and commercial pursuits, for the purposes of commercial education, may be made in cooperation with or through the Department of Commerce; such studies, investigations, and reports concerning the administration of vocational schools, courses of study and instruction in vocational subjects, may be made in cooperation with or through the Bureau of Education.

The Commissioner of Education may make such recommendations to the board relative to the administration of this Act as he may from time to time deem advisable. It shall be the duty of the chairman of the board to carry out the rules, regulations, and decisions which the board may adopt. The Federal Board for Vocational Education shall have power to employ such assistants as may be necessary to carry out the provisions of this Act.

## Further Resources

### BOOKS

Butts, R. Freeman, and Lawrence Cremin. *A History of Education in American Culture.* New York: Henry Holt, 1953.

Cremin, Lawrence A. *The Transformation of the School: Progressivism in American Education, 1876–1957.* New York: Alfred A. Knopf, 1961.

Gordon, Howard R. D. *The History and Growth of Vocational Education in America.* Boston: Allyn and Bacon, 1999.

Katznelson, Ira, and Margaret Weir. *Schooling for All: Class, Race, and the Decline of the Democratic Ideal.* New York: Basic Books, 1985.

McClure, Arthur F. et al. *Education for Work: The Historical Evolution of Vocational and Distributive Education in America.* Rutherford, N.J.: Fairleigh Dickinson University Press, 1985.

True, Alfred C. *A History of Agricultural Education in the United States, 1785–1925.* U.S. Department of Agriculture, Miscellaneous Publication No. 36. Washington, D.C.: U.S. Government Printing Office, 1929.

### PERIODICALS

Camp, W. G., and J. R Crunkilton. "History of Agricultural Education in America: The Great Individuals and Events." *The Journal of the American Association of Teacher Educators in Agriculture* 26, no. 1, 1985, 57–63.

Herren, R. "Controversy and Unification: The Passage of the Smith-Hughes Act." *The Journal of the American Association of Teacher Educators in Agriculture* 27, no. 1, 1986, 39–44.

Hillison, J. "Agricultural Teacher Education Preceding the Smith-Hughes Act." *The Journal of the American Association of Teacher Educators in Agriculture* 28 no. 2, 1987, 8–17.

# Cardinal Principles of Secondary Education
## Report

**By:** Commission on the Reorganization of Secondary Education

**Date:** 1918

**Source:** Bureau of Education, Department of the Interior. *Cardinal Principles of Secondary Education; A Report of the Commission on the Reorganization of Secondary Education, Appointed by the National Education Association.* Bulletin No. 35. Washington, D.C.: U.S. Government Printing Office, 1918.

**About the Commission:** The Commission on the Reorganization of Secondary Education, chaired by Clarence D. Kingsley, was appointed by the National Education Association in 1913 to determine the aims and direction of public, secondary education in the United States. The result, *Cardinal Principles of Secondary Education,* was released in 1918. ■

## Introduction

British philosopher Herbert Spencer, through his mid–nineteenth century essays on education, had a profound influence on American educational thinking. The purpose of education, for Spencer, was "to prepare us for complete living." He offered five categories that make up "complete living": activities regarding 1) "self-preservation," 2) "securing the necessaries of life," 3) "rearing and discipline of offspring," 4) "the maintenance of proper social and political relations," and 5) "gratification of the tastes and feelings." The question, "of what use is it," should always be asked, and the most useful area of study, for Spencer, is science. Spencer was critical of the classical, college-preparatory curriculum of nineteenth century American secondary schools.

As the end of the nineteenth century approached, American educational thought also was shaped by the progressive education movement. Gaining prominence by this time, it emphasized practical, relevant curricula, meaningful for students in their lives outside of school. In addition, the rapidly expanding industrial sector led some to turn to the schools to meet the growing need for skilled labor.

British philosopher Herbert Spencer had a profound influence on American education in the early twentieth century. © HULTON-DEUTSCH COLLECTION/CORBIS. REPRODUCED BY PERMISSION.

Beginning at the turn of the century, and accelerating after 1910, an increasing percentage of the high-school age population attended high school. This resulted in a more diverse student body, and a smaller proportion of college-bound students. Throughout the first two decades of the twentieth century, secondary schools gradually expanded the curriculum to meet the needs of this diverse group. Manual training, agricultural education, and commercial courses began to appear alongside traditional academic offerings.

In this context, the National Education Association (NEA) appointed the Commission on the Reorganization of Secondary Education in 1913 to determine "those fundamental principles that would be most helpful in directing secondary education." In its report, *Cardinal Principles of Secondary Education,* the Committee recommended a set of objectives, adhering closely to Spencer's view of education as preparation for complete living: "health," "command of fundamental processes," "worthy home-membership," "vocation," "citizenship," "worthy use of leisure," and "ethical character."

**Significance**

The Commission's report is often viewed as the catalyst for an expanded secondary curriculum, preparing students for life irrespective of their college plans. However, the report mainly confirmed and reinforced a trend already well underway at this time. Factors—including child labor laws, the growth of American industry, compulsory education laws, and new waves of immigration—forced schools to adapt. In addition, the ideas of Herbert Spencer and the progressive education movement had already impacted the type of curriculum offered in schools.

Yet the report marked a change in the official aims of public secondary education and the appearance of the "comprehensive high school," serving all students, which grew in popularity over the next several decades. The comprehensive high school, standard by the 1950s, serves the needs of college-bound students, as well as providing an array of vocational and technical programs for those who do not intend to continue past high school. Supporters of the comprehensive high school cite the benefits to American unity and inter-group understanding and cooperation. When the majority of children go to school together, rather than attending separate vocational and academic high schools, this unity grows.

Critics of the report, such as Richard Mitchell and John Gatto, charge that it represented a "dumbing-down" of the curriculum and a belief that many students cannot, or should not, reap the benefits of a broad, liberal course of studies. Others see in the report the beginnings of a scattered and unfocused curriculum, leaving little room for essentials or traditional academic studies. Nonetheless, the comprehensive high school is, today, the dominant model of secondary public schools.

**Primary Source**

*Cardinal Principles of Secondary Education*
[excerpt]

**SYNOPSIS:** In this excerpt from its report, the Commission outlines its arguments for the need to reorganize secondary education, citing changes in society, secondary students as a group, and educational theory. Seven objectives of education and the rationale behind them are discussed: health, command of fundamental processes, worthy home-membership, vocation, citizenship, worthy use of leisure, and ethical character.

**Cardinal Principles of Secondary Education**

**I. The Need for Reorganization**

Secondary education should be determined by the needs of the society to be served, the character of the individuals to be educated, and the knowledge of educational theory and practice available. These factors are by no means static. Society is always in process of development; the character of the secondary-school population undergoes modification; and the sciences on which educational theory and practice depend constantly furnish new information. Secondary education, however, like any other established agency of society, is conservative and tends to resist modification. Failure to make adjustments when the need arises leads to the necessity for extensive reorganization at irregular intervals. The evidence is strong that such a comprehensive reorganization of secondary education is imperative at the present time.

## 1. Changes in Society

Within the past few decades changes have taken place in American life profoundly affecting the activities of the individual. As a citizen, he must to a greater extent and in a more direct way cope with problems of community life, State and National Governments, and international relationships. As a worker, he must adjust himself to a more complex economic order. As a relatively independent personality, he has more leisure. The problems arising from these three dominant phases of life are closely interrelated and call for a degree of intelligence and efficiency on the part of every citizen that can not be secured through elementary education alone, or even through secondary education unless the scope of that education is broadened.

The responsibility of the secondary school is still further increased because many social agencies other than the school afford less stimulus for education than heretofore. In many vocations there have come such significant changes as the substitution of the factory system for the domestic system of industry; the use of machinery in place of manual labor; the high specialization of processes with a corresponding subdivision of labor; and the breakdown of the apprentice system. In connection with home and family life have frequently come lessened responsibility on the part of the children; the withdrawal of the father and sometimes the mother from home occupations to the factory or store; and increased urbanization, resulting in less unified family life. Similarly, many important changes have taken place in community life, in the church, in the State, and in other institutions. These changes in American life call for extensive modifications in secondary education.

## 2. Changes in the Secondary-School Population

In the past 25 years there have been marked changes in the secondary-school population of the United States. The number of pupils has increased, according to Federal returns, from one for every 210 of the total population in 1889–90, to one for every 121 in 1899–1900, to one for every 89 in 1909–10, and to one for every 73 of the estimated total population in 1914–15. The character of the secondary-school population has been modified by the entrance of large numbers of pupils of widely varying capacities, aptitudes, social heredity, and destinies in life. Further, the broadening of the scope of secondary education has brought to the school many pupils who do not complete the full course but leave at various stages of advancement. The needs of these pupils can not be neglected, nor can we expect in the near future that all pupils will be able to complete the secondary school as fulltime students.

At present only about one-third of the pupils who enter the first year of the elementary school reach the four-year high school, and only about one in nine is graduated. Of those who enter the seventh school year, only one-half to two-thirds reach the first year of the four-year high school. Of those who enter the four-year high school about one-third leave before the beginning of the second year, about one-half are gone before the beginning of the third year, and fewer than one-third are graduated. These facts can no longer be safely ignored.

## 3. Changes in Educational Theory

The sciences on which educational theory depends have within recent years made significant contributions. In particular, educational psychology emphasizes the following factors:

(a) *Individual differences in capacities and aptitudes among secondary-school pupils.* Already recognized to some extent, this factor merits fuller attention.

(b) *The reexamination and reinterpretation of subject values and the teaching methods with reference to "general discipline."* While the final verdict of modern psychology has not as yet been rendered, it is clear that former conceptions of "general values" must be thoroughly revised.

(c) *Importance of applying knowledge.* Subject values and teaching methods must be tested in terms of the laws of learning and the application of knowledge to the activities of life, rather than primarily in terms of the demands of any subject as a logically organized science.

(d) *Continuity in the development of children.* It has long been held that psychological changes at certain stages are so pronounced as to overshadow the continuity of development. On this basis secondary education has been sharply separated from elementary education. Modern psychology, however, goes to show that the development of the individual is in most respects a continuous process and that, therefore, any sudden or abrupt break between the elementary and the secondary school or between any two successive stages of education is undesirable.

The foregoing changes in society, in the character of the secondary school population, and in educational theory, together with many other considerations, call for extensive modifications of secondary education. Such modifications have already begun in part. The present need is for the formulation of a comprehensive program of reorganization, and its adoption, with suitable adjustments, in all the secondary schools of the Nation. Hence it is appropriate for a representative body like the National Education Association to outline such a program. This is the task entrusted by that association to the Commission on the Reorganization of Secondary Education.

## II. The Goal of Education in a Democracy

Education in the United States should be guided by a clear conception of the meaning of democracy. It is the ideal of democracy that the individual and society may find fulfillment each in the other. Democracy sanctions neither the exploitation of the individual by society, nor the disregard of the interests of society by the individual. More explicitly—

> The purpose of democracy is so to organize society that each member may develop his personality primarily through activities designed for the well-being of his fellow members and of society as a whole.

This ideal demands that human activities be placed upon a high level of efficiency; that to this efficiency be added an appreciation of the significance of these activities and loyalty to the best ideals involved; and that the individual choose that vocation and those forms of social service in which his personality may develop and become most effective. For the achievement of these ends democracy must place chief reliance upon education.

Consequently, education in a democracy, both within and without the school, should develop in each individual the knowledge, interests, ideals, habits, and powers whereby he will find his place and use that place to shape both himself and society toward ever nobler ends.

## III. The Main Objectives of Education

In order to determine the main objectives that should guide education in a democracy, it is necessary to analyze the activities of the individual. Normally he is a member of a family, of a vocational group, and of various civic groups, and by virtue of these relationships he is called upon to engage in activities that enrich the family life, to render important vocational services to his fellows, and to promote the common welfare. It follows, therefore, that worthy home membership, vocation, and citizenship demand attention as three of the leading objectives.

Aside from the immediate discharge of these specific duties, every individual should have a margin of time for the cultivation of personal and social interests. This leisure, if worthily used, will recreate his powers and enlarge and enrich life, thereby making him better able to meet his responsibilities. The unworthy use of leisure impairs health, disrupts home life, lessens vocational efficiency, and destroys civic-mindedness. The tendency in industrial life, aided by legislation, is to decrease the working hours of large groups of people. While shortened hours tend to lessen the harmful reactions that arise from prolonged strain, they increase, if possible, the importance of preparation for leisure. In view of these considerations, education for the worthy use of leisure is of increasing importance as an objective.

To discharge the duties of life and to benefit from leisure, one must have good health. The health of the individual is essential also to the vitality of the race and to the defense of the Nation. Health education is, therefore, fundamental.

There are various processes, such as reading, writing, arithmetical computations, and oral and written expression, that are needed as tools in the affairs of life. Consequently, command of these fundamental processes, while not an end in itself, is nevertheless an indispensable objective.

And, finally, the realization of the objectives already named is dependent upon ethical character, that is, upon conduct founded upon right principles, clearly perceived and loyally adhered to. Good citizenship, vocational excellence, and the worthy use of leisure go hand in hand with ethical character; they are at once the fruits of sterling character and the channels through which such character is developed and made manifest. On the one hand, character is meaningless apart from the will to discharge the duties of life, and, on the other hand, there is no guaranty that these duties will be rightly discharged unless principles are substituted for impulses, however well-intentioned such impulses may be. Consequently, ethical character is at once involved in all the other objectives and at the same time requires specific consideration in any program of national education.

This commission, therefore, regards the following as the main objectives of education:

1. Health
2. Command of fundamental processes
3. Worthy home membership
4. Vocation
5. Citizenship
6. Worthy use of leisure
7. Ethical character

The naming of the above objectives is not intended to imply that the process of education can be divided into separated fields. This can not be, since the pupil is indivisible. Nor is the analysis all-inclusive. Nevertheless, we believe that distinguishing and naming these objectives will aid in directing efforts; and we hold that they should constitute the principal aims in education.

## Further Resources

### BOOKS

Butts, R. Freeman, and Lawrence Cremin. *A History of Education in American Culture*. New York: Henry Holt, 1953.

Cremin, Lawrence A. *The Transformation of The School: Progressivism in American Education, 1876–1957*. New York: Alfred A. Knopf, 1961.

Kliebard, Herbert M. *The Struggle For the American Curriculum*. Boston: Routledge and Kegan Paul, 1986.

Mitchell, Richard. *The Graves of Academe*. Boston: Little, Brown, 1981.

Raubinger, F.M., et al. *The Development of Secondary Education*. New York: Macmillan, 1969.

Spencer, Herbert. *Herbert Spencer on Education*. Andreas M. Kazamias, ed. New York: Teachers College Press, 1966.

# "The Project Method"

Journal article

**By:** William Heard Kilpatrick

**Date:** 1918

**Source:** Kilpatrick, William Heard. "The Project Method." *Teachers College Record* 19, 1918, 319–323.

**About the Author:** William Heard Kilpatrick (1871–1965) earned degrees from Mercer University and the Johns Hopkins University, and he received his Ph.D. from Columbia University. He was a teacher and principal in the Georgia public schools. A student of the influential progressive educator John Dewey, Kilpatrick is credited with interpreting Dewey's theories for a wider audience. He taught at Mercer University, and then at Teachers College, Columbia University, until his retirement. He was the author of many books and articles. ■

## Introduction

William Heard Kilpatrick began his career in education during the progressive era. Although the progressive movement encompassed a variety of approaches and philosophies, progressive educators generally emphasized a scientific and experimental approach to educational problems. It focused on student interests, socialization, meaningful curriculum, freedom for students, and the needs of individual. Kilpatrick was a student, and later a colleague, of John Dewey, one of the most important figures in progressive education.

In Kilpatrick's project method, the student engages in "wholehearted purposeful activity proceeding in a social environment." The student, not the teacher, determined the goal, planned the procedure, carried it out, and evaluated the outcome. This occurred in a social environment, so that many projects were the work of a group, and community members evaluated all outcomes. The role of the teacher was "to guide the pupil through his present interests and achievement into the wider interests and achievement demanded by the wider social life. . . ."

In developing his project method, Kilpatrick sought to combine Dewey's emphases—on student motivation and the school as a true social community—with the "Laws of Learning" developed by Edward L. Thorndike. The most important of these laws was the law of effect: behaviors become stronger when followed by a satisfying effect, and weaker when followed by an annoying effect. Learning, for Thorndike, was the process of forming neural connections, based on the linking of a stimulus and a response. In the project method, the purpose served as the motivation for the student: a goal that the student genuinely wanted to achieve. Internal motivation, not external compulsion from a teacher, impelled the student toward the goal, solving problems and difficulties as they arose. Each successful step was satisfying to the student, because it leads toward the desired goal—skills and knowledge that the student learns in the process are thus reinforced and strengthened. In addition, purposeful activities carried on in a social environment will bring about moral learning, as the student's actions produce approval (a satisfying result) or disapproval (an annoying result) of the community of learners.

## Significance

Kilpatrick's article describing the project method received international attention, and it resulted in Kilpatrick's becoming a major spokesperson of progressive education. His work is viewed by many in the education field as a practical application of the philosophy of John Dewey. While there are common aspects between the ideas of Dewey and Kilpatrick, there are some key differences as well. Dewey's approach included the goal of guiding students from the interests they bring to school toward an organized curriculum. Kilpatrick, on the other hand, rejected all "fixed-in-advance" curriculum. Kilpatrick's more extreme "child-centered" approach has often been mistakenly attributed to Dewey.

Despite the diversity of the movement, Kilpatrick's approach came to be identified with the progressive education movement as a whole. While some credit him as the originator of current methods emphasizing student choice and group learning, others, such as E.D. Hirsch, view Kilpatrick as the source of an unfortunate lack of emphasis on content and core learning in modern schools.

## Primary Source

"The Project Method" [excerpt]

> **SYNOPSIS:** Kilpatrick defines "project" in terms of his project method as "wholehearted purposeful activity proceeding in a social environment." If education is (or should be) life, Kilpatrick argues, and life in a democracy ideally consists of purposeful acts, then the best preparation for that life is to live it. Thus, the unit of education is the project—an activity that the child is intrinsically motivated to do, plans himself or herself, and which takes place in a social context.

The word 'project' is perhaps the latest arrival to knock for admittance at the door of educational terminology. Shall we admit the stranger? Not wisely until two preliminary questions have first been answered in the affirmative: First, is there behind the proposed term and waiting even now to be christened a valid notion or concept which promises to render appreciable service in educational thinking? Second, if we grant the foregoing, does the term 'project' fitly designate the waiting concept? Because the question as to the concept and its worth is so much more significant than any matter of mere names, this discussion will deal almost exclusively with the first of the two inquiries. It is indeed entirely possible that some other term, as 'purposeful act', for example, would call attention to a more important element in the concept, and, if so, might prove superior as a term to the word 'project'. At the outset it is probably wise to caution the reader against expecting any great amount of novelty in the idea here presented. The metaphor of christening is not to be taken too seriously; the concept to be considered is not in fact newly born. Not a few readers will be disappointed that after all so little new is presented.

A little of the personal may perhaps serve to introduce the more formal discussion. In attacking with successive classes in educational theory the problem of method, I had felt increasingly the need of unifying more completely a number of important related aspects of the educative process. I began to hope for some one concept which might serve this end. Such a concept, if found, must, so I thought, emphasize the factor of action, preferably wholehearted vigorous activity. It must at the same time provide a place for the adequate utilization of the laws of learning, and no less for the essential elements of the ethical quality of conduct. The last named looks of course to the social situation as well as to the individual attitude. Along with these should go, as it seemed, the important generalization that education is life—so easy to say and so hard to delimit. Could now all of these be contemplated under one workable notion? If yes, a great gain. In proportion as such a unifying concept could be found in like proportion would the work of presenting educational theory be facilitated; in like proportion should be the rapid spread of a better practice.

But could this unifying idea be found? Here was in fact the age-old problem of effective logical organization. My whole philosophic outlook had made me suspicious of so-called 'fundamental principles'. Was there yet another way of attaining unity? I do not mean to say that I asked these questions, either in these words or in this order. Rather is this a retrospective ordering of the more important outcomes. As the desired unification lay specifically in the field of method, might not some typical unit of concrete procedure supply the need-some unit of conduct that should be, as it were, a sample of life, a fair sample of the worthy life and consequently of education? As these questionings rose more definitely to mind, there came increasingly a belief-corroborated on many sides-that the unifying idea I sought was to be found in the conception of whole-hearted purposeful activity proceeding in a social environment, or more briefly, in the unit element of such activity, the hearty purposeful act.

It is to this purposeful act with the emphasis on the word purpose that I myself apply the term 'project'. I did not invent the term nor did I start it on its educational career. Indeed, I do not know how long it has already been in use. I did, however, consciously appropriate the word to designate the typical unit of the worthy life described above. Others who were using the term seemed to me either to use it in a mechanical and partial sense or to be intending in a general way what I tried to define more exactly. The purpose of this article is to attempt to clarify the concept underlying the term as much as it is to defend the claim of the concept to a place in our educational thinking. The actual terminology with which to designate the concept is, as was said before, to my mind a matter of relatively small moment. If, however, we think of a project as a project, something pro-jected, the reason for its adoption may better appear.

Postponing yet a little further the more systematic presentation of the matter, let us from some typical instances see more concretely what is contemplated under the term project or hearty purposeful act? Suppose a girl makes a dress. If she did in hearty fashion purpose to make the dress, if she planned it, if she made it herself, then I should say the instance is that of a typical project. We have a wholehearted purposeful act carried on amid social surroundings. That the dressmaking was purposeful is clear; the purpose once formed dominated each succeeding step in the process and gave unity to the whole. That the girl was wholehearted in the work was assured in the illustration. That the activity proceeded in a social environment is clear; other girls at least are to see the dress. As another instance, suppose a boy undertakes to get out a school newspaper. If he is in earnest about it, we again have the effective purpose being the essence of the project. So we may instance a pupil writing a letter (if the hearty purpose is present), a child listening absorbedly to a story, Newton explaining the motion of the moon on the principles of terrestrial dynamics, Demosthenes trying to arouse the Greeks against Philip, Da Vinci painting the Last Supper, my writing this article, a boy solving with felt purpose an 'original' in geometry. All of the foregoing have been acts of individual purposing, but this is not to rule out group projects: a class presents a play, a group of boys organize a base-ball nine, three pupils prepare to read a story to their comrades. It is clear then that projects may present every variety that purposes present in life. It is also clear that a mere description of outwardly observable facts might not disclose the essential factor, namely the presence of a dominating purpose. It is equally true that there can be every degree of approximation to full projects according as the animating purpose varies in clearness and strength. If we conceive activities as ranging on a scale from those performed under dire compulsion up to those into which one puts his 'whole heart', the argument herein made restricts the term 'project' or purposeful act to the upper portions of the scale. An exact dividing line is hard to draw, and yields indeed in importance to the notion that psychological value increases with the degree of approximation to 'wholeheartedness'. As to the social environment element, some may feel that, however important this is to the fullest educative experience, it is still not essential to the conception of the purposeful act as here presented. These might therefore wish to leave this element out of the defining discussion. To this I should not object if it were clearly understood that the resulting concept—now essentially psychological in character—generally speaking, demands the social situation both for its practical working and for the comparative valuation of proffered projects.

With this general introduction, we may, in the first place, say that the purposeful act is the typical unit of the worthy life. Not that all purposes are good, but that the worthy life consists of purposive activity and not mere drifting. We scorn the man who passively accepts what fate or some other chance brings to him. We admire the man who is master of his fate, who with deliberate regard for a total situation forms clear and far-reaching purposes, who plans and executes with nice care the purposes so formed. A man who habitually so regulates his life with reference to worthy social aims meets at once the demands for practical efficiency and of moral responsibility. Such a one presents the ideal of democratic citizenship. It is equally true that the purposeful act is not the unit of life for the serf or the slave. These poor unfortunates must in the interest of the overmastering system be habituated to act with a minimum of their own purposing and with a maximum of servile acceptance of others' purposes. In important matters they merely follow plans handed down to them from above, and execute these according to prescribed directions. For them another carries responsibility and upon the results of their labor another passes judgment. No such plan as that here advocated would produce the kind of docility required for their hopeless fate. But it is a democracy which we contemplate and with which we are here concerned.

As the purposeful act is thus the typical unit of the worthy life in a democratic society, so also should it be made the typical unit of school procedure. We of America have for years increasingly desired that education be considered as life itself and not as a mere preparation for later living. The conception before us promises a definite step toward the attainment of this end. If the purposeful act be in reality the typical unit of the worthy life, then it follows that to base education on purposeful acts is exactly to identify the process of education with worthy living itself. The two become then the same. All the arguments for placing education on a life basis seem, to me at any rate, to concur in support of this thesis. On this basis education has become life. And if the purposeful act thus makes of education life itself, could we reasoning in advance expect to find a better preparation for later life than practice in living now? We have heard of old that "we learn to do by doing," and much wisdom resides in the saying. If the worthy life of the coming day is to consist of well-chosen purposeful acts, what preparation for that time could promise more than practice now, under discriminating guidance, in forming and executing worthy purposes? To this end must the child have within rather large limits the opportunity to purpose. For the issues of his act he must–in like limits–be held accountable. That the child may properly progress, the total situation–all the factors of life, including comrades-speaking, if need be through the teacher, must make clear its selective judgment upon what he does, approving the better, rejecting the worse. In a true sense the whole remaining discussion is but to support the contention here argued in advance that education based on the purposeful act prepares best for life while at the same time it constitutes the present worthy life itself.

A more explicit reason for making the purposeful act the typical unit of instruction is found in the utilization of the laws of learning which this plan affords. I am assuming that it is not necessary in this magazine to justify or even explain at length these laws.

## Further Resources

### BOOKS

Beineke, J. *And There Were Giants in the Land: The Life of William Heard Kilpatrick.* New York: P. Lang, 1988.

Cremin, Lawrence A. *The Transformation of The School: Progressivism in American Education, 1876–1957.* New York: Alfred A. Knopf, 1961.

Hirsch, E.D. *The Schools We Need and Why We Don't Have Them.* New York: Doubleday, 1996.

Kilpatrick, W.H. *The Educational Frontier.* New York: Arco Press, 1969.

———. *Foundations of Method: Informal Talks on Teaching.* New York: Arco Press, 1971.

———. *Group Education for a Democracy.* New York: Association Press, 1940.

### PERIODICALS

Bickel, Frank. "Student Assessment: The Project Method Revisited." *Clearing House* 68, no. 1, September–October 1994, 40–42.

Chipman, Donald D., and Carl B. McDonald. "The Historical Contributions of William Heard Kilpatrick." *Journal of Thought* 15, no. 1, Spring 1980, 71–83.

Waks, Leonard J. "The Project Method in Postindustrial Education." *Journal of Curriculum Studies* 29, no. 4, July–August 1997, 391–406.

# 4

# FASHION AND DESIGN

MILLIE JACKSON

*Entries are arranged in chronological order by date of primary source. For entries with one primary source, the entry title is the same as the primary source title. Entries with more than one primary source have an overall entry title, followed by the titles of the primary sources.*

**CHRONOLOGY**

Important Events in Fashion and Design,
   1910–1919 . . . . . . . . . . . . . . . . . . . . . . . . . . 188

**PRIMARY SOURCES**

Ford's Highland Park Plant
   Albert Kahn, 1910 . . . . . . . . . . . . . . . . . . . . . 190

"Craftsman Furniture Made by Gustav
   Stickley"
   Gustav Stickley, 1910 . . . . . . . . . . . . . . . . . . 191

"Five Pretty Ways to Do the Hair"
   *Ladies' Home Journal*, October 1911 . . . . . . . 193

"Flower Dresses for Lawn Fêtes"
   *Ladies' Home Journal*, 1911 . . . . . . . . . . . . . . 195

"What Is a Bungalow?"
   Phil M. Riley, 1912 . . . . . . . . . . . . . . . . . . . . 197

"Audacious Hats for Spineless Attitudes"
   *Dress & Vanity Fair*, September 1913 . . . . . . . 199

Woolworth Building . . . . . . . . . . . . . . . . . . . . . 202
"The Woolworth Building"
   Cass Gilbert, ca. 1913
*The Cathedral of Commerce*
   Edwin A. Cochran, 1916

"Proper Dancing-Costumes for Women"
   Irene Foote Castle, 1914 . . . . . . . . . . . . . . . . 207

"Whether at Home or Away, Your Summer
   Equipment Should Include a Bottle of
   Listerine"
   Lambert Pharmacal Company, 1915 . . . . . . . . 210

"Shopping for the Well-Dressed Man"
   *Vanity Fair*, July 1916 . . . . . . . . . . . . . . . . . 212

"A Woman Can Always Look Younger
   Than She Really Is"
   Elizabeth Arden, July 1916 . . . . . . . . . . . . . . 214

"Wealthiest Negro Woman's Suburban
   Mansion"
   *The New York Times Magazine*,
     November 4, 1917 . . . . . . . . . . . . . . . . . . . 216

"YWCA Overseas Uniform, 1918"
   House of Worth, 1918 . . . . . . . . . . . . . . . . . . 217

"Is There News in Shaving Soap?"
   J. Walter Thompson Company, May 29,
     1919 . . . . . . . . . . . . . . . . . . . . . . . . . . . . . 219

"Henry Ford in a Model T" . . . . . . . . . . . . . . . . 221

# Important Events in Fashion and Design, 1910–1919

## 1910

- Enormous hats festooned with ostrich plumes and fastened with long hat pins mark the end of the vogue for elaborate millinery creations that began in the nineteenth century.

- Elizabeth Arden (born Florence Nightingale Graham) opens a beauty salon in New York City. In 1915 she opens a branch in Washington, D.C., and by 1939 there are twenty-nine Elizabeth Arden salons.

- Ford Motor Company begins operations at Highland Park in the "Crystal Palace," a trailblazing factory complex designed by Albert Kahn and engineered by Edward Gray.

- Levi Strauss and Company begins making children's clothes, preparing the way for the adoption of casual play clothes for children.

- The first phonograph cabinet, with French cabriole legs and a mansard lid, is patented.

- Frank Lloyd Wright returns from Europe and begins construction on Taliesin, his new studio and house in the farm-lands of Wisconsin, where he had lived as a child.

- On July 13, the first issue of *Women's Wear Daily* is published in New York City.

- On September 8, Pennsylvania Station in New York City, the largest project ever undertaken by the architectural firm of McKim, Mead and White, is opened to commuter traffic from Long Island, linking the Pennsylvania and Long Island Railroads.

- In October, reacting to French fashions—such as the hobble skirt shown by French couturier Paul Poiret the previous spring—as unsuitable for American women's active lifestyles, the American Ladies' Tailors Association stages an exhibition of functional clothing at the Astor Hotel in New York City, showcasing such American originals as the suffragette suit with a divided skirt and aeroplane suits insulated with wool and fur.

## 1911

- C.H.K. Curtis, publisher of the *Saturday Evening Review* and *Ladies' Home Journal*, hires Charles Coolidge Parlin to conduct the first market research study, which alerts advertisers to the rise of women as consumers.

- Rayon, billed as "artificial silk," is introduced by the American Viscose Company. It does not become popular until

1915, when French couturiere Gabrielle "Coco" Chanel begins using it in her designs.

- On March 25, a fire at the Triangle Shirtwaist Factory, a sweatshop in New York's Lower East Side, kills 146 female workers.

- On May 23, fourteen years after breaking ground, the New York Public Library on Fifth Avenue, designed by the firm of Carrère and Hastings, is opened to the public. Partners John M. Carrère and Thomas Hastings are former employees of the architectural firm of McKim, Mead and White, well known for its Beaux-Arts buildings.

## 1912

- The dance team of Irene and Vernon Castle starts a craze for ballroom dancing. The simple, lightweight clothing that Irene Castle wears for ease of movement on the dance floor helps to increase the popularity of comfortable clothing among American women.

- Hoping to interest manufacturers in improving American industrial design, the Newark Museum of Art stages an exhibition of commercial productions designed by the Deutscher Werkbund of Germany.

- In December, *The New York Times* announces that it will sponsor a contest for American fashion designers, leading to the establishment of the Society of American Fashions.

- On December 22, the prestigious import and custom-design house Thurn of New York City admits it has been sewing French designer labels into its American-made dresses. "American women have been brainwashed into thinking French clothes are superior," complains a Thurn executive.

## 1913

- Designed by architect Cass Gilbert, the 792-foot-high Woolworth Building, nicknamed "The Cathedral of Commerce," opens on lower Broadway in New York City. Until 1930 it holds the record as the tallest building in the world.

- Midway Gardens, an amusement center and concert hall designed by Frank Lloyd Wright, opens in Chicago.

- The architectural firm of Cram, Goodhue and Ferguson completes two Gothic buildings, St. Thomas Church in New York City and the Graduate College at Princeton University.

- Henry Ford's Model T, originally available in a range of colors, is now available only in black.

- Grand Central Terminal, designed by the architectural firms of Reed and Stem and Warren and Wetmore, is completed in midtown Manhattan.

- The first face-powder compact, a cardboard box filled with powder and a puff, is introduced to American consumers.

- Formica is invented.

- On February 23, *The New York Times* announces the winning designs in its fashion contest. Included among the patriotic winners are a cotton-boll hat and a Quaker-style dress. Department stores trumpet their American-made designs, and *Ladies' Home Journal* claims credit for being first to promote American fashion.

- In March, *Ladies' Home Journal* features First Lady Ellen Wilson and her daughters modeling American designs.

## 1914

- The department store Lord & Taylor moves from Fifth Avenue and Nineteenth Street to Fifth Avenue and 38th Street in New York City.

- The Deutscher Werkbund exhibition in Cologne showcases the buildings of Walter Gropius, Josef Hoffman, and others whose work becomes influential in twentieth-century American architecture.

- In fall, anticipating that the outbreak of World War I will shut down the European fashion industry, *Vogue* editor Edna Woolman Chase prepares the New York Fashion Fete to take the place of the Paris shows, but the French couturiers manage to introduce new lines of clothing every season throughout the war. As the war continues, however, many women stop wearing lavish clothes and jewelry, and dress rules are relaxed in some venues. Also military styling becomes popular.

- In November, Mary Phelps Jacob (later Caresse Crosby) patents her design for the first brassiere. It does not become popular until the 1920s, after she sells the patent to Warner's corset company.

## 1915

- Helena Rubinstein launches her American cosmetics empire by opening the Maison de Beauté in New York City.

- Two expositions celebrating the opening of the Panama Canal are held in California. The Panama-California Exposition in San Diego, designed by Bertram Goodhue, features a Spanish theme and sparks a Spanish colonial revival. The Panama-Pacific Exposition in San Francisco has a Beaux-Arts Palace of Fine Arts designed by architect Bernard Maybeck, a former employee of the firm of Carrère and Hastings.

- Frank Lloyd Wright begins work on the Imperial Hotel in Tokyo (completed in 1922).

- Women's hemlines rise to mid-calf, shorter than ever before.

## 1916

- The Colburn Window-Glass Machine of the Libbey-Owens Sheet Glass Company turns out hundreds of square yards of glass in a continuous flow.

- The "hobble skirt" Coca-Cola bottle is introduced.

- Legislation in New York City addresses the problems created by skyscrapers—dark streets, congestion, traffic problems, and fire hazards—by requiring that buildings over a certain height be set back from the edges of their lots, and that the design include a stairstep feature.

- Bertram Goodhue begins work on the protomodern Nebraska State Capitol.

- The Massachusetts Institute of Technology moves to new buildings, designed by William Wells Bosworth, on the Charles River in Cambridge.

## 1917

- Construction begins on Harkness Memorial Tower at Yale University, designed by James Gamble Rogers and completed in 1921. It is one of many examples of a style that becomes known as "collegiate Gothic."

- The striking Hell's Gate Railroad Bridge, a cantilevered steel arch across the Harlem River, is completed in New York City.

- On February 23, the Smith-Hughes Act, promoting industrial education in America, is passed without any provision for education in aesthetics and design.

- Construction begins on Ford Motor Company's River Rouge plant in Michigan. In 1917, Albert Kahn completes Building B, which encloses an entire Ford assembly line. Ten years later, the plant consists of 90 miles of railroad tracks, 93 structures, 27 miles of conveyor belts, and employs 100,000 workers.

## 1918

- St. Bartholomew's Episcopal Church opens at Park Avenue and 50th Street in New York City. Designed by Goodhue, the Romanesque building incorporates the McKim, Mead and White portals from the congregation's previous church on Madison Avenue.

- The Hotel Commodore, designed by Warren and Wetmore, opens near Grand Central Terminal in New York City.

- The Hotel Pennsylvania, designed by McKim, Mead and White, opens near Pennsylvania Station in New York City.

- On November 11, a skyscraper at 27 West 43rd Street in New York City is the first building completed under the provisions of a 1916 zoning law that created a formula by which upper stories must be "stepped back" to allow more sunlight to reach the streets below.

## 1919

- William Randolph Hearst's San Simeon, designed by architect Julia Morgan, is begun 100 miles north of Santa Barbara, California.

- The Bauhaus, a design school directed by Walter Gropius, opens in Germany. Gropius becomes a major figure in American architecture after he flees Adolf Hitler's Germany in the 1930s.

- Ludwig Mies van der Rohe joins the Novembergruppe, directing its efforts to revive architecture in Germany, and undertakes the first of his glass skyscraper projects—a design that provides the basis for his history-making Seagram Building (1958) in New York City.

- Art-glass designer Louis Comfort Tiffany goes into semi-retirement.

## "Ford's Highland Park Plant"

Photograph

**By:** Albert Kahn

**Date:** 1910

**Source:** "Ford Motor Company Employees." 1916. Image no. IH161094. Available online at http://pro.corbis.com (accessed May 19, 2003).

**About the Architect:** Albert Kahn (1869–1942) was born in Rhaunen, Germany. He and his family immigrated to Detroit in 1880. Kahn began working as an architect in Detroit in 1884. In 1902, he started his own firm, and a year later he began working for Packard Automobile Company. In 1909, he was commissioned to design a new auto factory for Henry Ford; Kahn would eventually work on more than 1,000 projects for Ford. Kahn became America's foremost industrial architect, known for his functional designs. He designed some 2,000 factories in the United States and the Soviet Union. Kahn also designed numerous U.S. military installations and nonindustrial structures such as banks, office building, libraries, hospitals, and homes. ■

## Introduction

Detroit was booming in the early 1900s. Entrepreneurs, taking advantage of inexpensive land and a growing workforce, built auto factories and transformed Detroit into the Motor City.

Albert Kahn started designing factories almost by accident. In 1900, he designed a pneumatic-hammer factory and in 1903 was offered a job by the Packard Automobile Company. In 1906, he and his brother Julius, who was an engineer, designed a reinforced-concrete auto factory for Packard. It was a revolutionary structure that would change the future of automobile plants and industrial buildings, which until then had been timber framed. The concrete-reinforced building was strong, fireproof, inexpensive to build, and offered huge amounts of space unobstructed by columns.

In 1909, Henry Ford hired Kahn to build a new factory on a 230-acre lot in Highland Park, near Detroit. At first Kahn thought Ford's ideas were crazy, but he soon began seeing their possibilities. The final design was based on Kahn's previous work, but with significant improvements. The Highland Park Plant opened on New Year's Day 1910. Also called the "Crystal Palace," the building was four stories high and 860 feet long, with big windows that allowed for good lighting and ventilation. Like the Packard plant, it was made with reinforced concrete and did not have interior walls. The open structure would make a number of manufacturing innovations possible.

## Significance

Kahn was ahead of his time. Rather than building impractical, ornate buildings or concentrating on skyscrapers, he focused on what was needed by the industrialist. Kahn's relationship with Henry Ford was particularly significant and productive. Both men were self-made and pragmatic. Each cared more about efficiency than appearance. Together they devised a factory that would influence industrial architecture for the rest of the twentieth century. The Highland Park Plant was not perfect, but it was a testing ground for later manufacturing plants that Kahn would design and Ford would build.

The Highland Park Plant is probably most important for its role in the mass production of cars in the twentieth century. The plant was in large part responsible for the great number of Model Ts that were built at the time, because it enabled Henry Ford to introduce the assembly line at Highland Park in 1913. The center of the building was open and allowed the body of the car to be dropped in place. This new production method reduced the time it took to build a Model T from 728 minutes to 93 minutes. The conveyor belt was also introduced into the manufacturing process here.

By 1917, 700,000 Model Ts were being built each year at the Highland Park Plant, and it was time for Ford to expand again. The lessons learned at Highland Park would be used to build the River Rouge plant in 1917 and other Ford plants thereafter.

## Further Resources

### BOOKS

Bucci, Federico. *Albert Kahn: Architect of Ford.* New York: Princeton Architectural Press, 1993.

Ferry, W. Hawkins, ed. *The Legacy of Albert Kahn.* Detroit: Wayne State University Press, 1987.

Hildebrand, Grant. *Designing for Industry: The Architecture of Albert Kahn.* Cambridge, Mass.: The MIT Press, 1974.

### PERIODICALS

Sherman, Joe. "Like the Factories He Designed, Albert Kahn Lived to Work." *Smithsonian,* v. 25, September 1994, 48–50.

### WEBSITES

"Company Info/History." Albert Kahn Associates Inc. Available online at http://www.albertkahn.com/cmpny_history .cfm; website home page: http://www.albertkahn.com/ (accessed January 21, 2003).

## Primary Source

### "Ford's Highland Park Plant"

**SYNOPSIS:** Workers assemble outside of the Ford Motor Company plant in 1916. Architect Albert Kahn's groundbreaking Highland Park Plant for the Ford Motor Company changed factories forever. The assembly line was one of the important manufacturing developments made possible by the plant's innovative design. The Highland Park Plant was designated a National Historic Landmark in 1973. © CORBIS. REPRODUCED BY PERMISSION.

"Ford Motor Company: 100 Years." Ford Motor Company. Available online at http://www.ford.com/en/ourCompany /centennial/default.htm; website home page: http://www .ford.com/en/default.htm (accessed January 21, 2003).

## "Craftsman Furniture Made by Gustav Stickley"

Catalog

**By:** Gustav Stickley

**Date:** 1910

**Source:** Stickley, Gustav. *Catalogue of Craftsman Furniture Made by Gustav Stickley at The Craftsman Workshops.* Eastwood, N.J.: Gustav Stickley, 1910. Reprinted in *Stickley Craftsman Furniture Catalogs.* New York: Dover Publications, Inc., 1979.

**About the Designer:** Gustav Stickley (1858–1942) was born in Osceola, Wisconsin. In 1896, after years making furniture with his brothers and a trip to Europe where he met proponents of the Arts and Craft Movement, Stickley opened his own firm, Craftsman Workshops. It produced sturdy wood furniture that reflected the Arts and Crafts philosophy. In 1901, Stickley began publishing *The Craftsman,* a magazine that would become an important promoter of the Arts and Crafts Movement in the United States. Stickley's designs were very influential but he was not a successful businessman. His firm went bankrupt in 1915 and was purchased by his brothers. Stickley worked with them and as a consultant for the rest of his life. ■

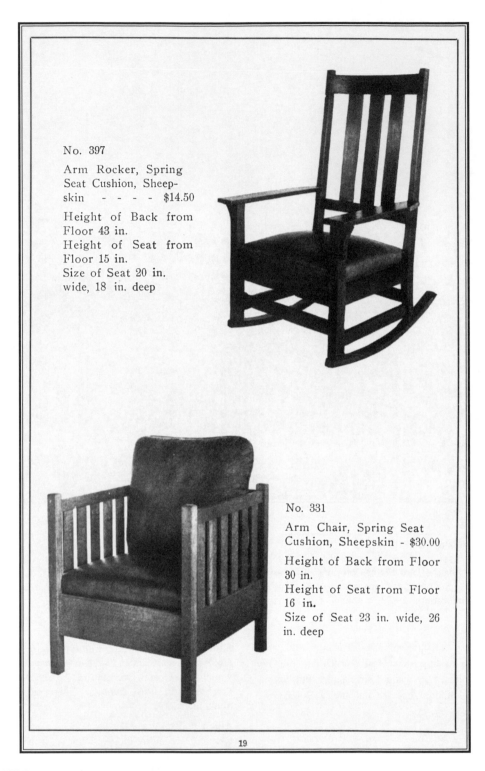

No. 397

Arm Rocker, Spring
Seat Cushion, Sheep-
skin  -  -  -  - $14.50

Height of Back from
Floor 43 in.
Height of Seat from
Floor 15 in.
Size of Seat 20 in.
wide, 18 in. deep

No. 331

Arm Chair, Spring Seat
Cushion, Sheepskin - $30.00

Height of Back from Floor
30 in.
Height of Seat from Floor
16 in.
Size of Seat 23 in. wide, 26
in. deep

19

## Primary Source

### "Craftsman Furniture Made by Gustav Stickley" [excerpt]

**SYNOPSIS:** The Craftsman chairs in Stickley's 1910 catalog are typical of his finely crafted Mission-style furniture. Made of American white oak, they have straight lines and a sturdy look. The wood was treated with ammonia because it resulted in the color and finish that Stickley desired. Even the leather was specially treated to last longer and wear well. REPRINTED FROM *STICKLEY CRAFTSMAN FURNITURE CATALOGS.* NEW YORK: DOVER PUBLICATIONS, INC., 1979.

## Introduction

Mission-style furniture, so named because it imitated the plain, rugged furniture found in the old California missions, became popular in the United States in the first decades of the twentieth century. This was due in part to the influence of the Arts and Crafts Movement, which began in England in the 1800s and was introduced in America at the end of the nineteenth century. The movement's philosophy stressed the importance of handcrafted furniture and buildings that were in harmony with their environment. Gustav Stickley, along with his brothers, who were also furniture makers, and Harvey Ellis, an architect, played major roles in establishing the popularity of Mission-style furniture and Craftsman homes in the United States.

Stickley's furniture, with its strong, simple lines, was very different from the ornate Victorian furniture that had been popular in the nineteenth century. His pieces were built to last several generations and to fit into many decorating schemes. All of his furniture was crafted from American white oak. Stickley sometimes added metal decoration and reinforcements to the wood pieces and later designed metal fixtures to complement the furniture.

Stickley's 1910 furniture catalog shows the variety of pieces available at the time. The catalog complemented *The Craftsman* magazine. Both were used to promote Stickley's furniture and his philosophy. Stickley's furniture was primarily sold via the catalog—only a few retailers carried it in the 1910s.

## Significance

Gustav Stickley did not just build furniture. His furniture was accompanied by a philosophy about the home and the environment in which people live. Stickley believed that the morals taught in the home were important, and that furniture both reflected and affected the character of the people who owned it. In his catalog he wrote, "I felt that badly constructed, over-ornate, meaningless furniture . . . was not only bad in itself, but that its presence in the homes of people was an influence that led directly away from the sound qualities which made an honest man and a good citizen."

Stickley was trying to sell his furniture, but he also provided plans so people could build his designs themselves. While it did not necessarily make good business sense, it embodied part of the Arts and Crafts philosophy, which promoted "self-sufficiency and joy in work."

The 1910 catalog is important because it is the beginning of a change in Stickley's work. Stickley had refined his style over the previous decade. The 1910 catalog reflects a retreat to an early style while it also looks to the future. Although Stickley's business went bankrupt in 1916, his style of furniture remains popular today. The influence of Stickley's clean and simple designs can also be seen in the steel and leather furniture of the modern era.

## Further Resources

### BOOKS

Bavaro, Joseph, et.al. *The Furniture of Gustav Stickley: History, Techniques and Projects.* New York: Van Nostrand Reinhold, 1982.

Sanders, Barry. *A Complex Fate: Gustav Stickley and the American Arts & Crafts Movement.* Washington, D.C.: Preservation Press, 1996.

Stickley, Gustav. *Craftsman Homes: Architecture and Furnishings of the American Arts and Crafts Movement.* New York: Dover Publications, Inc., 1979.

### PERIODICALS

*The Craftsman.* Eastwood, NY: United Crafts, 1901–1916.

### WEBSITES

"Gustav Stickley." The Arts & Crafts Society. Available online at http://64.66.180.31/archive/gstickley.shtml#bibliography, website home page: http://64.66.180.31/index.html (accessed January 27, 2003).

# "Five Pretty Ways to Do the Hair"

Hair style

**By:** *Ladies' Home Journal*

**Date:** October 1911

**Source:** Merritt, B.G., and M. Stokes. "Five Pretty Ways to Do the Hair." *Ladies Home Journal* 28, no. 15, October 1911, 35

**About the Publication:** *Ladies' Home Journal* had its beginnings in a newspaper column called "Women and Home" in the Philadelphia *Tribune and Farmer*. In 1883, the writers of the column, Cyrus Curtis and Louisa Knapp Curtis, began a supplement to the *Tribune and Farmer* called *Ladies' Journal*. He was the publisher, and she was the editor. The supplement quickly developed into a magazine, which was named *Ladies' Home Journal* and became a prototype for other women's magazines of its kind. It was still being published at the beginning of the twenty-first century. The authors of this article, Blanche G. Merritt and Maude Stokes, compose fashion articles and drawings for the magazine. ∎

## Introduction

While women had to fix their own hair in the nineteenth century, in the early twentieth century hairdressers

## Primary Source

"Five Pretty Ways to Do the Hair"

**SYNOPSIS:** The October 1911 issue of *Ladies' Home Journal* featured this article about the latest hairstyles. Illustrations showed various angles of the styles, so that readers could copy the looks themselves. LADIES HOME JOURNAL, OCTOBER 1911, were becoming more popular and available, so wealthier women could have their hair done by someone else. The readers of *Ladies' Home Journal* were lower- or middle-class white women, most of whom probably styled their own hair in 1911.

Women's hair was typical long at the beginning of the 1910s, but worn up on the head rather than hanging loose. "Five Pretty Ways to Do the Hair" is illustrated with photographs and drawings of women with hair that frames their faces and is swept up off their necks. Classic simplicity in hairstyles is stressed; the basic shapes of the styles depicted in the article are all similar, with variations on the twists. The article also emphasizes the importance of selecting the right style for the shape of a woman's face and for her age. It also recommends changing one's hairstyle from time to time to reduce strain on the scalp.

**Significance**

Articles such as this one were common in *Ladies' Home Journal* and other women's magazines in the 1910s—as they are today. Then, as now, a woman's hair was considered every bit as important to her appearance as her clothes or accessories. In 1911, women felt that it was their job to make the most of their appearance. The articles in women's magazines of the time supported and promoted that belief. *Ladies' Home Journal* often provided women with tips on increasing their femininity and appeal to men.

Hairstyles were becoming simpler and softer in the 1910s. Prior to 1911, women added pads, "rats," and other devices to make their hair look fuller. When this article was written, this practice was on the way out, in favor of easier styles that used women's own hair. The change in trends had to do with a moral issue—when women used hairpieces, they felt as though they were lying about their looks. *Ladies' Home Journal* encouraged women to rely on their own hair and to choose styles that flattered their particular features. As this article suggests, the newer hairstyles were designed to be shaped to the woman's head and to complement her face. By the end of the decade, bobs were popular for women who were daring enough to cut off their long hair.

**Further Resources**

**BOOKS**

Corson, Richard. *Fashions in Hair: The First Five Thousand Years.* London: Peter Owen, 2001.

Damon-Moore, Helen. *Magazines for the Millions: Gender and Commerce in the "Ladies' Home Journal" and the "Saturday Evening Post," 1880–1910.* Albany: State University of New York, 1994.

Ewing, Elizabeth. *History of Twentieth Century Fashion.* Revised and Updated by Alice Mackrell. London: B. T. Batsford, 1993.

**PERIODICALS**

"Anaesthetics and the Coiffure." *Scientific American Supplement,* v. 68, September 11, 1909, 163.

"Can a Woman's Hair Be Worn Simply?" *Ladies' Home Journal,* v. 28, January 15, 1911, 3.

Hard, Anna. "Beauty Business." *American Magazine,* v. 69, November 1909, 79–90.

**WEBSITES**

"Twentieth-Century Fashion: Women's Fashions—1910s." The Costume Gallery. Available online at http://www .costumegallery.com/1910.htm; website home page: http:// www.costumegallery.com (accessed January 22, 2003).

# "Flower Dresses for Lawn Fêtes"

## Clothing styles

**By:** *Ladies' Home Journal*

**Date:** July 1911

**Source:** Musselman, M.E., and the Editors, "Flower Dresses for Lawn Fêtes," *Ladies' Home Journal,* July 1911.

**About the Publication:** *Ladies' Home Journal* had its beginnings in a newspaper column called "Women and Home" in the Philadelphia *Tribune and Farmer*. In 1883, the writers of the column, Cyrus Curtis and Louisa Knapp Curtis, began a supplement to the *Tribune and Farmer* called Ladies' Journal. He was the publisher, and she was the editor. The supplement quickly developed into a magazine, which was named *Ladies' Home Journal* and became a prototype for other women's magazines. It was still being published at the beginning of the twenty-first century. M.E. Musselman may have been Emma Musselman, a fashion illustrator for *Ladies' Home Journal*. ∎

## Introduction

Edward Bok, the editor of *Ladies' Home Journal* from 1890 until 1919, had a narrow view of women's place in society. Women were supposed to provide a loving home and, as incomes increased, part of their responsibility included buying the right products. The magazine's articles and advertisements both advised women about what they should purchase.

In the 1910s, issues of *Ladies' Home Journal* regularly featured examples of dresses and other fashion accessories that women could buy or make for themselves. Women could adapt patterns to their own tastes through choices of fabrics and trims. Ready-to-wear fashions were becoming popular during this time period, but for some they were still too expensive.

# Flower Dresses for Lawn Fêtes
### Which May Also be Worn for Dances and Parties
#### Designs by the Editors
#### Drawings by M. E. Musselman

29

6209-6210-6207—Charming for an outdoor fête are dresses suggestive of the flowers. Such a dress is pictured on the right, the delicate maidenhair fern forming the trimming. Patterns (No. 6209) for the waist come in six sizes: 32 to 42 inches bust measure. Size 36 requires one yard and a half of 36-inch material. Patterns (No. 6210) for the skirt come in seven sizes: 22 to 34 inches waist measure. Size 24 requires five yards and three-quarters of 36-inch material, and one yard of 36-inch lining. Pattern (No. 6207) for the cap, including three styles, comes in one size and requires half a yard of 24-inch material.

6213-6207—This pink rose dress would be fascinating if made of voile or silk muslin with a design in full-blown roses. Pale pink satin could be used for the girdle with a rosette and sash ends fastening in the back. Point d'esprit net garlanded with roses would make a becoming cap. Patterns (No. 6213) for this dress—closing in back, with shirred waist and a straight, gathered skirt—come in six sizes: 32 to 42 inches bust measure. Size 36 requires four yards and three-quarters of 44-inch material. Pattern (No. 6207) for the cap, including three styles, comes in one size and requires five-eighths of a yard of 22-inch material.

6211-6207—Exceedingly becoming for a blonde type is the forget-me-not dress above. This would make a dainty dress which could be worn for evening parties later if made of a blue batiste with alternating bands in white with delicate pink flowers. This same intermingling of color is carried out in the twisted girdle, slippers and flower-basket. A wreath of forget-me-nots borders the bewitching tulle cap. Patterns (No. 6211) for this dress—with plaited waist and skirt—come in five sizes: 34 to 42 inches bust measure. Size 36 requires seven yards and a half of 44-inch material. Pattern (No. 6207) for the cap, including three styles, comes in one size and requires five-eighths of a yard of 22-inch material.

6206-6207—Dainty and modest is this gown made of violet figured lawn. It has a gathered waist and short puff sleeves, with the skirt tucked to simulate three sections, the simple lines making a foundation especially suited for the fringe of long-stemmed artificial violets which forms the trimming. The quaint cap, made of fine lawn with a deep frill at the back, and embroidered and trimmed with bunches of violets, adds a picturesque note to the costume. Patterns (No. 6206) come in six sizes: 32 to 42 inches bust measure. Size 36 requires six yards and three-quarters of 36-inch material. Pattern (No. 6207) for the cap, including three styles, comes in one size and requires three-quarters of a yard of 36-inch material.

6208—For a tall, slender brunette this sprightly little golden-eyed daisy costume would be especially becoming. It is made of white organdy with trimmings of yellow ribbon. The gathered waist is trimmed with a bertha shaped to form daisy petals, with a yoke and stock of daisy-patterned net. The skirt, cut in five gores with gathers at the waist, is trimmed with two petal flounces. In the shape of a daisy is the fetching little cap, with lawn petals and yellow satin top. Patterns (No. 6208) for this daisy dress—with high or round neck, and short puff or full-length sleeves, including also a pattern for the cap—come in six sizes: 32 to 42 inches bust measure. Size 36 requires eight yards of 36-inch material.

PATTERNS (including Guide-Chart) for these designs can be supplied at fifteen cents each, except No. 6207, which is ten cents. The amount of material required for the various sizes is printed on the pattern envelopes. Order from your nearest dealer in patterns; or by mail, giving number of pattern, bust measure for waist and costumes, waist measure for skirt, and inclosing the price to the Pattern Department, The Ladies' Home Journal, Philadelphia.

6209-6210 6207

6211-6207

6213-6207

6206-6207

6208

---

## Primary Source

"Flower Dresses for Lawn Fêtes"

**SYNOPSIS:** The July 1911 issue of *Ladies' Home Journal* featured an article describing the latest fashions in summer dresses—and how readers could buy the patterns to make the garments themselves. The article focuses on fabric selection and trim as much as the design of the dress. The implication was that extra attention to detail could enhance not only the dress, but also the wearer. LADIES HOME JOURNAL, JULY 1911, P. 29.

"Flower Dresses for Lawn Fêtes," which appeared in the July 1911 issue of the magazine, features dresses for outdoor parties. Lawn parties and garden parties were a part of life in the early twentieth century. On summer afternoons, men and women would gather for tea or for a light supper. Sometimes musical entertainment or games would be part of the festivities.

## Significance

By 1911, fashion had changed significantly since the Victorian era of the nineteenth century, and it would witness greater change by the end of the decade. Fashion had distorted women's figures for years, but in the 1910s women's fashions began to favor the natural line and a softer look. The dresses featured in the July 1911 issue of *Ladies' Home Journal* were long, dainty and feminine. Each dress had an accompanying hat or cap.

"Flower Dresses for Lawn Fêtes" is both an informational magazine article and an advertisement for dress patterns that readers could purchase. The article not only describes the garden party dresses in great detail, but also provides information about the patterns, which could be ordered through the magazine or purchased through a local pattern dealer.

*Ladies' Home Journal* often provided women with tips on increasing their femininity and appeal to men. By including colored drawings of the dresses worn by lovely girls, the pattern company and magazine hoped to increase sales. The text matched the gowns to the features of the potential wearer: "the slender brunette," "the blonde type." The magazine's target readers were white lower- and middle-class women, who presumably would be interested in saving money by making the charming new summer dresses rather than buying them in a store.

Advertisements for dress and accessory patterns were a regular feature in *Ladies' Home Journal*. Designed to appeal to the growing consumer class, this fashion advertising showed women how they should appear in the home and in society.

## Further Resources
### BOOKS
Damon-Moore, Helen. *Magazines for the Millions: Gender and Commerce in the "Ladies' Home Journal" and the "Saturday Evening Post" 1880–1910.* Albany: State University of New York, 1994.

Ewing, Elizabeth. *History of Twentieth Century Fashion.* Revised and updated by Alice Mackrell. London: B.T. Batsford, 1993.

Peacock, John. *The Chronicle of Western Fashion From Ancient Times to the Present Day.* New York: Harry N. Abrams, 1991.

### PERIODICALS
Clayton, R., and E.L. Phelps. "Size of Commercial Patterns." *Journal of Home Economics,* v. 18, March 1926, 150–151.

Daggett, M.P. "When *The Delineator* was Young: The Story of the First Butterick Pattern and How it Multiplied." *The Delineator,* v. 76, November 1910, 365–66.

### WEBSITES
"Patterns and Images from 1900–1919." Sense and Sensibility Patterns. Available online at http://www.sensibility.com/vintageimages/1900s/index.htm; website home page http://www.sensibility.com (accessed January 22, 2003).

# "What Is a Bungalow?"
Magazine article

**By:** Phil M. Riley

**Date:** July 1912

**Source:** Riley, Phil M. "What Is a Bungalow?" *Country Life in America,* July 15, 1912, 11–12.

**About the Publication:** *Country Life in America* was published from 1901 to 1917 by Doubleday, Page & Co. After that it changed titles a number of times (*New Country Life, Country Life in the War, Country Life and the Sportsman*) and finally ceased publication altogether in 1942. Geared for sportsmen and people who lived or spent time in the country, the magazine included articles on gardening, dogs, country houses, and similar subjects. ■

## Introduction

By 1912, bungalows had become a popular architectural style for American homes. The design of the American bungalow was an adaptation of the "true" bungalow style, which originated in India. Traditional Indian bungalows were designed in response to that continent's hot climate. The efficient one-story buildings had open roof areas that allowed air to circulate and cool the house. But architects and builders found that by adapting the style, the bungalow could fit the needs of American homeowners—American bungalows, for instance, sometimes had a second story.

The Arts and Crafts Movement, which began in the nineteenth century in England and moved to America at the end of the nineteenth century, was influential in the adaptation of the bungalow to the United States. The movement emphasized the importance of hand-crafted furniture and buildings that were in harmony with their environment. "Found" materials, or materials that were native to a particular region, were often used in the construction. Thus the architectural style of a bungalow was adapted to the region of the country in which it was built. As a result, several styles of American bungalows

This typical California bungalow was built around 1900–1915. Many bungalows were built in the early part of the century. They remained a popular choice of home into the twenty-first century. **THE LIBRARY OF CONGRESS.**

developed: Spanish Mission, Elizabethan cottage, Swiss chalet, Italian villa, Georgian, American Colonial, and Dutch Colonial.

Marketing of the bungalow was through magazines such as *The Craftsman,* published by noted Arts and Crafts furniture maker Gustav Stickley, and catalogs put out by Sears & Roebuck and Montgomery Ward. Plans or entire homes could be purchased through the national retailers as well as through smaller regional companies.

American bungalows in the 1910s generally cost between $5,000 and $10,000, within reach of people of relatively modest means. People with more money tended to build them as vacation homes, so the bungalows served both as inexpensive second homes as well as affordable primary homes.

### Significance

Residential design changed dramatically at the beginning of the twentieth century. Following the Victorian era, when large houses were the norm, people started to desire small, cozy homes. The relatively inexpensive bungalow made the American Dream—a single-family house on its own plot of land—a reality for the average family.

Bungalows could be nestled into spots where the larger Victorian-style home could not be built. The ar-

chitecture of the bungalow took advantage of its natural surroundings to enhance the home and the landscaping. For this reason, people began building bungalows as vacation or country homes. Bungalows were comfortable structures, even though they were small and generally had only one floor. Screened porches allowed for sleeping in good weather. Many American bungalows were built in the early part of the century—and the architectural style remains popular for homes today.

### Primary Source

"What Is a Bungalow?" [excerpt]

> **SYNOPSIS:** In this article, which appeared in the July 15, 1912, issue of *Country Life in America,* writer Phil M. Riley looks at the origins of the bungalow style of architecture and its growing popularity in the United States.

### The Bungalow of To-Day Not What Its Name Implies—What We Owe to the Bungalow Idea—Its Influence upon Domestic Architecture and Country Living

The bungalow is the thing, so it seems. Magazine sales prove conclusively that it is the most absorbing topic among prospective homebuilders who have from $5,000 to $10,000 to spend. It would be more truthful, though, to state frankly that it is the bungalow so-called which is increasingly popular.

Few words have achieved such widespread favor as "bungalow." Every year it appears more conspicuously in the annals of our domestic architecture, not through any inherent virtues of the true bungalow when placed on American soil, but because of the new meaning which time has given to the word. In fact, it becomes more and more apparent that it is the name rather than the thing which has caught the public fancy.

Constructed crudely of the rough materials at hand, there is little about the primitive Anglo-Indian bungalow, aside from its name, which we could possibly utilize in America, except the broad, low effect and the one-story idea. Its lofty rooms, ventilating windows under the eaves, many doors opening upon a broad veranda entirely surrounding the house, even the one-story idea, were solutions of the glaring sun and heat problem, in India, and are totally unsuited to our temperate climate with its extremes of winter and summer. Such characteristics make for comfort in temporary summer homes, but, except in southern California and Florida, which are sub-tropical, they find no logical place in our scheme of year-round architecture.

In its true sense, therefore, a bungalow is a one-story house with broad, extended lines, surrounded wholly or in part by a veranda. This was the form it first took in America, particularly in Southern California where this type of house has flourished chiefly. Happily, some of the earliest examples were simple, consistent, and, in appropriate settings, made most attractive pictures to look upon. Coming after the Victorian era with its hideous, cubical houses, the bungalow, always so friendly with its garden and grounds, was a great relief. By contrast with its predecessors it proved conclusively that the domination of one dimension makes for improved appearance; that an oblong house not only permits more exposure in the rooms, but possesses a peculiar charm of its own unknown to any other arrangement.

These facts furnished food for much thought, and opportunities for many experiments in design. The increased popular demand for small houses forced more and better architects into this field with the result that it was soon discovered that a house might be so designed as to give the *effect* of being low without actually being so; that while more grace of outline is secured by locating four or five rooms on

one floor, the addition of more than this number in the same way is detrimental to appearance in most styles and greatly increases cost. Then it was that the oblong story-and-a-half house with rambling single-story wings came into its own; then it was that the magic word bungalow became almost as popular east of the Rocky Mountains as it was west of them. The peasant cottages and small country houses of England and Continental Europe were studied, and it did not take long to show how, by means of dormers, gables and other devices, the second-story rooms could be made cozy and comfortable.

## Further Resources

### BOOKS

Duchscherer, Paul. *The Bungalow: America's Arts and Crafts Home.* New York: Penguin Studio, 1995.

Saylor, Henry H. *Bungalows: Their Design, Construction and Furnishing.* London: Grant Reehards, 1912.

White, Charles E., Jr. *The Bungalow Book.* New York: Macmillan, 1923.

### PERIODICALS

"Are You Building a Bungalow this Year?" *Ladies' Home Journal,* v. 37, February 1920, 50–51.

Waldron, Gertrude Luckey. "Seven Rooms and Simplicity." *Sunset,* Central West edition, v. 44, March 1920, 64–66.

### WEBSITES

*American Bungalow Magazine.* Available online at http://www.ambungalow.com/ (accessed January 22, 2003).

---

# "Audacious Hats for Spineless Attitudes"

**Magazine article, Clothing styles**

**By:** *Dress & Vanity Fair*

**Date:** September 1913

**Source:** "Audacious Hats for Spineless Attitudes." *Dress & Vanity Fair,* September 1913, 21.

**About the Publication:** The Vanity Fair Publishing Co. began publishing *Dress & Vanity Fair* in 1913. A year later, Condé Nast Publications took over the magazine and changed the name to *Vanity Fair.* The magazine sought to be the American counterpart of British magazines like *The Tatler* and *The Sketch,* which covered the arts, culture, and society as well as fashion, and aimed to attract both male and female readers. It was aimed at sophisticated and wealthy people. *Vanity Fair* was absorbed by *Vogue* magazine in 1936, but it reappeared in 1983. ∎

## Introduction

Hats were an important accessory in the 1910s. A women was not seen in public without one at this time.

## Primary Source

### "Audacious Hats for Spineless Attitudes": Clothing styles

**SYNOPSIS:** An illustration from a September 1913 *Dress and Vanity Fair* article. Hats were a part of every woman's wardrobe in the 1910s, with feathers and other elaborate decorations for those who could afford them. DRESS AND VANITY FAIR, SEPTEMBER 1913, P. 23.

Women who did not pay particularly close attention to fashion usually owned at least four hats, while fashion-conscious women might have had fifteen or more. Milliners and advertisers promoted hats as a fashion accessory that no woman should be without. A January 1917 *Ladies' Home Journal* article stated that "the woman who does not perpetually desire new hats has something lacking in her nature."

While wealthier women could afford a trip to the milliner for a new hat, middle-class women often designed their own hats. They could purchase the basic shape of the hat and use descriptions and drawings in magazines such as *Dress & Vanity Fair* and *Ladies' Home Journal* to try to replicate the latest fashions in headwear.

Hats came in all shapes and sizes for women in the 1910s. While many had large brims, a number of influences, such as the popularity of dancing and the changing lines of women's dresses and suits, were causing designers to create closer-fitting styles. The hats featured in *Dress & Vanity Fair* in 1913 were made from velvet, tulle, and ribbon and were trimmed with feathers, fur, and lace.

### Significance

"Audacious Hats for Spineless Attitudes," which appeared in the September 1913 issue of *Dress & Vanity Fair,* concentrates on the Parisian influences on fashion and caters to wealthy, upper-class women, rather than the lower- and middle-class readers that *Ladies' Home Journal* addressed. The author mentions several Parisian couturiers by name (Lucile, Georgette, Poiret) and describes their current styles.

*Dress & Vanity Fair* differed from most women's magazines of the time. It concentrated more on the designs of the clothing and hats themselves, than on the woman who would wear the garments. By focusing on Parisian fashions, *Dress & Vanity Fair* was trying to appeal to a select group of woman who could afford the styles and who would wear them. Wearing a hat that had been featured in *Dress & Vanity Fair* would signal that the woman was both fashionable and sophisticated.

The popularity of hats and the continuous changes in hat styles were good for business at this time. The larger department stores each employed as many as forty milliners to trim hats for the ready-to-wear departments as well as for custom orders.

The hat styles of this era, which featured exotic feathers and plumes, were not good for birds, however. The Massachusetts Audobon Society was been formed in 1896 to stop the widespread killing of birds so that their feathers could be used to adorn hats. Many more Audobon chapters were founded in subsequent years, and the Lacey Act of 1900 put some restrictions on hunting birds for fashion, but feathered hats were still in vogue more than a decade later.

### Primary Source

"Audacious Hats for Spineless Attitudes": Magazine article [excerpt]

> **SYNOPSIS:** The September 1913 issue of *Dress & Vanity Fair* included this report on the latest hats by Parisian fashion designers. Hats were an essential fashion accessory at the time, and upper-class women would soon be adding fashionable new feather-trimmed velvet and tulle toppers to their already large collections.

**Paris inclines toward the lackadaisical, sanctioning a carelessly picturesque pose of the body while capriciously capping herself with divers types—from the hat of a Pope to the wing of a humming-bird.**

The "mi-saison" in Paris always sees the birth of some new detail which later is introduced into the next season's models. This year, the "mi-saison" brought with it the vogue for velvet and tulle hats.

What was but a tentative effort in Paris became later an accomplished fact at Deauville, Trouville, and Ostend. Nine tenths of the headgear seen at these resorts—where congregate for a short three weeks all the elegance and beauty of three continents—were of velvet, or velvet and tulle.

The popularity of these materials once established, modistes devoted their attention to developing new shapes. These continue to be very diverse, especially in the smaller hats.

The varied types of the small hat range from a form not unlike the Greek Pope's "beret" down to the fascinating little arrangement which looks like a black taffeta handbag gathered into a wide supple band of velvet, drawn through a jet buckle in front. As a general rule the crowns are full, but not too full—and very supple. They are made without the stiff tulle lining formerly used for the foundation of all draped crowns.

Many little toques, shaped like a boudoir cap, are made of white or colored velvet, appliquéd with black Chantilly lace motifs. Others have a vivid red velvet crown and a curved black velvet brim.

The "beret" is also made of velvet, with a full crown gathered into the narrow velvet band which forms the brim. A narrow band of feather trimming, made of the plumage of the humming-bird, runs from the centre front to half way across the left front, where it ends in two semi-plucked feathers.

Feathers of different description continue to be the favorite trimming for the new hats.

## Further Resources

### BOOKS

Ewing, Elizabeth. *History of Twentieth Century Fashion.* Revised and updated by Alice Mackrell. London: B. T. Batsford, 1993.

McDowell, Colin. *Hats: Status, Style and Glamour.* London: Thames and Hudson, 1992.

### PERIODICALS

Balfour, Bruce J. "When a Plume Meant Aplomb." *Westways,* 1984, 76, 10, 46–48.

Katz, Elizabeth. "Feathers on Women's Hats." *Ladies' Home Journal,* v. 27, May 1910, 91.

### WEBSITES

"Vanity Fair." English Department of the University of Virginia. Available online at http://xroads.virginia.edu/~1930s /PRINT/vanity/fair.html (accessed January 22, 2003).

"The Feather Trade and the American Conservation Movement." A Virtual Exhibition from the Smithsonian Institution's National Museum of American History. Available online at http://www.americanhistory.si.edu/feather/index .htm; website home page: http://www.americanhistory.si .edu (accessed January 23, 2003).

# Woolworth Building

## "The Woolworth Building"

**Photograph**

**By:** Cass Gilbert

**Date:** ca. 1913

**Source:** "Woolworth Building and City Hall Park, Manhattan." ca. 1913. Corbis. Image no. IH059708. Available online at http://pro.corbis.com (accessed January 27, 2003).

**About the Architect:** Cass Gilbert (1859–1934) worked as an architect's assistant and as a surveyor before earning an architectural degree at the Massachusetts Institute of Technology. He then joined the prestigious architectural firm McKim, Mead and White in New York. In 1885, Gilbert and James Knox Taylor opened their own architectural firm in St. Paul, Minnesota. In 1899, Gilbert moved back to New York, and about a decade later he designed his most famous building, the Woolworth Building. Gilbert's buildings were distinguished by their ornamental facades and grand interiors. He and his firm built Gothic- and Classical-influenced buildings into the 1930s. Among Gilbert's other famous works are the United States Custom House and the New York Life Insurance Building, both in New York City; the Minnesota State Capitol; and the Supreme Court Building.

## *The Cathedral of Commerce*

**Booklet**

**By:** Edwin A. Cochran

**Date:** 1916

The Woolworth Building was built to be a striking symbol of the wealth and success of this businessman, Frank W. Woolworth. **THE LIBRARY OF CONGRESS.**

**Source:** Cochran, Edwin A. *The Cathedral of Commerce.* New York: Munder–Thomsen Company, 1916.

**About the Author:** Edwin A. Cochran wrote the gushing tribute to the "Cathedral of Commerce"—New York's Woolworth Building. ■

## Introduction

During the early years of the twentieth century, three new inventions—the airplane, the radio, and the skyscraper—were seen by many as a metaphor for man's soaring possibilities. For all three inventions seemed to tickle the heavens and along the way help liberate earthbound man by conquering both time and distance. Of the three, the skyscraper was the most physically impressive, a man-made mountain dominating everything that surrounded it, a daily reminder of mankind's commitment to material progress.

Cass Gilbert was already nationally known when he was approached in 1910 by Frank W. Woolworth, the owner of the national chain of stores that bore his name, to build a skyscraper office building in Manhattan. Two floors would be for the Woolworth Company headquarters and the rest of the floors would be rented out, thus providing income.

Gilbert and Woolworth spent two years considering various approaches and designs. The final design was a

## Primary Source

### "The Woolworth Building"

**SYNOPSIS:** The Woolworth Building towers over City Hall Park. Designed by architect Cass Gilbert, it was known as the "Cathedral of Commerce." Five-and-dime-store magnate Frank W. Woolworth paid $13.5 million in cash for the New York sky-scraper. Completed in 1913, it was the world's tallest building for 27 years. © CORBIS. REPRODUCED BY PERMISSION.

57-story structure with a steel frame, terra-cotta façade, and such ornate, Gothic-style features as gargoyles, arches, and flying buttresses. The building has high-speed elevators, a restaurant, an observation deck, a swimming pool, and a social club. The elaborately decorated Romanesque lobby features sculpted caricatures of Frank Woolworth, Cass Gilbert, and builder Louis Horowitz. The ornate design would lead to the building being nicknamed the Cathedral of Commerce.

Construction of the building, on Broadway between Barclay and Park Place, began in 1911 and was completed in 1913. The 792-foot skyscraper—New York's Woolworth Building—first opened its doors for business on April 24, 1913. At the time it was the world's tallest building. To commemorate the auspicious occasion, recently inaugurated United States President Woodrow Wilson, sitting in the White House, pressed a button that transmitted the signal to light up the entire Woolworth Building. The structure dominated the Manhattan skyline.

**Significance**

The Woolworth Building was the world's tallest building and most recognizable skyscraper from the time it was completed in 1913 until 1930, when the Chrysler Building and the Bank of Manhattan Tower were built, followed by the Empire State Building in 1931. The Woolworth Building, along with the other skyscrapers built in the same decade, brought a new energy to New York's expanding skyline.

By altering the skylines of America's cities, skyscrapers were symbolic of the changing world of the new century. In New York City, the new skyline reflected the city's growing economic life—office buildings began blocking out the steeples that had once dominated Manhattan. Gilbert viewed this as positive, writing, "the changing skyline of New York is one of the marvels of a marvelous age . . . skyscrapers were born of the necessities of time and space, under the urge of modern life, and they are expressive of its commercial conditions and the enterprise of our epoch."

Skyscrapers also reflected the wealth and ambition of their builders. These men were themselves a new breed of powerful businessmen, who saw themselves as the "captains of industry." With their huge business enterprises and skyscrapers they were leading the country into a new age of progress, prosperity, and happiness, or so they thought. Woolworth's publicity booklet on his skyscraper, *The Cathedral of Commerce*, reflects this view in its unreserved praise of the skyscraper and the man who made it possible. In truth, however, many Americans had already grown distrustful of big business and businessmen by the time this pamphlet was published. Optimism about the future and the inevitable

"progress" of mankind would be sorely tested by the terrible slaughter of World War I (1914–18). By the end of the century, few could agree with the sentiments expressed in *The Cathedral of Commerce*, but the Woolworth Building itself remains an architectural landmark, an ornate and stunning example of Manhattan's earliest skyscrapers.

**Primary Source**

*The Cathedral of Commerce* [excerpt]

**SYNOPSIS:** Author Edwin A. Cochran pays tribute to what was then the world's tallest office tower, New York's spectacular Woolworth Building. Dubbed the "Cathedral of Commerce" and opening for business in 1913, the skyscraper stood as a monument to man's soaring possibilities.

On the night of April 24, 1913, President Wilson pressed a tiny button in the White House and 80,000 brilliant lights instantly flashed throughout the Woolworth Building. The event marked the completion, the dedication and the formal opening of that regal edifice, the tallest and most beautiful building in all the world erected to commerce, so judged by the officials of the Panama-Pacific Exposition when they placed their seal of approval upon it and awarded it the gold medal. It also set in motion a vast machine called industry, whose influences and benefits forever will be felt in every corner of the globe. It was a memorable night. A profusion of light filled the twenty-seventh floor, which had been arranged for a superb banquet. And assembled there, was a great host of statesmen, captains of industry, merchants, journalists, scholars, poets— all representative Americans, proud to break bread with, and honor the man who had realized his dream and the gallant aides who tirelessly had labored with him to accomplish the stupendous task, the up-building of a monument to small things.

Yes, as a commercial institution the Woolworth Building is preeminent. Within its walls are housed great banking institutions, the executive and clerical staffs of giant industries, the New York representatives of America's big business enterprises and a great many leaders in the professions. Its tenants, with their employees, number 10,000 people—the population of a city—and only tenants of the highest standard are accepted. The Building could have been filled twice over had not Mr. Woolworth been so strict about the responsibility and personal integrity of every lessee. Altogether, these tenants rank among our country's most prosperous, most

The Woolworth Building under construction, on June 22, 1912. When completed it was the tallest building in the world. **THE LIBRARY OF CONGRESS.**

progressive and most reputable business and professional men.

Doctor Cadman, the noted divine, has called this Building "The Cathedral of Commerce," a term which fittingly describes it. It stands in magnificent splendor, a masterpiece of art and architecture, a Glorious Whole, quite beyond the power of human imagination. The true Gothic lines and tracery of the exterior are extremely impressive, and the proportions have been executed with such studious care and fidelity to detail that its enormous height is not realized from the street; yet it is by far the tallest building in the world, rising 792 feet 1 inch above the sidewalk, its summit piercing the heavens. The recessive Tower, gradually diminishing from base to pinnacle and appearing always in new lights and colors, forms a fascinating picture from every viewpoint, as it stands silhouetted against the sky.

Its location, too, is of supreme importance. It is in the very heart of things—the civic center of the world's great metropolis, in the midst of all transportation lines. It faces upon three streets and has nine entrances, including two direct communications with the subway system. It is within a stone's throw of City Hall, the Municipal Building, Brooklyn Bridge, the Post Office and Courts, as well as close by the great financial and banking center. No building could command a better location or one more advantageous to its tenants.

From the Observation Gallery, fifty-eight stories above the street, the view is marvelous, and the thrilling sensation which comes over the sightseer is never to be forgotten. It is indeed the most remarkable if not the most wonderful view in all the world. The scenic and color effects, with the sun shining on the multi-colored buildings around it, but far below, and on the water and land for twenty-five miles in every direction, make a landscape impossible of adequate description. The vast area spread out before the visitor's eye is inhabited by more than 7,500,000 souls. To the north lies the great City, with the Hudson River and the lordly Highlands beyond. To the east are Long Island and the mighty Atlantic Ocean, with its ships passing to and fro far distant on the horizon where sky and water seem to meet. To the south are the great Harbor of New York, the Narrows through which pass all ships entering and leaving the Port of New York, Governor's Island, the Statue of Liberty, and Staten Island in the distance. To the west we have again the Hudson River and the great expanses of meadow-land and mountainous country forming Eastern New Jersey. Look-

ing downward, the multitudes of people scurrying about the busy streets in close proximity to the Woolworth Building resemble an aggregation of pygmies—a crowd seen through the large end of a telescope. The view is bewildering. Every year upwards of 100,000 visitors from all parts of the world come here and the Register shows that these good people represent more than sixty different countries and thousands of cities. . . .

The wonders of the Woolworth Building are not confined to its exterior, for within will be found a wealth of things intensely interesting, and first among these should be mentioned the grand corridor with its tall, perfect lines rising and sweeping into graceful curves and arches. The marble, with its warm, golden, evenly matched colors of varied hues forming the corridor walls, was quarried on the Isle of Skyros off the coast of Greece, from the choicest of costly marbles obtainable there. It is richly carved in pure Gothic design, and blends perfectly with the magnificently decorated dome-ceiling. This ceiling is a masterpiece of glass mosaic, and its rare beauty is accentuated by the soft glow of artificial light concealed behind the lace-like marble cornice at the springing of the arches. It suggests a flood of dazzling jewels glittering in the sunlight—emeralds, rubies, sapphires, diamonds—a riot of harmonious colors, all spread out in golden settings, and arranged in exquisite designs. The whole effect is one of grandeur with which the corridor of no other building in the world may be compared; and it is, indeed, an appropriate entrance to this regal structure, "The Cathedral of Commerce." . . .

The Woolworth Building has been called "A Cathedral of Commerce"—a monument to small things, but it is even more—it is the colossal and enduring gift to civilization of a true-born, patriotic American, Frank W. Woolworth, and it stands unique in the history of great buildings throughout the world in that it is without a mortgage or dollar of indebtedness. Mr. Woolworth paid for this gigantic structure from start to finish from his own resources, accumulated through his business sagacity in establishing an entirely new line of merchandising through retail stores handling only five and ten cent goods. This wonderful enterprise, starting from one small store in 1879, has grown to a $65,000,000 corporation, operating over 870 stores throughout the United States, Canada, and Great Britain, with combined sales exceeding $80,000,000 in 1915—the largest retail business in the world.

Thus the name Frank W. Woolworth has been indelibly inscribed throughout the length and breadth of our land and abroad, and the Woolworth Building, symbolizing, as it truly does, the crowning achievement of a career of usefulness toward mankind, will long herald the march of progress down through the corridors of time.

## Further Resources

### BOOKS

Christen, Barbara S,. and Steven Flanders. *Cass Gilbert, Life and Work: Architect of the Public Domain.* New York: W. W. Norton, 2001.

Heilbrun, Margaret, ed. *Inventing the Skyline: The Architecture of Cass Gilbert.* New York: Columbia University Press, 2000.

*The Master Builders: A Record of the Construction of the World's Highest Commercial Structure.* New York: Hugh McAtamney and Company, 1913.

### PERIODICALS

Klaw, Spencer. "World's Tallest Building: The Woolworth Building." *American Heritage,* v. 28, February 1977, 86–98.

Tittle, Walter. "Creator of the Woolworth Tower." *World's Work,* v. 54, May 1927, 96–102.

### WEBSITES

Cass Gilbert Society. Available online at http://www.cass-gilbertsociety.org/index.htm (accessed August 20, 2002).

"Cass Gilbert." Skyscrapers.com. Available online at http://www.skyscrapers.com/english/company/0.9/101119/; website home page: http://www.skyscrapers.com (accessed February 4, 2003).

Dance proved to be a fashion liberator in the 1910s. Shown here are ballroom dance stars Vernon and Irene Castle. © CORBIS. REPRODUCED BY PERMISSION.

# "Proper Dancing-Costumes for Women"

Reference work

**By:** Irene Foote Castle

**Date:** 1914

**Source:** Irene Foote Castle. "Proper Dancing-Costumes for Women." In *Modern Dancing,* by Vernon and Irene Foote Castle. Special Edition. New York: The World Syndicate Co., 1914.

**About the Authors:** Mr. and Mrs. Vernon Castle, as they were known, were professional dance partners as well as co-authors and husband and wife. Vernon Castle (1887–1918) was born Vernon Blythe in England. He received a degree in engineering from Birmingham University, but his career took a different direction when he moved to New York and began appearing as a dancer in plays, using the stage name Vernon Castle. Irene Foote (1893–1969) was born in New Rochelle, New York. She studied dance as a child, and at the age of 16 she appeared in local theatricals, learning dance techniques that would become part of the "Castle style." Irene and Vernon met in 1910 and married in 1911. They performed together from 1912 to 1916, becoming one of the most famous exhibition ballroom teams of the century, known across the United States and in Europe. Vernon Castle died in a plane crash during World War I (1914–1918). Irene continued to perform after his death and married three more times. ■

## Introduction

The world of dancing underwent drastic changes in the 1910s. Dance moved from a social activity with set steps to a more competitive and performance-based activity. Exhibition ballroom dance teams, like the Castles, performed routines that pleased large crowds.

Dance manuals were one way that people learned the popular dance steps of the era. The Castles' manual, *Modern Dancing,* includes not only instruction on how to perform the steps, but also several photographs of the couple, and chapters on grace, beauty and etiquette in dance, and dancing attire. Through these photographs and descriptions, women could see what a proper and elegant dance costume looked like. Many women in this era still made their own clothes, and would use the photos to replicate and modify the costume for their own use and tastes.

## Significance

Clothing design of the late nineteenth and early twentieth century worked against women's freedom of movement. It was impossible for a woman to dance gracefully in the constrictive clothing and the tight corsets that were then popular. In the 1910s, the "modern" dance trends of the era began to influence fashion, and clothing for women became less constrictive. The move away from the "hobble skirt," which resembled a soda-pop bottle, to a looser cut was partially due to the needs and desires of women like Irene Castle.

Irene Castle believed in clothing that allowed the dancer to move and appear graceful. She also believed in comfort. Dance, she pointed out, was about movement and exercise. In order to move easily, a dancer's clothing had to be flowing and of the right material. Castle did not advocate improper exposure of dancers' bodies, but she did emphasize that women's clothes must allow them to perform the dance, enjoy it, and appear graceful while dancing.

Dance proved to be a fashion liberator, and Irene Castle was one of its leaders. She bobbed her hair. She wore flowing gowns that enhanced her ability to move. She wore smaller hats that fit the head tightly and didn't conflict with dance movements. Castle was a fashion trendsetter—her photographs appeared in magazines and newspapers throughout the country and women emulated her style.

## Primary Source

### "Proper Dancing-Costumes for Women" [excerpt]

**SYNOPSIS:** In this chapter from *Modern Dancing*, professional ballroom dancer and fashion trendsetter Irene Castle provides advice on what to wear for a *thé dansant* (tea dance) in the 1910s. Women should look for comfort as well as style in her dresses, she says, recommending "plaited" (pleated) skirts in soft fabrics and loose sleeves that allow the arms to be lifted above the head.

The costume for the modern dances is a very important feature. A gown that is stiff or bunchy in its lines and does not fall softly will make even the most graceful dancer seem awkward and uncouth, and no amount of skill in stepping intricate measures can obviate the ugliness of a pump slipping off at the heel in the pretty dips or twirls of the dance.

The plaited skirt of soft silk or chiffon, or even of cloth, is by far the most graceful to dance in, and the one which lends itself best to the fancy steps of these modern days. Therefore, while fashion decrees the narrow skirt, the really enthusiastic dancer will adopt the plaited one. A clever woman may, however, combine the two by the use of a split skirt, carefully draped to hide the split, and a plaited petticoat underneath. Thus when she dances the skirt will give and not form awkward, strained lines, and the soft petticoat, fluffing out, will lend a charming grace to the dancer's postures.

The openings in a skirt of this sort can be fastened with tiny glove-snaps, so that on the street the wearer may appear to have the usual narrow costume, while at the same time she has a practical one for the daily *thé dansant.*

The dancing-petticoats of the year are really lovely, and are quite a feature of the dancing-costumes at Castle House. Some are of crêpe de Chine, some of plaited chiffon with straight lace ruffles on the bottom, or tiny rosebuds as trimming; they should always match the costume and the stockings. Dark stockings showing through a filmy petticoat and a split skirt are very ugly. Under these petticoats the dancers are wearing the new combination of brassière and silk bloomers, finished with ruffles of lace or sometimes ending quite plainly at the knee. These, too, give full play in the various steps.

Of course, for some dances you may wear an ordinary skirt and blouse or a narrow afternoon frock. The Tango may be danced in the narrowest of skirts, because the feet are always close together; the Maxixe needs but a little more room, while the One Step and the Hesitation Waltz, with their longer glides and more intricate steps, require the regular plaited effect of which I have spoken.

Clothes are really a great aid to the woman in dancing, for the sweep of her soft skirts, the charm of her frock, lends her a grace that a man must inevitably lack. Often a man who dances far better than a lady will be considered only mediocre, while the lady who is properly dressed is applauded for her skill.

The waist-line in a dancing-frock should always be high enough to eliminate the harsh line of the hips. It need not necessarily be up under the arms, but it should be high enough to have a fullness over the hips so that one long, graceful line extends from the bust down to the ankle. This lends a supple ease to every movement of the body and tends to improve, from the artistic stand-point, the various measures of the dance. Added to this, the blouse should be loose— and in speaking of the blouse I mean especially the

MRS. VERNON CASTLE

Irene Castle provided advice about how a woman should dress to dance, looking for comfort as well as style in her frocks. Hats, too, were still important during this era. **THE LIBRARY OF CONGRESS.**

sleeve. Tight sleeves are too binding. Often the wide-armhole sleeve draws awkwardly when the arm is out-stretched to meet the partner's. Don't fasten the blouse down too tightly, and be sure, in selecting one of the transparent, filmy little affairs now so much in vogue for dancing, that you can stretch your arms right above your head without difficulty. If you can do that, the blouse is suitable for the *thé dansant.*

As to material, of course, it must be light.

## Further Resources

### BOOKS

Castle, Irene. *Castles in the Air.* Garden City, N.Y.: Doubleday & Co., 1953.

Malnig, Julie. *Dancing Till Dawn: A Century of Exhibition Ballroom Dance.* New York: Greenwood Press, 1992.

### PERIODICALS

Fields, Jill. "Fighting the Corsetless Evil: Shaping Corsets and Culture, 1900–1930." *Journal of Social History,* 33.2, 1999, 355–384.

"Selections by Our Shoppers." *Dress & Vanity Fair,* November 1913, 63.

### WEBSITES

"An American Ballroom Companion: Dance Instruction Manuals, ca. 1490–1920." Library of Congress, Music Division. Available online at http://memory.loc.gov/ammem/dihtml/dihome.html; website home page: http://memory.loc.gov (accessed January 14, 2003).

### AUDIO AND VIDEO MEDIA

*The Story of Vernon and Irene Castle.* Turner Home Entertainment. Videocassette, 2000.

---

# "Whether at Home or Away, Your Summer Equipment Should Include a Bottle of Listerine"

Magazine advertisement

**By:** Lambert Pharmacal Company

**Date:** 1915

**Source:** "Whether at home or away, your Summer equipment should include a bottle of Listerine." Magazine advertisement created for Lambert Pharmacal Company. 1915. Available online at Medicine and Madison Avenue: A Project of the National Humanities Center, the Digital Scriptorium, and the John W. Hartman Center for Sales, Advertising & Marketing History. Duke University Rare Book, Manuscript, and Special Collections Library. Database no. MM0596. http://scriptorium.lib.duke.edu/mma (accessed January 23, 2003).

**About the Organization:** In 1879, Dr. Joseph Lawrence and Jordan Wheat Lambert, a chemist, created a new disinfectant for surgical procedures. They named their new product Listerine, after the English physician Sir Joseph Lister, who developed the first antiseptic procedures for surgery. In 1884, Lambert formed the Lambert Pharmacal Company to manufacture and market Listerine to the medical community. In 1955, Lambert and the Warner-Hudnut company merged, creating Warner-Lambert. Listerine, now marketed as a mouthwash, was one of the main products for Lambert at the time of the merger, accounting for more than fifty percent of the company's sales. In 2000, Warner-Lambert merged with Pfizer, creating one of the world's largest

pharmaceutical companies, with 90,000 employees worldwide. ■

## Introduction

During the first decades of the twentieth century, magazine advertising increased significantly. Readership of the most popular women's magazines had grown during the closing years of the nineteenth century and into the new century. Consumers had more income, and advertisers and manufacturers began taking advantage of it.

At the same time, the beginning of the twentieth century saw a new focus on personal cleanliness, thanks in part to a greater scientific understanding of the role of microorganisms ("germs") in causing illness and infection. Products for personal hygiene and care were advertised in the pages of magazines and newspapers, and with more money to spend, people were more likely to take advantage of the products. Many of the new products were scams. Some, such as Listerine, were legitimate.

The Lambert Pharmacal Company, the makers of Listerine, capitalized on the new cleanliness craze. Up to this period Listerine had been sold as a disinfectant, but Gerald Lambert, Jordan's son, decided to promote it in a new way. The company invented the term "halitosis" ("bad breath"), and it was decided that Listerine would be the cure. The ads in the 1910s broadened the range of uses for Listerine—not only was it an antiseptic to be used in first aid, but it could also freshen your breath and "was excellent for personal hygiene"—just the thing to refresh and clean your body on a hot day.

## Significance

In its attempts to sell Listerine to a wider audience, the Lambert Pharmacal Company employed a number of innovative marketing techniques. The company took a product created for one specific purpose and invented new ways for people to use it. The Listerine advertisements were meant to appeal to people's social needs as well as their hygienic needs. By coining the term "halitosis," Lambert created a problem that people didn't even know existed—and then presented them with the solution. Listerine was now a product that could cure bad breath, and in the process lead to love, friendship, and success. Using the product became attached to social acceptance.

Lambert also employed a marketing technique that is now known as "branding." This is the process of creating a unique and recognizable identity for a product, and building a sense of loyalty to that product among consumers. Name brands and "branding" were not common in the early twentieth century. People did not hear the name "Listerine" and immediately think of mouth-

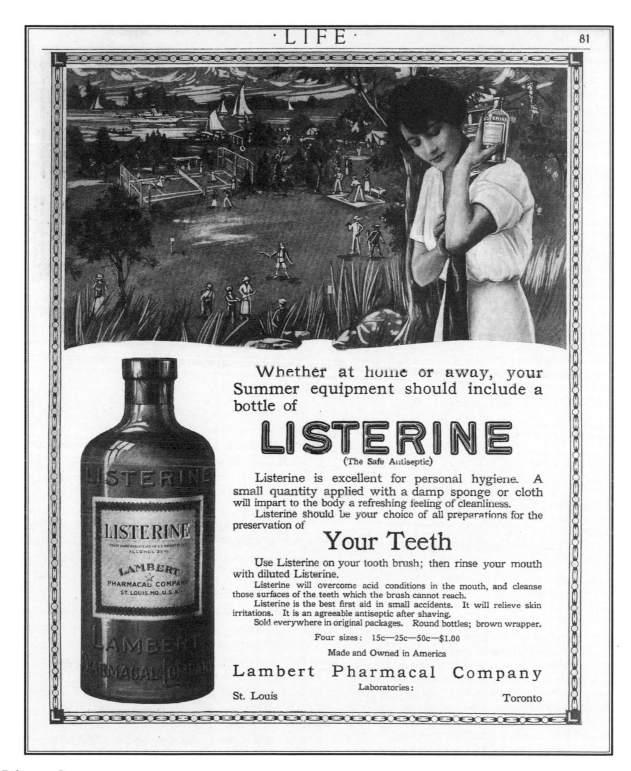

## Primary Source

### "Whether at Home or Away, Your Summer Equipment Should Include a Bottle of Listerine"

**SYNOPSIS:** In the 1910s, advertisements for Listerine were designed to appeal to the social needs of magazine readers as well as their desire for cleanliness and their practical need for an antisceptic for first aid. In this 1915 ad, Listerine was being sold as an indispensable product—something everyone should always have, both at home and on vacation. PFIZER, INC. REPRODUCED BY PERMISSION.

wash or fresh breath as they would today. The ad agencies and manufacturer worked together to build brand recognition. This kind of advertising increased in the 1920s. Listerine is an example of a product that might have disappeared if marketing techniques had not been applied to it. Listerine became one of Lambert Pharmacal's major products and remained so into the twenty-first century.

## Further Resources

### BOOKS

Vinikas, Vincent. *Soft Soap, Hard Sell: American Hygiene in an Age of Advertisement.* Ames, Iowa: Iowa State University Press, 1991.

### PERIODICALS

Sivulka, Juliann. "From Domestic to Municipal Housekeeper: The Influence of the Sanitary Reform Movement on Changing Women's Roles in America, 1860–1920." *Journal of American Culture* 22 no. 4, 1999, 1–7.

### WEBSITES

"Joseph Lister: Antiseptic Principle Of The Practice Of Surgery, 1867." Internet Modern History Sourcebook. Available online at http://www.fordham.edu/halsall/mod/1867lister.html; website home page http://www.fordham.edu/halsall/mod/modsbook.html (accessed January 31, 2003).

---

# "Shopping for the Well-Dressed Man"

## Clothing styles

**By:** *Vanity Fair*

**Date:** July 1916

**Source:** Trevor, Robert Lloyd. "Shopping for the Well-Dressed Man: Some Observations on a Standard Costume for Golfers." *Vanity Fair,* July 1916, 75.

**About the Publication:** The Vanity Fair Publishing Co. began publishing *Dress & Vanity Fair* in 1913. A year later, Condé Nast Publications took over the magazine and changed the name to *Vanity Fair.* The magazine sought to be the American counterpart of British magazines like *The Tatler* and *The Sketch,* which covered the arts, culture, and society as well as fashion, and aimed to attract both male and female readers. The magazine was aimed at sophisticated, wealthy people. *Vanity Fair* was absorbed by *Vogue* magazine in 1936, but it reappeared in 1983. Robert Lloyd Trevor, the author of this article, wrote a monthly column on men's fashions for *Vanity Fair* in the magazine's early years. ∎

## Introduction

"For the Well-Dressed Man" was a regular feature of *Vanity Fair* magazine. Written by Robert Lloyd Trevor, the column featured descriptions and photographs or drawings of trendsetting men's apparel. The articles were written in a chatty, narrative style.

To have a regular magazine column devoted to men's clothing was unusual in the 1910s. Men's clothing did not receive much attention because it changed very little. The suit, for example, had remained virtually the same style for more than 100 years. *Vanity Fair,* however, was a different kind of magazine. Its mission was to promote "modernism," and therefore it touched on all areas of its readers lives. It covered current fashions, but unlike the other fashion magazines of the day, it tried to attract both male and female readers. A column about male attire would, in theory, also draw men to a magazine that they might otherwise assume was for women. Males were a difficult audience to reach. On one hand they wanted to appear as if their attire did not matter; on the other hand, they knew that it did—enormously. The gentleman in particular wanted to be well groomed and well dressed. It is interesting to note that Trevor's column was accompanied by a box indicating that Trevor or a "*Vanity Fair* Shopper" would shop for any man who sent a specific request and a check.

## Significance

Though men's attire received less attention in the pages of magazines and newspapers in the 1910s, it was still important. Men of all classes knew that clothing could help them attain a higher standing in society. African American males and immigrants were particularly aware of this truth. While Trevor reaches out to men who have the time to play golf in this month's column, his other monthly columns often focus on items like topcoats or hats. Ready-to-wear clothing made fashionable attire more available to all men. Salesmen of the era were trained with a chart that told them what the correct dress was for the daytime and the evening.

Trevor's column in the July 1916 issue of *Vanity Fair* focuses on golf attire. This is revealing of the growing popularity of that sport. While the game of golf had been played for centuries, it took off as a popular sport in America around the turn of the century. Golf courses were being built across the country. Van Cortland Park, the oldest municipal golf course in the country, opened in 1895 in the Bronx, New York. The number of golf courses in America rose from 752 to 1,903 between 1916 and 1923. Of these, 543 were municipal courses.

Municipal courses, which were open to the public, made the game of golf accessible to the common man. Now men did not have to join an expensive private club to play golf; they could play a municipal course by paying a small fee per round. At the time, leisure clothing was generally considered to be for the well-to-do. But the golfers mentioned in the article are headed for a municipal golf course.

# Shopping for the Well-Dressed Man

*Some Observations on a Standard Costume for Golfers*

### By ROBERT LLOYD TREVOR

ONE night—but perhaps it would be more accurate to say morning—early last fall I entered the subway station at Columbus Circle, and boarded an uptown Broadway local. I had been to the theater earlier in the evening. I confess also to having attended a small, but respectable, supper party afterwards. However, I am telling you this, merely to account for my presence in the subway at an hour when everybody but the milkman is supposed to be at home and in bed, and also for the fact that I was in evening clothes. Everything else about my person was quite conventional; I was (needless to say) sober, self-contained, and in full possession of my faculties. Imagine my surprise, then, to find the car seats completely occupied by men who were attired in everything but what one would expect to find on a man at that hour in the morn-

Some new effects in French lisle hosiery. (upper) $2, (lower) $1.75

An English riding waistcoat of a heavy tweed, fancy pattern, $18.50

Two very smart summer designs in French silk hosiery, $5.00 each

High buckskin shoes for sport wear, $9.50

tailors just now, is illustrated by the accompanying sketch. The coat is made in a plain dark material such as a brown Shetland homespun. The knickers should be about the same weight and quality of material, but in a brown check; while the stockings should be conservative and should match the coat in shade. The cap is of a design similar to the knickers.

These effects can be carried out, of course, in grays or greens, but the coat should be a plain cloth without design.

NOTICE the sketch on the right hand side of this page. Someone has realized that the golfing enthusiast, being in many respects a perfectly human being, must find some means of protecting himself when it rains and at the same time not impede his movements with a clumsy sou'wester. Hence the Swithin rubberized silk golf coat. This is an admirable

A new idea for golfing costume, made to order. Coat and knickers, $45

guilty sensation of being so absolutely and wickedly *de trop*, I followed these men to the park; for there was a certain zest and novelty in the idea of watching daybreak golf that fascinated me.

Once at the golf links in the park, I was impressed with the enormous number of men who play golf, and amazed at the appalling lack of regard among them for suitable clothes.

Of course it could be argued that at such an hour, men would hardly be expected to dress as carefully as they would in the afternoon. Granted. But if you happen to have ten fingers on both of your hands, go out on the links any afternoon and count the men who look as though they had selected their clothes one half as carefully as they selected their caddy.

AN idea for a golfing costume which was brought out about six months ago, and is having considerable vogue with New York

*If you would like to buy any of the articles shown here, Mr. Trevor will gladly tell you where they may be had, or the Vanity Fair Shoppers will buy them for you. There is no extra charge for this service. Simply draw a check, to the order of the Vanity Fair Publishing Company, for the amount quoted under the picture of the article you want. Describe the article, tell on what page of which issue it appears, mail this information with your check or money-order to Vanity Fair and the article will be sent forward to you without delay*

Half-length Swithin rain coat for golfers. Rubberized silk, $10

ing. It was only through the fact that each clasped a golf bag that I recognized them to be golfers bound for Van Cortlandt Park.

IN spite of the embarrassing position in which my evening clothes placed me, and the

A very fine canvas and leather golf bag, with all-leather pocket for balls, $25

garment; cool, well ventilated, light, and easy to roll up and carry in the golf bag.

So much for golf clothes. As it is well on into June and approaching the time when one begins to think of buying one's second straw hat, I have illus- *(Continued on page 94)*

## Primary Source

## "Shopping for the Well Dressed Man" [excerpt]

**SYNOPSIS:** Golf was increasing in popularity during the 1910s, as new municipal courses made it affordable to the common man. Special clothing for golf was just coming into vogue in New York in 1916, when this article appear in *Vanity Fair* magazine. DRESS & VANITY FAIR MAGAZINE, JULY, 1916. COURTESY OF THE NEW YORK PUBLIC LIBRARY.

This article reflects the growing attention to men's clothing and the trend toward wearing particular costumes for leisure activities. Both trends would continue throughout the twentieth century. It also reflects the growing popularity of golf—and golf attire—among those outside the upper-class.

## Further Resources

### BOOKS

Joselit, Jenna Weissman. *A Perfect Fit: Clothes, Character, and the Promise of America.* New York: Metropolitan Books; Henry Holt, 2001.

Moss, Richard J. *Golf and the American Country Club.* Urbana, Ill.: University of Illinois Press, 2001.

### PERIODICALS

"Distinction of Golf." *Outlook,* v. 117, September 26, 1917, 116–117.

Moss, Richard. "Sport and Social Status: Golf and the Making of the Country Club in the United States, 1882–1920." *International Journal of the History of Sport,* 1993, 10, 1, 93–100.

### WEBSITES

"Golf at Van Cortland Park." Available online at http://www.bronx.com/5_96historyarch.html#anchor5398909; website home page http://www.bronx.com (accessed August 26, 2002).

Elizabeth Arden was one of the first women to encourage women to engage in a total beauty concept. **THE LIBRARY OF CONGRESS.**

## "A Woman Can Always Look Younger Than She Really Is"

**Magazine advertisement**

**By:** Elizabeth Arden

**Date:** July 1916

**Source:** "A Woman Can Always Look Younger Than She Really Is." Created for Elizabeth Arden. Published in *Vanity Fair,* July 1916.

**About the Author:** Elizabeth Arden (1878–1966) was born as Florence Nightingale Graham, the daughter of poor Canadian tenant farmers who had immigrated from England. She trained as a nurse, learning about skin care in the process, but instead of becoming a nurse moved to New York City. After working for a time with the E.R. Squibb pharmaceuticals company she took a job as a "treatment girl" at Eleanor Adair's beauty salon. In 1909, she opened a new salon on Fifth Avenue in partnership with Elizabeth Hubbard; the following year she changed her name to Elizabeth Arden and opened her own salon with that name. By her death in 1966, Arden had become one of the twentieth century's leading businesswomen, having built a worldwide beauty empire that encompassed 40,000 salons in 90 countries. ∎

## Introduction

Elizabeth Arden first learned about beauty treatments and techniques while working at the Eleanor Adair salon. She later acquired an understanding of various skin creams and other beauty products while working with her partner Elizabeth Hubbard, who had an expertise in that area. After the partnership dissolved, Arden took what she had learned from both women and began her own business. The Elizabeth Arden salon used and sold beauty products that were developed in a lab right on the premises.

When Elizabeth Arden opened her first salon on Fifth Avenue in 1910, beauty was just developing as a business, and there were very few women involved in it. (Helena Rubenstein, who opened her New York salon five years later, would be one of Arden's chief rivals throughout her life.) Prior to this time, skin care and beauty treatments were seen as pastimes for society women and also were considered slightly immoral.

Arden was determined to change that. She decorated her salon to be stylish and inviting, adopting her trademark red door as a way of making it look like a home in a fashionable neighborhood. She forged relationships with other businesses that could advance and legitimize her own. For example, she sublet space to the Ogilvie

# A Woman Can Always Look Younger Than She Really Is

My long experience and great success has positively convinced me that every skin requires an astringent tonic and a nourishing cream. Woman has always been searching for the Fountain of Youth, when, like the "Blue Bird," it is at home, and simply means ten minutes' care night and morning.

To have a wholesome skin is to keep it exquisitely clean. Many times the skin is not thoroughly cleansed and this is the real cause of blackheads and an impure complexion. For this there is nothing so important as a good Cleansing Cream. It must be light and very oily to properly remove all impurities and prevent the pores from becoming clogged. The *Venetian Cleansing Cream* ($2.00) is perfectly adapted to overcome this clogged condition of the skin.

Then if you are affected with coarse pores, one application of the *Pore Cream* ($1.00) will quickly refine the skin.

It is equally important to promote and stimulate the circulation and clear and firm the skin. This is easily accomplished by patting the skin well with *Venetian Ardena Skin Tonic* ($3.00). Learn not to over-massage the face which gives a lifeless looking skin. A wholesome, healthy skin, if wrongly treated can become gradually shrivelled, old and haggard.

The very best treatment for the face and throat is to firm the lines and muscles by a peculiar patting in of the *Venetian Special Herb Astringent* ($3.00). This particularly potent astringent firms as if by magic. Be taught to administer this treatment yourself. It is well worth learning how.

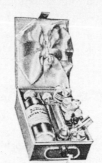

**$10 For Traveling**

Complete Set, including 8 preparations and eyebrow pencil and brush.
1. Venetian Ardena Skin Tonic
2. " Lille Lotion
3. " Muscle Oil
4. " Velva Cream
5. " Cleansing Cream
6. " Crystalline Eye Drops
7. " Rose Color
8. " Cream Amoretta
Also Eyebrow Pencil and Brush

Do not produce an artificial, unnatural look by doing too much to your skin. Just a few minutes each day is all that is required. And it is well to protect and soften the skin by using the *Venetian Amoretta Cream* ($2.00) before applying the new *Venetian Powder D'ILLUSION* ($2.50), a fascinating shade for sunburned faces.

## GET READY FOR THE HOT DAYS TO COME

Prepare your skin for July and August by taking a course of the *Venetian Muscle Strapping Treatment* at my Salon D'Oro. It will then be easy to keep it in perfect condition yourself by the methods which I have explained above.

The great lesson to learn about beauty charms is that no one method of treatment acts the same with all persons. It is because of this that I advise you to consult me before deciding which method to pursue.

### PROMPT ATTENTION GIVEN TO MAIL ORDERS

All Elizabeth Arden Venetian Preparations are shipped carefully packed with full instructions for use, immediately on receipt of cheque.

*Write for the "Quest of the Beautiful"*

# ELIZABETH ARDEN

SALON D'ORO. LARGEST AND FINEST IN THE WORLD 673 FIFTH AVENUE, ENTRANCE ON 53rd STREET NEW YORK

WASHINGTON, D. C., 1147 CONNECTICUT AVENUE

## Primary Source

### "A Woman Can Always Look Younger Than She Really Is"

**SYNOPSIS:** The July 1916 issue of *Vanity Fair* carried this advertisement for Elizabeth Arden's Venetian Ardena skin products. In addition to naming her products after herself, Elizabeth Arden wrote the copy for this and other ads in the early years of her business, because she wanted to control the image of her salon and her products. DRESS AND VANITY FAIR, JULY 1916, P. 88. COURTESY OF THE NEW YORK PUBLIC LIBRARY.

sisters, who did hair and scalp treatments, and referred clients to another sister, who had a hat-making business (and who referred her own clients to the salon). She added a mail order service to her salon business, and in 1914 opened a second salon in Washington D.C. Arden eventually formed a partnership with A. Fabian Swanson, a chemist who tested and made her products after she became too busy to do it herself.

## Significance

Elizabeth Arden was one of the first people to promote a total-body concept of beauty. Until the late 1910s, only hair and face treatments were seen as proper. Through her line of products and salons, and by forming alliances with other beauty-related businesses, she helped women see the connections between care for the face and the hair and their overall style and appearance.

Arden learned from both Adair and a visit to Paris that the image of a beauty product is as important as its

ingredients. She enhanced the women's perceptions of her beauty products through her glamorous salon; the names, aromas, and packaging her products were given; and through advertising. Advertisements in *Vogue, Vanity Fair,* and other chic fashion magazines were important to the growth of the Elizabeth Arden business. By 1916, Arden was incorporating her own name into the names of her products. Elizabeth Arden's Venetian Ardena Skin Tonic was the first beauty product to incorporate its maker's name.

Arden always tried to stay on top of beauty trends. After a trip to Paris in 1912, she introduced eye make-up, rouge, and tinted powders to American women. In 1918, she sent her sister and other trained treatment and demonstration girls out across the country to sell the Arden line, another marketing innovation.

The 1910s were the years in which Elizabeth Arden began building her empire. Between 1915 and 1920, she developed and introduced more products than anyone else in the beauty business at the time. She successfully sold beauty as a concept and as a product to a society that had until recently thought painted faces were immoral.

## Further Resources

### BOOKS

Lewis, Alfred Allen, and Constance Woodworth. *Miss Elizabeth Arden.* New York: Putnam Publishing Group, 1972.

Peis, Kathy. *Hope in a Jar: The Making of America's Beauty Culture.* New York: Metropolitan Books; Henry Holt and Co., 1998.

### PERIODICALS

Gehman, Richard B. "Elizabeth Arden, the Woman." *Cosmopolitan,* v. 140, June 1956, 69–73.

### WEBSITES

"Elizabeth Arden: Our Heritage." Elizabeth Arden. Available online at http://www.elizabetharden.com/heritage/early_start .asp#; website home page: http://www.elizabetharden.com (accessed January 21, 2003).

# "Wealthiest Negro Woman's Suburban Mansion"

Interview

**By:** *The New York Times Magazine*

**Date:** November 4, 1917

**Source:** "Wealthiest Negro Woman's Suburban Mansion," *The New York Times Magazine,* November 4, 1917, 6.

**About the Publication:** *The New York Times* began publication of a Sunday magazine supplement, called *The Times Illustrated Magazine,* on September 6, 1896. Prior to this, Sunday newspaper magazines consisted of comic strips and "yellow journalism" (stories that were sensational). Adolph S. Ochs, who purchased *The New York Times* in 1896, wanted to change the image of newspapers from scandal sheets to publications that featured serious news. With its high-caliber articles, the magazine became a popular addition to the Sunday edition of the newspaper, and is it was still published weekly in 2003. ■

## Introduction

Madame C.J. Walker (1867–1919) was born Sarah Breedlove in Delta, Louisiana. The daughter of slaves, she grew up in the South and worked as a domestic. She began her hair-products business in 1905. When her own hair began to thin, she experimented with various combinations of ingredients and developed a product that she called "Wonderful Hair." Walker began her business by experimenting on friends and by selling door-to-door.

By 1919, Walker's company was a huge success, providing work for 25,000 agents. Her company and its products encouraged women to become not only inde-

Madame C. J. Walker, creator of a chain of successful hair products, became one of the wealthiest African American women of her time. **THE GRANGER COLLECTION, NEW YORK. REPRODUCED BY PERMISSION.**

pendent, but also rich. Madame C. J. Walker, as she was by then called, was the first American woman of any race to become a self-made millionaire.

Walker's wealth allowed her to build a luxurious mansion in an "exclusive" village, New York's Irvington-on-Hudson, in 1917. At the time she already had a $90,000 Indiana limestone townhouse in New York City.

Walker frequently drew attention from the press because of her political activities. She was active in the National Association for the Advancement of Colored People (NAACP) and was a member of a committee that visited President Woodrow Wilson to protest riots in St. Louis. She provided philanthropic support to the African American community throughout her life; when she died in 1919, she left her fortune to various charities and educational institutions.

## Significance

Madame C.J. Walker's suburban estate was built with her personal wealth, a significant fact for a woman and an African American at the time. The mansion stood near the homes of two well-known industrialists of the day, Jay Gould and John D. Rockefeller. The Italianate

Neo-Palladian-style country house was designed by Vertner Woodson Tandy, the first licensed African American architect in New York State. He envisioned a villa that would inspire others to pursue their dreams as well. The luxurious mansion cost $250,000 to build, and furnishings cost an estimated $100,000. The thirty-four room house included a marble entryway, a Louis XV–style drawing room, and a dining room with hand-painted ceilings. It was decorated with a pipe organ, Persian rugs, oil paintings, and late-eighteenth- and early-nineteenth-century mahogany furniture.

Although her mansion was certainly a home that she enjoyed, Walker recognized its symbolic value. The mansion, named "Villa Lewaro" by Enrico Caruso, became a place for black people to gather for social events and for dinners. Walker hosted such luminaries of the time as author James Weldon Johnson and jazz composer and piano player Jelly Roll Morton in her home. Walker said that she wanted Villa Lewaro to be a place that made black people proud. The mansion was a symbol of how far she had come from poverty and how she had overcome the prejudices she had faced throughout her life.

## Primary Source

### "Wealthiest Negro Woman's Suburban Mansion" [excerpt]

> **SYNOPSIS:** Madame C. J. Walker began her hair-products business with almost nothing, but became America's first self-made woman millionaire. Like many other millionaires of the time, she used her money to support many philanthropic causes—and to build an impressive mansion. In this excerpt from a magazine article about her new home, Madame Walker reflects on her success.

"I was born forty-nine years ago," she said in speaking of her life, "was married at 14, and was left a widow at 20 with a little girl to support. If I have accomplished anything in life it is because I have been willing to work hard. I never yet started anything doubtingly, and I have always believed in keeping at things with a vim. When, a little more than twelve years ago, I was a washerwoman, I was considered a good washerwoman and laundress. I am proud of that fact. At times I also did cooking, but, work as I would, I seldom could make more than $1.50 a day. I got my start by giving myself a start. It is often the best way. I believe in push, and we mush push ourselves.

"I was at my tubs one morning with a heavy wash before me. As I bent over the washboard, and looked at my arms buried in soapsuds, I said to myself: 'What are you going to do when you grow old and you back gets stiff? Who is going to take care of your little girl?' This set me to thinking, but with all my thinking I couldn't see how I, a poor washerwoman, was going to better my condition.

"Now comes the part of my story that may sound strange, but it is the absolute truth. One night I had a dream, and something told me to start in the business in which I am now engaged. This I did. I went to Denver, Col., and began my business career on a capital of $1.25. I began, of course, in a most modest way. I made house-to-house canvasses among people of my race, and after awhile I got going pretty well, though I naturally encountered many obstacles and discouragements before I finally met with real success. I do not believe in taking chances, and I have never played the stock market. I am not a millionaire, but I hope to be some day, not because of the money, but because I could do so much then to help my race."

## Further Resources

### BOOKS
Bundles, A'Lelia. *On Her Own Ground: The Life and Times of Madam C.J. Walker.* New York: Scribner, 2001.

Peiss, Kathy. *Hope in a Jar: The Making of America's Beauty Culture.* New York: Metropolitan Books, Henry Holt & Co., 1998.

### PERIODICALS
Bundles, A'Lelia. "America's First Self-Made Woman Millionaire." *Radcliffe Quarterly,* December 1987, 11–12.

———. "Madame C.J. Walker—Cosmetics Tycoon." *Ms,* July 1983, 91–94.

### WEBSITES
Madam C.J. Walker. Available online at http://www.madamcjwalker.com/ (accessed January 26, 2003).

# "YWCA Overseas Uniform, 1918"

**Clothing style**

**By:** House of Worth

**Date:** 1918

**Source:** "YWCA Overseas Uniform." 1918. From the Costume Collection, House of Worth, Museum of the City of New York. Available online at http://www.mcny.org /Collections/costume/worth/costume29.jpg; website home page: http://www.mcny.org/ (accessed May 19, 2003).

## Primary Source

### "YWCA Overseas Uniform, 1918"

**SYNOPSIS:** American women who worked in the YWCA overseas units during World War I wore this uniform. It carried a designer label—House of Worth—that was more often found in evening gowns. In the background of the photograph is a typical YWCA recruitment poster from the era; they generally featured attractive young white women. © MUSEUM OF THE CITY OF NEW YORK, GIFT OF MRS. CORA GINSBURG, 80.117AB. REPRODUCED BY PERMISSION.

**About the Organization:** The House of Worth was established by Charles Worth (1825–1895), a noted fashion designer, in the late nineteenth century in Paris. When Worth died, his son Jean took over the business, which was still in operation in 2003. The House of Worth is known primarily for elegant gowns and dresses, but it designed this World War I YWCA uniform as a way of contributing to the war effort. ■

## Introduction

Women wore uniforms for many jobs during World War I (1914–1918). Train guards, police officers, mail carriers, and nurses all donned uniforms to help the Allies win the war. Women also contributed to the war effort through women's and voluntary organizations. The government relied heavily upon organizations like the Red Cross and the YWCA (Young Women's Christian Association) during the war. Workers for these organizations also wore uniforms.

The YWCA overseas corps uniform was the creation of Worth, a famous house of fashion better known for evening dresses. The blue-grey uniform included a long skirt, a belted jacket, a cape, and a brimmed hat. Women associated with the YWCA overseas worked as technicians and telephone operators in both paid and voluntary positions.

## Significance

Nearly 25,000 women served overseas during World War I. Women were provided with opportunities that they would not have had if the United States had not gone to war. This included being able to work in jobs that women previously had not been allowed to hold—and which would be taken away from them when the war ended. The jobs they held allowed women to realize that they could do "men's work" and eventually led American women to fight for voting rights.

Women's organizations grew and multiplied during the end of the nineteenth century and into the twentieth century. The YWCA, which had been imported to the United States from Great Britain, assisted working women and promoted social reform. Sending women overseas to help with the war was in keeping with those goals.

Women's uniforms served an important function during World War I. They made women visible as a group and validated their roles in the war as serious and worthy of respect.

## Further Resources

### BOOKS

Coppens, Linda Miles. *What American Women Did, 1789–1920.* Jefferson, N.C.: McFarland & Co., 2001.

Mankiller, Wilma, et al. *The Reader's Companion to U.S. Women's History.* Boston: Houghton Mifflin Company, 1998.

### PERIODICALS

Vining, Margaret, and Barton C. Hacker. "From Camp Follower to Lady in Uniform: Women, Social Class and Military Institutions before 1920." *Contemporary European History,* 10.3, 2001, 353–373.

### WEBSITES

"Women and War." Sparticus Educational. Available online at http://www.spartacus.schoolnet.co.uk/FWWwomen.htm; website home page http://www.spartacus.schoolnet.co.uk (accessed January 27, 2003).

"WWI: Thirty Thousand Women Were There." Military Women Veterans: Yesterday, Today, Today. Available online at http://userpages.aug.com/captbarb/femvets4.html; website home page http://userpages.aug.com/captbarb/ (accessed January 24, 2003).

"YWCA History." YWCA of the U.S.A. Available online at http://www.ywca.org/html/B5b.asp; website home page: http://www.ywca.org (accessed January 27, 2003).

# "Is There News in Shaving Soap?"

Magazine advertisement

**By:** J. Walter Thompson Company

**Date:** May 29, 1919

**Source:** J. Walter Thompson Company. "Is There News in Shaving Soap?" Advertisement in *Printer's Ink,* May 29, 1919. Reprinted online in Emergence of Advertising On-Line Project. John W. Hartman Center for Sales, Advertising & Marketing History. Duke University Rare Book, Manuscript, and Special Collections Library. Database no. J0075. http://scriptorium.lib.duke.edu/eaa/ (accessed January 26, 2003).

**About the Organization:** The J. Walter Thompson Company is one of the oldest advertising companies in the world. The company was founded in 1864 and purchased by J. Walter Thompson in 1878. Thompson tried many innovative ideas when advertising its clients' products. The agency placed advertisements in women's magazines in the early twentieth century, added a research department in 1915, and made groundbreaking use of testimonials in ads. ■

## Introduction

J. Walter Thompson introduced the American public to many products in the early twentieth century. Many of them, such as Listerine and Lux, were still household names a century later.

Soap ads were extremely common at the time. The 1910s saw a hygiene and cleanliness movement in the United States that helped soaps become good sellers. In addition, soap had a high profit margin, so to gain a share in the market helped a company tremendously. But this led to increased competion in the soap market; consumers found that they had several different soaps from which to choose,

8    PRINTERS' INK

PRINTERS' INK    9

What soaking in warm water for several minutes does to your finger nails, shaving soap must do instantly to the beard.

## Is there news in shaving soap?

"A new shaving soap—why?"

This headline introduced the new Woodbury's Shaving Stick to New Yorkers on May 22nd.

It not only announced a real achievement of the Andrew Jergens Company. It also summed up a big problem in advertising.

A new shaving stick, based on the famous Woodbury formula, was to be offered to New York men. It was different from other shaving sticks and splendidly adapted to its purpose.

How could these facts be used to make this soap stand out from others? How could it win a place in a field already over-crowded?

Out of the most commonplace thing in the world, a man's beard, a story was developed that tells concretely why Woodbury's Shaving Stick is superior to other soaps—a story that is intensely interesting human *news* to every man.

Your beard is of the same tough substance as your fingernails

Advertisements like these are carrying to New York men a news story which gives Woodbury's Shaving Stick a real individuality.

"Your beard is of the same tough substance as your finger-nails." This horn-like substance, *Keratin*, must be instantly softened by shaving soap lather.

"Which kind of beard is yours?" An average beard, with a tender skin—a heavy wiry beard—an ingrowing beard? For each of these three types of beard the correct method of using Woodbury's Shaving Stick has been perfected.

For this new shaving stick, a story of users has been worked out, which individualizes it just as the "Skin you love to touch" treatments have individualized Woodbury's Facial Soap.

Somewhere in every product—in every business—there is a story that can be developed into a genuine personality. By developing these stories and presenting them in compelling advertisements, the J. Walter Thompson Company is helping many clients build up rapid increase in sales and profits.

### J. WALTER THOMPSON COMPANY
*New York*

Chicago · Boston · Detroit · Cincinnati

5/29/19

## Primary Source

"Is There News in Shaving Soap?"

**SYNOPSIS:** How can shaving soap become news? J. Walter Thompson Company tried to attract new clients by creating house ads that touted successful advertising campaigns that they had created, such as the one for Woodbury's Shaving Stick. This house ad ran in the May 29, 1919, issue of *Printers Ink,* a trade magazine. COURTESY OF J. WALTER THOMPSON COMPANY. AD*ACCESS ON-LINE PROJECT - AD #J0075 JOHN W. HARTMAN CENTER FOR SALES, ADVERTISING & MARKETING HISTORY DUKE UNIVERSITY RARE BOOK, MANUSCRIPT, AND SPECIAL COLLECTIONS LIBRARY HTTP://SCRIPTORIUM.LIB.DUKE.EDU/ADACCESS/

not just the one they had grown up with. Soap companies tried to differentiate their products in consumers' minds, promoting particular varieties of soap for particular uses. The Andrew Jergens Company, for example, produced two types of Woodbury soap—a facial soap and shaving soap.

While the main business of the J. Walter Thompson Company was to produce advertisements for its clients' products, the agency also produced "house ads"—advertisements promoting its own work and talents. These innovative ads helped the ad agency attract more clients.

A house ad for the J. Walter Thompson Company appeared in the May 29, 1919, issue of *Printers Ink,* a

semimonthly trade magazine for marketing and communication management. The advertisement focuses on what J. Walter Thompson did to promote Woodbury's Shaving Stick. The partial ads reproduced in the two-page spread emphasized Thompson's innovative approach to advertising the new shaving stick by presenting it as a news story about a shaving soap breakthrough.

### Significance

J. Walter Thompson began using house ads in the 1880s. The ads were a good way to reach companies looking for advertising agencies. Advertising as a business was still in its infancy in the 1910s, and Thompson took steps to be different than other companies. With income on the rise and business growing in the United States, companies sought an advertising agency that could help a product gain a market share. J. Walter Thompson used its Woodbury ads as an example of one of its successful advertising campaigns in several house ads in the 1910s. The Woodbury campaign effectively used testimonials and narratives to create a real identity for Woodbury soaps in the minds of consumers.

Note that both the house ad and the Woodbury Shaving Stick ads that are reproduced in the house ad are extremely text-oriented. There is much more advertising copy than would appear in a modern magazine ads. Today the image is usually of primary importance in a magazine ad. But the story was the most important thing in both house ads and product ads in the 1910s.

## Further Resources

### BOOKS

Fox, Stephen. *The Mirror Makers. A History of American Advertising and Its Creators.* New York: Morrow, 1984.

Vinikas, Vincent. *Soft Soap, Hard Sell: American Hygiene in an Age of Advertisement.* Ames, Iowa: Iowa State University Press, 1991.

### PERIODICALS

"J. Walter Thompson Company." *Fortune,* November 1947, 95–101.

### WEBSITES

J. Walter Thompson Company Archives, John W. Hartman Center for Sales, Advertising & Marketing History, Duke University. Available online at http://scriptorium.lib.duke.edu/hartman/jwt/ (accessed January 26, 2003).

"The Jergens Story." Jergens. Available online at http://www.jergens.com/History1882.htm; website home page: http://www.jergens.com/main.htm (accessed January 26, 2003).

# "Henry Ford in a Model T"
Photograph

**Source:** "Henry Ford in a Model T." Corbis. Image no. BE036561. Available online at http://pro.corbis.com (accessed February 2, 2003).

**About the Inventor:** Henry Ford (1863–1947) grew up on a farm in what is now Dearborn, Michigan. At the age of sixteen he became an apprentice in the James Flower and Brothers Machine Shop. He continued learning about machines at the Detroit Drydock Company, a shipbuilding firm. In the late nineteenth century, Ford eventually developed a motorized automobile, and in 1899, he formed the Detroit Automobile Company, which later reorganized as the Cadillac Motor Car Company. In 1903, he founded the Ford Motor Company, which

he eventually transformed into a multinational conglomerate in thirty-three countries. His innovations in automobile manufacturing changed the automobile industry—and life in America. ∎

## Introduction

Henry Ford had been experimenting with automobiles for many years by the time the Model T was developed. The Model T was first sold to the public in 1908 and remained in production until 1927. The car became a best-seller by 1914. The Model T had a ten-gallon tank and four-cylinder/four-cycle motor; the early versions started with crankshafts. The Model T was available as a sedan, a truck, a convertible, a Deluxe Touring model, a two-seater Runabout, and a light delivery truck. But the Model T was available in only one color—black.

The appearance of the Model T remained relatively stable during the time it was built, although slight changes were introduced over the years to improve features or to save money. At one point, for example, the leather seats became "leatherette." The Model T remained a reliable car despite the cosmetic changes. It was a somewhat ugly car, but affordable to the general public.

The first Model Ts sold for between $825 and $1,000. The Model T of 1914 cost between $440 and $750, significantly less than previous models. Some parts were made of iron rather than aluminum on this model. The model retained the cherry dashboards and flat fenders for one more year. The front fenders were stronger than in previous models, however. The vanadium steel that was eventually used in the car made it even lighter in weight and more reliable.

Ford knew his audience and tailored not only the car itself but also advertising for the car to them. In a 1913 ad, the car was compared to "Old Dobbin," the family horse. The car weighed less and was stronger than the horse ever could be, according to the advertisement. A 1914 advertisement Ford introduced the "Coupelet," a car suitable for women to drive.

## Significance

The Model T was Ford's and the automobile world's biggest seller during its lifetime. Over the 19 years it was in production, 15 million Model Ts were built. In 1914 alone, almost 240,000 were made. Automobiles went from being a plaything of the rich to a common household possession during that time period. By 1921, Americans owned 10.5 million cars; by 1929, nearly half of all American families owned a car.

The Model T—nicknamed the "Tin Lizzie"—became a cultural icon, inspiring its own set of jokes. Despite the jokes about parts falling out and the car not starting in the cold, the Model T remained popular and a best-seller

## Primary Source

### "Henry Ford in a Model T"

**SYNOPSIS:** In this photograph, Henry Ford poses with his most famous invention. The car made automobiles accessible to people of modest means, and helped Ford build his automobile empire. © BETTMANN/CORBIS. REPRODUCED BY PERMISSION.

throughout the 1920s. Ford was quoted as saying, "The jokes about my car sure helped to popularize it. I hope they will never end."

Other innovations followed on the heels of the Model T. In 1913, Ford introduced the assembly line concept at the Ford Highland Park Plant. This efficient process would eventually be adopted by factories around the world. In 1914, Henry Ford implemented a five-dollar, eight-hour workday at his plant. This was during a time when other auto companies were paying $2.34 for a nine-hour workday.

The Model T changed the world. The style was consistent and the price continued to go down over the years, making a car affordable to the average family. The automobile made traveling significantly easier and made the world a smaller place. Trips to visit family and friends no longer took hours by horse-drawn buggies. The Model T, like many of the changes in society in the first few decades of the twentieth century, gave people greater freedom and autonomy.

### Further Resources

#### BOOKS

Bryan, Ford R. *Beyond the Model T: The Other Ventures of Henry Ford.* Detroit: Wayne State University Press, 1990.

Clymer, Floyd. *Henry's Wonderful Model T, 1908–1927.* New York: Bonanza Books, 1955.

Dammann, George H. *Illustrated History of Ford, 1903–1970.* Sarasota, Fl.: Crestline Publishers, 1971.

#### PERIODICALS

*Model T Times.* Elgin, Il. Model T Ford Club International, 1986–present.

**WEBSITES**

Ford Heritage. Available online at http://www.fordheritage.com/ (accessed January 23, 2003).

"The Model T." Henry Ford Museum & Greenfield Village. Available online at http://www.hfmgv.org/exhibits/showroom /1908/model.t.html; website home page: http://www.hfmgv .org (accessed January 23, 2003).

"Model T Ford Encyclopedia." The Model T Ford Club of America. Available online at http://www.mtfca.com/encyclo /index.htm; website home page http://www.mtfca.com/index .htm (accessed Jan. 28, 2003).

**AUDIO AND VIDEO RECORDINGS**

Dave Wretschko Orchestra. "The Model T Polka." *Cleveland-Style Polkas and Waltzes.* Fun City. LP, 1977.

*Model "T."* A & E Home Video, distributed by New Video Group. Produced and written by Michael Rose. Videocassette, 1996.

# 5

# GOVERNMENT AND POLITICS

PAUL G. CONNORS

*Entries are arranged in chronological order by date of primary source. For entries with one primary source, the entry title is the same as the primary source title. Entries with more than one primary source have an overall entry title, followed by the titles of the primary sources.*

**CHRONOLOGY**

Important Events in Government and Politics,
   1910–1919 . . . . . . . . . . . . . . . . . . . . . . . . . . . . 226

**PRIMARY SOURCES**

"The New Nationalism"
   Theodore Roosevelt, August 31, 1910 . . . . . . . . 232

"Henry Cabot Lodge: Corollary to the
   Monroe Doctrine"
   Henry Cabot Lodge Sr., August 2, 1912 . . . . . . 236

"Votes for Women"
   W.E.B. Du Bois, September 1912 . . . . . . . . . . 239

*The Yosemite*
   John Muir, 1912 . . . . . . . . . . . . . . . . . . . . . . . 241

"Composition and Characteristics of the
   Population for Wards of Cities of 50,000
   or More: Lawrence"
   Federal Bureau of the Census, 1913–1914 . . . . . 246

"Woodrow Wilson: *The Tampico Affair*"
   Woodrow Wilson, April 20, 1914 . . . . . . . . . . 249

*Family Limitation*
   Margaret Sanger, 1914 . . . . . . . . . . . . . . . . . . 252

The Zimmermann Telegram . . . . . . . . . . . . . . . . 254
Telegram from Arthur Zimmermann to
   Heinrich J.F. von Eckhardt
   Arthur Zimmermann, January 16, 1917
Telegram from U.S. Ambassador Walter
   Page to President Woodrow Wilson
   Walter Page, February 24, 1917

Woodrow Wilson's Declaration of War
   Message
   Woodrow Wilson, April 2, 1917 . . . . . . . . . . . 258

"Opposition to Wilson's War Message"
   George W. Norris, April 4, 1917 . . . . . . . . . . . 261

*"Over the Top": By an American Soldier
   Who Went*
   Arthur Guy Empey, 1917 . . . . . . . . . . . . . . . . 265

"Henry Cabot Lodge Speaks Out Against
   the League of Nations, Washington, D.C.,
   August 12, 1919"
   Henry Cabot Lodge Sr., August 12, 1919 . . . . . 267

"Statement by Emma Goldman at the Federal
   Hearing in Re Deportation"
   Emma Goldman, October 27, 1919 . . . . . . . . . 270

*Volstead Act of 1919*
   Andrew Volstead, October 28, 1919 . . . . . . . . . 273

## Important Events in Government and Politics, 1910–1919

### 1910

- On March 17, Congressman George W. Norris of Nebraska introduces a resolution to limit the power of Speaker of the House of Representatives Joseph G. Cannon of Illinois. Two days later the measure passes, an indication of the growing strength of Progressive Republicans against the "old guard" Republicans represented by President Taft and Representative Cannon.

- On March 26, Congress amends the Immigration Act of 1907 to prohibit criminals, paupers, anarchists, and diseased persons from entering the United States.

- On June 18, Congress passes the Mann-Elkins Act, which extends jurisdiction of the Interstate Commerce Commission to include telephone, telegraph, cable services, and wireless companies. It also augments ICC's power to regulate railroads.

- On June 20, Congress authorizes the citizens of the New Mexico and Arizona territories to form state governments and frame constitutions.

- On June 25, Congress establishes the Postal Savings Bank (PSB) system. People who deposit their money in savings accounts with the post office receive 2 percent interest. (The PSB is abolished in 1967.)

- On June 25, Congress passes the Publicity of Campaign Contributions Act, which requires members of Congress to report campaign contributions.

- On June 25, Congress passes the White Slave Traffic Act. Sponsored by Representative James R. Mann of Illinois, this law prohibits the transportation of women across state lines for "immoral purposes" (prostitution). Between 1910 and 1918 more than two thousand convictions for "white slavery" are obtained in the courts.

- On August 31, former President Theodore Roosevelt delivers his famous "New Nationalism" speech at Osawatomie, Kansas. Roosevelt calls for government regulation of trusts, tariff revision, graduated income tax, protection of labor, direct primary, and recall of elective officers. The speech is interpreted by many as a signal of Roosevelt's intention of challenging President William Howard Taft for the Republican Party nomination in 1912.

- On November 8, in the Congressional elections Democrats gain control of the House of Representatives for the first time since 1885. Republicans retain nominal control of the Senate because Democrats and Progressive Republicans form a bloc against conservative Republicans. Also, Victor L. Berger of Milwaukee, Wisconsin, is the first Socialist elected to Congress.

### 1911

- On January 21, the National Progressive Republican League, founded by Senator Robert M. La Follette of Wisconsin, issues its platform. It calls for direct election of United States senators, direct primaries, the initiative, the referendum, the recall, and other reforms. Senator Jonathan Bourne of Oregon is elected league president.

- On March 7, President Taft dispatches twenty thousand American troops and fifteen warships to the Mexican border to prevent fighting associated with the Mexican Revolution from spilling over into the United States.

- On May 15, citing the restraint of trade provision within the Sherman Antitrust Act of 1890, the United States Supreme Court rules that Standard Oil of New Jersey is a monopoly and therefore to be dissolved.

- On May 29, in *U.S.* v. *American Tobacco Company,* the United States Supreme Court finds the "tobacco trust" in violation of the Sherman Antitrust Act.

- On July 7, in a move to save seals from extinction, the United States joins Great Britain, Russia, and Japan in barring seal killing in the open seas north of the thirtieth parallel.

- On August 22, President Taft vetoes statehood for Arizona because its constitution allows for the recall of judges by popular vote. Arizona omits the offending clause, but after it gains statehood it adopts the recall provision.

- On October 16, the National Progressive Republican League endorses Robert M. La Follette of Wisconsin for president.

- On December 21, Congress passes a joint resolution abrogating the Russian Treaty of Commerce of 1832 because of Russia's unwillingness to recognize some United States passports, including those held by Jews and evangelical Protestant clergymen.

### 1912

- On January 6, New Mexico becomes the forty-seventh state.

- On January 19, amid the Chinese Revolution, American troops land in China to protect the important Peking-Tientsin Railroad.

- On February 10, seven Republican governors and seventy other Republican leaders representing twenty-four states endorse Theodore Roosevelt for president.

- On February 14, Arizona becomes the forty-eighth state.

- On February 24, Roosevelt, representing Progressive Republicans, announces his bid for the presidency.

- On April 27, Democratic Congressman Arsene Pujo of Louisiana begins House subcommittee hearings into J. Pierpont Morgan and the "money trust."

- On May 12, the Socialist Party Convention meeting at Indianapolis again nominates Eugene V. Debs of Indiana for president and Emil Seidel, mayor of Milwaukee, Wisconsin, for vice president.

- From June 18 to June 22, the Republican National Convention meeting in Chicago renominates William H. Taft for President and James S. Sherman for vice president.

- On June 22, convinced that the Republican National Convention's nomination process was fraudulent, Roosevelt supporters nominate him to lead the Progressive Party, or the "Bull Moose Party."

- From June 25 to July 3, the Democratic National Convention meeting in Baltimore nominates New Jersey Governor Woodrow Wilson for president on the forty-sixth ballot and Governor Thomas R. Marshall of Indiana for vice president.

- On July 10, the National Prohibition Party meeting at Atlantic City, New Jersey, nominates Eugene W. Chafin of Arizona for president and Aaron S. Watkins of Ohio for vice president.

- On August 5, the Progressive Party Convention meeting at Chicago nominates Theodore Roosevelt for president and Hiram W. Johnson of California for vice president.

- On September 2, President Taft creates the 39,969-acre Naval Oil Reserve at Elks Hills, California.

- On September 30, striking women garment workers riot at Lawrence, Massachusetts. On October 14, Theodore Roosevelt is shot and wounded by the assassin John Schrank in Milwaukee. Roosevelt delivers his scheduled speech before going to the hospital for treatment.

- On October 30, Vice-President James S. Sherman dies in Utica, New York. Columbia University President Nicholas Murray Butler replaces him as the Republican vice presidential candidate.

- On November 5, with the Republican vote split between Roosevelt and Taft, Democratic candidate Woodrow Wilson wins the presidential election, carrying forty of the forty-eight states. President Taft carries only Utah and Vermont. The Democrats win majorities in both houses of Congress.

## 1913

- On February 25, the Sixteenth Amendment to the Constitution, having been ratified by thirty-eight states, is adopted. The amendment legalizes the federal income tax.

- On February 28, the Pujo Committee issues its report implicating a few financial leaders of controlling the nation's money supply. The investigation leads to the creation of the Federal Reserve System in 1913 and the Clayton Antitrust Act of 1914.

- On March 1, Congress overrides President Taft's veto of the Webb-Kenyon Interstate Liquor Act, which prohibits the shipment of liquor into states where its sale is illegal.

- On March 4, Woodrow Wilson takes the oath of office and becomes the twenty-eighth president of the United States.

- On March 11, President Wilson announces that the United States will not recognize the Mexican government of General Victoriano Huerta, whose troops overthrew and assassinated President Francisco Madero in a coup from February 18 to February 22.

- On March 31, the financier John Pierpont Morgan, one of the richest and most powerful men in the world, dies while vacating in Rome, Italy, at the age of seventy-five.

- On April 8, President Wilson delivers a speech on tariff revision before Congress, becoming the first president since John Adams to appear before a joint session of the two houses.

- On May 3, the California Legislature passes a law preventing Japanese aliens from owning land. The act further damages United States-Japanese relations.

- On May 31, the Seventeenth Amendment to the Constitution, providing for the direct election of United States senators, is officially adopted following ratification by thirty-six states. Previously, senators were selected by state legislatures.

- On October 3, Congress passes the Underwood-Simmons Tariff Act, which lowers average duties to about 30 percent and allows some raw materials into the country tariff-free.

- On October 27, in a speech in Mobile, Alabama, President Wilson promises that the United States will "never again seek one additional foot of territory by conquest."

- On December 23, Congress passes the Federal Reserve Act, establishing the Federal Reserve Board and a system of twelve regional Federal Reserve Banks to control the money supply and regulate the national banking system.

## 1914

- On February 3, President Wilson lifts the arms embargo against Mexico in an effort to help the forces of Venustiano Carranza, who is working to overthrow the Huerta government.

- On April 9, an unarmed group of United States sailors from the USS *Dolphin,* is arrested in Tampico, Mexico after accidentally entering a restricted area while seeking to secure supplies. Without consulting Washington, D.C., Admiral Henry T. Mayo demands that the Mexicans formally apologize, raise the American flag on their soil, and give it a twenty-one-gun salute. Wilson backs these demands.

- On April 21, American forces bombard Veracruz, Mexico, and occupy the city as part of a general blockade of Mexico. The next day, Congress grants Wilson's request to use force against Mexico. Huerta breaks off diplomatic relations with the United States. By April 30, sixty-seven hundred American troops are engaging Huerta's forces. They do not withdraw from Mexico until November 23.

- On April 25, President Wilson accepts the mediation efforts of the "ABC Powers" (Argentina, Brazil, and Chile) in the dispute with Mexico.

- On July 24, meeting in Ontario, Canada, the United States, Mexico, and the ABC Powers decide the United States-Mexican dispute overwhelmingly in favor of the United States. Mediators recommend that Huerta resign, that Mexico establish a provisional government, and that the United States pay no indemnity for its invasion of Mexico. Rejected by Mexico, the plan nevertheless puts international pressure on Huerta, and he resigns on July 15.

- On August 4, in support of its allies Belgium and France, Great Britain declares war on Germany. The United States announces its neutrality.

• On August 5, Secretary of State William Jennings Bryan signs the Bryan-Chamorro Treaty with Nicaragua. In return for $3 million, the United States leases two Nicaraguan islands and receives the perpetual right to build a naval base and a canal across Nicaragua.

• On August 6, the USS *Tennessee* leaves for Europe with $6 million in gold to assist Americans stranded on the continent.

• On August 15, the United States announces that war loans to European nations by American bankers are "inconsistent with the true spirit of neutrality," but by October the State Department modifies its position, allowing some loans to be made.

• On August 15, the Panama Canal is officially opened to shipping.

• On September 26, Congress passes the Federal Trade Commission Act, which establishes a bipartisan five-member committee to replace the Bureau of Corporations and investigate the activities of corporations and individuals to prevent unfair business practices.

• On October 15, Congress passes the Clayton Antitrust Act, which prohibits interlocking business directorates.

## 1915

• On January 28, Congress establishes the United States Coast Guard by combining life saving and revenue cutting services.

• A German ship sinks the American merchant ship "William P. Frye" carrying wheat to Britain.

• On February 18, Germany announces that its submarines will sink neutral merchant vessels without warning that enter the British Isle war zone.

• On March 28, an American is killed when the Germans sink the British ship *Falaba.*

• On April 30, President Wilson creates the 9,481-acre Naval Oil Reserve No. 3 near Casper, Wyoming. Local residents believe that the reserve resembles a "Teapot Dome."

• On May 1, three Americans die when the Germans sink the United States tanker *Gulflight.*

• On May 7, the *Lusitania,* a British passenger liner, is sunk off the Irish coast by a German submarine. The dead include 114 Americans.

• On May 13, the first *Lusitania* note to Germany, written by President Wilson, demands that Germany stop its unrestricted submarine warfare and to make reparations to the families of United States citizens who died. Germany correctly asserts that the *Lusitania* was carrying rifles and bullets and therefore refuses to pay reparations.

• On June 8, Secretary of State William Jennings Bryan resigns after President Wilson asks him to sign a second *Lusitania* note. Bryan fears that the note will draw the United States into the war. Robert Lansing is appointed the new secretary of state.

• On July 21, President Wilson sends a third *Lusitania* note to Germany warning that similar actions in the future would be regarded as "deliberately unfriendly."

• On July 29, United States Marines go ashore in Haiti following the assassination of Haitian president Vilbrun Guillaume Sam.

• On August 10, the "Plattsburg idea"—military-preparedness training for civilians—begins in Plattsburg, New York.

• On August 19, two American citizens die when the British passenger ship *Arabic* is sunk by a German submarine.

• On September 7, Germany claims that it sank the *Arabic* in self-defense.

• On September 16, Haiti becomes a United States protectorate under the terms of a new ten-year treaty. The United States Senate ratifies the treaty on February 28, 1916. America retains Haiti until 1934.

• On October 5, Germany apologizes for sinking the *Arabic,* offers reparations, and promises that such incidents will not happen in the future.

• On October 19, the United States recognizes Venustiano Carranza as the president of Mexico.

• On December 4, Henry Ford with his delegation of peace advocates charters the *Oskar II,* known as the "peace ship," for Europe. Ford wants "to try to get the boys out of the trenches and back to their homes by Christmas day."

• On December 18, President Wilson marries Edith Boiling Gait at her home in Washington, D.C. (Wilson's first wife died in August 1914.)

## 1916

• On January 10, Pancho Villa and his band of outlaws kill eighteen American engineers at Santa Ysabel, Mexico.

• On February 10, Secretary of War Lindley M. Garrison resigns in protest to President Wilson's refusal to mobilize a four-hundred-thousand-man National Guard. Wilson prefers to rely on state militias to defend the nation.

• On March 9, Pancho Villa and his band raid Columbus, New Mexico, killing seventeen Americans.

• On March 15, six thousand American troops under the command of General John J. Pershing pursue Villa into Mexico.

• On April 18, in response to the German sinking of the *Sussex,* President Wilson threatens to sever diplomatic relations with Germany, if Germany does not end its campaign of submarine warfare against passenger and freight carrying vessels. On May 4, Germany agrees to Wilson's demands.

• On June 3, Congress passes the National Defense Act, which provides for the expansion of the regular army to 223,000 in five years, authorizes a National Guard of 424,800 men, establishes the Reserve Officers Training Corps (ROTC) at colleges and universities, and makes provisions for industrial preparedness.

• From June 7 to June 10, the Republican National Convention meeting in Chicago nominates Supreme Court Justice Charles Evans Hughes of New York for president and Charles W. Fairbanks of Indiana for vice president.

• From June 7 to June 9, the Progressive Party Convention meeting in Chicago nominates Theodore Roosevelt for president, but he declines the nomination and throws his support to Hughes.

- From June 14 to June 16, the Democratic National Convention meeting at St. Louis, Missouri renominates President Wilson and Thomas R. Marshall for vice president.

- On June 21, American troops are attacked at Carrizal, Mexico. Seven soldiers are killed, nine wounded, and twenty-two are taken prisoners. Thirty-eight Mexicans are killed in battle.

- On July 11, Congress passes the Federal Highway Act, authorizing federal assistance to states for road construction.

- On July 19, the National Convention of the Prohibition Party meeting in St. Paul, Minnesota, nominates J. Frank Hanly of Indiana for president and Ira D. Landrith of Tennessee for vice president.

- On July 30, German sabotage is believed to be the cause of an explosion of a munitions cache on Black Tom Island, New Jersey. The explosion causes $20 million in damages.

- On August 4, the United States purchases the Virgin Islands from Denmark for $25 million.

- On September 1, Congress passes the Keating-Owen Child Labor Act, which prohibits the interstate shipment of goods manufactured by children. The United States Supreme Court rules the act unconstitutional in 1918.

- On September 3, President Wilson signs the Adamson Act, which mandates an eight-hour day for railroad workers. As a result, a nationwide strike planned for September 4 is averted.

- On September 7, Congress passes the Workmen's Compensation Act, which provides compensation for injuries to half a million federal employees.

- On September 8, President Wilson signs the Emergency Revenue Act, which doubles the income tax rate on both individuals and corporations. In addition, the act imposes an inheritance tax.

- On October 7, the German submarine U-53 enters the Newport, Rhode Island, harbor. The next day, it sinks six merchant vessels off Nantucket Island and three more vessels on October 9.

- On November 7, Woodrow Wilson is reelected president in a close race.

- On November 29, the United States, acting under the Roosevelt Corollary, occupies the Dominican Republic. America retains the small Caribbean island until 1924.

- On December 18, President Wilson sends a "peace note" to the warring nations requesting that they state their war aims. Germany refuses to do so, and the Allies put forward a list of demands clearly unfavorable to Germany.

## 1917

- On January 19, in the famous "Zimmermann Telegram," the German foreign minister Arthur Zimmermann instructs German officials in Mexico to negotiate with Mexico. The note proposes that Mexico align itself with Germany and Japan against the United States in case of war. In return, Mexico will receive the territory it lost to the Americans in the United States-Mexican War of 1846. This territory consists of New Mexico, Texas, and Arizona.

- On January 31, the German ambassador delivers a diplomatic note to the United States State Department announcing that on February 1, Germany will renew unrestricted submarine warfare against neutral ships.

- On February 3, the United States severs diplomatic relations with Germany.

- On February 3, the United States steamer *Housatonic* is sunk by a German submarine.

- On February 5, Congress overrides President Wilson's veto to pass a law requiring new immigrants to pass a literacy test.

- On February 23, Congress passes the Smith-Hughes Act, which provides funding for agricultural and vocational education.

- On February 24, Great Britain turns over to the United States the "Zimmermann Telegram." The British had intercepted the telegram, but hesitated to inform the United States because Britain did not want to tip off the Germans that it had broken their secret code. Ultimately, the British turned over the note because it hoped that the Americans would disavow its neutrality and declare war against Germany.

- On March 2, Congress passes the Jones Act, making Puerto Rico an American territory and granting its inhabitants citizenship.

- On March 5, President Wilson is inaugurated for his second term in office.

- On March 12, the United States announces that merchant ships entering the submarine war zone will be armed and will fire on enemy submarines.

- On March 20, President Wilson's cabinet unanimously advises that he should ask Congress to declare war on Germany.

- On March 31, the Council of National Defense establishes the General Munitions Board to orchestrate the purchase of war materiel.

- On April 2, Jeannette Rankin of Montana is the first woman elected to the United States House of Representatives.

- On April 2, President Wilson addresses a special joint session of Congress to request a declaration of war against Germany. He concludes the speech by calling the American war effort an attempt to make the world "safe for democracy."

- On April 4, the United States Senate votes 82-6 in favor of the war declaration. The House passes the measure on a vote of 373-50.

- On April 14, President Wilson issues an executive order establishing the Committee on Public Information, headed by the journalist George Creel, to disperse propaganda in support of the American war effort.

- On April 24, Congress passes the Liberty Loan Act, authorizing the Secretary of the Treasury to issue $2 billion in war bonds at 3.5 percent interest. By the end of the war, American war bond drives have collected $21 billion.

- On May 18, Congress passes the Selective Service Act, which authorizes all men between the ages of twenty-one and thirty-one to enroll for military service.

- On June 15, Congress passes the Espionage Act, making it a crime to interfere with recruitment, foster disloyalty in the armed forces, or otherwise engage in disloyal acts. Crimes under the act are punishable by fines up to ten thousand dollars and twenty years imprisonment.

- On June 15, the anarchists Emma Goldman and Alexander Berkman are arrested for interfering with military conscription.

- On June 25, the first American troops arrive in Europe, landing at St. Nazaire, France.

- On July 7, the anarchists Goldman and Berkman are sentenced to two years imprisonment and fined ten thousand dollars. The United States Supreme Court sustains the decision in January 1918. Later the two anarchists, along with dozens of others, are exiled to the Soviet Union.

- On July 24, Congress passes the Aviation Act, which appropriates $640 million for the purchase and construction of airplanes. The aim is to build forty-five hundred planes by the spring of 1918.

- On July 28, the Council of National Defense (CND) creates the War Industries Board (WIB) to orchestrate government purchases and improve wartime efficiency.

- On August 10, Congress passes the Lever Act, authorizing the creation of a Food Administration and a Fuel Administration, headed by Herbert Hoover, to regulate the production, distribution, and costs of food and fuel.

- On October 3, the War Revenue Act doubles the income tax rates of 1916 and places excise taxes on many goods.

- On October 6, Congress passes the Trading with the Enemy Act, which authorizes the president to place an embargo on imports, forbids trade with enemy nations, and allows the government to censor foreign mail.

- On November 2, Secretary of State Lansing and Japanese Viscount Ishii Kikujiro sign the Lansing-Ishii Agreement, in which the United States recognizes Japan's special interests in China, and Japan agrees not to interfere with the "Open Door" policy.

- On November 3, American forces are involved in their first engagement of the war. While training near the Rhine-Marne Canal in France, three United States soldiers are killed by the German forces.

- On November 6, an amendment to the New York State constitution gives women the right to vote in state elections.

- On November 13, the Fuel Administration demands that all electric advertising signs be turned off on Thursdays and Sundays to conserve energy.

- On December 18, the Eighteenth Amendment to the Constitution—prohibiting the sale, manufacture, or transportation of alcohol—is passed by Congress and submitted to the states for ratification.

- On December 26, President Wilson places the railroads under the administration of the William G. McAdoo, Director General of Railroads.

## 1918

- On January 8, in an address before Congress, President Wilson puts forward his peace proposal (the Fourteen Points).

- On February 16, New Jersey passes the "anti-loafing" law, which requires all able-bodied men to get a job.

- On March 4, President Wilson names Bernard Baruch, a prominent Wall Street businessman, to head the War Industries Board.

- On March 19, to conserve energy during the war, Congress passes legislation that puts daylight savings time into effect.

- On March 21, the Railroad Control Act, authorizing federal control of the railroads, is passed by Congress.

- On April 5, Congress creates the War Finance Corporation and authorizes to make $3 billion dollars available in support of war industries.

- On April 8, the National War Labor Board (NWLB) is appointed as a final board of appeal for labor disputes.

- On April 10, Congress passes the Webb-Pomerene Trade Act, authorizing cooperation among American exporters by allowing them to work together for the duration of the war without fear of prosecution under antitrust statutes.

- On May 16, Congress amends the Espionage Act to provide penalties for false statements and reports made to hinder the war effort.

- From June 6 to June 25, in vicious fighting during the Battle of Belleau Wood, France, American forces halt a German advance. Almost eight thousand American soldiers die in the fight.

- On July 15, eighty-five thousand American troops participate in the bloody Second Battle of the Marne, helping to repel a German advance.

- From July 18 to August 6, the Aisne-Marne offensive, employing a quarter of a million American troops along with French forces, pushes the Germans from the Soissons-Rheims salient.

- On August 2, American troops are deployed near Archangel, Russia, in support of the anti-Communist White Russian army, which is mounting opposition to the radical Bolsheviks. American troops are withdrawn in June 1919.

- On August 16, American troops are dispatched to Siberia to aid the White Russian Army. They are withdrawn in April 1920.

- From September 12 to September 13, American forces at St. Mihiel, France capture about fifteen thousand German soldiers.

- On September 12, Eugene V. Debs, who has been the Socialist Party presidential candidate in 1900, 1904, 1908, and 1912, is found guilty of making seditious statements that impede recruitment efforts and is sentenced to ten years imprisonment under the Espionage Act of 1917.

- From September 26 to November 11, in the final major battle of the war for American troops, 1.2 million "Doughboys" join the Allied offensive at Meuse-Argonne.

- On November 3, the Allies sign an armistice with Austria-Hungary.

- On November 5, in congressional elections Republicans gain control of both houses of Congress. In the Senate, they have a 49-47 majority, and in the House of Representatives they have 240-190 majority (three seats are held by minor parties). The election results are a major political defeat for President Wilson.

• On November 11, on the eleventh hour of the eleventh day of the eleventh month of 1918, the armistice ending World War I goes into effect.

• On November 18, President Wilson announces that he will attend the peace conference in Europe. This is the first time that a president directly represents the United States during peace negotiations.

• On November 21, Congress passes the Food Production Act, banning the manufacture or sale of alcoholic beverages, except for export, during the demobilization.

• On December 4, President Wilson sails for France to attend the peace conference, arriving to a warm welcome by the French people on December 13.

## 1919

• On January 6, Theodore Roosevelt dies at home in Oyster Bay, Long Island, New York, at age sixty.

• On January 18, President Wilson attends the opening of the peace conference in Paris and urges the Allies to accept his Fourteen Points as the basis for an enduring peace.

• On January 29, the Eighteenth Amendment to the Constitution, banning alcoholic beverages, is ratified. It is repealed in 1933.

• On February 15, President Wilson sails for the United States to discuss treaty negotiations with Congress.

• On March 14, President Wilson returns to Paris to continue his efforts on behalf of the peace.

• On March 15, in Paris, units of the American Expeditionary Forces organize the American Legion.

• On June 28, the Treaty of Versailles is signed, officially ending World War I.

• On July 10, President Wilson presents the Treaty of Versailles and the League of Nations agreement to the United States Senate for ratification.

• On September 4, President Wilson begins a nationwide tour to promote the Treaty of Versailles and the League of Nations.

• On September 22, with wartime labor-management agreements dissolved, 268,710 United States Steel workers at Gary, Indiana, go on strike. The strike is broken in January 1920 with the aid of the military.

• On September 26, after making his fortieth speech in support of the League of Nations, President Wilson collapses in Pueblo, Colorado. Forced to return to the White House, Wilson suffers an incapacitating stroke from which he never fully recovers.

• On October 28, Congress passes the Volstead Act (the National Prohibition Act) to implement enforcement of the Eighteenth Amendment.

• On November 6, Congress confers citizenship on Native Americans who served honorably in the military.

• On November 6, Senator Henry Cabot Lodge announces his Fourteen Reservations to the League of Nations. Lodge believes that Article 10 of the covenant infringes upon American sovereignty because it dictates when and where American forces would be called into war. The Senate passes each of Lodge's reservations.

• On November 18, President Wilson instructs Democrats to vote against the amended treaty.

• On November 19, the United States Senate fails to ratify the Treaty of Versailles.

• On December 22, Attorney General A. Mitchell Palmer initiates the "Red Scare" with a series of raids against communists, anarchists, and other radicals.

# "The New Nationalism"

Speech

**By:** Theodore Roosevelt

**Date:** August 31, 1910

**Source:** Roosevelt, Theodore. "The New Nationalism." The Program in Presidential Rhetoric Speech Archive. Available online at http://www.tamu.edu/scom/pres/speeches/trnew.html; website home page: http://www.tamu.edu (accessed January 18, 2003).

**About the Author:** Theodore Roosevelt (1858–1919) was born in New York City, the seventh-generation Roosevelt to be born in Manhattan. He was a sickly child, suffering from chronic asthma, but he exhibited an iron-willed determination to lead "the Strenuous Life." A graduate of Harvard, he was an accomplished historian, boxer, cowboy, war hero, sportsman, reformer, and two-term president (served 1901–1909). ■

## Introduction

In 1901, following the death of William McKinley (served 1897–1901) by an anarchist's bullet, Theodore Roosevelt became the youngest president in the nation's history. Roosevelt believed that his handpicked successor, William Howard Taft (served 1909–1913), would continue his progressive policies. At the Republican convention in 1908, though, Roosevelt almost decided to run for another term. On the second day of the convention, an impromptu and disorderly forty-nine-minute demonstration supporting Roosevelt erupted. When Roosevelt finally sent word that he would not seek reelection, the delegates nominated Taft on the first ballot. After the convention, Roosevelt journeyed to Africa for a prolonged big-game hunt.

In some ways, Taft was more progressive than Roosevelt. His administration filed more antitrust lawsuits in one term than Roosevelt had in two terms. He supported the eight-hour workday and legislation to improve the working conditions of miners. He was also the first president to redistribute wealth by enacting the first tax on corporate profits. However, Taft angered Roosevelt when his administration filed an antitrust suit against United States Steel, owned by financier John Pierpont Morgan. During the lawsuit, documents surfaced showing that in

1907 Roosevelt agreed to allow Morgan's steel monopoly to grow larger with the acquisition of Tennessee Coal and Iron. Taft also signed the Payne-Aldrich Tariff Act, which further protected American monopolies and hurt consumers with higher prices on goods. Moreover, Taft fired Roosevelt's good friend Gifford Pinchot, the chief of the U.S. Forest Service who criticized the administration's gift of rich Alaskan coal lands to mining interests.

In March 1910 Roosevelt returned home from Africa and immediately plunged back into party politics. He concluded that Taft had failed to fight for progressive policies in Congress and that he supported the Old Guard faction of the Republican Party. In 1910 Roosevelt decided to unseat Taft and take back the presidency, setting up one of the most exciting and significant elections in American history.

## Significance

At first, Roosevelt made no attempt to publicize his problems with Taft or split from the Republican Party. In the summer of 1910, however, he set out on a sixteen-state, three-week tour of the West. Traveling in a private railway car, he gave a series of speeches to farmers and small businessmen, in which he challenged Taft and the Old Guard faction. On August 31, he visited Osawatomie, Kansas, to dedicate a new state park on a site where fifty years before the radical abolitionist John Brown had battled pro-slavery Missouri ruffians. Roosevelt's speech outraged his Republican opponents, who compared it to socialism, anarchism, and communism. Though the speech was hardly radical, Roosevelt foreshadowed the modern welfare state, which grew to fruition under his cousin President Franklin Delano Roosevelt (served 1933–1945) and the New Deal. In 1912 Taft won the Republican party nomination after a rowdy convention floor fight. Roosevelt left the party, forming the progressive Bull Moose Party. In the election, Roosevelt and Taft split the Republican vote, allowing progressive Democrat Woodrow Wilson (served 1913–1921) to win the election.

## Primary Source

"The New Nationalism" [excerpt]

> **SYNOPSIS:** Roosevelt's speech called for a New Nationalism of active democracy to replace the old nationalism characterized by corrupt special interests. His detractors accused him of betraying his aristocratic upbringing by denouncing "special privilege" and the "unfair money-getting" practices of "lawbreakers of great wealth."

We come here to-day to commemorate one of the epochmaking events of the long struggle for the rights of man—the long struggle for the uplift of humanity. Our country—this great Republic—means nothing unless it means the triumph of a real democracy, the triumph of popular government, and, in the long run, of an economic system under which each man shall be guaranteed the opportunity to show the best that there is in him. That is why the history of America is now the central feature of the history of the world; for the world has set its face hopefully toward our democracy; and, O my fellow citizens, each one of you carries on your shoulders not only the burden of doing well for the sake of your own country, but the burden of doing well and of seeing that this nation does well for the sake of mankind.

There have been two great crises in our country's history: first, when it was formed, and then, again, when it was perpetuated; and, in the second of these great crises—in the time of stress and strain which culminated in the Civil War, on the outcome of which depended the justification of what had been done earlier, you men of the Grand Army, you men who fought through the Civil War, not only did you justify your generation, not only did you render life worth living for our generation, but you justified the wisdom of Washington and Washington's colleagues. If this Republic had been founded by them only to be split asunder into fragments when the strain came, then the judgment of the world would have been that Washington's work was not worth doing. It was you who crowned Washington's work, as you carried to achievement the high purpose of Abraham Lincoln.

Now, with this second period of our history the name of John Brown will be forever associated; and Kansas was the theater upon which the first act of the second of our great national life dramas was played. It was the result of the struggle in Kansas which determined that our country should be in deed as well as in name devoted to both union and freedom; that the great experiment of democratic government on a national scale should succeed and not fail. In name we had the Declaration of Independence in 1776; but we gave the lie by our acts to the words of the Declaration of Independence until 1865; and words count for nothing except in so far as they represent acts. This is true everywhere; but, O my friends, it should be truest of all in political life. A broken promise is bad enough in private life. It is worse in the field of politics. No man is worth his salt in public life who makes on the stump a pledge which he does not keep after election; and, if he makes such a pledge and does not keep it, hunt him out of public life. I care for the great deeds of the past chiefly as spurs to drive us onward in the pre-

Theodore Roosevelt campaigned for president as a third party candidate for the Progressive Party. THE LIBRARY OF CONGRESS.

sent. I speak of the men of the past partly that they may be honored by our praise of them, but more that they may serve as examples for the future.

It was a heroic struggle; and, as is inevitable with all such struggles, it had also a dark and terrible side. Very much was done of good, and much also of evil; and, as was inevitable in such a period of revolution, often the same man did both good and evil. For our great good fortune as a nation, we, the people of the United States as a whole, can now afford to forget the evil, or, at least, to remember it without bitterness, and to fix our eyes with pride only on the good that was accomplished. Even in ordinary times there are very few of us who do not see the problems of life as through a glass, darkly; and when the glass is clouded by the murk of furious popular passion, the vision of the best and the bravest is dimmed. Looking back, we are all of us now able to do justice to the valor and the disinterestedness and the love of the right, as to each it was given to see the right, shown both by the men of the North and the men of the South in that contest which was finally decided by the attitude of the West. We can admire the heroic valor, the sincerity, the self devotion shown alike by the men who wore

The Progressive Party (Bull Moose), headed by Theodore Roosevelt, was wooed by both the Democrats and Republicans in the 1912 election.
© BETTMANN/CORBIS. REPRODUCED BY PERMISSION.

the blue and the men who wore the gray; and our sadness that such men should have had to fight one another is tempered by the glad knowledge that ever hereafter their descendants shall be found fighting side by side, struggling in peace as well as in war for the uplift of their common country, all alike resolute to raise to the highest pitch of honor and usefulness the nation to which they all belong. As for the veterans of the Grand Army of the Republic, they deserve honor and recognition such as is paid to no other citizens of the Republic; for to them the republic owes its all; for to them it owes its very existence. It is because of what you and your comrades did in the dark years that we of to-day walk, each of us, head erect, and proud that we belong, not to one of a dozen little squabbling contemptible commonwealths, but to the mightiest nation upon which the sun shines.

I do not speak of this struggle of the past merely from the historic standpoint. Our interest is primarily in the application to-day of the lessons taught by the contest of half a century ago. It is of little use for us to pay lip-loyalty to the mighty men of the past unless we sincerely endeavor to apply to the problems of the present precisely the qualities which in other crises

enable the men of that day to meet those crises. It is half melancholy and half amusing to see the way in which well-meaning people gather to do honor to the man who, in company with John Brown, and under the lead of Abraham Lincoln, faced and solved the great problems of the nineteenth century, while, at the same time, these same good people nervously shrink from, or frantically denounce, those who are trying to meet the problems of the twentieth century in the spirit which was accountable for the successful solution of the problems of Lincoln's time.

Of that generation of men to whom we owe so much, the man to whom we owe most is, of course, Lincoln. Part of our debt to him is because he forecast our present struggle and saw the way out. He said:

I hold that while man exists it is his duty to improve not only his own condition, but to assist in ameliorating mankind.

And again:

Labor is prior to, and independent of, capital. Capital is only the fruit of labor, and could never have existed if labor had not first existed. Labor is the superior of capital, and deserves much the higher consideration.

If that remark was original with me, I should be even more strongly denounced as a Communist agitator than I shall be anyhow. It is Lincoln's. I am only quoting it; and that is one side; that is the side the capitalist should hear. Now, let the working man hear his side.

> Capital has its rights, which are as worthy of protection as any other rights. . . . Nor should this lead to a war upon the owners of property. Property is the fruit of labor; . . . property is desirable; is a positive good in the world.

And then comes a thoroughly Lincoln-like sentence:

> Let not him who is houseless pull down the house of another, but let him work diligently and build one for himself, thus by example assuring that his own shall be safe from violence when built.

It seems to me that, in these words, Lincoln took substantially the attitude that we ought to take; he showed the proper sense of proportion in his relative estimates of capital and labor, of human rights and property rights. Above all, in this speech, as in many others, he taught a lesson in wise kindliness and charity; an indispensable lesson to us of today. But this wise kindliness and charity never weakened his arm or numbed his heart. We cannot afford weakly to blind ourselves to the actual conflict which faces us to-day. The issue is joined, and we must fight or fall.

In every wise struggle for human betterment one of the main objects, and often the only object, has been to achieve in large measure equality of opportunity. In the struggle for this great end, nations rise from barbarism to civilization, and through it people press forward from one stage of enlightenment to the next. One of the chief factors in progress is the destruction of special privilege. The essence of any struggle for healthy liberty has always been, and must always be, to take from some one man or class of men the right to enjoy power, or wealth, or position, or immunity, which has not been earned by service to his or their fellows. That is what you fought for in the Civil War, and that is what we strive for now.

At many stages in the advance of humanity, this conflict between the men who possess more than they have earned and the men who have earned more than they possess is the central condition of progress. In our day it appears as the struggle of freemen to gain and hold the right of self-government as against the special interests, who twist the methods of free government into machinery for defeating the popular will. At every stage, and under all circumstances, the essence of the struggle is to equalize opportunity, destroy privilege, and give to the life and citizenship of every individual the highest possible value both to himself and to the commonwealth. That is nothing new. All I ask in civil life is what you fought for in the Civil War. I ask that civil life be carried on according to the spirit in which the army was carried on. You never get perfect justice, but the effort in handling the army was to bring to the front the men who could do the job. Nobody grudged promotion to Grant, or Sherman, or Thomas, or Sheridan, because they earned it. The only complaint was when a man got promotion which he did not earn.

Practical equality of opportunity for all citizens, when we achieve it, will have two great results. First, every man will have a fair chance to make of himself all that in him lies; to reach the highest point to which his capacities, unassisted by special privilege of his own and unhampered by the special privilege of others, can carry him, and to get for himself and his family substantially what he has earned. Second, equality of opportunity means that the commonwealth will get from every citizen the highest service of which he is capable. No man who carries the burden of the special privileges of another can give to the commonwealth that service to which it is fairly entitled.

I stand for the square deal. But when I say that I am for the square deal, I mean not merely that I stand for fair play under the present rules of the games, but that I stand for having those rules changed so as to work for a more substantial equality of opportunity and of reward for equally good service. One word of warning, which, I think, is hardly necessary in Kansas. When I say I want a square deal for the poor man, I do not mean that I want a square deal for the man who remains poor because he has not got the energy to work for himself. If a man who has had a chance will not make good, then he has got to quit. And you men of the Grand Army, you want justice for the brave man who fought, and punishment for the coward who shirked his work. Is not that so?

Now, this means that our government, national and State, must be freed from the sinister influence or control of special interests. Exactly as the special interests of cotton and slavery threatened our political integrity before the Civil War, so now the great special business interests too often control and corrupt the men and methods of government for their own profit. We must drive the special interests out of politics. That is one of our tasks to-day. Every special interest is entitled to justice—full, fair, and complete—and, now, mind you, if there were any attempt by mob-violence to plunder and work harm to the special interest, whatever it may be, that I most dislike, and the wealthy man, whomsoever he may be, for whom I have the greatest contempt, I would fight for him, and you would if you were worth your salt. He should have justice. For every special interest is entitled to justice, but not one is entitled to a vote in Congress, to a voice on the bench, or to representation in any public office. The Constitution guarantees protections to property, and we must make that promise good. But it does not give the right of suffrage to any corporation. The true friend of property, the true conservative, is he who insists that property shall be the servant and not the master of the commonwealth; who insists that the creature of man's making shall be the servant and not the master of the man who made it. The citizens of the United States must effectively control the mighty commercial forces which they have themselves called into being.

There can be no effective control of corporations while their political activity remains. To put an end to it will be neither a short nor an easy task, but it can be done.

We must have complete and effective publicity of corporate affairs, so that people may know beyond peradventure whether the corporations obey the law and whether their management entitles them to the confidence of the public. It is necessary that laws should be passed to prohibit the use of corporate funds directly or indirectly for political purposes; it is still more necessary that such laws should be thoroughly enforced. Corporate expenditures for political purposes, and especially such expenditures by public-service corporations, have supplied one of the principal sources of corruption in our political affairs.

It has become entirely clear that we must have government supervision of the capitalization, not only of public-service corporations, including, particularly, railways, but of all corporations doing an interstate business. I do not wish to see the nation forced into the ownership of the railways if it can possibly be avoided, and the only alternative is thoroughgoing and effective regulation, which shall be based on a full knowledge of all the facts, including a physical valuation of property. This physical valuation is not needed, or, at least, is very rarely needed, for fixing rates; but it is needed as the basis of honest capitalization.

## Further Resources

**BOOKS**

Harbaugh, William H. *Power and Responsibility: The Life and Times of Theodore Roosevelt.* New York: Farrar, Straus, and Giroux, 1961.

Morris, Edmund. *Theodore Rex.* New York: Random House. 2001.

———. *The Rise of Theodore Roosevelt.* New York: Random House, 1979.

**PERIODICALS**

Dunne, Finley Peter. "Mr. Dooley's Friend: Theodore Roosevelt and Mark Twain." *Atlantic Monthly,* September 1963, 77–93.

Foerstel, Karen. "From Teddy Roosevelt On: A Century of Changes." *Congressional Weekly* 58, May 2000, 1090.

**WEBSITES**

"The Indomitable President." *The American President Series.* Available online at http://www.americanpresident.org/kotrain /courses/TR/TR_Life_After_the_Presidency.htm; website home page: http://www.americanpresident.org (accessed January 18, 2003).

Theodore Roosevelt Association. Available online at http://www .theodoreroosevelt.org (accessed January 18, 2003). *This site contains links to information about Theodore Roosevelt.*

---

# "Henry Cabot Lodge: Corollary to the Monroe Doctrine"

Congressional record

**By:** Henry Cabot Lodge Sr.

**Date:** August 2, 1912

**Source:** Lodge, Henry Cabot, Sr. "Henry Cabot Lodge: Corollary to the Monroe Doctrine." *Congressional Record,* 62nd Cong., 2d sess., 1912, 10045.

**About the Author:** Henry Cabot Lodge Sr. (1850–1924) was born in Boston, Massachusetts. He graduated from Harvard with a law degree and was the first Harvard student to earn a Ph.D. in political science. He was a prolific writer of historical, biographical, and political works. In 1884, he was elected to the U.S. House of Representatives. In 1893, he graduated to the Senate, where he headed the prestigious Senate Foreign Relations Committee. ■

## Introduction

The Monroe Doctrine is a cornerstone of American foreign policy. In December 1823, President James Monroe (served 1817–1825) used his annual message to Congress to confidently assert, "The American continents . . . are henceforth not to be considered as subjects for future colonization by any European powers." The Monroe administration was worried about two recent developments. In 1821, Russia had threatened to extend its empire in North America by proclaiming that all Alaskan waters were off limits to non-Russian vessels. Also, the administration feared that European monarchies were preparing to intervene on behalf of Spain to recapture its American colonies, which had recently won their independence. President Theodore Roosevelt extended the doctrine with his famous "corollary." In 1904, the Dominican Republic went bankrupt, and Roosevelt feared that its European creditors might intervene militarily to collect their debts. To keep the Europeans out of Latin America, Roosevelt announced that America would militarily and politically intervene on their behalf to ensure that all foreign debts were paid.

In 1912, the scope of the Monroe Doctrine was extended again. In 1911, an American syndicate had initiated negotiations to sell 4,000 acres of Pacific coast property at Magdalena Bay in Mexico to a Japanese corporation. The negotiations were controversial because if the property fell into the hands of a foreign power, it could pose a serious threat to the American-built Panama Canal, which was due to open in 1914. During negotiations, the Japanese government refused to allow the firm to complete the transaction because the U.S. Department of State, fearing the fortification of a foreign naval base on the bay, objected to the sale.

In 1912, unsubstantiated rumors appeared in the American press that Japan sought to secure a naval base at Magdalena Bay. In April, Mexican president Francisco Madero and Japanese prime minister Kimmochi Saionji, neither of whom had any interest in provoking the United States, categorically denied the rumors. Later in the month, the State Department announced that it had investigated the rumors and found no evidence that Japan had either directly or indirectly tried to acquire the property. Senator Henry Cabot Lodge Sr., chairman of the Senate Foreign Relations Committee, was wary of the executive branch report, so he launched his own investigation. Lodge, who had long distrusted Japanese intentions in Hawaii and advocated the expansion of the American navy, wondered why Japanese businessmen wanted to purchase land of questionable commercial value but of tremendous strategic military value. To Lodge, it seemed perfectly logical that the Japanese government wanted to establish a naval base at Magdalena Bay. To prevent this and other potential transactions in the future, Lodge, ignoring State Department protests that congressional action would cause diplomatic difficulties, introduced the Lodge Corollary resolution. On August 2, 1912, the Senate passed the resolution by a vote of 51 to 4.

This cartoon by Thomas E. Powers suggests the threat of aggression when Japan attempted to purchase land from Mexico. **THE LIBRARY OF CONGRESS.**

### Significance

The Lodge Corollary is important for several reasons. First, although the resolution clearly stated that there was no proof of a Japanese plot to establish a naval base on Magdalena Bay, it nevertheless showed the world that America was prepared to protect the approaches to the Panama Canal. Second, the resolution restricted the legitimate activities of foreign businesses in Latin America that had the potential to threaten American national security. Third, it was the first time that the Monroe Doctrine was specifically applied to an Asiatic power. Last, the resolution illustrated the power of the Senate to shape foreign policy, because its passage did not require the consent of President William Howard Taft (served 1909–1913) or the State Department.

### Primary Source

**"Henry Cabot Lodge: Corollary to the Monroe Doctrine"** [excerpt]

**SYNOPSIS:** Although the resolution does not mention Japan by name, it was understood that Lodge's admonition was directed against Japan. In addition, contrary to prevailing historical interpretation, the resolution states that it is not an extension of the Monroe Doctrine. For Lodge the resolution rested on the doctrine of self-preservation, which predated the Monroe Doctrine.

Resolved, that when any harbor or other place in the American continents is so situated that the occupation thereof for naval or military purposes might threaten the communications or the safety of the United States, the government of the United States could not see without grave concern the possession of such harbor or other place by any corporation or association which has such a relation to another government, not American, as to give that government practical power of control for national purposes. . . .

This resolution rests on a generally accepted principle of the law of nations, older than the Monroe Doctrine. It rests on the principle that every nation has a right to protect its own safety, and that if it feels that the possession by a foreign power, for military or naval purposes, of any given harbor or place is prejudicial to its safety, it is its duty as well as its right to interfere.

I will instance as an example of what I mean the protest that was made successfully against the occupation of the port of Agadir, in Morocco, by Germany. England objected on the ground that it threatened her communication through the Mediterranean. That view was shared largely by the European powers, and the occupation of that port was prevented in that way. That is the principle upon which the resolution rests.

It has been made necessary by a change of modern conditions, under which, while a government takes no action itself, the possession of an important place of the character I have described may be taken by a corporation or association which would be under the control of the foreign government.

The Monroe Doctrine was, of course, an extension in our own interests of this underlying principle— the right of every nation to provide for its own safety. The Monroe Doctrine, as we all know, was applied, so far as the taking possession of territory was concerned, to its being open to further colonization and naturally did not touch upon the precise point involved here. But without any Monroe Doctrine, the possession of a harbor such as that of Magdalena Bay, which has led to this resolution would render it necessary, I think, to make some declaration cov-

ering a case where corporation or association was involved.

In this particular case it became apparent from the inquiries made by the committee and by the administration that no government was concerned in taking possession of Magdalena Bay; but it also became apparent that those persons who held control of the Mexican concession, which included the land about Magdalena Bay, were engaged in negotiations, which have not yet been completed certainly but which have only been tentative, looking to the sale of that bay and the land about it to a corporation either created or authorized by a foreign government or in which the stock was largely held or controlled by foreigners.

The passage of this resolution has seemed to the committee, without division, I think, to be in the interest of peace. It is always desirable to make the position of a country in regard to a question of this kind known beforehand and not to allow a situation to arise in which it might be necessary to urge a friendly power to withdraw when that withdrawal could not be made, perhaps, without some humiliation.

The resolution is merely a statement of policy, allied to the Monroe Doctrine, of course, but not necessarily dependent upon it or growing out of it. When the message came in, I made a statement as to the conditions at Magdalena Bay which had led to the resolution of inquiry and which has now led to the subsequent action of the committee. It seemed to the committee that it was very wise to make this statement of policy at this time, when it can give offense to no one and makes the position of the United States clear.

Of course I need not say to the Senate that the opening of the Panama Canal gives to the question of Magdalena Bay and to that of the Galapagos Islands, which have been once or twice before considered, an importance such as they have never possessed, and I think it eminently desirable in every interest that this resolution should receive the assent of the Senate.

## Further Resources

### BOOKS

Curry, Roy Watson. *Woodrow Wilson and Far Eastern Policy, 1913–1921.* New York: Octagon, 1968.

Garraty, John A. *Henry Cabot Lodge: A Biography.* New York: Knopf, 1953.

Widenor, William C. *Henry Cabot Lodge and the Search for an American Foreign Policy.* Berkeley, Calif.: University of California Press, 1980.

**PERIODICALS**

Bailey, Thomas A. "The Lodge Corollary to the Monroe Doctrine." *Political Science Quarterly* 48, June 1933, 220–239.

Fischer, Robert. "Henry Cabot Lodge and the Taft Arbitration Treaties." *South Atlantic Quarterly* 78, 1979, 244–258.

**WEBSITES**

Ferraro, Vincent. "Documents Relating to Foreign Policy." Available online at http://www.mtholyoke.edu/acad/intrel /to1914.htm; website home page: http://www.mtholyoke .edu/acad/intrel/feros-pg.htm (accessed January 18, 2003).

"The Reluctant President: William Howard Taft." *The American President.* Available online at http://www.americanpresident .org/kotrain/courses/WHT/WHT_In_Brief.htm; website home page: http://www.americanpresident.org/presbios/presbios .htm (accessed January 18, 2003).

# "Votes for Women"

Editorial

**By:** W.E.B. Du Bois

**Date:** September 1912

**Source:** Du Bois, W.E.B. "Votes for Women." *The Crisis,* September 1912, 234. Available online at http://womhist .binghamton.edu/webdbtw/doc12.htm; website home page: http://www.womhist.binghamton.edu (accessed January 18, 2003).

**About the Author:** William Edward Burghart Du Bois (1868–1963) was an historian, sociologist, writer, and civil rights activist. Born in Great Barrington, Massachusetts, he was educated at Fisk University (1885–1888) and received a master's degree and a doctorate from Harvard (1888–1896). Du Bois became the first African American to earn a Ph.D. in history from Harvard. In 1910, he resigned as professor of history and economics at Atlanta University to accept a position with the National Association for the Advancement of Colored People (NAACP). ∎

## Introduction

In June 1866, Congress ratified the Fourteenth Amendment, which granted constitutional protection to the civil rights of African Americans by defining them as citizens. In February 1869, Congress ratified the Fifteenth Amendment, which stated that the right to vote could not be denied because of one's "race, color, or previous condition of servitude." One group of Americans that these amendments ignored was women, who had been striving for suffrage since the 1840s. Their constitutional exclusion greatly disappointed them because they thought that their service during the Civil War would convince Congress of their worthiness. As section two of the Fourteenth Amendment was being drafted, they fought to delete the word "male." Likewise, they battled to add the word "sex" to the Fifteenth Amendment. Afterward, they were dev-

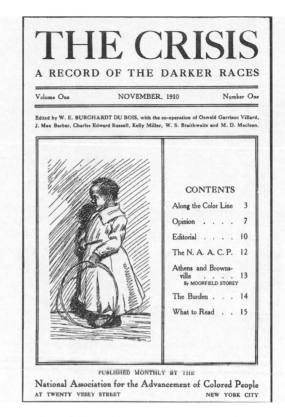

The cover for the first issue of *The Crisis,* a newspaper edited by W. E. B. Du Bois. **THE LIBRARY OF CONGRESS.**

astated that African American males were given the right to vote but not patriotic women. The omission of women was so troublesome to veteran suffragists Elizabeth Cady Stanton and Susan B. Anthony that it fractured their longtime abolitionist alliance with Frederick Douglass, who supported women's suffrage but did not sympathize with his female friends when he declared that this was the "Negro's hour." In turn Stanton proclaimed that uneducated African Americans were a "liability to the electorate and a danger to women."

In 1890, Stanton was elected president of the newly formed National American Woman Suffrage Association (NAWSA). Devoted entirely to winning the vote, the NAWSA strode a conservative political path and tried not to derail its mission by being identified with "radical" causes, such as the political rights of African American women. Stanton, still angered that African American men were enfranchised but women were not, abandoned her earlier insistence upon universal suffrage. Instead, the organization turned to racist tactics to achieve its ultimate goal. In order to gain suffrage, the NAWSA needed to build a strong base in the South. However, this was very difficult because white conservatives, who returned to political power following the end of Reconstruction, correctly associated the women's movement with abolitionism. In an effort to "bring in the South," NAWSA leaders advanced

The office of the NAACP where W. E. B. Du Bois (top right), the organization's founder, and others work on *The Crisis* magazine. © BETTMANN/ CORBIS. REPRODUCED BY PERMISSION.

the viewpoint that women's suffrage was not incompatible with white supremacy. In fact suffrage could be a useful and complementary tool of white bigotry. If women were given the right to vote subject to property and educational qualifications, most African American women would be disqualified. In turn eligible white women would use the power of the vote to further discriminate against African Americans. To implement the strategy, Stanton and Carrie Chapman Catt spent months crisscrossing the South, spreading their new philosophy. In the end, the cynical crusade failed. By 1903, southern male politicians rejected the strategy of using women as a façade for white supremacy. Racism could be further woven into the fabric of the South without also having to relinquish control over women by granting them the power to vote.

### Significance

The NAWSA's "southern strategy" angered many African Americans, including Du Bois. Prior to 1909, he was not an advocate for women's suffrage, though he sympathized with the plight of women and did not work against suffrage. He was certainly aware that if given the vote, southern white women threatened to use it to contribute to black oppression. In 1910, though, he became the editor of the NAACP magazine *The Crisis,* which gave him the opportunity to speak his mind in favor of women's suf-

frage. In fact, from 1910 to 1920, he published over fifty articles and editorials in full support of women's suffrage.

### Primary Source

#### "Votes for Women"

**SYNOPSIS:** In the September 1912 issue of *The Crisis,* which had a circulation of about 35,000, Du Bois included a symposium on women's suffrage. He also wrote an editorial in which he clearly articulated three reasons why he had changed his mind and supported the cause of women's suffrage.

Why should the colored voter be interested in woman's suffrage? There are three cogent reasons. First, it is a great human question. Nothing human must be foreign, uninteresting or unimportant to colored citizens of the world. Whatever concerns half mankind concerns us. Secondly, any agitation, discussion or reopening of the problem of voting must inevitably be a discussion of the right of black folk to vote in America and Africa. Essentially the arguments for and against are the same in the case of all groups of human beings. The world with its tendencies and temptations to caste must ever be asking itself how far may the governed govern? How far can the responsibility of directing, curbing and encouraging mankind be put upon mankind? When we face this vastest of human problems frankly, most of us, despite ourselves and half unconsciously, find ourselves strangely undemocratic, strangely tempted to exclude from participation in government larger and larger numbers of our neighbors. Only at one point, with disconcerting unanimity, do we pause, and that is with ourselves. That we should vote we cannot for a moment doubt even if we are willing to acknowledge, as most of us are, that we are neither all wise nor infinitely good.

This fact should give us pause; if we in our potent weakness and shortcomings see the vast necessity for the ballot not only for our own selfish ends, but for the larger good of all our neighbors, do not our neighbors see the same necessity? And is not the unanswerable congency of the argument for universal suffrage regardless of race or sex merely a matter of the point of view? Merely a matter of honestly putting yourself in the position of the disfranchised, and seeing the world through their eyes? The same arguments and facts that are slowly but surely opening the ballot box to women in England and America must open it to black men in America and Africa. It only remains for us to help the movement and spread the argument wherever we may.

Finally, votes for women mean votes for black women. There are in the United States three and a third million adult women of Negro descent. Except in the rural South, these women have larger economic opportunity than their husbands and brothers and are rapidly becoming better educated. One has only to remember the recent biennial convention of colored women's clubs with its 400 delegates to realize how the women are moving quietly but forcibly toward the intellectual leadership of the race. The enfranchisement of these women will not be a mere doubling of our vote and voice in the nation; it will tend to stronger and more normal political life, the rapid dethronement of the "heeler" and "grafter" and the making of politics a method of broadest philanthropic race betterment, rather than a disreputable means of private gain. We sincerely trust that the entire Negro vote will be cast for woman suffrage in the coming elections in Ohio, Kansas, Wisconsin and Michigan.

## Further Resources

### BOOKS

Gordon, Ann, ed. *African American Women and the Vote, 1837–1965.* Amherst, Mass.: University of Massachusetts Press, 1997.

Lewis, David Levering. *W.E.B. Du Bois: Biography of a Race.* New York: Henry Holt, 1993.

Manning, Marable. *W.E.B. Du Bois: Black Radical Democrat.* Boston: G.K. Hall, 1986.

### PERIODICALS

Green, Dan. "W.E.B. Du Bois: His Journalistic Career." *Negro History Bulletin* 40, 1977, 672–677.

Rudwick, Elliott. "W.E.B. Du Bois: In the Role of *Crisis* Editor." *Journal of Negro History* 43, 1958, 214–240.

### WEBSITES

Women and Social Movements. "How Did the Views of Booker T. Washington and W.E.B. Du Bois toward Woman Suffrage Change between 1900 and 1915?" Available online at http://womhist.binghamton.edu/webdbtw/doclist.htm; website home page: http://www.womhist.bingamton.edu/index .html (accessed January 18, 2003).

Rutgers University. "Stanton and Anthony Papers Project Online." Available online at http://ecssba.rutgers.edu/ (accessed January 18, 2003).

# *The Yosemite*
## Nonfiction work

**By:** John Muir

**Date:** 1912

**Source:** Muir, John. *The Yosemite.* New York: Century, 1912. Available online at http://www.yosemite.ca.us/john _muir_exhibit/writings/the_yosemite/; website home page: http://www.yosemite.ca.us/ (accessed May 19, 2003).

**About the Author:** John Muir (1838–1914) was born in Scotland, but when he was a young boy, his family moved to the Wisconsin wilderness. He was fascinated by nature's wonders. With little formal education, he enrolled at the University of Wisconsin and studied the natural sciences. In 1892, he founded the Sierra Club, which aimed to preserve the Sierra Nevada. ∎

## Introduction

The Hetch Hetchy Valley was once one of the most awe-inspiring natural wonders in the United States. Located within Yosemite National Park, it embraced the headwaters of the Tuolumne River, which flowed into the valley. The valley was surrounded by steep granite cliffs, which, rising to elevations of up to five thousand feet, stood quiet sentry over the waterfalls, giant sequoia groves, and lush meadows. The valley was very difficult to access, even in the summer, and early winter snows rendered it completely unreachable. In 1868, John Muir visited Hetch Hetchy, an Indian word meaning "grassy meadows." To preserve this unspoiled landscape, Muir urged the federal government to protect it. In 1890, Con-

The "high-lying natural landscape garden" of Hetch Hetchy Valley as seen before completion of the O'Shaughnessy Dam in 1923. **YOSEMITE NATIONAL PARK RESEARCH LIBRARY.**

gress passed the Yosemite National Park Act with the intent that this "great natural wonderland would be preserved in pure wilderness for all time for the benefit of the people of the United States."

Unfortunately for nature preservationists like Muir, the crystal-clear waters of the Tuolumne River, which ran through Hetch Hetchy, were coveted by the nearby city of San Francisco. For years, the city had received its water from the privately owned Spring Valley Water Company, which provided bad water and poor service at high rates. In 1901, Mayor James D. Phelan proposed that the city build a three-hundred-foot dam across Hetch Hetchy. The dam would cover 1,930 acres of land with water and extend the water back between seven and eight miles and about two miles wide at the widest point. It was estimated that the dam and reservoir in dry season would supply 250 gallons a day per capita for a million people. The Board of Public Works approved the plan because of the water's "absolute purity." At the mayor's urging, in 1901 Congress passed a bill that allowed cities adjacent to national parks to gain water rights-of-way for domestic and public uses. Subsequently, the city applied to the U.S. Department of Interior for the water rights to Hetch Hetchy. However, the secretary of the department, who was not in favor of public utility projects in national parks, rejected the plan in 1903 and again in 1905.

In May 1908, President Theodore Roosevelt favored granting San Francisco a permit, subject to congressional approval, to dam the Hetch Hetchy Valley. However, the permit was contingent upon the proposal's earning the support of city residents. In November 1908, seven out of eight city voters approved the referendum, but in February 1909, another resolution to dam the river died in Congress. In January 1910, the issue came before city voters again. Out of 30,000 votes cast, only 1,200 voters opposed the project. Nevertheless, subsequent congressional legislation died. In 1912, Representative John E. Raker of California sponsored the Raker Act. In December that year, President Woodrow Wilson signed it into law. In 1934, the Hetch Hetchy Dam was completed at a cost of $100 million.

## Significance

Hetch Hetchy was the first major issue that split the budding conservation movement. The issue divided longtime preservationist allies like John Muir and John Burroughs, the famous natural history writer. Moreover, the issue emphasized the growing rift between the preservationists and the utilitarians. Preservationists like Muir believed that Hetch Hetchy should remain untouched in its natural state. Utilitarians, like Gifford Pinchot, believed that the fundamental principal of "conservation policy is that of use, to take every part of land and its resources and put it to that use in which it will best serve the most people."

## Primary Source

*The Yosemite* [excerpt]

**SYNOPSIS:** In 1867, John Muir set out on a wilderness adventure to walk from Louisville, Kentucky, to the Amazon River. After contracting malaria in Florida, he wandered North America instead. In 1869, he ended up in Yosemite, which he made his home for eight years. Working as a nature guide, he chronicled his observations of Hetch Hetchy. The following excerpt is from Chapter 16 of his book.

Yosemite is so wonderful that we are apt to regard it as an exceptional creation, the only valley of its kind in the world; but Nature is not so poor as to have only one of anything. Several other yosemites have been discovered in the Sierra that occupy the same relative positions on the Range and were formed by the same forces in the same kind of granite. One of these, the Hetch Hetchy Valley, is in the Yosemite National Park about twenty miles from Yosemite and is easily accessible to all sorts of travelers by a road and trail that leaves the Big Oak Flat road at Bronson Meadows a few miles below Crane Flat, and to mountaineers by way of Yosemite Creek basin and the head of the middle fork of the Tuolumne.

It is said to have been discovered by Joseph Screech, a hunter, in 1850, a year before the discovery of the great Yosemite. After my first visit to it in the autumn of 1871, I have always called it the Tuolumne Yosemite, for it is a wonderfully exact counterpart of the Merced Yosemite, not only in its sublime rocks and waterfalls but in the gardens, groves and meadows of its flowery park-like floor. The floor of Yosemite is about 4000 feet above the sea; the Hetch Hetchy floor about 3700 feet. And as the Merced River flows through Yosemite, so does the Tuolumne through Hetch Hetchy. The walls of both are of gray granite, rise abruptly from the floor, are sculptured in the same style and in both every rock is a glacier monument.

Standing boldly out from the south wall is a strikingly picturesque rock called by the Indians, Kolana, the outermost of a group 2300 feet high, corresponding with the Cathedral Rocks of Yosemite both in relative position and form. On the opposite side of the Valley, facing Kolana, there is a counterpart of the El Capitan that rises sheer and plain to a height of 1800 feet, and over its massive brow flows

a stream which makes the most graceful fall I have ever seen. From the edge of the cliff to the top of an earthquake talus it is perfectly free in the air for a thousand feet before it is broken into cascades among talus boulders. It is in all its glory in June, when the snow is melting fast, but fades and vanishes toward the end of summer. The only fall I know with which it may fairly be compared is the Yosemite Bridal Veil; but it excels even that favorite fall both in height and airy-fairy beauty and behavior. Lowlanders are apt to suppose that mountain streams in their wild career over cliffs lose control of themselves and tumble in a noisy chaos of mist and spray. On the contrary, on no part of their travels are they more harmonious and self-controlled. Imagine yourself in Hetch Hetchy on a sunny day in June, standing waist-deep in grass and flowers (as I have often stood), while the great pines sway dreamily with scarcely perceptible motion. Looking northward across the Valley you see a plain, gray granite cliff rising abruptly out of the gardens and groves to a height of 1800 feet, and in front of it Tueeulala's silvery scarf burning with irised sun-fire. In the first white outburst at the head there is abundance of visible energy, but it is speedily hushed and concealed in divine repose, and its tranquil progress to the base of the cliff is like that of a downy feather in a still room. Now observe the fineness and marvelous distinctness of the various sun-illuminated fabrics into which the water is woven; they sift and float from form to form down the face of that grand gray rock in so leisurely and unconfused a manner that you can examine their texture, and patterns and tones of color as you would a piece of embroidery held in the hand. Toward the top of the fall you see groups of booming, comet-like masses, their solid, white heads separate, their tails like combed silk interlacing among delicate gray and purple shadows, ever forming and dissolving, worn out by friction in their rush through the air. Most of these vanish a few hundred feet below the summit, changing to varied forms of cloud-like drapery. Near the bottom the width of the fall has increased from about twenty-five feet to a hundred feet. Here it is composed of yet finer tissues, and is still without a trace of disorder—air, water and sunlight woven into stuff that spirits might wear.

So fine a fall might well seem sufficient to glorify any valley; but here, as in Yosemite, Nature seems in nowise moderate, for a short distance to the eastward of Tueeulala booms and thunders the great Hetch Hetchy Fall, Wapama, so near that you have both of them in full view from the same standpoint. It is the counterpart of the Yosemite Fall, but has a much greater volume of water, is about 1700 feet in height, and appears to be nearly vertical, though considerably inclined, and is dashed into huge outbounding bosses of foam on projecting shelves and knobs. No two falls could be more unlike—Tueeulala out in the open sunshine descending like thistledown; Wapama in a jagged, shadowy gorge roaring and plundering, pounding its way like an earthquake avalanche.

Besides this glorious pair there is a broad, massive fall on the main river a short distance above the head of the Valley. Its position is something like that of the Vernal in Yosemite, and its roar as it plunges into a surging trout-pool may be heard a long way, though it is only about twenty feet high. On Rancheria Creek, a large stream, corresponding in position with the Yosemite Tenaya Creek, there is a chain of cascades joined here and there with swift flashing plumes like the one between the Vernal and Nevada Falls, making magnificent shows as they go their glacier-sculptured way, sliding, leaping, hurrahing, covered with crisp clashing spray made glorious with sifting sunshine. And besides all these a few small streams come over the walls at wide intervals, leaping from ledge to ledge with birdlike song and watering many a hidden cliff-garden and fernery, but they are too unshowy to be noticed in so grand a place.

The correspondence between the Hetch Hetchy walls in their trends, sculpture, physical structure, and general arrangement of the main rock-masses and those of the Yosemite Valley has excited the wondering admiration of every observer. We have seen that the El Capitan and Cathedral rocks occupy the same relative positions in both valleys; so also do their Yosemite points and North Domes. Again, that part of the Yosemite north wall immediately to the east of the Yosemite Fall has two horizontal benches, about 500 and 1500 feet above the floor, timbered with golden-cup oak. Two benches similarly situated and timbered occur on the same relative portion of the Hetch Hetchy north wall, to the east of Wapama Fall, and on no other. The Yosemite is bounded at the head by the great Half Dome. Hetch Hetchy is bounded in the same way though its head rock is incomparably less wonderful and sublime in form.

The floor of the Valley is about three and a half miles long and from a fourth to half a mile wide. The lower portion is mostly a level meadow about a mile long, with the trees restricted to the sides and the river banks, and partially separated from the main, upper, forested portion by a low bar of glacier-polished granite across which the river breaks in rapids.

The principal trees are the yellow and sugar pines, digger pine, incense cedar, Douglas spruce, silver fir, the California and golden-cup oaks, balsam cottonwood, Nuttall's flowering dog-wood, alder, maple, laurel, tumion, etc. The most abundant and influential are the great yellow or silver pines like those of Yosemite, the tallest over two hundred feet in height, and the oaks assembled in magnificent groves with massive rugged trunks four to six feet in diameter, and broad, shady, wide-spreading heads. The shrubs forming conspicuous flowery clumps and tangles are manzanita, azalea, spiraea, brier-rose, several species of ceanothus, calycanthus, philadelphus, wild cherry, etc.; with abundance of showy and fragrant herbaceous plants growing about them or out in the open in beds by themselves—lilies, Mariposa tulips, brodiaeas, orchids, iris, spraguea, draperia, collomia, collinsia, castilleja, nemophila, larkspur, columbine, goldenrods, sunflowers, mints of many species, honeysuckle, etc. Many fine ferns dwell here also, especially the beautiful and interesting rock-ferns—pellaea, and cheilanthes of several species—fringing and rosetting dry rock-piles and ledges; woodwardia and asplenium on damp spots with fronds six or seven feet high; the delicate maidenhair in mossy nooks by the falls, and the sturdy, broad-shouldered pteris covering nearly all the dry ground beneath the oaks and pines.

It appears, therefore, that Hetch Hetchy Valley, far from being a plain, common, rock-bound meadow, as many who have not seen it seem to suppose, is a grand landscape garden, one of Nature's rarest and most precious mountain temples. As in Yosemite, the sublime rocks of its walls seem to glow with life, whether leaning back in repose or standing erect in thoughtful attitudes, giving welcome to storms and calms alike, their brows in the sky, their feet set in the groves and gay flowery meadows, while birds, bees, and butterflies help the river and waterfalls to stir all the air into music—things frail and fleeting and types of permanence meeting here and blending, just as they do in Yosemite, to draw her lovers into close and confiding communion with her.

Sad to say, this most precious and sublime feature of the Yosemite National Park, one of the greatest of all our natural re-sources for the uplifting joy and peace and health of the people, is in danger of being dammed and made into a reservoir to help supply San Francisco with water and light, thus flooding it from wall to wall and burying its gardens and groves one or two hundred feet deep. This grossly destructive commercial scheme has long been planned and urged (though water as pure and abundant can be got from outside of the people's park, in a dozen different places), because of the comparative cheapness of the dam and of the territory which it is sought to divert from the great uses to which it was dedicated in the Act of 1890 establishing the Yosemite National Park.

The making of gardens and parks goes on with civilization all over the world, and they increase both in size and number as their value is recognized. Everybody needs beauty as well as bread, places to play in and pray in, where Nature may heal and cheer and give strength to body and soul alike. This natural beauty-hunger is made manifest in the little window-sill gardens of the poor, though perhaps only a geranium slip in a broken cup, as well as in the carefully tended rose and lily gardens of the rich, the thousands of spacious city parks and botanical gardens, and in our magnificent National parks—the Yellowstone, Yosemite, Sequoia, etc.—Nature's sublime wonderlands, the admiration and joy of the world. Nevertheless, like anything else worth while, from the very beginning, however well guarded, they have always been subject to attack by despoiling gainseekers and mischief-makers of every degree from Satan to Senators, eagerly trying to make everything immediately and selfishly commercial, with schemes disguised in smug smiling philanthropy, industriously, shampiously crying, "Conservation, conservation, panutilization," that man and beast may be fed and the dear Nation made great. Thus long ago a few enterprising merchants utilized the Jerusalem temple as a place of business instead of a place of prayer, changing money, buying and selling cattle and sheep and doves; and earlier still, the first forest reservation, including only one tree, was likewise despoiled. Ever since the establishment of the Yosemite National Park, strife has been going on around its borders and I suppose this will go on as part of the universal battle between right and wrong, however much its boundaries may be shorn, or its wild beauty destroyed.

The first application to the Government by the San Francisco Supervisors for the commercial use of Lake Eleanor and the Hetch Hetchy Valley was made in 1903, and on December 22nd of that year it was denied by the Secretary of the Interior, Mr. Hitchcock, who truthfully said:

> Presumably the Yosemite National Park was created such by law because within its boundaries, inclusive alike of its beautiful small lakes, like Eleanor, and its majestic wonders, like Hetch Hetchy and Yosemite Valley. It is the aggregation of such natural scenic features that makes the Yosemite Park a wonder-land which the Congress of the United States sought by law to reserve for all coming time as nearly as practicable in the condition fashioned by the hand of the Creator—a worthy object of national pride and a source of healthful pleasure and rest for the thousands of people who may annually sojourn there during the heated months.

In 1907 when Mr. Garfield became Secretary of the Interior the application was renewed and granted; but under his successor, Mr. Fisher, the matter has been referred to a Commission, which as this volume goes to press still has it under consideration.

The most delightful and wonderful camp grounds in the Park are its three great valleys—Yosemite, Hetch Hetchy, and Upper Tuolumne; and they are also the most important places with reference to their positions relative to the other great features—the Merced and Tuolumne Cañons, and the High Sierra peaks and glaciers, etc., at the head of the rivers. The main part of the Tuolumne Valley is a spacious flowery lawn four or five miles long, surrounded by magnificent snowy mountains, slightly separated from other beautiful meadows, which together make a series about twelve miles in length, the highest reaching to the feet of Mount Dana, Mount Gibbs, Mount Lyell and Mount McClure. It is about 8500 feet above the sea, and forms the grand central High Sierra camp ground from which excursions are made to the noble mountains, domes, glaciers, etc.; across the Range to the Mono Lake and volcanoes and down the Tuolumne Cañon to Hetch Hetchy. Should Hetch Hetchy be submerged for a reservoir, as pro-posed, not only would it be utterly destroyed, but the sublime cañon way to the heart of the High Sierra would be hopelessly blocked and the great camping ground, as the watershed of a city drinking system, virtually would be closed to the public. So far as I have learned, few of all the thousands who have seen the park and seek rest and peace in it are in favor of this outrageous scheme.

One of my later visits to the Valley was made in the autumn of 1907 with the late William Keith, the artist. The leaf-colors were then ripe, and the great godlike rocks in repose seemed to glow with life. The artist, under their spell, wandered day after day along the river and through the groves and gardens, studying the wonderful scenery; and, after making about forty sketches, declared with enthusiasm that although its walls were less sublime in height, in picturesque beauty and charm Hetch Hetchy surpassed even Yosemite.

That any one would try to destroy such a place seems incredible; but sad experience shows that there are people good enough and bad enough for anything. The proponents of the dam scheme bring forward a lot of bad arguments to prove that the only righteous thing to do with the people's parks is to destroy them bit by bit as they are able. Their arguments are curiously like those of the devil, devised for the destruction of the first garden—so much of the very best Eden fruit going to waste; so much of the best Tuolumne water and Tuolumne scenery going to waste. Few of their statements are even partly true, and all are misleading.

Thus, Hetch Hetchy, they say, is a "low-lying meadow." On the contrary, it is a high-lying natural landscape garden, as the photographic illustrations show.

"It is a common minor feature, like thousands of others." On the contrary it is a very uncommon feature; after Yosemite, the rarest and in many ways the most important in the National Park.

"Damming and submerging it 175 feet deep would enhance its beauty by forming a crystal-clear lake." Landscape gardens, places of recreation and worship, are never made beautiful by destroying and burying them. The beautiful sham lake, forsooth, should be only an eyesore, a dismal blot on the landscape, like many others to be seen in the Sierra. For, instead of keeping it at the same level all the year, allowing Nature centuries of time to make new shores, it would, of course, be full only a month or two in the spring, when the snow is melting fast; then it would be gradually drained, exposing the slimy sides of the basin and shallower parts of the bottom, with the gathered drift and waste, death and decay of the upper basins, caught here instead of being swept on to decent natural burial along the banks of the river or in the sea. Thus the Hetch Hetchy dam-lake would be only a rough imitation of a natural lake for a few of the spring months, an open sepulcher for the others.

"Hetch Hetchy water is the purest of all to be found in the Sierra, unpolluted, and forever unpollutable." On the contrary, excepting that of the Merced below Yosemite, it is less pure than that of most of the other Sierra streams, because of the sewerage of camp grounds draining into it, especially of the Big Tuolumne Meadows camp ground, occupied by hundreds of tourists and mountaineers, with their animals, for months every summer, soon to be followed by thousands from all the world.

These temple destroyers, devotees of ravaging commercialism, seem to have a perfect contempt for Nature, and, instead of lifting their eyes to the God of the mountains, lift them to the Almighty Dollar.

Dam Hetch Hetchy! As well dam for water-tanks the people' cathedrals and churches, for no holier temple has ever been consecrated by the heart of man.

## Further Resources

### BOOKS

Fox, Stephen. *John Muir and His Legacy.* Boston: Little, Brown, 1981.

Sargent, Shirley. *Pioneers in Petticoats.* Yosemite, Calif.: Flying Spur Press, 1966.

Wolfe, Linnie Marsh. *Son of the Wilderness: The Life of John Muir.* New York: Knopf, 1945.

### PERIODICALS

Muir, John. "My First Summer in the Sierra." *The Atlantic Monthly,* January–April, 1911. Available online at http://www.theatlantic.com/unbound/flashbks/muir/muir.htm (accessed January 18, 2003).

Meyer, John M. "Gifford Pinchot, John Muir, and the Boundaries of Politics in American Thought." *Polity* 30, Winter 1997, 267–284.

### WEBSITES

Library of Congress. "American Memory: The Evolution of the Conservation Movement, 1850–1920." Available online at http://memory.loc.gov/ammem/amrvhtml/conshome.html; website home page: http://www.loc.gov/ (accessed January 18, 2003).

Yosemite Web Index. "John Muir Exhibit: The Writings of John Muir." Available online at http://www.yosemite.ca.us/john_muir_exhibit/writings/; website home page: http://www.yosemite.ca.us/ (accessed January 18, 2003).

# "Composition and Characteristics of the Population for Wards of Cities of 50,000 or More: Lawrence"

Table

**By:** Federal Bureau of the Census

**Date:** 1913–1914

**Source:** "Composition and Characteristics of the Population for Wards of Cities of 50,000 or More: Lawrence." In *Thirteenth Census of the United States Taken in the Year 1910,* Federal Bureau of the Census, U.S. Decennial Census Publications: Vol. II, Population 1910. Washington, D.C.: Government Printing Office, 1913–1914, 893. Available online at http://womhist.binghamton.edu/law/doc7.htm; website home page: http://www.binghamton.edu (accessed January 18, 2003).

**About the Organization:** The American census dates back

The 1912 strike in Lawrence, Massachusetts, was comprised of ten thousand woolen textile workers from nearly 40 different nationalities. **THE LIBRARY OF CONGRESS.**

to the early 1660s, when the British conducted a count of all people in the colonies. Acknowledging the importance of knowing the number of Americans, the nation's founders required in Article 1, Section 2 of the Constitution that a census be taken every ten years. In 1902, the Census Office was established in the Department of Interior. Ten years later, census tracts were added, allowing demographers to analyze cities by specific wards. ■

## Introduction

In 1912, Lawrence, Massachusetts, was a one-industry town. Out of about 86,000 inhabitants, 60,000 were dependent upon the textile mill payrolls. In January of that year, the American Woolen Company, to remain competitive with out-of-state textile mills, reduced workers' wages 3.5 percent, along with the number of work hours per week. These cutbacks, which lowered the standard of living considerably, were particularly hard on women and children, who made up nearly half the mill workers. Unfortunately, the workers were not unionized. The American Federation of Labor (AFL), the leading union in the nation, did not want to organize the workers for two reasons. First, there was little commonality among members of the workforce. Eighty-six percent of the people were either first- or second-generation Americans. Further, the workers consisted of almost forty different nationalities and ethnic groups that spoke at least twenty-

two different languages. Second, the mill workers were unskilled, which meant that they tended to be transients, frequently moving from one town to another. Nevertheless, by February 1912, 30,000 textile workers walked off the job demanding better wages and overtime pay. One union that was interested in organizing the workers was the Industrial Workers of the World or the "Wobblies."

The IWW was the nation's most radical and dangerous group of unionists. Unlike the mainstream AFL, which promoted conservative tactics to improve wages and working conditions, the IWW rejected political action. Instead, it advocated massive work slowdowns and sabotage and called on the world's workers to organize into one giant union that would force the capitalist class to surrender power. The leader of the IWW was "Big Bill" Haywood, a craggy-faced, one-eyed former miner, who six years earlier had been acquitted of murdering the antilabor governor of Colorado. The IWW, which welcomed all workers regardless of skill, gender, nationality, or race, united the fractious workers. Under IWW leadership, the workers formed a picket line around the entire mill district, twenty-four hours a day for ten weeks. In addition, the strikers, prohibited by law from parading on roadways, marched arm-in-arm down sidewalks, singing protest songs and waving signs that read "We Want Bread and Roses Too." The strike at times turned violent as local po-

| Subject | The City | Ward 1 | 2 | 3 | 4 | 5 | 6 |
|---|---|---|---|---|---|---|---|
| **Sex, color and nativity** | | | | | | | |
| Total population, 1910 | 85,892 | 14,186 | 13,571 | 14,236 | 13,581 | 16,180 | 14,138 |
| Male | 42,858 | 7,040 | 7,054 | 7,220 | 6,787 | 7,813 | 6,944 |
| Female | 43,034 | 7,146 | 6,517 | 7,016 | 6,794 | 8,367 | 7,194 |
| Native white-Native parentage | 11,699 | 1,693 | 1,814 | 1,212 | 1,483 | 2,505 | 2,992 |
| Native white-Foreign or mixed parentage | 32,553 | 4,991 | 4,576 | 5,129 | 5,160 | 6,545 | 6,152 |
| Foreign-born white | 41,319 | 7,475 | 7,168 | 7,858 | 6,864 | 6,983 | 4,971 |
| Negro | 265 | 21 | 6 | 27 | 51 | 145 | 15 |
| Chinese | 56 | 6 | 7 | 10 | 23 | 2 | 8 |
| **Foreign-born white: born in—** | | | | | | | |
| Austria | 1,450 | 915 | 137 | 181 | 161 | 41 | 15 |
| Belgium | 314 | 55 | 80 | 29 | 4 | 138 | 8 |
| Canada-French | 7,698 | 99 | 112 | 715 | 2,351 | 3,240 | 1,181 |
| Canada-Other | 1,800 | 340 | 206 | 168 | 264 | 405 | 415 |
| England | 5,659 | 755 | 591 | 597 | 1,158 | 1,428 | 1,130 |
| France | 788 | 178 | 117 | 124 | 32 | 248 | 89 |
| Germany | 2,301 | 1,489 | 380 | 133 | 152 | 41 | 106 |
| Greece | 171 | 2 | 5 | 32 | 107 | 20 | 5 |
| Ireland | 5,943 | 859 | 1,007 | 1,433 | 889 | 548 | 1,207 |
| Italy | 6,693 | 1,721 | 3,341 | 1,374 | 75 | 26 | 156 |
| Portugal | 389 | 4 | 48 | 323 | 4 | 4 | 6 |
| Russia | 4,366 | 725 | 771 | 950 | 1,346 | 448 | 126 |
| Scotland | 1,336 | 188 | 138 | 122 | 164 | 322 | 402 |
| Sweden | 121 | 13 | 15 | 6 | 9 | 20 | 58 |
| Turkey | 2,077 | 85 | 183 | 1,645 | 108 | 34 | 22 |
| Other foreign countries | 213 | 47 | 37 | 25 | 40 | 20 | 44 |
| **Males of voting age** | | | | | | | |
| Total number | 25,983 | 4,344 | 4,630 | 4,350 | 4,338 | 4,373 | 3,948 |
| Native white-Native parentage | 3,113 | 440 | 502 | 237 | 492 | 645 | 797 |
| Foreign white-Foreign or mixed parentage | 5,274 | 756 | 797 | 761 | 931 | 935 | 1,094 |
| Foreign-born white | 17,414 | 3,137 | 3,324 | 3,320 | 2,858 | 2,728 | 2,047 |
| Naturalized | 6,588 | 1,223 | 907 | 1,046 | 11,029 | 1,272 | 1,111 |
| Negro | 128 | 5 | 1 | 22 | 34 | 63 | 3 |
| **Illiteracy and school attendance** | | | | | | | |
| Total number 10 years and over | 68,928 | 11,509 | 11,109 | 11,326 | 11,178 | 12,669 | 11,137 |
| Number illiterate | 9,067 | 2,636 | 1,524 | 2,235 | 1,395 | 8,080 | 469 |
| Illiterate males of voting age | 3,852 | 1,144 | 738 | 771 | 598 | 442 | 159 |
| Total number 6 to 20 years, inclusive | 23,520 | 3,829 | 3,218 | 4,013 | 3,564 | 4,817 | 4,079 |
| Number attending school | 14,063 | 2,060 | 1,886 | 2,480 | 1,980 | 2,976 | 2,681 |
| **Dwellings and families** | | | | | | | |
| Dwellings, number | 10,413 | 1,657 | 1,457 | 1,296 | 1,354 | 2,366 | 2,283 |
| Families, number | 17,142 | 2,895 | 2,406 | 2,516 | 2,755 | 3,538 | 3,032 |

Note: This chart shows the ethnic makeup of the city of Lawrence in 1910 and the residence patterns of different nationalities by wards. Each group typically concentrated in a few ethnic enclaves across the city. Italians were concentrated in wards 1, 2, and 3; French Canadians in 4, 5, and 6; Russians in wards 3 and 4; Germans and Austrians in ward 1; and Turks in ward 3. Native-born residents were found in greatest numbers in wards 5 and 6.

SOURCE: Table V from *Thirteenth Census of the United States taken in the Year 1910*. Federal Bureau of the Census, U.S. Decennial Census Publications: Vol. II, Population 1910. Washington, D.C.: Government Printing Office, 1913–1914, p. 893.

## Primary Source

### "Composition and Characteristics of the Population for Wards or Cities of 50,000 or More: Lawrence"

**SYNOPSIS:** In 1910, Lawrence, Massachusetts, was one of the most ethnically diverse cities in America. Ethnic groups concentrated in tightly knit enclaves, where residents spoke the same language, practiced the same Old World customs, and worshipped in the same churches. The chart shows the residence patterns of the numerous ethnic groups by wards.

lice and protesters clashed. The workers gained national sympathy when the radical Elizabeth Gurley Flynn arranged to send some strikers' starving children to stay with out-of-town relatives. When the women and children said their tearful good-byes at the train station, police were photographed clubbing them unmercifully.

## Significance

On March 12, the IWW claimed victory when mill owners agreed to increase wages. The lowest paid received a 20 percent wage increase; the highest paid received a 5 percent increase. Further, the company agreed to pay overtime and promised not to discriminate against workers involved in the strike. The strike is important because unlike the Homestead strike, the Pullman strike, the Railroad strike of 1877, or other high-profile strikes, the exploited workers won. The strike is also important because thousands of unskilled workers put aside their ethnic, language, and religious differences long enough to prevail against the mill owners. The strike was also the last major victory for the IWW, which was unable to capitalize on its success to branch out and organize other stable local organizations. During World War I (1914–1918) the IWW came under vicious attack by vigilantes and the federal government. IWW-led strikes were seen as unpatriotic for undermining the war effort. Union leaders were arrested and charged with violating the espionage and sedition acts. By 1924, the union was nearly disbanded.

## Further Resources

### BOOKS

Cahn, William. *Mill Town: A Dramatic Pictorial Narrative of the Century-old Fight to Unionize an Industrial Town.* New York: Cameron & Kahn, 1954.

Cole, Donald. *Immigrant City: Lawrence, Massachusetts, 1945–1921.* Chapel Hill, N.C.: University of North Carolina Press, 1963.

Schinto, Jeanne. *Huddle Fever: Living in the Immigrant City.* New York: Knopf, 1995.

### PERIODICALS

Baker, Ray Stannard. "The Revolutionary Strike: A New Form of Industrial Struggle as Exemplified at Lawrence, Massachusetts." *American Magazine,* May 1912, 21.

Deland, Lorin F. "The Lawrence Strike: A Study." *The Atlantic Monthly,* May 1912, 694–705. Available online at http://www.theatlantic.com/issues/12may/deland.htm (accessed January 18, 2003).

### WEBSITES

Center for Historical Study of Women and Gender at the State University of New York at Binghamton. "The 1912 Lawrence Strike: How Did Immigrant Workers Struggle to Achieve an American Standard of Living? Document List." *Women and Social Movements in the United States, 1775, 2000.* Available online at http://womhist.binghamton.edu /about.htm (accessed January 18, 2003).

# "Woodrow Wilson: *The Tampico Affair*"
Speech

**By:** Woodrow Wilson

**Date:** April 20, 1914

**Source:** Wilson, Woodrow. "Woodrow Wilson: *The Tampico Affair.*" *Congressional Record.* 63rd Cong., 2d sess., 1914. Vol. 51, pt. 4. Available online at http://www.mtholyoke .edu/acad/intrel/tampico.htm; website home page: http://www .mtholyoke.edu (accessed January 19, 2003).

**About the Author:** Woodrow Wilson (1856–1924) was the twenty-eighth president of the United States (served 1913–1921). In 1910, he left his position as president of Princeton University to become the governor of New Jersey. In 1913, he became the first Democrat to occupy the White House since 1888. He called for limits on corporate campaign contributions, tariff reductions, a federal income tax, and the formation of the League of Nations. ∎

## Introduction

President Woodrow Wilson believed that the Monroe Doctrine gave America the right to intervene in the affairs of Latin America to spread the gospel of democracy. Displaying an attitude similar to that of nineteenth-century Christian missionaries, Wilson told a British diplomat, "I am going to teach the South American republics to elect good men." An important example of Wilson's "missionary diplomacy" occurred in Mexico. In 1910, the tyrant Porfiro Diaz ruled Mexico. Since coming to power in 1876, Diaz ruled the landless peons, the vast majority of the population, with an iron fist. His dictatorial control, however, provided economic and political stability, which was important to American business interests. In 1910, more than 40,000 American citizens lived in Mexico and more than $1 billion of American money was invested there.

In 1911, the revolutionary Francisco Madero toppled the corrupt Diaz regime and threatened to seize all land held by foreign investors. Madero, however, was overthrown and assassinated by General Victoriano Huerta, who had the support of American capitalists. Huerta aimed to restore law and order by crushing the revolutionaries. Most European governments recognized Huerta as the legitimate ruler of Mexico, but Wilson, against the advice of American business interests, refused to recognize the "government of butchers." Wilson's refusal was a departure from the traditional American foreign policy of recognizing all governments in power, regardless of how they had acquired power. He justified his actions on the grounds that by opposing dictatorship, he sought to promote democracy in Mexico and discourage other military uprisings in Latin America. When nonrecognition failed to remove Huerta from power, Wilson decided to intervene directly in Mexican internal affairs.

On April 9, 1914, a small whaleboat left the USS *Dolphin,* the flagship of the American squadron deployed at Tampico, Mexico's second largest port, to pick up fuel for the *Dolphin.* At the time, Tampico was controlled by the Huerta government but was under siege by the revolutionaries. Once ashore, the crew was arrested by the government for entering the area without permission. Within an hour of their arrest, however, the crew was released and the Mexican government apologized. The admiral of the squadron considered the crew's treatment a national insult and demanded that the Mexicans hoist the American flag onshore and honor it with a twenty-one-gun salute. Huerta rejected the demand as an assault on Mexican dignity. He wanted to use the incident to unite the revolutionaries behind him in a show of defiance against American arrogance. On April 19, Wilson learned that a German liner was due to deliver two hundred machine guns and 15 million cartridges to Veracruz. Wilson feared that the shipment would enable Huerta to stay in power. Determined to intercept the munitions, he ordered the *Dolphin* to invade the port city of Veracruz. Eight hundred marines soon captured the port and prevented the landing of the munitions. Before sending in the troops, President Wilson justified his actions in a speech to Congress on April 20.

### Significance

President Wilson's actions were important because they represented one of the few times the United States intervened against a dictator and in support of revolutionaries seeking radical reforms at the expense of American big business. Succeeding administrations resumed the traditional policy of supporting dictators who provided economic stability. Wilson's intervention is also important because it allowed the Mexican revolution to proceed independently along more democratic lines and not become overly influenced by the radical Bolshevik revolution of 1917.

### Primary Source

"Woodrow Wilson: *The Tampico Affair*"

**SYNOPSIS:** In his address President Wilson requests a resolution authorizing the use of armed forces. Although he admits that the *Dolphin* crew is safe, the nation needs to "enforce respect for our government." The House immediately passes the resolution, but the Senate wants stronger safeguards. While the administration and Senate negotiate, Veracruz is invaded without congressional consent.

It is my duty to call your attention to a situation which has arisen in our dealings with General Victoriano Huerta at Mexico City which calls for action, and to ask your advice and cooperation in acting upon it.

On the 9th of April a paymaster of the U.S.S. *Dolphin* landed at the Iturbide Bridge landing at Tampico with a whaleboat and boat's crew to take off certain supplies needed by his ship, and while engaged in loading the boat was arrested by an officer and squad of men of the army of General Huerta. Neither the paymaster nor anyone of the boat's crew was armed. Two of the men were in the boat when the arrest took place and were obliged to leave it and submit to be taken into custody, notwithstanding the fact that the boat carried, both at her bow and at her stern, the flag of the United States.

The officer who made the arrest was proceeding up one of the streets of the town with his prisoners when met by an officer of higher authority, who ordered him to return to the landing and await orders; and within an hour and a half from the time of the arrest, orders were received from the commander of the Huertista forces at Tampico for the release of the paymaster and his men. The release was followed by apologies from the commander and later by an expression of regret by General Huerta himself.

General Huerta urged that martial law obtained at the time at Tampico; that orders had been issued that no one should be allowed to land at the Iturbide Bridge; and that our sailors had no right to land there. Our naval commanders at the port had not been notified of any such prohibition; and, even if they had been, the only justifiable course open to the local authorities would have been to request the paymaster and his crew to withdraw and to lodge a protest with the commanding officer of the fleet. Admiral Mayo regarded the arrest as so serious an affront that he was not satisfied with the apologies offered, but demanded that the flag of the United States be saluted with special ceremony by the military commander of the port.

The incident cannot be regarded as a trivial one, especially as two of the men arrested were taken from the boat itself—that is to say, from the territory of the United States—but had it stood by itself it might have been attributed to the ignorance or arrogance of a single officer. Unfortunately, it was not an isolated case. A series of incidents have recently occurred which cannot but create the impression that the representatives of General Huerta were willing to go out of their way to show disregard for the

After American sailors were unlawfully held in Tampico, Mexico, these U.S. marines occupied Veracruz. **THE LIBRARY OF CONGRESS.**

dignity and rights of this government and felt perfectly safe in doing what they pleased, making free to show in many ways their irritation and contempt.

A few days after the incident at Tampico, an orderly from the U.S.S. *Minnesota* was arrested at Vera Cruz while ashore in uniform to obtain the ship's mail and was for a time thrown into jail. An official dispatch from this government to its embassy at Mexico City was withheld by the authorities of the telegraphic service until peremptorily demanded by our chargé d'affaires in person. So far as I can learn, such wrongs and annoyances have been suffered to occur only against representatives of the United States. I have heard of no complaints from other governments of similar treatment.

Subsequent explanations and formal apologies did not and could not alter the popular impression, which it is possible it had been the object of the Huertista authorities to create, that the government of the United States was being singled out, and might be singled out with impunity, for slights and affronts in retaliation for its refusal to recognize the pretensions of General Huerta to be regarded as the constitutional provisional president of the Republic of Mexico.

The manifest danger of such a situation was that such offenses might grow from bad to worse until something happened of so gross and intolerable a sort as to lead directly and inevitably to armed conflict. It was necessary that the apologies of General Huerta and his representatives should go much further, that they should be such as to attract the attention of the whole population to their significance, and such as to impress upon General Huerta himself the necessity of seeing to it that no further occasion for explanations and professed regrets should arise.

I, therefore, felt it my duty to sustain Admiral Mayo in the whole of his demand and to insist that the flag of the United States should be saluted in such a way as to indicate a new spirit and attitude on the part of the Huertistas. Such a salute General Huerta has refused, and I have come to ask your approval and support in the course I now purpose to pursue.

This government can, I earnestly hope, in no circumstances be forced into war with the people of Mexico. Mexico is torn by civil strife. If we are to accept the tests of its own constitution, it has no government. General Huerta has set his power up in the

City of Mexico, such as it is, without right and by methods for which there can be no justification. Only part of the country is under his control. If armed conflict should unhappily come as a result of his attitude of personal resentment toward this government, we should be fighting only General Huerta and those who adhere to him and give him their support, and our object would be only to restore to the people of the distracted republic the opportunity to set up again their own laws and their own government.

But I earnestly hope that war is not now in question. I believe that I speak for the American people when I say that we do not desire to control in any degree the affairs of our sister republic. Our feeling for the people of Mexico is one of deep and genuine friendship, and everything that we have so far done or refrained from doing has proceeded from our desire to help them, not to hinder or embarrass them. We would not wish even to exercise the good offices of friendship without their welcome and consent. The people of Mexico are entitled to settle their own domestic affairs in their own way, and we sincerely desire to respect their right. The present situation need have none of the grave implications of interference if we deal with it promptly, firmly, and wisely.

No doubt I could do what is necessary in the circumstances to enforce respect for our government without recourse to the Congress and yet not exceed my constitutional powers as President; but I do not wish to act in a matter possibly of so grave consequence except in close conference and cooperation with both the Senate and House. I, therefore, come to ask your approval that I should use the armed forces of the United States in such ways and to such an extent as may be necessary to obtain from General Huerta and his adherents the fullest recognition of the rights and dignity of the United States, even amidst the distressing conditions now unhappily obtaining in Mexico.

There can in what we do be no thought of aggression or of selfish aggrandizement. We seek to maintain the dignity and authority of the United States only because we wish always to keep our great influence unimpaired for the uses of liberty, both in the United States and wherever else it may be employed for the benefit of mankind.

## Further Resources

### BOOKS

Eisenhower, John S.D. *Intervention! The United States and the Mexican Revolution 1913–1917*. New York: Norton, 1993.

Grieb, Kenneth. *The United States and Huerta*. Lincoln, Neb.: University of Nebraska, 1967.

Knock, Thomas. *To End All Wars: Woodrow Wilson and the Quest for a New World Order*. Princeton, N.J.: Princeton University Press, 1995.

### PERIODICALS

Coletta, Paolo. "Bryan, Anti-Imperialism and Missionary Diplomacy." *Nebraska History* 18, September 1968, 167–187.

Katz, Friedrich. "Pancho Villa and the Attack on Columbus, New Mexico." *American Historical Review* 83, February 1978, 101–130.

### WEBSITES

Ferraro, Vincent. "Documents Relating to Foreign Policy." Available online at http://www.mtholyoke.edu/acad/intrel/to1914.htm; website home page: http://www.mtholyoke.edu (accessed January 18, 2003).

Public Broadcasting Service. "The Border: History." Available online at http://www.pbs.org/kpbs/theborder/history/index.html; website home page: http://www.pbs.org/ (accessed January 19, 2003).

University of Texas at El Paso. "The Borderlands Encyclopedia." Available online at http://www.utep.edu/border/ (accessed January 19, 2003).

# *Family Limitation*

## Pamphlet

**By:** Margaret Sanger

**Date:** 1914

**Source:** Sanger, Margaret. *Family Limitation*. New York, 1914. Reproduced in Katz, Esther, Cathy Moran Hajo, and Peter Engelman, eds. *The Margaret Sanger Papers Electronic Edition: Margaret Sanger and The Woman Rebel, 1914–1916*. Columbia, S.C.: Model Editions Partnership, 1999. Available online at http://adh.sc.edu/dynaweb/MEP/ms/@Generic__BookTextView/3454;td=2$^{\phi}$=0; website home page: http://.adh.sc.edu (accessed January 19, 2003).

**About the Author:** Margaret Sanger (1879–1966) was born in Corning, New York. Her mother, a devout Irish American Catholic, died at the age of fifty from tuberculosis. Margaret, the sixth of eleven children, blamed the premature death of her mother on her frequent pregnancies. In 1916, she opened the first birth control clinic. In 1921, she founded the American Birth Control League, which became Planned Parenthood. ∎

## Introduction

In 1873, a U.S. Post Office inspector named Anthony Comstock convinced Congress to pass the "Act of the Suppression of Trade in, and Circulation of, Obscene Literature and Articles of Immoral Use," commonly known as the Comstock Act. Comstock, who was a leader of the Society for the Suppression of Vice, wanted to combat obscenity. The act criminalized the publication, distribution, and possession of information about or devices or medications for unlawful abortion or contraception. Violators of the act could be imprisoned for up to five years at hard labor and fined up to $2,000. As postal inspector, Comstock estimated that from 1873 to 1914, he destroyed 160 tons of obscene literature and helped convict 3,760 criminals.

The Comstock laws had an enormous effect on Margaret Sanger. In 1910, she and her husband moved to New York City. To help support the family financially, she became a visiting obstetrical nurse among the Lower East Side poor. Influenced by the bohemian culture of nearby Greenwich Village, she became a radical feminist and was influenced by Emma Goldman, an anarchist who argued that working-class women could liberate themselves and improve their economic status by preventing unwanted pregnancies. As a nurse, Sanger witnessed firsthand the pain of frequent childbirth and miscarriage and deaths from dangerous, illegal abortions. To alleviate the suffering, Sanger gave up nursing and devoted her life to providing the poor with accurate information about birth control, contraception, and women's health. This was a bold move because public discussion of contraception was taboo. Such talk shocked Theodore Roosevelt, who equated birth control with "race suicide," warning that the "white" population was declining while immigrants and "undesirables" continued to breed.

In 1912, Sanger wrote a column entitled "What Every Girl Should Know" for the *New York Call,* which broadly discussed women's health issues. The government declared one article on venereal disease to be obscene and suppressed its circulation. Sanger remained convinced that women needed to control their pregnancies but was unsure of the best methods for doing so. She traveled to Europe to learn more about contraceptive techniques. Returning in 1914, she published the latest medical and scientific birth control studies from Europe in a short-lived magazine called *The Woman Rebel,* a radical feminist monthly. Consequently, three issues were banned and she was indicted for violating postal obscenity laws. In October 1914, she was unwilling to risk a possible forty-five-year prison term and jumped bail under the alias "Bertha Watson." While en route to England, she had "Big Bill" Haywood, leader of the International Workers of the World (IWW), a radical labor union, spread her views on birth control and contraception to the working poor by distributing 100,000 copies of her yet-to-be released pamphlet, *Family Limitation.*

### Significance

In October 1915, Sanger returned to the United States to stand trial. To her surprise, she learned that *Family Limitation* had been circulated among women

Margaret Sanger (seated on the left), in court with her sister Ethel Bryne, was on trial for mailing materials advocating birth control in 1916. © **BETTMANN/CORBIS. REPRODUCED BY PERMISSION.**

throughout the nation and that for the first time the merits of birth control had been publicly discussed. When her five-year-old daughter unexpectedly died in November, the government dropped all charges against her. Sanger promptly began a nationwide tour to promote the birth control cause. Although the birth rate had been in decline for decades, Sanger's crusade is partly responsible for the drop in family size from 3.6 children in 1900 to 2.5 in 1930.

### Primary Source

*Family Limitation* [excerpt]

> **SYNOPSIS:** In 1914, Sanger's pamphlet *Family Limitation* was published for the first time. Because it was against the law to print the document in America, Sanger arranged to have it printed in China. As a result of the pamphlet's publication, thousands of women for the first time learned or were given accurate information about birth control. The following is the pamphlet's introduction.

There is no need for any one to explain to the working men and women in America what this pamphlet is written for or why it is necessary that they should have this information. They know better than I could tell them, so I shall not try.

I have tried to give the knowledge of the best French and Dutch physicians translated into the simplest English, that all may easily understand.

There are various and numerous mechanical means of prevention which I have not mentioned here, mainly because I have not come into personal contact with those who have used them or could recommend them as entirely satisfactory.

I feel there is sufficient information given here, which if followed will prevent a woman from becoming pregnant unless she desires to do so.

If a woman is too indolent to wash and cleanse herself, and the man too selfish to consider the consequences of the act, then it will be difficult to find a preventive to keep the woman from becoming pregnant.

Of course, it is troublesome to get up to douche, it is also a nuisance to have to trouble about the date of the menstrual period. It seems inartistic and sordid to insert a pessary or a suppository in anticipation of the sexual act. But it is far more sordid to find yourself several years later burdened down with half a dozen unwished for children, helpless, starved, shoddily clothed, dragging at your skirt, yourself a dragged out shadow of the woman you once were.

Don't be over sentimental in this important phase of hygiene. The inevitable fact is that unless you prevent the male sperm from entering the womb, you are going to become pregnant. Women of the working class, especially wage workers, should not have more than two children at most. The average working man can support no more, and the average working woman can take care of no more in decent fashion. It has been my experience that more children are not really wanted, but that the women are compelled to have them either from lack of foresight or through ignorance of the hygiene of preventing conception.

It is only the workers who are ignorant of the knowledge of how to prevent bringing children in the world to fill jails and hospitals, factories and mills, insane asylums and premature graves, and who supply the millions of soldiers and sailors to fight battles for financiers and the ruling classes.

The working class can use direct action by refusing to supply the market with children to be exploited, by refusing to populate the earth with slaves.

It is also the one most direct method for you working women to help yourselves *today*.

Pass on this information to your neighbor and comrade workers. Write out any of the following information which you are sure will help her, and pass it along where it is needed. Spread this important knowledge!

## Further Resources

### BOOKS

Chesler, Ellen. *Woman of Valor: Margaret Sanger and the Birth Control Movement in American.* New York: Simon & Schuster, 1992.

Gordon, Linda. *Woman's Body, Woman's Right: A Social History of Birth Control in America.* New York: Penguin, 1990.

Kennedy, David. *Birth Control in America: The Career of Margaret Sanger.* New Haven, Conn.: Yale University Press, 1970.

### PERIODICALS

Katz, Esther. "Margaret Higgins Sanger." *American National Biography.* New Haven, Conn.: Yale University Press, 1999, 264–267.

Sanger, Margaret. "Comstockery in America." *International Socialist Review,* July 1915, 46–49.

### WEBSITES

New York University Department of History. "The Margaret Sanger Papers Project." Available online at http://www.nyu.edu/projects/sanger/index.html (accessed January 19, 2003). *This site contains links to numerous sources about Margaret Sanger.*

# The Zimmermann Telegram

## Telegram from Arthur Zimmermann to Heinrich J.F. von Eckhardt

Telegram

**By:** Arthur Zimmermann

**Date:** January 16, 1917

**Source:** Zimmermann, Arthur. "Telegram to Heinrich J.F. von Eckhardt, 16 January 1917." Available online at http://arcweb.archives.gov/arc/arch_results_detail.jsp?&pg;=4&si;=0&nh;=4&st;=b; U.S. National Archives and Records Administration home page: http://www.archives.gov (accessed January 20, 2003).

**About the Author:** Arthur Zimmermann (1864–1940) entered the German Foreign Office in 1902. Previously, he had been assigned to the consulate in China. Upon his recall to Germany, he landed in San Francisco. Crossing the continent by train to New York, Zimmermann was fascinated with America and considered himself an authority on its character. Zimmermann's knowledge of America, along with his support for U-boat submarines, was responsible for his promotion to foreign secretary in 1917.

# Telegram from U.S. Ambassador Walter Page to President Woodrow Wilson

Telegram

**By:** Walter Page

**Date:** February 24, 1917

**Source:** Page, Walter. "Telegram to Woodrow Wilson, 24 February 1917." Available online at http://arcweb.archives .gov/arc/arch_results_detail.jsp?&pg;=1&si;=0&st;=b&rp; =details&nh;=4; U.S. National Archives and Records Administration home page: http://www.archives.gov (accessed January 20, 2003).

**About the Author:** Walter Page (1855–1918) had a long and influential career as a journalist, working for the New York *World,* a newspaper, and the *Forum* and *Atlantic Monthly* magazines. He founded the magazine *The World's Work,* and was one of the founding partners of the publishing house Doubleday, Page, and Co. Appointed ambassador to Great Britain in 1913 by his friend President Woodrow Wilson (served 1913–1921), he served in that post until 1918. An admirer of Britain, he argued strenuously for U.S. aid to that country during Wold War I (1914–1918). ■

## Introduction

In 1916, President Woodrow Wilson was reelected president of the United States. The key issue in the political contest was American policy toward the war in Europe. Wilson and the Democrats campaigned on the slogan "He Kept Us Out of War." In 1915 and 1916, he sent an envoy on a secret mission to London, Paris, and Berlin to mediate a peaceful solution, but the gesture failed. By 1917, Germany had deployed over one hundred U-boats and threatened to sink without warning any neutral vessels that entered the war zone around the British Isles. Germany had long accused the United States of betraying its stance of neutrality by shipping food and munitions to the Allies, so the prospect of sinking neutral American merchant vessels did not overly concern the Germans. German foreign secretary Arthur Zimmermann believed that the United States would not enter the war against Germany because its 1.3 million Germans and 8 million Americans of German descent, along with 4.5 million Irish Americans who hated everything British, would revolt in protest. In addition Zimmermann believed that even if the United States entered the conflict, American troops were inferior and could not be trained and transported to Europe in time to seriously affect the outcome of the war.

Because of these beliefs, in 1916 Zimmermann enticed Mexican president General Venustiano Carranza to become a German ally. In the past Carranza had displayed pro-German sympathies and offered to provide a permanent base for U-boats. Zimmermann thought he could tempt Mexico into an alliance by playing upon Mexican anti-American sentiment, which had hardly subsided since the 1846 U.S.-Mexican War. In January 1917, he sent a telegram to the German minister to Mexico, instructing him to propose an alliance with the president of Mexico should the United States declare war on Germany. British cryptanalysts, who had previously captured German codebooks, intercepted the telegram at 10:30 A.M. on January 17. Consisting of a thousand numerical code groups, the message was addressed to the German minister to Mexico and was signed by Zimmermann.

When the British deciphered portions of the message, they found themselves in a difficult situation. If they alerted the Americans, it would influence the Wilson administration to declare war on Germany. But by passing on the decoded message, the British would signal to the Germans that they had cracked their secret codes. As a result, Germany would change its codes, depriving England of a valuable intelligence weapon. Another complicating factor was that disclosure of the message would reveal that the British were also monitoring U.S. coded telegrams. Finally, because the message was not fully decoded, there was a chance that their interpretation may not be fully accurate. Therefore, the British took no action, hoping that sooner or later America would declare war on Germany.

## Significance

In February 1917, there was no sign that America was ready to enter the war. Despite its threat to target American ships, Germany had not recently torpedoed a single American vessel. As a result, President Wilson was hesitant to call for war. In the meantime, France and England were locked in a bloody stalemate with Germany on the western front. England could wait no longer. Having finally cracked the entire code, the British revealed the Zimmermann telegram to President Wilson on February 22. On March 1, the administration leaked the telegram's contents to the press. Thus, the Zimmermann telegram became perhaps the most important single cryptanalysis in history. It helped push a reluctant America into war, allowed the Allies to defeat the Germans, and thrust the United States into a position of world leadership.

## Further Resources

**BOOKS**

Kahn, David. *The Codebreakers: The Story of Secret Writing.* New York: Macmillan, 1967.

Kennedy, David M. *Over Here: The First World War and American Society.* New York: Oxford University Press, 1980.

Tuchman, Barbara W. *The Zimmermann Telegram.* New York: Viking, 1968.

**PERIODICALS**

Kennedy, Ross. "Woodrow Wilson, World War I, and American National Security." *Diplomatic History* 25, 2001, 1–32.

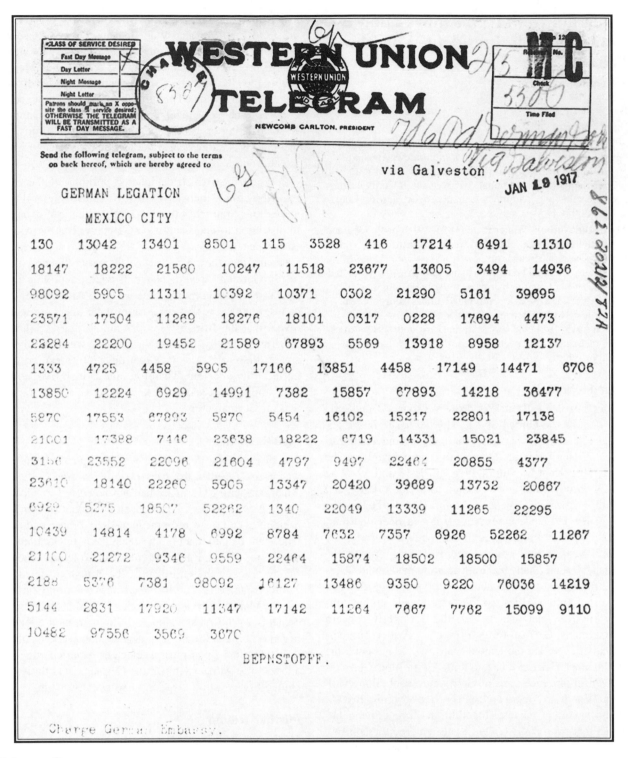

## Primary Source

### Telegram from Arthur Zimmermann to Heinrich J. F. von Eckhardt

**SYNOPSIS:** Arthur Zimmermann sent this telegram to Heinrich J.F. von Eckhardt, the German minister to Mexico, on January 16, 1917. After passing through a German ambassador in Washington, who translated it from one coding system to another, the encrypted message was received three days later. **NATIONAL ARCHIVES AND RECORDS ADMINISTRATION.**

## TELEGRAM RECEIVED.

CLAS... CANCELED
... ctor 1-8-58
... erson, State Dept.
By *Mark G Eckloff Archivist*
Date *Oct. 27, 1958*

FROM 2nd from London # 5747.

"We intend to begin on the first of February unrestricted submarine warfare. We shall endeavor in spite of this to keep the United States of America neutral. In the event of this not succeeding, we make Mexico a proposal of alliance on the following basis: make war together, make peace together, generous financial support and an understanding on our part that Mexico is to reconquer the lost territory in Texas, New Mexico, and Arizona. The settlement in detail is left to you. You will inform the President of the above most secretly as soon as the outbreak of war with the United States of America is certain and add the suggestion that he should, on his own initiative, ~~invite~~ Japan to immediate adherence and at the same time mediate between Japan and ourselves. Please call the President's attention to the fact that the ruthless employment of our submarines now offers the prospect of compelling England in a few months to make peace." Signed, ZIMMERMANN.

**Primary Source**

Telegram from U.S. Ambassador Walter Page to President Woodrow Wilson

**SYNOPSIS:** This excerpt from Page's February 24, 1917, telegram to President Wilson is the English translation of the decoded Zimmermann Telegram. That supposedly secret message from Germany to Mexico informed Mexico that Germany was prepared to launch unrestricted submarine warfare on the United States as of February 1, 1917. In case this strategy did not deter the Americans from declaring war, Germany offered an alliance with Mexico. In return for its assistance, Mexico would reclaim the lost territory of Texas, New Mexico, and Arizona. NATIONAL ARCHIVES AND RECORDS ADMINISTRATION.

Trow, Clifford W. "Woodrow Wilson and the Mexican Interventionist Movement of 1919." *Journal of American History* 58, June 1971, 46–72.

**WEBSITES**

Iavarone, Mike. "World War I: Trenches on the Web." Available online at http://www.worldwar1.com/index.html (accessed on January 20, 2003).

# Woodrow Wilson's Declaration of War Message

Speech

**By:** Woodrow Wilson

**Date:** April 2, 1917

**Source:** Wilson, Woodrow. "Address by the President of the United States." *Congressional Record,* 65th Congress, 1st sess., April 2, 1917, 102–104. Reprinted in Hyser, Raymond M., and J. Chris Arndt. *Voices of the American Past: Documents in U.S. History.* Vol. 2. Fort Worth, Tex.: Harcourt Brace, 1995, 122–124.

**About the Author:** Woodrow Wilson (1856–1924), born in Virginia, was the first post–Civil War president from the South. He earned a doctorate from Johns Hopkins University and became president of Princeton University in 1902. He was elected president of the United States in 1912 and reelected in 1916. He championed progressive reform, tariff reform, the Federal Trade Commission Act, and the Federal Reserve Act. ∎

## Introduction

George Washington's farewell address warned the nation against becoming involved in "entangling alliances," and throughout the nineteenth century the policy of the United States was to stay out of European affairs. The Monroe Doctrine, announced in 1823, warned European countries not to further colonize the Western Hemisphere; an unspoken corollary to this doctrine was that the United States would stay out of Europe. Thus, when World War I (1914–1918) began, the question arose as to what position the United States would take. Woodrow Wilson called for the United States to remain "impartial in thought as well as deed." Neutrality, though, proved to be difficult, for many Americans were first- or second-generation immigrants from Europe, and U.S. businesses did a thriving trade in Europe. Historically, the United States had been closer to Great Britain than to Germany and consequently made loans to Great Britain to help that nation finance its war effort.

Pressure for American intervention increased after the British bombarded the United States with stories, many of them fictitious, of German brutality in Belgium, which had been neutral in the conflict before Germany invaded it.

Wilson, however, was determined to remain neutral and in 1916 ran for reelection as president on a platform of neutrality; indeed, his campaign slogan was "He kept us out of war." A potential source of conflict with Germany was its submarine warfare, but after U.S. protests, Germany promised to attack only British ships, not American ones. Germany, though, was becoming desperate and needed to reduce the amount of supplies arriving in England, many of which were coming from the United States. For this reason, in early 1917, Germany resumed unrestricted submarine warfare, even though it knew that doing so would likely draw the United States into the conflict.

## Significance

The Germans believed that the United States could not fully mobilize in time to rescue the Europeans. This belief proved to be a mistake. In February 1917, President Wilson broke off diplomatic relations with Germany. He refused, though, to ask Congress to declare war in the absence of "actual overt acts" against American lives and property. Late in February, German submarines sank two American ships, then sank four more in March. On April 2, President Wilson asked Congress to declare war on Germany. Four days later, Congress passed the war resolution, with only six senators and fifty representatives voting to remain neutral.

Wilson's idealism is apparent throughout this message, including his goal that the world be "made safe for democracy." These idealistic goals for the war were later reflected in his Fourteen Points, his vision for a postwar Europe. This idealistic vision created tensions both at the Versailles Peace Conference, where the victorious European allies wanted to humiliate Germany, and during Senate deliberations on the Treaty of Versailles. The idealistic goals announced in Wilson's call for a declaration of war were never achieved, leading to a generation of disillusioned American fighting men and America's isolationism in the 1930s.

## Primary Source

Woodrow Wilson's Declaration of War Message [excerpt]

**SYNOPSIS:** Wilson first declares that human rights is the key issue in the conflict and that neutrality is no longer possible. The responsibility of the United States is to force civilized conduct between nations. He goes on to say that America's quarrel is not with the German people but with the German government, and that the goal of the United States in entering the conflict is to promote democracy throughout the world. He concludes by noting the "fiery trial and sacrifice ahead of us."

The present German submarine warfare against commerce is a warfare against mankind.

It is a war of all nations. American ships have been sunk, American lives taken, in ways which it has stirred us very deeply to learn of, but the ships and people of other neutral and friendly nations have been sunk and overwhelmed in the waters in the same way. There has been no discrimination. The challenge is to all mankind. Each nation must decide for itself how it will meet it. The choice we make for ourselves must be made with a moderation of counsel and a temperance of judgment befitting our character and our motives as a nation. We must put excited feeling away. Our motive will not be revenge or the victorious assertion of the physical might of the nation, but only the vindication of right, of human right, of which we are only a single champion. . . .

With a profound sense of the solemn and even tragical character of the step I am taking and of the grave responsibilities which it involves, but in un-hesitating obedience to what I deem my constitu-tional duty, I advise that the Congress declare the recent course of the Imperial German Government to be in fact nothing less than war against the gov ernment and people of the United States; that it for-mally accept the status of belligerent which has thus been thrust upon it; and that it take immediate steps, not only to put the country in a more thor-ough state of defense but also to exert all its power and employ all its resources to bring the Government of the German Empire to terms and end the war. . . .

Our object now, as then, is to vindicate the prin-ciples of peace and justice in the life of the world as against selfish and autocratic power and to set up among the really free and self-governed peoples of the world such a concert of purpose and of ac-tion as will henceforth ensure the observance of those principles. Neutrality is no longer feasible or desirable where the peace of the world is involved and the freedom of its peoples, and the menace to that peace and freedom lies in the existence of an autocratic government backed by an organized force which is controlled wholly by their will, not the will of their people. We have seen the last of neutrality in such circumstances. We are at the beginning of an age in which it will be insisted that the same standards of conduct and of responsibility for wrong done shall be observed among nations and their gov-ernments that are observed among the individual cit-izens of civilized states.

We have no quarrel with the German people. We have no feeling toward them but one of sympathy and friendship. It was not upon their impulse that their government acted in entering this war. It was

After President Wilson declared war on Germany, this poster appeared urging Americans to buy war bonds. **THE LIBRARY OF CONGRESS.**

not with their previous knowledge or approval. It was a war determined as wars used to be determined in the old, unhappy days when peoples nowhere [were] consulted by their rulers and wars were provoked and waged in the interest of dynasties or of little groups of ambitious men who were accustomed to use their fellowmen as pawns and tools. . . .

The world must be made safe for democracy. Its peace must be planted upon the tested foundations of political liberty. We have no selfish ends to serve. We desire no conquest, no domination. We seek no indemnities for ourselves, no material compensation for the sacrifices we shall freely make. We are but one of the champions of the rights of mankind. We shall be satisfied when those rights have been made as secure as the faith and the freedom of nations can make them. . . .

It will be all the easier for us to conduct our-selves as belligerents in a high spirit of right and fairness because we act without animus, not in en-mity toward a people or with the desire to bring any injury or disadvantage upon them, but only in armed opposition to an irresponsible government which has thrown aside all considerations of humanity and of right and is running amuck. We are, let me

President Woodrow Wilson gave his Declaration of War speech before a joint session of Congress April 2, 1917. **AP/WIDE WORLD PHOTOS. REPRODUCED BY PERMISSION.**

say again, the sincere friends of the German people, and shall desire nothing so much as the early reestablishment of intimate relations of mutual advantage between us—however hard it may be between them, for the time being, to believe that this is spoken from our hearts. We have borne with their present government through all these bitter months because of that friendship—exercising a patience and forebearance which would otherwise have been impossible. We shall, happily, still have an opportunity to prove that friendship in our daily attitude and actions toward the millions of men and women of German birth and native sympathy who live among us and share our life, and we shall be proud to prove it toward all who are in fact loyal to their neighbors and to the Government in the hour of test. They are, most of them, as true and loyal Americans as if they had never known any other fealty or allegiance. . . .

It is a distressing and oppressive duty, gentlemen of Congress, which I have performed in thus addressing you. There are, it may be, many months of fiery trial and sacrifice ahead of us. It is a fearful thing to lead this great peaceful nation into war, into the most terrible and disastrous of all wars, civ-

ilization itself seeming to be in the balance. But the right is more precious than peace, and we shall fight for the things which we have always carried nearest our hearts—for democracy, for the right of those who submit to authority to have a voice in their own governments, for the rights and liberties of small nations, for a universal dominion of right by such a concert of free peoples as shall bring peace and safety to all nations and make the world itself at last free. To such a task we can dedicate our lives and our fortunes, everything that we are and everything that we have, with the pride of those who know that the day has come when America is privileged to spend her blood and her might for the principles that gave her birth and happiness and the peace which she has treasured. God helping her, she can do no other.

## Further Resources

### BOOKS

Baker, Newton Diehl. *Why We Went to War.* New York: Harper, 1936.

Esposito, David M. *The Legacy of Woodrow Wilson: American War Aims in World War I.* Westport, Conn.: Praeger, 1996.

Gregory, Ross. *The Origins of American Intervention in the First World War.* New York: Norton, 1971.

Link, Arthur S., ed. *Woodrow Wilson and a Revolutionary World, 1913–1921.* Chapel Hill, N.C.: University of North Carolina Press, 1982.

Smith, Page. *America Enters the World: A People's History of the Progressive Era and World War I.* New York: McGraw-Hill, 1985.

Woodward, Robert Franklin Maddox. *America and World War I: A Selected Annotated Bibliography of English-Language Sources.* New York: Garland, 1985.

Wynn, Neil A. *From Progressivism to Prosperity: World War I and American Society.* New York: Holmes & Meier, 1986.

# "Opposition to Wilson's War Message"
Speech

**By:** George W. Norris

**Date:** April 4, 1917

**Source:** Norris, George W. "Opposition to Wilson's War Message." *Congressional Record.* 65th Cong., 1st sess., 1917. Vol. 55, pt. 1. Available online at http://www.mtholyoke.edu/acad/intrel/doc19.htm; website home page: http://www.mtholyoke.edu (accessed May 19, 2003).

**About the Author:** George W. Norris (1861–1942) was born on an Ohio farm. After earning a law degree from Valparaiso University in Indiana, he moved to Beaver City, Nebraska, to begin his law practice in 1885. In 1902, he was elected to Congress as a Republican; then in 1912, he was elected to the Senate. He sponsored the Twentieth Amendment to the Constitution and legislation to create the Tennessee Valley Authority. ■

## Introduction

Politically, George W. Norris was a Progressive. He believed that government must be made responsive to the will of ordinary people. He was not a radical, nor did he challenge the fundamental tenets of capitalism, but he believed that government must shed its laissez-faire (hands off) stance toward the business community. He believed that corporate America had a moral duty to ensure that it acted responsibly by looking out for the interests of women, children, and the poor. He also believed in reforming the political system, which allowed special interests to silence the voice of the common man. In 1910, Norris led the charge to strip the Speaker of the House of much of his power. He also gained control of the rules committee and allowed party caucuses to determine committee assignments. In 1913, he backed the Seventeenth Amendment, which allowed U.S. senators to be directly elected by voters rather than special-interest-dominated state legislatures.

Senator George Norris spoke out in opposition to the U.S. entry into WWI. THE LIBRARY OF CONGRESS.

Norris took his most controversial political position in 1917. On February 26, two American women were killed when the *Laconia* was torpedoed by a German U-boat. President Woodrow Wilson (served 1913–1921) asked Congress for the authority to arm American merchant ships, and on March 1, his bill, which was widely popular with the American people, came before the Senate. The matter was not debated because twelve antiwar senators, who believed that its passage would plunge the United States into war, successfully filibustered it until Congress's adjournment at noon on March 4. President Wilson characterized the antiwar senators as "a little groups of willful men, representing no opinion but their own." Later that day, Norris was flooded with telegrams from his home state condemning his behavior. Within forty-eight hours of the end of session, President Wilson announced that under executive power he had ordered the arming of American merchantmen.

## Significance

Wilson's executive decision to arm neutral vessels preserved the doctrine of freedom of the seas, but it failed to curb German belligerence. From March 7 to March 21, 1917, German submarines sank five American ships. With the support of the American people, on April 2, Wilson convened a special session of Congress, urging

Congress to declare war on Germany. Two days later, the war resolution came before the Senate. Unable to muster a filibuster, Senator Norris voted no because he felt that there was no immediate threat of war reaching American soil. The measure passed the Senate by a vote 82 to 6; two days later the House passed it 373 to 50. Afterward, Senator Norris believed that his civil liberties were trampled on. He maintained that some elements within the government, believing that he was "pro-German," kept him under surveillance and monitored his movements. Shadowy "investigators" appeared at his home when he was gone and made insulting inquiries to his wife. In 1918, Norris ran for reelection and narrowly defeated his Democratic nominee. He continued to serve in the Senate until 1942.

## Primary Source

"Opposition to Wilson's War Message" [excerpt]

**SYNOPSIS:** On April 4, 1917, two days after Wilson asked Congress to declare war on Germany, Norris argued that American munitions makers and banks that had loaned millions of dollars to the Allies had great financial interests in the war. Senator Gerald Nye's report (1934–1936) would later convince millions of Americans that "the interests" conspired to drag America into World War I.

While I am most emphatically and sincerely opposed to taking any step that will force our country into the useless and senseless war now being waged in Europe, yet, if this resolution passes, I shall not permit my feeling of opposition to its passage to interfere in any way with my duty either as a senator or as a citizen in bringing success and victory to American arms. I am bitterly opposed to my country entering the war, but if, notwithstanding my opposition, we do enter it, all of my energy and all of my power will be behind our flag in carrying it on to victory.

The resolution now before the Senate is a declaration of war. Before taking this momentous step, and while standing on the brink of this terrible vortex, we ought to pause and calmly and judiciously consider the terrible consequences of the step we are about to take. We ought to consider likewise the route we have recently traveled and ascertain whether we have reached our present position in a way that is compatible with the neutral position which we claimed to occupy at the beginning and through the various stages of this unholy and unrighteous war.

No close student of recent history will deny that both Great Britain and Germany have, on numerous occasions since the beginning of the war, flagrantly violated in the most serious manner the rights of neutral vessels and neutral nations under existing international law, as recognized up to the beginning of this war by the civilized world.

The reason given by the President in asking Congress to declare war against Germany is that the German government has declared certain war zones, within which, by the use of submarines, she sinks, without notice, American ships and destroys American lives. . . . The first war zone was declared by Great Britain. She gave us and the world notice of it on, the 4th day of November, 1914. The zone became effective Nov. 5, 1914. . . . This zone so declared by Great Britain covered the whole of the North Sea. . . . The first German war zone was declared on the 4th day of February, 1915, just three months after the British war zone was declared. Germany gave fifteen days' notice of the establishment of her zone, which became effective on the 18th day of February, 1915. The German war zone covered the English Channel and the high seawaters around the British Isles. . . .

It is unnecessary to cite authority to show that both of these orders declaring military zones were illegal and contrary to international law. It is sufficient to say that our government has officially declared both of them to be illegal and has officially protested against both of them. The only difference is that in the case of Germany we have persisted in our protest, while in the case of England we have submitted.

What was our duty as a government and what were our rights when we were confronted with these extraordinary orders declaring these military zones? First, we could have defied both of them and could have gone to war against both of these nations for this violation of international law and interference with our neutral rights. Second, we had the technical right to defy one and to acquiesce in the other. Third, we could, while denouncing them both as illegal, have acquiesced in them both and thus remained neutral with both sides, although not agreeing with either as to the righteousness of their respective orders. We could have said to American shipowners that, while these orders are both contrary to international law and are both unjust, we do not believe that the provocation is sufficient to cause us to go to war for the defense of our rights as a neutral nation, and, therefore, American ships and American citizens will go into these zones at their own peril and risk.

Fourth, we might have declared an embargo against the shipping from American ports of any merchandise to either one of these governments that persisted in maintaining its military zone. We might have refused to permit the sailing of any ship from any American port to either of these military zones. In my judgment, if we had pursued this course, the zones would have been of short duration. England would have been compelled to take her mines out of the North Sea in order to get any supplies from our country. When her mines were taken out of the North Sea then the German ports upon the North Sea would have been accessible to American shipping and Germany would have been compelled to cease her submarine warfare in order to get any supplies from our nation into German North Sea ports.

There are a great many American citizens who feel that we owe it as a duty to humanity to take part in this war. Many instances of cruelty and inhumanity can be found on both sides. Men are often biased in their judgment on account of their sympathy and their interests. To my mind, what we ought to have maintained from the beginning was the strictest neutrality. If we had done this, I do not believe we would have been on the verge of war at the present time. We had a right as a nation, if we desired, to cease at any time to be neutral. We had a technical right to respect the English war zone and to disregard the German war zone, but we could not do that and be neutral.

I have no quarrel to find with the man who does not desire our country to remain neutral. While many such people are moved by selfish motives and hopes of gain, I have no doubt but that in a great many instances, through what I believe to be a misunderstanding of the real condition, there are many honest, patriotic citizens who think we ought to engage in this war and who are behind the President in his demand that we should declare war against Germany. I think such people err in judgment and to a great extent have been misled as to the real history and the true facts by the almost unanimous demand of the great combination of wealth that has a direct financial interest in our participation in the war.

We have loaned many hundreds of millions of dollars to the Allies in this controversy. While such action was legal and countenanced by international law, there is no doubt in my mind but the enormous amount of money loaned to the Allies in this country has been instrumental in bringing about a public sentiment in favor of our country taking a course that would make every bond worth a hundred cents on the dollar and making the payment of every debt certain and sure. Through this instrumentality and also through the instrumentality of others who have not only made millions out of the war in the manufacture of munitions, etc., and who would expect to make millions more if our country can be drawn into the catastrophe, a large number of the great newspapers and news agencies of the country have been controlled and enlisted in the greatest propaganda that the world has ever known to manufacture sentiment in favor of war.

It is now demanded that the American citizens shall be used as insurance policies to guarantee the safe delivery of munitions of war to belligerent nations. The enormous profits of munition manufacturers, stockbrokers, and bond dealers must be still further increased by our entrance into the war. This has brought us to the present moment, when Congress, urged by the President and backed by the artificial sentiment, is about to declare war and engulf our country in the greatest holocaust that the world has ever known.

In showing the position of the bondholder and the stockbroker, I desire to read an extract from a letter written by a member of the New York Stock Exchange to his customers. This writer says:

> Regarding the war as inevitable, Wall Street believes that it would be preferable to this uncertainty about the actual date of its commencement. Canada and Japan are at war and are more prosperous than ever before. The popular view is that stocks would have a quick, clear, sharp reaction immediately upon outbreak of hostilities, and that then they would enjoy an old-fashioned bull market such as followed the outbreak of war with Spain in 1898. The advent of peace would force a readjustment of commodity prices and would probably mean a postponement of new enterprises. As peace negotiations would be long drawn out, the period of waiting and uncertainty for business would be long. If the United States does not go to war, it is nevertheless good opinion that the preparedness program will compensate in good measure for the loss of the stimulus of actual war.

Here we have the Wall Street view. Here we have the man representing the class of people who will be made prosperous should we become entangled in the present war, who have already made millions of dollars, and who will make many hundreds of millions more if we get into the war. Here we have the cold-blooded proposition that war brings prosperity to that class of people who are within the viewpoint of this writer.

He expresses the view, undoubtedly, of Wall Street, and of thousands of men elsewhere who see only dollars coming to them through the handling of stocks and bonds that will be necessary in case of war. "Canada and Japan," he says, "are at war, and are more prosperous than ever before."

To whom does war bring prosperity? Not to the soldier who for the munificent compensation of $16 per month shoulders his musket and goes into the trench, there to shed his blood and to die if necessary; not to the brokenhearted widow who waits for the return of the mangled body of her husband; not to the mother who weeps at the death of her brave boy; not to the little children who shiver with cold; not to the babe who suffers from hunger; nor to the millions of mothers and daughters who carry broken hearts to their graves. War brings no prosperity to the great mass of common and patriotic citizens. It increases the cost of living of those who toil and those who already must strain every effort to keep soul and body together. War brings prosperity to the stock gambler on Wall Street—to those who are already in possession of more wealth than can be realized or enjoyed.

Again this writer says that if we cannot get war, "it is nevertheless good opinion that the preparedness program will compensate in good measure for the loss of the stimulus of actual war." That is, if we cannot get war, let us go as far in that direction as possible. If we cannot get war, let us cry for additional ships, additional guns, additional munitions, and everything else that will have a tendency to bring us as near as possible to the verge of war. And if war comes, do such men as these shoulder the musket and go into the trenches?

Their object in having war and in preparing for war is to make money. Human suffering and the sacrifice of human life are necessary, but Wall Street considers only the dollars and the cents. The men who do the fighting, the people who make the sacrifices are the ones who will not be counted in the measure of this great prosperity that he depicts. The stockbrokers would not, of course, go to war because the very object they have in bringing on the war is profit, and therefore they must remain in their Wall Street offices in order to share in that great prosperity which they say war will bring. The volunteer officer, even the drafting officer, will not find them. They will be concealed in their palatial offices on Wall Street, sitting behind mahogany desks, covered up

with clipped coupons—coupons soiled with the sweat of honest toil, coupons stained with mothers' tears, coupons dyed in the lifeblood of their fellowmen.

We are taking a step today that is fraught with untold danger. We are going into war upon the command of gold. We are going to run the risk of sacrificing millions of our countrymen's lives in order that other countrymen may coin their lifeblood into money. And even if we do not cross the Atlantic and go into the trenches, we are going to pile up a debt that the tolling masses that shall come many generations after us will have to pay. Unborn millions will bend their backs in toil in order to pay for the terrible step we are now about to take.

We are about to do the bidding of wealth's terrible mandate. By our act we will make millions of our countrymen suffer, and the consequences of it may well be that millions of our brethren must shed their lifeblood, millions of brokenhearted women must weep, millions of children must suffer with cold, and millions of babes must die from hunger, and all because we want to preserve the commercial right of American citizens to deliver munitions of war to belligerent nations.

## Further Resources

### BOOKS

Crunden, Robert M. *Ministers of Reform: The Progressives' Achievement in American Civilization, 1889–1920*. Urbana, Ill.: University of Illinois Press, 1985.

Hofstadter, Richard. *The Age of Reform: From Bryan to F.D.R.* New York: Knopf, 1955.

Lowitt, Richard. *George W. Norris: The Making of a Progressive, 1861–1912*. Urbana, Ill.: University of Illinois Press, 1963.

### PERIODICALS

McClay, Wilfred M. "Croly's Progressive America." *The Public Interest* 137, Fall 1999, 56–72.

Schlesinger, Arthur M., Jr. "A Question of Power: Is the Time Ripe for a Progressive Revival." *American Prospect* 12, April 23, 2001, 26–29.

### WEBSITES

Bannister, Robert. "The United States in the Progressive Era: Guide to Resources." Available online at http://www.swarthmore.edu/SocSci/rbannis1/Progs/; website home page: http://www.swarthmore.edu (Accessed July 17, 2002).

Ferraro, Vincent. "Documents of World War I." Available online at http://www.mtholyoke.edu/acad/intrel/ww1.htm; website home page: http://www.mtholyoke.edu (accessed January 19, 2003).

Ohio State University. "Cartoons of the Gilded Age and Progressive Era." Available online at http://www.history.ohio-state.edu/projects/uscartoons/GAPECartoons.htm; website home page: http://www.history.ohio-state.edu (accessed January 20, 2003).

# *"Over the Top": By an American Soldier Who Went*

Memoir

**By:** Arthur Guy Empey

**Date:** 1917

**Source:** Empey, Arthur Guy. *"Over the Top": By an American Soldier Who Went.* New York: G. P. Putnam's Sons. 1917, 187–189.

**About the Author:** In May 1915, Arthur Guy Empey was in his office in Jersey City, New Jersey, when he read that a German U-boat had sunk the British passenger liner *Lusitania,* killing 1,198 people, including 128 Americans. Empey decided that because President Woodrow Wilson had not declared war on Germany, he would not enlist in the U.S. Army. Instead, he traveled to London, which was under attack by German zeppelins, and enlisted in the British army. ■

## Introduction

In August 1914, the uneasy peace of Europe was shattered. Once the Belgians refused to grant the Germans unopposed passage through their territory, the Germans implemented the Schlieffen Plan. First devised in 1905, the plan sought to end the encirclement of Germany by its two enemies—Russia and France—in a two-front war. The Germans believed that it would take underindustrialized Russia thirty days to mobilize its army, so they could hold Russia off with a minimum force of 200,000. The full weight of the German army, 1.5 million men, could then concentrate on France, its more dangerous foe. Instead of attacking the French along the Alsace, where the 1.7-million-man French army had mistakenly anticipated a German invasion, the German army would sweep down through Belgium, across northern France, and capture Paris. It would then roll up the French rear and pin French forces against German fortifications in Alsace. The Germans believed that the French army could be destroyed in forty-two days, allowing them to turn their attention to Russia. In August 1914, though, the small 200,000-man Belgian army delayed the German advance by two weeks, and 300,000 Russian troops advanced into East Prussia. The French shifted their forces northwestward in time to meet the invading Germans. Moreover, by August 21 the 150,000-man British Expeditionary Force reached the French frontier.

By the fall of 1914, the Allies had successfully blunted the German advance and the western front had stabilized. As a result, the war entered its next phase: trench warfare. By spring 1915, the Allies and the Germans had dug two lines of trenches that ran over four hundred miles across northern and eastern France. Between the two opposing armies lay No-Man's-Land, the term soldiers used to describe the virtual wasteland of mud, abandoned military equipment, smashed trees, and dismembered bodies between the opposing trenches. The width of No-Man's-Land varied. The average distance was 250 yards, but the narrowest stretch was twenty-one feet. Trench warfare was simply a battle of attrition. Typically, attacking troops climbed over their trenches and while advancing were decimated by heavy artillery and machine-gun fire. If one of the armies penetrated the one hundred yards of enemy barbwire that protected their frontline trenches, the enemy often counterattacked and reclaimed its territory. As a result, World War I was locked in a gruesome stalemate for nearly four long bloody years.

## Significance

Trench warfare inflicted frightful losses of life both outside and inside the maze of trenches. In 1915, the French launched numerous attacks against German lines but never gained more than three miles. In the process, they lost 1.4 million men. Life within the trenches was not a pleasant experience. Because most casualties were buried almost where they died, a large number of decomposing bodies were located just below the surface of the ground. These corpses attracted thousands of rats, which reproduced many hundredfold. Further, wounded men were particularly vulnerable to rats. Some were so large that they could eat an injured man if he could not adequately defend himself. With the collapse of government bureaucracies during the war, the precise number of men killed in trench warfare is difficult to calculate. It is estimated that one-third of all casualties on the western front were killed or wounded in the trenches.

## Primary Source

*"Over the Top": By an American Soldier Who Went* [excerpt]

**SYNOPSIS:** In 1917, Arthur Guy Empey joined the British army and volunteered to go to the western front to take a position in the trenches bordering No-Man's-Land. One day in the trench, Empey saw a greenish yellow cloud of chlorine gas drifting toward him. Though the gas smells like a mixture of pineapple and pepper, it destroys the respiratory organs and leads to a slow death by asphyxiation. The following is from Chapter 23, entitled "Gas Attacks and Spies."

Three days after we had silenced Fritz, the Germans sent over gas. It did not catch us unawares, because the wind had been made to order, that is, it was blowing from the German trenches towards ours at the rate of about five miles per hour.

Warnings had been passed down the trench to keep a sharp lookout for gas.

British soldiers, wearing gas helmets, fire a machine gun during the Battle of the Somme in 1916. More than nine million people died—many of them in the trenches—by the end of the war in 1918. © **HULTON-DEUTSCH COLLECTION/CORBIS. REPRODUCED BY PERMISSION.**

We had a new man at the periscope, on this afternoon in question; I was sitting on the fire step, cleaning my rifle, when he called out to me:

"There's a sort of greenish, yellow cloud rolling along the ground out in front, it's coming—"

But I waited for no more, grabbing my bayonet, which was detached from the rifle, I gave the alarm by banging an empty shell case, which was hanging near the periscope. At the same instant, gongs started ringing down the trench, the signal for Tommy to don his respirator, or smoke helmet, as we call it.

Gas travels quickly, so you must not lose any time; you generally have about eighteen or twenty seconds in which to adjust your gas helmet.

A gas helmet is made of cloth, treated with chemicals. There are two windows, or glass eyes, in it, through which you can see. Inside there is a rubber-covered tube, which goes in the mouth. You breathe through your nose; the gas, passing through the cloth helmet, is neutralized by the action of the chemicals. The foul air is exhaled through the tube in the mouth, this tube being so constructed that it prevents the inhaling of the outside air or gas. One helmet is good for five hours of the strongest gas.

Each Tommy carries two of them slung around his shoulder in a waterproof canvas bag. He must wear this bag at all times, even while sleeping. To change a defective helmet, you take out the new one, hold your breath, pull the old one off, placing the new one over your head, tucking in the loose ends under the collar of your tunic.

For a minute, pandemonium reigned in our trench—Tommies adjusting their helmets, bombers running here and there, and men turning out of the dugouts with fixed bayonets, to man the fire step.

Re-inforcements were pouring out of the communication trenches.

Our gun's crew were busy mounting the machine gun on the parapet and bringing up extra ammunition from the dugout.

German gas is heavier than air and soon fills the trenches and dugouts, where it has been known to lurk for two or three days, until the air is purified by means of large chemical sprayers.

We had to work quickly, as Fritz generally follows the gas with an infantry attack.

A company man on our right was too slow in getting on his helmet; he sank to the ground, clutching at his throat, and after a few spasmodic twistings, went West (died). It was horrible to see him die, but we were powerless to help him. In the corner of a traverse, a little, muddy cur dog, one of the company's pets, was lying dead, with his two paws over his nose.

It's the animals that suffer the most, the horses, mules, cattle, dogs, cats, and rats, they having no helmets to save them. Tommy does not sympathize with rats in a gas attack.

## Further Resources

### BOOKS

Lloyd, Alan. *The War in the Trenches.* New York: David McKay, 1976.

Tuchman, Barbara. *The Guns of August.* New York: Macmillan, 1962.

### PERIODICALS

Menichetti, David. "German Policy in Occupied Belgium, 1914–1918." *Essays in History* 39, 1997. Available online at http://etext.virginia.edu/journals/EH/EH39/menich39.html; website home page: http://etext.virginia.edu (accessed January 19, 2003).

"The Schlieffen Plan." *Army Quarterly* 18, no. 2, July 1929, 286–290. Available online at http://www.lib.byu.edu/~rdh /wwi/1914m/schlieffen.html; website home page: http://www .lib.byu.edu (accessed January 19, 2003).

### WEBSITES

Irwin, Will. "The German Army Disperses Chlorine Gas over Allied Lines at Ypres." *New York Tribune,* April 25–27, 1915. Available online at http://www.lib.byu.edu/~rdh /wwi/1915/chlorgas.html; website home page: http://www .lib.byu.edu (accessed January 19, 2003).

Iavarone, Mike. "World War I: Trenches on the Web." Available online at http://www.worldwar1.com/index.html; website home page: http://www.worldwar1.com (accessed January 19, 2003).

# "Henry Cabot Lodge Speaks Out Against the League of Nations, Washington, D.C., August 12, 1919"

Speech

**By:** Henry Cabot Lodge Sr.

**Date:** August 12, 1919

**Source:** Lodge, Henry Cabot, Sr. "Henry Cabot Lodge Speaks Out Against the League of Nations, Washington, D.C., August 12, 1919." *Congressional Record.* 66th Cong., 1st sess., 1919, p. 3784. Available online at "Great American

Speeches": http://www.pbs.org/greatspeeches/timeline (accessed January 19, 2003).

**About the Author:** Henry Cabot Lodge Sr. (1850–1924) was born in Boston, Massachusetts. He graduated from Harvard with a law degree and was the first Harvard student to earn a Ph.D. in political science. He was a prolific writer of historical, biographical, and political works. In 1884, he was elected to the U.S. House of Representatives; in 1893, he was elected to the Senate, where he headed the prestigious Senate Foreign Relations Committee. ■

## Introduction

On November 14, 1918, World War I ended, but the nature of the postwar world had yet to be determined. The French called for lasting peace but also wanted to punish Germany. Millions of civilians across the continent faced starvation. Others in Germany and the late Austro-Hungarian Empire were disillusioned with democracy and capitalism and were turning to communism. In January 1918, President Woodrow Wilson realized that if lasting peace was to reign, the victors must swallow their pride and offer relief to the vanquished. In a speech before Congress, he outlined his plan for postwar Europe, known as the Fourteen Points. The plan sought to make the world "fit and safe to live in" by negotiating peace in public, not behind closed doors. In part, the formula would guarantee freedom of the seas to all nations, tear down international trade barriers, provide a drastic reduction in military munitions, erase and reconfigure European borders so that ethnic and cultural groups had the right to self-determination, and accept peace with indemnities. To oversee this complicated undertaking, Wilson proposed to create the League of Nations, which would guarantee "political independence and territorial integrity to great and small states alike."

In January 1919, President Wilson made the unprecedented decision to attend the peace conference at Paris as a member of the United States Peace Commission. He failed, though, to include a prominent Republican member of the Senate on the negotiating team. This oversight was politically ruinous, since a Republican majority controlled the Senate and had veto power over any peace treaty. Once in Paris, the conference was directed by Wilson and the leaders of England, France, and Italy. In May, the conference drafted the Versailles Treaty. Wilson made numerous concessions to the Europeans, but he did not relent on the League of Nations. He believed that once the League was operational and arbitrating international disputes, it could undo the concessions he had made. The most important—and controversial—aspect of the League was Article 10, in which each member nation promised to protect the "territorial integrity" and "political independence" of all other members. This proviso raised the ire of Senate Republicans, and Wilson faced the daunting task of convincing them to ratify the peace

Senator Henry Cabot Lodge believed that membership in the League of Nations could put America's existence in jeopardy by mandating that the nation maintain world peace. THE LIBRARY OF CONGRESS.

treaty. In May 1919, he returned to the United States for a showdown.

### Significance

Wilson's battle with Lodge over the League of Nations is one of the classic political struggles in Senate history. Wilson could count on his fellow Democrats to support the treaty, but Republicans were split into three factions: absolute isolationists, "mild" reservationists, and "strong" reservationists, who were willing to accept the treaty as long as Article 10 completely safeguarded American sovereignty. The leader of the strong reservationists was Senator Lodge, the chairman of the Senate Foreign Relations Committee. Lodge crafted his own Fourteen Reservations. A reservation, unlike a treaty amendment, did not have to win the formal support of League members, who could accept the reservations without sacrificing their convictions. The most important of the Lodge reservations applied to Article 10. It stated that the article was void unless Congress acted to comply with it. Lodge had managed to gain the support of all three Republican factions but failed to gain the support of the president, who refused to compromise. In August, he reported out the treaty to the full Senate with reservations attached. In the

fall of 1919, President Wilson embarked on a nationwide tour to muster support for the League. However, in Colorado he collapsed, and after he returned home, he suffered a stroke. In November, an obstinate Wilson convinced Democrats to reject Lodge's version of the treaty. Though the United States did not join the League, it did not withdraw from world affairs. Moreover, if it had joined, its membership could not have prevented World War II.

### Primary Source

"Henry Cabot Lodge Speaks Out Against the League of Nations, Washington, D.C., August 12, 1919"

> **SYNOPSIS:** On August 12, 1919, Henry Cabot Lodge Sr. spoke out against the League of Nations. Although he opposed the League, Lodge was not an isolationist. In fact, he was one of the leading American expansionists. He feared, however, that membership in the League jeopardized America's very existence by mandating that the nation maintain world peace.

Mr. President:

The independence of the United States is not only more precious to ourselves but to the world than any single possession. Look at the United States today. We have made mistakes in the past. We have had shortcomings. We shall make mistakes in the future and fall short of our own best hopes. But none the less is there any country today on the face of the earth which can compare with this in ordered liberty, in peace, and in the largest freedom? I feel that I can say this without being accused of undue boastfulness, for it is the simple fact, and in making this treaty and taking on these obligations all that we do is in a spirit of unselfishness and in a desire for the good of mankind. But it is well to remember that we are dealing with nations every one of which has a direct individual interest to serve, and there is grave danger in an unshared idealism. Contrast the United States with any country on the face of the earth today and ask yourself whether the situation of the United States is not the best to be found. I will go as far as anyone in world service, but the first step to world service is the maintenance of the United States.

I have always loved one flag and I cannot share that devotion [with] a mongrel banner created for a League.

You may call me selfish if you will, conservative or reactionary, or use any other harsh adjective you see fit to apply, but an American I was born, an American I have remained all my life. I can never be anything else but an American, and I must think of the United States first, and when I think of the United States first in an arrangement like this I am thinking of what is best for the world, for if the United States fails, the best hopes of mankind fail with it. I have never had but one allegiance—I cannot divide it now. I have loved but one flag and I cannot share that devotion and give affection to the mongrel banner invented for a league. Internationalism, illustrated by the Bolshevik and by the men to whom all countries are alike provided they can make money out of them, is to me repulsive. National I must remain, and in that way I like all other Americans can render the amplest service to the world. The United States is the world's best hope, but if you fetter her in the interests and quarrels of other nations, if you tangle her in the intrigues of Europe, you will destroy her power for good and endanger her very existence. Leave her to march freely through the centuries to come as in the years that have gone. Strong, generous, and confident, she has nobly served mankind. Beware how you trifle with your marvelous inheritance, this great land of ordered liberty, for if we stumble and fall freedom and civilization everywhere will go down in ruin.

We are told that we shall 'break the heart of the world' if we do not take this league just as it stands. I fear that the hearts of the vast majority of mankind would beat on strongly and steadily and without any quickening if the league were to perish altogether. If it should be effectively and beneficently changed the people who would lie awake in sorrow for a single night could be easily gathered in one not very large room but those who would draw a long breath of relief would reach to millions.

We hear much of visions and I trust we shall continue to have visions and dream dreams of a fairer future for the race. But visions are one thing and visionaries are another, and the mechanical appliances of the rhetorician designed to give a picture of a present which does not exist and of a future which no man can predict are as unreal and short-lived as the steam or canvas clouds, the angels suspended on wires and the artificial lights of the stage. They pass with the moment of effect and are shabby and tawdry in the daylight. Let us at least be real. Washington's entire honesty of mind and his fearless look into the face of all facts are qualities which can never go out of fashion and which we should all do well to imitate.

Ideals have been thrust upon us as an argument for the league until the healthy mind which rejects cant revolts from them. Are ideals confined to this deformed experiment upon a noble purpose, tainted, as it is, with bargains and tied to a peace treaty which might have been disposed of long ago to the great benefit of the world if it had not been compelled to carry this rider on its back? 'Post equitem sedet atra cura,' Horace tells us, but no blacker care ever sat behind any rider than we shall find in this covenant of doubtful and disputed interpretation as it now perches upon the treaty of peace.

No doubt many excellent and patriotic people see a coming fulfillment of noble ideals in the words 'league for peace.' We all respect and share these aspirations and desires, but some of us see no hope, but rather defeat, for them in this murky covenant. For we, too, have our ideals, even if we differ from those who have tried to establish a monopoly of idealism. Our first ideal is our country, and we see her in the future, as in the past, giving service to all her people and to the world. Our ideal of the future is that she should continue to render that service of her own free will. She has great problems of her own to solve, very grim and perilous problems, and a right solution, if we can attain to it, would largely benefit mankind. We would have our country strong to resist a peril from the West, as she has flung back the German menace from the East. We would not have our politics distracted and embittered by the dissensions of other lands. We would not have our country's vigor exhausted or her moral force abated, by everlasting meddling and muddling in every quarrel, great and small, which afflicts the world. Our ideal is to make her ever stronger and better and finer, because in that way alone, as we believe, can she be of the greatest service to the world's peace and to the welfare of mankind.

## Further Resources

### BOOKS

Garraty, John A. *Henry Cabot Lodge: A Biography.* New York: Knopf, 1953.

Lederer, Ivo J. *The Legacy of the Great War: Peacemaking, 1919.* Boston: Houghton Mifflin, 1998.

Link, Arthur. *Wilson: The Struggle for Neutrality.* Princeton, N.J.: Princeton University Press, 1960.

### PERIODICALS

Cooper, John Milton. "Progressivism and American Foreign Policy: A Reconsideration." *Mid-America* 51, October 1968, 260–277.

Garraty, John A. "Spoiled Child of American Politics." *American Heritage* 6, August 1955, 55–59.

### WEBSITES

Library of Congress. "Today in History: Henry Cabot Lodge." Available online at http://memory.loc.gov/ammem/today /may12.html; website home page: http://memory.loc.gov/ (accessed January 19, 2003).

# "Statement by Emma Goldman at the Federal Hearing in Re Deportation"

Statement

**By:** Emma Goldman

**Date:** October 27, 1919

**Source:** Goldman, Emma. "Statement by Emma Goldman at the Federal Hearing in Re Deportation." United States National Archives, Record Group 165. Reproduced in the Emma Goldman Papers. Available online at http://sunsite.berkeley .edu/Goldman/Exhibition/plea.html; website home page: http://www.sunsite.berkeley.edu (accessed January 20, 2003).

**About the Author:** Emma Goldman (1869–1940) was born in the poor Jewish ghetto in Kovno, Russia. In 1889, she moved to New York City and joined the anarchist movement, which rejected the authority of the state, church, and family and believed that morality was relative. Goldman also advocated free speech, free love, birth control, and unionism. She died in exile in Canada but was buried in Chicago next to the Haymarket anarchists whose deaths led her to anarchism. ∎

## Introduction

A young J. Edgar Hoover of the Federal Bureau of Investigation once called Emma Goldman one of the most dangerous women in America. In 1892, she assisted her lifelong friend Alexander Berkman in the attempted assassination of the industrialist Henry Clay Frick. Frick was responsible for crushing the 24,000-member ironworkers union during the Homestead Strike in Pittsburgh, Pennsylvania. Goldman hoped that the death of one of the nation's leading capitalists would inspire the working class to rise up and overthrow the political system. In 1901, she was implicated and temporarily jailed in connection with the assassination of President William McKinley (served 1897–1901) by anarchist Leon Czolgosz. Goldman was later jailed in 1916, 1918, 1919, and 1921 on allegations ranging from inciting to riot to opposing World War I (1914–1918).

In 1902, Goldman organized the nation's first Free Speech League, a precursor to the American Civil Liberties Union (ACLU). In March 1906, she founded the magazine *Mother Earth,* a forum for socialists, anarchists, and liberal thinkers to promote birth control, eugenics, the "free motherhood movement," and other progressive causes. In 1917, in response to the government's military preparation for World War I, the magazine focused almost solely on antiwar agitation. Particularly disturbing to Goldman was President Woodrow Wilson's (served 1913–1921) support for the military draft. As an anarchist who believed that everyone must follow his or her individual conscience, she objected to government-imposed mandatory conscription. In May 1917, she organized the No-Conscription League to encourage conscientious objectors to resist the draft. Within four weeks, the league had distributed 100,000 anticonscription pamphlets to youths across the country. In June, the U.S. attorney general ordered a raid on the office of *Mother Earth* and the arrest of Goldman and Berkman. After deliberating for just thirty-nine minutes, a jury found them guilty of conspiring to prevent the draft and advocating violence. The two were sentenced to two years in federal prison. After an unsuccessful appeal to the U.S. Supreme Court, Goldman began serving her term at the Missouri State Penitentiary. Also in 1917, the government ruled that because of its political content, *Mother Earth* was unmailable and ordered all issues to be completely destroyed.

In 1919, the nation was wracked with labor protest, as four out of every five workers went on strike. As anarchist pamphlets threatened a violent overthrow of American democracy, over two dozen handmade bombs were mailed to financier J.P. Morgan, John D. Rockefeller of Standard Oil, and other capitalist enemies of the radicals. Fortunately, the bombs did not detonate because the packages were held by New York postal officials for insufficient postage. However, six bombs did explode in Pittsburgh, one blew off the hands of a maid who worked for a U.S. senator, and another exploded outside the home of U.S. Attorney General A. Mitchell Palmer.

## Significance

Believing that foreign radicals were behind domestic terrorism, Palmer sought to locate and deport them. Because of her radical associations, Goldman was among the first to be deported. With still a month to serve in prison, Palmer had her rearrested and stripped of her naturalized citizenship. The so-called Palmer Raids followed Goldman's rearrest. For the next four months, thousands of presumed communists and anarchists were arrested, though the majority were released for lack of evidence. On December 21, 1919, however, Goldman and 249 other radicals left Ellis Island onboard the SS *Buford,* dubbed the "Red Ark," bound for the Soviet Union. Standing guard were 250 armed soldiers. This display of force was intended to send a message to remaining anarchists that they were enemies of the state.

## Primary Source

"Statement by Emma Goldman at the Federal Hearing in Re Deportation"

**SYNOPSIS:** On October 27, 1919, in a New York federal hearing concerning her deportation to the Soviet Union, Emma Goldman dismissed the "star chamber" proceedings, comparing them to tactics used in czarist Russia. Her principal complaints against American democracy were its use of the

Alien Act of 1918 to suppress free speech and the government's alliance with powerful capitalists whose aim was to crush labor.

At the very outset of this hearing I wish to register my protest against these star chamber proceedings, whose very spirit is nothing less than a revival of the ancient days of the Spanish Inquisition or the more recently defunct Third Degree system of Czarist Russia.

This star chamber hearing is, furthermore, a denial of the insistent claim on the part of the Government that in this country we have free speech and a free press, and that every offender against the law—even the lowliest of men—is entitled to his day in open court, and to be heard and judged by a jury of his peers.

If the present proceedings are for the purpose of proving some alleged offense committed by me, some evil or anti-social act, then I protest against the secrecy and third degree methods of this so-called "trial." But if I am not charged with any specific offense or act, if—as I have reason to believe—this is purely an inquiry into my social and political opinions, then I protest still more vigorously against these proceedings, as utterly tyrannical and diametrically opposed to the fundamental guarantees of a true democracy.

Every human being is entitled to hold any opinion that appeals to her or him without making herself or himself liable to persecution. Ever since I have been in this country—and I have lived here practically all my life—it has been dinned into my ears that under the institutions of this alleged Democracy one is entirely free to think and feel as he pleases. What becomes of this sacred guarantee of freedom of thought and conscience when persons are being persecuted and driven out for the very motives and purposes for which the pioneers who built up this country laid down their lives?

And what is the object of this star chamber proceeding, that is admittedly based on the so-called Anti-Anarchist law? Is not the only purpose of this law, and of the deportations en masse, to suppress every symptom of popular discontent now manifesting itself through this country, as well as in all the European lands? It requires no great prophetic gift to foresee that this new Governmental policy of deportation is but the first step towards the introduction into this country of the old Russian system of exile for the high treason of entertaining new ideas of social life and industrial reconstruction. Today so-called aliens are deported, tomorrow native Americans will be banished. Already some patrioteers are suggesting that native American sons to whom Democracy is not a sham but a sacred ideal should be exiled. To be sure, America does not yet possess a suitable place like Siberia to which her exiled sons might be sent, but since she has begun to acquire colonial possessions, in contradiction of the principles she stood for over a century, it will not be difficult to find an American Siberia once the precedent of banishment is established.

The Anti-Anarchist law confuses the most varied social philosophies and isms in order to cover with the same blanket, so to speak, every element of social protest, so that under the guise of this single law, striking steel workers, railroad men, or any other class of workers, may be corralled wholesale and the most active of the strikers hurried out of the country, in order to serve the interests of our industrial kings.

Collective bargaining for the workers is now an admitted right, recognized by the highest officials of the land and accepted by the most reactionary elements. Yet when the steel workers of this country, after a quarter of a century of desperate struggle for the right to bargain collectively, have mustered enough spirit and cohesion to enter into a struggle with the steel barons for that fundamental right, the entire machinery of government, State and Federal, is put in operation to crush that spirit and to undermine the chance of establishing humane conditions in the industry where conditions have been worse than those that existed under the most brutal feudalism. The workers in the steel industry have expressed no particular social philosophy. They are certainly not on strike to "overthrow the government by a force or violence," yet the Anti-Anarchist law is used as a means to reach out for these simple, hard-driven and hard-pressed human beings, who have endangered life and limb to build up this devouring monster—the Steel Trust. A reign of terror has been established in the strike region. American Cossacks, known as the State Constabulary, ride over men, women and children; deputies of the Department of Justice break into the strikers' homes, violating the sacred Anglo-Saxon tradition that a man's home is his castle and may not be entered except by due warrant of law; and to add the finishing touch to this picture of American "freedom," the Immigration authorities, the men of your department, take the strikers off secretly and order them deported by such proceedings as I am being subjected to today, without having committed even the slightest offense against American institutions,

Emma Goldman and Alexander Berkman—pictured here during their 1917 trial—were convicted of conspiracy to obstruct the draft and sentenced to two years in prison. Both were deported to Russia in December 1919. **NATIONAL ARCHIVES AND RECORDS ADMINISTRATION.**

save the one that is the greatest crime today—the right of the workers to life, liberty and the pursuit of happiness—a right that was made in America, and not imported by these hated aliens.

A commission, appointed by your department, finds that eighty per cent of the wealth in this country is produced by these aliens themselves or the sons of these aliens. In return for this, they are hounded and persecuted as criminals and enemies.

Under the mask of the same Anti-Anarchist law every criticism of a corrupt administration, every attack on Governmental abuse, every manifestation of sympathy with the struggle of another country in the pangs of a new birth—in short, every free expression of untrammeled thought may be suppressed utterly, without even the semblance of an unprejudiced hearing or a fair trial. It is for these reasons, chiefly, that I strenuously protest against this despotic law and its star chamber methods of procedure. I protest

against the whole spirit underlying it—the spirit of an irresponsible hysteria, the result of the terrible war and of the evil tendencies of bigotry and persecution and violence which are the epilogue of five years of bloodshed.

Under these circumstances it becomes evident that the real purpose of all of these repressive measures—chief among them the Anti-Anarchist law—is to support the capitalist status quo in the United States. Vain is the pretence that the safety of the country or the well-being of the American people demands these drastic Prussian methods. Nay, indeed, the people can only profit by a free discussion of the new ideas now germinating in the minds of thinking men and women in society. The free expression of the hopes and aspirations of a people is the greatest and only safety in a sane society. In truth, it is such free expression and discussion alone that can point the most beneficial path for human progress and development. But the object of deportations and of the Anti-Anarchist law, as of all similar repressive measures, is the very opposite. It is to stifle the voice of the people, to muzzle every aspiration of labor. That is the real and terrible menace of the star chamber proceedings and of the tendency of exiling and banishing everyone who does not fit into the scheme of things our industrial lords are so eager to perpetuate.

With all the power and intensity of my being I protest against the conspiracy of imperialist capitalism against the life and the liberty of the American people.

## Further Resources

### BOOKS

Avrich, Paul. *Anarchist Portraits.* Princeton, N.J.: Princeton University Press, 1988.

Drinnon, Richard. *Rebel in Paradise: A Biography of Emma Goldman.* Chicago: University of Chicago Press, 1961.

Wexler, Alice. *Emma Goldman in Exile: From the Russian Revolution to the Spanish Civil War.* Boston: Beacon Press, 1989.

### PERIODICALS

Oz, Frank. "What Happened to Red Emma?" *Journal of American History* 83 (December 1996), 903–943.

Weisberger, Bernard A. "Terrorism Revisited." *American Heritage* 44 (November 1993), 25.

### WEBSITES

Berkeley Digital Library Sunsite. "Emma Goldman Papers." Available online at http://sunsite.berkeley.edu/Goldman (accessed January 20, 2003).

Center for the Historical Study of Women and Gender at the State University of New York at Binghamton. "Women and Social Movements in the United States, 1775–2000." Available online at http://womhist.binghamton.edu/index.html (accessed January 20, 2003).

# *Volstead Act of 1919*
## Law

**By:** Andrew Volstead

**Date:** October 28, 1919

**Source:** Volstead, Andrew. *Volstead Act of 1919.* U.S. House. 66th Cong., 1st sess., H.R. 6810.U.S. Statutes at Large 41 (1919): 305–323. Available online at "Documents of American History II." http://tucnak.fsv.cuni.cz/~calda/Documents/1920s/Volstead.html; website home page: http://www.tucnak.fsv.cuni.cz (accessed January 19, 2003).

**About the Author:** Andrew Volsted (1860–1947) was a second-generation Norwegian American from Minnesota. In 1903, the Republican was elected to Congress for the first of ten terms. On May 19, 1919, as chairman of the House Judiciary Committee, he sponsored the National Prohibition Act—more commonly known as the Volstead Act—prohibit-

ing the manufacture, transportation, or sale of intoxicating beverages. ■

## Introduction

Public concern over alcohol consumption is almost as old as the country itself. In the early years of the Republic, the consumption of whiskey, rum, and hard cider, which generally were 80 proof, or 40 percent alcohol, was widespread. The annual per capita consumption of pure alcohol by the drinking-age population was 7.1 gallons. This figure does not take into account that many adult men did not drink and that women, children, and slaves did not consume their per capita share. In 1826, the American Temperance Society was established, and in a decade the organization grew to more than 200,000 members. Alcohol consumption fell considerably as the organization pressured stores not to sell "demon rum" and convinced municipalities to issue fewer tavern licenses.

In 1840, a Maine businessman named Neal Dow took the prohibition movement to the next level. Attributing family violence and poverty to excessive drinking, Dow successfully lobbied the legislature to prohibit the manufacture and sale of intoxicating alcohol. In 1851, the "Maine Law" had been enacted in thirteen of the thirty-one states. In 1869, the Prohibition Party was organized in Michigan. The party was concerned with the phenomenal growth of the liquor business, the Whiskey Ring frauds of President Ulysses Grant's (served 1869–1877) administration, and the belief that neither the Democratic nor Republican party would pass and strictly enforce prohibition. In 1884, the Prohibitionist candidate drew enough support from Republican presidential nominee James G. Blaine in New York to ensure that Democrat Grover Cleveland won the state's electoral votes and ultimately the national election. In 1892, the party reached its peak when its presidential nominee received 270,000 votes, or 2.5 percent of the total.

The Prohibition Party had the longstanding support of the National Woman's Christian Temperance Union (NWCTU), founded in 1874 in Cleveland, Ohio. At this time, Americans spent over a billion dollars annually on alcoholic beverages, more than on meat and public education. Frustrated by their inability to vote, these middle-class Protestant women nevertheless flexed their political muscles. The NWCTU urged women to combat drunkenness though prayer, hymn singing, petitions, and mass marches on saloons. Both the Prohibition Party and the NWCTU supported the National Anti-Saloon League (ASL), founded in Washington, D.C., in 1895. The interdenominational Protestant church-based group sought to ban alcoholic beverages on the county level by campaigning for "dry" Republicans and Democrats who supported its cause. In 1913, the ASL changed its focus to national prohibition. By 1916, twenty-one states had banned saloons, and congressional dry

H. R. 6810.

## Sixty-sixth Congress of the United States of America;

### At the First Session,

Begun and held at the City of Washington on Monday, the nineteenth day of May, one thousand nine hundred and nineteen.

### AN ACT

To prohibit intoxicating beverages, and to regulate the manufacture, production, use, and sale of high-proof spirits for other than beverage purposes, and to insure an ample supply of alcohol and promote its use in scientific research and in the development of fuel, dye, and other lawful industries.

*Be it enacted by the Senate and House of Representatives of the United States of America in Congress assembled,* That the short title of this Act shall be the "National Prohibition Act."

#### TITLE I.

##### TO PROVIDE FOR THE ENFORCEMENT OF WAR PROHIBITION.

The term "War Prohibition Act" used in this Act shall mean the provisions of any Act or Acts prohibiting the sale and manufacture of intoxicating liquors until the conclusion of the present war and thereafter until the termination of demobilization, the date of which shall be determined and proclaimed by the President of the United States. The words "beer, wine, or other intoxicating malt or vinous liquors" in the War Prohibition Act shall be hereafter construed to mean any such beverages which contain one-half of 1 per centum or more of alcohol by volume: *Provided,* That the foregoing definition shall not extend to dealcoholized wine nor to any beverage or liquid produced by the process by which beer, ale, porter or wine is produced, if it contains less than one-half of 1 per centum of alcohol by volume, and is made as prescribed in section 37 of Title II of this Act, and is otherwise denominated than as beer, ale, or porter, and is contained and sold in, or from, such sealed and labeled bottles, casks, or containers as the commissioner may by regulation prescribe.

## Primary Source

### Volstead Act of 1919

**SYNOPSIS:** One distinctive feature of the National Prohibition Act was that it did not go into effect for one year in order to protect the liquor industry. Nevertheless, the act ruined the liquor industry, which was the seventh largest industry in the nation. Only the Thirteenth Amendment, which ended slavery, had a greater impact on property rights. NATIONAL ARCHIVES AND RECORDS ADMINISTRATION.

United States officials pose outside of the Brownsville, Texas, Custom House after destroying a large quantity of illegal liquor on December 20, 1920.
THE ROBERT RUNYON PHOTOGRAPH COLLECTION, IMAGE NUMBER 08690, COURTESY OF THE CENTER FOR AMERICAN HISTORY, THE UNIVERSITY OF TEXAS AT AUSTIN.

members outnumbered "wets" two to one. Along with the combined power of the Prohibitionist Party, the NWCTU, and the ASL, World War I (1914–1918) tipped the balance in favor of prohibition. Due to the increasing need for grain, Congress passed the Lever Act of 1917, which outlawed the use of grain in the manufacture of alcoholic beverages, primarily as a conservation measure. Further, because most of America's beer brewers were of German ancestry, prohibition was associated with patriotism.

## Significance

By 1917, state and local laws had combined to ban the sale and manufacture of alcohol across a major portion of the nation. Nevertheless, the prohibitionists rallied enough support for the states to ban alcohol nationally with the Eighteenth Amendment, which was ratified in early 1919. The Volstead Act was passed to implement and enforce the amendment. The new amendment, though, was nearly impossible to enforce, and illegal drinking was extensive. One of the consequences of prohibition was the rise of gangsterism. The increase in criminal behavior, along with a projected tax revenue boon from liquor sales

during the Great Depression, caused public opinion to shift, and prohibition was repealed in 1933.

## Further Resources

### BOOKS

Coffey, Thomas M. *The Long Thirst: Prohibition in America, 1920–1933.* New York: Norton, 1975.

Rorabaugh, W.J. *The Alcoholic Republic: An American Tradition.* Oxford, U.K.: Oxford University Press. 1981.

Timberlake, James H. *Prohibition and the Progressive Movement: 1900–1920.* Cambridge, Mass.: Harvard University Press, 1963.

### PERIODICALS

Rudin, Max. "Democracy's Drink: What Beer Tells Us About America." *American Heritage,* July 2002, 28–38.

Thornton, Mark. "Alcohol Prohibition Was a Failure." *Policy Analysis,* July 1991, 1–16.

### WEBSITES

Shaffer Library of Drug Policy. "History of Alcohol Prohibition." Available online at http://www.druglibrary.org/schaffer/Library/studies/nc/nc2a.htm; website home page: http://www.druglibrary.org/schaffer/index.htm (accessed January 19, 2003).

# 6

# LAW AND JUSTICE

SCOTT A. MERRIMAN

*Entries are arranged in chronological order by date of primary source. For entries with one primary source, the entry title is the same as the primary source title. Entries with more than one primary source have an overall entry title, followed by the titles of the primary sources.*

**CHRONOLOGY**

Important Events in Law and Justice,
1910–1919 . . . . . . . . . . . . . . . . . . . . . . . . . . . 278

**PRIMARY SOURCES**

*New York Worker's Compensation Act*
New York State Legislature, 1910 . . . . . . . . . 281

*Standard Oil Co. of New Jersey v. U.S.*
Edward D. White and John Marshall
Harlan, 1911 . . . . . . . . . . . . . . . . . . . . . . . . . 283

*Hoke v. U.S.*
Joseph McKenna, February 24, 1913 . . . . . . . . 287

*Weeks v. U.S.*
William R. Day, February 24, 1914 . . . . . . . . . 292

*Houston, East & West Texas Railway Co. v.
U.S.*
Charles Evans Hughes, June 8, 1914 . . . . . . . . 294

*Bunting v. Oregon*
Joseph McKenna, April 9, 1917 . . . . . . . . . . . 298

*Buchanan v. Warley*
William R. Day, November 5, 1917 . . . . . . . . . 301

*"Dissent During World War I: The Kate
O'Hare Trial: 1919"*
Kate Richards O'Hare and Martin J. Wade,
December 1917 . . . . . . . . . . . . . . . . . . . . . . 304

*Selective Draft Law Cases*
Edward D. White, January 7, 1918 . . . . . . . . . 310

The Lynching of Robert P. Prager
"German Is Lynched by an Illinois Mob";
"Cabinet Discusses Prager's Lynching";
"Prager Asked Mob to Wrap Body in
Flag"; "Tried for Prager Murder"; "The
Prager Case"
*New York Times, April 5–June 3, 1918* . . . . . . . 313

*Schenck v. U.S.*
Oliver Wendell Holmes Jr., March 3,
1919 . . . . . . . . . . . . . . . . . . . . . . . . . . . . . . . 316

*Debs v. U.S.*
Oliver Wendell Holmes Jr., March 10,
1919 . . . . . . . . . . . . . . . . . . . . . . . . . . . . . . . 319

*Abrams v. U.S.*
Oliver Wendell Holmes Jr., November
10, 1919 . . . . . . . . . . . . . . . . . . . . . . . . . . . . 322

# Important Events in Law and Justice, 1910–1919

## 1910

• On January 3, Supreme Court Justice Horace H. Lurton is sworn in.

• On March 28, David J. Brewer, associate justice of the Supreme Court, dies.

• On May 1, the National Association for the Advancement of Colored People (NAACP) is founded. Six months later it begins to publish the journal, *The Crisis,* under the editorship of W.E.B. Du Bois.

• On May 2, Charles Evans Hughes, former governor of New York, is nominated to the U.S. Supreme Court. He serves on the High Court until 1916 when he is chosen to be the Republican Party's presidential candidate.

• On October 1, an explosion destroys a portion of the *Los Angeles Times* building, killing twenty-one people. The publisher of the newspaper blames labor radicals who have been attempting to unionize the newspaper's employees. Union organizers James and John McNamara are arrested and charged with the crime.

• On October 10, Charles E. Hughes is sworn in as an associate justice of the Supreme Court.

• On November 20, William H. Moody, associate justice of the Supreme Court, retires.

• On December 10, Edward D. White, a member of the Confederate army during the Civil War, former senator from Louisiana, and a Supreme Court associate justice, is nominated by President William Howard Taft to be chief justice. He is sworn in on December 19.

• On December 12, Willis Van Devanter is nominated by President Taft to succeed former associate justice Edward White on the Supreme Court. His nomination is confirmed by the Senate on December15.

## 1911

• On January 3, the Supreme Court rules in *Bailey* v. *Alabama,* that the Thirteenth Amendment's prohibition of involuntary servitude was violated when the defendant, an African American, was sentenced to hard labor for breaking an employment contract.

• On January 3, Willis Van Devanter and Joseph R. Lamar are sworn in as associate justices of the Supreme Court.

• On January 18, Bill Miner robs the Southern Railroad Express of $3,500 near White Sulphur Springs, Georgia. The famous train robber is tracked down and at sixty-six years of age is sentenced for life to the Georgia State Penitentiary, where he dies in 1913.

• On January 24, Judge Kenesaw Mountain Landis begins an investigation of the beef trust in Chicago. The investigation was initiated by complaints of rising meat prices and the abusive business practices of the National Packing Company, among others.

• On March 25, a fire that lasts only half an hour traps 850 people in a New York City garment district factory. Fire and smoke kill 146 employees, mostly women.

• On April 11, the owners of the Triangle Shirtwaist Company are indicted on charges of manslaughter stemming from the deaths of 146 of their employees who were trapped in the company's factory by a raging fire.

• On May 1, in the case of *United States* v. *Grimaud,* the U.S. Supreme Court rules that the federal government, not the states, controls the nation's great forest preserves.

• On May 15, in the case of *Standard Oil Company of New Jersey* v. *United States,* the U.S. Supreme Court rules that Standard Oil violated the Sherman Antitrust Act and the company must be dissolved.

• On June 11, under pressure brought by the Justice Department, the directors of the American Tobacco Company, which controls 80 percent of the cigarette production in the nation, agree to divide their company into fourteen smaller and independent business entities.

• On August 22, a bill granting Arizona statehood is vetoed by President William Howard Taft because its proposed constitution permits the recall of judges by popular election, a measure the president considers a threat to the traditional independence of the judiciary. Arizona amends its constitution and is admitted to the Union on February 14, 1912.

• On October 14, John M. Harlan, Supreme Court associate justice since 1877, dies.

## 1912

• On March 18, Mahlon Pitney is sworn in as an associate justice of the Supreme Court.

• On March 14, the Department of Justice announces the beginning of an investigation into the merger of the Southern Pacific and Union Pacific railroads, triggered by the Union Pacific's purchase of 46 percent of the stock issued by its rival, the Southern Pacific.

• On July 15, gambler and police informant Herman "Beansie" Rosenthal is shot and killed by four assassins in New York City. New York City Police Lieutenant Charles Becker, head of a graft and kickback ring protecting gambling dens in Manhattan, is suspected of ordering the hit because Rosenthal refused to pay for police protection. The killers are quickly apprehended, tried, and sentenced to the electric chair. Becker is executed in Sing Sing prison on July 7, 1915.

• On October 14, Theodore Roosevelt, the Progressive Party's candidate for president, is shot in the chest while campaigning in Milwaukee, Wisconsin. The bullet is deflected by a manuscript the former president had placed in his coat pocket.

## 1913

• On September 4, Henry B. Brown, retired Supreme Court associate justice, dies. He served on the high court from 1890 to 1906.

## 1914

• On January 13, a bitter feud over airplane patents is settled by the U.S. Circuit Court of Appeals in favor of Wilbur and Orville Wright and against Glenn Curtiss, the brothers' chief competitor in the fledgling airplane industry.

• On January 20, Wisconsin's circuit court declares the state's marriage law, based on eugenic principles, unconstitutional.

• On February 13, the American Society of Composers, Authors, and Publishers (ASCAP) is organized to improve copyright laws and to protect its members from infringements upon their work.

• On February 24, the constitutionality of the Mann Act is upheld by the Supreme Court in the case of *Hoke* v. *United States*.

• On February 24, the Supreme Court finds that entering and searching a person's home without a search warrant violates the Fourth Amendment, in *Weeks* v. *United States*.

• On April 20, National Guardsmen and security forces employed by coal-mining companies shoot into the tents of mine workers near Ludlow, Colorado, killing an estimated twenty people, including women and children. The workers began striking in September 1913. Federal troops are eventually required to restore order.

• On July 12, Justice Horace H. Lurton dies.

• On August 19, James Clark McReynolds is nominated to succeed Lurton on the Supreme Court. McReynolds previously served as an assistant attorney general in charge of the Justice Department's antitrust division and was serving as Attorney General under President Wilson at the time of his appointment.

• On October 12, James C. McReynolds is sworn in as an associate justice of the Supreme Court.

## 1915

• On January 25, in the case of *Coppage* v. *Kansas* the Supreme Court rules unconstitutional a Kansas state law forbidding employers from requiring that employees be nonunion.

• On May 15, the U.S. Supreme Court finds unconstitutional laws in the states of Oklahoma and Maryland that exempt some voters from the states' literacy requirements. The law was intended to permit whites to vote while disenfranchising African Americans.

• On July 2, a bomb destroys the U.S. Senate's reception room. It was placed there by Erich Muenter, a German instructor at Cornell University. The following day Muenter

shoots and wounds J. Pierpont Morgan in New York. Morgan's company represents the British government in the negotiation of wartime contracts. Muenter commits suicide on July 6.

• On July 13, New York State's workmen's compensation law is ruled valid by the New York Court of Appeals. The law had become effective in May.

• On July 15, Secret Service agents discover evidence of German espionage in the United States. Agents come into possession of a portfolio belonging to Dr. Heinrich F. Albert, which reveals Albert is the head of a German propaganda and espionage ring and implicates several German Americans, members of the German Embassy staff, and officials of a German American steamship line.

• On August 17, Leo M. Frank, age twenty-nine, is lynched for the April 26, 1913, murder of Mary Phagan, age thirteen, in Atlanta, Georgia. Frank was charged with the murder after the girl's body was found on the factory premises where he was superintendent. After a sensational trial full of racial and anti-Semitic overtones, an enraged mob took Frank from a jail in Marietta, Georgia, and hanged him.

• On November 19, Joe Hill, a composer of radical and labor songs and an organizer for the Industrial Workers of the World, is hanged for a murder to which there are no witnesses and for which there is no motive. President Woodrow Wilson, besieged by pleas for clemency, attempts unsuccessfully to save Hill from execution.

## 1916

• Margaret Sanger, a well-known advocate of birth control, is charged with violating New York City's obscenity laws through the distribution of her book, *Family Limitation* (1914), and is found guilty for actions the court finds "contrary not only to the law of the state, but to the law of God."

• On January 2, Joseph R. Lamar, associate justice of the Supreme Court, dies.

• On January 24, in the case of *Brushaber* v. *Union Pacific Railroad Company* the U.S. Supreme Court rules that the new federal income tax is constitutional.

• On January 28, Louis D. Brandeis is nominated to the Supreme Court to succeed Justice Lamar. The Senate confirms his appointment on June 1 after considerable debate.

• On June 5, Louis D. Brandeis is sworn in as an associate justice of the Supreme Court.

• On June 10, Charles E. Hughes resigns as an associate justice of the Supreme Court in order to run for president. He makes his way back to the Supreme Court when President Hoover nominated him as chief justice in 1930.

• On July 16, John H. Clarke is nominated by President Wilson to become an associate justice of the Supreme Court. Clarke resigns from the Supreme Court in 1922 to promote American participation in the League of Nations.

• On July 22, a bombing in San Francisco during a parade kills ten people and wounds forty. Labor organizer Tom Mooney is sentenced to hang, and his alleged co-conspirator, Warren K. Billings, is sentenced to life imprisonment. President

Wilson commutes Mooney's sentence to life imprisonment in 1918.

• On October 9, John H. Clarke, associate justice of the Supreme Court, is sworn in.

## 1917

• An antiprostitution drive in San Francisco attracts huge crowds to public meetings held throughout the month of January. Within weeks the police close nearly two hundred houses of prostitution.

• On April 9, the Supreme Court upholds an Oregon state law that prescribes a ten-hour workday for men and women, and requires time and a half for up to three hours of overtime a day. The court rules in *Bunting* v. *Oregon* that the law does not interfere with liberty of contract protected by the Fourteenth Amendment.

• On July 2, William H. Moody, former associate justice on the Supreme Court, dies. Moody had served on the high court from 1906 until 1910, when ill health forced his retirement.

• On August 28, ten suffragist picketers are arrested in front of the White House.

• On September 5, federal agents, assisted by local police, raid the offices of the Industrial Workers of the World in twenty-four cities and seize the union's records while arresting ten of its leaders, including William Haywood, the organizer of the textile workers' strike in Lawrence, Massachusetts.

## 1918

• On January 7, the U.S. Supreme Court rules in the case of *Arver* v. *United States* that wartime conscription is constitutionally valid.

• On June 3, the Federal Child Labor Law of 1916 is declared unconstitutional by the Supreme Court in the case of *Hammer* v. *Dagenhart* on the ground that it violates rights reserved to the states under the Tenth Amendment. The Court also holds that Congress, in blocking interstate shipments of goods made by underage children, exceeded its power to regulate interstate commerce.

• On July 25, Annette Adams begins her term in California as the first woman in the United States to serve as a district attorney.

• On September 14, Eugene V. Debs, four times the Socialist candidate for the presidency, is sentenced to ten years' imprisonment for violating the Espionage Act of 1917. Debs

was arrested on June 30, 1918 for making allegedly seditious statements. His sentence is commuted in 1921.

## 1919

• On March 3, in *Schenck* v. *United States,* the Supreme Court upholds the conviction of Schenck under the Espionage Act for speech critical of the war. The court reasons that utterances permissible in peacetime can be punished during times of war.

• On March 10, the conviction of Eugene V. Debs, Socialist Party leader and presidential candidate, for violating the Espionage Act is upheld by the Supreme Court.

• On June 2, an anarchist places a bomb on the front steps of the home of Attorney General A. Mitchell Palmer in Washington, D.C., but the bomb explodes prematurely, killing the anarchist. Palmer then supports "red raids," which result in the arrests of thousands of dissenters across the country and the deportation of some five hundred aliens.

• From July 28 to July 30, a seventeen-year-old African American youth swims into waters reserved for whites on Chicago's South Side. Whites allegedly throw stones, and the boy drowns. The incident, hot weather, and racial tensions from African Americans moving into traditionally white neighborhoods, leads to violence that leaves twenty-two African Americans and fourteen whites dead, and more than five hundred others wounded. Two days later, with assistance of the state militia, peace is restored.

• On August 14, the *Chicago Tribune,* after a much-reported trial, is found to have libeled Henry Ford when it called him an anarchist.

• On September 9, the Boston City Police go on strike, with 1,117 out of 1,544 patrolmen refusing to report to work. The strike results in widespread looting, which forces Governor Calvin Coolidge to deploy the state's National Guard until police replacements can be hired. Coolidge's action catapults him into the national limelight.

• On October 10, in *Abrams* v. *U.S.* the Supreme Court finds that amendments to the Espionage Act are constitutional, and thereby upholds convictions of persons charged with inciting resistance to the war effort and urging curtailment of production of essential war materials.

• On November 11, members of the Industrial Workers of the World in Idaho fight back when their union hall is attacked by a mob that includes American Legionnaires and members of the Citizen's Protective League. Three legionnaires are killed, and the body of one union member is found hanging from a tree. Many of the union's members are arrested and jailed.

cal, labor unions had fallen into some disrepute in the late nineteenth century, but by 1910, this perception had begun to fade. The Progressive movement in American politics was aiming the spotlight on poor labor conditions, and many states decided to act by passing worker's compensation acts. These laws ended the fellow servant rule and offered the worker guaranteed compensation for injuries without the need to sue the employer.

## New York Worker's Compensation Act

Law

**By:** New York State Legislature

**Date:** 1910

**Source:** New York State Legislature. *New York Worker's Compensation Act* (1910). Reprinted in Hall, Kermit, William M. Wiecek, and Paul Finkelman. *American Legal History: Cases and Materials,* 2nd ed. New York: Oxford University Press, 1996, 359–361.

**About the Organization:** New York formed its state legislature in 1777 but has frequently reshaped it, with changes occurring as recently as 1982. The legislature currently has 211 members, 150 in the Assembly and 61 in the Senate. ■

### Introduction

Until the twentieth century, the American workplace was largely unregulated. Growth of the factory system, combined with an American belief in freedom, produced an atmosphere ripe for corporate abuse of workers in nineteenth-century factories. Legal theorists argued that "liberty of contract" gave both workers and companies freedom to agree to wages and working conditions, such as the length of the work week. This view, however, assumed equal bargaining power between the worker and the company, which did not exist in practice. The main recourse for workers injured on the job was the courts and the legislatures. In the courts, a number of legal doctrines prevented workers from receiving compensation for on-the-job injuries, including the "fellow servant rule," which held that if an accident was caused by a fellow workman, the workman was the one to be sued, not the employer. Another doctrine was "assumption of risk," meaning that a worker assumed the risks inherent in any job and so could not sue if injured. The legislatures, like the courts, offered injured workers little relief, for they were generally sympathetic to employers.

By the beginning of the twentieth century, many states had banned child labor and had limited the number of hours women could be required to work. In a few professions, some states had limited hours for both men and women. Because they were often perceived as radi-

### Significance

Worker's compensation acts were advantageous to workers, but many employers welcomed them as well. For the employer, they provided predictability. Employers paid into a general fund from which awards were paid, so they did not have to run the risk of paying a ruinous award in the event an employee sued and won. Under the *New York Worker's Compensation Act,* as under laws, employers paid a certain amount to the state, an expense they could plan into their budgets. Additionally, employees surrendered the right to sue corporations, and the cap on liability was low. Payments to workers, regardless of the extent of their injury or the event of death, could continue only for eight years, and the amount paid could not exceed ten dollars a week, a relatively small sum even in the early twentieth century.

Some railroad workers made up to a thousand dollars a year, or twenty dollars a week, which was twice what was recoverable. These systems were sometimes challenged, and the New York act was struck down in *Ives v. South Buffalo Railway Co.* (1911), but a new worker's compensation law was soon adopted. The system has been improved in years since. Worker's compensation awards have been supplemented by Social Security, which allows most employees who have worked five years or more to receive disability payments when totally disabled. Worker's compensation laws in the early twentieth century thus laid the groundwork for more recent laws.

### Primary Source

*New York Worker's Compensation Act* [excerpt]

**SYNOPSIS:** The act only applies to dangerous labor activities. It holds the employer liable when the risk is inherent in the employment or when the employer is required to exercise "due care." It defines the compensation, limiting it to 1,200 days' pay if the worker was married and died; if the worker was disabled, the act provided payment of 50 percent of his wages for up to eight years, but no more than $10 a week.

AN ACT to amend the labor law, in relation to workmen's compensation in certain dangerous employments.

Memorial parade for employees who perished in the Triangle Shirtwaist fire, April 5, 1911. **THE LIBRARY OF CONGRESS.**

Application of article. This article shall apply only to workmen engaged in manual or mechanical labor in the following employments, each of which is hereby determined to be especially dangerous, in which from the nature, conditions or means of prosecution of the work therein, extraordinary risks to the life and limb of workmen engaged therein are inherent, necessary or substantially unavoidable, and as to each of which employments it is deemed necessary to establish a new system of compensation for accidents to workmen. . . .

[The statute then itemized eight categories of dangerous labor, including demolition, blasting, tunneling, electrical construction, and railroad operation.]

Sec. 217. Basis of liability. If, in the course of any of the employments above described, personal injury by accident arising out of and in the course of the employment after this article takes effect is caused to any workman employed therein, in whole or in part, or the damage or injury caused thereby is in whole or in part contributed to by

a. A necessary risk or danger of the employment or one inherent in the nature thereof; or

b. Failure of the employer of such workman or any of his or its officers, agents or employees

to exercise due care, or to comply with any law affecting such employment; then such employer shall . . . be liable to pay compensation at the rates set out in section two hundred and nineteen-a of this title; provided that the employer shall not be liable in respect of any injury which does not disable the workman for a period of at least two weeks from earning full wages at the work at which he was employed, and provided that the employer shall not be liable in respect of any injury to the workman which is caused in whole or in part by the serious and willful misconduct of the workman. . . .

Sec. 219-a. Scale of compensation. The amount of compensation shall be in case death results from injury:

a. If the workman leaves a widow or next of kin at the time of his death wholly dependent on his earnings, a sum equal to twelve hundred times the daily earnings of such workman at the rate at which he was being paid by such employer at the time of the injury subject as hereinafter provided, and in no event more than three thousand dollars. Any weekly pay-

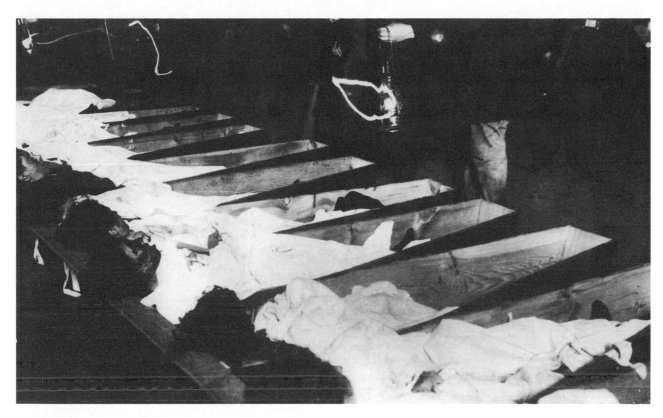

The Triangle Shirtwaist fire, which killed 146 people, demonstrated the need for worker's compensation. © **CORBIS. REPRODUCED BY PERMISSION.**

ments made under this article shall be deducted in ascertaining such amount. . . .

■ ■ ■

2. Where total or partial incapacity for work at any gainful employment results to the workman from the injury, a weekly payment commencing at the end of the second week after the injury and continuing during such incapacity . . . equal to fifty per centum of his average weekly earnings when at work on full time during the preceding year during which he shall have been in the employment of the same employer[.] . . .

In no event shall any compensation paid under this article exceed the damage suffered, nor shall any weekly payment payable under this article in any event exceed ten dollars a week or extend over more than eight years from the date of the accident.

### Further Resources

**BOOKS**

Horwitz, Morton J. *The Transformation of American Law, 1780–1860.* New York: Oxford University Press, 1992.

Karsten, Peter. *Heart Versus Head: Judge-Made Law in Nineteenth-Century America.* Chapel Hill, N.C.: University of North Carolina Press, 1997.

Novokov, Julie. *Constituting Workers, Protecting Women: Gender, Law, and Labor in the Progressive Era and New Deal Years.* Ann Arbor, Mich.: University of Michigan Press, 2001.

**WEBSITES**

Bonney, Doug. "A Brief and Incomplete Tour of U.S. Labor Law: Where We Are, How We Got Here, and Who Drove the Bus." Available online at http://www.kclabor.org/bonney623talk.htm; website home page: http://www.kclabor.org/index.html (accessed January 22, 2003).

Lause, Mark. "American Labor History: An Online Study Guide." Available online at http://www.geocities.com/CollegePark/Quad/6460/AmLabHist/; website home page: http://www.geocities.com (accessed January 22, 2003).

# Standard Oil Co. of New Jersey v. U.S.

**Supreme Court decision**

**By:** Edward D. White and John Marshall Harlan

**Date:** 1911

**Source:** White, Edward D., and John Marshall Harlan. *Standard Oil Co. of New Jersey v. U.S.,* 221 U.S. 1 (1910). Available online at http://caselaw.lp.findlaw.com/scripts

/getcase.pl?court=us&vol=221&invol=1; website home page: http://caselaw.lp.findlaw.com (accessed May 15, 2003).

**About the Authors:** Edward D. White (1845–1921) fought in the Confederate army in the Civil War. President Grover Cleveland appointed him associate justice of the U.S. Supreme Court in 1894, and President William Howard Taft elevated him to chief justice in 1911.

John Marshall Harlan (1833–1911) was born in Kentucky and began his career as a lawyer and politician. He served on the Supreme Court from 1877 to 1911 and was famous for his dissenting opinions, including his lone dissent in *Plessy v. Ferguson,* which established the "separate but equal" racial segregation doctrine. ∎

## Introduction

During the Industrial Revolution in the United States in the late 1800s, many large corporations grew into monopolies and many captains of industry were monopolists. Monopolies drove many small businesses out of the marketplace, and calls for reform were widespread. States were faced with two obstacles when they tried to regulate monopolies. First, many state legislators were heavily influenced by industrialists, who had the money to defeat legislation they did not like. Second, many of these industries were involved in interstate commerce, so state attempts to control them were struck down by the courts as violating the federal government's exclusive right to

John D. Rockefeller, head of the Standard Oil Company. **ARCHIVE PHOTOS. INC.**

regulate interstate commerce. To address the jurisdictional question, Congress passed the 1890 *Sherman Anti-Trust Act* to prohibit monopolies. The act was not self-executing, though, and the federal government had to bring suit against a monopolist. The first major suit brought under the act dealt with the sugar trust, which controlled 94 percent of sugar manufacturing in the United States. In 1895, the case reached the Supreme Court, which held that the Sherman Act did not apply to the sugar trust or any other trust that was involved only in manufacturing, which the Court did not regard as "commerce."

President Theodore Roosevelt (served 1901–1909) promised to break up trusts and had success against United States Steel and the Northern Securities Company, which controlled most of the railroad traffic in the Northwest. His successor, William Howard Taft (served 1909–1913), took on International Harvester and Standard Oil—one of the world's largest companies, and, under John D. Rockefeller, one of the most ruthless. Muckraking journalists such as Ida Tarbell had exposed Rockefeller's business practices, so Standard Oil became an important target for the Taft administration.

## Significance

This case had two major impacts. First, it broke up Standard Oil, creating a number of subsidiary oil companies, such as Standard Oil of Ohio. Second, the Court's ruling modified the ruling in the Northern Securities case by applying the Sherman Act only to "unreasonable" combinations. Through the remainder of the twentieth century, Congress and the courts continued to wrestle with the questions of what a monopoly is and when certain business practices constitute an unreasonable restraint of trade. To correct some of the weaknesses in the Sherman Act, Congress passed the Clayton Act and the Federal Trade Commission Act, both in 1914. The Clayton Act banned specific business practices, but only where they lessened competition. The Federal Trade Commission Act set up the Federal Trade Commission (FTC), which held hearings and issued rulings that defined unfair trade practices. President Franklin Roosevelt's (served 1933–1945) administration continued the FTC's policy of using administrative agencies to regulate competition. More recent court rulings have frequently reflected general beliefs about the role of the government in relation to business. During the 1960s, the Warren Court generally opposed any one business controlling more than a certain percentage of a given market. It tended to regard all business concentrations as suspect, seeing a need to protect the public. The Burger and Rehnquist Courts tended to apply the "rule of reason" articulated in *Standard Oil.* These Courts were more trusting of business (and more pro-business) and therefore allowed businesses more latitude. The dispute over what exactly constitutes a monopoly continued in the early twenty-first century as the government attempted to break up the Microsoft Corporation.

## Primary Source

*Standard Oil Co. of New Jersey v. U.S.* [excerpt]

**SYNOPSIS:** White argues that the exhaustive list of monopoly practices enumerated in the *Sherman Anti-Trust Act* merely stated that any type of monopoly could be regulated under the act. He goes on to note that common law and the act read as a whole indicate that only monopolies that "unreasonably" restrain trade are banned. In his dissent, Harlan notes that Congress had intended to ban all monopolies that restrain trade, not just "unreasonable" ones. In his view, the majority opinion was "judicial legislation," meaning that the Supreme Court was creating law.

Chief Justice White delivered the opinion of the Court. . . .

As to the 1st section, the words to be interpreted are: "Every contract, combination in the form of trust or otherwise, or conspiracy in restraint of trade or commerce . . . is hereby declared to be illegal." As there is no room for dispute that the statute was intended to formulate a rule for the regulation of interstate and foreign commerce, the question is, What was the rule which it adopted?

In view of the common law and the law in this country as to restraint of trade, which we have reviewed, and the illuminating effect which that history must have under the rule to which we have referred, we think it results: . . .

b. That in view of the many new forms of contracts and combinations which were being evolved from existing economic conditions, it was deemed essential by an all-embracing enumeration to make sure that no form of contract or combination by which an undue restraint of [221 U.S. 1, 60] interstate or foreign commerce was brought about could save such restraint from condemnation. The statute under this view evidenced the intent not to restrain the right to make and enforce contracts, whether resulting from combinations or otherwise, which did not unduly restrain interstate or foreign commerce, but to protect that commerce from being restrained by methods, whether old or new, which would constitute an interference—that is, an undue restraint. . . .

. . . And, of course, when the 2d section is thus harmonized with and made, as it was intended to be, the complement of the 1st, it becomes obvious that the criteria to be resorted to in any given case

John D. Rockefeller, "King of the World," was accused of having a monopoly over the oil industry. © **BETTMANN/CORBIS. REPRODUCED BY PERMISSION.**

for the purpose of ascertaining whether violations of the section have been committed is the rule of reason guided by the established law and by the plain duty to enforce the prohibitions of the act, and thus the public policy which its restrictions were obviously enacted to subserve. . . .

. . . The error involved lies in assuming the matter to be decided. This is true, because, as the acts which may come under the classes stated in the 1st section and the restraint of trade to which that section applies are not specifically enumerated or defined, it is obvious that judgment must in every case be called into play in order to determine whether a particular act is embraced within the statutory classes, and whether, if the act is within such classes, its nature or effect causes it to be a restraint of trade within the intendment of the act. To hold to the contrary would require the conclusion either that every contract, act, or combination of any kind or nature, whether it operated a restraint on trade or not, was within the statute, and thus the statute would be destructive of all right to contract or agree to combine in any respect whatever as to subjects embraced in interstate trade or commerce, or, if this conclusion were not reached, then the contention would require it to be held that, as the statute did not define the things to which it related, and excluded resort to the only means by which the acts to which it relates could be ascertained—the light of reason—the enforcement of the statute was impossible because of its uncertainty. The merely generic enumeration which the statute makes of the acts to which it refers, and the absence of any definition of restraint of trade as used in the statute, leaves room for but one conclusion, which is, that it was expressly designed not to unduly limit the application of the act by precise definition, but, while clearly fixing a standard, that is, by defining the ulterior boundaries which could not be transgressed with impunity, to leave it to be determined by the light of reason, guided by the principles of law and the duty to apply and enforce the public policy embodied in the statute, in every given case whether any particular act or contract was within the contemplation of the statute. . . .

Our conclusion is that the decree below was right and should be affirmed, except as to the minor matters concerning which we have indicated the decree should be modified. Our order will therefore be one of affirmance, with directions, however, to modify the decree in accordance with this opinion. The court below to retain jurisdiction to the extent necessary to compel compliance in every respect with its decree.

And it is so ordered.

Mr. Justice Harlan, concurring in part and dissenting in part:

A sense of duty constrains me to express the objections which I have to certain declarations in the opinion just delivered on behalf of the court.

I concur in holding that the Standard Oil Company of New Jersey and its subsidiary companies constitute a combination in restraint of interstate commerce, and that they have attempted to monopolize and have monopolized parts of such commerce—all in violation of what is known as he anti-trust act of 1890. 26 Stat. at L. 209, chap. 647, U. S. Comp. Stat. 1901, p. 3200. The evidence in this case overwhelmingly sustained that view and led the circuit court, by its final decree, to order the dissolution of the New Jersey corporation and the discontinuance of the illegal combination between that corporation and its subsidiary companies.

In my judgment, the decree below should have been affirmed without qualification. But the court,

while affirming the decree, directs some modifications in respect of what it characterizes as "minor matters." It is to be apprehended that those modifications may prove to be mischievous. In saying this, I have particularly in view the statement in the opinion that "it does not necessarily follow because an illegal restraint of trade or an attempt to monopolize or a monopolization resulted from the combination and the transfer of the stocks of the subsidiary corporations to the New Jersey corporation that a like restraint of trade or attempt to monopolize or monopolization would necessarily arise from agreements between one or more of the subsidiary corporations after the transfer of the stock by the New Jersey corporation." Taking this language, in connection with other parts of the opinion, the subsidiary companies are thus, in effect, informed—unwisely, I think—that although the New Jersey corporation, being an illegal combination, must go out of existence, they may join in an agreement to restrain commerce among the states if such restraint be not "undue". . .

. . . It is now with much amplification of argument urged that the statute, in declaring illegal every combination in the form of trust or otherwise, or conspiracy, in restraint of trade or commerce, does not mean what the language used therein plainly imports, but that it only means to declare illegal any such contract which is in unreasonable restraint of trade, while leaving all others unaffected by the provisions of the act; that the common-law meaning of the term "contract in restraint of trade" includes only such contracts as are in unreasonable restraint of trade; and when that term is used in the Federal statute it is not intended to include all contracts in restraint of trade, but only those which are in unreasonable restraint thereof. . . . By the simple use of the term "contract in restraint of trade," all contracts of that nature, whether valid or otherwise would be included, and not alone that kind of contract which was invalid and unenforceable as being in unreasonable restraint of trade. When, therefore, the body of an act pronounces as illegal every contract or combination in restraint of trade or commerce among the several states, etc., the plain and ordinary meaning of such language is not limited to that kind of contract alone which is in unreasonable restraint of trade, but all contracts are included in such language, and no exception or limitation can be added without placing in the act that which has been omitted by Congress. . . . If only that kind of contract which is in unreasonable restraint of trade be within the meaning of the statute, and declared therein to be illegal, it is at once apparent that the subject of what is a reasonable rate is attended with great uncertainty. . . . To say, therefore, that the act excludes agreements which are not in unreasonable restraint of trade, and which tend simply to keep up reasonable rates for transportation, is substantially to leave the question of reasonableness to the companies themselves. . . . But assuming that agreements of this nature are not void at common law, and that the various cases cited by the learned courts below show it, the answer to the statement of their validity now is to be found in the terms of the statute under consideration. . . . The arguments which have been addressed to us against the inclusion of all contracts in restraint of trade, as provided for by the language of the act, have been based upon the alleged presumption that Congress notwithstanding the language of the act, could not have intended to embrace all contracts, but only such contracts as were in unreasonable restraint of trade. Under these circumstances we are, therefore, asked to hold that the act of Congress excepts contracts which are not in unreasonable restraint of trade, and which only keep rates up to a reasonable price, notwithstanding the language of the act makes no such exception. In other words, we are asked to read into the act by way of judicial legislation an exception that is not placed there by the lawmaking branch of the government, and this is to be done upon the theory that the . . . legislation is so clear that it cannot be supposed Congress intended the natural import of the language it used. This we cannot and ought not to do. . . .

. . . Is it to be supposed that any point escaped notice in those cases when we think of the sagacity of the justice who expressed the views of the court, or of the ability of the profound, astute lawyers who sought such an interpretation of the act as would compel the court to insert words in the statute which Congress had not put there, and the insertion of which words would amount to "judicial legislation?" Now this court is asked to do that which it has distinctly declared it could not and would not do, and has now done what it then said it could not constitutionally do. It has, by mere interpretation, modified the act of Congress, and deprived it of practical value as a defensive measure against the evils to be remedied. . . . In effect the court says that it will now, for the first time, bring the discussion under the "light of reason," and apply the "rule of reason" to the questions to be decided. I have the authority of this court for saying that such a course of proceeding on its part would be "judicial legislation". . .

. . . When Congress prohibited every contract, combination, or monopoly, in restraint of commerce, it prescribed a simple, definite rule that all could understand, and which could be easily applied by everyone wishing to obey the law, and not to conduct their business in violation of law. But now, it is to be feared, we are to have, in cases without number, the constantly recurring inquiry—difficult to solve by proof—whether the particular contract, combination, or trust involved in each case is or is not an "unreasonable" or "undue" restraint of trade. Congress, in effect, said that there should be no restraint of trade, in any form, and this court solemnly adjudged many years ago that Congress meant what it thus said in clear and explicit words, and that it could not add to the words of the act. But those who condemn the action of Congress are now, in effect, informed that the courts will allow such restraint of interstate commerce as are shown not to be unreasonable or undue. . . .

For the reasons stated, while concurring in the general affirmance of the decree of the Circuit Court, I dissent from that part of the judgment of this court which directs the modification of the decree of the Circuit Court, as well as from those parts of the opinion which, in effect, assert authority in this court to insert words in the antitrust act which Congress did not put there, and which, being inserted, Congress is made to declare, as part of the public policy of the country, what it has not chosen to declare.

## Further Resources

### BOOKS

Bringhurst, Bruce. *Antitrust and the Oil Monopoly: The Standard Oil Cases, 1890–1911*. Westport, Colo.: Greenwood, 1979.

Chernow, Ron. *Titan: The Life of John D. Rockefeller, Sr.* New York: Random House, 1998.

Klein, Henry H. *Rockefeller or God, Who Will Rule?* New York: Loder Appeal, 1938.

Nevins, Allan. *John D. Rockefeller: The Heroic Age of American Enterprise.* New York: Scribner's, 1941.

Tarbell, Ida M. *The History of the Standard Oil Company.* London: William Heineman, 1912.

# *Hoke v. U.S.*

### Supreme Court decision

**By:** Joseph McKenna

**Date:** February 24, 1913

**Source:** McKenna, Joseph. *Hoke v. U.S.*, 227 U.S. 308 (1913). Available online at http://caselaw.lp.findlaw.com

/cgi-bin/getcase.pl?court=US&vol=227&invol=308; website home page: http://caselaw.lp.findlaw.com (accessed January 22, 2003).

**About the Author:** Joseph McKenna (1843–1926) served as a representative from California to the U.S. House of Representatives and as judge for the Ninth Circuit Court of Appeals. In 1897, he served briefly as attorney general before President William McKinley (served 1897–1901) appointed him associate justice of the Supreme Court. He resigned from the Court in 1925. ■

## Introduction

Public morality has long been a concern in the United States. Soon after the Puritans landed in the New World, the first morality laws were passed and violators were prosecuted. The colonies, and later, the states—rather than the British Crown or the U.S. federal government—governed morality. In the 1800s, though, concern over morals permeated several federal acts. Much of the debate over immigration policy, for example, was rife with questions of "decency." In 1873, Congress passed the Comstock Act, which banned the sending through the mail of "obscene materials," including information about birth control and abortion. Indeed, many states passed acts banning the distribution of birth control material on moral grounds, and Connecticut made the use of contraceptives illegal.

Adding to this mix was the development of large cities, where prostitution thrived and police forces seemed unable or unwilling to cope with the problem. Around 1907, concern grew that women were being kidnapped, drugged, and forced into brothels. Though the fears were inflated, Congress responded to them with the Mann White Slave Traffic Act of 1910, which banned the transportation of women across state lines for immoral purposes. The fine for a violation was up to $5,000 and five years in jail. Effie Hoke and Basil Economides were convicted of violating the Mann Act. They appealed their convictions to the U.S. Supreme Court.

## Significance

The Court in *Hoke v. U.S.* upheld Hoke's and Economides' convictions, and therefore the Mann White Slave Traffic Act as well. The challenge to the Mann Act in this case was based largely on the ground of "states' rights"; in other words, the defendants argued that the federal Mann Act interfered with the rights of the states to legislate their own affairs. The Supreme Court, however, rejected this view. The Court expanded the scope of the Mann Act the next year to allow prosecution for traveling across state lines for the intent of immoral purposes, holding that the act was violated even if the immoral purpose was never accomplished. In 1917, the Court extended the act even further in a case involving the conviction of a congressman's son for private, rather than commercial,

abuse of the law. He had taken his nineteen-year-old girl-friend across state lines and was captured when his wife set the police on his trail. In upholding the conviction, the Court interpreted the Mann Act to mean that any man taking a woman not his wife across state lines, even if she was willing, could be prosecuted. Many men fell victim to extortion as professional women lured them across state lines and then presented them with the choice of paying up or facing the law. During the Roaring Twenties, more liberal juries made convictions harder to achieve, but the Department of Justice continued to chase any man whom it deemed had crossed state lines for immoral purposes, including musician Chuck Berry, who served twenty months after conviction, and actor Charlie Chaplin, whose main offense was being a communist (the jury acquitted him on the Mann Act charge).

Sexism was always a problem with the act, and the Supreme Court eventually narrowed its reading of it but never overturned it. Recent amendments have narrowed it to focus on commercial exploitation of minors of either sex. Annual prosecutions have also dropped from the hundreds to the teens, with fourteen in 1980. Congress, though, never repealed the act, for representatives and senators always desire to remain on the side of morality.

## Primary Source

*Hoke v. U.S.* [excerpt]

**SYNOPSIS:** McKenna reviews the charges against the two defendants, describes the claims made by defense counsel, and notes that the determining factor will be whether Congress exceeded its authority under the commerce clause of the Constitution. The opinion then discusses other items Congress had legitimately banned from interstate commerce. McKenna notes that only Congress could have banned such trade, and thus this law does not interfere with the power of the states.

Mr. Justice McKenna delivered the opinion of the Court:

Error to review a judgment of conviction under the act of Congress of June 25, 1910, entitled, "An Act to Further Regulate Interstate and Foreign Commerce by Prohibiting the Transportation Therein for Immoral Purposes of Women and Girls, and for Other Purposes." . . . It is commonly known as the white slave act.

The constitutionality of the act was assailed by demurrer, and as its sufficiency otherwise was not questioned, a brief summary of its allegations is all that is necessary.

The charge against Effie Hoke is that she "did, on the 14th day of November, A.D. 1910, in the city of New Orleans and state of Louisiana, unlawfully, feloniously, and knowingly persuade, induce, and entice one Annette Baden, alias Annette Hays, a woman, to go from New Orleans, a city in the state of Louisiana, to Beaumont, a city in the state of Texas, in interstate commerce, for the purpose of prostitution," etc.

The charge against Basil Economides is that he "did unlawfully, feloniously, and knowingly aid and assist the said Effie Hoke to persuade, induce, and entice the said Annette Baden . . . to go in interstate commerce . . . for the purpose of prostitution," with the intent and purpose that the said woman "should engage in the practice of prostitution in the said city of Beaumont, Texas."

The second and third counts make the same charge against the defendants as to another woman, the one named in the third count being under eighteen years.

The demurrers were overruled, and after trial the defendants were convicted and sentenced, each to two years' imprisonment on each count. . . .

The grounds of attack upon the constitutionality of the statute are expressed by counsel as follows:

1. Because it is contrary to and contravenes art. 4, 2, of the Constitution of the United States, which reads: "The citizens of each state shall be entitled to all the privileges and immunities of citizens in the several states."

2. Because it is contrary to and contravenes the following two amendments to the Constitution: Art. 9. The enumeration in the Constitution of certain rights shall not be construed to deny or disparage others retained by the people. Art. 10. The powers not delegated to the United States by the Constitution, nor prohibited by it to the states, are reserved to the states respectively, or to the people.

3. Because that clause of the Constitution which reserves to Congress the power (art. 1, 8, subdiv. 2) "to regulate commerce with foreign nations, and among the several states," etc., is not broad enough to include the power to regulate prostitution or any other immorality of citizens of the several states as a condition precedent (or subsequent) to their right to travel interstate, or to aid or assist another to so travel.

4. Because the right and power to regulate and control prostitution, or any other immoralities of

citizens, comes within the reserved police power of the several states, and under the Constitution Congress cannot interfere therewith, either directly or indirectly, under the grant of power "to regulate commerce between the states."

We shall discuss at length but one of these grounds; the others will be referred to incidentally. The power of Congress under the commerce clause of the Constitution is the ultimate determining question. If the statute be a valid exercise of that power, how it may affect persons or states is not material to be considered. It is the supreme law of the land, and persons and states are subject to it.

Congress is given power "to regulate commerce with foreign nations and among the several states." The power is direct; there is no word of limitation in it, and its broad and universal scope has been so often declared as to make repetition unnecessary. And, besides, it has had so much illustration by cases that it would seem as if there could be no instance of its exercise that does not find an admitted example in some one of them. Experience, however, is the other way, and in almost every instance of the exercise of the power differences are asserted from previous exercises of it and made a ground of attack. The present case is an example.

Commerce among the states, we have said, consists of intercourse and traffic between their citizens, and includes the transportation of persons and property. There may be, therefore, a movement of persons as well as of property; that is, a person may move or be moved in interstate commerce. And the act under consideration was drawn in view of that possibility. What the act condemns is transportation obtained or aided, or transportation induced, in interstate commerce, for the immoral purposes mentioned. But an objection is made and urged with earnestness. It is said that it is the right and privilege of a person to move between states, and that such being the right, another cannot be made guilty of the crime of inducing or assisting or aiding in the exercise of it, and "that the motive or intention of the passenger, either before beginning the journey, or during or after completing it, is not a matter of interstate commerce." The contentions confound things important to be distinguished. It urges a right exercised in morality to sustain a right to be exercised in immorality. It is the same right which attacked the law of Congress which prohibits the carrying of obscene literature and articles designed for indecent and immoral use from one state to another. . . . It is the same right which was excluded as an element as affecting the constitutionality of the act for the suppression of lottery traffic through national and interstate commerce. . . . It is the right given for beneficial exercise which is attempted to be perverted to and justify baneful exercise, as in the instances stated, and which finds further illustration in *Reid v. Colorado*. . . . This constitutes the supreme fallacy of plaintiffs' error. It pervades and vitiates their contentions.

Plaintiffs in error admit that the states may control the immoralities of its citizens. Indeed, this is their chief insistence; and they especially condemn the act under review as a subterfuge and an attempt to interfere with the police power of the states to regulate the morals of their citizens, and assert that it is in consequence an invasion of the reserved powers of the states. There is unquestionably a control in the states over the morals of their citizens, and, it may be admitted, it extends to making prostitution a crime. It is a control, however, which can be exercised only within the jurisdiction of the states, but there is a domain which the states cannot reach and over which Congress alone has power; and if such power be exerted to control what the states cannot, it is an argument for—not against—its legality. Its exertion does not encroach upon the jurisdiction of the states. We have examples; others may be adduced. The pure food and drugs act is a conspicuous instance. In all of the instances a clash of national legislation with the power of the states was urged, and in all rejected.

Our dual form of government has its perplexities, state and nation having different spheres of jurisdiction, as we have said; but it must be kept in mind that we are one people; and the powers reserved to the states and those conferred on the nation are adapted to be exercised, whether independently or concurrently, to promote the general welfare, material and moral. This is the effect of the decisions; and surely, if the facility of interstate transportation can be taken away from the demoralization of lotteries, the debasement of obscene literature, the contagion of diseased cattle or persons, the impurity of food and drugs, the like facility can be taken away from the systematic enticement to and the enslavement in prostitution and debauchery of women, and, more insistently, of girls.

This is the aim of the law, expressed in broad generalization; and motives are made of determining consequence. Motives executed by actions may make it the concern of government to exert its powers. Right purpose and fair trading need no restrictive regulation, but let them be transgressed, and penalties and prohibitions must be applied. We may illustrate again by the pure food and drugs act. Let an article be debased by adulteration, let it be misrepresented by false branding, and Congress may exercise its prohibitive power. It may be that Congress could not prohibit the manufacture of the article in a state. It may be that Congress could not prohibit in all of its conditions its sale within a state. But Congress may prohibit its transportation between the states, and by that means defeat the motive and evils of its manufacture. How far-reaching are the power and the means which may be used to secure its complete exercise we have expressed in *Hipolite Egg Co. v. United States*. . . . There, in emphasis of the purpose of the law, are denominated adulterated articles as "outlaws of commerce," and said that the confiscation of them enjoined by the law was appropriate to the right to bar them from interstate transportation, and completed the purpose of the law by not merely preventing their physical movement, but preventing trade in them between the states. It was urged in that case, as it is urged here, that the law was an invasion of the power of the states.

Of course it will be said that women are not articles of merchandise, but this does not affect the analogy of the cases; the substance of the congressional power is the same, only the manner of its exercise must be accommodated to the difference in its objects. It is misleading to say that men and women have rights. Their rights cannot fortify or sanction their wrongs; and if they employ interstate transportation as a facility of their wrongs, it may be forbidden to them to the extent of the act of July 25, 1910, and we need go no farther in the present case.

The principle established by the cases is the simple one, when rid of confusing and distracting considerations, that Congress has power over transportation "among the several states;" that the power is complete in itself, and that Congress, as an incident to it, may adopt not only means necessary but convenient to its exercise, and the means may have the quality of police regulations. . . . We have no hesitation, therefore, in pronouncing the act of June 25, 1910, a legal exercise of the power of Congress.

There are assignments of error based upon rulings on the admission and rejection of evidence and upon the instructions to the jury and the refusing of instructions. The asserted errors are set forth in twenty-five bills of exceptions, and the special assignment of errors in this court occupy twenty-eight pages of the record, and present the constitutional objections to the law in all the aspects that counsel's ingenuity can devise. A like ingenuity has been exercised to represent the many ways in which the conduct of the accused can be viewed and shown to be inconsistent with guilty purpose. To discuss them all is unnecessary. We shall pass more or less rapidly over those we consider to be worthy of attention.

1. It is contended that there is variance between the indictment and the proof, in that the indictment charges that the women were transported over the Texas & New Orleans Railroad Company's road, and that the government failed to prove that such road was a line extending from New Orleans to Beaumont, Texas, these places marking the beginning and end of the transportation of the women. Further, that the proof showed that their tickets were purchased over the Southern Pacific Road. The indictment alleges that the Texas & New Orleans Railroad was a part of the Southern Pacific System, and was commonly known as the "Sunset Route," and there was through transportation. The variance is not much more than verbal, and that it prejudiced their defense in any way is not shown. If it is error at all, it does not appear to have caused even embarrassment to the defense. But was it error? See *Westmoreland v. United States.* . . .

2. The evidence does not show that the defendants or either of them induced, etc., the women to become passengers in interstate commerce. The particulars are recited wherein it is contended that the evidence is deficient. It is not necessary to review them. It was for the jury to consider and determine the sufficiency of the evidence, and we cannot say they were not justified by it in the judgment they pronounced.

3. It is contended that Florence Baden persuaded her sister Gertrude to go to Beaumont, and an instruction of the court is attacked on the ground that it declared the charge of the indictment was satisfied against the defendants if Florence acted for them. There was no error in the instruction under the circumstances shown by the record.

4. Error is assigned on the refusal of the court to give certain instructions requested by defendants. To consider them in detail would require a lengthy review of the evidence, for they present arguments on certain phases of it as to the degree of persuasion used or its sufficiency to induce or entice the women. There was no error in refusing the instructions.

5. The court permitted the women to testify as to the acts of Effie Hoke at her house at Beaumont, restraining the liberty of the women, and coercing their stay with her. Such testimony was relevant. The acts illustrated and constituted a completion of what was done at New Orleans. They were part of the same scheme and made clear its purpose.

There were other instructions asked by which the jury was charged that they could not convict Effie Hoke for the character of the house she kept or Economides for the business he conducted. The charge of the court sufficiently excluded both views. It explained the act of Congress and the offenses it condemned and directed the attention of the jury to them.

6. Defendants complain that they were not permitted to show that the women named in the indictment were public prostitutes in New Orleans. Such proof, they contend, was relevant upon the charge of persuasion or enticement. This may be admitted, but there was sufficient evidence, as the court said, of the fact of the immorality of their lives, and explicitly ruled that they could be shown to be public prostitutes. The court, however, excluded certain details sought to be proved. Under the circumstances there was no error in the ruling.

In conclusion we say, after consideration of all errors assigned, that there was no ruling made which was prejudicial to defendants.

Judgment affirmed.

## Further Resources

### BOOKS

Bell, Ernest Albert. *Fighting the Traffic in Young Girls or, War on the White Slave Trade: A Complete and Detailed Account of the Shameless Traffic in Young Girls.* Nashville, Tenn.: Southwestern, 1911.

Glickman, Nora. *The Jewish White Slave Trade and the Untold Story of Raquel Liberman.* New York: Garland, 2000.

Langum, David J. *Crossing Over the Line: Legislating Morality and the Mann Act.* Chicago: University of Chicago Press, 1994.

McDevitt, Matthew. *Joseph McKenna: Associate Justice of the United States.* New York: Da Capo, 1974.

# *Weeks v. U.S.*

Supreme Court decision

**By:** William R. Day

**Date:** February 24, 1914

**Source:** Day, William R. *Weeks v. U.S.,* 232 U.S. 383 (1914). Available online at http://caselaw.lp.findlaw.com/us /232/383.html; website home page: http://caselaw.lp.findlaw .com (accessed January 22, 2003).

**About the Author:** William R. Day (1849–1923), born in Ravenna, Ohio, served briefly (and unwillingly) as U.S. attorney general in 1898. In 1899, he was appointed to the U.S. Court of Appeals for the Sixth Circuit. In 1903, President Theodore Roosevelt (served 1901–1909) appointed him to the Supreme Court, where he served as an associate justice until his resignation in 1922. ■

## Introduction

Many Anti-Federalists opposed the U.S. Constitution because they believed it granted too much power to the federal government. To quiet their fears, and to protect the citizenry, the first Congress proposed twelve amendments to the Constitution in 1789. Ten, the Bill of Rights, were quickly ratified by the states and became part of the Constitution in 1791. The Bill of Rights protects both civil liberties and a defendant's rights when tried in a court of law. These provisions, however, are not self-enforcing, and the question quickly arose as to what would happen if they were violated. Because there were few federal criminal laws in the nation's early years, the Supreme Court had few chances to answer this question.

The Embargo Act of 1807 raised questions of what the federal government could search and seize, but the Supreme Court never ruled on this question. In an early case that finally addressed the issue, *Boyd v. U.S.,* the Supreme Court prohibited the use of evidence seized without a warrant. The Court, however, did not explicitly state that *all* evidence seized without a warrant could not be used—an issue raised in *Weeks.* In *Barron v. Baltimore,* the Court again ruled that the federal government could not use evidence seized without a search warrant, but it specified no penalty for the government should it use such evidence in a trial until the *Weeks* case.

## Significance

The penalty that the Supreme Court imposed in *Weeks* for using evidence obtained without a search warrant was a heavy one: the overturning of convictions. This ruling put teeth into the Fourth Amendment. As the Court noted, if illegally seized documents are allowed, "the Fourth Amendment . . . might as well be stricken from the Constitution." The prohibition on using illegally seized evidence has come to be known as the "exclusionary rule." Even with this decision, the issue was not settled, though, as the question remained whether the exclusionary rule applied not only to the federal government but also to the states through the Fourteenth Amendment, which prohibits states from violating a person's liberty without due process of law. If "liberty" included the Fourth Amendment right against search and seizure without a warrant, then the exclusionary rule applied. In 1937, the Supreme Court ruled that some of the Bill of Rights applied to the states, but only those amendments that were part of what the court called "ordered liberty." The Court held illegal those practices that violated what Justice Felix Frankfurter called "accepted notions of justice." In 1949, the Supreme Court applied this theory to refuse to overturn a state conviction based on evidence obtained by an illegal search. In 1952, the Court did find illegal evidence obtained by a stomach pump, even while allowing, five years later, a blood sample taken from an unconscious person. Throughout the 1940s and 1950s, therefore, no clear standard emerged.

In 1961, the Warren Court finally set a clear precedent. In *Mapp v. Ohio,* it held that the Fourth Amendment did apply to the states and that the Supreme Court would hold them to the "exclusionary rule." The Court in *Mapp* noted that over half of the states already used the federal standard. Since *Mapp,* though, the Supreme Court has limited that ruling, allowing states to use some illegally seized evidence. The Court severely reformulated the *Mapp* formula in *U.S. v. Leon* (1984), deciding to weigh the benefit to society against a particular suspect's rights. Under the Rehnquist Court, the Fourth Amendment has continued to be narrowed. Thus, the width and applicability of the Fourth Amendment has varied significantly since the *Weeks* decision, but *Weeks* set the precedent for overturning convictions obtained through illegal search and seizure.

## Primary Source

*Weeks v. U.S.* [excerpt]

> **SYNOPSIS:** Day first lays out Weeks's claim that his Fourth Amendment rights had been violated. He next cites the *Boyd* case, which held that the federal government cannot use illegally seized evidence, as that would violate the Fourth Amendment. He goes on to say that the illegally seized evidence should not have been used, and thus Weeks was wrongfully convicted. He concludes by reversing the conviction.

Mr. Justice Day delivered the opinion of the Court.

An indictment was returned against the plaintiff in error, defendant below, and herein so designated, in the district court of the United States for the western district of Missouri, containing nine counts. The seventh count, upon which a conviction was had, charged the use of the mails for the purpose of transporting certain coupons or tickets representing chances or shares in a lottery or gift enterprise, in violation of 213 of the Criminal Code [35 Stat. at L. 1129, chap. 321, U. S. Comp. Stat. Supp. 1911, p. 1652]. Sentence of fine and imprisonment was imposed. This writ of error is to review that judgment.

The defendant was arrested by a police officer, so far as the record shows, without warrant, at the Union Station in Kansas City, Missouri, where he was employed by an express company. Other police officers had gone to the house of the defendant, and being told by a neighbor where the key was kept, found it and entered the house. They searched the defendant's room and took possession of various papers and articles found there, which were afterwards turned over to the United States marshal. Later in the same day police officers returned with the marshal, who thought he might find additional evidence, and, being admitted by someone in the house, probably a boarder, in response to a rap, the marshal searched the defendant's room and carried away certain letters and envelopes found in the drawer of a chiffonier. Neither the marshal nor the police officer had a search warrant. . . .

The defendant assigns error, among other things, in the court's . . . permitting the papers to be used at the trial.

It is thus apparent that the question presented involves the determination of the duty of the court with reference to the motion made by the defendant for the return of certain letters, as well as other papers, taken from his room by the United States marshal, who, without authority of process, if any such could have been legally issued, visited the room of the defendant for the declared purpose of obtaining additional testimony to support the charge against the accused, and, having gained admission to the house, took from the drawer of a chiffonier there found certain letters written to the defendant, tending to show his guilt. These letters were placed in the control of the district attorney, and were subsequently produced by him and offered in evidence against the accused at the trial. The defendant contends that such appropriation of his private correspondence was in violation of rights secured to him by the 4th and 5th Amendments to the Constitution of the United States. We shall deal with the 4th Amendment, which provides:

> The right of the people to be secure in their persons, houses, papers, and effects, against

## The Exclusionary Rule

The "exclusionary rule" does not just require a search warrant in order for seized property to be used against a defendant in court. It also requires probable cause for the search that produces the seizure. A drug raid in 1981 resulted in the arrests of four dealers, including Alberto Leon, who protested that the search warrant under which the paraphernalia had been seized had not been issued with probable cause. The Supreme Court heard the case but determined that, as the four plainly were guilty, the rights of society outweighed any rights Leon and his compatriots were asserting.

unreasonable searches and seizures, shall not be violated, and no warrants shall issue but upon probable cause, supported by oath or affirmation, and particularly describing the place to be searched, and the persons or things to be seized. . . .

The effect of the 4th Amendment is to put the courts of the United States and Federal officials, in the exercise of their power and authority, under limitations and restraints as to the exercise of such power and authority, and to forever secure the people, their persons, houses, papers, and effects, against all unreasonable searches and seizures under the guise of law. This protection reaches all alike, whether accused of crime or not, and the duty of giving to it force and effect is obligatory upon all intrusted under our Federal system with the enforcement of the laws. The tendency of those who execute the criminal laws of the country to obtain conviction by means of unlawful seizures and enforced confessions, the latter often obtained after subjecting accused persons to unwarranted practices destructive of rights secured by the Federal Constitution, should find no sanction in the judgments of the courts, which are charged at all times with the support of the Constitution, and to which people of all conditions have a right to appeal for the maintenance of such fundamental rights. . . .

What, then, is the present case? . . . The case in the aspect in which we are dealing with it involves the right of the court in a criminal prosecution to retain for the purposes of evidence the letters and correspondence of the accused, seized in his house in his absence and without his authority, by a United States marshal holding no warrant for his arrest and none for the search of his premises. The accused, without awaiting his trial, made timely application to the court for an order for the return of these letters, as well or other property. This application was denied, the letters retained and put in evidence, after a further application at the beginning of the trial, both applications asserting the rights of the accused under the 4th and 5th Amendments to the Constitution. If letters and private documents can thus be seized and held and used in evidence against a citizen accused of an offense, the protection of the 4th Amendment, declaring his right to be secure against such searches and seizures, is of no value, and, so far as those thus placed are concerned, might as well be stricken from the Constitution. The efforts of the courts and their officials to bring the guilty to punishment, praiseworthy as they are, are not to be aided by the sacrifice of those great principles established by years of endeavor and suffering which have resulted in their embodiment in the fundamental law of the land. The United States marshal could only have invaded the house of the accused when armed with a warrant issued as required by the Constitution, upon sworn information, and describing with reasonable particularity the thing for which the search was to be made. Instead, he acted without sanction of law, doubtless prompted by the desire to bring further proof to the aid of the government, and under color of his office undertook to make a seizure of private papers in direct violation of the constitutional prohibition against such action. Under such circumstances, without sworn information and particular description, not even an order of court would have justified such procedure; much less was it within the authority of the United States marshal to thus invade the house and privacy of the accused. . . . To sanction such proceedings would be to affirm by judicial decision a manifest neglect, if not an open defiance, of the prohibitions of the Constitution, intended for the protection of the people against such unauthorized action. . . .

We therefore reach the conclusion that the letters in question were taken from the house of the accused by an official of the United States, acting under color of his office, in direct violation of the constitutional rights of the defendant; that having made a seasonable application for their return, which was heard and passed upon by the court, there was involved in the order refusing the application a denial of the constitutional rights of the accused, and that the court should have restored these letters to the accused. In holding them and permitting their use upon the trial, we think prejudicial error was committed. As to the papers and property seized by the po-

licemen, it does not appear that they acted under any claim of Federal authority such as would make the amendment applicable to such unauthorized seizures. The record shows that what they did by way of arrest and search and seizure was done before the finding of the indictment in the Federal court; under what supposed right or authority does not appear. What remedies the defendant may have against them we need not inquire, as the 4th Amendment is not directed to individual misconduct of such officials. Its limitations reach the Federal government and its agencies. . . . It results that the judgment of the court below must be reversed, and the case remanded for further proceedings in accordance with this opinion.

## Further Resources

### BOOKS

Adams, James A. *Prosecutor's Manual for Arrest, Search, and Seizure.* Charlottesville, Va.: Lexis, 1998.

McLean, Joseph Erigina. *William Rufus Day, Supreme Court Justice from Ohio.* Baltimore, Md.: Johns Hopkins Press, 1946.

United States Congress, House Committee on the Judiciary Subcommittee on Crime. *Taking Back Our Streets Act of 1995: Hearings Before the Subcommittee on Crime of the Committee on the Judiciary, House of Representatives.* 104th Congress, 1st sess., H.R. 3, 1995. Washington, D.C.: U.S. Government Printing Office, 1996.

United States Department of Justice, Office of Legal Policy. *Report to the Attorney General on the Search and Seizure Exclusionary Rule.* Washington, D.C.: Government Printing Office, 1988.

Wilson, Bradford P. *Enforcing the Fourth Amendment: A Jurisprudential History.* New York: Garland, 1986.

# Houston, East & West Texas Railway Co. v. U.S.

Supreme Court decision

**By:** Charles Evans Hughes

**Date:** June 8, 1914

**Source:** Hughes, Charles Evans. *Houston, East & West Texas Railway Co. v. United States,* 234 U.S. 342 (1914). Available online at http://caselaw.lp.findlaw.com/us/234/342.html; website home page: http://caselaw.lp.findlaw.com (accessed January 22, 2003).

**About the Author:** Charles Evans Hughes (1862–1948), born in New York, is one of the few U.S. Supreme Court justices to join the Court twice. After serving as governor of New York starting in 1906, President William Howard Taft (served 1909–1913) appointed Hughes to the Supreme Court in 1910. He left the Court to run unsuccessfully for president against

Woodrow Wilson (served 1913–1921) in 1916. He served as secretary of state under Warren Harding (served 1921–1923) and returned to the Court in 1930 as its chief justice. ■

## Introduction

In the 1860s and 1870s, railroads enabled farmers in the West to get their goods to market and to remain in contact with the outside world. The railroads, though, tended to charge the farmers high rates, which caused considerable protest and led, in the late 1880s and early 1890s, to the emergence and growth of the Populist Party, which demanded railroad pricing equity. Pressure from the Populist Party led to the Interstate Commerce Act of 1887, which established the Interstate Commerce Commission (ICC) to create "fair and reasonable" railroad rates.

In certain circumstances, the ICC set railroad rates. In *Interstate Commerce Commission v. Cincinnati, New Orleans and Texas Pacific Railway Co.* (1897), however, the Supreme Court held that the ICC could not legally set railroad rates because it was part of the executive branch and only the legislative branch had power to set rates. In another decision that year, the Supreme Court weakened the ICC's fact-finding authority. Progressives in the early 1900s resurrected the railroad issue and succeeded in passing the Hepburn Act of 1906 and the Mann-Elkins Act of 1910, which granted rate-setting authority to the ICC. In 1910, in *ICC v. Illinois Central Railroad Company*, the Supreme Court upheld the ICC's rate-setting powers and granted greater discretion to the commission. It also took a broader view of the Constitution than the 1897 decisions had by holding that Congress could legally delegate rate-setting power to the commission. The net effect of this decision was that in future cases, the Supreme Court would review only whether or not the ICC had the power to issue a given order rather than whether or not the issuance of that order was a wise exercise of the ICC's power.

## Significance

In *Houston, East & West Texas Railway Co.*, commonly called the Shreveport case, the Court allowed the ICC to raise intrastate rates, or rates within a state's borders. This decision expanded the scope of the ICC's power and established the ICC's superiority over state and local regulatory commissions. After Shreveport, the ICC continued to monitor rates and generally worked to keep rates low. However, it did not generally consider the relationship of the railroads to the economy as a whole. Some ICC members pushed for higher rates, which would lead to stronger railroads and improved services. The railroads, of course, wanted high rates, but the ICC as a whole did not.

The ICC suspended its antimonopoly rules during World War I, and after the Transportation Act of 1920, it worked to create a number of railroad cartels across the nation. These powers were upheld in several 1920 court cases. The ICC did not exercise all of its powers in the 1920s, though, following the belief of the period's Republican presidents that less government was better government. After the 1920s, the ICC's powers expanded beyond railroads to include all commercial carriers except airplanes. The ICC also had the responsibility for managing labor disputes on railroads. In the 1950s and 1960s, it enforced desegregation orders in interstate transportation. In the 1960s, its oversight of safety issues was transferred to the Department of Transportation. Slowly the ICC's other powers were also curtailed, in accordance with Ronald Reagan's (served 1981–1989) administration's belief in deregulation. In the early 1990s, the Republicans disbanded the ICC, transferring its few remaining powers to the National Surface Transportation Board.

## Primary Source

*Houston, East & West Texas Railway Co. v. U.S.*
[excerpt]

**SYNOPSIS:** Hughes first notes the railroad's complaint that intrastate, not interstate, rates were being affected. The opinion answers that complaint by noting Congress's complete power over interstate commerce and stating that that power extends to all activities having a "close and substantial" relationship to interstate commerce. Since inter- and intrastate commerce both have that relationship, intrastate rates can be raised. Any discrimination that burdens interstate commerce can be regulated by Congress, and thus by the ICC.

Justice Hughes delivered the opinion of the Court.

The point of the objection to the order is that, as the discrimination found by the Commission to be unjust arises out of the relation of intrastate rates, maintained under state authority, to interstate rates that have been upheld as reasonable, its correction was beyond the Commission's power. Manifestly the order might be complied with, and the discrimination avoided, either by reducing the interstate rates from Shreveport to the level of the competing intrastate rates, or by raising these intrastate rates to the level of the interstate rates, or by such reduction in the one case and increase in the other as would result in equality. But it is urged that, so far as the interstate rates were sustained by the Commission as reasonable, the Commission was without authority to compel their reduction in order to equalize them with the lower intrastate rates. The holding of the commerce court was that the order relieved the appellants from further obligation to observe the intrastate

Trains like this one crossing a bridge over the Pecos River near Langtry, Texas, precipitated the need to set rates for interstate railroad travel. **THE LIBRARY OF CONGRESS.**

rates, and that they were at liberty to comply with the Commission's requirements by increasing these rates sufficiently to remove the forbidden discrimination. The invalidity of the order in this aspect is challenged upon two grounds:

1. That Congress is impotent to control the intrastate charges of an interstate carrier even to the extent necessary to prevent injurious discrimination against interstate traffic; and

2. That, if it be assumed that Congress has this power, still it has not been exercised, and hence the action of the Commission exceeded the limits of the authority which has been conferred upon it.

First. It is unnecessary to repeat what has frequently been said by this court with respect to the complete and paramount character of the power confided to Congress to regulate commerce among the several states. It is of the essence of this power that, where it exists, it dominates. Interstate trade was not left to be destroyed or impeded by the rivalries of local government. The purpose was to make impossible the recurrence of the evils which had overwhelmed the Confederation, and to provide

the necessary basis of national unity by insuring "uniformity of regulation against conflicting and discriminating state legislation." By virtue of the comprehensive terms of the grant, the authority of Congress is at all times adequate to meet the varying exigencies that arise, and to protect the national interest by securing the freedom of interstate commercial intercourse from local control. . . .

Congress is empowered to regulate,—that is, to provide the law for the government of interstate commerce. . . . Its authority, extending to these interstate carriers as instruments of interstate commerce, necessarily embraces the right to control their operations in all matters having such a close and substantial relation to interstate traffic that the control is essential or appropriate to the security of that traffic, to the efficiency of the interstate service, and to the maintenance of conditions under which interstate commerce may be conducted upon fair terms and without molestation or hindrance. As it is competent for Congress to legislate to these ends, unquestionably it may seek their attainment by requiring that the agencies of interstate commerce shall not be used in such manner as to cripple, retard, or destroy it. The fact that carriers are instruments of intrastate commerce, as well as of interstate commerce, does not derogate from the complete and paramount authority of Congress over the latter, or preclude the Federal power from being exerted to prevent the intrastate operations of such carriers from being made a means of injury to that which has been confided to Federal care. Wherever the interstate and intrastate transactions of carriers are so related that the government of the one involves the control of the other, it is Congress, and not the state, that is entitled to prescribe the final and dominant rule, for otherwise Congress would be denied the exercise of its constitutional authority, and the state, and not the nation, would be supreme within the national field. . . .

While these decisions sustaining the Federal power relate to measures adopted in the interest of the safety of persons and property, they illustrate the principle that Congress, in the exercise of its paramount power, may prevent the common instrumentalities of interstate and intrastate commercial intercourse from being used in their intrastate operations to the injury of interstate commerce. This is not to say that Congress possesses the authority to regulate the internal commerce of a state, as such, but that it does possess the power to foster and protect interstate commerce, and to take all measures necessary or appropriate to that end, although intrastate transactions of interstate carriers may thereby be controlled.

This principle is applicable here. We find no reason to doubt that Congress is entitled to keep the highways of interstate communication open to interstate traffic upon fair and equal terms. That an unjust discrimination in the rates of a common carrier, by which one person or locality is unduly favored as against another under substantially similar conditions of traffic, constitutes an evil, is undeniable; and where this evil consists in the action of an interstate carrier in unreasonably discriminating against interstate traffic over its line, the authority of Congress to prevent it is equally clear. It is immaterial, so far as the protecting power of Congress is concerned, that the discrimination arises from intrastate rates as compared with interstate rates. The use of the instrument of interstate commerce in a discriminatory manner so as to inflict injury upon that commerce, or some part thereof, furnishes abundant ground for Federal intervention. Nor can the attempted exercise of state authority alter the matter, where Congress has acted, for a state may not authorize the carrier to do that which Congress is entitled to forbid and has forbidden.

It is to be noted—as the government has well said in its argument in support of the Commission's order—that the power to deal with the relation between the two kinds of rates, as a relation, lies exclusively with Congress. It is manifest that the state cannot fix the relation of the carrier's interstate and intrastate charges without directly interfering with the former, unless it simply follows the standard set by Federal authority. . . . It is for Congress to supply the needed correction where the relation between intrastate and interstate rates presents the evil to be corrected, and this it may do completely, by reason of its control over the interstate carrier in all matters having such a close and substantial relation to interstate commerce that it is necessary or appropriate to exercise the control for the effective government of that commerce. . . .

In conclusion: Reading the order in the light of the report of the Commission, it does not appear that the Commission attempted to require the carriers to reduce their interstate rates out of Shreveport below what was found to be a reasonable charge for that service. So far as those interstate rates conformed to what was found to be reasonable by the Commission, the carriers are entitled to maintain them, and they are free to comply with the order by so adjusting the other rates, to which the order relates, as to remove the forbidden discrimination. But this result they are required to accomplish.

The decree of the Commerce Court is affirmed in each case.

Affirmed.

Mr. Justice Lurton and Mr. Justice Pitney dissent.

## Further Resources

### BOOKS

Hendel, Samuel. *Charles Evans Hughes and the Supreme Court.* New York: Russell & Russell, 1968.

Hoogenboom, Ari Arthur. *A Short History of the ICC: From Panacea to Palliative.* New York: Norton, 1976.

Pusey, Merlo John. *Charles Evans Hughes.* New York: Macmillan, 1951.

Stone, Richard D. *The Interstate Commerce Commission and the Railroad Industry: A History of Regulatory Policy.* New York: Praeger, 1991.

Thomas, William G. *Lawyering for the Railroad: Business, Law, and Power in the New South.* Baton Rouge, La.: Louisiana State University Press, 1999.

United States Interstate Commerce Commission, Bureau of Transport Economics and Statistics. *Interstate Commerce Commission Activities, 1887–1937.* Washington, D.C.: Government Printing Office, 1937.

# *Bunting v. Oregon*

Supreme Court decision

**By:** Joseph McKenna

**Date:** April 9, 1917

**Source:** McKenna, Joseph. *Bunting v. State of Oregon,* 243 U.S. 426 (1917). Available online at http://caselaw.lp.findlaw .com/us/243/426.html; website home page: http://caselaw.lp .findlaw.com (accessed January 22, 2003).

**About the Author:** Joseph McKenna (1843–1926) served as a representative from California to the U.S. House of Representatives and as judge for the Ninth Circuit Court of Appeals. In 1897, he served briefly as attorney general before President William McKinley (served 1897–1901) appointed him associate justice of the Supreme Court, where he served until his resignation in 1925. ∎

## Introduction

Throughout the nineteenth century, employers in the United States were allowed to treat workers in ways that, by modern standards, seem outrageous. Employees were expected to work at least six days a week, ten or twelve hours a day. Steel workers had to labor seven days a week, twelve hours a day, with a twenty-four hour shift every two weeks to switch shifts. Attempts to unionize were met with strong resistance, and government attempts to regulate hours and wages were generally fruitless, for industry lobbies were generally stronger than those for labor. Even when state and local laws regulating the workplace were passed, they did not always take effect. In the late 1800s and early 1900s, the Supreme Court struck down many such laws because, the Court maintained, they interfered with interstate commerce, which was regulated solely by the federal government, or for interfering with individual property rights.

During these years, the Supreme Court developed a doctrine known as "freedom of contract," which held that legislatures had no right to interfere with an individual's freedom to make contracts, such as the contract between a worker and an employer. This freedom of contract, the Court said, was protected by the Fourteenth and Fifteenth Amendments to the Constitution. This doctrine shaped several Supreme Court decisions, including its decision in *Lochner v. New York* (1905) striking down a New York law limiting bakers' work weeks to sixty hours. The proponents of a limited work week were not daunted, however, and the first successful hours limit was upheld by the Supreme Court in *Muller v. Oregon* (1908). The case involved an Oregon law that limited the workday for women to ten hours a day. It is noteworthy in part because future Supreme Court justice Louis D. Brandeis defended the Oregon law before the Court by citing a wealth of scientific "evidence" that women were weaker than men and that long work hours limited their reproductive

capacity—the first time the Supreme Court had taken such extralegal data into consideration in rendering a decision. The law in question in *Bunting,* though, went much further than the law in *Muller.* It limited the workday for both men and women to ten hours and mandated time-and-a-half pay for work over ten hours a day.

## Significance

The Supreme Court upheld the Oregon law in *Bunting v. Oregon,* another step toward allowing government regulation of the workplace. This case is unique in that it was one of the first that upheld wage regulations in addition to hours regulations. In 1917 the Supreme Court went further when it upheld a worker's compensation act. Many at the time thought that the doctrine of freedom of contract expressed in *Lochner* was dead, but this belief proved to be premature, for in *Adkins v. Childrens Hospital* (1923), the Supreme Court struck down a minimum wage law for women in the District of Columbia. The *Adkins* decision, and the general belief in liberty of contract, proved troublesome for the Franklin D. Roosevelt (served 1933–1945) administration in the 1930s, when the Supreme Court struck down several of his New Deal initiatives attempting to create programs to stimulate the economy and help the country during the Great Depression. The issue of wage and hours regulation was finally decided in 1941 in *U.S. v. Darby,* when the Court upheld the Fair Labor Standards Act which had created both a federal minimum wage and a maximum hours work week.

## Primary Source

*Bunting v. State of Oregon* [excerpt]

**SYNOPSIS:** Justice McKenna summarizes Bunting's complaint: that the law regulates wages and is an attempt by the state to fix prices. McKenna counters by stating that as the law does not fix a specific minimum wage, it cannot be considered price-fixing. He goes on to say that the requirement of time-and-a-half for overtime represents a method of forcing employers to abide by the law while still allowing them to require employees to work extra hours in emergency situations.

Justice McKenna delivered the opinion of the Court.

Indictment charging a violation of a statute of the state of Oregon, 2 of which provides as follows:

No person shall be employed in any mill, factory or manufacturing establishment in this state more than ten hours in any one day, except watchmen and employees when engaged in making necessary repairs, or in case of emergency, where life or property is in immi-

Government wage regulations, requiring time-and-a-half pay for overtime, entered the workplace in 1917. **THE LIBRARY OF CONGRESS.**

nent danger; provided, however, employees may work overtime not to exceed three hours in any one day, conditioned that payment be made for such overtime at the rate of time and one half of the regular wage. . . .

The consonance of the Oregon law with the 14th Amendment is the question in the case, and this depends upon whether it is a proper exercise of the police power of the state, as the supreme court of the state decided that it is.

That the police power extends to health regulations is not denied, but it is denied that the law has such purpose or justification. It is contended that it is a wage law, not a health regulation, and takes the property of plaintiff in error without due process. The contention presents two questions: (1) Is the law a wage law, or an hours-of-service law? And (2) if the latter, has it equality of operation?

Section 1 of the law expresses the policy that impelled its enactment to be the interest of the state in the physical well-being of its citizens and that it is injurious to their health for them to work "in any mill, factory or manufacturing establishment" more than ten hours in any one day; and § 2, as we have seen, forbids their employment in those places for a longer time. If, therefore, we take the law at its word, there can be no doubt of its purpose, and the supreme court of the state has added the confirmation of its decision, by declaring that "the aim of the statute is to fix the maximum hours of service in certain industries. The act makes no attempt to fix the standard of wages. No maximum or minimum wage is named. That is left wholly to the contracting parties.". . .

It is, however, urged that we are not bound by the declaration of the law or the decision of the court. In other words, and to use counsel's language, "the legislative declaration of necessity, even if the act followed such declaration, is not binding upon this court." . . . Of course, mere declaration cannot give character to a law nor turn illegal into legal operation, and when such attempt is palpable, this court necessarily has the power of review.

But does either the declaration or the decision reach such extreme? Plaintiff in error, in contending for this and to establish it, makes paramount the provision for overtime; in other words, makes a limitation of the act the extent of the act—indeed, asserts that it gives, besides, character to the act —illegal character.

To assent to this is to ascribe to the legislation such improvidence of expression as to intend one thing and effect another; or artfulness of expression to disguise illegal purpose. We are reluctant to do either, and we think all the provisions of the law can be accommodated without doing either.

First, as to plaintiff in error's attack upon the law. He says: "The law is not a ten-hour law; it is a thirteen-hour law designed solely for the purpose of compelling the employer of labor in mills, factories, and manufacturing establishments to pay more for labor than the actual market value thereof." And further: "It is a ten-hour law for the purpose of taking the employer's property from him and giving it to the employee; it is a thirteen-hour law for the purpose of protecting the health of the employee." To this plaintiff in error adds that he was convicted, not for working an employee during a busy season for more than ten hours, but for not paying him more than the market value of his services. . . .

There is a certain verbal plausibility in the contention that it was intended to permit thirteen hours' work if there be fifteen and one-half hours' pay, but the plausibility disappears upon reflection. The provision for overtime is permissive, in the same sense that any penalty may be said to be permissive. Its purpose is to deter by its burden, and its adequacy

for this was a matter of legislative judgment under the particular circumstances. It may not achieve its end, but its insufficiency cannot change its character from penalty to permission. Besides, it is to be borne in mind that the legislature was dealing with a matter in which many elements were to be considered. It might not have been possible, it might not have been wise, to make a rigid prohibition. We can easily realize that the legislature deemed it sufficient for its policy to give to the law an adaptation to occasions different from special cases of emergency for which it provided, occasions not of such imperative necessity, and yet which should have some accommodation—abuses prevented by the requirement of higher wages. Or even a broader contention might be made that the legislature considered it a proper policy to meet the conditions long existent by a tentative restraint of conduct rather than by an absolute restraint, and achieve its purpose through the interest of those affected rather than by the positive fiat of the law.

We cannot know all of the conditions that impelled the law or its particular form. . . .

But we need not cast about for reasons for the legislative judgment. We are not required to be sure of the precise reasons for its exercise. . . . It is enough for our decision if the legislation under review was passed in the exercise of an admitted power of government; and that it is not as complete as it might be, not as rigid in its prohibitions as it might be, gives, perhaps, evasion too much play, is lighter in its penalties than it might be, is no impeachment of its legality. This may be a blemish, giving opportunity for criticism and difference in characterization, but the constitutional validity of legislation cannot be determined by the degree of exactness of its provisions or remedies. New policies are usually tentative in their beginnings, advance in firmness as they advance in acceptance. They do not at a particular moment of time spring full-perfect in extent or means from the legislative brain. Time may be necessary to fashion them to precedent customs and conditions, and as they justify themselves or otherwise they pass from militancy to triumph or from question to repeal.

But passing general considerations and coming back to our immediate concern, which is the validity of the particular exertion of power in the Oregon law, our judgment of it is that it does not transcend constitutional limits.

This case is submitted by plaintiff in error upon the contention that the law is a wage law, not an hours-of-service law, and he rests his case on that contention. To that contention we address our decision and do not discuss or consider the broader contentions of counsel for the state that would justify the law even as a regulation of wages.

There is a contention made that the law, even regarded as regulating hours of service, is not either necessary or useful "for preservation of the health of employees in mills, factories, and manufacturing establishments." The record contains no facts to support the contention, and against it is the judgment of the legislature and the supreme court, which said: "In view of the well-known fact that the custom in our industries does not sanction a longer service than ten hours per day, it cannot be held, as a matter of law, that the legislative requirement is unreasonable or arbitrary as to hours of labor. Statistics show that the average daily working time among workingmen in different countries is, in Australia, 8 hours; in Britain, 9; in the United States, 9 ¾; in Denmark, 9 ¾; in Norway, 10; Sweden, France, and Switzerland, 10 ½; Germany, 10 ¼; Belgium, Italy, and Austria, 11; and in Russia, 12 hours."

Further discussion we deem unnecessary.

Judgment affirmed.

The Chief Justice, Mr. Justice Van Devanter, and Mr. Justice McReynolds, dissent.

Mr. Justice Brandeis took no part in the consideration and decision of the case.

## Further Resources

### BOOKS

Frankfurter, Felix, and Josephine Goldmark. *Franklin O. Bunting, Plaintiff in Error, Vs. the State of Oregon, Defendant in Error. In Error to the Supreme Court of the State of Oregon. Brief for the Defendant in Error.* New York: C.P. Young, 1915.

————. *The Case for the Shorter Work Day, Franklin O. Bunting, Plaintiff in Error, vs. the State of Oregon, Defendant in Error. Brief for Defendant in Error. Felix Frankfurter, of Counsel for the State of Oregon. Assisted by Josephine Goldmark.* New York: National Consumer's League, 1916.

Frankfurter, Felix. *Supplemental Brief for Defendant-in-Error upon Reargument, vs. the State of Oregon, Defendant in Error [in the] Supreme Court of the United States, October Term, 1916, no. 38.* New York: National Consumer's League, 1917.

### WEBSITES

Bannister, Robert. "The United States in the Progressive Era: Guide to Resources." Available online at http://www.swarthmore.edu/SocSci/rbannis1/Progs/; website home page: http://www.swarthmore.edu (accessed January 22, 2003).

# Buchanan v. Warley
## Supreme Court decision

**By:** William R. Day

**Date:** November 5, 1917

**Source:** Day, William R. *Buchanan v. Warley,* 245 U.S. 60 (1917). Available online at http://caselaw.lp.findlaw.com /us/245/60.html; website home page: http://caselaw.lp .findlaw.com (accessed January 23, 2003).

**About the Author:** William R. Day (1849–1923), born in Ravenna, Ohio, served briefly (and unwillingly) as U.S. attorney general in 1898. In 1899, he was appointed to the U.S. Court of Appeals for the Sixth Circuit. In 1903, President Theodore Roosevelt (served 1901–1909) appointed him to the Supreme Court, where he served as an associate justice until his resignation in 1922. ∎

## Introduction

After the Civil War, much of the South failed to extend civil rights to freed slaves. Most southern governments enacted "Black Codes" to maintain African Americans' status as second-class citizens. After a brief period of relief in the 1870s, many southern states again adopted discriminatory laws in the 1880s and 1890s. The U.S. Supreme Court sanctioned these laws in the landmark case *Plessy v. Ferguson* (1896), which upheld "separate but equal" railroad cars in Louisiana. The South followed this up with separate facilities of many types, but they were never equal. In particular, many cities forced segregation in housing with municipal ordinances that prohibited African Americans from moving into white neighborhoods. Louisville, Kentucky, was no exception, and it was this segregation that was challenged in *Buchanan v. Warley.*

African Americans organized to protest this segregation and to protect themselves. One of the leading organizations was the National Association for the Advancement of Colored People (NAACP), founded in 1909 by W.E.B. Du Bois and others after a race riot in Springfield, Illinois, the hometown of Abraham Lincoln. The NAACP filed lawsuits in the federal courts to challenge discrimination. One of its first victories was in *Guinn v. U.S.,* which challenged Oklahoma's "grandfather clause" granting the right to vote to anyone descended from a voter qualified to vote in 1866 (the year before Reconstruction governments began to register African American voters), even if he could not pass the literacy test required of all others. However, the NAACP only filed *amicus curae* (friend of the court) briefs in *Guinn,* so *Buchanan v. Warley* represented the first NAACP appearance before the Supreme Court to argue a case. The Kentucky Court of Appeals had ruled that the state could use its police power to prevent intermingling of the races, arguing that if all African Americans were kept together, then the more well-educated and able among them could, in the words of the court, help "their less fortunate fellows" improve their living conditions. The NAACP's chief argument in its appeal to the Supreme Court was that the Fourteenth Amendment granted African Americans the same right to own property as whites.

## Significance

The Supreme Court overturned the Kentucky Court of Appeals decision, holding that a city could not prohibit people from buying houses wherever they chose. The forces of segregation were not finished, though. Instead of cities passing municipal ordinances, property owners frequently placed restrictive covenants into their housing deeds, which stated that they would sell or lease their property only to other whites. Today, such covenants would violate the Fourteenth Amendment, but the Supreme Court in *Corrigan v. Buckley* (1926) ruled that these covenants, because they were made by private individuals and were not state action, were not illegal. It was not until 1948 that the Supreme Court, in *Shelley v. Kraemer,* ruled that restrictive covenants could not be enforced in courts of law, finally resulting in some semblance of equality. It took even longer, until the 1960s, for the federal government to pass equal housing laws and end discrimination in federal housing programs. Thus, *Buchanan v. Warley* was a first step toward the ending of housing discrimination.

This decision also illustrates the ways attitudes and vocabularies have changed since 1910. Note, for instance, the Court's use of the term "colored," now considered offensive. Note also that Louisville justified its housing law because it was designed to maintain "racial purity." But rather than questioning such a goal, the Supreme Court simply notes that the same city allows white households to employ African American servants and that the ordinance does not prohibit African Americans from buying land on nearby blocks. It evades the larger issue of segregation by stating that the current case does not deal with an attempt to prevent racial amalgamation. However, its acceptance of the "separate but equal" doctrine indicates that this Court still reflected the attitudes of the pre–civil rights era. The doctrine would not be overruled until 1954 in the landmark case *Brown v. Board of Education of Topeka.*

## Primary Source

### *Buchanan v. Warley* [excerpt]

**SYNOPSIS:** Justice Day establishes that property rights include the right to buy, own, and sell property. Louisville claimed that housing segregation was needed to minimize racial hostilities. However, Day emphasizes twice that peace between the races

cannot be kept by depriving people of their constitutional right to property. Since the Thirteenth and Fourteenth Amendments to the Constitution guarantee property rights to all citizens, the Court overturned the Kentucky Court of Appeals and ruled in favor of Buchanan.

Mr. Justice Day delivered the opinion of the Court.

. . . This drastic [ordinance] is sought to be justified under the authority of the state in the exercise of the police power. It is said such legislation tends to promote the public peace by preventing racial conflicts; that it tends to maintain racial purity; that it prevents the deterioration of property owned and occupied by white people, which deterioration, it is contended, is sure to follow the occupancy of adjacent premises by persons of color.

The authority of the state to pass laws in the exercise of the police power, having for their object the promotion of the public health, safety and welfare is very broad as has been affirmed in numerous and recent decisions of this court. Furthermore the exercise of this power, embracing nearly all legislation of a local character is not to be interfered with by the courts where it is within the scope of legislative authority and the means adopted reasonably tend to accomplish a lawful purpose. But it is equally well established that the police power, broad as it is, cannot justify the passage of a law or ordinance which runs counter to the limitations of the federal Constitution; that principle has been so frequently affirmed in this court that we need not stop to cite the cases.

The Federal Constitution and laws passed within its authority are by the express terms of that instrument made the supreme law of the land. The Fourteenth Amendment protects life, liberty, and property from invasion by the states without due process of law. Property is more than the mere thing which a person owns. It is elementary that it includes the right to acquire, use, and dispose of it. The Constitution protects these essential attributes of property. Property consists of the free use, enjoyment, and disposal of a person's acquisitions without control or diminution save by the law of the land.

True it is that dominion over property springing from ownership is not absolute and unqualified. The disposition and use of property may be controlled in the exercise of the police power in the interest of the public health, convenience, or welfare. . . .

The concrete question here is: May the occupancy, and, necessarily, the purchase and sale of

The Supreme Court's decision in *Buchanan v. Warley* was a minor step in housing rights for African Americans. **GETTY IMAGES. REPRODUCED BY PERMISSION.**

property of which occupancy is an incident, be inhibited by the states, or by one of its municipalities, solely because of the color of the proposed occupant of the premises? That one may dispose of his property, subject only to the control of lawful enactments curtailing that right in the public interest, must be conceded. The question now presented makes it pertinent to inquire into the constitutional right of the white man to sell his property to a colored man, having in view the legal status of the purchaser and occupant. . . .

The statute of 1866, originally passed under sanction of the Thirteenth Amendment, 14 Stat. 27, and practically re-enacted after the adoption of the Fourteenth Amendment, 16 Stat. 144, expressly provided that all citizens of the United States in any state shall have the same right to purchase property as is enjoyed by white citizens. Colored persons are citizens of the United States and have the right to purchase property and enjoy and use the same without laws discriminating against them solely on account of color. These enactments did not deal with the social rights of men, but with those fundamental rights in property which it was intended to secure upon the same terms [to citizens of every race and color]. . . .

That there exists a serious and difficult problem arising from a feeling of race hostility which the law is powerless to control, and to which it must give a measure of consideration, may be freely admitted. But its solution cannot be promoted by depriving citizens of their constitutional rights and privileges.

As we have seen, this court has held laws valid which separated the races on the basis of equal accommodations in public conveyances, and courts of high authority have held enactments lawful which provide for separation in the public schools of white and colored pupils where equal privileges are given. But in view of the rights secured by the Fourteenth Amendment to the federal Constitution such legislation must have its limitations, and cannot be sustained where the exercise of authority exceeds the restraints of the Constitution. We think these limitations are exceeded in laws and ordinances of the character now before us.

It is the purpose of such enactments, and, it is frankly avowed it will be their ultimate effect, to require by law, at least in residential districts, the compulsory separation of the races on account of color. Such action is said to be essential to the maintenance of the purity of the races, although it is to be noted in the ordinance under consideration that the employment of colored servants in white families is permitted, and nearby residences of colored persons not coming within the blocks, as defined in the ordinance, are not prohibited.

The case presented does not deal with an attempt to prohibit the amalgamation of the races. The right which the ordinance annulled was the civil right of a white man to dispose of his property if he saw fit to do so to a person of color and of a colored person to make such disposition to a white person.

It is urged that this proposed segregation will promote the public peace by preventing race conflicts. Desirable as this is, and important as is the preservation of the public peace, this aim cannot be accomplished by laws or ordinances which deny rights created or protected by the federal Constitution.

It is said that such acquisitions by colored persons depreciate property owned in the neighborhood by white persons. But property may be acquired by undesirable white neighbors or put to disagreeable though lawful uses with like results.

We think this attempt to prevent the alienation of the property in question to a person of color was not a legitimate exercise of the police power of the state, and is in direct violation of the fundamental law enacted in the Fourteenth Amendment of the Constitution preventing state interference with property rights except by due process of law. That being the case, the ordinance cannot stand. . . .

[I]t follows that the judgment of the Kentucky Court of Appeals must be reversed, and the cause remanded to that court for further proceedings not inconsistent with this opinion.

## Further Resources

### BOOKS

Hill, Herbert, and James E. Jones. *Race in America: The Struggle for Equality.* Madison, Wis.: University of Wisconsin Press, 1993.

Nieman, Donald G. *Black Southerners and the Law: 1865–1900.* New York: Garland, 1994.

### PERIODICALS

Bernstein, David E. "Philip Sober Controlling Philip Drunk: *Buchanan v. Warley* in Historical Perspective." *Vanderbilt Law Review* 51, no. 4, 1998, 797–879.

Ely, James W., Jr. "Reflections on *Buchanan v. Warley,* Property Rights, and Race." *Vanderbilt Law Review* 51, no. 4, 1998, 953–75

Tushnet, Mark V. "Progressive Era Race Relations Cases in Their 'Traditional' Context." *Vanderbilt Law Review* 51, no. 4, 1998, 993–1003.

### WEBSITES

Kentucky Educational Television. "Kentucky Civil Rights Timeline." *Living the Story: The Civil Rights Movement in Kentucky.* Available online at http://www.ket.org/civilrights /timeline.htm; website home page: http://www.ket.org (accessed January 23, 2002).

# "Dissent During World War I: The Kate O'Hare Trial: 1919"

Court case

**By:** Kate Richards O'Hare and Martin J. Wade

**Date:** December 1917

**Source:** O'Hare, Kate Richards, and Martin J. Wade. "Dissent During World War I: The Kate O'Hare Trial: 1919." Reprinted in Marcus, Robert D., and Anthony Marcus. *On Trial: American History Through Court Proceedings and Hearings.* Vol. 2. St. James, N.Y.: Brandywine Press, 1998, 96–105.

**About the Authors:** Kate Richards O'Hare (1877–1948) joined the Socialist Party in 1901 and was a prominent Socialist in the early twentieth century. She ran for the U.S. Senate from Missouri and the House of Representatives from Kansas, though she never polled more than 5 percent of the vote. She campaigned against poverty and in favor of prison reform. After divorcing Francis P. O'Hare, she married Charles Cunningham in 1928 and lived the remainder of her life in California.

Martin J. Wade (1861–1931) as a judge was distinguished by his patriotic fervor. He was known for lecturing bootleggers about the importance of law and for his opinion that draft dodgers were public enemies. ■

## Introduction

The American Socialist Party was divided on whether or not to support American involvement in World War I (1914–1918). Many Socialists viewed it as a war for money and Wall Street profiteers, while others chose to support their country, or, at the very least, to adopt the more prudent course and support the war. O'Hare belonged to the former group; throughout 1917, she made

Kate Richards O'Hare, pictured with her husband and children, was sentenced to a five-year prison term under the Espionage and Sedition Acts of World War I. **REPRINTED FROM SALLY MILLER, *FROM PRAIRIE TO PRISON: THE LIFE OF SOCIAL ACTIVIST KATE RICHARD O'HARE,* COLUMBIA: UNIVERSITY OF MISSOURI PRESS, 1993.**

many speeches across the country opposing the war, including speeches in North Dakota. North Dakota's situation, though, was unique, for socialism in North Dakota had long been popular, and that popularity had boosted the socialist Nonpartisan League into power. The Democratic Party, looking for a way to unseat the Nonpartisan Leaguers, used the war issue, and O'Hare was one of the casualties of its efforts. The Sedition Act, which made illegal any false speech that impeded the war effort, had been passed as an amendment to the 1917 Espionage Act, and O'Hare was one of the first well-known people to be convicted under it. People watched the O'Hare trial closely to see if she would be convicted, and when she was, what sentence she would receive.

At the trial, O'Hare battled against predominant societal perceptions. Her activism clashed with Judge Wade's position and certainly affected the sentence she received. The judge's comments in the case demonstrated that his animosity toward O'Hare came in large part from his opposition to radical politics.

### Significance

Over two thousand people were eventually indicted under the Espionage and Sedition Acts, and six hundred of those were convicted, including such well-known figures as labor leaders "Big Bill" Haywood and Eugene V. Debs and socialist congressman Victor Berger. Nearly all of their convictions were upheld by the higher courts, and

## Socialists Convicted Under the Espionage and Sedition Acts

"Big Bill" Haywood and Victor Berger were two of the better-known socialist activists convicted under the Espionage and Sedition Acts. Haywood was a radical labor organizer who campaigned for the eight-hour workday. For a time, he was president of the Western Federation of Miners, but he joined the Industrial Workers of the World (IWW) in 1908. Convicted of violating the Espionage and Sedition Acts for calling a strike during World War I, he was sentenced to Leavenworth prison in Kansas. However, he remained free on appeal, and in 1921 jumped bail and moved to Moscow, Russia.

Victor Berger was a Milwaukee socialist and politician. Publishing his socialist paper *The Milwaukee Leader* became difficult after his second-class mailing privileges were revoked under the Espionage Act. He and four other socialists were convicted under the act for attempting to cause insubordination in the military. Though Berger won a seat as Wisconsin's fifth district representative to Congress in 1918, Congress refused to seat him because of his conviction. The governor held a special election, which Berger once more won, and when Congress again refused to allow him his seat, the governor left it empty until 1921.

the Supreme Court held the Espionage Act constitutional all six times it heard cases on the issue. The O'Hare case served as a rallying cry for radicals. Debs stated that if O'Hare was guilty, then so was he. Many people wrote letters to the president and attorney general, urging that she be pardoned and her sentence be commuted.

O'Hare remained free on bail while her lawyers appealed her case. In October 1918, the circuit court of appeals upheld her conviction, and, in March 1919, the Supreme Court refused to hear her case. She was sent to prison in April 1919 and served time in the Missouri State Penitentiary. The time she spent in prison shaped the rest of her life. Though she wanted to study the prison itself as her work assignment, she was instead assigned to a sewing room. She studied the prison for her own benefit, however, and in 1923 published a book, *In Prison,* to expose what in her view was the prison system's abusive nature. Also while in prison, she befriended other women radicals who were imprisoned, including Mollie Steimer and Emma Goldman. O'Hare was released in 1920, when her sentence was commuted, and she eventually received a full pardon from President Calvin Coolidge (served 1923–1929). For most of the rest of her life, she worked

for prison reform. She remained active in other radical causes as well, campaigning for Upton Sinclair in his gubernatorial campaign of 1934. O'Hare was one of the few women ever tried under the Espionage and Sedition Acts, and her social activism before, during, and after her prison term makes her a unique figure from this period.

## Primary Source

**"Dissent During World War I: The Kate O'Hare Trial: 1919"** [excerpt]

**SYNOPSIS:** In this excerpt from the court record, O'Hare makes a passionate argument for neutrality in lawmaking and directly addresses the wartime hysteria that surrounded the Sedition Acts. She argues that her conviction was unjust, saying it resulted from such hysteria. Judge Wade argues that her speeches, because they were defiant, bred anarchism and carried "the seed of discontent," making them seditious.

**Judge Wade:** Is there anything to be said now why sentence should not be imposed upon this defendant?

**Mrs. O'Hare:** Yes, your Honor: I was taught in high school that law was pure logic. Abstract law may be pure logic but the application of the law of testimony in this case seems to have gone far afield from logic. As your Honor knows, I am a professional woman, following the profession of delivering lectures whereby I hope to induce my hearers to study the philosophy of socialism. In the regular course of my profession and work I delivered during this year lectures all over the United States—in North Carolina when the draft riots were at their height; in Arizona two or three days following the deportations from Bisbee, and on the day when the strike vote was taken, when excitement ran high and passions were having their sway; in San Francisco during the Mooney case, and in Portland, Idaho, and the Northwestern lumber regions during the great I. W. W. [Industrial Workers of the World] excitement; and at all of these lectures conditions were as tense as conditions could be. The men who were in the employ of the United States in the Department of Justice were present at my meetings. These men were trained, highly efficient, and highly paid, detectors of crime and criminals. In all these months, when my lecture was under the scrutiny of this kind of men, there was no suggestion at any time that there was anything in it that was objectionable, treasonable or seditious. It was the custom of my meetings to send complimentary tickets to the district attorney and the marshal and deputy marshals of the district in order that they might hear the lecture.

And then in the course of the trip I landed at Bowman—a little, sordid, wind-blown, sun-blistered, frost-scarred town on the plains of Western Dakota. There was nothing unusual in my visit to Bowman, except the fact that it was unusual to make a town of this size. The reason I did was because there was one man whose loyalty and faithfulness and unselfish service to the cause to which I had given my life wanted me to come, and I felt he had a right to demand my services. I delivered my lecture there just as I had delivered it many, many times before. There was nothing in the audience that was unusual except the fact that it was a small audience—a solid, substantial, stolid type of farmer crowd. There was not the great enthusiasm that had prevailed at many of my meetings. There was nothing to stir me or arouse me or cause me to make a more impassioned appeal than usual. There was nothing at all in that little sordid, wind-blown town, that commonplace audience, that should have for a moment over-balanced my reason and judgment and common sense and have caused me to have been suddenly smitten with hydrophobia of sedition. But I found there were peculiar conditions existing at Bowman, and they are common to the whole state of North Dakota. In this State in the last year and a half the greatest and most revolutionary social phenomena that has occurred since the foundation of this Government, has taken place. The story is one that is so well known that I need spend little time on it. Here to these wind-blown, frost-scarred plains came men hard of face and feature and muscle who subdued this desert and made it bloom and produce the bread to feed the world; and these men, toiling in their desperate struggle with adverse conditions and with nature, gradually had it forced on their minds that in some way they were not receiving a just return for the labor expended; that after their wheat was raised and garnered in the processes of marketing, men who toiled not and suffered none of the hardships of production were robbing them of the product of their labor. . . .

And your Honor, it seems to me one of those strange grotesque things that can only be the outgrowth of this hysteria that is sweeping over the world today that a judge on the bench and a jury in the box and a prosecuting attorney should attempt to usurp the prerogatives of God Almighty and look down into the heart of a human being and decide what motives slumber there. There is no charge that if my intent or my motive was criminal that that intent or motive ever was put into action—only the charge that in my heart there was an intent, and on that strange charge of an intent so securely buried in a human heart that no result and no effect came from it, I went to trial. . . .

Your Honor, there are 100,000 people in the United States who know me personally. They have listened to my voice, looked in my face and have worked side by side with me in every great reform movement of the last twenty years. My life has been an open book to them. They know down to this time I have given all that I am, all that I have, from my earliest girlhood, my girlhood, my young womanhood, even my motherhood. And, your Honor, no judge on earth and no ten thousand judges or ten thousand juries can ever convince these hundred thousand people who know me and have worked with me, and these millions who have read my writings, that I am a criminal, or that I have ever given anything to my country except my most unselfish devotion and service. You cannot convince the people who know me that I am dangerous to the United States Government. They are willing to admit I am dangerous to some things in the United States, and I thank God that I am. I am dangerous to the invisible government of the United States; to the special privileges of the United States; to the white-slaver and the saloonkeeper, and I thank God that at this hour I am dangerous to the war profiteers of this country who rob the people on the one hand and rob and debase the Government on the other, and then with their pockets and wallets stuffed with the blood-stained profits of war, wrap the sacred folds of the Stars and Stripes about them and shout their blatant hypocrisy to the world. You can convince the people that I am dangerous to these men; but no jury and no judge can convince them that I am a dangerous woman to the best interests of the United States. . . .

Judge Wade: It is never a pleasant duty for me to sentence any one to prison, and it certainly is not a pleasant duty to send a woman to prison; in the course of a trial, in all the years I have been on the bench in the State and Federal courts, I have made it a rule to try to find out who I am sending to prison, because we all make mistakes in this world at times. On the spur of the moment and under excitement, sometimes people are misled and commit offenses, and I have a hard time to reconcile my view of things with heavy sentences in those cases. Therefore, when this case was closed, I made up my mind that I would find out before imposing sentence in this case what were the activities of this defendant.

She testified here to her loyalty, and her support of the President, and I was hoping in my heart that somewhere I would find out that after all, she was such a woman as she has here pictured herself today, and that thus a small penalty for this offense might be adequate, because I realize this is a serious business. The Nation is at war. Every sane man and woman knows that there is only one way that this war can be won, and that is by having men and money and spirit. Those three things are necessary—spirit in the men, in the service, and spirit in the men and women behind the men. And it was because of these absolute essentials that Congress enacted the Espionage law, to reach out and take hold of those who are trying to kill the spirit of the American people, in whole or in part; trying to put in their hearts hate toward this Government and towards the officials of this Government conducting the war. And realizing that this was such a grave matter, I investigated it as far as possible to find out really what character of woman this defendant is, and has been, in her work. I heard the evidence in this case. I had nothing to do with the question of whether she was guilty or innocent. The jury settled that question, and in my judgment, settled it right.

I received information from another town in North Dakota, and this information was given in the presence of counsel for the defendant that at Garrison, in her lecture there, she made the statement that mothers who reared sons to go into the army, were no better than animals on a North Dakota farm; that this war was in behalf of the capitalists, and that if we had loaned our money to Germany instead of to the allies, we would be now fighting with Germany instead of with the allies. That she had boys, but that they are not old enough to to go to war, but that if they were, they would not go. That the way to stop the war was to strike, and if the laboring men of this nation would strike, the war would soon be ended. Of course that was an *ex parte* matter. I have heard enough of testimony in my life, and I have seen enough of human nature to know that sometimes these things are stretched because of the feeling on one side or another of the question. So I thought I would go back and see what she had been doing. I wired the Postoffice Department at Washington, and I received a telegram which states:

> Party is on editorial staff of publication, *Social Revolution,* Saint Louis, Missouri, which has been barred from the mails for gross violations of Espionage Act, and is successor to *Ripsaw.* The party appears to be of the extreme type who have attempted to handicap the Government in every way in the conduct of the present war.

That was only a statement of an opinion. I tried to get copies of the *Social Revolution,* and have not succeeded in getting either the number for June or July. At some period during that time the Postmaster General barred this from the mails. I have the April and May numbers. In April they publish from Eugene Debs this statement:

> As we have said, the bankers are for bullets—for the fool patriots that enlist at paupers' wages to stop the bullets, while the bankers clip coupons, boost food prices, increase dividends, and pile up millions and billions for themselves. Say, Mr. Workingman, suppose you have sense enough to be as patriotic as the banker, but not a bit more so. When you see the bankers on the firing line with guns in their hands ready to stop bullets as well as start them, then it is time enough for you to be seized with the patriotic itch and have yourself shot into a crazy-quilt for their profit and glory. Don't you take a fit and rush to the front until you see them there. They own the country and if they don't set the example of fighting for it, why should you?

This was in April, before the war was declared. Up to that time I realize that every person in this country had the right to discuss the war, express their opinions against the war, give any reasons they might have against the war. But you will find here in this statement the note which rings out from the statement of the defendant here in court this afternoon and which forms the foundation of the entire gospel of hate which she and her associates are preaching to the American people: That the Nation is helpless, prostrate, down-trodden by a few capitalists, and that the average man has not a chance on earth; that this war is a war of capitalism; that it was brought about by capital and in the interest of capital; that 100, 200. Or 300 millionaires and billionaires if you please, in these United States dominate the souls and consciences of the other 99,000,000 American people. . . .

The Department of Justice furnishes me the following resolutions adopted at a meeting of the extreme wing of the Socialist Party, to which the defendant belongs, at their St. Louis convention after war was declared. The Secret Service, in sending in their report, says in a letter:

> We have been unable to secure anything specific on her that would be a violation of the Federal law in this district, but we have placed her in a class whose hearts and souls we are morally certain are for Germany against our country.

This defendant was chairman of the committee that brought in these resolutions. A newspaper of the city of St. Louis, in describing this convention, states:

> The Socialist Party, in a national convention at the Planters' Hotel last night, adopted resolutions proclaiming its unalterable opposition to the war just declared by the Government of the United States. The majority report of the committee on war and militarism containing the resolutions received 140 votes. An even more radical report by Louis Boudin, of New York, received 31 votes. The conservative minority report of John Spargo, of New York, declaring that Socialists should support the war, received only 5 votes. The vote was taken after hours of speech-making. Thomas William, of California, was hissed when he said he was an American, charged the delegates with being pro-German, and declared they did not represent the true sentiment of American Socialists. Mrs. Kate Richards O'Hare, of St. Louis, defied the Government and civil authorities. She declared that Socialists would not be molested in St. Louis for what they said because the city was against war, and the authorities were afraid to molest them.

Fine stuff for the boys and girls of the United States to be reading at this hour!

Mrs. O'Hare: May I make a statement to your Honor?

The Court: No, no; I have heard you. . . .

> This defendant does not take pride in her country. She abhors it. From the Atlantic to the Pacific there is nothing she can approve; she can only condemn. She is the apostle of despair, and carries only a message of hate and defiance. She is sowing the seed of discontent. She preaches defiance of authority. She poses as a Socialist, but she is breeding anarchy. Even in those sad times of bitter stress she cannot refrain from inspiring class hatreds. She asserts here today that if at liberty she could aid the Government. "Aid the Government!" Why every day she is at liberty she is a menace to the Government. She proclaims that if she is punished her followers will assert themselves and that the cause she represents will gain in strength and power. Let them "assert themselves"; they will find that while this Nation is kind and generous, she is also powerful, and that when the loyal people of the country are fully aroused, traitors will receive the reward of their treachery.

> Every person sentenced by a court must not only serve to expiate his own wrong, but he must serve as a warning to others. For these reasons the judgment of the court is that you, Kate Richards O'Hare, shall serve a period of five years in the Federal prison at Jefferson City, Missouri, and pay the costs of this suit.

## Further Resources

### BOOKS

American Civil Liberties Union. *The Conviction of Mrs. Kate Richards O'Hare and North Dakota Politics.* New York: National Civil Liberties Bureau, 1918.

Foner, Philip S., and Sally M Miller. *Kate Richards O'Hare: Selected Writings and Speeches.* Baton Rouge, La.: Louisiana State University Press, 1982.

Kennedy, Kathleen. *Disloyal Mothers and Scurrilous Citizens: Women and Subversion During World War I.* Bloomington, Ind.: Indiana University Press, 1999.

Miller, Sally M. *From Prairie to Prison: The Life of Social Activist Kate Richards O'Hare.* Columbia, Mo.: University of Missouri Press, 1993.

O'Hare, Kate Richards. *In Prison.* Seattle, Wash.: University of Washington Press, 1976.

### PERIODICALS

Mallach, Stanley. "Red Kate O'Hare Comes to Madison: The Politics of Free Speech." *Wisconsin Magazine of History* 53, no. 3, Spring 1970, 204–222.

Sannes, Erling N. "Queen of the Lecture Platform: Kate Richards O'Hare and North Dakota Politics, 1917–1921." *North Dakota History* 58, no. 4, Fall 1991, 2–19.

**WEBSITES**

Elwyn B. Robinson Department of Special Collections, University of North Dakota. "Kate Richards O'Hare Papers." Available online at http://www.und.edu/dept/library/Collections /og220.html; website home page: http://www.und.edu/dept /library/ (accessed January 22, 2003). *This site contains a biographical sketch of Kate Richards O'Hare.*

# Selective Draft Law Cases

Supreme Court decision

**By:** Edward D. White

**Date:** January 7, 1918

**Source:** White, Edward D. *Selective Draft Law Cases,* 245 U.S. 366 (1918). Reprinted in Kutler, Stanley I., ed. *The Supreme Court and the Constitution: Readings in American Constitutional History,* 3rd ed. New York: Norton, 1984, 321–323.

**About the Author:** Edward D. White (1845–1921), born in 1845 in Louisiana to a slaveholder, fought for the Confederacy in the Civil War. He served on the Louisiana Supreme Court and ran for a seat in the U.S. Senate. President Grover Cleveland (served 1885–1889; 1893–1897) appointed him associate justice to the U.S. Supreme Court in 1894, and President William Howard Taft (served 1909–1913) elevated him to chief justice in 1911. ■

## Introduction

During the nineteenth century, the United States prided itself on raising armies through volunteers. Although most soldiers in the Civil War (1861–1865) were volunteers, Congress passed an unpopular draft law in March 1863, leading to antidraft riots in New York City in July of that year. The Conscription Act, as the act was known, was challenged in court, but the Supreme Court never ruled on the case and lower courts did not present a unified opinion. The Spanish American War (1898) was fought primarily by volunteers and National Guard units provided by local areas.

In the early twentieth century, public opinion was deeply divided about American participation in World War I (1914–1918). Some fifty congressional representatives voted against the war, and President Woodrow Wilson (served 1913–1921) believed he needed a national draft to raise a large enough army. Statistics proved him correct: Only two million men joined the army as volunteers, while three million were drafted. This law, called the Selective Draft Law, required registration for the draft and set up mechanisms for conducting the draft.

Its legality rested upon the Congress's constitutional power to "raise and support Armies," and "to declare War." At least 337,000 men dodged the draft, but most were never prosecuted. *Selective Draft Law Cases* is the name given to the Supreme Court case that consolidated the appeals of some of the ten thousand men who were prosecuted.

## Significance

The Supreme Court faced a dilemma in this case. Those convicted under the law argued that Congress did not have a constitutional right to draft soldiers. Conscription, they argued, was slavery, and therefore unconstitutional. If the Court ruled against the law, however, then Congress and the president may very well have ignored the ruling. Such behavior would not have been without precedent: President Andrew Jackson, for example, ignored the Supreme Court in relocating Native Americans and famously remarked about the Court's chief justice, "John Marshall has made his decision. Now let him enforce it." This potential outcome might have been one reason the Supreme Court upheld the constitutionality of the Draft Law. The Court also held that the powers to raise an army and to declare war gave Congress the power to create a draft. It reasoned that when America first sought its independence, the British Crown had the power to enforce military service but American colonists, under the Articles of Confederation, did not, so the framers of the Constitution wished to grant America's new government the power to enforce military service. Accordingly, the Court ruled in favor of the government in the Draft Law cases.

By the Vietnam conflict in the 1960s and 1970s, the Court was less supportive of the federal government, giving increased rights to conscientious objectors to the draft. Nonetheless, the initial decisions supporting the draft have had a lasting impact on the United States. The government used the draft to raise armies in World War I, World War II (1939–1945), and the Vietnam conflict (1964–1975). In the 1970s, one of the key arguments in favor of lowering the voting age to eighteen was that a person old enough to die in war should be considered old enough to vote. In recent years, questions have arisen about the gender bias of the draft. Though all men are still required to register with the Selective Service when they turn eighteen, women are exempt. Some argue that this practice is sexist and that women should be subject to the draft.

## Primary Source

*Selective Draft Law Cases* [excerpt]

**SYNOPSIS:** White first notes that Congress has the power to create an army, which allows it to raise

The selective draft of World War I demonstrated the power of the federal government to compel military service. NATIONAL ARCHIVES AND RECORDS ADMINISTRATION.

men for that army. He then examines the forced nature of the selective service, reasoning that just as government has obligations to its citizens, citizens have obligations to their government, including military service. He also observes that the Constitution corrected the weakness of the Articles of Confederation, which did not allow a draft.

Chief Justice White delivered the opinion of the Court.

The possession of authority to enact the statute must be found in the clauses of the Constitution giving Congress power "to declare war; . . . to raise and support armies, but no appropriation of money to that use shall be for a longer term than two years; . . . to make rules for the government and regulation of the land and naval forces." Article I, § 8. And of course the powers conferred by these provisions like all other powers given carry with them as provided by the Constitution the authority "to make all laws which shall be necessary and proper for carrying into execution the foregoing powers." Article I, § 8.

As the mind cannot conceive an army without the men to compose it, on the face of the Constitution the objection that it does not give power to

provide for such men would seem to be too frivolous for further notice. It is said, however, that since under the Constitution as originally framed state citizenship was primary and United States citizenship but derivative and dependent thereon, therefore the power conferred upon Congress to raise armies was only coterminous with United States citizenship and could not be exerted so as to cause that citizenship to lose its dependent character and dominate state citizenship. But the proposition simply denies to Congress the power to raise armies which the Constitution gives. That power by the very terms of the Constitution, being delegated, is supreme. Article VI. In truth the contention simply assails the wisdom of the framers of the Constitution in conferring authority on Congress and in not retaining it as it was under the Confederation in the several States. Further it is said, the right to provide is not denied by calling for volunteer enlistments, but it does not and cannot include the power to exact enforced military duty by the citizen. This however but challenges the existence of all power, for a governmental power which has no sanction to it and which therefore can only be exercised provided the citizen consents to its exertion is in no substantial sense a power. It is argued, however, that although this is abstractly true, it is not concretely so because as compelled military service is repugnant to a free government and in conflict with all the great guarantees of the Constitution as to individual liberty, it must be assumed that the authority to raise armies was intended to be limited to the right to call an army into existence counting alone upon the willingness of the citizen to do his duty in time of public need, that is, in time of war. But the premise of this proposition is so devoid of foundation that it leaves not even a shadow of ground upon which to base the conclusion. Let us see if this is not at once demonstrable. It may not be doubted that the very conception of a just government and its duty to the citizen includes the reciprocal obligation of the citizen to render military service in case of need and the right to compel it. Vattel, Law of Nations, Book III, c. 1 & 2. To do more than state the proposition is absolutely unnecessary in view of the practical illustration afforded by the almost universal legislation to that effect now in force. . . .

In the Colonies before the separation from England there cannot be the slightest doubt that the right to enforce military service was unquestioned and that practical effect was given to the power in many cases. Indeed the brief of the Government contains a list of Colonial acts manifesting the power and its enforcement in more than two hundred cases. And this exact situation existed also after the separation. Under the Articles of Confederation it is true Congress had no such power, as its authority was absolutely limited to making calls upon the States for the military forces needed to create and maintain the army, each State being bound for its quota as called. But it is indisputable that the States in response to the calls made upon them met the situation when they deemed it necessary by directing enforced military service on the part of the citizens. In fact the duty of the citizen to render military service and the power to compel him against his consent to do so was expressly sanctioned by the constitutions of at least nine of the States. . . . While it is true that the States were sometimes slow in exerting the power in order to fill their quotas—a condition shown by resolutions of Congress calling upon them to comply by exerting their compulsory power to draft and by earnest requests by Washington to Congress that a demand be made upon the States to resort to drafts to fill their quotas—that fact serves to demonstrate instead a challenge to the existence of the authority. A default in exercising a duty may not be resorted to as a reason for denying its existence.

When the Constitution came to be formed it may not be disputed that one of the recognized necessities for its adoption was the want of power in Congress to raise an army and the dependence upon the States for their quotas. In supplying the power it was manifestly intended to give it all and leave none to the States, since besides the delegation to Congress of authority to raise armies the Constitution prohibited the States, without the consent of Congress, from keeping troops in time of peace or engaging in war. . . .

Thus sanctioned as is the act before us by the text of the Constitution, and by its significance as read in the light of the fundamental principles with which the subject is concerned, by the power recognized and carried into effect in many civilized countries, by the authority and practice of the colonies before the Revolution, of the States under the Confederation and of the Government since the formation of the Constitution, the want of merit in the contentions that the act in the particulars which we have been previously called upon to consider was beyond the constitutional power of Congress, is manifest. . . .

Finally, as we are unable to conceive upon what theory the exaction by government from the citizen of the performance of his supreme and noble duty of contributing to the defense of the rights and honor of the nation, as the result of a war declared by the great representative body of the people, can be said to be the imposition of involuntary servitude in violation of the prohibitions of the Thirteenth Amendment, we are constrained to the conclusion that the contention to that effect is refuted by its mere statement.

Affirmed.

## Further Resources

### BOOKS

Central Committee for Conscientious Objectors. *Attorneys' Guide to Selective Service and Military Case Law.* Philadelphia: Central Committee for Conscientious Objectors, 1969.

Chambers, John Whiteclay. *To Raise an Army: The Draft Comes to Modern America.* New York: Free Press, 1987.

Clifford, J. Garry. *The First Peacetime Draft.* Lawrence, Kan.: University Press of Kansas, 1986.

Keene, Jennifer D. *Doughboys, The Great War, and the Remaking of America.* Baltimore, Md.: Johns Hopkins University Press, 2001.

Kennedy, David M. *Over Here: The First World War and American Society.* New York: Oxford University Press, 1980.

Murdock, Eugene Converse. *Patriotism Limited, 1862–1865: The Civil War Draft and the Bounty System.* Kent, Ohio: Kent State University Press, 1967.

Pearlman, Michael. *To Make Democracy Safe for America: Patricians and Preparedness in the Progressive Era.* Urbana, Ill.: University of Illinois Press, 1984.

# The Lynching of Robert P. Prager

## "German Is Lynched by an Illinois Mob"; "Cabinet Discusses Prager's Lynching"; "Prager Asked Mob to Wrap Body in Flag"; "Tried for Prager Murder"; "The Prager Case"

Newspaper articles

**By:** *The New York Times*

**Date:** April 5–June 3, 1918

**Source:** "German Is Lynched by an Illinois Mob," *The New York Times,* April 5, 1918, 4; "Cabinet Discusses Prager's Lynching," *The New York Times,* April 6, 1918, 15; "Prager Asked Mob to Wrap Body in Flag," *The New York Times,* April 11, 1918, 10; "Tried for Prager Murder," *The New York Times,* May 14, 1918, 24; "The Prager Case," *The New York Times,* June 3, 1918, 10.

**About the Organization:** Founded in 1850 as the *Daily Times, The New York Times* was originally a relatively obscure local paper. By the early twentieth century, however, it had grown into a widely known, widely read news source. Its banner, "All the News That's Fit to Print," is recognized across the United States and throughout the world. ∎

## Introduction

Vigilante violence has long been a part of American history. Threatened lynchings, tarrings and featherings, and arson were all part of the protests against the Stamp Act before the American Revolution. Supporters of slavery burned the headquarters of abolitionists in Philadelphia in 1834, and Elijah Lovejoy, an abolitionist publisher, was killed trying to defend his press from attacks. Violence did not abate after the Civil War, as the Ku Klux Klan (KKK) used lynchings to suppress the black population, and in the 1890s, the nation averaged 187 lynchings annually. Though most of these occurred in the South, they were not unheard of in the rest of the nation, especially as the KKK began to expand its influence in the early twentieth century. The lynching of Robert P. Prager was therefore not an isolated incident.

This vigilantism was part of the backdrop as the United States considered its role in World War I (1914–1918). Though the country's announced purpose in the war was a noble one, many of its supporters used

ignoble methods to silence or sway opponents. Houses were vandalized with yellow paint because their owners failed to contribute enough to the war, people were fired from their jobs for not buying enough war bonds, and towns ostracized opponents of the war. Tarrings and featherings and beatings (sometimes with a horsewhip) were common. In Montana in 1917, vigilantes seized Frank Little, an organizer for the radical union the Industrial Workers of the World (IWW), and hanged him from a railroad trestle. The government did little to contain this violence other than issue tepid condemnations of vigilantism, and this hands-off attitude set the stage for Prager's lynching.

## Significance

For many people, what set the lynching of Prager, a German-born socialist, apart from other World War I violence was the finality of it and the fact that Prager had done nothing wrong. (Many people believed that Frank Little had brought the lynching upon himself by organizing for the IWW.) There was an immediate outcry against the lynching from many newspapers, and the federal government took notice. The government's first reaction, however, was not to go after the lynchers or to try to prevent a repeat but to enact a stronger "antidisloyalty" act so that the government rather than vigilante mobs would punish any antiwar speech. Indeed, the guilty parties were all acquitted rapidly, and the lynching was one of the contributing factors to the creation of the Sedition Act, designed to punish "any disloyal" speech about the government. President Woodrow Wilson (served 1913–1921) finally spoke out against the lynching nearly four months later.

After World War I, the nation's attention turned to radicals during the "Red Scares" of the 1920s, and wanton violence was carried out against many striking workers. The growth of the KKK also contributed to the violence. Many in the nation tried to persuade Congress to pass an antilynching statute, but southern opposition killed the effort. Lynchings decreased in numbers as efforts to keep the spotlight on the issue continued. Not until the 1960s, though, did lynching became a federal crime. Some observers believe that the vigilante tradition in America continues today, as many people feel the need to carry a gun, not only for protection, but also to "right a wrong" when "the system fails."

## Primary Source

The Prager Case

**SYNOPSIS:** Together, these five articles tell the story of Prager's lynching and his murderers' subsequent trial. After Prager was lynched at the hands of an angry mob, charges were brought against those responsible. Though the lynchers were quickly acquitted, the case garnered national attention, and authorities used it as a justification for stronger laws against sedition.

### German Is Lynched by an Illinois Mob

Had Made Speeches to Miners on Socialism and Uttered Disloyal Sentiments.

### Police Tried to Save Him

Mob Stormed City Hall to Get Him and Then Hanged Him After Wrapping Him In an American Flag.

St. Louis, Mo. April 4—Robert P. Prager, a German born Socialist, was dragged from the basement of the Collinsville, Ill., City Hall, twelve miles from St. Louis, tonight by leaders of a mob of from three to four hundred men, marched barefooted to a point one-half mile outside of the Collinsville limits and lynched. He was accused of having made disloyal remarks to Maryville, Ill. miners.

His capture by the mob and lynching came after he had been hidden by the Collinsville police among a lot of tiling in the basement of the City Hall while Mayor Siegel made a speech to the mob from the steps of the City Hall, pleading with his hearers to give the prisoner the right of trial. The police previously had rushed the mob and captured Prager while he was being marched through the main street of the city with an American flag tied about him.

Twice before the mob wreaked its vengeance on the man it appeared that he would have escaped from it—once when he fled from Maryville to Collinsville, a distance of four miles and again when the police, after hiding their prisoner, told the mob he had been spirited out of the city. But the mob leaders each took up the march for their victim and stayed with it until they found him.

The lynching took place on the old National Road leading toward St. Louis. While police were rushing toward the scene in an automobile from East St. Louis, Prager, who was a baker and miner, 32 years old, was strung up to a tree. The lynching took place about 12:30 o'clock Friday morning. The body was found a few minutes later and the Coroner of Edwardsville, Madison County, notified.

The trouble started at Maryville when Prager was employed there in the Bruno Bakery. Recently he made application to join the Miners' Union and sought work in the coal mines. He said he had worked as a miner in Germany.

While his application for membership in the union was pending, Prager is said to have harangued some of the miners on socialism. In the course of his remarks he made statements they interpreted as disloyal and pro-German. When a recent wave of patriotism swept over many Illinois towns the miners and others at Maryville organized a committee to deal with Prager.

The committee was to have taken him in custody yesterday afternoon. Prager heard of it and fled to Maryville.

The committee followed and searched for him. He was found in a house there in which he formerly resided and dragged into the street. His shoes were stripped off and members of the mob began pulling off his clothes when some one produced an American flag. It was wrapped about him and tied.

With the prisoner bareheaded and stumbling every few steps a parade was started up the main street of the city. It had proceeded several blocks when a policeman led a squad of other officers in a dash into the crowd. They captured the prisoner. He was hurried to the police station, members of the mob following. Later, he was retaken by the mob.

### Cabinet Discusses Prager's Lynching

Holds Congress at Fault for Failing to Pass Pending Bills Against Sedition.

### No Federal Interference

German at Collinsville, Ill., Avowed Loyalty, It Is Said—Tried to Enlist in Navy.

Washington, April 5—The lynching of Robert P. Prager at Collinsville, Ill. for alleged pro-German utterances and activities caused considerable concern among Federal officials in Washington and was the subject of discussion at the regular meeting of the Cabinet this afternoon. From what was said after the meeting, it was apparent that the President and his advisors decided that the Federal Government had no warrant for interference.

After the Cabinet meeting Attorney General Gregory said that the Federal Government would be obliged to let the State of Illinois handle the case. The Department of Justice, it was indicated, probably would send some of its agents in the State to investigate but this was as far as the Government could go.

Members of the Cabinet said that while the lynching was to be deplored the fact remained that the slowness of Congress in enacting pending legislation dealing with enemy aliens was in a measure responsible for such occurrences. One Cabinet officer said that if Congress would not enact the nec-

Vigilantes such as these showed the hysteria existing on the home front during World War I. THE LIBRARY OF CONGRESS.

essary laws similar attacks on enemy aliens would happen. Officials believe that other outbreaks against Germans are likely.

The lynching of Prager Is regarded here as an instance of an aroused feeling among the American people since the beginning of the German offensive in Picardy. This feeling is observed in occurences all over the country.

### Prager Asked Mob to Wrap Body in Flag

Witness Also Tells the Coroner That Boys of 12 to 16 Helped to Hang Alleged Pro-German.

Collinsville, Ill., April 10.—A request that his body be wrapped in the American flag formed the last words of Robert B. [sic] Prager, hanged here by a mob early last Friday, according to testimony given today before the Coroner's inquest by Joseph Riegel, it was said tonight by persons who were present at the inquiry, which was held behind closed doors. Riegal, according to these persons, admitted he was a leader of the mob.

Riegel said that en route to the scene of the hanging several persons were met in automobiles and Prager was forced to sing and kiss the flag for them. At the tree members of the mob questioned Prager for twenty minutes regarding his alleged pro–Germanism.

"Somebody tied the rope around Prager's neck," Riegel continued, "and several boys, from 12 to 16 years old, pulled him up. His hands were not tied and he grabbed at the rope. They let him down and we said: "Now are you going to tell whether anybody is mixed up with you? We told him we were going to kill him if he did not tell us everything.

"All the time the crowd kept getting more excited and angry. Some one shouted: 'Well, if he won't come in with anything, string him up.' A boy produced a handkerchief and his hands were tied. I might have been the man who did the thing. I was drunk and because I had been in the army the crowd made me the big man in the affair and I guess I was sort of puffed up over that.

"Just as we were about to string him up Prager said: 'All right, boys! Go ahead and kill me, but wrap me in the flag when you bury me.' Then they pulled the rope."

The inquest was continued tonight in an attempt to conclude it by tomorrow night. No arrests will be made until after the inquest, according to W.M. Trautmann, Assistant Attorney General of Illinois, who is in charge of the proceedings.

### Tried for Prager Murder

Eleven Men Face Court for Hanging of Enemy Alien.

Edwardsville, Ill., May 13.—Three talesmen [jurors] had been accepted tentatively by the State at adjournment tonight of the first day's session in the trial of eleven men charged with the murder of Robert Paul Prager, enemy alien. Prager, who was accused of disloyal utterances, was hanged by a mob at Collinsville, Ill., on April 5.

Motions by the defense for a quashing of the indictments, based on alleged technical errors, were overruled late this afternoon by Judge Bernreuter and up to adjournment twenty-five veniremen [jurors] had been interrogated by attorneys for the prosecution. All save the three tentatively seated were excused because they said they had formed opinions after reading newspaper accounts of the lynching.

The eleven defendants joked with bystanders and whistled as they crossed the street from the jail to the courthouse when their cases were called. Each wore a red, white, and blue rosette in his coat lapel.

### The Prager Case [June 3, 1918]

The acquittal of the murderers of ROBERT PAUL PRAGER was evidently a gross miscarriage of justice. PRAGER was a German and a Socialist who, it is said, was guilty of anti-American talk about the war in the Illinois mining district where he lived and worked. His talk was violently resented by his fellow-miners, and for his own protection, he was placed in jail. The jail was broken into by a mob and PRAGER was lynched.

Eleven men were placed on trial for this crime, and have been acquitted. The reports indicate that their defense was not that they did not lynch PRAGER, but that he deserved what he got. "A new unwritten law" is said to have been pleaded by their counsel. The present "unwritten law" is that any woman may kill any man whose conduct displeases her for any reason, and that any man may kill any other man provided there is a woman in the case. The new unwritten law appears to be that any group of men may execute justice, or what they consider justice, in any case growing out of the war. Both "unwritten laws" are recognitions of murder as a defensible and even legal American institution. The old unwritten law is a disgrace and a scandal, and the new one is nothing less.

## Further Resources

**BOOKS**

Mock, James R. *Censorship 1917.* Princeton, N.J.: Princeton University Press, 1941.

Preston, William. *Aliens and Dissenters: Federal Suppression of Radicals, 1903–1933.* Urbana, Ill.: University of Illinois Press, 1994.

Tolzmann, Don H., Carl Wittke, and Franziska Ott Munchen. *German-Americans in the World Wars: Volume I: The Anti-German Hysteria of World War One.* New Providence, N.J.: K.G. Saur, 1995.

**WEBSITES**

Burnett, Paul. "The Red Scare." Available online at http://www.law.umkc.edu/faculty/projects/ftrials/SaccoV/redscare.html (accessed January 23, 2003).

Center for History and New Media. "Listening to Anti-German Hysteria: The War at Home: The War on German Americans." Available online at http://chnm.gmu.edu/features/voices/ww1german/warongerman.html; website home page: http://chnm.gmu.edu (accessed January 23, 2003).

Ellis Island Immigration Museum. "Ellis Island History: Closing the Open Door." Available online at http://www.ellisisland.com/closing.html; website home page: http://www.ellisisland.com/history.html (accessed January 23, 2003).

# *Schenck v. U.S.*

**Supreme Court decision**

**By:** Oliver Wendell Holmes Jr.

**Date:** March 3, 1919

**Source:** Holmes, Oliver Wendell, Jr. *Schenck v. U.S.*, 249 U.S. 47 (1919). Available online at http://caselaw.lp.findlaw.com/us/249/47.html; website home page: http://caselaw.lp.findlaw.com (accessed January 23, 2003).

**About the Author:** Oliver Wendell Holmes Jr. (1841–1935) served in the Union army during the Civil War (1861–1865) from 1861 to 1864. He joined the Massachusetts Supreme Court as an associate justice in 1883, rising to chief justice in 1899. In 1902, President Theodore Roosevelt (served 1901–1909) appointed him associate justice of the U.S. Supreme Court, where he served until age ninety-one. ■

## Introduction

Free speech restrictions were relatively few, especially on the federal level, before World War I (1914–1918). The first federal restrictions were the Alien and Sedition Acts, enacted in 1798 during a crisis involving France. These acts were usually used by the Federalist government against political opponents, and in response to them, Virginia and Kentucky passed resolutions announcing that states had the right to nullify acts of Congress. These acts expired early in the nineteenth century, but free speech became a federal issue again during the Civil War. During the war, the writ of habeas corpus (which forbids the government from indefinitely imprisoning people) was suspended, and many people lost their liberties. The Supreme Court never specifically addressed the suspension of habeas corpus, but it indirectly supported President Lincoln's authority by allowing him to respond to the emergency of the Civil War. The Court also refused to exercise jurisdiction over military tribunals, but it did hold that neither Congress nor the president had power to empower military commissions to try civilians when the civil courts were open. In the few cases in which it ruled on free speech issues before World War I, the Court generally favored the government's position.

Before the United States entered World War I, dissent over possible U.S. involvement in the war was widespread. In response, Congress passed several laws designed to quell dissent. These included the Draft Act, which made it a crime to oppose the draft, and the Espionage Act, which made it a crime to engage in espionage that interfered with the war effort. Charles T. Schenck was the first person charged with violating the Espionage Act whose case came before the Supreme Court. Schenck had been tried, convicted, and sentenced to six months in prison for circulating a variety of materials opposing military conscription, including a pamphlet labeled *Long Live the Constitution of the United States*, but he was free on bail pending his appeal.

## Significance

The Supreme Court upheld Schenck's conviction. In doing so, the Court created a standard by which to judge restrictions on free speech: the "clear and present danger" standard (although since the 1960s the Court has not applied this standard). The decision also generated one of the most quoted statements in court history: "the most stringent protection of free speech would not protect a man in falsely shouting fire in a theatre and causing a panic." After Schenck, the "clear and present danger" standard was applied to uphold five more convictions under the Espionage and Sedition Acts. Two of those decisions were unanimous, but Holmes and Louis Brandeis dissented in three later cases, arguing that the criminalized speech did not create a clear and present danger.

Free speech was expanded in 1925 when the Supreme Court extended the First Amendment to protect some speech against state action. It was not until the 1960s, though, that the Warren Court held that speech could not be banned unless it was aimed to produce "imminent lawless action" and such action was likely to occur.

## Primary Source

*Schenck v. U.S.* [excerpt]

**SYNOPSIS:** Holmes first establishes that Schenck was responsible for conspiring to mail a Socialist flyer deemed illegal for mailing because of its content. Then, he states that the flyer was indeed mailed illegally and with the intent to cause hysteria. During peacetime, he says, such literature would be legal, but mailing it in wartime is equivalent to "falsely shouting fire in a theatre and causing a panic."

Mr. Justice Holmes delivered the opinion of the Court.

This is an indictment in three counts. The first charges a conspiracy to violate the Espionage Act of June 15, 1917, . . . by causing and attempting to cause insubordination, &c., in the military and naval forces of the United States, and to obstruct the recruiting and enlistment service of the United States, when the United States was at war with the German Empire, to-wit, that the defendant willfully conspired to have printed and circulated to men who had been called and accepted for military service under the Act of May 18, 1917, a document set forth and alleged to be calculated to cause such insubordination and obstruction. The count alleges overt acts in pursuance of the conspiracy, ending in the distribution of the document set forth. . . . The defendants were found guilty on all the counts. They set up the First Amendment to the Constitution forbidding Congress to make any law abridging the freedom of speech, or of the press, and bringing the case here on that ground have argued some other points also of which we must dispose.

It is argued that the evidence, if admissible, was not sufficient to prove that the defendant Schenck was concerned in sending the documents. According to the testimony Schenck said he was general secretary of the Socialist party and had charge of the Socialist headquarters from which the documents were sent. . . . Without going into confirmatory details that were proved, no reasonable man could doubt that the defendant Schenck was largely instrumental in sending the circulars about. As to the defendant Baer there was evidence that she was a member of the Executive Board and that the minutes of its transactions were hers. The argument as to the sufficiency of the evidence that the defendants conspired to send the documents only impairs the seriousness of the real defence. . . .

The document in question upon its first printed side recited the first section of the Thirteenth Amendment, said that the idea embodied in it was violated by the conscription act and that a conscript is little better than a convict. In impassioned language it intimated that conscription was despotism in its worst form and a monstrous wrong against humanity in the interest of Wall Street's chosen few. It said, "Do not submit to intimidation," but in form at least confined itself to peaceful measures such as a petition for the repeal of the act. The other and later printed side of the sheet was headed "Assert Your Rights." It stated reasons for alleging that any one violated the Constitution when he refused to recognize "your right to assert your opposition to the draft," and went on, "If you do not assert and support your rights, you are helping to deny or disparage rights which it is the solemn duty of all citizens and residents of the United States to retain." It described the arguments on the other side as coming from cunning politicians and a mercenary capitalist press, and even silent consent to the conscription law as helping to support an infamous conspiracy. It denied the power to send our citizens away to foreign shores to shoot up the people of other lands, and added that words could not express the condemnation such cold-blooded ruthlessness deserves, &c., &c., winding up, "You must do your share to maintain, support and uphold the rights of the people of this country." Of course the document would not have been sent unless it had been intended to have some effect, and we do not see what effect it could be expected to have upon persons subject to the draft except to influence them to obstruct the carrying of it out. The defendants do not deny that the jury might find against them on this point.

But it is said, suppose that that was the tendency of this circular, it is protected by the First Amendment to the Constitution. Two of the strongest expressions are said to be quoted respectively from well-known public men. . . . We admit that in many places and in ordinary times the defendants in saying all that was said in the circular would have been within their constitutional rights. But the character of every act depends upon the circumstances in which it is done. . . . The most stringent protection of free speech would not protect a man in falsely shouting fire in a theatre and causing a panic. It does not even protect a man from an injunction against uttering words that may have all the effect of force. . . . The question in every case is whether the words used are used in such circumstances and are of such a nature as to create a clear and present danger that they will bring about the substantive evils that Congress has a right to prevent. It is

a question of proximity and degree. When a nation is at war many things that might be said in time of peace are such a hindrance to its effort that their utterance will not be endured so long as men fight and that no Court could regard them as protected by any constitutional right. It seems to be admitted that if an actual obstruction of the recruiting service were proved, liability for words that produced that effect might be enforced. The statute of 1917 in section 4 punishes conspiracies to obstruct as well as actual obstruction. If the act, (speaking, or circulating a paper,) its tendency and the intent with which it is done are the same, we perceive no ground for saying that success alone warrants making the act a crime. . . .

It was not argued that a conspiracy to obstruct the draft was not within the words of the Act of 1917. The words are "obstruct the recruiting or enlistment service," and it might be suggested that they refer only to making it hard to get volunteers. Recruiting heretofore usually having been accomplished by getting volunteers the word is apt to call up that method only in our minds. But recruiting is gaining fresh supplies for the forces, as well by draft as otherwise. It is put as an alternative to enlistment or voluntary enrollment in this act. The fact that the Act of 1917 was enlarged by the amending Act of May 16, 1918, c. 75, 40 Stat. 553, of course, does not affect the present indictment and would not, even if the former act had been repealed.

Judgments affirmed.

## Further Resources

### BOOKS

Alonso, Karen. *Schenck v. United States: Restrictions on Free Speech.* Springfield, N.J.: Enslow, 1999.

Chafee, Zechariah. *Free Speech in the United States.* Cambridge, Mass.: Harvard University Press, 1946.

Kohn, Stephen M. *American Political Prisoners: Prosecutions Under the Espionage and Sedition Acts.* Westport, Conn.: Praeger, 1994.

Mauro, Tony. *Illustrated Great Decisions of the Supreme Court.* Washington, D.C.: CQ Press, 2000.

Peterson, H.C., and Gilbert C. Fite. *Opponents of War, 1917–1918.* Madison, Wis.: University of Wisconsin Press, 1957.

### WEBSITES

Supreme Court Historical Society. "History of the Court: The White Court: 1910–1921." Available online at http://www.supremecourthistory.org/02_history/subs_history/02_c09.html; website home page: http://www.supremecourthistory.org/index.html (accessed January 23, 2002).

University of Montana School of Journalism. "The Sedition Cases." Available online at: http://www.umt.edu/journalism /student_resources/class_web_sites/media_law/sedition.html; website home page: http://www.umt.edu (accessed January 23, 2003).

# *Debs v. U.S.*

Supreme Court decision

**By:** Oliver Wendell Holmes Jr.

**Date:** March 10, 1919

**Source:** Holmes, Oliver Wendell, Jr. *Debs v. U.S.*, 249 U.S. 211 (1919). Available online at http://caselaw.lp.findlaw.com /cgi-bin/getcase.pl?court=US&vol=249&invol=211; website home page: http://caselaw.lp.findlaw.com (accessed January 23, 2003).

**About the Author:** Oliver Wendell Holmes Jr. (1841–1935) served in the Union army in the Civil War (1861–1865) from 1861 to 1864. He joined the Massachusetts Supreme Court as an associate justice in 1883, rising in 1899 to chief justice. In 1902, President Theodore Roosevelt (served 1901–1909) appointed him associate justice to the U.S. Supreme Court, where he served until he resigned in 1932 at the age of ninety-one. ∎

## Introduction

In the late nineteenth century, Eugene V. Debs was a well-known labor leader and supporter of workers' rights. As president of the American Railway Union, he supported the Pullman Strike when George Pullman, owner of the Pullman Palace Car Company, cut his employees' wages but not their rent at his company town outside of Chicago. In response, Debs's union refused to handle Pullman cars, so rail transportation came to a halt. The government, arguing that the strike restrained trade, obtained an injunction against Debs under the Sherman Anti-Trust Act. He violated the injunction and was jailed, and in 1895 the U.S. Supreme Court upheld his conviction. Debs continued to fight for workers' rights after leaving prison as a leader in the American Socialist Party. In 1900, he was nominated for the first of four successive times as the party's presidential candidate, winning six percent of the popular vote in 1912. When Debs took a strong stand against American participation in World War I (1914–1918), the American Socialist Party followed his lead.

During the war, Congress enacted a number of laws designed to deal with opposition to the war. One of these, the Espionage Act, criminalized espionage activities that harmed the war effort. An amendment to that act, the Sedition Act, made illegal any false statements that hindered the war effort. In 1918, when Debs attended the Ohio Socialist Convention, three Ohio Socialists were in jail for opposition to the draft. Debs rose at the convention and delivered an impassioned defense of pacifism, of the three jailed men, and of others who had been jailed for opposition to the war. Agents of the Department of Justice were in the crowd creating a transcript of Debs's speech, and he was soon arrested and indicted. The Department of Justice did not find any one particular part of his speech objectionable. Rather, they indicted him for his whole speech, correctly assuming the jury would find at least one criminal phrase in it. Debs was convicted in 1918, and his conviction was affirmed by the Supreme Court in 1919.

## Significance

After his conviction, Debs rose in popularity and status. He was sent originally to Moundsville State Prison in West Virginia, but because of his high profile, he was moved to Atlanta Federal Penitentiary. As soon as he entered prison, many supporters called for his release, though many more opposed any reduction in his sentence. President Woodrow Wilson (served 1913–1921) and A. Mitchell Palmer, the U.S. attorney general, were both opposed to leniency. Debs did not help his own cause, for he refused to apply for executive clemency, believing that by doing so he would be admitting that he had done something wrong. While still in jail in 1920, Debs was nominated again for president on the Socialist ticket and received 900,000 votes, 3.4 percent of the total popular vote. During the term of the winner, Warren G. Harding (served 1921–1923), the clemency issue returned to the forefront. Harding did not want to make a martyr out of Debs, so in 1921, he solicited an opinion from his attorney general, Harry M. Daugherty. Daugherty believed that Debs had clearly violated the Espionage Act, but he also felt that Debs should be released because of his advanced age. Harding followed this advice and released Debs on December 25, 1921. By today's standards, many people would conclude that Debs's freedom of speech was violated, but at the time, his arrest was legal. His case demonstrates how definitions of freedom of speech have evolved over the past decades.

## Primary Source

*Debs v. U.S.*

**SYNOPSIS:** Holmes notes that Debs's advocacy of socialism is protected by the First Amendment but that the amendment does not protect his antiwar statements. Homes then notes that the jury was correct in finding Debs guilty of attempting to prevent military recruitment. Since he was guilty of this charge and serving his sentence, Holmes saw no reason to examine the charge that Debs's speech attempted to cause insubordination within the armed forces.

Eugene Debs, delivering an antiwar speech on June 16, 1918, was convicted under the Espionage and Sedition Acts used during World War I to silence opposition. © **BETTMANN/CORBIS. REPRODUCED BY PERMISSION.**

Mr. Justice Holmes delivered the opinion of the Court.

This is an indictment under the Espionage Act of June 15, 1917, c. 30, tit. 1, 3, 40 Stat. 219, as amended by the Act of May 16, 1918, c. 75, 1, 40 Stat. 553 (Comp. St. 1918, 10212c). It has been cut down to two counts, originally the third and fourth. The former of these alleges that on or about June 16, 1918, at Canton, Ohio, the defendant caused and incited and attempted to cause and incite insubordination, disloyalty, mutiny and refusal of duty in the military and naval forces of the United States and with intent so to do delivered, to an assembly of people, a public speech, set forth. The fourth count alleges that he obstructed and attempted to obstruct the recruiting and enlistment service of the United States and to that end and with that intent delivered the same speech, again set forth. There was a demurrer to the indictment on the ground that the statute is unconstitutional as interfering with free speech, contrary to the First Amendment, and to the several counts as insufficiently stating the supposed offence. This was overruled, subject to exception. There were other exceptions to the admission of evidence with which

we shall deal. The defendant was found guilty and was sentenced to ten years' imprisonment on each of the two counts, the punishment to run concurrently on both.

The main theme of the speech was Socialism, its growth, and a prophecy of its ultimate success. With that we have nothing to do, but if a part or the manifest intent of the more general utterances was to encourage those present to obstruct the recruiting service and if in passages such encouragement was directly given, the immunity of the general theme may not be enough to protect the speech. The speaker began by saying that he had just returned from a visit to the workhouse in the neighborhood where three of their most loyal comrades were paying the penalty for their devotion to the working class—these being Wagenknecht, Baker and Ruthenberg, who had been convicted of aiding and abetting another in failing to register for the draft. *Ruthenberg v. United States,* 245 U.S. 480, 38 Sup. Ct. 168. He said that he had to be prudent and might not be able to say all that he thought, thus intimating to his hearers that they might infer that he meant more, but he did say that those persons were paying the penalty for standing erect and for seeking to pave the way to better conditions for all mankind. Later he added further eulogies and said that he was proud of them. He then expressed opposition to Prussian militarism in a way that naturally might have been thought to be intended to include the mode of proceeding in the United States.

After considerable discourse that it is unnecessary to follow, he took up the case of Kate Richards O'Hare, convicted of obstructing the enlistment service, praised her for her loyalty to Socialism and otherwise, and said that she was convicted on false testimony, under a ruling that would seem incredible to him if he had not had some experience with a Federal Court. We mention this passage simply for its connection with evidence put in at the trial. The defendant spoke of other cases, and then, after dealing with Russia, said that the master class has always declared the war and the subject class has always fought the battles—that the subject class has had nothing to gain and all to lose, including their lives; that the working class, who furnish the corpses, have never yet had a voice in declaring war and never yet had a voice in declaring peace. "You have your lives to lose; you certainly ought to have the right to declare war if you consider a war necessary." The defendant next mentioned Rose Pastor Stokes, convicted of attempting to cause insubordination and refusal of duty in the military forces of the United States and obstructing the recruiting service. He said that she went out to render her service to the cause in this day of crises, and they sent her to the penitentiary for ten years, that she had said no more than the speaker had said that afternoon; that if she was guilty so was he, and that he would not be cowardly enough to plead his innocence; but that her message that opened the eyes of the people must be suppressed, and so after a mock trial before a packed jury and a corporation tool on the bench, she was sent to the penitentiary for ten years.

There followed personal experiences and illustrations of the growth of Socialism, a glorification of minorities, and a prophecy of the success of the international Socialist crusade, with the interjection that "you need to know that you are fit for something better than slavery and cannon fodder." The rest of the discourse had only the indirect though not necessarily ineffective bearing on the offences alleged that is to be found in the usual contrasts between capitalists and laboring men, sneers at the advice to cultivate war gardens, attribution to plutocrats of the high price of coal, &c., with the implication running through it all that the working men

are not concerned in the war, and a final exhortation, "Don't worry about the charge of treason to your masters; but be concerned about the treason that involves yourselves." The defendant addressed the jury himself, and while contending that his speech did not warrant the charges said, "I have been accused of obstructing the war. I admit it. Gentlemen, I abhor war. I would oppose the war if I stood alone." The statement was not necessary to warrant the jury in finding that one purpose of the speech, whether incidental or not does not matter, was to oppose not only war in general but this war, and that the opposition was so expressed that its natural and intended effect would be to obstruct recruiting. If that was intended and if, in all the circumstances, that would be its probable effect, it would not be protected by reason of its being part of a general program and expressions of a general and conscientious belief.

The chief defences upon which the defendant seemed willing to rely were the denial that we have dealt with and that based upon the First Amendment to the Constitution, disposed of in *Schenck v. United States,* 249 U.S. 47, 39 Sup. Ct. 247. His counsel questioned the sufficiency of the indictment. It is sufficient in form. *Frohwerk v. United States,* 249 U.S. 204, 39 Sup. Ct. 249. The most important question that remains is raised by the admission in evidence of the record of the conviction of Ruthenberg, Wagenknecht and Baker, Rose Pastor Stokes, and Kate Richards O'Hare. The defendant purported to understand the grounds on which these persons were imprisoned and it was proper to show what those grounds were in order to show what he was talking about, to explain the true import of his expression of sympathy and to throw light on the intent of the address, so far as the present matter is concerned.

There was introduced also an "Anti-War Proclamation and Program" adopted at St. Louis in April, 1917, coupled with testimony that about an hour before his speech the defendant had stated that he approved of that platform in spirit and in substance. The defendant referred to it in his address to the jury, seemingly with satisfaction and willingness that it should be considered in evidence. But his counsel objected and has argued against its admissibility at some length. This document contained the usual suggestion that capitalism was the cause of the war and that our entrance into it "was instigated by the predatory capitalists in the United States." It alleged that the war of the United States against Germany could not "be justified even on the plea that it is a war in defence of American rights or American 'honor'." It said:

> We brand the declaration of war by our Governments as a crime against the people of the United States and against the nations of the world. In all modern history there has been no war more unjustifiable than the war in which we are about to engage.

Its first recommendation was, "continuous, active, and public opposition to the war, through demonstrations, mass petitions, and all other means within our power." Evidence that the defendant accepted this view and this declaration of his duties at the time that he made his speech is evidence that if in that speech he used words tending to obstruct the recruiting service he meant that they should have that effect. The principle is too well established and too manifestly good sense to need citation of the books. We should add that the jury were most carefully instructed that they could not find the defendant guilty for advocacy of any of his opinions unless the words used had as their natural tendency and reasonably probable effect to obstruct the recruiting service, &c., and unless the defendant had the specific intent to do so in his mind.

Without going into further particulars we are of opinion that the verdict on the fourth count, for obstructing and attempting to obstruct the recruiting service of the United States, must be sustained. Therefore it is less important to consider whether that upon the third count, for causing and attempting to cause insubordination, &c., in the military and naval forces, is equally impregnable. The jury were instructed that for the purposes of the statute the persons designated by the Act of May 18, 1917, c.15, 40 Stat. 76 (Comp. St. 1918, 2044a–2044k), registered and enrolled under it, and thus subject to be called into the active service, were a part of the military forces of the United States. The Government presents a strong argument from the history of the statutes that the instruction was correct and in accordance with established legislative usage. We see no sufficient reason for differing from the conclusion but think it unnecessary to discuss the question in detail.

Judgment affirmed.

## Further Resources

### BOOKS

Ginger, Ray. *The Bending Cross: A Biography of Eugene Victor Debs.* New Brunswick, N.J.: Rutgers University Press, 1949.

Salvatore, Nick. *Eugene V. Debs: Citizen and Socialist.* Urbana, Ill: University of Illinois Press, 1982.

Schneirov, Richard, Shelton Stromquist, and Nick Salvatore, eds. *The Pullman Strike and the Crisis of the 1890s: Essays on Labor and Politics.* Chicago: University of Illinois Press, 1999.

### PERIODICALS

Sterling, David. "In Defense of Debs: The Lawyers and the Espionage Act Case." *Indiana Magazine of History* 83, March 1987, 17–42.

### WEBSITES

Indiana State University Library. "Rare Books and Special Collections Quick Links: Databases and Lists: Debs Collection." Available online at http://odin.indstate.edu/level1.dir /cml/rbsc/rare2.html#Debs; website home page: http://www .odin.indstate.edu/home.html (accessed January 23, 2003). *This site contains links to numerous sites about Debs.*

---

# Abrams v. U.S.

Supreme Court decision

**By:** Oliver Wendell Holmes Jr.

**Date:** November 10, 1919

**Source:** Holmes, Oliver Wendell, Jr. *Abrams v. U.S.,* 250 U.S. 616 (1919). Available online at http://caselaw.lp.find-law.com/us/250/616.html; website home page: http://caselaw.lp.findlaw.com (accessed January 23, 2003).

**About the Author:** Oliver Wendell Holmes Jr. (1841–1935) served in the Union army in the Civil War (1861–1865) from 1861 to 1864. He joined the Massachusetts Supreme Court as an associate justice in 1883, rising to chief justice in 1899. In 1902, President Theodore Roosevelt (served 1901–1909) appointed him associate justice of the U.S. Supreme Court, where he served until he resigned in 1932 at age ninety-one. ■

## Introduction

Public opinion was deeply divided over U.S. participation in World War I. In response to this dissent, Congress passed a number of measures. These included the Draft Act, which forbade interfering with the draft; the Espionage Act, which made espionage that interfered with the war effort a crime; and the Sedition Act (an amendment to the Espionage Act), which made illegal false statements that interfered with the war effort. Many people were convicted under these laws, and the U.S. Supreme Court unanimously upheld convictions in three Espionage Act cases in early 1919. In *Schenck v. U.S.,* for example, in a case involving the distribution of flyers urging resistance to the draft, the Court declared that free speech could be restricted when a statement posed a "clear and present danger."

Other international events had implications for free speech rights during this time. Russia had undergone two revolutions, first by anticzarist forces, then by communists. The United States, like many other countries, opposed communism and sent forces to defeat them. In response, Jacob Abrams, Hyman Lachowsky, Samuel Lipman, Jacob Schwartz, and Mollie Steimer, anarchists and socialists who had all immigrated to the United States from Russia in the early twentieth century, protested U.S. involvement in Russian affairs by printing a brochure calling upon all "workers of the world" to "awake" in a general protest strike. After they were arrested for distributing these pamphlets, confessions were beaten out of some and they were indicted for violating the Sedition Act. Before trial, Jacob Schwartz died of a heart condition aggravated by police brutality. The others were tried and convicted in federal court; Abrams, Lachowsky, and Lipman were sentenced to twenty years in prison, while Steimer was given a fifteen-year sentence. They were released on bail pending an appeal to the Supreme Court.

### Significance

The Supreme Court majority upheld the convictions. Abrams, Lachowsky, and Lipman were imprisoned in the Atlanta Federal Penitentiary, while Steimer went to a state prison in Jefferson City, Missouri. All served about a year and ten months in prison before their sentences were commuted and they were deported to Russia. Holmes's dissent in *Abrams* was an early indication that the belief that the government should be allowed to enact sweeping restrictions on free speech was not universal. The dissent led to an expansion of free speech's definition in later years. In 1925, the Supreme Court extended the First Amendment to protect some speech against state action. In the 1960s, free speech was widely expanded when the Warren Court ruled that speech could not be banned unless it was aimed to produce "imminent lawless action" and that action was likely to occur.

### Primary Source

*Abrams v. United States* [excerpt]

**SYNOPSIS:** In his dissent, Holmes defends the government's right to curtail speech in wartime, but he also says Congress cannot forbid all dissident speech. He argues that the pamphlet could not possibly have produced a revolution. Moreover, as the defendants' sympathies were not with Germany but were opposed to American intervention in Russia, Holmes does not see them as having violated the Espionage and Sedition Acts.

Mr. Justice Holmes dissenting.

This indictment is founded wholly upon the publication of two leaflets which I shall describe in a moment. . . .

No argument seems to be necessary to show that these pronunciamentos in no way attack the

Jacob Abrams (far right), along with Sameul Lipman, Hyman Lachowsky, and Mollie Steimer, were deported after World War I for violating the Espionage and Sedition Acts. **REPRINTED FROM RICHARD POLENBERG, *FIGHTING FAITHS: THE ABRAMS CASE, THE SUPREME COURT, AND FREE SPEECH*, NEW YORK. VIKING, 1987.**

form of government of the United States, or that they do not support either of the first two counts. What little I have to say about the third count may be postponed until I have considered the fourth. With regard to that it seems too plain to be denied that the suggestion to workers in the ammunition factories that they are producing bullets to murder their dearest, and the further advocacy of a general strike, both in the second leaflet, do urge curtailment of production of things necessary to the prosecution of the war within the meaning of the Act of May 16, 1918. But to make the conduct criminal that statute requires that it should be "with intent by such curtailment to cripple or hinder the United States in the prosecution of the war." It seems to me that no such intent is proved. . . .

It seems to me that this statute must be taken to use its words in a strict and accurate sense. They would be absurd in any other. A patriot might think that we were wasting money on aeroplanes, or making more cannon of a certain kind than we needed, and might advocate curtailment with success, yet even if it turned out that the curtailment hindered and was thought by other minds to have been obviously likely to hinder the United States in the prosecution of the war, no one would hold such conduct a crime. I admit that my illustration does not answer all that might be said but it is enough to show what I think and to let me pass to a more important aspect of the case. I refer to the First Amendment to the Constitution that Congress shall make no law abridging the freedom of speech.

I never have seen any reason to doubt that the questions of law that alone were before this Court in the Cases of Schenck, Frohwerk, and Debs, were rightly decided. I do not doubt for a moment that by the same reasoning that would justify punishing persuasion to murder, the United States constitutionally may punish speech that produces or is intended to produce a clear and imminent danger that it will bring about forthwith certain substantive evils that the United States constitutionally may seek to prevent. The power undoubtedly is greater in time of war than in time of peace because war opens dangers that do not exist at other times.

But as against dangers peculiar to war, as against others, the principle of the right to free speech is always the same. It is only the present danger of immediate evil or an intent to bring it about that warrants Congress in setting a limit to the expression of opinion where private rights are not concerned. Congress certainly cannot forbid all effort to change the mind of the country. Now nobody can suppose that the surreptitious publishing of a silly leaflet by an unknown man, without more, would present any immediate danger that its opinions would hinder the success of the government arms or have any appreciable tendency to do so. Publishing those opinions for the very purpose of obstructing, however, might indicate a greater danger and at any rate would have the quality of an attempt. . . . It is necessary where the success of the attempt depends upon others because if that intent is not present the actor's aim may be accomplished without bringing about the evils sought to be checked. An intent to prevent interference with the revolution in Russia might have been satisfied without any hindrance to carrying on the war in which we were engaged.

I do not see how anyone can find the intent required by the statute in any of the defendant's words. The second leaflet is the only one that affords even a foundation for the charge, and there, without invoking the hatred of German militarism expressed in the former one, it is evident from the be-

ginning to the end that the only object of the paper is to help Russia and stop American intervention there against the popular government—not to impede the United States in the war that it was carrying on. To say that two phrases taken literally might import a suggestion of conduct that would have interference with the war as an indirect and probably undesired effect seems to me by no means enough to show an attempt to produce that effect. . . .

In this case sentences of twenty years imprisonment have been imposed for the publishing of two leaflets that I believe the defendants had as much right to publish as the Government has to publish the Constitution of the United States now vainly invoked by them. Even if I am technically wrong and enough can be squeezed from these poor and puny anonymities to turn the color of legal litmus paper; I will add, even if what I think the necessary intent were shown; the most nominal punishment seems to me all that possibly could be inflicted, unless the defendants are to be made to suffer not for what the indictment alleges but for the creed that they avow—a creed that I believe to be the creed of ignorance and immaturity when honestly held, as I see no reason to doubt that it was held here but which, although made the subject of examination at the trial, no one has a right even to consider in dealing with the charges before the Court.

Persecution for the expression of opinions seems to me perfectly logical. If you have no doubt of your premises or your power and want a certain result with all your heart you naturally express your wishes in law and sweep away all opposition. To allow opposition by speech seems to indicate that you think the speech impotent, as when a man says that he has squared the circle, or that you do not care whole heartedly for the result, or that you doubt either your power or your premises. But when men have realized that time has upset many fighting faiths, they may come to believe even more than they believe the very foundations of their own conduct that the ultimate good desired is better reached by free trade in ideas—that the best test of truth is the power of the thought to get itself accepted in the competition of the market, and that truth is the only ground upon which their wishes safely can be carried out. That at any rate is the theory of our Constitution. It is an experiment, as all life is an experiment. Every year if not every day we have to wager our salvation upon some prophecy based upon imperfect knowledge. While that experiment is part of our system I think that we should be eternally vigilant against attempts to check the expression of opinions that we loathe and believe to be fraught with death, unless they so imminently threaten immediate interference with the lawful and pressing purposes of the law that an immediate check is required to save the country. I wholly disagree with the argument of the Government that the First Amendment left the common law as to seditious libel in force. History seems to me against the notion. I had conceived that the United States through many years had shown its repentance for the Sedition Act of 1798, by repaying fines that it imposed. Only the emergency that makes it immediately dangerous to leave the correction of evil counsels to time warrants making any exception to the sweeping command, "Congress shall make no law abridging the freedom of speech." Of course I am speaking only of expressions of opinion and exhortations, which were all that were uttered here, but I regret that I cannot put into more impressive words my belief that in their conviction upon this indictment the defendants were deprived of their rights under the Constitution of the United States.

## Further Resources

### BOOKS

Chafee, Zechariah. *Free Speech in the United States.* Cambridge, Mass.: Harvard University Press, 1946.

Polenberg, Richard. *Fighting Faiths: The Abrams Case, the Supreme Court, and Free Speech.* New York: Viking, 1987.

Political Prisoners Defense and Relief Committee. *Abrams Sentenced to Twenty Years Prison.* New York: Political Prisoners Defense and Relief Committee, 1919.

Steimer, Mollie, Simon Fleshin, and Abe Bluestein. *Fighters for Anarchism: Mollie Steimer and Senya Fleshin: A Memorial Volume.* London: Libertarian Publications Group, 1983.

### WEBSITES

Linder, Doug. "Exploring Constitutional Conflicts: The 'Clear and Present Danger' Test. Available online at http://www.law.umkc.edu/faculty/projects/ftrials/conlaw/clear&pdanger.htm; website home page: http://www.law.umkc.edu (accessed January 23, 2003).

Urofsky, Melvin I. "Introduction to Justice Holmes' Dissenting Opinion on the *Abrams v. United States* Case." *Basic Readings in Democracy.* Available online at http://usinfo.state.gov/usa/infousa/facts/democrac/43.htmwebsite home page: http://www./usinfo.state.gov (accessed January 23, 2003).

# 7

# LIFESTYLES AND SOCIAL TRENDS

JONATHAN MARTIN KOLKEY

*Entries are arranged in chronological order by date of primary source. For entries with one primary source, the entry title is the same as the primary source title. Entries with more than one primary source have an overall entry title, followed by the titles of the primary sources.*

**CHRONOLOGY**

Important Events in Lifestyles and Social
  Trends, 1910–1919 . . . . . . . . . . . . . . . . . . . . 328

**PRIMARY SOURCES**

*The Conflict of Colour*
  B. L. Putnam Weale, 1910 . . . . . . . . . . . . . . 333

"The Woman Shopper: How to Make Her
  Buy"
  Isaac F. Marcosson, 1910 . . . . . . . . . . . . . . . 335

*The Social Evil in Chicago*
  The Vice Commission of Chicago, 1911 . . . . . . 340

*The Immigration Problem*
  Jeremiah W. Jenks and W. Jett Lauck,
  1912 . . . . . . . . . . . . . . . . . . . . . . . . . . . . . . 342

"On the Imitation of Man"
  Ida M. Tarbell, 1913 . . . . . . . . . . . . . . . . . . . 345

America's Sex Hysteria . . . . . . . . . . . . . . . . . . . 347
"Sex O'Clock in America"
  *Current Opinion*, 1913
"Popular Gullibility as Exhibited in the New
  White Slavery Hysteria"
  *Current Opinion*, 1914

"Making Men of Them"
  Thornton W. Burgess, 1914 . . . . . . . . . . . . . . 351

"The Next and Final Step"
  P.A. Baker, 1914 . . . . . . . . . . . . . . . . . . . . . . 354

"The Flapper"
  Henry L. Mencken, 1915 . . . . . . . . . . . . . . . . 357

"How We Manage"
  E.S.E., 1915 . . . . . . . . . . . . . . . . . . . . . . . . . 359

*The Passing of the Great Race*
  Madison Grant, 1916 . . . . . . . . . . . . . . . . . . . 362

"Are the Movies a Menace to the Drama?"
  Brander Matthews, 1917 . . . . . . . . . . . . . . . . 364

*The Individual Delinquent*
  William Healy, 1918 . . . . . . . . . . . . . . . . . . . 367

Dark Side of Wartime Patriotism . . . . . . . . . . . . 370
Woodrow Wilson's Memorandum to His
  Secretary, Joseph Tumulty
  Woodrow Wilson, 1918
"Chicagoans Cheer Tar Who Shot Man"
  1919

"The Negro Should Be a Party to the
  Commercial Conquest of the World"
  Marcus Garvey, 1919 . . . . . . . . . . . . . . . . . . . 372

purposes. The law results from growing public concern over "white slavery," especially the importation of European girls for work as prostitutes in American brothels.

- On July 20, Missouri's Christian Endeavor Society calls for a ban on all motion pictures that depict kissing between people who are not related.

- In July, the tango, sweeping Europe with its South American flavor, begins to catch on in New York City ballrooms.

- On September 2, Blanche Stuart becomes the first American woman to fly an airplane.

## Important Events in Lifestyles and Social Trends, 1910–1919

### 1910

- The average American worker earns less than fifteen dollars per week and works fifty-four to sixty hours per week.

- Life expectancy in the United States reaches 48.4 years for men and 51.8 years for women.

- Seventy percent of bread consumed in the United States is baked at home, compared with 80 percent in 1890.

- After approval by an act of Congress, the U.S. Post Office inaugurates parcel post service to carry packages up to four hundred pounds.

- Over ten thousand nickelodeons in cities across the nation provide entertainment, mainly for the poor. For an admission fee of five to ten cents, customers can sit in wooden seats and watch an hour of one-reel movies, vaudeville, and sometimes a dog act.

- In Ohio, fifty-eight of the state's eighty-eight counties vote to ban the sale of liquor.

- Among the new products available this year are electric kitchen ranges (with three settings) and iodine.

- On February 6, Chicago publisher William Boyce founds the Boy Scouts of America.

- On March 17, Dr. and Mrs. Luther Halsey Gulick, Mr. and Mrs. Ernest Thompson Seton, and others found the Camp Fire Girls.

- On March 26, Congress amends the 1907 Immigration Act, barring criminals, paupers, anarchists, and carriers of disease from settling in the United States.

- On April 18, suffragists present a petition with five hundred thousand signatures to Congress, asking that women be granted the right to vote.

- On May 18, Halley's Comet reaches its closest point to Earth. "Comet pills," a supposed antidote to the lethal gases believed to be present in the comet's tail, sell briskly across the nation. Farm families take shelter in cyclone cellars and caves to avoid the poisonous vapors. City dwellers board up their windows for the same reason. Con artists seize on the public hysteria.

- On June 19, Mrs. John B. Dodd of Spokane, Washington, celebrates the first Father's Day with the support of the Ministerial Association and the YMCA.

- On June 25, Congress passes the Mann Act, which makes it illegal to transport women across state lines for immoral

### 1911

- The Sante Fe Railroad's Sante Fe Deluxe cuts travel time between Chicago and Los Angeles to sixty-three hours.

- Summer camps and conferences are the rage. Some 40 million people attend "Chautauquas," which feature opera singers and Hawaiian crooners, orchestras and yodelers, American Indians, and inspirational speakers.

- In February, General Motors adapts an electric motor used in cash registers to start the engine in its Cadillac automobiles. Cadillac owners will no longer have to use hand cranks to start their cars.

- On March 25, a fire sweeps through the Triangle Shirtwaist Factory in lower Manhattan. The only exit door is locked, trapping about 850 employees in the building. Some 146 workers, most of them young girls, are killed. The tragedy arouses a nationwide demand for better working conditions.

- On April 17, a one-day record twelve thousand immigrants arrive at New York's Ellis Island.

- On May 7, three thousand women demanding the right to vote march down New York's Fifth Avenue. Only a few hundred women marched the previous year. In 1915, fifteen thousand march.

### 1912

- The ragtime fad spawns numerous dances named for animals: fox-trot, horse trot, crab step, kangaroo dip, camel walk, fish walk, chicken scratch, lame duck, snake, grizzly bear, turkey trot, bunny hug.

- The National Biscuit Company tempts America's sweet tooth with a new cookie—two chocolate wafers with a cream filling in between—that it calls the Oreo Biscuit.

- For those who can afford it, the Hamburg-American line offers a 110-day cruise around the world for $650.

- On March 12, inspired by the efforts of Sir Robert Baden-Powell, founder of the Boy Scouts in Great Britain, Juliet Gordon Lowe organizes the first American Girl Guides, a forerunner of the Girl Scouts, in Savannah, Georgia.

- On April 15, the *Titanic* sinks on its maiden voyage, killing 1,517 passengers and crew, including members of some of America's most prominent families.

- On May 1, the elegant Beverly Hills Hotel opens in what had once been a bean field. Its bar becomes a famous Hollywood rendezvous.

- On September 17, Calbraith Rogers takes off from Sheepshead Bay, New York, in a Burgess-Wright biplane.

About six weeks later, on November 5, he reaches Pasadena, California, to complete the first crossing of the continent by plane. Total flying time is 82 hours.

- On October 1, a New York law limits the work week in the state to a maximum of 54 hours.

- On October 9, crowds swarm New York's Times Square to see the World Series score on the new electric bulletin board of the *Times*.

- In November, women gain the right to vote in Arizona, Kansas, and Oregon. However, the proposal is defeated in Michigan. Women now enjoy voting rights in nine states. Women's suffrage has reached the ballot in six other states since 1896. Each time it lost by a wide margin.

## 1913

- Formal and restrained cotillion dancing gives way to the waltz and the two-step.

- The *New York World* publishes the first crossword puzzle.

- The first drive-in service station opens in Pittsburgh.

- In Chicago the first female police officers take to the streets.

- To combat declining chocolate sales during the summer, Cleveland candy maker Clarence Crane introduces a peppermint candy with a hole in its center. Because they remind him of a ship's life preserver, he calls his new candies LifeSavers. Also new to Americans this year are hot dog stands, Chesterfield and Camel cigarettes, Quaker Puffed Rice and Puffed Wheat.

- On February 2, Grand Central Terminal opens in New York City, and 150,000 visitors barrage attendants with questions about train locations and departures.

- On February 25, the Sixteenth Amendment to the U.S. Constitution takes effect, allowing Congress to levy a tax on people's incomes. On October 3, Congress imposes a graduated tax on personal incomes of three thousand dollars or more (four thousand dollars for married couples).

- On March 1, Congress passes the Webb-Kenyon Interstate Liquor Act over President Taft's veto. The act prohibits shipment of liquor into states where its sale is illegal.

- On May 31, the Seventeenth Amendment takes effect, allowing the people of each state to directly elect their two U.S. senators.

- On June 7, Socialist journalist John Reed and a crew of labor organizers, anarchists, and Greenwich Village socialites produce the Paterson Strike Pageant at Madison Square Garden. Hundreds of striking workers from the Paterson, New Jersey, silk industry perform a dramatization about their struggle.

- On July 1, the first state minimum wage law takes effect in Massachusetts.

- On October 7, Henry Ford opens the first assembly line in Highland Park, Michigan. It can produce a Model T in three hours.

- On October 10, President Woodrow Wilson pushes a button that ignites eight tons of dynamite, opening the Panama Canal and linking the waters of the Atlantic and Pacific Oceans.

- On November 5, the Los Angeles Owens River Aqueduct opens, a feat of engineering that rivals the Panama Canal. It brings water 234 miles, using only gravity, to parched southern California. Critics charge that the government duped Owens Valley farmers into signing away their water rights by promising them an irrigation project.

## 1914

- Hollywood, California, becomes the center of motion picture production in the United States when filmmaker Cecil B. DeMille establishes his studio there, and other producers follow.

- A censorship board is created in Chicago to shorten or cut movie scenes of beatings and dead bodies.

- The cost of a year at Harvard is seven hundred dollars. An education at Columbia University is five hundred dollars a year. About two-thirds of the costs at each school are for room and board.

- The number of new immigrants between 1910 and 1914 totals 4.1 million people.

- On January 1, New Jersey sets the minimum wage for women at nine dollars a week.

- On January 5, Henry Ford announces that he will pay his employees a minimum of five dollars per day and inaugurate three eight-hour shifts, rather than two nine-hour shifts, to keep his factories running around the clock. To qualify for the new wage, however, workers must answer questions about their home lives and habits from Ford's new Sociological Department.

- On May 7, Congress passes a resolution to celebrate Mother's Day on the second Sunday in May. President Woodrow Wilson calls on Americans to display flags to express love and reverence.

- On August 19, President Wilson, calls on Americans to be "impartial in thought as well as in deed" toward World War I, which erupted in Europe earlier in the month.

- On December 14, to please his terminally ill daughter Marcella, John Gruelle draws a face on a faceless rag doll she has found in their attic. Mrs. Gruelle restuffs the doll and puts a heart-shaped piece of candy, with the words "I love you," on its chest. The family names the tattered doll Raggedy Ann.

- In December, the first full-length feature comedy motion picture, *Tillie's Punctured Romance,* stars Marie Dresser, Mabel Normand, and newcomer Charlie Chaplin.

## 1915

- The United States population passes 100 million.

- Birth control activist Margaret Sanger is arrested on obscenity charges in connection with her book *Family Limitation.* Taken to court by the New York Society for the Suppression of Vice, she is found guilty of circulating a work "contrary not only to the law of the state, but to the law of God" and jailed.

- The Victor Talking Machine Company introduces a phonograph called the Victrola, which soon becomes a generic name. By 1919 Americans spend more on phonographs and recordings than on musical instruments, books and periodicals, or sporting goods.

- The taxicab becomes an established mode of transportation. Short rides cost a nickel, or a jitney. Drivers are known as hackers or hackies in the East and as cabbies in the Midwest.

- Vice President Thomas R. Marshall, during a tedious debate in the Senate, quips, "What this country really needs is a good five-cent cigar."

- On February 23, an easy-divorce law requiring only six months of residence is passed in Nevada.

- On March 3, D. W. Griffith's controversial three-hour film epic, *The Birth of a Nation,* opens in New York. Tickets cost an astronomical two dollars. The film idealizes plantation life in the antebellum South and perpetuates harmful stereotypes of African Americans.

- On April 19, President Wilson describes the United States as a "great melting pot." But with war raging in Europe, many Americans are more concerned about immigrants who do not "melt." A popular song, *Don't Bite the Hand That's Feeding You,* expresses this increasing nativism when it warns "If you don't like your Uncle Sammy, then go back to your home over the sea."

- On May 15, the Supreme Court strikes down laws in Maryland and Oklahoma that employ a "grandfather clause" to bar African Americans from voting. The Court says that it is unconstitutional to deny someone suffrage just because his grandfather could not vote.

- On July 1, the cost of a telephone call in New York City is reduced to five cents. But a call to San Francisco costs $20.70.

- On October 10, in Chicago a new law restricting liquor sales on Sunday takes effect. On November 7, over forty thousand men march in protest against the law.

- In November, William J. Simmons, a failed preacher and salesman, gathers a handful of supporters for a cross-burning outside Atlanta and revives the long-dormant Ku Klux Klan.

- On December 4, Henry Ford charters the "Peace Ship" for an expedition to Europe to end the war. The ship bears the slogan "Out of their trenches and back to their homes by Christmas." The attempt to find a diplomatic solution to the war quickly collapses.

## 1916

- Auto and truck production in the United States exceeds one million new models this year. The average cost of a new car is slightly more than $600, but Ford's Model T sells for $360. Half a million Model Ts roll off the lines in 1916. There are more than 3.5 million cars on the road.

- At nine hundred dollars, the cost of the new "mechanized" home refrigerator is higher than the price of most cars. Mechanical windshield wipers and washing machines with agitators are other improvements that become available this year.

- The son of architect Frank Lloyd Wright invents Lincoln Logs so kids can make their own buildings.

- Trade both within the United States and with foreign countries sets all-time highs. Domestic commerce generates $45 billion, and exports top $8 billion.

- African-American self-help advocate Marcus Garvey returns to New York City to establish an American headquarters for his United Negro Improvement Association.

- On July 22, a bomb explodes along a preparedness parade route in San Francisco, killing six and injuring many more. A Finnish sailor who rushed to the scene and screamed "This is nothing!" is arrested.

- On September 1, after years of calls for reform, Congress finally bars from interstate trade any product made by child labor. Many children still work twelve to fourteen hours a day. However, South Carolina has raised the age for working in mills, factories, and mines from twelve to fourteen years old.

- On September 8, President Woodrow Wilson addresses a suffrage rally in Atlantic City, New Jersey, and tells the cheering crowd that he is on their side, that women will have the right to vote "in a little while."

- On October 16, the first birth control clinic is opened in Brooklyn, New York, by Margaret Sanger, Fania Mindell, and Ethel Burne. The clinic is publicized by pamphlets written in English, Italian, and Yiddish.

## 1917

- More than four hundred thousand southern African Americans have come north in search of jobs in war industries. Although most find work, they receive lower wages and pay higher rents in northern cities than do white Americans.

- Americans save tons of fruit pits, especially of peaches, to be used in the manufacture of charcoal filters for gas masks.

- Storyville, a section of New Orleans known for its honky-tonks and brothels, is closed at the insistence of the U.S. Navy. The closing drives many jazz musicians out of the city, thus helping to spread this music form around the nation.

- On February 5, Congress overrides Wilson's veto, and an act requiring all immigrants to pass a literacy test becomes law. The law also bars Asian workers, except for Japanese, from entering the United States.

- On April 6, the United States declares war on Germany. George M. Cohan writes the song "Over There" to rally public support for sending American troops overseas.

- On May 18, the Selective Service Act passes, authorizing federal conscription and requiring registration of all-male U.S. citizens from ages twenty-one to thirty. Although some predict draft riots, more than ten million men are processed without incident.

- On June 27, Major General John J. "Black Jack" Pershing arrives in France with the first contingent of the American Expeditionary Forces (AEF) to enter the war in Europe.

- On July 8, President Woodrow Wilson declares absolute government control over food, fuel, and war materiel exports.

- On August 10, Wilson puts Herbert Hoover in charge of the nation's wartime food program. To conserve resources for the war effort, Hoover calls for wheatless (breadless) Mondays and Wednesdays, meatless Tuesdays, and porkless Thursdays and Saturdays.

• On August 19, the War Department announces that the cost of providing each soldier with a uniform, arms, bedding, and eating utensils is $156.30, which people find a startlingly high amount.

• On September 23, fifty thousand striking workers from twenty-five unions in factories, shipyards, and machine shops on the Pacific Coast agree to return to work after a special plea from President Woodrow Wilson. The new Shipbuilding Labor Adjustment Board works to resolve the wage disputes that led to the strike.

• On November 6, a constitutional amendment passes the New York state legislature, mandating women's suffrage.

• On December 18, Congress passes the Eighteenth Amendment, prohibiting the manufacture, sale, or transportation of alcoholic beverages. It is later ratified by the states on January 29, 1919.

## 1918

• For one of the few times in American history, the United States population declines. The decline of fifty thousand people is attributed to war casualties, postponed marriages, the lack of immigration, and a devastating influenza epidemic.

• The American Civil Liberties Union is founded, an outgrowth of the Committee Against Militarism and the Committee Against Preparedness.

• A New York toy firm begins manufacturing the Raggedy Ann doll; the doll soon grows into a $20-million-a-year business.

• On March 29, government officials announce that since the nation entered World War I, some 1.4 million women are doing jobs once held by men. In addition, more than 10,000 women have volunteered for the U.S. Navy and are performing secretarial duties for the military.

• On March 31, the nation adopts Daylight Savings Time. Clocks are set ahead one hour from April through October to provide more daylight during working hours, reduce electricity needs, and thereby conserve fuel for the war effort.

• On May 11, the New York City superintendent of schools asks the board of education to ban the teaching of German in high schools.

• On May 15, airmail service is launched by the War Department. After taking off from Washington, D.C., with mail for Philadelphia, the first flight crashes near Waldorf, Maryland. On August 12, the Post Office Department takes control of air mail and service improves.

• On May 16, Congress passes the Sedition Act. People can now be arrested for criticizing the flag, government, draft, or war production. More than two thousand are jailed for hindering the war effort. They include Socialist and labor leader Eugene Debs, who is sentenced to ten years in prison for defending a radical labor union and pacifism.

• On May 24, in New York City 284,114 women register to vote.

• On June 4, New York Harbor is closed after nine ships are sunk by U-boats off the Atlantic coast.

• On July 26, sugar rations are reduced to two pounds a month per person by the U.S. Food Board.

• From September 3 to September 6, the American Protective League conducts massive "Slacker Raids" in New York City, rounding up fifty thousand suspected draft dodgers. Sixteen thousand are found to have violated the Selective Service Act in ways ranging from administrative matters to draft evasion.

• On September 18, a massive drive to recruit women for farmwork begins, in an effort to compensate for the loss of farm labor that results when large numbers of male farmworkers join the military.

• On October 31, U.S. public health officials predict that the worldwide influenza epidemic will kill twenty million people. By this date, eighty thousand deaths in the United States alone are attributed to the epidemic. In the United States the death toll from influenza eventually reaches between four hundred thousand and five hundred thousand, far exceeding the fifty-three thousand American combat deaths in World War I.

• On November 11, World War I ends. After a parade, 150 tons of paper have to be cleared off the streets of New York City. U.S. combat casualties total fifty-three thousand, with deaths from other causes numbering more than sixty-three thousand. The cost to American taxpayers is $21 billion, in addition to the cost of loans to the Allies.

• On December 22, the federal government ends the last ban on consumption of foodstuffs judged necessary to the war effort.

## 1919

• Since World War I ended, wheat prices have fallen from $2.20 to 60¢ per pound. A pound of cotton that brought farmers forty cents during wartime now sells for a nickel. In addition, pent-up wartime labor unrest has produced a wave of strikes in the transportation, coal, steel, and construction industries now that the war is over.

• The Ku Klux Klan is active in twenty-seven states. Membership has grown to some one hundred thousand since its revival in 1915.

• On January 29, the Eighteenth Amendment, adopted by the required three-quarters of the states, is proclaimed to be part of the Constitution as of January 16, 1920. Americans have one year to drink legally; some begin stockpiling liquor in anticipation of Prohibition.

• On April 27, the National Association of the Motion Picture Industry volunteers to submit films for censorship.

• On June 2, bombs damage the homes of several leading government officials in Washington, D.C., including those of Attorney General A. Mitchell Palmer and Assistant Secretary of the Navy Franklin D. Roosevelt. Three days later, sixty-seven anarchists are arrested; they face deportation.

• On July 20, roaming bands of soldiers, sailors, and marines attack African Americans on the streets of Washington, D.C. The bands claim that African Americans had been attacking white women in the city during the past month.

• On July 30, U.S. troops are called to help end race riots in Chicago, where whites have burned and pillaged African

American sections of the city for two weeks. The riots start when white youths begin throwing rocks at an African American youth swimming near a segregated beach on Lake Michigan. By the time troops are called in, thirty-one people are dead; more than five hundred people have been injured.

• In August, after race riots in Washington, D.C., and Chicago, similar riots occur in Norfolk, Virginia; Knoxville, Tennessee; Blaine, Arkansas; Omaha, Nebraska, and twenty other cities. By summer's end, hundreds of people are dead, mostly African Americans, about one hundred of whom have been lynched.

• On August 14, to help stem rampant inflation, the Wilson administration seizes and distributes food that had been stored in warehouses in several cities. Producers had stored the food as a way of keeping food prices high.

• On September 15, Massachusetts officials begin hiring replacement workers for striking police in the city of Boston. The state militia had already been called out to help control mobs of looters. Gov. Calvin Coolidge takes the lead in condemning the striking police, thereby catapulting himself into the national spotlight.

• On October 26, it is reported that nine thousand tractors are in use in the state of Iowa, an indication of the mechanization of farm labor.

• On October 28, Congress passes the Volstead Act over Wilson's veto. The act defines intoxicating liquor as anything with more than 0.5 percent alcohol and provides for the enforcement of the Eighteenth Amendment, passed on January 29.

• On November 16, since the passage of the child labor provision in the federal tax code in April, child labor has been reduced by 40 percent, particularly in the coal mining and canning industries.

• On December 17, after meetings among members of Congress, the administration, and motion picture executives, the industry announces it will fight the spread of Bolshevism and anti-Americanism with "all that is within our power."

• On December 21, nearly 250 Russian immigrants accused of holding radical political beliefs are deported on a ship labeled the "Soviet Ark" to the newly formed Soviet Union.

# The Conflict of Colour

Nonfiction work

**By:** B. L. Putnam Weale

**Date:** 1910

**Source:** Weale, B L. (Bertram Lenox) Putnam. *The Conflict of Colour: The Threatened Upheaval Throughout the World.* New York: The Macmillan Company, 1910, 228–232, 234–235.

**About the Author:** B.L. (Bertram Lenox) Putnam Weale (1877–1930) was a prominent American author who wrote about the emerging non-Western world—especially China and Japan. Throughout his writings, he warned of the dangers that the rise of strong non-white nations would pose for the United States. ■

NIGGER MILK.

An image from a 1916 wall calendar. Caricatures depicting African Americans or other dark-skinned people as different and inferior to whites were a part of everyday life in the 1910s. **THE LIBRARY OF CONGRESS.**

## Introduction

It became apparent by 1910 that the era of imperialism—with its driving belief in the White Man's Burden—had mostly come to an end. With little remaining Third-World lands to divide up among themselves, the imperial powers seemed content to administer and develop the possessions that they had already acquired, rather than seeking fresh conquests. There was also pressure from critics back home to develop these new lands, in part to demonstrate that these territories had been in fact worth obtaining and now holding.

Elsewhere, other elements entered the equation. As early as 1896, the Ethiopians had shocked the world by defeating Italy in a war. Meanwhile, Japan, the first non-Western nation to attempt to play the modern imperial game, burst on the scene with a stunning triumph in the Russo–Japanese War of 1904–1905. Suddenly, with the arrival of Japan, the imperial game was no longer simply the whites against everyone else. Also, colonial development (both economic and social) actually served to make the natives even more restless by opening their eyes to the larger world around them. In addition, by 1910 a new generation of Western-educated native elites began nationalist movements against their colonial masters. By 1910 there was a heightened white anxiety that the Third World was seething with unrest, and that the non-whites would soon counterattack. Indeed, this concern had

reached such a peak following World War I that it elevated to classic status Lothrop Stoddard's otherwise undistinguished book, *The Rising Tide of Color Against White World-Supremacy.*

## Significance

At the time that Weale's book was published, this Third-World revolt was just beginning. Great anxiety surfaced, now that the age of naked imperialism was over. Perhaps the whites from Europe remained dangerously overexposed—especially so in the tropical regions. In those regions, the whites constituted a distinct minority in an overwhelming sea of color. Of course, this concern would be worsened after the bloodletting of World War I, which left a much weaker Europe less able to fend off vigorous nationality claims arising from increasingly restless subjugated peoples.

By 1910, Americans began linking this worldwide upheaval by people of color with events at home. By 1910 the twenty-year Jim Crow counter-revolution had finished sweeping the South, disenfranchising and segregating blacks, who were just a generation or two removed from slavery. Also, the American South (in particular, Mississippi and Alabama) furnished the segregationist

Jesse Washington, a young African American man, was burned alive by this lynch mob in front of the Waco, Texas, city hall on May 15, 1916. Lynchings such as this were common in the 1910s, a terrible sign of white Americans' fear and hatred of African Americans. None of the people involved in Washington's death were ever prosecuted. **THE LIBRARY OF CONGRESS.**

model for the apartheid system of white racial supremacy that South Africa began instituting around 1910.

At home, many "Old-Stock" Americans feared that they would lose control of the United States as the result of overbreeding by perceived "inferiors." This fear resulted in intense anxiety and negativity toward various races, including Asian, black, and even southern and eastern European immigrants, although these immigrants were technically white.

## Primary Source

*The Conflict of Colour* [excerpt]

> **SYNOPSIS:** Author B.L. (Bertram Lenox) Putnam Weale analyzes the link between the unrest against white colonial rule that was sweeping through the Third World and the serious internal tensions raised by the still-subjugated American black population. This selection places America's race problem in a worldwide context.

### The Black Problem

There is perhaps nothing quite so cruel in the whole world as the strange law which has given to so many scores of millions of human beings coal-

black faces and bodies, thus so distinguishing them from the rest of the human family that this singular colour—together with the unalterable odour which accompanies it, and the simian features which accentuate it—is held to be the mark of the beast.

In European climes, where the black man—the African native—is generally only a creature imagined and not seen or understood, and where, if he does happen to wander, he is so submerged in the flood of whites that he cannot possibly count, it may sound like a grievous and foolish overstatement to speak of the negro is such harsh and uncompromising terms. But in the two Americas, in Africa and along the vast Asiatic coast-line, as well as in the world of island outposts along each of these continents, the coal-black native is almost universally considered as a man utterly separated from the rest of the world's inhabitants, and therefore not far removed from being accursed. . . .

Yet though this is so, many people are so ignorant to-day as to imagine that the whites of the Southern States of the American Union are cruel to despair in their treatment of the black man—in the way they segregate him and then lynch him if he shows the slightest signs of the great lust with which he is popularly credited. But people in Europe think this only because they do not understand those primitive impulses which are indissolubly mixed with all racial questions. The anxiety to preserve racial purity is a natural and commendable one; it is common to all the higher peoples of the world; and since it is one of nature's most jealously-guarded laws that purity means life, to descend to the level of those pulpit orators who blindly advocate the removal of barriers which can never be properly removed, is really to descend to a level which even brute beasts do not understand. Those who advocate wholesale cross-breeding as a sensible method of solving racial antagonism undoubtedly talk of things about which they are not qualified to speak. Such a movement, if it could be started, would destroy the world. And this is exactly what all who have some practical acquaintance with the problem but too well know.

Thus the whites of the Southern States, as everyone who has lived in Asia or Africa understands, when they do everything they can to prevent all mixing of blood, are simply obeying natural laws, which, if they ignored, would quickly lead to their own undoing. In these Southern States miscegenation is rightly held to be an offence far worse than manslaughter, and when the guilty couple have gone through the formality of marriage it is punished by life-imprisonment. It is felt that unless the greatest restraints are imposed, the position of the whites, who are too often in the minority, would speedily become intolerable from an inter-breeding which would perforce drag all down to the mixed white level of certain parts of South America, notably Brazil—where the black man has bred not only with whites, but with Indians, thus producing dreadful hybrids. . . .

Nor must it be forgotten that in the case of man there is good reason for this profound aversion on other grounds. The black man has given nothing to the world. He has never made a nation—he belongs to nothing but a subject race. He has no architecture of his own, no art, no history, no real religion, unless animism be a religion. His hands have reared no enduring monuments, save when they have been forcibly directed by the energies of other races. . . .

It is not strange, then, that the negro should always have been held to be a perfect example of arrested development. He has never yet made a nation—he has never dreamed of anything greater than a tribe. Though he has for three thousand years been in contact with other peoples, he has never learnt much—in any case he forgets more quickly

than he learns—and consequently he has very naturally remained where he still is, despised, rejected, and ill-treated, whenever possible. Such, in a few words, is his tragic and featureless history. . . .

For the black man is a great breeder of men, and in a few scores of years, when he has in the whole of the Dark Continent the same ease and security of life as, for instance, he has to-day in the Southern States of America or in South Africa, he will be multiplying prodigiously. How to keep races pure from his contact will then certainly be an acute problem: for as he scatters far and wide he will leave—in spite of all precautions—some traces of his blood. Nobody really knows how many negroes there are already in the world; it is roughly calculated that with the cross-breeds there are about one hundred millions. Accepting this figure as correct, and accepting also the calculation that White doubles in eighty years, Yellow or Brown in sixty years, but Black in forty years, then it is evident that even by the close of the present century the Blacks will have so greatly multiplied that, like the Japanese of the present day, who maintain that emigration has become a vital necessity for their continued existence, they may attempt to force themselves where they are not wanted. For that there will be some day an overflow, an overspilling of black men, seems tolerably certain. By the end of the present century there should certainly be three hundred million negroes in the world—a number terrifying in its possibilities, in view of certain special and very peculiar considerations.

## Further Resources
### BOOKS
Grant, Madison. *The Passing of the Great Race; or, The Racial Basis of European History.* New York: Charles Scribner, 1916.

Stoddard, Lothrop. *The Rising Tide of Color Against White World-Supremacy.* New York: Charles Scribner, 1920.

# "The Woman Shopper: How to Make Her Buy"
Magazine article

**By:** Isaac F. Marcosson
**Date:** 1910
**Source:** Marcosson, Isaac F. "The Woman Shopper: How to Make Her Buy." *The Saturday Evening Post* 183, no. 8, August 20, 1910.

**About the Author:** Isaac Frederick Marcosson (1876–1961), a prolific writer on various business-related issues, was one of America's leading advertising and marketing authorities during the first half of the twentieth century. ∎

## Introduction

A debate has engaged historians regarding which came first: the chicken or the egg. In this case, the discussion revolves around an intriguing question: Did the women's liberation movement of the 1960s create an increased consciousness among working women, or did the working women themselves create the women's liberation movement? Similarly, the feminist movement earlier in the century appears to have been largely the result of the changing attitudes among working women as early as 1910. This movement culminated in 1920 with the passage of the Nineteenth Amendment to the U.S. Constitution, which granted American women the right to vote.

Indeed, it seems clear that the emergence around 1910 of a new generation of actualized women—who made their mark in the workplace, in the professions, in the universities, and in business—helped to set the stage for the birth of the strong, politically oriented feminist movement later in the decade. In addition, the 1910s witnessed the arrival of the American woman as a consumer—not simply as the matriarch of the household shopping for her family but as a full participant in the American consumer culture with plenty of discretionary income to lavish on herself.

## Significance

The early 1900s was a transitional period during which the pre-feminist world was decaying but the modern feminist world had not yet emerged. In the midst of these changes, the woman consumer presented a unique set of challenges to marketers trying to sell their goods and services. Meanwhile, the 1910s saw the transformation of mass marketing into science. Marketing was a skillful blend of advertising, salesmanship, and public relations, and during this period it shed much of its intuitive approach to deciphering consumer trends in favor of hard survey research. The goal of this research was to precisely measure public tastes. The 1920s saw the full flowering of this trend toward the science of marketing—replete with consulting firms dispensing advice to clients from atop Madison Avenue office suites in New York City—but its outline was clearly evident by 1910.

Older attitudes—especially toward women—die hard. Indeed, marketers often engaged in open and shameless manipulation when trying to woo newly liberated female consumers. The industry often embraced traditional stereotypes that portrayed women as unthinking emotional creatures who could be tricked routinely by various clever marketing ploys. However, in the end, although marketers retained a generally low opinion of female shoppers, the hard dollars now bulging out of these women's purses forced marketers to devise innovative strategies to reach this group of consumers.

## Primary Source

**"The Woman Shopper: How to Make Her Buy"**
[excerpt]

> **SYNOPSIS:** Isaac F. Marcosson, one of America's most knowledgeable merchandising experts, explains how savvy marketers can successfully attract women shoppers.

"If Women only bought what they set out to buy there would be fewer department stores," said the house manager as he watched the ebb and flow of the tide of shoppers in a great New York drygoods establishment. He summed up in a sentence the state of mind that has made the whole many-sided science of merchandising for the sex possible. In the profitable encouragement of the feminine buying instinct lies the secret of the successful conduct of a vast part of the retail business in the United States, because the average woman not only shops for herself, but, by reason of her position in the household, shops for the entire family, husband often included. The winning trade appeal must be to her. A. T. Stewart recognized this many years ago, for his first published advertisement was addressed to "the ladies of New York." Perhaps in no commercial activity does human nature play so big a part or is competition so keen. In the explanation of some of the methods employed there is a helpful lesson in retailing for the shopkeeper, no matter whether he sells pins or pianos.

The problem of merchandising for women is peculiar and universal. Temperament enters largely into the transaction. A man who goes out to buy something for himself usually knows just what he wants and he almost invariably gets it without delay. He hasn't the time to shop. Merchandising for him is comparatively easy. A woman, on the other hand, does not always know exactly what she wants when she goes forth; she waits to see what is offered. Style, suggestion, environment, even atmospheric conditions, contribute to the choice and the extent of her buying, and she has the leisure to pick and choose. Just as you find a Tartar when you scratch a Russian so do you instantly uncover the born shopper when you offer a woman goods across the counter. It is the instinct of her sex and in the main it knows no creed or caste. . . .

The famous New York City department store Macy's, around 1908. The success of Macy's and other stores like it relied heavily on their ability to sell to women. **THE LIBRARY OF CONGRESS.**

Though this genius for shopping is universal, you find on comparison that the American woman is the best shopper in the world. One reason is that, where the French woman, for example, looks only for effect when she shops, the American woman scrutinizes the details that combine to cause this effect. The seeking out of these many little things comprises the perfect art of her buying. In brief, she knows everything that she is getting and she is particular about what she gets. . . .

Since the instinct of woman is to shop, it follows that the first step in successful merchandising for her is to make the place where she can shop as accessible as possible. The way to her buying must be the easiest way. You find that almost all of the stores that attract begin on a corner, because a corner is a beacon-light for business. Women naturally gravitate toward one. When you have a corner and

perfect transportation facilities you get the ideal combination for drawing a woman's trade. The general rule to be laid down, which may be followed by any kind of retail merchant, is, "Get near the densest traffic." If the store is to be kept open day and night it should be located where traffic does not cease in the evening. Such a store should not be near a bank or group of banks, because they close early and are dark and deserted at night. This tends to give the whole block a dead appearance. . . .

Assuming that the merchant has the properly accessible site, what is he to do to make the woman buy the moment she gets into the store? The whole secret, after having seasonable, reasonable and dependable goods, is to make the main floor as attractive and alluring as possible. It is at this point that one result of a careful study of the feminine temperament comes in, because the really successful

The interior of Traub Brothers, a department store in Detroit, Michigan, in the early 1900s. **THE LIBRARY OF CONGRESS.**

main floor is so arranged as to stimulate the shopping instinct and make the woman buyer feel that she "simply must have" the articles displayed.

That fascinating psychological institution—the power of suggestion—does the job. The shrewd merchandiser simply turns it loose when he fills the main floor with "pickups," little articles that attract the eye and make the woman pause and examine them. They may be jewelry, belts, belt-buckles, silver or gilt picture frames, toilet articles, notions, hatpins, leather goods, fans, veils, combs, umbrellas, hosiery—all the things that appeal to feminine fancy, that arouse instant interest and make a swift and unexpected appeal for purchase. The woman will buy them impulsively because they fascinate her. This starts the buying machinery and gives the shopper the feeling that she is getting just what she wants. The chances are that she will buy more than she ever expected to buy on that trip.

This naturally leads to what might be called the geography of merchandising for women. By having the small, highly suggestive and quickly salable articles, whose buying requires no forethought, at the entrance and near by on the main floor, the merchant is enabled to place the less attractive goods, and the stocks that require time and thought in buying, farther back and higher up. A woman who starts out to buy a suit or a long coat or a brass bedstead, or even a pair of shoes, is willing to go to the third or fourth floor after them. She has made up her mind to get this particular article and needs no power of suggestion to guide her. You can see that one reason why some retail merchants for women have failed is simply because they put the wrong kind of stock on their main floors, and especially near the doors.

There is still another good business reason behind the grouping of enticing articles on the main floor. It creates quick buying, and a busy counter is one of the first and best aids to merchandising for women. Crowds of women shoppers have been likened to flocks of sheep. Experience shows that if a woman stops at a counter and says out loud, "I think this is a real bargain," nearly every other woman within the range of her voice will at once think the same thing and rally around the goods. Many of them will buy. Thus to the power of suggestion must be added the potent influence of the power of example in inducing women to buy. The whole machinery that stirs the far-flung American bargain line into action operates on this theory. Bargains are good bait, for they bring people into the store. Women will buy them because they think they are cheap, whether they need them or not. Then they stir around to find some place or use for them.

The very origin of bargain day indicates its best value today. Formerly Friday was the poorest business day of the week. It was the lull after the rush of the first part of the week and the calm before Saturday, which was the general payday, when many people did their buying. How to make this a profitable day was the problem. A clever man said to himself, "Why not have a big volume of business at a very small profit rather than no business at all?" He marked down a pile of goods, advertised them and called Friday "bargain day." Women, being by instinct shoppers and bargain-hunters, flocked to the store. Friday is now as big a day as any other, and sometimes bigger.

Every great merchandiser has his own peculiar system of creating bargains. Often bargains are the result of opportunities. The shrewd merchant will buy a stock that may be slightly out of date and sell it at a small margin of profit. The article is unusual and it brings a lot of new people into the store. In short, it is one form of publicity.

There are many clever devices to get women into the stores. One is the "rainy-day special." It is a well-known fact that unless there is some very special inducement the average woman shopper will not rush out to buy on a rainy day. One far-sighted New York merchant hit upon an idea to make this inducement. He said, "Why not make the store so attractive on rainy days that the women will make it a point to come to my store every time it rains?" He planned a series of special bargains, which would not be advertised and which would be available only on rainy days. Thus the women would have to come to the shop to see just what they were. The element of surprise added interest to the performance. . . .

All the genius of providing the right kind of store and the right kind of stock will be unavailing, however, if there are not intelligence and selling ability behind the counter. Although rules for employees are made every day by the score, experience shows that the whole science of reaching the woman customer lies in two simple things—attention to the customer and knowledge of the stock.

Clerks who study the merchandise they handle roll up big sales, and it is easy to see why. Take a girl at the lace counter. A woman happens to be strolling through the store and sees an attractive pattern of lace, and stops. Without being intrusive the intelligent clerk can engage in conversation with the woman. If she can tell her, for example, that this particular lace was woven by some nuns in a French convent the chances are that she will at once interest the woman. She invests her stock with a story interest that wins. So with any kind of goods. The very moment that a clerk, by reason of investigation or study, can impart interesting facts about what she sells she plays a strong card for business. Thus that much-worked institution—human interest—performs its labor at the drygoods counter as it does in the larger sphere of wholesale salesmanship and in that still greater activity—the whole work of the world. . . .

You have now seen this many-sided drama of merchandising unfold in some of its myriad details. What of the men behind it? They are the owners and managers who sit in their offices with their fingers on the pulse of trade, their eyes on the stocks of the world. Their task is best summed up, perhaps, by one of the veterans—a wiry, gray-haired, keen-eyed little man, who owns a chain of stores that extends from Boston to Chicago. He said to me:

> In popular merchandising for women no man has a right to call a customer his own. This means that, no matter how long you have been in business, you must regard each day as if it were the day you started, with every resource you have put to the test. It's the price you must pay for a woman's trade.

## Further Resources

### BOOKS

Bronner, Simon J., ed. *Consuming Visions: Accumulation and Display of Goods in America, 1880–1920.* New York: Norton, 1989.

Garvey, Ellen Gruber. *The Adman in the Parlor: Magazines and the Gendering of Consumer Culture, 1880s to 1910s.* New York: Oxford University Press, 1996.

Hill, Daniel Delis. *Advertising to the American Woman, 1900–1999.* Columbus, Ohio: Ohio State University Press, 2002.

# *The Social Evil in Chicago*

Report

**By:** The Vice Commission of Chicago

**Date:** 1911

**Source:** The Vice Commission of Chicago. *The Social Evil in Chicago.* Chicago: Gunthorp-Warren Printing Company, 1911, 25–27, 31, 45, 47.

**About the Organization:** A distinguished citizens' body formed to investigate crime and "social evil" in the city of Chicago in the early twentieth century. ∎

## Introduction

Much civic concern focused on prostitution, often dubbed the "world's oldest profession," during the early twentieth century. Aside from the usual moral questions raised by the practice, a growing awareness of public health issues, such as controlling the spread of venereal disease, helped fuel the debate. In addition, the size and scope of government expanded at all levels of American life during the Progressive era. The public was also increasingly willing to allow the state's police power to interfere with many areas of daily activity; these included areas of life that had previously been private.

Indeed, the Progressive era featured a good deal of what later came to be known as "social engineering." Along with Prohibition, the anti-narcotics crusade, and the war on pornography, the assault on prostitution definitely displayed coercive aspects. But resorting to the heavy hand of government flew directly in the face of America's longstanding tradition of volunteerism (and moral persuasion) as the remedy for social ills. By 1910, though, America's numerous social maladies seemed to demand more drastic remedies.

## Significance

Twentieth-century Chicago has always sported a well-earned "blue-collar" reputation. Indeed, poet Carl Sandburg labeled Chicago the city with "big shoulders." The notorious downtown stockyards served as a metaphor for the Windy City. Chicago's rough edges were on prominent display during the 1920s when arch-gangster Al Capone rode herd over businessmen and public officials and in 1968 when Mayor Richard Daley played host to the disastrous 1968 Democratic National Convention.

But Chicago has always sported another side and has produced a string of able urban reformers who, from time to time, have sought to uplift urban life by tackling assorted social ills. Regarding prostitution, the legendary 1910 Chicago Vice Commission was perhaps the most respected public commission of the entire Progressive era—indeed, it often served as a model for other public

commissions established across the country. On a more practical level, the Chicago Vice Commission's work helped to galvanize public opinion supporting the Mann Act, the sweeping 1910 national anti-prostitution measure.

## Primary Source

*The Social Evil in Chicago* [excerpt]

**SYNOPSIS:** During the Progressive era, investigative journalism and citizens' commissions were two of the most effective vehicles for focusing public attention on economic, social, and political problems and for galvanizing support for efforts to remedy the problems. In this excerpt, the 1910 Chicago Vice Commission took a hard, yet thoughtful, look at prostitution.

The honor of Chicago, the fathers and mothers of her children, the physical and moral integrity of the future generation demand that she repress public prostitution.

Prostitution is pregnant with disease, a disease infecting not only the guilty, but contaminating the innocent wife and child in the home with sickening certainty almost inconceivable; a disease to be feared with as great horror as a leprous plague; a disease scattering misery broadcast, and leaving in its wake sterility, insanity, paralysis, the blinded eyes of little babes, the twisted limbs of deformed children, degradation, physical rot and mental decay. . . .

We believe that Chicago has a public conscience which, when aroused, cannot be easily stilled—a conscience built upon moral and ethical teachings of the purest American type—a conscience which when aroused to the truth will instantly rebel against the Social Evil in all its phases. . . .

The immensity of the Social Evil problem is no excuse for us to stand idly by and do nothing in an attempt to solve it. The sin of impurity may not be cured in a day, a year, or perhaps in generations. But that prostitution as a commercialized business or anything akin to it, is necessary, can never be conceded. We assume that by earnest, wise, united, and persistent effort on the part of individuals and organized groups in society, we can do something—how much we can only discover by trial. To say we can do nothing may be left to the morally inert; of course, they can do nothing—but evil.

As plagues, epidemics and contagious diseases old as the world have given way before the onslaught of medical science; as slavery in this country has been rooted out by the gradually growing conviction of an American conscience; so may the Social Evil be repressed proportionately as the American people grow in righteousness and in the knowledge of this curse, which is more blasting than any plague or epidemic; more terrible than any black slavery that ever existed in this or any other country; more degenerating to the morals and ideals of the nation than all other agencies against decency combined.

We may enact laws; we may appoint Commissions; we may abuse Civic administrations for their handling of the problem; but the problem will remain just as long as the public conscience is dead to the issue or is indifferent to its solution.

The law is only so powerful as the public opinion which supports it. It is the habit of Americans when they make laws to insist on ethical ideals. They will not compromise. they have been endowed, however, with a fine ability to be inconsistent, and having once declared their ideals to find no difficulty, when it comes to the administration of the laws, to allow officials to ignore them; to do things not in the laws; and to substitute a practice which is a de facto law, though technically illegal. This is the basis of graft and the greatest evil in Municipal government.

Commissions may be appointed. However valuable their findings and recommendations may be, unless the public insist no changes in the situation will obtain.

The Social Evil in its worst phases may be repressed. So long as there is lust in the hearts of men it will seek out some method of expression. Until the hearts of men are changed we can hope for no absolute annihilation of the Social Evil. Religion and education alone can correct the greatest curse which today rests upon mankind. For this there is a mighty work for agencies and institutions of righteousness in our land. . . .

## Two Standards of Morality

Unfortunately there are two standards of morality in Chicago. One standard permits and applauds dances by women almost naked in certain public places under the guise of art, and condemns dances no worse before audiences from the less prosperous walks of life. This same hypocritical attitude drives the unfortunate and often poverty stricken prostitute from the street, and at the same time tolerates and often welcomes the silken clad prostitute in the public drinking places of several of the most pretentious hotels and restaurants of the city. Houses of prostitution patronized by the lowly are closed at various times for various reasons, but the gilded palaces of sin patronized by the wealthy are immune from punishment, even to the extent of being saved the humiliation of appearing upon a police list. . . .

## Causes Which Lead to Downfall

Any plan of reformation must take into consideration the causes which lead to the downfall of these unfortunates. After an exhaustive study of the whole field the Commission feels that among the causes which influence girls and women to enter upon a life of semi-professional and professional prostitution are the following: First, lack of ethical teaching and religious instruction; second, the economic stress of industrial life on unskilled workers, with the enfeebling influences on the will power; third, the large number of seasonal trades in which women are especially engaged; fourth, abnormality; fifth, unhappy home conditions; sixth, careless and ignorant parents; seventh, broken promises; eighth, love of ease and luxury; ninth, the craving for excitement and change; tenth, ignorance of hygiene. . . .

## To Men—A Closing Word

In closing this introduction the Commission desires to say one more word to those who support this business of women's souls, whether as barterers of the body, or those who demand the service— the Man. There is only one moral law—it is alike for men and women. Again, there is a contract called matrimony which is a solemn contract made between those who love. It carries with it the elements of vested rights—even a solemn promise before God. A signature represents honor—it is there—likewise a promise—it is there. Has this contract been kept inviolate? If not, why not?

To one who hears the ghastly life story of fallen women it is ever the same—the story of treachery, seduction and downfall—the flagrant act of man— the ruin of a soul by man.

It is a man and not a woman problem which we face today—commercialized by man—supported by man—the supply of fresh victims furnished by men— men who have lost that fine instinct of chivalry and that splendid honor for womanhood where the destruction of a woman's soul is abhorrent, and where the defense of a woman's purity is truly the occasion for a valiant fight.

## Further Resources

**BOOKS**

Connelly, Mark Thomas. *The Response to Prostitution in the Progressive Era.* Chapel Hill, N.C.: The University of North Carolina Press, 1980.

Hobson, Barbara Meil. *Uneasy Virtue: The Politics of Prostitution and the American Reform Tradition.* New York: Basic Books, 1987.

Langum, David J. *Crossing Over the Line: Legislating Morality and the Mann Act.* Chicago: The University of Chicago Press, 1994.

# The Immigration Problem

Nonfiction work

**By:** Jeremiah W. Jenks and W. Jett Lauck

**Date:** 1912

**Source:** Jenks, Jeremiah W. and W. Jett Lauck *The Immigration Problem.* New York: Funk & Wagnalls Company, 1912, 198–203.

**About the Author:** Jeremiah Whipple Jenks (1856–1929) and William Jett Lauck (1879–1949) were both well-known economists who frequently wrote on the subject of immigration. ∎

## Introduction

By 1910 immigration (and all of its ramifications) had become one of the most pressing public issues in American life. Indeed, after a full decade of discussion on the matter, the United States wound up completely reorienting its national policy. The United States abandoned its opengate in 1921 in favor of tight restrictions that remained in place, virtually unchanged, until 1965.

During normal times, the immigration issue had pitted American business against American organized labor. The business community favored unlimited immigration in order to provide a huge pool of workers that would act to hold down wages and forestall unionization. In contrast, organized labor wanted to limit the immigration that created an oversupply of workers, thus depressing wages and hindering unionization efforts. (Incidentally, throughout American history many newly arrived immigrant groups, having gained a foothold in the American economic system, were more than willing to slam shut the doors on newcomers who they viewed as competition.) Since the business community was much stronger politically than organized labor, the gates remained wide open.

However, as early as the 1890s, the demand for limitations on immigration increased. Indeed, this decade saw the advent of the Immigration Restriction League. Aside from the usual economic arguments, those favoring closing the border now mentioned differences in religion, language, ethnic background, and even social class. By 1921, this broader concern over the non-economic impact of immigration had produced a potent political coalition of various interests determined to reverse America's centuries-old policy of virtually unlimited immigration.

## Significance

While much of the literature surrounding the immigration debate of 1910 was strikingly negative, some voices advocated a more balanced approach. Observers such as economists Jeremiah W. Jenks and William Jett Lauck retained the idea that America still needed immigrants. Indeed, they recognized the great contributions of many groups including, significantly enough, the then-small number of high-end immigrants. This foretold the future. For when immigration revived in 1965, the percentage of upscale immigrants was higher than in any other period in American history.

Besides, many of the maladies that seemed to afflict the bulk of the immigrant population of 1910 did not necessarily have to be permanent. America, after all, was widely known as the land of the fresh start. And many sincerely believed in America's power to redeem the otherwise wretched of the earth. Franz Boas, a famous anthropologist, claimed to find in a study that even a short exposure to the healthy American environment made pronounced physical changes in the bodies of immigrants—including altering the shape of their heads to look more "American." Jenks and Lauck reminded readers that the then-despised Italians were the heirs to the magnificent ancient Roman and Renaissance civilizations.

In another insight, Jenks and Lauck understood that America's white/black race problem—especially the residual effects of slavery—affected the way that the United States welcomed European newcomers. In addition, Jenks and Lauck questioned why America offered citizenship and landowning opportunities to immigrants from numerous countries that did not afford newcomers such generous opportunities. Such issues arise today as Americans are asked to abide by one set of rules accommodating newcomers while the rest of the world adheres to its traditional restrictive policies.

## Primary Source

*The Immigration Problem* [excerpt]

**SYNOPSIS:** In this analysis of the impact of widespread immigration on the United States in 1912, economists Jenks and Lauck raise issues that are still major concerns today.

### European and Mexican Immigrants on the Pacific Coast

. . . When the immigrants are members of races widely different from Americans, as are the Chinese, the Japanese, the Hindus, the question of race and race prejudice becomes an extremely important problem.

The untrained man is likely to assume that those people who differ widely from himself in appearance, in habits of living or of working, are members of a lower and not merely of a different race. He is accustomed to speak of the Italian, for example, with contempt, as a "dago." Still more emphatic is he in his denouncement of the Chinese, the Japanese, and the Hindus as members of an inferior race. Of course, the cultivated man, especially one who has traveled widely, knows better. As Professor Steiner has so well reminded us, the first immigrant to America was a dago named Columbus, a man of learning and of the highest cultivation. Moreover, when at the present day Americans go to Europe to study art and architecture they are very likely to go to the land of the great dagoes, Michelangelo, Giotto, Raffael, Leonardo da Vinci, and others of similar rank. Nowhere in the world have we been able to find in centuries past, or do we find in the world to-day, people of higher cultivation than the Italians. Moreover, if instead of turning our eyes to Europe, we go to the Far East, and visit the Chinese and Japanese, we are equally imprest, as we meet members of the wealthier and more cultivated classes in society, with their high degree of intelligence, with their intellectual training, and especially, perhaps, with the personal qualities which have made them the world over models of courtesy and of manners that characterize the gentleman. . . .

It is hardly to be expected, however, that people who have not traveled and who have not read widely should recognize that the ordinary working men from the Orient with whom they come into keen competition, and who often underbid them in wages, especially in doing work of the most arduous type, belong to races of cultivation; and it is natural that they should look upon them as inferior people. Moreover, whether they recognize this fact or not, whether or not we ourselves believe that race prejudice is something to be heartily condemned, we must still recognize the actual existence of this feeling as an important political fact.

### Race Feeling Elsewhere

The feeling against the negroes has forced us to recognize that race feeling is an extremely important political question, and may well become a social question.

Moreover, we should recognize the fact that the feeling on the Pacific Coast against the Chinese, the

The early twentieth century was a period of massive immigration into the United States. These immigrant children are being examined for disease at Ellis Island, New York, before admission into the country in 1911. **CORBIS-BETTMANN. REPRODUCED BY PERMISSION.**

Japanese and the Hindus is not in itself exceptional. A similar feeling against these same races is found in Canada, in Australia, in South Africa, in every place where these oriental races have come into immediate contact with the white race, and especially when they have come into active competition with it in ordinary labor. We must recognize this feeling, then, as a natural one and one that must be counted upon when it comes to political action.

### Orientals not Easily Assimilated

Altho these races may not be considered in any way inferior to ourselves, it is a fact that they are materially different: that they are not so easily assimilated as are the members of the European races; that they do not readily marry with our people nor our people with them.

### Form a Separate Class

On the Pacific Coast they have, as a matter of fact, usually made an entirely separate working class. Generally speaking, when they have entered largely into a business, or when they have under-

One sign of the difficulty Asian immigrants had in joining mainstream culture was that the mostly male immigrants were unable or unwilling to find American wives. A Japanese man generally had to order a "picture bride," like these women, from a catalog of Japanese women willing to come to the United States and marry a stranger. **UPI/CORBIS-BETTMANN. REPRODUCED BY PERMISSION.**

taken certain classes of work, there has been a rapid separation between them and the American workingmen, they taking the harder kinds and the members of the white races taking types of work entirely different. In this way they have become, to a considerable extent, almost a separate caste. Indeed, there is a feeling on the part of many people who have carefully observed conditions in that region that they have almost made a servile caste; and many of the most thoughtful, most cultivated, most kindly people on the Coast have thought that, inasmuch as these are facts, and must be recognized, it is wise for us to take action accordingly.

### Governmental Action of China and Japan

The Governments of China and Japan have really no reason to object to our wishing not to admit the working people of their races in large numbers. As a matter of fact, Americans are not admitted to China or to Japan on even terms with the natives there. They can go into the country as residents only in very limited communities; they are not permitted to buy land; and they are not admitted to citizenship in those countries. As a matter of fact, our country has treated the members, particularly, of the Japanese race, more liberally than the Japanese have treated the Americans. The Japanese have been allowed to buy land, in many instances in large tracts; and tho at the present time we are taking rather active measures to exclude them from coming in large numbers, up to date, at any rate, we have treated them more liberally than they have treated us.

It may be well said, then, that it is better for them, better for us, better for the civilization of the world at large, that each country attempt to work out its own problems independently instead of each working them out in the country of the other. . . .

We should not fail to recognize, nevertheless, the great advantage that comes from intimate association with people who are different from ourselves. One of the mistakes that we often make in our social intercourse, as well as in our political relations, in associating with people of similar tastes and habits, is to form a little clique or society of persons like ourselves, forgetting that in our intimate intercourse with them, while we may derive enjoyment, we obtain very few new ideas. In talking with men trained as we have been trained, meeting the same people, thinking along lines similar to our own habits of thinking, it is not likely that we shall give them many new thoughts, or that we shall derive much from them. On the other hand, when we meet with people of a different type from ourselves, from them we gather many new ideas, if we are thoughtful and can free ourselves from prejudice. It is they, rather than our most intimate associates, perhaps, from whom we learn most and to whom we owe most in our advancement. Indeed, it is often true, that from people who are really opposed to ourselves, we learn the most. By opposing our ideas, they rouse us to activity.

## Advantage of Association with Educated Orientals

We ought, then, not to fail to get the benefit from associating with foreigners, especially those whose racial customs differ widely from ours. In order, however, to secure this advantage, it is not necessary that they come in large numbers, and especially that they come as people of the unskilled laboring classes. Rather should we encourage our own people to travel in foreign countries; to get the ideas that come from the study of different civilizations; and to encourage the coming to our shores of people of the more intelligent classes, travelers, scientists, students, merchants, and others from whom we can gather new plans of work. While it may, for economic as well as for social reasons, be wise to exclude the common laborer, it can not but be unwise to exclude trained men and women who come to us usually merely for a temporary sojourn, and from whom we may learn much that will tend to benefit our own civilization. Moreover, by exchanging ideas and giving to them the benefit of our civilization, which differs from theirs, we may give to them an equal advantage, and thus the civilization of the world will be promoted.

## Further Resources

### BOOKS

Grant, Madison. *The Passing of the Great Race; or, The Racial Basis of European History.* New York: Charles Scribner, 1916.

Guterl, Matthew Pratt. *The Color of Race in America, 1900–1940.* Cambridge, Mass.: Harvard University Press, 2001.

Nash, Gary B. and Richard Weiss, eds. *The Great Fear: Race in the Mind of America.* New York: Holt, Rinehart and Winston, 1970.

# "On the Imitation of Man"

Essay

**By:** Ida M. Tarbell

**Date:** 1913

**Source:** Tarbell, Ida M. "On the Imitation of Man" in *The Business of Being a Woman.* New York: The Macmillan Company, 1913, 30–36.

**About the Author:** Ida Minerva Tarbell (1857–1944) became America's most famous investigative journalist of the late nineteenth century and early twentieth century. The daughter of an independent oil refiner who was driven out of business by the ruthless tactics of Standard Oil Company's John D. Rockefeller, Tarbell gained her revenge with *The History of the Standard Oil Company* (1904), a devastating book that exposed Rockefeller. The piece also helped to launch her career as a muckraker (someone who exposes misconduct of a prominent individual). ∎

## Introduction

By 1920 the first phase of the American Feminist Movement had triumphed. Women received the right to vote with the ratification of the Nineteenth Amendment to the U.S. Constitution that year. Moreover, as women entered the workforce in significant numbers (especially in more prestigious professional positions), their incomes increased.

By 1920 support for women's suffrage, once thought radical, had become mainstream. Women had achieved the vote due to a fortuitous set of circumstances that had little to do directly with women themselves. All of the usual reasons advanced by women for the vote—that it would be fair, just, decent, democratic, indeed American—failed to carry the day.

Instead, women received the vote from men because of a pair of powerful political and social movements—one liberal, the other conservative. The liberal peace movement, which viewed American entry into World War I as a significant step toward a world without war, favored women's suffrage, thinking this would guarantee peace. After all, they reasoned, what woman wants her husband or son marching off to war? Conversely, the normally conservative Prohibitionists favored women's suffrage, expecting to find in newly enfranchised females a reliable ally to enforce the restrictions on alcoholic beverages. After all, what woman, they reasoned, wanted her husband or son staggering home drunk from the neighborhood saloon?

Despite the progress made in women's suffrage, many men (including many advocates of women's suffrage) who had no problem granting women the right to vote still disliked the idea of social equality. Feminine equality represented uncharted waters. And some sort of power adjustments would have to be worked out between

Ida M. Tarbell in 1915. A successful author and journalist, Tarbell exemplifies the sort of women that she describes in *The Business of Being a Woman* as being interested, and good at, tradionally male subjects and pursuits. UPI/CORBIS-BETTMANN. REPRODUCED BY PERMISSION.

men and women—at the expense of men's traditional prerogatives. Some men hardly relished the prospect.

And what of the American woman once completely liberated? Would she lose much of her individuality—indeed her special status—only to become a pale imitation of man? From this perspective, the issue of women's suffrage was merely the tip of a much larger iceberg.

### Significance

Meawhile, at every stage of the feminist movement, the female ranks were bitterly divided. Not all women favored granting women the right to vote—doubtless on the basis of the slippery slope argument that once the voting threshold had been pierced, the feminist movement (no matter how originally limited in scope) would ultimately careen out of control.

Similar concerns lay behind much of the female opposition to the controversial Equal Rights Amendment, which cleared Congress in 1972 but fell three states short of the necessary thirty-eight required for ratification. Even President Reagan, who endorsed full legal female equality, sought a statute-by-statute review of all laws rather than letting mischievous judges unfavorably inter-

pret the unclear language of the Equal Rights Amendment. By century's end, Reagan's position seems to be the latest word on the subject of feminine equality, for no pressure currently exists to revive the Equal Rights Amendment.

### Primary Source

"On the Imitation of Man"

**SYNOPSIS:** Pioneering woman journalist Ida M. Tarbell (herself, curiously enough, not a feminist) discusses the problems of female social equality—especially if women wind up as mere pale imitation of men.

Go to-day into many a woman's club house, into many a drawing-room or studio at, let us say, the afternoon tea hour, and what will you see? One or probably more women in mannish suits and boots calmly smoking cigarettes while they talk, and talk well, about things in which women are not supposed to be interested, but which it is apparent they understand.

Look the exhibit over. It is made, you at once recognize, by women of character, position, and sense. They have simply found certain masculine ways to their liking and adopted them. The probability is that if anybody should object to their habits, many of them would be as bewildered as are the great majority of Americans by the demonstration that "nice" women can smoke and think nothing of it!

The cigarette, the boot, and much of the talk are only by-products of the woman's invasion of the man's world. She did not set out to win these spoils. They came to her in the campaign!

The objects of her attack were things she considered more fundamental. She was dissatisfied with the way her brain was being trained, her time employed, her influence directed. "Give us the man's way," was her demand, "then we shall understand real things, can fill our days with important tasks, will count as human beings."

There was no uncertainty in her notion of how this was to be accomplished. A woman rarely feels uncertainty about methods. She instinctively sees a way and follows it with assurance. Half her irritation against man has always been that he is a spendthrift with time and talk. Madame Roland, sitting at her sewing table listening to the excited debate of the Revolutionists in her salon, mourned that though the ideas were many, the resulting measures were few. It is the woman's eternal complaint against discussion—nothing comes of it. In a country like our own, where reflection usually follows action, the woman's natural mental attitude is exaggerated. It is one reason why we have so few houses where there is anything like conversation, why with us the salon as an institution is out of question. The woman wants immediately to incorporate her ideas. She is not interested in turning them over, letting her mind play with them. She has no patience with other points of view than her own. They are *wrong*—therefore why consider them? She detests uncertainties— questions which cannot be settled. Only by man and the rare woman is it accepted that talk is a good enough end in itself.

The strength of woman's attack on man's life, apart from the essential soundness of the impulse which drove her to make it, lay then in its directness and practicality. She began by asking to be educated in the same way that man educated himself. Preferably she would enter his classroom, or if that was denied her, she would follow the "just-as-good" curriculum of the college founded for her. In the last sixty or seventy years tens of thousands of women have been students in American universities, colleges, and technical schools, taking there the same training as men. In the last twenty years the annual crescendo of numbers has been amazing; over ten thousand at the beginning of the period, over fifty-two thousand at the end. Over eight thousand degrees were given to women in 1910, nearly half as many as were given to men. Fully four fifths of these women students and graduates have worked side by side with men in schools which served both equally.

Here, then, is a great mass of experience from which it would seem that we ought to be able to say precisely how the intellects of the two sexes act and react under the stimulus of serious study, to decide definitely whether their attack on problems is the same, whether they come out the same. Nevertheless, he would be a rash observer who would pretend to lay down hard-and-fast generalizations. Assert whatever you will as to the mind of woman at work and some unimpeachable authority will rise up with experience that contradicts you. But the same may be said of the mind of man. The mind— *per se*—is a variable and disconcerting organ.

But admitting all this—certain generalizations, on the whole correct, may be made from our experience with coeducation.

One of the first of these is that at the start the woman takes her work more seriously than her mas-

culine competitor. Fifty years ago there was special reason for this. The few who in those early days sought a man's education had something of the spirit of pioneers. They had set themselves a lofty task: to prove themselves the equal of man—to win privileges which they believed were maliciously denied their sex. The spirit with which they attacked their studies was illumined by the loftiness of their aim. The girl who enters college nowadays has rarely the opportunity to be either pioneer or martyr. She is doing what has come to be regarded as a matter of course. Nevertheless, to-day as then, in the co-educational institution she is more consciously on her mettle than the man.

### Further Resources

**BOOKS**

Brady, Kathleen. *Ida Tarbell: Portrait of a Muckraker*. New York: Seaview/Putnam, 1984.

Camhi, Jane Jerome. *Women Against Women: American Anti-Suffragism, 1880–1920*. Brooklyn, N.Y.: Carlson Publishers, 1994.

# America's Sex Hysteria

## "Sex O'Clock in America"

**Magazine article**

**By:** *Current Opinion*

**Date:** 1913

**Source:** "Sex O'Clock in America." *Current Opinion,* August 1913, 113–114.

## "Popular Gullibility as Exhibited in the New White Slavery Hysteria"

**Magazine article**

**By:** *Current Opinion*

**Date:** 1914

**Source:** "Popular Gullibility as Exhibited in the New White Slavery Hysteria," *Current Opinion*. February 1914, 129. ∎

### Introduction

By all accounts, 1913 was the year when cracks first developed in the carefully constructed nineteenth-century Victorian façade of sexual prudery. In time, this edifice would be replaced by today's media-driven titillation. That first wave of sexual liberation was abruptly stamped out. Indeed, it barely survived the First World War when the heavy hand of wartime government censorship, combined with the fear engendered by the Red Scare (1919–20), drove open displays of sexuality deeply underground. For instance, the once-vibrant silent-movie industry buckled under pressure from government coercion, industry self-regulation, and the consolidation of small independent companies into large, conservative, profit-driven studios.

The second phase of this sexual liberation surfaced in 1964, the year in which the topless bathing suit made its American debut and sex became once again a subject of popular interest. Meanwhile, this sexual liberation soon merged with the larger political and cultural rebellion of the 1960s. Since 1964, sex has become a permanent fixture in American life.

### Significance

In the midst of this hoopla about sex during the earlier part of the century, the White Slavery Panic of 1913–14 remains quite fascinating. Without question, organized rings of kidnappers did lure some young girls into prostitution. But reports of widespread White Slavery are exceedingly difficult to verify. America has experienced many instances where various sorts of dangers were wildly exaggerated. For example, there were the Salem Witchcraft Trials of the 1690s, as well as the rampant fear of child molestation permeating American society during the 1980s.

The United States Congress, under intense pressure from the public, must have taken the White Slavery threat seriously, for the 1910 Mann Act passed swiftly. Also, the mass media helped to fuel the concern over White Slavery in silent movies such as "Damaged Goods." These films probably terrified millions of Americans (mostly rural folks) who seemed more than willing to believe that America's cities—already teaming with immigrants, alcohol, and narcotics—were cesspools of crime and vice, like White Slavery.

In 1913–14, young girls were afraid of going out in public alone. And many parents admonished their children to look out for the "white slavers."

Today the trafficking in human beings constitutes a worldwide problem. America held slaves until 1865 and today often overlooks not only virtual slavery (forced labor) in factories that manufacture products destined for sale in the American markets, but also sexual slavery that caters to the tourist and adult-entertainment industries.

### Primary Source

"Sex O'Clock in America" [excerpt]

**SYNOPSIS:** This article notes the growing willingness of Americans to discuss sex publicly, while lamenting the uninformed, even hysterical, opinions being put forward.

### Sex O'Clock in America

A wave of sex hysteria and sex discussion seems to have invaded this country. Our former reticence on matters of sex is giving way to a frankness that would even startle Paris. Prostitution, as *Life* remarks, is the chief topic of polite conversation. It has struck "sex o'clock" in America, to use William Marion Reedy's memorable phrase. The White Slave appears in the headlines of our newspapers. Reginald Wright Kauffman and a tribe of other scribes are making capital out of the victims of Mrs. Warren's profession. Witter Bynner in *The Forum* exploits the White Slave in blank verse. *Leslie's Weekly* points out her lesson in short stories. *The Smart Set* makes her the subject of a novelette: In the theater, "Damaged Goods," a play of which the action springs from venereal disease, marks an epoch of new freedom in sex discussion. The story of Brieux' drama is being "adapted" to *Physical Culture* readers by Upton Sinclair. Mr. Rockefeller's young men in Chicago, Philadelphia and New York, have made exhaustive studies of the lupanar and its inmates. Vice reports leap into print. Vice commissions meet and gravely attempt to rebuild in a fortnight the social structure of the world. Is this overemphasis of sex a symptom of a new moral awakening or is it a sign that the morbidity of the Old World is overtaking the New? Does it indicate a permanent change in our temper or is it merely the concomitant of the movement for the liberation of woman from the shackles of convention that will disappear when society has readjusted itself to the New Woman and the New Man? Has it struck sex o'clock permanently or will time soon point to another hour?

One writer in the St. Louis *Mirror,* James F. Clark, asserts that we must grant to-day to woman the same promiscuity that society tacitly grants to the male. This statement has aroused a storm of discussion and protest. Mr. Reedy himself, tho a radical, strongly dissents from the attitude of his aggressive contributor. He points out that Clark's point of view is the logical outcome of the hideously materialistic theory that disregards spiritual values altogether. "I do not believe," he says, "that given the prophylactic and remedy, women, under the new dispensation, are to abandon themselves to promiscuity. I cannot see that emancipation tends that way. It seems rather to me that emancipated woman, knowing good and evil, will choose her man rather than be chosen." . . .

Dr. Cecile L. Greil, a Socialist writer, welcomes the fact that society is drawing its head out of the sand of prudery where it had hidden it, ostrich-like. But she, too, fears the hysteria of sex discussion. She especially warns the members of her own sex. The pendulum with women swings more rapidly to extreme degrees, she asserts. This may be because of her highly sensitized nervous organism, which fastens with almost hysterical tenacity to anything which produces an emotional appeal. And surely nothing that has come to her for study or reflection in all the ages has been as important to her, and through her to posterity, as is this freedom of sex knowledge, which guards the citadel of society and makes for a better, finer race of citizens. "But one danger lurks in her midst. Sex freedom is frequently hysterically interpreted into meaning sex license. And the science which shall give her the right to freer, happier motherhood entails all the responsibilities that freedom in any other sense does." The modern social system, the writer continues in *The Call,* is a terrific endurance test against the forces within ourselves and the forces that attack us without. Vanity and love and sport she admits, quoting a Judge of one of the Night Courts, make more prostitutes than economic pressure and exploitation. . . .

The necessity of sex education is generally recognized. Yet there are also evidences of reaction. Thus the Chicago Board of Education rescinded the order issued by Mrs. Ella Flagg Young, in whose hands rests the school system of Chicago, providing for lectures on sex hygiene in the schools. *The Ecclesiastical Review,* a Roman Catholic publication, maintains that whatever warning and instruction may be necessary should be left in the hands of the priest. Nevertheless, the editor, tho grudgingly, prints a list of books on eugenics for the use of Roman Catholic teachers and priests to aid them in following intelligently the trend of public opinion. Another Roman Catholic publication, *America,* asks for the suppression of vice reports and of vice commissions, except for restricted particular investigations. The publication attacks Doctor Eliot's championship of the Society of Sanitary and Moral Prophylaxis. Eliot has no right, in the opinion of *America,* to declare that before the advent of the Society and its head, Dr. Morton, the policy of the world was "absolute silence" with regard to sex hygiene. "There is," we are told, "a world of difference between absolute silence and the wise and prudent discretion which bids father and mother and teacher refrain from handling the topic in public and without discriminating sense, whilst it at the same time inspires them to say at the fitting time the right word which

A woman, holding a bouquet of flowers, is embraced by her sweetheart, c. 1910. GETTY IMAGES. REPRODUCED BY PERMISSION.

shall safeguard their children, and to say it with a circumspection not likely to destroy the sense of shame, which is the best natural protection of the innocence of these little ones."

Radicals and conservatives, Freethinkers and Catholics, all seem to believe in solving the sex problem by education, but as to the method that is to be followed there are abysmal differences of opinion.

## Primary Source

"Popular Gullibility as Exhibited in the New White Slavery Hysteria" [excerpt]

> **SYNOPSIS:** This article examines the widespread fear of "White Slavery" across America in 1914. During the 1910s many Americans were convinced that young, white, women were frequently being kidnapped, drugged, or otherwise forced into prostitution. As the article notes, fear of White Slavery was far out of proportion to its actual occurence.

"White slavery," as a popular catchword to cover a multitude of crimes, real and imaginary, has for the past year been greatly developed and strengthened by sensational "stories" printed by the daily newspapers. It has remained for the newspapers themselves to calm the frenzied hysteria for which they themselves are partially responsible. The New York *World* editorially characterizes "white slavery" as a "new witchcraft mania," comparing popular gullibility to-day with that of the witchcraft days in old Salem. "When harmless old women lost their lives," comments the *World,* referring to a recent exploded "poisoned needle" case, "for commerce with the Evil One, a mysterious pricking with pins was one of the charges frequently brought against them by hysterical girls, some of whom later recanted. How nearly history repeats itself in a country which has grown, of course, much too intelligent to believe in witchcraft!"

Dailies like the Chicago *Record-Herald,* the Albany *Press,* the Baltimore *American,* the Baltimore *Evening Sun,* the Pittsburgh *Dispatch,* the New York *Sun,* and many others, have attacked the power of the catchword, "white slavery," and have attempted to extinguish the conflagration of hysteria which has in many American cities followed the vague but sensational accounts of mysterious poisoning and abductions of young girls. Simultaneously with these efforts, however, "white slave" plays and "white slave" films are attractions which crowd theaters and have become a source of substantial revenue to theatrical managers. It seems evident that the idea of "white slavery" is not only strongly established in the popular mind, but is one in which the public veritably revels.

"How far is this ridiculous delusion to go?" asks the *World,* editorially:

> If the popular imagination is to become heated to a point where it discerns an attempt at abduction in every dizzy feeling of momentary illness suffered by a young woman in a public place, it will be unsafe for a man to offer the slightest civility to any person of the other sex whom he does not happen to know. To assist a woman into a car will subject him to suspicion, and to go to her aid if she faints in the street will render him liable to arrest as a white slaver.

> Are we losing our senses over white slavery? Anatole France says somewhere that one result of getting rid of old delusions is that they are often replaced with others of worse aspect. This present phase of popular credulity on the subject would deserve to be regarded as merely silly if it were not for the tendency

of an exaggeration of the fancied dangers of the evil to confuse the public mind about its real dangers.

The tidal wave of "white slavery" excitement, according to the Chicago *Record-Herald,* will soon recede, leaving many of us abashed and mortified by the manifestations it has produced. "In the case of the unexplained and often temporary disappearance of a young woman," this paper points out, "it is unfair and cruel both to her and to her family to jump immediately at the most offensive and improbable of explanations." The New York *Sun* thinks that the "poisoned needle" case may be of value as acting as a corrective on popular gullibility as to the class of alleged crimes with which it has been associated. "Its discussion has elicited a wealth of authoritative opinion testifying to the practical impossibility of drugging a human being by the means described that should ease the minds of all who have been disturbed by these tales."

> That such wild yarns should obtain wide circulation is much to be lamented, but the cause of the credulity which sustains them is not difficult to find. The community has lately been deluged with printed and spoken matter on the relations of the sexes which has prepared the careless to believe anything that may be said on the subject. It is a reason for profound regret that the unselfish labors of a number of disinterested persons to mitigate a grave evil should have opened the flood gates for a stream of obscenity which can do no good and has already done not a little injury.

> A few years ago, had we been asked if any creature more despicable than the pimp drew breath, we should have answered "No" with absolute positiveness. When we contemplate the foul brood gathered around the moral autopsy a few intelligent and unselfish souls undertook when they attacked the race old evil of prostitution; when we watch them distort honest purpose to lascivious intent; when we see their ugly leers and hear their thick chucklings as they count the gains they reap from exploiting the weak and the vicious, we unhesitatingly revise our previous opinion and assert that they are viler than the degraded beings on whose misfortunes they fatten.

A correspondent of the New York *World* declares that his wife returned home from a lecture on "white slavery" and regaled him with the shocking information that 50,000 young women disappear each year between Chicago and New Year. "It was with the greatest difficulty," he says, "that I persuaded her that not more than half of the men in the country are engaged in the traffic of the 'white slaver,' and she is still of the opinion that there is an organization as formidable as the Steel Trust working day and night in the interest of vice."

The San Francisco *Bulletin* points out that there is a real and profound white slavery flourishing in the community and ravaging society quite apart from the sentimental "white slavery" of the fictitious "poisoned needle case." The public love of the exaggerated and the sensational and its care-free avoidance of facts and cruel truths, thinks the *Bulletin,* is responsible in part for this slavery. Says the *Bulletin:* "The translation of the whole matter is that the white slavery enforced by a community's attitude of mind is far more destructive in its effects than the white slavery, real or mythical, enforced by a few wretched individuals."

## Further Resources

**BOOKS**

Connelly, Mark Thomas. *The Response to Prostitution in the Progressive Era.* Chapel Hill, N.C.: The University of North Carolina Press, 1980.

Hobson, Barbara Meil. *Uneasy Virtue: The Politics of Prostitution and the American Reform Tradition.* New York: Basic Books, 1987

Langum, David J. *Crossing Over the Line: Legislating Morality and the Mann Act.* Chicago: The University of Chicago Press, 1994.

## "Making Men of Them"

Magazine article

**By:** Thornton W. Burgess

**Date:** 1914

**Source:** Burgess, Thornton W. "Making Men of Them." *Good Housekeeping Magazine,* July 1914, 3–6, 12.

**About the Author:** Thornton Waldo Burgess (1874–1965) was a well-known author of children's books and a lifelong amateur naturalist. ∎

## Introduction

The Boy Scouts were founded in Britain by the highly eccentric Anglo–Boer War hero General Robert (Lord) Baden-Powell. The organization reinforced very conservative social and political values. Swiftly transported to the United States, the Boy Scouts continued to emphasize traditional fidelity to God, country, and morality.

Scouting grew in the United States because many Americans around 1910 felt anxious over the condition of the nation's youth. With sex, alcohol, narcotics, and other pleasures seemingly all too readily available, scouting was seen as a means of channeling youthful energies

into a more wholesome direction. Scouting was also widely viewed as a method of Americanizing the wave of immigrants then coming ashore by influencing the newcomers' children with traditional American values. Finally, with its emphasis on nature, scouting was an antidote to the soft, sedentary life that seemed to plague urban inhabitants. Indeed, as Americans moved from rural to urban areas, and as strapping farm lads relocated to cities, a strong physical fitness movement (of which scouting was one important element) swept the nation.

## Significance

Lord Baden-Powell had launched scouting in Britain partly to help turn boys into men. He wanted to reinvigorate the British military, which seemed to have weakened, as demonstrated by its relatively poor performance in the Anglo–Boer War (1899–1902). Despite the urging of men like Theodore Roosevelt, America remained a far less militaristic society than did Britain. So in the United States, scouting was much less concerned with preparation for war and more concerned with fostering the proper moral development of young boys. Indeed, the goal was to transform boys into good citizens and good fathers.

To some extent, the deliberate exposure of impressionable young boys to the wholesome effects of mentoring through scouting represented a bit of Progressive-era "social engineering"—albeit on a much milder scale than, say, the more coercive Prohibition Movement. Consequently, although scouting was seen as a welcome antidote to the negative effects of magazines, cinema, and other popular diversions, it still retained its commitment to a kind of volunteerism that had long shaped the American reform tradition.

## Primary Source

"Making Men of Them"

> **SYNOPSIS:** Veteran children's author Thornton W. Burgess discusses the positive impact that Boy Scout leaders can make on young men who require strong role models in order to develop into solid adults.

How can you make a good man of the average boy? Precept and command will fail except in a negligible number of instances. But there are millions of boys—all of them worth making men of. Then some surer method must be sought for. Have you considered the Boy Scouts? Of course you know their organization, but do you know what it does for the inner boy? What about Scouting makes men like Daniels and Lindsey wish that every boy might be a Scout? The movement is no longer an experiment; it is possible now to point to results. That is the

Boy Scouts from the New York City area saw wood while camping out in 1912. **THE LIBRARY OF CONGRESS.**

purpose of this article—that and to offer help in the very serious problem everywhere of bringing up the boys to be the right kind of men

Recently the mother of a boy of thirteen asked me if I could suggest some way of overcoming the opposition of a certain political organization to the Boy Scout movement. This organization is very strong in her town, and its local leaders had attacked the movement so bitterly that any attempt to organize Boy Scout patrols there had been deemed unwise.

"Why do you care whether or not this movement is given a foothold in your neighborhood?" I asked.

"Because I want my own boy to be a Boy Scout," was the prompt reply.

"And why? Because the boy happens to be interested and thinks it would be fun?" I persisted.

"No," she responded, "no, it isn't that, though he is interested, and I know that he would thoroughly enjoy Scout activities. I want him to be a Boy Scout because I have studied the work of the organization, have watched the results in other neighborhoods where patrols have been established, and have become convinced that it is the greatest aid I can find outside the immediate home circle for the physical,

moral, and spiritual development of my boy. He is just at the hero-worshiping, gang-loving age. As a member of a Boy Scout patrol, under the right kind of a scout master, he will have these two natural cravings of boy nature gratified, and at the same time guided in the right direction. I will not have to worry when he slips the apron-strings at the garden-gate."

That mother is blessed with a clear vision. She understands boy nature, and she appreciates, and is willing to acknowledge, the fact that to a certain extent the apron-strings are slipped at the garden-gate; that the first faint stirring of the man within demands fellowship with his kind, hence the "gang," and that in his new-found emancipation a leader, a "hero" whose merest nod is a law by the simple virtue of masculine superiority, is inevitable. The boy has become a citizen of the world, a world in which petticoats are scorned and an attempt at petticoat rule is resented.

This is a viewpoint that all too few mothers get—simply because they never were boys themselves. It is a wise mother who can extend her gentle rule to the ball-field and the playground; and to do this successfully, the effort must not be apparent. It is with a realization of this that many mothers are watching with the keenest interest, in some cases not unmixed with distrust, the growth of the Boy Scout movement, and are asking: "What is its real significance? What does it mean to our boys? What does it mean to us mothers? Is the movement to be welcomed or shunned?" . . .

Broadly speaking, the Boy Scouts of America constitute a brotherhood of boys of from twelve to eighteen years of age banded together for the purpose of developing under wise leadership, sound bodies, clean morals, self-reliant characters and the ability to think quickly and do things at the right time and in the right way. The organization is founded on a thorough understanding of boy nature during its formative period, and full recognition of a boy's divine right to worship a "hero" and belong to a "gang." It aims to supply the "hero" in the person of the scout master, a man who understands and loves boys, whose personality can win boys, and whose character boys will instinctively recognize as of the highest type—a man, in short, whom boys will seek to emulate. In the "patrol" and the "troop" it meets the demand of the gang spirit. Thus it instantly appeals to the average boy through frank recognition of two of the strongest attributes of his nature, and these two attributes it uses constantly to develop and strengthen those quali ties which every mother desires her son to possess— manliness, chivalry, courage, honor, thoughtfulness for others, moral and physical stamina, integrity and independence in thought and deed.

A boy normally belongs to his mother until he is ten or twelve years old; but from that time on he wants and needs the companionship and direction of a man. Instinctively he turns from mother to father, because he feels that there are many things mother doesn't understand, cannot understand, whereas father does understand, because he is a man, is what the boy is going to be, what subconsciously, he feels that he is already beginning to be. Unfortunately, however, the great majority of fathers are not available to their sons at this time when they are most needed. They are chained to business through the hours when their boys are free of the restraint of school, which is just the time when they most need wise guidance in finding a proper outlet for their accumulated energy and surcharged spirits. So the boy seeks some other man to tell him things and show him things, for at this age a boy is naturally inquisitive and wonderfully acquisitive.

All too often this other "man" is not a man at all save in the eyes of his young admirer. He is simply an older boy, himself in need of wise direction. He is the leader of the gang—though this word here is not meant necessarily to imply badness or even mischievousness; merely a loosely bound group of boys playing and acting together in that strong loyalty of youth which is their code, and which passes among them for honor.

You mothers of boys of twelve and over know all about this, and it has caused many of you many anxious hours. You have seen the slipping of the apron-strings and have realized the futility of trying to hold your old dominant place in the affairs of your boys, not through a feeling of incompetence on your part, but because you know that the boys themselves hold that attitude. Your rule is still direct and unchallenged in the home; but beyond the home can you govern and direct the unseen forces molding the characters of your boys there? Not by direct methods, certainly. But by indirect methods, yes; by cooperation with every movement looking to the betterment of boy life; by finding out who the associates of your boys are, and then diplomatically leading them voluntarily to choose the good from the bad.

It is just here that the Boy Scout movement comes to your aid as a powerful ally. It takes up and applies to the life of your boys beyond the home the very precepts you have sought to inculcate in the home, and it does it in a way that to the boys themselves appears to be of their own initiative. This is a very vital factor in the successful handling of boys, for instead of violating that spirit of independence which has so suddenly sprung into being, and which is so precious to them, it cherishes it. The movement also provides a wholesome outlet for that restless activity which demands active expression. It "blazes the trail" to the highest type of manhood, while leading the boy to think that he is finding it himself. It so presents the nobler qualities of manhood that the boy voluntarily chooses them. It affords him a chance to express his own individuality in the accomplishment of things in which he is most interested, and at the same time it leads him to appreciate the accomplishments and talents of his fellows. It elevates his inherent sense of personal loyalty to the highest plane. It gives to him the feeling that he is an integral, necessary, and important part of the scheme of things, and as such has responsibilities in the affairs of life. . . .

Will it benefit your boy to have him a Boy Scout? I believe it will, physically, mentally, morally. Will it aid you as a mother? Yes, directly and indirectly. Will it benefit the community? Most emphatically, yes! The solution of the world's great problems, every one of them, is in your hands and mine in the shaping of the characters of the present generation of young people. The boy of today is the most potent force for good or evil in the man of tomorrow. The Boy Scouts of America furnish a tremendously effective medium through which to aid in the development of that master creation, high-principled, clean and clear-thinking, independent manhood.

## Further Resources

### BOOKS

Mechling, Jay. *On My Honor: Boy Scouts and the Making of American Youth.* Chicago: University of Chicago Press, 2001.

Pendry, Elizabeth Ruth. *Organizations for Youth; Leisure Time and Character Building Procedures.* New York: McGraw-Hill Book Company, 1935.

Rosenthal, Michael. *The Character Factory: Baden–Powell and the Origins of the Boy Scout Movement.* New York: Pantheon Books, 1986.

# "The Next and Final Step"

## Statement

**By:** P.A. Baker

**Date:** 1914

**Source:** Baker, P.A. "The Next and Final Step." In *The Anti-Saloon League Year Book.* Westerville, Ohio: The American Issue Press, 1914, 16–17.

**About the Author:** P. (Purley) A. Baker (1858–1924) served as general superintendent of the Anti-Saloon League of America from 1903 until his death in 1924. During his tenure, the Anti-Saloon League successfully lobbied Congress in 1917 to pass the Eighteenth Amendment to the United States Constitution mandating national Prohibition. The measure was eventually ratified by the requisite number of states in 1919. ∎

## Introduction

The Anti-Saloon League, one of the most effective (indeed single-minded) pressure groups in American political history, can take a great deal of the credit for the surprising passage of the Eighteenth Amendment to the United States Constitution. This amendment mandated the national Prohibition of alcoholic beverages. Founded in 1893, the Anti-Saloon League wisely avoided targeting individual drinkers and instead concentrated its fire on the business end of the liquor industry—saloon owners, brewers, and distillers. In this fashion, the Prohibition Movement coincided with the anti-corporate thrust of the Progressive era, which included assaults on businesses that were seen as harming the public, such as meat-packing plants selling tainted beef.

The urban saloon epitomized all that was deemed wrong with American life around 1910. Barely Ameri-

canized immigrants frequented saloons that swarmed with prostitutes and gamblers, while the police and local politicians were routinely bribed to look the other way. In this manner, the saloon became a key element in the political machine that held many American cities in the grip of municipal corruption.

Alcohol was viewed as the primary cause of wasted youth. The Physical Fitness Movement branded alcohol as a poison. In the racist South, whites feared that alcohol rendered blacks disrespectful to whites and made them "uppity." On a practical political level, the Women's Suffrage Movement reinforced Prohibition, and vice-versa. Indeed, President Woodrow Wilson saw fit to endorse both measures simultaneously.

Despite the aggressive tactics of the Anti-Saloon League, the Eighteenth Amendment would probably have never passed without the sense of urgency that was created when America entered World War I. The need to keep soldiers on the battlefield sharp and munitions workers back home sober doubtless induced many men and women to support Prohibition as a wartime measure. The pressing need for food conservation also played a role, for huge amounts of grain that might have yielded nutritious bread wound up as empty calories in beer and spirits. Finally, the Prohibitionists shamelessly exploited the anti-German sentiment unleashed by the war, since so many visible members of the nation's brewing and distilling industry were German–Americans.

## Significance

The Anti-Saloon League disbanded in 1933 when the Eighteenth Amendment was repealed by the passage of the Twenty-First Amendment.

Why did Prohibitionists secure a huge (if temporary) political victory for their cause? Perhaps the secret of the Anti-Saloon League's stunning success stemmed from the fact that the organization managed to adopt a strictly non-partisan stance. Prohibitionists could be found in both the Republican and Democratic Parties. History seems to indicate that the chances for success are immeasurably greater if a movement avoids being exclusively identified in the American public's mind with a single political party and all of its accompanying baggage.

## Primary Source

"The Next and Final Step"

> **SYNOPSIS:** Purley A. Baker, longtime head of the Anti-Saloon League, outlines his organization's ambitious plans to implement the nationwide Prohibition of alcoholic beverages. At the time this manifesto was published in 1914, most Americans did not take the movement seriously.

Members of the Anti-Saloon League of America at their 15th annual national convention in Columbus, Ohio, November 10–13, 1913. It was at this convention that the League decided to start lobbying for an amendment to the Constitution outlawing alcohol throughout the United States. THE LIBRARY OF CONGRESS.

The policy of the Anti-Saloon League since its inception has been to go just as fast and just as far as public sentiment would justify. It confines its efforts to law enforcement and sentiment building where that is the only policy public sentiment will sustain. It is for local Prohibition where that policy meets the requirements of the most advanced public demand. It always has favored the adoption of state and national Prohibition just as quickly as an enlightened public conscience warrants. We believe the time is fully ripe for the launching of a campaign for national Prohibition—not by any party or parties, but by the people. This does not mean that we are to relax our efforts one iota for law enforcement, local Prohibition and Prohibition by states, but it is a recognition of the fact that the task begun more than a hundred years ago should speedily be completed.

### The Character of the Traffic

Every defense the liquor traffic has erected has been battered down except the defenseless appeal to greed and appetite. It no longer has advocates: it must depend for its existence upon partisans. It is united with the white slave traffic. The offspring of this unholy union are robbery, bribery, cruelty, debauchery and murder. The martyred Senator Carmack but uttered an accepted truth when he said, "The liquor traffic would rather die than obey law." It is an enemy to everything that is good in private and public life. It is the friend of everything that is bad. In the name of decent civil government and for the sake of humankind the manufacture and sale of this despoiler of the race should be abolished.

### The Peril We Face

The vices of the cities have been the undoing of past empires and civilizations. It has been at the point where the urban population outnumbers the rural people that wrecked Republics have gone down. There the vices have centered and eaten out the heart of the patriotism of the people, making them the easy victims of every enemy. The peril of this Republic likewise is now clearly seen to be in her cities. There is no greater menace to democratic institutions than the great segregation of an element which gathers its ideas of patriotism and citizenship from the low grogshop and which has proved its enmity to organized civil government. Already some of our cities are well-nigh submerged with this unpatriotic element, which is manipulated by the still baser element engaged in the un-American drink traffic and by the kind of politician the saloon creates. The saloon stands for the worst in political life. All who stand for the best must be aggressively against it. If our Republic is to be saved the liquor traffic must be destroyed.

### What Has Been Accomplished

More than half the counties of the Republic, multitudes of the incorporated villages and cities, and nine entire States containing upwards of forty-six millions of people—50 per cent of the population—embracing above two-thirds of the entire territorial area of the country, have outlawed the saloon. The traffic has been driven from the army and navy, from immigrant stations and from the National Capitol; but the greatest triumph of the temperance forces of the nation was the passage of the Webb-Kenyon bill over President Taft's veto, not only for the service it will render the cause of law enforcement, but for the demonstrated fact that Congress is responsive to the organized, expressed will of the people on this as on other important moral issues.

### National Prohibition—How Secured

National Prohibition can be secured through the adoption of a constitutional amendment by Con-

## Must These Go Down To a Drunkard's Grave In Order That We the Streets May Pave?

—(Chcago Boys' Club.)

"Pave today the broad highway
With something not so white as the souls
Of the innocent boys at play?
Why can't men pave the business marts
With something harder than women's hearts?
Is there no gold that will serve their turn,
Save the shining gold of the heads that rest
Soft on a mother's loving breast?
Must these go down to a drunkard's grave
In order that we the streets may pave?"

SERIES G. No. 22.

THE AMERICAN ISSUE PUBLISHING CO.,
Westerville, Ohio.

Opponents of prohibition often argued that the government couldn't afford to outlaw alcohol, as alcohol taxes were one of the primary sources of federal revenue at the time. This poster from the late 1910s attacks that position. **THE LIBRARY OF CONGRESS.**

gress and ratification of the same by the necessary three-fourths—thirty-six—States. A State once having ratified the amendment cannot rescind its action, but a State failing in its effort to ratify may do so at any future time.

### The Opportune Time

The time for a nation-wide movement to outlaw the drink traffic is auspicious. Organization is now established and in operation in all parts of the country. The forces that definitely oppose the traffic are in accord as at no time in the past. The moral, scientific and commercial aspects of the problem are being more intelligently put before the public than hitherto. The narrow, acrimonious and emotional appeal is giving way to a rational, determined conviction that the traffic being the source of so much evil and economic waste and the enemy of so much good has no rightful place in our modern civilization.

Abraham Lincoln reluctantly consented to the levying of an Internal Revenue tax as a war measure only when assured by members of his cabinet and leaders in Congress that it would be repealed at the close of the war. When the war was ended and the broken fortunes of the Republic were manifest, the liquor traffic, with that serpent-like wisdom for which it is noted, was the first to urge the continuation of this tax, knowing the force of the bribe upon the public conscience. From that time to the present the chief cry against national Prohibition has been that the government must have the revenue. The adoption of the income tax amendment to the federal constitution furnishes an answer to the revenue problem.

We appeal to every church, to all organized philanthropies and to every individual, of every race and color, who loves his country and his kind, to join in this crusade for a saloonless nation. We depend for success upon the same Leader who commanded Moses to "speak to the children of Israel that they go forward."

## Further Resources

### BOOKS

Kerr, K. (Kathel) Austin. *Organized for Prohibition: A New History of the Anti-Saloon League.* New Haven, Conn.: Yale University Press, 1985.

Odegard, Peter H. *Pressure Politics: The Story of the Anti-Saloon League.* New York: Octagon Books, 1966.

Sinclair, Andrew. *Prohibition, The Era of Excess.* Boston: Little, Brown, 1962.

# "The Flapper"

**Magazine article**

**By:** Henry L. Mencken

**Date:** 1915

**Source:** Mencken, Henry L. "The Flapper." *The Smart Set: A Magazine of Cleverness,* February 1915, 1–2.

**About the Author:** Henry L. (Louis) Mencken (1880–1956) was a longtime figure in American journalism and literary crit-

icism. In addition, his biting social commentaries, which cover an extraordinarily wide variety of topics, are legendary. ∎

## Introduction

The term "Flapper" is associated in the American public's mind with the decade of the Roaring 20s along with bootleg gin, Al Capone, Charles Lindbergh, and the Stock Market craze. But the word "Flapper" comes from the pre-World War I period when humorist and social satirist Henry L. Mencken popularized the term (already in use in Britain) in a cheeky piece in *The Smart Set: a Magazine of Cleverness,* a New York-based, avant garde publication.

Evidently, the magazine's name was intended to be a self-conscious parody of itself. But despite the obvious humorous intent of Mencken's piece, the name "Flapper" stuck—in large measure because the time was ripe for a fresh term to describe what was happening to young American women. As mentioned above, the label appears to have originated in Britain. In cultural terms, much of Europe was several steps ahead of the United States in the cultural liberation of its women.

## Significance

Meanwhile, the prevailing German term "der Backfisch" seemed a bit too harsh (not to mention foreign) for the American ear. In like fashion, the French term "l'Ingenue" seemed a bit too sophisticated (indeed racy) for the oftentimes provincial American sensibilities. Instead, the English word "Flapper" had a no-nonsense, practical quality about it, not to mention a reassuring wholesomeness.

As a matter of fact, the term "Flapper" denotes strength coupled with a touch of youthful defiance. It has a sturdy Anglo-Saxon feel to it. One can envision a self-confident young woman standing tall while braving the elements as her short skirt flaps in the breeze. The word recalls the yearling—a neophyte waiting to flap her wings as she embarks upon her maiden flight of discovery.

Indeed the term "Flapper" evokes a veritable forest of images. No wonder the word caught the American public's fancy so rapidly. (Perhaps the closest recent parallel was the 1984 acceptance of the descriptive word "Yuppie" to describe the Young Upscale Professional phenomenon.) At any rate, the swift spread of the term "Flapper" after its introduction into America in 1915 furnishes a clear-cut demonstration of the power of language, not only to reflect behavior, but to shape it.

## Primary Source

"The Flapper"

> **SYNOPSIS:** In this historic piece, social satirist and humorist Henry L. Mencken introduces to America the British term "Flapper" to describe the modern young American woman.

Two young women dressed in the flapper style. **HARVARD THEATRE COLLECTION. REPRODUCED BY PERMISSION.**

The American language, curiously enough, has no name for her. In German she is *der Backfisch,* in French she is *l'Ingénue,* in English she is the Flapper. But in American, as I say, she is nameless, for Chicken will never, never do. Her mother, at her age, was a Young Miss; her grandmother was a Young Female. But she herself is no Young Miss, no Young Female. Oh, dear, no! . . .

Observe, then, this nameless one, this American Flapper. Her skirts have just reached her very trim and pretty ankles; her hair, newly coiled upon her skull, has just exposed the ravishing whiteness of her neck. A charming creature! Graceful, vivacious, healthy, appetizing. It is a delight to see her bite into a chocolate with her pearly teeth. There is music in her laugh. There is poetry in her drive at tennis. She is an enchantment through the plate glass of a limousine. Youth is hers, and hope, and romance, and—

Well, well, let us be exact: let us not say innocence. This Flapper, to tell the truth, is far, far, far from a simpleton. An Ingénue to the Gaul, she is actually as devoid of ingenuousness as a newspaper reporter, a bartender or a midwife. The age she lives in is one of knowledge. She herself is educated. She

is privy to dark secrets. The world bears to her no aspect of mystery. She has been taught how to take care of herself.

For example, she has a clear and detailed understanding of all the tricks of white slave traders, and knows how to circumvent them. She is on the lookout for them in matinée lobbies and railroad stations—benevolent-looking old women who pretend to be ill, plausible young men who begin business with "Beg pardon," bogus country girls who cry because their mythical brothers have failed to meet them. She has a keen eye for hypodermic needles, chloroform masks, closed carriages. She has seen all these sinister machines of the devil in operation on the screen. She has read about them in the great works of Elizabeth Robins, Clifford G. Roe and Reginald Wright Kauffman. She has followed the war upon them in the newspapers.

Life, indeed, is almost empty of surprises, mysteries, horrors to this Flapper of 1915. She knows the exact percentage of lunatics among the children of drunkards. She has learned, from *McClure's Magazine,* the purpose and technique of the Twilight Sleep. She has been converted, by Edward W. Bok, to the gospel of sex hygiene. She knows exactly what the Wassermann reaction is, and has made up her mind that she will never marry a man who can't show an unmistakable negative. She knows the etiology of ophthalmia neatorum. She has read Christobel Pankhurst and Ellen Kay, and is inclined to think that there must be something in this new doctrine of free motherhood. She is opposed to the double standard of morality, and favors a law prohibiting it. . . .

This Flapper has forgotten how to simper; she seldom blushes; it is impossible to shock her. She saw "Damaged Goods" without batting an eye, and went away wondering what the row over it was all about. The police of her city having prohibited "Mrs. Warren's Profession," she read it one rainy Sunday afternoon, and found it a mass of platitudes. She has heard "Salomé" and prefers it to "Il Trovature." She has read "Trilby," "Three Weeks" and "My Little Sister," and thinks them all pretty dull. She slaved at French in her finishing school in order to read Anatole France. She admires Strindberg, particularly his "Countess Julie." She plans to read Havelock Ellis during the coming summer.

As I have said, a charming young creature. There is something trim and trig and confident about her. She is easy in her manners. She bears herself with dignity in all societies. She is graceful, rosy, healthy, appetizing. It is a delight to see her sink her pearly teeth into a chocolate, a macaroon, even a potato. There is music in her laugh. She is youth, she is hope, she is romance—she is wisdom!

## Further Resources

### BOOKS

Curtiss, Thomas Quinn. *The Smart Set: George Jean Nathan and H.L. Mencken* New York: Applause, 1998.

Inness, Sherrie A., ed. *Delinquents and Debutantes: Twentieth-Century American Girls' Cultures.* New York: New York University Press, 1998.

Teachout, Terry. *The Skeptic: A Life of H.L. Mencken.* New York: HarperCollins, 2002.

# "How We Manage"

Magazine article

**By:** E.S.E. (pseudonym)

**Date:** 1915

**Source:** E.S.E. (pseudonym), "How We Manage." *American Cookery,* August–September 1915, 132–135.

## Introduction

Although the economic, political, and social trends of an era highlight the larger currents in any society, the vast majority of people rarely, if ever, give much thought to such weighty matters. Instead, the average citizen fills up his or her day with the mundane tasks of earning a living and budgeting for the family. State policies matter far less than everyday practical concerns. Elsewhere, despite laments emanating from the educated classes, this arrangement of priorities doubtless makes perfect sense for the vast bulk of the population.

Nevertheless, it remains difficult for historians to reconstruct with accuracy the texture of day-to-day life. For such knowledge has an inherent elusive (indeed ethereal) quality about it. Unlike, say, high politics, mundane affairs rarely draw the attention of observers—even at the time. That said, the following excerpt from American Cookery titled "How We Manage" does provide a revealing glimpse at what the typical middle-class American family encountered as they struggled to make the optimal use of their time and money.

## Significance

The 1910s witnessed the advent of a new hybrid academic discipline—home economics—the science of rational household management. To a considerable degree, the rise of home economics coincided with other Progressive-era trends, including the increasing profes-

sionalism demanded of various aspects of the workforce (in particular, involving the government) as well as an expanded emphasis on learned skills such as planning and budgeting. In this vein, the household served as a symbol of the larger society. Progressive-era social engineering on a micro scale triumphed inside the home, which was to be managed scientifically just like other facets of society.

Meanwhile, scholars are not sure what to make of the relationship between the burgeoning science of home economics and the emerging Feminist Movement. On the one hand, home economics sought to provide a measure of dignity to what had heretofore always been considered the female realm—the household. Now home economics replaced ordinary "housework" as the central purpose in a woman's life. On the other hand, by reemphasizing the traditional female role of household manager—albeit a more scientifically oriented one—home economics kept women in a traditional subservient position. In this instance, perhaps the truth lies somewhere in between.

## Primary Source

"How We Manage" [excerpt]

**SYNOPSIS:** This piece provides an instructive glimpse at how a typical American family prepared the yearly household budget. It is interesting to note the curiously low 1915 prices for various everyday living expenses.

My husband is a New York City High School teacher, with the maximum salary of $2650. We are the average American family of four. Our boy is ten years old and our girl is eight. We look upon our marriage partnership as an economic success as we have two highly satisfactory children and have, each year, laid aside a substantial cash surplus. In the early years some of this was devoted to self improvement by paying the expenses of two European trips. After our children arrived this was laid aside as a fund with which to purchase a home when we should find exactly what we wanted in that line.

Three years ago we purchased a $9500 house. Since that time we have paid $1500 toward the house and, as we needed more furniture for our larger quarters, we have added to our collection of antique furniture and oriental rugs a few articles of sufficiently high quality as to make them an important asset.

At first glance, perhaps, our house might be considered extravagant in proportion to our salary, but as time goes on we are proving that it is not extravagant. In the path of a coming subway it is a

A living room typical of a well-off American family's house in 1910. **THE LIBRARY OF CONGRESS.**

piece of real estate that promises an excellent investment. Already we could not purchase another house like it for less than $10,500. In fact our builder is offering houses like ours, but less desirably located, at that price. The ideal neighborhood, broad street, sunny rooms add to our health and happiness. My husband is a few minutes' walk from his school and saves carfare as well as the nervous energy wasted by a long car-ride. He has more time to spend in enjoying his home and in doing the health-giving, happy tasks required in keeping up the place. A house constructed of brick and limestone requires very little in the line of repairs other than those which the "handy man" can do himself. Our coal bill is the marvel of our friends who live in detached suburban houses and also of our neighbors who employ an Italian boy to run their furnaces for them. Our wall treatment, woodwork, etc., is exactly as we want it and will not need changing for a long

time. The house was purchased in such an early stage of its construction that we were able to make many changes which add to its beauty and convenience. I am able to do my own housework with no more assistance than I had in an apartment. This I consider of especial advantage, not only because of the money saved, but because I consider it of especial advantage in the training of my children. Their home tasks, to which they are held responsible, are far easier to provide in a servantless home. These responsibilities do much toward the building of character. . . .

Fifty dollars a month, $600 a year, is set aside from our incomes as a saving fund. We might be forced to break into this by sickness or we might decide that sometime a vacation of travel was a wise investment for it. Usually, however, our budget, as we estimate it at the beginning of the year, is sufficiently large to provide for extras in the line of emergencies.

We consider the careful planning of our yearly budget an important part of good homemaking.

Our budget for the year 1915 is as follows:

Savings . . . . . . . . . . . . . . . . . . . . . . $600.00

Life insurance . . . . . . . . . . . . . . . . . . 220.00

Fire insurance . . . . . . . . . . . . . . . . . . . 5.00

Burglar insurance . . . . . . . . . . . . . . . . 6.00

Interest on mortgage (Months of July,
    August and Sept. only, $4750 at 5%) . . . 237.50

Taxes . . . . . . . . . . . . . . . . . . . . . . . . 150.00

Water tax . . . . . . . . . . . . . . . . . . . . . . 9.00

Telephone . . . . . . . . . . . . . . . . . . . . . 35.00

Coal (5 tons) . . . . . . . . . . . . . . . . . . . 35.00

Gas (All cooking, laundry, hot water
    heater) . . . . . . . . . . . . . . . . . . . . . . 10.00

Electricity (Lighting, vacuum cleaner,
    flat-iron) . . . . . . . . . . . . . . . . . . . . . 15.00

Woman helper . . . . . . . . . . . . . . . . . . 34.00

Man helper . . . . . . . . . . . . . . . . . . . . . 5.00

Papers and magazines . . . . . . . . . . . . 15.00

Laundry . . . . . . . . . . . . . . . . . . . . . . . 25.00

Church . . . . . . . . . . . . . . . . . . . . . . . 52.00

Benevolences . . . . . . . . . . . . . . . . . . 25.00

Clubs . . . . . . . . . . . . . . . . . . . . . . . . 30.00

Husband's advanced study . . . . . . . . . . 25.00

Amusements . . . . . . . . . . . . . . . . . . . 50.00

Gifts . . . . . . . . . . . . . . . . . . . . . . . . . 40.00

Doctors, dentists and oculists . . . . . . . . 35.00

Travel, including carfare . . . . . . . . . . . 120.00

Food . . . . . . . . . . . . . . . . . . . . . . . . 459.00

Clothing (Including upkeep, pressing,
    glove-cleaning, etc.) . . . . . . . . . . . . . 320.00

House supplies . . . . . . . . . . . . . . . . . 50.00

Emergency fund . . . . . . . . . . . . . . . . . 42.50

Total . . . . . . . . . . . . . . . . . . . . . . $2,650.00

. . .

All of the cooking is done in the house, with the exception of bread, an occasional cake, and occasionally canned articles and preserves. I make my own grape jelly and can a few of the strawberries and peaches of which my family are particularly fond. For these the children delight in looking over the grapes and hulling the strawberries and I find that the result pays for the small amount of effort. We use very few canned vegetables in our home. We enjoy winter vegetables in winter and summer vegetables in summer and rarely attempt to reverse the seasons. We are exceedingly fond of fresh fruit and that with candy often furnishes our desserts. Our butter, eggs, apples, potatoes, hams, sausages, chickens and maple syrup and honey are sent to us directly from the country. I hunt the markets through for fruit and vegetable bargains and watch the advertisements for bargains in groceries. There is no waste of food-supplies. Even the vegetable waters, which many housewives throw in the sink, go into my soups. I find a fireless cooker a faithful servant. I plan our table at a dollar a day plus my husband's $.25 lunch. The estimate as given provides amply for guests, for my husband eats his lunch away from home five days a week for 40 weeks. During the summer our fish, berries, cheap milk, fruits and vegetables make our cost of food very much smaller than $1.25 a day.

Our cost of clothing is considerably smaller than that of most families who dress as well. Shoes are an expensive item. For instance, my shoes and the children's are seconds purchased at a factory where a high-grade of shoes is made. If carefully selected their defects do not in any way decrease their wear. I do much of the sewing for myself and daughter and find that a cheap tailor and a cheap dressmaker perform wonders when carefully and tactfully supervised. Our materials are always of fine quality and we insist upon having them modeled along conservative lines. I watch for bargain sales in clothing. However, I value my time and strength and consider a morning spent struggling at a bargain counter to procure a bargain night-gown much harder work than making one quietly at home. . . .

In the business of homemaking, as in any other business, it is necessary that all the members of the firm do their part, that waste shall be eliminated, that the business manager shall study the markets, read the papers, and in all ways be alive to every available means of improving her business, and it is, also, necessary that finances shall be arranged on a business partnership basis. We have found a joint checking account a good solution of the problem. Many of our bills are always paid by check, and at the beginning of the month, when my husband receives his monthly check, we each make an estimate of the amount of cash we will probably require to carry us through the month. By having a joint account, if for any reason I require money, I can draw a check without asking my husband for more money in the time-honored fashion.

In the good old days the women spun and wove their clothing and raised and manufactured their food-supplies. They literally "traded" on the rare occasions, when they went to the stores, exchanging some commodity for desired articles. Thus there was little need for them to handle money. They were partners in the firm without it. As conditions have changed, men have been slow to recognize the need of treating their wives as business partners in the handling of the family funds. Women have been slow to adapt themselves to changed conditions, but men have been slower. This lack of financial partnership I believe to be one of the chief reasons why women fail to conduct their homes in an efficient, business-like fashion.

## Further Resources

### BOOKS

Stage, Sarah and Virginia B. Vincenti, eds. *Rethinking Home Economics: Women and the History of a Profession.* Ithaca, N.Y.: Cornell University Press, 1997.

Strasser, Susan. *Never Done: A History of American Housework.* New York: Pantheon Books, 1982.

# The Passing of the Great Race

Nonfiction work

**By:** Madison Grant

**Date:** 1916

**Source:** Grant, Madison. *The Passing of the Great Race or The Racial Basis of European History.* New York: Charles Scribner's Sons, 1916, 14–16, 42–45, 47.

**About the Author:** Madison Grant (1865–1937), amateur anthropologist and president of the New York Zoological Society, wrote and spoke extensively in favor of immigration restriction in order to preserve the traditional Anglo character of the United States. ∎

## Introduction

By 1916 many Americans were consumed by anxiety over the demographic future of the United States. The "Old-Stock" Americans, primarily of Anglo descent, had long since adopted measures to control family size. This included the partial liberation of their women, which served to empower them somewhat in family reproductive matters. In contrast, most newcomers—the recent immigrants pouring into the United States in record numbers—often used little or no birth control.

A pair of suggestions surfaced regarding how to deal with this battle of the birthrates. The first, Eugenics, a movement designed to discourage the supposed "less desirable" people from breeding, advocated drastic steps including, if deemed necessary, forced sterilization. Despite the fact that many thousands of citizens were ultimately sterilized without their consent, that number would have had to multiply into the millions to have been truly effective. This level of forced sterilization was not politically feasible. The United States, for all its faults, was still never as bad as Nazi Germany.

Meanwhile, a milder form of reproductive coercion was Prohibition, which sought to eliminate the immigrants' alcohol so that their men would, presumably, no longer attack their women out of drunken lust. The second suggestion, immigration restriction, remained a more practical alternative. The gates of America would in fact be virtually slammed shut in 1921.

## Significance

Madison Grant's landmark work, *The Passing of the Great Race,* first published in 1916, perfectly mirrors this "Old-Stock" siege mentality regarding the impact of birthrates and unfettered immigration. Grant's book exhibits an extreme racial bias, placing the whites at the forefront of virtually all of civilization's higher achievements. So the declining Anglo birthrate, coupled with a population upsurge among recent immigrants and non-whites, constitutes a catastrophe for the nation.

To Grant, the lessons of history are abundantly evident: racial amalgamation never works. For instead of the superior race elevating the lower one, the lower one invariably drags down the superior. In short, no society can "solve" its race problem by producing a horde of mixed offspring.

Clearly Grant's philosophy represents a complete rejection of the idea of America as a healthy "melting pot." Of course, such unabashedly racist notions are not considered legitimate today. Indeed, such talk is rarely expressed openly in universities, in the media, or in government. Nevertheless, these racist ideas doubtless lurk just below the radar screen in the minds of many citizens.

## Primary Source

The Passing of the Great Race

**SYNOPSIS:** Madison Grant laments the decline of "Old-Stock" Americans who founded the United States and describes the dangers posed by the rapid increase of then-recent immigrants.

There exists to-day a widespread and fatuous belief in the power of environment, as well as of education and opportunity to alter heredity, which arises from the dogma of the brotherhood of man, derived in turn from the loose thinkers of the French Revolution and their American mimics. Such beliefs have done much damage in the past, and if allowed to go uncontradicted, may do much more serious damage in the future. Thus the view that the negro slave was an unfortunate cousin of the white man, deeply tanned by the tropic sun, and denied the blessings of Christianity and civilization, played no small part with the sentimentalists of the Civil War period, and it has taken us fifty years to learn that speaking English, wearing good clothes, and going to school and to church, does not transform a negro into a white man. Nor was a Syrian or Egyptian freedman transformed into a Roman by wearing a toga, and applauding his favorite gladiator in the amphi-theatre. We shall have a similar experience with the Polish Jew, whose dwarf stature, peculiar mentality, and ruthless concentration on self-interest are being engrafted upon the stock of the nation. . . .

What the Melting Pot actually does in practice, can be seen in Mexico, where the absorption of the blood of the original Spanish conquerors by the native Indian population has produced the racial mixture which we call Mexican, and which is now engaged in demonstrating its incapacity for self-government. The world has seen many such mixtures of races, and the character of a mongrel race is only just beginning to be understood at its true value.

It must be borne in mind that the specializations which characterize the higher races are of relatively recent development, are highly unstable and when mixed with generalized or primitive characters, tend to disappear. Whether we like to admit it or not, the result of the mixture of two races, in the long run, gives us a race reverting to the more ancient, generalized and lower type. The cross between a white man and an Indian is an Indian; the cross between a white man and a negro is a negro; the cross between a white man and a Hindu is a Hindu; and the cross between any of the three European races and a Jew is a Jew.

In the crossing of the blond and brunet elements of a population, the more deeply rooted and ancient dark traits are prepotent or dominant. This is matter of everyday observation, and the working of this law of nature is not influenced or affected by democratic institutions or by religious beliefs. . . .

**The Competition of Races**

Where two races occupy a country side by side, it is not correct to speak of one type as changing into the other. Even if present in equal numbers one of the two contrasted types will have some small advantage or capacity which the other lacks toward a perfect adjustment to surroundings. Those possessing these favorable variations will flourish at the expense of their rivals, and their offspring will not only be more numerous, but will also tend to inherit such variations. In this way one type gradually breeds the other out. In this sense, and in this sense only, do races change.

Man continuously undergoes selection through social environment. Among native Americans of the Colonial period a large family was an asset, and social pressure and economic advantage both counselled early marriage and numerous children. Two hundred years of continuous political expansion and material prosperity changed these conditions and children, instead of being an asset to till the fields and guard the cattle, became an expensive liability. They now require support, education, and endowment from their parents, and a large family is regarded by some as a serious handicap in the social struggle.

These conditions do not obtain at first among immigrants, and large families among the newly arrived population are still the rule, precisely as they were in Colonial America, and are to-day in French Canada, where backwoods conditions still prevail.

The result is that one class or type in a population expands more rapidly than another, and ultimately replaces it. This process of replacement of one type by another does not mean that the race changes, or is transformed into another. It is a replacement pure and simple and not a transformation.

The lowering of the birth rate among the most valuable classes, while the birth rate of the lower classes remains unaffected, is a frequent phenomenon of prosperity. Such a change becomes extremely injurious to the race if unchecked, unless nature is allowed to maintain by her own cruel devices the relative numbers of the different classes in their due proportions. To attack race suicide by encouraging indiscriminate breeding is not only futile, but is dangerous if it leads to an increase in the undesirable elements. What is needed in the community most of all, is an increase in the desirable classes, which are of superior type physically, intellectually, and morally, and not merely an increase in the absolute numbers of the population. . . .

The small birth rate in the upper classes is, to some extent, offset by the care received by such children as are born, and the better chance they have to become adult and breed in their turn. The large birth rate of the lower classes is, under normal conditions, offset by a heavy infant mortality, which eliminates the weaker children.

Where altruism, philanthropy, or sentimentalism intervene with the noblest purpose, and forbid nature to penalize the unfortunate victims of reckless breeding, the multiplication of inferior types is encouraged and fostered. Efforts to indiscriminately preserve babies among the lower classes often result in serious injury to the race.

Mistaken regard for what are believed to be divine laws and a sentimental belief in the sanctity of human life, tend to prevent both the elimination of defective infants and the sterilization of such adults as are themselves of no value to the community. The laws of nature require the obliteration of the unfit, and human life is valuable only when it is of use to the community or race.

It is highly unjust that a minute minority should be called upon to supply brains for the unthinking mass of the community, but it is even worse to burden the responsible and larger, but still overworked, elements in the community with an ever increasing number of moral perverts, mental defectives, and hereditary cripples. . . .

Efforts to increase the birth rate of the genius producing classes of the community, while most desirable, encounter great difficulties. In such efforts we encounter social conditions over which we have as yet no control. It was tried two thousand years ago by Augustus, and his efforts to avert race suicide and the extinction of the old Roman breed were singularly prophetic of what some far seeing men are attempting in order to preserve the race of native Americans of Colonial descent.

Man has the choice of two methods of race improvement. He can breed from the best, or he can eliminate the worst by segregation or sterilization. The first method was adopted by the Spartans, who had for their national ideals, military efficiency and the virtues of self control, and along these lines the results were completely successful. Under modern social conditions it would be extremely difficult in the first instance to determine which were the most desirable types, except in the most general way, and even if a satisfactory selection were finally made, it would be, in a democracy, a virtual impossibility to limit by law the right to breed to a privileged and chosen few.

## Further Resources

### BOOKS

Guterl, Matthew Pratt. *The Color of Race in America, 1900–1940.* Cambridge, Mass.: Harvard University Press, 2001.

Nash, Gary B. and Richard Weiss, eds. *The Great Fear: Race in the Mind of America.* New York: Holt, Rinehart and Winston, 1970.

Stoddard, Lothrop. *The Rising Tide of Color Against White World-Supremacy.* New York: Charles Scribner, 1920.

# "Are the Movies a Menace to the Drama?"

Essay

**By:** Brander Matthews

**Date:** 1917

**Source:** Matthews, Brander. "Are the Movies a Menace to the Drama?" *North American Review,* March 1917, 447–451, 453–454.

**About the Author:** Brander Matthews (1852–1929) was a prolific essayist, as well as a literary and drama critic. ■

## Introduction

Before 1915, the silent motion picture had posed little threat to the popularity of the theater. Grand drama (even the lowly farce) had hardly anything to fear from carnival nickelodeons or from dimly lit, poorly ventilated movie houses in seedy neighborhoods. Besides, silent films had an exceedingly unsavory reputation, exacerbated by the fact that pornography flourished early on alongside legitimate films. "Proper" middle-class Americans left moviegoing to sleazy sailors and poor immigrants.

However, the breakthrough silent film, D.W. Griffith's "Birth of a Nation," revolutionized America moviegoing habits. Perhaps the first silent film worth watching by today's standards, "Birth of a Nation" was vastly superior to anything that had been filmed and released previously. Now, with screen epics like Griffith's masterpiece playing in local cinemas across the country, the silent film had finally arrived as a serious art form and as a competitor for the live stage production.

## Significance

By 1917, perceptive observers such as essayist Brander Matthews recognized that the motion picture had evolved to the point where it told a story in superior fashion than did the traditional stage play. What appeared to grant a reprieve to the live drama was the indisputable fact that the silent film could never match the stage pro-

Frederick Warde, a popular Shakesperean theatre actor, in a 1912 silent film adaptation of Shakespeare's "Richard III." AP/WIDE WORLD PHOTOS. **REPRODUCED BY PERMISSION.**

duction in the quality of dialogue—notwithstanding the use in silent films of written titles interspersed throughout the film to convey a semblance of dialogue.

However, the motion picture remained very much a work in progress. And lovers of live stage productions, such as drama critic Matthews, seem to have grossly underestimated the ability of filmmakers to add sound to their products at some point in the not-too-distant future. Indeed by 1927, the "Talkie" had been introduced, to the enthusiastic acclaim of audiences everywhere.

By century's end, the live production, while not mortally wounded, had been completely eclipsed by the dominant motion picture. Actually, the stage play lives on as a relic of the past, barely viable in an economic sense and often heavily dependent on various subsidies.

## Primary Source

"Are the Movies a Menace to the Drama?"

**SYNOPSIS:** Essayist and drama critic Brander Matthews discusses the threat posed to the live stage production by the advent of a new art form—the silent motion picture.

. . . In the opening years of the twentieth century there has been invented a new method of picturesque story-telling, which has already exhibited wholly unsuspected possibilities. At the present moment the art of the moving-picture is in process of rapid evolution; and we cannot yet foresee what its ultimate limitations will prove to be. What we can perceive clearly is that it has already been accepted by not a few observers as a dangerous rival of the drama; it has captured many theatres; it has enlisted in its service an army of actors and actresses; and it has captivated a host of men and women and children of whom many have probably been more or less habitual playgoers. How far is this apparent rivalry of the wordless moving-picture and the spoken drama to extend? Are the movies actually a menace to the drama? Is there any real danger that the primary art of the play-wright and the secondary art of

A boy stands outside of Havlin's movie theatre in St. Louis, Missouri, in 1910. © CORBIS. REPRODUCED BY PERMISSION.

the player will be damaged if not destroyed by the continuous and increasing competition of the cinematograph? . . .

This is a good occasion therefore to point out once more that the theatre and the drama are not the same thing; the moving-picture might take over half the playhouses in the United States and still exert scarcely any influence upon the drama itself. The drama is an art, perhaps the loftiest and most powerful of the arts; and the theatre is a commercial enterprise. Of course, the drama cannot prosper unless it is on a sound economic basis; and for this it must always depend on the theatre. But the theatre can get along without the drama; it can for example rely on the review, the so-called comic opera, the summer song-show in which there is little or no trace of the essentially dramatic; it can fill out its programme with song and dance, with acrobatics, with trained animals, with sidewalk conversationalists, with jugglers and conjurers, and wit all the other possibilities of the variety-show. In so far as the moving-picture has forced itself into a prominent place among these non-dramatic entertainments, it is not in any way invading the field of the drama, and therefore it is not to be considered as a competitor.

But the moving-picture has done more than this: it has of late been bold enough to "picturize"—if that is to be the new world describing a new thing—popular plays, popular novels, and popular operas. It has made these picturizations long enough to provide entertainment for a whole evening. And it has discovered that it can present a story with an amplitude of effect not possible in the theatre. It has at its command resources impossible to the regular drama. Where the dramatist has to content himself by telling the audience how the hero saved the heroine's life by catching her runaway horse or by snatching her from before the locomotive or bringing her down from the burning building, the director of the moving-picture is able to show the heroic deed itself, visible to all the spectators. . . .

One swift result of the advent of the moving-picture was the demise of the ultra-sensational melodrama, a tissue of thrilling adventures, often ingeniously contrived but nearly always devoid of any direct relation to human life as it really is. . . .

Perhaps it is going a little too far to assert that the disappearance of the ultra-sensational melodrama is due solely to the competition of the moving-picture which can present the same kind of story with a far greater wealth of detail. Yet it is beyond question that the movie can satisfy the ruder likings of the mob for coarse-grained happenings far more successfully than the most inventive and ingenious stage-manager can ever hope to do. But while melodrama has had a long and interesting history, it is not one of the higher and more important forms of the drama. Indeed, it is frankly an inferior form because it contents itself with story-telling for its own sake, never hesitating to sacrifice character to situation. Its appeal is to the emotions but mainly to the senses, and more especially to the nerves, whereas true drama, the drama comic or serious, which is really worth while, appeals both to the emotions and to the intellect; it uses situation mainly to reveal character.

In a melodrama or in a farce we are interested very much in what happens and very little in the persons to whom these misadventures happen. In a comedy or in a tragedy we are interested mainly in the persons themselves, in what they are rather than in what they do. However powerful the situations may be in which they are immeshed, we are always watching them to see how their characters are going to react and to reveal themselves under the stress of unforeseen circumstance. In melodrama and in farce we are quite satisfied to find characters painted in the primary colors, by a few bold strokes, presented in profile as it were, whereas in comedy and tragedy we expect the rotundity of real life, the complexity, the delicate colors and the finer shadings of a subtler art. We demand from the dramatist who essays the higher forms that he shall be able to "convince the taste and console the spirit." And Mr. Howells was right when he declared that this was precisely what the moving picture could not do. So long therefore as it labors under this total disability the moving picture can never be a real rival of the drama. . . .

It is because the moving-picture has perforce to do without the potent appeal of the spoken word that it can never be really a rival of the drama. It is only by the aid of dialogue and soliloquy that we can peer into the recesses of the human soul. The Greeks, so the late Professor Butcher told us in his luminous essay on "The Written and the Spoken Word," held that not only the drama, but the epic also (which was originally composed for oral delivery), "depended, if not for their existence, at least for their vitality on the living voice and the listening crowds." Even today we do not really possess a poem until we have heard it; it demands the test of the ear; and it does not reveal its hidden beauties to the eye alone. When we listen to a pregnant speech of one of Shakespeare's characters, spoken on the stage by an actor who has a noble voice and who knows how to use it, the words take on a richer meaning and have a vitality and a significance unsuspected before.

As the moving-picture is deprived of the aid of words, it cannot be literature. As it is deprived of the aid of the human voice, it takes from the actor his most powerful resource. It demands only that its performers shall be able to make the gestures indicate and to "register" the emotions called for; and although it is luring to its aid not a few actors of prominence, it is often finding that they are not always as satisfactory when seen on the screen as novices young enough to be able to respond to the summary training which the movie-directors can bestow hurriedly in their own studios. . . .

It is likely that the differentiation between the real play (which must have a story, no doubt, but which has also a soul) and the picture-play (which can never be more than a story told in pictures) will increase and become more obvious as the managers of the movies cease to borrow the plots of plays and devote themselves to stories compounded in accord with the possibilities and the limitations of their own special art. As they accept these limitations and as

they develop these possibilities the apparent rivalry between the drama and the moving-picture will lessen, and each will be left in possession of its own special field.

## Further Resources

### BOOKS

Everson, William K. *American Silent Film.* New York: Da Capo Press, 1998.

MacCann, Richard Dyer. *The Silent Screen.* Iowa City, Iowa: Scarecrow Press, 1997.

Slide, Anthony. *Early American Cinema.* Metuchen, N.J.: Scarecrow Press, 1994.

# *The Individual Delinquent*
## Nonfiction work

**By:** William Healy

**Date:** 1918

**Source:** Healy, M.D, William. in *The Individual Delinquent: A Text-Book of Diagnosis and Prognosis For All Concerned in Understanding Offenders.* Boston: Little, Brown, and Company, 1918, 308 310.

**About the Author:** William Healy, M.D., born in 1869, was a recognized authority on adolescent criminal psychology. ■

## Introduction

The Progressive era exhibited an obsession with what could be characterized as "social engineering." Eschewing America's longstanding libertarian tradition and its reliance on voluntary self-improvement and moral persuasion to produce changes in individual behavior, the period circa 1910 saw an increased emphasis on the use of state police power to alter individual behavior. The problem of handling what appeared to be an epidemic of juvenile delinquency fits this pattern perfectly.

In the nineteenth century, the issue of inappropriate underage conduct was treated as a moral problem. Even the rise of scouting in the United States around 1910 still reflected this more gentle volunteer tradition. But the Progressive era was well aware of environmental factors that might contribute to juvenile delinquency and intended to use the power of government to tackle harmful influences on youngsters. In the case of juvenile delinquency, censorship of motion pictures might well prove fruitful in preventing wayward behavior in impressionable boys and girls.

Meanwhile, in the Progressive era various social sciences, such as anthropology, psychology, and sociology, became widely accepted as valuable resources for solving social problems. College-trained psychology graduates

A gang of boys hangs out on a Springfield, Massachusetts, street corner on June 27, 1916. Several are smoking, and one has an air rifle. **THE LIBRARY OF CONGRESS.**

became therapists while college-trained sociologists joined the ranks of social workers. This dovetailed with the increasing professionalism and emphasis on credentials during the period around 1910.

Hence the problem of juvenile delinquency in the United States required a scientific approach using insights gleaned from psychology and sociology. The power of the government was also employed in order to implement solutions. This potent combination, for instance, helped ensure the triumph of the Prohibition crusade.

### Significance

Regarding juvenile delinquency, experts such as William Healy, M.D. placed the blame for the proliferation of wayward children squarely at the door of negative societal influences—in this case, the newly introduced motion picture which, while mild when compared with films today, shocked any Victorian sensibilities that were still lingering by 1915.

Progressive-era anxiety led to government and entertainment industry self-censorship of motion pictures— a policy that put a chill on the creative filmmaking

community until well into the 1960s. Unfortunately, as with many of the moral-oriented reforms of the 1910s, the anti-juvenile delinquency movement overplayed its hand. The implementation of sensible liquor restrictions has always been hampered by the memory of the Prohibition fiasco. And similarly the alarming cry of "censorship" has dogged advocates who today press for some sort of reasonable regulation regarding children's entertainment.

### Primary Source

*The Individual Delinquent* [excerpt]

> **SYNOPSIS:** William Healy, M.D., a renowned expert of adolescent psychology, analyzes the alleged baneful effects that motion pictures have on impressionable developing boys.

We have had much evidence, sometimes in remarkable ways, that moving pictures may be stimulating to the sex instinct. We should expect pictures of love-making and similar scenes to have this effect on young adults or older adolescents, but we have very strikingly heard of it in children. The effect is not only felt at the moment, but also there is the establishment of memory pictures which come up at other quiet times, such as when the individual is in bed. We have found that bad sex habits sometimes center around these pictures. In some instances a very definite mental conflict ensues, with production of delinquency along other lines.

(No one considering the effect of moving pictures can neglect the possibilities for bad behavior which occur through the darkness of the hall in which the pictures are shown. Under cover of dimness evil communications readily pass and bad habits are taught. Moving picture theatres are favorite places for the teaching of homosexual practices.)

There can be no fair consideration of the whole subject of moving pictures unless we remember that, after all, the amount of delinquency produced by them corresponds but slightly to the immense number of pictures which are constantly shown. This partly tends to show the innocuousness of the greater number of these pictures, but it also brings us back to our old question of personal equation. Some individuals are susceptible to pictorial suggestions and others are not. However, there is no excuse for showing pictures which damage the morals of any one.

The main hope for the prevention of these undesirable effects will be found in rigorous censorship of perverting pictures, and in radical prosecution of those who produce and deal in obscene and other demoralizing pictorial representations. Never have we heard one word indicating that bad effects have arisen from representations that could in any way be interpreted as productions of art. The type of thing we mean is altogether unsavory, and obviously manufactured for its appeal to the passions, or to other unhealthy interests. . . .

The effect of moving pictures in starting criminalistic tendencies in children is almost always along such conspicuous lines that it is not necessary to cite cases. It is nearly always a boy who is affected, and the impulse started is an imitative one. He proceeds to get weapons and cowboy clothes, and wants to make off for the plains. Or else he desires to become a soldier and get into warfare. The stealing suggestion is much more rarely taken up with.

In considering the total social results of the introduction of moving pictures one must not forget the astonishing appetite which is created for the particular mental pabulum which they supply. In many instances the stealing has taken place in order that the individual shall have his fill of going to such shows. Often we have heard of a perfect orgy in this direction—the delinquent staying away from home and going from one show to another during the entire day and evening. Several possible features of the whole situation are brought out in the following instances.

### Case 48.—William J.

This is the interesting case of a very charming little boy, not yet 11 years old, who is in good physical condition and of supernormal mental ability. He belongs to an exceptionally nice family of immigrants. His father and mother are decidedly rational people who have been willing to do much for him, but he has caused them an excessive amount of trouble for about a year. He has very repeatedly stolen, and very curiously, in the light of his physical delicacy and mental ability, often stayed away from home all night. He sleeps in boxes or under porches even in cold weather. Punishment has done no good, and even when he has been promised money to stay at home, he has jumped out of the window. When he is away from home he begs for his meals. At home he is very reticent. The only causes for his misconduct which his mother can think of are that he was taught bad sex things by a girl when he was four years of age, and that later on he was caught at the same thing with other boys, but there has been frankness in the family and his parents are sure he is not given to an excess of sex habits. He does go with bad companions, first one and then another, but when he is out all night he is always by himself. He wants to go to nickel shows every day. Neither in hereditary nor in developmental history do we hear of items of great importance.

We had reason to see this little boy on a number of occasions, and we and others found him a very open-hearted and charming boy. One can hardly believe that he carries on the life that he does. He frankly acknowledges his stealing, and his perfect craze for moving pictures. He goes practically every night to them and stays all evening in one show. In the winter he stays out until 11 or 12 o'clock, and in the summer until 2 or 3 in the morning. Sometimes he sleeps in a box, or under a porch, before going home. Sometimes he does not go home at all during the night. He is fondest of cowboys and Indians, and with a poor show of talent he draws many pictures of Indians for us. He runs away because his mother does not want him to go to the shows. He says he does not want to be a cowboy. He would rather be a soldier or an engineer. When he steals he spends it for shows, and perhaps treats other boys. Some of these boys are pretty bad and have initiated him into sex affairs, but his father has counselled with him about it. He finds sex stimulation in the nickel shows when he sees lovers' pictures, "when they kiss theirselves," but he likes cowboys better. He thinks about sex affairs and sometimes practices masturbation afterwards. Often he does not get his supper, eating nothing between noon and breakfast the next morning. He stays away from home at supper time so that he may go to shows.

After a long trial in his old environment it was finally found impossible for him to succeed there. Old associations connected with the shows had too strong a hold upon him. He repeatedly stole several dollars at a time, and finally had to be put in an institution.

## Further Resources

### BOOKS

Donovan, Frank Robert. *Wild Kids: How Youth Has Shocked Its Elders—Then and Now.* Harrisburg, Pa.: Stackpole Books, 1967.

Healy, William and Mary Tenney Healy. *Pathological Lying, Accusation, and Swindling; a Study in Forensic Psychology.* Montclair, N.J.: Patterson Smith, 1969.

# Dark Side of Wartime Patriotism

## Woodrow Wilson's Memorandum to His Secretary, Joseph Tumulty

Memo

**By:** Woodrow Wilson

**Date:** 1918

**Source:** Baker, Ray Stannard, ed. *Woodrow Wilson: Life and Letters: Armistice, March 1–November 11, 1918.* New York: Doubleday, Doran & Company, Inc., 1939, 362.

**About the Author:** Woodrow Wilson (1856–1924), political scientist and president of Princeton University, served as President of the United States from 1913–1921. Wilson led America to victory over Imperial Germany in the First World War, but failed to reconstruct the international political order when the United States Senate rejected his ambitious plans for America to join the newly formed League of Nations.

## "Chicagoans Cheer Tar Who Shot Man"

Newspaper article

**Date:** 1919

**Source:** "Chicagoans Cheer Tar Who Shot Man," Washington Post, May 7, 1919. ■

## Introduction

On the eve of American entry into World War I against Imperial Germany, United States President Woodrow Wilson met in the White House with his old friend, newspaperman Frank Cobb, editor-in-chief of *New York World.* About to send Congress a message asking for a declaration of war, Wilson expressed to Cobb in private his strong reservations about his decision. In fact, Wilson wondered aloud if he was about to commit the worst blunder of his life. The American homefront during the conflict, Wilson predicted, would explode with hatred. Various groups would attack each other, Wilson warned, and they would use the war as an excuse to press their own private agendas and to settle old scores.

In Wilson's own words, the American people would quickly "forget there ever was such a thing as tolerance. To fight you must be brutal and ruthless, and the spirit of ruthless brutality will enter into the very fibre of our national life, infecting the Congress, the courts, the policeman on the beat, the man in the street. . . . the [United States] Constitution would not survive it . . . free speech would have to go."

Indeed with so much at stake and with the risks so apparent, one wonders why Wilson actually plunged ahead with his intended course of action and got America involved in the conflict. Meanwhile as expected, all hell broke loose on the homefront during the First World War.

## Significance

Wilson initially sought to restrain the worst tendencies in America come wartime. Unfortunately, he eventually lost control of the situation. Meanwhile, the advent of war rendered people a bit nutty, as reason and common sense often flew out the window. Wilson himself clearly expressed annoyance after receiving a letter from noted symphony conductor Leopold Stokowski, who wondered if the music of Bach, Beethoven, and other long-dead German composers should be banned for the duration of the struggle—as if performing this music would somehow undermine America's war effort against Germany.

But this nonsense turned out to be only the tip of the mighty iceberg of intolerance. By 1919, in the aftermath of the November 11, 1918 Armistice, the country was gripped with the so-called Red Scare. Vigilantes (self-

The crowd at Chicago's first Victory Loan Day fair and aerial circus, 1917. **THE LIBRARY OF CONGRESS.**

styled patriots) took the law into their own hands. One of the most celebrated incidents occurred at a rally to sell victory bonds held in Chicago on May 6, 1919 when a sailor calmly shot a spectator in the back who had refused to stand for the Star Spangled Banner.

## Primary Source

Woodrow Wilson's Memorandum to His Secretary, Joseph Tumulty [excerpt]

> **SYNOPSIS:** In this memo, President Wilson discusses with his personal secretary Joseph Tumulty the proper response (if any) to a bizarre request from famed symphony conductor Leopold Stokowski, who was looking for presidential guidance regarding whether or not long-dead German composers Bach and Beethoven should be banned during World War I (1914–18).

### Woodrow Wilson: Life and Letters. Armistice, March 1—November 11, 1918

Won't you write a kind letter to Mr. Stokowski, pointing out to him how impossible it is for me to decide a question of this sort and suggesting this to him: It is not a question which can be decided on its merits, but only by the feelings and present thoughts of the audiences to whom the Philadelphia Orchestra and the other orchestras of the country play. It would be unwise to attempt 'a settlement' of the question, because feeling changes and will no doubt become perfectly normal again after the abnormal experiences through which we are passing. Please express my appreciation of his confidence in my judgment.

## Primary Source

"Chicagoans Cheer Tar Who Shot Man"

> **SYNOPSIS:** In this article *The Washington Post* describes an incident where, at a rally held for government war bonds ("Victory Bonds") in Chicago, an enraged sailor methodically gunned down a spectator who refused to stand up when the Star Spangled Banner was played. The reaction of the thousands of witnesses is described as favorable.

Sailor Wounds Pageant Spectator
Disrespectful to Flag

Chicago, May 6.—Disrespect for the American flag and a show of resentment toward the thousands who participated in a victory loan pageant here tonight may cost George Goddard his life. He was shot down by a sailor of the United States navy when he did not stand and remove his hat while the band was playing the "Star-Spangled Banner."

Goddard had a seat of vantage in the open amphitheater. When he failed to stand he was the most conspicuous figure among the throng. When he fell at the report of the "sailor's" gun the crowd burst into cheers and handclapping. When Goddard failed to respond to the first strains of the national anthem Samuel Hagerman, sailor in the guard of honor, asked him to get up.

"What for?" demanded Goddard.

Hagerman touched him with his bayonet.

"Get up. Off with your hat."

Goddard muttered, and drew a pistol.

With military precision Hagerman stepped back a pace and slipped a shell into his gun.

Goddard started away. As the last notes of the anthem sounded the sailor commanded him to halt. Then he fired into the air.

"Halt!"

Goddard paid no attention.

The sailor aimed and fired three times. Goddard fell wounded. Each shot found its mark.

When he was searched, an automatic pistol, in addition to the one he had drawn, was found. Another pistol and fifty cartridges were found in a bag he carried. He said he was a tinsmith, out of work. Papers showed he had been at Vancouver and Seattle and it was believed by the authorities he had come here for the I. W. W. convention.

## Further Resources

### BOOKS

Ferrell, Robert H. *Woodrow Wilson and World War I, 1917–1921.* New York: Harper & Row, 1985.

Smith, Gene. *When the Cheering Stopped: The Last Years of Woodrow Wilson.* New York: Morrow, 1964.

Vigilante, David. *The Constitution in Crisis: The Red Scare of 1919–1920: A Unit of Study For Grades 9–12.* Los Angeles: National Center for History in the Schools, University of California. Los Angeles, 1991.

# "The Negro Should Be a Party to the Commercial Conquest of the World"

### Editorial

**By:** Marcus Garvey

**Date:** 1919

**Source:** Hill, Robert A., ed. "The Negro Should be a Party to the Commercial Conquest of the World: Wake Up You Lazy Men of the Race—This is the Time of Preparation for All." In *The Marcus Garvey and Universal Negro Improvement Association Papers.* Berkeley: University of California Press, 1983, 351–353.

**About the Author:** Marcus Garvey (1887–1940), a Jamaican-born political and social leader, was America's first true black nationalist. In 1914 Garvey founded the Universal Negro Improvement Association (UNIA) in Jamaica. Two years later he brought the UNIA to the United States. He preached black pride, black power, and black economic self-sufficiency, and sought to link the struggle of American blacks with the worldwide uprising of colored people against their white oppressors. ∎

## Introduction

America after 1916 was shocked and disturbed by the rise to prominence of Marcus Garvey and his organization, the United Negro Improvement Association (UNIA). As the nation's first major Black Nationalist leader, Garvey naturally rejected the second-class status to which American blacks had been reduced as a result of the two-decade-long Jim Crow counterrevolution in the South that had reduced the blacks (still struggling mightily to enjoy their recently granted emancipation from slavery) back to a virtual condition of peonage. But Garvey also rejected the goodwill of well-intentioned liberal whites, who had hoped for a measure of integration. Both approaches were unsatisfactory for Garvey. Instead, he recommended a Black Nationalist solution.

Garvey was undoubtedly influenced by the worldwide agitation of blacks against their white overlords; this state of affairs had become part of international political life by 1910. Indeed perceptive white authors had published books warning against this agitation. These titles included B.L. Putnam Weale's *The Conflict of Colour: The Threatened Upheaval Throughout the World* (1910). Later, after the First World War had weakened Europe's ability to fend off such challenges to its authority, author Lothrop Stoddard, in his best-selling *The Rising Tide of Color Against White World-Supremacy* (1920), analyzed the increasing anxiety felt by both white Europeans and Americans. Nevertheless, most of this discontent appeared to center in the Third World. Evidently, the last thing white Americans wanted to contemplate was a link between the United States' domestic race problems and this worldwide agitation.

Yet most American whites were surely living in a dream world regarding the race issue. Like it or not, the United States circa 1916 was definitely part of the larger world community. For instance, South Africa modeled its own apartheid system instituted after 1910 on the Jim Crow racial segregation that had earlier been created in Southern states such as Mississippi and Alabama. The Garvey movement provided an unwelcome alternative model for the economic and political development of America's black community that clashed head-on with cherished notions of gradual accommodation through liberal pluralism. Instead, Garvey advocated that blacks reject participation in the larger American society in favor of separate (indeed parallel) development. In whites' eyes, this strategy proved unwelcome (even threatening) as it provided an alternative course of action for the black community that did not render blacks beholden in any manner to the white majority—and thus far less likely to be controlled. In short, blacks would fulfill their own destiny without white patronage or approval.

### Significance

Marcus Garvey, the Jamaican-born American Black Nationalist leader, entertained specific thoughts regarding the importance of blacks gaining control of their own economic destiny. By 1919, with the First World War now finally ended and with more or less normal peacetime conditions ready to resume, Garvey saw the entire planet as a giant playing field where African Americans might compete on equal footing with whites. Of course, Garvey acknowledged obstacles to his grand vision of widespread black entrepreneurship. This included an appalling lack of self-confidence among American blacks that naturally hindered their ability to seize the initiative. Garvey also blasted the many lazy men among his own race.

On a practical level, Garvey's interest in economic self-sufficiency spurred him to found a steamship company, the Blue Star Line, that entertained plans to connect American blacks directly with their West African roots. Sadly, mismanagement, an overly optimistic projection of revenues, and perhaps a bit of sabotage courtesy of the white community, contributed to Garvey's corporate failure. His personal demise ensued. He found himself tried and convicted of mail fraud, imprisoned, and subsequently deported. But the impact of Marcus Garvey remained. Indeed his memory was resurrected by a new generation of American Black Nationalists during the tumultuous 1960s.

Marcus Garvey around 1920. He is wearing his uniform as commander-in-chief of the Universal African Legion, a paramilitary branch of his U.N.I.A. ARCHIVE PHOTOS, INC. REPRODUCED BY PERMISSION.

### Primary Source

"The Negro Should be a Party to the Commercial Conquest of the World"

SYNOPSIS: In an editorial letter dated January 31, 1919 and published in Marcus Garvey's own newspaper, The Negro World, America's foremost Black Nationalist leader outlines his ambitious agenda to enable blacks to control their own economic destiny and to take full advantage of the tremendous possibilities for trade and commerce that beckoned, now that peace had finally returned after the end of World War I (1914–18).

Fellowmen of the Negro Race:

Greeting:—It is expected that the Peace Conference will adjourn about late spring, at which time the representatives of the various nations of the world, now in France, will return to their respective countries. They will take back with them the new thought, the new hope—industrial and commercial expansion and conquest.

England is preparing for a great commercial warfare; so is America, Japan, France, Germany and the other nations. The next twenty-five year[s] will be a period of keen competition among people. It will be an age of survival of the fittest. The weaker elements will totter and fall. They will be destroyed for the up-building of the greater powers.

As a Negro, I would be untrue to myself and would be untrue to you, if I, from my observation, fail to prepare the mind of the race for this titanic industrial and commercial struggle that is in the making. This era has forced out the best races and nations. The white people have risen to the occasion. In Europe they are presenting to the world their keenest and best intellects. In Asia, the Japanese and Chinese are presenting on the stage of world affairs, men, who are as big as the age. America is also presenting extraordinary big men to meet the situation. The Negro can do no less than rise also to the occasion to produce of his best.

This commercial rivalry that I speak of will send the representatives of all these people into all parts of the world to conquer trade. As Germany sent out her commercial agents to conquer the trade of the world and had become so successful up to the time when war was declared in 1914, so must the Negro be prepared to play . . . [remainder of sentence missing]. If we are to rise as a great [people?] to become a great national force, we must start business enterprises of our own; we must build ships and start trading with ourselves between America, the West Indies and Africa. We must put up factories in all the great manufacturing centers of this country, to give employment to the thousands of men and women who will be thrown out of work as soon as the nation takes on its normal attitude. In these factories we must manufacture boots, clothing and all the necessaries of life, those things that the people need, not only our people in America, the West Indies and Africa, but the people of China, of India, of South and Central America, and even the white man. He has for hundreds of years made a market for his goods among Negroes and alien races; therefore, Negroes have the same right to make a market among white people for his manufactured goods.

The time has come when the Negro must take his stand as a man. If the white man is manly enough to put up a factory, the Negro ought to be manly enough to do the same thing. If he can, as a white man, manufacture things that other people need, then Negroes ought to be able to do the same thing. There is absolutely no monopoly in knowledge today. The equality of men has been proved and in this recent bloody conflict, and in this period of reconstruction, when all men are endeavoring to take their

stand as equals, the Negro would be less than [a] man if he were to allow all the other races within another generation to present to the world the results of their efforts in rising to the ordinary human plane without his achieving a modicum of success.

The vision of some of us today is as penetrating as that of the great economists of Europe and Asia. When we can as a race settle down to business with honesty of purpose, we will be on the way to the founding of a permanent and strong position among the nations and races of the world. Commerce and industry were the forces that pushed the great German Empire to the front. As it can be remembered, during the first Napoleonic era, Germany was regarded as the pauper nation of Europe, whilst England and France had reached a high state in commerce and industry, having their merchant marines sailing to and anchoring [in] every port of the world; Germany was without steamships. The German was looked down on then, even as the Negro of the South is looked down on today; but the Germans of . . . [mutilated] about and applied themselves assiduously to the [mutilated] of these two forces. They . . . [several words missing] [Bisma]rck From then up to 1914 . . . [several words missing] that two hours before war was declared German manufactured goods, were underselling in England goods manufactured in England, America, Japan, Canada and Australia.

These are fair examples of how a people can rise to greatness when they apply themselves to any one good thing without faltering. The Negro should not falter, and, economically and industrially today, he should endeavor to lay a good foundation and continue to build and until the structure becomes impregnable.

In a word, my message to you for this week is: "Develop yourselves into a commercial and industrial people, and you will have laid the foundation for racial greatness."

*Your[s] fraternally,*
*Marcus Garvey*

## Further Resources

**BOOKS**

Cronon, Edmund D. *Black Moses: The Story of Marcus Garvey and the Universal Negro Improvement Association.* Madison: University of Wisconsin Press, 1969.

Martin, Tony. *The Pan–African Connection: From Slavery to Garvey and Beyond.* Dover, Mass.: Majority Press, 1983.

Vincent, Theodore G. *Black Power and the Garvey Movement.* Berkeley, Calif.: Ramparts Press, 1971.

# 8

# THE MEDIA

DAN PROSTERMAN

*Entries are arranged in chronological order by date of primary source. For entries with one primary source, the entry title is the same as the primary source title. Entries with more than one primary source have an overall entry title, followed by the titles of the primary sources.*

**CHRONOLOGY**

Important Events in the Media, 1910–1919 . . . . . . 376

**PRIMARY SOURCES**

Photographs by Lewis Hine
    Lewis Hine, 1908–1912 . . . . . . . . . . . . . . . . . . 379

National American Woman Suffrage
    Association Broadsides . . . . . . . . . . . . . . . . . 383
    "Votes for Women"; "Why Women Want
    to Vote"; "Women in the Home"
    National American Woman Suffrage
    Association, 1910, 1912

Early Baseball Cards . . . . . . . . . . . . . . . . . . . . . 387
    "Chicago Cubs Baseball Card"; "Tris
    Speaker Baseball Card"; "Cy Young
    Baseball Card"
    Liggett & Myers, Co.; American Tobacco
    Company, 1913; 1911; 1911

"Fun's Word Cross Puzzle"
    Arthur Wynne, December 21, 1913 . . . . . . . . . 390

*The Woman Rebel*
    Margaret Sanger, March 1914 . . . . . . . . . . . . . 392

The First Pulitzer Prizes . . . . . . . . . . . . . . . . . . 395
"The Anniversary"
    *New York Tribune*, May 7, 1916
"Germany Keen for Peace, but Expects and
    is Ready to Battle for Years"
    Herbert Bayard Swope, 1917

"Warning: The Deadly Parallel"
    Industrial Workers of the World, 1916 . . . . . . . 400

Letters to the Chicago *Defender*
    Chicago *Defender*, 1916–1918 . . . . . . . . . . . . . 403

"For Freedom and Democracy"
    *North American Review*, March 30, 1917 . . . . . 407

*Sedition Act, 1918*
    Woodrow Wilson, May 16, 1918 . . . . . . . . . . . 410

Chicago Race Riots . . . . . . . . . . . . . . . . . . . . . . 413
"A Crowd of Howling Negroes"
    *Chicago Tribune*, July 28, 1919
"Ghastly Deeds of Race Rioters Told"
    Chicago *Defender*, August 2, 1919

*The Brass Check*
    Upton Sinclair, 1919 . . . . . . . . . . . . . . . . . . . 419

# Important Events in Media, 1910–1919

## 1910

- Robert R. McCormick, known after World War I as the Colonel, becomes editor and publisher of the *Chicago Tribune,* turning it into the most consistently ultraconservative paper for the next several decades.

- Oswald Garrison Villard, at work as a reporter for his father's *New York Evening Post,* investigates the Republican majority leader of the New York state legislature. His exposés lead to the first conviction of a legislator for graft in New York history.

- Rheta Childe Dorr publishes *What Eight Million Women Want,* an account of the suffrage movements in Great Britain and the United States.

- On March 10, the *Pittsburgh Courier* begins publication.

- On June 18, Congress gives the Interstate Commerce Commission (ICC) regulatory authority over the nation's telephone, telegraph, cable, and wireless communications companies. The move is applauded by those industries, which feared the development of a wide variety of regulations by individual states.

- On July 13, the first issue of *Women's Wear Daily* appears, under the editorship of journalist Edmund Fairchild.

- On October 1, a bomb explodes at the offices of the *Los Angeles Times,* killing twenty. Two union leaders, John and James McNamara, later confess to planting the bombs to protest the conservative antilabor policies of the paper's owners, the Chandler family.

- In November, the first issue of *The Crisis,* the monthly publication of the new National Association for the Advancement of Colored People (NAACP), is published, with W. E. B. Du Bois as editor.

- On December 1, the city of Miami, with a population of under six thousand, gets its first daily newspaper, the *Miami Herald.*

## 1911

- The Curtis Publishing Company, publisher of the *Saturday Evening Post,* builds new headquarters on Washington Square in Philadelphia.

- Hearst Magazines acquires the household monthly *Good Housekeeping* from newspaper publisher Charles W. Bryan. Hearst begins emphasizing fiction, publishing name authors

such as W. Somerset Maugham, James Hilton, Sinclair Lewis, Daphne du Maurier, and John P. Marquand.

- Victor Berger founds the *Milwaukee Leader.* During World War I its third-class mail privileges are suspended under the Espionage Act.

- James R. Quirk founds *Photoplay,* the first motion picture fan magazine. It includes articles, interviews, and photographs of stars, but its film reviews are honestly critical.

- In January, the socialist weekly *The Masses* is founded. In 1912 Max Eastman becomes editor and lines up contributors such as Randolph Bourne, Floyd Dell, and John Reed. The publication is suppressed by the government in 1918 for opposition to the war.

- *Collier's* begins publication of the fourteen-part landmark series by Will Irwin, "The American Newspaper."

- On September 28, the *Chicago Day Book* is founded by E. W. Scripps as an experimental tabloid, taking no advertising. It comes near to financial success until increased newsprint costs due to World War I bankrupt it.

- In October, with the death of Joseph Pulitzer, Frank I. Cobb becomes editor of the *New York World.*

## 1912

- The School of Journalism opens at Columbia University with a $2 million bequest from Joseph Pulitzer. It becomes one of thirty universities offering courses in journalism.

- Gertrude Battles Lane becomes editor in chief of the *Woman's Home Companion,* a post she will hold until 1941.

- On March 16, a record is set for a wireless transmission—fifty-five minutes from London to New York.

- On April 15, the *Titanic* sinks after striking an iceberg, killing 1,517 people. Seven hundred people are saved because another ship, the *Carpathia,* receives a radio distress call and steams to the site of the disaster. A closer ship misses the call because its radio operator is asleep.

- In October, the magazine *Poetry: A Magazine of Verse* is founded in Chicago by Harriet Monree. Carl Sandburg, Hilda Doolittle (H. D.), Amy Lowell, Ezra Pound, T. S. Eliot, Vachel Lindsay, and Hart Crane are among its early contributors.

## 1913

- *Southern Women's Magazine* is founded.

- *Dress and Vanity Fair* is founded in New York City by Condé Nast as a sophisticated monthly. In 1914 Frank Crowninshield becomes editor and shortens the name to *Vanity Fair,* making it at least the fourth publication with that name.

- The Associated Press inaugurates the first teletypes, which print the news automatically, replacing the telegraph.

- Bell Syndicate is founded by John N. Wheeler, featuring "Mutt and Jeff," the first daily cartoon strip, first drawn by H. C. "Bud" Fisher of the *San Francisco Chronicle* in 1907.

- Cartoonist George Herriman introduces a spinoff to his popular "The Dingbat Family" comic strip called "Krazy Kat," which will prove to be one of the most popular and influential strips in the history of the art.

## 1914

* The number of newspapers in the United States reaches a record high of fifteen thousand.

* Thirteen hundred foreign-language newspapers are published in the United States, including 160 dailies. There are 55 in German; 12 each in French, Italian, and Polish; 10 each in Japanese and Yiddish; and 8 each in Bohemian and Spanish. Total circulation is 2.6 million, with more than 800,000 German and more than 750,000 Yiddish readers. The largest daily is the *New Yorker Staats-Zeitung* with 250,000 readers.

* King Features Syndicate, the first major distributor for comic strips, is founded by William Randolph Hearst. The "Katzenjammer Kids" is its leading color comic.

* H. L. Mencken and George Jean Nathan become coeditors of *The Smart Set.*

* *Pearson's* publishes muckraker Charles Edward Russell's series on the business pressures that brought an end to muckraking.

* On January 3, a direct wireless connection is established between the United States and Germany.

* On February 13, the American Society of Composers, Authors, and Publishers (ASCAP) is founded in New York with Victor Herbert as director.

* In March, *The Little Review* is founded in Chicago by Margaret Anderson to showcase experimental art, literature, and music. Its serial publication of James Joyce's *Ulysses* leads to Anderson's conviction for publishing obscenity.

* On July 3, the first telephone line is completed between New York and San Francisco.

* On September 9, *The New York Times* establishes its *Mid-Week Pictorial* featuring pictures of the European war.

* On November 7, *The New Republic* is founded by Herbert Croly, Walter Weyl, and Walter Lippmann with financial backing from Willard and Dorothy Straight. Croly serves as editor in chief of this liberal journal of public affairs until 1930.

## 1915

* The Associated Press allows members to subscribe to other news services for the first time.

* Five hundred U.S. correspondents cover the war in Europe, with another fifty covering the American Expeditionary Forces after they are formed in 1917.

* In January, *Midland,* a significant review featuring work about the Midwest and the West, is founded.

* On June 27, the first direct wireless service between the United States and Japan is established.

* In June, the *Texas Review* is founded.

* On October 21, American Telephone and Telegraph Company sends a radio signal across the Atlantic from the naval station at Arlington, Virginia, to the Eiffel Tower in Paris.

## 1916

* William Randolph Hearst inaugurates the *City Life* arts supplement to his Sunday newspapers.

* Norman Rockwell, art director of the Boy Scouts' magazine *Boy's Life,* publishes his first illustration in the *Saturday Evening Post.*

* Lee De Forest commences daily music broadcasts from his home in New York City.

* The experimental radio station 8XK begins broadcasting in Pittsburgh but is shut down for the duration of the war. It will reopen in 1919 and receive the first Department of Commerce commercial radio license in 1920, as KDKA.

* In November, David Sarnoff, the commercial manager of the American Marconi Company, predicts that the future of commercial broadcasting will be in homes rather than for point-to-point communication.

* On November 7, De Forest broadcasts presidential election returns, incorrectly reporting the victory of Charles Evans Hughes over Woodrow Wilson.

## 1917

* The first *World Book* encyclopedia is published.

* On February 17, Floyd Gibbons of the *Chicago Tribune* sails for England on the *Laconia.* When the ship is torpedoed only thirteen passengers perish, and Gibbons' account of the sinking and rescue establish his reputation as a brave and vivid reporter.

* On April 6, the United States enters the war in Europe. All nongovernmental radio operations are closed for the duration.

* On April 14, President Wilson establishes the Committee on Public Information, known as the Creel Committee because of its chairman George Creel. It promulgates official information and a voluntary censorship code. Creel signs up some 100,000 "four-minute men" to give short speeches and write literature to strengthen support for the war and stir anti-German sentiment.

* On June 4, the first Pulitzer Prizes are awarded to the *New York Tribune* for its editorial on the first anniversary of the sinking of the Lusitania and to Herbert Bayard Swope of the *New York World* for his series "Inside the German Empire."

* On June 15, the Espionage Act enables prosecution of people opposed to the war, including those who make statements that undermine morale. In its first year seventy-five publications lose mailing privileges or agree to change their editorial positions.

* In September, John Reed and Louise Bryant arrive in Petrograd, Russia, in time to witness the October Revolution.

* On September 15, Bertie Charles Forbes founds the general interest business weekly *Forbes.*

* In October, the president establishes a Censorship Board to monitor foreign communication.

## 1918

* Max and Crystal Eastman found *The Liberator.*

* In February, the price of Sunday papers in New York rises from five cents to seven cents and shortly thereafter to ten cents. Each hike is followed by a brief dip in circulation.

- On February 3, *The New York Times* begins home delivery.

- On February 18, *Stars and Stripes* is founded in France for the American Expeditionary Forces and continues until June 1919 with Harold Ross, later of *The New Yorker,* as editor.

- On May 16, the Sedition Act amends the Espionage Act of 1917, making it a crime to publish writing opposed to the government of the United States.

- On August 25, the War Industries Board declares moving pictures an "essential industry."

- On November 11, the United Press International (UPI) falsely reports an armistice.

## 1919

- Upton Sinclair publishes *The Brass Check,* a novel replete with criticism of the newspaper industry.

- In January, Bruce Barton, Roy Durstine, and Alex Osborn start the Barton, Durstine, and Osborn Advertising Agency in New York City and meet with almost instant and overwhelming success.

- On January 18, *Justice,* the largest labor magazine, a publication of the International Ladies' Garment Worker's Union, is founded. It reaches a peak circulation of almost four hundred thousand.

- In February, *The Watch on the Rhine* newspaper is founded for the Army of Occupation in Germany.

- In May, Bernarr Macfadden, publisher of *Physical Culture,* founds the confessional magazine *True Story* with the motto "Truth is Stranger than Fiction."

- On June 26, Cousins Robert R. McCormick and Joseph Medill Patterson found the tabloid *New York Illustrated Daily News,* soon dropping the word *Illustrated* from the title. It becomes the most widely read paper in the country.

- In August, the *Chicago Tribune* is found guilty of libeling Henry Ford.

- In October, encouraged by the navy, American Telephone and Telegraph, Westinghouse, General Electric, and United Fruit together found the Radio Corporation of America to prevent foreign control of American broadcasting. David Sarnoff becomes commercial manager.

# Photographs by Lewis Hine

Photographs

**By:** Lewis Hine

**Date:** 1908–1912

**Source:** "Lewis Hine Photographs for the National Labor Committee, ca. 1912." Record Group 102: Records of the Children's Bureau, 1908–1969. Still Picture Records LICON, Special Media Archives Services Division (NWCS-S), National Archives at College Park, MD. Available online at http://arcweb.archives.gov/arc/arch_results_detail.jsp?&pg;=1&si;=0&nh;=100&st;=b; website home page: http://www.nara.gov (accessed October 11, 2002).

**About the Author:** Lewis Wickes Hine (1874–1940) was born in Wisconsin but moved to New York City to teach at the turn of the century. Within the next few years, he became closely associated with several reform organizations, especially the National Child Labor Committee (NCLC), and began to take some of his most influential photographs. These pictures depicted the human impact of industrialization. He took his most famous and significant pictures of child laborers in textile mills, mines, factories, and farms. During the Great Depression, he undertook projects for various New Deal agencies. ∎

## Introduction

The first two decades of the twentieth century brought a growing concern about the impact of industrialization and massive immigration in the United States. Progressives focused their energies on reforming the practice of industrial capitalism to ease the burdens of working-class life. As the medium of photography increased in popularity at the turn of the twentieth century, many social reformers recognized the documentary qualities that photographs could bring to their activism. Jacob Riis' pioneering "How the Other Half Lives" combined text and photographs to depict the squalor of tenement life in New York City in 1890. That work contributed to the passage of tenement reform laws that increased safety standards in housing.

Popular support for the outlawing of child labor grew throughout the early years of the twentieth century. Progressive reformers, primarily from middle- and upper-

## The National Child Labor Committee

Progressive reformers organized in the early twentieth century to combat the employment of young children. The National Child Labor Committee (NCLC), launched in 1904, included social welfare advocates Felix Adler, Jane Addams, Florence Kelley, and Lillian Wald. The NCLC sought minimum age requirements of fourteen in manufacturing and sixteen in mining. It also wanted documentary proof of age, a maximum eight-hour workday, and an end to night work. No state met these standards at the NCLC's founding, but by 1914, more than thirty states had put some or all of these principles into law. Eventually, public reaction contributed to the Child Labor Act of 1916, which set minimum ages for work in mining (sixteen) and manufacturing (fourteen). In spite of this, the reformers did not achieve uniform federal regulation for all aspects of child labor. It was not until the New Deal of the 1930s that Congress—despite prior constitutional objections—enacted strict prohibitions on child labor.

class families, argued that child labor threatened the safety of the young workers but also stunted their potential. Most, if not all, poor immigrant families relied upon the work of children simply to make ends meet. The abolition of child labor posed a very real concern to millions of impoverished families who needed this extra source of income to survive.

## Significance

In the mold of Riis, Lewis Hine's photographs of child workers influenced ongoing Progressive campaigns for social reform. Hine took many of the pictures for the National Child Labor Committee, formed in 1904 for the primary purpose of ending child labor in the United States. The pictures revealed to many Americans the large population of children who toiled in factories in unsafe conditions. Akin to the muckraking exposés in the 1900s and the Farm Service Agency photographs of rural American in the 1930s, Hine's work presented the country with the human faces of poverty and struggle. The boys and girls seen in these photographs could not be ignored.

Though Jessie Tarbox Beals isn't as well known as many of her contemporaries, her photographs convey the complex social fabric of the period. The picture shown here brings to mind the overcrowded, urban tenements captured by Jacob Riis two decades before. Though city, state, and national legislators had passed numerous laws aimed at improving living conditions for the poor, Beals'

## Primary Source

### Photographs by Lewis Hine (1 OF 6)

**SYNOPSIS:** These pictures present the wide range of employment performed by children. Youths served as newspaper and clothing sellers, coal miners, messengers, and mill workers, among other professions. Hine wrote the captions for each of these pictures, paying particular attention to the specific tasks assigned to the children. The various locations, from rural to urban settings, provide a sense of how pervasive child labor was in the United States in the 1910s. "A common case of 'team work.' Smaller boy, Joseph Bishop, goes into saloons and sells his last paper. Then comes out and his brother gives him more. Joseph said, 'Drunks are me best customers. I sell more's me bruder does. Dey buy me out so I kin go home.'"—*Lewis Hine,* March 4, 1909. NATIONAL ARCHIVES AND RECORDS ADMINISTRATION.

## Primary Source

### Photographs by Lewis Hine (2 OF 6)

"Rose Bido, Philadelphia, 10 years old. Working 3 summers, minds baby and carries berries, two pecks at a time. Whites Bog, Brown Mills, N.J. This is the fourth week of school and the people expect to remain here two weeks more."—*Lewis Hine,* September 28, 1910. NATIONAL ARCHIVES AND RECORDS ADMINISTRATION.

## Primary Source

### Photographs by Lewis Hine (3 OF 6)

"At the close of day. Just up from the shaft. All work below ground in Shaft #6 Pennsylvania, Coal Co. Clement Tiskie, (smallest boy next to right hand end) is a nipper. Arthur Harvard, (on Clement's right hand) is a driver. Jo Puma, (on Arthur's right) is a nipper. Jo's mother showed me the passport which shows Jo to be 14 years old, but he has no school certificate although working inside mine. . . . Works a mile underground from the shaft which is 500 ft. down. South Pittston, Pa."—*Lewis Hine,* January 6, 1911. NATIONAL ARCHIVES AND RECORDS ADMINISTRATION.

## Primary Source

### Photographs by Lewis Hine (4 OF 6)

"Hiram Pulk, 9 years old, cuts some in a canning company. 'I ain't very fast only about 5 boxes a day. They pay about 5 [cents] a box.' Eastport, Me."—*Lewis Hine,* August 14, 1911. NATIONAL ARCHIVES AND RECORDS ADMINISTRATION.

## Primary Source

### Photographs by Lewis Hine for the National Child Labor Committee (5 OF 6)

"Photograph of Wilbur H. Woodward, Western Union Messenger 236, is one of the youngsters on the border line. He is 15 years old and works until 8 P.M. only."—*Lewis Hine,* April 11, 1912. NATIONAL ARCHIVES AND RECORDS ADMINISTRATION.

## Primary Source

### Photographs by Lewis Hine for the National Child Labor Committee (6 OF 6)

". . .7-year-old Tommie Noonan demonstrating the advantages of the Ideal Necktie Form in a store window. . . His father said proudly, 'He is the youngest demonstrator in America. Has been doing it for several years from San Francisco to New York. . . .' The remarks of appreciation from the by-standers were not having the best effect on Tommie."—*Lewis Hine,* April 13, 1912. NATIONAL ARCHIVES AND RECORDS ADMINISTRATION.

*Room in a Tenement Flat* by Jessie Tarbox Beals, 1910. Many poor, urban Americans, living in tenement houses like these, needed the income from putting their children to work. © **BETTMANN/CORBIS. REPRODUCED BY PERMISSION.**

photograph reveals the extent to which city workers, primarily immigrants, continued to endure unsafe home environments.

## Further Resources

**BOOKS**

Curtis, Posever, and Stanley Mallach. *Photography and Reform: Lewis Hine and the National Child Labor Committee.* Milwaukee, Wisc.: Milwaukee Art Museum, 1981.

Riis, Jacob A. *How the Other Half Lives: Studies Among the Tenements of New York.* New York: Scribner's, 1890.

Rosenblum, Walter, et al. *America and Lewis Hine: Photographs 1904–1940.* New York: Aperture, 1977.

Trachtenberg, Alan. *Reading American Photographs: Images as History, Mathew Brady to Walker Evans.* New York: Noonday Press, 1990.

**PERIODICALS**

Gutman, Judith Mara. "Lewis Hine's Last Legacy," *The New York Times Magazine,* April 17, 1983

Seixas, Peter. "Lewis Hine: From 'Social' to 'Interpretive' Photographer." *American Quarterly* 39, no. 3, 1987, 381–409.

**WEBSITES**

Hine, Lewis W. "Tennessee Valley." *New Deal Photo Gallery.* Available online at http://newdeal.feri.org/library/h_3b.htm (accessed April 9, 2003).

Seixas, Peter. "Hine, Lewis Wickes." Available online at http://www.anb.org/articles/17/17-00411.html; website home page: http://www.anb.org/ (accessed April 9, 2003).

# National American Woman Suffrage Association Broadsides

## "Votes for Women"; "Why Women Want to Vote"; "Women in the Home"

**Broadsides**

**By:** National American Woman Suffrage Association
**Date:** 1910, 1912
**Source:** National American Woman Suffrage Association Broadsides. American Memory. *An American Time Capsule: Three Centuries of Broadsides and Other Printed Ephemera.* Available online at http://memory.loc.gov/ (accessed April 10, 2003).

**About the Organization:** From its founding in 1890 until ratification of the Nineteenth Amendment in 1920, the National American Woman Suffrage Association (NAWSA) led the campaign for women's suffrage in the United States. The organization formed through the merger of two competing groups: the American Woman Suffrage Association (AWSA) and the National Woman Suffrage Association (NWSA). This coalition featured several of the most influential women's rights advocates in American history, including Susan B. Anthony, Elizabeth Cady Stanton, Carrie Chapman Catt, and Lucy Stone. Following the victory in 1920, the NAWSA restructured its objectives to focus on ongoing political issues relating to women. The group changed its name to the League of Women Voters, which would continue to campaign for policies beneficial to women for the rest of the twentieth century. ∎

## Introduction

The campaign for women's suffrage in the United States began with the writing of the Constitution. Women such as Abigail Adams urged her husband, future president John Adams, to "remember the ladies." Yet equal voting rights for women would not be granted for nearly 150 years. Throughout this period, women's rights activists debated the proper strategy for obtaining the vote, disagreeing over whether campaigns should be waged at a statewide basis (AWSA) or on a national level (NWSA). The formation of the NAWSA, which dedicated itself to the passage of a constitutional amendment, strengthened the movement toward national suffrage.

When the NASWA produced the following broadsides in 1910 and 1912, statewide suffrage had only been granted west of the Mississippi River. Before 1910, only Wyoming (1869), Utah (1870), Colorado (1893), and Idaho (1896) provided women with the right to vote. Washington (1910), California (1912), Kansas (1912), Oregon (1912), and Arizona (1912) more than doubled

# VOTES FOR WOMEN!
## THE WOMAN'S REASON.
### BECAUSE

**BECAUSE** women must obey the laws just as men do,
> They should vote equally with men.

**BECAUSE** women pay taxes just as men do, thus supporting the government,
> They should vote equally with men.

**BECAUSE** women suffer from bad government just as men do,
> They should vote equally with men.

**BECAUSE** mothers want to make their children's surroundings better,
> They should vote equally with men.

**BECAUSE** over 5,000,000 women in the United States are wage workers and their health and that of our future citizens are often endangered by evil working conditions that can only be remedied by legislation,
> They should vote equally with men.

**BECAUSE** women of leisure who attempt to serve the public welfare should be able to support their advice by their votes,
> They should vote equally with men.

**BECAUSE** busy housemothers and professional women cannot give such public service, and can only serve the state by the same means used by the busy man—namely, by casting a ballot,
> They should vote equally with men.

**BECAUSE** women need to be trained to a higher sense of social and civic responsibility, and such sense developes by use,
> They should vote equally with men.

**BECAUSE** women are consumers, and consumers need fuller representation in politics,
> They should vote equally with men.

**BECAUSE** women are citizens of a government **of** the people, **by** the people and **for** the people, **and women are people.**
> They should vote equally with men.

### EQUAL SUFFRAGE FOR MEN AND WOMEN.

WOMEN Need It.
MEN Need It.
The STATE Needs It.

# WHY?

# BECAUSE

Women Ought To GIVE Their Help.
Men Ought To HAVE Their Help.
The State Ought To USE Their Help.

## National American Woman Suffrage Association

### Headquarters: 505 FIFTH AVENUE, NEW YORK

 11

## Primary Source

### "Votes for Women!"

**SYNOPSIS:** Coming in the midst of the Progressive movement, the following publications highlight not only the desire of women to possess political power but also the belief that the government must serve the people as a mechanism of social reform. The suffrage movement mobilized millions of women to join the political system in the hopes of creating policies that would fundamentally alter the relationship of government and the people. The NAWSA campaign stressed the government's responsibility to improve health care, education, housing, sanitation, and employment for its citizens. These broadsides reveal the extensive connections between women's activism, suffrage, and reform in the United States during the 1910s. THE LIBRARY OF CONGRESS.

JUSTICE                            EQUALITY

## Why Women Want to Vote.

# WOMEN ARE CITIZENS,

### AND WISH TO DO THEIR CIVIC DUTY.

WORKING WOMEN need the ballot to regulate conditions under which they work. Do working men think they can protect themselves without the right to vote?

HOUSEKEEPERS need the ballot to regulate the sanitary conditions under which they and their families must live. Do MEN think they can get what is needed for their district unless they can vote for the men that will get it for them?

MOTHERS need the ballot to regulate the moral conditions under which their children must be brought up. Do MEN think they can fight against vicious conditions that are threatening their children unless they can vote for the men that run the district?

TEACHERS need the ballot to secure just wages and to influence the management of the public schools. Do MEN think they could secure better school conditions without a vote to elect the Mayor who nominates the Board of Education?

BUSINESS WOMEN need the ballot to secure for themselves a fair opportunity in their business. Do business MEN think they could protect themselves against adverse legislation without the right to vote?

TAX PAYING WOMEN need the ballot to protect their property. Do not MEN know that "Taxation without representation" is tyranny?

ALL WOMEN need the ballot, because they are concerned equally with men in good and bad government; and equally responsible for civic righteousness.

ALL MEN need women's help to build a better and juster government, and

WOMEN need MEN to help them secure their right to fulfil their civic duties.

## National American Woman Suffrage Association

### Headquarters: 505 FIFTH AVENUE, NEW YORK

---

**Primary Source**

"Why Women Want to Vote"
"Why Women Want to Vote" broadside published in 1910. THE LIBRARY OF CONGRESS.

# WOMEN IN THE HOME

We are forever being told that the place for women is in the HOME. Well, so be it. But what do we expect of her in the home? Merely to stay in the home is not enough. She is a failure unless she does certain things for the home. She must make the home minister, as far as her means allow, to the health and welfare, moral as well as physical, of her family, and especially of her children. She, more than anyone else, is held responsible for what they become.

SHE is responsible for the cleanliness of her house.

SHE is responsible for the wholesomeness of the food.

SHE is responsible for the children's health.

SHE, above all, is responsible for their morals, for their sense of truth, of honesty and decency, for what they turn out to be.

## How Far Can the Mother Control These Things?

She can clean her own rooms, BUT if the neighbors are allowed to live in filth, she cannot keep her rooms from being filled with bad air and smells, or from being infested with vermin.

She can cook her food well, BUT if dealers are permitted to sell poor food, unclean milk or stale eggs, she cannot make the food wholesome for her children.

She can care for her own plumbing and the refuse of her own home, BUT if the plumbing in the rest of the house is unsanitary, if garbage accumulates and the halls and stairs are left dirty, she cannot protect her children from the sickness and infection that these conditions bring.

She can take every care to avoid fire, BUT if the house has been badly built, if the fire-escapes are insufficient or not fire-proof, she cannot guard her children from the horrors of being maimed or killed by fire.

She can open her windows to give her children the air that we are told is so necessary, BUT if the air is laden with infection, with tuberculosis and other contagious diseases, she cannot protect her children from this danger.

She can send her children out for air and exercise, BUT if the conditions that surround them on the streets are immoral and degrading, she cannot protect them from these dangers.

ALONE, she CANNOT make these things right. WHO or WHAT can?

THE CITY can do it—the CITY GOVERNMENT that is elected BY THE PEOPLE, to take care of the interest of THE PEOPLE.

And who decides what the city government shall do?

FIRST, the officials of that government; and,

SECOND, those who elect them.

DO THE WOMEN ELECT THEM? NO, the men do. So it is the MEN and NOT THE WOMEN that are really responsible for the

UNCLEAN HOUSES                          BAD PLUMBING
UNWHOLESOME FOOD                   DANGER OF FIRE
RISK OF TUBERCULOSIS AND OTHER DISEASES
IMMORAL INFLUENCES OF THE STREET.

In fact, MEN are responsible for the conditions under which the children live, but we hold WOMEN responsible for the results of those conditions. If we hold women responsible for the results, must we not, in simple justice, let them have something to say as to what these conditions shall be? There is one simple way of doing this. Give them the same means that men have. LET THEM VOTE.

Women are, by nature and training, housekeepers. Let them have a hand in the city's housekeeping, even if they introduce an occasional house-cleaning.

## National American Woman Suffrage Association

### Headquarters: 505 FIFTH AVENUE, NEW YORK

 11

---

**Primary Source**

"Women in the Home"

"Women in the Home" by the National Woman Suffrage Association, 1910. THE LIBRARY OF CONGRESS.

Suffragettes Mrs. Stanley McCormick and Mrs. Charles Parker pose with a banner for the National Woman Suffrage Association, April 22, 1913. © CORBIS. REPRODUCED BY PERMISSION.

the number of states with such provisions by 1912. Although several states provided partial ballot access, not a single state east of the Mississippi granted women equal voting rights until New York did so in 1917.

### Significance

The three documents displayed here convey both the message and the medium used by suffragists in the 1910s. The broadside format allowed for the large sheets of paper to be posted for public display or folded like a pamphlet for distribution by hand. The NAWSA, headquartered in New York City, printed thousands of these broadsides in its call for equal voting rights for women in New York City, New York State, and throughout the United States.

As each of these texts made clear, the NAWSA's primary argument was that women deserved the vote because of their contributions to American society as citizens and as women. Not only do women "pay taxes" and "obey the laws just as men do," women possess a unique role in the social development of the country by the very nature of their sex. The broadsides emphasize women's work from a broader context than hourly wages. As mothers and wives, women possess a keen sense of what government must do to reform society. Rather than deriding women's

responsibilities as "housemothers," these documents praise women for all of their economic, social, and maternal contributions to the nation's prosperity. Foreshadowing the relatively moderate impact female voters would cause during the 1920s, the NAWSA's campaign literature concludes that women's participation in democracy will strengthen the existing political order through "an occasional house-cleaning" rather than a radical overhaul.

### Further Resources

#### BOOKS

Chafe, William Henry. *The Paradox of Change: American Women in the 20th Century.* New York: Oxford University Press, 1991.

Flexner, Eleanor. *Century of Struggle: The Woman's Rights Movement in the United States.* New York: Atheneum, 1974.

Kraditor, Aileen S. *The Ideas of the Woman Suffrage Movement, 1890–1920.* New York, Columbia University Press, 1965.

#### WEBSITES

*The History of the Suffrage Movement.* Available online at http://www.pbs.org/onewoman/suffrage.html; website home page: http://www.pbs.org (accessed April 10, 2003).

*History of Women's Suffrage.* Available online at http://www.rochester.edu/SBA/history.html; website home page: http://www.rochester.edu (accessed April 10, 2003).

Public Broadcasting Service. *Not for Ourselves Alone: The Story of Elizabeth Cady Stanton and Susan B. Anthony.* Available online at http://www.pbs.org/stantonanthony/; website home page: http://www.pbs.org/ (accessed April 10, 2003).

---

# Early Baseball Cards
Baseball cards

## "Chicago Cubs Baseball Card"; "Tris Speaker Baseball Card"; "Cy Young Baseball Card"

**By:** Liggett & Myers Co.; American Tobacco Company
**Date:** 1913; 1911; 1911
**Source:** "Chicago Cubs Baseball Card"; "Tris Speaker Baseball Card"; "Cy Young Baseball Card". American Memory: Historical Collections for the National Digital Library. "Baseball Cards, 1887–1914." Available online at http://memory.loc.gov/ammem/bbhtml/bbhome.html; website home page: http://www.memory.loc.gov (accessed April 9, 2003).
**About the Organization:** The American Tobacco Company (ATC) was formed in 1890 when five of the nation's largest cigarette producers merged. North Carolina industrialist James Buchanan Duke headed ATC and used his revamped cigarette-rolling machine to take virtually complete control of the tobacco industry in the United States. As the Progressive

movement ushered in a wave of antimonopoly reforms, the U.S. Justice Department concentrated its efforts on breaking up ATC in the 1900s. In 1911, the corporation dissolved. Duke cut his losses and moved from tobacco production to philanthropy. Shortly before his death in 1925, he agreed to contribute more than $100 million from his multibillion-dollar estate to Trinity College. Trinity changed its name to Duke University, which would become one of the nation's elite universities. ∎

## Introduction

The invention of a mechanical cigarette roller in 1880 and James B. Duke's revisions of the machine in the 1880s, irrevocably altered Americans' desire for cigarettes. Duke's company alone produced more than 100,000 cigarettes a day by the end of the decade. With increased production came unprecedented nationwide advertising campaigns selling brand-name tobacco on billboards and in print media. Marketers devoted an increasingly significant portion of ad investments to the production of tobacco cards. From the 1880s into the twenty-first century, these cards evolved into a multimillion-dollar industry of their own—trading cards.

## Significance

Much smaller than modern sports cards, tobacco cards were about two-and-a half inches tall by one-and-a-half inches wide. After years of using blank cards to strengthen soft cigarette packs, tobacco manufacturers decided to use this valuable space as a means of advertising their product with the images of professional "base ball" players. Tobacco companies almost always included only a single card per cigarette pack. As baseball increased in popularity at the turn of the century, so too did the use and variety of tobacco cards.

The American Tobacco Company's troublesome litigation with trust-busters in the U.S. government did not deter it from producing hundreds of cards in the 1910s. The Tris Speaker and Cy Young cards reprinted here incorporated design elements similar to modern sports cards. The front of the cards offered a dynamic visual of the player. Cy Young, the most successful pitcher in history, is shown throwing from the mound. The reverse of Tris Speaker's card gave fans a summary of his career, complete with statistics for games played, batting average, and fielding percentage. Cards such as these adver-

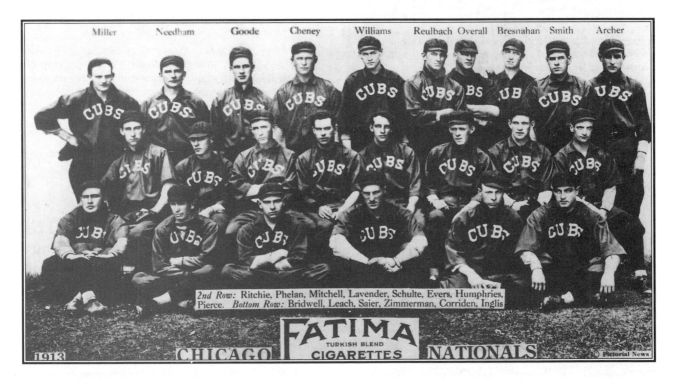

## Primary Source

### Chicago Cubs Baseball Card

**SYNOPSIS:** The front of Fatima Cigarettes' 1913 card featuring the team photo of the Chicago Cubs. For collectors, these turn-of-the-century cards represent a treasure trove of investment opportunities. The expansion of the modern trading card industry has turned some of these throwaway additions to cigarette packs into some of the most valuable collectibles in the world. The most sought-after item, the 1909 card of Pittsburgh Pirates shortstop Honus Wagner, produced by the American Tobacco Company, sold at auction for over $1.25 million in 2000. In addition to carrying a steep market value, the following cards of Hall of Famers Tris Speaker and Cy Young convey an important strategy by which advertisers sought to market cigarettes for over a half-century. THE LIBRARY OF CONGRESS.

**TRIS SPEAKER**

Tris Speaker, the Boston Americans' hard hitting out-fielder, came from Texas, where he batted .318 for the Houston team in 1907. For the 1908 season the Boston management sent him to Little Rock, where he batted .350. Recalled to Boston in 1909 he made 165 hits that year for a total of 242 bases, and in 1910 hit safely 183 times, for 252 bases. He is fast on his feet both in the field and when base-running.

|  | G. | B. | F. |
|---|---|---|---|
| 1908 | 127 | .350 | .967 |
| 1909 | 143 | .309 | .973 |
| 1910 | 141 | .340 | .957 |

2-87-204, 529

**BASE BALL SERIES 400 DESIGNS**

*HASSAN* CORK TIP CIGARETTES
*The Oriental Smoke*
FACTORY Nº 649 1ST DIST N.Y.

LOT 13163-25, NO. 117

**Primary Source**

Tris Speaker Baseball Card (1 OF 2)
Boston Red Sox outfielder Tris Speaker's baseball card, 1911. THE LIBRARY OF CONGRESS.

**Primary Source**

Tris Speaker Baseball Card (2 OF 2)
Statistics from the back of Tris Speaker's baseball card from Hassan Cigarettes, 1911. THE LIBRARY OF CONGRESS.

tised not only the product being sold but the sport of baseball to a growing number of fans across the country.

If sometimes not displayed in the front visual, the primary function of these cards as advertisements for cigarettes usually appeared on their backs. Contrary to the relatively small Hassan emblem on the Speaker card, many card backs simply featured a large company logo without space for any additional information. Enticing smokers, and perhaps a few nonsmoking fans, the Young card's reverse side listed seventy-six different pictures of baseball players and athletes such as heavyweight boxers Jack Johnson and James Jeffries. Using a marketing tactic still used today, the manufacturer offered one photo

in exchange for proofs of purchase coupons from 10 to 25 cigarette packs.

Far from the lowly franchise that occupied the National League cellar for much of the twentieth century, the Chicago Cubs actually experienced great success during the early 1900s, winning the World Series in 1907 and 1908. The 1913 team card displayed here focused the attention of Fatima Cigarettes buyers squarely on the ballplayers as well as the boldfaced type of the brand name. Like many of the tobacco cards of the period, this card's back provided an even larger advertisement for Fatima rather than further information on the Cubs. In addition, this card offered a common incentive for greater

## Primary Source

**Cy Young Baseball Card (1 OF 2)**
Cy Young baseball card issued by the American Tobacco Company. THE LIBRARY OF CONGRESS.

sales: "Special Offer: On receipt of 40 'FATIMA' Cigarette coupons, we will send you an enlarged copy (size 13 x 21) of this picture (without advertising) or of any other picture in this series (National League and American League teams). This picture is mounted, and ready for framing. Write plainly your name and address, stating picture desired."

## Further Resources

### BOOKS

Alexander, Charles C. *Our Game: An American Baseball History.* New York: Henry Holt, 1991.

Rudd, David E. *Illustrated History of Baseball Cards, 1900–1915.* Seattle, Wash.: Cycleback Press, 1999.

Slocum, Frank. *Classic Baseball Cards: The Golden Years, 1886–1956.* New York: Warner, 1987.

### PERIODICALS

Lemke, Bob. "History of Tobacco Trading Cards." *Sports Collectors Digest,* August 21, 1998, 60–63.

---

N°. 42
**PROMINENT BASE BALL PLAYERS & ATHLETES**
ORDER BY NUMBER ONLY

| | | |
|---|---|---|
| 1 M. Brown, Chicago Nat'l | 26 McGraw, New York Nat'l | 51 Jem Driscoll |
| 2 Bergen, Brooklyn | 27 Mathewson, N. Y. Nat'l | 52 Abe Attell |
| 3 Leach, Pittsburg | 28 H. McIntyre, Brooklyn | 53 Ad. Wolgast |
| 4 Bresnahan, St. Louis Nat'l | 29 McConnell, Boston Amer. | 54 Johnny Coulon |
| 5 Crawford, Detroit | 30 Mullin, Detroit | 55 James Jeffries |
| 6 Chase, New York American | 31 Magee, Philadelphia Nat'l | 56 Jack (Twin) Sullivan |
| 7 Camnitz, Pittsburg | 32 Overall, Chicago National | 57 Battling Nelson |
| 8 Clarke, Pittsburg | 33 Pfeister, Chicago National | 58 Packey McFarland |
| 9 Cobb, Detroit | 34 Rucker, Brooklyn | 59 Tommy Murphy |
| 10 Devlin, New York Nat'l | 35 Tinker, Chicago National | 60 Owen Moran |
| 11 Dahlen, Brooklyn | 36 Speaker, Boston American | 61 Johnny Marto |
| 12 Donovan, Detroit | 37 Sallee, St. Louis National | 62 Jimmie Gardner |
| 13 Doyle, New York National | 38 Stahl, Boston American | 63 Harry Lewis |
| 14 Dooin, Philadelphia Nat'l | 39 Waddell, St. Louis Amer. | 64 Wm. Papke |
| 15 Elberfeld, Washington | 40 Willis, St. Louis National | 65 Sam Langford |
| 16 Evers, Chicago National | 41 Wiltse, New York National | 66 Knock-out Brown |
| 17 Griffith, Cincinnati | 42 Young, Cleveland | 67 Stanley Ketchel |
| 18 Jennings, Detroit | 43 Out at Third | 68 Joe Jeannette |
| 19 Joss, Cleveland | 44 Trying to Catch Him Nap'g | 69 Leach Cross |
| 20 Jordan, Brooklyn | 45 Jordan and Herzog at First | 70 Phil. McGovern |
| 21 Kleinow, New York Amer. | 46 Safe at Third | 71 Battling Hurley |
| 22 Krause, Philadelphia Amer. | 47 Frank Chance at Bat | 72 Honey Mellody |
| 23 Lajoie, Cleveland | 48 Jack Murray at Bat | 73 Al Kaufman |
| 24 Mitchell, Cincinnati | 49 A Close Play at Second | 74 Willie Lewis |
| 25 M. McIntyre, Detroit | 50 Chief Myers at Bat | 75 Philadelphia Jack O'Brien |
| | | 76 Jack Johnson |

Any one of the above named pictures given in exchange for 10 Coupons taken from Turkey Red Cigarettes or 25 Coupons from either Old Mill or Fez Cigarettes. Send coupons by Mail or express, charges prepaid to

**BASE BALL AND ATHLETE PICTURE DEPT.**
DRAWER S.       JERSEY CITY, N.J.
THIS OFFER EXPIRES JUNE 30-1911.

## Primary Source

**Cy Young Baseball Card (2 OF 2)**
Back of Cy Young Baseball card, listing baseball players whose photo can be ordered in exchange for Turkey Red Cigarette coupons, 1911. THE LIBRARY OF CONGRESS.

### WEBSITES

*The Illustrated History of Baseball Cards: The 1800s.* Available online at http://www.cycleback.com/1800s/index.html; website home page: http://www.cycleback.com (accessed April 9, 2003).

---

# "Fun's Word Cross Puzzle"

Crossword puzzle

**By:** Arthur Wynne

**Date:** December 21, 1913

**Source:** Wynne, Arthur. "Fun's Word Cross Puzzle," *World* (New York), December 21, 1913. Available online at http://www.crosswordtournament.com/more/wynne.html; website home page: http://www.crosswordtournament.com (accessed April 9, 2003).

**About the Author:** Arthur Wynne, molding existing word game and puzzle styles, created the newspaper crossword

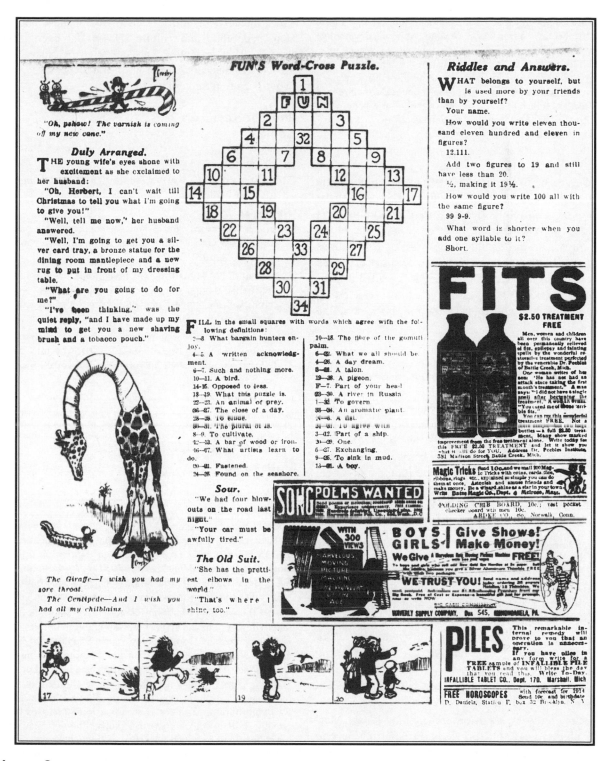

## Primary Source

### "Fun's Word Cross Puzzle"

**SYNOPSIS:** Arthur Wynne's first Word Cross featured a diamond shape and did not include any black space squares. Rather than having Across and Down directions, each clue offered numbers for the first and last letter of the word to be solved. The literacy needed to complete the puzzle varied broadly, with easy items (F-7: four-letter word starting with F meaning "Part of your head.") and more difficult terms (23-30: A river in Russia). NEW YORK WORLD SUNDAY SUPPLEMENT, DECEMBER 21, 1913.

puzzle in December 1913. As the editor of the Sunday "Fun" section in the New York *World,* Wynne's job was developing games such as "Word Cross" for the publication. Wynne immigrated to the United States from Liverpool, England. He probably relied upon a children's game published in Great Britain at the turn of the century, Magic Square, which required readers to arrange a given set of words in a pattern. Although Wynne left the *World* to fight in World War I, the paper continued to run "Word Cross." ■

## Introduction

Print media in the United States grew rapidly in the early decades of the twentieth century. To stave off the boredom of commuting to their workplaces, commuters consumed as much reading material as possible. In the 1910s, more and more publications offered word games and puzzles to an increasingly literate workforce. Games such as Arthur Wynne's Word Cross provided a measure of distraction from the daily grind, a service crosswords would continue to perform for the rest of the century.

## Significance

Published the last Sunday before Christmas in 1913, Wynne's Word Cross accompanied several pages of games, puzzles, and advertisements in the pull-out "Fun" section of the *World.* Puzzles not only distracted tired workers but also increased the connection between newspapers and readers that drove circulation. Just as newspapers offered an easily digestible summary of world events, they also offered readers entertainment. The puzzle pages did not include the tawdry sensationalism of the era's tabloids, but they appealed to a growing population of addicted word gamers who welcomed the daily challenge of a good puzzle.

The crossword boom that followed Word Cross built a publishing empire. Recent college graduates Lincoln Schuster and Richard L. Simon formed the Simon and Schuster publishing firm in 1924. Their first book was a collection of crossword puzzles from the New York *World.* By the end of the year, *The Cross-Word Puzzle Book* had sold a half-million copies and made the new publishers $100,000. Within the next decade, Simon and Schuster sold 1.5 million crossword collections.

Following Wynne's departure from the *World,* Margaret Petherbridge (Petherbridge Farrar after marriage to John Farrar in 1926) began editing the crossword section in 1920. Upon her arrival at *The New York Times* in 1942, she began developing a weekly puzzle for the Sunday magazine. The first Sunday *Times* puzzle appeared on February 15, 1942, and is reprinted here accompanied by its solution printed the following week. This newspaper's crossword selections required an extensive vocabulary, as well as knowledge of current events. Printed two months after the United States entered World War II, the

clues included several references to Japanese and German geography and culture. Down-103 even offered readers "Port on Zuider Zee, occupied by Nazis," with the correct answer: Amsterdam. The *Times* daily crossword began on September 11, 1950.

## Further Resources

### BOOKS

Augarde, Tony. *The Oxford Guide to Word Games.* New York: Oxford University Press, 1984.

Millington, Roger. *Crossword Puzzles: Their History and Their Cult.* Nashville, Tenn.: Thomas Nelson, 1974.

### WEBSITES

American Crossword Puzzle Tournament. Available online at http://www.crosswordtournament.com/more/wynne.html (accessed April 9, 2003).

Lemelson-MIT Awards Program Invention Dimension. Available online at http://web.mit.edu/invent/iow/crosswordhome .html; website home page: http://web.mit.edu/invent/ (accessed April 9, 2003).

Taub, Mel. "Farrar, Margaret Petherbridge." Available online at http://www.anb.org/articles/20/20-01547.html; website home page: http://www.anb.org/ (accessed April 9, 2003).

# *The Woman Rebel*
Newsletter

**By:** Margaret Sanger

**Date:** March 1914

**Source:** Sanger, Margaret. *The Woman Rebel,* vol. 1, no. 1. In Katz, Esther, Cathy Moran Hajo, and Peter Engelman, eds. *The Margaret Sanger Papers Electronic Edition: Margaret Sanger and "The Woman Rebel," 1914–1916.* Columbia, S.C.: Model Editions Partnership, 1999. Available online at http://adh.sc.edu/ms/ms-table.html (accessed April 9, 2003).

**About the Author:** Margaret Sanger (1883–1966), born Margaret Higgins, was the sixth of eleven children born to Irish Catholic parents in Corning, New York. She attended Claverack College and Hudson River Institute before entering the White Plains Hospital nursing program. She married architect William Sanger, with whom she had three children. In 1910, the Sangers moved to New York City. When William gave up architecture for a career as an artist, Margaret used her nursing skills to help support the family. She saw firsthand the tribulations, risk, and mortality of frequent pregnancies, miscarriages, and back-alley abortions—and was reminded of her own mother's suffering. She devoted the rest of her life to the legalization of birth control in the United States. ■

## Introduction

The 1910s saw enormous struggles for women's rights in the United States. At the beginning of the decade, women possessed full voting power in only four sparsely populated western states: Idaho, Wyoming,

Utah, and Colorado. By 1920, suffragists had successfully campaigned for the Nineteenth Amendment to the Constitution, which provided women with equal voting privileges throughout the country. As reformers campaigned for female political independence, a smaller, more radical group of women called for women's sexual liberation as well. A variety of state and federal laws prevented legal access to contraceptive devices and information. While suffragists called for the vote in order to improve the existing government structure, radical feminist Margaret Sanger's *The Woman Rebel* declared that the entire social, economic, sexual hierarchy of the American capitalist system must be overthrown—violently, if necessary.

Sanger's protests consistently brought government prosecution. She fled to Europe for thirteen months after being charged with violating postal codes by publishing the radical journal *The Woman Rebel* in 1914. Although Sanger returned to face trial, prosecutors dropped the case after the death of her five-year-old daughter, Peggy. Sanger established the first birth control clinic in the United States in 1916, for which she served a thirty-day prison sentence. She founded the American Birth Control League in 1921 and the Birth Control Clinical Research Bureau in 1923. These organizations later merged and in 1942 the new organization became Planned Parenthood of America. Following World War II, she devoted her resources to international effort and helped found the International Planned Parenthood Federation in 1952. During the last years of her life, she funded research used to develop the birth control pill.

**Significance**

The excerpts below from the first issue of *The Woman Rebel* represent the radical, militant nature of the monthly journal's advocacy for total female independence. According to "The Aim," *The Woman Rebel* strived "to stimulate working women to think for themselves and to build up a conscious fighting character." In order to increase women's power in American society, the balance of power must be altered from the boardroom to, most importantly, the bedroom. Only by demystifying sex and removing its negative, scandalous connotations could women achieve greater authority over their lives. The newsletter's desire "to advocate the prevention of conception" proved critical to its strategy of sexual and economic liberation. Through the use of contraceptive methods, sex could be separated from motherhood with the ultimate objective being complete independence. Motherhood meant dependence upon child rearing and marriage to a man. As Emma Goldman noted sarcastically in the article "Love and Marriage," "the marriage institution is our safety valve against the pernicious sex-awakening of woman." *The Woman Rebel* found mar-

Margaret Sanger, reading a magazine, January 18, 1916. Sanger was an outspoken and controversial feminist and birth control advocate.
© BETTMANN/CORBIS. REPRODUCED BY PERMISSION.

riage and motherhood to be critical components of the existing social hierarchy predicated upon unequal male-female relations. As the subtitle, "No Gods; No Masters," declared, women must be freed from all external forces—economic, sexual, religious, and emotional.

At its core, *The Woman Rebel* reflected Sanger's belief that class inequality harmed working-class and poor women to a greater extent that other groups. The publication specifically challenged the middle- and upper-class women who directed the suffrage movement and participated in the Progressive reform movement. According to *The Woman Rebel*, "The freedom which the new feminists expound can only be obtained through a greater reenslavement of the already enslaved working-women. . . ." Such class distinctions explain the journal's support of the Industrial Workers of the World (IWW), which agitated for class warfare as the only means for the working masses to gain power in the global capitalist system. In "Why Wait?" Marion Howard called for immediate action by the workers of the world.

Elizabeth Kleen defined a true woman rebel when "her social and marital arrangements are free, flexible and original; the things that are unchangeable, are her principles, her ideals." At the same time that *The Woman Rebel* urged women to defy social norms and expectations, its

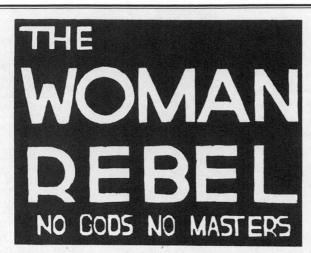

# THE WOMAN REBEL

## NO GODS NO MASTERS

VOL I.                    MARCH 1914                    NO. 1.

## THE AIM

This paper will not be the champion of any "ism."

All rebel women are invited to contribute to its columns.

The majority of papers usually adjust themselves to the ideas of their readers but the WOMAN REBEL will obstinately refuse to be adjusted.

The aim of this paper will be to stimulate working women to think for themselves and to build up a conscious fighting character.

An early feature will be a series of articles written by the editor for girls from fourteen to eighteen years of age. In this present chaos of sex atmosphere it is difficult for the girl of this uncertain age to know just what to do or really what constitutes clean living without prudishness. All this slushy talk about white slavery, the man painted and described as a hideous vulture pouncing down upon the young, pure and innocent girl, drugging her through the medium of grape juice and lemonade and then dragging her off to his foul den for other men equally as vicious to feed and fatten on her enforced slavery — surely this picture is enough to sicken and disgust every thinking woman and man, who has lived even a few years past the adolescent age. Could any more repulsive and foul conception of sex be given to adolescent girls as a preparation for life than this picture that is being perpetuated by the stupidly ignorant in the name of "sex education"?

If it were possible to get the truth from girls who work in prostitution to-day, I believe most of them would tell you that the first sex experience was with a sweetheart or through the desire for a sweetheart or something impelling within themselves, the nature of which they knew not, neither could they control. Society does not forgive this act when it is based upon the natural impulses and feelings of a young girl. It prefers the other story of the grape juice procurer which makes it easy to shift the blame from its own shoulders, to cast the stone and to evade the unpleasant facts that it alone is responsible for. It sheds sympathetic tears over white slavery, holds the often mythical procurer up as a target, while in reality it is supported by the misery it engenders.

If, as reported, there are approximately 35,000 women working as prostitutes in New York City alone, is it not sane to conclude that some force, some living, powerful, social force is at play to compel these women to work at a trade which involves police persecution, social ostracism and the constant danger of exposure to venereal diseases. From my own knowledge of adolescent girls and from sincere expressions of women working as prostitutes inspired by mutual understanding and confidence I claim that the first sexual act of these so-called wayward girls is partly given, partly desired yet reluctantly so because of the fear of the consequences together with the dread of lost respect of the man. These fears interfere with mutuality of expression —the man becomes conscious of the responsibility of the act and often refuses to see her again, sometimes leaving the town and usually denouncing her as having been with "other fel-

lows." His sole aim is to throw off responsibility. The same uncertainty in these emotions is experienced by girls in marriage in as great a proportion as in the unmarried. After the first experience the life of a girl varies. All these girls do not necessarily go into prostitution. They have had an experience which has not "ruined" them, but rather given them a larger vision of life, stronger feelings and a broader understanding of human nature. The adolescent girl does not understand herself. She is full of contradictions, whims, emotions. For her emotional nature longs for caresses, to touch, to kiss. She is often as well satisfied to hold hands or to go arm in arm with a girl as in the companionship of a boy.

It is these and kindred facts upon which the WOMAN REBEL will dwell from time to time and from which it is hoped the young girl will derive some knowledge of her nature, and conduct her life upon such knowledge.

It will also be the aim of the WOMAN REBEL to advocate the prevention of conception and to impart such knowledge in the columns of this paper.

Other subjects, including the slavery through motherhood; through things, the home, public opinion and so forth, will be dealt with.

It is also the aim of this paper to circulate among those women who work in prostitution; to voice their wrongs; to expose the police persecution which hovers over them and to give free expression to their thoughts, hopes and opinions.

And at all times the WOMAN REBEL will strenuously advocate economic emancipation.

## THE NEW FEMINISTS

That apologetic tone of the new American feminists which plainly says "Really, Madam Public Opinion, we are all quite harmless and perfectly respectable" was the keynote of the first and second mass meetings held at Cooper Union on the 17th and 20th of February last.

The ideas advanced were very old and time-worn even to the ordinary church-going woman who reads the magazines and comes in contact with current thought. The "right to work," the "right to ignore fashions," the "right to keep her own name," the "right to organize," the "right of the mother to work"; all these so-called rights fail to arouse enthusiasm because to-day they are all recognized by society and there exist neither laws nor strong opposition to any of them.

It is evident they represent a middle class woman's movement; an echo, but a very weak echo, of the English constitutional suffragists. Consideration of the working woman's freedom was ignored. The problems which affect the

## Primary Source

### The Woman Rebel

**SYNOPSIS:** "The Aim," an article by Margaret Sanger on page 1 of *The Woman Rebel,* March 1914, shows the controversial nature of the newsletter's content, given the federal Comstock law, passed in 1873, that forbade the distribution of contraceptive information. On April 2, 1914, the U.S. Postmaster wrote Sanger informing her that the publication was unmailable under the provisions of the criminal code. Two future editions would also be banned and Sanger was arrested. Her escape to Europe, year-long exile, and return to the United States cemented her standing as the nation's leading advocate of birth control. *THE WOMAN REBEL,* VOLUME 1, MARCH 1914, #1. MARGARET SANGER PAPERS. SOPHIA SMITH COLLECTION, SMITH COLLEGE. REPRODUCED BY PERMISSION.

writers asserted that woman's ideals and values must be inculcated from within. In other words, "Let her be herself and live for her ideal and her convictions not for the approval or the applause of fashionable feminism. If she does it, however, for some secondary reason, from vanity or worldly ambition, she may become a beggar in more sense than one."

## Further Resources

### BOOKS

Chesler, Ellen. *A Woman of Valor: Margaret Sanger and the Birth Control Movement in America.* New York: Simon and Schuster, 1992.

Gordon, Linda. *Woman's Body, Woman's Right: A Social History of Birth Control in America.* New York: Grossman, 1976.

Katz, Esther, ed. *The Selected Papers of Margaret Sanger,* Vol. 1: *The "Woman Rebel" 1900–1928.* Urbana, Ill.: University of Illinois Press, 2002.

Sanger, Margaret. *Margaret Sanger: An Autobiography.* New York: W.W. Norton, 1938.

———. *My Fight for Birth Control.* New York: Farrar & Rinehart, 1931.

### PERIODICALS

"Margaret Sanger" (obituary). *The New York Times,* September 7, 1966.

### WEBSITES

Katz, Esther. "Sanger, Margaret." Available online at http://www.anb.org/articles/15/15-00598.html; website home page: http://www.anb.org (accessed April 9, 2003).

*Margaret Sanger Papers Project.* Available online at http://www.nyu.edu/projects/sanger/ (accessed April 9, 2003).

# The First Pulitzer Prizes

## "The Anniversary"

**Editorial**

**By:** *New York Tribune*
**Date:** May 7, 1916
**Source:** "The Anniversary." *New York Tribune,* May 7, 1916.

## "Germany Keen for Peace, but Expects and is Ready to Battle for Years"

Newspaper article

**By:** Herbert Bayard Swope
**Date:** 1917
**Source:** Swope, Herbert Bayard. "Germany Keen for Peace, but Expects and Is Ready to Battle for Years," *New York*

*World,* November 4, 1916. Reprinted in Swope, Herbert Bayard. *Inside the German Empire: 1916.* New York: Century, 1917. ■

## Introduction

The Pulitzer Prize originated with Joseph Pulitzer (1847–1911) who was born in Hungary and is perhaps the most influential journalist in American history. His brand of newspaper publishing, dubbed "yellow journalism," first gained appeal during his ownership of *St. Louis Post-Dispatch* and later the *New York World.* His style offered readers titillating accounts of trials, trysts, and tragedy, but its foundation rested in investigative reporting and sharp editorials that advocated social, political, and economic reform. Before his death, Pulitzer arranged for a $2 million contribution to Columbia University for the formation of a graduate school of journalism and the establishment of the Pulitzer Prizes. First awarded in 1917, the prizes soon became the most prestigious awards in journalism, letters, drama, and, later, music, poetry, and photography.

The events surrounding the sinking of the *Lusitania* and the U.S. entry into World War I, led to the first Pulitzer Prize awards. The assassination of the heir to the throne of the Austro-Hungarian Empire in 1914 drove the major European powers into war. Russia, Great Britain, and France allied with one another against the Central Powers of Germany, Austria-Hungary, and the Ottoman Empire. Although the United States officially remained neutral, Americans aided the Allies economically and militarily with transatlantic shipments primarily to Britain. In response, Germany declared unrestricted warfare on all vessels traveling into Allied waters. German submarines patrolling Atlantic sea routes from the United States to Great Britain threatened to fire upon any vessel taking this course. In May 1915, the German navy fired upon and sank the British passenger liner *Lusitania,* killing 124 Americans and 1,198 total civilians. Although the Wilson administration denounced this and other attacks, the United States remained neutral.

## Significance

In 1916, the United States still had not entered World War I. The *New York Tribune* marked the first anniversary of the *Lusitania* sinking with an editorial that would win the first Pulitzer Prize in Journalism for editorial writing. In stirring, visceral language, "The Anniversary" excoriated those who opposed U.S. entrance into the conflict. It portrayed the Great War in almost exactly the same terms as other prowar publications and President Wilson in his eventual call to Congress for a declaration of war on April 2, 1917. The editorial characterized the sinking of the *Lusitania* as

An illustration of the *Lusitania* sinking. The British passenger liner was torpedoed by German submarines and sank on May 7, 1915, killing over 1,000, including 124 Americans. © BETTMANN/CORBIS. REPRODUCED BY PERMISSION.

part of a "war between civilization and barbarism, between humanity and savagery." Enraged by the "wanton murder" of this "supreme atrocity," the *Tribune* called for intervention as the only method of protecting the nation, preserving its honor, and saving all of mankind. The newspaper accompanied this edition with a special section devoted to the *Lusitania.* These pages included several pictures of the Americans who died in the attack, particularly children, as well as the drawing reproduced here that captures the essence of the editorial's argument.

Herbert Bayard Swope's *Inside the German Empire* series won the first Pulitzer Prize for reporting. Appearing in the *New York World* for three consecutive weeks in November 1916, these articles provided a fascinating glimpse into the nation depicted so maliciously in the *Tribune* editorial. The hundreds of interviews quoted in these articles conveyed the massive sweep of Swope's investigation. In fact, the reporter wrote so many articles as part of this series that he later published them as a book-length collection. From the lead sentence of the first article on, readers gained a sense of the complexities involved in the war from a German perspective: "The desire for peace is strong in Germany, but from top to bottom there is no belief that it is near."

## Primary Source

"The Anniversary" [excerpt]

**SYNOPSIS:** The first Pulitzer Prize for editorial writing was awarded to this bitter denunciation of Germany in the *New York Tribune* and call for Americans to join World War I (1914–18). The editorial's occasion was the first anniversary of the sinking of the *Lusitania,* a British passenger liner, by German submarines, an attack that killed over a hundred Americans and more than a thousand people total.

On the anniversary of the sinking of the Lusitania it is natural and fitting that Americans should review all that has happened since wanton murder first brought to this side of the Atlantic a nascent realization of the issue that was being decided on a world battlefield.

There will be no anger and no passion in American minds. We have never asked, never desired, that the slaughter should be avenged. No portion of the American people or the American press has clamored for vengeance, no man or political party has demanded that there should be German lives taken because American lives had been ended.

It is not too difficult to reconstitute our own minds as we stood in the presence of that supreme atrocity. The horror that seized a whole nation in that moment has no counterpart in our history. We have known war, we have fought Great Britain twice, we have fought Spain and Mexico: within our own boundaries we have conducted the most desperate civil war in human history.

But it was not the emotion provoked by war or the acts of war which moved Americans. It was not even the emotion stirred by the sinking of the Maine nearly two decades ago. It was certainly something utterly remote from the feelings of our fathers and grandfathers on the morrow of the firing on Fort Sumter.

The Lusitania Massacre was not an act of war. The victims were not soldiers, only a portion of them were men. Essentially the thing was a new phenomenon to the American people. It was at first incomprehensible, unbelievable. Despite the solid and inescapable evidences of death, men's intelligence doubted what their senses told them.

So for days and weeks the American people stood doubtful and puzzled. They waited for that evidence they expected, they believed would come, that there had been an accident, a mistake, the blunder of a subordinate which would be repudiated by a government, the crime of a navy which would be disavowed by a people. But instead far borne across the seas they heard the songs of triumph of thousands of German men and women, who hailed the crime as a victory, the eternal disgrace as an everlasting honor.

Day by day, week by week, we Americans have since then been learning what Europe has known for nearly two years. We have been learning that we are not in the presence of a war between nations, a conflict between rival powers: that we are not the agonized witnesses of one more conflagration provoked by conflicting ambitions of hereditary enemies. We have been learning that what is going forward remorselessly, steadily, is a war between civilization and barbarism, between humanity and savagery, between the light of modern times and the darkness of the years that followed the collapse of Rome

Time and again Americans have been murdered, time and again our government, our people, have had recourse to the ordinary machinery and the ordinary conceptions of civilized life. But each time we have beheld the utter collapse of every appeal based upon reason, justice, and common humanity. The Germans who slew our women and our children flung us back the challenge that they and not we possessed the true civilization, and that their civilization, their Kultur was expressed in their works, which were altogether good and right.

Slowly, steadily we have been learning. We still have much to learn, but the primary truth is coming home to many day by day. This German phenomenon which fills the world is a new thing and an old thing; it is new in our generation, it is new in recent centuries; but it is as old as that other barbarism which, descending upon the Roman civilization, beat upon it and spread destruction until it was conquered and tamed amidst the ruins and the desert it had created

The French who see things as they are have beheld and appraised the German phenomenon justly. The British, like ourselves, have partially and temporarily failed to understand the nature of the German assault; we have insisted upon applying to the German mind our own standards and upon believing that the Germans thought as we thought, believed as we believed, but were temporarily and terribly betrayed by a military spirit and by dynastic madness.

Nothing is less true, nothing more fatal to a just appreciation of the essential fact in the world in which we live. These things which we name crimes are neither accidents nor excesses; they are not regretted or condemned by a majority or even a minority of the German people. They are accepted by Kaiser and present: they are practiced by Crown Prince and private soldiers; they are a portion of what Germany holds to be her right and her mission.

The Lusitania Massacre should have been a final illumination for us. Blazing up as it did, it should have revealed to us the ashes of Belgium and the ruins of Northern France. We should have seen in our slain women and children the sisters and fellows in misfortune of those who died more shamefully in Louvain and a score more of Belgian cities. We should have seen the German idea working here as there and revealing in each incident the same handiwork, the same detail. All those things were similar as the different impressions left by a single stamp.

We did not see. We have not yet as a nation, or as a people, perceived that the German phenomenon is an attack upon civilization by barbarism. A barbarism which combines the science of the laboratory with the savagery of the jungle, but a

Newspaper tycoon Joseph Pulitzer. He established the endowment for the Pulitzer Prize in 1911. HULTON/ARCHIVE. REPRODUCED BY PERMISSION.

barbarism because it denies those doctrines and principles which have been accepted after long years as the proof of human progress and the glory of mankind's advance.

In France the people will show you the atrocities of Germany committed not upon human beings, but upon inanimate things, the destruction of the village church and the Rheims Cathedral, of the little thing of beauty quite as well as the larger and more famous thing with far more emphasis then they will recount the horrors suffered by women and children. In the assault upon things beautiful because they are beautiful, an assault provoked neither by lust nor by passion, they recognize the revelation of that which is essential barbarism.

For us the Lusitania Massacre was a beginning. It was only a beginning, but it was not possible then, it is hardly possible now, for men and women, living in peace under the protection of laws framed to protect human liberty and human rights living in the full sunlight of this Twentieth Century, to believe that suddenly there has broken out from the depths the frightful and all-destroying spirit of eras long forgotten.

We have been learning—we must continue to learn. The road of suffering and humiliation is still long. But the Lusitania was a landmark and it will endure in American history. Our children and our children's children recalling this anniversary will think of it as did the Romans over long generations, after the first inroads of the barbarians had reached their walls.

Today is not a day for anger or passion. It is not in anger or in passion that civilized men go forth to deal with wild animals, to abolish the peril which comes from the jungle or out of the darkness. We do not hate Germans and we shall not hate Germans because on this day a year ago, American men, women and children were slain, willfully, wantonly, to serve a German end, slain without regard to sex or condition, slain in the broad daylight by German naval officers and men whose countrymen hailed the killing as the supreme evidence of German courage, manhood, Kultur.

But as we view the thing without passion we must see it without illusion. If the German idea prevails all that we believe in government, in humanity in the thing we call civilization is doomed. If Germany succeeds in this war then it is not again time, as Pitt said after Austerlitz, "to roll up the map of Europe," but it is time to burn our ancient parchments and dismiss our hard won faith. All that there is in the German ideas was expressed in the Lusitania Massacre, it was expressed in the killing of women and children, innocent of all offense, entitled to all protection as helpless, unoffending as the children of a race not at war, at least entitled to immunity which hitherto was reckoned the right of women and children, neutral or belligerent.

The war that is being fought in Europe is a war for civilization. The battle of Great Britain, of France, of Russia, is our battle. If it is lost we are lost. If it is lost we shall return to the standards and the faiths of other centuries. The truth of this is written for us in the Lusitania, it is written in the wreck of Belgium and desert of Northern France for those who may see. Where the German has gone he has carried physical death, but he has done more, he has carried spiritual death to all that is essential in our own democratic faith, which derives from that of Britain and France.

This war in Europe is going on until the German idea is crushed or conquers. The world cannot now exist half civilized and half German. Only one of two conceptions of life, of humanity, can subsist. One of the conceptions was written in the Lusitania Massacre, written clear beyond all mistaking. It is this writing that we should study on this anniversary; it is this fact that we should grasp today, not in anger, not in any spirit that clamors for vengeance, but as the citizens of a nation which has inherited noble ideals and gallant traditions, which has inherited liberty and light from those who died to serve them and now stand face to face with that which seeks to extinguish both throughout the world.

## Primary Source

"Germany Keen for Peace, but Expects and Is Ready to Battle on for Years" [excerpt]

> **SYNOPSIS:** This is the first in a series of *New York World* articles called *Inside the German Empire*. The series gave Americans a detailed first-hand description of conditions inside of wartime Germany and the state of mind of its people. It won the first ever Pulitzer Prize for reporting.

*What of Germany to-day? How does she stand? How are her sons maintaining her far-flung battle line? Are her people despairing? When do they see the end? Do they starve? What of her allies? What is her attitude toward America—her hopes of peace, her fears of defeat, her plans for the future?*

*These are a few of the questions The World's special correspondent, Herbert Bayard Swope, sought to answer in the trip he has just made to Germany, where unusual opportunities for observation were afforded him. A trained reporter, he saw matters objectively, and the information he gained forms a valuable contribution to the history of the last phases of the war.*

*Not that the end is near—no one but a prophet could make such a pronouncement; but it is evident that Germany and the central powers have now settled down, in plan and preparation, to the final lines that will lead them to victory, compromise or defeat.*

*They have reached the ultimate in their resources and the utilization thereof, and, come what may, their mental, spiritual and physical attitudes will not differ much when the end is reached from what they are now. That is why it is proper to say that Germany is to-day in her last phase. She has done almost all that can be done, and now she waits for the successive moves of those aligned against her.*

*Because the Kaiser's realm is becoming more and more difficult for foreigners to enter, because of the rigidity of the censorship has become increasingly great, because the allies have interrupted* *mail and cable communications, Germany and the truth about the Germans become less and less known to the world.*

*That is why The World, since the beginning of the war, has made it a practice to send members of its staff to the empire to set down their freshly gathered facts and impressions with atmosphere, color and detail—apart from the work of Karl H. von Wiegand, who is regularly stationed in Berlin for The World, and with whose communications, sent by wireless and cable, readers of The World are familiar.*

*Mr. Swope, the writer of the series The World is about to publish, was in Germany for several months at the outbreak of the war. He revisited the country after two years. One of the valuable results of his journey was the striking despatch he wirelessed from the Frederik VIII., on which he and Ambassador Gerard returned on Tuesday, Oct. 10, in which he brought home to America in direct, concrete form, and for the first time, the grave menace existing in the imminent possibility of Germany's resumption of a ruthless, Lusitania type of U boat warfare.*

*Now The World is about to print a carefully written series of reports in which, without bias or prejudgment, the author treats of all phases of Germany's condition to-day. . . .*

The desire for peace is strong in Germany, but from top to bottom there is no belief that it is near. German hopes and expectations of the end are indefinite as to time—the most optimistic can see no real prospects within another two years, and from that period the conjectures run up to ten years. And in their economic and military planning the Kaiser's subjects are preparing to enact their motto of "durchalten" (stick it out) for years to come.

As a striking illustration of how far away is the idea of any peace that Germany herself does not make, I can submit this news of secret diplomacy, which may meet denial, but which is unqualifiedly true: Within the last eighteen months no fewer than eleven separate interrogatories have been submitted to the German Government as to Belgium. The question has been asked, by the United States, Spain, Denmark, Holland, Sweden, Switzerland, Norway and other neutrals, if Germany will give a formal assurance of the restoration of Belgian entity at the end of the war—and *not once has this assurance been given*, nor has the Kaiser's Government, in its most affable moments, permitted even inferentially the idea to gain ground that it regarded Belgium's re-establishment, according to the status quo ante as an essential.

## Further Resources

**BOOKS**

Boylan, James, ed., *The World and the 20's: The Golden Years of New York's Legendary Newspaper.* New York: Dial, 1973.

Kennedy, David. *Over Here: The First World War and American Society.* New York: Oxford University Press, 1980.

Sloan, W. David, ed. *Pulitzer Prize Editorials: America's Best Editorial Writing, 1917–1979.* Ames, Iowa: Iowa State University Press, 1980.

**WEBSITES**

Pfaff, Daniel W. "Pulitzer, Joseph." Available online at http://www.anb.org/articles/16/16-01333.html; website home page: http://www.anb.org/ (accessed April 10, 2003).

"The Pulitzer Prizes." Available online at http://www.pulitzer.org/index.html (accessed April 10, 2003).

# "Warning: The Deadly Parallel"

Poster

**By:** Industrial Workers of the World

**Date:** 1916

**Source:** Industrial Workers of the World. "Warning: The Deadly Parallel." Special Collections AZ 114, box 1, folder 1, exhibit 2. Available online at http://digital.library.arizona.edu/bisbee/main/iww.php; website home page: http://digital.library.arizona.edu (accessed April 10, 2003).

**About the Organization:** The Industrial Workers of the World (IWW) formed in 1905 in opposition to the American Federation of Labor. Throughout its tumultuous history, the IWW agitated for a worldwide revolution against capitalism. The group's rallying cry called for the creation of "One Big Union," incorporating the working classes from every corner of the globe. The IWW believed that an international worker coalition could institute a strike and overthrow the existing class hierarchy. The organization argued that workers should control the product of their labor, rather than higher profits going to middle- and upper-class businessmen. Government prosecution during World War I decimated the IWW, and the group never again reached its prewar membership levels of over 100,000. ■

## Introduction

Few expected the assassination of the heir to the throne of the Austro-Hungarian Empire to engulf Europe in war. Yet this attack in 1914 fostered the rapid degeneration of peaceful relations between what came to be known as the Central Powers (Germany, Austria-Hungary, and the Ottoman Empire) and the Allies (primarily Great Britain, France, and Russia). Struggling to avoid sending U.S. troops to the ghastly trench warfare that consumed millions of Europeans between 1914 and 1916, President Woodrow Wilson gained reelection in 1916 on the platform of maintaining the country's neutral status toward the conflict. When Wilson began to alter his stance in early 1917, activists heightened their campaigns against the war. The president's call for a declaration of war on April 2, 1917, enraged millions of Americans opposed to joining the conflict.

## Significance

From the moment war erupted in Europe in 1914, the IWW argued that the United States must avoid the clash. "The Deadly Parallel" provided viewers with the group's central interpretation of the war and its ongoing opposition to the more moderate American Federation of Labor. Given the figures displayed and the content of the argument, this poster almost certainly appeared in March 1917, just weeks before the Wilson administration brought the nation into the Great War. The IWW framed the war as part of a global competition between the capitalist elite for greater territorial control and profits. From this perspective, the conflict's victims on both sides were common laborers thrust into the trenches without hope of survival. The IWW's view that class similarities outweighed national distinctions characterized the core of radical antiwar dissent during the 1910s.

The political cartoon displayed here from *The Masses* echoed this attitude. The original drawing encompassed the entire back page of the journal's July 1916 edition. The artist, Robert Minor, provided no attributes that could distinguish the "Army Medical Examiner" by nationality. The drawing's grotesque, headless brute of a soldier conveyed the antiwar critique of war's ultimate dehumanization. The perfect soldier was mindless and removed of all individuality. In the context of the horrifying trench warfare that caused hundreds of thousands of deaths in a matter of days, this soldier simply provided yet another corpse to be thrown into the heap.

Both the IWW and *The Masses* suffered greatly because of their antiwar publications. The federal government prosecuted both organizations for violating the Espionage and Sedition Acts of 1917 and 1918. These laws prohibited Americans from questioning the war effort and resulted in the arrests of more than 1,500 radicals nationwide. Federal officials arrested more than one hundred members of the IWW, sentencing many to stiff prison terms. William Haywood, the union's leader, received the maximum twenty-year sentence and a fine of $30,000. After the war, membership dwindled rapidly and the group survived as merely a shell of its former strength. By the end of 1917, postal officials and the Wilson administration's Committee on Public Information

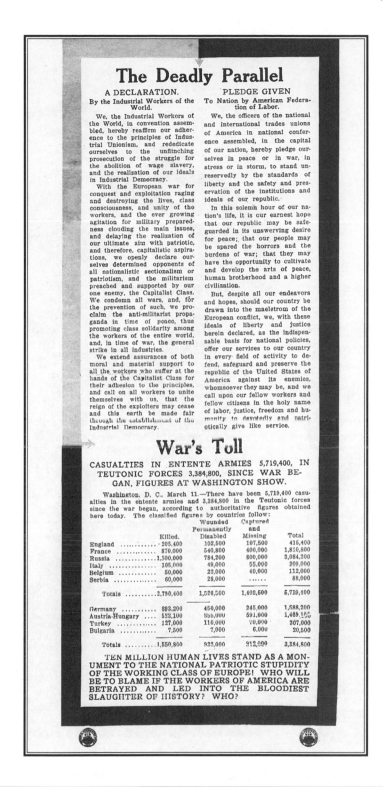

## Primary Source

### "Warning: The Deadly Parallel"

**SYNOPSIS:** This poster appeared just as the United States prepared to finally enter World War I. Although President Wilson's call to arms came within a matter of days, the American press continued to debate the war's merits in much the same way as depicted in the poster. Radicals called for massive action to hinder the war effort. Moderate groups, such as the AFL, appeared to oppose joining the conflict but ultimately supported America as a force for "justice, freedom and humanity. . . ." The antiwar and anticapitalist dissent expressed here and through other media brought great consequences to leftist groups once the U.S. committed to the war. SPECIAL COLLECTIONS, UNIVERSITY OF ARIZONA LIBRARY, BISBEE DEPORTATION LEGAL PAPERS AND EXHIBITS, 1919, AZ114, BOX 1, FOLDER 1. REPRODUCED BY PERMISSION.

Army Medical Examiner: ⁊"At last a perfect soldier!"

A cartoon by Robert Minor from the back cover of *The Masses* magazine, July 1916. It implies that the militaries fighting World War I do not care about their soldiers as human beings, only as brute, and expendable, fighting machines. **COURTESY OF THE NEW YORK PUBLIC LIBRARY.**

succeeded in banning *The Masses,* which began in 1911. Though the journal ceased publication with the December 1917 issue, its editors created *The Liberator* in March 1918 and managed to sustain the publication until October 1924.

## Further Resources

### BOOKS

Buhle, Mari Jo, Paul Buhle, and Dan Georgakas. "International Workers of the World" and "*The Masses.*" *Encyclopedia of the American Left.* New York: Oxford University Press, 1998.

Kennedy, David. *Over Here: The First World War and American Society.* New York: Oxford University Press, 1980.

Peterson, H.C., and Gilbert Fite. *Opponents of War, 1917–1918.* Seattle: University of Washington Press, 1968.

Vaughn, Stephen. *Holding Fast the Inner Lines: Democracy, Nationalism, and the Committee on Public Information.* Chapel Hill, N.C.: University of North Carolina Press, 1980.

### WEBSITES

"History of the International Workers of the World." Available online at http://www.spartacus.schoolnet.co.uk/USAiww.htm; website home page: http://www.spartacus.schoolnet.co.uk (accessed April 10, 2003).

"History of 'The Masses.'" Available online at http://www.spartacus.schoolnet.co.uk/ARTmasses.htm; website home page: http:///www.spartacus.schoolnet.co.uk (accessed April 10, 2003).

## Letters to the Chicago *Defender*

Letters

**By:** Chicago *Defender*

**Date:** 1916–1918

**Source:** Chicago *Defender.* "Letters of Negro Migrants of 1916–1918." *Journal of Negro History* 4, no. 3, 1919, 291, 293. "Additional Letters of Negro Migrants of 1916–1918." *Journal of Negro History* 4, no. 4, 1919, 412–413, 418, 420, 442–443, 457–460. Available online at http://azimuth .harcourtcollege.com/history/ayers/chapter22/22.3.migrants .html; website home page: http://www.azimuth.harcourtcollege .com (accessed April 9, 2003).

**About the Publication:** The Chicago *Defender,* founded by Robert S. Abbott in 1905, was a conduit for African American social change through much of its history. By World War I, the weekly paper was the most widely read source of information for African Americans in all regions of the country. It actively promoted the Great Migration of African Americans away from the South during the 1910s and 1920s, playing a pivotal role in the movement of well over one and a half million people. Author Langston Hughes and others contributed to the publication and aided its calls for

economic and political justice. Becoming a daily paper in 1956, the *Defender* continues to advocate progress for African Americans. ■

## Introduction

As the nation entered the Great War in Europe in April 1917, nearly six million American men, primarily of European descent, left their jobs and enlisted in the armed services. The transfer of a significant portion of the country's industrial workforce, combined with the war's reduction in the flow of immigrants from Europe, created an enormous demand for labor. Employment opportunities opened primarily in northern cities such as Detroit, Pittsburgh, Cleveland, Chicago, and New York. The main beneficiaries of these job openings proved to be African Americans, who left the prejudice and bigotry of the South to the seemingly endless opportunities of life in the North and West.

More than half a million African Americans moved from the South during the 1910s, most during the war years (1917–1919). Newspapers published for African-American audiences provided critical means of communication for employers advertising jobs in attempts to convince southern blacks to move north. At the same time, nationally syndicated papers such as the Chicago *Defender* published letters penned by southerners eager for work and transplantation from the South.

## Significance

The letters excerpted below provide a glimpse of how Americans from across the country communicated with one another via the press to, in effect, create the Great Migration. They also reveal the crucial role played by the African American press in facilitating the migration from the South. Each of these letters originated in the former Confederacy, in Cotton Belt states such as Mississippi, Alabama, South Carolina, Arkansas, and Louisiana. The texts offer passionate pleas for work and extensive descriptions of job experience. One writer from Texas described the horrors of southern living, imploring anyone reading to offer immediate assistance: "Our southern white people are so cruel we collord people are almost afraid to walke the streets after night. So please let me hear from you by return mail."

One person who had recently moved to Chicago conveyed the jubilance of receiving a daily wage. "We get $1.50 a day and we pack so many sausages we don't have much time to play but it is a matter of a dollar with me and I feel that God made the path and I am walking therein." The author noted that "work is plentiful here" and offered assistance in finding work and housing to any friend in need. As this writer noted in a postscript, the *Defender* had become so popular that it printed "extras two and three times a day."

The dates of these letters are also important. Nearly all came after the passage of the Selective Service Act of April 1917, during a period of massive instability in the nation's economy as millions of workers learned that they must leave their jobs immediately and report for military duty. Signed shortly after President Woodrow Wilson's declaration of war in April 1917, Selective Service created the first national draft. More than three million Americans would be drafted during the war. News of job openings spread quickly and resulted in the flood of entreaties represented below.

While the Great Migration provided opportunities for hundreds of thousands of African Americans, the move did not end their hardships. The concluding letter from Pittsburgh in May 1917 exemplifies the distress encountered by many. While the writer appreciated the money he earned, he lamented the changes experienced in living in such a dramatically different place. "I like the money O.K. but I like the South betterm for my Pleasure this city is too fast for me they gie you big money for what you do but they charge you big things for what you get and people are coming by cal Loads every day its just pack out the people are Begging for some whears to sta." The transfer of so many people so quickly created an entirely new set of problems concerning work, home, and family life. The return of three million soldiers from the war would further heighten tensions in the urban North in 1919. Competition over housing, employment, and access to public facilities would spark major riots in nearly two dozen cities.

## Primary Source

Letters to the Chicago *Defender* [excerpts]

> **SYNOPSIS:** Serving as a networking catalyst for African Americans migrating from the South, the *Defender* received countless letters such as those reprinted below. This correspondence depicts the goals and fears of people attempting to reshape their lives in the midst of war abroad and dramatic change at home. Far from presenting a picture of ease in the North, these letters convey the complex realities faced by those who uprooted themselves, moved across the country, and reshaped urban America.

Dallas, Tex., April 23, 1917

Dear Sir:

Having been informed through the Chicago Defender paper that I can secure information from you. I am a constant reader of the Defender and am contemplating on leaving here for some point north. Having your city in view I thought to inquire of you about conditions for work, housing, wages and everything necessary. I am now employed as a laborer in a structural shop, have worked for the firm five years.

I stored ears for Armour packing co. 3 years, I also claims to know something about candy making, am handy at most anything for an honest living. I am 31 yrs. Old have a very industrious wife, no children. If chances are available for work of any kind let me know. Any information you can give me will be highly appreciated.

Mobile, Ala., April 27, 1917

Sir:

Your advertisement appearing in the Chicago Defender have influenced me to write to you with no delay. For seven previous years I bore the reputation of a first class laundress in Selma. I have much experience with all of the machines in this laundry. This laundry is noted for its skillful work of neatness and ect. We do sample work for different laundries of neighboring cities, viz. Montgomery, Birmingham, and Mobile once or twice a year. At present I do house work but would like to get in touch with the Chicago . . . . I have an eager desire of a clear information how to get a good position. I have written recommendation from the foreman of which I largely depend upon as a relief. You will do me a noble favor with an answer in the earliest possible moment with a description all about the work.

Marcel, Miss., 10/4/17

Dear Sir:

Although I am a stranger to you but I am a man of the so called colored race and can give you the very best or reference as to my character and ability by prominent citizens of my community by both white and colored people that knows me although am native of Mississippi. Now I am a reader of your paper the Chicago Defender. After reading your writing ever week I am compell[ed] & persuade to say that I know you are a real man of my color you have I know heard of the south land & I need not tell you any thing about it. I am going to ask you a favor and at the same time beg you for your kind and best advice. I wants to come to Chicago to live. I am a manof a family wife and I child can do just any work in the line of common labor & I have for the present sufficient means to support us till I can obtain a position. Now should I come to your town, would you please to assist me in getting a position I am willing to pay whatever you charge I don't want you to loan me not 1 cent but help me to find an occupation there in your town now I has a present position that will keep me employed till the first of Dec. 1917. now please give me your best advice on this subject. I enclose stamp for reply.

Jacksonville, Fla., April 4, 1917

Dear Sir:

I have been taking defender for sevel months and I have seen that there is lots of good work in that section and I want to say as you are the editor of that paper I wish that you would let me know if there is any wheare up there that I can get in with an intucion that I may get my wife and my silf from down hear and can bring just as miney more as he want we are suffing to hear all the work is giveing to poor white peples and we can not get anything doe at all I will go to pennsylvania or n y state or N J or Ill. Or any wheare that I can surport my wife I am past master of son of light in Mass. Large Royal arch and is in good standing all so the good Sancer large no.18. I need helpe my wife cant get any thing to due eather can I so please If you can see any body up there that want hands let me no at once I can get all they need and it will allow me to get my wife away from down hear so please remember and ans I will appreciate it.

Looking for ans at once. Please let me no some thing thease crackers is birds in south.

Alexandria, La., June 6, 1917

Dear Sirs:

I am writing to you all asking a favor of you all. I am a girl of seventeen. School has just closed I have been going to school for nine months and now I feel like I aught to go to work. And I would like very well for you all to please forward me to a good job. But there isn't a thing here for me to do, the wages here is from a dollar and a half a week. What could I earn Nothing. I have a mother and father my father do all he can for me but it is so hard. A child with any respect about her self or his self wouldn't like to see there mother and father work so hard and earn nothing I feel it my duty to help. I would like for you all to get me a good job and as I haven't any money to come in please send me a pass and I would work and pay every cent of it back and get me a good quite place to stay. My father have been getting the defender for three or four months but for the last two weeks we have failed to get it. I don't

know why. I am tired of down hear in this . . . I am afraid to say. Father seem to care and then again don't seem to but Mother and I am tired of all of this. I wrote to you all because I believe you will help I need your help hopeing to here from you all very soon.

Sumter, S.C., May 12, 1917

Dear Sir:

Courd you get me a job in the . . . Tin Plate Factory at . . . , Pa. A job for (3) three also a pass from here for (3) I am a common laborer and the other are the same. If you could we will be ever so much ablige and will comply with your advertisement. If you can't get a job where we wish to go we will thank you for a good job any where in the state of Pa. or Ohio. I am in my 50 the others are my sons just in the bloom of life and I would wish that you could find a place where we can make a living and I also wish that you could find a place where we all three can be together. If you will send us a pass we will come just as soon as I receive it. If you find a place that you can send us please let us hear what the job will pay. Nothing more. I am yours respectfully.

Troy, Al., 3/24/17

Dear Sir:

I received you of Feb. 17 and was very delighted to hear from you in regards of the matter in which I writen you about. I am very anxious to get to Chicago and realy believe that if I was there I would very soon be working on the position in which I writen you about. Now you can just imagine how it is with the colored man in the south. I am more than anxious to go to Chicago but have not got the necessary fund in which to pay my way and these southern white peoples are not paying a man enough for his work down here to save up enough money to leave here with. Now I am asking you for a helping hand in which to assist me in getting to Chicago. I know you can do so if you only will.

Hoping to hear from you at an early date and looking for a helping hand and also any information you choose to inform me of, I remain as ever yours truly.

Palestine, Tex., 1/2/17

Dear Sir:

I hereby enclose you a few lines to find out some few things if you will be so kind to word them to me. I am a southerner lad and has never ben in the north no further than Texas and I has heard so much talk about the north and how much better the colard people are treated up there than they are down here and I has ben strieving so hard in my coming up and now I see that I cannot get up there without the ade of some one and I wants to ask you Dear Sir to please direct me in your best manner the stept that I shall take to get there and if there are any way that you can help me to get there and if there are any way that you can help me to get there I am kindly asking you for your ade. And if you will ade me please notify me by return mail because I am sure ancious to make it in the north because these southern white people are so mean and they seems to be getting worse and I wants to get away and they won't pay enough for work for a man to save up enough to get away and live to. If you will not ade me in getting up there please give me some information how I can get there I would like to get there in early spring, if I can get there if posible. Our southern white people are so cruel we collord people are almost afraid to walke the streets after night. So please let me hear from you by return mail. I will not say very much in this letter I will tell you more about it when I hear from you please ans. Soon to Yours truly

Chicago, Illinois

My dear Sister:

I was agreeably surprised to hear from you and to hear from home. I am well and thankful to say I am doing well. The weather and everything else was a surprise to me when I came. I got here in time to attend one of the greatest revivals in the history of my life over 500 people joined the church. We had a Holy Ghost shower. You know I like to have run wild. It was snowing some nights and if you didn't hurry you could not get standing room. Please remember me kindly to any who ask of me. The people are rushing here by the thousands and I know if you come and rent a big house you can get all the roomers you want. You write me exactly when you are coming. I am not keeping house yet I am living with my brother and his wife. My sone is in California but will be home soon. He spends his winter in California. I can get a nice place for you to stop until you can look around and see what you want. I am quite busy. I work in Swifts packing co. in the sausage department. My daughter and I work for the same company-We get $1.50 a day and we pack so many sausages we don't have much time to play but it is a matter of a dollar with me and I feel that God made the path and I am walking therein.

Tell your husband work is plentiful here and he won't have to loaf if he want work. I know unless old man A—— changed it was awful with his sould and G—— also.

Well I am always glad to hear from my friends and if I can do anything to assist any of them to better their condition. Please remember me to Mr. C———and his family I will write them all as soon as I can. Well, I guess I have said about enough. I will be delighted to look into your face once more in my life. Pray for me for I am heaven bound. I have made too many rounds to slip now. I know you will pray for prayer is the life of any sensible man or woman. Well goodbye from your sister in Christ.

P.S. My brother moved the week after I came. When you fully decide to come write me and let me know what day you expect to leave and over what road and if I don't meet you I will have some ther to meet you and look after you. I will send you a paper as soon as one come along they send out extras two and three times a day.

Pittsburg, Pa., May 11, 1917

My dear Pastor and wife:

It affords me great pleasure to write you this leave me well & O.K. I hope you & sis Hayes are well & no you think I have forgotten you all but I never will how is ever body & how is the church getting along well I am in this great city & you no it cool here right now the trees are just peeping out. fruit trees are now in full bloom but its cool yet we set by big fire over night. I like the money O.K. but I like the South betterm for my Pleasure this city is too fast for me they give you big money for what you do but they charge you big things for what you get and the people are coming by cal Loads every day its just pack out the people are Begging for some whears to sta. If you have a family or children & come here you can buy a house easier than you can rent one if you rent one you have to sign up for 6 months or 12 month so you see if you don't like it you have to stay you no they pass that law because the People move about so much I am at a real nice place and stay right in the house of a Rve.—— and family his wife is a state worker I mean a missionary she is some class own a plenty rel estate & personal Property they has a 4 story home on the mountain, Piano in the parlor, organ in the sewing room, 1 daughter and 2 sons but you no I have to pay $2.00 per week just to sleep and pay it in advance.

## Further Resources

### BOOKS

American Social History Project. *Who Built America? Working People and the Nation's Economy, Politics, Culture, and Society.* Volume 2: *Since 1877.* New York: Worth Publishers, 2000.

Grossman, James R. *Land of Hope: Chicago, Black Southerners, and the Great Migration.* Chicago: University of Chicago, 1989.

Tuttle, William M., Jr. *Race Riot: Chicago in the Red Summer of 1919.* New York: Atheneum, 1970.

### WEBSITES

*Newspapers: The Chicago "Defender."* Available online at http://www.pbs.org/blackpress/news_bios/defender.html; website home page: http://www.pbs.org (accessed April 9, 2003).

# "For Freedom and Democracy"

Editorial

**By:** *North American Review*

**Date:** March 30, 1917

**Source:** "For Freedom and Democracy." *North American Review,* March 30, 1917, 482–488. Available online at http://historymatters.gmu.edu/d/4939 (accessed April 10, 2003).

**About the Publication:** The *North American Review* is one of the oldest published journals in American history. First published in 1815 in Boston, it ran continuously until 1940, evolving from a focus on literature to a stronger concentration on current events from a distinctly American perspective. Following a lengthy hiatus, the publication restarted in Iowa in 1964 and has been published continuously since. ∎

## Introduction

With the assassination of the heir to the throne of the Austro-Hungarian Empire in 1914, Europe soon became engulfed in the Great War. Russia, Great Britain, and France were the allies, opposed by the Central Powers of Germany, Austria-Hungary, and the Ottoman Empire (modern-day Turkey). Although President Woodrow Wilson campaigned successfully to keep the United States out of the war through the end of 1916, his views toward the conflict shifted significantly. The sinking of the British passenger liner *Lusitania* in May 1915 and discovery of the Zimmerman Telegram in January 1917 dramatically increased domestic opposition to the Central Powers. The German submarine attack on the *Lusitania* resulted in the deaths of 1,198 civilians, including 124 Americans. The telegram, intercepted by British intelligence officers who delivered it to the Wilson administration, revealed a possible alliance between

"MISGUIDED LADY" PUTTING UP POSTER.

This cartoon shows a thinly disguised German soldier putting up isolationist posters in America. The implication is that isolationists are helping Germany to win World War I. © CORBIS. REPRODUCED BY PERMISSION.

Germany and Mexico. The message called for Mexico to aid Germany by invading the United States from the south.

## Significance

"For Freedom and Democracy" represented the core argument offered by public officials and the press who favored U.S. military intervention in the Great War. Foreshadowing the language of Wilson's call for a congressional declaration of war the next week, this article characterized America as the force behind freedom and democracy throughout the world. The title echoed the ideals of the Constitution and the Declaration of Independence, as well as previous arguments behind the use of force abroad. The idea of "manifest destiny," coined by editor John O'Sullivan in the context of westward expansion before the Civil War, justified national growth as a divine duty thrust upon the American people. Manifest destiny called on a solemn obligation that must be met by all citizens to aid in the development of liberty and civilization throughout the world. This idyllic

A 1918 poster encouraging the purchase of war bonds, by Henry Patrick Raleigh. During World War I, the Germans were commonly portrayed as barbarians bent on destroying democratic civilization, like the ancient Huns did to the Roman Empire. © CORBIS. REPRODUCED BY PERMISSION.

portrait of American foreign policy objectives justified participation in the Mexican and Spanish-American Wars in the nineteenth century.

This editorial in the *North American Review* relied upon a similar characterization of American purpose. From this perspective, World War I "is the last of the great battles for Freedom and Democracy," and the United States must naturally participate in a struggle similar to the one "America fought . . . a century and forty years ago." This nation must go to war not to gain greater wealth and territory "but eager and fearless in support of free life and full liberty the world over. . . ." This idea of the United States' unique position as the world's defender of freedom and democracy would remain the cornerstone of foreign policy for the rest of the twentieth century.

## Primary Source

"For Freedom and Democracy"

**SYNOPSIS:** Less than a week after this editorial's publication, on April 2, 1917, President Wilson called for Congress to declare war against Germany

and the Central Powers. The president's argument reflected many of the justifications offered by the review's editors and other prowar journals. Wilson asserted that the German submarine attacks on noncombatant vessels represented "warfare against all mankind." This conclusion relied upon the idea expressed by the *Review* that the war represented a contest between civilization and barbarism. Almost exactly as stated in "For Freedom and Democracy," he concluded that the United States must enter the war to "make the world safe for democracy."

Just as Thomas Jefferson experienced difficulty in compressing a multitude of complaints against a German king of Britain into a modest "Declaration of Independence," so will President Wilson, when the time comes, find himself overwhelmed by a sense of the grievances which this country has endured at the will of the madman of Prussia. We shall await with grimmest zest his recital of treaties broken, of wrongs to be done, of lies told, of treacheries bared, of insults borne, of murders committed, of all the most shameful shocking, mean and low practices against civilization, humanity and common decency recorded even in the history of barbarism, in the face of forbearance for the sake of peace unprecedented in the chronicles of governing Powers. . . .

The issue is in doubt no longer. We know now, if we have not known before, what this war is. It is the last of the great battles for Freedom and Democracy. America fought the first a century and forty years ago. France followed through seas of blood and tears. But lately the Great Charter has passed in its entirety from the barons to the people of England. Japan has ceased to be a monarchy except in name. China as a Republic defies the power of might. Portugal, freed by a bloodless revolution stands with the Allies. Personal government has disappeared forever from every part of the Western hemisphere. And now Russia, autocracy of autocracies, casts off the yoke and takes her place in the sun of civilization. Can anyone doubt that the beginning of the end of absolutism is at hand; that the thrones of Hapsburgs and Mahomeds are crumbling; that the whole clan Hohenzollern, no less of Greece and Bulgaria than of Prussia, is doomed beyond recall; that liberty for the patient German people is as certain as freedom for downtrodden Hungary, for despoiled Serbia and for bleeding Armenia?

So mighty a change cannot be wrought in a month or likely in a year—and not at all unless and until the rulers of Central Europe shall yield to a world of freemen. Wholly aside, then, from the injuries and insults which America had endured at the hands of the War Lord and which she is expected to advance as technical grounds for action, does not America's higher duty, her greater opportunity, lie along the path of the shot heard 'round the world? Are we to permit others to finish the glorious work which we began, according to even the infidel Allen, in the name of Almighty God? Shall we renounce our own professed ideals so completely that, at the end of the war, we may not deny as a matter of fitness and right, the transshipment of Liberty Enlightening the World from the harbor of New York to that of Hong Kong or Vladivostock? Must even China be allowed to forge ahead of America in defense of democracy?

We are for war; of course, we are; and for reasons good and plenty, to wit:

1. Because we have reached and passed the limit of forbearance in trying to maintain amicable relations with a barbaric brute who has presumed so far upon our good intent as to treat our most conciliatory and helpful suggestions with glaring contempt, who has incited all manner of treasonable activities and damnable outrages within our borders, has gloated over his avowed assassination of our innocent and harmless citizens of both sexes and all ages upon the high seas and has missed no opportunity to deceive, to sneer at and to lie to our constituted authorities; because to conserve our own self-respect we are driven finally to the point where we must fight or forfeit the decent opinion of all mankind; because we cannot even seem to condone the breaking of treaties, the burning of villages to no purpose except to deprive the poor and helpless of shelter essential to mere existence, the enslavement of men who alone could save their families from destitution and death from starvation, the violating of women and young girls, the bayoneting of little children, the approved indiscriminate slaughter by the unspeakable Turks of thousands of helpless Christians in Armenia, and God only knows what else and what more that has stamped the Hun for more than one generation to come as the sublimated hero of the shambles of humanity; because, in a word, we cannot acknowledge the supremacy of might and frightfulness over right and righteousness without denying our faith in the living God.

2. Because we owe it to our forefathers who founded the Republic and to our fathers who saved the Union to prove ourselves not merely worthy of the happiness which flows from prosperity but eager and fearless in support of free life and full liberty the world over, to the end that the noble example set by them may not be degraded in gluttonous realization by us; because as a practical matter if spies and traitors infest our land now is the time to smoke them out; if a few scattering undersea waifs can break down our defenses and damage our cities, let them do their utmost that we may discover what might be anticipated from a fleet and prepare accordingly; if our navy is lopsided and deficient, our provision for a defensive army unfulfilled and unrealizable, our stores of ammunition insufficient, our air-machines and submarines but samples, today when only negligible harm can come to us is the day to acquaint ourselves with the facts; and if, as we are told, so many of us are pro-this or pro-that and so many more are putting self above patriotism and so many more should be feeding off our own fat instead of mulcting lean Chautauquans, then what we need is a test—a test of body, of mind and of spirit— a trying-out by fire while yet there is time to make America fit for any real emergency; yes, and able, through universal service; because simply and finally, in such a case, war is curative, not destructive, a blessing not a curse.

3. Because our going into the great conflict at this psychological moment would not only complete the ring of democracies around the doomed autocracy and so render the ultimate result certain to the dullest and the blindest, but also from that very fact would infect all Germany, all Austria and all Hungary without the new spirit of Russia, and so by surely shortening and perhaps quickly ending the war would save millions of precious finer perceptions as a being altogether worthy of our worshipful lives, certain else to be sacrificed to no purpose other than impoverishment of the human race for centuries to come.

## Further Resources

### BOOKS

Kennedy, David. *Over Here: The First World War and American Society.* New York: Oxford University Press, 1980.

Stephanson, Anders. *Manifest Destiny: American Expansionism and the Empire of Right.* New York: Hill and Wang, 1995.

### WEBSITES

*North American Review.* Available online at http://webdelsol .com/NorthAmReview/NAR/narneed.htm; website home page: http://www.webdelsol.com (accessed April 10, 2003).

# *Sedition Act, 1918*
Law

**By:** Woodrow Wilson

**Date:** May 16, 1918

**Source:** Wilson, Woodrow. *Sedition Act, 1918. United States Statutes at Large,* vol. 40, April 1917–March 1919. Washington, D.C.: U.S. Government Printing Office, 1919, 553–554. Available online at http://azimuth.harcourtcollege.com/history/ayers/chapter22/22.2.sedition.html; website home page: http://www.azimuth.harcourtcollege.com (accessed April 9, 2003).

**About the Author:** Woodrow Wilson (1856–1924), the twenty-eighth president of the United States and former president of Princeton University, was drafted as head of the Democratic ticket in 1912 and won against a split Republican Party with just over 40 percent of the vote. Progressive legislation at home, the Great War abroad, and the Versailles peace treaty shaped Wilson's presidency. Wilson won the Nobel Peace Prize in 1919. ∎

## Committee on Public Information

In order to strengthen popular support of the war, the Wilson administration created the Committee on Public Information (CPI), headed by journalist George Creel. The CPI began operations within ten days of U.S. entry into the war and eventually published some 75 million pamphlets defending the government's actions before the Armistice of 1918. The CPI organized the first daily government bulletin, sponsored tens of thousands of public addresses, and deluged the American public with arguments for American involvement in the war. This propaganda machine was unprecedented and laid the foundation for carefully orchestrated government public relations campaigns that soon became a staple of American politics.

## Introduction

President Woodrow Wilson campaigned for reelection in 1916 on the slogan "He Kept Us Out of the War"— that is, he had successfully prevented America's entrance into World War I (1914–18). His certitude about the war, though, had begun to waver with the sinking of the British passenger ship *Lusitania* in May 1915 and discovery of the infamous Zimmerman Telegram in January 1917. The German submarine attack on the *Lusitania* resulted in the deaths of 124 Americans (1,198 total deaths). The telegram, intercepted by British intelligence officers, revealed a possible plot between Germany and Mexico to invade the United States from the south.

Less than five months after winning reelection, Wilson altered his position on the conflict and called for Congress to declare war on the Central Powers (Germany, Austria-Hungary, and the Ottoman Empire) in April 1917. The president argued that the German submarine attacks on noncombatant vessels represented "warfare against all mankind." Facing such a threat, and in spite of his own opposition to women's suffrage at home, Wilson concluded that the United States must enter the war to "make the world safe for democracy." One month after U.S. entry, the Wilson administration passed the Selective Service Act in May 1917 and faced enormous public protest. For millions of antiwar activists, the president's change of heart struck them as duplicitous. Moreover, the draft instituted with Selective Service created an outpouring of antiwar sentiment.

The Wilson administration crafted the Espionage Act of June 1917 to quell popular dissent. The Espionage Act broadly defined treasonous activity. Prohibited actions included hindering military recruitment and disclosing secret defense information to the enemy. As the war continued into 1918, with just under one thousand people arrested under the Espionage Act, Congress passed the Sedition Act, of May 1918.

## Significance

The Sedition Act forbade published material that called for an end to the war. The language of the act, though, provided an expansive view of what specific acts could be prevented by the government. The law was geared not only at silencing critical media; its language seemed to suppress all antiwar protest. Moreover, the language also prohibited any protests against the government that might hinder the war effort, even if the protests did not explicitly concern the war.

With penalties up to a fine of $10,000 and twenty years imprisonment, the law forbade anyone who "shall willfully utter, print, write or publish any disloyal, profane, scurrilous, or abusive language about the form of government of the United States or the Constitution of the United States, . . . or shall willfully utter, print, write, or publish any language intended to incite, provoke, or encourage resistance to the United States, . . . or shall willfully by utterance, writing, printing, publication, or language spoken, urge, incite, or advocate any curtailment of production in this country. . . ." Thus, the act expanded the provisions of the Espionage Act to target directly rights many believed to be protected by the First Amendment to the Constitution. According to the wording of this measure, sedition encompassed any speech or writing that criticized the government. Attorney General A. Mitchell Palmer used the Sedition and Espionage Acts to arrest 1,500 radicals and left-wing protesters, as well as deport more than two hundred suspected Communists to the Soviet Union.

These laws spurred the creation of the American Civil Liberties Union, and the Supreme Court would decide the constitutionality of both within two years of their passage. In *Schenck v. U.S.* (1919) and *Abrams v. U.S.* (1919), the Supreme Court ruled that the acts provided constitutional methods of preserving national security during times of war. Just as "free speech would not protect a man in falsely shouting fire in a theatre and causing a panic," Justice Oliver Wendell Holmes ruled in *Schenck,* Congress possesses the right to prevent "words . . . of such a nature as to create a clear and present danger" that "substantive evils" will be committed.

By the time he dissented in *Abrams,* though, Holmes had changed his mind concerning civil liberties during times of war. Then, he argued that "the principle of the right to free speech is always the same," regardless of whether the speech comes during war or peace. While the majority of the Court ruled that the Sedition Act legally prevented speech that threatened security during wartime, Holmes' ringing declaration against the law remains one of the strongest endorsements of the freedom of speech ever offered by a Supreme Court Justice.

Debate over the basic issues covered in the Sedition Act continued long after the end of World War I. The question of whether antigovernment protest should be prohibited during war sparked massive divisions in the coming years, especially during the Vietnam War.

AS GAG-RULERS WOULD HAVE IT.
—Satterfield in the Jersey City *Journal.*

Anti-sedition legislation cartoon by Robert W. Satterfield, 1920. **LITERARY DIGEST, FEBRUARY 7, 1920. COURTESY OF THE NEW YORK PUBLIC LIBRARY.**

## Primary Source

*Sedition Act, 1918*

**SYNOPSIS:** When Congress passed the Sedition Act, in May 1918, the United States had been involved in World War I for just over one year. Hundreds of thousands of antiwar demonstrators had argued vehemently against American participation in the conflict. During the Russian Revolution of 1917, Communists seized power there in part on an antiwar platform, and the Wilson administration feared similar revolts at home. The war would soon end with the armistice agreement of November 11, 1918. But the core arguments raised by the law remain. Should the U.S. government forbid antiwar protests? What forms of protest should be prohibited to protect national security?

Sec. 3. Whoever, when the United States is at war, shall willfully make or convey false reports or false statements with intent to interfere with the operation or success of the military or naval forces of the United States, or to promote the success of its enemies, or shall willfully make or convey false reports or false statements, or say or do anything except by way of bona fide and not disloyal advice to an investor or investors, with intent to obstruct the sale by the United States of bonds or other securities of the United States or the making of loans by or to the United States, and whoever when the United States is at war, shall willfully cause or attempt to cause, or incite or attempt to incite, insubordination, disloyalty, mutiny, or refusal of duty, in the military or naval forces of the United States, or shall willfully obstruct or attempt to obstruct the recruiting or enlistment services of the United States, and whoever, when the United States is at war, shall willfully utter, print, write or publish any disloyal, profane, scurrilous, or abusive language about the form of government of the United States or the Constitution of the United States, or the military or naval forces of the United States, or the flag of the United States, or the uniform of the Army or Navy of the United States into contempt, scorn, contumely, or disrepute, or shall willfully utter, print, write, or publish any language intended to incite, provoke, or encourage resistance to the United States, or to promote the cause of its enemies, or shall willfully display the flag of any foreign enemy, or shall willfully by utterance, writing, printing, publication, or

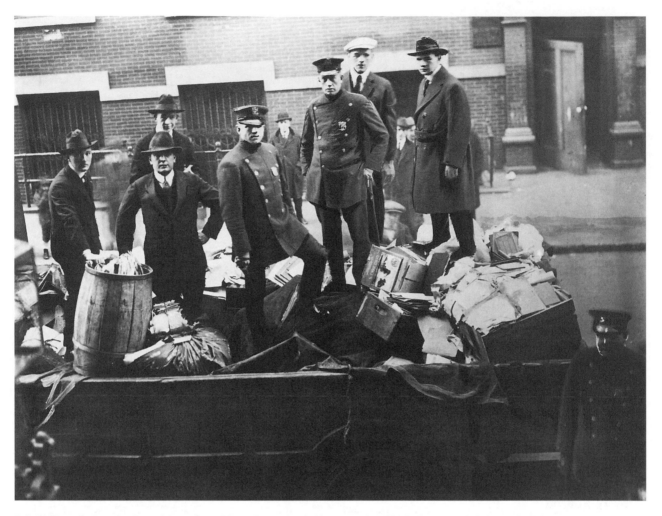

Police officers display printed materials confiscated from Communists in November 1919. The Sedition Act of 1918 gave the federal government the power to seize any publications considered to be critical of the government. © HULTON-DEUTSCH COLLECTION/CORBIS. REPRODUCED BY PERMISSION.

language spoken, urge, incite, or advocate any curtailment of production in this country of any thing or things, product or products, necessary or essential to the prosecution of the war in which the United States may be engaged, with intent by such curtailment to cripple or hinder the United States in the prosecution of war, and whoever shall willfully advocate, teach, defend, or suggest the doing of any of the acts or things in this section enumerated, and whoever shall by word or act support or favor the cause of any country with which the United States is at war or by word or act oppose the cause of the United States therein, shall be punished by a fine of not more than $10,000 or the imprisonment for not more than twenty years, or both: Provided, That any employee or official of the United States Government who commits any disloyal act or utters any unpatriotic or disloyal language, or who, in an abusive and violent manner criticizes the Army or Navy or the flag of the United States shall be at once dismissed from the service. . . .

Sec. 4. When the United States is at war, the Postmaster General may, upon evidence satisfactory to him that any person or concern is using the mails in violation of any of the provisions of this Act, instruct the postmaster at any post office at which mail is received addressed to such person or concern to return to the postmaster at the office at which they were originally mailed all letters or other matter so addressed, with the words 'Mail to this address undeliverable under Espionage Act' plainly written or stamped upon the outside thereof, and all such letters or other matter so returned to such postmasters shall be by them returned to the senders thereof under such regulations as the Postmaster General may prescribe.

Approved, May 16, 1918.

## Further Resources

**BOOKS**

Clements, Kendrick A. *The Presidency of Woodrow Wilson.* Lawrence, Kan.: University Press of Kansas, 1992.

Creel, George. *How We Advertised America.* New York: Harper, 1920.

Irons, Peter. *A People's History of the Supreme Court.* New York: Penguin Books, 2000.

Kennedy, David. *Over Here: The First World War and American Society.* New York: Oxford University Press, 1980.

Tulis, Jeffrey. *The Rhetorical Presidency.* Princeton, N.J.: Princeton University Press, 1987.

Vaughn, Stephen. *Holding Fast the Inner Lines: Democracy, Nationalism, and the Committee on Public Information.* Chapel Hill: University of North Carolina Press, 1980.

**WEBSITES**

Ambrosius Lloyd E. "Wilson, Woodrow." Available online at http://www.anb.org/articles/06/06-00726.html; website home page: http://www.anb.org (accessed April 9, 2003).

# Chicago Race Riots

## "A Crowd of Howling Negroes"

Newspaper article

**By:** *Chicago Tribune*
**Date:** July 28, 1919
**Source:** "A Crowd of Howling Negroes." *Chicago Daily Tribune,* July 28, 1919. Available online at http://historymatters.gmu.edu/d/4975 (accessed April 9, 2003).
**About the Publicaton:** The *Chicago Daily Tribune* began publication in 1847 and established itself by the turn of the century as the Midwest's most influential daily newspaper. At the time of the Chicago race riots in July 1919, cousins Robert R. McCormick and Joseph Medill Patterson were the paper's copublishers. McCormick's influence proved critical to the paper's opposition to liberalism. In June 1919, Patterson started the nation's first tabloid-style paper, the *New York Illustrated Daily News,* which reached a circulation of over one million by the mid-1920s.

## "Ghastly Deeds of Race Rioters Told"

Newspaper article

**By:** Chicago *Defender*
**Date:** August 2, 1919
**Source:** "Ghastly Deeds of Race Rioters Told," Chicago *Defender,* August 2, 1919. Available online at http://historymatters.gmu.edu/d/4975 (accessed April 9, 2003).
**About the Publication:** The Chicago *Defender,* founded by Robert S. Abbott in 1905, was a conduit for African Ameri-

can social change. By World War I, the weekly paper stood as the most widely read source of information for blacks in all regions of the country. It actively promoted the Great Migration of African Americans away from the South during the 1910s and 1920s. Becoming a daily paper in 1956, the *Defender* continues to advocate progress for African Americans. ∎

## Introduction

Competition between white and black Americans for jobs and housing contributed to the rash of riots that occurred in the summer of 1919. Across the country, about two dozen violent clashes erupted as Americans of all races struggled to structure their lives after the end of the Great War. With millions of soldiers returning from Europe, and hundreds of thousands of African Americans migrating north, citizens fought for dwindling employment options. On July 27, 1919, the Chicago riot erupted after a white threw a rock and killed a black youth who was swimming near a segregated, whites-only beach by Lake Michigan. Blacks and whites fought one another for several days after the initial attack, causing the deaths of thirty-eight (twenty-three black and fifteen white) and injuring more than five hundred.

## Significance

Far from calming the situation, both the *Tribune* and the *Defender* likely kindled greater animosity and suspicion with their sensational coverage. The *Tribune*'s reporting of the first day of the riot probably sparked further violence. The story began by describing the deaths of two blacks and injuries of whites and blacks totaling fifty. But the article's language shifted greatly in tone, depending upon the race of the group discussed. Time after time, the article described groups of blacks as "mobs." The paper noted that policeman John O'Brien "was attacked by a mob . . . after he tried to rescue a fellow cop from a crowd of bawling Negroes." In response to several shots apparently fired in his direction, the officer returned into the "mob" and "[t]hree colored men dropped." The report included vivid descriptions of how "Negroes who were found in street cars were dragged to the street and beaten." The paper acknowledged the violent attacks against blacks but framed these outbursts as attempts "to avenge the beatings their brethren had received." For the *Tribune,* "blacks added to the racial feeling by carrying guns and brandishing knives." Overall, the *Tribune*'s coverage implied the existence of an unruly mob of blacks far outnumbering whites and threatening to cause even greater damage.

In its August 2 article, the *Defender* perceived "racial antagonism" as the cause of the conflict. The paper offered horrifying descriptions of the violence that rivaled, and perhaps exceeded, the *Tribune*'s reporting in drama and sensationalism. According to the *Defender,* the riot

One of the many homes damaged during race riots in Chicago, July 31, 1919. © BETTMANN/CORBIS. REPRODUCED BY PERMISSION.

became an "orgy of hate," "a carnival of death," with people "infected by the insanity of the mob." Possibly the most lurid, and unsubstantiated, report described how a "young woman and a 3 month old baby were found dead on the street." According to the reporter, a mob of whites had apparently "seized her, beat her, slashed her body into ribbons and beat the Baby's brains out against a telegraphic pole." The journalist provided no source for this scene, leaving the contemporary reader with one more reason to join the fray. This report also described the African American rioters as a "mob" seeking to exact revenge upon white Chicagoans. The article's closing scene even featured the reporter switching to first person and relating his own involvement in a police standoff.

## Primary Source

### "A Crowd of Howling Negroes"

**SYNOPSIS:** This Chicago *Tribune* article describes the race riots that broke out in Chicago on July 27, 1919. The story, carried in a conservative paper intended for a white audience, mirrors the polarization of the city, providing dramatic reports of the brutality without care for objectivity. It also shows how newspaper journalists in the age before television attempted to express the sights, sounds, and emotions they encountered.

### Report Two Killed, Fifty Hurt, in Race Riots

Bathing Beach Fight Spreads to Black Belt

### All Police Reserves Called to Guard South Side

Two colored men are reported to have been killed and approximately fifty whites and negroes injured, a number probably fatally, in race riots that broke out at south side beaches yesterday. The rioting spread through the black belt and by midnight had thrown the entire south side into a state of turmoil.

Among the known wounded are four policemen of the Cottage Grove avenue station, two from west side stations, one fireman of engine company No. 9, and three women.

One Negro was knocked off a raft at the Twenty-ninth street beach after he had been stones by whites. He drowned because whites are said to have frustrated attempts of colored bathers to rescue him. The body was recovered, but could not be identified.

A colored rioter is said to have died from wounds inflicted by Policeman John O' Brien, who fired into a mob at Twenty-ninth street and Cottage Grove avenue. The body, it is said, was spirited away by a colored man.

## Drag Negroes from Cars

So serious was the trouble throughout the district that Acting Chief of Police Alcock was unable to place an estimate on the injured. Scores received cuts and bruises from flying stones and rocks, but went to their homes for medical attention.

Minor rioting continued through the night all over the south side. Negroes who were found in street cars were dragged to the street and beaten.

They were first ordered to the street by white men and if they refused the trolley was jerked off the wires.

Scores of conflicts between the whites and blacks were reported at south side stations and reserves were ordered to stand guard on all important street corners. Some of the fighting took place four miles from the scene of the afternoon riots.

When the Cottage Grove avenue station received a report that several had drowned in the lake during the beach outbreak, Capt. Joseph Mullen assigned policemen to drag the lake with grappling hooks. The body of a colored man was recovered, but was not identified.

## Boats Scour Lake

Rumors that a white boy was a lake victim could not be verified. The patrol boats scoured the lake in the vicinity of Twenty-ninth street for several hours in a vain search.

John O' Brien, a policeman attached to the Cottage Grove avenue station, was attacked by a mob at Twenty-ninth and State streets after he had tried to rescue a fellow cop from a crowd of bawling Negroes. Several shots were fired in his direction and he was wounded in the left arm. He pulled his revolver and fired four times into the gathering. Three colored men dropped.

## Man Cop Shot Dies

When the police attempted to haul the wounded into the wagon the Negroes made valiant attempts to prevent them. Two were taken to the Michael Reese hospital but the third was spirited away by the mob. It was later learned that he died in a drug store a short distance from the shooting.

Fire apparatus from a south side house answered an alarm of fire which was turned in from a drug store at Thirty-fifth and State streets. It was said that more than fifty whites had sought refuge here and that a number of Negroes had attempted to "smoke them out." There was no semblance of

a fire when the autos succeeded in rushing through the populated streets. . . .

## Shot at His Window

Charles Cromier was sitting in his window at 2839 Cottage Grove avenue watching the clashing mobs. A stray bullet lodged in his head and he fell back into the room. Spectators saw him being helped to a chair by a woman.

Racial feeling, which had been on a par with the weather during the day took fire shortly after 5 o'clock when white bathers at the Twenty-ninth street improvised beach saw a colored boy on a raft paddling into what they termed "white" territory.

A snarl of protest went up from the whites and soon a volley of rocks and stones were sent in his direction. One rock, said to have been thrown by George Stauber of 2904 Cottage Grove avenue, struck the lad and he toppled into the water.

## Cop Refuses to Interfere

Colored men who were present attempted to go to his rescue, but they were kept back by the whites, it is said. Colored men and women, it is alleged, asked Policeman Dan Callahan of the Cottage Grove station to arrest Stauber, but he is said to have refused.

Then, indignant at the conduct of the policeman, the Negroes set upon Stauber and commenced to pummel him. The whites came to his rescue and then the battle royal was on. Fists flew and rocks were hurled. Bathers from the colored Twenty-fifth street beach were attracted to the scene of the battling and aided their comrades in driving the whites into the water.

## Negroes Chase Policeman

Then they turned on Policeman Callahan and drove him down Twenty-ninth street. He ran into a drug store at Twenty-ninth street and Cottage Grove avenue and phoned the Cottage Grove avenue police station.

Two wagon loads of cops rolled to the scene, and in a scuffle that ensued here Policeman John O' Brien and three blacks were shot.

Riot calls were sent to the Cottage Grove avenue station and more reserves were sent into the black belt. By this time the battling had spread along Cottage Grove avenue and outbreaks were conspicuous at nearly every corner.

Meanwhile the fighting continued along the lake. Miss Mame McDonald and her sister, Frances, had been bathing with a friend, Lieut. Runkie, a convalescing soldier. A colored woman walked up to the trio and made insulting remarks, it is said.

Runkie attempted to interfere, but the colored woman voiced a series of oaths and promptly struck the soldier in the face. Negroes in the vicinity hurled stones and rocks at the women and both were slightly injured.

### Reserves Called Out

In less than a half hour after the beach outbreak, Cottage Grove avenue and State street from Twenty-ninth south to Thirty-fifth were bubbling caldrons of action.

When the situation had gotten beyond the control of the Cottage Grove police, Acting Chief of Police Alcock was notified. He immediately sent out a call to every station in the city to rush all available men to the black belt.

Before they arrived colored and white men were mobbed in turn. The blacks added to the racial feeling by carrying guns and brandishing knives. It was not until the reserves arrived that the rioting was quelled.

### Whites Arm Selves

News of the afternoon doings had spread through all parts of the south side by nightfall, and whites stood at all prominent corners ready to avenge the beatings their brethren had received. Along Halsted and State streets they were armed with clubs, and every Negro who appeared was pommeled.

Lewis Phillips, colored, was riding in a Thirty-ninth street car, when a white man took a pot shot from the corner as the car neared Halsted street. Phillips was wounded in the groin and was taken to the provident hospital. Melvin Davies, colored, of 2816 Cottage Grove avenue, was waiting for a Thirty fifth street car at Parnell avenue when he was slugged from behind. His assailant disappeared.

### Primary Source

"Ghastly Deeds of Race Rioters Told"

**SYNOPSIS:** This article describes Chicago in the grip of its fourth straight day of race rioting. Written for the *Defender,* a primarily African-American paper, it takes the side of African Americans in the conflict, much as the Chicago *Tribune* does for whites.

For fully four days this old city has been rocked in a quake of racial antagonism, seared in a blaze of red hate flaming as fiercely as the heat of day—each hour ushering in new stories of slaying, looting, arson, rapine, sending the awful roll of casualties to a grand total of 40 dead and more than 500 wounded, many of them perhaps fatally. A certain madness distinctly indicated in reports of shootings, stabbings and burning of buildings which literally pour in every minute. Women and children have not been spared. Traffic has been stopped. Phone wires have been cut.

### Stores and Offices Shut

Victims lay in every street and vacant lot. Hospitals are filled: 4,000 troops rest in arms, among which are companies of the old Eighth regiment, while the inadequate force of police battles vainly to save the city's honor.

### Fear to Care for Bodies

Undertakers on the South Side refused to accept bodies of white victims. White undertakers refuse to accept black victims. Both for the same reason. They feared the vengeance of the mobs without.

Every little while bodies were found in some street, alley or vacant lot—and no one sought to care for them. Patrols were unable to accommodate them because they were being used in rushing live victims to hospitals. Some victims were dragged to a mob's "No Man's Land" and dropped.

The telephone wires in the raging districts were cut in many places by the rioters as it became difficult to estimate the number of dead victims.

### Hospitals Filled with Maimed

Provident hospital, 36th and Dearborn streets, situated in the heart of the "black belt," as well as other hospitals in the surrounding districts, are filled with the maimed and dying. Every hour, every minute, every second finds patrols backed up and unloading the human freight branded with the red symbol of this orgy of hate. Many victims have reached the hospitals, only to die before kind hands could attend to them. So pressing has the situation become that schools, drug stores and private houses are being used. Trucks, drays and hearses are being used for ambulances.

### Monday Sees "Reign of Terror"

Following the Sunday affray, the red tongues had blabbed their fill, and Monday morning found the

Mounted police escort an African American man to safety during race riots in Chicago, July 31, 1919. © BETTMANN/CORBIS. REPRODUCED BY PERMISSION.

thoroughfares in the white neighborhoods throated with a sea of humans—everywhere—some armed with guns, bricks, clubs and an oath. The presence of a black face in their vicinity was a signal for a carnival of death, and before any aid could reach the poor, unfortunate one his body reposed in some kindly gutter, his brains spilled over a dirty pavement. Some of the victims were chased, caught and dragged into alleys and lots, where they were left for dead. In all parts of the city, white mobs dragged from surface cars, black passengers wholly ignorant of any trouble, and set upon them. An unidentified man, young woman and a 3 month old baby were found dead on the street at the intersection of 47th street and Wentworth avenue. She had attempted to board a car there when the mob seized her, beat her, slashed her body into ribbons and beat the Baby's brains out against a telegraph pole. Not sat-

isfied with this, one rioter severed her breasts and a white youngster bore it aloft on pole, triumphantly, while the crowd hooted gleefully. All the time this was happening, several policemen were in the crowd, but did not make any attempt to make rescue until too late.

### Kill Scores Coming from Yards

Rioters operating in the vicinity of the stock yards, which lies in the heart of white residences west of Halsted street, attacked scores of workers—women and men alike returning form work. Stories of these outrages began to fluster into the black vicinities and hysterical men harangued their fellow to avenge the killings—and soon they, infected with the insanity of the mob, rushed through the streets, drove high powered motor cars or waited for street cars which they attacked with gunfire and stones.

Shortly after noon all traffic south of 22nd street and north of 55th street, west of Cottage Grove avenue and east of Wentworth avenue, was stopped with the exception of trolley cars. Whites who entered this zone were set upon with unmeasurable fury.

Policemen employed in the disturbed sections were wholly unable to handle the situation. When one did attempt to carry out his duty he was beaten and his gun taken from him. The fury of the mob could not be abated. Mounted police were employed, but to no avail.

**35th Vortex of Night's Rioting**

With the approach of darkness the rioting gave prospects of being continued throughout the night. Whites boarded the platforms and shot through the windows of the trains at passengers. Some of the passengers alighting themselves from cars were thrown from the elevated structure, suffering broken legs, fractured skulls, and death.

The block between State street and Wabash avenue on East 35th street was the scene of probably the most shooting and rioting of the evening and a pitched battle ensued between the police, whites and blacks.

The trouble climaxed when white occupants of the Angelus apartments began firing shots and throwing missiles from their windows. One man was shot through the head, but before his name could be secured he was spirited away. The attack developed a hysterical battling fervor and the mob charged the building and the battle was on.

Police were shot. Whites were seen to tumble out of automobiles, from doorways, and other places, wounded or suffering from bruises inflicted by gunshots, stones or bricks. A reign of terror literally ensued. Automobiles were stopped, occupants beaten and machines wrecked. Street cars operating in 35th street were wrecked as well as north and south bound State street cars. Windows were shattered and white occupants beaten.

Trolley cars operating east and west on 35th street were stopped, since they always left the vicinity in a perforated state. Shortly after 8 o'clock all service was discontinued on 43rd, 47th, and 51st streets.

**Stores Looted: Homes Burned**

Tiring of street fights rioters turned to burning and looting. This was truly a sleepless night and a resume on the day's happenings nourished an in-clination for renewed hostilities from another angle. The homes of blacks isolated in white neighborhoods were burned to the ground and the owners and occupants beaten and thrown unconscious in the smoldering embers. Meanwhile rioters in the "black belt" smashed windows and looted shops of white merchants on State street.

Other rioters, manning high powered cars and armed, flitted up and down the darkened streets, chancing shots at fleeting whites on the street and those riding in street cars.

Toward midnight quiet reigned along State street under the vigilance of 400 policemen and scores of uniformed men of the 8th Regiment.

**Rioting Extends Into Loop**

Tuesday dawned sorrowing with a death toll of 20 dead and 300 injured. In early morning a 13-year-old lad standing on his porch at 51st and Wabash avenue was shot to death by a white man who, in an attempt to get away, encountered a mob and his existence became history. A mounted policeman, unknown, fatally wounded a small boy in the 48th block on Dearborn street and was shot to death by some unknown rioter.

Workers thronging the loop district to their work were set upon by mobs of sailors and marines roving the streets and several fatal casualties have been reported. Infuriated white rioters attempted to storm the Palmer house and the post offices, where there are a large number of employees, but an adequate police force dispersed them and later the men were spirited away to their homes in closed government mail trucks and other conveyances. White clerks have replaced our clerks in the main postoffice temporarily and our men have been shifted to outlying postoffices. The loop violence came as a surprise to the police. Police and reserves had been scattered over the South Side rioting districts, as no outbreaks had been expected in this quarter. Toward noon stations therein were overwhelmed with calls.

Frederick Smith, 33 years old, who spent three years in the Canadian army overseas and bears three wound chevrons, was attacked by a mob of hoodlums as he was passing Harrison street on S. State street. Smith had just stepped from the train, here to visit relatives, and was wholly ignorant of the disturbance. Monroe Gaddy, 3712 S. State street, and Halbert L. Bright, 3005 S. State street both employees of the custodians office in the Federal building, were attacked and severely beaten by a crowd of whites at Jackson boulevard and S. State street.

Excitement ran high all through the day July 28. Groups of men whose minds were inflamed by rumors of brutal attacks on men, women and children crowded the public thoroughfares in the South Side district from 27th to 39th streets. Some voicing sinister sentiments, others gesticulating and the remainder making their way home to grease up the old family revolver.

Added to the already irritable feeling was the fact that some whites had planned to make a "fore day" visit to the South Side homes with guns and torches. This message was conveyed to a group of men who were congregated near 36th street, on State. I elbowed my way to the center of the maddened throng as a man with his face covered with court plaster recited the story of his experience at the hands of a mob which had pounced upon him unannounced at 31st street and Archer ave. His story proved convincing enough to hasten the death of Casper Kazzourman (Greek), a peddler who was struck down form his wagon in front of 3618 South State street. It was men from this crowd who stole silently away and knifed the peddler to death.

## Bullets Fly Thick

But hell was yet to break loose, and by fate I was destined to be present. It occurred at Wabash avenue and 35th street at 8:10 o'clock at night, when over fifty policemen, mounted and on foot, while in the attempt to disperse a mob that was playing havoc with every white face, drew their revolvers and showered bullets into the crowd. The officers' guns barked for fully ten minutes. Seeing no way to escape and at the same time thinking of the obituary column, I immediately decided that my best move was to fall face downward to the pavement and remain there til the air cleared. This I did at the expense of a perfectly new "straw bonnet." But it was worth it.

## Four Wounded

During the reign of terror four citizens fell wounded; one a woman. She voiced her distress after a bullet had pierced her left shoulder. A man of slender proportions stumbled over my body in the hurried attempt to escape and plunged head first into the ground. A stream of blood gushed from a wound in the back of his neck. The bullet from an officer's revolver had found its mark. Blood from his fatal wound trickled down the pavement until it had reached me and heated corpuscles bathed my left cheek as I awaited the cessation of hostilities. The pavement about me was literally covered with splin-

tered glass which had been torn from a laundry window by the fusillade of shots, and several times I was tempted to brush the broken fragments from my back, when some had fallen, but I dreaded making a move. I had a reason. It was a case of eventuality, but not now.

Beads of perspiration rolled off my forehead as a bullet passed over the back of my coat, burning a path near the collar as it sped on its deathly mission. I arose reluctantly as a cop yelled: "Get up, everybody." He said it in the 200-point type we use on the front page of extras. His command was obeyed.

The wounded were whisked away in automobiles to nearby hospitals for treatment. Shortly after the guns had ceased firing the telephone on the managing editor's desk at the office tinkled. He answered.

"Have you heard of the shooting at 35th and Wabash avenue?" queried a mellow tone voice on the other end. The rejoinder came, evidenced in clear tones: "Yes, madam, a Defender reporter was passing."

## Further Resources

### BOOKS

Grossman, James R. *Land of Hope: Chicago, Black Southerners, and the Great Migration.* Chicago: University of Chicago, 1989.

Tuttle, William M., Jr. *Race Riot: Chicago in the Red Summer of 1919.* New York: Atheneum, 1970.

Wendt, Lloyd. *Chicago Tribune: The Rise of a Great Newspaper.* Chicago: Rand McNally, 1979.

### WEBSITES

O'Brien, Ellen, and Lyle Benedict. *Deaths, Disturbances, Disasters and Disorders in Chicago.* Available online at http://www.chipublib.org/004chicago/disasters/riots_race.html; website home page: http://www.chipublib.org/cpl.html (accessed April 9, 2003).

# The Brass Check

**Nonfiction work**

**By:** Upton Sinclair

**Date:** 1919

**Source:** Sinclair, Upton. *The Brass Check: A Study of American Journalism.* Pasadena, Calif.: Author, 1919, 436–439, 440–440, 443.

**About the Author:** Upton Sinclair (1878–1968) entered City College of New York in 1892. After joining the Socialist

Party a decade later, he embarked upon a career in muckraking journalism and leftist political activism. His most famous exposé, *The Jungle* (1905), investigated the meat-packing industry in Chicago and aided the passage of the Pure Food and Drug Act and the Meat-Inspection Act of 1906. He continued to investigate corruption in business and government for the next several decades. In 1934, he lost a campaign for the governorship of California but received more than 40 percent of the vote. He wrote more than two thousand published works and established himself as the quintessential radical activist/journalist. ∎

## Introduction

Upton Sinclair wrote *The Brass Check* as an investigative report on the downfall of the press. Following the heyday of muckraking, activist journalism in the 1900s, Sinclair saw the 1910s as a period of decline for journalism as a public service. American society exited the 1910s, according to Sinclair, "passing through one of the greatest crises of its history." The continued rise in sensationalist coverage certainly concerned the author. But the antiradicalism spawned by World War I may have further influenced the author's analysis of the news media at the end of the decade. Although the press involved itself on both sides of the debate about entering World War I, the official entry into the conflict in April 1917 resulted in curtailment of press freedoms. Under the Espionage and Sedition Acts (1917, 1918) and supported by two Supreme Court rulings, federal prosecutors arrested more than 1,500 antiwar activists and banned several publications that argued against American participation in the war. The signing of the armistice ending the war in 1918 brought even greater repression as the Red Scare began in the conflict's immediate aftermath.

## Significance

*The Brass Check* is an attack upon the media profession and those who Sinclair sees as its primary manipulators. He charged that corrupt links between politics, big business, and the reporters and editors who cover the newsmakers prevented substantive investigations of public malfeasance. This complicity resulted in a form of prostitution, according to Sinclair, that made mainstream journalists impotent. As described by Sinclair, patrons in houses of prostitution would purchase a "BRASS CHECK" from a cashier, then give it to a prostitute in exchange for services. This check symbolized shame, and Sinclair employed the analogy to conclude that the industrial elite had purchased the news media's moral compass. As conveyed in the book's preliminary subtitle, "A Study of the Whore of Journalism," big business had corrupted journalism and destroyed its independence and sense of social justice. This book's ultimate significance lies in its unflinching attacks upon the very institution de-

signed to defend society against fraud. If one accepted Sinclair's premise that American journalism provided only a mouthpiece for conniving politicians and businessmen, then the future would appear grim indeed.

## Primary Source

*The Brass Check* [excerpt]

**SYNOPSIS:** In the following excerpts, Sinclair proposed his strategy for improving the news media. He called for the removal of direct connections between government, financial interests, and journalists. He argued that only this degree of separation could enable journalists to independently investigate public and private vice. The labor disputes described here rose in frequency after the Great War as the economy entered a recession. Wages dropped, workers protested, and, in some cases, private employers and government agencies joined forces to quash the protests with lethal force.

Sometimes people criticize my books as being "destructive." Well, here is a book with a constructive ending. Here is something to be done; something definite, practical, and immediate. Here is a challenge to every lover of truth and fair dealing in America to get busy and help create an open forum through which our people may get the truth about their affairs, and be able to settle their industrial problems without bloodshed and waste. Will you do your share? . . .

## Conclusion

When I first talked over this book with my wife, she gave me a bit of advice: "Give your facts first, and then call your names." So throughout this book I have not laid much stress on the book's title. Perhaps you are wondering just where the title comes in!

What is the Brass Check? The Brass Check is found in your pay-envelope every week—you who write and print and distribute our newspapers and magazines. The Brass Check is the price of your shame—you who take the fair body of truth and sell it in the market-place, who betray the virgin hopes of mankind into the loathsome brothel of Big Business. And down in the counting-room below sits the "madame" who profits by your shame; unless, perchance, she is off at Palm Beach or Newport, flaunting her jewels and her feathers.

Please do not think that I am just slinging ugly words. Off and on for years I have thought about this book, and figured over the title, and what it means; I assert that the Brass Check which serves in the house of ill-fame as "the price of a woman's shame" is, both in its moral implications and in its social effect, precisely and identically the same as the gold and silver coins and pieces of written paper that are found every week in the pay-envelopes of those who write and print and distribute capitalist publications.

The prostitution of the body is a fearful thing. The young girl, trembling with a strange emotion of which she does not know the meaning, innocent, confiding and tender, is torn from her home and started on a road to ruin and despair. The lad, seeking his mate and the fulfilment of his destiny, sees the woman of his dreams turn into a foul harpy, bearer of pestilence and death. Nature, sumptuous, magnificent, loving life, cries: "Give me children!" And the answer comes: "We give you running sores and bursting glands, rotting lips and festering noses, swollen heads and crooked joints, idiot gabblings and maniac shrieks, pistols to blow out your brains and poisons to still your agonies." Such is the prostitution of the body.

But what of the mind? The mind is master of the body and commands what the body shall do and what it shall become; therefore, always, the prostitution of the mind precedes and causes the prostitution of the body. Youth cries: "Life is beautiful, joyous! Give me light, that I may keep my path!" The answer comes: "Here is darkness, that you may stumble, and beat your face upon the stones!" Youth cries: "Give me Hope." The answer comes: "Here is Cynicism." Youth cries: "Give me understanding, that I may live in harmony with my fellow-men." The answer comes: "Here are lies about your fellow-men, that you may hate them, that you may cheat them, that you may live among them as a wolf among wolves!" Such is the prostitution of the mind.

When I planned this book I had in mind a subtitle: "A Study of the Whore of Journalism." A shocking sub-title: but then, I was quoting the Bible, and the Bible is the inspired word of God. It was surely one of God's prophets who wrote this invitation to the reading of "The Brass Check":

Come hither; I will shew unto thee the judgment of the great whore that sitteth upon many waters;

With whom the kings of the earth have committed fornication, and the inhabitants of the earth have been made drunk with the wine of her fornication.

For eighteen hundred years men have sought to probe the vision of that aged seer on the lonely isle of Patmos. Listen to his strange words:

Upton Sinclair in 1916. A famous journalist, writer, and activist, Sinclair's thousands of published works include the *The Brass Check*, a critique of the 1910s news media. © BETTMANN/CORBIS. REPRODUCED BY PERMISSION.

So he carried me away in the spirit into the wilderness: and I saw a woman sit upon a scarlet colored beast, full of names of blasphemy, having seven heads and ten horns. And the woman was arrayed in purple and scarlet color, and decked with gold and precious stones and pearls, having a golden cup in her hands full of abominations and filthiness of her fornication:

And upon her forehead was a name written, MYSTERY, BABYLON THE GREAT, THE MOTHER OF HARLOTS AND ABOMINATIONS OF THE EARTH.

Now, surely, this mystery is a mystery no longer! Now we know what the seer of Patmos was foreseeing—Capitalist Journalism! And when I call upon you, class-conscious workers of hand and brain, to organize and destroy this mother of all iniquities, I do not have to depart from the language of the ancient scriptures. I say to you in the words of the prophet Ezekiel:

So the spirit took me up, and brought me into the inner court; and behold, the glory of the Lord filled the house.

And I heard him speaking unto me out of the house:

Now let them put away their whoredom, and the carcases of their kings, far from me, and I will dwell in the midst of them forever.

## A Practical Program

As I am about to send this book to press, I take one last look at the world around me. Half a million coal-miners have struck, a court injunction has forced the leaders to call off the strike, the miners are refusing to obey their leaders—and the newspapers of the entire United States are concealing the facts. For a week it has been impossible for me to learn, except from vague hints, what is happening in the coal-strike. And at the same time, because of false newspaper stories from Centralia, Washington, a "white terror" reigns in the entire West, and thousands of radicals are beaten, jailed, and shot.

I have pleaded and labored long to avoid a violent revolution in America; I intend to go on pleading and laboring to the last hour. I know that thousands of my readers will, like myself, be desperately anxious for something they can do. I decided to work out a plan of action; something definite, practical, and immediate.

I propose that we shall found and endow a weekly publication of truth-telling, to be known as "The National News." This publication will carry no advertisements and no editorials. It will not be a journal of opinion, but a record of events pure and simple. It will be published on ordinary news-print paper, and in the cheapest possible form. It will have one purpose and one only, to give to the American people once every week the truth about the world's events. It will be strictly and absolutely nonpartisan, and never the propaganda organ of any cause. It will watch the country, and see where lies are being circulated and truth suppressed; its job will be to nail the lies, and bring the truth into the light of day. I believe that a sufficient number of Americans are awake to the dishonesty of our press to build up for such a paper a circulation of a million inside of a year. . . .

I picture a publication of sixty-four pages, size nine inches by twelve, with three columns of ordinary newspaper type. The paper will have special correspondents in several of the big cities, and in the principal capitals of Europe, and will publish telegraphic news from these correspondents. It will obtain the names of reliable men in cities and towns throughout America, and in case of emergency it can telegraph, say to Denver, ordering five hundred words about the Ludlow massacre, or to Spokane, ordering the truth about the Centralia fight. The editor of the "National News" will sit in a watch-tower with the world spread before him; thousands of volunteers will act as his eyes, they will send him letters or telegrams with news. He and his staff will consider it all according to one criterion: Is the truth being hidden here? Is this something the American people ought to know? If so, the editor will send a trusted man to get the story, and when he has made certain of the facts he will publish them, regardless of what is injured, the Steel Trust or the I. W. W., the Standard Oil Company or the Socialist Party— even the "National News" itself.

Our editor will not give much space to the news that all other papers publish. The big story for him will be what the other papers let alone. He will employ trained investigators, and set them to work for a week, or maybe for several months, getting the facts about the lobby of the Beef Trust in Washington, the control of our public schools in the interest of militarism, the problem of who is paying the expenses of the American railway mission in Siberia. Needless to say the capitalist press will provide the "National News" with a complete monopoly of this sort of work. Also it will provide the paper with many deliberate falsehoods to be nailed. When this is done, groups of truth-loving people will buy these papers by the thousands, and blue-pencil and distribute them. So the "National News" will grow, and the "kept" press will be moved by the only force it recognizes—loss of money.

There are in America millions of people who could not be persuaded to read a Socialist paper, or a labor paper, or a single tax paper; but there are very few who could not be persuaded to read a paper that gives the news and proves by continuous open discussion that it really does believe in "the truth, the whole truth, and nothing but the truth." I do not think I am too optimistic when I say that such a publication, with a million circulation, would change the whole tone of American public life.

What would such a paper cost? To be published without advertisements, it would have to charge a high subscription price, two dollars a year at least; and there are not enough who will subscribe to a paper at that price. It would be better for the people to go without shoes than without truth, but the people do not know this, and so continue to spend their money for shoes. If the "National News" is to succeed, the few who do realize the emergency must pay more than their share; in other words, the paper must have a subsidy, and the subsidy must be large enough to make success certain—otherwise, of course, no one ought to give anything.

## Further Resources

**BOOKS**

Harris, Leon. *Upton Sinclair: American Rebel.* New York: Crowell, 1975.

Sinclair, Upton. *The Jungle.* New York: Doubleday, Page, 1906.

———. *The Autobiography of Upton Sinclair.* New York: Harcourt, Brace & World, 1962.

**PERIODICALS**

Obituary of Upton Sinclair. *The New York Times,* November 26, 1968.

**WEBSITES**

Gale, Robert L. "Sinclair, Upton." Available online at http://www.anb.org/articles/16/16-01510.html; website home page: http://www.anb.org (accessed April 10, 2003).

# 9

# MEDICINE AND HEALTH

JONATHAN MARTIN KOLKEY

*Entries are arranged in chronological order by date of primary source. For entries with one primary source, the entry title is the same as the primary source title. Entries with more than one primary source have an overall entry title, followed by the titles of the primary sources.*

**CHRONOLOGY**

Important Events in Medicine and Health,
　　1910–1919; . . . . . . . . . . . . . . . . . . . . . . . . 426

**PRIMARY SOURCES**

"Nursing as a Profession for College Women"
　　Edna L. Foley, May 1910. . . . . . . . . . . . . . . . 429

"How Physical Training Affects the Welfare
　　of the Nation"
　　Baroness Rose Posse, October 1910 . . . . . . . . 432

*Changes in Bodily Form of Descendants of*
　　*Immigrants*
　　Immigration Commission; Franz Boas, 1910 . . . 434

"Tobacco: A Race Poison"
　　Daniel Lichty, January 1914. . . . . . . . . . . . . . 437

*Painless Childbirth*
　　Henry Smith Williams, 1914 . . . . . . . . . . . . . 439

"The Endowment of Motherhood"
　　John F. Moran, January 9, 1915 . . . . . . . . . . . 441

"How the Drug Dopers Fight"
　　George Creel, January 30, 1915 . . . . . . . . . . . 443

"The Heart of the People"
　　Randolph Bourne, July 3, 1915. . . . . . . . . . . . 447

"Progress in Pediatrics"
　　Philip Van Ingen, September 1915 . . . . . . . . . 449

"Orthopedic Surgery in War Time"
　　Robert B. Osgood, 1916. . . . . . . . . . . . . . . . . 452

"War and Mental Diseases"
　　Pearce Bailey, October 19, 1917. . . . . . . . . . . 454

"Some Considerations Affecting the
　　Replacement of Men by Women Workers"
　　Josephine Goldmark, October 19, 1917 . . . . . . 457

Influenza Epidemic . . . . . . . . . . . . . . . . . . . . . . 460
"100 Sailors at Great Lakes Die of Influenza"
　　*Chicago Tribune*, September 23, 1918
"Find Influenza Germ"
　　*Washington Post*, September 21, 1918

"The Fight Against Venereal Disease"
　　Raymond B. Fosdick, November 30, 1918. . . . . 463

"The Next War"
　　Harvey Washington Wiley, January 1919 . . . . . 465

# Important Events in Medicine and Health, 1910–1919

## 1910

- The drug salvarsan comes into use against syphilis.
- The New York School of Chiropody opens in New York City.
- On January 15, the directory of the Rockefeller Sanitary Commission for hookworm prevention holds its first meeting.
- In March, the National Association for the Study and Prevention of Infant Mortality is formed, leading to the creation of baby clinics.
- In June, the American Medical Association's Council on Medical Education and Hospitals issues the Flexner Report on medical education, leading many inadequate medical schools to close and others to merge.
- In June, the University of Michigan awards the first American degree in public health.
- In September, the School of Medicine of the University of Pennsylvania establishes the nation's first medical research chair.
- In September, Columbia University offers the country's first course in optics and optometry.
- On October 3, the Ohio College of Dental Surgery in Cincinnati offers the first U.S. course for dental assistants and nurses.
- In November, the Hospital of the Rockefeller Institute opens.

## 1911

- Measles is discovered to be a viral infection.
- On February 6, the first Old Age Home for Pioneers opens in Prescott, Arizona.
- On May 3, Wisconsin enacts the nation's first workmen's compensation insurance law.
- On June 30, the first U.S. Army flight surgeon reports for duty.
- In July, London physician William Hill develops the gastroscope, which allows physicians to see the stomach and digestive track and their contents.

## 1912

- Phenobarbital, a sedative and anticonvulsant that suppresses epileptic seizures, is introduced.

- Local medical boards form a voluntary association, the Federation of State Medical Boards.
- On March 6, Congress passes the Sherley Amendment to the 1906 Pure Food and Drug Act. The amendment empowers the U.S. Justice Department to prosecute fraudulent claims of patent medicine effectiveness.
- On April 9, Congress creates the Children's Bureau to investigate and report on "all matters pertaining to the welfare and child life among all classes of people."
- On June 13, the University of Minnesota in Minneapolis holds the first graduation ceremony of a university school of nursing.
- In July, the Progressive Party includes a proposal in its platform requiring employers to offer health insurance to workers. The party's presidential candidate, Theodore Roosevelt, loses in November to Democratic candidate Woodrow Wilson, who did not promote health care.
- On August 12, Congress establishes the Dental Corps of the U.S. Navy.
- On September 30, the Cooperative Safety Congress holds its first national convention, in Milwaukee.
- In October, the National Organization for Public Health Nursing is founded.
- On November 25, the American College of Surgeons is incorporated in Springfield, Illinois.
- On December 7, James B. Herrick publishes the first diagnosis of a heart attack in a living patient in the *Journal of the American Medical Association.*
- On December 10, Alexis Carrel, who immigrated to the United States from France in 1904, becomes the first American to win the Nobel Prize in medicine or physiology.

## 1913

- The Association of Experimental Pathology is founded.
- Mammography, an X-ray technique for detecting breast cancer, is developed.
- Pellagra kills 1,192 in Mississippi.
- The U.S. Children's Bureau publishes a pamphlet on prenatal care.
- On February 25, the Rockefeller Foundation is chartered in New York.
- In April, Hungarian American Béla Schick develops the "Schick test" for diagnosing diphtheria.
- On April 19, Congress again amends the Pure Food and Drug Act of 1906 to broaden its power to regulate the quality of food and drugs imported from foreign companies.
- In May, the American Cancer Society is founded.
- On May 5, the American College of Surgeons organizes in Washington, D.C.
- In June, Johns Hopkins Medical School in Baltimore, Maryland appoints professors of medicine, surgery, and pediatrics. These appointments are the country's first full-time clinical professorships.
- In June, the National Safety Council is created.

- On June 19, the first immunology society, the American Association of Immunologists, organizes in Minneapolis.

- In September, the Phipps Psychiatric Clinic at Johns Hopkins Hospital opens.

- On November 13, the first annual convention of the American College of Surgeons meets in Chicago.

- On November 17, the first course in the U.S. for dental hygienists begins at the A. C. Fones Clinic in Bridgeport, Connecticut.

## 1914

- The Council of Medical Education of the American Medical Association (AMA) sets minimum standards for medical schools. To receive the AMA's Class A rating, medical schools must require at least one year of college as a prerequisite for admission.

- The AMA publishes its first listing of hospital internships.

- The hookworm control program begun in the South by the Rockefeller Foundation reaches its peak of activity, but in many areas barefoot victims are reinfected.

- The Life Extension Institute, an insurance association, begins offering preventive health examinations.

- The pasteurization of milk begins in large cities.

- The American Public Health Association adds an Industrial Hygiene section.

- The American College of Surgeons admits its first women members.

- On February 6, Congress passes the Harrison Anti-Narcotic Act.

- In June, the Mayo family opens its Mayo Clinic building in Rochester, Minnesota.

- On June 22, the first annual meeting of the American Association of Immunologists opens in Atlantic City, New Jersey.

- In August, the Association of Immunologists is founded.

- In December, Elmer V. McCollum, a scientist at the Wisconsin Agricultural Experiment Station, discovers the first vitamin, which he names vitamin A.

## 1915

- The U.S. Bureau of the Census begins to record births and infant mortality rates.

- Death certificates come into general use.

- Joseph Goldberger demonstrates that pellagra is the result of a dietary deficiency rather than a bacteria-borne disease.

- Thyroxin, an iodine-containing hormone later used to treat thyroid disorders, is isolated and identified.

- Modern virology is born with the development of a simple procedure for culturing and assaying viruses that attack bacteria.

- In January, the first issue of the *International Journal of Orthodontia* is published in St. Louis, Missouri.

- In March, the American College of Physicians is incorporated.

- In April, the Mayo family gives $1.5 million to endow the Mayo Foundation for Medical Education and Research.

- On May 19, Connecticut enacts the first state legislation to regulate dental hygienists.

- On June 14, the first Protestant Church for Lepers is dedicated in Carville, Louisiana.

- On July 2, the United States Public Health Service creates a Division of Industrial Hygiene and Sanitation.

- On September 20, Temple University opens the first chiropody school (a system of healing involving spinal manipulation) as a regular division of a university.

## 1916

- Physician and chemist William T. Bull develops an antitoxin to treat gas gangrene.

- Medical student William H. Howell discovers the anticoagulant property of the drug heparin, making it useful in preventing blood clots during transfusion.

- The practice of refrigerating blood for transfusion is begun.

- To relieve angina pectoris, sympathectomy, or the surgical interruption of sympathetic nerve pathways, is performed for the first time.

- The National Board of Medical Examiners holds its first examinations in Washington, D.C.

- In May, the American Association of Industrial Physicians and Surgeons is incorporated.

- On May 2, the Harrison Drug Act requires all persons licensed to sell narcotic drugs to file an inventory of their stocks with the Internal Revenue Service.

- On June 5, the U.S. Supreme Court rules that users and sellers of opium are liable for prosecution.

- On June 18, President Woodrow Wilson creates the Medical Division of the Council of National Defense.

- From June to September, a polio epidemic strikes 28,767 victims, killing about 6,000 and crippling thousands.

- On October 16, Margaret Sanger, Ethel Byrne, and Fania Mindell open the first birth control clinic in the United States in Brooklyn, New York.

## 1917

- On February 23, the American Society of Orthodontists, the first for the profession, is incorporated.

- In June, Harvard Medical School establishes a Department of Applied Physiology.

- In June, the AMA House of Delegates approves a report endorsing health insurance.

- In June, General John J. Pershing, commander of U.S. forces in World War I, announces that U.S. medical personnel will care for any wounded soldier, irrespective of nationality. He warns Germany, however, that the U.S. will cease care of German wounded soldiers should German troops launch a chemical attack on U.S. forces.

- From June to August, U.S. medical personnel establish field hospitals in France along the entire Western front and begin treating casualties.

• In October, General John J. Pershing, commander of U.S. forces in World War I, forbids troops on leave from visiting Paris, France after French commanders brief him on the prevalence of syphilis and gonorrhea in Parisian brothels.

## 1918

• S. R. Benedict devises a test to measure the basal metabolism rate.

• The American Medical Association increases the prerequisite for Class A medical school admission from one to two years of college.

• Some 46 percent of fractures in the U.S. Army cause permanent disability, chiefly by amputation; 12 percent of fractures cause death.

• In February, the French government issues a citation commending the U.S. Nursing Corps for its heroism and quality of care in treating wounded French soldiers.

• On March 9, Congress passes the Chamberlain-Kahn Act for the study and control of venereal diseases.

• In May, the American College of Surgeons begins a program to evaluate hospital standards.

• In May, the *Journal of Industrial Hygiene* publishes its first issue.

• On May 25, the Secretary of War authorizes the U.S. Army to establish the Army School of Nursing.

• In June, Germany announces its intent to classify captured U.S. medical personnel, including nurses, as prisoners of war. General John Pershing responds by dispatching U.S. Marines to guard U.S. field hospitals.

• On August 27, the "Spanish" influenza epidemic hits the U.S. in Boston. Nearly 25 percent of Americans contract the flu, and some 500,000 die.

• On October 1, the Johns Hopkins School of Hygiene and Public Health, the first of its kind, opens in Baltimore.

## 1919

• The curative effect of sunlight on rickets is discovered.

• The Battle Creek Toasted Corn Flakes Company introduces Kellogg's All-Bran as a source of dietary fiber.

• On January 16, the states ratify the Eighteenth Amendment to the Constitution prohibiting the sale of alcoholic beverages. The amendment will go into effect January 16, 1920, one year after ratification.

• On February 27, the first national social organization for the hearing impaired, the American Association for the Hard of Hearing, is formed in New York City.

• On June 15, the Ohio General Assembly enacts the first law for statewide care of handicapped children.

• On December 2, President Woodrow Wilson convenes the White House Conference on the Care of Dependent Children.

• On December 23, the first ambulance ship, the *Relief,* designed and built as a hospital, is launched.

the entire health-care industry, evidently one of the nation's more conspicuous exploiters of female labor.

## Significance

In this climate, the nursing profession came under intense scrutiny. Reformers advocated transforming nursing into a more established, prestigious, and well-paying profession that would attract the women college graduates who around 1910 were starting to pour out of America's colleges and universities in record numbers. Accordingly, nursing needed to remake itself. Nurses would require better education and training—especially in the swiftly evolving science of modern medicine—so that they might be able to interact with predominately male doctors on a more equal basis. Indeed, under this new regimen, which featured enhanced education coupled with the traditional hands-on experience, nurses might come to rival the knowledge base of the physicians themselves. In short, the nurse would be less like an orderly (or a maid) and more like a skilled health professional liberated from the menial aspects of patient care.

Finally, reformers sought to sever nursing from its traditional orientation as a female "helping profession." Since for centuries hospitals had been essentially run by churches—and hence staffed with nuns and female community volunteers—a lingering "nonmaterialistic" ethos pervaded nursing. In fact, some men who ran large hospitals believed that by refusing to pay decent wages, the nursing field eliminated women who were not "truly devoted" to the cause. The hope in the 1910s was that increased pay, responsibilities, and prestige would serve to attract higher-caliber, middle-class college-educated women into the field.

## Primary Source

**"Nursing as a Profession for College Women"**
[excerpt]

> **SYNOPSIS:** In these excerpts, Edna L. Foley, the Supervising Nurse at the Chicago Tuberculosis Institute, exhorts college-educated women to consider nursing as a worthy career path.

After college what? So many and such various employments are opening their doors to women now, that your choice is a large one. One may be anything from a strike-breaker to a learned Don, though the first takes a socialistic temperament, and the last takes many years of study. One may teach or go into a library school, take up domestic science, or enter a settlement. There is no lack of things to do; perhaps that is the reason why nursing has been, heretofore, overlooked as a profession for college

# "Nursing as a Profession for College Women"
Journal article

**By:** Edna L. Foley
**Date:** May 1910
**Source:** Foley, Edna L. "Nursing as a Profession for College Women." *American Journal of Nursing,* 10, no. 8, May 1910, 533, 534, 535, 536.
**About the Author:** Edna L. Foley, who received her bachelor's degree at Smith College in 1901, was the supervising nurse at the Chicago Tuberculosis Institute. ■

## Introduction

Alongside traditional occupational categories such as "white collar" or "blue collar," historians and sociologists are increasingly identifying the so-called pink collar occupational realm that features female-dominated jobs that are accorded low pay and little social status. This was clearly the case with nursing, perhaps the most "pink collar" career field of all. Centuries of staffing largely with nuns and community volunteers had served to render nursing a lowly, chronically underappreciated line of work.

Meanwhile, by 1910 the entire medical profession itself was changing. Medicine had once been an unregulated frontier, but the early 1900s witnessed the rapid spread of state certification for doctors and pharmacists. In short, the Progressive-era thrust of championing government intervention into areas of life that had been considered purely private preserves impacted the practice of medicine in numerous ways, including enhanced educational requirements for licensing.

In response to this change, the medical profession itself decided to become more professional. It began to make efforts to weed out incompetent practitioners—a reform that also reduced competition and in so doing raised the salaries of doctors and pharmacists. Slowly but surely, the female-dominated nursing profession took note of these trends. In addition, the rise of the feminist movement after 1910, which exerted pressure to increase the power and prestige of women generally, took aim at

A 1917 poster encourages women to take up the nursing occupation. **THE LIBRARY OF CONGRESS.**

graduates. Not only overlooked, but rather looked at askance, as if the work of healing sick bodies and preventing more ill ones was interesting, "Oh, very," and endlessly self-sacrificing, but "hardly the work for a college woman."

Why not? A certain training school superintendent, a woman of international experience, says that college women are too unwilling to work, too anxious for long vacations, too dreamy and self-centred to be trusted in matters of life and death. Another says that they are "not strong enough." The college girl replies that the work is not interesting, that it is all drudgery, leading to nothing but reddened hands and aching feet. Now who is to be believed? There is a little truth in all of these statements but one, and that is the college girl's mistaken idea that nursing is not interesting. It is the most live, fascinating, complex, and vitally interesting work that the world offers to women, and it is a field open only to women. Male nurses are misnomers, save in rare instances, and these only serve as exceptions to prove the rule. It is a work, too, so full of the joy of service that only those who have entered it realize what it means to them. To help save a human life, to assist at the birth of a new born soul, to make the going out of a tired life easier, to get into close touch with the realities, the mysteries of life, to be able to help rather than to hinder at times like these, is more than sufficient recompense for hours of study and hard work.

And other opportunities in nursing work are unlimited. In the last few years, so many different lines have opened to nurses that the supply does not begin to equal the demand. School nursing, tuberculosis visiting nursing, social service and welfare work, children's nursing, and last, but not least, institutional nursing, all offer excellent positions with generous compensation to nurses. The desire for the "right woman in the right place" is sometimes so great that the nurse may usually arrange her own terms. Especially is this true in children's institutions. The medical profession and the public at large have been slow in recognizing the fact that nurses, as well as teachers, must receive special training if they are going to care for little children, but now children's institutions and hospital wards are clamoring for supervisors and head nurses, who have had this preparation. . . .

All hospitals now offer a broad three years' training to their pupil nurses, and it has been found best for both nurse and patient to give the first six months of this training to preliminary study and practice. Instructors and lecturers for this course are needed, but they must be nurses, for it has been demonstrated very often that nurses must teach nurses. And if these instructors have, besides their general training, a college education, they will be all the better prepared to give this teaching the important place which, in the past, it has sometimes lacked. . . .

Besides just as the child leaves the kindergarten and enters the primary, so the nurse leaves this sort of work in her probation and advances to other, but she must realize its importance, and not consider it "infra dig" if she is to be entrusted with the care of human life and the training of younger nurses. The whole secret of the training lies in learning when, how, and why to do things; to do things in a given time, to keep her head in an emergency, to be, in short, a tower of strength in time of trouble. We consider nothing too good for the sick. We call in the best physicians, the most expensive specialists,—and the nurse. The doctors consult, advise, prescribe, and leave the house. On the nurse rests a tremendous responsibility; a life, very near and dear to us, is in her hands. Thanks to that very discipline and drudgery, which suddenly seems to have grown so small and petty, she is able to accept the responsibility; to keep the atmosphere of the sick-room cool and unruffled; to reassure the family; to placate the cook; and to wheedle the children into playing less noisily. We cease to worry, we forget the bad symptoms of the day before, the nurse has come and all will be well. That is as it should be with our ideal of a nurse. Unfortunately, we sometimes get a different stamp of a woman, but who is to blame—the hospital who accepted her for want of more promising applicants, the superintendent who trained her, or the indifference to the profession of the better educated women, who refuse to enter the work themselves, and so make it necessary to recruit many of our nurses from a certain class of unsocialized women, earnest and sincere, doubtless, but handicapped by their previous training, as well as by their inability to grasp essentials in their hospital course? Our work is what we make it, and to any college woman who enters nursing with the desire to forget herself in ministering to others, the training itself will be full of pleasant surprises, and the possibilities for big constructive work in the future, boundless.

## Further Resources
### BOOKS

Bullough, Vern I., and Bonnie Bullough. *History, Trends and Politics of Nursing*. Norwalk, Conn.: Appleton-Century-Crofts, 1984.

Nelson, Sioban. *Say Little, Do Much: Nurses, Nuns, and Hospitals in the Nineteenth Century.* Philadelphia: University of Pennsylvania Press, 2001.

Roberts, Joan I., and Thetis Group. *Feminism and Nursing: An Historical Perspective on Power, Status, and Political Activism in the Nursing Profession.* Westport, Conn.: Praeger, 1995.

# "How Physical Training Affects the Welfare of the Nation"

Journal article

**By:** Baroness Rose Posse

**Date:** October 1910

**Source:** Posse, Baroness Rose. "How Physical Training Affects the Welfare of the Nation." *American Physical Education Review,* 15, no. 7, October 1910, 493–494, 496–497, 498, 499.

**About the Author:** Baroness Rose Posse, founder of the Posse Gymnasium of Boston, Massachusetts, was one of the nation's leading advocates of physical education for the country's boys and girls. ■

## Introduction

The physical education movement burst onto the American scene in the early years of the twentieth century. The cause of physical education was a solid idea on its own merits; no one could argue against the benefits of physical fitness. But other motives drove the movement, which reflected some of the deeper anxieties present in American life around 1910.

In an earlier age, when America was predominately a rural country, the notion of encouraging physical fitness seemed preposterous. With strapping farm lads pitching heavy bales of hay, there was no need for an exercise program, or concern for eating "natural foods" for that matter. But by the dawn of the twentieth century, a growing percentage of Americans had already shifted from farms and small towns to the cities. If projections proved correct, America was clearly on its way to becoming an urban nation. To compound the problem, the experience of England and parts of continental Europe that had industrialized a generation or two ahead of the United States provided a disturbing glimpse of an urban future that many Americans hardly welcomed.

## Significance

Meanwhile, by 1910 many "old stock" Americans had expressed concern about birthrates and immigration figures. The birthrate of old-stock Anglo-Saxon descended Americans had declined, while other groups in America had yet to lower significantly their own rates. Simultaneously, the unprecedented wave of immigrants flooding into America boded ill for the prospect of continued Anglo dominance.

Thus, the physical education movement was part of larger crusade to improve the health of the "breeding stock"—in particular, among Anglos—as well as to provide a wholesome outlet for youngsters of all groups, who might otherwise fall victim to urban vices including crime; gambling; prostitution; and alcohol, drug, and tobacco abuse. Moreover, self-professed advocates of the "strenuous life," such as physical fitness buff President Theodore Roosevelt (served 1901–1909), viewed physical weakness as a crime committed against society. It not only inhibited an individual's reproductive obligations but it lowered the fighting capabilities of the country's soldiers come wartime. Some supporters of the physical education movement viewed war as the ultimate test of a nation.

Finally, as an interesting sidelight, the physical education movement made sure to appeal to women—in keeping with feminist ideas then beginning to take hold. Physical fitness advocates fully intended to include girls in their program.

## Primary Source

"How Physical Training Affects the Welfare of the Nation" [excerpt]

**SYNOPSIS:** Baroness Rose Posse, a leading advocate of physical education for America's youngsters, extols the virtues of fitness and health in an increasingly urban and oftentimes sedentary society.

It has been said that the future will belong to the best educated nation. I would make this proviso, that this education has been of the body as well as of the mind.

The very first essential of power is stamina. A nation that has no endurance can not clinch the nails it drives. A nation that is in physical decay is doomed. No matter how widespread its interests, how great its commerce, how learned its scientists, or how wonderful its inventions, when there are many deaths, few marriages and less births, it is but a question of arithmetical ratio as to how soon such a nation loses its power.

America has always been in the front rank in mental ability, and mediocre in physical power. The average limit of life for the American man is fifty

Members of the Gamma Epsilon Club take a physical education class around 1910. Formal physical education was of growing concern in early twentieth century America, as people moved to large cities and away from strenuous farm living. © SCHENECTADY MUSEUM; HALL OF ELECTRICAL HISTORY FOUNDATION/CORBIS. REPRODUCED BY PERMISSION.

years, women live somewhat longer. The conditions now surrounding the American people are frightful from a hygienic point of view. Among many evils are the capricious climate, the greed of gold with its mad race for fortune that develops conditions leading to suicide, insanity and death, the increasing appetite for pleasurable excitement which is accompanied by too much theatre going, too much eating, too much drinking, too little sleep and too much nerve strain. These last conditions attend the lives of many club women, actors, journalists and others much in public life, who grow accustomed to sleeping with one eye open, and who eat when they can. Moreover, a serious evil that is growing in our midst is the inordinate rage for athletics among growing boys, which, unless checked, can only result in harm. Boys or girls should not indulge in violent exercise unless they are in systematic physical training. By this I mean physical training supervised by an expert, by one who knows what exercises to give to strengthen the heart and lungs, and to induce all the vital organs to perform their functions normally and regularly, without overstrain on any one part. Too often, as athletics are practiced to-day, very little attention is paid to the result of overexercise on the heart and

it is pitiable to see small boys weakening themselves by immoderate exertion, thus planting the seeds of future ill health. . . .

One of the greatest needs of the American people is a better condition of health, and a prominent factor in producing this improved condition should be physical training.

What is physical training? It is putting into use all parts of the body so that no one part shall be used at the expense of any other part, but so that all shall receive a sufficient amount of exercise to enable all the functions of the vital organs to be performed harmoniously and healthfully. . . .

America needs to pay more attention to gymnastics and less to athletics. Americans have always been prominent in special deeds. We have had the swift runners, the fast walkers, the high jumpers and the winners in any sport that calls for a quick spurt and a sudden nervous effort. But in the great race of life our men fall by the wayside. Their limit of life is brief. They die long before they ought and they fail to show resistance to a supreme call for endurance.

What we need is to begin with the boys and girls and give them gymnastic training as faithfully as we give them food and clothing. Boston and other large cities have done much in this respect but there is still more to be done. We have gymnasia in the high schools but there should be a gymnasium in every school. Children cannot obtain a great amount of benefit from exercise taken in the schoolroom. They should have a place properly equipped, where the whole atmosphere is different, and where there is no limitation or constraint.

After the child grows out of the days when Nature can guard him against the bad conditions of civilized life, he begins to get in ruts, he uses one side more than the other, he uses certain sets of muscles continually and certain other sets not at all. As he grows to manhood he becomes a bookkeeper and sits all day at a desk, or a salesman and stands all day behind the counter, or a worker in a mill, where he uses his arms in one continuous motion all the day, or he may break stone on the road, or he may even be a school teacher, using his head and brain to the exclusion of the rest of his body. When any of these workers go home at night they are tired, but it is only a part of them that is tired. They should take gymnastic exercise to draw the blood away from the overworked parts and to distribute it over the body. Then the congestion relieved, they would feel rested. They may not feel like going through gymnastic exercises, but they like to eat, they like to sleep, they like to do other things that custom calls necessary, and if the habit of gymnastics be once established, it will be reckoned as one of the most essential of all the things to be done, if one wishes to live long and happily, and to have the proper efficiency for work. . . .

We must awake to the fact that it is due our children that they should have a proper development of their bodies, and not, as now, too often leave the whole matter to chance. It has been said that everyone carries with him for many years before his death the seeds of disease that will finally end his life, although the disease may not develop for twenty years. This need not be true. If proper attention to well living is persisted in, diseases may be averted and old age indefinitely deferred. . . .

The ancient Greeks were once the most powerful nation on earth. That was the time when they practiced physical training as faithfully as they ate and slept. Their culture and attainments along certain lines have never been equaled. Their influence upon the history of the world can never be effaced. But what happened? They allowed their bodies to become weakened. They stopped their gymnastic exercises, and it sounded the death knell of their power.

So, if we would become the most powerful as well as the best educated of nations, we must have physical training made compulsory for every child up to a certain age, and we must cultivate the love of exercise so that after it has ceased to be compulsory it will be practiced from a sense of duty, of duty to ourselves, to our country and to the coming race.

## Further Resources

### BOOKS

Lee, Mabel. *A History of Physical Education and Sports in the U.S.A.* New York: Wiley, 1983.

Welch, Paula D., and Harold A. Lerch. *History of American Physical Education and Sports.* Springfield, Ill.: C.C. Thomas, 1981.

Weston, Arthur. *The Making of American Physical Education.* New York: Appleton-Century-Crofts, 1962.

# *Changes in Bodily Form of Descendants of Immigrants*

Report

**By:** Immigration Commission; Franz Boas

**Date:** 1910

**Source:** The Immigration Commission. "Introductory." *Changes in Bodily Form of Descendants of Immigrants,* 61st Congress, 2d sess. Washington, D.C.: U.S. Government Printing Office, 1910, 5; Boas, Franz. *Changes in Bodily Form of Descendants of Immigrants,* 61st Congress, 2d sess. Washington, D.C: U.S. Government Printing Office, 1910, 7–8.

**About the Author:** Franz Boas (1858–1942) was one of America's leading anthropologists and experts on race and ethnicity. Born and educated in Germany, he emigrated to the United States in 1886 and became a professor at Columbia University. ∎

## Introduction

From its founding in the seventeenth century, there was to many something remarkably special about America. Newcomers quickly realized that the streets were not paved with gold, but the land seemed uniquely blessed. Doubtless this prospect attracted millions of immigrants from Europe and elsewhere over time. And the material abundance was so evident that historian David Potter saw fit to title his classic work on Americans *People of Plenty.*

This ethos of plenty played itself out in various ways. Many observers contrasted the healthy, chubby-cheeked American children with those wretched youngsters often found in other lands, exemplified by the dwarfish chimney sweeps of Charles Dickens' England or the prematurely aged children who toiled in Thomas Carlyle's "satanic mills." Indeed many noted that the American-born children of immigrants seemed far more healthy (indeed robust) than did their own parents. Clearly, the wholesome American environment served as a most welcome tonic for newcomers.

## Significance

Nonetheless, this almost universally accepted view that the American environment was the most beneficial on earth often led observers to unwarranted conclusions. Such was the fate of the otherwise reputable anthropologist Franz Boas.

Boas had been invited by the congressional Dillingham Immigration Commission (1907–1910) to present his dubious findings that the American environment had a dramatic, almost immediate, impact on newcomers. The children of immigrants, upon inspection, were born with heads that appeared to be shaped more like the heads of "regular Americans." His view constituted an extreme example of environmentalism, which, incidentally, sought to refute the suggestion that the latest wave of immigrants to come ashore circa 1910 were hopelessly unassimilable, as many people at the time thought. In addition, his conclusions that physical changes could occur so quickly misrepresents the dynamics of Darwinian evolution. But in 1910, Charles Darwin's theories were still relatively fresh and intellectually exciting, and often imperfectly understood. Boas' blunders may well have reflected, in part, this overenthusiasm.

Finally, Boas' material highlights the dangers of science influenced by ideology. Far from being value free, twentieth-century science has often been used for the benefit of various causes—many of them highly political. A century ago, the latest science, although relying on little data, "proved" that, for instance, the white race was superior. What passes for scientific knowledge is often disputed and likely will forever be used for ideological ends.

## Primary Source

### Changes in Bodily Form of Descendants of Immigrants [excerpt]

**SYNOPSIS:** Franz Boas, one of the country's leading anthropologists, presents a report to the Dillingham Immigration Commission offering alleged proof of a highly dubious theory that the wholesome American environment actually served to change the head shapes of the children of recent immigrants. This theory may have been intended to neutralize then-fashionable anti-immigrant sentiment regarding the supposed inability of newcomers to adapt to American conditions. The otherwise normally reliable Boas produced data purporting to demonstrate that im-

Anthropologist Franz Boas. **THE LIBRARY OF CONGRESS.**

migrant children were in fact swiftly Americanizing because their head shapes appear to be more "American."

### Introductory.

The question of the assimilation of immigrants under American conditions has long been looked upon as vital, and it has been much discussed, but heretofore with little accurate information. Speaking from general personal observation, people have thought that under the influence of the existing educational, social, and political conditions, the immigrants gradually change their habits of life and their ways of thinking, and thus become Americans. Little or no thought has been given to the possible effect of these conditions on the physical type of descendants of immigrants.

Shortly after the beginning of the Immigration Commission's work the possibility of getting a more accurate and more scientific test of the influence of the American environment upon our immigrants and their descendants was considered. It was thought that if measurements of the bodies of European immigrants and of their descendants at different ages and under differing circumstances could be made in the careful way followed by scientific anthropometrists,

A family of Italian immigrants on Ellis Island, New York, awaiting entry to the United States, c. 1910. **THE LIBRARY OF CONGRESS.**

valuable results might be reached. One of the best experts on this question, Prof. Franz Boas, of Columbia University, was invited to direct the investigation and was put in general charge. A small appropriation was made to test the question and see if the promise of results was sufficient to warrant the continuance of the investigation. Almost immediately it became evident that there might be much value in such a study, and the work has therefore been continued, although as yet only on a small scale. The investigation has been carried on only in New York City and its immediate vicinity, much of the material being furnished by the public schools. The results so far are based entirely upon the measurements of Sicilians and east European Hebrews. There is much material in hand, but not yet worked out, regarding the Bohemians, Hungarians, and Scotch.

The results, in the opinion of Professor Boas, are much more far-reaching than was anticipated. It is probably not too much to say that they indicate a discovery in anthropological science that is fundamental in importance. The report seems to indicate that the descendant of the European immigrant "changes his type even in the first generation almost entirely. Children born not more than a few years after the arrival of the immigrant parents in America develop in such a way that they differ in type essentially from their foreign-born parents. These differences seem to develop during the earliest childhood and persist throughout life. It seems that every part of the body is influenced in this way, and even the form of the head, which has always been considered as one of the most permanent hereditary features, undergoes considerable changes.

"The importance of this entirely unexpected result lies in the fact that even those characteristics which modern science has led us to consider as most stable are subject to thorough changes under the new environment." This would indicate the conclusion "that racial physical characteristics do not survive under the new social and climatic environment of America." The adaptability of the various races coming together on our shores seems, if these indications shall be fully borne out in later study, to be much greater than had been anticipated. If the American environment can bring about a modification of the head forms in the first generation, may it not be that other characteristics may be as easily modified, and that there may be a rapid assimilation of widely varying nationalities and races to something that may well be called an American type?

The commission feels that it is too early to pronounce absolutely upon this question. The investigation is by no means complete, and moreover, considering the importance of the subject, it should clearly be carried on on a larger scale and in different surroundings in various parts of the country, and perhaps also be checked up by certain investigations made upon the same races elsewhere. Without venturing, therefore, to pronounce as yet a definite judgment, the commission expresses its confidence in the training and ability of Professor Boas, in charge of the work, and urges strongly the desirability of continuing this most important investigation on an extended scale.

### Changes in Bodily Form of Descendants of Immigrants

#### General Results Of The Investigation.

The anthropological investigation had for its object an inquiry into the assimilation of the immigrants by the American people, so far as the form of the body is concerned. . . .

An attempt was made to solve the following questions:

1. Is there a change in the type of development of the immigrant and his descendants, due to his transfer from his home surroundings to the congested parts of New York?

2. Is there a change in the type of the adult descendant of the immigrant born in this country as compared to the adult immigrant arriving on the shores of our continent?

The investigation has shown much more than was anticipated; and the results, so far as worked out, may be summarized as follows:

1. The head form, which has always been considered as one of the most stable and permanent characteristics of human races, undergoes far-reaching changes due to the transfer of the races of Europe to American soil. The east European Hebrew, who has a very round head, becomes more long-headed; the south Italian, who in Italy has an exceedingly long head, becomes more short-headed; so that both approach a uniform type in this country, so far as the roundness of the head is concerned. . . .

This fact is one of the most suggestive ones discovered in our investigation, because it shows that not even those characteristics of a race which have proved to be most permanent in their old home remain the same under our new surroundings; and we are compelled to conclude that when these features of the body change, the whole bodily and mental make-up of the immigrants may change.

## Further Resources

### BOOKS

Hyatt, Marshall. *Franz Boas, Social Activist: The Dynamics of Ethnicity.* New York: Greenwood, 1990.

Williams, Vernon J. *Rethinking Race: Franz Boas and His Contemporaries.* Lexington, Ky.: University Press of Kentucky, 1996.

# "Tobacco: A Race Poison"

## Presentation

**By:** Daniel Lichty

**Date:** January 1914

**Source:** Lichty, Daniel. "Tobacco: A Race Poison." *Proceedings of the First National Conference on Race Betterment*, Battle Creek, Mich.: Race Betterment Foundation, 1914, 222–224, 225, 226, 229, 230, 232.

**About the Author:** Daniel Lichty, M.D. was a vigorous antitobacco crusader who brought his firsthand experience with lung diseases—especially tuberculosis—to bear on the prob-

lems of smoking. ■

## Introduction

During the Progressive era, while the crusade to prohibit the consumption of alcoholic beverages was a major issue, a lesser campaign targeted yet another perceived public-health menace—tobacco. While the opponents of alcohol scored a spectacular political victory with the passage of the Eighteenth Amendment to the Constitution mandating at least a partial national prohibition (the manufacture, sale, and transportation were outlawed, while the purchase and consumption continued to be legal), the opponents of tobacco achieved no such comparable triumph.

Nonetheless, the antismoking movement of the 1910s, while hardly successful, served as a harbinger of the antismoking campaign that has been conducted since the publication of the Surgeon General's landmark Report of 1964. After the nation's largely failed experiment with alcohol prohibition (1920–1933), no such similar effort was ever again attempted. Meanwhile, the antismoking campaign of today has adopted a zero-tolerance policy that, in some respects, went far beyond what the proponents of the earlier partial alcohol ban had ever contemplated.

## Significance

The relative success of the alcohol prohibition movement of the Progressive era and the corresponding failure of the campaign against tobacco can be attributed to a number of factors. The alcohol prohibition movement became a potent vehicle for others intent on furthering their own interests. For instance, soft drink manufactures like Coca-Cola supported alcohol prohibition as a means of crippling a rival in the highly competitive beverage industry. Some beer brewers mistakenly assumed that the prohibitionists would be content to target only hard liquor and wine—thus leaving an open field for beer. In contrast, tobacco never faced a comparable rival for consumer allegiance.

Fortunately for the alcohol prohibitionists, the United States's entry into World War I (1914–1918) against Germany in April 1917 permitted opponents to link the foreign enemy with German Americans on the home front. German Americans were among the most conspicuous members of the nation's brewing and distilling industry. Of course, the tobacco trade suffered no such negative association with a hostile foreign power. The first English colonial settlement in Virginia survived primarily by tobacco cultivation. Lastly, the anti-alcohol effort in the southern states was connected with efforts to keep increasingly restless blacks in check. The belief was widespread that when sober, blacks respected whites; but when drunk, it was alleged, blacks became "uppity." No such claim could be made against tobacco.

Then, too, opponents pushed alcohol prohibition by linking it in the public mind with the hated saloon, which around 1914 had come to epitomize all that some people thought was wrong with urban America—it was in their minds a den of inequity frequented by barely Americanized immigrants. The saloon fostered prostitution, gambling, civic corruption, and an overall loosening of moral standards. But although tobacco posed a serious personal health risk, one could not make a similar charge against it.

The strong antismoking movement that has burgeoned since 1964 has avoided many of the political mistakes that plagued the alcohol prohibition crusade. Today's tobacco adversaries take pains not to present the issue in moral terms. Instead, tobacco is almost always presented as a purely individual and public health concern.

## Primary Source

"Tobacco: A Race Poison" [excerpt]

**SYNOPSIS:** Dr. Daniel Lichty, a physician with extensive experience in lung diseases, describes the various health risks associated with smoking in this paper originally delivered at the First National Conference on Race Betterment and reprinted in the conference's proceedings. His indictment reflects a strong antismoking movement that flourished in America during the first two decades of the twentieth century.

Man, generic man, is the greatest asset of the age, and of the world. It is the duty of those who dwell on the heights to conserve this asset.

It should not be necessary to put the subject of tobacco on the defensive, yet, in its almost universal use, to openly declare it a *race poison* demands this; it requires the courage and sacrifice of a martyr to do it.

However, as Abraham Lincoln said of his opposition to human slavery, "If the end brings me out wrong, ten angels swearing I was right would make no difference."

Tobacco is a poison, a narcotic poison, an acronarcotic; it is so classed in every text-book on poisons, in every book on botany. Every chemistry so classes its alkaloids, and every dictionary, medical or otherwise, so defines it. Every part of the plant is poisonous. Even the sweet secretion of its flowers is stupefying. Only a few poisonous plants excel it in deadliness. In Germany tobacco is fittingly called *teufel kraut,* "devil's weed."

Tobacco alone possesses the fascinating flavor and aroma that lures the world. Eighty per cent of the adolescent and adult male population are enamored of its narcotic and lethal potency. How some are poisoned and others are immune is the paradox of human physiology and pathology. Here heredity and education, maternal and filial affection, are all deposed and dumped into a common mire of tobacco debauchery. . . .

Man the world over has sought and possessed a sense obtunder. Tobacco, alcohol, opium, cocaine, are all narcotics which make all races adverse to ethnic as well as ethical progress. No substance has become so universal as tobacco. Through his stupor he severs connection with the real source of joy and power—fresh air, pure water, right food, and wins false force through intoxication and narcosis. . . .

The doctor, the research student, the biological engineer seem timid, lax or indifferent to the ethnic blight of tobacco.

Occasionally articles appear in scientific medical or other highly ethical and literary magazines deploring the spreading use, economic waste, and bane of tobacco and its racial wreckage. In other more popular magazines, whose circulation is measured by millions (and their readers by tens of millions), with front and back full-page covers in four colors we find display lines of illustrated advertisement extolling the merits of their respective tobacco manufactures, each with positive declaration and loud boasting that their product has neither "bite" nor "sting," nor poisonous nicotine. A score of pipes are patented every year claiming to prevent the acrid smoke and toxic oil and deadly nicotine from reaching the consumer. The anxious, hurried reader does not recognize between the lines the admissions of the cunning advertiser of both pipe maker and tobacco mixer that there is poison in his product, in the substance and in the advertisement. A chewing gum is now advertised to relieve the dryness of the mouth after smoking. No trust is so conscienceless in its advertising as the tobacco trust. A hundred or two human lives may be burned to death or horrible disfigurement in shirtwaist factories; another several hundred destroyed in burning hotels; ships may be set on fire, mines burned, hospitals, homes, morgues and graves be filled, while widows wail and children's cries fill the saddened air, but the news press must not tell that these grewsome and grief-laden tragedies were all caused by stupefied cigar, cigarette, and pipe smokers, indifferent and carelessly criminal with their matches and embers and stubs. . . .

Epilepsy, insanity, idiocy, imbecility and all the collateral grades of mental infirmities are on the increase. The statistics of increase of positive defectives over population are appalling—to say nothing of the criminals, substandards and repeaters of common society. To enumerate them would be wearisome. Let this suffice: In Illinois the increase of insanity is 667 per cent, while population increase was only 50 per cent, census 1900. That these unfortunates, wrecks, and derelicts have been cast upon the moaning beach of the Sea of Life in regularly increasing winrows, *parallel* with the *increasing use of tobacco,* is a graphic and significant presentation that cannot be ignored nor denied. There may be comfort in this reflection, however, that blocking this blight on humanity in part, is absolute sterility in the male, which is also on the increase, in the original, in the secondary and tertiary issues of the tobacco user. . . .

Nicotine begets very decidedly neuropathic stock. The heredity of nicotine tainted stock is never on the right side. Nicotine is an ethical as well as a race poison. Heredity as a science has made rapid progress and is advancing. Humans are entitled to equal consideration with plants and animals. Propagation should be made selective from both sides. There might well be a parent inspection before there is the child and pupil inspection, before the "Better Babies" enter their contests. There needs be a standard of narcotic-free fatherhood before a standard of childhood and scholarship is demanded. Prophylaxis should precede prosecution and segregation. It is realized that statistics are the mystics of argument. The aggregate of life is made up of vicissitudes of transmigration, climate, environment, vocational disease and accidents, habit and habit-heredity, disease and disease-heredity, alcohol, syphilis, and tobacco. Alcohol is in almost universal use. Syphilis is all too prevalent; its spirochetæ leave their unmistaken trail in rural and mural "Damaged Goods." But there is a bane as prevalent as *all these combined.* It is the Race Poison, Tobacco; it is running a neck-and-wreck race with syphilis and alcohol for supremacy. No athletic or scholarship test has ever been made in which non-smokers did not excel the smokers; a similar comparison would militate against progeny. . . .

Temples and tombs survive, but the earth is fertile with the bones of extinct races. No monument is so favored of God as that which in His image con-

tinues achievement in His name, through Race Betterment.

## Further Resources

### BOOKS
Ferrence, Roberta G. *Deadly Fashion: The Rise and Fall of Cigarette Smoking in North America.* New York: Garland, 1989.

Sullum, Jacob. *For Your Own Good: The Anti-Smoking Crusade and the Tyranny of Public Health.* New York: Free Press, 1998.

Tate, Cassandra. *Cigarette Wars: The Triumph of "The Little White Slaver."* New York: Oxford University Press, 1999.

# Painless Childbirth
### Nonfiction work

**By:** Henry Smith Williams

**Date:** 1914

**Source:** Williams, Henry Smith. *Painless Childbirth.* New York: Goodhue, 1914, 10, 14, 18, 19–20, 36, 43, 90–91.

**About the Author:** Henry Smith Williams (1863–1943), a physician and pathologist, was one of America's foremost advocates of the so-called new "Twilight Sleep" method for inducing painless childbirth in women. ■

## Introduction

The pain of childbirth has been something that women, and women alone, have always had to endure. Moreover, childbirth induces a particular type of pain that is not easily treated. Throughout labor, the woman must remain conscious in order to push, hold back, or engage in whatever other actions the birth process may require. Hence, the nineteenth-century introduction of safe general anesthetic, which rendered the patient totally unconscious, was really not an option with labor. Meanwhile, other pain remedies presented the threat that the newborn might be exposed to harmful, even life-threatening, drugs.

However, by 1910 a new pain-management option had arrived in the United States from Germany that went by the name "twilight sleep:" With the use of small doses of narcotics, such as morphine or opium derivatives, a pleasant dreamlike state could be induced while the woman remained fully conscious and hence capable of participating in the birthing process, but all the while remaining devoid of any physical discomfort. One would have expected that this new "twilight-sleep" method of painless childbirth would be embraced universally as a more perfect solution to an age-old problem.

## Significance

Nonetheless, the twilight sleep method engendered much heated opposition from the public on a number of fronts. First, the use of a narcotic, any narcotic, raised fears. The decade of the 1910s witnessed a "war on drugs," and the introduction of twilight sleep method coincided with the powerful antinarcotics thrust of the Progressive era. Then too, the ancient idea lingered that by experiencing pain the woman bonded more effectively with her offspring. Finally, many argued that maternal pain was natural and thus the entire delivery process should not be tampered with.

Arrayed against the traditionalists were feminists and their allies, especially men who took an interest in women's health issues generally. Elsewhere, the declining birthrate among "old stock" American of Anglo ancestry was viewed by some as the understandable result of the reluctance of many middle and upper-class women to undergo the pain of childbirth. Conversely, an unspoken assumption held that immigrant and minority women, being allegedly less "delicate" or "refined," were better equipped by nature to handle the pain—hence their continued high birthrates. As with any social movement that ultimately succeeds, such as the campaign for painless childbirth, numerous groups—each pursuing its own distinct agenda—somehow manage to coalesce in order to enact reform.

## Primary Source

*Painless Childbirth* [excerpt]

**SYNOPSIS:** Henry Smith Williams, a physician and pathologist, presents a convincing case for the widespread adoption the revolutionary method of pain management for women during childbirth first introduced in Germany and commonly known as the "twilight sleep."

## The Twilight Sleep

So firmly established had the tradition become that the pains of childbirth represent a primal curse to be expiated anew by each and every mother, that when Dr. Morton gave the blessing of anæsthesia to humanity toward the middle of the nineteenth century, there was an outcry from many a pulpit against the use of this blessing to assuage the sorrows of childbirth.

And while the outcry was disregarded by many a practitioner, yet its echoes are heard to this day, and I make no doubt that the prejudice thus engendered is in good part responsible for the fact that even in this second decade of the twentieth century the generality of women bring forth their children in sorrow, quite after the ancient fashion, unsolaced by even a single whiff of those beneficent anæsthetic vapors through the use of which, in the poetic phrasing of Dr. Oliver Wendell Holmes, the agonies of tortured humanity may be "steeped in the waters of forgetfulness."

How many millions of women, I wonder, first and last, when in the utter extremity of anguish they have pled for an anæsthetic, have been met with a cold-blooded quotation of the malevolent phrase that the Ancient scribe sent down to us, paraphrased, perhaps, or supplemented with the assurance that the suffering of childbirth is a natural phenomenon that "does good" to both mother and child?

A "natural phenomenon"! In a sense, yes; since these agonizing pains are the regular attendant of childbirth with the vast majority of civilized women. But to say that this suffering does good, in any ordinary interpretation of the words, is to travesty language. . . .

And what, then, is the Freiburg method, which brings forth such enthusiastic comment from those who have shared its benefactions?

Stated in the fewest words, this method consists essentially in the hypodermic administration of certain drugs, given just at the incipiency of the acute pains of childbirth, and calculated to render the patient oblivious of the pains—or, to be quite accurate, to modify her consciousness in such a way that she has no recollection of suffering when the ordeal is over.

The treatment does not give entire unconsciousness, like the narcosis of ether or chloroform. Just what it does accomplish will be explained in some detail in a moment.

The drug chiefly depended on to produce this condition of painless childbirth at Freiburg is known as scopolamin. With it is associated, in the first dose, the more familiar drug morphine, or, more recently, another opium derivation called nacrophin. . . .

The essence of the matter is that when drugs are given in just the right quantity, the patient retains consciousness, and (except that she may fall asleep between pains) is at all times more or less cognizant of what is going on about her, but is singularly lacking in the capacity to remember any of the happenings that she observes.

She may seem to be conscious of the birth of her child, and may give evidence of apparent suffering. Yet when a few moments later the child is brought in by the nurse from the neighboring room where it has been cared for, and placed in the mother's arms, the patient does not recognize the child as her own, or realize that she has yet been delivered. . . .

This, obviously, is a very curious condition of sleep-waking. In some ways it suggests the hypnotic state. . . .

. . . In the English language, the condition is characterized as the "Twilight Sleep."

Twilight sleep! A pleasing and suggestive term, is it not? To scores of English-speaking women it has come to be a synonym for painless childbirth. And enthusiasts are not lacking who express the hope that in future it may become a household word throughout the English-speaking world.

Thousands of women have experienced the blessing of having the agonies of childbirth assuaged to the point of annulment by the Freiburg method. Why should not their millions of suffering sisters throughout the world be given also the boon and blessing of the twilight sleep or its equivalent?

Why not, indeed? . . .

### What Is Pain and Why?

. . . That question answers itself. For clearly, if every woman brought to childbed were to make such interpretation of the warning, and never repeat the experiment of motherhood, the human race would dwindle at a geometrical ratio, and incur every probability of elimination; . . .

So here we are confronted with a fine paradox. The purpose of pain in general we seem clearly to know. Yet the pain of childbirth—the most intense, perhaps, to which a human being can be subjected—can only be interpreted in a directly inverted sense.

Suppose we state the matter thus: Nature desires that woman shall bear a large number of children. Nature provides pain as a warning against repetition of a pain-engendering experience. . . .

### Labor Pains

. . . But as to this, as well as to the main question at the moment under consideration, let Dr. Krönig speak for himself:

"Of late," he says, "the demand made of us obstetricians to diminish or abolish suffering during delivery has become more and more emphatic. The modern woman, on whose nervous system nowadays quite other demands are made than was formerly the case, responds to the stimulus of severe pain more rapidly with nervous exhaustion and paralysis of the will to carry the labor to a conclusion. The sensitiveness of those who carry on hard mental work is much greater than that of those who earn their living by manual labor. . . ."

### What the Average Layman Can Do

. . . Moreover, the cultured woman of to-day has a nervous system that makes her far more susceptible to pain and to resultant shock than was her more lethargical ancestor of remote generations.

Such a woman not unnaturally shrinks from the dangers and pains incident to child-bearing; yet such cultured women are precisely the individuals who should propagate the species and thus promote the interests of the race.

The problem of making child-bearing a less hazardous ordeal and a far less painful one for these nervous and sensitive women is a problem that concerns not merely the women themselves, but the coming generations. Let the robust, phlegmatic, nerveless woman continue to have her children without seeking the solace of narcotics or the special attendance of expert obstetricians, if she prefers. But let her not stand in the way of securing such solace and safety for her more sensitive sisters.

### Further Resources

#### BOOKS

Edwards, Margot. *Reclaiming Birth: History and Heroines of American Childbirth Reform.* Trumansburg, N.Y.: Crossing Press, 1984.

Sandelowski, Margarete. *Pain, Pleasure, and American Childbirth: From the Twilight Sleep to the Read Method, 1914–1960.* Westport, Conn.: Greenwood, 1984.

Wertz, Richard W. *Lying-in: A History of Childbirth in America.* New Haven, Conn.: Yale University Press, 1989.

# "The Endowment of Motherhood"

Speech

**By:** John F. Moran

**Date:** January 9, 1915

**Source:** Moran, John F. "The Endowment of Motherhood." Presidential Address read at a meeting of the Washington, D.C., Obstetrical and Gynecological Society, January 9, 1915. In *Journal of the American Medical Association* 64, no. 2, January–June, 1915, 122–126.

**About the Author:** John Francis Moran, M.D. (1885–1929), president of the Washington (D.C.) Obstetrical and

Gynecological Society and a longtime critic of traditional home-childbirth midwives, sought to promote hospital childbirth under physician care for all American women. ■

## Introduction

There has always existed a tension between the idea of medicine as a healing art and as a business. Over the last two centuries, physicians—sometimes more loyal to the business end of the health-care industry than to its actual practice on patients—have waged a turf battle with other health-related professions that physicians viewed as rivals. Nurses and pharmacists, osteopaths, homeopaths, and chiropractors have all found it hard to resist the economic, political, and social power exerted by physicians backed by the authority of the state.

One example is the relationship between physicians and druggists. Self-medication had been the norm before physicians became the gatekeepers over a whole range of substances through the prescription system. Meanwhile, by banishing competitors from the field, physicians increased their compensation. Further, by convincing the government to mandate standardized credentials and licensing, the status and prestige of physicians likewise increased.

## Significance

One health-care turf battle during the Progressive era pitted obstetricians against midwives. At stake was primacy in the childbirth realm. Allied with obstetricians in this fight were hospital administrators who wanted to end the age-old practice of women giving birth at home and replace it with a more modern way of delivery under hospital conditions. In this fashion, physician care would replace the midwives, whom physicians thought of as amateurs. In fact, within a generation, the traditional at home-birth experience was largely forgotten, and the hospital stay became the norm for many (and eventually most) American women. In a historical footnote, Jimmy Carter (born in 1924) appears to have been the first U.S. president delivered in a hospital.

In addition, the midwife controversy became entangled with the larger feminist movement then emerging during this period. Midwifery had long represented a traditional bastion of female power in an otherwise largely male-dominated world. As part of the antifeminist backlash that accompanied women's demands for enhanced professional opportunities (especially in nursing or the agitation to permit women themselves to become physicians), men struck back.

Elsewhere, as part of the obstetricians' opposition to midwifery, the abortion issue surfaced. One of the major selling points for transferring child delivery responsibilities from midwives to physicians centered around the alleged ease with which women midwives routinely performed abortions—a practice that came under intense scrutiny during the early years of the twentieth century. Male doctors, presumably less sympathetic than females to the practice of abortion, would therefore cut down this increasingly unpopular practice. Thus, the restrictions enacted in many states on abortions were an ancillary repercussion of the campaign that male obstetricians pursued against female midwives.

## Primary Source

**"The Endowment of Motherhood"** [excerpt]

**SYNOPSIS:** Dr. John F. Moran takes aim at midwives, who were a long-standing rival in the childbirth field. Moran presents the case to entrust all maternal care and baby deliveries solely to physicians.

In this day, when the laity is discussing eugenics and legislatures are enacting laws for the betterment of the race, it behooves us as medical men to consider the value of the potential mother and her unborn baby as a national asset and ascertain wherein their status can be benefited. The crux of the situation is the safety of the mother during pregnancy, labor and the puerperium.

The latest reports of the Bureau of Census on mortality statistics show that slightly more than 42 percent of the infants dying under one year in the registration area in 1911 did not live to complete the first month of life, and that of these 42 per cent, almost seven-tenths died as the results of conditions existing before they were born, or of injury and accident and birth. Of those that lived less than one week about 83 per cent died of such causes, and of the number that lived less than one day 94 per cent died of these causes. . . .

Why women at this day are permitted to entrust themselves to the hands of ignorant and untrained persons at the most important period of their lives would seem incredible but for the fact that it is actually true. It is not that we are more capable than our predecessors, for comparatively few epoch-making measures have been evolved in obstetrics in the last half century, but it is the immense advantage we possess in the added knowledge of asepsis and antisepsis and preventive medicine, owing to the developments in modern bacteriology. . . .

It is over fifty years since that grand savant, Pasteur, established the correlation of germs with disease and proved that wound infection and puerperal infection were identical; and yet, notwithstanding these epoch-making advances of knowledge in the prevention of infection, the mortality and morbidity in parturition and the puerperium, in the general practice of obstetrics, has been but little diminished since the advent of the antiseptic era.

That thousands of women die every year from puerperal infection and accidents of childbirth, that many thousands more pass into the care of the gynecologists, and that one-third of the blindness in the world is the result of ophthalmia neonatorum are true and convincing proofs that obstetrics is wofully lacking in the careful study and attention it so rightly deserves.

How shall we lessen this frightful mortality and morbidity? To use a commercial phrase let us take stock and see wherein we can minimize the dangers that beset pregnancy, labor and the puerperium. While much of the etiology and pathology of the diseases of pregnancy are unknown, yet we have many measures of prevention at our command that lack universal application because of ignorance, carelessness and faulty judgment. . . .

Why is the standard of obstetrics in general practice so low? The following have been imputed to be the responsible agents: ignorance and indifference of the laity; that pregnancy and labor are normal processes and do not require experienced help; the midwife and her bargain counter inducement, and the laxity of the medical profession. While these are admittedly factors in the final analysis, lack of training of the medical graduate in practical obstetrics is the principal cause. . . .

Many of the schools are inadequately equipped for the teaching of obstetrics properly, only one having an ideal clinic; many of the professors are poorly prepared for their duties and have little conception of the obligations of a professorship; many of the teachers admit that their students are not prepared to practice obstetrics on graduation; one-half of the answers state that ordinary practitioners lose proportionately as many women from puerperal infection as do midwives and that reform is urgently needed, and can be more readily accomplished by radical improvement in medical education than by the almost impossible task of improving midwives. . . .

The most glaring default of medical teaching is the paucity of time and attention that is given to obstetrics. Its present standard is so low that it is a disgrace. To err from ignorance when human life and health are involved is lamentable, but when we possess the light and neglect to avail ourselves of the knowledge it is inexcusable, aye, often criminal. . . .

The college curriculum should be revised so as to fit men to do the greatest good to the race. Obstetrics and general medicine should be intensively taught in the graduate course, and the practice of surgery and gynecology, which are largely elective, should be restricted to postgraduate teaching. . . .

Obstetrics is the most arduous, least appreciated, least supported, and least compensated of all the branches of medicine. Its dignity and importance will never be recognized as long as the incompetent female and male midwives with their bargain counter inducements are placed on an equality with the trained practitioner. That statistics may show that the results of the general profession are little if any better than those of the midwives is beside the question and proves that the standard of teaching of obstetrics is low, very low, and needs to be radically improved.

## Further Resources

### BOOKS

Ehrenreich, Barbara, and Deirdre English. *Witches, Midwives, and Nurses: A History of Women Healers.* Old Westbury, N.Y.: Feminist Press, 1973.

Rooks, Judith. *Midwifery and Childbirth in America.* Philadelphia: Temple University Press, 1997.

Rothman, Barbara Katz. *In Labor: Women and Power in the Birthplace.* New York: Norton, 1982.

# "How the Drug Dopers Fight"

Magazine article

**By:** George Creel

**Date:** January 30, 1915

**Source:** Creel, George. "How the Drug Dopers Fight." *Harper's Weekly,* January 30, 1915, 110–112.

**About the Author:** George Creel (1876–1953), a crusading investigative journalist, was a vehement critic of the patent-medicine industry. Shifting gears, he served the Wilson administration during World War I (1914–1918) as chairman of the highly controversial Committee on Public Information, a government agency designed to promote support for the conflict. ∎

## Introduction

Most of the laws prohibiting the sale, possession, and use of narcotics and other controlled substances are barely a century old. Throughout the earlier part of the nation's history, a libertarian attitude prevailed regarding these matters, which were once deemed private, not pub-

Shoppers look in at a promotion for the patent medicine "Digestit" at Brown's Drug Store, April 9, 1915. In addition to elaborate signs and displays for Digestit there is a pianist, "Mr. Thomas," who has been performing for more than sixty hours straight to promote the drug. Mr. W.L. Brown stands behind him. THE LIBRARY OF CONGRESS.

lic, concerns. Self-medication had been the norm. Only during the Progressive era did this traditional libertarian sentiment shift enough to allow the acceptance of the idea that personal habits might be subject to public regulation.

The nineteenth-century pharmacy was a wide-open and completely unregulated frontier where druggists routinely sold tonics laced with large doses of alcohol, cocaine, opium, or morphine to anyone, even children, often causing addiction. A bottled "rheumatism cure" contained enough narcotics to be illegal today. Even more alarming, on the fringes of legitimate drugstores, dwelt the traveling medicine shows that saw hustlers peddling "snake-oil" potions and assorted home concoctions to gullible men and women.

The landmark national Pure Food and Drug Act of 1906 gave the federal government authority to regulate much of the medicine manufactured and sold in the United States. A strict system of physician-controlled prescriptions was instituted to keep the use of drugs firmly under the auspices of responsible health practitioners. As a result, many now-banned substances disappeared from over-the-counter remedies. Meanwhile, narcotics were banished from other corners of American life. For instance, in response to growing public pressure, the Coca-Cola Company in 1904 quietly changed its formula to eliminate active cocaine. American opinion shifted dramatically: Within a single generation, the tolerant attitudes toward personal drug use changed to permit increased government police powers to control it, if not stamp it out altogether.

## Significance

Nonetheless, many pharmaceutical makers and their allies waged an effective rearguard action against these new government controls. Some sought exemptions for their products; others disguised or reformulated their products. Fatiguing administrative or court challenges were waged in an effort to confuse the issue, circumvent the law, or stall for time. In other cases, illegal substances simply moved underground, as a thriving black market appeared that, in hindsight, served as a precursor of the illegal American drug market today. Finally, pharmaceutical firms often engaged in a public-relations campaign of obvious deception, often even contradicting scientific evidence demonstrating that their products either failed to work or were harmful. It required a generation, if not longer, of crusading investigative journalists to expose these tactics.

## Primary Source

### "How the Drug Dopers Fight" [excerpt]

**SYNOPSIS:** Investigative journalist George Creel describes some of the tactics that pharmaceutical manufacturers and their business allies used to avoid government efforts to keep harmful "patent medicines" off the shelves of American pharmacies and drugstores.

There is no interest in the United States than can wage a more bitter, cunning and plausible resistance to inimical legislation than the so-called "patent medicine" industry. Anyone attempting to protect the public health against lies and fraud, whether he be a member of Congress, high state official or local commissioner, must be prepared to run a continuous gauntlet of attack and misrepresentation.

A business of huge returns, it is in the division of these returns that the poisoners have gained their strength. Of every dollar derived from the sale of a nostrum at least one-half goes to some unscrupulous newspaper proprietor in the shape of advertising payments, so that, in the last analysis, a large portion of the press is the working partner of the quack. An attack upon the patent medicine evil, therefore, not only arouses the hatred of those primarily responsible, but may be depended upon to earn the ill will, passive or active, of the newspapers that share in the profits of fraud. It is this absence of helpful sympathetic publicity that makes the way of the patent medicine reformer so hard and thankless. To illustrate:

On December 31, 1914, Dr. S. S. Goldwater, commissioner of health for New York city, issued an order that after December 31, 1915, all patent medicines sold locally must either bear the names of the ingredients on the label, or else have such a state-

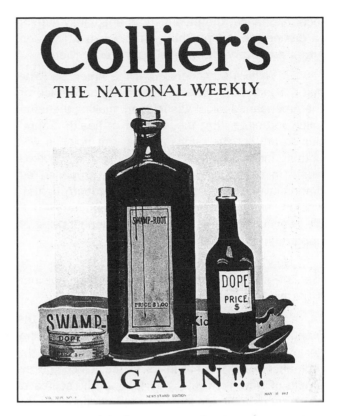

Cover of the May 1912 edition of *Collier's*, featuring an exposé article on patent medicines. **GETTY IMAGES. REPRODUCED BY PERMISSION.**

ment on file in the health department. In plain words, it was Dr. Goldwater's idea that the purchasers of these medicines should be given a chance to *know* what they were buying.

This simple theory of open dealing, however, was straightway branded as an outrage by the manufacturers and sellers of such nostrums as depend upon secrecy for their success. The cry of "oppression" and "confiscation" was raised, and upon these representations Mayor Mitchell requested Dr. Goldwater to grant a public hearing at which opponents of the regulation could be heard. This hearing was held January 6, and the large council chamber in the city hall was packed and jammed. Several morning papers reported the meeting in such manner as to give the impression that there was a "medical trust," and that the developments of the hearing had placed Dr. Goldwater in a somewhat sorry and even untenable position.

The true story is interesting, not only as a disproof of these inferences, but because the proceedings throughout were so completely expositional of the claims and defenses of the whole patent medicine business. Although held in New York on a local ordinance, the meeting had absolutely nothing to distinguish it from the hearings with which Congress and every state legislature are familiar.

Dr. William C. Anderson, of the American Druggists' Syndicate, opened with the usual attack on the American Medical Association, making the usual mildewed claim that the attempt of health authorities to protect the public from secret poisons was nothing more than a scheme to perfect a "doctor's trust." In its essence, he declared, the proposed regulation involved "the confiscation of property rights," was an "assault on personal liberty" and turned people over to rapacious practitioners by destroying all opportunity for self-medication.

"How?" interrupted Dr. Goldwater. "Do you mean that the public will refuse to buy patent medicines if the contents are printed on the label?"

Albert Plaut, a wholesale druggist engaged in the manufacture of proprietary preparations, put his finger on the real sore spot when he insisted that the ordinance was national in its scope, since the example of New York would be followed by scores of other communities, each eager to improve upon the model.

"Why not?" Dr. Goldwater asked. "Why should any community be asked to permit secret traffic in medicines?"

"If a man makes a valuable discovery," explained Mr. Plaut, "he has no protection except in secrecy."

"Isn't it a fact," insisted Dr. Goldwater, "that the constituents of these valuable discoveries are changed quite often?"

"Yes."

"Do you regard this switching of ingredients, done in secrecy and without public knowledge, as a legitimate practice?"

"I can't give a general answer to that," Mr. Plaut replied. Continuing, he praised the high honor of the drug trade, insisted that druggists were responsible for the Food and Drugs act, asserted that the task of remedial legislation was a national function, and pledged aid to the enactment of congressional measures, in the event that local attempts should be discontinued.

■ ■ ■

All of which is ancient buncombe. The Food and Drugs act was passed over the strenuous opposition of the nostrum manufacturers, and every attempt to give it proper amendment has brought out the same money-spending, power-wielding patent medicine influences. When Congress proposes to act, the dopers cry that it is an infringement of states' rights, when a legislature considers remedies it becomes a "local matter," and when communities agitate, there is insistence that the entire matter is "federal."

Dr. J. H. Rehfuss, of the New York Pharmaceutical Association, trotted Personal Liberty into the show ring, and made that venerable nag perform until its bones ached.

"If any member of my family wants to take a laxative," he cried in clear, ringing tones, "why should I have to send to some doctor for a prescription? The ordinance is an attack on personal liberty. I have a right to take what I please."

"You will still have that right," Dr. Goldwater soothed. "All that we are trying to do is to let people know what it is they are buying. "Surely you do not wish poisonous and injurious substances in the mouths of the unwitting?"

"Certainly not," Dr. Rehfuss replied. "I am willing at all times to aid you in driving out the vicious patent medicines."

"How?"

"Well," hesitantly, "I would want time to consider that." . . .

Peter Diamond, a New York retail druggist of the old school, was the one witness of the afternoon, as a matter of fact, that struck a new note.

"Fifty per cent of the prescriptions that I fill," he said, "are for proprietary medicines of which the physicians writing the prescriptions know nothing."

"Do you know anything about them?" Dr. Goldwater asked.

"No," Mr. Diamond replied. "I want to know nothing about them."

"Yet you sell them, Mr. Diamond," insisted Dr. Goldwater. "Many druggists have come to me and confessed the same ignorance. They are selling secret remedies that may contain death instead of health, and they have said that this ordinance, which lets them know what they are handing out to the sick, will take a load off their consciences."

Again the crowded room rocked to hisses, catcalls and derisive laughter, yet when quiet was restored at last, Mr. Diamond answered "Yes, Doctor, you are right. I do not want to sell them at all," he continued. "I want patent medicines separated entirely from pharmacy. And let me say here and now that we will never have the absolutely necessary standards in medicines and drugs until the municipality itself takes over the business." . . .

Let the Goldwater regulation be enforced by all means, and let other communities follow the good example, but the ultimate goal will not be reached until the public is afforded a protection that does not rest upon the initiative of the individual. Disclosure of ingredients will kill the sale of injurious compounds to persons of intelligence, perhaps, but it will not do to forget the large percentage of ignorant, careless or reckless purchasers who will still persist in the use of health-destroying preparations. This is the problem.

## Further Resources

### BOOKS

Anderson, Ann. *Snake Oil, Hustlers and Hambones: The American Medicine Show*. Jefferson, N.C.: McFarland, 2000.

Hechtlinger, Adelaide. *The Great Patent Medicine Era: or, Without Benefit of Doctor*. New York: Galahad Books, 1970.

Natenber, Maurice. *The Legacy of Doctor Wiley and the Administration of His Food and Drug Act*. Chicago: Regent House, 1957.

---

# "The Heart of the People"

Movie review

**By:** Randolph Bourne

**Date:** July 3, 1915

**Source:** Bourne, Randolph. "The Heart of the People." *The New Republic*, July 3, 1915.

**About the Author:** Randolph Bourne (1886–1918), an essayist and social critic, was one of the nation's outstanding young intellectuals during the pre-World War I period. A fervent opponent of American intervention in the conflict, Bourne is famous for his aphorism "War is the health of the state." He died prematurely during the influenza epidemic of 1918. ∎

## Introduction

The second decade of the twentieth century saw the American motion picture come of age. Prior to 1915, the movies had largely been the preserve first of carnival arcades with their nickelodeons and later of small movie houses located in seedy neighborhoods frequented by poor immigrants and minorities. But all that changed in 1915 with the release of D.W. Griffith's epic drama, *The Birth of a Nation*—the first truly great silent-screen clas-

sic. Now for the first time, going to the movies became an accepted middle-class pastime.

In addition, by 1915 the increasingly sophisticated motion-picture industry had become a vehicle for the discussion of social issues. Movies often exhibited a gritty reality—often taking great delight in depicting the seamy side of life. In contrast, after 1920, as giant studios consolidated and many independent production companies went out of business, Hollywood played it safe and projected an economic, political, and social conservatism that avoided treatment of controversial matters

## Significance

Nonetheless, the movie industry had witnessed a period of vibrant experimentation and innovation for American filmmakers. One previously taboo subject that found its way onto the silver screens was venereal disease, which became the focus of several films. Similarly, the unpleasant topic of tuberculosis—known as the "white death"—made its appearance on the screen.

One tuberculosis film came to the attention of essayist and social critic Randolph Bourne, one of the leading writers of the period. Bourne, like other observers, seriously wondered whether or not the public could handle such a delicate, if distasteful, subject as tuberculosis. Indeed the question whether the motion picture itself could serve as a suitable medium for the dissemination of information was even raised. One concern raised by Bourne about the use of cinema as an educational medium revolved around the problem inherent in any dramatization: The public expected movies in a conventional dramatic format. But perhaps a pure documentary style would be a more effective means of presenting information. Indeed, this long-standing dependence on following the requirements of dramatic construction has doubtless prevented the motion picture from supplanting, say, books as the principal vehicle for the public discussion of serious ideas.

## Primary Source

"The Heart of the People" [excerpt]

**SYNOPSIS:** Randolph Bourne, noted essayist and social critic, explores the question whether or not the cinema can be employed as an effective medium for the presentation of controversial information for public discussion. In this selection, Bourne analyzes his experience viewing a silent motion picture, *The White Terror*, dealing with the subject of tuberculosis.

As a would-be democrat, I should like to believe passionately in the movies. I am told constantly of their great educational possibilities. By the innocent

A volunteer from the Community Service of New York speaks with an immigrant family about tuberculosis prevention. A poster about the "White Plague" helps illustrate her point. GETTY IMAGES. REPRODUCED BY PERMISSION.

and ubiquitous movies we are to be made over, insensibly led to higher things. Buoyed by such hopes, I go with ever-renewed courage. But into that democrat that I long to be I shall never be made by such exhibitions as "The White Terror," "an educational feature film in four reels," sponsored by the National Association for the Prevention of Tuberculosis. Experience it seems has proved that the public does not take kindly to pure "education" in the movies. The "education" has had to be smeared on in the spots where was thought it would best stick. The first object of the deviser of this film had been

to tell a dramatic story, and from the meticulous care with which it was presented one could not doubt that every detail had been ingeniously arranged to meet some deep public hunger.

It was exciting. Love, crime, political corruption, industrial exploitation, social service, redemption, pathos and personal hygiene were woven into an unforgettable work of art. The climax came when, after a long and blissful kiss between the happily healed and reconciled daughter of the ruthless but reformed patent-medicine magnate and her valiant lover, this hopeful quotation from Pasteur was thrown upon our gaze: "It is possible to banish from the earth all such parasitic germ diseases within a generation." Although our sophisticated social-worker group burst into unanimous glee, there lingered the horrible suspicion that that fifty per cent of the public who would see it were not supposed to laugh. . . .

Swift upon the crime follows nemesis. The lovely daughter contracts the dread disease. I hope the movies don't see many such scenes of bathos as this in which the father comes with a touching smile and presents his daughter with a bottle of his interesting compound of opium and arsenic. Fortunately the doctor intervenes. Enter "education," with its sanatoriums and open-air schools and all the proper ways to cure consumption. The father falls upon his desk, a broken man, while lines of skeletons poring over his advertisements pass before his eyes, and serried rows of gravestones haunt him, each marking the effect of a bottle of his poison. But presto! all is redeemed. A sumptuous banquet is given the reconciled pair, the father announces a gift of a tuberculosis sanatorium to the city, the bad man is redeemed into a philanthropist, the daughter is healed, the lover rewarded, and excellent moral and hygienic lessons are implanted in the heart of the American people. . . .

I have to take "The White Terror" seriously, because it is as scientific a record as a statistical graph. Like the popular novel, it marks the norm of what happy and hearty America is attending to. Melodrama used to be bad form, but the movies are good form for almost all classes. This is the great public of a generation which has had universal common school education, free libraries, museums, cheap journals, and books, on a scale known to no generation in history. This is what we get out of it all.

## Further Resources

**BOOKS**

Bates, Barbara. *Bargaining for Life: A Social History of Tuberculosis, 1876–1938.* Philadelphia: University of Pennsylvania Press, 1992.

Dormandy, Thomas. *The White Death: A History of Tuberculosis.* New York: New York University Press, 2000.

Ott, Katherine. *Fevered Lives: Tuberculosis in American Culture Since 1870.* Cambridge, Mass.: Harvard University Press, 1996.

# "Progress in Pediatrics"
Journal article

**By:** Philip Van Ingen
**Date:** September 1915
**Source:** Van Ingen, Philip. "Progress in Pediatrics: Recent Progress in Infant Welfare Work." *American Journal of Diseases of Children* 10, September 1915, 212, 213–214, 219.
**About the Author:** Philip Van Ingen, M.D. (1875–1953), was one of the nation's outstanding practicing pediatricians. He maintained a lifelong interest in promoting science-based education among parents so as to enable them to appreciate better the medical and nutritional needs of their children. He played a major role in promoting and popularizing the childhood health movement. ∎

## Introduction

The early years of the twentieth century witnessed a dramatic growth in government power throughout the United States that featured extensive state involvement in many areas of life that had previously been considered strictly private matters. Measures appeared regulating personal conduct, including alcohol and drug use and sexual behavior. Older, more libertarian-oriented ideas that unsavory personal conduct could be corrected either by voluntary efforts or by moral pressure gave way to more government-oriented solutions.

Meanwhile, government authority was enhanced in other significant ways. Stricter credential and license requirements made physicians the sole dispensers of most medicines. All in all, the Progressive era saw the rise of greatly enlarged state that could enforce its authority in unprecedented fashion.

## Significance

While enhanced state power sometimes had unfavorable consequences, it also had obvious benefits, particularly in the public-health sector, including disease control and the growing campaign to upgrade the overall health of America's youngsters. The period after 1910 saw the rise of a vigorous (often state supported) children's health movement. Children benefited immensely from this newfound attention.

By 1910, much scientific knowledge had accumulated demonstrating how to raise a healthy baby. Impressive breakthroughs occurred in the field of childhood nutrition, sanitary practices, and immunizations. As a result, the period witnessed a dramatic decrease in infant mortality. Meanwhile, all these breakthroughs reinforced the emerging practice of pediatrics.

Of course, this knowledge explosion alone was not enough. For America was populated with poor, uneducated women, both native-born and immigrant, who

NEW JERSEY MUST FIGHT ON
THAT THESE SHALL NOT
HAVE DIED IN VAIN

THAT THESE SHALL NOT
BE BORN IN VAIN

© 1919 DEPARTMENT OF HEALTH
OF THE STATE OF NEW JERSEY

A poster from the Department of Health of the State of New Jersey, c. 1919. It likens the battle to improve child health care to that of World War I. Scientific child-rearing and health care methods were widely promoted by government in the 1910s. THE LIBRARY OF CONGRESS.

sometimes did not know what to make of this information. Many foreigners remained wedded to folk remedies used in their old countries, and folk remedies were no stranger to many less advanced regions of America either. Thus, the childhood health awareness campaign contained a large educational component that sought to instruct parents in modern practices. Some cities sponsored "Baby Week" when a concerted effort was waged to spread useful information. New York City in particular spearheaded efforts to spread this knowledge and became a model for the rest of the nation.

## Primary Source

### "Progress in Pediatrics" [excerpt]

**SYNOPSIS:** Philip Van Ingen, M.D., one of America's best known pediatricians, describes the progress of the children's health movement in educating parents on new scientific ideas regarding medicine and nutrition. In particular, he discusses New York City's highly successful "Baby Week" campaign.

### Recent Progress in Infant Welfare Work

During the past year, in spite of unfavorable conditions, financial and political, infant welfare work has steadily increased in extent and efficiency. Even from war-cursed Europe a few reports of progress have been received. . . .

Probably the most extensive campaign carried on was in New York. As a preliminary a letter was sent out by the Commissioner of Health to all health officers in the state asking for their cooperation, and for information as to the needs in their particular localities. The objects of the campaign were, "to educate the mother in the care and feeding of her child, to arouse the community to the necessity for child welfare work, to point out the fact that a high infant mortality was unnecessary and should be considered a disgrace, to establish infant welfare centers with the employment of nurses, and to improve the general milk supply." Three special exhibits were prepared and those of the Rochester department of health and the Russell Sage Foundation were borrowed. During April, May and June these exhibits were shown in forty-five cities and large villages, over 150 public meetings had been held in connection with them and over 79,000 people had been reached. Three additional exhibits were prepared dealing especially with rural hygiene and, with the other exhibits, were shown during August and September at fifty-five county fairs, the State Fair, and the Rochester Industrial Exhibition. Ten requests for them had to be refused.

All exhibits were in charge of a trained nurse or specially trained person. Advice and literature were given, and, in addition, special meetings were held for mothers and prospective mothers. The older girls in the public and parochial schools were given talks and demonstrations, and, when requested, the nurse did a certain amount of home instructive visiting. In certain places two moving picture films were used in connection with the exhibit, on the care of the baby and on the subject of pure milk.

Wherever the exhibits were shown an attempt was made to arouse public interest and to try to secure the establishment of infant welfare stations. In 1913 there were thirty-two such stations in twelve localities outside of New York City. As a result of this campaign, by the end of 1914 there were sixty-seven stations already established in thirty-two different localities.

This was only a part of the activities of the department. Among others may be mentioned a campaign to establish a state organization of "Little Mothers' League," sending its pamphlet "How to Save the Babies" to the mother of every baby whose birth was registered, with a letter from the commissioner, and within the last few weeks the organization of a State-wide Baby Welfare Sunday.

How much good is accomplished by the distribution of literature is still something of an open question. That it does have some effect and is appreciated is shown from the following letters.

Locust Valley, N. Y., Dec. 21, 1914.
New York State Department of Health, Albany, N. Y.
Gentlemen:

A few days ago my wife received from you the "Baby Book." We cannot begin to express our gratitude to you for this little book. It is a Godsend to any mother with a little baby. It is being the means of saving thousands of lives and untold hours of care and worry.

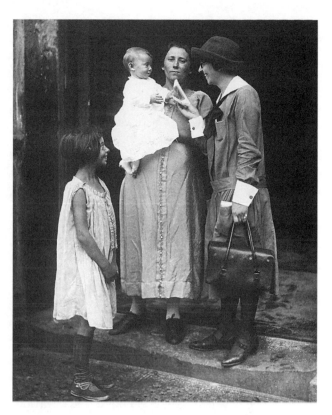

A public health nurse from the Henry Street settlement house visits a young mother in a slum district in New York City. © BETTMANN/CORBIS. REPRODUCED BY PERMISSION.

I have two sisters. One has a baby several months old, and the other will be a mother this coming spring. If it is not asking too much, I would like two more baby books—one for each of these women.

Thanking you again, I remain

*Yours very truly,*
———

Yonkers, N. Y., Dec. 5, 1914.
Dear Sir:

Recently one of my young mothers received a pamphlet from you, the title of which, I believe, was "Your Baby—How to Keep It Well." I would like to ask if each mother is to get one? I was much pleased with the pamphlet and would like one myself.

*Yours sincerely,*
*Dr.*———

P. S. It seems to me that if the doctors, nurses and midwives were included in the distribution of the pamphlet it would be of value. . . .

■ ■ ■

During the summer of 1914 a very extensive campaign of education was carried out in New York City through holding a "Baby Week." The mayor of the city issued the call. Practically every organization in the city was called upon to take part in carrying out the program and all responded willingly. A letter was sent by the mayor, which was read in many of the churches and synagogues throughout the city. A similar letter was read to the children of every public school on the Monday of "Baby Week," followed by appropriate ceremonies in many of the schools. The rest of the week was given up to demonstrating the needs of the babies of the city and the work that was being done to meet those needs. The milk stations, day nurseries, hospitals, outing associations and other activities all came in for their share of attention. During the week the final baby contest was held, at which was selected the prize baby of the city. Previous contests had been held during the winter and spring and the winners of all these preliminary contests competed. The final ceremony was a parade of milk station babies with their mothers in Fifth Avenue motor busses, private automobiles and taxicabs, all of which were donated for the occasion, which parade was reviewed by the mayor, commissioner of health and other city officials and the prize baby and the winners of other prizes were presented by the mayor with their diplomas, after which the children and their mothers were given a ride through the park. There was a tremendous response from every side to this plan for stimulating interest. Department stores held special baby week sales. The newspapers gave much space to a description of the proceedings. The advertising companies donated space on their bill boards. The results of such a campaign is hard to judge, but from the requests for information received from all over the country, it may be said that "Baby Week" was a success in calling attention to the needs of the baby. Similar work has been carried on since in a number of other places and during the first week of July, a local "Baby Week" is to be celebrated in the Borough of Richmond, New York.

## Further Resources

### BOOKS

Colon, A.R., with P.A. Colon. *Nurturing Children: A History of Pediatrics*. Westport, Conn.: Greenwood, 1999.

King, Charles R. *Children's Health in America: A History*. New York: Twayne, 1993.

Stern, Alexandra Minna, and Howard Markel. *Formative Years: Children's Health in the United States, 1880–2000*. Ann Arbor, Mich.: University of Michigan Press, 2002.

# "Orthopedic Surgery in War Time"

Presentation

**By:** Robert B. Osgood

**Date:** 1916

**Source:** Osgood, Robert B. "Orthopedic Surgery in War Time." Paper presented at the 67th Annual Session of the American Medical Association, Detroit, Michigan, June 13–16, 1916. Published in *Transactions of the Section on Orthopedic Surgery*. Chicago: American Medical Association Press, 1916, 143–144, 148, 149, 150.

**About the Author:** Robert Bailey Osgood (1873–1956), one of America's leading orthopedic surgeons, practiced in Boston. He was a recognized expert on diseases of the bones and joints and an author of a standard reference book on the subject. ∎

## Introduction

One of the consequences of war is the large number of men maimed in combat. In the past, the seriously wounded veteran was more often than not the object of pity. He faced a lifetime of difficult rehabilitation with uncertain prospects for recovery, as well as relentless pain and grief. While those killed in action are in time forgotten, the disabled survivor remains a constant reminder to the community of the human cost of war.

## Significance

By World War I, medical science had made great strides treating many once life-threatening battlefield wounds. Although the advent of antibiotics was still a generation into the future, other antiseptics were proving reasonably effective in treating war injuries. Hence, American society had to come to grips with a basic change: Men now survived war wounds that had once proved fatal.

Of particular note was the extraordinary progress made in the field of orthopedic surgery and rehabilitation as well as in the manufacture of effective prosthetic devices to replace shattered or missing body parts. In addition, there occurred a recognition of the importance of returning the injured veteran to the ranks of productive workers. In the words of one of the nation's leading orthopedic surgeons, Dr. Robert B. Osgood, his profession's task was to ensure that "war cripples may become happy, productive, wage earning citizens, instead of boastful, consuming, idle derelicts."

## Primary Source

"Orthopedic Surgery in War Time" [excerpt]

**SYNOPSIS:** With the First World War raging in Europe, and with the prospect looming of eventual

A World War I veteran whose arm was amputated due to battlefield injuries rehabilitates at Walter Reed Hospital in Washington, D.C., 1918. The government is training him, and thousands of other war amputees, for jobs that they can perform despite their injuries, such as painting toys. © BETTMANN/CORBIS. REPRODUCED BY PERMISSION.

American participation in the conflict, famed orthopedic surgeon Robert B. Osgood seeks to reassure the public with upbeat news of the remarkable medical progress that had recently been made in the field of reconstructive surgery to repair war wounds.

In a physical conflict such as war, the goal of both sides is set. To attain it each must conserve the physical energy of its soldiers in order to increase their strength in battle. Each must strive for the complete recovery of its wounded in order that the ranks may be kept as full as possible. Finally, but perhaps most important of all in any long conflict, each must see to it that those large numbers who do not lose their lives, but who by reason of their mutilating wounds lose their fighting power, do not become a burden on the industrial community already depleted and vastly overburdened by the necessity of support of the armies in the field. The few left at home are doing intensive work, and the wounded heroes, if the national strength is to be conserved, must have a still further test of their heroism and be made to contribute their remaining energy to help maintain their still efficient comrades.

Our thesis is to be that orthopedic surgery has a very large part to play in (1) assuring physical efficiency in the ranks; (2) in conserving and restoring the function of the locomotive apparatus of the wounded; (3) in providing the physical possibility and perhaps reorganizing the means by which the war cripples may become happy, productive, wage earning citizens, instead of boastful, consuming, idle derelicts. . . .

Many limbs are saved now that formerly would have been amputated, both because it is more possible to save them and save life as well, and also because the supply of artificial limbs bids fair to be so inadequate for some time to come. In these limbs, position has often been sacrificed to life, and realinement will be necessary. A further task and opportunity for orthopedic surgery is thus presented. These are only a few of the tasks and opportunities. . . .

The cripple has a right to look to the orthopedic surgeon for an amelioration of his condition. Much may be done by preventive and restorative surgery alone; much more may be accomplished by the added use of apparatus of one sort or another, supportive, retentive or corrective. . . .

## A Successful Workman

This man who lost an arm in an industrial accident in Cleveland, invented a good substitute arm, wears it at work, and uses it in earning his living. He has made good by his own unaided efforts. The average man, however, needs a lift in the way of training.

This Red Cross poster from 1919 shows a man who lost his arm in an industrial accident, wearing a prosthetic device of his own design. Medical advances had made relatively sophisticated prostheses like these possible by the 1910s. The poster urges that those who need them be trained in their use. **THE LIBRARY OF CONGRESS.**

This brings us to the consideration of the occupational training of cripples. It is fitting that orthopedic surgeons should take the lead in organizing this work, as they have done in the past and are doing now in Europe.

Here in America, although much has been accomplished, most of the cripples throughout the country are cripples still, and idlers instead of special wage earners. There can be no question as to which state of being is of greater use to the nation, or as to which state is the happier state for the individual. We should surely appreciate the importance of devoting much energy in our several communities to a rounding up of these interesting people and providing them, probably by state legislation, with vo-

cational training. This is a form of preparedness of which every pacifist must approve. . . .

We believe orthopedic surgery in times of peace is a most comprehensive specialty; in war time the possibilities of its helpfulness are still greater. The fact that these possibilities are not always recognized should make orthopedic surgeons seek opportunities to demonstrate them. If this opportunity is accepted it may well mark an epoch in the history of the specialty.

## Further Resources

### BOOKS

Le Vay, David. *A History of Orthopaedics: An Account of the Study and Practice of Orthopaedics from the Earliest Times to the Modern Era.* Park Ridge, N.J.: Parthenon, 1990.

Rang, Mercer. *The History of Orthopaedics.* Philadelphia: W.B. Saunders, 2000.

# "War and Mental Diseases"

**Presentation**

**By:** Pearce Bailey

**Date:** October 19, 1917

**Source:** Bailey, Pearce. "War and Mental Diseases." Address given to General Sessions, American Public Health Association, Washington, D.C., October 19, 1917. Reprinted in *American Journal of Public Health* 8, no. 1, January 1918, 1–5, 7.

**About the Author:** Pierce Bailey (1865–1922), a major in the U.S. Medical Reserve Corps, was a recognized authority on the mental and psychological aspects of war. He also wrote a comprehensive study of the various diseases of the nervous system resulting from accidents or injuries. ∎

## Introduction

The task of overcoming fear has always been a problem for military commanders. Various solutions have been tried—usually involving a training regimen designed to mold troops into cohesive units where the spirit of teamwork acts as a unifying force intended to overcome normal fear. The legendary eighteenth-century armies of Prussian king Frederick the Great operated on the basis of raw terror, for officers were stationed to the rear of the men with orders to shoot deserters. In essence, Frederick sought to instill in his men more dread of their own superiors than of the battlefield enemy.

The study of the psychological impact of war on fighting men received some scientific credibility with the publication of the work of French colonel Charles Jean Jacques Joseph Ardant du Picq (1821–1870). Du Picq, who was killed during the opening days of the Franco-Prussian War (1870–1871), explored the psychological dimension of war. In particular, he wished to discover why some armies trudged on despite the terror while others cracked. In a world where armies had become increasing mechanized, the decisive difference separating victory or defeat, Du Picq reasoned, would no longer be primarily the martial prowess of the soldiers but rather their psychological "will"—especially in a war of mass armies where civilians found themselves abruptly thrust into the front lines as never before.

Elsewhere, the late nineteenth-century Freudian revolution also served to focus attention on psychology in general. Not surprisingly, insights from this discipline found their way into the study of soldiers under fire. Thus, when the First World War erupted in 1914, the groundwork had already been laid for a more searching examination of the "mental" aspects of war than had ever been undertaken previously.

## Significance

After the United States entered the First World War against Germany in April 1917, the nation had to deal with this psychological dimension. It was deemed essential to keep the troops mentally "fit" for this in some ways unprecedented struggle. Then, too, trench warfare placed a punishing level of strain on soldiers. Psychological trauma from "shell shock" became common.

In actuality, this newfound appreciation for the mental aspects of military combat came relatively late for Americans. With the exception of the Civil War (1861–1865), Americans had never fought anything like the struggles that had routinely visited Europe for centuries. The United States, perhaps more than any other nation, clung to a heroic vision of war long after most of the civilized world had become thoroughly disillusioned. Perhaps this factor accounts for the seeming lack of interest in the treatment of war-induced psychological maladies. It focused attention on the "fear factor," which made war appear less heroic and less romantic. And it speaks of weakness and defeat, something that the United States had never experienced in the modern world.

## Primary Source

"War and Mental Diseases" [excerpt]

**SYNOPSIS:** Major Pearce Bailey, an expert on the mental and psychological impact of combat on soldiers, discusses some of the mental-health problems associated with American participation in the First World War.

Among the general problems of public health, the subject of mental hygiene has not received the attention it merits. It is among the more recent developments in preventive medicine, but it is an extremely important one and its importance, I think, is going to be very much emphasized and clarified by the conditions in this war. . . .

As I suppose everyone knows, the chances of recovery from insanity developed during war time are very much greater than from insanity developed in peace. A favorable hospital rate of recovery among civilians during peace is 20 per cent or 25 per cent. The psychoses developed in war time have a higher recovery rate. . . .

The history of past wars makes it imperative for the modern army to have a psychiatric department. The frequency of insanity in military forces may be found in army reports, in the Surgeon-General's reports of our navy or our army or of the medical departments of England and France, and of Germany as long as they were accessible, and you will find just about the same thing in all, namely that the discharge rate in practically all armies, is three men in every thousand every year. That is during peace. Now during war, that rate increases to six per thousand, or ten per thousand, varying with different wars. It increases much more rapidly in expeditionary wars, that is, wars in foreign countries. . . .

But the present conflict has made all the above mentioned conditions seem academic. The discharges due to nervous conditions in this war are enormous. . . .

Of course you all know that shell-shock, which is a disabling but recoverable form of nervous disturbance, has been enormously frequent in the expeditionary forces of England and Canada, and that probably is included in these high figures I have given. At the outbreak of the war the nervous casualties absolutely overwhelmed the British and French surgeons. Prior to that time, special physicians had not been prominent in either of the armies, and special hospitals had not been organized for the purpose of caring for nervous diseases. They had to make special efforts in England and all over France, had to build special centers for the special care of these cases, and now today one-fourth of all of the neurologists in England—25 per cent of all the men who are neurologists—have gone to the colors. With these considerations in mind, namely, the army reports and the results of this present war, the Surgeon-General before the actual outbreak of war foresaw the necessity of creating a

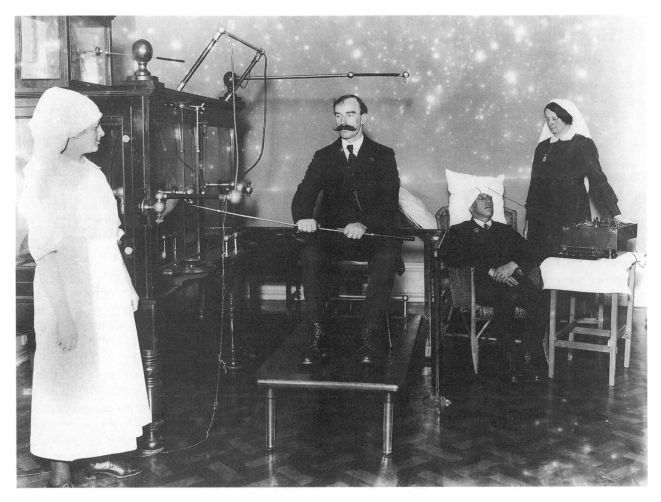

Nurses at a British hospital treat shell-shocked soldiers in 1915. Shell-shock (now called post-traumatic stress disorder) was a common problem among soldiers in World War I and began to be systematically studied and treated then. © HULTON-DEUTSCH COLLECTION/CORBIS. REPRODUCED BY PERMISSION.

special department in the army to take care of this kind of disability.

Now the question might naturally be asked, why was not this department created before? It had practically been created in no army before. I think one of the reasons was that before the advent of preventive medicine as a general sanity measure the armies had had to contend with such terrible and fatal diseases that surgeons had no time to contend with the mental disabilities. . . .

Armies have not adopted the specialty of nervous and mental diseases because also it is a young specialty. . . .

Almost every branch of the service is being or has now been examined by these specialists, and whenever we hear—as we only hear in a very indirect kind of way—that some organization, some division, some regiment, is about to sail that has not been examined, a number of officers are immedi-

ately ordered with the idea of examining them quickly before they go, and this, of course, is extremely important in view of the extra high percentage of neurologic conditions in expeditionary forces. Every man that goes abroad and breaks down uses up six tons of bottom for two months, you might say. It is very poor economy to let men go abroad who are going to break down from nervous diseases.

The diseases most frequently encountered, in the order of their importance are: First, the mental deficients. The stupid ones cause the same trouble in the army that the backward and feebleminded children do to the schools. It is not a question at all of education, because a man may be absolutely illiterate and still not be feebleminded at all. . . .

That man was entirely illiterate, but still perfectly competent in his immediate environment and as such gave promise of making a good soldier. It is not probable that a man who is mentally defective can make a good soldier. . . .

It is extraordinary how little some of these nervous affections are noticed in times of peace. The mental defective in peace time is the stupid fellow called a boob; but in war, he becomes delinquent or forgets his command or fails to appear. Then if he is at the front, he is shot for cowardice. The English found very soon that they were having so many cases at the front where a man seemed to be a coward with the result that he would be summarily court-martialed and shot, that they had to keep alienists and neurologists at the front for the purpose of determining, in cases of breach of discipline under fire, whether the man was responsible or not; and since they have done that the executions have fallen off very much in number. Epilepsy, another scourge of the army, may occur only as slight attacks during peace, but in war the attacks get worse. We endeavor to eliminate all epileptics. . . .

Now we talk so much about the evil of armies and the perils of war and all that, that sometimes we forget that armies do good and that good does come, in a large, sociological sense, from wars. . . . They have the picked medical men of the country, the latest equipment—I won't say the best, but all necessary equipment. There is a scientific spirit down there, and an interest in each other and in their work that is really extraordinary and very fine. I think their administration is going to teach all of us a good deal. The army has shown us how well it can take care of sickness in wooden buildings, that I hope our own brick piles and stone piles, built at such great expense, will give place to simple structures which can be burned up at the end of five years to meet new conditions; and that the extra money will be spent on the men that are going to manage them. And the army, in this particular branch I am interested, is going to do great good to the civil community because it will send back to the civil community after the war many trained psychiatrists and neurologists.

## Further Resources

### BOOKS

Becker, Harry. *Men, War, and Madness: A Psychoanalytic Study.* New York: Carleton, 1989.

Gillespie, Robert Dick. *Psychological Effects of War on Citizen and Soldier.* New York: W.W. Norton, 1942.

Kardiner, Abram, and Herbert Spiegel. *War Stress and Neurotic Illness.* New York: Hoeber, 1947.

# "Some Considerations Affecting the Replacement of Men by Women Workers"

Speech

**By:** Josephine Goldmark

**Date:** October 19, 1917

**Source:** Goldmark, Josephine. "Some Considerations Affecting the Replacement of Men by Women Workers." Address given to Industrial Hygiene Section, American Public Health Association, Washington, D.C., October 19, 1917. Reprinted in *American Journal of Public Health* 8, no. 4, April 1918, 270, 272, 273, 275, 276.

**About the Author:** Josephine Goldmark (1877–1950) served in various capacities as an officer of the National Consumers' League of New York City. She became a recognized authority on the problems both of women and child labor. ∎

## Introduction

During the Progressive era, many states and localities passed laws mandating worker protection. These statutes included health and safety measures designed to protect women from a variety of hazards, including exposure to toxic substances—especially while pregnant. Other laws limited, for instance, the amount of weight that a woman might be required to lift as part of her job. Ironically, at the moment when the long-standing efforts of industrial reformers were coming to fruition, the emerging feminist movement oftentimes exerted pressure in the opposite direction. Some, but not all, feminists argued that if women desired rough equality with men, and wished to enter the workforce in order to obtain jobs held exclusively by men, then why should they be given special protections. This split in the movement was clearly visible by 1915 and has continued right down to the present day.

## Significance

This issue turned from a theoretical dispute to an intensely practical one soon after America entered the First World War in April 1917. With millions of working men called to active military duty, gaping holes in the industrial workforce needed to be filled, and America's women were the most likely candidates. Hence, the problem of women replacing men on the front lines of American industry drew the attention of the public after 1917.

Those concerned with women's health paid close attention to this development. Again, observers were divided on how it would impact women. On one hand, this change opened new opportunities for women. Enhanced workplace opportunities not only meant better pay and

FOR EVERY FIGHTER A WOMAN WORKER

Y·W·C·A·

BACK OUR SECOND LINE OF DEFENSE
UNITED WAR WORK CAMPAIGN

A 1918 Y.W.C.A. poster promoting women in the workplace to meet the labor demand created by sending young men off to fight World War I. **THE LIBRARY OF CONGRESS.**

increased prestige but might finally convince men to grant women their full political rights, including the right to vote. On the other hand, the old fears surfaced about women's health, especially those regarding exposure of women of child-bearing age to harmful materials. Some suggested that because women were allegedly less aggressive and more easily intimidated, they would be exploited by their employers. In fact, the specter of women strikebreakers or even the outright feminization of entire sections of the workforce in order to stave off unionization was discussed. Women might simply constitute a vast new pool of cheap labor.

In the end, the pressing manpower needs of American industry dictated the outcome of events. Women were brought into the industrial workforce, although mainly as a stopgap measure. When peace returned, most women were encouraged to return to their previous pursuits or else let go to make way for returning men. But the short-lived experiment of 1917–1918 served as a source of in-

spiration for the women's liberation movement a half-century later.

## Primary Source

### "Some Considerations Affecting the Replacement of Men by Women Workers" [excerpt]

> **SYNOPSIS:** Josephine Goldmark, an expert on occupational problems encountered by females in the workplace, discusses the pros and cons of women replacing men in various industrial jobs as a result of the severe U.S. labor shortage during World War I when men were suddenly mustered into military service.

Among the many new and urgent problems of industry in wartime, none challenges our best thought more sharply than the replacement of men by women workers. This movement which has gone far abroad, is still in its infancy in this country; yet it is not too soon, it is, indeed, high time to gauge the tendencies and consequences of so radical a change. The replacement of men by women, proceeding in many industries and occupations in every state of the union, must of necessity react for good or for ill not only upon the girls and women so employed, but upon far wider circles, upon their families, their children, and upon the whole standard of living of their communities.

In this country it is too soon as yet to hazard an estimate of the numbers of women who are entering upon new occupations and taking men's places. The number of the women so employed is not yet numerically great; their employment is in many cases still experimental, but we are undoubtedly on the threshold of great innovations. Girls and women as messengers and elevator operators, as section hands and towermen on railroads, running drills and presses, working in powder-mills and sawmills, cleaning the outsides of railroad coaches and wiping engines, in the machine shop, in the munitions plant, in the airplane factory—these are some of the new figures in industry.

### Benefits of the Change

Among the benefits from the new widening of women's employment one of the most important is the breakdown of prejudices. Women have in the past been hampered in advancing industrially by the prejudices of both employers and their fellow workmen, organized and unorganized. Women's sex and inexperience has been made the excuse not only for all manner of exploitation but for the refusal of employers to advance them to positions of responsibility and trust. . . .

If the achievements of women workers challenge the world's admiration, we cannot neglect the obverse side of the picture. We have not yet learned the cost, the wastage of woman power. There is no doubt that both abroad and in this country unmistakable dangers are inherent in many of the new occupations. Some indeed are totally unfit for women; some may be rendered fit by changes in method of management; in all of them the indispensable prerequisite is a new scrutiny of the workers and the effect of the work, a kind of intelligent supervision known hitherto in only a very small number of the most enlightened establishments but needed now wherever women are employed in new lines of activity if we are to preserve our national energies. . . .

Of the specific dangers to be guarded against, one of the most obvious is the lifting of excessive weights. This has long been recognized as a source of injury for women. . . .

Another obvious danger calling for close observation in some of the new occupations is that of industrial poisoning. . . .

In all of the new occupations as in the old, too much emphasis cannot be laid upon the factor of fatigue in predisposing to illness and exhaustion. . . .

In regard to the general replacement of men by women workers, no single consideration is more important than the matter of wages. This is, moreover, not a social or economic question alone. It is primarily a question of health and must be of the first importance to all those concerned with public health issues. . . .

Another medical opinion on the relation between wages and health has recently been well put in a study of Occupation and Mortality: "We believe," say Doctors Wynne and Guilfoy, "that wages have a most important bearing upon the morbidity and mortality of any occupation, because, where real wages are high, the standard of living is correspondingly high, housing is better, food is more plentiful and more nourishing; and, in short, conditions are more favorable to physical and mental well-being, which results in greater resistance to disease, more recuperative power, and a healthier enjoyment of life, all of which stimulates the worker to preserve his health and makes him more alert to guard against accidents; whereas when wages are low, home conditions are of necessity unfavorable, and if in addition shop con-

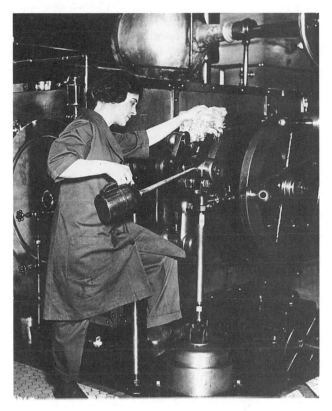

A female employee oils machinery at a Colt Firearms plant in Hartford, Conn., during World War I (1914–18). THE LIBRARY OF CONGRESS.

ditions are also bad, as they frequently are, the hazards of any occupation are increased manifold."

The great danger from the stand-point of health is that the employment of women should be resorted to merely in order to obtain cheap labor. As a matter of public health we must see to it that women are paid equal wages for equal work. Otherwise their employment can be and is daily being made the excuse for undercutting the standard wage of men and so reducing the whole standards of living in the community. . . .

There are many other pressing health problems in women's new employment needing wise consideration, which cannot even be enumerated here. Instances are beginning to multiply of the lack of decencies and sanitary provisions for women employed in railroad yards and round houses; the housing of women who must leave home is a pressing problem; the matter of clothing is highly important; women obviously cannot do men's work in ill adapted clothes such as skirts which are usually too full or too tight for safety and which are dust gathering in the dangerous trades, or in high-heeled shoes, more quickly inducing fatigue. Separate entrances should be provided for men and women especially in occupations involving heat and grime; the nutrition of the workers, and the provision of restaurants or lunch counters, is a chapter of immense importance. . . .

In summing up this brief survey of a large topic, emphasis should be laid upon three essential safeguards for girls and women entering upon men's occupations: equal wages, additional legislation and adequate medical supervision. I am aware that in making a plea for this last requisite, I am treading upon very difficult ground. The pressure for physicians for military and civilian needs is so great that a plea for new industrial supervision may appear ill-timed. Yet if any one truth has emerged from three years of warfare it is the indispensable nature of our industrial contribution. To preserve that is a part of the nation's self preservation.

## Further Resources

### BOOKS

Hepler, Allison L. *Women in Labor: Mothers, Medicine, and Occupational Health in the United States, 1890–1980.* Columbus, Ohio: Ohio State University Press, 2000.

Messing, Karen. *One-eyed Science: Occupational Health and Women Workers.* Philadelphia: Temple University Press, 1998.

# Influenza Epidemic

## "100 Sailors at Great Lakes Die of Influenza"

Newspaper article

**By:** *Chicago Tribune*
**Date:** September 23, 1918
**Source:** "100 Sailors at Great Lakes Die of Influenza." *Chicago Tribune,* September 23, 1918, 1.

## "Find Influenza Germ"

Newspaper article

**By:** *Washington Post*
**Date:** September 21, 1918
**Source:** "Find Influenza Germ." *Washington Post,* September 21, 1918. ∎

## Introduction

The word *plague* conjures up horrific images of centuries past when deadly diseases ravaged entire continents.

The mid-fourteenth-century bubonic plague ("black death"), when 25 percent of Europe's population was killed, is the most famous example. Thankfully, over the past several centuries, advances in medicine, public health, and personal hygiene have diminished, if not altogether eliminated, most plagues, or "pandemics," as they are called today. Perhaps the reason the AIDS epidemic is so frightening is that modern medical research has failed to find a cure despite its best efforts. It serves as a chilling reminder that microbes can still wreak havoc on the human population.

## Significance

Influenza, usually called the flu, is a common disease and is generally not life-threatening. However, the disease mutates rapidly, and occasionally a particularly powerful strain of the disease breaks out. The 1918–1919 influenza outbreak, called Spanish influenza at the time because it was thought to have originated in Spain, stands as the most significant pandemic to afflict mankind over the last several centuries. An estimated 20 million men and women died worldwide, including a half million in the United States. This figure includes victims who were killed by the influenza virus itself and those who, severely weakened by this disease, succumbed from complications.

Wartime conditions at home and abroad contributed to the swift spread of the contagion. The outbreak seems to have started at military bases before spreading throughout the general populace. Soldiers and sailors seemed particularly afflicted, for close quarters in makeshift army camps and on cramped ships enabled the disease to spread rapidly. In retrospect, the outbreak occurred at the worst possible moment, when waging a world war necessitated packing large numbers of people in confined spaces.

The influenza pandemic required people to adjust their daily routines. Many avoided crowds in order to minimize the risk of infection. Others donned surgical masks to stave off the disease. The deployment of troops throughout the nation contributed to the rapid spread of the affliction. America, already having spread its resources thin by the need to fight a major war overseas, had few resources to spare. The nation was forced to muddle through at home against yet another, unseen, enemy.

## Primary Source

"100 Sailors at Great Lakes Die of Influenza" [excerpt]

> **SYNOPSIS:** The "Spanish influenza" pandemic of 1918–19 struck soldiers and sailors particularly hard, as demonstrated by this article about deaths at the Great Lakes Naval Training station. The base commandant emphasizes in his statement that the disease is under control there, that the

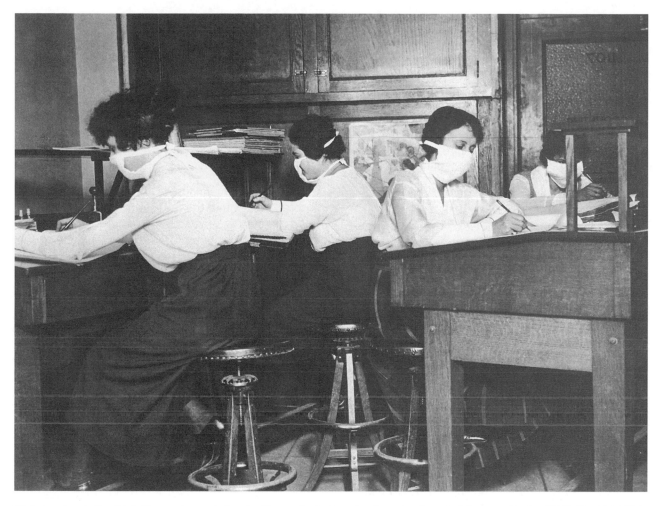

Clerical workers in New York City wearing surgical masks. They are hoping to protect themselves from the influenza epidemic of 1918–20, which killed more than 20 million people worldwide. © CORBIS. REPRODUCED BY PERMISSION.

sick are being cared for and the healthy sailors and surrounding civilian population are being protected. He goes on to describe methods for treating the disease.

### 4,500 Cases now under Treatment, 1,000 Serious

There are 4,500 cases of Spanish influenza at the Great Lakes Naval Training station, and there have been more than a hundred deaths since Sept. 9, according to a statement issued last night by Capt. William A. Moffett, commandant, to allay the fears of relatives of men in training and to set at rest sensational rumors of the ravages of the malady. The death rate is given at 1¾ per cent, based on a total of 7,000 cases that have been reported since the beginning of the epidemic.

Capt. Moffett declared the situation well in hand, there being now only about 1,000 cases sufficiently serious to warrant their transfer to the base hospital. In support of this assertion he cited the fact that

it had not been deemed necessary to close the station to visitors.

Liberty of the men had been restricted, he explained, only as a precautionary measure to protect the surrounding civilian population. The number of cases is decreasing at the rate of 10 per cent a day, Capt. Moffett said.

### Daily Reports to Relatives

The nearest of kin of the men are informed immediately when they are taken to the hospital, the captain added, and daily reports on their progress are given. The captain's statement follows:

Spanish influenza first appeared at Great Lakes Sept. 9. The total population at the station today is 45,000, and there are about 4,500 cases of Spanish influenza. About one thousand cases have been transferred to the base hospital.

The use of a nasal spray and other precautionary measures taken is not only reducing the number of cases but is reducing the virulence of the disease and the consequent number of deaths. Two regiments—the Fifth and Tenth—so far have not lost a single case, and the situation in general is much improved.

### Death Rate 1.5 Per Cent

The death rate has been about 1½ per cent, which is below the death rate in the east, which has been about 2½ per cent. Since the advent of warmer weather admissions are much less and the progress of the disease is very favorably influenced.

The number of new cases on the station today is about half what it was yesterday. The disease reached its highest point on the 19th and has been steadily decreasing since.

The families of men suffering from the disease, living in this vicinity, have been greatly aided by the Red Cross and the navy relief society. Liberty has been restricted in the hope that this will partially protect the civil communities against the disease or at least give them the opportunity to prepare for its inevitable arrival.

### Most Potent Treatment

According to Lieutenant Commander Owen J. Mink, medical corps, U.S.N., the experience at Great Lakes has shown that the most potent measure in the prevention of the disease is the use of nasal sprays or douches of Dobell's solution or other mild antiseptics. Those contracting the disease should be put to bed immediately and kept there until they are entirely recovered. The treatment meeting with the best results is the regular use of cathartics, hot drinks, soup, with Dover's powders and aspirin for the relief of pain.

Station authorities have not deemed it necessary to close the station to visitors.

## Primary Source

"Find Influenza Germ" [excerpt]

**SYNOPSIS:** This *Washington Post* article demonstrates the scope and deadly power of the 1918–19 influenza pandemic. While scientists in New York study the disease, hundreds across the United States are dying each day.

### Find Influenza Germ

New York Scientists' Discovery May Help Fight Malady.

### New England Deaths Heavy

2,000 Workers in Bay State Shipyards Afflicted—Hospitals are Improvised—15

Deaths at Camp Devens—Suspected Cases Reported in Washington.

New York, Sept. 20—Examination of Spanish influenza germs by bacteriologists of the department of health has resulted in the discovery of a new organism, Health Commissioner Copeland announced today. Further tests will be made to establish the identity of the organism, which, it is hoped, will throw more light on the nature of the malady and enable physicians to deal with it more effectively.

Eighteen new cases of the disease have been located here within the last 24 hours, as against 47 yesterday: 172 seamen on a receiving ship in the harbor are under quarantine, and 75 cases are under surveillance at Ellis Island.

### 2,000 Ship Workers Afflicted

Boston, Sept. 20—More then 129 deaths from influenza and pneumonia, 55 of them in this city, were reported in New England during the 24 hours ending at 10 o'clock tonight. Although the mortality was the greatest in several days, the health authorities said they were confident that the worst was passed.

A marked increase in the number of new cases of influenza was noted on the South Shore today. In Quincy the number of sufferers had reached nearly 3,000, almost 2,000 of them shipbuilding workers. There were four deaths from the disease. Two new dormitories for shipyard workers were hastily converted into hospitals.

### Fifteen Deaths at Camp Devens

There were fifteen deaths today at Camp Devens, sixteen among the sailors in the First naval district and three in the Second district. The Rev. Simon A. O'Rourke, chaplain at the Boston navy yard, is seriously ill of pneumonia at his home in Fall River. Several deaths of children were recorded today in this and surrounding cities. Somerville, with 600 cases, closed its schools. There are 258 cases among the school children of Boston.

The State board of health today issued a warning to employers to send home all employees showing any indication of having influenza.

### Two More Regiments Suffer

Atlanta, Ga., Sept. 20—Spanish influenza has made its appearance in two additional regiments of infantry at Camp Gordon, it became known today, and as a result practically half the soldiers at the camp have had restrictions placed on their movements.

### Ship Brings Eleven Cases

New Orleans, La., Sept. 20—Eleven cases of Spanish influenza were found among 101 passengers on a vessel which reached quarantine here today for a Central American port. Four of the cases were United States soldiers. The soldiers were taken to Jackson barracks and placed in strict quarantine.

### Further Resources

**BOOKS**

Crosby, Alfred W., Jr. *Epidemic and Peace, 1918.* Westport, Conn.: Greenwood, 1976.

Kolata, Gina Bari. *Flu: The Story of the Great Influenza Pandemic of 1918 and the Search for the Virus That Caused It.* London: Macmillan, 2000.

Osborn, June E., ed. *History, Science, and Politics: Influenza in America, 1918–1976.* New York: PRODIST, 1977.

# "The Fight Against Venereal Disease"

**Magazine article**

**By:** Raymond B. Fosdick

**Date:** November 30, 1918

**Source:** Fosdick, Raymond B. "The Fight Against Venereal Disease." *The New Republic,* November 30, 1918, 132–133, 134.

**About the Author:** Raymond Blaine Fosdick (1883–1972), a lawyer and social activist, served as chairman of the Commission on Training Camp Activities of the Army and Navy Departments during World War I. In this capacity, Fosdick fought to maintain high moral standards among the military recruits. ∎

## Introduction

Of all the various public health concerns, the subject of venereal disease, particularly syphilis, was the most difficult to bring up in public. For unlike other contagious diseases that were more or less randomly transmitted, syphilis carried the stigma of sin, for the disease was contracted by personal behavior and reflected poorly on the victim.

Nonetheless, by 1910 the once-taboo subject was at long last becoming a proper topic of public debate. For instance, Norwegian playwright Henrik Ibsen's breakthrough drama *Ghosts* (1881) brought a new awareness of syphilis to the stage. Elsewhere, the American press began publishing articles about the disease. The widespread adoption of the Wassermann test furnished a reliable weapon in the battle to identify syphilis

as a key first step in treatment. Finally, a number of semi-effective remedies were available, although none would prove as effective as antibiotics developed a generation later.

## Significance

In this atmosphere of increased awareness coupled with a more aggressive American government committed to improving public health, the United States entered World War I in April 1917. The nation's participation in this conflict came to resemble a crusade with its intense moral fervor and utopian promises for the creation of a new and better world.

Consequently, the subject of syphilis became intertwined with this crusading aspect of the war. Families were sometimes reluctant to permit their sons to be drafted into the military if the sometimes loose wartime climate presented opportunities for exposure to syphilis. They were reassured by the administration of President Woodrow Wilson that their sons would be supervised closely. In the same fashion, prohibitionists extracted a pledge from the U.S. government to ban alcohol from navy ships and forbid liquor to be sold adjacent to military bases. In short, the American fighting man, in the eyes of many, was embarking on a moral crusade to remake humanity and must therefore himself remain pure and chaste.

Of course, prostitutes followed armies throughout history. The "camp follower" was an integral part of war. The intended destination of American troops, France, raised suspicions throughout the nation's heartland, for France had a "racy" image in the eyes of some Americans. In the final analysis, the wartime fight against syphilis became a fight against sex itself.

## Primary Source

"The Fight Against Venereal Disease" [excerpt]

> **SYNOPSIS:** Raymond B. Fosdick, chairman of the Commission on Training Camp Activities of the Army and Navy Departments during World War I, points with pride to the concerted efforts of the U.S. government to protect the country's young servicemen from exposure to the dreaded venereal disease syphilis.

When the history of America's participation in the great war comes to be written, no finer achievement will be recorded to her credit than the unending battle against sex indulgence and venereal disease in the army. The success of the efforts to repress prostitution on this side of the Atlantic are already fairly well known. Now that peace is at hand, some account can be given of the measures taken

You kept fit and defeated the Hun

Now— set a high standard A CLEAN AMERICA !

STAMP OUT VENEREAL DISEASES-

THE H.C. MINER LITHO. CO. N.Y.

A late 1910s poster calls on American men returning from war to set a high standard and prevent the spread of venereal disease. While treatment was available for syphilis by this time, its effectiveness was limited, hence this poster's underlying message of chastity. **THE LIBRARY OF CONGRESS.**

by General Pershing to protect the American Expeditionary Forces from this menace.

"The federal government has pledged its word that as far as care and vigilance can accomplish the result, the men committed to its charge will be returned to the homes and communities that so generously gave them with no scars except those won in honorable conflict." These were the words of President Wilson in April, 1918. Through the Surgeon General of the Army and the War Department Commission on Training Camp Activities the government has carried out a programme for combating prostitution and venereal diseases without parallel in any other country. It was founded on the proved principle that sexual continence was not only possible for soldiers, but was also highly desirable from the standpoint of physical efficiency, morals and morale. Its chief features were education of the men; repression of disorderly resorts; provision of healthful, interesting and constructive recreation; prophylaxis,

or early treatment, for men who had exposed themselves; punishment for those exposed who failed to take prophylaxis; and, finally, expert treatment for those who either came into the army already infected or broke through all the barriers set up by the military authorities.

On the other side of the water a similar programme was instituted, but an exception had to be made of the feature of law enforcement—repression of prostitution. The foreign governments with which it was necessary for us to deal held views about prostitution very different from ours. The French believed in "toleration" and "regulation." For generations they had been used to licensed brothels and registered prostitutes, inspected with greater or less care by medical officers. They felt that an army could not get along without sexual indulgence and that to attempt to carry out such a policy was to court discontent, a lowering of morale and health standards, and perhaps even mutiny. So sincerely did they hold this belief that prostitution facilities for our soldiers were officially offered to the American High Command. A further reason for this offer was the conviction among the French that without such facilities the venereal rate would be much higher both among the soldiers and among the civilian population around their billets and training areas.

It is perfectly evident that this attitude and this offer were both entirely honest and sincere. The French thought that General Pershing's repudiation of the former and refusal of the latter were an expression of most naive idealism. "America has the noblest official moral aspirations," said a high official of the French Surgeon-General's Office in a report on the situation, "but can our ally guarantee the arrangement?" In any event it is evident that such an attitude precluded any possibility of establishing in France a system of repression comparable with that which has been established and carried out in this country.

The only alternative was to prevent our soldiers as far as possible from coming into contact with prostitutes, either public or clandestine. One of the first general orders issued after our early contingents landed in France impressed upon American line and medical officers the danger of such contact and their responsibility towards their men. Whereas in America punishment involving court martial was imposed upon men who became infected with venereal diseases only in case they had not taken the prophylactic treatment, in France the contraction of such a disease was made per se an offense against military regulations. A second order soon followed urging sexual continence and the maintenance of high moral standards of living, and requiring men reaching Paris and other cities in France to live in barracks or hotels designated by the Provost Marshal in which prophylactic stations had been installed. In order to prevent deliberate venereal infection on the part of any slackers who might think that they would thus escape military duty, this order also provided that venereal cases should be treated while on duty status at dispensaries within their own organizations instead of being evacuated to hospitals where they would use space and medical facilities needed for the care of the wounded. As a result, loss of effectives was prevented, and, instead of having three 1,000-bed hospitals filled with venereal patients by a given date, as had been expected and prepared for, the Americans had by that date no venereal hospitals and only about 300 non-effective hospitalized cases, mostly in regimental and field infirmaries.

In the meantime, both at ports of embarkation and in the training areas, careful search was made for houses of prostitution and they and the surrounding districts were placed out of bounds for our troops, military police being used to enforce the orders.

Complaints having been brought to the attention of the American authorities that some of our men who had been venereally infected just before sailing were debarking and spreading their infection among the civilian population at the base ports, another order was issued providing for strict physical examination of all troops before debarkation, prohibiting shore leave to all troops held on shipboard, restricting debarked troops to the port camps, placing out of bounds all houses of prostitution and such cafés as had been found selling heavy liquors to our troops, and renewing directions to officers to enforce strictly the rules for prophylactic treatment. One very remarkable provision of this order was that requiring venereal disease statistics of all organizations to be filed at General Headquarters *"to be used as a basis in determining the commander's efficiency and the suitability of his continuing in command."* This served of course as a very strong stimulus to greater efforts on the part of officers to promote continence among their troops and to keep down the venereal disease rate of their organizations. . . .

The victory over Germany is won. When the members of the American Expeditionary Forces return to their homes, they will come "with no scars except those won in honorable conflict" because America has been far-sighted enough, idealistic enough, to undertake to fight an unseen enemy, and win, in the face of tremendous odds, a victory over it as notable, in proportion, as the victory forced from the Central Powers.

## Further Resources

### BOOKS

Andreski, Stanislav. *Syphilis, Puritanism, and Witch Hunts: Historical Explanations in the Light of Medicine and Psychoanalysis with a Forecast about AIDS.* New York: St. Martin's Press, 1989.

Ziporyn, Terra Diane. *Disease in the Popular American Press: The Case of Diphtheria, Typhoid Fever, and Syphilis, 1870–1920.* New York: Greenwood, 1988.

# "The Next War"

### Magazine article

**By:** Harvey Washington Wiley

**Date:** January 1919

**Source:** Wiley, Harvey Washington. "The Next War." *Good Housekeeping,* January 1919, 44–45.

**About the Author:** Dr. Harvey Washington Wiley (1844–1930), was a major figure in the campaign to induce the U.S. government to enact the 1906 Pure Food and Drug Act, which established the Food and Drug Administration (FDA). President Theodore Roosevelt appointed Wiley to be the first commissioner of the FDA, which he headed from 1907 until 1912. ■

## Introduction

The First World War served as a watershed event in American history in a variety of ways. The Wilson administration presented the struggle to the public as a moral crusade to "make the world safe for democracy." For many ordinary citizens, the war was a reason to remake American society to render the country a fitting place for returning heroes.

The war also proved a milestone in the evolution of power and responsibility for American governments at every level. Efforts to eliminate venereal disease, for instance, were viewed as a means of ensuring the health and productivity of both troops in the field and workers at home. The same could be said for the campaign to eliminate the consumption of alcoholic beverages. Prohibition was seen not only as a way to elevate public health and morals but as part of the war effort against the foreign enemy, Germany. Then too, the massive response to the killer influenza pandemic of 1918–1919 high-

Dr. Harvey Washington Wiley, the first head of the Food and Drug Administration and an advocate for public health. **THE LIBRARY OF CONGRESS.**

lighted the need for better coordination of public health resources in the United States. A sobering statistic was that the United States had lost up to ten times as many people to the virus as to war wounds.

## Significance

One of the most disturbing aspects of the war mobilization was the poor physical condition of many recruits. The conflict provided a unique opportunity to take an inventory of American young men, a large number of whom were rejected as unfit for military service. This information alarmed the American public, but it did shine a spotlight on a variety of health-related issues. The requirements of total war meant that every soldier and civilian be considered a valuable piece of "human capital" and thus an asset that needed to be maintained properly.

Some reformers, such as Dr. Harvey Wiley, the driving spirit behind the passage of the Pure Food and Drug Act of 1906 and first commissioner of the Food and Drug Administration (FDA) from 1907 until 1912, advocated an ambitious program to institutionalize many of these wartime public-health innovations. Wartime advances would become permanent parts of the American landscape. In this fashion, the United States, a nation that wel-

comed back its wartime heroes, would become a better place fit for them.

## Primary Source

"The Next War" [excerpt]

> **SYNOPSIS:** Dr. Harvey Washington Wiley, crusading reformer and the first commissioner of the Food and Drug Administration, advocated that the public-health measures enacted during the First World War as part of the campaign to help the nation win the struggle be made a permanent part of American life.

We have been fighting for worldwide democracy. The autocratic military power that stood in the road has crumbled. We see the light of the morning of victory bright in the east. But we should not relax in any way our efforts until the sun of democracy is fully risen. There is another problem of almost equal importance. When we have at last a democratic world, shall we have democrats who are fit to live in it? What matter justice, right, and autonomy to the democrat with a sunken chest, a bleary eye, syphilitic blood, and spindle shins? The democrat fit to enjoy democracy is full-blooded, full-chested, robust, and free of taint. We should have a well-rounded biological democrat as well as a well-environed political democracy. In our zeal for the ideal political conditions, we should not lose sight of the ideal individual inhabitant. The world is full of imperfect biological beings. The figures from the draft returns are not collated, but apparently some fifty percent of the adult Americans whose ages were suitable for military service were found physically unfit. A campaign for health should go hand in hand with any war for democracy.

The medical records of the Civil War show in round numbers that for every soldier killed in battle or dead of wounds two died of disease. . . . Daily we have had spread before us the casualties of the great war in which we have been engaged. General Pershing reported November 23, 1918, the following casualties in the American Expeditionary Forces: Killed in action or died of wounds, 36,154. Died of disease, 14,811. This is a surprising contrast to the records of the Civil War. Two and two-fifths men were killed in battle or died of wounds where one died of disease. This is a triumph of modern medical science. The soldier who dies of disease is worthy of just as much respect and honor as one who dies in battle. But the soldier does not go into war to die in a hospital, but to die on the battle-field for

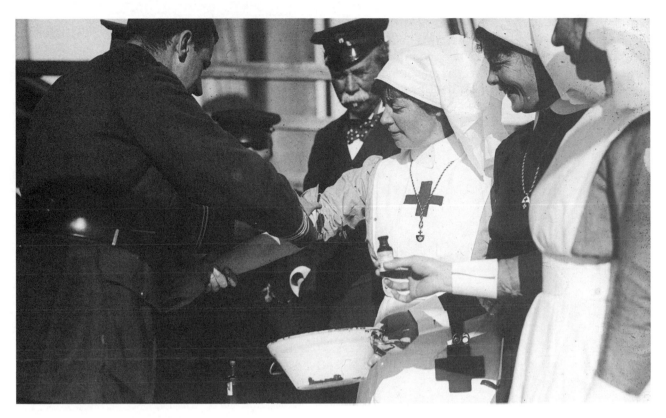

A nurse is inoculated against typhoid fever in 1915. GETTY IMAGES. REPRODUCED BY PERMISSION.

his country. Disease robs the dead soldier of the glory of the supreme sacrifice.

What is the principal cause of the increasing immunity of the soldier? The answer is simple: sanitation and immunization. By immunization I do not mean alone the prevention of smallpox. I refer particularly to the prevention of typhoid fever. Typhoid fever was one of the chief factors in the mortality of the soldiers of the Civil and Spanish Wars. This great scourge, which so loved the camp, has practically been banished therefrom. . . . It is not idle to hope that other germ and infectious diseases, especially pneumonia, may finally be conquered in a similar way. Unhappily this has not yet been accomplished, and pneumonia has succeeded typhoid as the most dangerous enemy of the soldier. . . .

Among the diseases which have undoubtedly become more prevalent as a result of war conditions, pneumonia holds first place. Medical science is practically helpless in the presence of pneumonia. The mortality of this disease is no less than it was a quarter of a century ago. Tuberculosis is a hopeful disease as compared with pneumonia. We know that a sanitary outdoor life, free from business and other troubles, based upon a very wholesome, nutritious diet, is capable of arresting tuberculosis.

Pneumonia apparently loves the strongest and most robust. The epidemic of influenza which has scattered such disaster among our people has been feared chiefly because of the supervening pneumonia. Undoubtedly the death rate among the civil population from this disease has been increased as a result of the war. The epidemic of influenza which has swept over the country is not necessarily a war epidemic. In times of peace similar epidemics have occurred. The part the war has played in the matter has been in furnishing the foci of infection. The epidemic had started and grown to huge proportions in our camps before spreading to the civil population. An epidemic of this kind, happily, is of short duration. Before medical science has time to discover its causes and methods of distribution it has passed. The term "epidemic" is a particularly happy one. It means "upon the people." No one is safe. We feel the disease is spread rapidly in crowds. We keep out of the street cars and other public conveyances and avoid public assemblies as much as possible. Happily, aside from the supervention of pneumonia, the disease is not a deadly one, and the mortality is comparatively low. But even with a low rate of mortality, when so many thousands of people are ill, the total of deaths is threatening. We see daily the names of a hundred or more brave Americans who met death on the battle-field. During the past few months there have been thousands who have met death from influenza, directly or indirectly. We have cheered ourselves constantly by feeling that in this country we would not be subjected to the barbarity of the Hun. We scarcely realize that we have been visited by a greater scourge in so far as the loss of life is concerned.

## Further Resources

### BOOKS

Coppin, Clayton A. *The Politics of Purity: Harvey Washington Wiley and the Origins of Federal Food Policy*. Ann Arbor, Mich.: University of Michigan Press, 1999.

Natenberg, Maurice. *The Legacy of Doctor Wiley and the Administration of His Food and Drug Act*. Chicago: Regent House, 1957.

Wiley, Harvey Washington. *An Autobiography*. Indianapolis, Ind.: Bobbs-Merrill, 1930.

# 10

# RELIGION

DENNIS A. CASTILLO

*Entries are arranged in chronological order by date of primary source. For entries with one primary source, the entry title is the same as the primary source title. Entries with more than one primary source have an overall entry title, followed by the titles of the primary sources.*

**CHRONOLOGY**

Important Events in Religion, 1910–1919 . . . . . . . 470

**PRIMARY SOURCES**

*A Living Wage: Its Ethical and Economic Aspects*
John A. Ryan, 1906 . . . . . . . . . . . . . . . . . . . 474

"The Church and the Labor Question"
Washington Gladden, May 6, 1911 . . . . . . . . . 476

"Cardinal's Golden Jubilee"
James Cardinal Gibbons, October 1, 1911 . . . . . 478

*America in the Making*
Lyman Abbott, 1911 . . . . . . . . . . . . . . . . . . . 481

*Acres of Diamonds*
Russell H. Conwell, 1915 . . . . . . . . . . . . . . . . 484

*Prisoners of Hope and Other Sermons*
Rev. Charles H. Brent, 1915 . . . . . . . . . . . . . . 486

"What the Bible Contains for the Believer"
Rev. George F. Pentecost, 1915 . . . . . . . . . . . . 489

*A Theology for the Social Gospel*
Walter Rauschenbusch, 1917 . . . . . . . . . . . . . . 492

*The Churches of Christ in Time of War*
Federal Council of the Churches of
Christ in America, 1917 . . . . . . . . . . . . . . . . 494

Cardinal Gibbons' Letter to the U.S.
Archbishops
James Cardinal Gibbons, May 1, 1919 . . . . . . . 498

"A Program for the Reconstruction of Judaism"
Mordecai M. Kaplan, August 1920 . . . . . . . . . 500

"Interchurch World Movement Report"
Interchurch World Movement, 1920 . . . . . . . . 502

*Leaves From the Notebook of a Tamed Cynic*
Reinhold Niebuhr, 1929 . . . . . . . . . . . . . . . . 505

# Important Events in Religion, 1910–1919

## 1910

- The Presbyterian General Assembly adopts a declaration of "essential" doctrines, to be used in examining theology professors and students for doctrinal orthodoxy. The "five points" included in the declaration are the inerrancy of Scripture, the Virgin Birth of Christ, his substitutionary atonement (the idea that his death provided forgiveness of sins), his bodily resurrection, and the authenticity of the miracles.

- A census records 540,000 Jews living in New York City, with most on the Lower East Side. This figure represents approximately 25 percent of the country's total Jewish population.

- Jane Addams, whose Chicago settlement house had provided the model for many Social Gospel churches and missions, publishes a retrospective, *Twenty Years at Hull House*.

- In February, the Fundamentalist movement in American Protestantism begins to take shape with the publication of the first volume, edited by Amzi C. Dixon, of *The Fundamentals: A Testimony to the Truth*.

- In June, John R. Mott of the Student Volunteer Movement presides over the World Missionary Conference in Edinburgh, Scotland, attended by more than twelve hundred delegates.

- On June 8, Stephen Theobald, the first African American diocesan priest to be accepted and trained in a seminary in the United States, is ordained by Archbishop John Ireland in Saint Paul, Minnesota.

- From September 25 to September 28, the National Conference of Catholic Charities holds its first meeting, at the Catholic University of America. Bishop Thomas Shahan, the rector of the Catholic University, is elected president. The conference, organized largely by lay members of the St. Vincent de Paul Society, is designed to coordinate the efforts of lay and diocesan social work agencies nationwide.

- On October 9, Charles Taze Russell, founder of the International Bible Students' Association (later known as Jehovah's Witnesses), delivers a speech before thousands of Jews at the Hippodrome in New York City advocating the return of the Jews to Palestine. His prophetic interpretation of the Bible had led him to support Zionism, gaining him the support of many Jews.

## 1911

- On April 27, the Catholic Foreign Mission Society of America, popularly known as Maryknoll, is approved by American archbishops in Washington, D.C. The Society will be authorized by Pope Pius X on 29 June. Maryknoll priests and nuns are most active in mission work in Central America and South America.

- On June 6, the city of Baltimore honors James Cardinal Gibbons, Catholic archbishop, in a jubilee celebrating the twenty-fifth anniversary of his elevation to the cardinalate and the fiftieth anniversary of his ordination to the priesthood. Twenty thousand people attend the celebration, including President Taft and Theodore Roosevelt.

- In Summer, William Jennings Bryan, three-time Democratic nominee for president, delivers an address titled "The Old-Time Religion" at the annual interdenominational Winona Bible Conference in Indiana. The speech marks Bryan's continuing commitment to evangelical Christianity in the face of progressive trends.

- On November 29, Archbishops John Farley of New York and William O'Connell of Boston are named cardinals by Pope Pius X.

## 1912

- The Methodist General Conference issues a statement asserting that lynching, which has been a persistent problem for twenty years, should become a federal crime.

- Jacob Schiff, a prominent Jewish industrialist, donates fifteen thousand volumes of Hebraic literature to the Library of Congress.

- Father Divine, an enigmatic African American preacher about whose background almost nothing is known, launches his first preaching mission in Americus, Georgia.

- On March 7, Zionist Henrietta Szold founds Hadassah, the Jewish welfare organization, in New York City.

- On April 14, Abdul Baha, the major purveyor of the Baha'i faith (a Persian offshoot of Islam) to the United States, delivers a sermon on the "fundamental unity of all religions" at the Church of the Ascension in New York City. The sermon is part of Abdul Baha's tour of the United States, which culminates in the breaking of ground for the massive Baha'i Mother Temple in Wilmette, Illinois, a suburb of Chicago. The temple is not dedicated until 1953.

- In Fall, at the opening meeting of the Princeton Seminary, J. Gresham Machen, a rising star among conservative Presbyterians, calls on scholars to reassert the intellectual foundations of the faith, which he feels have been neglected by advocates of the Social Gospel.

## 1913

- Under the leadership of Solomon Schechter and Mordecai Kaplan, twenty-two congregations leave Orthodox Judaism and unite to form the United Synagogue.

- The Jewish Anti-Defamation League is founded.

- Moderate conservative Baptists establish the Northern Baptist Seminary in Chicago to combat the liberal influence of the Divinity School at the University of Chicago.

- On August 26, Leo Frank, president of B'nai B'rith in Atlanta, is sentenced to death for the murder of fourteen-year-old Mary Phagan, who worked in his pencil factory. Many suspect that anti-Semitism played a major role in his conviction and sentencing, and his conviction elicits worldwide protest. In June 1915, the governor of Georgia commutes Frank's sentence, but two months later he is abducted from the state penitentiary by a band of armed men and hanged.

- In October, Father John A. Ryan and Morris Hillquit begin a series of debates on socialism in *Everybody's Magazine*. The series runs for seven issues, concluding in April 1914. The debates are excerpts of a book, *Socialism: Promise or Menace*, published in 1914.

- On December 20, Eudorus N. Bell, in an article in *Word and Witness*, calls for the establishment of a national organization of Pentecostals.

## 1914

- The Philadelphia Yearly Meeting of the Society of Friends (Quakers) goes on record as the only U.S. religious body to endorse women's suffrage.

- On January 11, Charles Taze Russell's "Photo-Drama of Creation," a multimedia production that includes motion pictures, slides, music, and phonograph recordings, opens at the International Bible Students' Association Temple in New York City with five thousand people in attendance. By the end of the year, the Photo-Drama has toured the United States, Europe, Australia, and New Zealand.

- In February, the Church Peace Union is created with a $2 million endowment from philanthropist Andrew Carnegie. Its initial board of twenty-nine trustees include Protestant, Catholic, and Jewish leaders. Carnegie writes a clause into the deed of this endowment stating that if "the time shall come when peace is fully established, and no more need be done in that cause, the income of the grant may be spent for the alleviation of poverty or other good causes."

- In April, at a conference in Hot Springs, Arkansas, a new Pentecostal denomination is organized as the Assemblies of God. Only sixty-eight delegates sign the charter of incorporation, but by the end of the year most white ministers of the Church of God in Christ, as well as many independent Pentecostal ministers, join the Assemblies.

- On August 20, Pope Pius X dies in Rome. He is succeeded by Giacomo Cardinal della Chiesa as Benedict XV.

- On August 30, the Federation of American Zionists (FAZ) convention takes place at the Hotel Marseilles in New York City. Louis D. Brandeis is chosen as chairman of the Provisional Executive Committee. FAZ membership rises from 12,000 in 1914 to 176,000 in 1919.

- On October 4, at the request of the Federal Council of Churches of Christ in America, President Woodrow Wilson declares a day of prayer. In cooperation with the Church Peace Union, standard prayer texts are issued, along with a "peace hymn" written by Unitarian minister John Haynes Holmes. By 1917, Holmes will be widely denounced for his pacifist beliefs.

## 1915

- Patrick Henry Callahan, director of the Roman Catholic fraternal organization the Knights of Columbus, works with Rev. John A. Ryan, the famous Catholic economist and reformer, to develop a profit-sharing plan for the Louisville Varnish Company, of which Callahan is the president. Under the plan the company's surplus revenues are divided between stockholders and employees.

- In January, the Church Peace Union issues a questionnaire to ten thousand ministers, asking their opinion on a military build-up in preparation for the possibility of U.S. entry into the European war. When the results of the survey are published in May, 95 percent of the clergy polled are on record as opposing an arms build-up as a threat to peace.

- On June 9, William Jennings Bryan's strict pacifist beliefs lead him to resign as President Woodrow Wilson's secretary of state when the two men clash over how the United States should respond to German submarine attacks on American ships and citizens.

- On July 8, Baptist theologian Walter Rauschenbusch and Congregational pastor Charles Aked publish *Private Profit and the Nation's Honor: A Protest and a Plea*. They call for the prohibition of arms shipments to any party involved in World War I. The book receives a strong negative reaction for its failure to support military preparedness wholeheartedly.

- On September 9, two African American Baptist ministers, Rev. Richard H. Boyd and Rev. C. H. Clark, split from the National Baptist Convention U.S.A., Inc., to form the National Baptist Convention of America. At issue is the control of the National Baptist Publishing Board, which plays a major role in the success of the new African American Baptist denomination.

- On December 4, the Ku Klux Klan is revived in Atlanta, Georgia, by William J. Simmons, under a charter granted by the state. Anti-Catholicism and anti-Semitism are joined with the original Klan's white supremacist views, and for the first time the Klan has chaplains and specially adapted Protestant hymns. The revival is spurred in part by the case of Leo Frank; members of the Knights of Mary Phagan, who had lynched Frank, join with Simmons in the revived Klan.

## 1916

- Martha G. M. Avery and David Goldstein found the Catholic Truth Guild in Boston, which becomes the most extensive lay mission movement in American Catholicism.

- From January 4 to January 6, Representatives of fifteen Protestant denominations convene in Garden City, New York, for the Conference on Faith and Order for North America. Participants discuss the nature and functions of the church in modern America, as well as issues of doctrine and the administration of missionary and social functions.

- On January 28, President Woodrow Wilson nominates Louis D. Brandeis for the position of associate justice of the Supreme Court. Following his confirmation by the Senate, Brandeis becomes the Court's first Jewish justice.

- In March, eighty-three ministers from various Christian denominations sign a letter, published in *The New York Times*, expressing support for American military preparedness. The letter is intended as a rebuttal to a Church Peace Union petition against the build-up in armaments.

- In May, representatives of three different Norwegian Lutheran bodies (the Norwegian Synod, Hauge's Synod, and the United Norwegian Synod) meet in Minneapolis to unite as the Norwegian Lutheran Church in America. The new denomination serves 3,000 churches with 1,300 ministers and 310,000 communicants.

- On May 13, in a parade for military preparedness in New York City, 130 clergymen march as a division. The following day, many other ministers preach on the event and the topic of preparedness in their pulpits.

- On August 21, the National Committee on Public Morals, a division of the American Federation of Catholic Societies, condemns "alien radicalism," meaning socialism, divorce, and immoral films.

## 1917

- The Mennonite Church of North America votes to withdraw from the Federal Council of Churches of Christ in America when its pacifist beliefs clash with the council's growing involvement in the war effort.

- On April 14, the Supreme Board of Directors of the Knights of Columbus meets in Washington, D.C., and pledges to provide volunteer recreational and religious workers in army camps. The Knights had performed similar services during the Mexican border campaign the previous year.

- On April 26, the War Department's Commission on Training Camp Activities meets and officially places the Young Men's Christian Association in charge of recreational activities in U.S. Army camps.

- On April 30, representatives of various Society of Friends (Quaker) meetings hold a conference in Philadelphia to discuss the possibilities for Quaker service in wartime. The conference results in the founding of the American Friends Service Committee, officially named at a 4 June meeting. Rufus Jones is appointed chair of the committee, which focuses on opportunities for noncombatant service and support for conscientious objectors.

- From May 8 to May 9, the Federal Council of Churches calls a special meeting in Washington, D.C., in conjunction with the YMCA, the YWCA, the American Bible Society, several mission boards, and other organizations, to discuss cooperative war work. A total of some thirty-five Protestant denominational and interdenominational bodies are represented at the session.

- On August 11, John Burke, a Paulist priest and the editor of *Catholic World*, calls a meeting at the Catholic University of America in Washington, D.C., to discuss coordinating Catholic war efforts. Delegates from forty dioceses, twenty-eight lay organizations, and the Catholic press attend. The meeting results in the organization of the National Catholic War Council.

- On September 20, the General War-Time Commission of the Federal Council of Churches meets for the first time in New York City.

## 1918

- The Central Conference of American Rabbis (Reform Judaism) argues for a "fundamental reconstruction of our economic organization." They advocate workers' compensation insurance, labor's right to organize and bargain collectively, social insurance for the elderly, establishment of a minimum wage, and the abolition of child labor.

- Edward T. Demby of Arkansas becomes the first African American bishop in the Episcopal Church.

- Aimee Semple McPherson arrives in Los Angeles with $100, a tambourine, and a car with a sign reading "Jesus is Coming Soon—Get Ready." Her dynamic preaching leads to the founding of the Church of the Foursquare Gospel in 1927.

- On March 1, the first government-run school for the training of army chaplains opens at Fort Monroe, Virginia.

- From May 28 to May 30, at the Philadelphia Prophecy Conference, premillennialists speak on how the events of World War I represent "signs of the times" that correspond to biblical prophecies about the coming of the millennium.

- On May 30, President Woodrow Wilson declares Decoration Day to be a day of fasting and prayer for victory in the war.

- In June, at a convention in Pittsburgh, the Federation of American Zionists adopts a policy regarding the future Jewish state in Palestine. The platform calls for public ownership of land, cooperative economic development, and political equality for all inhabitants.

- On June 21, Seven "Russellites," or Jehovah's Witnesses, are sentenced to twenty years each in the federal penitentiary in Atlanta for circulating and teaching the doctrines laid out by founder Charles Taze Russell in *The Finished Mystery*, published earlier that year. Their actions are held to be in violation of the Espionage Act of 1917. In the book Russell argues that he found no biblical support for patriotism as a duty, and he denounces the coercion of citizens into participating in wars. A substantial number of Witnesses had applied for conscientious objector status at the beginning of the war.

- On September 5, the United War Work Campaign, a massive fund-raising effort to benefit all Protestant, Catholic, and Jewish war work organizations, is announced by President Wilson. The drive kicks off on November 11, Armistice Day, but nonetheless pledges a total of $205 million by November 20. Of those pledges, a total of $188 million are ultimately collected and distributed.

## 1919

- Wentworth Arthur Matthew, a former Pentecostal minister who was active in Marcus Garvey's Universal Negro Improvement Association, founds the Commandment Keepers Congregation of the Living God, an African American Jewish group in New York. He argues that the Hebrew patriarchs were African American, making African Americans representatives of the "true" Jewish race. Matthew also denounces Christianity as a "white man's religion" and adheres to Orthodox Jewish practices, including the use of Hebrew in the services and the keeping of kosher laws.

- Father Divine establishes a mission in Sayville, Long Island, with his wife and about twenty followers. He preaches hard work, honesty, sobriety, racial and gender equality, and sexual abstinence. The mission, later named the Peace Mission Movement, provides food and shelter to anyone in need and opens its membership to whites as well as African Americans.

- At an "All American Convention" in Pittsburgh, Pennsylvania, the Russian Orthodox Church in America declares that it will be independent of the Russian Orthodoxy in the newly formed Soviet Union, in order to distance itself from the Bolsheviks.

- In May, the first conference of the World's Christian Fundamentals Association is held in Philadelphia. Speakers denounce the "Great Apostasy" and the rejection of biblical doctrines by liberal Protestants. The association was founded by William Bell Riley, the pastor of a prominent Baptist church in Minneapolis, Minnesota.

- Methodist minister and suffragist Anna Howard Shaw is awarded the Distinguished Service Medal for her work as chair of the Women's Committee of the Council of National Defense, a position she had held since 1917. She is the first American woman to receive this honor.

- On September 24, the National Catholic Welfare Council is established in response to a call from Pope Benedict XV for American bishops to "join him in working for the cause of peace and social justice in the world." The Council represents the transformation of the National Catholic War Council into a peacetime organization devoted to social action.

# A Living Wage: Its Ethical and Economic Aspects

Nonfiction work

**By:** John A. Ryan

**Date:** 1906

**Source:** Ryan, John A. *A Living Wage: Its Ethical and Economic Aspects.* New York: Macmillan, 1906. Reprint, New York: Macmillan, 1912, 324–326.

**About the Author:** John A. Ryan (1869–1945) was ordained a priest in 1898. He continued his studies at the Catholic University of America in Washington, D.C., where he was influenced by Pope Leo XIII's encyclical *Rerum Novarum* (1891), which promoted the rights of labor. Ryan advocated social justice through his writings and his position in the Social Action Department of the National Catholic Welfare Conference (NCWC). He composed the pamphlet "Social Reconstruction," which was adopted by the NCWC in 1919 and anticipated much of the legislation of the New Deal. ∎

## Introduction

In his 1891 encyclical *Rerum Novarum,* Pope Leo XIII provided a Catholic response to the Industrial Revolution and began a new tradition in Catholic social teaching. He rejected Karl Marx's ideas of class conflict and defended the right to own private property. Leo critiqued capitalism as well, however, and advocated labor's right to organize unions and the worker's right to a living wage. He defined a living wage as enough money for a worker to support a family in reasonable comfort and, through hard work and sacrifice, to eventually become a property owner.

Leo's encyclical, however, came forty-three years after Marx's *Communist Manifesto* (1848), so it didn't impact the working class in Western Europe, which had become attracted to socialism. The American labor movement developed later, however, and while *Rerum Novarum* may have appeared too late for Europe, it was just in time for the American working class, which had a high proportion of Catholic immigrants in its ranks.

Still, the influence of *Rerum Novarum* on the American labor movement was not automatic. James Cardinal Gibbons had defended one of the earliest labor movements, the Knights of Labor, but there still needed to be

someone who could effectively apply Leo's social teachings to the American context. This person would be John A. Ryan. Inspired by Leo's encyclical and his advocacy for the rights of labor, Ryan titled his dissertation *A Living Wage: Its Ethical and Economic Aspects,* which argued that a living wage is a moral right that employers are morally obligated to provide.

## Significance

Partly because of his dissertation, Ryan gained a reputation as a leading Catholic social theorist. From 1902 to 1915, he taught at St. Paul Seminary in Minneapolis. In his teachings and writings, he advocated the following reforms: a minimum wage; an eight-hour working day; the right for labor to organize and strike; the development of agencies to assist the unemployed; social insurance for unemployment, disability, and old age; public ownership of utilities, mines, and forests; and progressive income and inheritance taxes. In 1915, he went to Washington, D.C., to teach at Catholic University of America.

Ryan arrived in Washington just prior to the founding of the NCWC. As a result of his reputation on social issues, he was asked to head its Social Action Department. Soon thereafter, he wrote the pamphlet "Social Reconstruction: A General Review of the Problems and Survey of Remedies," which was inspired by his dissertation. In 1919, he showed this document to the committee of bishops overseeing the Social Action Department. These bishops liked it so much that they signed their names to it and issued it in the name of the NCWC. Popularly known as the 1919 Bishop's Plan, it advocated for minimum-wage legislation; regulation of child labor; labor's right to organize; public housing; national employment service; and unemployment, industrial accident, and old-age insurance. With a few exceptions, the recommendations of the 1919 plan became part of the New Deal legislation of the early years of President Franklin Roosevelt's administration (served 1933–1945).

Ryan remained active in the Social Action Department of the NCWC until his death on September 16, 1945, at the age of seventy-six. By that time, an impressive body of social teachings had been developed. Unlike its counterparts in Western Europe, the Catholic Church in the United States, because of its actions on behalf of labor, was successful in retaining the loyalty of the industrial class.

## Primary Source

*A Living Wage: Its Ethical and Economic Aspects* [excerpt]

> **SYNOPSIS:** Ryan was a key figure in the development of American Catholic social teaching in the

twentieth century. The views he expressed in *A Living Wage,* evident in the following excerpt, were adopted by the NCWC and influenced Roosevelt's New Deal, which had a lasting, decades-long impact on the country.

The main argument of this volume may be summarized as follows: the laborer's right to a Living Wage is the specific form of his generic right to obtain on reasonable conditions sufficient of the earth's products to afford him a decent livelihood. The latter right is, like all other moral rights, based on his intrinsic worth as a person, and on the sacredness of those needs that are essential to the reasonable development of personality. Among the things to which these needs point there is included a certain amount of material goods. A man's right to this indispensable minimum of the bounty of nature is as valid as his right to life: the difference is merely in degree of importance. Now when the man whose social and economic function is that of a wage earner has expended all his working time and energy in the performance of some useful task, he has fulfilled the only condition that in his case can be regarded as a reasonable prerequisite to the actual enjoyment of his right to a decent livelihood. The *obligation* of providing him with the material means of living decently rests in a general way upon all his fellow men. That is to say, they are all under moral restraint not to do anything that would be an unreasonable interference with his access to these means. However, it is only those persons who are in control of the goods and opportunities of living that are practicably within his reach, who can effectively hinder or promote his enjoyment of the right in question. When they prevent him from peaceably getting possession of the requisite amount of goods, they are morally responsible for his failure to obtain a decent livelihood. Their action is as unjust as that of the majority of the first occupants of a No-man's Land who should force the minority to work for a bare subsistence. This specific obligation of the class of persons that we are considering falls primarily upon the employer; for his economic position as direct beneficiary of the laborer's exertion and as payer of wages, renders this the only practicable outcome of any reasonable division of the community's opportunities of living and of the corresponding responsibilities. Nor can the employer escape this duty of paying a Living Wage by taking refuge behind the terms of a so-called free contract. The fact is that the underpaid laborer does not *willingly* sell his labor for less than the equivalent of a decent liveli-

Robber barons ransack a village in a drawing by the Master of the House Book. In *A Living Wage* (1906) John Ryan likened the superior economic force an employer uses to pay a worker less than a living wage to the force of a highwayman waylaying a traveler and stealing his money.
© BETTMAN/CORBIS. REPRODUCED BY PERMISSION.

hood, any more than the wayfarer willingly gives up his purse to the highwayman. It is the superior *economic force* (which consists essentially in the ability to wait, while the laborer must go to work to-day or starve) possessed by the employer that enables him to hire labor for less than a Living Wage. And the employer who can afford to pay a Living Wage is no more justified in using his superior economic strength in this way than he would be justified in using superior physical strength to prevent the laborer from taking possession of a sack of flour or a suit of clothes that the latter had bought and paid for. In both cases the laborer is deprived by superior strength of something to which he has a right. As a determinant of rights, economic force has no more validity or sacredness than physical force. The other economic classes in the community, the landowner, the loan-capitalist, the consumer, and the man of wealth, share the responsibility of providing the laborer with a decent livelihood in a secondary degree, and in accordance with the nature and possibilities of their several economic positions. Finally, the State is morally bound to compel employers to pay a Living

Wage whenever and wherever it can, with a moderate degree of success, put into effect the appropriate legislation.

## Further Resources

### BOOKS

Beckley, Harlan R., ed. *Economic Justice: Selections From Distributive Justice and a Living Wage.* Louisville, Ky.: Westminster John Knox Press, 1996.

Broderick, Francis L. *Right Reverend New Dealer.* New York: Macmillan, 1963.

Gearty, Patrick William. *The Economic Thought of Monsignor John A. Ryan.* Washington, D.C.: Catholic University of America Press, 1953.

Kennedy, Robert G. *Religion and Public Life: The Legacy of Monsignor John A. Ryan.* Lanham, Md.: University Press of America, 2001.

---

# "The Church and the Labor Question"

Magazine article

**By:** Washington Gladden

**Date:** May 6, 1911

**Source:** Gladden, Washington. "The Church and the Labor Question." *The Outlook* 98, no. 1, May 6, 1911, 36.

**About the Author:** Washington Gladden (1836–1918), a Congregationalist clergyman, was born on February 11, 1836, in Pennsylvania. Gladden ministered to various congregations in New York, Massachusetts, and Ohio. Often called the father of the Social Gospel movement, he became an early advocate of connecting Christian principles to contemporary social problems. He died on July 2, 1918, in Columbus, Ohio, where he had been serving as pastor and pastor emeritus at First Congregationalist Church. ■

## Introduction

Washington Gladden, one of the founders of the Social Gospel movement, began working at the *Owego Gazette* and wrote local news. He resumed his education in 1855, graduated from Williams College in 1859, and was ordained a minister in the Congregationalist Church in 1860. He furthered his theological training by attending lectures at Union Theological Seminary and reading the works of the liberal theologian Horace Bushnell.

While serving as the pastor of the Congregational church in North Adams, Massachusetts, from 1866 to 1871, he returned to his earlier involvement in journalism, contributing as a writer and editor to various periodicals. Gladden focused on Bushnell's New Theology views and the social issues resulting from the rapid industrialization of the United States, which had been

spurred on by the enormous demands for steel by the Union during the Civil War (1861–1865).

Gladden's most original contribution was to take the liberal insights of New Theology and combine them with the growing problems of labor and industry, thereby giving rise to a new movement in American Protestant social ethics known as the Social Gospel. The dominating theme of New Theology was God's presence in the world and in human culture—which meant that the world and human culture needed to be redeemed as well, not just individuals. Gladden believed it was the duty of Christians to move beyond concerns for individual morality by addressing social injustices. The most obvious social problem that Gladden saw was the poor condition of labor in American industry. A major issue in Gladden's time was whether labor had the right to organize. Conservative ministers either supported a pro-capitalistic view that favored the factory owners or believed that it was not appropriate for the churches to be involved in such economic issues. In his 1911 article, "The Church and the Labor Question," Gladden argues that it is in fact the obligation of the churches to become involved in economic issues.

## Significance

As a founder of the Social Gospel movement, Gladden criticized the American free enterprise system throughout his career. While he rejected socialism, Gladden did advocate government ownership of public utilities, as well as the right of labor to organize and form unions. The early years of the labor movement were often violent, and while sympathetic to the workers, Gladden was opposed to the use of force by either side. Furthermore, Gladden did not endorse any specific economic program. Rather, he believed that the present social order could be Christianized by application of one of the Ten Commandments: "Thou shalt love thy neighbor as thyself." Gladden called on the churches, by word and by example, to encourage individuals to apply this teaching to the social arena.

Many of Gladden's theological battles were with the conservative Christians, many of whom were influenced by the pro-capitalist Gospel of Wealth. A common criticism was that ministers should only focus on issues of personal morality and that attention to social issues was outside the sphere of their proper responsibilities. Gladden responded to this view in "The Church and the Labor Question." In this article, he contended that "all economic questions are fundamentally religious questions." This view remained a cornerstone of liberal Protestant social ethics. While not ignoring the issues of personal morality, such as the commandment prohibiting theft, liberal Protestants eventually began to challenge the morality of an economic system that overworked the impoverished working class. Gladden's work was echoed by other reformers, such as Walter Rauschenbusch, who further developed it as a theological system. It also inspired the liberal leadership of the short-lived Interchurch World Movement, which threw its support behind the steel strike of 1919.

## Primary Source

"The Church and the Labor Question" [excerpt]

> **SYNOPSIS:** Gladden was among the first to broaden Protestantism's ethical concerns beyond individual sin to social sin. In the following excerpt, he called on the churches to accept the responsibility of challenging economic inequities in American society, particularly in the area of heavy industry and labor.

Briefly, then, we may say that the labor question is an economic question, and that all economic questions are fundamentally religious questions; that there are no purely spiritual interests, since the spiritual forces all incarnate themselves in the facts of everyday life, and can be known only as they are there manifested; that there is indeed danger that the Church will make mistakes in dealing with such questions, but that the greatest of all her mistakes is in ignoring them; that there are no souls that more need saving than the souls that are getting entangled in the materialisms that undervalue manhood; and that there are no people who need moral guidance more than those who are grappling with the manifold phases of the labor question. That some of them resent the truth about this matter is a sad fact, but that is not a good reason for suppressing the truth; and there must be many among them who are ready to know the truth and from whom it would be a crime to conceal it. While, therefore, the preacher knows that to some of his hearers the truth, no matter how wisely and kindly spoken, will be "a savor of death unto death," it is his business to tell the truth for the sake of those to whom it will be "a savor of life unto life."

It is sometimes said that the Church cannot deal in any explicit and concrete fashion with these labor problems; that the utmost she can do is to enunciate ethical principles; that she must not venture to apply them. But if Scriptural examples are of any validity, it is clear that Amos and Hosea and Micah and Isaiah and Jeremiah knew how to apply principles to concrete cases. All these Hebrew prophets dealt in the most direct and explicit manner with the social injustices then prevailing. They did not content themselves with enunciating ethical principles, they made the application in the most pungent fash-

Washington Gladden, an American Congregational minister, believed religious principles should be applied to contemporary social problems and published several works in helping lead the Social Gospel movement. © CORBIS. REPRODUCED BY PERMISSION.

ion. "Forasmuch therefore," cries Amos, "as your treading is upon the poor, and ye take from him burdens of wheat; ye have built houses of hewn stone, but ye shall not dwell in them; ye have planted pleasant vineyards, but ye shall not drink wine of them. For I know your manifold transgressions and your mighty sins; they afflict the just, they take a bribe, and they turn aside the poor in the gate from their right." "Woe to them," echoes Micah, "that devise iniquity, and work evil upon their beds! when the morning is light, they practice it, because it is in the power of their hand. And they covet fields, and take them by violence; and houses, and take them away: so they oppress a man and his house, even a man and his heritage." It is hardly too much to say that the burden of these Hebrew prophets was the social inequality of their time, and that it was in their struggle against the oppression of the weak by the strong that they came to their clear consciousness of a righteous God. Doubtless these were disturbing messages; doubtless many of the well-to-do were alienated from the Church by this trenchant testimony; but it was spoken nevertheless, and it remains to the world an imperishable legacy.

Much of Christ's preaching on social topics has no lack of definiteness, and the concluding chapters of most of the Epistles would be suggestive reading for those who think that the Church must avoid the application of Christian principles to actual human conditions. James, the brother of our Lord, may be supposed to be familiar with our Lord's point of view. His words recall the old prophets: "Go to now, ye rich, weep and howl for your miseries that are coming upon you. Your riches are corrupted and your garments are moth-eaten. Your gold and your silver are rusted; and their rust shall be for a testimony against you, and shall eat your flesh as fire. Ye have laid up your treasure in the last days. Behold, the hire of the laborers who mowed your fields, which is of you kept back by fraud, crieth out; and the cries of them that reaped have entered into the ears of the Lord of Sabaoth. Ye have lived delicately on the earth, and taken your pleasure; ye have nourished your hearts in a day of slaughter. Ye have condemned, ye have killed the righteous one; he doth not resist you." If we faithfully expound the Scripture, we shall surely be compelled to do a good deal of preaching of a very direct and concrete sort on the labor question.

It will be admitted that the chief interest of the Church is in character. Its business in the world is primarily the production of good character, the building up of sound, clean, upright, neighborly men. In this commercial age such character is mainly made or lost in the pursuits of industry. Whether a business man becomes a good man or not depends mainly on the way in which he manages his business. He may be a good husband and father, charitable to the poor, and a devout church member, but if in his business he is greedy, hard-hearted, unjust, and tyrannical, the core of his character is bad. In the prevailing interest of his life his conduct is defective, and it makes him essentially a bad man. Now the Church has in her membership hundreds of thousands of men whose characters are being formed by their business practices. She owes to these men the instruction and the moral guidance by which they may be saved from the fatal loses of manhood to which they are exposed, and established in virtue and honor. She must not say that she has no knowledge of these questions. She has no right to be ignorant concerning practices that are blunting the consciences and destroying the souls of millions of her own members. In truth, this ignorance is largely feigned. The ethical principles involved in all these transactions are clear, and there is no more danger of error in dealing with them than is involved in any attempt to apply the principles of

morality to the conduct of life. Always there is need of caution, of discretion, of just and balanced treatment of such problems, but this is not a reason why they should be ignored. Even bungling attempts to help men into the right way—if they are only honest and sincere—are far less dangerous than a cowardly avoidance. When the Church, in the person of the priest and the Levite, passed by the wounded man on the Jericho road, it may have pleaded that it was not expert in caring for such cases. The Church can better afford to make many mistakes in enforcing the Christian law of industrial relations than to give the impression that the Christian law has nothing to do with industrial relations. In fact, it has everything to do with them, and the Church is not dealing fairly with a great multitude of its own members when it fails to show them just how the Christian law does apply to those relations with their fellowmen in which, more than in any other portion of their lives, the great values of character are gained or lost.

## Further Resources

### BOOKS

Fry, C. George. *Pioneering a Theology of Evolution: Washington Gladden and Pierre Teilhard de Chardin.* Lanham, Md.: University Press of America, 1988.

Knudten, Richard D. *The Systematic Thought of Washington Gladden.* New York: Humanities, 1968.

# "Cardinal's Golden Jubilee"

Sermon

**By:** James Cardinal Gibbons

**Date:** October 1, 1911

**Source:** Gibbons, James Cardinal. "Cardinal's Golden Jubilee." October 11, 1911. Reprinted in Gibbons, James Cardinal. *A Retrospective of Fifty Years.* Baltimore, Md.: Murphy, 1916.

**About the Author:** James Gibbons (1834–1921) was the son of Irish immigrants and born in Baltimore, Maryland. An intelligent and industrious man, he was ordained a Catholic priest in 1861 and rapidly rose up the American Catholic hierarchy. Gibbons was ordained a bishop in 1868, became archbishop of Baltimore in 1877, and was made cardinal by Pope Leo XIII in 1886. A tolerant and gracious man, Gibbons was the most influential American Catholic leader of the early twentieth century. ■

## Introduction

James Gibbons was the eldest son of Thomas and Bridget Gibbons, who had emigrated from Ireland. As immigrants, the Gibbons family was part of a great trans-

James Cardinal Gibbons believed that Catholic immigrants should assimilate into predominantly Protestant American society, yet retain their Catholicism. As the Catholic population grew rapidly, he wrote and spoke extensively on the subject. © CORBIS. REPRODUCED BY PERMISSION.

formation in American religious life. At the time of American Revolution (1775–1783), the American Catholic community numbered approximately twenty-five thousand—less than 1 percent of the population of the new nation. By the mid-nineteenth century, great waves of immigration to the United States from Europe began to dramatically change this situation. First came the Irish, who fled famine, then the Germans, Italians, and Poles began to arrive. The Catholic Church grew rapidly in the United States, and there was a great deal of concern over whether such an ethnically diverse community would be able to become a part of American society. This would become one of the major objectives of the future American cardinal.

As a young man, Gibbons embarked initially in the field of business and did quite well. In time, however, he discerned a vocation to the Catholic priesthood and was ordained in 1861. His intellectual and leadership abilities gained him attention, and he was ordained a bishop seven years later at the age of thirty-two. In 1872, he was ap-

pointed bishop of Richmond. His tolerant character and gracious personality helped him to be very successful in this predominantly Protestant area. Whenever possible, he cooperated with other faiths in areas of common concern, such as Prohibition. Gibbons was appointed archbishop of Baltimore in 1872 and named a cardinal in 1886.

In addition to the challenges posed by immigration, another issue confronting Gibbons was the labor movement. These two movements were actually connected, since the bulk of those working for low wages in the dangerous factories were Catholic immigrants. The central economic and political issue in Gibbons' day was whether labor had the right to organize.

## Significance

Gibbons' major concern was to integrate Catholic immigrants into American society, while at the same time help them retain their Catholic identity and beliefs. Gibbons' views regarding assimilation conflicted with those of conservatives and the majority of the German

American bishops. Conservatives were concerned that accommodation with American culture, which was predominantly Protestant, would be injurious to the Catholic faith. The Germans feared the loss of both their German heritage and their Catholic faith, which they believed went hand in hand.

Conservatives were successful in communicating their concerns to Rome. In 1899, Leo XIII issued his *Testem Benevolentiae* condemning the heresy of "Americanism," which was defined as the belief that the American style of church-state relations should be the norm for the whole church and that church doctrines should be altered in order to make converts. Rather than being widely distributed, this letter was sent only to Gibbons to act on as he saw fit. Gibbons responded in a letter on March 17, 1899, asserting the loyalty of the American Catholic Church and assuring Leo XIII that no such heresies were to be found in the United States.

In the area of the labor movement, Gibbons was guided by the teachings of Leo XIII's 1891 encyclical *Rerum Novarum,* which supported the right of labor to organize. Gibbons supported the first national labor union, the Knights of Labor, and, through the National Catholic Welfare Conference (NCWC), advocated for more just compensation and better working conditions for factory workers. He lived long enough to see the NCWC adopt in 1919 a comprehensive program promoting social security, workman's compensation, and a minimum wage. Gibbons died two years later on March 24, 1921, at the age of eighty-six.

## Primary Source

"Cardinal's Golden Jubilee" [excerpt]

**SYNOPSIS:** In the following excerpt, Gibbons touches on the great growth that took place in the Catholic community during his episcopate. He also refers to the theme that was central to his work, that is, of the need for the immigrants of his denomination to be Catholic and American at the same time.

It may be interesting as well as consoling to institute a comparison between the Church of 1861 and its present situation after half a century.

In 1861 the Archbishops and Bishops of the United States numbered 48. The priests were 2,064. The number of churches with priests attached was 2,042, and the Catholic population was estimated at 1,860,000.

The number of Archbishops and Bishops today in charge of Sees amounts to 96. Just twice as many as existed in 1861. The priests amount to 17,000, an increase of over eightfold. There are

13,500 churches, nearly a sevenfold increase. We have about 15 millions of Church members, over four times as many as existed in the United States in 1861.

But the progress of religion in our country is to be estimated not only by the augmentation of the numbers of its communicants, but also by its more efficient co-ordination and discipline. The clergy in 1861, were as detached squadrons compared to the compact and well-marshalled army of today. Half a century ago, the Prelates and clergy labored under many adverse circumstances. In widely extended parts of the country, they had to minister to the faithful scattered over a vast expanse of territory, without organized parishes, often without churches wherein to worship, and without Catholic schools. They had but scant resources to sustain them. Frequently they had to contend with deep-rooted prejudices.

Now, thank God, we have in most places parishes well organized. Churches have multiplied from the Atlantic to the Pacific. Parochial schools have become the rule instead of the exception in the large centers of population. A generous laity are usually able and always willing to aid our missionaries. An unfriendly feeling indeed still exists in some quarters, as the result of long-standing traditions and a biased education. But the mists of prejudice are gradually disappearing before the sunlight of truth.

Let me address you, my junior brethren of the Episcopate and the clergy. Oh! you who are now in the full tide of physical and intellectual vigor, I congratulate you; your lines are fallen in pleasant places. What a rich field is open to your apostolic zeal! You represent the highest authority in the world, the Lord of Hosts Himself. You go forth as the envoys not of an earthly potentate, but of the King of kings and Lord of lords. To be an ambassador of Christ is a heavy charge. It means the giving up of one's whole life, the bending of one's every energy to the cause for which we have enrolled ourselves, for the subject of our embassy is nothing short of eternal life, and the work of our embassy is nothing less than the salvation of souls.

Your mission is to an enlightened American people who are manly and generous, open to conviction, and who will give you a patient hearing. The American race form the highest type of a Christian nation when their natural endowment of truth, justice and indomitable energy are engrafted on the supernatural virtues of faith, hope and charity.

But, my brethren of the laity, the mightiest efforts of your Bishops and Clergy will be of no avail without your generous co-operation. If the genius of a Washington, a Wellington, and a Napoleon would be exerted in vain without the help of their armies, so the zeal of a Peter and a John the Baptist and the eloquence of a Paul would be fruitless without the active concurrence of their devoted disciples. But when the prelates, the clergy and people are united in the cause of religion and humanity, there is no such word as fail. We form an impregnable phalanx which cannot be pierced. We constitute a triple alliance far more formidable and enduring than the alliance of kings and potentates, for ours is not a confederation of flesh and blood, but an alliance cemented by divine charity.

You will always be loyal in the profession and faithful in the practice of your religion. You will take an active, personal interest in all that concerns the welfare of Holy Church. You will rejoice in her growth and prosperity, and will grieve at any adversity that may befall her. You will be animated by the spirit of the Prophet, when he mourned over the destruction of Jerusalem and besought God to have mercy upon her and deliver her from her enemies.

And as citizens of the United States you should take a patriotic part in every measure that contributes to the progress of the Commonwealth. No man liveth to himself alone, nor can any man shirk his responsibility. No matter how humble may be our station, our country will be either a little better or a little worse because we have lived.

## Further Resources

### BOOKS

Ellis, John Tracy. *The Life of James Cardinal Gibbons.* Milwaukee, Wisc.: Bruce, 1963.

Newcomb, Covelle. *Larger Than the Sky: A Story of James Cardinal Gibbons.* London: Longmans, Green, 1945.

Smith, Albert Edward. *Cardinal Gibbons: Churchman and Citizen.* Baltimore, Md.: O'Donovan Brothers, 1921.

# *America in the Making*

Theological work

**By:** Lyman Abbott

**Date:** 1911

**Source:** Abbott, Lyman. *America in the Making.* New Haven, Conn.: Yale University Press, 1911, 195–201.

**About the Author:** Lyman Abbott (1835–1922) was a Congregationalist minister, author, and editor. He was born on December 18, 1835, in Roxbury, Massachusetts, and relocated to New York City with his family at the age of eight. After first practicing law, Abbott was ordained in 1860 and eventually became a leader in liberal Protestantism in the late nineteenth and early twentieth centuries. He died on October 22, 1922. ∎

## Introduction

Lyman Abbott gave a series of lectures at Yale University on the responsibilities of American citizenship. These were published in 1911 in a book entitled *America in the Making.* One of Lyman's gifts, as demonstrated in this book, was the ability to promote liberal ideas while preserving core religious beliefs. As a religious liberal, he supported the separation of church and state and opposed any amendments to the Constitution that would incorporate any particular religious beliefs. Yet, he also believed that a religious spirit was necessary for the progressive development of the American people, as well as to define its role in world affairs.

As a child, Abbott dreamed of becoming a minister; instead, he followed more secular pursuits. After graduation in 1853, he joined his brothers' New York–based law firm. After six relatively successful years of practicing law, he decided to return to his childhood ambition. He was ordained in 1860 and assumed the pastorate of the Congregational church in Terre Haute, Indiana.

Abbott's option for the ministry did not mean, however, turning his back to the world. In addition to comforting those who lost loved ones in the Civil War (1861–1865), he also labored to explain the issues related to the conflict. In 1865, he became the corresponding secretary of the American Union Commission, an organization dedicated to assisting the South during Reconstruction.

During this period, he began writing book reviews that were published in *Harper's* magazine, thus beginning his literary career. In 1870, he was appointed as editor of the new periodical *The Illustrated Christian Weekly.* In 1876, he became associated with Henry Ward Beecher's journal *Christian Union,* and in 1881, he became editor in chief of the journal, which changed its name to the *Outlook* in 1893. Abbott also succeeded Beecher as pastor of Plymouth Congregational Church in Brooklyn in 1887.

## Significance

Abbott combined his ministerial, writing, and editorial work to become one of the most influential religious liberals in the late nineteenth- and early twentieth-century United States. He supported the liberal view of evolution, popularizing the line of an earlier writer named John Fiske, that "evolution is God's way of doing things." Abbott had a dynamic, rather than static, view of God, cre-

Dr. Lyman Abbott in 1919. Abbott was a liberal Congregationalist minister who believed strongly in separation of church and state, but also insisted that a religious spirit was necessary for the development of American citizens. **THE LIBRARY OF CONGRESS.**

ation, and Christianity. In his book *The Evolution of Christianity* (1892), he spoke of the evolution of the Bible, the church, Christian society, and the soul.

Abbott was a big supporter of social reform. In *America in the Making,* he expressed his view that religion should be an active part of the political process in order to obtain the needed changes in society. The year following its publication, during the 1912 presidential campaign, he and the *Outlook* supported the candidacy of Theodore Roosevelt and the platform of the Progressive Party, despite the loss in subscribers this action caused. So strong was his support that religious historian Sydney E. Ahlstrom calls Abbott "the virtual chaplain of Theodore Roosevelt's Progressivism."

Despite his liberalism and support of social causes, Abbott shared many of the prejudices of his day. He defended the view that it was the duty of the Anglo-Saxon race to confer the gifts of civilization, through law, commerce, and education, on the uncivilized people of the world. Like other religious liberals, Abbott supported Woodrow Wilson during World War I (1914–1918), viewing the conflict as a twentieth-century crusade, a struggle of civilization against barbarism. While these latter views have been rejected, Abbott's legacy continues

today in liberal Protestantism in the areas of modernism and social justice.

## Primary Source

*America in the Making* [excerpt]

> **SYNOPSIS:** Abbott's support for evolution was deemed irreligious by conservatives, and his support for progressive politics was viewed as inappropriate for a minister, even though he saw no inconsistency. Far from minimizing religion, the following excerpt shows that Abbott also sought a religious revival in the United States, albeit on the foundations of liberal, and not conservative, Christianity.

The question is not Should the Nation give its support or even its recognition to a Church? For Americans the absolute separation of Church and State may be regarded as settled. Nor is it a question whether the State should have a theology; whether a creed, however simple, should be incorporated in the Constitution, as for example a declaration of belief in the Bible, or in Christ, or in God. This is indeed proposed by some of our fellow-citizens, but this is not the question which I desire here to discuss. I do not think the Constitution is a proper place for the insertion of a system of theology or even an article of religious belief, however simple. The function of a constitution is to define and limit the powers of the various departments of the government, not to declare the religious belief of the people who constitute the government. Nor is it the question whether the individual citizens who constitute the Nation should be religious individuals; whether they should possess religious beliefs, be inspired by religious motives, and controlled in their actions by religious principles. It is not the question whether in their political action as citizens they should be governed by the same religious considerations by which they are governed in their domestic, their business, and their church lives; whether they should carry their religions into their politics. This will not be a question to any one who really believes in religion at all. Religion is nothing if it is not a rule of life and of the whole life; a man is not religious at all if he is not religious in every part of his nature, at all times, and in all relations of life.

The question is whether the life of the Nation can be and should be a religious life. Is religion solely a matter of individual conviction and experience? Or is it true that a Nation also has a religious life which must be influential in determining National questions, must control the National policy, and must find expression in National legislation? Or is the Nation as a Nation a purely unreligious organization?

There are not a few who entertain the latter opinion. This is partly because they have not thought deeply on the subject, and have confounded religion with theology (that is, with the philosophy of religion), or with the church (that is, with the institutional forms of religion); partly because they do not see how it is possible that a Nation made up of individuals of such various, and even antagonistic, faiths as the American people can yet possess a common religious life, partly because they see the curse which has fallen on other nations, who either have been separated into hostile camps by hostile religious faiths, as Ireland into Roman Catholics and Orangemen, or have been oppressed by the despotism of a hierarchy, as Spain in the fifteenth century by the power of a Papal priesthood, or Massachusetts in the seventeenth century by the power of a Protestant autocracy. They believe that religion is the inspired guide of the individual, that it should govern the citizen, that it is the bond of the family, that in his religious rights the person should be protected by the State, but also that the State itself not only need not but cannot be religious, that to treat all forms of religion with impartiality it must itself ignore religion altogether. I, on the contrary, believe that the Nation must as a Nation be pervaded by the religious spirit and that among the responsibilities of your citizenship in the making of America you have no responsibilities more important than inspiring it with a true religious spirit. And to make my meaning clear I will take as my definition of the religious spirit one with which we are all familiar—that of the prophet Micah: Doing justly, loving mercy, and walking humbly with God. My thesis then is this: The spirit of justice, mercy, and reverence is essential to the peace, the prosperity, and even the perpetuity of the American Republic as a self-governing, cooperative commonwealth.

What is the primary object of a State? Why do we, ninety millions of people of various races, nationalities and temperaments and religious faiths unite in a common political and industrial organization called a State or a Nation? Why do we maintain not only harbors for our foreign commerce, and railways and navigable rivers for our domestic commerce, and army and navy and police for our mutual protection, and factories and stores for the interchange of the products of our industry, and lawyers and courts for the administration of justice, and schools for public education, and homes for our refuge and our enjoyment and the rearing and training of our young?

*The School of Athens,* by Raphael. In 350 B.C.E., the Greek philosopher Aristotle (left) argued that the object of the state is to promote the virtue of its citizens. This argument formed the basis of Dr. Abbott's assertion that the object of the state is the promotion of religion. © BETTMANN/ CORBIS. REPRODUCED BY PERMISSION.

What ultimate purpose gives significance to all this elaborate machinery of life? To this question Aristotle in his Politics has given an answer which subsequent reflection of political students has not superseded. It is, he argues, not merely to protect property: in that case the owner's share in the government should be proportioned to his property, as, to use a modern illustration, is the share of the stockholder in the government of the corporation. Nor is it merely to protect life and promote industry. In that case the lower animals might form a State, whereas this is impossible. An ant-hill or a beehive is not a State. Nor is a mere military alliance for the purpose of protection from foreign aggression a State. Such military alliances are often formed between different States; but they do not lose their independent existence and become one State. Nor is a combination of men to promote trade and commerce a State: a trust is something very different from a State. And treaties between independent States are often formed for the purpose of promoting trade and commerce, but such commercial treaty does not make the contracting parties into a State. Nor yet is it the function of the State merely to secure justice and peace between the various citizens. For this may be and is secured by international treaties by which different States agree to leave the controversies which may arise between them or between their citizens to a Court appointed for the purpose. There may be an International Court as well as a National Court; the existence of such a Court does not therefore constitute a Nation. The object of a State is, Aristotle says, to promote the virtue of its citizens.

> The State is not merely a local association or an association existing to prevent mutual injury and to promote commercial exchange. . . . A State on the contrary is the association of families and villages in a complete and independent existence, or, in other words, according to our definitions, in a life of felicity and nobleness. . . . We must assume that the object of the political association is not merely a common life but noble action.

If this be true, then the object of the State is a religious object: for the preservation of virtue and of noble action is the precise object of religion. To be inspired in all our life by virtue, to act in all our conduct nobly,—this is religion. What Aristotle calls virtue and noble action, Jesus calls eternal life. For eternal life, as he uses the term, does not mean an unknown life in an unknown world to come. It means a certain quality of life—the kind of life which untoward circumstances cannot destroy or even impair; and that is precisely the life of virtue and noble action. Thus the object of the State is seen to be the promotion of religion; or, if any of you think this a too narrow definition of religion, then the promotion of a certain phase or aspect of religion.

## Further Resources

### BOOKS

Ahlstrom, Sydney E. *A Religious History of the American People.* New Haven, Conn.: Yale University Press, 1972.

Brown, Ira V. *Lyman Abbott, Christian Evolutionist: A Study in Religious Liberalism.* Westport, Conn.: Greenwood, 1970.

### PERIODICALS

Parsons, Edward Smith. "Lyman Abbott." *Religious Life,* August 1978.

Roberts, Robert R. "The Social Gospel and the Trust Busters." *Church History,* September 1956.

# Acres of Diamonds
## Speech

**By:** Russell H. Conwell

**Date:** 1915

**Source:** Conwell, Russell H. *Acres of Diamonds.* New York: Harper and Brothers, 1915, 20–22.

**About the Author:** Russell H. Conwell (1843–1925), an American Baptist minister, lecturer, and founder of Temple University, was born in Worthington, Massachusetts. After first practicing law, he was ordained a minister in 1879 and moved to Philadelphia. There he founded Temple University in 1884 and served as its first president. Conwell was also a popular lecturer, with his most famous speech being "Acres of Diamonds." ■

## Introduction

Russell H. Conwell earned his law degree at Albany Law School and went into practice. In 1879, he was consulted about the disposal of a run-down church in Boston. Rather than selling it, he advised the congregation to restore the building. Not only did he convince it to save the church, but after being ordained he became the congregation's minister. Soon, his reputation as a preacher led to his appointment in 1882 at Grace Baptist Church in Philadelphia.

A man of great energy, Conwell founded Temple University in 1884 and served as its first president in addition to doing his ministerial duties. He authored forty books, wrote hymns, founded a hospital, and lectured extensively.

His most popular lecture was his "Acres of Diamonds" speech. According to Conwell, during a trip in the Middle East in 1870, a tour guide told him a legend about a prosperous Persian farmer. The farmer had heard of a mythical field of diamonds and spent the rest of his life searching for it. He eventually died poor and far away from home, not knowing that acres of fabulous diamonds were buried within the fields he left behind. Conwell became convinced that wealth was not to be found in far-off lands but was present in people's own backyards if only they would put forth the effort.

The connection Conwell made between wealth and religion can be traced back to the belief in predestination, that is, that people are predestined before birth to go to Heaven or to Hell. While people could not know for certain whether they were part of the elect or the damned, there was a strong feeling that if they were blessed in this life, it could be a sign that they were blessed in the next.

## Significance

"Acres of Diamonds" is a classic example of the Gospel of Wealth, the view that possessing wealth was

Socialites relax at a Philadelphia, Pennsylvania, country club. According to the Gospel of Wealth, the accumulation of great wealth is not viewed negatively as the product of greed and selfishness, but rather as a sign of God's favor. © **BETTMANN/CORBIS. REPRODUCED BY PERMISSION.**

not only acceptable for Christians, but also that it was their duty to become rich. Conwell stated that the pursuit of wealth was not a rejection of the gospel, but that "to make money honestly is to preach the gospel." This was a clear rejection of the medieval virtue of poverty, which saw material possessions as an obstacle to the spiritual life.

The Gospel of Wealth flourished in the late nineteenth and early twentieth centuries. Theologically, it saw wealth not only as the result of hard work, but also of God's blessings. The accumulation of great wealth was not viewed negatively as the product of greed and selfishness, but rather as a sign of God's favor. Conwell disagreed with those who believed that only the dishonest or corrupt became rich: "The men who get rich may be the most honest men you find in the community . . . ninety-eight out of one hundred of the rich men of America are honest. That is why they are rich."

In contrast to the view of wealth being religiously edifying, poverty on the other hand was seen as sinful. Therefore, the condition of the poor was the result of their

moral failings and not the responsibility of society. Such a view was countered by the Social Gospel movement, which was active at the same time as the Gospel of Wealth.

Conwell reached millions of listeners and readers who, not surprisingly, welcomed his frank equation of wealth and godliness. Like Bruce Barton in the following decade, Conwell saw a natural relationship between religion and business. This message was extremely popular in American religion until disillusionment with big business followed the stock market crash of 1929 and the Great Depression.

## Primary Source

*Acres of Diamonds* [excerpt]

**SYNOPSIS:** Conwell's famous "Acres of Diamonds" speech is one of the best examples of the Gospel of Wealth teaching in American Protestantism. In it, he argued that it was the duty of all Christians to accumulate wealth. As for the poor, their condition was largely due to their own lack of initiative. This attitude toward wealth contrasted not only with traditional views of Christianity, but also with the Social Gospel movement, which saw the poor as victims of corrupt economic systems.

For a man to have money, even in large sums, is not an inconsistent thing. We preach against covetousness, and you know we do, in the pulpit, and oftentimes preach against it so long and use the terms about *"filthy lucre"* so extremely that Christians get the idea that when we stand in the pulpit we believe it is wicked for any man to have money—until the collection-basket goes around, and then we almost swear at the people because they don't give more money. Oh, the inconsistency of such doctrines as that!

Money is power, and you ought to be reasonably ambitious to have it. You ought because you can do more good with it than you could without it. Money printed your Bible, money builds your churches, money sends your missionaries, and money pays your preachers, and you would not have many of them, either, if you did not pay them. I am always willing that my church should raise my salary, because the church that pays the largest salary always raises it the easiest. You never knew an exception to it in your life. The man who gets the largest salary can do the most good with the power that is furnished to him. Of course he can if his spirit be right to use it for what it is given to him.

I say, then, you ought to have money. If you can honestly attain unto riches in Philadelphia, it is your Christian and godly duty to do so. It is an awful mistake of these pious people to think you must be awfully poor in order to be pious.

Some men say, "Don't you sympathize with the poor people?" Of course I do, or else I would not have been lecturing these years. I won't give in but what I sympathize with the poor, but the number of poor who are to be sympathized with is very small. To sympathize with a man whom God has punished for his sins, thus to help him when God would still continue a just punishment, is to do wrong, no doubt about it, and we do that more than we help those who are deserving. While we should sympathize with God's poor—that is, those who cannot help themselves—let us remember there is not a poor person in the United States who was not made poor by his own shortcomings, or by the shortcomings of some one else. It is all wrong to be poor, anyhow. Let us give in to that argument and pass that to one side.

A gentleman gets up back there, and says, "Don't you think there are some things in this world

that are better than money?" Of course I do, but I am talking about money now. Of course there are some things higher than money. Oh yes, I know by the grave that has left me standing alone that there are some things in this world that are higher and sweeter and purer than money. Well do I know there are some things higher and grander than gold. Love is the grandest thing on God's earth, but fortunate the lover who has plenty of money. Money is power, money is force, money will do good as well as harm. In the hands of good men and women it could accomplish, and it has accomplished, good.

## Further Resources

### BOOKS

Burr, Agnes Rush. *Russell H. Conwell and His Work: One Man's Interpretation of Life.* Philadelphia: Winston, 1926.

Shackleton, Robert. *Conwell's Life and Achievements.* Joshua Tree, Calif.: Tree of Life Publications, 1993.

Stokes, John Wesley. *The Man Who Lived Two Lives,* 2nd ed. New York: Vantage, 1980.

### PERIODICALS

Carlson, Cheree A. "Narrative As the Philosophic Stone: How Russell H. Conwell Changed Lead into Diamonds." *Western Journal of Speech Communication,* Fall 1989.

### WEBSITES

Carter, Joseph C. "Temple University's Founder." Available online at http://www.temple.edu/about/temples_founder.html; website home page: http://www.temple.edu (accessed December 8, 2002).

---

# *Prisoners of Hope and Other Sermons*
## Sermon

**By:** Rev. Charles H. Brent

**Date:** 1915

**Source:** Brent, Rev. Charles H. *Prisoners of Hope and Other Sermons.* New York: Longmans, Green, 1915, 35–41.

**About the Author:** Charles H. Brent (1862–1929) was a noted American Episcopalian clergyman and ecumenist. While serving as a bishop in the Philippines and New York State, Brent spent a great deal of his energy in the cause of Christian unity. He eventually became one of the major leaders in the establishment of the Faith and Order Conference in 1927, which helped lead to the formation of the World Council of Churches in 1948. ∎

## Introduction

Charles H. Brent was an Episcopalian clergyman who first worked in the slums of Boston. In 1901, he was appointed the first Protestant Episcopal missionary bishop of the Philippines, which had been acquired by the United States in the Spanish-American War (1898). It was in this work that Brent's abilities in interfaith cooperation and statesmanship became recognized.

Brent could have limited his efforts to simply serve the U.S. officials in Manila or to take advantage in the change of government to proselytize the local Roman Catholic population. He did not believe, however, in increasing one church at the expense of another, "The effort to expand is a requisite of health, but the expansion must be of a unified church, not of sectarian fragments." Instead, he showed both his missionary zeal and concern for Christian unity by directing his efforts toward the non-Christian peoples of his territory. In the area of social change, Brent served on several international commissions devoted to eliminating narcotics. His reputation as an advocate of Christian unity led to his participation in the 1910 World Missionary Conference in Edinburgh. This gathering of different churches became the first building block of the World Council of Churches. The major achievement of this conference was a call to end competition among Christians in the mission field, a practice in which Brent had demonstrated leadership.

Brent's experiences in the Philippines inspired him to struggle against religious bigotry and to promote Christian unity. He wrote, "The unity of Christendom is not a luxury, but a necessity. The world will go limping until Christ's prayer that all may be one is answered. We must have unity, not at all costs, but at all risks. A unified Church is the only offering we dare present to the coming Christ, for in it alone will He find room to dwell."

## Significance

A major obstacle to cooperation among churches was competition for converts. Many church leaders operated on the assumption that evangelization necessarily meant demonstrating the superiority of one's church over others, thus fostering tension between denominations. Brent became a major figure in the ecumenical movement by demonstrating that evangelization and ecumenism could go hand in hand. In his sermon "Whole Man for Whole God," Brent stated, "Fragments can only do fragmentary work. Do not be deceived; without unity the conversion of great nations is well-nigh hopeless. The success of Missions is inextricably bound up with unity."

Despite serious health problems, Brent continued to labor hard in the area of church unity. Significant gains had been made in the cause of Christianity in missionary work and social action. Work was still needed, however, in addressing the differences in beliefs and practices. This was the task to which Brent dedicated himself. In 1920,

Charles Henry Brent. Brent was a leading proponent for Christian unity and much of his work, including his famous "Whole Man for Whole God" sermon, centered on this topic. **THE LIBRARY OF CONGRESS.**

he presided over a planning meeting for the first World Conference on Faith and Order. Seven years later, the first World Conference on Faith and Order met in Lausanne, Switzerland. Brent was elected president of the conference by the representatives of the 127 Christian churches present. Brent returned to Lausanne two years later for additional administrative work and died there in 1929.

The establishment of the Faith and Order Conference was a major step in the formation of the World Council of Churches, founded in 1948. In 2002, a celebration marking the seventy-fifth anniversary of the Faith and Order Commission of the World Council of Churches was held in Lausanne. The ceremony began with the laying of a wreath on Brent's grave, which acknowledged the pivotal role of this American in the cause of Christian unity and religious tolerance.

## Primary Source

*Prisoners of Hope and Other Sermons* [excerpt]

**SYNOPSIS:** Brent was one of the leading ecumenists of the twentieth century. As demonstrated in the following excerpt, he addressed a major issue of denominational friction by stating that ecumenism and evangelization could go hand in hand. The fact that he practiced what he preached enhanced his reputation as an advocate for Christian unity.

Whole man for whole God—this means a corporate offering. Mere individualism is a thing of yesterday. The written record of revelation begins with a garden and ends with a city; it begins with a man and ends with man; it begins with an individual and ends with a society; it begins with a unit and ends with a unity. These days in which we live are not the beginning—they are the end. We must therefore offer God for His foothold a unified Church and an evangelized race. Unity in Christendom is the prayer and purpose of Jesus Christ. Its desirability is beyond dispute. The need of it those who, like myself, belong to a Christian Communion none too numerous or strong, and who, like myself, wear the proud title of missionary, alone can fully appreciate. Fragments can do only fragmentary work. Do not be deceived; without unity the conversion of great nations is well-nigh hopeless. The success of Missions is inextricably bound up with unity. It has been said by some one that we need not more but better Christians. Such antitheses are unfortunate. You cannot have better Christians without having more. The effort to expand is a requisite of health, but the expansion must be of a unified Church, not of sectarian fragments.

There are four main obstacles in the way of promoting unity. First, acquiescence in the broken order. Satisfaction with the moderate success of things as they are, the acceptance of mediocrity as a necessity, is fatal in the Christian life. We have fleeting glimpses of Christ, when we ought to have a glowing vision. A mutilated Christendom can never have anything better than a mutilated conception of our Lord and an impoverished influx of His power. Our broken Christendom is wholly inadequate to meet the needs of society. We have rather settled down in the conviction that unity is not a possibility, and that we must therefore make the best of the situation as we find it. Unity is possible only so far as we believe it to be so, and there can be no realization of it or any other ideal until we crown our desire for it with our conviction that it must be. Secondly, the sense of security among great dominating Churches like the Church of England, the Roman Catholic Church, and the Orthodox Churches of the East. It is their misfortune rather than their fault if they fail to recognize the imperative need of unity. They are apt to be prejudiced in their own favor by their prestige and position. They rejoice in their strength and mistake their local for universal influence. Endowed as each is with a body of systematic theology all its own, they are in danger of worshipping their idea of God instead of God, and invoking the presence of their idea of Christ rather than Christ. Ideas are noble, but at best they contain only a cupful of nourishment and are soon wrung dry.

Thirdly, the misuse of the word "Church." So far as I am aware, there is no warrant except perverted use for the application of the word Church to any existing Christian Communion in the sense it is commonly intended. The word is so majestic in what it connotes that it cannot bear the restraint of adjectival qualification beyond what has been attached to it in the language of the Creeds. A distinguishing word linked to it—like Protestant or Episcopal, for instance—is apt to contradict the essential meaning of the word. The utmost it can bear is a territorial or a national characterization, and only then if it is applied with understanding. Its careless use obscures the catholicity of its sweep, caging men in sectarianism and removing the stinging rebuke which it for ever carries to a city that is not at unity with itself. My preference would be to term the various organic groups of Christians indiscriminately as Communions. Not one is to-day worthy of a better title. Then we could reserve "Church" for the Bride of Christ, that glorious Church, holy, without blemish, not having spot, or wrinkle, or any such thing.

Fourthly, substitutes for unity, of which there are two principal ones, called respectively Undenominationalism and Uniformity. Undenominationalism at best can only hope to bring about a federative patch-work, "a glueing of the Churches together at the edges." At worst it will lead us into the slough of unreality by slurring over those distinctions of conviction which call for a treatment, not of obliteration, but of preservation and synthesis. The other substitute—Uniformity—is equally disastrous. At best it is capable only of creating structural dignity and formal completeness. At worst it would rob us of our royal liberties by an imperialistic tyranny. It is organic unity that we are reaching for, not reunion. The former is from within; the latter from without. The one is fundamental, the other artificial. It is a mistake to suppose that it is desirable to reproduce the imperialistic unity of ancient times, good as it was for the moment. It is no more desirable or possible than it would be to regain the civilization that is past. That which is to be can be built only on that which is. There is a simple unity and a synthetic unity. . . .

The Communion which I represent, less than two months ago in its Representative Council, composed of upwards of three hundred picked presbyters and laymen and more than a hundred Bishops, adopted, without a dissenting voice, this resolution:

"We believe that the time has now arrived when representatives of the whole family of Christ, led by the Holy Spirit, may be willing to come together for the consideration of questions of Faith and Order. We believe, further, that all Christian Communions are in accord with us in our desire to lay aside self-will, and to put on the mind which is in Jesus Christ our Lord. We would heed this call of the Spirit of God in all lowliness and with singleness of purpose. We would place ourselves by the side of our fellow-Christians, looking not only on our own things, but also on the things of others, convinced that our one hope of mutual understanding is in taking personal counsel together in the spirit of love and forbearance. It is our conviction that such a conference for the purpose of study and discussion, without power to legislate or to adopt resolutions, is the next step towards unity. With grief for our aloofness in the past and for other faults of pride and self-sufficiency which make for schism, with loyalty to the truth as we see it, and with respect for the convictions of those who differ from us, holding the belief that the beginnings of unity are to be found in the clear statement and full consideration of those things in which we differ, as well as of those things in which we are at one, we respectfully submit the following resolution:—*Whereas,* there is to day among all Christian people a growing desire for the fulfilment of our Lord's prayer that all His disciples may be one, that the world may believe that God has sent Him, *Resolved,* That a Joint Commission be appointed to bring about a Conference for the consideration of questions touching faith and order, and that all Christian Communions throughout the world which confess our Lord Jesus Christ as God and Saviour be asked to unite with us in arranging for and conducting such a conference."

"What a risk!" I hear some one say. Yes, I reply, a glorious risk. It were better far for a Christian Communion to risk the loss of its distinctive character in a brave effort toward unity than to sit in idle contemplation of a shattered Christendom. At worst it would lose its eccentricities and prejudices; at best it would lose itself entirely in the splendor of unity according to the mind of Christ. But let there be what peril there may, peril for God's sake is the only safe condition for Church or Churchmen. It is more reasonable to be in peril than in security if the best things lie a hair's-breadth beyond the peril. Everything worth having is found only on the yonder side

of a risk. We must have unity, not at all costs, but at all risks. A unified Church is the only offering we dare present to the coming Christ, for in it alone will He find room to dwell. Whole man for whole God is our watchword. Let us expect unity, let us think unity, let us pray for unity, let us work for unity. If we fail, it will be better to fail because we have dared great things than because we have not dared at all, so that men can say that we aimed at—

The high that proved too high, the heroic for earth too hard.

The passion that left the ground to lose itself in the sky.

## Further Resources

### BOOKS

Kates, Frederick Ward. *No Other Wealth: The Prayers of a Modern-Day Saint,* Nashville, Tenn.: Upper Room, 1965.

Zabriskie, Alexander Clinton. *Bishop Brent: Crusader for Christian Unity.* Philadelphia: Westminster, 1948.

### PERIODICALS

Norbreck, Mark D. "The Legacy of Charles Henry Brent." *International Bulletin of Missionary Research,* October 1996.

### WEBSITES

"Faith and Order Marks 75th Anniversary." Available at http://www.wcc-coe.org/wcc/news/press/02/08info-e.html; website home page: http://www.wcc-coe.org (accessed December 8, 2002).

# "What the Bible Contains for the Believer"
Essay

**By:** Rev. George F. Pentecost

**Date:** 1915

**Source:** Pentecost, Rev. George F. "What the Bible Contains for the Believer." In Amzi C. Dixon, Louis Meyer, and Reuben A. Torrey, eds., *The Fundamentals: A Testimony to the Truth,* vol. 10. Chicago: Testimony, 1914(?). Reprint in Marsden, George M. *The Fundamentals.* Vol. 4. Fundamentalism in American Religion, 1880–1950, ed. Joel A. Carpenter. New York: Garland, 1988, 97–99.

**About the Author:** George Frederick Pentecost (1842–1920) was an American clergyman and author who was recognized as a strong supporter of biblical authority and a compelling preacher whose sermons featured both deep feeling and unusual breadth. In addition to serving various congregations in Indiana, Kentucky, New York, Massachusetts, and Pennsylvania, he undertook evangelistic campaigns to Europe and Asia and spent six years as pastor of a London church. His most popular writings included *The Angel in the Marble* (1875), *In the Volume of the Book* (1879), *Out of Egypt* (1884), and the twelve-volume set *Bible Studies* (1880–1889). ∎

## Introduction

The teachings of liberal preachers and theologians such as Horace Bushnell, Washington Gladden, and Walter Rauschenbusch were unsettling to many Protestants. This was particularly the case with the New Theology's use of biblical criticism, which questioned such things as the authorship of certain books of the Bible. This provoked a response from a group of conservative Protestants known as Fundamentalists. (The label "Fundamentalist" was coined by Curtis Lee Laws, the Baptist editor of the *Watchman-Examiner* in 1920. According to Laws, a Fundamentalist was one who was prepared to fight for the fundamentals of the Christian faith. Most of this rested on accepting the authority of the Bible.) The Fundamentalists believed that liberal theology had surrendered too much of the core beliefs of Christianity to modernism, that the essentials of the faith had to be preserved, and that the Bible was the sole, unerring, and unchanging source of authority for Christianity.

Lyman Stewart was a wealthy Presbyterian who gave generously to the Fundamentalist cause in Los Angeles. A major financier for the Bible Institute of Los Angeles, which was modeled on the Moody Bible Institute in Chicago, Stewart recruited Reuben Archer Torrey from Moody to serve as the dean. He then financed, with the help of his brother Milton, the publication of a twelve-volume collection of ninety essays known as *The Fundamentals: A Testimony to the Truth.* Together, the brothers established a $250,000 fund to make certain that every pastor, evangelist, minister, theology professor, seminarian, Sunday school director, and YMCA and YWCA director in the English-speaking world would be provided with this body of conservative literature. Eventually, three million copies were distributed. Many date the origin of the Fundamentalist movement, which has ever since been a major force in American Protestantism, with the appearance of these tracts.

## Significance

At the heart of the controversy was the issue of liberal theology and biblical criticism. Liberal theology believed that the inherited faith needed to be adapted to modern times. Conservatives felt this undermined traditional Christian beliefs. They insisted on the preservation of traditional understandings of doctrines and rejected any attempt to dissect the sources of those doctrines, especially the Bible.

Most of the explicit criticisms of liberal theology in *The Fundamentals* were directed at its use of higher criticism in the study of the Bible. Liberal theologians believed that new scientific methods of research needed to be applied to traditional sources, in particular the Bible. Furthermore, they claimed that the Bible was not the sole source for truth, but rather that truth was to be found in religious experience. Fundamentalists responded by asserting that the Bible was the unerring source of all theology.

Fundamentalism operated on two fronts: externally in society and internally within the churches. Externally, Fundamentalists resisted scientific theories, such as evolution, that were deemed to contradict traditional interpretations of the Bible. Within the denominations, Fundamentalism resisted the spread of liberal theology and modern scholarship. The Fundamentalist controversy was strongest in those denominations where neither liberals nor conservatives dominated. The Congregationalists, dominated by liberals, experienced no conflict. Neither did the conservative Southern Baptist Convention. The greatest conflict took place in the northern Baptist and Presbyterian churches, where the proportion of liberal and conservative members was more balanced.

The appearance of *The Fundamentals* galvanized conservative opposition to liberal theology and secular learning. At times, such as in the *Scopes* trial, the struggle gained national headlines. Often, it is confined to teaching appointments in seminaries. The struggle continues to this day.

## Primary Source

**"What the Bible Contains for the Believer"**
[excerpt]

> **SYNOPSIS:** The appearance of *The Fundamentals* represented the conservative counterattack to the perceived threat of liberal theology to traditional Christian beliefs. As stated by the following excerpt, "What the Bible Contains for the Believer," the most important element of this struggle was the role, interpretation, and authority of the Bible.

### I. The Bible is the Only Book That Can Make Us Wise unto Salvation

The Bible is not a book to be studied as we study geology and astronomy, merely to find out about the earth's formation and the structure of the universe; but it is a book revealing truth, designed to bring us into *living union* with God. We may study the physical sciences and get a fair knowledge of the facts and phenomena of the *material* universe; but what difference does it make to us, as *spiritual* beings, whether the Copernican theory of the universe is true, or that of Ptolemy? On the other hand, the eternal things of God's Word do so concern us. Scientific knowledge, and the words in which that knowledge is conveyed, have no power to change our characters, to make us better, or give us a living hope of a blessed immortality; but the Word of God has in it a vital power, it is "quick and powerful"—living and full of Divine energy (Heb. 4:12)—and when received with meekness into our understanding and heart is able to save our souls (Jas. 1:18, 21), for it is the instrument of the Holy Spirit wherewith He accomplishes in us regeneration of character. The Word of God is a living seed containing within itself God's own life, which, when it is received into our hearts, springs up within us and "brings forth fruit after its kind;" for Jesus Christ, the eternal Word of God, is the living germ hidden in His written Word. Therefore it is written, "The words that I speak unto you, they are spirit and they are life" (John 6:63), and so it is that "he that heareth My words"—that is, receiveth them into good and honest hearts—that heareth the Word and understandeth it, *"hath everlasting life"* (John 5:24). Of no other book could such things as these be said. Hence we say, the Word of God is the instrument in His hand to work in us and for us regeneration and salvation; "for of His own will begat He us with the Word of truth, the engrafted Word, which is able to save your souls" (Jas. 1:18, 21).

This leads us to say that we are related to God and the eternal verities revealed in this Book, not through intellectual apprehension and demonstration, but by *faith.* Not by reasoning, but by simple faith, do we lay hold on these verities, resting our faith in God, who is under and in every saving fact in the Book. (See 1 Pet. 1:21.) It seems to me, therefore, to be the supreme folly for men to be always speculating and reasoning about these spiritual and revealed things; and yet we meet constantly even good people who are thus dealing with God's Word. First of all, they treat the revelation as though it were only an *opinion* expressed concerning the things revealed, and so they feel free to dissent from or receive it with modification, and deal with it as they would with the generalizations and conclusions. more or less accurate, of the scientists, and the theories, more or less true, of the philosophers. If the Word commends itself to their judgment they accept it; thus making *their judgment* the criterion of truth, instead of submitting their opinions to the infallible Word of God. It is not seldom that we hear a person say they believe the Word of God to be true; and then the very next instant, when pressed by some statement or declaration of that Word, they say, "Ah! but then *I* believe so and so"—something entirely different from what God has declared. Then again, many people who profess to believe God's Word seem never to think of putting themselves into practical and saving relation to it. They believe that

Jesus Christ is the Saviour of the world, but they never believe *on* Him or *in* Him; in other words, that He is a Saviour to *them.*

God's Book is full of doctrines and promises. We declare them, and some one says, "You must prove that doctrine or that promise to be true." The only way to prove a doctrine to be true is by a personal experience of it through faith in Jesus Christ. Jesus Christ says, "Ye must be born again." Should you attempt to master the meaning and power of that doctrine by mere speculation, you would presently land just where Nicodemus did, and say, "How can these things be?" Instead of doing so, suppose you attend further to what is said, namely, "Whosoever believeth is born of God" (1 John 5:1; John 1:12, 13). In obedience to this Divine teaching, not knowing how it is to be done in us, we take that Word and yield ourselves to Jesus Christ; and lo! there dawns upon us an experience that throws light upon all that which before was a mystery. We have experienced no *physical shock,* but a great change is wrought in us, especially in our relation to God. "Old things are passed away, and behold all things are become new" (2 Cor. 5:17). Thus we come into an experimental understanding of the doctrine of the new birth. So every other doctrine pertaining to the spiritual life is by God's grace transmuted into experience. For just as a word stands for an idea or thought, so the doctrines of God stand for experiences; but the doctrine must be received before the experience can be had. And, moreover, we are to receive all doctrines, all truth, through faith in Him, for Christ and His Word are inseparable, just as a man's *note* is only current and valuable because the *man* is good. A bank-note is received in the faith of the *bank* it represents. Should the bank fail, the note instantly becomes worthless.

## Further Resources

### BOOKS

Marsden, George. *Fundamentalism and American Culture: The Shaping of Twentieth Century Evangelicalism.* New York: Oxford University Press, 1980.

———. *Understanding Fundamentalism and Evangelicalism.* Grand Rapids, Mich.: Eerdmans, 1991.

### WEBSITES

"The Fundamentals Homepage." Available at http://www.xmission.com/~fidelis/; website home page: http://www.xmission.com (accessed December 8, 2002).

# A Theology for the Social Gospel

Theological work

**By:** Walter Rauschenbusch

**Date:** 1917

**Source:** Rauschenbusch, Walter. *A Theology for the Social Gospel.* Macmillan, 1917. Reprint, Nashville, Tenn.: Abingdon, 1981, 4–9.

**About the Author:** Walter Rauschenbusch (1861–1918) was a Baptist minister, a professor of church history, and a writer on the social responsibilities of Christianity. Born in Rochester, New York, he was the son of German immigrants who fled Germany in 1848. Rauschenbusch was an influential supporter of the Social Gospel movement and promoted this social view of Christianity in his many writings. ∎

## Introduction

The American Civil War (1861–1865) commenced about the time of Walter Rauschenbusch's birth. The enormous demands of the Union war effort brought about a great surge in industrial production—so much so that, by the turn of the century, the United States had become an industrial giant. But this growth came at great human cost. The small workshops that had close contact between owners and workers were replaced by far larger plants that employed thousands and were controlled by distant management. While in the earlier system workers could negotiate with owners who were aware of the workers' skills and needs, individual workers were powerless in the large industrial plants. The development of labor unions was seen as a way of countering the increasing power of the factory owners with the collective power of the workers.

Such efforts at collective bargaining were seen as subversive, even by many members of the clergy. Regardless, liberal Protestants called for a reform of the modern social order, a reform rooted in the Old Testament prophets and the Gospel. This modern Christian response to the Industrial Revolution became known as the Social Gospel movement. A leading figure in this movement was Walter Rauschenbusch.

In 1886, Rauschenbusch was ordained a minister of the German Baptist Church. After his ordination, Rauschenbusch declined a more comfortable, middle-class pastorate to become the minister at Second German Baptist Church, located near a destitute section of New York City called Hell's Kitchen. While serving the spiritual needs of his congregation, which consisted largely of German immigrants, Rauschenbusch also became familiar with the plight of the urban poor.

## Significance

In 1897, Rauschenbusch left New York City to teach at the Rochester Theological Seminary. While his experience as a minister put him in touch with urban social ills, Rauschenbusch's work in the seminary afforded him the opportunity to reflect on the theological implications of religion and society.

In April 1917, Rauschenbusch was invited by the Nathaniel W. Taylor Foundation to give four lectures before the annual convocation of the Yale School of Religion. The focus of the Taylor Lectures had traditionally been in the field of doctrinal theology, but the faculty at Yale indicated in their invitation that they would prefer it if Rauschenbusch changed the focus to a discussion of Christianity and the social problem. He complied, and the fundamentals of his lecture are contained in *A Theology for the Social Gospel,* published later in 1917. The book represents Rauschenbusch's most theological analysis of the relationship between Christianity and social issues, and it remains a classic work in the field of Protestant social ethics. In contrast to traditional Christian ethics, which focused on individual sins and individual salvation, Rauschenbusch emphasized that Jesus preached a social gospel for the salvation of society. The view that social structures can be sinful and in need of redemption continues to animate modern liberal Protestantism.

In *A Theology for the Social Gospel,* Rauschenbusch brought together themes he had raised in his earlier books, *Christianity and the Social Crisis* (1907) and *Christianizing the Social Order* (1912), and incorporated the experience of World War I (1914–1918) to connect these themes to the international situation.

## Primary Source

*A Theology for the Social Gospel* [excerpt]

**SYNOPSIS:** *A Theology for the Social Gospel* was Rauschenbusch's most important writing on the relationship between Christianity and social issues. In the following excerpt, Rauschenbusch calls for the Social Gospel movement to be expanded beyond economic reform, to include a "christianizing of international relations."

The Great War has dwarfed and submerged all other issues, including our social problems. But in fact the war is the most acute and tremendous social problem of all. All whose Christianity has not been ditched by the catastrophe are demanding a christianizing of international relations. The demand for disarmament and permanent peace, for the rights of the small nations against the imperialistic and colonizing powers, for freedom of the seas and of trade routes, for orderly settlement of grievances,—these are demands for social righteousness and fraternity on the largest scale. Before the War the social gospel dealt with social classes; to-day it is being translated into international terms. The ultimate cause of the war was the same lust for easy and unearned gain which has created the internal social evils under which every nation has suffered. The social problem and the war problem are fundamentally one problem, and the social gospel faces both. After the War the social gospel will "come back" with pent-up energy and clearer knowledge.

The social movement is the most important ethical and spiritual movement in the modern world, and the social gospel is the response of the Christian consciousness to it. Therefore it had to be. The social gospel registers the fact that for the first time in history the spirit of Christianity has had a chance to form a working partnership with real social and psychological science. It is the religious reaction on the historic advent of democracy. It seeks to put the democratic spirit, which the Church inherited from Jesus and the prophets, once more in control of the institutions and teachings of the Church.

The social gospel is the old message of salvation, but enlarged and intensified. The individualistic gospel has taught us to see the sinfulness of every human heart and has inspired us with faith in the willingness and power of God to save every soul that comes to him. But it has not given us an adequate understanding of the sinfulness of the social order and its share in the sins of all individuals within it. It has not evoked faith in the will and power of God to redeem the permanent institutions of human society from their inherited guilt of oppression and extortion. Both our sense of sin and our faith in salvation have fallen short of the realities under its teaching. The social gospel seeks to bring men under repentance for their collective sins and to create a more sensitive and more modern conscience. It calls on us for the faith of the old prophets who believed in the salvation of nations.

Now, if this insight and religious outlook become common to large and vigorous sections of the Christian Church, the solutions of life contained in the old theological system will seem puny and inadequate. Our faith will be larger than the intellectual system which subtends it. Can theology expand to meet the growth of faith? The biblical studies have responded to the spiritual hunger aroused by the social gospel. The historical interpretation of the Bible has put the religious personalities, their spiritual struggles, their growth, and their utterances, into social connection with the community life of which they were part. This method of interpretation has given back the Bible to men of modernized intelligence and has made it the feeder of faith in the social gospel. The studies of

In his *Theology for the Social Gospel* (1917), Baptist reformer Walter Rauschenbusch calls for the Social Gospel movement to be expanded beyond economic reform, to include a "christianizing of international relations." **THE LIBRARY OF CONGRESS.**

"practical theology" are all in a process of rejuvenation and expansion In order to create competent leadership for the Church, and most of these changes are due to the rise of new ideals created by the social gospel. What, then, will doctrinal theology do to meet the new situation? Can it ground and anchor the social gospel in the eternal truths of our religion and build its main ideas into the systematic structure of christian doctrine?

Theology is not superior to the gospel. It exists to aid the preaching of salvation. Its business is to make the essential facts and principles of Christianity so simple and clear, so adequate and mighty, that all who preach or teach the gospel, both ministers and laymen, can draw on its stores and deliver a complete and unclouded Christian message. When the progress of humanity creates new tasks, such as world-wide missions, or new problems, such as the social problem, theology must connect these with the old fundamentals of our faith and make them Christian tasks and problems.

The adjustment of the Christian message to the regeneration of the social order is plainly one of the most difficult tasks ever laid on the intellect of religious leaders. The pioneers of the social gospel have had a hard time trying to consolidate their old faith and their new aim. Some have lost their faith; others have come out of the struggle with crippled formulations of truth. Does not our traditional theology deserve some of the blame for this spiritual wastage because it left these men without spiritual support and allowed them to become the vicarious victims of our theological inefficiency? If our theology is silent on social salvation, we compel college men and women, workingmen, and theological students, to choose between an unsocial system of theology and an irreligious system of social salvation. It is not hard to predict the outcome. If we seek to keep Christian doctrine unchanged, we shall ensure its abandonment.

Instead of being an aid in the development of the social gospel, systematic theology has often been a real clog. When a minister speaks to his people about child labour or the exploitation of the lowly by the strong; when he insists on adequate food, education, recreation, and a really human opportunity for all, there is response. People are moved by plain human feeling and by the instinctive convictions which they have learned from Jesus Christ. But at once there are doubting and dissenting voices. We are told that environment has no saving power; regeneration is what men need; we can not have a regenerate society without regenerate individuals; we do not live for this world but for the life to come; it is not the function of the church to deal with economic questions; any effort to change the social order before the coming of the Lord is foredoomed to failure. These objections all issue from the theological consciousness created by traditional church teaching. These half-truths are the proper product of a half-way system of theology in which there is no room for social redemption. Thus the Church is halting between two voices that call it. On the one side is the voice of the living Christ amid living men to-day; on the other side is the voice of past ages embodied in theology. Who will say that the authority of this voice has never confused our Christian judgment and paralysed our determination to establish God's kingdom on earth?

Those who have gone through the struggle for a clear faith in the social gospel would probably agree that the doctrinal theology in which they were brought up, was one of the most baffling hindrances in their spiritual crisis, and that all their mental energies were taxed to overcome the weight of its traditions. They were fortunate if they promptly discovered some recent theological book which showed them at least the possibility of conceiving Christian doctrine in social terms, and made them conscious of a fellowship of faith in their climb toward the light. The situation would be much worse if Christian thought were nourished on doctrine only. Fortunately our hymns and prayers have a richer consciousness of solidarity than individualistic theology. But even to-day many ministers have a kind of dumb-bell system of thought, with the social gospel at one end and individual salvation at the other end, and an attenuated connection between them. The strength of our faith is in its unity. Religion wants wholeness of life. We need a rounded system of doctrine large enough to take in all our spiritual interests.

In short, we need a theology large enough to contain the social gospel, and alive and productive enough not to hamper it.

## Further Resources

### BOOKS

Fishburn, Janet Forsythe. *The Fatherhood of God and the Victorian Family: The Social Gospel in America.* Philadelphia: Fortress, 1981.

Jaehn, Klaus Juergen. *Rauschenbusch: The Formative Years.* Valley Forge, Pa.: Judson, 1976.

Minus, Paul M. *Walter Rauschenbusch: American Reformer.* New York: Macmillan, 1988.

Ramsay, William M. *Four Modern Prophets: Walter Rauschenbusch, Martin Luther King, Jr., Gustavo Gutiérrez, Rosemary Radford Ruether.* Atlanta: John Knox, 1986.

Smucker, Donovan E. *The Origins of Walter Rauschenbusch's Social Ethics.* Montreal: McGill-Queen's University Press, 1994.

# The Churches of Christ in Time of War

Handbook

**By:** Federal Council of the Churches of Christ in America

**Date:** 1917

**Source:** Federal Council of the Churches of Christ in America. *The Churches of Christ in Time of War.* Charles S. MacFarland, ed. New York: Missionary Education Movement of the United States and Canada, 1917, 6–9.

**About the Organization:** The Federal Council of the Churches of Christ in America (FCC) was founded in 1908. It originally consisted of thirty-three Protestant denominations representing eighteen million members. While there had been cooperation among churches on specific issues before, the founding of the FCC was a major step toward ecumenism (worldwide cooperation among different churches), as it was the first permanent interdenominational organization in the United States. It exists today as the National Council of Churches, which is itself a part of the World Council of Churches. ■

## Introduction

A significant proportion of the American population is of German descent. Many of the great American religious thinkers have been German American, such as Walter Rauschenbusch and Reinhold Niebuhr. In fact, for a full century before World War I (1914–1918), Germany profoundly influenced American intellectual life and educational institutions. Liberal Protestantism, in particular, was indebted to German theology. American theologians studied German ideas on biblical criticism, as well as the theological and social ideas that would eventually give rise to the Social Gospel movement. Despite this, with very few exceptions, American churches—whether conservative or liberal, Protestant or Catholic—got swept up in the patriotic fervor of World War I, condemning the Germans as untamed barbarians.

It is not surprising that many American church leaders and members supported the Allies in World War I, since the majority of American Protestant churches are of British origin. This includes not only the Congregationalists, Presbyterians, and Episcopalians, but also their offshoot churches, the Baptists and Methodists. Still, there are also many Protestant denominations of German origin. This includes the Lutherans, as well as the smaller German Baptist and Reformed congregations. German Americans also compose a large part of the Roman Catholic Church in the United States, second only to the Irish.

What is surprising is how dramatically churches got swept up by patriotic sentiment when the United States entered the war in April 1917 and adopted a strong anti-German stance. Religious leaders of every denomination joined their voices in a chorus of support for the war. The influential Lyman Abbott spoke for the majority of American Christians in calling the war a "twentieth-century crusade," a struggle of civilization against barbarism. Even liberal intellectuals got behind the war effort. Shailer Mathews wrote in his 1918 book, *Patriotism and Religion*, "For an American to refuse to share in the present war . . . is not Christian."

## Significance

Allied propaganda depicting Germans as villainous Huns was repeated from pulpits across the nation. According to Sydney E. Ahlstrom, one minister in Washington, D.C., claimed, "It is God who has summoned us to this war. . . . This conflict is indeed a crusade. The greatest in history—the holiest. It is in the profoundest

and truest sense a Holy War. . . . Yes, it is Christ, the King of Righteousness, who calls us to grapple in deadly strife with this unholy and blasphemous power." The minister of Plymouth Church in Brooklyn, New York, went so far as to speak in favor of exterminating the German people.

Amid American churches' general support for the war, the FCC's stance is interesting. While it would have been too much to expect it to follow the lead of the "peace" churches (such as the Amish, Mennonites, and Quakers, who refused to speak in favor of the war), it could have adopted a more neutral position that was not anti-German. The leaders of the FCC, after all, owed a great intellectual debt to the liberal theology of such German thinkers as Albrecht Ritschl. Furthermore, German American liberals such as Walter Rauschenbusch refused to lay blame for the war exclusively on the German people but, rather, laid it on the internal social evils found in every nation. Despite this, the FCC followed the more patriotic line when it issued its 1917 handbook, *The Churches of Christ in Time of War*. Even though it certainly adopted a milder tone in its statements, the FCC nonetheless chose to lend its support to the conflict, stating, "The war for righteousness will be won! Let the Church do her part." The document demonstrates how even the most progressive religious groups could get caught up in war fever.

## Primary Source

*The Churches of Christ in Time of War* [excerpt]

**SYNOPSIS:** The following excerpt is taken from *The Churches of Christ in Time of War*, a handbook issued in 1917 by the Federal Council of the Churches of Christ in America (FCC). It outlines the FCC's position on World War I to its member denominations. Less vitriolic than statements by other religious organizations, it does share the view, promoted by President Woodrow Wilson, that this was a just war to defend freedom and democracy.

Washington appealed to heaven: "That the happiness of the people of these states, under the auspices of liberty, may be made complete, by so careful a preservation and so prudent a use of this blessing (the liberties guaranteed by the Constitution) as will acquire to them the glory of recommending it to the applause, the affection, and the adoption of every nation which is yet a stranger to it."

Lincoln, in his immortal words, half appeal to the people, half prayer to Almighty God, heartened for fresh effort the struggling nation: "It is rather for us to be dedicated to the great task remaining before us, that from these honored dead we take in-

*The Cross and the Crusaders!!* by Alexander Oscar Levy, 1917. Through the use of the figure of Liberty and the crucifix this lithograph allegorically represents support of religious groups for the Allies in World War I. **THE LIBRARY OF CONGRESS.**

creased devotion to that cause for which they gave the last full measure of devotion, that we here highly resolve that these dead shall not have died in vain, that this nation, under God, shall have a new birth of freedom, and that government of the people, by the people, for the people, shall not perish from the earth."

Wilson, worthy of this great fellowship, in that recent hour upon which focused the thought of the whole world, declared: "The right is more precious than peace, and we shall fight for the things which we have always carried nearest our hearts—for democracy, for the right of those who submit to authority to have a voice in their own governments, for the rights and liberties of small nations, for a universal dominion of right by such a concert of free peoples as shall bring peace and safety to all nations and make the world itself at last free. To such a task we can dedicate our lives and our fortunes, everything that we are and everything that we have, with the pride of those who know that the day has come when America is privileged to spend her blood and her might for the principles that gave her birth and happiness and the peace which she has treasured. God helping her, she can do no other!"

These three great utterances ring with a common note. It vibrates through twelve decades of the nation's life—the indefeasible right of human liberty.

One greater than these declared, before the nations of this day were born, the one eternal principle of liberty for man and nation: "If the Son shall make you free, ye shall be free indeed."

Because the messages of the churches, because the prayers which rise from their altars, ring with this note, we who represent the churches have a place here in this vital hour. We come at the nation's crisis because at the burning center of each of these compelling statements of a great truth is the luminous heart of that which sixty generations of men have held to be the gospel of Jesus Christ, the Redeemer, the Liberator of the world.

The Constitution of the United States guarantees to the churches the right of freedom of worship. It as well protects them in the privilege of freedom for service. The separation of church and state is the very condition of the sacrificial devotion of the churches to the common welfare of community or nation. That devotion we are here to offer. War, however just and unselfish in its aims, places upon the nation an incalculable moral strain. To the individual it brings startling opportunities both for the most exalted heroism and the basest degradation.

The churches will, with fresh enthusiasm, consecrate their resources of courage, of sacrifice, of service, of prayer, to the uses of the nation as it steadies itself for the travail and the triumph of war. They will press as close as they may to the side of those who bear arms on land or sea. They will bring their reserves of mercy and kindness to the sick and wounded and desolate. They will give their youth, their manhood's strength, their woman's sympathy and skill, to the armies, to the farms and shops, to the hospitals. They will surrender their most tireless workers, their best trained students, their strongest ministers, for the common service and the highest spiritual tasks in the camps at home or with the forces at the front. They will resist with all their power the sordid influences of selfishness and materialism which war so surely fosters and will strive, with the Divine power, to keep pure the springs of motive and to renew from day to day the moral and spiritual vitality of the nation without which the victory of its arms would be the defeat of its ideals. And when the glad hour comes for which all are eager, we of the churches will stand in close ranks with all the grateful citizens of the Republic, to challenge the peoples of the world to the splendid enterprises of peace, of peace upon the unshaken basis of righteousness and liberty, ready, let us trust, then as now for whatever contest or renunciation the Master of Life who is the Lord of Love may appoint us.

We are here to-day, members of the Federal Council, not to stimulate our patriotism, nor to assert our loyalty, but to accept our responsibility, to define our task, and to determine our program. To these ends may the Spirit of God abide in us throughout these significant days.

## Further Resources
### BOOKS

Ahlstrom, Sydney E. *A Religious History of the American People.* New Haven, Conn.: Yale University Press, 1972.

Bundy, Edgar C. *Collectivism in the Churches: A Documented Account of the Political Activities of the Federal, National, and World Councils of Churches.* Wheaton, Ill.: Church League of America, 1958.

Mathews, Shailer. *Patriotism and Religion.* New York: Macmillan, 1918.

McIntire, Carl. *Twentieth Century Reformation.* New York: Garland, 1988.

# Cardinal Gibbons' Letter to the U.S. Archbishops

Letter

**By:** James Cardinal Gibbons

**Date:** May 1, 1919

**Source:** Gibbons, James Cardinal. Letter to the U.S. Archbishops, May 1, 1919. Reprinted in Ellis, John Tracy, ed. *Documents of American Catholic History.* 2nd ed. Milwaukee, Wis.: Bruce, 1962, 604–607.

**About the Author:** James Gibbons (1834–1921) was born in Baltimore, Maryland. The son of Irish immigrants, Gibbons was ordained a Catholic priest in 1861. A bright and energetic clergyman, he was ordained bishop in 1868 and became archbishop of Baltimore in 1877. In 1886, he was made cardinal by Pope Leo XIII. A man of great charm and intelligence, Gibbons supported the rights of labor and encouraged immigrant Catholics to fit into American society. ∎

## Introduction

James Gibbons was born on July 23, 1834, in Baltimore, the eldest son of Thomas and Bridget Gibbons. Initially, Gibbons did well in the field of business, but he felt a call to the Catholic priesthood. He excelled at his studies and was ordained in 1861. His intelligence and vigor were soon recognized. Becoming a priest at the age of thirty-two, he was eventually appointed bishop of Richmond in 1872. Five years later, he was appointed archbishop of Baltimore, and in 1886 he was named a cardinal by Leo XIII.

Gibbons' work as a young bishop in North Carolina and Virginia exposed him to many non-Catholics. It was through these experiences that he developed a broadly tolerant outlook that, combined with his intelligence and pleasant personality, was to characterize his work. Gibbons believed in cooperating with Protestants whenever possible on issues of common concern, such as Prohibition. He was far from timid in expounding the Catholic faith, however, and his book *The Faith of Our Fathers* has been called one of the most successful Catholic apologetics written in the English language.

By the time Gibbons became archbishop of Baltimore, the Catholic Church had surpassed the Methodists to become the largest denomination in the United States. This growth was largely the result of immigration. In the early nineteenth century, Irish immigrants dominated this new growth, followed in the mid-nineteenth century by the Germans. In the later nineteenth and early twentieth centuries, large numbers of Italian and Polish immigrants also arrived. This created a Catholic community that was not only large, but also diverse, with differing languages and customs.

## Significance

A major concern of Gibbons was to help the Catholic community in the United States become mainstreamed into American life, while at the same time holding on to its traditional Catholic beliefs. This dual objective of being fully Catholic and fully American, or in other words, of being faithful simultaneously to Rome and to the U.S. Constitution, had in fact been faced by American church leaders since John Carroll, the first bishop of the United States. It was, of course, the major charge of the anti-Catholic Nativist movement that Catholicism and American principles were incompatible. In 1889, on the one hundredth anniversary of the establishment of the diocese of Baltimore, Gibbons reaffirmed Bishop Carroll's vision that Catholic clergy and laity, regardless of their nation of origin, should become grounded in American customs, laws, and political institutions and thoroughly assimilated into American society.

Cardinal Gibbons was a liberal in the area of church-state relations. Unlike traditionalists who believed that the church needed to be established to prosper, Gibbons believed that American Catholics could flourish without the official support of the government. At the time of the Second Vatican Council (1962–1965), when the Roman Catholic Church officially promoted the idea of religious liberty as a civil right, the United States was the best example of how Catholicism could flourish in a pluralistic society.

Cardinal Gibbons died on March 24, 1921, at the age of eighty-six. The following excerpt touches on the great growth that took place in the Catholic community during his episcopate. He also refers to the theme that was central to his work, that is, of the need for the immigrants of his denomination to be Catholic and American at the same time.

## Primary Source

Cardinal Gibbons' Letter to the U.S. Archbishops

**SYNOPSIS:** In this letter to the U.S. Archbishops, Cardinal Gibbons argues for greater cooperation between Catholic leaders. A firm believer in the compatibility of Catholicism and American culture, he was concerned that Catholics were not as prominent in national affairs as their numbers warranted. Gibbons believed the establishment of a national organization of Catholic bishops would resolve this problem.

May 1, 1919

Baltimore

My Dear Archbishop:

After the celebration of my Episcopal Jubilee which was honored by the gracious presence of so many of the Hierarchy, there was a general meeting of all the Prelates who had participated. At this meeting there were present nearly all the Archbishops and Bishops of the country.

On this occasion, the Prelates present unanimously adopted three important resolutions, to which I desire to call your attention.

The first was that we should take extraordinary measures to aid the Holy Father in his present financial straits occasioned by the war.

The second measure adopted by the assembled Prelates was that annually all the Bishops, including Auxiliaries and the Rector of the University,—if he is a Bishop,—shall be invited to be present in Washington at the annual meeting of the Metropolitans.

The third measure adopted was that the Archbishop of Baltimore name a committee of five Prelates to be known hereafter as "The Committee on General Catholic Interests and Affairs."

These measures were all suggested and urged in an address to the Bishops who attended my Jubilee, by the special Representative of our Holy Father, Most Reverend Archbishop Cerretti.

I assure you that, great as was my joy in being permitted to commemorate my fifty years in the Episcopate, and my gratitude to Almighty God for His many blessings, the pleasure of the celebration was enhanced by knowing that it had been made the occasion for this meeting of the Hierarchy and for the inauguration of these measures which I regard as the most important since the Third Plenary Council of Baltimore.

The appointment of "The Committee on General Catholic Interests and Affairs" is especially gratifying to me. Hitherto, through the courtesy of my Confrères in the Episcopate and largely because the center of our National Government is within the limits of the Baltimore Archdiocese, the burden of the Church's general interests has in great measure rested on me. My experience has made me feel keenly the necessity of such a committee which with adequate authority and the aid of sub-committees could accomplish more than any individual, however able and willing he might be.

It is recognized by all that the Catholic Church in America, partly through defective organization, is not exerting the influence which it ought to exert in proportion to our numbers and the individual prominence of many of our people. Our diocesan units indeed are well organized. But the Church in America as a whole has been suffering from the lack of a unified force that might be directed to the furthering

Cardinal James Gibbons slaps former President Theodore Roosevelt on the back, Baltimore, Maryland, 1918. Cardinal Gibbons was responsible for the formation of the National Catholic Welfare Conference, the first national bishops conference in the United States. THE CATHOLIC UNIVERSITY OF AMERICA.

of those general policies which are vital to all. It was the general opinion of the Prelates present that we need a committee of the Hierarchy which shall be representative, authoritative and directive. It should be representative in the sense that it would stand for and express the views of the whole Hierarchy. It should be authoritative in as much as it would possess the confidence and have the support of the whole Hierarchy. Probably, too, it should be empowered to act when any emergency arises for which no provision has been made, but when immediate action is imperative and it would be impossible for lack of time to obtain the views of the individual members of the Hierarchy. Such a committee will unify our forces if entrusted with the powers above outlined.

I was asked by the Prelates who were present at the meeting to appoint the members of this committee, and I have named the committee to act until the next meeting of the Hierarchy. For the permanent and regular method of choosing this committee, however, it will, I think, be more satisfactory to all the Hierarchy, and more authoritative, if the committee be elected by secret ballot by all the members present at our annual meeting. It might be understood that those who are unable to attend the annual meeting should send their votes before the meeting.

The committee so chosen would naturally be composed of Prelates representing as far as possible all the interest of the Church at large, as well as the various sections of our country.

If this plan for organizing the committee is agreeable to you, we shall at our next annual meeting elect in the way I have suggested four Prelates by ballot. In the meantime, as a temporary measure, I have asked the four Prelates of the National Catholic War Council, who were selected, with the consent of the majority of the Hierarchy, to serve on the "Committee on General Catholic Interests and Activities"; and as I was Chairman of the War Council I will act as chairman of the new Committee until our next general meeting.

A meeting of the Committee will be held during the month of May. Several very important matters naturally impose themselves for consideration:

The collection for the Holy Father;

The continuation of the activities of the National War Council as far as may be deemed expedient;

Measures to safeguard general Catholic interests in National Legislation;

The vital interests of Catholic education;

The awakening of concern about the needs of home and foreign missions.

Suggestions concerning these or any other matters of general Catholic interest will be greatly appreciated by myself and the other members of the Committee.

*Faithfully yours in Xto.*
*J. Card. Gibbons*

## Further Resources

### BOOKS

Ellis, John Tracy. *The Life of James Cardinal Gibbons.* Milwaukee, Wis.: Bruce, 1963.

Newcomb, Covelle. *Larger Than the Sky: A Story of James Cardinal Gibbons.* London: Longmans, Green, 1945.

Smith, Albert Edward. *Cardinal Gibbons: Churchman and Citizen.* Baltimore, Md.: O'Donovan Brothers, 1921.

# "A Program for the Reconstruction of Judaism"

Journal article

**By:** Mordecai M. Kaplan

**Date:** August 1920

**Source:** Kaplan, Mordecai M. "A Program for the Reconstruction of Judaism." *The Menorah Journal* 6, no. 4, August 1920, 183–184. Reprinted in Emanuel S. Goldsmith, and Mel Scult, eds. *Dynamic Judaism: The Essential Writings of Mordecai M. Kaplan.* New York: Fordham University Press/The Reconstructionist Press, 1985, 39–40.

**About the Author:** Mordecai M. Kaplan (1881–1983), founder of the Jewish Reconstructionist movement, was born in Lithuania. In 1889, his family immigrated to the United States, where he earned a bachelor's degree from the City College of New York and a master's from Columbia University. After completing his education, Kaplan became a rabbi and taught at New York's Jewish Theological Seminary. He also authored numerous books, the most famous being *Judaism as a Civilization* (1934). ∎

## Introduction

Mordecai M. Kaplan was one of the most significant figures in American Judaism in the twentieth century. He taught at the Jewish Theological Seminary in New York, a center for Conservative Judaism. Kaplan was active in promoting Jewish identity and believed that Jewish life meant more than just Judaism. He sought a means to create a sense of Jewish identity that would include all Jews, religious and nonreligious. This would lead him eventually to establish the Reconstructionist movement in American Judaism.

Kaplan was born into an Orthodox Jewish family. In the course of his studies, Kaplan deemed Orthodox Judaism to be too conservative, but he did not adopt Reform Judaism. Instead, he became associated with Conservative Judaism, which strove to find a middle point between the liberal, pro-assimilationist Reform and the traditional, separatist Orthodox. For the time being, this middle-path approach to Judaism worked for Kaplan, but he still felt there was something missing.

In 1909, Kaplan became principal of the Teacher's Institute at the Jewish Theological Seminary, and in 1910, he also began teaching homiletics (the study of religious homilies) at the seminary. In this work, he began to ponder the question of Judaism and Jewishness. An important step in Kaplan's development came in 1918, when he founded the Jewish Center in New York City. It was at the Jewish Center that Kaplan began to formulate the new understanding of what it meant to be Jewish that would later be expressed in "A Program for the Reconstruction of Judaism."

## Significance

On the surface, the Jewish Center appeared to be simply an attempt to make the synagogue more attractive by adding a variety of nonreligious activities to the house of worship and the school. But Kaplan's vision was broader than this. He did not see the synagogue's involvement in additional activities to be supplementing its main task of providing religious services. Rather, Kaplan believed that the purpose of the synagogue was to promote *all* aspects of Jewish identity, both religious and nonreligious. His aim was a new type of Jewish community, with its focus not on religion but on "Jewishness." While Judaism was certainly an important part of this, Kaplan's plan would give equal emphasis to other aspects of Jewish life, including political, cultural, intellectual, and philanthropic activities. The synagogue was to be the rallying center for the Jewish people and culture, even for those who did not feel strongly about Judaism.

Kaplan served as rabbi of the Jewish Center from 1918 to 1922. During this period, his views became more fully developed. This can be seen in his article, "A Program for the Reconstruction of Judaism," published in *The Menorah Journal* in 1920.

In 1922, Kaplan left his position with the Jewish Center to head the Society of the Advancement of Judaism, which he led until 1944. In 1934, he published *Judaism as a Civilization,* in which he argued that Judaism was not a religion, as the term was generally understood, but rather a religious civilization. He described the breakdown of the Jewish community in the United States and argued for the reconstruction of central Jewish communities, which would coordinate the various activities being performed by Jewish organizations, both secular and religious. Nonreligious Jews were to have as much a place in such a community as Orthodox, Reform, and Conservative Jews. Kaplan's advocacy of Judaism as a distinct civilization within American culture set him against Reform Judaism. The fact that his definition of Judaism included non-practicing Jews set him against the Orthodox, as well. In time, his views would also conflict with the Conservatives, who also continued to see Judaism primarily as a religion.

To further spread his program, Kaplan founded the magazine *Reconstructionist* in 1935. Although Reconstruction originated within Conservative Judaism, it gradually emerged as a fourth distinct branch of American Judaism.

## Primary Source

### "A Program for the Reconstruction of Judaism"

**SYNOPSIS:** In this article from the August 1920 issue of *The Menorah Journal,* Kaplan demonstrates the distinction between his movement and Reform Judaism. In particular, he focuses on the importance of the distinctiveness of the Jewish community. This emphasis on a separate, unique Jewish community ran counter to the Reform view of accommodation with American culture. The fact that Kaplan saw this separate, unique Jewish community as including non-practicing Jews distinguished his views from those of the Orthodox.

## A Critique of Reform Judaism

Our dissent from Reform Judaism is even more pronounced than that from Orthodoxy. If we have been content to put up with much in Orthodoxy that we do not approve of, it is that we might not be classed with the "Reformers." The reason for this attitude of ours toward Reform is that we are emphatically opposed to the negation of Judaism. The principles and practices of Reform Judaism, to our mind, make inevitably for the complete disappearance of Jewish life. Reform Judaism represents to us an absolute break with the Judaism of the past, rather than a development out of it. In abrogating the hope for a national restoration, it has shifted the center of spiritual interests from the Jewish people to the individual Jew. Reform Judaism has as little in common with historic Judaism as has Christianity or Ethical Culture. Although it insists that the Jews are a religious community and not a nation, it has never taken the trouble to develop the full implications either of the term "religious" or of the term "community." It overlooks the fact that a community implies living in common and not merely believing in common. A community is not merely a society. It is because we refuse to sublimate the Jewish people into a philosophical society that we object to the Reform movement. While the Reform movement gives free scope to the intellectual inquiry, it does not take full advantage of that freedom. Being opposed to ancient ideas is not the same as having acquired modern ideas. There is as much credulity in gulping down ill-understood modern slogans as in blindly accepting ancient dogmas. If the Reform movement had learned from the recent studies of the history and nature of religion, it would have abandoned its attempt to reduce Judaism to a few anemic platitudes.

The untenability of the Reform position is never so apparent as in its attempt to find in the mission idea a substitute for the national aspiration of the Jewish people. On the face of it the mission idea appears more absurd than the belief in the personal Messiah. The belief in the personal Messiah at least has an air of poetry and romanticism to it, and until recently no one thought of questioning its literalness; whereas the mission idea, as entertained by Reform Judaism, represents a half-hearted attempt at self-hypnotization. So far as making the Jews understood to the rest of the world is concerned, which is after all the avowed aim of the Reform movement, the so-called mission idea is certainly a failure, for it does more to accentuate the alleged megalomania of the Jews than the most extravagant Messianic doctrine.

## Further Resources

### BOOKS

Berkovitz, Eliezer. *Major Themes in Modern Philosophies of Judaism.* New York: Ktav, 1975.

Breslauer, S. Daniel. *Mordecai Kaplan's Thought in a Postmodern Age.* Atlanta, Ga.: Scholars, 1994.

Caplan, Eric. *From Ideology to Liturgy: Reconstructionist Worship and American Liberal Judaism.* Cincinnati, Ohio: Hebrew Union College Press, 2002.

Cohn, Jack J. *Guides for an Age of Confusion: Studies in the Thinking of Avraham Y. Kook and Mordecai M. Kaplan.* New York: Fordham University Press, 1999.

Goldsmith, Emanuel S., Mel Scult, and Robert M. Seltzer, eds. *The American Judaism of Mordecai M. Kaplan.* New York: New York University Press, 1990.

Gurock, Jeffrey S., and Jacob J. Schacter. *A Modern Heretic and a Traditional Community: Mordecai M. Kaplan, Orthodoxy, and American Judaism.* New York: Columbia University Press, 1997.

Libowitz, Richard. *Mordecai M. Kaplan and the Development of Reconstructionism.* Lewiston, N.Y.: E. Mellen, 1984.

Scult, Mel. *Judaism Faces the Twentieth Century: A Biography of Mordecai M. Kaplan.* Detroit: Wayne State University Press, 1993.

# "Interchurch World Movement Report"
Report

**By:** Interchurch World Movement

**Date:** 1920

**Source:** Interchurch World Movement. "Interchurch World Movement Report." In *The Steel Strike of 1919,* ed. Colston E. Warne. Boston: D.C. Heath, 1963, 90–97.

**About the Organization:** The Interchurch World Movement (IWM) was a Christian interfaith organization founded in 1918. It represented one of the most ambitious projects of American Protestantism, with its goals being to coordinate the resources of the American churches to evangelize the world and to tackle a variety of other religious and social objectives. Its goals were too varied, however, and discord over its objectives led members to begin leaving in 1920. Thereafter, it soon dissolved and the churches resumed their individual activities. ■

## Introduction

During World War I (1914–1918), Protestant denominations in the United States raised $200 million by working together in the United War Work Campaign. John R. Mott, a noted ecumenist and later Nobel Prize winner, called it "the Largest Voluntary Offering in History." In 1918, at the conclusion of the war, it was decided to use this experience to create a new organization that would harness the power of the churches to address the needs of the postwar world.

On December 17, 1918, representatives from various denominations met in New York City. Their vision was that a united church could unite a divided world. Thus was born the IWM, a religious cross between the League of Nations and the United Way. The IWM was seen as a great peacetime crusade that would coordinate all the charitable and missionary agencies of American Protestantism, including raising the money for these activities. It was to include every phase of church work, both at home and abroad.

While the new organization began to study needs in the world and at home, much of its effort focused on the need to raise the enormous sums required for its work. One nationwide campaign in April 1920 called on American Protestants to give generously to the "biggest business of the biggest man in the world":

Christ was big, was He not? None ever bigger.

Christ was busy, was He not? None ever busier.

He was always about His Father's business.

Christ needs big men for big business.

The original goal set by the IWM was $300 million. This was soon deemed insufficient for its many objectives, so the goal was eventually raised to $1 billion. It was a truly impressive undertaking.

## Significance

Since ecumenism was a longtime goal for liberal Protestants, it is not surprising that liberals dominated the leadership of the IWM. In addition to ecumenism, Protestant liberals also supported the right of labor to organize. When the steel strike of 1919 took place, the leadership of the new IWM threw the support of the new organization behind it.

In June 1918, the American Federation of Labor decided to organize the steel industry, an action which was strongly resisted by corporate management. President Woodrow Wilson (served 1913–1921) failed to resolve the dispute, and the workers went on strike on September 22, 1919. The IWM tried to mediate the dispute between November 28 and December 5, 1919, but failed to gain an agreement. The strike was called off January 5, 1920. The "Conclusions and Recommendations of Interchurch World Movement Report" on the strike was adopted by the IWM on June 28, 1920. This report was highly critical of the steel companies and decidedly pro-labor.

The big fund-raising goals for the IWM relied heavily on wealthy businessmen who thought the IWM was about missionary work, not forming unions. These indi-

Steel workers on the job, circa 1920. Low wages, long hours, and atrocious working conditions led to a national steel strike in 1919. The newly formed Interchurch World Movement attempted to mediate the strike, but disagreement over its conclusions led to its sudden collapse. © CORBIS. REPRODUCED BY PERMISSION.

viduals were shocked by the early pro-labor stance of the IWM report and refused to contribute. The prominence of liberals in the leadership of the organization led conservatives to question their denomination's membership. In 1920, the Northern Presbyterians and Northern Baptists pulled out of the IWM. Others quickly followed and soon the IWM collapsed.

The controversy over the IWM's support for the 1919 strike shows how difficult it is to maintain unity among diverse religious groups. This support also shows how strongly liberal Protestantism supported the right of labor to organize. The following excerpt is taken from the report issued by the commission that the IWM appointed to investigate the 1919 steel strike. The document is not a theological piece, as it focuses mostly on economic issues and contains many statistics. In its report, the commission was very critical of U.S. Steel and took such a pro-labor position that the commission, as well as the IWM, was accused of advocating socialism. Such criticism made those churches already rethinking their membership in the IWM even more uneasy.

## Primary Source

"Interchurch World Movement Report" [excerpt]

SYNOPSIS: This excerpt demonstrates the concern for labor among Protestant liberals. Such a concern was not shared by all, however, and the controversial support for the strike was one reason for the dissolution of the IWM. Liberal Protestants were able to continue their advocacy for labor through the Federal Council of Churches.

The annual earnings of over one-third of all productive iron and steel workers were, and had been for years, below the level set by government experts as the *minimum of subsistence* standard for families of five. The annual earnings of 72 per cent of all workers were, and had been for years, below the level set by government experts as the *minimum of comfort* level for families of five.

This second standard being the lowest which scientists are willing to term an "American standard of living," it follows that nearly three-quarters of the steel workers could not earn enough for an American standard of living. The bulk of unskilled steel labor earned less than enough for the average family's minimum subsistence; the bulk of semi-skilled labor earned less than enough for the average family's minimum comfort.

Skilled steel labor was paid wages disproportionate to the earnings of the other two-thirds, thus binding the skilled class to the companies and creating divisions between the upper third and the rest of the force. Wage rates in the iron and steel industry as a whole are determined by the rates of the U.S. Steel Corporation. The Steel Corporation sets its wage rates, the same as its hour schedules, without conference (or collective bargaining), with its employees.

Concerning the financial ability of the Corporation to pay higher wages the following must be noted (with the understanding that the Commission's investigation did not include analysis of the Corporation's financial organization): the Corporation vastly increased its undistributed financial reserves during the Great War. In 1914 the Corporation's total undivided surplus was $135,204,471.90. In 1919 this total undivided surplus had been increased to $493,048,201.93. Compared with the wage budgets, in 1919, the Corporation's final surplus after paying dividends of $96,382,027 and setting aside $274,277,835 for Federal taxes payable in 1919, was $466,888,421,—a sum large enough to have paid a second time the total wage and salary budget for 1918 ($452,663,524), and to have left a surplus of over $14,000,000. In 1919 the undivided surplus was $493,048,201.93, or $13,000,000 more than the total wage and salary expenditures.

Increases in wages during the war in no case were at a sacrifice of stockholders' dividends.

Extreme congestion and unsanitary living conditions, prevalent in most Pennsylvania steel communities, were largely due to underpayment of semi-skilled and common labor. . . .

■ ■ ■

It is an epigram of the industry that "steel is a man killer." Steel workers are chiefly attendants of gigantic machines. The steel business tends to become, in the owners' eyes, mainly the machines.

Steel jobs are not easily characterized by chilly scientific terms. Blast furnaces over a hundred feet high, blast "stoves" a hundred feet high, coke ovens miles long, volcanic Bessemer converters, furnaces with hundreds of tons of molten steel in their bellies, trains of hot blooms, miles of rolls end to end hurtling white hot rails along,—these masters are attended by sweating servants whose job is to get close enough to work but to keep clear enough to save limb and life. It is concededly not an ideal industry for men fatigued by long hours.

To comprehend precisely what the twelve-hour day meant, the Inquiry gathered data from steel mill officials and from the workers themselves. Mr. Gary's testimony was:

> It is not an admitted fact that more than eight hours is too much for a man to labor per day. . . . I had my own experience in that regard (on a farm); and all our officers worked up from the ranks. They came up from day laborers. They were all perfectly satisfied with their time of service; they all desired to work longer hours . . . the employees generally do not want eight hours. . . . I do not want you to think that for a moment.

> *(Senate Testimony, Vol. I, p. 180.)*

Mr. H.D. Williams, president of the Carnegie Steel Company, said that he had worked fourteen hours a day and did not feel he was any the worse for it. . . .

First, what exactly is the schedule of the twelve-hour worker? Here is the transcript of the diary of an American worker, the observations of a keen man on how his fellows regard the job, the exact record of his own job and hours made in the spring of 1919, before the strike or this Inquiry, and selected here because no charge of exaggeration could be made concerning it. It begins:

> Calendar of one day from the life of a Carnegie steel workman at Homestead on the open hearth, common labor:

> 5:30 to 12 (midnight)—Six and one-half hours of shoveling, throwing and carrying bricks and cinder out of bottom of old furnace. Very hot.

> 12:30—Back to the shovel and cinder, within few feet of pneumatic shovel drilling slag, for three and one-half hours.

> 4 o'clock—Sleeping is pretty general, including boss.

> 5 o'clock—Everybody quits, sleeps, sings, swears, sighs for 6 o'clock.

> 6 o'clock—Start home.

> 6:45 o'clock—Bathed, breakfast.

7:45 o'clock—Asleep.

4 P.M.—Wake up, put on dirty clothes, go to boarding house, eat supper, get pack of lunch.

5:30 P.M.—Report for work. . . .

None can dispute the demoralizing effects on family life and community life of the inhuman twelve-hour day. As a matter of arithmetic twelve-hour day workers, even if the jobs were as leisurely as Mr. Gary says they are, have absolutely no time for family, for town, for church or for self-schooling; for any of the activities that begin to make full citizenship; they have not the time, let alone the energy, even for recreation. . . .

## Further Resources

### BOOKS

Carpenter, Joel A. *The Fundamentalist-Modernist Conflict: Opposing Views on Three Major Issues.* New York: Garland, 1988.

Ernst, Eldon G. *Moment of Truth for Protestant America: Interchurch Campaigns Following World War One.* Missoula, Mont.: American Academy of Religion, 1974.

Olds, Marshall. *Analysis of the Interchurch World Movement Report on the Steel Strike.* New York: Da Capo, 1971.

### WEBSITES

Townsley, D. L. "The Interchurch World Movement." Available online at http://www.yale.edu/divinity/case_teaching /inter.html; website home page: http://yale.edu (accessed June 2002).

# *Leaves From the Notebook of a Tamed Cynic*
Diary

**By:** Reinhold Niebuhr

**Date:** 1929

**Source:** Niebuhr, Reinhold. *Leaves From the Notebook of a Tamed Cynic.* 1929. Reprint, San Francisco: Harper and Row, 1980, 14–16.

**About the Author:** Reinhold Niebuhr (1892–1971), an Evangelical Synod minister and theologian, was born in Wright City, Missouri. Niebuhr served as a pastor for thirteen years in Detroit and then taught social ethics at Union Theological Seminary in New York City. He was the author of numerous books, including *Moral Man and Immoral Society* (1932) and the two-volume *The Nature and Destiny of Man: A Christian Interpretation* (1941–1943). ∎

## Introduction

Reinhold Niebuhr served as pastor of Bethel Evangelical Church in Detroit from 1915 to 1928, during which time he learned much about human nature. These experiences were published in his diary *Leaves From the Notebook of a Tamed Cynic.* Niebuhr wrote extensively on social issues, but he rejected liberal views regarding the perfectibility of humanity and human institutions. While an advocate of social reform, he nonetheless believed that the reality of human sin also needed to be taken into consideration.

Niebuhr was not yet twenty-five years old and had been a pastor only two years when the United States entered World War I (1914–1918). American religious groups, whether Protestant, Catholic, or Jewish, generally supported the U.S. military effort, and many did so with enthusiasm. Allied propaganda was accepted uncritically, and the American cause was blessed from various pulpits as a just war against German barbarism. Even liberal Christians supported President Woodrow Wilson's crusade.

Not all religious leaders, however, gave their blessing. The peace churches, such as the Amish, Quakers, and Mennonites, adhered to their historical pacifist beliefs and condemned the war. A few others from more mainline religious groups also spoke out against it. Unitarian minister John Haynes Holmes in 1915 denounced all war as a "foul business." Rabbi Stephen Wise wrote President Wilson to condemn the build-up of a war mentality. The liberal Baptist Harry Emerson Fosdick in 1917 condemned all talk of the "glory of war." He claimed that anyone who spoke of war that way was "morally unsound." Quoted in Edwin Scott Gaustad's book, Fosdick said war is not glorious, but rather "is dropping bombs from aeroplanes and killing women and children in their beds; it is shooting, by telephonic orders, at an unseen place miles away and slaughtering invisible men; it is murdering innocent travelers on merchant ships with torpedoes from unknown submarines."

## Significance

In the following excerpt from Niebuhr's diary, we can see how the young minister was struggling in that middle ground between those calling for a crusade to crush the barbarous Huns and the pacifists who condemned the war as an unmitigated evil. While the liberal Niebuhr sympathized with Wilson's aims for international peace, he was still uncomfortable with the ministers' close association with the military that he found in the camps.

Niebuhr's inner turmoil was resolved after the war when much of the Allied propaganda was proven to be untrue. In 1923, he noted in his diary, "Gradually the whole horrible truth about the war is being revealed. Every new book destroys some further illusion." Later that year, he visited the French occupation zone in the Ruhr Valley: "One would like to send every sentimental spellbinder of war days into the Ruhr. This, then, is the glorious issue

Soldiers engage in bayonet practice at a U.S. war training camp, circa 1918. Visiting camps like this one made Reinhold Niebuhr question how a good Christian could support World War I. © CORBIS. REPRODUCED BY PERMISSION.

for which the war was fought! I didn't know Europe in 1914, but I can't imagine that the hatred between peoples could have been worse than it is now. This is as good a time as any to make up my mind that I am done with the war business. . . . For my own part I am not going to let my decision in regard to war stand alone. I am going to try to be a disciple of Christ, rather than a mere Christian, in all human relations and experiment with the potency of trust and love much more than I have in the past."

The horrors of the war, with its ten million dead, caused many religious leaders to feel the same revulsion, which led to a renewed interest in pacifism. The Fellowship of Reconciliation and the Fellowship for a Christian Social Order were founded to promote peace. Over twenty thousand clergy petitioned President Warren Harding (served 1921–1923) to call a conference on international disarmament. Eventually held in Washington on November 12, 1921, the conference resulted in limitations being placed on the number and size of warships in the world's navies.

## Primary Source

*Leaves From the Notebook of a Tamed Cynic*
[excerpt]

**SYNOPSIS:** As both a liberal and a German American, Niebuhr was uncomfortable with the churches'

strong support for the war with Germany. He expressed this discomfort in his diary, later published under the title *Leaves From the Notebook of a Tamed Cynic*.

## 1918

**(After a trip through the war training camps.)**

I hardly know how to bring order out of confusion in my mind in regard to this war. I think that if Wilson's aims are realized the war will serve a good purpose. When I talk to the boys I make much of the Wilsonian program as against the kind of diplomacy which brought on the war. But it is easier to talk about the aims of the war than to justify its methods.

Out at Funston I watched a bayonet practice. It was enough to make me feel like a brazen hypocrite for being in this thing, even in a rather indirect way. Yet I cannot bring myself to associate with the pacifists. Perhaps if I were not of German blood I could. That may be cowardly, but I do think that a new nation has a right to be pretty sensitive about its unity.

Some of the good old Germans have a hard time hiding a sentiment which borders very closely on hatred for this nation. Anyone who dissociates himself from the cause of his nation in such a time as this ought to do it only on the basis of an unmistakably higher loyalty. If I dissociated myself only slightly I would inevitably be forced into the camp of those who romanticize about the Kaiser. And the Kaiser is certainly nothing to me. If we must have war I'll certainly feel better on the side of Wilson than on the side of the Kaiser.

What makes me angry is the way I kowtow to the chaplains as I visit the various camps. Here are ministers of the gospel just as I am. Just as I they are also, for the moment, priests of the great god Mars. As ministers of the Christian religion I have no particular respect for them. Yet I am overcome by a terrible inferiority complex when I deal with them. Such is the power of a uniform. Like myself, they have mixed the worship of the God of love and the God of battles. But unlike myself, they have adequate symbols of this double devotion. The little cross on the shoulder is the symbol of their Christian faith. The uniform itself is the symbol of their devotion to the God of battles. It is the uniform and not the cross which impresses me and others. I am impressed even when I know that I ought not be.

What I dislike about most of the chaplains is that they assume a very officious and also a very masculine attitude. Ministers are not used to authority and revel in it when acquired. The rather too obvious masculinity which they try to suggest by word and action is meant to remove any possible taint which their Christian faith might be suspected to

have left upon them in the minds of the he-men in the army. H—— is right. He tells me that he wants to go into the army as a private and not as a chaplain. He believes that the war is inevitable but he is not inclined to reconcile its necessities with the Christian ethic. He will merely forget about this difficulty during the war. That is much more honest than what I am doing.

## Further Resources
### BOOKS

Brown, Charles C. *Niebuhr and His Age: Reinhold Niebuhr's Prophetic Role and Legacy.* Harrisburg, Penn.: Trinity Press International, 2002.

Clark, Henry B. *Serenity, Courage, and Wisdom: The Enduring Legacy of Reinhold Niebuhr.* Cleveland, Ohio: Pilgrim, 1994.

Dibble, Ernest F. *Young Prophet Niebuhr: Reinhold Niebuhr's Early Search for Social Justice.* Washington, D.C.: University Press of America, 1977.

Gaustad, Edwin Scott. *A Religious History of America.* Rev. ed. San Francisco: Harper and Row, 1990.

Harries, Richard, ed. *Reinhold Niebuhr and the Issues of Our Time.* London: Mowbray, 1986.

Kegley, Charles W. *Reinhold Niebuhr: His Religious, Social, and Political Thought.* New York: Pilgrim, 1984.

Landon, Harold R., ed. *Reinhold Niebuhr, a Prophetic Voice in Our Time: Essays in Tribute, by Paul Tillich, John C. Bennett and Hans J. Morgenthau.* Plainview, N.Y.: Books for Libraries, 1974.

Scott, Nathan Jr. *The Legacy of Reinhold Niebuhr.* Chicago: University of Chicago Press, 1975.

# 11

# SCIENCE AND TECHNOLOGY

*Entries are arranged in chronological order by date of primary source. For entries with one primary source, the entry title is the same as the primary source title. Entries with more than one primary source have an overall entry title, followed by the titles of the primary sources.*

**CHRONOLOGY**

Important Events in Science and Technology,
　　1910–1919 . . . . . . . . . . . . . . . . . . . . . . . . . . . 510

**PRIMARY SOURCES**

*The Future of Electricity*
　　Charles Proteus Steinmetz, 1910 . . . . . . . . . . . . 513

*The Mind of Primitive Man*
　　Franz Boas, 1911 . . . . . . . . . . . . . . . . . . . . . . . 516

"Manufacture of Gasolene"
　　William Burton, January 7, 1913 . . . . . . . . . . . 520

"On the Constitution of Atoms and
　　Molecules"
　　Niels Bohr, 1913 . . . . . . . . . . . . . . . . . . . . . . . 525

"Psychology as the Behaviorist Views It"
　　John B. Watson, 1913 . . . . . . . . . . . . . . . . . . . 527

"A Direct Photoelectric Determination of
　　Planck's '$h$'"
　　Robert A. Millikan, March 1916 . . . . . . . . . . . 530

*Psychology of the Unconscious*
　　Carl Jung, 1916 . . . . . . . . . . . . . . . . . . . . . . . . 534

"The Atom and the Molecule"
　　Gilbert N. Lewis, 1916 . . . . . . . . . . . . . . . . . . 537

"Globular Clusters and the Structure of the
　　Galactic System"
　　Harlow Shapley, February 1918 . . . . . . . . . . . 541

*Report on the Relativity Theory of Gravitation*
　　Arthur Eddington, 1918 . . . . . . . . . . . . . . . . . . 546

*The Physical Basis of Heredity*
　　Thomas Hunt Morgan, 1919 . . . . . . . . . . . . . . 550

*A General Introduction to Psycho-Analysis*
　　Sigmund Freud, 1920 . . . . . . . . . . . . . . . . . . . 553

# Important Events in Science and Technology, 1910–1919

## 1910

- The availability of electricity in American homes spurs the purchase of electric washing machines.

- American electrical engineer and mathematician Charles Steinmetz publishes *Future of Electricity*, warning that industry and technology can create air and water pollution. In addition, Steinmetz sees the potential of electricity to revolutionize the home, work, and transportation.

- On May 13, Halley's comet makes its closest approach to Earth. The comet completes its elliptical orbit every seventy-six years, next visiting Earth in 1986.

- In June, Major Frank Woodbury of the U.S. Army introduces tincture of iodine as a disinfectant for wounds.

- In December, the number of telephones in the United States exceeds seven million.

## 1911

- In February, physicists from around the world meet at the first Solvay Physics Conference—named for the Belgian industrial chemist and philanthropist who founded the Solvay Institutes in Brussels. They discuss the atom's structure and adopt Ernest Rutherford's solar-system model.

- In February, Columbia University embryologist Thomas Hunt Morgan publishes a paper with the first plot of a gene on a chromosome. The gene and chromosome are of *Drosophila*, the common fruit fly, which Morgan had begun breeding in 1909 to study the transmission of genes from generation to generation.

- In March, U.S. scientists begin to study superconductivity after Dutch scientist H. Kamerlingh Onnes discovers that some metals, when cooled to low temperatures, allow electrons to flow through them without resistance.

- In March, Columbia University anthropologist Franz Boas publishes *The Mind of Primitive Man,* in which he argues that human beliefs, norms, and ethics vary from culture to culture. This is called "cultural relativism."

- In March, A. A. Campbell Swinton conceives of a television as a large cathode-ray tube. The tube would emit a stream of electrons and deflect them to cover the entire wall opposite the point of emission; this wall would be the television screen.

- In May, engineers complete the Roosevelt Dam on the Salt River. Its reservoir supplies a quarter-million acres of land surrounding Phoenix, Arizona, with fresh water.

- In June, the world's first escalators open at London's Earl's Court subway station.

- In June, British physicist Ernest Rutherford announces that the atom has a positively charged nucleus surrounded by negatively charged electrons. During the 1920s, physicists will determine that electrons do not orbit the nucleus; rather, they occupy regions of the atom and move such that one cannot predict their location at any instant.

- In July, Charles Franklin Kettering invents an electric starter for automobiles. The electric starter allows a driver to start a car with a switch or key instead of turning a crank in front of the car.

- In August, the Bell Telephone Company creates a research and development division. During the decade, universities and other corporations found laboratories where scientists and engineers aim to develop practical technologies.

- On December 14, Norwegian explorer Roald Amundsen becomes the first person to reach the South Pole. A month later, the British explorer Robert Scott and his party also reach the South Pole, but they perish on the return journey.

## 1912

- Dr. Sidney Russell invents the electric heating pad.

- The Morse code SOS (. . . - - - . . .) is adopted internationally as the universal signal for a ship in distress.

- German scientist Alfred L. Wegener publishes *The Origins of Continents and Oceans*, which asserts that continents ride on top of "plates" that move at the rate of only a few centimeters a century. In 1962, American oceanographer Harry Hess will amass evidence to support the idea of continental drift.

- In January, American inventor Lee De Forest uses three of his triode tubes to amplify sound 120 times.

- In April, British lawyer and amateur archeologist Charles Dawson announces the discovery of a skull in Piltdown, England; he christens his find Piltdown Man. Henry Fairfield Osborn, president of the American Museum of Natural History in New York City, heralds Piltdown Man as the "missing link," the evolutionary link between apes and humans. In 1953, a French anatomist exposes Piltdown Man as a forgery.

- In April, astronomer Henrietta Swan Leavitt proposes that stars may vary in brightness. She made this discovery while studying clusters of stars in the Southern Hemisphere's Magellanic Cloud.

- On April 15, the SS *Titanic,* believed "unsinkable" because of its compartmentalized interior design, sinks on its maiden voyage after striking an iceberg and sustaining a three-hundred-foot gash.

- In July, the Corona Company begins selling portable typewriters in the U.S.

- In July, Albert Einstein publishes a paper which announces that a concentrated beam of light would have enough energy to bore through solids. This idea is the foundation of the laser.

• In December, American astronomer Vesto M. Slipher asserts that some star clusters are moving away from earth, implying that the universe is expanding.

## 1913

• American inventor Lee De Forest's amplifier boosts the quality of telephone signals, improving telephone communications between New York and Baltimore.

• John B. Watson publishes *Behaviorism*, which defines psychology as the study of behavior. He rejects the study of interior mental states as part of psychology because scientists can have no evidence of such states.

• Stainless steel, which has a high tensile strength and is resistant to abrasion and corrosion, is developed in England by adding a chromium to steel, an alloy of iron and carbon.

• In January, William Burton invents a new process for refining oil, "thermal cracking," that uses high temperature and pressure to convert petroleum to gasoline by "cracking" large molecules into the smaller molecules of gasoline, without the aid of catalysts.

• In January, American astronomer Henry N. Russell publishes his theory of stellar evolution, which announces that stars, like organisms, are born, mature, and die.

• In February, Edouard Belin introduces the "Belino," or portable facsimile machine.

• In March, American inventor Elmer Ambrose Sperry receives a patent for his gyroscope.

• In March, British scientist Henry Gwyn-Jeffreys discovers that the number of electrons in an element is the same as its atomic number. That is, the number of protons (positively charged particles) equals the number of electrons (negatively-charged particles). Because positive and negative charges balance, an atom is electrically neutral.

• In April, Hungarian American Béla Schick develops the "Schick test" for diagnosing diphtheria.

• In May, engineers complete the Los Angeles aqueduct, which carries fresh water 215 miles from the Owens Valley high in the Sierra Nevada to Los Angeles.

• In May, Alfred H. Sturtevant, a graduate student working with Thomas Hunt Morgan at Columbia University in New York City, publishes the first chromosome map of an organism, in this case of *Drosophila,* the common fruit fly.

• In June, Russian-American aeronautical engineer Igor Sikorsky builds and flies the first plane with more than one engine.

• In June, American inventor Irving Langmuir lengthens the lightbulb's lifespan by introducing tungsten filaments and inert gas.

• In June, French physicist Charles Fabry discovers the ozone layer in Earth's stratosphere. The ozone layer shields humans from most of the ultraviolet light the sun emits.

• In July, engineers complete the 792-foot-tall Woolworth Building in New York City, then the world's tallest building.

## 1914

• The first transcontinental telephone line is completed.

• A near-perfect vacuum is created by American scientist Irving Langmuir's mercury-vapor pump.

• The red-green traffic light is introduced in Cleveland, Ohio.

• In February, Harvard University astronomer Harlow Shapley establishes an inverse relationship between luminosity and distance in Cepheid variable stars, a class of stars that regularly brighten and dim. That is, the nearer a star, the brighter it appears. The farther a star, the dimmer it appears.

• In February, the Boston Wire Stitcher Company introduces the modern stapler.

• On May 8, Congress passes the Smith-Lever Act, establishing an extension service at each land-grant college. Through the extension service, scientists would teach farmers how to apply scientific knowledge to improve the growth of crops and livestock.

• From May to July, Tony Jannus pilots his plane in Florida on scheduled flights between Saint Petersburg and Tampa, establishing the first passenger airline.

• In June, Edwin H. Armstrong, while a student at Columbia University in New York City, patents a receiver with regeneration (positive feedback) that improves radio reception.

• On August 14, the fifty-one-mile Panama Canal opens to ships, saving them from the need to travel around the southern tip of South America.

• In September, Robert Goddard begins work on the design of a liquid-fuel rocket.

• In December, Elmer V. McCollum, a scientist at the Wisconsin Agricultural Experiment Station, discovers the first vitamin, which he names vitamin A.

## 1915

• Detroit, Michigan, blacksmith August Fruehauf invents the tractor-trailer, a truck with its cab and engine separate from the main cargo body.

• In January, German aviators and engineers build the first all-metal airplane for use in World War I.

• On January 25, American inventor Alexander Graham Bell makes the first transcontinental telephone call, from New York to San Francisco, to his assistant Thomas A. Watson.

• In February, American electrical engineer Manson Benedicks uses a germanium crystal to convert alternating current into direct current. Alternating current travels a greater distance than direct current per volt of electricity.

• In May, French scientist Paul Langevin invents sonar to detect icebergs and other objects submerged in water.

• In June, chemists at the Corning Glass Works in New York create Pyrex, a glass with 80 percent silicon oxide and 12 percent boron oxide. The new glass is soon used in kitchens and laboratories.

• In July, Albert Einstein publishes his General Theory of Relativity, which establishes that the more massive an object the greater it curves or distorts space. What British polymath Isaac Newton called gravity Einstein calls the curvature of space.

• In October, the British develop the first tank, a vehicle that could surge through barbed wire, as infantry could not, on the western front during World War I.

- On October 21, the first transatlantic radiotelephone conversation is held between the Eiffel Tower in Paris and Arlington, Virginia.

## 1916

- The Dodge Motor Company builds the first all-steel automobile body.

- Ford manufactures the first cars with windshield wipers.

- In March, American physicist and 1923 Nobel laureate Robert Andrews Millikan uses Albert Einstein's photoelectric effect to confirm Planck's constant, a theory, posited by German physicist Max Planck, that states that energy is not a continuum but instead comes in small packages.

- In July, Gilbert Newton Lewis, professor of physical chemistry at the University of California, discovers that some elements bond by equally sharing a pair of electrons. Chemists call this bond a covalent bond.

- In October, German astronomer Karl Schwarzschild, working from Albert Einstein's theory of relativity, posits the existence of "black holes," intense gravitational fields from which nothing, not even light, can escape.

## 1917

- American inventor Clarence Birdseye develops a technique for preserving foods, the beginning of the frozen food industry.

- The first commercial use is made of the plastic Bakelite. It is soon used to make handles for frying pans and in other home and industry applications.

- In February, American astronomer Herbert D. Curtis calculates the distance from Earth to the Andromeda galaxy.

- In October, Dutch astronomer Willem de Sitter announces that Albert Einstein's General Theory of Relativity implies that the universe is expanding. The General Theory of Relativity asserts that space is curved, but a curved universe ought to collapse upon itself; because it does not, it must be expanding.

- On November 1, American astronomer George Ellery Hale uses the Hooker Telescope, a reflecting telescope with a one-hundred-inch mirror installed at Mount Wilson Observatory in Pasadena, California, for the first time.

## 1918

- Electric mixers for the kitchen are marketed.

- The nation's first three-color traffic light (red, amber, green) is installed in New York City.

- The first diamond-edged drills for oil exploration go into production.

- In March, Alexander Graham Bell develops a sixty-foot-long high-speed hydrofoil, the HD-4, that can achieve seventy miles per hour.

- In May, Harlow Shapley plots the shape and dimensions of our galaxy, the Milky Way.

- In June, American geneticist Herbert Evans claims that each human cell contains forty-eight chromosomes. The correct number is forty-six.

- In June, American inventor Edwin H. Armstrong develops a superheterodyne circuit, which lowers the frequency of electromagnetic waves and amplifies them. This invention makes amplitude modulation (AM) reception as easy as turning a dial.

## 1919

- Shortwave radio is invented, and amateur radio "hams" begin to take to the airwaves.

- Lockheed produces the hydraulic braking system for cars.

- Thomas Hunt Morgan publishes *The Physical Basis of Heredity,* which summarizes Morgan's work with *Drosophila,* the common fruit fly: namely, that adults pass chromosomes to offspring.

- In February, Clark University physicist Robert Goddard announces the possibility that a rocket might one day reach the moon. The National Aeronautics and Space Administration (NASA) will land the first men on the moon in 1969.

- In March, Charles F. Jenkins of Dayton, Ohio, patents a system for transmitting television pictures.

- On May 29, astronomers confirm Albert Einstein's General Theory of Relativity by observing the bending of a star's light as it passes the sun during a total eclipse.

- In June, the Radio Corporation of America (RCA) is founded.

- In July, British physicist Ernest Rutherford confirms the existence of the proton, a positively-charged particle in the nucleus of an atom.

- On December 6, American Theodore W. Richards delivers his Nobel Lecture. He had won the 1914 Nobel Prize in chemistry for determining the atomic weights of elements, but only in 1919 did he receive the award.

## The Future of Electricity

Lecture

**By:** Charles Proteus Steinmetz

**Date:** 1910

**Source:** Steinmetz, Charles. *The Future of Electricity.* New York: Electrical Trade School, 1910.

**About the Author:** Charles Proteus Steinmetz (1865–1923) was born in Prussia. Like his father, he was very short in stature, about four feet three inches. He attended the University of Breslau but left just before he would have been granted his degree with honors. Fearful of being persecuted for socialist activities, he emigrated to America, where he prospered as an electrical engineer at General Electric Co. and a professor at Union College in Schenectady, New York. ∎

## Introduction

In 1910, when Charles Steinmetz spoke to students at the New York Electrical Trade School, the electric industry was still relatively young. Most electric power generated in America was used for lighting and for electric streetcars. Later in the decade, however, new electric appliances, such as the vacuum cleaner, the toaster, and the iron, would create a huge demand for electric power and catalyze the buildup of the electric distribution system across the nation. Large electric generating power plants were being built by companies such as the Edison Electric Illuminating Company and the Westinghouse Electric Company. Power plants burned vast amounts of coal to boil water and produce steam, which was then used to spin an electric generating turbine.

Steinmetz was a prominent, popular, and brilliant electrical engineer at General Electric. He was instrumental in the development of the electric transmission network, "the grid," in America. He developed several theories about magnetism and alternating current (AC), which were used to build the grid.

Steinmetz' lecture at the New York Electrical Trade School is a mark of his visionary brilliance. He predicted several events, many of which came to pass: that the United States would begin to consume enormous amounts of coal, that a coal shortage would come about, that the soils of the earth would be unable to support crops

without fertilizer, that electricity would become as cheap as a few cents per kilowatt hour, and that the use of coal and other fuels would contribute to pollution.

## Significance

The Steinmetz lecture is significant because many of Steinmetz' predictions have come true. His predictions about the impact of electricity use are especially insightful. More than 50 percent of all the electricity generated in the United States today is produced at coal-fired power plants. These plants have changed little since Steinmetz' day. Coal is still burned to heat water and produce steam, causing a turbine to spin. The turbine is attached to a magnet, and the magnet spins around copper wires and thereby generates electricity. When coal is burned, carbon dioxide and smaller amounts of sulfur dioxide, nitrogen oxides, and mercury are emitted. In 1970, though, the federal government enacted the Clean Air Act. As a result of this law and several others since then, coal-fired power plants are required to control and reduce their emissions of several pollutants. The percentage of electricity generated by burning coal, though still large, has decreased since Steinmetz' time.

## Primary Source

*The Future of Electricity* [excerpt]

**SYNOPSIS:** In these excerpts from his lecture at the New York Electrical Trade School, Steinmetz warns about several environmental impacts from the production of electricity.

The subject of the lecture is the prospective future development of electrical engineering.

On a subject like this it obviously is not possible to make any very definite statements. We do not know what the future will bring. A single year's development may reverse the trend of progress and turn it into an entirely different direction. All we can do is to see what is going on at the present time, and study the development of electrical engineering, to understand in which direction it trends at present, and estimate whereto it will lead when progressing in the way it progresses at present.

We can, however, see a number of problems before our nation and the world at large—problems which have no immediate connection with electricity, but which the electrical engineer will have to take up and solve. I also desire to speak on the personal relations of all of us here assembled, and its change with the advance and progress in electrical engineering. . . .

New York Edison Company power plant. East River, New York City. **THE LIBRARY OF CONGRESS.**

We use coal whenever we produce electric power by steam engine, but there will be a time when we will not have any more coal to use, and that is in the not very far future. The anthracite coal will not last very long. Very many of us will probably see the last hard coal. Then the only coal will be soft coal. The next generations will see the time when even the soft coal will be exhausted. Possibly we may not, because there is very much more soft coal than hard coal, and it is more widely distributed. But we have already approached the end of wood as a fuel. The forests are destroyed, wasted. Wood does not come into consideration any more, except very locally, as fuel. Oil is too insignificant in its available supply to come into much consideration. Also, when coal has gone, what are you going to do then in the winter time to keep from freezing? It is a rather serious problem which the next generations will have to meet.

By that time the United States will have awakened to the viciousness of poisoning the air by burning soft coal. Whenever you go into one of those regions, as around Pittsburgh, where soft coal is used, look around where you can see pine trees. The pine is the best indicator of the effect of the poisoning of the air by soft coal smoke. When you find that the pine trees are dying it is time to call a halt. These evergreen trees share with us the feature that they have only one set of lungs. The tree which gets new leaves every year gets a new set of lungs, and so can stand poisoning much better than the evergreen tree, as the pine, which has to get along with the same set of lungs throughout all its life, and so soon is killed, suffocated by smoke and coal gas. If you go where soft coal is being used very much you see no pine trees. Probably even before the soft coal is used up we will have awakened to the viciousness of poisoning nature and ourselves with smoke and coal gas.

When we reach the end of our resources in coal, in the not very far distant future, then the only remaining source of power, the only thing which will keep us from freezing will be the water power, which we will have to utilize electrically. At the present time, with all our so-called development of water power, the available supply is hardly touched. In a single New England state water power is running to waste many times greater than the power of Niagara. The water power that we use now is power that is collected in the waterfall, and as electric current it is sent out, but we have not yet started to collect the power. Now let us look at any of these water powers, like our Hudson, for instance. The Hudson River water power is being developed. In this state we now have some of these big falls where there is a considerable amount of power available used for lighting and for supplying railroads in towns and cities. There is now an unbroken line of electric transmissions from beyond Cleveland in Ohio and Toronto in Canada, far beyond Niagara Falls down to near Poughkeepsie. These are all joined together in circuits. So the railroads in Syracuse are run from Niagara Falls, but if the transmission line of Niagara Falls fails, breaks down, we have available and can receive the power from the Hudson River.

We are gradually extending the use of water power, but what we have done so far is very little. Consider the case of the Hudson River. We probably use up altogether from its falls something like 150 feet head. We do not make an attempt to get the enormous power which runs to waste through the spring floods, or in all the creeks and the rivers that feed into the big stream. Practically all that water comes down from elevations of two to three thousand feet above the ocean level. And of that power, practically all is wasted in all the little creeks and rivers which go to make up the big stream, all except 150 feet head. We cannot use that power at present, but methods will have to be developed, new ways of collecting the joined powers of all these little streams, creeks and rivers so as to gather the power together. We will have to do all this when we are at the end of our resources, when the escape from freezing and starvation depends upon our getting the power.

There is an enormous field for the electrical engineer, and without him there would be hard times coming for future generations, much harder than we dream of now. We will then have to develop all that power that is now being wasted. We can see in which direction it can be done, only at present it would not be worth while doing it, because we can still use our capital in coal, but we will not always be able to use that. When that time comes we will have to economize; we will not be able to go haphazardly; we may even have to collect the rays of the sun, whenever it shines, to get that heat, because it takes a lot of electric power to produce very little heat.

There is still an enormous, far vaster problem, confronting the nations of the earth, which at the present time only electricity seems to be able to solve. In bygone ages all civilization started in the Far East, in the big river valleys of Asia, in countries which are deserts now. These large, dense populations earned their living by tilling the soil. That soil does not bring any crops now. It is exhausted, has been exhausted a long time ago. You cannot get any crops there without putting back in the soil in some way whatever you take out in crops. There is no capital any more in the soil there. And it is the same all over Europe. In America we have been more fortunate. We have had an enormous capital in the soil here. First, in the eastern states. Well, New England is a farming country no more. It was once, but the farms are exhausted. There is still the west, with its vast resources, but it is only a question of time when all those farms of the west will reach the same end as the farms of New England, as the farms of Europe and of the Euphrates valley, and when that time comes we will not be able to do as we have done in former ages—go west. No, for as we get farther west we meet the Pacific Ocean, beyond which are the countless millions of China, whose lands have all reached that stage long ago. So the last capital is just being used up now, but when that is gone whatever we take out as crops will have to be put back in the soil as fertilizer. For ages there were accumulating stores of fertilizer on earth. There was guano, bird manure. We have long ago used this up. It is not now available as fertilizer, because it is gone. There is saltpetre. Saltpetre in Chili is still available, but the supply will be exhausted in less than ten years. It is already so far exhausted that the price is beyond reach for general use. There is nothing further in view. The capital is gone in that direction. We have to produce fertilizer now.

All what we take out of the soil as crops we now dump in the rivers to pollute the streams. But soon it will not be a mere sanitary question any more of polluting the rivers. We are sending millions and millions worth of fertilizer down to the sea lost forever, but in the future we will have to use that waste to keep from starvation, and all that refuse, all the waste of the cities and towns and farms must go back to the farm, to the soil from which it was taken. But all that which we now waste, when collected and returned to the farms will not replace what you take out, because there is a very large unavoidable loss in the spontaneous self-destruction of nitrogen compounds, and electric power apparently is the only

Charles Proteus Steinmetz, electrical engineer who was also a prolific researcher and inventor. THE LIBRARY OF CONGRESS.

efficient means which at present seems to be able to combine these elements of the air, nitrogen and oxygen, which are necessary as a fertilizer, and which cannot completely be recovered.

At present we do not use electric power for this purpose, to any extent, because we still have our capital of virgin soil, and the cost of electric power is too high, but every year we can see the necessity increasing of producing by electric power a method of restoring the capital to our farms. That problem is a very urgent one, and will have to be met within our lifetime.

But now that we have so many uses for electric power, and the only available supply is from water power, what we will need is a method of completely and successfully collecting all the power which there is in the water courses of this country. When that is done there will be no more rapid creeks and rivers, and these streams which furnish electric power will be slow-moving pools, connected with one another by power stations, and the creeks will be empty, because their water power will be needed to maintain our life. There will then be no more question of saving the beauty of nature when it becomes a question of saving our lives, and that takes precedence

over the beauty of nature. We will need electric power then for heating, cooking, keeping ourselves warm, and for restoring the fertility of our farms. You see that power will have to be saved, and we will no more be able to waste it as now.

These are the problems which we electrical men will have to meet in the future, as well as in a short time, and we all will have to cooperate so as to organize all those forces which can be used for developing power. We must use electricity economically, find out how we can spread the use over the twenty-four hours of the day and all the days of the year, so as to get the highest possible load factor, the most efficient use from our available power. Likewise, we must furnish power at the lowest cost. In other words, we must get the greatest benefit out of electricity that we can.

## Further Resources

**BOOKS**

Grey, Jerry. *The Race for Electric Power.* Philadelphia: Westminster Press, 1972.

Leonard, Jonathan Norton. *Loki, the Life of Charles Proteus Steinmetz.* Garden City, N.Y.: Doubleday, Doran, 1929.

**PERIODICALS**

Corcoran, Elizabeth. "Cleaning Up Coal." *Scientific American,* May 1991, 106–116.

Platt, Harold, L. "Technology and Transformation in the American Electric Utility Industry." *Journal of American History* 77, no. 4, March 1991, 1412.

**WEBSITES**

"Electricity–Electronics." Available online at http://inventors .about.com/library/inventors/blelectric.htm; website home page: http://inventors.about.com (accessed May 15, 2003).

Union of Concerned Scientists. "Coal generates 54% of our electricity, and is the single biggest air polluter in the U.S." Available online at http://www.ucsusa.org/CoalvsWind/c01 .html; website home page: http://www.ucsusa.org (accessed February 16, 2003).

# *The Mind of Primitive Man*

Nonfiction work

**By:** Franz Boas

**Date:** 1911

**Source:** Boas, Franz. *The Mind of Primitive Man.* Rev. ed. New York: Macmillan, 1938, 3–6, 15–18.

**About the Author:** Franz Boas (1858–1942) was born in Minden, Germany, but moved to the United States at age twenty-eight. His first job in New York was as editor of the prestigious journal *Science.* He later went on to serve as president of the American Association for the Advancement of Science, the governing body that still publishes the journal today. He filled several teaching posts before settling at Columbia University. He established the *International Journal of American Linguistics* and was one of the founders of the American Anthropological Association. ■

## Introduction

In *The Mind of Primitive Man,* Boas examines in detail what was meant by the terms race and culture in the early twentieth century. Culture includes language, art, religion, morals, laws, ceremonies, and any other capability or habit acquired by man as a member of society. The concept of culture is primarily seen as unique to human beings and sets us apart from all other animals.

In the nineteenth and early twentieth centuries, anthropology was largely ethnocentric. Most anthropologists were white Europeans or North Americans and tended to evaluate other cultures in relation to their own. Other cultures, such as those of the Chinese, Africans, Native Americans, and New Zealanders, were considered primitive merely because they were different in their physical attributes and their ways of thinking.

In *The Mind of Primitive Man,* Boas attempted to prove that there is no fundamental difference in the ways of thinking between so-called primitive people and civilized people, that there is not a close connection between race and culture, that the concept of race is misleading, and that cultures could not be evaluated or graded as higher and lower, superior or inferior. He presents the results of several scientific studies showing that anatomical features exhibit significant variability within one ethnic group and overlap between different ethnic groups. Boas contended that the biological development of humans is influenced by too many uncontrollable conditions to predict a biological form based on heredity. He believed in the plasticity of both human races and human cultures.

## Significance

*The Mind of Primitive Man* is a classic. It represents the legacy of a man who did more than any other to fight the scientific racism prevalent in the early twentieth century. Scientific racism was the practice of using scientific data to claim the superiority of one race over another. For example, in Boas' time, the general view was that white Europeans had larger brains and therefore were more intelligent and the superior race. In *The Mind of Primitive Man,* Boas exposed the difficulty in defining race and the impracticality in trying to link race and culture.

Boas' last paragraph in *The Mind of Primitive Man* is still relevant today: "Freedom of judgment can be attained only when we learn to estimate an individual ac-

Franz Boas, noted ethnologist, who pioneered the use of a scientific approach to anthropology. © BETTMANN/CORBIS. REPRODUCED BY PERMISSION.

cording to his own ability and character. Then we shall find, if we were to select the best of mankind, that all races and nationalities would be represented."

## Primary Source

*The Mind of Primitive Man* [excerpt]

**SYNOPSIS:** In these excerpts from the introduction, Boas describes the issue—that white Europeans see themselves as superior and more civilized than other so-called primitive races. Then he sets forth the reasons why this perception is ungrounded. Finally, he presents the fundamental question that his book focuses on, that is, "whether the cultural character of a race is determined by its physical characteristics."

A survey of our globe shows the continents inhabited by a great diversity of peoples different in appearance, different in language and in cultural life. The Europeans and their descendants on other continents are united by similarity of bodily build, and their civilization sets them off sharply against all the people of different appearance. The Chinese, the native New Zealander, the African Negro, the American

Indian present not only distinctive bodily features, but each possesses also his own peculiar mode of life. Each human type seems to have its own inventions, its own customs and beliefs, and it is very generally assumed that race and culture must be intimately associated, that racial descent determines cultural life.

Owing to this impression the term "primitive" has a double meaning. It applies to both bodily form and culture. We are accustomed to speak both of primitive races and primitive cultures as though the two were necessarily related. We believe not only in a close association between race and culture; we are also ready to claim superiority of our own race over all others. The sources of this attitude spring from our every-day experiences. Bodily form has an aesthetic value. The dark color, the flat and wide nose, the thick lips and prominent mouth of the Negro; the slanting eye and prominent cheekbones of the East Asiatic do not conform to those ideals of human beauty to which we of West European traditions are accustomed. The racial isolation of Europe and the social segregation of races in America have favored the rise of the so-called "instinctive" aversion to foreign types, founded to a great extent on the feeling of a fundamental distinctiveness of form of our own race. It is the same feeling that creates an "instinctive" aversion to abnormal or ugly types in our own midst, or to habits that do not conform to our sense of propriety. Furthermore such strange types as are members of our society occupy, very generally, inferior positions and do not mingle to any great extent with members of our own race. In their native land their cultural life is not as rich in intellectual achievement as our own. Hence the inference that strangeness of type and low intelligence go hand in hand. In this way our attitude becomes intelligible, but we also recognize that it is not based on scientific insight but on simple emotional reactions and social conditions. Our aversions and judgments are not, by any means, primarily rational in character.

Nevertheless, we like to support our emotional attitude toward the so-called inferior races by reasoning. The superiority of our inventions, the extent of our scientific knowledge, the complexity of our social institutions, our attempts to promote the welfare of all members of the social body, create the impression that we, the civilized people, have advanced far beyond the stages on which other groups linger, and the assumption has arisen of an innate superiority of the European nations and of their descendants. The basis of our reasoning is obvious: the higher a civilization, the higher must be the ap-

titude for civilization; and as aptitude presumably depends upon the perfection of the mechanism of body and mind, we infer that the White race represents the highest type. The tacit assumption is made that achievement depends solely, or at least primarily, upon innate racial ability. Since the intellectual development of the White race is the highest, it is assumed that its intellectuality is supreme and that its mind has the most subtle organization.

The conviction that European nations possess the highest aptitude supports our impressions regarding the significance of differences in type between the European race and those of other continents, or even of differences between various European types. Unwittingly we pursue a line of thought like this: since the aptitude of the European is the highest, his physical and mental type is also highest, and every deviation from the White type necessarily represents a lower feature.

This unproved assumption underlies our judgments of races, for other conditions being equal, a race is commonly described as the lower, the more fundamentally it differs from our own. We interpret as proof of a lower mentality anatomical peculiarities found in primitive man which resemble traits occurring in lower forms of the zoological series; and we are troubled by the observation that some of the "lower" traits do not occur in primitive man, but are rather found in the European race.

The subject and form of all such discussions show that the idea is rooted in the minds of investigators that we should expect to find in the White race the highest type of man.

Social conditions are often treated from the same point of view. We value our individual freedom, our code of ethics, our free art so highly that they seem to mark an advancement to which no other race can lay claim.

The judgment of the mental status of a people is generally guided by the difference between its social status and our own, and the greater the difference between their intellectual, emotional and moral processes and those which are found in our civilization, the harsher our judgment. It is only when a Tacitus deploring the degeneration of his time finds the virtues of his ancestors among foreign tribes that their example is held up to the gaze of his fellow-citizens; but the people of imperial Rome probably had only a pitying smile for the dreamer who clung to the antiquated ideals of the past.

In order to understand clearly the relations between race and civilization, the two unproved assumptions to which I have referred must be subjected to a searching analysis. We must investigate how far we are justified in assuming achievement to be primarily due to exceptional aptitude, and how far we are justified in assuming the European type—or, taking the notion in its extreme form, the Northwest European type—to represent the highest development of mankind. It will be advantageous to consider these popular beliefs before making the attempt to clear up the relations between culture and race and to describe the form and growth of culture. . . .

Several races have developed a civilization of a type similar to the one from which our own has sprung, and a number of favorable conditions have facilitated its rapid spread in Europe. Among these, similar physical appearance, contiguity of habitat and moderate difference in modes of manufacture were the most potent. When, later on, Europeans began to spread over other continents, the races with which they came into contact were not equally favorably situated. Striking differences of racial types, the preceding isolation which caused devastating epidemics in the newly discovered countries, and the greater advance in technical processes made assimilation much more difficult. The rapid dissemination of Europeans over the whole world destroyed all promising beginnings which had arisen in various regions. Thus no race except that of eastern Asia was given a chance to develop independently. The spread of the European race cut short the growth of the existing germs without regard to the mental aptitude of the people among whom it was developing.

On the other hand, we have seen that no great weight can be attributed to the earlier rise of civilization in the Old World, which is satisfactorily explained as due to chance. In short, historical events appear to have been much more potent in leading races to civilization than their innate faculty, and it follows that achievements of races do not without further proof warrant the assumption that one race is more highly gifted than another.

After having thus found an answer to our first problem, we turn to the second one: In how far are we justified in considering those anatomical traits in regard to which foreign races differ from the White race as marks of inferiority? In one respect the answer to this question is easier than that to the former. We have recognized that achievement alone is no satisfactory proof of an unusual mental ability of the White race. It follows from this, that anatomical differences between the White race and others can be interpreted as meaning superiority of the for-

mer, inferiority of the latter, only if a relation between anatomical form and mentality can be proved to exist.

Too many investigation relating to mental characteristics of races are based on the logical fallacy of first assuming that the European represents the highest racial type and then interpreting every deviation from the European type as a sign of lower mentality. When the formation of the jaws of the Negroes is thus interpreted without proof of a biological connection between the forms of the jaw and the functioning of the nervous system an error is committed that might be paralleled by a Chinaman who would describe Europeans as hairy monsters whose hirsute body is a proof of a lower status. This is emotional, not scientific reasoning.

The question that must be answered is: In how far do anatomical traits determine mental activities? By analogy we associate lower mental traits with theriomorphic, brutelike features. In our naive, everyday parlance, brutish features and brutality are closely connected. We must distinguish here, however, between the anatomical characteristics of which we have been speaking and the muscular development of the face, trunk and limbs due to habits of life. The hand, which is never employed in activities requiring those refined adjustments which are characteristic of psychologically complex actions, will lack the modeling brought about by the development of each muscle. The face, the muscles of which have not responded to the innervations accompanying deep thought and refined sentiment will lack in individuality and expressiveness. The neck that has supported heavy loads, and has not responded to the varied requirements of delicate changes of position of head and body, will appear massive and clumsy. These physiognomic differences must not mislead us in our interpretations. We are also inclined to draw inferences in regard to mentality from a receding forehead, a heavy jaw, large and heavy teeth, perhaps even from an inordinate length of arms or an unusual development of hairiness. A careful consideration of the relation of such traits to mental activities will be required, before we can assume as proven their significance.

It appears that neither cultural achievement nor outer appearance is a safe basis on which to judge the mental aptitude of races. Added to this is the one-sided evaluation of our own racial type and of our modern civilization without any close inquiry into the mental processes of primitive races and cultures which may easily lead to erroneous conclusions.

The object of our inquiry is therefore an attempt to clear up the racial and cultural problems involved in these questions. Our globe is inhabited by many races, and a great diversity of cultural forms exists. The term "primitive" should not be applied indiscriminately to bodily build and to culture as though both belonged together by necessity. It is rather one of the fundamental questions to be investigated whether the cultural character of a race is determined by its physical characteristics. The term race itself should be clearly understood before this question can be answered. If a close relation between race and culture should be shown to exist it would be necessary to study for each racial group separately the interaction between bodily build and mental and social life. If it should be proved not to exist, it will be permissible to treat mankind as a whole and to study cultural types regardless of race.

We shall thus have to investigate primitiveness from two angles. First of all we shall have to inquire whether certain bodily characteristics of races exist that doom them to a permanent mental and social inferiority. After we have cleared up this point we shall have to discuss the traits of the mental and social life of those people whom we call primitive from a cultural point of view, and see in how far they coincide with racial groups and describe those features that distinguish their lives from those of civilized nations.

## Further Resources

**BOOKS**

Hughes, Langston. *Langston Hughes and the Chicago Defender: Essays on Race, Politics, and Culture, 1942–62.* Christopher C. De Santis, ed. Urbana, Ill.: University of Illinois Press, 1995.

Takaki, Ronald. *Iron Cages: Race and Culture in 19th-Century America.* New York: Oxford University Press, 2000.

**PERIODICALS**

Briggs, Charles, L. "Linguistic Magic Bullets in the Making of a Modernist Anthropology." *American Anthropologist* 104, no. 2, June 2002, 481–498.

Nicholas, George, P. "On Representations of Race and Racism." *Current Anthropology* 42, no. 1, February 2001, 140–142.

**WEBSITES**

"History of Race in Science." Available online at http://www.racesci.org (accessed March 12, 2003).

"The Idea of Race." The Kennewick Man Virtual Exhibit: The Burke Museum of Natural History and Culture at the University of Washington. Available online at http://www.washington.edu/burkemuseum/kman/the_idea_of_race.htm; website home page: http://www.washington.edu/burkemuseum/index_v4.html (accessed May 15, 2003).

# "Manufacture of Gasolene"

**Patent application**

**By:** William Burton

**Date:** January 7, 1913

**Source:** Burton, William. "Manufacture of Gasolene." U.S. patent 1,049,667. 1913. Available online at http://www.uspto.gov/patft/index.html (accessed March 20, 2003).

**About the Author:** William Merriam Burton (1865–1954) was born in Cleveland, Ohio. He received a B.S. from Western Reserve University in 1886 and a Ph.D. from Johns Hopkins University in 1889. Following his education Burton went to work for the Standard Oil Company. At Standard Oil he went from chemist to refinery superintendent, company director, vice president, and finally in 1918, president. He served as president of Standard Oil from 1918 until he retired in 1927. ■

## Introduction

Petroleum is one of the most important natural resources in the world. Petroleum and other fossil fuels were made millions of years ago from decaying plant material. Petroleum is a complex mixture of hydrocarbons (molecules made of carbon and hydrogen). When it comes from out of the ground it is often called crude oil. It can be red, green, yellow, brown, or black and can be as thick as paste or as thin as water.

The uses for petroleum in America have evolved over the years. One of the first uses for petroleum was as a medicinal "cure-all" in the middle of the nineteenth century. It was skimmed off the salty waters from salt mines and bottled. Later, the value of petroleum was linked to kerosene. Kerosene was used for lighting in kerosene lamps. It had become valuable because of a whale shortage brought about by heavy hunting (whale oil had been used to light lamps).

In the mid to late 1800s, American refineries were set up to separate kerosene from the rest of the petroleum. Refineries were called distilleries or just "stills." Distillation separates complex chemical mixtures into their component parts based on boiling point. Each compound in the mixture has a unique boiling point. When the mixture is heated as the temperature increases, each component will begin to vaporize (convert into a gas) as its boiling point is reached. By simply cooling and re-liquefying the vapor (condensing) and then collecting the condensate at different times, the mixture can be separated into its different components. Early stills were known as "tea kettle" stills and consisted of a large iron drum heated by a coal fire. A long iron tube acted as the condenser. Three fractions were obtained during the distillation process. The first component to boil off was the low-temperature boiling (volatile) gasoline (originally

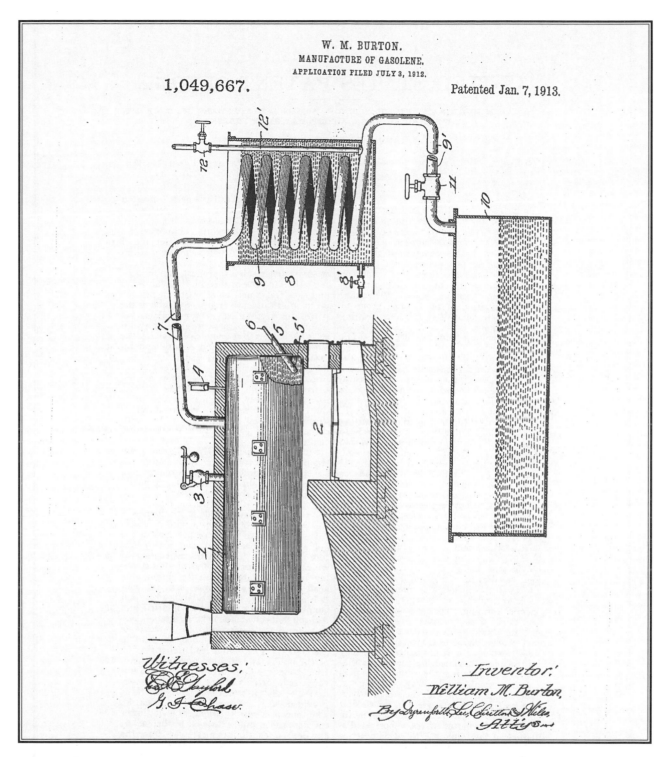

W. M. BURTON.
MANUFACTURE OF GASOLENE.
APPLICATION FILED JULY 3, 1912.

1,049,667.

Patented Jan. 7, 1913.

Witnesses:
E. B. Taylor
G. F. Chase.

Inventor:
William M. Burton,
By Dyrenforth Lee, Chritton & Wiles
Att'ys

## Primary Source

### "Manufacture of Gasolene" (1 OF 3)

**SYNOPSIS:** In his 1913 patent application, W. M. Burton describes the specifics of a new refining process, called thermal cracking, which leads to an increased yield of gasoline from petroleum. COURTESY OF THE U.S. GOVERNMENT PATENT OFFICE.

# UNITED STATES PATENT OFFICE.

WILLIAM M. BURTON, OF CHICAGO, ILLINOIS, ASSIGNOR TO STANDARD OIL COMPANY, OF WHITING, INDIANA, A CORPORATION OF INDIANA.

## MANUFACTURE OF GASOLENE.

**1,049,667.**   Specification of Letters Patent.   **Patented Jan. 7, 1913.**

Application filed July 3, 1912. Serial No. 707,424.

*To all whom it may concern:*

Be it known that I, WILLIAM M. BURTON, a citizen of the United States, residing at Chicago, in the county of Cook and State of
5   Illinois, have invented a new and useful Improvement in the Manufacture of Gasolene, of which the following is a specification.

My invention relates to an improvement in the treatment of the high boiling-point re-
10  sidual portions, and particularly the residue of the distillation of the paraffin group or series of petroleum after the lower boiling point distillates have been removed to obtain a low boiling-point product of the same
15  group or series.

The great and growing demand during the past ten years for gasolene has induced a large increase in the supply by improvements in the method of distilling from crude
20  petroleum the naphthas, the boiling points of which range from about 75° F. to 350° F. This leaves the illuminating oils, the boiling points of which range from about 350° F. to about 600° F., and the lubricating oils and
25  waxes and, as residue, fuel-oil and gas-oil, with boiling-points ranging from about 600° F. to 700° F. The increasing demand for gasolene has induced attempts to obtain it from this residue; but these attempts, while
30  successful in producing gasolene, have invariably, so far as I am aware, as the result of lowering the boiling point, changed the general formula of the paraffin group $(C_nH_{2n}+2)$ to that of the ethylene group
35  $(C_nH_{2n})$, rendering the product unmarketable because undesirable by reason of its offensive odor, for the removal of which no suitable treatment has been found.

A known method of treating the fuel and
40  gas oils, forming the aforesaid residue of distillation of the paraffin series of petroleum, for obtaining therefrom a low boiling-point product involves subjecting the liquid to be treated to a temperature sufficiently
45  high to secure so-called destructive distillation, and conducting the resultant vapors through a condenser by way of a pipe or conduit connecting it with the still, but having a loaded valve interposed in the conduit
50  between the condenser and still to maintain pressure in the latter of the vapors of distillation on the liquid. While this practice produces the desired effect of lowering the boiling point of the liquid, the condensed
55  product, for reasons which I do not attempt

to explain, is found to have been converted into distillates belonging to the objectionable ethylene group, referred to.

The object of my invention is to provide a
60  method of treating the aforesaid residue of the paraffin group of petroleum by distillation and condensation of the vapors thereof, whereby the resultant product of low boiling-points shall be of the same paraffin series
65  and thus free from the objection mentioned or, in other words, whereby conversion of the petroleum of that series into products belonging to the ethylene series shall be avoided. This object I accomplish by raising the
70  boiling point of the liquid residue and increasing the heat-influence thereon while undergoing distillation by maintaining back-pressure on said liquid of the vapors arising therefrom by distillation, as has hitherto
75  been done as aforesaid, and also maintaining the vapors themselves under pressure throughout their course from the still through the condenser and while undergoing condensation.
80  Suitable apparatus devised for the practise of my improvement is illustrated in the accompanying drawing by a broken view in vertical longitudinal section, diagrammatic in character, showing parts in elevation.
85  A boiler-like holder 1 for the liquid residue to be treated surmounts a fire-chamber 2 and is shown to be equipped with a safety-valve 3 to relieve excessive pressure in the holder; a pressure-gage 4, and a tempera-
90  ture-gage 5, the preferable construction of which is that illustrated of a tube 5¹ extending inclinedly into the holder through its head and closed at its inner end, for containing mercury, or by preference oil, and
95  adapted to have withdrawably inserted into it through its outer, open end a suitable thermometer 6 for immersion into the contents of the tube under subjection to the heat in the holder. A conduit 7 leads from the top
100  of the holder and inclines upwardly therefrom, to induce the return-flow into it of unvaporized portions of the liquid, to a condenser 8, the tank of which is shown to be provided with a lower draw-off cock 8¹.
105  The condenser-coil 9 discharges at its lower end through a pipe-extension 9¹ thereof, of any desired length, into a receiver 10 for the products of condensation. In this pipe, and thus beyond the discharge-end of the coil, is
110  contained a shut-off valve 11, and it is desir-

---

**Primary Source**

"Manufacture of Gasolene" (2 OF 3)

Second page of W. M. Burton's patent application for the manufacture of gasoline. COURTESY OF THE U.S. GOVERNMENT PATENT OFFICE.

**2**                              1,049,667

able to equip the coil with a relief-valve 12, shown on the upper end of a pipe 12¹ rising from near the lower end of the coil through the top of the condenser-tank, for relieving
5 the gas-pressure which is liable to accumulate in the coil and obstruct the action of the apparatus.

The valve 11 is normally closed. From a supply of the aforesaid liquid residue con-
10 tained in the holder 1, heat from the fire-chamber distills the volatile constituents, and the resultant vapors course through the conduit 7 and coil 9, wherein they are condensed. With the valve 11 tightly closed
15 against the escape of the products of condensation, the vapors of distillation accumulate and thereafter exert a high pressure amounting from about 4 to about 5 atmospheres upon the liquid in the holder or still,
20 raising the boiling-point from 500° F.–600° F. to 750°F.–800° F.; and this pressure of the vapors combined with their contained heat greatly enhances the conversion of the high boiling members of the paraffin series
25 into low boiling members of the same series. The valve 11 is opened from time to time to draw off the products of condensation into the receiver 10. In fact, the intervals of drawing off should be sufficiently frequent to
30 avoid filling the coil with liquid, for the most satisfactory operation of the apparatus. The resultant gasolene is a product belonging to the paraffin series, the same as the petroleum residue from which it was dis-
35 tilled. I do not herein account for the effect of the back-pressure from the extreme end of the condenser-coil upon the contents of the holder 1 in preventing transformation of

the paraffin series into the objectionable ethylene series, but it is the fact that such 40 effect ensues.

What I claim as new and desire to secure by Letters Patent is:—

1. The method of treating the liquid-portions of the paraffin-series of petroleum-dis- 45 tillation having a boiling point upward of 500° F. to obtain therefrom low-boiling-point products of the same series, which consists in distilling at a temperature of from about 650 to about 850° F. the volatile con- 50 stituents of said liquid, conducting off and condensing said constituents, and maintaining a pressure of from about 4 to about 5 atmospheres on said liquid of said vapors throughout their course to and while undergoing 55 condensation.

2. The method of treating the liquid-portions of the paraffin-series of petroleum-distillation having a boiling point of upward of 500° F. to obtain therefrom low-boiling- 60 point products of the same series, which consists in distilling off at a temperature of from about 650 to about 850° F. the volatile constituents of said liquid, conducting off and condensing said constituents, maintaining 65 a pressure of from about 4 to about 5 atmospheres on said liquid of said vapors throughout their course to and while undergoing condensation, and releasing from time to time accumulations of gas from the products 70 of condensation.

WILLIAM M. BURTON.

In presence of—
O. C. AVISUS,
R. A. SCHAEFER.

## Primary Source

"Manufacture of Gasolene" **(3 OF 3)**
Third page of W. M. Burton's patent application for the manufacture of gasoline. COURTESY OF THE U.S. GOVERNMENT PATENT OFFICE.

A refinery near Sapulpa, Oklahoma, 1909. AP/WIDE WORLD PHOTOS. REPRODUCED BY PERMISSION.

spelled "gasolene"). Next came the kerosene, and lastly came the heavy oils and tar which were simply left in the bottom of the drum.

At first, the gasoline fraction and the heavy fraction left in the drum were simply discarded. But later, all the fractions of petroleum became useful and valuable, especially gasoline. With the introduction of gasoline-powered automobiles, gasoline started to usurp kerosene as the most valuable component of petroleum. Henry Ford introduced the Model T in 1908 and invented the first conveyor-belt assembly line in 1913. As Ford started selling millions of Model Ts, the need for gasoline soared.

In the same year that Henry Ford began using his conveyor-belt assembly line, William Burton applied for a patent for an improved technique to manufacture gasoline. Burton's technique was called thermal cracking. Thermal cracking is the application of steady heat and pressure to crack (break down) the heavy hydrocarbon oils into the lighter ones which comprise gasoline. By applying pressure to the still system Burton and his partner William Humphreys found a way to produce low-boiling gasoline from the heavier fractions, thus greatly increasing the yield of gasoline.

In January 1913, at the Standard Oil of Indiana's Whiting refinery, the first set of twelve Burton stills went into operation producing gasoline. By 1925, 23 million barrels of gasoline were produced from Burton stills. The use of Burton stills in the refining industry more than doubled the yield of gasoline obtained from petroleum, and Standard Oil's profits sky-rocketed.

## Significance

Today petroleum is one of the most valuable commodities on earth. Petroleum refining is the physical, thermal, and chemical separation of petroleum into its major distillation fractions, which are then further processed into finished products. The primary products of the industry fall into three major categories: fuels, non-fuel products, and chemical feed-stocks. Fuels derived from petroleum are gasoline, diesel fuel, jet fuel, kerosene, and coke. Non-fuel petroleum products include lubricating oils, greases, petroleum wax, petroleum jelly, and asphalt. Petroleum chemical feed-stocks are used to produce a vast number of products, including fertilizers, pesticides, paints, cleaning fluids, detergents, refrigerants, resins, latex, rubber compounds, hard plastics, plastic sheeting, and myriad other compounds.

Thermal cracking, first introduced to the refining industry with Burton's stills in 1913 is still a major component of modern petroleum refineries.

## Further Resources

### BOOKS

Enos, John L. *Petroleum Progress and Profits: A History of Process Innovation.* Cambridge: MIT Press, 1962.

Haynes, William. *This Chemical Age: The Miracle of Man-Made Materials.* New York: Alfred A. Knopf, 1942.

### PERIODICALS

Houdry, Eugene. "Catalytic Cracking, and World War II Aviation Gasoline." *Journal of Chemical Education* 61, August 1984, 655–656.

Vartanian, Paul. F. "The Chemistry of Modern Petroleum Product Additives." *Journal of Chemical Education* 68, December 1991, 1015–1020.

### WEBSITES

"Distillation." The Distillation Group, Inc. Available online at http://www.distillationgroup.com/distill.htm (accessed February 16, 2003).

Pafco, Wayne. "Case Study: Petroleum Origins of the Industry." Available online at http://www.pafko.com/history //h_petro.html (accessed November 25, 2002).

---

# "On the Constitution of Atoms and Molecules"

Journal article

**By:** Niels Bohr

**Date:** 1913

**Source:** Niels Bohr. "On the Constitution of Atoms and Molecules." *Philosophical Magazine* series 6, vol. 26, July 1913, 1–25, 476–502, 857–875. Available online at http://dbhs .wvusd.k12.ca.us/Chem-History/Bohr/Bohr-1913a.html (accessed March 1, 2003).

**About the Author:** Niels Henrik David Bohr (1885–1962) was born in Copenhagen, Denmark. Upon graduation from high school in 1903, Bohr entered the University of Copenhagen, where he majored in physics. He conducted a research project on the surface tension of water as evidenced in a vibrating jet stream. He received his Ph.D. in 1911. His thesis centered on the electron theory of metals. Bohr was awarded numerous prizes for his scientific achievements, such as the Hughes Medal from the Royal Society, 1921; Nobel Prize in physics, 1922; and Atoms for Peace Award from the Ford Foundation, 1957. Bohr married Margarethe Norlund in 1912, and they had six children. ∎

## Introduction

In the early twentieth century, the fundamental nature of the building blocks of matter and energy were coming into view. The electron was discovered in 1897, and many scientists were putting their efforts into determining the electron's location in the atom.

Around this time, physicist Ernst Rutherford proposed a theory on atomic structure. Rutherford's solar sys-

Niels Bohr, notable theoretical physicist and Nobel Prize winner. © BETTMANN/CORBIS. REPRODUCED BY PERMISSION.

tem theory had a positively charged nucleus surrounded by a relatively distant system of orbiting electrons.

Niels Bohr attempted to reconcile Rutherford's model with Newton's and Kepler's laws of motion, which predicted that electrons would occupy elliptical orbits around the positively charged nucleus, as in our solar system. However, based on experimental observations relating to the line spectrum of the hydrogen atom, Bohr concluded that such a system was impossible. When bombarded by light, each element in the periodic table absorbs certain wavelengths and emits certain wavelengths. The emitted wavelengths are called the line spectrum of the element. Line spectrums are unique for each element and are like a fingerprint. Rutherford's model seemed impossible under the accepted physical laws governing matter.

Bohr did not abandon Rutherford's atomic theory. Rather, he abandoned the classic physical laws. In "On the Constitution of Atoms and Molecules," he applied a revolutionary new approach to Rutherford's atomic structure, introducing a mathematical constant proposed by Max Planck in 1900.

When Bohr introduced Planck's constant, "h," into Rutherford's atomic theory, everything seemed to make sense. Using Planck's constant to describe the interaction between light and matter and Rutherford's atomic theory

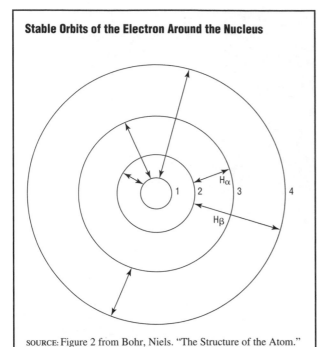

**Stable Orbits of the Electron Around the Nucleus**

SOURCE: Figure 2 from Bohr, Niels. "The Structure of the Atom." Nobel Lecture, December 11, 1922. Available online at http://www.nobel.se/physics/laureates/1922/bohr-lecture.html. (Accessed December 18, 2002).

provided an explanation for the line spectrum of the hydrogen atom.

Bohr's combination of Planck's constant with Rutherford's model described in "On the Constitution of Atoms and Molecules" contained three postulates. First, the electrons in an atom are normally restricted to specific orbits based on the orbital radii. Bohr called the state when the electrons are in their allowed orbits the "stationary state" of the atom. Second, when the electrons are in a stationary state, the atom does not emit radiation. Third, when the atom is bombarded with light of certain wavelengths, certain electrons will "jump" to other orbits and a quantum of energy (photon) is released or absorbed.

As it turned out, Rutherford's atomic solar-system model was wrong, but it was a stepping-stone that eventually led others to deduce the correct atomic structure.

**Significance**

Bohr's atomic theory was a huge step toward the elucidation of the correct atomic structure. His incorporation of Planck's constant and the concept of a stationary, or ground state, for electrons, as well as electrons "jumping" between orbitals and emitting quantized amounts of energy, are entirely in keeping with the correct structure of atoms. However, the solar-system model of electrons orbiting the nucleus is incorrect. Electrons are said to occupy orbitals. But these orbitals are not solar-system-type circular orbits. Rather, they are variously shaped clouds of electronic probability.

Bohr's use of Planck's constant was a key part of the development of quantum mechanics. Quantum mechanics describes the behavior of energy and matter within the infinitely small space of the atom. Bohr's model explained the frequency of atomic line spectra as resulting from different energy levels within an atom. This explanation provided a basis for the development of quantum mechanics by Erwin Schrodinger, W. Heisenberg, Louis V. de Broglie, Max Born, P. A. M. Dirac, and others.

**Primary Source**

"On the Constitution of Atoms and Molecules" [excerpt]

**SYNOPSIS:** In the present document, Bohr outlines the quantum structure of the atom.

In order to explain the results of experiments on scattering of α rays by matter, Prof. Rutherford has given a theory of the structure of atoms. According to this theory, the atoms consist of a positively charged nucleus surrounded by a system of electrons kept together by attractive forces from the nucleus; the total negative charge of the electrons is equal to the positive charge of the nucleus. Further, the nucleus is assumed to be the seat of the essential part of the mass of the atom, and to have linear dimensions exceedingly small compared with the linear dimensions of the whole atom. The number of electrons in an atom is deduced to be approximately equal to half the atomic weight. Great interest is to be attributed to this atom-model; for, as Rutherford has shown, the assumption of the existence of nuclei, as those in question, seems to be necessary in order to account for the results of the experiments on large angle scattering of the α rays.

In an attempt to explain some of the properties of matter on the basis of this atom-model we meet, however, with difficulties of a serious nature arising from the apparent instability of the system of electrons: difficulties purposely avoided in atom-models previously considered, for instance, in the one proposed by Sir J. J. Thomson. According to the theory of the latter, the atom consists of a sphere of uniform positive electrification, inside which the electrons move in circular orbits.

The principal difference between the atom-models proposed by Thomson and Rutherford consists in the circumstance the forces acting on the electrons in the atom-model of Thomson allow of certain configurations and motions of the electrons for which the system is in a stable equilibrium; such configurations, however, apparently do not exist for the second atom-model. The nature of the difference in question will perhaps be most clearly seen by noticing that among the quantities characterizing the first atom a quantity appears—the radius of the positive sphere—of dimensions of a length and of the same order of magnitude as the linear extension of the atom, while such a length does not appear among the quantities characterizing the second atom, viz. the charges and masses of the electrons and the positive nucleus; nor can it be determined solely by help of the latter quantities.

The way of considering a problem of this kind has, however, undergone essential alterations in recent years owing to the development of the theory of the energy radiation, and the direct affirmation of the new assumptions introduced in this theory, found by experiments on very different phenomena such as specific heats, photoelectric effect, Röntgen &c. The result of the discussion of these questions seems to be a general acknowledgment of the inadequacy of the classical electrodynamics in describing the behavior of systems of atomic size. Whatever the alteration in the laws of motion of the electrons may be, it seems necessary to introduce in the laws in question a quantity foreign to the classical electrodynamics, i.e. Planck's constant, or as it often is called, the elementary quantum of action. By the introduction of this quantity the question of the stable configuration of the electrons in the atoms is essentially changed as this constant is of such dimensions and magnitude that it, together with the mass and charge of the particles, can determine a length of the order of magnitude required.

This paper is an attempt to show that the application of the above ideas to Rutherford's atom-model affords a basis for a theory of the constitution of atoms. It will further be shown that from this theory we are led to a theory of the constitution of molecules.

In the present first part of the paper the mechanism of the binding of electrons by a positive nucleus is discussed in relation to Planck's theory. It will be shown that it is possible from the point of view taken to account in a simple way for the law of the line spectrum of hydrogen. Further, reasons are given for a principal hypothesis on which the considerations contained in the following parts are based.

I wish here to express my thanks to Prof. Rutherford for his kind and encouraging interest in this work.

## Further Resources

### BOOKS

Bohr, Niels. *Atomic Physics and Human Knowledge.* New York: Wiley, 1958.

———. *Atomic Theory and the Description of Nature.* New York: Macmillan, 1961.

———. *Collected Works.* L. Rosenfeld, ed. Amsterdam: North-Holland, 1972.

———. "The Structure of the Atom." Noble Prize in Physics Award Address. Elsevier Cie and the Nobel Foundation. Reprinted in Jefferson H. Weaver. *The World of Physics,* vol. 2. New York: Simon and Schuster, 1987, 315–338.

———. *The Theory of Spectra and Atomic Constitution: Three Essays.* Cambridge, England: The University Press, 1922.

Pais, Abraham. *Niels Bohr's Times: In Physics, Philosophy, and Polity.* Oxford, England: Clarendon Press, 1991.

Petruccioli, Sandro. *Atoms, Metaphors, and Paradoxes: Niels Bohr and the Construction of a New Physics.* New York: Cambridge University Press, 1993.

Whitaker, Andrew. *Einstein, Bohr, and the Quantum Dilemma.* New York: Cambridge University Press, 1996.

### PERIODICALS

Kragh, Helge. "J.J. Thomson, the Electron, and Atomic Architecture." *The Physics Teacher* 35, September 1997, 328–332.

### WEBSITES

"Niels Bohr Archives." Available online at http://www.nba.nbi.dk/ (accessed February 16, 2003).

"Niels Henrik David Bohr." Available online at http://www-history.mcs.st-andrews.ac.uk/history/Mathematicians/Bohr_Niels.html; website home page: http://www-maths.mcs.st-andrews.ac.uk (accessed May 15, 2003).

"A Science Odyssey—Peoples and Discoveries—Niels Bohr." Available online at http://www.pbs.org/wgbh/aso/databank/entries/bpbohr.html; website home page: http://www.pbs.org/ (accessed February 16, 2003).

# "Psychology as the Behaviorist Views It"

Journal article

**By:** John B. Watson

**Date:** 1913

**Source:** John B. Watson. "Psychology As the Behaviorist Views It." *Psychological Review* 20, 1913, 158–177. Available online at http://psychclassics.yorku.ca/Watson/views.htm; website home page: http://psychclassics.yorku.ca (accessed May 15, 2003).

John Watson, behaviorist, wears a Santa Claus mask to test the reaction of an infant he conditioned to fear white furry objects. **PHOTOGRAPH BY BENJAMIN HARRIS, PH.D. REPRODUCED BY PERMISSION.**

**About the Author:** John Broadus Watson (1878–1958) was born in Greenville, South Carolina. He received his master's degree from Furman College in 1900 and his Ph.D. from the University of Chicago in 1903. Watson remained at this school to teach and study the behavior of rats. In 1908, he moved to Johns Hopkins University in Baltimore, Maryland. Here Watson set up a laboratory to run psychological experiments, and he continued to study animal behavior as well as the behavior of small children. ■

## Introduction

John B. Watson was responsible for forming and popularizing the behaviorist school of thought in psychology. His article "Psychology As the Behaviorist Views It" represents the first major statement of the behaviorist position.

Psychology is the scientific study of human and animal behavior. Its goals are to describe, understand, predict, and control behavior. All psychology attempts to answer the question, "How can we step outside ourselves and look at how we live, think, and act?"

Behaviorism was one of five schools of thought vying for supremacy in early twentieth-century American psychology. The others were structuralism, functionalism, Gestalt psychology, and psychoanalysis. Each school had had its own particular convictions about what the study of psychology should endeavor to

do and what methods were best used in the study of psychology.

In "Psychology As the Behaviorist Views It," Watson puts forward the fundamental concepts of behaviorism. In addition he shows his general opposition to using subjective and introspective data, which was part of the dogma of all the other schools. Behaviorism concerned itself exclusively with measurable and observable data and excluded using any data from inner mental experiences such as ideas and emotions. In this way, psychology was to become like chemistry and physics, "a purely objective experimental branch of natural science."

By excluding conscious awareness of self, Watson did not differentiate human behavior from animal behavior. Rather, the behavior of all living things (even, according to Watson, the simple organism the amoeba) is based on a stimulus. Behaviorism is based on the belief that behind every response is a stimulus, either external or internal, that caused it. Behaviorism is best exemplified by the work of the Russian scientist Ivan Pavlov and his experiments with dogs.

## Significance

Watson's paper is considered the first treatise on classic behaviorism. The American period of classic behaviorism started with Watson in 1913 and lasted until roughly the 1930s. Classic behaviorism was tied very tightly to the personality and image of its organizer.

In later years, however, others would develop and add to the behaviorist position, and after World War II, behavior therapy became popular. Behavior therapy was the behaviorists' answer to psychoanalysis. It focused on changing a patient's behavior rather than on the thoughts and feelings of the patient (as in psychoanalysis). B. F. Skinner, a popular behaviorist around this time, introduced the concept of positive and negative reinforcement.

The behaviorist view that the study of the mind should be purely objective and experimental, much the way chemistry or physics is studied, has had a revolutionary influence on modern psychology. In the fall of 1957, Watson received the American Psychological Association Distinguished Service Award. The plaque read, "To Dr. John B. Watson, whose work has been one of the vital determinants of the form and substance of modern psychology. He initiated a revolution in psychological thought, and his writings have been a point of departure for continuing lines of fruitful research."

## Primary Source

"Psychology As the Behaviorist Views It" [excerpt]

**SYNOPSIS:** The 1913 article by Watson excerpted here is regarded as the "first manifesto of the behaviorist movement" and thus ranks as one of the most influential psychological papers of all time.

Psychology as the behaviorist views it is a purely objective experimental branch of natural science. Its theoretical goal is the prediction and control of behavior. *Introspection* forms no essential part of its methods, nor is the scientific value of its data dependent upon the readiness with which they lend themselves to interpretation in terms of consciousness. The behaviorist, in his efforts to get a unitary scheme of animal response, recognizes *no dividing line between man and brute*. The behavior of man, with all of its refinement and complexity, forms only a part of the behaviorist's total scheme of investigation. . . .

## Summary

Human psychology has failed to make good its claim as a natural science. Due to a mistaken notion that its fields of facts are conscious phenomena and that introspection is the only direct method of ascertaining these facts, it has enmeshed itself in a series of speculative questions which, while fundamental to its present tenets, are not open to experimental treatment. In the pursuit of answers to these questions, it has become further and further divorced from contact with problems which vitally concern human interest.

Psychology, as the behaviorist views it, is a purely objective, experimental branch of natural science which needs introspection as little as do the sciences of chemistry and physics. It is granted that the behavior of animals can be investigated without appeal to consciousness. Heretofore the viewpoint has been that such data have value only in so far as they can be interpreted by analogy in terms of consciousness. The position is taken here that the behavior of man and the behavior of animals must be considered on the same plane; as being equally essential to a general understanding of behavior. It can dispense with consciousness in a psychological sense. The separate observation of 'states of consciousness', is, on this assumption, no more a part of the task of the psychologist than of the physicist. We might call this the return to a non-reflective and naive use of consciousness. In this sense consciousness may be said to be the instrument or tool with which all scientists work. Whether or not the tool is properly used at present by scientists is a problem for philosophy and not for psychology.

From the viewpoint here suggested the facts on the behavior of amoebæ have value in and for themselves without reference to the behavior of man. In biology studies on race differentiation and inheritance in amoebæ form a separate division of study which must be evaluated in terms of the laws found there. The conclusions so reached may not hold in any other form. Regardless of the possible lack of generality, such studies must be made if evolution as a whole is ever to be regulated and controlled. Similarly the laws of behavior in amoebæ, the range of responses, and the determination of effective stimuli, of habit formation, persistency of habits, interference and reinforcement of habits, must be determined and evaluated in and for themselves, regardless of their generality, or of their bearing upon such laws in other forms, if the phenomena of behavior are ever to be brought within the sphere of scientific control.

This suggested elimination of states of consciousness as proper objects of investigation in themselves will remove the barrier from psychology which exists between it and the other sciences. The findings of psychology become the functional correlates of structure and lend themselves to explanation in physicochemical terms.

Psychology as behavior will, after all, have to neglect but few of the really essential problems with which psychology as an introspective science now concerns itself. In all probability even this residue of problems may be phrased in such a way that refined methods in behavior (which certainly must come) will lead to their solution.

## Further Resources

### BOOKS

O'Donnell, J.M. *The Origins of Behaviorism: American Psychology, 1870–1920.* New York: New York University Press, 1985.

Watson, J.B. *Behavior: An Introduction to Comparative Psychology.* New York: Holt, 1914.

———. *Behaviorism.* New York: Norton, 1924.

———. *Psychology from the Standpoint of a Behaviorist.* Philadelphia: Lippincott, 1919.

### PERIODICALS

Bergmann, G. "The Contributions of John B. Watson." *Psychological Review* 63, 1956, 265–276.

Samuelson, F. "Struggle for Scientific Authority: The Reception of Watson's Behaviorism, 1913–1920." *Journal of the History of the Behavioral Sciences* 17, 1981, 225–228.

Watson, J.B., and R. Rayner. "Conditioned Emotional Responses." *Journal of Experimental Psychology* 3, 1920, 1–14.

Watson, J.B. "Is Thinking Merely the Action of Language Mechanisms?" *British Journal of Psychology* 11, 1920, 87–104.

Yerkes, R.M., and S. Morgulis. "The Method of Pavlov in Animal Psychology." *Psychological Review* 6, 1909, 257–273.

### WEBSITES

"John B. Watson." Available online at http://www.furman.edu/~einstein/watson/watson5.htm (accessed February 16, 2003).

---

# "A Direct Photoelectric Determination of Planck's '*h*'"

Journal article

**By:** Robert A. Millikan

**Date:** March 1916

**Source:** Millikan, Robert, A. "A Direct Photoelectric Determination of Planck's '*h*'." *Physical Review* 7, March 1916, 355–357, 359, 360–361, 374–375, 383, 388.

**About the Author:** Robert A. Millikan (1868–1953) was born in Morrison, Illinois. He received his doctorate from Columbia University and taught physics at the University of Chicago (1896–1921) and at the California Institute of Technology from 1921 until 1945. Among Millikan's many achievements, he was president of the American Physical Society, director of the National Research Council, and Nobel laureate for Physics in 1923. ∎

## Introduction

Robert A. Millikan's contributions to science include three important verifications of the wave-particle duality. The wave-particle duality is the principle that subatomic particles possess some wavelike characteristics and that electromagnetic waves, such as light, possess some particle-like characteristics. Evidence for the wave-particle duality accumulated from 1900 to 1920. However, it was not until 1923 that Louis De Broglie postulated the wave-particle theory. Millikan's contributions toward the development of the theory were threefold and involved providing conclusive evidence that electrons are particles, proving the validity of the photoelectric effect, and using the photoelectric effect to determine the precise value of Planck's constant. Millikan recieved a Nobel Prize in 1923 "for his work on the elementary charge of electricity and on the photoelectric effect."

Through his famous oil-drop experiment, Millikan provided the first irrefutable evidence that electrons were fundamental, discrete units, that is, particles. The electron was the first subatomic particle discovered. Many scientists believed that electrons consisted of continuous waves rather than discrete particles. Using an excellent experimental setup, which used oil droplets instead of water droplets, Millikan determined the exact value of the electron charge.

Millikan's second and third contributions to the wave-particle duality were exemplified in "A Direct Photoelectric Determination of Planck's '*h*,'" published in 1916. This paper describes the first measurement of Planck's constant *h* and was part of a set of experiments in which Millikan proved the photoelectric effect. The photoelectric effect proposed by Albert Einstein asserted that light, and other electromagnetic radiation, possessed particle-like characteristics. It was based on the observation that charged particles are emitted from matter when it absorbs light or any other radiant energy.

German physicist Max Planck proposed *h* based on his observations of "blackbody radiation." A blackbody is black because all visible light is absorbed without reflection, making the surface appear black. Planck found that any object with a higher temperature than its surroundings loses heat by radiation. The hotter the object, the more radiation it produces. Planck found that rather than emitting all frequencies of radiation equally, blackbodies emit larger quantities of some wavelengths rather than others. This led Planck to propose that radiant heat energy is emitted in definite discrete amounts called quanta. Planck theorized that the energy emitted (E) is released according to the following equation: $E = h\mu$, where $\mu$ is the frequency of light. He called this equation the quantum theory. Planck's quantum theory implied that energy was not a continuous flow of waves but an ensemble of discrete packets.

Millikan determined Max Planck's *h* using an ingenious device he described as being a "machine shop in a vacuum." Millikan was an astute experimentalist. He took note of all the inherent difficulties involved in determining Planck's constant and designed an experimental method to avoid these errors. One error he noted involved the presence of a surface film, which exerted an effect on escaping electrons. His experimental design eliminated this error. Additionally, having an accurate value for the electron charge, which he obtained in his oil-drop experiment, proved critical for Millikan in this experiment.

Millikan determined *h* to have the value $6.57 \times 10^{-27}$ erg-sec to "a precision of about 0.5 per cent," a value much superior to what had been obtained in previous attempts.

### Significance

In the early twentieth century, physicists were discovering the fundamental nature of the building blocks of matter and energy. There was much scientific debate concerning whether matter, such as atoms and subatomic particles, possessed wavelike characteristics and whether energy, such as electromagnetic radiation, possessed particle-like characteristics. That matter and energy could consist of both wave- and particle-like characteristics (the wave-particle duality) was not compatible with classical, or Newtonian physics, which was sacrosanct at the time.

Millikan's 1916 article was significant in that it provided experimental evidence for Planck's constant and the photoelectric effect, both of which were important in the development of the wave-particle duality and eventually to quantum mechanics. Quantum mechanics is the physical science that applies to the interaction of energy and matter on the scale of atoms and subatomic particles. On this infinitely small scale, the classical physics that rule the macromolecular world break down. The cornerstone of quantum mechanics is Planck's quantum theory, expressed as $E = h\mu$.

In the equation, Max Planck's *h* plays a central role. This constant ($h = 6.626 \times 10^{-34}$ joule-second) is one of the most important in all of physics. Einstein used Planck's quantization-of-energy principle to explain the photoelectric effect, which involves the emission of electrons from certain materials when exposed to light, a phenomenon that could not be explained by classical models. "A Direct Photoelectric Determination of Planck's 'h'" provided the most accurate measurement of *h* at the time. Additionally, it was part of a set of experiments in which Millikan proved the validity of the photoelectric effect.

---

**Experimental Photoelectric Measurements used to Determine Value of Planck's Constant**

| Wave-length compared with 5,461 | Slope in volt-frequencies |
|---|---|
| 3,126 | $4.11 \times 10^{-16}$ |
| 3,650 | $4.14 \times 10^{-16}$ |
| 3,126 | $4.10 \times 10^{-16}$ |
| 3,650 | $4.12 \times 10^{-16}$ |
| 3,126 | $4.24 \times 10^{-16}$ |
| 4,047 | $3.98 \times 10^{-16}$ |
| 2,535 | $4.04 \times 10^{-16}$ |
| 3,126 | $4.24 \times 10^{-16}$ |
| 4,047 | $4.21 \times 10^{-16}$ |
| | Mean = $4.131 \times 10^{-16}$ |

SOURCE: Table 2 from Millikan, Robert A. "A Direct Photoelectric Determination of Planck's 'h'." *Physical Review*, Vol. VII, March 1916, p. 375.

---

## Primary Source

"A Direct Photoelectric Determination of Planck's 'h'" [excerpt]

**SYNOPSIS:** In these excerpts, Millikan describes the significance of Einstein's photoelectric effect and Planck's constant, *h*. He also describes some experimental observations and finally provides the experimentally determined value for *h*.

### 1. Introductory

Quantum theory was not originally developed for the sake of interpreting photoelectric phenomena. It was solely a theory as to the mechanism of absorption and emission of electromagnetic waves by resonators of atomic or subatomic dimensions. It had nothing whatever to say about the energy of an escaping electron or about the conditions under which such an electron could make its escape, and up to this day the form of the theory developed by its author has not been able to account satisfactorily for the photoelectric facts presented herewith. We are confronted, however, by the astonishing situation that these facts were correctly and exactly predicted nine years ago by a form of quantum theory which has now been pretty generally abandoned.

It was in 1905 that Einstein made the first coupling of photo effects and with any form of quantum theory by bringing forward the bold, not to say the reckless, hypothesis of an electro-magnetic light corpuscle of energy $h\mu$, which energy was transferred upon absorption to an electron. This hypothesis may well be called reckless first because an electromagnetic disturbance which remains localized in space seems a violation of the very conception of an electromagnetic disturbance, and

Robert Millikan, physicist and Nobel Prize winner, working in his laboratory. He made numerous momentous discoveries, chiefly in the fields of electricity, optics, and molecular physics. © BETTMANN/CORBIS. REPRODUCED BY PERMISSION.

second because it flies in the face of the thoroughly established facts of interference. The hypothesis was apparently made solely because it furnished a ready explanation of one of the most remarkable facts brought to light by recent investigations, viz., that the energy with which an electron is thrown out of a metal by ultra-violet light or X-rays is independent of the intensity of the light while it depends on its frequency. This fact alone seems to demand some modification of classical theory or, at any rate, it has not yet been interpreted satisfactorily in terms of classical theory.

While this was the main if not the only basis of Einstein's assumption, this assumption enabled him at once to predict that the maximum energy of emission of corpuscles under the influence of light would be governed by the equation

$$\tfrac{1}{2}mv^2 = V.\ e = hv - p_1 \qquad (1)$$

in which $hv$ is the energy absorbed by the electron from the light wave, which according to Planck contained just the energy $hv$, $p$ is the work necessary to get the electron out of the metal and $\tfrac{1}{2}mv^2$ is the energy with which it leaves the surface, an energy evidently measured by the product of its charge $e$ by the P.D. [Potential Difference] against which it is just able to drive itself before being brought to rest.

At the time at which it was made this prediction was as bold as the hypothesis which suggested it, for at that time there were available no experiments whatever for determining anything about how P.D. varies with $v$, or whether the hypothetical $h$ of equation (1) was anything more than a number of the same general magnitude as Planck's $h$. Nevertheless, the following results seem to show that at least five of the experimentally verifiable relationships which are actually contained in equation (1) are rigorously correct. These relationships are embodied in the following assertions:

1. *That there exists for each exciting frequency $v$, above a certain critical value, a definitely determinable maximum velocity of emission of corpuscles.*

2. *That there is a linear relation between V and $v$.*

3. *That dV/dv or the slope of the V v line is numerically equal to $h/e$.*

4. *That at the critical frequency $v_0$ at which $v= 0$, $p = hv_0$, i.e., that the intercept of the V v line on the v axis is the lowest frequency at which the metal in question can be photoelectrically active.*

5. *That the contact E.M.F. [Electromotive Force] between any two conductors is given by the equation*

   Contact E.M.F. $= h/e(v_0 - v_0') - (V_0 - V_0')$.

No one of these points except the first had been tested even roughly when Einstein made his prediction and the correctness of this one has recently been vigorously denied by Ramsauer. As regards the fourth Elster and Geitel had indeed concluded as early as 1891, from a study of the alkali metals, that the more electro-positive the metal the smaller is the value of $v$ at which it becomes photo-sensitive, a conclusion however which later researches on the non-alkaline metals seemed for years to contradict.

During the ten years which have elapsed since Einstein set up his equation the fifth of the above assertions has never been tested at all, while the third and fourth have never been subjected to careful experimental test under conditions which were even claimed to permit of an exact and definite answer, nor indeed can they be so subjected without simultaneous measurements *in vacuo* of both contact potentials and photo-potentials *in the case of metals which are sensitive throughout a long range of observable frequencies.* . . .

The work at the Ryerson Laboratory on energies of emission began in 1905. How the present investigation has grown out of it will be clear from the following brief summary of its progress and its chief results.

1. It was found first that these energies are independent of temperature, a result unexpected at the time but simultaneously discovered by Lienhop and thoroughly confirmed by others later. This result showed *that photoelectrons do not share in the energies of thermal agitation as they had commonly been supposed to do,* and this result still stands. . . .

6. The relation between V and $v$ was tested with spark sources without bringing to light at first anything approaching a linear relationship. These results were reported by Dr. Wright. A question as to their validity was, however, raised by my subsequent proof of the insufficiency of such screening devices as had been used in the case of spark sources. Accordingly Dr. Kadesch took up again the relation between V and $v$ with powerful spark sources, using film-free sodium and potassium surfaces, and obtained results which spoke definitely and strongly in favor of a linear relation between the maximum P.D. and $v$. The range of wave lengths studied was from 3,900 Å. to 2,200 Å. These results have been published since Pohl and Pringsheim wrote their critique, else I think they would not have felt that the common assumption since 1905 of a linear relation between V and $v$ rested upon so insecure an experimental basis.

7. At the same time I undertook to investigate with as much exactness as possible, using as a source the monochromatic radiations of the quartz-mercury arc, the third, fourth and fifth of the above assertions of Einstein's equation, and in the vice-presidential address before the American Association for the Advancement of Science in December, 1912, expressed the hope that we should soon be able to assert whether or not Planck's $h$ actually appeared in photoelectric phenomena as it has been usually assumed for ten years to do. At that time the papers of Hughes and of Richardson and Compton had just appeared, though the latter paper I had unfortunately not seen at the time of writing and hence made no reference to it. These authors found the value of $h$ in the Einstein photoelectric equation varying in the eight metals studied from $3.55 \times 10^{-27}$ to $5.85 \times 10^{-27}$. Planck's $h$ was $6.55 \times 10^{-27}$, a difference which Hughes tried to explain by assuming either that only a fraction of the energy $hv$ was absorbed or that the energy of emission against the

direction of the incident light was less than that in the direction of the incident light. . . .

Having placed beyond a doubt, however, the fact of the linear relation between V and $\nu$, it was possible to determine the slope of the line in the highest attainable vacuum by locating two distant points on it in rapid succession. Wave-length 5,461 was always chosen for one of these points because its great intensity and large wave-length *i.e.*, steep slope, adapt it admirably to an accurate determination of the intercept on the potential axis. This intercept was determined a few minutes after shaving, while the molecular pump was kept running and the McLeod gauge showed a pressure of perhaps a ten millionth of a millimeter, then the intercept of the other chosen line was found as quickly as possible by the method used above, after which the intercept of 5,461 was again taken. If the contact E.M.F. was changing uniformly this change should be eliminated by taking the mean intercept of line 5,461. The results of nine different determinations of slope made in this way on different days and with different wavelengths to compare with 5,461 are given . . . . [See table "Experimental Photoelectric Measurements used to Determine Planck's Constant."]

The estimated uncertainties in these slopes, as set down at the time of taking, range from 1 per cent. to 4 per cent., those corresponding to lines 3,650 and 3,120 being most reliable. I have not, however, attempted to weight the individual observations in taking the mean. ... We may conclude then that the slope of the volt-frequency line for sodium is the mean of 4.124 and 4.131, namely $4.128 \times 10^{-15}$ which, with my value of $e$, yields

$$h = 6.569 \times 10^{-27} \text{ erg. sec.}$$

. . .

### 9. Theories of Photo Emission

Perhaps it is still too early to assert with absolute confidence the general and exact validity of the Einstein equation. Nevertheless, it must be admitted that the present experiments constitute very much better justification for such an assertion than has heretofore been found, and if that equation be of general validity, then it must certainly be regarded as one of the most fundamental and far reaching of the equations of physics; for it must govern the transformation of all short-wave-length electromagnetic energy into heat energy. . . .

### 10. Summary

1. Einstein's photoelectric equation has been subjected to very searching tests and it appears in every case to predict exactly the observed results.

2. Planck's $h$ has been photoelectrically determined with a precision of about .5 per cent. and is found to have the value
$$h = 6.57 \times 10^{-27}.$$

## Further Resources

### BOOKS
Mundlak, Max. *The Consequences of Philosophy: A Reply to Planck and Einstein.* London: J Bale, Sons, and Danielsson, Ltd, 1936.

Planck, Max. *Scientific Autobiography, and Other Papers.* New York: Greenwood, 1968.

Rosenthal-Schneider, Ilse. *Reality and Scientific Truth: Discussions with Einstein, von Laue, and Planck.* Detroit, Mich.: Wayne State University Press, 1980.

### PERIODICALS
Chen, Chun Xiao, and Chang Geng Zhang. "New Demonstration of Photoelectric Effect." *The Physics Teacher* 37, no.7, October 1999, 442.

Gebelle, Ronald. "A Comment on Waves and Particles." *The Physics Teacher* 31, December 1993, 525.

### WEBSITES
"Robert Andrew Millikan 1868–1953." Center for the History of Physics: Selected Papers of Great American Physicists. Available online at http://www.aip.org/history/gap/Millikan/Millikan.html; website home page: http://www.aip.org/history/gap/index.html (accessed May 16, 2003).

Holton, Gerald. "Centennial Focus: Millikan's Measurement of Planck's Constant." *Physical Review Focus*, April 22, 1999. Available online at http://focus.aps.org/story/v3/st23; website home page: http://focus.aps.org (accessed May 16, 2003).

Millikan, Robert, A. "The Electron and the Light-Quant from the Experimental Point of View." Nobel Lecture, May 23, 1924. Nobel e-museum. Nobel Lectures, Physics 1922–1941. Available online at http://www.nobel.se/physics/laureates/1923/millikan-lecture.html; website home page: http://www.nobel.se/ (accessed February 13, 2003).

# *Psychology of the Unconscious*

Nonfiction work

**By:** Carl Jung

**Date:** 1916

**Source:** Jung, Carl G. *Psychology of the Unconscious: A Study of the Transformations and Symbolism of the Libido.* Beatrice M. Hinkle, trans. 1916. Reprint, New York: Dodd, Mead, 1965, 37–41.

**About the Author:** Carl Jung (1875–1961), the son of a Protestant clergyman, was born in Kesswil, Switzerland. He studied at the University of Basel from 1895 to 1900, receiving his medical degree from the University of Zurich in 1902. He later studied psychology in Paris, but had an interest in many subjects such as biology, zoology, paleontology, and the history of religion. In 1903, he married Emma Rauschenbach. The couple had five children and lived in Kusnacht on the Lake of Zurich, where he died on June 6, 1961. ■

## Introduction

*Psychology of the Unconscious: A Study of the Transformations and Symbolisms of the Libido* was the first work Carl Jung published after his split with Sigmund Freud. From about 1909 until about 1912, Jung and Freud were close collaborators, Jung having even been called a Freud disciple. However, Jung disagreed with some of the particulars of Freud's psychoanalytic theory in the latter's *Psychology of the Unconscious*. Primarily, he did not agree that libido (sexual desire) lay beneath all human mechanisms. Rather, Jung believed that there is some "energy of life" that includes sexuality and hunger and all human interests and activities.

In this work, Jung used an American woman's recorded fantasies to illustrate some of his broad theories on the nature of the unconscious mind and what compels humans to act as they do. In about 1907, a Miss Frank Miller, an American woman studying in Switzerland, wrote an article outlining many of her fantasies. The article, "Some Instances of Subconscious Creative Imagination," was subsequently published in the *Journal of the American Society for Psychical Research*. Jung used Miss Miller's vivid fantasies to redefine the concept of Freud's libido.

Jung demonstrated the concept of religious and mythical symbolism. In many of Miss Miller's fantasies, she identifies herself with various characters from religious, historical, and mythological stories. Additionally, Jung himself used innumerable legends, myths, and religious accounts to convey his points. Dionysius, Moses, and Hiawatha all show up in the pages of *The Psychology of the Unconscious*.

Jung drew upon Miss Miller's fantasies to show that libido is more precisely defined as a psychic energy rather than an exclusively sexual desire. He believed the psychic energy could be represented by the idea of the collective unconscious and archetypes (primordial images or patterns). For instance, he observed that the "myths and fairy tales of world literature contain definite motifs which crop up everywhere." Furthermore Jung observed that "we meet these same motifs in the fantasies, dreams, deliria, and delusions of individuals living today." Jung believed the psychic energy emerges from deep within our unconscious and appears as symbols in our conscious thoughts, dreams, or fantasies.

## Significance

Jung's book was a milestone because it represents his break with Sigmund Freud. Following this work, Jung went on to formulate and refine what was to be called Jungian psychology. He revised *Psychology of the Unconscious* in 1952, and this edition was one of his most popular and significant books.

Jung's concept of the collective unconscious is first introduced in *Psychology of the Unconscious*. The concept of the collective unconscious was an entirely new concept in 1912. He establishes the meaning of archetypes, specifically discussing the archetypes of the hero and the mother. His concept of archetypes and the collective unconscious influenced many scholars and literary figures. Joseph Campbell, a celebrated American author, was heavily influenced by Jung. Campbell theorized that all myths are linked in the human psyche and that they are cultural manifestations of the universal need to explain social, cosmological, and spiritual realities. His classic book, *The Hero with a Thousand Faces* (1949), was a study of the "myth of the hero." Campbell believed that "hero myths" from all cultures contain a shared pattern of a heroic journey. In his book, Campbell presents the stages in the journey of the hero archetype.

## Primary Source

*Psychology of the Unconscious* [excerpt]

> **SYNOPSIS:** In this excerpt from *Psychology of the Unconscious*, Jung discusses myths and the unconscious by using as an example the story of Abbe Oegger written by Anatole France. Later in the book, Jung used Miss Frank Miller's fantasies to illustrate many of his concepts on myths, archetypes, and a collective unconscious.

Our foregoing explanations show wherein the products arising from the unconscious are related to the mythical. From all these signs it may be concluded that the soul possesses in some degree historical strata, the oldest stratum of which would correspond to the unconscious. The result of that must be that an introversion occurring in later life, according to the Freudian teaching, seizes upon regressive infantile reminiscences taken from the individual past. That first points out the way; then, with stronger introversion and regression (strong repressions, introversion psychoses), there come to light pronounced traits of an archaic mental kind which, under certain circumstances, might go as far as the re-echo of a once manifest, archaic mental product.

This problem deserves to be more thoroughly discussed. As a concrete example, let us take the

Carl Jung, founder of analytical psychology, who emphasized the importance of social and cultural archetypes in the collective unconscious as a means to understanding human psychology. © **BETTMANN/ CORBIS. REPRODUCED BY PERMISSION.**

history of the pious Abbé Oegger which Anatole France has communicated to us. This priest was a hypercritical man, and much given to phantasies, especially in regard to one question, viz., the fate of Judas; whether he was really damned, as the teaching of the church asserts, to everlasting punishment, or whether God had pardoned him after all. Oegger sided with the intelligent point of view that God, in his all-wisdom, had chosen Judas as an instrument, in order to bring about the highest point of the work of redemption by Christ. This necessary instrument, without the help of which the human race would not have been a sharer in salvation, could not possibly be damned by the all-good God. In order to put an end to his doubts, Oegger went one night to the church, and made supplication for a sign that Judas was saved. Then he felt a heavenly touch upon his shoulder. Following this, Oegger told the Archbishop of his resolution to go out into the world to preach God's unending mercy.

Here we have a richly developed phantasy system before us. It is concerned with the subtle and perpetually undecided question as to whether the legendary figure of Judas is damned or not. The Ju-

das legend is, in itself, mythical material, viz., the malicious betrayal of a hero. I recall Siegfried and Hagen, Balder and Loki. Siegfried and Balder were murdered by a faithless traitor from among their closest associates. This myth is moving and tragic—it is not honorable battle which kills the noble, but evil treachery. It is, too, an occurrence which is historical over and over again. One thinks of Cæsar and Brutus. Since the myth of such a deed is very old, and still the subject of teaching and repetition, it is the expression of a psychological fact, that envy does not allow humanity to sleep, and that all of us carry, in a hidden recess of our heart, a deadly wish towards the hero. This rule can be applied generally to mythical tradition. *It does not set forth any account of the old events, but rather acts in such a way that it always reveals a thought common to humanity, and once more rejuvenated.* Thus, for example, the lives and deeds of the founders of old religions are the purest condensations of typical, contemporaneous myths, behind which the individual figure entirely disappears.

But why does our pious Abbé torment himself with the old Judas legend? He first went into the world to preach the gospel of mercy, and then, after some time, he separated from the Catholic church and became a Swedenborgian. Now we understand his Judas phantasy. *He was the Judas* who betrayed his Lord. Therefore, first of all, he had to make sure of the divine mercy, in order to be Judas in peace.

This case throws a light upon the mechanism of phantasies in general. The known, conscious phantasy may be of mythical or other material; it is not to be taken seriously as such, for it has an indirect meaning. If we take it, however, as important per se, then the thing is not understandable, and makes one despair of the efficiency of the mind. But we saw, in the case of Abbé Oegger, that his doubts and his hopes did not turn upon the historical problem of Judas, but upon his own personality, which wished to win a way to freedom for itself through the solution of the Judas problem.

*The conscious phantasies tell us of mythical or other material of undeveloped or no longer recognized wish tendencies in the soul.* As is easily to be understood, an innate tendency, an acknowledgement of which one refuses to make, and which one treats as non-existent, can hardly contain a thing that may be in accord with our conscious character. It concerns the tendencies which are considered immoral, and as generally impossible, and the strongest resentment is felt towards bringing them into the consciousness. What would Oegger have said had he been told confidentially that he was preparing himself for the Judas rôle? And what in ourselves do we consider immoral and non-existent, or which we at least wish were non-existent? It is that which in antiquity lay widespread on the surface, viz., sexuality in all its various manifestations. Therefore, we need not wonder in the least when we find this at the base of most of our phantasies, even if the phantasies have a different appearance. Because Oegger found the damnation of Judas incompatible with God's goodness, he thought about the conflict in that way; that is the conscious sequence. Along with this is the unconscious sequence; because Oegger himself wished to be a Judas, he first made sure of the goodness of God. To Oegger, Judas was the symbol of his own unconscious tendency, and he made use of this symbol in order to be able to meditate over his unconscious wish. The direct coming into consciousness of the Judas wish would have been too painful for him. *Thus, there must be typical myths which are really the instruments of a folk-psychological complex treatment.* Jacob Burckhardt seems to have suspected this when he once said that every Greek of the classical era carried in himself a fragment of the Oedipus, just as every German carries a fragment of Faust.

The problem which the simple story of the Abbé Oegger has brought clearly before us confronts us again when we prepare to examine phantasies which owe their existence this time to an exclusively unconscious work. We are indebted for the material which we will use in the following chapters to the useful publication of an American woman, Miss Frank Miller, who has given to the world some poetical unconsciously formed phantasies under the title, "Quelque faits d'imagination créatrice subconsciente."

## Further Resources

### BOOKS

Campbell, Joseph. *The Hero with a Thousand Faces.* 2nd ed. Princeton, N.J.: Princeton University Press, 1968.

Jung, C.G. *The Collected Works of C.G. Jung.* Vol. 1–20. Bollingen Series XX. Sir Herbert Read et al., eds. Princeton, N.J.: Princeton University Press, 1979.

———. *Two Essays on Analytical Psychology.* New York: Pantheon Books, 1966.

———. *The Undiscovered Self.* R.F.C. Hull, trans. Boston: Little, Brown, 1958.

McGuire, William, ed. *The Freud-Jung Letters: the Correspondence between Freud and Jung.* Princeton, N.J.: Princeton University Press, 1974.

### PERIODICALS

Mather, Ronald. "On the Mythology of the Reflexive Subject." *History of the Human Sciences* 10, no. 4, November 1997, 65–82.

Pietikainen, Petteri. "Dynamic Psychology, Utopia, and Escape from History: The Case of C.G. Jung." *Utopian Studies* 12, no. 1, 2001, 41–55.

### WEBSITES

"Archetypes as Defined by Carl Jung." Available online at http://www.acs.appstate.edu/~davisct/nt/jung.html (accessed February 16, 2003).

C.G. Jung Page. Available online at http://www.cgjungpage .org/ (accessed May 16, 2003). *Abstracts of the Collected Works of C.G. Jung and Much More.*

# "The Atom and the Molecule"
## Journal article

**By:** Gilbert N. Lewis

**Date:** 1916

**Source:** Lewis, Gilbert, N. "The Atom and the Molecule." *Journal of the American Chemical Society* 34, 1916, 763–785.

**About the Author:** Gilbert Newton Lewis (1875–1946) was born in Weymouth, Massachusetts. His early education was a bit informal, as he was home-schooled until the age of thirteen. While still in his teens, he took courses from the University of Nebraska and received a bachelor's degree in chemistry and a Ph.D. from Harvard. Lewis spent a long and distinguished career at the University of California, Berkeley. ∎

## Introduction

The nature of a chemical bond is of utmost importance in chemistry. The strength and character of the bonds that join one atom with another determines such fundamental chemical properties as reactivity, boiling and melting points, and color.

There are two main types of chemical bonds, ionic and covalent. An ionic bond joins two polar atoms together. It is much more prevalent in inorganic compounds like salts, minerals, and metals. In an ionic bond, electrons are transferred from one atom to another atom.

The counterpart of the ionic bond is the covalent bond. Covalent bonds typically join two nonpolar atoms together. The covalent bond is the bond of organic chemistry, which has to do primarily with the element carbon and the molecules of life: proteins and DNA (deoxyribonucleic acid). In covalent bonds, neither atom completely "lets go" of the bonding electrons. Rather, in a covalent bond, electrons are shared between the two atoms. Covalent bonds are much stronger than ionic bonds.

In 1916, two papers were published within about a month of each other that explained the nature of both types of bonds. First, Walter Kossel published a paper in Germany that discussed the ionic bond. A month later, Gilbert Lewis in America proposed the concept of shared electron bonding in "The Atom and the Molecule."

Fundamental to both Lewis's and Kossel's work was the theory of valence electrons. Valence electrons are the electrons in the outer shell of the atom that are involved in bonding. In 1904, German chemist Richard Abegg proposed a rule that said the difference between the maximum negative and positive valences of an atom always results in the number eight. This idea was expanded by Lewis in "The Atom and the Molecule" and by others to become an important theory of chemical bonding. The octet rule says that in order to achieve eight electrons in their outer shell (called a noble-gas electron configuration), atoms either transfer electrons, as in an ionic bond, or share electrons, as in a covalent bond.

In "The Atom and the Molecule," Lewis proposed and discussed the covalent bond. He explained when and why atoms would share electrons rather than completely transfer them. He said that polar compounds are composed mostly of ionic bonds and nonpolar compounds are composed mostly of covalent bonds. Polarity is a fundamental property of chemical compounds. It conveys the electrical homogeneity of a chemical compound. In polar compounds, positive and negative charges are separated. One-half of the compound tends to be electrically negative while the other half is electrically positive. On the other hand, nonpolar compounds tend to carry the same level of electro-negativity throughout.

Lewis also presented a method to depict the number of electrons shared between the two atoms. A Lewis structure represents the atom and its eight valence electrons. The valence electrons are represented by dots. In a Lewis structure. it is easy to count electrons and visualize the number of electrons shared between two atoms.

## Significance

The discovery of the covalent bond was a significant milestone in chemistry. Knowledge about the structure and nature of the covalent bond is of fundamental importance in organic chemistry. The stability of biological molecules such as proteins and DNA is conferred in large part by the strength of the covalent bond.

In "The Atom and the Molecule," Lewis proposed a systematic way to indicate the electronic configuration of atoms bonded together. His Lewis Dot Configuration is still taught in sophomore organic chemistry classes today.

Scanning any college level organic chemistry textbook reveals the importance of Lewis's proposals. Organic chemistry students learn about Lewis structures, Lewis bonding theory, Lewis dot notation, and Lewis formulas.

## Primary Source

**"The Atom and the Molecule" [excerpt]**

> **SYNOPSIS:** In this excerpt from "The Atom and the Molecule," Lewis discusses the concept of a polar-to-nonpolar continuum. He says that most molecules lie in the middle of the continuum and contain characteristics of polarity and nonpolarity. He also introduces the Lewis Dot Formula Notation. Finally, Lewis presents his theory of covalent bonding.

### Molecular Structure

I shall now attempt to show how, by a single type of chemical combination, we may explain the widely varying phenomena of chemical change. With the original assumption of Helmholtz, which has been used by some authors under the name of the electron theory of valence, and according to which a given electron either does or does not pass completely from one atom to another, it is possible to give a very satisfactory explanation of compounds which are of distinctly polar type, but the method becomes less and less satisfactory as we approach the nonpolar type. Great as the difference is between the typical polar and nonpolar substances, we may show how a single molecule may, according to its environment, pass from the extreme polar to the extreme nonpolar form, not *per saltum* but by imperceptible gradations, as soon as we admit that an electron may be the common property of two atomic shells.

Let us consider first the very polar compounds. Here we find elements with but few electrons in their shells tending to give up these electrons altogether to form positive ions, and elements which already possess a number of electrons tending to increase this number to form the group of eight. Thus $Na^+$ and $Ca^{++}$ are kernels without a shell, while chloride ion, sulfide ion, nitride ion (as in fused nitrides) may each be represented by an atom having in the shell eight electrons at the corners of a cube.

As an introduction to the study of substances of slightly polar type we may consider the halogens. [The illustration attempts] to show the different forms of the iodine molecule $I_2$. *A* represents the molecule as completely ionized, as it undoubtedly is to a measurable extent in liquid iodine. Without ionization we may still have one of the electrons of one atom fitting into the outer shell of the second atom, thus completing its group of eight as in *B*. But at the same time an electron of the second atom may fit into the shell of the first, thus satisfying both groups of eight and giving the form *C* which is the predominant and characteristic structure of the halogens. Now, notwithstanding the symmetry of the form *C*, if the two atoms are for any reason tending to separate, the two common electrons may cling more firmly sometimes to one of the atoms, sometimes to the other, thus producing some dissymmetry in the molecule as a whole, and one atom will have a slight excess of positive charge, the other of negative. This separation of the charges and the consequent increase in the polar character of the molecule will increase as the atoms become separated to a greater distance until complete ionization results. [When the separation occurs in a nonpolar environment the atoms may separate in such a way that each retains one of the two common electrons, as in the thermal dissociation of iodine gas.] Thus between the perfectly symmetrical and nonpolar molecule *C* and the completely polar and ionized molecule represented by *A* there will be an infinity of positions representing a greater or lesser degree of polarity. Now in a substance like liquid iodine it must not be assumed that all of the molecules are in the same state, but rather that some are highly polar, some almost nonpolar, and others represent all gradations between the two. When we find that iodine in different environments shows different degrees of polarity, it means merely that in one medium there is a larger percentage of the more polar forms. So bromine, although represented by an entirely similar formula, is less polar than iodine. In other words, in the average molecule the separation of the charge is less than in the case of iodine. Chlorine and fluorine are less polar than either and can be regarded as composed almost completely of molecules of the form *C*.

I wish to emphasize once more the meaning that must be ascribed to the term tautomerism. In the simplest case where we deal with a single tautomeric change we speak of the two tautomers and sometimes write definite formulae to express the two. But we must not assume that all of the molecules of the substance possess either one structure or the other, but rather that these forms represent the two limiting types, and that the individual molecules range all the way from one limit to the other. In certain cases where the majority of molecules lie very near to one limit or to the other, it is very convenient and desirable to attempt to express the percentage of the molecules belonging to the one or to

the other tautomeric form; but in a case where the majority of molecules lie in the intermediate range and relatively few in the immediate neighborhood of the two limiting forms such a calculation loses most of its significance.

With the halogens it is a matter of chance as to which of the atoms acquires a positive and which a negative charge, but in the case of a binary compound composed of different elements the atoms of

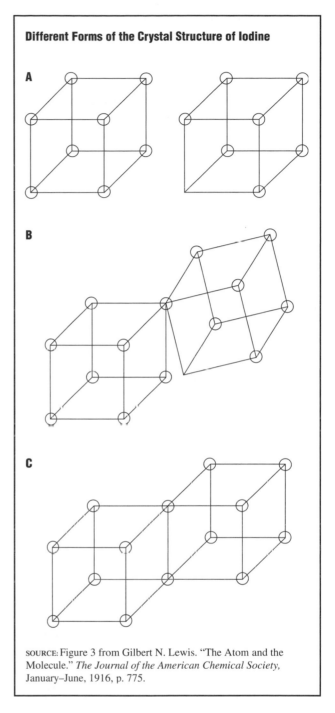

**Different Forms of the Crystal Structure of Iodine**

A

B

C

SOURCE: Figure 3 from Gilbert N. Lewis. "The Atom and the Molecule." *The Journal of the American Chemical Society*, January–June, 1916, p. 775.

one element will be positive in most, though not necessarily all, of the molecules. Thus in $Br_2$ the bromine atom is as often positive as negative, but in BrCl it will be usually positive and in IBr usually negative, although in all these substances which are not very polar the separation of charges in the molecule will be slight, whereas in the metallic halides the separation is nearly complete and the halogen atoms acquire almost complete possession of the electrons.

In order to express this idea of chemical union in symbols I would suggest the use of a colon, or two dots arranged in some other manner, to represent the two electrons which act as the connecting links between the two atoms. Thus we may write $Cl_2$ as Cl : Cl. If in certain cases we wish to show that one atom in the molecule is on the average negatively charged we may bring the colon nearer to the negative element. Thus we may write Na :I, and I :Cl. Different spacings to represent different degrees of polarity can of course be more freely employed at a black-board than in type.

It will be noted that, since in the hydrogen-helium row we have the rule of two in the place of the rule of eight, the insertion of one electron into the shell of the hydrogen atom is entirely analogous to the completion of the cube in the case of the halogens. Thus we may consider ordinary hydrogen as a hydride of positive hydrogen in the same sense that chlorine may be regarded as a chloride of positive chlorine. But $H_2$ is far less polar even than $Cl_2$. The three main types of hydrogen compounds may be represented therefore by H :Cl, H : H, and Na :H.

We may go further and give a complete formula for each compound by using the symbol of the kernel instead of the ordinary atomic symbol and by adjoining to each symbol a number of dots corresponding to the number of electrons in the atomic shell. Thus we may write H : H, H :Ö: H, H :Ï:, :Ï:Ï:, but we shall see that in many cases such a formula represents only one of the numerous extreme tautomeric forms. For the sake of simplicity we may also use occasionally formulae which show only those electrons concerned in the union of two atoms, as in the preceding paragraphs. . . .

Let us turn now to a problem in the solution of which the theory which I am presenting shows its greatest serviceability. The electrochemical theories of Davy and Berzelius were overshadowed by the "valence" theory when the attention of chemists was largely drawn to the nonpolar substances of organic chemistry. Of late the electrochemical theories have come once more into prominence, but there has always been that antagonism between the two views which invariably results when two rival theories are mutually exclusive, while both contain certain elements of truth. Indeed we may now see that with the interpretation which we are now employing the two theories need not be mutually exclusive, but rather complement one another, for the "valence" theory, which is the classical basis of structural organic chemistry, deals with the fundamental structure of the molecule, while electrochemical considerations show the influence of positive and negative groups in minor distortions of the fundamental form. Let us consider once for all that by a negative element or radical we mean one which tends to draw towards itself the electron pairs which constitute the outer shells of all neighboring atoms, and that an electropositive group is one that attracts to a less extent, or repels, these electrons. In the majority of carbon compounds there is very little of that separation of the charges which gives a compound a polar character, although certain groups, such as hydroxyl, as well as those containing multiple bonds, not only themselves possess a decidedly polar character, but increase, according to principles already discussed, the polar character of all neighboring parts of the molecule. However, in such molecules as methane and carbon tetrachloride, instead of assuming, as in some current theory, that four electrons have definitely left hydrogen for carbon in the first case, and carbon for chlorine in the second, we shall consider that in methane there is a slight movement of the charges toward the carbon so that the carbon is slightly charged negatively, and that in carbon tetrachloride they are slightly shifted towards the chlorine, leaving the carbon somewhat positive. We must remember that here also we are dealing with averages and that in a few out of many molecules of methane the hydrogen may be negatively charged and the carbon positively.

In a substance like water the electrons are drawn in from hydrogen to oxygen and we have in the limiting case a certain number of hydrogen atoms which are completely separated as hydrogen ion. The amount of separation of one of the hydrogen atoms, and therefore the degree of ionization, will change very greatly when the other hydrogen atom is substituted by a positive or negative group. As a familiar example we may consider acetic acid, in which one hydrogen is replaced by chlorine, $H_2$ ClCCOOH. The electrons, being drawn towards the chlorine, permit the pair of electrons joining the methyl and carboxyl groups to approach nearer to the methyl carbon. This pair of electrons, exercising therefore a smaller repulsion upon the other electrons of the hydroxyl oxygen, permit these also to shift in the same direction. In other words, all the electrons move toward the left, producing a greater separation of the electrons from the hydrogen of the hydroxyl, and thus a stronger acid. This simple explanation is applicable to a vast number of individual cases. It need only be borne in mind that although the effect of such a displacement of electrons at one end of a chain proceeds throughout the whole chain it becomes less marked the greater the distance, and the more rigid the constraints which hold the electrons in the intervening atoms.

This brief account of the theory of atomic and molecular structure could be extended almost indefinitely by illustrations of its application to numerous types of compounds, but I believe enough has been said to show how, through simple hypotheses, we may explain the most diverse types of chemical union and how we may construct models which illustrate the continuous transition between the most polar and the most nonpolar of substances. I shall therefore conclude this paper with a brief discussion of a phenomenon which bears closely upon the ideas which have been presented here.

## Further Resources

### BOOKS

Coulson, C.A. *The Shape and Structure of Molecules.* Oxford: Clarendon Press, 1973.

Gillespie, Ronald J., and Paul L.A. Popelier. *Chemical Bonding and Molecular Geometry from Lewis to Electron Densities.* New York: Oxford University Press, 2001.

### PERIODICALS

Davenport, Derek A. "Gilbert Newton Lewis: 1875–1946." *Journal of Chemical Education* 61, 1984, 2.

Seaborg, Glenn. "The Research Style of Gilbert N. Lewis." *Journal of Chemical Education* 61, 1984, 93.

Tiernan, N.F. "Gilbert Newton Lewis and the Amazing Electron Dots." *Journal of Chemical Education* 62, July 1985, 569.

### WEBSITES

Nave, Rod. "Chemical Bonding." Hyperphysics. Available online at http://hyperphysics.phy-astr.gsu.edu/hbase/chemical /bond.html (accessed February 16, 2003).

Steinberg, June, B. "Chemical Bonds." Available online at http://faculty.nl.edu/jste/bonds.htm (accessed February 16, 2003).

# "Globular Clusters and the Structure of the Galactic System"

Journal article

**By:** Harlow Shapley

**Date:** February 1918

**Source:** Shapley, Harlow. "Globular Clusters and the Structure of the Galactic System." *Publications of the Astronomical Society of the Pacific* 30, no. 173, February 1918, 42, 46–48, 50–51, 54. Available online at http://adsabs.harvard.edu/ (accessed March 12, 2003).

**About the Author:** Harlow Shapley (1885–1972) was born on a farm near Nashville, Missouri. At age fifteen, Shapley attended a business school in Kansas for several months, then spent a year as a newspaper crime reporter and a police reporter. Wanting more education, he entered the Presbyterian Carthage Collegiate Institute, finishing the equivalent of six years of high school in a year and a half. He next attended the University of Missouri. Intending to major in journalism but finding that department not yet open, he chose astronomy. He was hired as a teaching assistant during his third year, and obtained a M.A. degree in 1911. During his fourth year he won a fellowship to Princeton University, where he was awarded his Ph.D. degree in 1913. Shapley married Martha Betz in 1914, and they had five children ■

## Introduction

The first solid evidence pinpointing the location of the sun in the Milky Way was assembled by Harlow Shapley and reported in "Globular Clusters and the Structure of the Galactic System." In this work, Shapley calculated the distance from the Earth of several "globular clusters," which are congregations of a great number of stars (ten thousand to one million) held together by gravity, all clustered in a relatively small space and orbiting around the center of the Milky Way.

Shapley used a method developed by the American astronomer Henrietta Leavitt to calculate the distances of the globular clusters. The tremendous distances of objects very far out in space are difficult to comprehend let alone to calculate. The method Shapley used is based on measuring the pulses of light that come from stars called cepheids. Cepheids are young stars whose brightness, or luminosity, fluctuates. By measuring the time between fluctuations, the distance of the star can be calculated. This is based on Leavitt's determination that if one knows the actual and the apparent brightness of an object, its distance can be calculated.

When Shapley published this article, the accepted model of the Milky Way was that our sun was very close to the galactic center. Prominent astronomers such as Thomas Wright in the late eighteenth century, William Herschel in the early nineteenth century, and J. C. Kapteyn

Harlow Shapley, astronomer who first determined the size and structure of our galaxy. AP/WIDE WORLD PHOTOS. REPRODUCED BY PERMISSION.

later in the nineteenth century had provided a picture of a flattened disk-shaped galaxy with our sun, and hence our solar system, near its center.

However, when Shapley plotted the locations of the globular clusters, he found we were not at the center of the Milky Way. He determined that the globular clusters appeared to form a group that was centered on a point about thirty thousand light-years from the Earth. Shapley postulated that the clusters were orbiting around the center of the galaxy, which appeared to be in the direction of the constellation Sagittarius. Shapley was correct. The center of the Milky Way is in the direction of Sagittarius, and our solar system is located closer to the edge of the galaxy rather than near its center.

### Significance

In 1610, Galileo, upon observing our galaxy the Milky Way with his new telescope, wrote in his pamphlet *Siderus Nuncius* (The Starry Messenger): "For the Galaxy is nothing else than a congeries of innumerable stars distributed in clusters."

Some three hundred years later, Shapley used these starry clusters to discern the position of our solar system within our galaxy. In "Globular Clusters and the Structure of the Galactic System," he provided conclusive ev-

idence that the Earth, the sun, and our solar system lie closer to the outer reaches of our galaxy rather than near the galactic center. His conclusion was opposite to what many astronomers of the time believed. However, no one could refute Shapley's calculations. Star clusters (there are three different types: globular clusters, open clusters, and stellar associations) have told astronomers much about the organization of stars in our galaxy and the evolution of the galaxy itself.

As of July 2002, there were 150 known globular clusters in the Milky Way. Of the 150 known clusters, 137 (91.3 percent) are concentrated in the hemisphere centered on the Sagittarius constellation. Most globular clusters move beyond the limits of the Milky Way.

The present picture of the Milky Way is for the most part still based on Shapley's conclusions. Shapley was wrong about the size of the Milky Way, yet he was correct about the structure of our galaxy and the position of our solar system within it. Based on Shapley's work and that of many other astronomers, we now know the Milky Way is a flattened disk of stars with a central bulge. It has a diameter of 25 kiloparsecs and is 1 kiloparsec thick. (A parsec is equal to 3.26 light-years, or $3.085678 \times 10^{13}$ kilometers. It is the distance at which a star would have a parallax—the apparent change in the position of a star that is caused by the motion of the Earth—of 1 second of arc. A kiloparsec is 1,000 parsecs.) The sun is approximately 8 kiloparsecs from its center and approximately 4 kiloparsecs from its edge.

### Primary Source

"Globular Clusters and the Structure of the Galactic System" [excerpt]

**SYNOPSIS:** In the paper from which the following excerpts are taken, Shapley presents the methods he used in the analysis of globular clusters and the bold conclusions he arrived at regarding the dimensions of our galaxy and the location of its center.

The continuation of my work on clusters has yielded information that seems to have some significance in the problem of the extent and arrangement of the general sidereal system. During the past two years the magnitudes of several thousand stars in thirty globular clusters have been measured, some rather extensive studies of variable stars and open clusters have been carried out, and methods have been investigated for the determination of the distances of clusters and variables. The results are discussed at length in several contributions from the Mount Wilson Solar Observatory, which are now in process of publication and will appear within a few

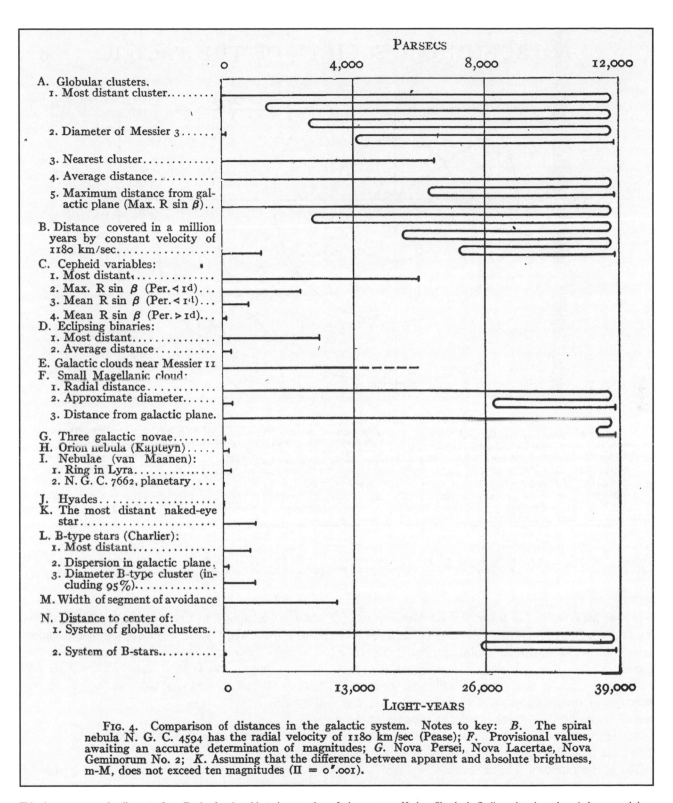

FIG. 4. Comparison of distances in the galactic system. Notes to key: *B*. The spiral nebula N. G. C. 4594 has the radial velocity of 1180 km/sec (Pease); *F*. Provisional values, awaiting an accurate determination of magnitudes; *G*. Nova Persei, Nova Lacertae, Nova Geminorum No. 2; *K*. Assuming that the difference between apparent and absolute brightness, m-M, does not exceed ten magnitudes (Π = 0″.001).

This chart compares the distances from Earth of major objects in our galaxy. It demonstrates Harlow Shapley's findings that the galaxy is larger, and the Earth less central in it, than scientists believed prior to 1918. **THIS FIGURE ORIGINALLY APPEARED IN THE PUBLICATIONS OF THE ASTRONOMICAL SOCIETY OF THE PACIFIC (SHAPLEY, H. 1918, PASP, 30, 42), COPYRIGHT 1918, ASTRONOMICAL SOCIETY OF THE PACIFIC. IT IS REPRODUCED WITH PERMISSION OF THE EDITORS.**

## ASTRONOMICAL SOCIETY OF THE PACIFIC    53

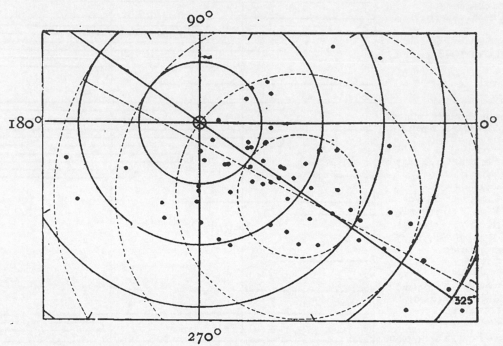

FIG. 5.   The system of globular clusters projected on the plane of the galaxy.  The galactic longitude is indicated for every thirty degrees.  ·The "local system" is completely within the smallest full-line circle, which has a radius of a thousand parsecs.  The larger full-line circles, which are also heliocentric, have radii increasing by intervals of 10,000 parsecs.  The broken line indicates the suggested major axis of the system, and the broken circles are concentric about its center.  The dots are about four times the actual diameters of the clusters on this scale.  Nine clusters more distant from the plane than 15,000 parsecs are not included in the diagram.

months. Meanwhile the more striking features may be briefly outlined, omitting, as is necessary for an article of this kind, the computations and numerical tables. In fact, the present announcement can be little more than a summary of methods, observations, and conclusions, and indulgence must be asked for presenting these results in advance of the observational material upon which they are based. The accompanying diagrams, however, may partially serve in the place of tabular data.

### A. Methods of Determining the Distances of Globular Clusters

1. The parallaxes of stellar systems that are too remote for direct trigonometrical measurement are best determined from the luminosities of the individual stars they contain. To give such a method ac-

curacy, we must first find stars both near the Sun and in the distant system having intrinsic luminosities which, within allowable uncertainties, are comparable, and in the second place we must be able to derive the absolute magnitudes of such stars near the Sun. . . .

### B. The Distribution in Space of 69 Globular Clusters

1. The survey of the distances and space distribution of globular clusters may be considered complete except for some whose brightest stars are fainter than the 16th photographic magnitude; that is, complete up to a distance of 30,000 parsecs from the sun.

2. The nearest globular clusters, ω *Centauri* and 47 *Tucanae,* are just less than 7,000 parsecs distant;

the average distance of 69 systems is 23,000 parsecs. The parallax of the most distant now known, N. G. C. 7006, was first found from diameter measurement alone to be 0'.000015, corresponding to a distance of 67,000 parsecs; within the last month magnitude observations have been secured, giving $\pi = 0'.000014$—a highly satisfactory confirmation. One-fourth of the clusters are more distant than 100,000 light-years (30,000 parsecs).

3. North of the galactic plane are 32 recognized clusters; south of it are 37. Their average distance from the plane is 6,900 parsecs, and the algebraic mean of the distances is only −100 parsecs. There can be no doubt that the galactic plane is the fundamental and symmetrical plane in the system of globular clusters.

4. The apparent concentration of globular clusters in the direction of the richest part of the galaxy has been known since the time of the Herschels. More than half of them have galactic longitudes between 300° and 350°, with a conspicuous maximum at 325°, while between longitudes 45° and 190° there is none.

5. Two clusters, N. G. C. 7006 and 4147, are separated by a distance of 100,000 parsecs, which may be taken for the present as the diameter of the system of clusters. The center of the system appears to be at a distance of about 20,000 parsecs, but there is considerable uncertainty in this estimate because of the probable lack of complete data for clusters more distant than 30,000 parsecs. The center, which lies in the region of the rich star clouds of *Sagittarius* near the boundary of *Scorpio* and *Ophiuchus,* has the coördinates R. A. = $17^h$ $30^m$, Decl. = −30°. . . .

### D. Notes on the Structure of the Galactic System

1. A consideration of the foregoing results leads naturally to the conclusion that the globular clusters outline the extent and arrangement of the total galactic organization.

2. Adopting this view of the stellar universe, all known sidereal objects become a part of a single enormous unit, in which the globular clusters and Magellanic Clouds, tho extensive and massive systems, are clearly subordinate factors. Its volume is more than a hundred thousand times that commonly assigned to the stellar universe. The distance to its center is more than 200 times the distance to the center of our local group. ... [see Fig. 4.]

3. A striking characteristic of the general system is the equatorial region avoided by globular clusters. Its width is between 3,000 and 4,000 parsecs—less than one twenty-fifth its probable extent in the galactic plane. But between the planes adopted as its boundary are the open clusters, the planetary nebulae, the diffuse nebulosities, the naked-eye stars, and, in fact, nearly all the stars of our catalogs.

4. Outside the region of avoidance are the globular clusters, the Magellanic Clouds, a few isolated cluster-type variables, and probably the spiral nebulae—all of which appear to be objects of exceptionally high average velocity. Very likely other isolated stars are scattered throughout this extra-galactic domain, and occasionally a very faint open cluster (N. G. C. 7492).

5. The equatorial segment is untenanted by globular clusters perhaps thru their inability to form in an intense gravitational field, and thru impossibility of existence as compact organizations if they enter that region from without. The cluster nearest to the galactic plane, Messier 22, is one of the least compact of globular systems. . . .

9. The general system of clusters appears to be somewhat ellipsoidal . . . [See Fig. 5], the longest axis lying in the galactic plane and passing the Sun at a distance of some 3,000 parsecs. Its nearest point is in galactic longitude 240°, approximately coincident with the direction of the center of the local system of stars.

10. The center of the complete galactic system, including globular clusters, is in the general direction of (a) the richest star clouds of the Milky Way; (b) the most numerous open clusters, planetary nebulae, O-type stars; (c) the vertex of the second star stream; (d) the region most conspicuously avoided by spiral nebulae, and in which lies the roughly determined antapex of their radial velocities.

11. With the plan of the sidereal system here outlined, it appears unlikely that the spiral nebulae can be considered separate galaxies of stars. In addition to the evidence heretofore existing the following points seem opposed to the "island universe" theory: (a) the dynamical character of the region of avoidance; (b) the size of the galaxy; (c) the maximum luminosity attainable by a star; (d) the increasing commonness of high velocities among other sidereal objects, particularly those outside the region of avoidance. In favor may be urged the

suggestive ratio of width to extent for the equatorial segment of the galactic system. The matter can not be discussed in this summary, but we may state that the cluster work strongly suggests the hypothesis that spiral nebulae, while not closely related in history or dynamical development to the average star, are, however, members of the galactic organization, appearing to avoid the regions of enormous masses and forces more widely than do the globular clusters. The most generally accepted explanation of galactic novae is the penetration of nebulosity by a star with considerable velocity. Inverting this, the novae in spirals may be considered as the engulfing of a star by rapidly moving nebulosity; and the frequency of novae in spirals becomes a function of the dimensions of the nebula, its velocity in space, and the stellar density of its neighborhood—that is, the distance from the galactic plane.

12. The Sun is very eccentrically situated in the general system, being some 20 parsecs north of the plane and about a hundred parsecs from the center of a very open, perhaps ill-defined, local aggregation. The local group is about half way from the center to the edge of the galaxy, the thinnest part of the Milky Way lying between galactic longitudes 90° and 180°.

13. Throughout the whole extent of the region of avoidance the star density probably averages as great as near the Sun. The rich galactic clouds possibly represent depth more than star density. Stars of the 15th apparent magnitude are at the distance of the center if they have absolute magnitudes as bright as −1.5. A few blue stars of this apparent magnitude are already recorded from the neighborhood of Messier 11. Ultimately we may derive a check of the extent of the system from such stars.

14. Globular clusters supply a valuable "base line in time" for the observational study of the speed of the evolution of stars. Eddington's computations show that the duration of the total giant stage of a star, if contraction is its source of energy, can scarcely exceed 100,000 years. From the study of light that left the nearest clusters some twenty or thirty thousand years ago, we find for giant stars a well-known relation of color to luminosity. The light from the most distant globular cluster left its source nearly 200,000 years earlier. But the color-luminosity relation, so far as present results show, is identical.

*Mount Wilson Solar Observatory,*
*December, 1917.*

## Further Resources

**BOOKS**

Shapley, H. *Star Clusters.* New York: McGraw-Hill, 1930.

———. "Thirty Deductions from a Glimmer of Star Light." In *Beyond the Observatory.* New York: Scribner's, 1967, 127–133.

———. *Through Rugged Ways to the Stars.* New York: Scribner's, 1969.

———. *The View from a Distant Star: Man's Future in the Universe.* New York: Basic Books, 1963.

Shapley, H., and Helen E. Howarth. *A Source Book in Astronomy.* New York: McGraw-Hill, 1929.

**PERIODICALS**

Shapley, H. "On the Existence of External Galaxies." *PASP* 31, 1919, 261–268.

———. "On the Nature and Cause of Cepheid Variation." *ApJ* 40, 1914,, 448–465.

———. "The Scale of the Universe." *Bulletin of the National Research Council,* Vol. 2, part 3, No. 11., 1921, 171–217. Also available online at http://antwrp.gsfc.nasa.gov/htmltest /gifcity/cs_nrc.html (accessed May 16, 2003).

**WEBSITES**

Harvard University Archives. "Papers of Harlow Shapley, 1906–1966." Available online at http://oasis.harvard.edu /html/hua03998frames.html (accessed May 16, 2003).

"Zoom Astronomy Dictionary." Available online at http://www.enchantedlearning.com/subjects/astronomy; website home page: http://www.enchantedlearning.com/home .html (accessed May 16, 2003).

# *Report on the Relativity Theory of Gravitation*
Report

**By:** Arthur Eddington

**Date:** 1918

**Source:** Eddington, Arthur. *Report on the Relativity Theory of Gravitation.* London: Fleetway Press, 1918, v, 82–84.

**About the Author:** Arthur Eddington (1882–1944) was born at Kendal, Westmoreland, England. Before he was sixteen years old, he won a scholarship to Owen's College, where he studied mathematics and physics. He graduated with a degree in physics in 1902 and won a scholarship to Trinity College in Cambridge, where he concentrated in mathematics. Eddington was the head of his class in 1904 and graduated in only three years. Following graduation, Eddington was appointed chief assistant at the Royal Observatory at Greenwich. From 1906 to 1913 he received training in astronomy and made two research voyages. He eventually became professor of astronomy and the director of the observatory. ■

## Introduction

Early in the twentieth century, Newtonian physics dominated scientific thinking. Isaac Newton, perhaps one of the most brilliant scientists in history, put forth theories on motion and gravity in the late seventeenth century. The famous story goes that Newton conceived the law of gravity when an apple fell from a tree and hit him on the head. He deduced that the apple fell to the earth because an "attractive force" was acting on the apple. Newton postulated that the attractive force was gravity and that it existed between all objects of matter.

Newton proposed a mathematical equation for the gravitational force. His equation, though, did not involve a variable for time. Therefore, time was supposed to be absolute. According to Newtonian physics, no matter where a clock was placed in the universe, a second was a second was a second.

For some 250 years Newton's law of gravity was taken as an indisputable fact. It explained the orbits of planets around the sun and the moon around the earth. However, there were subtle inconsistencies. Certain observable phenomena, such as a slight variation in the orbit of Mercury, could not be explained by Newtonian physics. No one was able to explain why Newton's law could not account for these observations.

However, this changed when Albert Einstein proposed two monumental theories, in which he introduced the concept of "relativity." The special theory of relativity (1905) and the general theory of relativity (1915) proposed that nothing in the universe could travel faster than the speed of light (186,000 miles per second) and that light always travels at 186,000 miles per second. This implied that time could not be absolute, marching on at the same rate for everyone, everywhere. According to the theories of relativity, time is relative.

A key idea of general relativity is that the gravity of any mass has an effect on the space and time around it. The sun's mass, through gravity, curves nearby space and time, leading to the elliptical orbits of the Earth and other planets. It even explains the slight shift in the orbit of Mercury, which is the closest planet to the sun. Hence, space-time is more distorted near Mercury. Even our bodies bend space and time, albeit to an insignificant amount.

The mathematics involved in Einstein's general theory of relativity were extremely complicated. Even other scientists found the theory hard to grasp. Einstein is quoted as saying that there were not more than twelve people in the whole world who could understand his theory. One scientist who did understand it was Sir Arthur Eddington.

Eddington was extremely impressed by the elegance of Einstein's general theory. He immediately began promoting it to English scientists. His *Report on the Rela-*

Sir Arthur Eddington was a key proponent of Albert Einstein's general theory of relativity. © HULTON-DEUTSCH COLLECTION. REPRODUCED BY PERMISSION.

*tivity Theory of Gravitation* written for the Physical Society of London in 1918 was the first complete report of the general theory in the English language.

In his report, Eddington emphasized the importance of testing the general theory. He realized that a total eclipse of the sun provided the best opportunity to do this. According to Einstein's theory, starlight just grazing the sun's surface would be deflected or "bent" by a very small but measurable amount due to the distortion of space-time by the sun's gravity. During a total eclipse, when the sun's light is blotted out for a few minutes, you can see distant stars appearing close to the Sun in the sky. The Sun is normally so bright that these stars are unseen. If the general theory was right, the sun's gravity would shift these stars to slightly different positions, compared to where they are seen in the night sky or at other times of the year when they are farther away from the sun.

Eddington measured the deflection of light during a total eclipse of the sun, which was viewable in the Southern Hemisphere on May 29, 1919. It took several months of data analysis for Eddington to arrive at a conclusion. But in November 1919, he reported that he had verified Einstein's theory.

## Significance

Eddington was a firm believer in the truth of the general theory, and he was pivotal in the world's acceptance of it. His report and verification of the general theory led to its widespread acceptance. In 1919, headlines appeared in newspapers all over the world reporting the event, and Einstein became an instant celebrity. It has been said that the general theory appealed to the world's masses because it brought a certain order to a world spiritually emptied from the horrors of one of the bloodiest wars in history, World War I.

## Primary Source

*Report on the Relativity Theory of Gravitation*
[excerpt]

**SYNOPSIS:** This report was the first description of Einstein's Theory of General Relativity in English. In the preface Eddington discusses Einstein's theory of relativity in terms of its placement in the current day's scientific spectrum. In the final chapter of his Report, Eddington introduced one of the ramifications of relativity, namely that space and time combine to make a space-time continuum, and the space-time continuum bends.

## Preface

The relativity theory of gravitation in its complete form was published by Einstein in November 1915. Whether the theory ultimately proves to be correct or not, it claims attention as one of the most beautiful examples of the power of general mathematical reasoning. The nearest parallel to it is found in the applications of the second law of thermo-dynamics, in which remarkable conclusions are deduced from a single principle without any inquiry into the mechanism of the phenomena; similarly, if the principle of equivalence is accepted, it is possible to stride over the difficulties due to ignorance of the nature of gravitation and arrive directly at physical results. Einstein's theory has been successful in explaining the celebrated astronomical discordance of the motion of the perihelion of Mercury, without introducing any arbitrary constant; there is no trace of forced agreement about this prediction. It further leads to interesting conclusions with regard to the deflection of light by a gravitational field, and the displacement of spectral lines on the sun, which may be tested by experiment.

■■■

## The Curvature of Space and Time

We have now presented the laws of gravitation, of hydromechanics, and of electromagnetism, in a form which regards all systems of co-ordinates as on an equal footing. And yet it is scarcely true to say that all systems are equally fundamental; at least we can discriminate between them in a way which the restricted principle of relativity would not tolerate.

Imagine the earth to be covered with impervious cloud. By the gyro-compass we can find two spots on it called the Poles, and by Foucault's pendulum-experiment we can determine an angular velocity about the axis through the Poles, which is usually called the earth's absolute rotation. The name "absolute rotation" may be criticised; but, at any rate, it is a name given to something which can be accurately measured. On the other hand, we fail completely in any attempt to determine a corresponding "absolute translation" of the earth. It is not a question of applying the right name—there is no measured quantity to name. It is clear that the equivalence of systems of axes in relative rotation is in some way less complete than the equivalence of axes having different translations; and this may perhaps be regarded as a failure to reach the ideals of a philosophical principle of relativity.

This limitation has its practical aspect. We might suppose that from the expression ... for the field of a particle at rest it would be possible by a transformation of co-ordinates to deduce the field of a particle, say, in uniform circular motion. But this is not the case. We may, of course, reduce the particle to rest by using rotating axes; but we find it necessary to take an entirely different solution of the partial differential equations, satisfying different boundary conditions.

We have not hitherto paid any attention to the invariance of the boundary conditions; and it is here that the breakdown occurs. The axes ordinarily used in dynamics are such that as we recede towards infinity in space the $g_\mu^\nu$ approach the special set of values ... . On transforming to other co-ordinates the differential equations are unaltered; but usually the boundary values of the $g_\mu^\nu$, and consequently the appropriate solutions of the equations, are altered. We can, therefore, discriminate between different systems of co-ordinates according to the boundary values of the $g_\mu^\nu$'s; and those which at infinity pass into Galilean co-ordinates may properly be considered the most fundamental, since the boundary values are most simple. The complete relativity for uniform translation is due to the boundary values as well as the differential equations remaining unaltered.

We have based our theory on two axioms—the restricted principle of relativity and the principle of equivalence. These taken together may be called the *physical* principle of relativity. We have justified, or explained, them by reference to a *philosophical* principle of relativity, which asserts that experience is concerned only with the relations of objects to one another and to the observer and not to the fictitious space-time framework in which we instinctively locate them. We are now led into a dilemma; we can save this philosophical principle only by undermining its practical application. The measurement of the rotation of the earth detects something of the nature of a fundamental frame of reference—at least in the part of space accessible to observation. We shall call this the "inertial frame." Its existence does not necessarily contradict the philosophical principle, because it may, for instance, be determined by the general distribution of matter in the universe; that is to say, we may be detecting by our experiments relations to matter not generally recognised. But having recognised the existence of the inertial frame, the philosophical principle of relativity becomes arbitrary in its application. It cannot foretell that the Michelson-Morley experiment will fail to detect uniform motion relative to this frame; nor does it explain why the acceleration of the earth relative to this frame is irrelevant, but the rotation of the earth is important.

The inertial-frame may be attributed (1) to unobserved world-matter, (2) to the aether, (3) to some absolute character of space-time. It is doubtful whether the discrimination between these alternatives is more than word-splitting, but they lead to rather different points of view. The last alternative seems to contradict the philosophical principle of relativity, but in the light of what has been said the physicist has no particular interest in preserving the philosophical principle. In this chapter we shall consider two suggestions towards a theory of the inertial frame made by Einstein and de Sitter respectively. These should be regarded as independent speculations, arising out of, but not required by, the theory hitherto described.

The inertial frame is distinguished by the property that the $g_\mu^\nu$ referred to it approach the limiting Galilean values ... as we recede to a great distance from all attracting matter. This is verified experimentally with considerable accuracy; but it does not follow that we can extrapolate to distances as yet unplumbed, or to infinity. If it is assumed that the Galilean values still hold at infinite distances, the in-

ertial frame is virtually ascribed to conditions at infinity, and its explanation is removed beyond the scope of physical theory. We may, however, suppose that observational results relate to only a minute part of the whole world, and that at vaster distances the $g_\mu^\nu$ tend to zero values which would be invariant for all finite transformations. In that case all frames of reference are alike at infinity, and the property of

---

## LIGHTS ALL ASKEW IN THE HEAVENS

---

Men of Science More or Less Agog Over Results of Eclipse Observations

---

### EINSTEIN THEORY TRIUMPHS

---

Stars Not Where They Seemed or Were Calculated to be, but Nobody Need Worry

---

### A BOOK FOR 12 WISE MEN

---

No More in All the World Could Comprehend It, Said Einstein When His Daring Publishers Accepted It.

---

Special Cable to *The New York Times*.

LONDON, Nov 10—Efforts made to put in words intelligible to the nonscientific public the Einstein theory of light proved by the eclipse expedition so far have not been very successful. The new theory was discussed at a recent meeting of the Royal Society and Royal Astronomical Society. Sir Joseph Thomson, President of the Royal Society, declares it is not possible to put Einstein's theory into really intelligible words, yet at the same time Thomson adds:

"The results of the eclipse expedition demonstrating that the rays of light from the stars are bent or deflected from their normal course by other aerial bodies acting upon them and, consequently the inference that light has weight, form a most important contribution to the laws of gravity given us since Newton laid down his principles."

Thomson states that the difference between theories of Newton and those of Einstein are infinitesimal in a popular sense, and as they are purely mathematical and can only be expressed in strictly scientific terms, it is useless to endeavor to detail them for the man in the street. . . .

Source: Excerpted from "Lights All Askew in the Heavens," *The New York Times*, November 10, 1919, page 17.

---

the inertial frame arises from conditions within a finite distance. In that case physical theories of the inertial frame may be developed.

The ascription of the inertial frame to boundary conditions at infinity may also be avoided by abolishing the boundary. This is really only another aspect of the vanishing of the $g_{\mu}^{\nu}$ at infinity. Our four-dimensional space-time may be regarded as a closed surface in a five-dimensional continuum; it will then be unbounded but finite, just as the surface of a sphere is unbounded.

We have seen . . . that wherever matter exists space-time has a curvature. It might seem that if there were sufficient matter the continuum would curve round until it closed up; but it has not been found possible to eliminate the boundary so simply. I think the difficulty arises because time is not symmetrical with respect to the other co-ordinates; in general matter moves with small velocity, so that the different components of the energy-tensor $T_{\mu}^{\nu}$ are not of the same order of magnitude.

## Further Resources

### BOOKS

Chandrasekhar, S. *Eddington: The Most Distinguished Astrophysicist of His Time.* New York: Cambridge University Press, 1983.

Collins, Harry M., and Trevor Pinch. *The Golem: What You Should Know about Science.* New York: Cambridge University Press, 1998.

Eddington, A.S. *The Mathematical Theory of Relativity.* 3rd ed. Cambridge, England: Cambridge University Press, 1963.

————. *The Nature of the Physical World.* New York: Macmillan, 1928.

————. *Space, Time, and Gravitation: An Outline of the General Relativity Theory.* Cambridge, England: Cambridge University Press, 1987.

Jacks, L.P. *Sir Arthur Eddington: Man of Science and Mystic.* Cambridge, England: Cambridge University Press, 1949.

Kilmister, C.W. *Eddington's Search for a Fundamental Theory: A Key to the Universe.* New York: Cambridge University Press, 1994.

Whittaker, E.T. *From Euclid to Eddington: A Study of Conceptions of the External World.* Cambridge, England: Cambridge University Press, 1949.

### PERIODICALS

Collins, Graham, P. "Revising Relativity." *Scientific American,* November 2002, 27–28.

Panek, Richard. "And Then There Was Light: Einstein's Universe Is Subtle, but No Longer beyond the Reach of Ordinary Common Sense." *Natural History,* November 2002, 46–51.

### WEBSITES

Coles, Peter. "Eclipse That Changed the Universe." Available online at http://www.firstscience.com/site/articles/coles.asp; website home page: http://www.firstscience.com/site/ (accessed May 16, 2003).

"Einstein's Relativity Theory of Gravitation." Available online at http://leiwen.tripod.com/eingra.htm (accessed February 16, 2003).

---

# The Physical Basis of Heredity

Nonfiction work

**By:** Thomas Hunt Morgan

**Date:** 1919

**Source:** Morgan, Thomas Hunt. *The Physical Basis of Heredity.* Philadelphia: J. B. Lippincott, 1919. Reproduced online at http://www.esp.org/books/morgan/physical-basis/facsimile/title3.html; website home page: http://www.esp.org (accessed May 16, 2003).

**About the Author:** Thomas Hunt Morgan (1866–1945) was born in Kentucky. He received the B.S. degree in 1886 from the State College of Kentucky, and then attended Johns Hopkins University for graduate work. Morgan did research on the regeneration of earthworms and in 1890 received the Ph.D. degree with a thesis on the embryology of sea spiders. In 1891, he was appointed associate professor of biology at Bryn Mawr College, and later in 1904 acted as professor of experimental zoology at Columbia University. Morgan carried out an outstanding amount of research and published over 400 papers and fifteen books. ■

## Introduction

The concept of a gene was first discussed in the late 1860s by Gregor Mendel, an Augustinian monk. Mendel crossbred different types of pea plants and made note of the characteristics of the offspring. He observed that some traits were dominant, in that they appeared often in offspring, and some were recessive, in that they appeared less often. These experiments led him to discover the heritability of traits, the idea that "discrete factors" (later known as genes), inherited from parents, determine an individual's traits.

Later, American scientist Thomas Hunt Morgan provided evidence that the traits of an individual are related to chromosomes. At the turn of the century, a few researchers had postulated that chromosomes are the bearers of heredity. But it was Morgan's 1919 book *The Physical Basis for Heredity* that for the first time clearly correlated Mendel's laws with the physical behavior of chromosomes.

Morgan's famous research was based on noting the differences between successive generations of *Drosophila melanogaster,* the fruit fly. The choice of the fruit fly turned out to be a good one: Fruit flies reproduce extremely quickly in large numbers, and each offspring displays myriad and observable variations in traits, such as eye color or wing shape. Additionally, Morgan and his colleagues could easily observe fruit fly chromosomes under a light microscope.

Through the work of Morgan and a team of researchers, the genes for certain traits were associated with certain of the fruit fly's four chromosomes. For example, they found that the gene producing white eyes in fruit flies was always associated with the X-chromosome.

*The Physical Basis for Heredity* established several fundamental concepts and rules of heredity. First, Morgan proposed the rule that separate genes associated with different chromosomes will show up in offspring in an independent manner. However, genes that are on the same chromosome will remain together in the offspring.

Morgan found a twist on the above rule with the concept of "crossing-over," or recombination. Sometimes, genes that were on the same chromosome did not remain together in the offspring. This led Morgan to surmise that chromosomes might exchange pieces of themselves to create new combinations of genes.

The culmination of Morgan's studies provided three more rules of heredity. First, genes are arranged in a linear order with the members of a gene pair usually occupying the same relative position on homologous chromosomes (the same chromosome from different individuals). Second, recombination, or crossing over, will occur only between homologous chromosomes from each parent. Third, the frequency with which two different gene pairs will cross over together (as a bundle) is a function of how close they are on the chromosome.

**Significance**

Morgan's book was a milestone in the study of heredity and genes. Along with Mendel's research, it provided the underlying principles on which the study of genetics is based. It would move heredity from an abstract idea to reality. *The Physical Basis of Heredity* provided the first tangible link between chromosomes and observable physical traits in an organism. Thus, Morgan linked Mendelian genetics, which is the statistical analysis of the inheritance of individual traits, with genes, the carriers of those traits. Morgan was rewarded with a Nobel Prize for Medicine in 1933 for the work he published in *The Physical Basis of Heredity.*

Other major discoveries in genetics would come later. Morgan linked specific physical traits with specific genes and then linked the genes with certain chromo-

somes. Later, the chemical composition of chromosomes and genes would become known. In 1944, three scientists—Oswald Avery, Colin MacLeod, and Maclyn McCarty—discovered that DNA was the heritable factor. Then in 1953, the chemical structure of DNA was determined by James Watson and Francis Crick.

**Primary Source**

*The Physical Basis of Heredity* [excerpt]

**SYNOPSIS:** In this excerpt from *The Physical Basis of Heredity,* Morgan articulates the results of his research and experiments on the *Drosophila* fruit fly and shows the central role played by chromosomes in heredity.

**Introduction**

That the fundamental aspects of heredity should have turned out to be so extraordinarily simple supports us in the hope that nature may, after all, be entirely approachable. Her much-advertised inscrutability has once more been found to be an illusion due to our ignorance. This is encouraging, for, if the world in which we live were as complicated as some of our friends would have us believe we might well despair that biology could ever become an exact science. Personally I have no sympathy with the statement that "the problem of the method of evolution is one which the biologist finds it impossible to leave alone, although the longer he works at it, the farther its solution fades into the distance." On the contrary, the evidence of recent years and the methods by means of which this evidence is obtained have already in a reasonably short time brought us nearer to a solution of some of the important problems of evolution than seemed possible only a few years ago. That new problems and developments have arisen in the course of the work—as they are bound to do in any progressive science, as they do in chemistry and in physics for example—goes without saying, but only a spirit of obscurantism could pretend that progress of this kind means that we see the solution of our problem fading away into the distance.

Mendel left his conclusions in the form of two general laws that may be called the law of segregation and the law of independent assortment of the genes. They rest on numerical data, and are therefore quantitative and can be turned into mathematical form wherever it seems desirable. But though the statements were exact, they were left without any suggestion as to how the processes involved take place in the living organism. Even a purely mathematical formulation of the principles of segregation and of free assortment would hardly satisfy the botanist and zoölogist for long. Inevitably search would be made for the place, the time, and the means by which segregation and assortment take place, and attempts would sooner or later be made to correlate these processes with the remarkable and unique changes that take place in the germ-cells. Sutton, in 1902, was the first to point out clearly how the chromosomal mechanism, then known, supplied the necessary mechanism to account for Mendel's two laws.

The knowledge to which Sutton appealed, had been accumulating between the years 1865, when Mendel's work was published, and 1900, when its importance became generally known. An account of the chromosomal mechanism may be deferred, but I have spoken of it here in order to call attention to a point rarely appreciated, namely, that the acceptance of this mechanism at once leads to the logical conclusion that Mendel's discovery of segregation applies not only to hybrids, but also to normal processes that are taking place at all times in all animals and plants, whether hybrids or not. In consequence we find that we are dealing with a principle that concerns the actual composition of the material that carries one generation over to the next.

Segregation and independent assortment were the two fundamental principles of heredity discovered by Mendel. Since 1900, four other principles have been added. These are known as linkage, the linear order of the genes, interference, and the limitation of the linkage groups. In the same sense in which in the physical sciences it is customary to call the fundamental generalizations of the science the "laws" of that science, so we may call the foregoing generalizations, the six laws of heredity known to us at present. Despite the fact that the use of this word "law" has been much abused in popular biological writing we need not apologize for using it here, because the postulates in question have been established by the same scientific procedure that chemists and physicists make use of, viz., by deductions from quantitative data. Excepting for the sixth law they can be stated independently of the chromosomal mechanism, but on the other hand they are also the necessary outcome of that mechanism.

The theory of the constitution of the germ-plasm, to which Mendel's discoveries led him, not only failed to receive any recognition for fifty years, but the principle of particulate inheritance to which it ap-

peals has met with a curious reception even in our own time, leading a recent writer to state that particulate theories in general "do not help us in any way to solve any of the fundamental problems of biology," and another writer to affirm that if the chromatin of the sperm is "pictured" as composed of individual units that represent "some specific unit-characters of the adult," then we should expect it to be extremely complex, "more complex indeed than any chromatin in the body, since it is supposed to represent them all," but "as a matter of fact chemical examination shows the chromatin in the fish sperm to be the simplest found anywhere." Were our knowledge of the chemistry of the "chromatin" as advanced as these very positive statements might lead one to suppose, the objection raised might appear to be serious, but there is no evidence in favor of the statement that the sperm-chromatin should be expected to be more complex than the same chromatin in the cells of the embryo or adult. And even were it different in the germ-tract and soma the criticism would miss its mark, because heredity deals with the constitution of the chromatin of the germ-tract and not with that of the soma. Until physiological chemists are in position to furnish more complete information concerning the composition of the chromosomes, or more illuminating criticism of the situation as it exists, we need not, I think, be over-much troubled by such views so long as we handle our own data in a manner consonant with the recognized methods of scientific procedure.

Other critics object for one reason or another to all attempts to treat the problem of heredity from the stand-point of the factorial hypothesis. It has been said, for instance, that since the postulated genetic factors are not known chemical substances the assumption that they are such bodies is presumptuous, and gives a false analogy with chemical processes. Such critics claim that the procedure is at best only a kind of symbolism. Again, it has been said, that the factorial hypothesis is not a real scientific hypothesis, for it merely restates its facts in terms of factors, and then by juggling with numbers pretends that something is being explained. It has been argued that Mendelian phenomena relate to unnatural conditions and that they have nothing to do with the normal process of heredity in evolution that takes place in "nature." It has been objected that such a hypothesis assumes that genetic factors are fixed and stable in the same sense that molecules are stable, and that no such hard lines are to be found in the organic world. And finally it has been urged that the hypothesis rests on discontinuous variation which, it is said, does not exist.

If the implications in any or in all of these objections were true, the attempt to explain the traditional problem of heredity by the factorial hypothesis would appear fantastic in the extreme. An attempt will be made in the following chapters to present the evidence on which our present views concerning heredity rest, in the hope that an understanding of this evidence will go far towards removing these *a priori* objections, and will show that they have no real foundation in fact.

## Further Resources

### BOOKS

Allen, G. *Thomas Hunt Morgan: A Biography.* Princeton, N.J.: Princeton University Press, 1978.

Morgan, T.H. *Embryology and Genetics.* New York: Columbia University Press, 1934.

———. *The Theory of the Gene.* New Haven, Conn.: Yale University Press, 1928.

Morgan, T.H., et al. *The Genetics of the Drosophila.* New York: Garland, 1988.

Sturtevant, A.H. *A History of Genetics.* New York: Harper & Row, 1965.

### PERIODICALS

Crow, Ernest, W., and James F. Crow. "100 Years Ago: Walter Sutton and the Chromosome Theory of Heredity." *Genetics* 160, no.1, January 2002, 1–4.

Sturtevant, A.H. "Reminiscences of T.H. Morgan." *Genetics* 159, no.1, September 2001, 1–5.

### WEBSITES

"APS Library Collection: History of Genetics and Eugenics." Available online at http://www.AMPHILSOC.org/library/guides/glass/ (accessed February 16, 2003).

Lewis, Edward B. "Thomas Hunt Morgan and His Legacy." Available online at http://www.nobel.se/medicine/articles/lewis/index.html; website home page: http://www.nobel.se (accessed February 16, 2003).

"Thomas Hunt Morgan—Biography." Available online at http://www.nobel.se/medicine/laureates/1933/morgan-bio.html; website home page: http://www.nobel.se (accessed February 16, 2003).

# A General Introduction to Psycho-Analysis

Lecture

**By:** Sigmund Freud

**Date:** 1920

**Source:** Freud, Sigmund. *A General Introduction to Psycho-Analysis: A Course of Twenty-Eight Lectures Delivered at the University of Vienna.* 1920. Reprint. New York: Liveright, 1935, 17–24.

**About the Author:** Sigmund Freud (1856–1939) was born in Freiberg, Moravia (now Czechoslovakia). He was the son of a wealthy Jewish wool merchant and was raised in Vienna. Freud attended the local elementary school and attended high school from 1866 to 1873. He studied Greek and Latin, mathematics, history, and the natural sciences. A superior student, he entered the University of Vienna and received his doctor of medicine degree. Freud was a physically small man. He loved to read, travel, and was a collector of archeological oddities. He valued the companionship of friends and enjoyed playing cards. Freud married Martha Bernays in 1887, and they had six children. ■

## Introduction

*A General Introduction to Psycho-Analysis* contains twenty-eight lectures Freud delivered to psychology students at the University of Vienna during the period 1915–1917. These lectures constituted the first textbook on the theory of psychoanalysis.

Freud's psychoanalytic theory grew out of his treatment of neurotic patients as well as his own self-analysis. His theory was based on the influence that unconscious thoughts, impulses, and desires have on behavior. He theorized that we commonly repress our unconscious thoughts because they are sexual or aggressive but that these thoughts are revealed by dreams, emotions, or slips of the tongue (Freudian slips). Freud believed that unsatisfied libido is the root cause of neurosis and that libido lies beneath all normal human mechanisms. Libido generally refers to sexual desire, but Freud considered libido in very broad terms to signify all tender feelings and emotions in addition to physical expression.

As a part of the theory of psychoanalysis, Freud developed a method, or therapy, for treating "nervous disorders." The method involves digging down into the hidden depths of the psyche to bring to the surface the unconscious tendencies that lie behind behavior. The aim of the method is, as Freud says, to "change something unconscious into something conscious." Freud believed that if a person became aware of repressed thoughts and feelings, the symptoms of neuroses would cease. Today, when people refer to "psychoanalysis," they often mean the method Freud developed to treat neurosis. However, psychoanalysis properly refers to both the treatment and the theory underlying it.

In the first of the lectures in *A General Introduction to Psycho-Analysis,* Freud warned students of the difficulties inherent in the field of psychoanalysis. Many of the difficulties had to do with the subjective nature of psychoanalysis. In the first two decades of the twentieth century, mainstream psychology was leaning toward the behaviorist school of thought, which was objective, scientific, and experimental. Freud's psychoanalytic theory departed as far from this as is possible. As a result, Freud's theory was at first unpopular and was attacked. Freud alludes to this overt resistance to psychoanalysis when he tells his students, "not only would the choice of such a career (as a psychoanalyst) put an end to all chances of academic success, but, upon taking up work as a practitioner, such a man would find himself in a community which misunderstood his aims and intentions, regarded him with suspicion and hostility, and let loose upon him all the latent evil impulses harbored within it."

## Significance

Psychoanalysis is regarded by many scholars as one of the most significant intellectual developments of the twentieth century. Many of Freud's concepts as presented in *A General Introduction to Psycho-Analysis,* which were met with antagonism in the early twentieth century, are now widely accepted. Freud was the first to recognize the importance of unconscious influences on human behavior. Through his work with his patients and through his own self-analysis, he showed that many factors which influence thoughts and behavior exist in the unconscious, outside of awareness.

The development of psychoanalysis has had an enormous impact on the field of psychology. Freud's theory captivated and spawned many new psychologists. Psychologists such as Erich Fromm, Karen Horney, and Freud's daughter Anna followed after Freud and applied his core principles in their work. Hence, they are called Neo-Freudians. Other psychologists believed in the general outline of Freud's theory but disagreed with many of its basic principles. Most notable of the latter group was Carl Jung, who was one of Freud's students. Jung's chief disagreement was with the principle that libido, or sexual desire, lies beneath all normal human mechanisms. Jung felt that the underlying stimulus of behavior was much larger and encompassing than libido.

Psychoanalysis has had a significant impact on society in general. Freud's theories captured the imagination of Americans throughout the twentieth century. Many concepts in *A General Introduction to Psycho-Analysis* have become securely embedded in American thought and culture: the ego, repression, the Oedipal complex, and Freudian slips.

Psychoanalysis has continued to grow and develop as a general psychological theory. Psychoanalysts today still look to the power of the unconscious in unlocking the underlying reasons behind human behavior. Current psychologists view the psychoanalytic theory as a sophisticated tool for increasing self-awareness and freeing patients from suffering.

## Primary Source

*A General Introduction to Psycho-Analysis* [excerpt]

**SYNOPSIS:** In the first of a series of lectures, Freud discusses the specifics of his psychoanalytic theory and warns his audience about the difficulties to be expected and some of the misconceptions typically encountered with regard to his approach.

### First Lecture

#### Introduction

I do not know what knowledge any of you may already have of psycho-analysis, either from reading or from hearsay. But having regard to the title of my lectures—Introductory Lectures on Psycho-Analysis—I am bound to proceed as though you knew nothing of the subject and needed instruction, even in its first elements.

One thing, at least, I may pre-suppose that you know—namely, that psycho-analysis is a method of medical treatment for those suffering from nervous disorders; and I can give you at once an illustration of the way in which psycho-analytic procedure differs from, and often even reverses, what is customary in other branches of medicine. Usually, when we introduce a patient to a new form of treatment we minimize its difficulties and give him confident assurances of its success. This is, in my opinion, perfectly justifiable, for we thereby increase the probability of success. But when we undertake to treat a neurotic psycho-analytically we proceed otherwise. We explain to him the difficulties of the method, its long duration, the trials and sacrifices which will be required of him; and, as to the result, we tell him that we can make no definite promises, that success depends upon his endeavours, upon his understanding, his adaptability and his perseverance. We have, of course, good reasons, into which you will perhaps gain some insight later on, for adopting this apparently perverse attitude.

Now forgive me if I begin by treating you in the same way as I do my neurotic patients, for I shall positively advise you against coming to hear me a second time. And with this intention I shall explain to you how of necessity you can obtain from me only an incomplete knowledge of psycho-analysis and also what difficulties stand in the way of your forming an independent judgment on the subject. For I shall show you how the whole trend of your training and your accustomed modes of thought must inevitably have made you hostile to psycho-analysis, and also how much you would have to overcome in

Sigmund Freud's study, where much of his early psychoanalytic work took place. ARCHIVE PHOTOS, INC. REPRODUCED BY PERMISSION.

your own minds in order to master this instinctive opposition. I naturally cannot foretell what degree of understanding of psycho-analysis you may gain from my lectures, but I can at least assure you that by attending them you will not have learnt how to conduct a psycho-analytic investigation, nor how to carry out a psycho-analytic treatment. And further, if any one of you should feel dissatisfied with a merely cursory acquaintance with psycho-analysis and should wish to form a permanent connection with it, I shall not merely discourage him, but I shall actually warn him against it. For as things are at the present time, not only would the choice of such a career put an end to all chances of academic success, but, upon taking up work as a practitioner, such a man would find himself in a community which misunderstood his aims and intentions, regarded him with suspicion and hostility, and let loose upon him all the latent evil impulses harboured within it. Perhaps you can infer from the accompaniments of the war now raging in Europe what a countless host that is to reckon with.

However, there are always some people to whom the possibility of a new addition to knowledge will prove an attraction strong enough to survive all such

inconveniences. If there are any such among you who will appear at my second lecture in spite of my words of warning they will be welcome. But all of you have a right to know what these inherent difficulties of psycho-analysis are to which I have alluded.

First of all, there is the problem of the teaching and exposition of the subject. In your medical studies you have been accustomed to use your eyes. You see the anatomical specimen, the precipitate of the chemical reaction, the contraction of the muscle as the result of the stimulation of its nerves. Later you come into contact with the patients; you learn the symptoms of disease by the evidence of your senses; the results of pathological processes can be demonstrated to you, and in many cases even the exciting cause of them in an isolated form. On the surgical side you are witnesses of the measures by which the patient is helped, and are permitted to attempt them yourselves. Even in psychiatry, demonstration of patients, of their altered expression, speech and behaviour, yields a series of observations which leave a deep impression on your minds. Thus a teacher of medicine acts for the most part as an exponent and guide, leading you as it were through a museum, while you gain in this way a direct relationship to what is displayed to you and believe yourselves to have been convinced by your own experience of the existence of the new facts.

But in psycho-analysis, unfortunately, all this is different. In psycho-analytic treatment nothing happens but an exchange of words between the patient and the physician. The patient talks, tells of his past experiences and present impressions, complains, and expresses his wishes and his emotions. The physician listens, attempts to direct the patient's thought-processes, reminds him, forces his attention in certain directions, gives him explanations and observes the reactions of understanding or denial thus evoked. The patient's unenlightened relatives—people of a kind to be impressed only by something visible and tangible, preferably by the sort of 'action' that may be seen at a cinema—never omit to express their doubts of how "mere talk can possibly cure anybody." Their reasoning is of course as illogical as it is inconsistent. For they are the same people who are always convinced that the sufferings of neurotics are purely "in their own imagination." Words and magic were in the beginning one and the same thing, and even to-day words retain much of their magical power. By words one of us can give to another the greatest happiness or bring about utter despair; by words the teacher imparts his knowledge to the student; by words the orator sweeps his audience with him and determines its judgements and decisions. Words call forth emotions and are universally the means by which we influence our fellow-creatures. Therefore let us not despise the use of words in psycho-therapy and let us be content if we may overhear the words which pass between the analyst and the patient.

But even that is impossible. The dialogue which constitutes the analysis will admit of no audience; the process cannot be demonstrated. One could, of course, exhibit a neurasthenic or hysterical patient to students at a psychiatric lecture. He would relate his case and his symptoms, but nothing more. He will make the communications necessary to the analysis only under the conditions of a special affective relationship to the physician; in the presence of a single person to whom he was indifferent he would become mute. For these communications relate to all his most private thoughts and feelings, all that which as a socially independent person he must hide from others, all that which, being foreign to his own conception of himself, he tries to conceal even from himself.

It is impossible, therefore, for you to be actually present during a psycho-analytic treatment; you can only be told about it, and can learn psycho-analysis, in the strictest sense of the word, only by hearsay. This tuition at second hand, so to say, puts you in a very unusual and difficult position as regards forming your own judgement on the subject, which will therefore largely depend on the reliance you can place on your informant.

Now imagine for a moment that you were present at a lecture in history instead of in psychiatry, and that the lecturer was dealing with the life and conquests of Alexander the Great. What reason would you have to believe what he told you? The situation would appear at first sight even more unsatisfactory than in the case of psycho-analysis, for the professor of history had no more part in Alexander's campaigns than you yourselves; the psycho-analyst at least informs you of matters in which he himself has played a part. But then we come to the question of what evidence there is to support the historian. He can refer you to the accounts of early writers who were either contemporaries or who lived not long after the events in question, such as Diodorus, Plutarch, Arrian, and others; he can lay before you reproductions of the preserved coins and statues of the king, and pass round a photograph of the mosaic at Pompeii representing the battle at Issus. Yet, strictly speaking, all these documents only prove that the existence of Alexander and the reality of his deeds were already believed in by former generations of men, and your criticism might begin anew at this point. And then you would find that not everything reported of Alexander is worthy of belief or sufficiently authenticated in detail, but I can hardly suppose that you would leave the lecture-room in doubt altogether as to the reality of Alexander the Great. Your conclusions would be principally determined by two considerations: first, that the lecturer could have no conceivable motive for attempting to persuade you of something which he did not himself believe to be true, and secondly, that all the available authorities agree more or less in their accounts of the facts. In questioning the accuracy of the early writers you would apply these tests again, the possible motives of the authors and the agreement to be found between them. The result of such tests would certainly be convincing in the case of Alexander, probably less so in regard to figures like Moses and Nimrod. Later on you will perceive clearly enough what doubts can be raised against the credibility of an exponent of psycho-analysis.

Now you will have a right to ask the question: If no objective evidence for psycho-analysis exists and no possibility of demonstrating the process, how is it possible to study it at all or to convince oneself of its truth? The study of it is indeed not an easy matter, nor are there many people who have thoroughly learned it; still, there is, of course, some way of learning it. Psycho-analysis is learnt first of all on oneself, through the study of one's own personality. This is not exactly what is meant by introspection, but it may be so described for want of a better word. There is a whole series of very common and well-known mental phenomena which can be taken as material for self-analysis when one has acquired some knowledge of the method. In this way one may obtain the required conviction of the reality of the processes which psycho-analysis describes, and of the truth of its conceptions, although progress on these lines is not without its limitations. One gets much further by submitting oneself to analysis by a skilled analyst, undergoing the working of the analysis in one's own person and using the opportunity to observe the finer details of the technique which the analyst employs. This, eminently the best way, is of course only practicable for individuals and cannot be used in a class of students.

The second difficulty you will find in connection with psycho-analysis is not, on the other hand, inherent in it, but is one for which I must hold you yourselves responsible, at least in so far as your medical studies have influenced you. Your training will have induced in you an attitude of mind very far removed from the psycho-analytical one. You have been trained to establish the functions and disturbances of the organism on an anatomical basis, to explain them in terms of chemistry and physics, and to regard them from a biological point of view; but no part of your interest has ever been directed to the mental aspects of life, in which, after all, the development of the marvellously complicated organism culminates. For this reason a psychological attitude of mind is still foreign to you, and you are accustomed to regard it with suspicion, to deny it a scientific status, and to leave it to the general public, poets, mystics, and philosophers. Now this limitation in you is undoubtedly detrimental to your medical efficiency; for on meeting a patient it is the mental aspects with which one first comes into contact, as in most human relationships, and I am afraid you will pay the penalty of having to yield a part of the curative influence at which you aim to the quacks, mystics, and faith-healers whom you despise.

I quite acknowledge that there is an excuse for this defect in your previous training. There is no auxiliary philosophical science that might be of service to you in your profession. Neither speculative philosophy nor descriptive psychology, nor even the so-called experimental psychology which is studied in connection with the physiology of the sense-organs, as they are taught in the schools, can tell you anything useful of the relations existing between mind and body, or can give you a key to comprehension of a possible disorder of the mental functions. It is true that the psychiatric branch of medicine occupies itself with describing the different forms of recognizable mental disturbances and grouping them in clinical pictures, but in their best moments psychiatrists themselves are doubtful whether their purely descriptive formulations deserve to be called science. The origin, mechanism, and interrelation of the symptoms which make up these clinical pictures are undiscovered: either they cannot be correlated with any demonstrable changes in the brain, or only with such changes as in no way explain them. These mental disturbances are open to therapeutic influence only when they can be identified as secondary effects of some organic disease.

This is the lacuna which psycho-analysis is striving to fill. It hopes to provide psychiatry with the missing psychological foundation, to discover the common ground on which a correlation of bodily and mental disorder becomes comprehensible. To this end it must dissociate itself from every foreign preconception, whether anatomical, chemical, or physiological, and must work throughout with conceptions of a purely psychological order, and for this very reason I fear that it will appear strange to you at first.

For the next difficulty I shall not hold you, your training or your mental attitude, responsible. There are two tenets of psycho-analysis which offend the whole world and excite its resentment; the one conflicts with intellectual, the other with moral and æsthetic prejudices. Let us not underestimate these prejudices; they are powerful things, residues of valuable, even necessary, stages in human evolution. They are maintained by emotional forces, and the fight against them is a hard one.

The first of these displeasing propositions of psycho-analysis is this: that mental processes are essentially unconscious, and that those which are conscious are merely isolated acts and parts of the whole psychic entity. Now I must ask you to remember that, on the contrary, we are accustomed to identify the mental with the conscious. Consciousness appears to us as positively the characteristic that defines mental life, and we regard psychology as the study of the content of consciousness. This even appears so evident that any contradiction of it seems obvious nonsense to us, and yet it is impossible for psycho-analysis to avoid this contradiction, or to accept the identity between the conscious and the psychic. The psycho-analytical definition of the mind is that it comprises processes of the nature of feeling, thinking, and wishing, and it maintains that there are such things as unconscious thinking and unconscious wishing. But in doing so psycho-analysis has forfeited at the outset the sympathy of the sober and scientifically minded, and incurred the suspicion of being a fantastic cult occupied with dark and unfathomable mysteries. [Literally: "that wishes to build in the dark and fish in murky waters."—Tr.] You yourselves must find it difficult to understand why I should stigmatize an abstract proposition, such as "The psychic is the conscious," as a prejudice; nor can you guess yet what evolutionary process could have led to the denial of the unconscious, if it does indeed exist, nor what advantage could have been achieved by this denial. It seems like an empty wrangle over words to argue whether mental life is to be regarded as co-extensive with consciousness or whether it may be said to stretch beyond this limit, and yet I can assure you that the acceptance of unconscious mental processes represents a decisive step towards a new orientation in the world and in science.

As little can you suspect how close is the connection between this first bold step on the part of psycho-analysis and the second to which I am now coming. For this next proposition, which we put forward as one of the discoveries of psycho-analysis, consists in the assertion that impulses, which can only be described as sexual in both the narrower and the wider sense, play a peculiarly large part, never before sufficiently appreciated, in the causation of nervous and mental disorders. Nay, more, that these sexual impulses have contributed invaluably to the highest cultural, artistic, and social achievements of the human mind.

In my opinion, it is the aversion from this conclusion of psycho-analytic investigation that is the most significant source of the opposition it has encountered. Are you curious to know how we ourselves account for this? We believe that civilization has been built up, under the pressure of the struggle for existence, by sacrifices in gratification of the primitive impulses, and that it is to a great extent for ever being re-created, as each individual, successively joining the community, repeats the sacrifice of his instinctive pleasures for the common good. The sexual are amongst the most important of the instinctive forces thus utilized: they are in this way sublimated, that is to say, their energy is turned aside from its sexual goal and diverted towards other ends, no longer sexual and socially more valuable. But the structure thus built up is insecure, for the sexual impulses are with difficulty controlled; in each individual who takes up his part in the work of civilization there is a danger that a rebellion of the sexual impulses may occur, against this diversion of their energy. Society can conceive of no more powerful menace to its culture than would arise from the liberation of the sexual impulses and a return of them to their original goal. Therefore society dislikes this sensitive place in its development being touched upon; that the power of the sexual instinct should be recognized, and the significance of the individual's sexual life revealed, is very far from its interests; with a view to discipline it has rather taken the course of diverting attention away from this whole field. For this reason, the revelations of psycho-analysis are not tolerated by it, and it would greatly prefer to brand them as æsthetically offensive, morally reprehensible, or dangerous. But since such objections are not valid arguments against conclusions which claim to represent the objective results of scientific investigation, the opposition must be translated into intellectual terms before it can be expressed. It is a characteristic of human nature to be inclined to regard anything which is disagreeable as untrue, and then without much difficulty to find arguments against it. So society pronounces the unacceptable to be untrue, disputes the results of psycho-analysis with logical and concrete arguments, arising, however, in affective sources, and clings to them with all the strength of prejudice against every attempt at refutation.

But we, on the other hand, claim to have yielded to no tendency in propounding this objectionable theory. Our intention has been solely to give recognition to the facts as we found them in the course of painstaking researches. And we now claim the right to reject unconditionally any such introduction of practical considerations into the field of scientific investigation, even before we have determined whether the apprehension which attempts to force these considerations upon us is justified or not.

These, now, are some of the difficulties which confront you at the outset when you begin to take an interest in psycho-analysis. It is probably more than enough for a beginning. If you can overcome their discouraging effect, we will proceed further.

## Further Resources

### BOOKS

Bettelheim, Bruno. *Freud and Man's Soul.* New York: Knopf, 1982.

Cavell, M. *The Psychoanalytic Mind: From Freud to Philosophy.* Cambridge, Mass.: Harvard University Press, 1993.

Frosh, S. *The Politics of Psychoanalysis: An Introduction to Freudian and Post-Freudian Theory.* New Haven, Conn.: Yale University Press, 1987.

Jones, E. *Sigmund Freud: Life and Work.* 3 vols. New York: Basic Books, 1953–1957.

Vaughan, Susan. *The Talking Cure: The Science Behind Psychotherapy.* New York: Putnam's Sons, 1997.

### WEBSITES

Freud Museum—London. Available online at http://www.freud .org.uk/ (accessed May 15, 2003).

Library of Congress. "Sigmund Freud—Conflict and Culture." Available online at http://www.loc.gov/exhibits/freud/; website home page: http://www.loc.gov/ (accessed May 15, 2003).

The New York Freudian Society. Available online at http:// www.nyfreudian.org (accessed February 16, 2003).

Sigmund Freud and the Freud Archives. Available online at http://users.rcn.com/brill/freudarc.html (accessed February 16, 2003).

# 12

# SPORTS

COREY SEEMAN

*Entries are arranged in chronological order by date of primary source. For entries with one primary source, the entry title is the same as the primary source title. Entries with more than one primary source have an overall entry title, followed by the titles of the primary sources.*

**CHRONOLOGY**

Important Events in Sports, 1910–1919 . . . . . . . . 562

**PRIMARY SOURCES**

"University Athletics"
  Simon Newcomb, 1907 . . . . . . . . . . . . . . . . . 566

"Johnson Wins in 15 Rounds; Jeffries Weak"
  John L. Sullivan, July 5, 1910 . . . . . . . . . . . . 570

"Burman Lowers Speedway Records"
  *The New York Times*, May 30, 1911 . . . . . . . . 574

"Are Athletics Making Girls Masculine?"
  Dudley A. Sargent, March 1912 . . . . . . . . . . . 577

"The Amateur"
  Lyman Abbott, Hamilton W. Mabie, and
    Theodore Roosevelt, February 8, 1913 . . . . . . 581

"Baseball and the National Life"
  Henry Addington Bruce, May 17, 1913 . . . . . . . 585

"Ouimet World's Golf Champion"
  *The New York Times*, September 21, 1913 . . . . . 591

Page from George Weiss's scrapbook
  George Weiss, 1916 . . . . . . . . . . . . . . . . . . . 595

*You Know Me Al: A Busher's Letters*
  Ring Lardner, 1916 . . . . . . . . . . . . . . . . . . . . 597

*Girls and Athletics*
  Mary C. Morgan, 1917 . . . . . . . . . . . . . . . . . 600

Memorandum to Colonel Bruce Palmer,
  Elwood S. Brown, October 15, 1918 . . . . . . . . 603

*Basket Ball: for Coach, Player and
  Spectator*
  E.D. Angell, 1918 . . . . . . . . . . . . . . . . . . . . 607

"Boxers Spend Last Night Under Guard"
  George R. Pulford, July 4, 1919 . . . . . . . . . . . 611

*Pioneer in Pro Football*
  Jack Cusack, 1963 . . . . . . . . . . . . . . . . . . . . 614

Interview with Edd Roush
  Edd Roush, 1966 . . . . . . . . . . . . . . . . . . . . . 619

# Important Events in Sports, 1910–1919

## 1910

- On March 16, Barney Oldfield driving a Benz automobile sets a new land speed record of 131.7 mph at Daytona Beach, Florida.

- On April 14, William Howard Taft becomes the first president to throw out the first ball of the baseball season at a game between the Washington Senators and the Philadelphia Athletics.

- On April 7, Jack Johnson successfully defends his world heavyweight boxing title against Jim Jeffries in a fifteenth-round technical knockout.

- On April 19, Fred L. Cameron of Amherst, Nova Scotia, wins the fourteenth Boston Marathon in 2:28:52.

- On May 7, Jockey R. Estep rides Layminster to victory in the thirty-fifth annual Preakness Stakes.

- On May 10, Robert Herbert rides Donau to victory in the thirty-sixth annual Kentucky Derby.

- On May 19, Cy Young earns his 500th career victory, beating the Washington Senators 5–4 in eleven innings.

- On May 30, Jimmy Butwell rides Sweep to victory in the forty-third annual Belmont Stakes.

- On June 18, Alex Smith wins the U.S. Open golf tournament in an eighteen-hole playoff after regulation play had ended in a three-way tie with Smith, John J. McDermott, and McDonald Smith.

- On June 26, Hazel Hotchkiss wins the women's singles at the U.S. Lawn Tennis Association Championship.

- On September 2, William A. Larned wins the men's singles at the U.S. Lawn Tennis Association Championship.

- From October 17 to October 23, the Philadelphia Athletics win the World Series, defeating the Chicago Cubs four games to one.

## 1911

- On April 19, Clarence H. DeMar, defying doctor's orders not to race because of a heart murmur, wins the fifteenth annual Boston Marathon in the record time of 2:21:39. DeMar, who would not race again until 1917, would win the event six more times.

- On May 13, Meridian, ridden by jockey George Archibald, wins the Kentucky Derby.

- On May 30, Ray Harroun driving a six-cylinder Marmon Wasp wins the first Indianapolis 500 automobile race with an average speed of 74.59 mph.

- On June 17, Hazel Hotchkiss repeats as the women's singles champion of the U.S. Lawn Tennis Association Championship.

- On June 24, John J. McDermott wins the U.S. Open golf tournament, defeating Michael Brady and George Simpson in a play-off round to become the first American-born champion.

- On September 3, William A. Larned becomes the oldest men's singles champion by winning the U.S. Lawn Tennis Association Championship.

- From October 14 to October 26, the Philadelphia Athletics win the World Series, defeating the New York Giants four games to two.

- On November 11, in one of the greatest upsets in gridiron history, the unranked Carlisle Indian School football team, led by Jim Thorpe, defeats the powerhouse Harvard University team 18–15.

## 1912

- Robert A. Gardner of Yale University becomes first pole vaulter to surpass 13′ with a vault of 13′1′.

- The Amateur Fencers League of America holds its first women's national fencing championship, won by Adelaide Baylis. The women's competition is limited to foils only.

- On February 9, the U.S. Lawn Tennis Association rules that the defending men's singles champion must play through the entire tournament rather than gaining a bye until the challenger was decided.

- On February 22, in San Francisco, Johnny Kilbane outpoints Abe Attell in twenty rounds for the world featherweight boxing title.

- On April 11, Rube Marquard and the New York Giants defeat the Brooklyn Dodgers 18-3, the first of Marquard's nineteen consecutive wins that season.

- On April 19, Michael J. Ryan of New York City smashes Clarence DeMar's year-old record by twenty-one seconds to win the sixteenth annual Boston Marathon in 2:21:18.

- On April 20, Fenway Park opens in Boston. In the first game played in the new stadium, the Red Sox defeat the New York Highlanders 7–6 before a crowd of 27,000.

- On April 20, Tiger Stadium opens in Detroit. However, baseball has been played at that location since 1896, five years before the Tigers or the American League existed.

- On May 5, the 1912 Olympic Games begin in Stockholm, Sweden. The Americans won twenty-three events, including Jim Thorpe's victories in the decathlon and pentathlon

- On May 11, Carroll Hugh Shilling rides Worth to victory in the Kentucky Derby.

- George Horine of Stanford University sets a world record of 6′ 7′ in the high jump using the newly developed western roll technique.

- On May 30, Joe Dawson wins the Indianapolis 500 and a purse of twenty thousand dollars, averaging 78.72 mph.

- On July 20, at the Stockholm Olympics, Hawaiian swimmer Duke Kahanamoku establishes a world record of 61.2 seconds in the 100-meter freestyle.

- On August 2, John J. McDermott wins the U.S. Open golf tournament.

- On August 26, in the U.S. Lawn Tennis Association Championships, Maurice E. McLoughlin wins the men's title and Mary K. Browne wins the women's.

- On September 7, Eddie Collins of Philadelphia Athletics steals six bases against the Detroit Tigers, a post-1900 record. On September 22, he repeats the feat against the St. Louis Browns.

- On October 8, the Boston Red Sox win the World Series, defeating the New York Giants four games to three.

- On November 9, the Carlisle Indian School football team, led by Jim Thorpe's twenty-two points, defeats Army 27–6. The Army defense, which included future President Dwight Eisenhower, only gave up a total of thirty-three points in its other seven games that year.

- On November 28, Willie Ritchie wins the world lightweight boxing title in sixteen rounds on a foul by Ad Wolgast in San Francisco.

## 1913

- On February 5, the New York State Athletic Commission votes unanimously to prohibit interracial boxing competition, in part because of racial disturbances caused by the victory of Jack Johnson, an African American fighter, over former champion Jim Jeffries.

- On March 5, Frank Klaus wins the world middleweight title over Billy Papke in fifteen rounds.

- On April 19, the Swedish-born Fritz Carlson of Minneapolis wins the seventeenth Boston Marathon in 2:25:14.

- On May 10, Roscoe Goose rides Donerail, a 91–1 long shot, to victory in the Kentucky Derby.

- On May 15, Walter Johnson of the Washington Senators sees his fifty-six consecutive scoreless innings streak end against the St. Louis Browns.

- On May 26, the International Olympic Committee strips Jim Thorpe of his medals in the 1912 games. Thorpe had played professional baseball prior to the Olympics.

- On May 30, Jules Goux of France wins the third annual Indianapolis 500, averaging 75.93 mph.

- On June 13, Mary K. Browne wins the women's title at the U.S. Lawn Tennis Association Championship.

- On July 18, Christy Mathewson of the New York Giants sees his streak of sixty-eight consecutive innings without allowing a base on balls end. The record is not broken until 1962 by Chicago White Sox pitcher Bill Fisher.

- From July 25 to July 28, the United States wins the Davis Cup for the first time since 1902, defeating Great Britain three matches to two.

- On August 14, the "California Comet" Maurice E. McLoughlin wins the men's title at the U.S. Lawn Tennis Association Championship.

- In September, Coal magnate James A. Gilmore becomes president of the minor Federal League and plans to challenge the National and American Leagues for the best baseball players.

- On September 20, Francis Ouimet, a twenty-year-old amateur, defeats two British professionals, Harry Vardon and Ted Ray, in an eighteen-hole play-off round to win the U.S. Open golf tournament.

- From October 7 to October 11, the Philadelphia Athletics win the World Series, defeating the New York Giants four games to one.

- On November 1, the first Army-Notre Dame game is played, with the Irish winning 35–13.

- On December 23, George Chip knocks out Frank Klaus in five rounds to win the world middleweight title in Pittsburgh.

## 1914

- On March 21, in the first U.S. Figure Skating Championship Norman N. Scott of Montreal, Canada, wins the men's division, Theresa Weld of Boston wins the women's division, and Jeannie Chevalier and Scott win the pair's competition.

- On March 30, the Portland, Oregon Rosebuds, the first American professional hockey team, lose to the Montreal Canadiens in the Stanley Cup Finals.

- On April 7, in Brooklyn Al McCoy knocks out George Chip in the first round for the world middleweight title.

- On April 13, after constructing eight new stadiums in three months, the Federal League opens with the Baltimore Terrapins defeating Buffalo 3–2 before 27,140 fans.

- On April 20, James Duffy of Hamilton, Ontario, wins the eighteenth Boston Marathon in 2:25:01.

- On May 5, E. G. "Cannonball" Baker, riding his V-twin 1000c Stutz Indian motorcycle, begins his cross-country trip. He completes the journey in 11 days, 12 hours, 10 minutes.

- On May 9, John McCabe rides Old Rosebud to victory in the fortieth annual Kentucky Derby.

- On May 16, the Grand League of American Horseshoe Players Association organizes in Kansas City, Kansas, and standardizes equipment, procedures, and rules for the sport.

- On May 30, Rene Thomas, averaging 82.47 mph, wins the fourth annual Indianapolis 500.

- On June 9, Kid Williams takes the world bantamweight title by knocking out Johnny Coulon in three rounds in Los Angeles, California.

- On June 19, Honus Wagner of the Pittsburgh Pirates collects his 3,000th hit.

- On July 4, eight men from Harvard win the Grand Challenge Cup at the Henley Royal Regatta in England, marking the first victory of an American crew in the event. The Union Boat Club of Boston takes second place.

- On July 11, twenty-year old George Herman "Babe" Ruth of the Boston Red Sox debuts as a pitcher, beating Cleveland 4–3.

- On August 15, Australia defeats the United States in Davis Cup competition, three matches to two.

- On August 21, twenty-one year old Walter Hagen wins the U.S. Open golf tournament, defeating amateur Charles Evans Jr.

- On September 1, Mary K. Browne wins the women's division of the U.S. Lawn Tennis Association Championship, and Richard Norris Williams wins the men's title.

- On September 22, Cleveland Indian Nap Lajoie collects his 3,000th hit against St. Louis.

- From October 9 to October 13, the Boston Braves, who had risen from last place to win the pennant, defeated the Philadelphia Athletics four games to none in the World Series.

- On November 21, the Yale Bowl, a new stadium capable of accommodating sixty-one thousand spectators, opens in New Haven, Connecticut.

## 1915

- Most Valuable Player Ty Cobb sets a major league record of 96 stolen bases in a season, which stood until Maury Wills stole 104 bases in 1962.

- On April 5, Jess Willard knocks out Jack Johnson in the twenty-sixth round for the world heavyweight boxing championship in Havana, Cuba.

- On April 19, Edouard Fabre of Montreal, Canada, wins the nineteenth annual Boston Marathon in 2:31:41.

- On May 6, Babe Ruth hits the first home run of his career against the New York Yankees at the Polo Grounds.

- On May 8, Joe Notter rides Regret to victory in the forty-first Kentucky Derby.

- On May 31, Ralph De Palma, averaging 89.84 mph, wins the fifth annual Indianapolis 500.

- On June 12, Molla Bjurstedt Mallory, a Norwegian, wins the women's division of the U.S. Lawn Tennis Association Championship. She is the first non-American to win the title.

- On June 18, Jerome D. Travers becomes the second amateur to win the U.S. Open golf tournament.

- On July 16, Norman Taber establishes a world record of 4:12.6 for the mile.

- On July 27, the American Lawn Bowls Association organizes in Buffalo, New York.

- On September 8, William M. Johnston wins the men's division of the U.S. Lawn Tennis Association Championship. The event moves from Newport, Rhode Island, to the West Side Tennis Club in Forest Hills, New York.

- In fall, football teams from Toledo, Youngstown, Akron, and Dayton join Canton, Massillon, and Columbus in the Ohio League. The league champion was unofficially recognized as the world champion of professional football. In 1922, the league became the National Football League (NFL).

- From October 8 to October 13, the Boston Red Sox win the World Series, defeating the Philadelphia Phillies four games to one.

- On December 21, U.S. District Court Judge Kenesaw Mountain Landis rules against the Federal League in its antitrust suit against the American and National Leagues. The Federal League goes out of existence as its star players sign with its older competitors.

## 1916

- On January 1, in the second Tournament of Roses Association football game (first played in 1902), Washington State University defeats Brown University 14–0.

- On January 17, the Professional Golfers' Association (PGA) is organized.

- On April 1, the Amateur Athletic Union (AAU) holds both the first women's indoor and outdoor national swimming championships.

- On April 19, Arthur V. Roth of Roxbury, Massachusetts wins the Boston Marathon in 2:27:16.

- On April 20, the Chicago Cubs play the first game in Weeghman Park. The park was renamed Wrigley Field in 1926.

- On May 13, Johnny Loftus rides George Smith to victory in the Kentucky Derby.

- On May 30, Dario Resta, averaging 84 mph, wins the Indianapolis 500, the distance of which was reduced to three hundred miles. The race is not held in 1917 and 1918 because of World War I.

- On June 12, Molla Bjurstedt Mallory wins the women's division of the U.S. Lawn Tennis Association Championship.

- On June 30, Charles "Chick" Evans Jr., an amateur, wins the U.S. Open golf tournament. His 286 total stood as a record until 1936. Competition was suspended because of World War I and resumed in 1919.

- On July 30, *The New York Times* reports that women golfers are allowed only restricted access to most courses in New York and New Jersey.

- On September 6, Richard Norris Williams wins the men's division of the U.S. Lawn Tennis Association Championship.

- On September 30, the Boston Braves took the second game of a double header from the New York Giants 8–3, ending the longest winning streak in major league baseball history at twenty-six games.

- On October 7, Georgia Tech defeats Cumberland College of Lebanon, Tennessee, 222–0, the most lopsided college football game in history.

- From October 7 to October 12, the Boston Red Sox win the World Series, defeating the Brooklyn Dodgers four games to one.

- On October 24, in Boston "Battling Levinsky" outpoints Jack Dillon in twelve rounds to win the world light heavyweight boxing title.

- On November 29, the Women's National Bowling Association organizes in St. Louis.

- On December 21, *The New York Times* reports rapid growth in trapshooting. The sport attracts 675,000 participants, members of some five thousand clubs nationwide, who spend $12 million a year on ammunition.

## 1917

- On January 1, the University of Oregon defeats the University of Pennsylvania, 14–0, in the third annual Rose Bowl.

- The Seattle Metropolitans capture the Stanley Cup, the first U.S. professional hockey team to accomplish the feat, when they defeat the Montreal Canadiens.

- On April 19, the thirty-five year old bricklayer William K. Kennedy is the oldest person to date to win the Boston Marathon in 2:28:37.

- On May 2, Jim Vaughn of the Chicago Cubs and Fred Toney of the Cincinnati Reds pitch no-hitters for nine innings against each other. The Reds win in the tenth inning 1-0 when the Cubs commit two errors.

- On May 12, Charles Borel rides Omar Khayyam to victory in the forty-third annual Kentucky Derby.

- On May 28, Benny Leonard wins the lightweight boxing championship, knocking out British title-holder Freddy Welsh in the ninth round of a bout in New York City. Leonard held the title until he retired in 1924. He fought 209 times and lost only five bouts in his career.

- On May 31, the Indianapolis 500 is cancelled due to World War I.

- On June 23, Molla Bjurstedt Mallory wins the women's title at the U.S. Lawn Tennis Association Championship.

- On June 23, Babe Ruth is ejected from the game for protesting a call that walked the lead off batter. Eddie Shore replaces Ruth and throws a no-hitter.

- On August 19, John McGraw, manager of the New York Giants, and Christy Mathewson, manager of the Cincinnati Reds, are arrested when their teams violate a New York prohibition against playing baseball on Sunday.

- From October 6 to October 15, the Chicago White Sox win the World Series, defeating the New York Giants four games to two.

- On November 14, Mike O'Dowd knocks out Al McCoy in six rounds for the middleweight boxing title in Brooklyn

## 1918

- On January 1, the Mare Island Marines defeat the Camp Lewis Army Team, 19–7, in the fourth annual Rose Bowl.

- On March 7, in the U.S. Figure Skating Championships, Nathaniel W. Niles of Boston wins the men's singles division and the pairs division with Theresa Weld of Boston. Rosemary Beresford of Great Britain wins the women's singles division.

- On May 11, Willie Knapp rides Exterminator to victory in the Kentucky Derby.

- On May 15, the forty-third annual Preakness Stakes is run in two sections. The first is won by War Cloud, with a time of 1:53.6. The jockey was Johnny Loftus. The second is won by Jack Hare Jr., with a time of 1:53.4. The jockey was C. Peak.

- On June 22, Molla Bjurstedt Mallory wins the women's title at the U.S. Lawn Tennis Association Championship.

- On August 2, Secretary of War Newton D. Baker orders major league baseball to end its season on September 1 but permits the World Series to be played.

- On September 3, Robert Lindley Murray wins the men's title of the U.S. Lawn Tennis Association Championship.

- From September 5 to September 11, the Boston Red Sox win the World Series, defeating the Chicago Cubs four games to two. In the series, Babe Ruth earned two wins and extended his postseason consecutive scoreless innings to a record 29 2/3.

- On December 16, William Harrison "Jack" Dempsey knocks out Carl Morris in fourteen seconds of the first round in a heavyweight bout in New Orleans. On July 27, Dempsey had knocked out Fred Fulton in eighteen seconds.

## 1919

- With World War I just ending and attendance down in 1918, Major League baseball owners decide to save money by reducing the 154 game schedule to 140 games..

- Babe Ruth of the Boston Red Sox sets a new major league baseball home run record of twenty-nine in a single season. He also had a batting average of .322 and 114 RBIs

- Sir Barton, ridden by Johnny Loftus, becomes the first Triple Crown champion, winning the Kentucky Derby, the Preakness Stakes, and the Belmont Stakes.

- The 1919 influenza epidemic causes the cancellation of the Stanley Cup championship series between the Seattle Metropolitans and the Montreal Canadiens.

- On January 1, the Great Lakes Naval Training Station defeats the Mare Island Marines, 17–0 in the fifth annual Rose Bowl.

- On March 17, Jack Britton knocks out Ted Lewis in nine rounds in Canton, Ohio, to capture the world welterweight boxing title, which he will retain until 1922.

- On April 19, Carl W. A. Linder wins the twenty-third Boston Marathon in 2:29:13.

- On May 31, after a two-year lapse, Howard Wilcox, averaging 88.05 mph, wins the seventh Indianapolis 500.

- On June 11, Walter Hagen wins the U.S. Open golf tournament in a play-off against Michael Brady.

- On June 21, Hazel Hotchkiss Wightman wins the women's title at the U.S. Lawn Tennis Association Championship.

- On July 4, in Toledo, Ohio, Jack Dempsey defeats Jess Willard in three rounds for the world heavyweight boxing championship.

- On September 4, William M. Johnston wins the men's title at the U.S. Lawn Tennis Association Championship.

- On September 14, the Green Bay Packers defeat the Menominee North End A. E. 53–0 in their first game.

- On September 20, Jim Barnes defeats Fred McLeod in the final round of the PGA tournament.

- From October 1 to October 9, the Cincinnati Reds win the World Series, defeating the Chicago White Sox five games to three. The series would soon become the focus of the infamous "Black Sox" scandal.

# "University Athletics"

Essay

**By:** Simon Newcomb

**Date:** 1907

**Source:** Newcomb, Simon. "University Athletics." *North American Review,* 185, June 21, 1907, 353–364. Reprinted as Chapter 8 in *College and the Future: Essays for the Undergraduate on Problems of Character and Intellect.* Richard Rice Jr., ed. New York: Charles Scribner's Sons, 1915, 115–130.

**About the Author:** Simon Newcomb (1835–1909) was a leading figure in American higher education in the late nineteenth and early twentieth century. An American astronomer, educator, and author, Newcomb taught in Maryland for three years and worked for a short time for the American Nautical Survey before entering Harvard University. In 1861, Newcomb became a professor of mathematics at the Naval Observatory in Washington, D.C., a position he held for thirty-six years. His achievements in the field of astronomy included successful negotiation for the construction of a twenty-six-inch equatorial telescope. In addition to more than twenty-five books on mathematics, astronomy, general science, and economics, Newcomb wrote one science fiction novel, *His Wisdom, The Defender* (1900). ∎

## Introduction

If one were to think about college athletics today, one would likely think of the National Collegiate Athletic Association's (NCAA) biggest sports of football, basketball, baseball, and hockey. However, at the beginning of the twentieth century, the role of athletics in college life was much different. For one, there was no gender equity in sports, so women's teams were primarily located at women-only schools, such as Vassar and Bryn Mawr. Also, the variety of sports offered at the college level was far more limited. In the 1910s, the biggest college sport was football, which even far outpaced professional football for the fans' interest. Few, if any, other sports drew more than a passing interest from spectators and students alike. The role of athletics on campus was designed to make students able to compete physically, as well as mentally. In the early twentieth century, many schools developed recreational and athletic programs to promote a better learning environment.

Richard Rice was the editor of *College and the Future: Essays for the Undergraduate on Problems of Character and Intellect.* Rice chose essays that would illustrate all of the elements necessary to educate the youth of America. He assembled essays by leaders in the educational community on a number of topics. Included in that list is President Woodrow Wilson (served 1913–1921), who wrote two essays, "What is a College For?" and "The Training of Intellect," drawing upon his experience as the President of Princeton University. Other authors also included Robert Louis Stevenson and President Theodore Roosevelt (served 1901–1909). Simon Newcomb addressed university athletics and its role in developing well-rounded students for the collection. Its inclusion in this book of essays was indicative of the perceived importance of the growing role of sports in collegiate life.

## Significance

Newcomb defined different ways that a student athlete can contribute to his own education. Newcomb asserted that a "physically lazy man is not apt to be mentally active," and he encouraged athletics to promote a more complete student. However, Newcomb viewed the role of athletics primarily as a means to physical fitness. He questioned the role of intercollegiate contests and offered examples from classical Greek and Roman mythology to illustrate his point. Every student reading the essay would be familiar with the names Minerva, the Roman goddess of wisdom, and Ajax, a warrior who fought with Achilles and Odysseus against the soldiers of Troy during the Trojan War. Newcomb attributed to Ajax the activities of attending the football games and standing in awe of the athletic prowess displayed on the playing field. Newcomb attributed to Minerva the knowledge that the brain, not the brawn, does the "world's work." While Newcomb saw the role of physical fitness as powerful, he found little value in following or watching sports at the collegiate level. This, he thought, developed inferior values and did not contribute to the overall education and improvement of the college student.

While supporting the need of a physical life to complement an intellectual one, Newcomb stated that athletic contests between schools were not the means to meet this end. In the early twentieth century, many sports rivalries developed that remain to this day. These rivalries are based on physical proximity or an intellectual rivalry. Most notable in this regard is the annual Harvard-Yale football game—a passionate event between two of the nation's elite institutions. Newcomb stated that "the energy displayed in these contests is misdirected, and that a wise adaptation of means to ends requires athletic exercises to be a personal matter," focusing on self-improvement rather than the ability to outdo others. While the role of and interest in college sports was

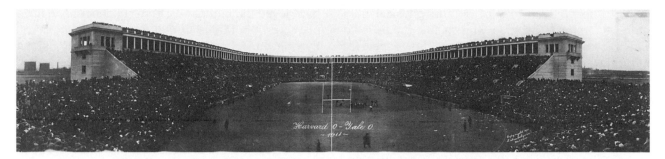

Harvard-Yale Football game of 1911 held at Harvard. Simon Newcomb encouraged athletics to promote a more complete student. **THE LIBRARY OF CONGRESS.**

rising at the time, Newcomb encouraged students to focus on the element of sports that improved well-being, not the role of the spectator and fan.

## Primary Source

### "University Athletics" [excerpt]

**SYNOPSIS:** Simon Newcomb offers an analysis of the role of both participatory and spectator athletics in colleges and universities. Newcomb primarily explores the developing role of college athletics as a spectator sport, one that does not encourage the majority of students to participate in a meaningful way. Newcomb sees the growing interest in college athletics as a potential distraction to the true value of athletics, enhancing physical well being as an element of an excellent college education.

"The greatest nation is the one that can send most men to the top of the Matterhorn." This reply to the question which we should deem the greatest nation was probably regarded by the guests who heard it as a euphonious paradox rather than a serious opinion. And yet, if not taken too literally, it suggests a direction in which progress is now tending. With the decay of asceticism, naturally commences the growth of the opposite idea, embodied in the familiar phrases, "muscular Christianity" and "the physical basis of life." This idea is supported by modern physiological investigation, which brings out in clear relief that physical health and vigor are qualities to be cultivated, not merely from a selfish desire for amusement and to secure freedom from pain, but as a means toward the attainment of our highest ethical ends. Experience shows the general rule to be that the physically lazy man is not apt to be mentally active, though the mentally active man may be so absorbed in his work as to have little time or energy to spend in outdoor exercise. The names of the few hundred persons who since Whymper's memorable and disastrous adventure have as-

cended the Matterhorn would be more than a miscellaneous list of people endowed with bodily vigor and a propensity to climb. They would include a President of the United States, a goodly list of leaders in science and literature, and more than a due proportion of men who have made their mark in various fields of effort. The general trend of evidence recently collected by students of hygiene is toward the view that there is something toxic in the air of even the best houses, and that he who would command the best measure of physical health must, so far as he can, live and sleep in the open air. He cannot do this well unless he is in motion during most of his waking hours; and in this we have a completely rational incentive to bodily exercise.

Having said this by way of preface, let us proceed to our task. We wish to bring about peace and amity between lusty Ajax, who attends all the football games, admires the manly qualities there displayed, and sees in the actors the men who are to do the real work of the world—and wise Minerva, who has learned that brain and not muscle does the world's work, and that the best physical health and mental vigor are quite compatible with inability to climb a hill or fight a burglar. We fancy that the goddess is already beginning to ply us with questions, whether we are not confounding causes and effect, whether men do not play football because they are already strong and active, rather than the reverse, whether the qualities they display in the game are really those most required by modern society, and whether Whymper would not have done as good work, and Leslie Stephen become as effective a writer, if neither of them had ever seen a mountain. But, with all the deference due her sex, we shall ask her to postpone her questions and remain a spectator while Ajax has his innings.

The world, he tells us, has no need of the weakling, who shrinks from personal combat and is disturbed by the fear of a little physical pain and discomfort. The man who in the future is to win the admiration and command the respect of his fellow men by his works must possess the robust qualities of the body, as well as the finer qualities of the intellect. In no way are such qualities more readily acquired and displayed than in the roughest of the games played by university students in intercollegiate contests. The large majority of men who are to be leaders in this and the next generation will be trained at colleges and in universities. It is essential to their efficiency that they shall not be mere scholars and book-worms, but physically strong and courageous, ready to sacrifice ease and comfort to the exigencies of their work. Therefore, let them engage in manly contests, the rougher the better.

Now, dear Ajax, I am delighted that you take this ground. I take much the same view as you do, though I might state our case a little differently. We wish the men of our nation to be capable of carrying on great works. The best and most effective work cannot be done unless the doer enjoys good physical health. Human experience, as a whole, shows that life and motion in the open air are among the agents most conducive to vigor. Let us, therefore, cultivate this life in the nation at large, especially in that fraction of it which is to take the lead. Open-air games are an excellent means toward this end, therefore we wish to encourage them. I look for your cordial assent to my statement of the problem before us, which is to devise that course of action best adapted to imbue our intellectual young men with a warm love for the green fields, the blue sky, and the varied beauties of nature and such a fondness of physical movement that they shall look forward with pleasure many months in advance to the moment when they can escape from their daily routine to engage in country walking or in mountain climbing. Let us now put our heads together and map out the course of action best adapted to our purpose. To do this we must begin with a survey of the situation, and study the problem which it offers from our poi nt of view.

A body of several hundred young men enter college. The first step in deciding how to secure them the full measure of the manly qualities we admire will be to classify them as to their present possession of such qualities. We divide them into three groups. At the head will be the vigorous and courageous young men, already possessing in the highest degree the manly qualities we desire to cultivate. Born of strong and healthy parents, they have loved the outdoor air from childhood, and have played on the teams of their respective schools till they have reached the college age. If any of us can claim them as children or grandchildren, we are glad to do so.

The second and much larger group will comprise a middle class, possessing fair or excellent health and a due amount of every manly quality, but taking no special pleasure in bestowing their car-fares upon the shoemaker, more interested in study than in sport and fonder of seeing others lead the strenuous life than of leading it themselves.

The third will take in the weaklings; the men who shrink from strenuous physical effort, are not strong enough to engage in a rough-and-tumble game, fear they would get hurt if they tried, will not incur even a slight risk of a few bruises without some more serious reason than love of excitement, deem it the part of wisdom to go through life with a minimum of physical pain, and prefer a sphere of activity in which the sacrifice of comfort will be as small as possible. Perhaps many of them watch the games with as much eagerness as any of their fellows and hurrah for their teams as loudly as their weak lungs will permit. But this adds little to their physical vigor. . . .

There still stands in a corner of the Harvard University grounds a small, low, old-fashioned brick building, offering in its proportions a striking contrast to the buildings of to-day. It was the first gymnasium erected for the use of Harvard students. In it those who aimed at increasing the physical strength took as much pleasure in nothing their improvement every week as does the football player of to-day in his contests. This continual gain, coupled with the real pleasure of physical activity, which perhaps many experienced there for the first time, was the sufficient motive to gain the full measure of physical energy attainable by the constitution of each individual student. We never know how interesting the simplest exercise may be unless we have had the experience. I never saw an outing more enjoyed than that of a poor widow of a Tyrolese schoolmaster, who once arranged a picnic for a small party on a slope of one of her native mountains. I could see nothing in it but cooking and eating a meal out-of-doors instead of in the house; but it gave her a pleasure and a distraction which lightened her labors for days to come. In the light of a modern athletic contest, the interest taken by the students of forty years ago in their exercises may seem quite childish. Who but a child could be amused, as students then were, by seeing his fellows lean backward and walk under a barrier slowly lowered day by day until it was little more than knee-high? The youth who was looking forward to increasing the weight of his dumb-bells from sixty to eighty pounds, who could walk to the end of a vibrating spar without falling, and who was hoping soon to be able to mount up the peg-studded pole while hanging by his hands, were all interested by the sight of what the others could do in these various lines. It cannot be denied that all gained the greatest of the benefits that come from physical exercise; and, if we would secure the same advantage to our children, we can do it by inciting them to action on similar lines. Instead of each trying to excel his fellows, which he knows is vain unless he is one of the strongest of the class, each person must try to be stronger to-day than he was yesterday. Even if we cannot move every one by this motive, we shall certainly move more than we do under our present system.

Let us temper a little our admiration for the manly qualities displayed in an athletic contest, by recognizing the confusion between cause and effect which we find involved. Probably nearly all of our readers would share with the writer the pleasure which he would feel in seeing a son win a boat-race. But why? Because the winning made him stronger? No, but because winning proved him to be a strong man to begin with. Success was the effect, not the cause, of strength. The same remark will apply to the manly qualities displayed in an athletic game. Psychologists will tell us that it is very doubtful whether innate qualities can be improved in any great degree in this way. But, apart from this, as we are now in a critical mood, let us inquire whether the manly qualities at play in a contest are really those which the world most needs to-day and will need in the future.

It is a characteristic of human nature that the sentiments and ideas which we inherit from our ancestors may continue through many generations after they have ceased to be needed. It is of especial interest that such sentiments are strongest in the boy, and tend to diminish with age. In former times, cities, villages, nations, and empires were so exposed to aggressions from their neighbors that not only their prosperity, but even the lives of their people, depended upon the prowess and courage of their fighting population. Hence arose an admiration for these qualities, which we may expect to continue, not only as long as war is permitted, but even after conditions are so improved that no one will ever be

obliged to place himself voluntarily in danger for the benefit of his fellow men. Every well-endowed boy of to-day admires the brave fighter as the highest type of humanity and shows his budding patriotism by delighting in the battles which our soldiers have won. But, as he grows up, he is from time to time surprised to find social regulations at seeming variance with his ideas. He learns that the man who jumps off the Brooklyn Bridge, or risks life and limb otherwise than in the performance of the greatest public or private duty, instead of receiving the reward of a hero is haled before the courts, to be dealt with as an offender against the law. His traditional ideas of the qualities essential in a soldier include readiness to take offense and to engage in mortal combat with his personal enemy. He is therefore surprised when he finds that duelling is prohibited by the regulations governing modern armies, and that the officer of to-day need not be quick of temper to prove his courage. The writer was once told by a distinguished officer of the past generation that it was a disappointment to the average citizen when he first found that the naval officer of our time was an educated gentleman, who did not interlard his conversation with sea slang. As the boy grows to manhood, he finds that fear is strongest in his boyhood and that physical courage is the rule and not the exception among grown men.

In the same category with physical courage we may place readiness to engage in personal combat. The boy who possesses this quality has a decided advantage among his fellows. But, as he grows older, he finds that the requirements of social life render it an undesirable quality among grown men. The boy who is not ready to defend himself is liable to be imposed upon by his fellows. But the grown man trusts for his protection to public opinion and to the agents of the law; and, although the latter may not always be at hand when needed, it is not likely that an occasion will ever arise during his life in which he will have to maintain his rights in the manner employed by primitive mankind. How much soever he would be pleased to down a burglar, he might live through a score of lives without once enjoying the opportunity.

If the argument here submitted is sound, the wisest policy on the part of believers in physical training as a basis of intellectual efficiency is to discourage and, if possible, abolish that special form of intercollegiate contests which has assumed such striking proportions during the past ten years. We should not lose sight of the fact that the energy displayed in these contests is misdirected, and that a wise adaptation of means to ends requires athletic exercises to be a personal matter, in which each individual shall be interested in his own improvement rather than in his ability to outdo his fellows.

## Further Resources

### BOOKS

Duderstadt, James J. *Intercollegiate Athletics and the American University: A University President's Perspective.* Ann Arbor, Mich.: University of Michigan Press, 2000.

Sperber, Murray *Onward to Victory: The Crises That Shaped College Sports.* New York: H. Holt, 1998.

### PERIODICALS

Bachin, Robin F. "Courage, Endurance and Quickness of Decision: Gender and Athletics at the University of Chicago, 1890–1920." *Rethinking History,* March 2001, 93–116.

Cowley, W.H. "Athletics in American Colleges." *Journal of Higher Education,* September/October 1999, 494–503.

### WEBSITES

"National Collegiate Athletic Association (NCAA)." NCAA. Available online at http://www.ncaa.org (accessed April 8, 2003).

# "Johnson Wins in 15 Rounds; Jeffries Weak"

Newspaper article

**By:** John L. Sullivan

**Date:** July 5, 1910

**Source:** Sullivan, John L. "Johnson Wins in 15 Rounds; Jeffries Weak." *The New York Times,* July 5, 1910, 1–2.

**About the Author:** John L. Sullivan (1858–1918) was a boxer born in Boston Massachussets. Nicknamed the "Boston Strong Boy," and "the Great John L.," he was the last bare-knuckles heavyweight champion. In 1892, after 21 rounds, Sullivan, soft and wasted from drinking and an undisciplined life that left no time for training, was defeated by James J. Corbett. Wisely, Sullivan never staged a comeback but sustained his popularity on the vaudeville stage and, after reforming in 1905, as a temperance lecturer. Sullivan was inducted into the International Boxing Hall of Fame in 1990. ∎

## Introduction

When Jack Johnson and Jim Jeffries met for the heavyweight championship on July 4, 1910, the stage was set for one of the most significant boxing matches in the history of the sport. The boxing match reportedly received more coverage in British newspapers than did the Boer War (1899–1902), fought between Great Britain and the Boers in South Africa. The fight had more reporters covering it than any previous sports contest.

Johnson, an African American born in Texas, defeated all of the African American heavyweights who fought him in 1904. Johnson then challenged then-heavyweight champion Jim Jeffries to a fight. Jeffries, a white man, opted not to fight someone of a different race, and the bout was never held. When Jeffries retired in 1905 as undefeated champion, Tommy Burns became the new heavyweight champion and he accepted Johnson's challenge to fight. In 1908, after defeating Burns, Johnson became the first African American heavyweight champion of the world.

Many whites sought a fighter who would reclaim the crown from Johnson. Finally, Jim Jeffries was convinced to return to the ring as the "great white hope" and reestablish himself as the true heavyweight champion of the world. In a society that accepted and, at times, encouraged racial inequality, fans all over the world looked to Jeffries to reclaim the "honor of the white people." On July 4, 1910, in the sleepy town of Reno, Nevada, the fight was held. Jack Johnson, who embraced his role as a boxer and entertainer on vaudeville circuits, was up to the challenge. A crowd of twenty-five thousand attended the match. The crowd was overwhelmingly supportive of Jeffries, as was most of the white population in the country. Jack Johnson had very few fans in attendance, but he had tremendous confidence that he would carry the day. The fight was scheduled for forty-five rounds, but Johnson knocked out his opponent in fifteen.

## Significance

The fight between Jack Johnson and Jim Jeffries was one of the greatest fights of the twentieth century. While the boxing was fine, the real significance of the fight lay in pitting the two races against one another. That race was at the front and center of this story was accepted at the time and reflected attitudes in the United States. This fight took place thirty-seven years before Jackie Robinson played for the Brooklyn Dodgers and broke the most famous color barrier in American sports. The coverage of this fight, by former champion John Sullivan, was surprisingly candid in its assessment of the race issue.

Sullivan opens up his coverage with a simple statement: "The fight of the century is over and a black man is the undisputed champion of the world." He lamented that the fight only lasted fifteen of the forty-five rounds, a mark of a one-sided contest. And while he spent a fair amount of time discussing the fight itself—which was not memorable as a sporting event—the true story of this fight is the victory of a person of color over a white legend. Sullivan added later that "By this time the crowd was realizing that Johnson had won out, but there was very little cheering. Jeff[ries] had been such a decided favorite they could hardly believe that he was beaten. . . ." Sullivan, though writing as a special reporter for *The New*

*York Times,* also did not hide (or even attempt to hide) his dislike of Johnson because of his race. It is hard to believe that a newspaper writer could so disparage a person because of race, but this was part of the culture of 1910. Despite not having the fans or the support that Jeffries had, at the end of the fight, Johnson had what he really wanted—the heavyweight boxing crown, which he kept until losing to Jess Wiliard in 1915 in Havana, Cuba.

## Primary Source

### "Johnson Wins in 15 Rounds; Jeffries Weak"

> **SYNOPSIS:** This is one of a series of lengthy articles covering the World Championship fight between Jack Johnson and Jim Jeffries to unify the World Heavyweight Boxing Crown. The fight took place in Reno, Nevada on July 4, 1910, and it established Jack Johnson as one of the greatest boxers of all times. Sullivan includes a great deal of information on how the partisan crowd that favored Jeffries reacted to his defeat.

### Johnson Wins in 15 Rounds; Jeffries Weak

#### " I Couldn't Come Back," Says Former Champion, Helpless After Third Knockdown.

#### Poor Fight, Says Sullivan

White Man Outclassed by His Opponent from the First Tap of the Gong.

#### Crowd's Sympathy Aroused

Yells to Referee to Save Jeffries from a Knockout and His Seconds Jump Into the Ring.

#### Johnson's Share, $70,600

While Jeffries Takes $50,400 from the Purse—The Moving-Picture Rights Bring Them More Thousands.

Reno, Nev. July 4.—The fight of the century is over and a black man is the undisputed champion of the world.

It was a poor fight as fights go, this less than fifteen-round affair between James J. Jeffries and Jack Johnson. Scarcely ever has there been a championship contest that was so one-sided.

All of Jeffries's much-vaunted condition and the prodigious preparations that he went though availed him nothing. He wasn't in it from the first bell tap to the last, and as he fell bleeding, bruised and weakened in the twenty-seventh second of the third minute of the fifteenth round, no sorrier sight has

Jack Johnson (right) became the first African American to hold the World Heavyweight title by defeating Jim Jeffries on July 4, 1910.
© BETTMANN/CORBIS. REPRODUCED BY PERMISSION.

ever gone to make pugilistic history. He was practically knocked out twice in this round.

Johnson's deadly left beat upon his unprotected head and neck, and he went down for the count just before the second minute had gone in the fifteenth round. As Johnson felled him the first time he was conscious, but weakened. He tactfully waited for the timekeeper's call of nine before he rose. When he did, Johnson caught him flush on the jaw again and he fell almost in the same spot but further out, and as he leaned against the lower rope his great bulk crashed through outside the ring.

His seconds and several newspaper men hauled him into the ring again and he staggered weakly over to the other side. Johnson slowly followed him, measured his distance carefully, and as Jeff's head always hangs forward, struck him hard in the face and again that terrible left hand caught him, sending him reeling around to a stooping posture.

Johnson pushed his right hand hard as Jeffries wheeled around, and quick as a flash whipped his left over again, and Jeff went down for the last time. His seconds had given it up.

They didn't wait for the ten seconds to be counted, but jumped into the ring after their man. Billy Delaney, Johnson's chief second, always watchful for the technicalities, yelled his claim for the fight for his man on the breach of the rules by Jeff's handlers. Tex Rickard, in the meantime, was trying to make himself heard, and he was saying that the fight was Johnson's.

### Result Left the Crowd Dazed.

By this time the crowd was realizing that Johnson had won out, but there was very little cheering. Jeff had been such a decided favorite they could hardly believe that he was beaten and that there wouldn't still be a chance for him to reclaim his lost laurels. The crowd was not even willing to leave the arena, and as poor old Jeff sat in his corner being sprayed with water and other resusitating liquids, he was pitied from all sides.

The negro had few friends but there was no real demonstration against him. They could not help but admire Johnson because he was the type of prize fighter that is regarded highly by sportsmen. He played fairly at all times and fought fairly. He gave in wherever there was a contention and he demanded his rights only up to their limits, but never beyond them.

### Had Picked Johnson to Win.

I have never witnessed a fight where I was in such a peculiar position. I all along refused to announce my choice as to the winner. I refused on Jeff's account because he was sensitive and I wanted to be with him some time during his training. I refused on Johnson' account because of my well-known antipathy to his race, and I didn't want him to think that I was favoring him from any other motive than a purely sporting one. He might have got this impression, although since I know him better in the last few weeks, I am rather inclined to believe that he hasn't many of the petty meanness of human character.

You will deduce from the foregoing that I really had picked Johnson as the winner. My personal friends all know it, and even Jeffries accused me of it one day, but I denied it in this way. I said:

"Jeff, I have picked the winner, but I haven't done it publicly. A few personal friends know who I think will win and I am not going to tell you before the fight. I don't want you to get any wrong impression."

However, the fact remains that three weeks ago I picked Johnson to win. It seems almost too much

to say but I did say inside of fifteen rounds. It's all over now and it does not matter who I picked to win to either Jeff or Johnson, but the main theory I based my decision on was the old one that put me out of the game. Jeff could not come back. Jeffries was mere shell of his former self. All the months of weight reducing, involving great feats of exercise had come to naught.

The experts who figured that a man must receive his reward for such long, conscientious, muscle-wearing and nerve-racking work figured that he must get it even providentially.

It seemed only just to human nature that Jeffries must win, even in the face of all the features resting on the other side of the argument. For it is true, and probably would only be denied by Johnson himself that the big colored champion did not train conscientiously. As subsequent events proved, he didn't have to train more than he did, but nevertheless he took a chance, and by his manner and deportment, seemed perfectly willing to stand the consequences, whatever they were. The result was success for him in its fullest meaning.

Johnson got scarcely a hard knock during the whole encounter and was never bothered by Jeffries's actions one little bit. He came out of the fray without a mark if one except the cut lip he got in the third round which proved to be only the opening of the old cut that George Cotton gave him the other day when Gov. Dickerson was out at his training quarters.

Never before has there been a fight for the championship of the world with so many peculiar ends to it because never before has a black man been a real contender for the championship. Johnson, of course, was the credited champion even before to-day's fight by virtue of his defeat of Tommy Burns, but just the same the rank and file of sporting people never gave him the full measure of his title. Jeffries has always been the bugaboo of Johnson's championship career, and it seemed to many that if only the big boilermaker would go back into the fighting game and get himself into condition he could obliterate this so-called blot on the pugilistic map.

Jeffries was persuaded against his will and he went to work with a willingness and determination that brought about wonderful results, but that couldn't bring back outraged old nature.

### Johnson Never in Doubt.

Probably never before was a championship so easily won as Johnson's victory to-day. He never showed the slightest concern during the fifteen rounds and from the fourth round on his confidence was the most glaring thing I ever saw in any fighter. He was the one person in the world at that moment who knew that Jeffries's best blow was packed away in his last fight and on the road and by the running brooks from which he lured the fish during his preliminary training for his fight.

He was a perfect picnic for the big negro, who seemed to be enjoying himself rather than fighting for 50 per cent of a $101,000 purse. It could not have been all assumed either as his remarks during the contest to me while I sat below and near him at the ringside showed that he had honestly a good opinion of himself.

Once in the interval between the fifth and sixth rounds, he leaned over and said: "John, I thought this fellow could hit."

I said: "I never said so, but I believe he could have six years ago."

Johnson continued with conversation when he should have been paying attention to the advice his seconds were giving him and said: "Yes, five or six years ago ain't now, though."

By that time the bell had rung and he was up and at it again.

My, what a crafty, powerful, cunning left hand he has. He leads with it, of course, but he does most of his work in close and some of his blows look as though he were trying to lead with his right while his left is traveling to its goal.

He is one of the craftiest, cunningest boxers that ever stepped into the ring, and poor old Jeffries could not get set or anywhere near him for an effective punch.

As a matter of fact, he didn't have any. They both fought closely all during the fifteen rounds. It was just the sort of a fight that Jeffries wanted. There was no running around and ducking like Corbett did with me in New Orleans.

Jeffries didn't miss so many blows because he hardly started any. Johnson was on top of him all the time, and he scarcely attempted a blow that didn't land. There wasn't a full swing during the whole fifteen rounds, something unusual in the latter-day fighting.

The only thing that wasn't actual fighting to-day was the many clinches that occurred and here instead of Jeff getting in the fatal work it was Johnson. None of the plans that all of the experts and critics have been talking about for this last six months materialized.

Jeffries's fearful rushes were not there. The awful wallops that he was going to land on Johnson's body, where were they?

Johnson didn't receive a blow during the whole encounter that would have hurt a 16-year-old boy. From the time Jeff got his right eye closed in the sixth round it was all over as far as I was concerned. I felt that if Jeffries had all this power behind that had been claimed for him, he would get mad and he would at least have taken a desperate chance. Probably he had some such idea in mind himself, for he did step in viciously in the next round, but a gloved first always stopped his onward way.

When I saw Johnson throw Jeffries away from him in one of the many clinches in the eighth or ninth round, I was still further convinced that the negro was the winner.

This had been one of his favorite stunts during his training, and he was expected to at least attempt it here. He didn't get gay at all with Jeffries in the beginning and it was always the white man who clinched but Johnson was very careful and he backed away and took no chances, and was good-natured with it all.

**Probably the Last Big Fight Here.**

There were those in the throng to-day who will probably say it was the greatest fight the world ever saw, but that is because it was the most peculiar fight crowd the world ever saw, for half of them never saw a fight before. It was the greatest fight this class ever saw, but as a matter of fact it was about the poorest fight that has ever been fought for the championship. It will probably be the last big fight in this country, notwithstanding the crowd's enthusiastic reception of Billy Muldoon's sentimental speech. "Let us give three cheers for the great broad-minded State of Nevada and its great broad-minded Governor," because it will be hard to work up the fervor that has existed all through the arrangements for this fight.

It will go down in history as the greatest fight that ever took place in some respects, and from a purely sporting point of view, the very worst.

Nevertheless, the best man won, and I was one of the first to congratulate him, and also one of the first to extend my heartfelt sympathy to the beaten man.

## Further Resources

### BOOKS

Hietala, Thomas. *The Fight of the Century: Jack Johnson, Joe Louis, and the Struggle for Racial Equality*. Armonk, N.Y.: M.E. Sharpe, 2002.

Roberts, Randy. *Papa Jack: Jack Johnson and the Era of White Hopes*. New York: Free Press, 1983.

### PERIODICALS

Bennett, Lerone, Jr. "Jack Johnson and the Great White Hope." *Ebony*, April 1994, 86–92.

Gilmore, Al-Tony. "Black Athletes in an Historical Context: The Issue of Race." *Negro History Bulletin*, October/December 1995, 7–14.

### WEBSITES

"Cyber Boxing Champion Jack Johnson." Cyber Boxing Zone. Available online at http://www.cyberboxingzone.com/boxing/jjohn.htm; website home page http://www.cyberboxingzone.com (accessed March 30, 2003).

"Cyber Boxing Champion James J. Jeffries." Cyber Boxing Zone. Available online at http://www.cyberboxingzone.com/boxing/jeffries.htm; website home page http://www.cyberboxingzone.com (accessed March 30, 2003).

### AUDIO AND VISUAL MEDIA

*Great White Hope*. Directed by Martin Ritt. Twentieth Century Fox, 1970, VHS.

*Legends of the Ring: Jack Johnson—Breaking Barriers*. MPI Home Video, 2001, VHS.

# "Burman Lowers Speedway Records"

Newspaper article

**By:** *The New York Times*

**Date:** May 30, 1911

**Source:** "Burman Lowers Speedway Records." *The New York Times*, May 30, 1911.

**About the Author:** A *New York Times* sportswriter wrote this unsigned article. The coverage of the first Indianapolis 500 automobile race was in the general sports section, and it did not make the front page. It was quite common for newspapers to have unsigned articles covering lesser events in the nation and the world. ∎

## Introduction

The Indianapolis 500 is one of the most famous automobile races in the United States and the world. Though the Daytona 500—featuring NASCAR stock cars, a fixture since 1959—has been more popular lately in the United States, the Indy 500 (as it is known) has the longest tradition in American motor sports history. The race is held every year on Memorial Day weekend at the track known as the "Brickyard," just northwest of downtown Indianapolis. The Indianapolis Motor Speedway was built in 1909 as a two-and-a-half-mile rectangular track, with a surface of crushed rock and tar. In the same year, the speedway hosted its first race, a disastrous five-mile dash that saw the deaths of six people, including two spectators. Later that year, the owners of the speedway resurfaced the track with over three million bricks, laid on their side and fixed with mortar, giving the track its famous nickname—and making it far safer for racing.

After three lackluster events in 1910 failed to draw fans to the speedway, the promoters of the track decided to host a single event during the year, hoping that it would draw national and international attention. The promoters were hopeful that one major event would draw fans and attention greater than a number of lesser events held at the speedway. Their plan was to have a single race of five hundred miles (or two hundred laps of the track). It initially would be held on May 30, 1911. The length of the race was unprecedented in motor sports and attracted interest by itself. In the initial five-hundred-mile race, the winner was Ray Harroun, driving a car owned by Marmon, besting the field of forty drivers with an average speed of 74.59 miles per hour, finishing in six hours forty-two minutes. Today's race car attain speeds well over two hundred miles per hour and, even with caution laps, complete the race in about half the time of the initial contest.

While it is expected that the cars would be faster now than they were when the race started in 1911, the cars were fundamentally different. They carried both the driver and a mechanic. Early racing automobiles had a mechanic on board to fix problems as they occurred during the race. What remains similar is the open cockpit nature of the car that has remained to this day. During the initial race of 1911, there was one fatality, when driver, Arthur Greiner, along with mechanic, S. P. Dickson, had an accident only thirteen miles into the race. When one of the front wheels of their car fell off, the car flipped, hurling both people from the car. While Grenier only fractured his arm, Dickson was thrown against a fence twenty feet from the car and died instantly. Over the next few years, the mechanic would no longer drive in the car, which placed fewer people on the track and improved safety. The growing popularity of these types of race cars spread throughout the country. They have been traditionally called Indy cars, in reference to the famous race on that circuit.

## Significance

Despite a desire to have one major event at the Indianapolis Motor Speedway that would gain international

Ray Harroun races his car to victory in the inaugural Indianapolis 500. He won the race with an average speed of 74.602 miles per hour, finishing in 6 hours, 42 minutes, 8 seconds. AP/WIDE WORLD PHOTOS. REPRODUCED BY PERMISSION.

attention, *The New York Times* did not cover this race as they would in later years after the event became more prominent. The coverage below reflects the interest in the preliminaries of the race. This provides some indication of the impact that the Indianapolis Speedway would have on motor sports in the country. In just a few years, the coverage of the Indy 500 in *The New York Times* and other out-of-town newspapers would grow and make it to the front page with great consistency.

The author here provided the background information on the 500-mile race that was to take place that day. Of note in the article is the discussion of the lowering of the speedway record, the early methods of driving evident in the qualifying for the race, and the interest of fans in the event. The speed record was particularly important in billing the event at the Indianapolis Speedway as being one of international importance. Bob Burman broke four records that day, including one held by Barney Oldfield, one of the early prominent figures in automobile

racing and holder of the record speed for the mile. Breaking speed records at the Indy 500 would be a common occurrence, as cars improved and became faster. Also, the writer noted the time trials that would be very different then they are now. The drivers, as described for Bob Burman's run, would raise their right arm to indicate that they were ready to be timed, not the opposite where drivers are told during time trials that they should start. Also, the event was intended to be run completely without stops. The "race, once started, will not be stopped until finished, it is understood, no matter what the weatherman may decide to do." However, when Greiner and Dickson crashed their car just a few miles into the race, they naturally had to stop the race as fans ran on the track to see the status of the driver and mechanic.

The interest of fans in this event was possibly the most interesting element of all. As the promoters had hoped, having one major event during the year would draw more fans to the Indianapolis Motor Speedway than a number of smaller events. Not only were the fans interested in the event, but they came from all over the country to view the race. Most interesting is the author's description of the elderly man and wife who were looking for the "best surgeon" in town as he waited in the lobby of the Hotel Claypool in Indianapolis. They apparently were involved in an automobile accident and abandoned their car some five miles from town in an effort to make sure that they would be able to attend the race. The writer goes on to add that these people "will most likely witness the race to-morrow, with the assistance of a few bandages and plasters." Like with other great events of its day, the writer describes the large arrival of people to see the race and the fact that "hundreds of homes have been thrown open for the accommodation of the overflow crowds from the hotels." Very few cities had the infrastructure to fully support the influx of huge crowds of fans, so creative residents opened their homes to earn a bit of money.

## Primary Source

### "Burman Lowers Speedway Records"

**SYNOPSIS:** This newspaper account relays the time trials and interest in the initial Indy 500 automobile race. The writer provides detailed descriptions of the time trials, with the times for the miles and kilometer marks, as well as the activities of the spectators of the event.

### Oldfield's Mile Dash Goes by Board—Forty Cars to Start in 500-Mile Race

Indianapolis, May 20.—As a curtain raiser to tomorrow's great 500-mile international automobile sweepstakes on the Speedway "Bob Burman, the "speed king," today lowered four records. Driving his 300 horsepower Blitzen Benz car he established a new slate of Speedway records. He drove the mile in 35.25 seconds, the kilometer in 21.40 seconds, the half-mile in 16.53 seconds, and the quarter mile in 8.16 seconds. The previous record for the kilometer was 21.45 seconds, for the half-mile, 17 seconds, and the mile 35.63 seconds. The quarter-mile record is a new one.

Ideal weather conditions favored the trial, which was driven by Burman in masterly fashion. He started his first trial shortly after 10 o'clock, but after driving three laps of the track pulled down because his engine was not working quite right.

After working over his engine for fifteen minutes Burman again got into his seat and started on his record-breaking journey. He drove one lap and came thundering down the stretch with right arm raised as a signal to judges and timers that he was ready. The big white Benz flashed around the brick oval just once and the new slate of records had been established. The timing was done with an electrical timer, which caught Burman at the quarter, half, kilometer, and mile distances.

Barney Oldfield, who held the previous mile record, watched Burman's feat from the grand stand. Following Burman's record drive and the speed qualification trials a score of the entries in tomorrow's big race lineup for a practice start. The drivers ran their machines on "tuning up" trials until noon, when the track was closed for the day.

There will be forty starters in the Memorial Day contest. Six cars, in addition to the thirty-four, which qualified Friday, successfully met the elimination trials today. Bert Adams, (McFarlan:) Howard Hall, (Velle:) Charles Bigelow, (Mercer:) W. H. Turner, (Amplex:) Ralph de Palma, (Simplex,) and Ernest Delaney, (Cutting.) This list comprises the largest field in the history of automobile racing cars withdrew and the remainder failed to qualify at the elimination trials.

The heat today was intense, which probably accounted for the lack of interest manifested by the spectators that visited the track. Except that the track is raised on the outer edge the scene in front of the judges' stand greatly resembles the same scene on the Vanderbilt Cup course on Long Island. Perhaps the one thing that impresses the New Yorker and makes him feel completely at home is the countless number of machines parked in the grounds and forming an endless procession to and from the track.

The lobby of the Hotel Claypool brings visions of the Garden City Hotel set down on Broadway. Men begrimed with dirt and grease mix with fashionably clad women. One little happening which occurred in the animated lobby showed the price which any automobilist must stand ready to pay. An elderly man, in cap and duster, inquired in the most matter-of-fact way for the best surgeon in town. His arm was in an improvised splint and a shield covered the remains of a battered and sightless eye. His machine had been abandoned in a ditch five miles from the city. Still, he and his wife, who was also injured in the accident, will most likely witness the race to-morrow, with the assistance of a few bandages and plasters.

Shortly after daylight the advance guard of the New York contingent began to arrive, and from that time throughout the day every train from the East brought additions to the Broadway delegation.

Promptly at 10 o'clock to-morrow Carl G. Fisher, President of the Speedway, will take the starters in the 500-mile race around the track for one lap, acting as pacemaker and giving the racers a flying start. The first lap will not exceed forty miles an hour, and will not count.

The race, once started, will not be stopped until finished, it is understood, no matter what the weather man may decide to do. If it is raining tomorrow, however, it may be postponed until Wednesday.

During the race seven warning stations will be maintained about the course. By means of flag signals the drivers will be warned if there is any trouble ahead, just where the trouble is located, and its nature. If any car in the race shows signs of giving trouble that may cause an accident, or if any driver becomes so worn out or so disabled by the long grind that he is not capable of managing his car, it will be flagged from the course.

With the arrival yesterday and to-day of large crowds of racing enthusiasts from all over the country, interest in the big event has reached a high pitch in Indianapolis. Hundreds of homes have been thrown open for the accommodation of the overflow crowds from the hotels, and there is little doubt but that the 100,000 visitors will be well cared for while in the city. Large numbers are making preparations to start as early as 7 A.M. for the Speedway in order to avoid the crowds and the jams of autos on the road.

## Further Resources

**BOOKS**

Life Magazine. *American Speed: From Dirt Tracks to NASCAR.* New York: Time-Life Books, 2002.

**PERIODICALS**

Fenster, J.M. "Indy." *American Heritage,* May/June 1992, 66–78.

**WEBSITES**

"History of the Indianapolis 500." *Indianapolis Star.* Available online at http://www.indystar.com/library/factfiles/sports /autoracing/indy500.html; website home page: http://www .indystar.com (accessed April 4, 2003).

"Indianapolis 500." Brickyard Network. Available online at http://my.brickyard.com/500; website home page: http:// www.brickyard.com (accessed April 4, 2003).

**AUDIO AND VISUAL MEDIA**

"Voices of the 500 (Audio & Video Clips)." Brickyard Network. Available online at http://iq-ims-indybox1.iquest.net /brickyard/mybrickyard/500/multimedia/radioclips; website home page: http://www.brickyard.com (accessed April 4, 2003).

# "Are Athletics Making Girls Masculine?"

**Magazine article**

**By:** Dudley A. Sargent

**Date:** March 1912

**Source:** Sargent, Dudley A. "Are Athletics Making Girls Masculine? A Practical Answer to a Question Every Girl Asks." *Ladies' Home Journal,* March 1912.

**About the Author:** Dr. Dudley A. Sargent (1849–1924) was a prominent figure in early physical education, and he served as the Director of the Hemenway Gymnasium at Harvard University from 1879 to 1919. He was one of the pioneers of research into physical fitness, a science now called kinesiology. He studied the human body, seeking the most perfect proportions for both men and women, by collecting the measurements of almost all of his students. As a contributor to *Ladies' Home Journal,* his academic credentials helped influence number of people to accepts his arguments. ∎

## Introduction

As one of the leading figures in physical education in the United States, Dudley Sargent earned a great respect for his opinions on the role of athletics in culture. He researched the human body on a quest to use exercise and sport to build the perfect physical form. In his articles for *Ladies' Home Journal,* Sargent examines the issues still raised by the media, both for and against women in sport, and offers a scientific approach to the issue. Sargent worked extensively with women at the Sanatory Gymnasium, and he had strong opinions on the role of athletics in women's lives.

In "Are Athletics Making Girls Masculine? A Practical Answer to a Question Every Girl Asks," Sargent states that "that there is a change taking place in our American girls and women is unquestioned. And it is so elusive, so baffling of description that it is proving the most attractive of subjects for discussion in the newspaper and magazine." In the media, Sargent notes, all the commentaries were written to sensationalize the expanding role of women in society in every area. Through his background with physical education, he hoped to use science and research to provide the real answers to the question on the potential role of athletics in making girls masculine.

## Significance

As one of the leading figures in contemporary physical education and a respected scholar, Dr. Sargent created what was perceived to be a definitive work on the role of athletics in shaping the female body. Subjects taken up in "Are Athletics Making Girls Masculine? A Practical Answer to a Question Every Girl Asks" include: what athletics are doing for girls; the difference between

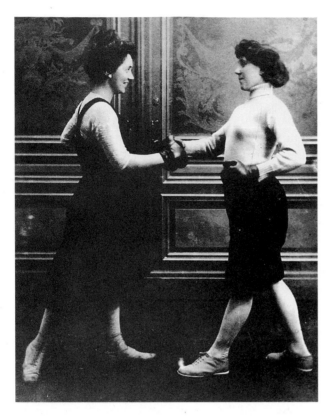

Two women engage in the sport of boxing in 1912. According to Dudley Sargent, boxing was a sport that tended to make women objectionably masculine. **THE LIBRARY OF CONGRESS.**

athletics for women and men; whether women need to exercise as much as men; whether any sports should be prohibited for women; the best sports for girls; which sports make women more masculine; and modifying men's sports for women. He asserts a much different point of view than Mary Morgan in her piece, "Girls and Athletics," also found in this chapter. Through scientific examinations, Sargent asserted that athletics had an important role in women's social and recreational life. But Sargent felt strongly about the choosing sports to prevent women from becoming too masculine.

Sargent offered much information for the reader on selecting sports for women. According to Sargent, a woman can be affected by the sport that she chooses to play. This is a common theme in his article, and one of the main differences between him and Morgan. While he claims that women should be able to participate in any sport, he also adds that "women who are able to excel in the rougher and more masculine sports have either inherited or acquired masculine characteristics." He also notes that there are "no sports that tend to make women masculine in an objectionable sense, except boxing, baseball, wrestling, basket-ball, ice hockey, water polo and Rugby football." These are better left to the men because they are so "rough and strenuous." (Of that list, Mary

Morgan included baseball, basketball, ice hockey and water polo in the list of sports she included in her book five years later.) Sargent also promoted the idea of modifying the sports for women, to reduce the "prolonged mental or physical strain."

While focusing on the actual sports with the potential to make women more masculine, Sargent also looked at the basic role of exercise and sport moving women in this direction. While supporting physical activity, he states that "all forms of athletic sports and most physical exercises tend to make women's figures more masculine, inasmuch as they tend to broaden the shoulders, deepen the chest, narrow the hips and develop the muscles of the arms, backs and legs, which are masculine characteristics." To this end, according to Sargent, there is little that a woman could do that would allow her the pleasure and health benefits of physical activity without becoming more masculine.

## Primary Source

### "Are Athletics Making Girls Masculine?" [excerpt]

**SYNOPSIS:** Sargent acknowledges that all athletic activity, by its very nature, will result in an increasingly masculine physical appearance as well as behavior for women. While Sargent fully supports the role of athletics in a woman's life, he sees the problem of increasing masculinity as something that they must face.

That there is a change taking place in our American girls and women is unquestioned. And it is so elusive, so baffling of description that it is proving the most attractive of subjects for discussion in the newspaper and magazine. Every journalistic wind that blows either moans or shrieks, according to its source, of feminine activities, and we are forced to listen whether we will or not. Much of the reading matter put forth in certain somewhat sensational papers so utterly disregards truth and reason that we are in danger of half believing that womankind has already become a distorted Amazon creation, to be talked about and wondered at, but no longer to be loved and admired.

### What It Is Believed Athletics Are Doing for Girls

There is really nothing in the present state of women's development, either mental or physical, which calls for the pen of a Jeremiah. As a nation we are probably deteriorating physically, and in enlarging upon this topic the alarmist might find much material to his liking. But this statement applies no more to women than to men, and perhaps not as much. Heretofore women have been more creatures of the kitchen and fireside than of the great outdoors, and the present generation of young women who will become the mothers of the next generation have more muscle and more lung capacity than their own mothers. The growth of athletics for girls is largely responsible for this. Colleges for women have more or less grudgingly made room in their curricula for gymnastics and athletics, and the noncollegiate world has followed suit and made athletic sports accessible to women.

Any one who practices gymnastics or engages in athletics with regularity must find a change in certain organs and muscles of the body: the waist-line is enlarged, the chest expansion is increased, the muscles of the back are strengthened. These are some of the results in both men and women. They are not regarded as alarming as men but when we mention them in connection with our young women we are interpreted as claiming that our girls are becoming masculine.

Many persons honestly believe that athletics are making girls bold, masculine and overassertive; that they are destroying the beautiful lines and curves of her figure, and are robbing her of that charm and elusiveness that has so long characterized the female sex. Others, including many physicians, incline to the belief that athletics are injurious to the health. This double charge, of course, gives a serious aspect to the whole question, and it should be met. . . .

### Athletics for Men and Athletics for Women

All the highly specialized athletic sports and games have been developed to meet the requirements of men, but many of our girls and women have entered into them, and hence the query: "Are our women becoming masculine?" From the biologist's point of view, men and women, like the males and females of most animals, show by their organization that they have been evolved from a type in which both sexes were combined in the same individual. The separation of the sexes did not destroy this dual nature, as is demonstrated by the development of secondary male characteristics in women in extreme age and of feminine characteristics in aged men. This contention may also be supported by the structure of the body's tissue cells, the nuclei of which are made up of paternal and maternal parts.

It is in consequence of this dual structure that secondary sexual characters are latent in both males and females, which may make their appearance in abnormal individuals or under certain conditions of habit and surroundings. In the early history of mankind

men and women led more nearly the same life, and were therefore more nearly alike physically and mentally than in the subsequent centuries of civilization. This divergence of the sexes is a marked characteristic among highly civilized races. Co-education and participation in occupations and recreations of certain kinds may have a tendency to make the ideals and habits of women approximate those of men in these highly civilized races. But such approximation would not belong to the progressive stages of the evolution of mankind.

### Do Women Need As Much Exercise As Men?

Such changes would be convergences in structure and character, and while they might lead to what we should now consider an advancement this condition would not in any way alter the fact that the tendency would be for women to become virile and men to become effeminate, and both sexes would approximate each other, which would mean the retrogressive period of the evolution of the sexes. These biological theories, although usually considered in connection with the evils of co-education, are equally applicable to the consideration of the evils which have followed the entrance of women into commercial life, and must follow them into competitive athletics which are regulated according to men's rules and standards.

From a physiological point of view woman needs physical exercise as much as man. She has the same kind of brain, heart, lungs, stomach and tissues, and these organs in her are just as responsive to exercise as in men. Fundamentally both sexes have the same bones and muscles. They are much larger, however, in the average male than in the average female.

The average male weighs about one hundred and thirty-five pounds without clothes and is about five feet seven inches in height, while the female weighs about one hundred and fifteen pounds and is about five feet two inches in height. The male has broad, square shoulders, the female narrow, sloping ones. The male has a large, muscular chest, broad waist, narrow hips and long and muscular legs, while the female has little muscle in the chest, a constricted waist, broad hips, short legs and thighs frequently weighted with adipose tissue. The ankles, waist, feet and hands in the male are much larger than those in the female. In point of strength the female is only about one-half as strong as the male; and the average lung capacity of the male is two hundred and forty cubic inches, of the female one hundred and sixty cubic inches. To these average conditions there are, of course, many exceptions. . . .

## No Athletic Sport Prohibitive to Women

I have no hesitation in saying that there is no athletic sport or game in which some women cannot enter, not only without fear of injury but also with great prospects of success. In nearly every instance, however, it will be found that the women who are able to excel in the rougher and more masculine sports have either inherited or acquired masculine characteristics. This must necessarily be so, since it is only by taking on masculine attributes that success in certain forms of athletics can be won. For instance, a woman could not hope to be successful in the practice of heavy gymnastics where she has to handle her own weight without reducing the girth of her hips and thighs and increasing the development of her arms, chest and upper back. She could not hope to succeed in rowing or in handling heavy weights without broadening the waist and shoulders and strengthening the muscles of the back and abdomen. Her relatively short legs and heavy hips and thighs would handicap her severely in all running, jumping and vaulting contests, and render it practically impossible for her to make records in these events comparable to those made by men.

These athletic limitations do not apply only to women as women, but also to men who have women's physical characteristics. Nor do the limitations which I have mentioned apply to young girls from ten to fifteen years of age, who, if properly trained, will often surpass boys of the same age in any kind of game or athletic performance. But it is at these ages that girls have neat, trim and boyish figures. If girls received the same kind of physical training as boys throughout their growing and developing period they could make a much more creditable showing as athletes when they become adult women. The interesting question is: Would such girls become more womanly women, and the boys more manly men?

## The Best Sports for Girls

The athletics in which girls most frequently indulge are lawn tennis, running, jumping, hurdling, swimming, skating, field hockey, cricket, basket-ball, rowing, canoeing, fencing, archery, bowling, vaulting and certain forms of heavy gymnastics. Some girls also play ice hockey, lacrosse, baseball, polo and association football, while others box and wrestle and play Rugby football just as their brothers do. There is really no such thing as sex in sport, any more than there is sex in education. All sports are indulged in by most men, and most sports are enjoyed by some women.

There are no sports that tend to make women masculine in an objectionable sense except boxing, baseball, wrestling, basket-ball, ice hockey, water polo and Rugby football. These sports are thought better adapted to men than to women, because they are so rough and strenuous. They afford opportunity for violent personal encounter, which is distasteful to many men as well as to most women. That is the real objection to all antagonistic sports, and that is the reason why it Is so difficult for a lady or a gentleman to indulge in them. But we must bear in mind that all athletic sports are of the nature of a contest, and in this very fact lies much of their physical, mental and moral value.

## These Make Women More Masculine

Physically all forms of athletic sports and most physical exercises tend to make women's figures more masculine, inasmuch as they tend to broaden the shoulders, deepen the chest, narrow the hips, and develop the muscles of the arms, back and legs, which are masculine characteristics. Some exercises, like bowling, tennis, fencing, hurdling and swimming, tend to broaden the hips, which is a feminine characteristic. But archery, skating and canoeing, which are thought to be especially adapted to women, tend to develop respectively broad shoulders, long feet and deep muscular chests, which are essentially masculine; while rowing, which is thought to be the most masculine of all exercises, tends to broaden the hips, narrow the waist, develop the large front and back thighs and give many of the fines of the feminine figure.

Just how all-round athletics tend to modify woman's form may be judged by comparing the conventional with the athletic type of woman. The conventional woman has a narrow waist, broad and massive hips and large thighs. In the athletic type of woman sex characteristics are less accentuated, and there is a suggestion of reserve power in both trunk and limbs. Even the mental and moral qualities that accompany the development of such a figure are largely masculine, but this is because women have not yet had as many opportunities to exercise them. . . .

## Modify Men's Athletics for Women

Any one who has had much experience in teaching or training women must have observed these facts in regard to them: Women as a class cannot stand a prolonged mental or physical strain as well as men. Exact it of them and they will try to do the work, but they will do it at a fearful cost to themselves and eventually to their children. Give women frequent intervals of rest and relaxation and they will often accomplish as much in twenty four hours as men accomplish. So firmly have I become convinced of this fact that I have arranged the schedule of work at both the winter and summer Normal Schools at Cambridge so that periods of mental and physical activity follow each other alternately, and both are interspersed with frequent intervals of rest.

The modifications that I would suggest in men's athletics so as to adapt them to women are as follows: Reduce the time of playing in all games and lengthen the periods of rest between the halves. Reduce the heights of high and low hurdles and lessen the distance between them. Lessen the weight of the shot and hammer and all other heavy-weight appliances. In heavy gymnastics have bars, horses, swings, ladders, etc., adjustable so that they may be easily adapted to the requirements of women. In basket-ball, a favorite game with women and girls, divide the field of play into three equal parts by lines, and insist upon the players confining themselves to the space prescribed for them. This insures that every one shall be in the game, and prevents some players from exhausting themselves. If the field of play is large enough seven or nine players on a side are preferable to the five required by the men's rules. As the game is played today by men, with only five on a side and without lines, it brings a harder strain on the heart, lungs and nervous system than the game of football does.

I am often asked: "Are girls overdoing athletics at school and college?" I have no hesitation in saying that in many of the schools where basket-ball is being played according to rules for boys many girls are injuring themselves in playing this game. The numerous reports of these girls breaking down with heart trouble or a nervous collapse are mostly too well founded. Other instances are recorded where schoolgirls have broken down in training for tennis tournaments, or for running, jumping and swimming contests. These instances generally occur in schools or colleges where efforts are made to arouse interest in athletics by arranging matches between rival teams, clubs and institutions, and appealing to school pride, loyalty, etc., to furnish the driving power. Under the sway of these powerful impulses the individual is not only forced to do her best, but to do even better than her best, though she breaks down in her efforts to surpass her previous records.

There will be little honor or glory in winning a race, playing a game or doing a "stunt" which every other girl could do. It is in the attempt to win distinction by doing something that others cannot do that the girl who is over-zealous or too ambitious is likely to do herself an injury. For this reason girls who are ambitious to enter athletic contests should be carefully examined and selected by a physician or trained woman expert, and the usual method of trying out unprepared candidates by actual contests in order to determine "the survival of the fittest" should not be allowed.

## Further Resources

### BOOKS
Guttmann, Allen. *Women's Sports: A History.* New York: Columbia University Press, 1991.

Sparhawk Ruth M., et. al., comp. *American Women in Sport, 1887–1987: A 100-Year Chronology.* Metuchen, N.J.: Scarecrow Press, 1989.

### PERIODICALS
Cottrell, Debbie Mauldin. "The Sargent School for Physical Education." *The Journal of Physical Education, Recreation & Dance,* March 1994, 32–37.

Lupcho, Paula Rogers. "The Harvard Summer School of Physical Education." *The Journal of Physical Education, Recreation & Dance,* March 1994, 43–46.

### WEBSITES
"History of Women in Sports Timeline." St. Lawrence County Branch of the American Association of University Women. Available online at http://www.northnet.org/stlawrenceaauw /timeline.htm; website home page: http://www.northnet.org /stlawrenceaauw (accessed March 19, 2003).

"Dr. Thomas Chats with Dr. Dudley Sargent." Iowa Health and Physical Readiness Alliance. Available online at http://www .ihpra.org/sargent_chat.htm; website home page: http://www .ihpra.org (accessed March 19, 2003).

# "The Amateur"

### Editorial

**By:** Lyman Abbott, Hamilton W. Mabie, and Theodore Roosevelt

**Date:** February 8, 1913

**Source:** Abbott, Lyman, Hamilton W. Mabie, and Theodore Roosevelt. "The Amateur." *Outlook,* February 8, 1913, 293–295.

**About the Publication:** An ordained minister, Lyman Abbott (1835–1922) was the editor of the weekly magazine the *Outlook,* which started in 1876 as the *Christian Union.* In the

*Outlook,* Abbott promoted the views of the moderate Protestant progressivism movement and solicited the help of President Theodore Roosevelt (served 1901–1909) to serve as an associate editor. It was one of the most influential magazines of its day. ∎

### Introduction

Jim Thorpe (1888–1953), a Native American from Sauk and Fox descent, was arguably the finest athlete in American history. As a young man, he gained national fame and notoriety playing football for the Carlisle Indian School in Carlisle, Pennsylvania. In 1912, Thorpe won two gold medals at the Stockholm Olympics of 1912 in the pentathlon and decathlon. But Thorpe had to forfeit those medals after revealing that he played semi-professional baseball in 1909 and 1910 and received payment for his services. He went on to a career in professional baseball and football, but would never again possess the medals he won in Stockholm.

In the 1912 Olympics, Thorpe easily won the pentathlon and decathlon, events testing an athlete's skills in many areas. These events featured five and ten different tests of skills, respectively, of general fitness and athleticism. Ironically, these events were added to the

Jim Thorpe warms up before a game in 1912. He scored 25 touchdowns and 198 points that year, leading the Carlisle Indian School to the national collegiate championship. **AP/WIDE WORLD PHOTOS. REPRODUCED BY PERMISSION.**

Olympics in 1912 at the request of European athletes. European teams had complained that American athletes focused on one area and did not share their love for general fitness. Both of these events combined different track and field events, including running, the javelin throw, and the discus throw. Besides the gold medals Thorpe won for both events, the King of Sweden and the Czar of Russia honored him with trophies and other accolades.

Within months after his return from Stockholm, Thorpe revealed that he accepted a small amount of money while playing semi-professional baseball in 1909 and 1910 for the Rocky Mount Railroaders of the Carolina League. Semi-pro baseball was much more common in the early twentieth century than it is now, and players often were paid under the table. Many players assumed fake names, more to protect their reputations than to retain amateur athletic eligibility. When the news broke that he was not a pure "amateur" and had accepted money in exchange for his athletic services, the Amateur Athletic Union demanded that Thorpe return all of the awards and medals won at the 1912 Olympics.

### Significance

When the Associated Press polled sports writers in 1950 to determine the greatest athlete of the first half of the twentieth century, Jim Thorpe was the clear choice, winning 252 of 393 first-place votes. (Babe Ruth garnered eighty-six first-place votes, the second highest total.) While his fame has faded in recent years, Jim Thorpe remains one of the best, if not the best, athlete of the twentieth century. What is also clear is that he suffered one of the great injustices in sports history when stripped of his Olympic medals. Thorpe was forced to relinquish these prizes, though they were returned to his family in 1982, long after his death. He played professional baseball and football through the 1910s and 1920s, but Thorpe never personally recovered from losing these medals.

There were many issues associated with the Thorpe debacle. First, there was tremendous confusion between the amateur and professional athlete in the early part of the twentieth century. Only three sports—baseball, boxing, and horse racing—were recognized as professional sports, and even those three had a number of gray areas. Baseball at the lower levels, such as semi-pro, allowed many chances to play in relative obscurity. Second, Thorpe's race, as a Native American, (and possibly his class) clearly did not help his cause. Racism in the early twentieth century created equally hostile environments for both Jim Thorpe and heavyweight boxing champion, Jack Johnson. Third, Thorpe represented a precursor to today's student-athlete, who needed to balance financial needs with the standards of amateur competition. In today's environment, what constitutes amateur and professional status is much clearer.

Illustration by Paul Schroeder of James E. Sullivan, Secretary of the Amateur Athletic League holding knife over "Jim Thorpe" goat, while other goats, "Summer Ball Players," huddle together, 1913. **THE LIBRARY OF CONGRESS.**

## Primary Source

"The Amateur"

**SYNOPSIS:** The editorial authors of the *Outlook* chose Jim Thorpe's exposure as a professional athlete as an opportunity to criticize American sports and its commercialism. The writers advocate a more European approach to sports, supporting the virtues of athletics for athletics' sake. The article supports the decision of the Amateur Athletic Union to strip Thorpe of his Olympic medals because Thorpe was not technically an amateur when he competed. The editors also find problems with the growing commercialism of American sport, and a desire to win at any cost.

When an American Indian, who had won the championship as the best all-round athlete in America, established his right in the Olympic Games at Stockholm last July to be regarded as the greatest amateur athlete in the world, and was so declared by the King of Sweden, there was widespread gratification in America. Now that that great Indian athlete, James Thorpe, has been stripped of his honors because, by his own confession, he had received money for playing baseball, and therefore was not an amateur but a professional and had no right to enter into competition with amateur athletes, the humiliation is not confined to him; it extends to all who value their country's reputation for fairness in sport as in all other matters.

Every such incident lends aid and comfort to those who are constantly looking for proof of their assertions that Americans are constitutionally devoted to the doctrine that nothing should stand in the way of winning. This incident in particular will afford an opportunity to those unfriendly to this country to declare again their opinion that the ideals of the gentleman are beyond the comprehension of American athletes, and that American sport is thoroughly commercialized. The fact that these aspersions are unjust and ill founded only makes it the more humiliating for such an incident as this to occur: for the fact that in this conspicuous instance the standards of amateur athletics have been ignored makes it all the more difficult to persuade foreign critics to regard these aspersions as ill founded and unjust.

James Thorpe is a student at the Carlisle Indian School. He is of the Sac and Fox tribe, and, like many other Indians, has sufficient property to afford him support. The Carlisle School is well known for its athletes and its athletic teams. In particular, the Carlisle football team has established a reputation for a peculiar skill and brilliance. Thorpe has been the best-known football player at the School and one of the greatest football players in the country. He is almost as well known as a player of baseball. "In the summer of 1909 and 1910" (this is his own phrase) he played baseball in North Carolina, and for this received money. In the fall of 1911 he was readmitted to the Carlisle Indian School. He took part not only in the sports of the School but also in the athletic meets of the Amateur Athletic Union. Last summer he went with the rest of the American team to Stockholm and competed in the Olympic Games. His achievements there astonished the whole world of athletes. In particular, he took part in two great series of athletic events. One, known as the Pentathlon, is a series of five athletic events; the other, the Decathlon, is a series of ten athletic events. In the first series, out of a possible five firsts he won four; in the Decathlon he registered 8,412 points as against the 7,724 of his nearest competitor, a Swede. Thus the two events which he won required specialized skill in many varieties of sport, such as sprinting, long-distance running, high and broad jumping, weight-throwing, casting the javelin, and the like. As a result of his extraordinary achievements in the Olympic Games he received among his prizes the sculptured Viking ship given by the Czar of Russia and the bronze bust of the King of Sweden presented by the King. These and other trophies which he has secured as an amateur athlete will be his no longer, and such of them as he secured at the Olympic Games must be returned to the Olympic Committee to be redistributed to those who rightfully won them.

This is a subject that concerns American public opinion.

In the first place, American public opinion should cordially support the officials of the Amateur Athletic Union, whose action was so prompt and sure in this matter that the repudiation of Thorpe as an amateur was officially made simultaneously with the news of the discovery of his offenses. There was a chance for the representatives of organized amateur sport in America to make clear to the world that their standards of amateur sport were inexorable; and they used that chance to the best advantage. They might have allowed a very legitimate sympathy for this Indian student, and their recognition that he had done only what others had done with impunity, to cloud their judgment and to obscure their sense of duty toward the cause of pure athletics. This they did not do. Like everybody else who thinks about this, they must from the first have seen that there was a large element of individual injustice to Thorpe himself in the consequences that followed his acts as a boy. For a young man to be humiliated before the whole world simply because be played baseball one summer and thoughtlessly accepted money for his playing, as others were doing and as a great many professional players do without any disgrace whatever, seems to be an extraordinarily disproportionate punishment. It might be said that his punishment came from the fact that he concealed his having received money; but the fact that he played for the fun of it and not for the sake of the money may well have led him to believe thoroughly in his own amateur spirit and standing. He was mistaken; but the consequence to him is a very severe penalty for such a mistake. These considerations must have been in the minds of Mr. James E. Sullivan, the American Commissioner to the Olympic Games and Secretary of the Amateur Athletic Union; Mr. G. T. Kirby, the President of the organization, and Mr. Bartow S. Weeks, the legal adviser; but such considerations did not govern their decision. Humiliating, therefore, as the experiences is in one respect, it is emphatically encouraging in another, for it has afforded evidence to the whole world that organized amateur athletics in this country will not countenance disregard of amateur standards. These officials should, and we believe will, receive unmistakable signs of the applause of American public sentiment.

There is another matter in connection with this as to which American public sentiment should express itself unmistakably. In the course of his letter to Mr. Sullivan acknowledging that he had received money for baseball-playing, Thorpe writes:

On the same teams I played with were several college men from the North who were earning money by ball-playing during their vacations and who were regarded as amateurs at home. I did not play for the money there was in it, because my property brings me in enough money to live on, but because I liked to play ball. I was not very wise to the ways of the world and did not realize that this was wrong and it would make me a professional in track sports, although I learned from the other players that it would be better for me not to let any one know that I was playing, and for that reason I never told any one at the School about it until to-day. . . . I never realized until now what a big mistake I made by keeping it a secret about my ball-playing, and I am sorry I did so. I hope I will be partly excused by the fact that I was simply an Indian school-boy and did not know all about such things. In fact, I did not know that I was doing wrong because I was doing what I knew several other college men had done: except that they did not use their own names.

To every college in the land these words of this Indian student should come as a sermon. To some they should bring shame and contrition. The colleges of the country should be the repositories of the best traditions and standards of amateur sport. It is because they have not been that this humiliation has come upon an Indian athlete, and indeed upon the whole country. Every college alumnus who is influential in any respect in athletics should search his conscience to see if he, through word or influence, has been in any way responsible for maintaining the low standards regarding fairness and candor in athletics that led James Thorpe to this pass.

## Further Resources

### BOOKS

Wheeler, Robert. *Jim Thorpe, World's Greatest Athlete.* Norman, Okla.: University of Oklahoma Press, 1979

### PERIODICALS

Gould, Stephen Jay. "The Athlete of the Century." *American Heritage,* October 1998, 14–16.

Koehler, Michael. "Jim Thorpe's Grandson on School Athletics." *Education Digest,* February 1995, 40–44.

### WEBSITES

"Biography of Jim Thorpe." Jim Thorpe Association. Available online at http://www.jimthorpeassoc.org/biography.htm; website home page: http://www.jimthorpeassoc.org (accessed March 31, 2003).

"Jim Thorpe: Athlete of the Century Campaign." National Environmental Coalition Of Native Americans. Available online at http://www.alphacdc.com/necona/jimthorp.html; website home page: http://www.alphacdc.com/necona (accessed April 6, 2003).

### AUDIO AND VISUAL MEDIA
*Thorpe's Gold.* Directed by David Putnam. VCI Home Video, 1984, VHS.

# "Baseball and the National Life"
Essay

**By:** Henry Addington Bruce

**Date:** May 17, 1913

**Source:** Bruce, H. Addington. "Baseball and the National Life." *Outlook,* May 17, 1913, 104–107.

**About the Author:** Henry Addington Bruce (1874–1959) was a Canadian-born author and newspaper journalist who graduated from the University of Toronto and attended Harvard University. He specialized in psychical research and wrote extensively on this subject with works such as *Adventurings in the Psychical* (1914), *Riddle of Personality* (1908) and *Psychology and Parenthood* (1915). ∎

## Introduction

One of the most interesting debates that takes place in today's sports environment is whether baseball is America's national pastime. Many critics point to the growing popularity of NASCAR stock-car racing and the overwhelming interest in professional football as proof that baseball no longer can claim its place as the national pastime. While it is clear that baseball does not stand alone among professional sports today, no sport has been able, or will be able, to completely dominate the sporting world as baseball did in the late-nineteenth century and early-twentieth century. This notion of baseball as the national pastime was solidified in the 1900s and 1910s through a series of books and articles extolling the virtues of the game while making the connections back to the very nature of American society. For many of the commentators early in the twentieth century, there was no question that baseball was the national pastime. It also manifested many of the great aspects of American culture.

## Significance

Bruce extolled the virtues of baseball in American society and made the connection between the sport and its country's culture. In large part, Bruce focused on a few basic areas where baseball had made a positive impact on American culture, teamwork and "team spirit," quick thinking, and physical activity. In the process, Bruce offered anecdotal accounts of the role of baseball in our culture—such as the Supreme Court justices' demanding updates on the score from the World Series, and the tremendous increase in gate revenue from the championship games between 1858 and 1912 ($750 to $490,833 respectively). Had his audience been unsympathetic, he might have required additional proof to the role of baseball as the national pastime. It is clear that in 1913, that was all the convincing needed.

The three areas of influence Bruce discussed when writing "Baseball and the National Life" were very important in the unique nature of American society in the early twentieth century. Bruce emphasized the role of baseball in developing a team spirit and camaraderie needed by society. He was particularly fascinated with the "unselfish co-operation" of the "sacrifice hit" and the notion of a player stepping out of the spotlight for the betterment of all. In the role of quick thinking, Bruce took a quote from A.G. Spalding on the role that baseball plays in developing a way of working through problems. His article cites Spalding's lessons from the bleachers as representing the highest level of criticism that anyone can expect: "If that doesn't train him to think quickly, nothing can."

Finally, baseball played a great role in keeping the nation engaged in physical activity. While he might have been a bit naïve in thinking that participation in baseball would promote sobriety and self-control, Bruce was accurate in seeing it as a way of "gaining momentary relief from the strain of an intolerable burden, and at the same time finding a harmless outlet for pent-up emotions." While recognizing its defects, Bruce cites at the end of the document the power of both baseball and the "Little Red Schoolhouse" as being parallel in making the American society great.

## Primary Source

"Baseball and the National Life"

> **SYNOPSIS:** In this essay from the *Outlook,* H. Attington Bruce offers his assessment of the role of baseball as a positive force in American society. Rather than spend a great deal of time talking about how people felt about the sport, he focused on the attributes in baseball that improve American culture and society. Of these areas, Bruce writes about baseball's attributes such as promoting teamwork and "team spirit," developing a sense of quick thinking that became the earmark of the American entrepreneur, and ensuring physical activity that provided a much needed "pressure valve" for young men in American society.

On July 20, 1858, there was played the first recorded game of baseball to which an admission fee was charged. The opposing teams were made up of carefully selected players representing New York and Brooklyn; the scene of the game was the old Fashion Race Course on Long Island; and some fifteen hundred people paid $750 to see New York win by four runs.

October 16, 1912, or little more than fifty years later, another New York team, playing in Boston, lost by a single run the last of a series of inter-league games for the title of "World's Champions." The newspapers of the country reported the game in the most minute detail, and incidentally announced that the eight games of the series had been attended by more than 250,000 persons, whose admission fees aggregated $490,833, or an average in excess of 30,000 spectators and average receipts of about $60,000 per game. Than these contrasting figures nothing could exhibit more impressively the tremendous growth in popularity of baseball in the comparatively short interval between the earliest and the latest championship game.

When, in the late summer of last year, the Boston "Red Sox" returned from a Western tour which virtually assured to them the championship of the American League, it has been estimated that nearly 100,000 people assembled in the streets of Boston to give them a welcome home. And later, when they played the New York "Giants" in the "World's Series," the course of every game was followed with the most eager attention not alone by the thousands in grand stand and "bleachers," but by many, many thousands more standing in compact masses before the bulletin boards of city newspapers, or in little groups at the telegraph offices of remote and isolated villages. So widespread, in fact, was the interest that the day after the deciding game the newspapers were able to print this astonishing item of news from Washington:

> Unprecedented procedure was permitted to day in the Supreme Court of the United States when the Justices, sitting on the bench hearing the Government's argument in the "bathtub trust" case, received bulletins, inning by inning of the "World's Championship" baseball game in Boston. The progress of the playing was closely watched by the members of the highest court in the land, especially by Associate Justice Day, who had requested the baseball bulletins during the luncheon recess from 2 to 2:30 P.M. The little slips giving the progress of the play went to him not only during the luncheon recess, but when the Court resumed its sitting. They were passed along the bench from Justice to Justice.

Veritably baseball is something more than the great American game—it is an American institution having a significant place in the life of the people, and consequently worthy of close and careful analysis.

Fully to grasp its significance, however, if is necessary to study it, in the first place, as merely a game, and seek to determine wherein lie its peculiar qualities of fascination. As a game, as something that is "playable," it of course must serve the ordinary ends of play. These, according to the best authorities on the physiology and psychology of play, are threefold: the expenditure of surplus nervous energy in a way that will not be harmful to the organism, but, on the contrary, will give needed exercise to growing muscles; the development of traits and abilities that will afterwards aid the player in the serious business of life; and the attainment of mental rest through pleasurable occupation.

Until recently it has been customary to emphasize one or another of these purposes and motives as affording the sole reason for play. But scientists are beginning to appreciate that all of them may be operant in determining the action of the play impulse, one motive being influential in one instance, the second in another, the third in yet another, or all three in combination. As between the three, though, the preparation motive would seem to be uppermost, at all events in the play of childhood and youth, children instinctively favoring those games which, although they are completely unconscious of the fact, tend most strongly to form and establish the characteristics that will be most serviceable to them in later years. Or, as stated by Professor Karl Gross, the first to dwell on this aspect of play:

> Play is the agency employed to develop crude powers and prepare them for life's uses, and from the biological standpoint we can say: From the moment when the intellectual development of a species becomes more useful in the 'struggle for existence' than the most perfect instinct, will natural selection favor those individuals in whom the less elaborated faculties have more chance of being worked out by practice under the protection of parents—that is to say, those individuals that play.

Now, in all civilized countries of the modern world, and especially in countries of advanced economic development and of a form of government like that of the United States, success and progress depend chiefly on the presence of certain personal characteristics. Physical fitness, courage, honesty, patience, the spirit of initiative combined with due respect for lawful authority, soundness and quickness of judgment, self-confidence, self-control, cheeriness, fair-mindedness, and appreciation of the importance

Baseball card of Frederick C. Snodgrass, center fielder for the New York Giants, 1911. **THE LIBRARY OF CONGRESS.**

of social solidarity, of "team play"—these are traits requisite as never before for success in the life of an individual and of a nation. They are traits developed to some extent by all outdoor games played by groups of competitors. But it is safe to say that no other game—not even excepting football—develops them as does baseball.

One need attend only a few games, whether played by untrained school-boys or by the most expert professionals, to appreciate the great value of baseball as a developmental agent. Habits of sobriety and self-control are established in the players if only from the necessity of keeping in good condition in order to acquit one's self creditably and hold

Baseball card of Jacob G. Stahl, manager/first-baseman for the Boston Red Sox, 1911. THE LIBRARY OF CONGRESS.

a place on the team. Patience, dogged persistence, the pluck that refuses to acknowledge either weariness or defeat, are essential to the mastery of the fine points of batting, fielding, or pitching—a mastery which in turn brings with it a feeling of self confidence that eventually will go far in helping its possessor to achieve success off as well as on the "diamond." It takes courage of a high order to play infield positions, as, for example, they ought to be played when "stolen bases" are imminent; and, for that matter, it takes courage to "steal" them when the runner knows that he is likely to be "blocked off" by some courageous infielder of the type of the two Wagners of "Pirate" and "Red Sox" fame.

So, too, courage, and plenty of it, is needed at the bat—courage not simply to face the swiftly moving ball, but to "crowd" the "plate" so as to handicap the pitcher in his efforts to perform successfully and expeditiously the work of elimination. I well remember, in connection with the "World's Series" of 1911, the boldness in this respect displayed by the New York player Snodgrass, when batting against the pitching of the mighty Bender. Time after time Snodgrass stood so close to the "plate" as to draw vehement protests from his opponent, with whom, as an American League partisan, I heartily sympathized. But at the same time I could not withhold some slight measure of admiration for the courage of the batsman, typical of the spirit which, pervading the whole team, had no small share in winning for the "Giants" the National League honors in 1911 and again last year.

As an agent in the development of the "team spirit" baseball is no less notable. The term "sacrifice hit" eloquently expresses one phase of the game which must leave on all playing it an indelible impression of the importance in all affairs of life of unselfish co-operation. The extent, indeed, to which baseball tends to inculcate the lesson of subordination of self for the common good is well shown by a little story I heard not long ago regarding two professional baseball players. One was the shortstop, the other the second baseman, of a "major" league team, and consequently they were required by the duties of their positions to work more closely together than any other members of the team except the pitcher and catcher. One day, the story goes, they had a quarrel so bitter that for the remainder of the season they did not address a word to each other when off the "diamond." But, once the umpire had cried "Play ball!" their antagonism was temporarily dropped, and they fought the common foe in as complete accord as though they had been the best of friends. Surely a game that can develop such a social consciousness—and conscience—is a game of which any nation may be proud, and to which it may well feel indebted.

And, besides aiding powerfully in physical and moral development baseball is also a splendid mindbuilder. The ability to think, and to think quickly, is fostered by the duties of its every position as well as by the complicated problems that are constantly arising in its swiftly changing course of events. Time and again games have been won, or the way has been cleared to victory, by the quickness of a player or a manager in appreciating the possibilities of a critical situation and planning a definite plan of campaign to meet the emergency. It was thus, to give a single illustration, with the final game of last year's "World's Series."

That game was won by the "Red Sox" by the score of three runs to two, an extra inning being necessary, as the score stood one to one in the ninth. The newspapers next day gave unenviable prominence to two New York fielders, to whose errors in the tenth inning the loss of the game was ascribed. Actually the turning-point came in the seventh inning, when New York led by one run to none for Boston.

From the start of the game Mathewson, the premier pitcher of the National League, had been disposing of the "Red Sox" batsmen with all his old-time skill. Bedient, his young rival, had been doing almost equally well, although New York had earned a run off him in the third inning. In Boston's half of the seventh, with two men out and a man on first base, the manager of the "Red Sox"—who also, as it happened, was the man then on first base—made the move that undoubtedly saved the game for his team. It was Bedient's turn to bat, but instead Manager Stahl sent to the "plate" a utility outfielder, Henriksen, who until that moment had not once been at bat in the series. Mathewson, utterly in the dark as to his weaknesses as a batsman, tried him with a variety of pitches. One proved so much to his liking that he drove it past third base for a hit that brought in the tying run. Stahl's judgment, plus Henriksen's ability to "make good," had turned impending defeat into possible victory.

So incessant and so varied are the demands made on the ball-player's intelligence that any one who really knows the game will be inclined to indorse unreservedly the published declaration of that most successful baseball-player and most successful business man. Mr. Albert G. Spalding:

> I never struck anything in business that did not seem a simple matter when compared with complications I have faced on the baseball field. A young man playing baseball gets into the habit of quick thinking in most adverse circumstances and under the most merciless criticism in the world—the criticism from the 'bleachers.' If that doesn't train him, nothing can. Baseball in youth has the effect in later years of making him think and act a little quicker than the other fellow.

To-day this is even more the case than in the days when Mr. Spalding led his Boston and Chicago teams to victory, for with the passage of time the technique of the game has been improved to an ex-

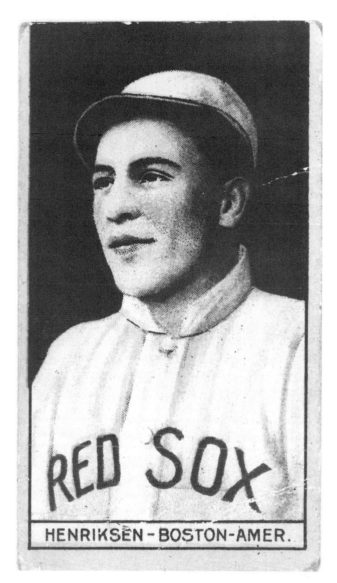

Baseball card of Olaf Henriksen, outfielder for the Boston Red Sox 1912. THE LIBRARY OF CONGRESS.

tent that makes it more of a developmental agent than it was even ten years ago. Lacking the strength, skill, and experience of the professional player, the school-boy whose efforts are confined to the "diamond" of the vacant lot or public park plays the game under precisely the same rules as the professional, and with no less zest and earnestness, and profits correspondingly. To be sure, in playing it he does not dream for an instant that he is thereby helping to prepare himself for the important struggles of maturity. He plays it merely because he finds it "good fun"—merely because, in its variety and rapidity of action, in the comparative ease with which its fundamental principles may be learned and in its essentially co-operative yet competitive character, it affords an intensely pleasurable occupation. It is, in truth, a game which makes an irresistible appeal to the instincts of youth precisely because it so admirably meets the principal objects of play—mental rest through enjoyment, exercise for the muscles, the healthy expenditure of surplus nervous energy, and practice and preparation for life's work.

This, of course, does not explain its popularity with the non-playing American public of mature years, a popularity which seems to many the more surprising and reprehensible in view of the fact that to-day, when baseball games are drawing larger crowds than in all the previous history of the sport, the Nation is burdened to an appalling extent by economic and social evils. But in reality this phenomenon is neither so unusual nor so ominous as alarmists would have us believe. "Give us games!" was the cry of the Roman populace in time of disaster many centuries ago, and it has since been unconsciously echoed by many another people under the stress of some great crisis.

Baseball itself, it is worth noting, was a product of the period of anti-slavery agitation that preceded the crisis of the Civil War, having been invented in 1839, two years after the murder of the abolitionist Elijah P. Lovejoy, and one year after the burning of Pennsylvania Hall, in Philadelphia, by a mob of pro-slavery sympathizers; and its first rise into favor as a public spectacle was but a year or so before North and South met in their epochal conflict.

What this means is simply an instinctive resort to sport as a method of gaining momentary relief from the strain of an intolerable burden, and at the same time finding a harmless outlet for pent-up emotions which, unless thus gaining expression, might discharge themselves in a dangerous way. It also means, there is reason to believe, a continuance of the play impulse as an aid in the rational and efficient conduct of life. It is no mere coincidence that the great sport-loving peoples of the world—the Americans, the English, the Canadians, and the Australians—have been pre-eminent in the art of achieving progress by peaceful and orderly reform. There have been times, as in the case of the Civil War, when the issues involved have been such as to make absolutely necessary the arbitrament of arms. But evolution, not revolution, has been the rule in the development of these nations—these nations which above all others respond to the impulse to play.

Baseball, then, from the spectator's standpoint, is to be regarded as a means of catharsis, or, perhaps better, as a safety-valve. And it performs this service the more readily because of the appeal it makes to the basic instincts, with resultant removal of the inhibitions that ordinarily cause tenseness and restraint. For exactly the same reason it has a democratizing value no less important to the welfare of society than is its value as a developmental and tension-relieving agent. The spectator at a ball game is no longer a statesman, lawyer, broker, doctor, merchant, or artisan, but just a plain every-day man, with a heart full of fraternity and good will to all his fellow-men—except perhaps the umpire. The oftener he sits in grand stand or "bleachers," the broader, kindlier, better man and citizen he must tend to become.

Finally, it is to be observed that the mere watching of a game of baseball, as of football, lacrosse, hockey, or any other game of swift action, has a certain beneficial physical effect. It is a psychological commonplace that pleasurable emotions, especially if they find expression in laughter, shouts, cheers, and other muscle-expanding noises, have a tonic value to the whole bodily system. So that it is quite possible to get exercise vicariously, as it were; and the more stimulating the spectacle that excites feelings of happiness and enjoyment, the greater will be the resultant good. Most decidedly baseball is a game well designed to render this excellent service.

Like every virile, vigorous game, it has its defects. But its qualities far outweigh its shortcomings, and it must be accounted a happy day for America when the first players met on the first "diamond" laid out on American soil. The little red school-house has long been extolled as a prime factor in the Republic's progress. I for one am firmly convinced that the lessons taught in it would have lacked much of their potency had it not been for the reinforcement they received from the lessons learned on the baseball field near by. Long may Uncle Sam play ball!

## Further Resources

### BOOKS

National Baseball Hall of Fame and Museum. *Baseball As America: Seeing Ourselves Through Our National Game.* Washington, D.C.: National Geographic, 2002.

Spalding, A. G. *America's National Game* Lincoln, Neb.: University of Nebraska Press, 1992.

### PERIODICALS

Messenger, Christian K. "Baseball and the Meaning of America." *Humanities,* July/August 1994, 13–18.

Regan, F. Scott. "The Might Casey: Enduring Folk Hero of Failure." *Journal of Popular Culture,* Summer 1997, 91–110.

### WEBSITES

"The National Game: Baseball and American Culture." NationalPastime.com. Available online at http://www

.nationalpastime.com/the_national_game.html; website home page: http://www.nationalpastime.com (accessed April 4, 2003).

**AUDIO AND VISUAL MEDIA**

*Baseball.* Directed by Ken Burns. Warner Home Video, 1994, VHS.

---

# "Ouimet World's Golf Champion"

**Newspaper article**

**By:** *The New York Times*

**Date:** September 21, 1913

**Source:** "Ouimet World's Golf Champion." *The New York Times,* September 21, 1913. ■

## Introduction

The history of golf in the United States has changed with every generation in the twentieth century. The game came to America primarily from the Scottish and British, who dominated the professional championships in the late nineteenth and early twentieth centuries. In America, high membership fees at country clubs placed golf out of the reach of most Americans. Consequently, the sport was played exclusively by the wealthy. With many public golf courses, smaller golf clubs, and increased leisure time, golf now is accessible to millions of Americans. Even with the game out of reach for most children in the early twentieth century, many kids dreamed of a career in golf—or just a chance to play on a regular basis.

In 1913 Francis Ouimet was a clerk in a sporting-goods store. He had caddied since he was eleven at Brookline (Massachusetts) Country Club in a suburb of Boston. He played Brookline from time to time, and he won the Massachusetts State Amateur Championship. He was offered a spot in the U.S. Open, played at Brookline that year, and Ouimet decided to ask for the day off. With a ten-year-old caddie, his first two holes to start the tournament were awful. After the horrid start, he began to play exceptionally well. By the end of the second round of golf, he was within four shots of the lead. He played a great third round and ended tied for the lead with two British golf legends: Harry Vardon and Ted Ray–winners of a combined six British Open titles. These three golfers—two greats from England and a young former caddie—were set to play eighteen holes to determine the championship. News of the local boy playing for the championship caused almost ten thousand people to show up at Brookline and cheer on Ouimet. Ouimet defeated the two English golfers with a final round of seventy-two. The win put the golf championship on the front pages of newspapers everywhere.

## Significance

Long before Tiger Woods, Jack Nicklaus, Arnold Palmer, and Ben Hogan, the name synonymous with excellence in American golf was Francis Ouimet; his fame came from his stunning U.S. Open victory in September 1913 at the Brookline Country Club. In the previous day's newspaper, *The New York Times* claimed that the battle between Ouimet and the two British champions "ceased to be a purely golf competition and developed into an international contest between the representatives of Uncle Sam and John Bull." When he defeated the two British champions, it was another victory of the new world over the old world in the transplanted game of golf. With the interest given to the coverage of the young American winning the championship, more Americans were exposed to golf.

While significant as a golf event, the real interest in this story was the reaction by the spectators at Brookline. This article provides a detailed description of the activities of the spectators, and how they followed Ouimet and cheered loudly when he was poised to win. The author describes it as such: "When Ouimet holed his final stroke on the home green of the Country Club this afternoon, the 8,000 persons who had tramped through the heavy mist and dripping grass behind the trip of players for almost three hours realized what the victory meant to American golf and the scenes of elation which followed were pardonable under the circumstances." Additionally, the writer takes great pains to compare Ouimet and his accomplishments to American champions in tennis, polo, and track. These were the games and sports that the European countries had dominated. The writer does not compare Ouimet's skills to those of baseball greats Ty Cobb or Christy Mathewson, since at the time there was no question of the American dominance in baseball. However, the United States had not had a true golf champion until Ouimet's victory over the Europeans showed the country that the Americans could compete in any sport. Many historians have seen Ouimet's victory to be very influential in promoting golf in America—equally important to what Tiger Woods is doing in the early twenty-first century to further expand access to and interest in golf.

## Primary Source

**"Ouimet World's Golf Champion"** [excerpt]

> **SYNOPSIS:** This article includes coverage of the last day of the 1913 U.S. Open tournament, a three-way eighteen-hole play-off between Francis Ouimet, Harry

Vardon, and Ted Ray. The article also includes a great description of the spectators during the last round. Many of these fans were there only to root for Ouimet and had never attended a professional golf tournament before.

## Ouimet World's Golf Champion

Twenty-Year-Old Amateur Defeats Famous British Professionals for Open Title.

### Remarkable Golf Feat

Covers the 18-Hole Course at Brookline in 72 Strokes—Vardon 77, Ray 78.

### Splendid Display of Nerve

First Amateur to Win American Open Championship—Big Gallery Makes Demonstration at Finish.

Brookline, Mass., Sept. 20.—Another name was added to America's list of victors in international sport here today when Francis Ouimet, which for the benefit of the uninitiated is pronounced we-met, a youthful local amateur, won the nineteenth open championship of the United States Golf Association.

The winning of this national title was lifted to an international plane, due to the sensational circumstances of the play and to the calibre of the entrants whom Ouimet defeated during his four-day march to victory. Safely berthed in his qualifying round, the boy trailed the leaders in the first half of the championship round: tied with Harry Vardon and Edward Ray, the famous English professionals, for the first place in the final round, then completely outplayed them to-day in the eighteen-hole extra round which was necessary to decide the 1913 championship.

Ouimet won with the score of 72 strokes, two under par for one of the hardest courses in the country. Vardon finished five strokes behind Ouimet with 77; Ray took third place with 78.

### Ouimet's Rank in Sport

It was not the actual defeat of this famous pair of golfers so much as the manner of that defeat that entitles Ouimet's name to rank with that of Maurice E. McLoughlin, champion in tennis; Harry Payne Whitney, leader in polo, and James Thorpe, victor in athletics. Ouimet, a tall, slender youth, just past his teens, outplayed and outnerved not only Vardon and Ray in the play-off, a wonderful fact in itself, but succeeded in battling his way through the largest and most remarkable field of entrants that ever played for an American title. When the qualifying rounds began last Tuesday the lists contained 170 names, including in addition to Vardon and Ray, those of Wilfred Reid, another well-known English player; Louis Tellier, a French professional of note; a few high class amateurs, and a host of American and foreign professional playing for United States and Canadian clubs.

When Ouimet holed his final stroke on the home green of the Country Club this afternoon the 8,000 persons who had tramped through the heavy mist and dripping grass behind the trio of players for almost three hours realized what the victory meant to American golf and the scenes of elation which followed were pardonable under the circumstances.

### The Winner's Perfect Form

The pride in the young American's victory was all the more justified because of the fact that he had won without fluke or flaw in his play, responding in perfect form to a test of nerve, stamina and knowledge of golf never before required of a player in a national tournament. All through the crucial journey around the 18-hole course Ouimet never faltered. In fact his play might be termed mechanical, so perfect was it under the trying weather and course conditions. He appeared absolutely without nerve, playing from tee to fairway, from fairway to green, and finishing each hole with a splendid exhibition of putting. His veteran opponents, tried players of many a hard-won match in various parts of the world, broke under the strain, leaving Ouimet to finish as coolly as he had started.

The very fact that Vardon and Ray could not hold up under the stress of the struggle shows the titanic form and strain of the final round of the championship. Vardon has five times won the English open championship, and in 1900 won the American open at Wheaton, Ill., defeating J. H. Taylor, England's greatest golfer and present champion.

Before the tournament began Ray, Vardon, and Reid were 2 to 1 favorites to win over the remainder of the field. Even after Ouimet had tied with his two opponents of to-day, wagers were laid at 5 to 4 that one of the two Englishmen would defeat him and even money on Ray or Vardon against Ouimet alone.

The scenes of jubilation on the home green after the match had been won were, therefore, but natural expressions of pride and pleasure at Ouimet's success in retaining a championship for America, which was considered earlier in the week destined to cross the Atlantic.

### Ray and Vardon Cheered

Thousands of dripping rubber-coated spectators massed about Ouimet, who was hoisted to the shoulders of those nearest to him, while cheer after cheer rang out in his honor. Excited women wore bunches of flowers from their bodices and hurled them at the youthful winner. Hundreds of men strove to reach him in order to pat him on the back or shake his hand.

Ray and Vardon, whose fight for the Open championship brought out the possibilities of Ouimet as a golfer, were now forgotten in the celebration of victory. Each Englishman got a three times three before the parade started for the dressing quarters, where the recent competitors changed to dry clothing for the presentation of the medals and other prizes.

During this ceremony, in which Secretary John Reid, Jr., acted as master of ceremonies, both Ray and Vardon took the opportunity to praise Ouimet as a sportsman and golfer. Ray said that Ouimet had played the best golf during the four-day struggle that he had ever seen in America and that it had been an honor to play with him and no dishonor to lose to him. Vardon brought cheers from the gallery when he frankly stated that they had never had a chance to win with Ouimet, during the play-off, because he had played better golf and never gave them an opening at one of the eighteen holes. He congratulated Ouimet and America the victory and proved a popular speechmaker as well as golfer. Secretary Reid, in awarding the championship medal to Ouimet, the trophy to the Woodland Club of Auburndale, Mass., which he represented, and cash prizes to Vardon and Ray, took occasion to apologize "in a slight way" as he put it for the outbursts of cheering at inopportune times.

This was a delicate reference to a picture of to-day's play which is quite likely to be a subject of international comment by the golfing contingents of England and the United States. The management of the tournament has been the subject of much praise, but to-day the gallery several times violated the keen ethics of the sport, by cheering wildly whenever Ouimet gained a point. The same outbursts occurred yesterday, but Ouimet was then playing with George Sargent, who had no chance for first place in the final half of his round. To-day it was different, for both Ray and Vardon were playing shots either just before or after Ouimet and it was plainly evident that these outbreaks annoyed them. Approaching the seventeenth hole, Ray deliberately stopped in the midst of a swing and refused to play until the cheer-

Francis Ouimet, first amateur to win the US Open, 1913.
© BETTMANN/CORBIS. REPRODUCED BY PERMISSION.

ing ceased. This action of the gallery had little or no effect on the result of the match, but a number of golfers publicly voiced their regret that cheering like that at boat races or football games should have occurred, although they realized and stated that it was impossible to check these national outbursts of enthusiasm when Ouimet made particularly good plays.

### How the Strokes Were Made

It was exactly 10 o'clock when the trio of players teed up in the drizzle for the start. The fairways and greens were watersoaked and in many places churned to the consistency of the muddy paste by the trampling of hundreds of feet during the last three days of rain. Overhead low-hanging gray clouds appeared to be part of the mist which would have made the most ardent Scotch golfer feel perfectly at home. The first and second holes were recorded in fives and fours for all three players.

Both Ray and Vardon outdrove Ouimet from the tees, but both sliced and pulled slightly, while the ultimate winner held true to the course.

The first break came at the third hole, where Ray took a five, while the other two players holed in four. There was no advantage either way in the fourth and fifth, but Vardon took the lead in the sixth with a three, while Ray and Ouimet required four. Ray drove furthest, but Vardon's approach was right on the green and he holed a comparatively easy putt, while Ray and Ouimet needed two.

Vardon and Ouimet took four for the short seventh, approaching indifferently, while Ray was on the green in two and holed a brilliant put for three, drawing up even with Ouimet. Vardon lost his head in the eighth, when, after getting on the green in two, he putted badly, requiring two to hole. Ouimet's second was within a foot of the pin, and he scored an easy three. Ray arose to the occasion with a beautiful 23-foot put for a three also. All took fives on the ninth, the longest and hardest hole of the course, being 520 yards of hill and dale, known as the Himalayas.

It therefore came about that the two Englishmen and the American youth played the greatest match in the history of golf on this continent, turning for home all square at 38.

Ouimet immediately jumped to the fore with a three on the short tenth. All were on the green in one, but Ray and Vardon each needed three putts to hole, while Ouimet, from his more favorable lie, scored with two. This gave him a lead of a stroke and marked the beginning of the end.

The eleventh was halved in four, but Ouimet picked up another stroke on the twelfth. He outdrove both opponents from the tee and his approach was within eight feet of the hole, but he took two putts for a four. Ray and Vardon both had trouble in getting to the edge of the green in twos, and putting poorly, halved in five. All landed on the thirteenth green with their second shots, but Vardon's perfect putt gave him a three while Ouimet and Ray took two for fours.

The fourteenth was halved in five, and with but four holes to play Ouimet was leading by the narrow margin of one stroke. Vardon stayed with him on the fifteenth, each getting a four, but Ray, after hitting a spectator with his sliced drive, reached the sand trap in the mashie shot. He required two to get on the green and two putts for a six. He was now four strokes behind Ouimet and three behind Vardon, and his experience appeared to break his playing nerve.

On the sixteenth, the shortest hole of the course, all played the 125-yard iron shot to the green. Vardon and Ouimet made par threes, but Ray required three putts for a four so off was he on his game.

Ouimet won the match and title on the seventeenth, when he got a three for his opponents' fives. The youngster drove far down the fairway, was on the green in two, and holed a short putt, one stroke below par. Vardon, who had been showing signs of the strain, hooked his drive into a trap, took three to the green, and two putts to hole. Ray was in deep grass and, playing as though he had given up hope, halved the hole with his countryman. He rallied and scored a three on the home hole with a long putt, while Ouimet, playing safe, had a par four. Vardon's second shot was short, landing in the mud of the race course, and when he finally holed for the last time of the match his card showed a six.

A resume of the play shows that while Ouimet was frequently outdriven with iron and wood, his game was far steadier and more consistent than that of Ray or Vardon. The two Englishmen showed a tendency to slice and pull their first and second shots, which got them into trouble frequently. While Ouimet did not get the distance of this competitors, he played line shots all during the match, his direction being little short of remarkable, considering the soft, muddy condition of the turf. In putting, too, he was steadier and more accurate than either Ray or Vardon.

## Further Resources

### BOOKS

Frost, Mark. *The Greatest Game Ever Played: Harry Vardon, Francis Ouimet, and the Birth of Modern Golf* New York: Hyperion, 2002.

### PERIODICALS

Reilly, Rick. "The Longest Long Shot." *Sports Illustrated,* November 29, 1999, 124–125.

Entrust, P. "Links With History." *American Heritage,* April 1991, 52–54.

### WEBSITES

"Francis Ouimet." Francis Ouimet Scholarship Fund. Available online at http://www.ouimet.org/Pages/francis.htm; website home page: http://www.ouimet.org (accessed April 6, 2003).

# Page from George Weiss's Scrapbook

**Scrapbook**

**By:** George Weiss

**Date:** 1916

**Source:** George Weiss Papers. National Baseball Hall of Fame and Museum, Cooperstown, N.Y.

**About the Author:** George Weiss (1895–1972) was a baseball executive for both the New York Yankees and New York Mets. During his tenure with the Yankees (1932–1960) as farm team director and general manager, the Yankees were one of the most successful franchises in the game. His career earned him a place in the National Baseball Hall of Fame, where he was inducted in 1971. ∎

## Introduction

At the age of nineteen, George Weiss became a national figure in baseball without a nasty curve ball or a home-run swing. He gained notoriety through the exploits of the semi-pro team he managed, the New Haven Colonials. When Weiss graduated high school in 1914, he sought to continue to manage his teammates at New Haven's Hillhouse High School. With a two-dollar investment in letterhead, the New Haven Colonials were born; they soon stole the spotlight from that city's Eastern League team in organized baseball. Weiss became a national figure when he obtained a lease at a ballpark outside the city limits. Weiss's ballpark was not regulated by blue laws that prevented teams in New Haven and other cities from hosting baseball games on Sunday. Beginning in 1915, Weiss scheduled games with major league teams and other semi-pro teams on Sundays. These games were very popular and attracted major league players, whose teams could not play on Sunday. In September and October of 1916, Weiss brought in the New York Giants, Brooklyn Dodgers, and Chicago White Sox to play his Colonials. To increase attendance for these Sunday games, Weiss invited major leaguers, including Hall of Fame outfielder Ty Cobb and Yankee pitcher Ray Keating, to play for the Colonials.

## Significance

While barnstorming teams was not unique to the New Haven Colonials and George Weiss, Weiss had an aggressive approach to bringing baseball to his city and he incorporated innovative ideas that bent the rules of baseball. George Weiss's biggest coup was scheduling the world champion Boston Red Sox for a game just after the 1916 World Series. The National Commission, baseball's governing body at the time, had strict rules that all teams must disband after the World Series. Hoping to bypass the rule, Weiss signed the Red Sox play-

ers individually. The game was played at the Lighthouse on Sunday, October 15, only three days after the World Series ended. The pitcher for the Red Sox was Babe Ruth, who had won game two of the World Series with a fourteen-inning complete game the previous Monday. A crowd of twenty-seven hundred braved the cold weather to watch the Colonials play the Red Sox to a three-three tie. Ruth pitched a complete game, giving up six hits and three runs. Despite the success of the game, Weiss took a loss, with practically all the proceeds going to the visiting Red Sox (who received nearly thirty-nine hundred dollars each) and Cobb. After the game the American League President, Ban Johnson, fined the participating members of the Red Sox an amount equal to their appearance fee and stripped them of their World Series medals.

Johnson was trying in vain to exert his control over the major league players. The National Commission, which governed major league baseball during the first twenty years of the twentieth century, was a three-member panel that included the presidents of the American and National Leagues and an additional member. This structure was replaced with the Commissioner system after the Black Sox Scandal of 1919. But to a greater degree, these barnstorming games, even at the risk of fines, represented a substantial percentage of the player's salaries. They could earn large sums in the off-season by participating on one of these tours. Besides being financially attractive to the players, the fans in these cities relished the chance to see the stars of baseball in person. Long before the days of television and radio, the only way to see these players was to travel to watch them play. Despite this setback, barnstorming remained a very lucrative proposition for baseball players and hugely popular for baseball fans across the country.

## Further Resources

**BOOKS**

Seymour, Harold. *Baseball: The People's Game.* New York: Oxford University Press, 1990.

**WEBSITES**

"George Weiss." National Baseball Hall of Fame and Museum. Available online at http://www.baseballhalloffame.org/hofers_and_honorees/hofer_bios/weiss_george.htm; website home page http://www.baseballhalloffame.org (accessed April 7, 2003).

"New Haven Ravens." New Haven Ravens. Available online at http://www.ravens.com (accessed April 7, 2003).

## WORLD'S CHAMPION BOSTON RED SOX TO PLAY AT LIGHTHOUSE WITH COLONIALS ON SUNDAY

### Cobb To Lead Local Team nd Jack Barry To Have Charge of Champions in Great Exhibition Game Here —"Babe" Ruth To Pitch and Cady Catch.

#### (By H. M. ROBINSON.)

The Boston Red Sox, champion of the world, fresh from the world's series in which they outpointed the Brooklyn Nationals in four out of five games, which declared them the undisputed rulers in the kingdom of baseball are coming to Lighthouse Point Sunday afternoon to play the Colonials. This startling and very important announcement came from the lips of Manager George Weiss this morning after he had been in conference for some time with Jack Barry and other members of the world champion outfit. The announcement of the coming of the Red Sox will be hailed with delight by every man, woman and child in New Haven who knows or pretends to know anything about the great national game and it means Lighthouse Point will accommodate a gathering Sunday never before equal in numbers. The Champion Red Sox and Colonials will start this great exhibition at 3 o'clock Sunday afternoon with Hugh J. Rorty of Hartford as the umpire.

#### LOOK WHO'S COMING.

The lineup of the Red Sox as given to Manager Weiss will be Henriksen, right field; Janvrin, second base. Shorten, center field; Hoblitzel, first base; Lewis, left field; Kardner or McNally third base; Scott, shortstop; Cady catcher and Ruth, pitcher, Hooper leaves today on a hunting trip and so will not be able to be here and there is some doubt about Gardner being able to take part in this exhibition but the other world's stars have promised to be on hand and give the New Haven fans an exhibition of the very highest class of baseball possible for any promoter to provide. "Babe" Ruth, hero of the notable 14-inning victory for the Red Sox on Monday in the second world's series game, will do the pitching Sunday and is slated to twirl the entire game for the champions.

#### KEATING TO PITCH.

The Colonials will have Ray Keating, famous New York Yankee star, on the slab and the team will be strengthened greatly for this exhibition. As Catcher Clyde Waters is out of the game with a broken thumb, Kelliher will probably be sent behind the bat on Sunday.

#### COBB VS. BARRY.

Just size up the respective team leaders for Sunday. The Red Sox will be in charge of Jack Barry, while Ty Cobb will be leader of the Colonials and will play first base. This will bring two of the greatest baseball generals in the world together in a battle which will afford a sight never before seen in New Haven. Cobb is in love with George Weiss' Colonials. He figures the college stars will be able to surprise the world's champions and give them a good battle. He will do all in his power to help the local boys in this great exhibition and tells Manager Weiss the Red Sox will k

#### WEISS PULLS NEW ONE.

In securing the world's champions to come to New Haven for an exhibition game, fresh from their sensational victory in the world's series, Manager Weiss, accomplishes something never known before in the history of baseball and perhaps will never occur again. Never has a winning team in the world's series played an exhibition game upon the closing of the big event. The National Commission will stand for no such thing so Manager Bill Carrigan would not consent to bringing his club here to play the Colonials. Manager Weiss however did not give up hopes when he learned that the club could not be sent out for an exhibition game. He consulted his old friend Jack Barry, who came to the rescue. Jack gets around the ruling of the "comish" by dealing individually with each one of the world's champions and will bring the boys here as Barry's Red Sox and not as the Boston American league club. Manager Weiss is doing business directly with Barry and not with the officials of the club. Manager Weiss is certainly showing a true sportsman spirit in this big undertaking as it will cost him over $2,000 to open the gates to the Lighthouse Point park on Sunday afternoon. But he figures the fans of New Haven and the vicinity will appreciate this great treat and his venture will not go to waste. The fact of New Haven being the scene of the first exhibition game played by a world's championship club directly after winning the title, means a big boost to the city as well as to the manager of the Colonials.

### CHAMPION RED SOX PLAY COLONIALS HERE S[U]

#### Famous World's Champions To Be Seen At Lighthouse In Greatest Exhibition Game Ever Staged In This Country—Brilliants of Baseball World Including Ty Cobb To Be Seen.

The greatest exhibition game of baseball arranged in any city in many, many years is that just signed up for the Lighthouse Point grounds Sunday afternoon, which will bring together the 1916 World's Champions who clinched the pennant yesterday afternoon at Boston, and George Weiss' famous Colonials. New Haven fans are talking of nothing else now that the coming here of the most famous players the game has seen in years and years is absolutely assured.

During the course of the world's series games this week Manager Weiss made his headquarters at the same hotels the Boston Americans did and was noticed several times in close conference with the management of the American leaguers. When he was seen by the Register sporting scribe at the St. Andrew's hotel in New York apparently completing details for a game Weiss enjoined secrecy until the final details could be arranged.

Captain Jack Barry of the Red Sox will be in charge of the team here,

### WORLD'S CHAMPION RED SOX PLAY COLONIALS IN EXHIBI[TION] GAME TODAY AT LIGHT[HOUSE]

#### Ty Cobb Will Lead Local Team Against Champions and Record Crowd Is Provided For At East Shore Attraction;

#### (By H. M. ROBINSON.)

The most brilliant array of baseball talent ever gathered on one field will be seen this afternoon at the Lighthouse Point park when the Boston Americans, world's champions of 1915 and 1916 and fresh from their great and sensational four victories over the Brooklyn Nationals, will line up for competition against George Weiss' All-Star Colonials, led by Ty Cobb, of the Detroit Americans, and one of the greatest ball stars that ever shone on the diamond. It is needless to spend much space in introducing the World's champions. They have been introduced from coast to coast and back again during the past two seasons and the wonderful performances of every member of the team

membered by those who visit the park for years to come.

The Red Sox will introduce from the mound, 'Babe' Ruth, the young fellow, who was hero of the 14 inning victory over Brooklyn on Monday which was the longest game ever palyed in a world's series. It will be recalled that Ruth allowed the Dodgers only six safe hits in 14 innings and Boston won 2 to 1. Ruth is slated to pitch the entire game for the champions. Ray Keating, former Yankee pitcher, and the Bridgeport boy who expects to shine in the major league again next season, will be on the mound for the Colonials, so the fans can look for a pitchers' battle from the start to finish. Ruth will be held up by Cady, who caught in four of the world's series games in 1915, and who caught, in the final game this season that gave Boston the title. The Colonials will have Bill Kelleher behind the bat. He is the former Princton star and later a New York Yankee catcher, who is to-day, considered one of the finds of the

#### Cleveland Section (right column, partial)

New Haven ... ing town in the proven yesterda paid their way enclosure to see attraction before conditions on as worse than yes 3,800 fans on see Rabbit Ma

The Yale Ne terview from the Brooklyn whys of the will never get alibis.

Scott to Jar very much in terday. Cobb predominating

With the ba closed, place Colonials, amo has provided best baseball to be regrette was not a fin

Out-of-town have carried Saturday. M

That has always Janvrin, who place at second Barry was injur this afternoon, Bobby Watt of fellow who led season with the ed right into pro the Virginia sta at second base. It is doubtful able to play th so Mcally is sla Joe Dugan, form school player, and the young Barry wants to Sox has been a for the Colonia assigned to thir Bobby Stow at Texas league in last season and went for a try association. Th at Short. Scott actors in the 19 The Colonial

---

**Primary Source**

## Page from George Weiss's scrapbook

**SYNOPSIS:** This article from a page of George Weiss's scrapbook discusses the plans in place for the Red Sox players, recently crowned World Champions of baseball, to play the New Haven Colonials just a few days after the World Series. Never shy about his business practices, George Weiss felt he was in the right by signing the players individually to play in the contest.

# *You Know Me Al: A Busher's Letters*

### Fictional work

**By:** Ring Lardner

**Date:** 1916

**Source:** Lardner, Ring. *You Know Me Al: A Busher's Letters.* New York: Charles Scribner's Sons, 1916; 1925, 9–18.

**About the Author:** Ring Lardner (1885–1933), a journalist and author, was one of the greatest sportswriters of all time. He wrote for many newspapers including *The Chicago Tribune, The Sporting News,* and *The Saturday Evening Post.* The National Baseball Hall of Fame selected Lardner in 1963 as the second recipient of the J.G. Taylor Spink Award for "for meritorious contributions to baseball writing." The first person to receive the award was J.G. Taylor Spink himself. ∎

## Introduction

Ring Lardner gained notoriety in the twentieth century as both one of the world's best sports writers and one of its finest satirists. Lardner combined these two attributes in a memorable series of columns in *The Saturday Evening Post.* They started in 1914 and portrayed the life of a fictitious young ballplayer, Jack Keefe. Lardner portrayed Keefe as an ignorant young man who, by virtue of his ability to play baseball, rose in stature and fame far beyond his intellectual capacities. These letters became the basis of the 1916 book, *You Know Me Al,* as well as a series of other books describing Keefe's life—his army experience during World War I (1914–1919), and life upon his return from the war. Lardner also created the character, "Alibi Ike," a baseball player who shared Keefe's lack of intellect, and who had an excuse for everything that happen to him.

Lardner used Jack Keefe's letters to his friend, Al, to satire the praise and notoriety society paid to the professional athletes. Lardner referred to Keefe as a "busher," indicating a young ballplayer who acted like a minor (or bush) leaguer. While Keefe started out as a minor leaguer about to make a splash with the Chicago White Sox, Keefe was ignorant about the important issues of his day. His lack of an appreciation about his own privileged position cemented the "busher" label. Lardner, like many other social commentators at the time, questioned openly the role that sports played in society. One's station in life could elevate quickly by virtue of his ability to play a professional sport.

## Significance

In the 1910s, the role of the professional athlete was changing in society. Before the age of radio and television, the exploits of the professional athlete, especially baseball players, were described in every newspaper in the land. Through this national attention, baseball players became national celebrities, though many of them came from modest backgrounds. In many of these ballplayers, the fame that they had on the baseball diamond did not necessarily come with the intelligence and maturity of most national figures. In Jack Keefe, Lardner had a country bumpkin thrust into the sports world's limelight by virtue of a strong pitching arm. And through Jack Keefe, Lardner was able to poke fun at such ball players, and the society that held them up as heroes.

Lardner's style in writing these pieces for the *Post,* and then in book form, drew upon a certain contempt for the success and notoriety given to these players. Lardner routinely had Keefe misspell words in these letters to a friend and use slang to indicate his lack of education and social status. Keefe also threw out salary figures that would have been far more than the income of most people at the time. Long before Babe Ruth would comment that he deserved a higher salary than President Herbert Hoover (served 1929–1933) because Ruth had had a better year, baseball players were being paid far more money in salaries than they ever would have earned doing anything else.

## Primary Source

*You Know Me Al: A Busher's Letters* [excerpt]

**SYNOPSIS:** Ring Lardner devotes much of the first chapter introducing Jack Keefe to readers and describing his contract negotiations with Charlie Comiskey, owner of the Chicago White Sox. Lardner freely incorporates real people in the work, allowing him to provide a more realistic story, and to poke fun at Comiskey, who was notoriously cheap. He also talks about Kid Gleason, the coach who eventually took over the team for the 1919 season.

### Chapter I

### A Busher's Letters Home

Terre Haute, Indiana, September 6

Friend Al:

Well, Al old pal I suppose you seen in the paper where I been sold to the White Sox. Believe me Al it comes as a surprise to me and I bet it did to all you good old pals down home. You could of knocked me over with a feather when the old man come up to me and says Jack I've sold you to the Chicago Americans.

I didn't have no idea that anything like that was coming off. For five minutes I was just dum and couldn't say a word.

Author Ring Lardner criticized American society's glorification of professional athletes through fiction. **THE LIBRARY OF CONGRESS.**

He says We aren't getting what you are worth but I want you to go up to that big league and show those birds that there is a Central League on the map. He says Go and pitch the ball you been pitching down here and there won't be nothing to it. He says All you need is the nerve and Walsh or no one else won't have nothing on you.

So I says I would do the best I could and I thanked him for the treatment I got in Terre Haute. They always was good to me here and though I did more than my share I always felt that my work was appresiated. We are finishing second and I done most of it. I can't help but be proud of my first year's record in professional baseball and you know I am not boasting when I say that Al.

Well Al it will seem funny to be up there in the big show when I never was really in a big city before. But I guess I seen enough of life not to be scared of the high buildings eh Al?

I will just give them what I got and if they don't like it they can send me back to the old Central and I will be perfectly satisfied.

I didn't know anybody was looking me over, but one of the boys told me that Jack Doyle the White Sox scout was down here looking at me when Grand Rapids was here. I beat them twice in that serious. You know Grand Rapids never had a chance with me when I was right. I shut them out in the first game and they got one run in the second on account of Flynn misjuging that fly ball. Anyway Doyle liked my work and he wired Comiskey to buy me. Comiskey come back with an offer and they excepted it. I don't know how much they got but anyway I am sold to the big league and believe me Al I will make good.

Well Al I will be home in a few days and we will have some of the good old times. Regards to all the boys and tell them I am still their pal and not all swelled up over this big league business.

*Your pal, Jack.*

Chicago, Illinois, December 14.

Old Pal:

Well Al I have not got much to tell you. As you know Comiskey wrote me that if I was up in Chi this month to drop in and see him. So I got here Thursday morning and went to his office in the afternoon. His office is out to the ball park and believe me its some park and some office.

I went in and asked for Comiskey and a young fellow says He is not here now but can I do anything for you? I told him who I am and says I had an engagement to see Comiskey. He says The boss is out of town hunting and did I have to see him personally?

I says I wanted to see about signing a contract. He told me I could sign as well with him as Comiskey and he took me into another office. He says What salary did you think you ought to get? and I says I wouldn't think of playing ball in the big league for less than three thousand dollars per annum. He laughed and says You don't want much. You better stick round town till the boss comes back. So here I am and it is costing me a dollar a day to stay at the hotel on Cottage Grove Avenue and that don't include my meals.

I generally eat at some of the cafes round the hotel but I had supper downtown last night and it cost me fifty-five cents. If Comiskey don't come back soon I won't have no more money left.

Speaking of money I won't sign no contract unless I get the salary you and I talked of, three thousand dollars. You know what I was getting in Terre Haute, a hundred and fifty a month, and I know it's going to cost me a lot more to live here. I made inquiries round here and find I can get board and room for eight dollars a week but I will be out of town half the time and will have to pay for my room when I am away or look up a new one when I come back. Then I will have to buy cloths to wear on the road in places like New York. When Comiskey comes back I will name him three thousand dollars as my lowest figure and I guess he will come through when he sees I am in ernest. I heard that Walsh was getting twice as much as that.

The papers says Comiskey will be back here sometime to-morrow. He has been hunting with the president of the league so he ought to feel pretty good. But I don't care how he feels. I am going to get a contract for three thousand and if he don't want to give it to me he can do the other thing. You know me Al.

*Yours truly, Jack.*

Chicago, Illinois, December 16.
Dear Friend Al:

Well I will be home in a couple of days now but I wanted to write you and let you know how I come out with Comiskey. I signed my contract yesterday afternoon. He is a great old fellow Al and no wonder everybody likes him. He says Young man will you have a drink? But I was to smart and wouldn't take nothing. He says You was with Terre Haute? I says Yes I was. He says Doyle tells me you were pretty wild. I says Oh no I got good control. He says Well do you want to sign? I says Yes if I get my figure. He asks What is my figure and I says three thousand dollars per annum. He says Don't you want the office furniture too? Then he says I thought you was a young ball-player and I didn't know you wanted to buy my park.

We kidded each other back and forth like that a while and then he says You better go out and get the air and come back when you feel better. I says I feel O. K. now and I want to sign a contract because I have got to get back to Bedford. Then he calls the secretary and tells him to make out my contract. He give it to me and it calls for two hundred and fifty a month. He says You know we always have a city serious here in the fall where a fellow picks up a good bunch of money. I hadn't thought of that so I signed up. My yearly salary will be fifteen hundred dollars besides what the city serious brings me. And that is only for the first year. I will demand three thousand or four thousand dollars next year.

I would of started home on the evening train but I ordered a suit of cloths from a tailor over on Cottage Grove and it won't be done till tomorrow. It's going to cost me twenty bucks but it ought to last a long time. Regards to Frank and the bunch.

*Your Pal, Jack.*

Paso Robles, California, March 2.
Old Pal Al:

Well Al we been in this little berg now a couple of days and its bright and warm all the time just like June. Seems funny to have it so warm this early in March but I guess this California climate is all they said about it and then some.

It would take me a week to tell you about our trip out here. We came on a Special Train De Lukes and it was some train. Every place we stopped there was crowds down to the station to see us go through and all the people looked me over like I was a actor or something. I guess my hight and shoulders attracted their attention. Well Al we finally got to Oakland which is across part of the ocean from Frisco. We will be back there later on for practice games.

We stayed in Oakland a few hours and then took a train for here. It was another night in a sleeper and believe me I was tired of sleepers before we got here. I have road one night at a time but this was four straight nights. You know Al I am not built right for a sleeping car birth.

The hotel here is a great big place and got good eats. We got in at breakfast time and I made a B line for the dining room. Kid Gleason who is a kind of asst. Manager to Callahan come in and sat down with me. He says Leave something for the rest of the boys because they will be just as hungry as you. He says Ain't you afraid you will cut your throat with that knife. He says There ain't no extra charge for using the forks. He says You shouldn't ought to eat so much because you're overweight now. I says You may think I am fat, but it's all solid bone and muscle. He says Yes I suppose it's all solid bone from the neck up. I guess he thought I would get sore but I will let them kid me now because they will take off their hats to me when they see me work.

Manager Callahan called us all to his room after breakfast and give us a lecture. He says there would be no work for us the first day but that we must all take a long walk over the hills. He also says we must not take the training trip as a joke. Then the colored trainer give us our suits and I went to my room and tried mine on. I ain't a bad looking guy in the White Sox uniform Al. I will have my picture taken and send you boys some.

My roommate is Allen a lefthander from the Coast League. He don't look nothing like a pitcher but you can't never tell about them dam left handers. Well I didn't go on the long walk because I was tired out. Walsh stayed at the hotel too and when he seen me he says Why didn't you go with the bunch? I says I was too tired. He says Well when Callahan comes back you better keep out of sight or tell him you are sick. I says I don't care nothing for Callahan. He says No but Callahan is crazy about you. He says You better obey orders and you will git along better. I guess Walsh thinks I am some rube.

When the bunch come back Callahan never said a word to me but Gleason come up and says Where was you? I told him I was too tired to go walking. He says Well I will borrow a wheel-barrow some place and push you round. He says Do you sit down when you pitch? I let him kid me because he has not saw my stuff yet.

Next morning half the bunch mostly vetrans went to the ball park which isn't no better than the one we got at home. Most of them was vetrans as I say but I was in the bunch. That makes things look pretty good for me don't it Al? We tossed the ball round and hit fungos and run round and then Callahan asks Scott and Russell and I to warm up easy and pitch a few to the batters. It was warm and I felt pretty good so I warmed up pretty good. Scott pitched to them first and kept laying them right over with nothing on them. I don't believe a man gets any batting practice that way. So I went in and after I lobbed a few over I cut loose my fast one. Lord was to bat and he ducked out of the way and then throwed his bat to the bench. Callahan says What's the matter Harry? Lord says I forgot to pay up my life insurance. He says I ain't ready for Walter Johnson's July stuff.

Well Al I will make them think I am Walter Johnson before I get through with them. But Callahan come out to me and says What are you trying to do kill somebody? He says Save your smoke because you're going to need it later on. He says Go easy with the boys at first or I won't have no batters. But he was laughing and I guess he was pleased to see the stuff I had.

There is a dance in the hotel to-night and I am up in my room writing this in my underwear while I get my suit pressed. I got it all mussed up coming out here. I don't know what shoes to wear. I asked Gleason and he says Wear your baseball shoes and if any of the girls gets fresh with you spike them. I guess he was kidding me.

Write and tell me all the news about home.

*Yours truly, Jack.*

## Further Resources

### BOOKS

Evans, Elizabeth. *Ring Lardner.* New York: F. Ungar, 1979.

Yardley, Jonathon. *Ring: A Biography of Ring Lardner.* New York: Random House, 1977.

### PERIODICALS

Goodman, Walter. "Ring Lardner Understood Baseball, and Life, Too." *The New York Times,* July 18, 2000, E2.

Staudohar, Paul. "Baseball Short Stories: From Lardner to Asinof to Kinsella." *Culture, Sport and Society,* Summer 2000, 44–55

### WEBSITES

"Ring Lardner." Baseballlibrary.com. Available online at http://www.pubdim.net/baseballlibrary/ballplayers/L/Lardner_Ring.stm; website home page: http://www.pubdim.net (accessed March 14, 2003).

"Ring Lardner." National Baseball Hall of Fame and Museum. Available online at http://www.baseballhalloffame.org/hofers_and_honorees/spink_bios/lardner_ring.htm; website home page: http://www.baseballhalloffame.org (accessed March 14, 2003).

### AUDIO AND VISUAL MEDIA

*Eight Men Out.* Directed by John Sayles. Orion Pictures, 1988, VHS.

# Girls and Athletics
## Handbook

**By:** Mary C. Morgan

**Date:** 1917

**Source:** Morgan, Mary C., ed. *Girls and Athletics.* New York: American Sports Publishing, 1917, 7–10.

**About the Author:** Mary C. Morgan was a graduate of the Bryn Mawr College in 1915, and she was associated with the Lansdowne Country Club of Philadelphia. She edited *Girls and Athletics,* a book that was part of the Spalding's Athletic Library, one of the most prominent publishing endeavors in the early history of sport. Its titles encouraged participation in sport and supported Spalding's own sporting goods company. ∎

## Introduction

The role of women in society changed a great deal in the early part of the twentieth century. Women made strides to increase their participation in society and gain rights held only by men. As with the suffrage movement (culminating in 1920 when the Nineteenth Amendment granted women the right to vote), women worked hard to break societal barriers. One area where women moved into new territory was sport. In preparing *Girls and Athletics,* Mary Morgan sent a questionnaire to three hundred schools and colleges surveying the role of women

Minnesota students watch a girls' basketball game, c. 1910. © MINNESOTA HISTORICAL SOCIETY/CORBIS. REPRODUCED BY PERMISSION

and sport in education. Of the 237 responses she received, only one school noted an opposition to providing athletic programs for women. While some of these schools did little to support women's athletics, the majority provided some level of programming for this new type of activity. Additionally, this fundamental change in the offering of programs was amplified by the roles that women played in the expansion of sports. In her acknowledgements for the book, Morgan thanked a number of contributors, including women who held key athletic positions at Vassar College, the New Haven Normal School of Physical Training, Smith College and the Public Schools Athletic League of New York.

**Significance**

Mary Morgan's introduction to this book is a wonderful piece that provided the information for women exploring athletics for the first time. What is also wonderful about the book as a whole is that a woman wrote it for a female audience, unlike Dudley Sargent's "Are Athletics Making Girls Masculine?" Rather than discussing issues specifically as they relate to women, Morgan views athletics as possessing a gender-neutral benefit to the participant. In her introduction, instead of extolling the virtues of sport as a way to move towards equality of the sexes, she focuses on the types of issues women looking

to play sports faced, possibly for the first time. Morgan's discussion of sport's virtues was as valid for men as women when the book was published. She stresses three concepts: that athletics build character; what to wear when participating in sports; and that athletes at the time lacked a clear source and guide for training.

On these three topics, Morgan addresses athletes of either gender. On character, she writes, "Athletics as a builder of character are just as important as a builder of physical strength." She adds that being called a "good sportswoman" has no higher compliment. On training, she touches upon the generational issue facing girls wishing to pursue athletics. While a boy might be able to get assistance from his father on training and athletics, few girls would have mothers who could assist on such a program. Women from the previous generation did not have the opportunity to participate in sports and could offer little guidance to their daughters. However, they could offer encouragement, which Morgan promoted. Finally, on what to wear, Morgan advised girls to "dress sensibly." Most girls did not have access to athletic wear and naturally did not know what to wear for athletic training and contests. While today these issues seem intuitive, Morgan saw this information as necessary for a generation of girls who had no experience with such issues.

## Primary Source

*Girls and Athletics* [excerpt]

**SYNOPSIS:** Morgan offers an overview of how girls should be approaching sports in the latter part of the 1910s. She reminds readers that the values of sport include character and physical well-being, then suggests that girls follow basic elements of training for athletic contests and dress logically when participating in sports. As sports become more common for girls and women, they need to have a source for basic information, such as learning a game, what to eat, and how to exercise.

In gathering information for this volume a *questionaire* was sent to some three hundred schools and colleges. Replies were received from two hundred and thirty-seven of these. Of this number only one school went on record as opposed to athletics for girls and women. All of the others make provision for athletics or some form of physical education. Some schools provide little or no supervision, it is true, but the great majority provide for or realize the necessity for provision of adequate control of this form of training.

The impression one receives from scanning the replies to the *questionaire* is undoubtedly that general athletics for girls are becoming more and more popular, and that development is slowly but surely broadening out to include eventually almost every form of athletics for almost every girl.

From the physical standpoint, any exercise under favorable circumstances is beneficial in that it develops and brings into play the muscles of the body and stimulates the whole system. But all forms of athletics should be carefully supervised, particularly for growing girls. Every participant should have a thorough physical examination and if any limitations are placed upon her athletics, the reasons for such restrictions should be carefully explained. It is natural that some people are more delicate than others—absolutely unfit for some of the more strenuous games—but there are always less strenuous exercises which may be indulged in.

The physical condition being assured, the girl should be watched so that she does not enter into the sports or games with too much intensity. It is a common tendency of the average American girl to throw her whole soul into the particular matter at hand. If it happens to be athletics, often her enthusiasm helped out by a thoroughly admirable spirit and by quite a lot of "grit"—as her brothers term it—keeps her playing when she is really tired out physically. This is the time where a coach—or if there is no coach, friendly advice—will show the girl that she is not getting any benefit out of the exercise, and she is running the risk of injuring herself.

This excess is as wrong in athletics as it is in anything else. Be temperate.

My advice to every girl is: Know your physical condition; use common sense and gauge the amount of exercise you take by your physical condition and stamina.

Athletics as a builder of character *are* just as important as a builder of physical strength. *Fair play* and *good sportsmanship* are the two maxims kept constantly before the eye. A girl who has won the reputation of being a clean, square player is happy herself and is admired by all with whom she comes in contact. There is no higher compliment than to be called a "good sports-woman." A girl who can lose and smile, or win and not exult over her opponent's defeat, is quite apt to get something bigger than mere physical development out of her athletics.

### Training

A few girls have asked me, "How can I learn to play this or that game well?" Athletics are just like almost every phase of life; it requires practice and experience before one becomes skilled. If, then, a girl wishes to be successful it is best to make a thorough study of the branch of sport she is going to take up and practice, assimilating each detail carefully. The amount of time it takes to become proficient depends upon the natural ability of the person—some people are much more talented in athletics than others.

The best advice I can give is to know your game thoroughly, so that you may play with your head as well as your body. Practice until you have confidence in your ability. Do not practice so constantly and continually that you become "stale." A little practice taken regularly is often more beneficial than a lot of practice which tires you out so that you are unfit for more the next day. Do a little bit, so that you are not tired, increasing the practice slowly.

Some people believe in set training rules; others do not. It is best to be in good physical condition all the time if it is possible; it stands to reason, however, that for especial speed and endurance the physical condition should be nearly perfect. Sleep is a very necessary factor; therefore, every athlete should have a long and sound sleep every night. As for diet, there is a difference of opinion. It seems reasonable that no heavy food, nor rich food that is indigestible, should be eaten. In particular, just before a contest, a light meal should be eaten with the proper time for digestion allowed before playing. Some people make the mistake of eating heavily and then playing immediately afterward. The most sensible training seems to be, eat the most nourishing and easily digested food.

## What to Wear

Dress sensibly. For track and field games, basket ball and other games that require speed, agility and the freest play of all muscles, by all means wear bloomers and a middy blouse. For tennis, golf and the other less strenuous games, wear shirtwaist or middy blouse and a skirt wide enough and short enough to give the most play of the leg muscles. For instance, there is nothing so ridiculous as to see a girl athlete togged with more regard for the impression she is making on the male part of the gallery than for getting the most physical benefit out of her game. I have great sympathy for every girl who takes pride in her appearance at all times. I maintain that it is both possible to present a neat and an agreeable appearance and at the same time to dress sensibly for the business at hand. In each of the following chapters on the various forms of sports I have endeavored to say a word about dress specifically for that sport, unless it is evident what costume is suitable. Back of it all I will repeat this fundamental: Dress sensibly.

## Further Resources

### BOOKS

Guttmann, Allen. *Women's Sports: A History.* New York: Columbia University Press, 1991.

Sparhawk, Ruth M., et. al., comp. *American Women in Sport, 1887–1987: A 100-year Chronology.* Metuchen, N.J.: Scarecrow Press, 1989.

### WEBSITES

"History of Women in Sports Timeline." St. Lawrence County Branch of the American Association of University Women. Available online at http://www.northnet.org/stlawrenceaauw/timeline.htm; website home page: http://www.northnet.org/stlawrenceaauw (accessed April 7, 2003).

# Memorandum to Colonel Bruce Palmer

**Memo**

**By:** Elwood S. Brown

**Date:** October 15, 1918

**Source:** Brown, Elwood S. Memorandum to Colonel Bruce Palmer, October 15, 1918. In *The Inter-Allied Games: Paris 22nd June to 6th July, 1919.* Paris, France: Games Committee, Inter-Allied Games, 1919, 17–20.

**About the Author:** Elwood S. Brown was an athletic director for the Young Men's Christian Association (YMCA) of the American Expeditionary Forces during World War I. He had gained notoriety previously as the physical director of the American YMCA in Manila, Philippines for many years. In that position, he introduced basketball and volleyball to the people of the Philippines and created athletic competitions between United States soldiers and local residents. His role in introducing volleyball to the Philippines was one of the key factors in the internationalization of the sport. ■

## Introduction

In late 1918, World War I (1914–1918) was coming to an end. After years of stalemate and trench warfare in northeast France, German lines were broken and they were in retreat. The fighting ceased on November 11, 1918, when an armistice was reached on the western front between German and Allied troops. The United States had many soldiers fighting in the war after entering the war in 1917. This force, known as the American Expeditionary Forces (AEF), helped turn the tide on the western front and led to the defeat of Germany. In all, the different Allied countries including the United States, France, Italy, Great Britain and a number of smaller nations had two million soldiers. What these soldiers would do after the hostilities ended was the primary concern of Elwood Brown.

Less than a month before the armistice, Elwood S. Brown was named Director of Athletics for the American Expeditionary Forces (AEF) YMCA. On the same day, Brown sent a memorandum to the Headquarters of the AEF, citing the need for an activity after the hostilities of the war ended. This memorandum outlined his concerns for what these soldiers, who were "engaged in the strenuous game of beating the Hun," would do after the fighting stopped. Brown proposed that upon victory by the Allied troops, the attention of the soldiers should be directed to physical activities. This would remove the "moral temptations" that still could exist in the minds of the two million or so soldiers, and prevent bigger problems they might encounter, including prostitution, drinking and other activities that might be drawn out through a long demobilization period. Through sport, Brown could redirect the attention of the soldiers and create a more positive post-war experience. This event would be the first international games since the 1912 Stockholm Olympics and give the soldiers something to work toward while waiting to return to their home country.

## Significance

Through the vision of Brown, and with the full support of the Allied Generals, the Inter-Allied Games were held from June 22 to July 6, 1919. The games were held in a stadium built for the event—and named after U.S. General John Pershing, commander in chief of the AEF. The games featured soldiers from eighteen Allied countries including the United States, France, Great Britain, Australia, Canada, Portugal, Italy, and others. These games were known as the Military Olympics because they, in some regards, took the place of the 1920 Olympics. The games were a tremendous success for the United States team. In an international showcase for the relatively new American sport of basketball, the United States team, led by Basketball Hall of Famer Marty Friedman, crushed the French team 93-8 in the championship game—played outdoors on a court placed in the middle of the stadium. Ultimately, the games were a great success in achieving their initial goal; they provided soldiers with a positive, recreational activity that focused their energies when the fighting stopped.

Brown proposed the redirection of the physical activity from war to sport, finding a common element to these two seemingly dissimilar activities. In today's sporting environment, the linguistic ties between the aggressions of war and the athletic competitions are easy to find. We describe athletic contests as rumbles, battles, conflicts, and with other military terms. In Brown's memorandum, we find the origins for this type of association. He refers to the AEF force in France as a "physical machine" and felt that only focused physical activity through games and play (both informal and competitive) would sufficiently replace the mental stress of battle.

Additionally, Brown sought to create a environment where these contests could be played by the greatest number of people. He proposed as his first point that the AEF sponsor a great mass games as "Athletics for everybody." The other points raised included creating official AEF championships, creating physical pageants, and creating the actual Inter-Allied games. For each of these points, Brown spells out what steps needed to be undertaken by the YMCA to support these programs. The costs involved in proposing these events were very substantial, and show the commitment made by both the YMCA and AEF in making these games possible. Simply in the matter of recreation, the YMCA proposed spending a total of $1,585,000 on athletic equipment, just over seventy-five cents per soldier. Additionally, the Army needed to commit noncoms (noncommissioned officers) to assist in the effort to train and organize these activities. Brown's memo reflects the need and role of sports in ensuring a healthy focus for the attentions and activities of the post-hostilities soldier.

## Primary Source

### Memorandum to Colonel Bruce Palmer

**SYNOPSIS:** Elwood Brown prepared this memorandum on his first day as Director of the Department of Athletics for the YMCA of the AEF. Brown addresses the conditions that will exist in the inevitable post-war period, together with his suggestions for four activities that would create both an informal and a competitive athletic play program. This memorandum set into motion the planning that led to the Inter-Allied Games of 1919.

October 15, 1918

From: Elwood S. Brown, Department of Athletics, Y.M.C.A., Paris.
To: Colonel Bruce Palmer.
Subject: Proposed Athletic Program for Demobilization Period.

### Conditions

Peace, whether it comes tomorrow or many months from now, should find us in a state of preparedness against the inevitable period of relaxation that must be met when hostilities cease. This period will bring about an increased danger from moral temptations, will be a time of impatient waiting for the day of departure for America and will call for very constructive and interesting bodily activity if the dangers of disorderly physical expression are to be avoided.

Fundamentally our Army in France is a physical machine. Physical vitality is the chief element, the most important asset. Two million men are now engaged in the strenuous game of beating the Hun. They are in hard daily labor, intensive military training or engaged in actual fighting—physical expression, nearly all of it. When this is suddenly taken away no mental, moral or social program however extensive will meet the need. Physical action will be the call; games and play, informal and competitive, will be the answer. It is assumed that a certain amount of military work will be continued but it is not believed that this will be found either sufficient or the best way to offset the certain reaction that will come about when the fighting is over.

### Suggestions

Four activities are suggested below for which in co-operation and conjunction with the necessary army committees the Y.M.C.A. through its Department of Athletics is prepared to assume the initial responsi-

An American soldier wins a track event during the Inter-Allied games at Pershing Stadium, France, 1919. © CORBIS. REPRODUCED BY PERMISSION.

bility in promotion and organization. It should be said that the underlying principle would be to conduct a two-sided effort coordinating the athletic play program, both informal and competitive, for which the Association would be primarily responsible, with the strictly military effort looking towards the accomplishment of the same results and for which it is recognized the Army will have a program.

## Items

1. Great mass games and play for every possible man—"Athletics for everybody."

2. Official A.E.F. championships in a wide variety of competitive sports including military events, beginning with elimination regimental contests, ranging upwards through the divisions, possibly the army corps, and culminating in great finals in Paris.

3. Physical pageants and demonstrations to be held in many centers demonstrating to our allied friends America's best in sport, her great play spirit and incidentally her finest in physical manhood.

4. Interallied athletic contests—open only to soldiers of the Allied Armies—a great set of military Olympic games.

## Item No. 1

This item represents the major portion of the program and unquestionably the most important part. The Y.M.C.A. is in a strong position to handle a purely recreative effort of this kind. It would introduce the play spirit and would keep the activities free from a strictly military aspect; that is, its recreative work could be semivolunteer in character and hence would not be regarded by the men as one more duty in the military day's order.

*This item involves for the Association:*

1. The immediate arrangement with at least one hundred of its strongest and best trained experts in mass play now in France to remain for the entire demobilization period. Most of these men are now on contracts reading "for the duration of the war."

2. The placing of an order by cable for at least $500,000 worth of additional athletic supplies. An order amounting to $1,085,000 for 1919 has already been placed.

3. The immediate preparation of the necessary instruction handbooks and other technical printed matter that would be required.

*For the Army is involved:*

1. Plans to detail a considerable group of non-coms whom our trained athletic directors could instruct in the promotion, organization and conduct of the groups games adopted.

2. The detailing, after hostilities cease, of a number of trained athletic directors now in the Army who would supplement the efforts of, and work in cooperation with, the Association directors.

3. The appointment of a committee of officers with which and through which the Association representatives could work.

## Item No. 2.

Division rivalry of every sort is characteristic of our Army and is a wholesome incentive to better effort. This is particularly true in competitive athletics and, it is understood, in purely military sports as well. It is believed this rivalry can be most constructively capitalized through official A.E.F. championships sanctioned and recognized as such by the Commander-in-Chief.

*This item involves for the Association:*

1. Technical direction of the elimination athletic contests within the regiments and divisions of their equivalent units.

2. The securing of suitable grounds, equipment and the necessary prizes for the finals.

3. The general responsibility for the handling of the many details such as entry lists, arrangements of heats, events, officials and the like.

*For the Army is involved:*

1. Committees of athletic officers within the divisions to conduct the strictly military events desired and to coordinate these with the athletic events.

2. A group of officers to sit as members of a representative A.E.F. Championships Committee in general charge of the finals.

## Item No. 3.

The French soldiers as well as the civilian population are keenly interested in American sports and the fine play spirit that permeates them. There is also unusual interest in American calisthenic drills and a number of other of our best-known activities. There is particular interest in baseball and track and field sports. Through the Foyer du Soldat baseball has been quite generally introduced in the French Army. The American Army could make a lasting impression on French sports as well as a most definite contribution to them by demonstrating in various great centers in France our popular National games, and by putting on great pageants such as are frequently used in our municipalities at home to typify the spirit and traditions of the community. If military band concerts or competitions together with male chorus singing could be added, the net result would be at once physically stimulating and strongly artistic.

*This would involve for the Association:*

1. Bringing over from America a number of specialists on events of this kind.

2. The drilling of many large groups of men in the various pageants. The general conduct of the games and demonstrations.

3. Furnishing of the necessary suits for the athletic activities and costumes for the pageants.

*For the Army is involved:*

1. Committee with authority to treat with the French officials in the locations decided upon as to the use of buildings or fields, permission for parades and other required items about which it would be necessary to deal with local authorities.

2. A general committee of officers to work in conjunction with a similar Association committee.

## Item No. 4.

A Military "Olympic" would bring together the best athletes in every sport from all of the Allied Armies and would undoubtedly be the greatest gathering of athletes ever seen. Entry would be restricted to men who had seen military service in the present war. The amateur-professional question would be ignored. Such an athletic meeting would unquestionably be a great factor in cementing on the field of sport those friendly ties between the men of the Allied Armies that have sprung up on the common field of battle. International sports of this kind have always developed mutual respect and understanding.

*For the Association this involves:*

1. Securing and arranging a suitable stadium.

2. The general responsibility for the technical details.

3. The furnishing of symbolic and artistic prizes.

*For the Army is involved:*

1. Responsibility for the training of its men entered in these International events.

2. As the initiative in promoting the Games would be taken by the American Army, the meet should be of an invitation nature and therefore it is suggested that if this item is approved, the Commander-in-Chief formally invite the Commanders of the Allied Armies to send entries and to participate extensively in the contests.

3. The organization of a suitable Interallied-Army Committee to work with a technical committee from the Association forming a general operating unit for the games.

It will be observed that the adoption of any or all of the above items calls for immediate and definite plans and also financial appropriations by the Association. These things it is prepared to do, as well as to supply further details whenever necessary, if the general outline is approved by the Army authorities and the definite responsibility now placed upon the Association by the Commander-in-Chief for the operation of the volunteer athletic program with the A.E.F. be continued to include the period under discussion and the items suggested.

An early reply will be appreciated.

*Respectfully submitted,*
*Elwood S. Brown,*
*Department of Athletics.*

## Further Resources

### BOOKS

Daniles, George G. *The V & VI Olympiads: Stockholm 1912, Inter-Allied Games 1919.* Volume 6 of *The Olympic Century.* Los Angeles: World Sport Research & Publications, 2000.

### PERIODICALS

Buchanan, Ian. "Elwood S. Brown: Missionary Extraordinary." *Journal of Olympic History,* Fall 1998.

Lewis, G. "Military Olympics at Paris, France, 1919." *Physical Educator* 31, no. 4, December 1974, 172–175.

### WEBSITES

"Inter-Allied Games." International Games Archive. Available online at http://www.internationalgames.net/interallied.htm; website home page: http://www.internationalgames.net (accessed April 7, 2003).

# Basket Ball: for Coach, Player and Spectator

Reference work

**By:** E.D. Angell

**Date:** 1918

**Source:** Angell, E.D. *Basket Ball: for Coach, Player and Spectator.* Chicago: Thomas E. Wilson, 1918, 7–12.

**About the Author:** E.D. Angell was a lieutenant in the United States Navy Medical Corps and an expert sports coach. In the introduction to *Basket Ball: for Coach, Player and Spectator,* Chris Steinmetz, captain of the 1905 University of Wisconsin baseball team, wrote that Angell never had a losing baseball team and "instilled in the men the determinator to fight to the very end and never to quit." He is also the author of the sporting book *"Play"* on various sports. Angell coached both basketball and baseball at the University of Wisconsin. ∎

## Introduction

In the late nineteenth century, two sports were invented in the YMCAs of Massachusetts to solve pressing issues with recreational programs. Baseball was the most popular sport played in the country, but it was suited to neither cold weather nor small, urban facilities. The games invented to solve these problems were volleyball, coming from the YMCA in Holyoke, Massachusetts, and basketball, coming from the YMCA in Springfield, Massachusetts. Invented in 1892 by James Naismith, basketball could claim its place as America's "great national indoor game" by 1917. Indoor baseball, played with a "dead ball" designed not to go very far, was popular, but soon lost out to basketball and volleyball. Also, these games could be seen as an American invention, as opposed to baseball, which evolved from the British game of rounders.

A large number of books came out in the early twentieth century offering the rules and setup for basketball. As a relatively new and growing sport, supporters of basketball needed to promote the game as a perfect recreational alternative for the winter months. While basketball is played very differently than it is today, the rules of the game are fundamentally the same as they were almost one hundred years ago.

## Significance

Angell wrote about the training of a basketball team and offered ideas on what players should do when practicing. Early in the chapter, Angell noted the contrast between training for basketball and training for baseball. Angell contended that baseball was so much a part of the culture that boys did not need to learn the game when they were trying out. Practically every child trying out for the team had played baseball in grade school, on the playground or elsewhere. Basketball was different early in its history, as most boys had only a passing knowledge of the game at best. Twenty-six years after being invented, basketball had gained acceptance as a popular American sport. Angell stated that most students came to the team with a good an understanding of the sport—just as players had for baseball. Also implied in this piece are the different physical requirements for the two sports. Baseball permitted a fair amount of resting—both in the field and when batting. Basketball was a far different sport, with competitors playing both offense and defense and remaining on the court for minutes at a time. For this reason, training and conditioning were essential to the success of any team.

Angell also discussed the importance of diet and the "training table," a food program established by the club's trainer. Angell offered a story of runners being forced to "dry out" twenty-four hours before a race; they did not get any water, but rather were given raw meat and eggs. Angell, years ahead of his time, offered four simple rules for athletes to follow: do not overeat; do not eat between meals; be careful on days when you compete; and eat lightly if competing in the evening. Though not related to diet, Angell mentioned the food of the soul, music! He stressed the need for people who could lighten the atmosphere around the club, in addition to athletic skills. He stated that good teams were cheerful, with that joy coming from "some one or two fellows in the squad [that] had unconscious ability as entertainers." His simple dietary rules and thoughts on having people on the team who can entertain provided a vision of the teams not as cloistered athletes, but of a group of players who approach the sport with joy and moderation.

## Primary Source

*Basket Ball: for Coach, Player and Spectator*
[excerpt]

**SYNOPSIS:** Angell offers a very levelheaded approach to training basketball players. He states that since basketball is twenty-six years old in 1918, coaches do not need to introduce all of the players to the fundamentals, and that the athlete's background in the sport is as strong as their background in baseball. Additionally, he offers advice on training, diet, and the composition of the team.

### Training of a Basket Ball Team

In training we consider those matters that pertain to the development and conditioning of the individual members of the team and of the team as a whole. It is really a physical training proposition plus diet, hygiene and some psychology. We shall consider the conditioning of a team without any par-

ticular reference to the development of their skill in the playing of the game; and the methods utilized in bringing a university team to top form and holding them there until their schedule is completed would indicate in a general way the kind of policy that would bring a non-collegiate team to the same degree of fitness. There was a time, in the early history of basket-ball, when a coach found it necessary to teach the members of his team many of the fundamentals of the game, the handling of the ball, the proper way of tossing it toward the basket and many other details that led up to efficiency. In baseball this was not so true as every American boy, before competing for a position on the varsity team had already lived through a very large experience in the grade school, in the high school, and on the playground. It is a well known belief that corner lots have developed more major league baseball players than have been developed in any organized school of instruction. This was not true in the early days of basket-ball because the very newness of the game meant that it had no traditions behind it and very few boys had developed the unconscious co-ordinated understanding that permitted them to handle with facility the basket-ball as a playing device.

Basket-ball is now 26 years old and has been an important part of the play life of the American boy for many years, so we now have, as candidates for our varsity teams, young men who have the same sort of preliminary basket-ball experience as we find in candidates on the diamond for the baseball team. In other words they have the feel of the game before they ever report to the coach, and considerable youthful experience back of them. In training men for the varsity team it is better to go too slow than too fast, because in the rigor of competition it is possible for a team of men who have trained too strenuously early in the season to go "stale," become listless, disinterested, and incapacitated for the "ginger and pep" that is essential in practice. The men must like the game and they must enjoy the practice scrimmages. If a point is reached in their training when they look upon it as drudgery their playing suffers and games will be lost. In the early season it is wise to emphasize the amount of scrimmage work and possibly it is better to omit all scrimmages for the first couple of weeks, during which time the work of the squad is limited to fundamentals. Floor passing and shooting for baskets may be improved and the team carefully conditioned up to a point where scrimmages may be readily introduced. From a training standpoint the writer disapproves of

The basketball team of Aspen High School in Colorado, 1911. **WESTERN HISTORY/GENEALOGY DEPARTMENT, DENVER PUBLIC LIBRARY. REPRODUCED BY PERMISSION.**

the method utilized by some trainers of having the men brought to condition by adding to their floor practice a lot of running, supposedly for the purpose of increasing wind and endurance. It is much better to get this endurance and this respiratory capacity incidentally as a part of the actual practice of the game itself. Through this early conditioning period physical defects may be noted; players who have weak ankles or weak knees that should be protected from further injury are noted.

There have been many peculiar notions in the handling of athletes. There was a time in the old days when it was deemed advisable, prior to an athletic contest, to "dry out" the competitor for 24 hours before a race. For example, the runners were deprived of all water and were fed on raw meat or raw eggs and half a glass of sherry. They were deprived of all kinds of food that might be attractive to them and punished by a diet that was deemed to have some mysterious value. Up to 8 or 10 years ago every university in the country supported a training table where the men were provided with plain sub-

stantial food more or less modified by the eccentricities of the trainer in charge of the table. It was supposed that a team could not be developed to a high degree of efficiency without a training table. Training tables, however, became more or less of a menace. They became an excuse for petty graft and men in college subsidized as athletes were kept on the training table throughout the year and fed at the expense of the association. A careful study of the athletic life of our colleges resulted in the abolition of training tables in a great many institutions, and it is interesting to note that the records made by the athletes are just as fine and the efficiency of the teams under a no-training-table regime is just as marked. Of recent years the diet schemes of men who have made a close study of athletic endeavor have been very much normalized and it is now believed that the kind of food that a man would get in his own home, the ordinary everyday diet, permits of just as much skill, endurance and efficiency as if the diet was planned and schemed out for the man. There are certain fundamental rules, that if observed, will take care of the diet problem of the athlete.

Over-eating should be avoided.

Eating between meals should be prohibited.

On the day of a game a man should eat more carefully than at other times.

If a game is played in the evening the evening meal should be light.

As there is considerable uniformity in the judgment of trainers, the evening meal indicated will be found on many an athlete's table the night of an important game:

2 pieces of toast.

1 poached egg.

1 cup of weak tea.

However, there is some compensation for this starvation diet at 6 o'clock as most coaches see that the men get a pretty good square meal after the game. Before hard scrimmages or games it is advisable to avoid any foods that have a distinct flavor as experience has shown that some vegetables and highly seasoned items of the diet, during the progress of a hard game result in enough gastric disturbance so that the taste of the food is noted by the player. Of course, it is unnecessary to emphasize that the use of tobacco and liquor in any form is a poor preparation for training. It is very true that many men can play wonderful games even though they dissipate to a certain extent, but as a rule the average athlete will not play up to his best form if he smokes during the training season.

The efficiency of a basket-ball player depends upon individual co-ordination and a fine degree of accuracy, and as many games are lost by one point it may be that the very defect in the training of some one athlete may mean the loss of a point or two that may lose the game. In training one is aiming at physical efficiency, striving for as close an approximation to physical perfection as is possible, and so it is good to taboo anything that may interfere even slightly with the highest efficiency of the competing athlete. Another important value found in the giving up of some pet vice is in the psychological value. If a man gives up something for the team on which he plays he feels a deeper sense of responsibility and feels more completely a part of the organization because of the fact that he has sacrificed some one thing for it. This is a value in itself, not less important than the physical value that may come from such sacrifice.

Men recuperate while they sleep and so it is important that during the training period men of the team should have plenty of sleep. That means a sacrifice of a good many social engagements, but as in all games the main fun is in winning it is worth while to sacrifice somewhat socially that one may be more efficient.

In training a team all minor injuries should be properly cared for. It is especially necessary that the feet of a player be in good condition. If his running gear is out of order he is absolutely incapacitated. All foot injuries should be properly cared for to avoid the possibility of infection. In training a team it is sometimes found that one man on the team becomes listless and plays indifferently. The coach may note this and figure that the man is "stalling," but it is quite often true that a listless player has simply gone "stale" on his game. One of the very best treatments for a man who has lost interest in the game is to order him out of the gymnasium and tell him not to come around for three or four days. This takes his attention away from the game and gives him a needed rest, and when he returns he puts a tremendous amount of "pep" and enthusiasm into his play. Sometimes it is a good thing to allow the whole squad to rest for a day or two and keep them away from all practice and when they return, as a team, they will respond with renewed energy and vigor in their play.

It was mentioned that psychology had something to do with the efficient training of a team. All coaches will recall certain teams that they have had in their charge that were cheerful and happy and contented throughout the season and a large part of this contentment may be due to the fact that some one or two fellows in the squad had unconscious ability as entertainers. It is always good to have singers on a basketball team or some one or two fellows that play musical instruments. It keeps the team occupied and interested and they get a lot more fun out of their trips and during the training season. A team should be well disciplined, should stop at good hotels and should have the very best treatment, and equipment that they are not ashamed of, and this discipline plus contentment is a happy combination that leads toward the winning of games.

## Further Resources

### BOOKS

Peterson, Robert. *Cages to Jump Shots: Pro Basketball's Early Years.* New York: Oxford University Press, 1990.

Wolff, Alexander. *Basketball: A History of the Game.* New York: Bishop Books, 1997.

### PERIODICALS

Nelson, Murry. "The Original Celtics and the 1926–27 American Basketball League." *Journal of Popular Culture,* Fall 1996, 87–100.

### WEBSITES

"Hoop Hall History Page." Basketball Hall of Fame. Available online at http://www.hoophall.com/history/history.htm; website home page: http://www.hoophall.com (accessed April 7, 2003).

### AUDIO AND VISUAL MEDIA

*It Started with a Peach Basket: the History of College Basketball.* Presented by Norwegian Cruise Line. Produced in association with the National Association of Basketball Coaches. Louisville, Kent.: AdCraft Associates, 1992, VHS.

# "Boxers Spend Last Night Under Guard"

Newspaper article

**By:** George R. Pulford

**Date:** July 4, 1919

**Source:** Pulford, George, "Boxers Spend Last Night Under Guard." *Toledo Blade,* July 4, 1919, 14.

**About the Publication:** The *Toledo Blade* was first published on December 19, 1835, and it is the city's oldest continuous business—predating Toledo's incorporation as a city in 1837. The *Blade* covers fourteen counties in northwest Ohio and southeast Michigan. The *Blade* is owned by Block Communication, and it is headquartered in Toledo. ■

## Introduction

The city of Toledo, Ohio, fifty miles south of Detroit, was prosperous in large part because of two major industries: glass and automobiles. The city also was on the train line between New York City and Chicago, making it an easy travel destination. In 1919, a fight for boxing's world heavyweight championship came to Toledo. These events transformed a community into a global stage. Fans and newspapermen came from all over the country and the world to watch and report on the events. Like today, local boosters supported these events strongly. First, the event brought money into the local economy. Second, boosters used these events to showcase the city and increase its name recognition. Third, by hosting an event like this, the boosters exhibited a "can-do" attitude that created a positive perception of the community in the nation and the world. For a medium-sized city like Toledo, these reasons justified the expense and inconvenience of hosting an event of world-wide interest.

The match featured the reigning champion, Jess Willard, who defeated African American boxer, Jack Johnson, in Havana Cuba a few years prior. Willard took the role of the "great white hope" and was very popular for beating Johnson. Boxing was one of the few interracial sports in American society in the early twentieth century. Many viewed Jack Johnson as a usurper for the heavyweight crown because of his race. Newspapers all over the country sought a white fighter to regain the crown, and Willard had done just that. But in the shadows was a young boxer from Colorado: Jack Dempsey. Dempsey won the championship that day in 1919 and went on to become one of the best boxers in the history of the sport. While this match lacked the racial intrigue of the 1910 bout between Jack Johnson and Jim Jeffries, it had tremendous significance in the sporting world because it was a heavyweight championship fight.

## Significance

For the July 4th edition of the *Toledo Blade,* the editors wanted to provide an idea of what was happening in their city the evening before the heavyweight championship fight between Jack Dempsey and Jess Willard. "Boxers Spend Last Night Under Guard" provided a snapshot of four separate activities, all related to the next day's championship fight. These activities included the activities of the boxers, the conditions for Toledo's visitors, laments of scalpers trying to sell tickets to the fight, and the betting that was taking place. All of these events enhanced the fight culture in Toledo and transformed the city. For a few days, there existed in Toledo a sporting frenzy that no city could sustain for long.

These four activities each offered a glimpse into an international sporting event in the early twentieth century. First, with slower transportation methods, boxers spent far more time training in the city where the boxing match was to be held. This was important to ensure no loss in conditioning during a long train ride immediately prior to the bout. Today's boxers can fly into a city after training wherever they choose. Dempsey, from Colorado, trained for six weeks in Toledo prior to the match. Second, a substantial number of visitors came to Toledo. Pulford noted that Toledo was "surging over the rim with humanity" and that every hour, trains arrived filled to capacity. While some residents took it in stride, the presence of one hundred thousand to 150,000 visitors could not be missed in a mid-sized American city. Third, despite the huge number of visitors to Toledo, ticket scalpers were scrambling on the night before the fight to sell their tickets. Many people came to Toledo to be in the city of the fight with no intention of attending the fight. The fourth activity mentioned on the night before the fight was the betting that was taking place on the match. Pulford describes the activities of the gamblers, and that Dempsey did not emerge as a favorite in the match. These activities described the transformation of Toledo when hosting this important prizefight.

## Primary Source

"Boxers Spend Last Night Under Guard"

**SYNOPSIS:** Pulford, a staff writer for the *Toledo Blade,* describes events that take place in the city of Toledo, Ohio, on the evening before the prize fight between Jack Dempsey and Jess Willard on July 4, 1919. He writes about the restful evening that the boxers have, the influx of people into Toledo, the large number of unsold tickets, and the gambling activities taking place. Jack Dempsey would win that fight in Toledo, but the focal point of the article is the effect of the fight and the national spotlight focused on Toledo.

Out on Parkwood avenue where Champion Jess Willard has lived since he came to Toledo, and down at the Overland club on the bay shore, where Jack Dempsey has trained and lived for six weeks, smiling his way into the heart of the multitude, everything was quiet and peaceful Thursday night.

Around the buildings where the champion and his challenger reposed constant guard was maintained throughout the night. Men, armed and ready to shoot, if necessary, watched over the sleeping giants, that their rest might be undisturbed—that they would have the benefit of restful repose, to enter the arena Friday in complete possession of every ounce of energy and nerve force.

Both Willard and Dempsey kept out of sight Thursday. Willard absented himself from the Secor where he has held noon day levee for weeks, and Dempsey, who has been seen about the city only at widely separated intervals, spent the day in company with Trainer Jimmy De Forest, who has been his constant companion for weeks.

Dempsey was not out of De Forest's sight at any time during the last 48 hours. Even while he slept, during the afternoon as he has each day, De Forest stood guard, that the siesta might be uninterrupted.

Thursday night the watch was doubled and tripled and no one not a member of the camp was permitted to approach the Overland club. Never was thoroughbred watched more solicitously as the boy who on Friday throws down his gage for Jess Willard to pick up.

At the Neuhausel home on Parkwood silence reigned. Willard's guards paced back and forth, conversing in subdued tones. No word of their low talk reached the ears of the champion as he slept peacefully through night and they saw to it that no others in any way interfered with the perfect rest so essential to a complacent mind—if a champion's mind can be complacent on the eve of battle.

Toledo is full of visitors. In fact it is surging over the rim with humanity. Every hour brings additional trains filled to capacity with men and women, here to attend the spectacle of two men boxing for supremacy.

Any two men might box for any other title in the world save that immortal if mythical crown that once decorated the classic brow of John L. Sullivan, and the world at large, while it might care a tinker's damn or two, would not travel as it has travelled to see Friday's spectacle.

There's something about the heavyweight championship, something about such names as Sullivan, Corbett, Fitzsimmons, Jeffries, that throws a mantle of romance over the sordid details incident to staging an actual bout, that appeals to everyone, in whose veins red blood courses.

And that's why the men of the sporting world gathered here in Toledo today. It answers the crowded hotel lobbies, the jammed lodging houses, the densely packed streets and the general appearance of a too well filled basket which Toledo offers the camera men and the world at large.

It has been estimated that there is 100,000 or 150,000 strangers within the gate. A mere matter of ten or twelve thousands at this particular stage meaning nothing to the average citizen.

No one will deny that the crowd is big enough to suit everyone save the promoters and the speculators, who will be disappointed of course if the arena is not sold out. The promoters will lose nothing, because the sale long ago passed the point where profit was reached. But the speculators will be sorry dudes unless they can sell the pasteboards they bought on the idea that they would reap a harvest.

Speaking of speculators, the frantic efforts of the scalpers to unload their accumulated tickets was laughable, as early as Thursday afternoon.

The straw cracked the camel's back, otherwise the speculator's back was the announcement a few days ago that 28,000 tickets were unsold and that no one need stay away from Toledo through fear of disappointment in obtaining seats.

Shortly after the word went around that a large number of seats were unsold scalpers who had been holding their bits of pasteboard at a premium, started to sell them at the legal price. First one man, then another and finally a rush marked the announcement that plenty of good seats could be obtained and almost every street corner downtown had its peddler.

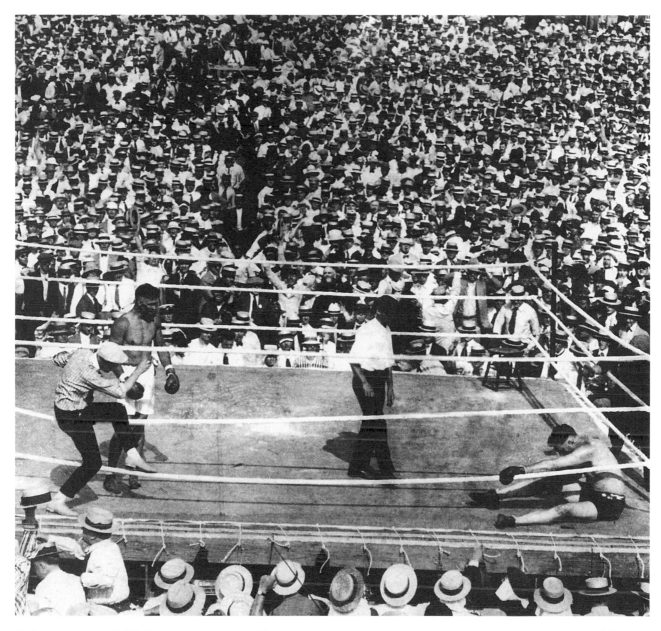

The Fourth of July, 1919, fight between Jack Dempsey and Jess Willard drew a huge crowd of spectators despite the heat, said to be a hundred degrees that day. © BETTMANN/CORBIS. REPRODUCED BY PERMISSION.

Offices were also opened in stores by the men who faced a heavy loss if they failed to unload.

In front of the Willard-Dempsey headquarters, Thursday afternoon, Fred Martin and Benny Baum, of the Rail-Light, were selling tickets at $5 off the price asked by the promoters.

The tickets were said to be some of those purchased by the Doherty interests early in the sale, on the theory that employes of other Doherty companies would want them. At the last moment, finding themselves unable to come, the men for whom the tickets were purchased, released them.

When the tickets were taken to headquarters with a request that they be bought back, a refusal was met with, on the ground that it was taken for granted they had been purchased for speculative purposes.

When Baum and Martin were disposing of their tickets several plain clothes men approached and ordered them to desist, but their activity did not decrease noticeably and they were still disposing of their tickets at last accounts.

Speculators were hit hard, it is believed and unless the sale Thursday night and Friday reaches undreamed of proportions it is believed thousands of tickets were bought and paid for by them, that have not been unloaded—certainly not at advanced rates. At sight the heavyweight championship appears to be a poor bet for the ticket pirates.

In sporting resorts downtown Thursday night, the atmosphere was filled with words. More money was bet verbally than the Victory loan figured.

How much actual cash was put up would be difficult to say, but it has been estimated that a quarter of a million is just about top figure at this time. There will be more betting Friday perhaps. They always step on the Throttle on the final lap.

Dempsey at this distance does not appear to be able to enter the ring favorite, as was predicted some weeks ago by Billy McCarney. The appearance of large sums of Willard money, following the occular evidence that the champion is in condition, cut down the enthusiasm of Dempsey supporters materially, although there has been no time that bets were not being offered and taken.

Thursday night the betting was even, with scads of money offered that Dempsey would win with knockout. These offers were at 100 to 500 or longer and the Willard men did not seem to feel like taking the long end, although apparently confident that Dempsey would not turn the trick. They preferred to bet even money that Willard would win the bout.

One of the features of the championship bout that has not attracted much outside attention is the program, published by Rickard, Flournoy and Byrne, which contains a history of the heavyweight championship by Bob Edgren, photographs of many prominent boxers and much other interesting data.

When the program first appeared little effort was made to push its sale and then Billy McCarney and Tom Bodkin conceived the idea of bringing the silvery tongued Campbell onto the ground. Since "Doc" who shakes up the English language like a man making a Ramoos fizz, put on the grandoldspeil the books have been selling like hotcakes, the public paying tribute to the enticing elements of the human voice, which in this case literally talked the loose change out of the pickets of the people who came within sound of his vocal efforts.

## Further Resources

### BOOKS

Bacho, Peter. *Boxing in Black and White.* New York: H. Holt & Co., 1999.

Dempsey, Jack, with Myron Stearns. *Round by Round: An Autobiography.* New York, McGraw-Hill, 1940.

### PERIODICALS

Nack, William. "The Long Count." *Sports Illustrated,* September 22, 1997, 72–83.

Robinson, Ray. "The Prizefighter." *American Heritage,* September 2001, 34–36.

### WEBSITES

"Dempsey and Willard: The Worst Beating in Boxing History." East Side Boxing. Available online at http://www.eastside-boxing.com/DempseyvsWillard.html; website home page: http://www.eastsideboxing.com (accessed April 7, 2003).

"Jack Dempsey." International Boxing Hall of Fame. Available online at http://www.ibhof.com/dempsey.htm; website home page: http://www.ibhof.com (accessed April 7, 2003).

Seltzer, Louis B. Chapter 12 of *The Years Were Good: The Autobiography of Louis B. Seltzer.* Reproduced in the Cleveland Memory Project. Available online at http://web.ulib.csuohio.edu/SpecColl/press/tywg/chapt12.html; website home page: http://www.clevelandmemory.org (accessed April 7, 2003).

### AUDIO AND VISUAL MEDIA

*Greatest Rounds Ever: Part I.* NBC Sports. GoodTimes Home Video, 1990, VHS.

# *Pioneer in Pro Football*
## Memoir

**By:** Jack Cusack

**Date:** 1963

**Source:** Cusack, Jack. *Pioneer in Pro Football.* Fort Worth, Tx.: Self-published, 1963, 11–12, 13–15, 16–17.

**About the Author:** Jack Cusack (1890–1973) was one of the prominent early figures in professional football in Ohio. At the age of twenty-one, Cusack became the manager of the Canton Bulldogs, one of the leading teams of the day. During his six years with the Canton Bulldogs, Cusack led the team to two championships (in 1916 and 1917), and was responsible for bringing Jim Thorpe into professional football. In 1918, Cusack left football to enter the oil and gasoline business in Oklahoma. He later worked as an independent oil operator in Fort Worth, Texas. ∎

## Introduction

The location of the Pro Football Hall of Fame in Canton, Ohio, is logical given the strong role that Canton and Ohio had in the early days of professional football. The first professional football league in the state was the Ohio League, which was formed in 1903 and lasted until the end of the 1919 season. The stronger Ohio teams then joined the new American Professional Football Association, the league that eventually became today's National Football League (NFL). The leading teams of the day included the Canton Bulldogs, the Akron Indians, and the Massillon Tigers (champions from 1903 to 1907). Massillon is a small city ten miles west of Canton. The proximity of the two cities created a tremendous rivalry between the two clubs that set the stage for the 1915 season.

Jack Cusack took over the Canton Bulldogs in 1912, at the young age of twenty-one years old. Cusack remained committed to bring a championship to Canton. To compete with Massillon, Cusack looked all over for players to sign and made an attempt to contact every All-American college player. Many refused to play professional football. In a move that would become commonplace among today's sports owners, Cusack committed a huge amount of money to sign the best player of professional football, if not the best athlete in the first half of the twentieth century, Jim Thorpe. Thorpe signed just before the first game with Massillon for $250 dollars a week. The move paid immediate dividends, raising the attendance from twelve hundred to six thousand. While Thorpe made a tremendous impact, Cusack also signed a tackle from Michigan, Charlie Smith, who was one of the first African American players in professional football. Three hard-fought seasons ensued. The Canton Bulldogs won the championship of the Ohio League in 1916 and 1917.

### Significance

Cusack's memoir provides a glimpse of early professional football in Ohio, the state that provided much of its nascent history. The early days of professional football in the 1900s and 1910s developed unlike early baseball. Baseball grew as a community and professional sport, later making an impact at the college level. Football grew first as a college sport, with the professional version creating much less of an impact. While there are a number of reasons for this, the focus of professional football in Ohio did not lend itself to national interest. However, in Ohio, professional football became a tremendous passion for its communities. In the fan culture that evolved, followers of the leading teams (Canton, Massillon, and Akron) developed a natural rivalry between cities so close geographically.

The "Mystery of the Phantom Policeman" is an interesting story about the frenzy that took place at these early games. In the second game that season between Canton and Massillon, which was the last game of the season, one play secured the victory for Canton and a share of an Ohio League crown. The Massillon player, Briggs, would have scored a touchdown on a play to tie the game at six; but a spectator in the standing-room-only section knocked the ball out of Briggs's hands. Charlie Smith caught the ball for a touchback. Briggs insisted it was a policeman who knocked the ball out of his hands, and huge arguments between the players and fans ensued. Fans of both teams swarmed onto the field. When the dust settled, the officials determined that the ball was

rightly fumbled and that the possession, and eventually the game, belonged to Canton.

Another important element touched on in *Pioneer in Pro Football* is the role of race and diversity that existed in professional sports. While Jim Thorpe played professional baseball, he was not embraced by that sport like he was in professional football. Thorpe, a Native American Indian of Sauk and Fox descent, and Charlie Smith, an African American, played side by side for the Canton team long before any people of color were allowed to play in Major League Baseball. In searching for talent, Cusack was driven only by abilities on the field, and not by the color of the player's skin. In this regard, football followed boxing (with Jack Johnson) in creating a racially diverse playing field years ahead of baseball, the leading sport in the country in terms of popularity.

### Primary Source

*Pioneer in Pro Football* [excerpt]

**SYNOPSIS:** Jack Cusack offers his account of the 1915 season with the Canton Bulldogs, the team that would later win the Ohio League championships of 1916 and 1917. He discusses bringing Jim Thorpe, the Carlisle graduate and former all-American who won the 1912 pentathlon and decathlon at the Stockholm Olympics, to Canton to play football. Cusack also talks about the playing conditions, the role of the fans, and the support that they received in the Canton community after signing Thorpe.

The year 1915 brought the beginning of the big-time era in professional football, and happily it brought Massillon back into play. A group of Massillon business men, headed by Jack Whalen and Jack Donahue, invited me to a meeting to discuss details, and they were now willing to agree with the principals I held out for the year before. Their decision to field a team brought back the old rivalry that all of us needed so badly and furnished the drawing power that meant good gates. With the return of Massillon, another pleasant thing occurred—the sports writers, having all but forgotten the 1906 scandal, began referring to the old rivals again as the Canton Bulldogs and the Massillon Tigers. We were back in business once more at the old stand.

I knew that in order to compete properly with Massillon we had to secure for Canton the best available talent, so I contacted every All-American I could locate, either by mail or personally, but found the response somewhat reluctant. The colleges and most sports writers around the country were opposed to professional football, as were many of the coaches and graduate players, and many of those I contacted

The Canton Bulldog's Jim Thorpe (20) brings down a Buffalo player in a game at the Polo Grounds, New York, December 4, 1920. © BETTMANN/ CORBIS. REPRODUCED BY PERMISSION.

refused to play. Some of those who did agree to consider playing jobs insisted on the use of assumed names, particularly the coaches, who wanted to protect their jobs. The various clubs booked the strongest teams possible from around the nation but only four were outstanding in 1915—Canton, Massillon, Youngstown and Columbus. Peggy Parratt withdrew from Akron at this time but did place a fine team in Cleveland the following year.

The Canton Bulldogs opened the 1915 season with Wheeling, W. Va., and racked up a 75-0 victory, and on October 18 we defeated the Columbus Pan-

handles, 7-0. Meanwhile, I succeeded in strengthening the Bulldogs with some of the star players of that era, one of the best recruits being Bill Gardner, a great tackle or end from Carlisle, the government's famous Indian school in Pennsylvania. Another was Hube Wagner, an All-American end and former captain at Pitt who had been picked second All-American by sports writers 26 times during his college career. I also signed Greasy Neale, then coach at West Virginia Wesleyan, an outstanding end and halfback with considerable All-American mention. I also acquired John Kelleson, a fine tackle, assistant coach to Neale.

On October 25 we lost, 3-9, to the Detroit Heralds in a hard-fought game on their home grounds. This was our first defeat by the Heralds, with whom we had contested during the two previous seasons. On November 1 we defeated the Cincinnati Colts, 41-12; the Colts had a better team than the score indicates because their players were largely former college stars. And on November 8 we took a 38-0 victory over the Altoona Indians, composed mainly of Carlisle stars and self-styled "champions of Pennsylvania."

Then, just in time for Canton's first game with the newly revived Massillon Tigers, I hit the jackpot by signing the famous Jim Thorpe, the Sac and Fox Indian from Oklahoma who was rated then (and still is today) as the greatest footballer and all-around athlete that the world of sports has ever seen!

He had first won world acclaim as the one-man track team who swept the 1912 Olympics for the United States at Stockholm, Sweden; he had been the backbone of the Carlisle football team during his school years there, a powerfully built halfback who was unequalled anywhere as a line smasher, kicker and runner; and he was destined to become, at a later time, a top-rated baseball outfielder with the New York Giants, the Boston Braves, and the Cincinnati Reds.

In 1915, when I conceived the idea of hiring this already living legend of sportdom, Jim already had lost his amateur standing (and his Stockholm medals) because he had played a little semi-pro baseball for $25 a week, and at the moment he was doing backfield coaching at the University of Indiana. I sent Bill Gardner, his old Carlisle teammate, over to Indiana to see him, and shortly thereafter I had Thorpe under contract to play for the Canton Bulldogs for $250 a game. The signing also marked the start of a warm friendship between us that lasted until Jim died of a heart attack, in 1953.

Some of my business "advisers" frankly predicted that I was leading the Bulldogs into bankruptcy by paying Jim the enormous sum of $250 a game, but the deal paid off even beyond my greatest expectations. Jim was an attraction as well as a player, and whereas our paid attendance averaged around 1,200 before we took him on, we filled the Massillon and Canton parks for the next two games—6,000 for the first and 8,000 for the second. All the fans wanted to see the big Indian in action. . . .

In order for the reader of this narrative to have the full import of the first 1915 Canton-Massillon game, I quote from the writeup of Warren Cross, a highly respected sports scribe for *The Canton Repository,* who recently retired after half a century of reporting:

> Only the slippery surface of the field kept the Indian (Thorpe), ideal in build and a finished football man, from scoring at least one touchdown. In the second period he broke through the Massillon defense and headed for the goal, with only Dorias in his path. In attempting to get by the Massillon luminary he lost his footing and slipped, going out of bounds on the eight-yard line. On another occasion, after skirting Massillon's left end, he slipped with almost a clear field in front of him. He was the only Canton man feared by the Massillon defense. He showed the 6,000 yelling fans the reason for this fear.

> Fisher (Greasy Neale), the unknown halfback from the East, and Carp Julian were the only other Canton men able to accomplish anything. For Massillon, in addition to Dorias, there stood out Fullback Hanley and Ed Kagy, Captain. The first scoring came in the first quarter when Dorias of Massillon dropped the ball over from the 28-yard line. Just before the close of the period, Thorpe trotted onto the field, heralded by cheers from 6,000 throats. He took left half.

> Early in the second quarter, a pass from Dorias to Kagy took the ball to the Canton two-yard line. Canton held for three downs. On the fourth attempt, Hanley plunged through. Fleming booted the goal. Score: Massillon 10, Canton 0.

> After the next kickoff and the exchange of punts that followed, Canton made its best showing. Gardner intercepted a pass on Canton's 41-yard line. Thorpe grabbed a short pass over the line for nine yards and then shot outside of Massillon's left tackle for the longest run of the game. He covered 40 yards before he slipped and went out of bounds on the 8-yard line. Massillon's line held, Canton making only 4 yards in three attempts. On the fourth down Julian shot a pass over center, the ball was batted down by a Massillon forward and into the arms of Guard Drumm. He pushed through and over the goal line, but the touchdown was not allowed, Umpire Durfee ruling that a Canton man had touched the ball before it was batted down by the Massillon lineman. Protest was unavailing, Although it appeared to be a legal touchdown for Canton. Not until late in the third quarter could Massillon score again. Then Dorias scored a dropkick from the 42-yard line. An intercepted pass by Massillon paved the way for the last scoring, another Dorias dropkick from the 45-yard line.

After a lapse of nine years barren of the intense rivalry that has always been the outstanding feature of the athletic relations between the two cities, the same old Massillon Jinx still holds its mystic power over Canton. Massillon and the Jinx conquered, 16 to 0.

In preparation for our second game with Massillon, to be played at Canton on November 29, I further bolstered the Bulldogs with the addition of Robert Butler, Walter Camp's All-American tackle from the University of Wisconsin; Abel, another Camp All-American tackle from Colgate; and Charlie Smith, a fine tackle from the Michigan Aggies, and to my knowledge the first Negro to play professional football. Jim Thorpe was now serving as the Canton captain. . . .

Our Canton park would hold as many as 8,000 people, but on this November afternoon we had an overflow crowd of spectators. Not wanting to lose any gate admissions, we sold standing room in the end zones and, in agreement with Massillon, adopted ground rules providing that any player crossing the goal line into the crowd must be in possession of the ball when he emerged from the crowd—and as things turned out, this proved to be a lucky break for Canton.

The contest was a hard-fought, nerve-knotting game with both teams about equally matched on line play. We were able to make but two first downs on line play, while Massillon was held to one. We made several forward pass attempts without completing one, while Massillon completed four. Jim Thorpe succeeded in making a dropkick from the 18-yard line and later followed up with a placement kick from the 45, giving Canton a 6-0 advantage. Massillon was held scoreless in the first three quarters, but in the final quarter the visitors opened their stock of passes and the situation began to look bad for Canton.

At this juncture I saw that something was wrong with Abel, our new tackle. Our opponents were making far too much yardage through his position, and when Captain Thorpe made no move to replace him I took it upon myself to do so—in keeping with an agreement I had with Thorpe that it would be my right to substitute from the bench if I felt it to be necessary. (I might mention, too, that Jim was sometimes hesitant to substitute, especially as to replacing a player with All-American qualifications.) I found that Abel was ill with a heavy cold, and I replaced him with Charlie Smith, the Negro from Michigan Aggies.

Then, with only a few minutes left to play, the fireworks really started. Briggs, right end for Massillon, caught a forward pass on our 15-line and raced across our goal line right into the midst of the "Standing Room Only" customers. Briggs fumbled—or at least he was said to have fumbled—and the ball popped out of the crowd right into the hands of Charlie Smith, the Canton substitute who had been following in hot pursuit. Referee Conners, mindful of the ground rules made before the game, ruled the play a touchback, but Briggs had something to say about that.

"I didn't fumble!" protested the Massillon end. "That ball was kicked out of my hands by a policeman—a uniformed policeman!"

That was ridiculous on the face of it. Briggs was either lying or seeing things that didn't happen to be there—for most everybody knew that Canton had no uniformed policemen in those days. But Briggs was unable to accept this solid fact.

"It *was* a policeman!" he insisted. "I saw the brass buttons on his coat."

Both teams had a lot going on this end-zone play. The 1915 championship of the so-called Ohio League was at stake, along with "championship of the world," as the sports writers called it. If Referee Conners' decision were allowed to stand, Canton had the title wrapped up by 6-0, while if Briggs' touchdown had been completed the score would have been 6-6, giving Massillon the undisputed championship.

The spectators, brightly aware of all this, could stand the strain and tension no longer. With only three minutes left to play, the fans—of both Massillon and Canton persuasion—broke down the fences surrounding the playing area and swarmed across the field by the thousands, the Massillon fans protesting the referee's decision, the Canton citizens defending it. The officials strove manfully to clear the field and resume play but found the task impossible and called the game.

It wasn't all over yet, however. The Massillon team and its loyal supporters demanded that the game officials settle the matter conclusively by making a statement on the referee's decision, and at last they agreed to do so—on the condition that the statement be sealed and given to Manager Langford of the Courtland Hotel, to be opened and read by him at thirty minutes after midnight. This arrangement was made in order to give the officials plenty of time to get out of town and escape any wrath that might descend upon them from either side. Tension remained high throughout the evening, and the hotel lobby was filled with a bedlam of argument until Manager Langford read the statement at 12:30 a.m. It backed Referee Conners' touchback decision, saying that it was proper under the ground rules, and the Canton Bulldogs and Massillon tied for the championship.

The "Mystery of the Phantom Policeman" who had caused Briggs of Massillon so much unhappiness was solved about ten years later, long after I had left professional football and had gone to live in Oklahoma. While on a visit back to Canton I had occasion to ride a street car, on which I was greeted by an old friend, the brass-buttoned conductor. We began reminiscing about the old football days, and the conductor told me what had happened during that crucial final quarter play back in 1915. Briggs, when he plunged across the goal line into the end zone spectators, fell at the feet of the conductor, who promptly kicked the ball from Briggs' hands into the arms of Canton's Charlie Smith.

"Why on earth did you do a thing like that?" I asked.

"Well," he said, "it was like this—I had thirty dollars bet on that game and, at my salary, I couldn't afford to lose that much money."

And that's how the Canton Bulldogs tied for the 1915 championship—on Jim Thorpe's two field kicks, with assists from a streetcar conductor and a lucky catch by Charlie Smith.

## Further Resources

### BOOKS

Carroll, Bob. *The Ohio League, 1910–1919.* N. Huntingdon, Penn.: Professional Football Researchers Association, 1997.

### WEBSITES

"Chronology of Professional Football." Pro Football Hall of Fame. Available online at http://www.profootballhof.com /history/mainpage.cfm?cont_id=90353; website home page: http://www.profootballhof.com (accessed April 7, 2003).

"The Ohio League." Professional Football Researchers Association. Available online at http://www.footballresearch.com /articles/frpage.cfm?topic=ohiolgue; website home page: http://www.footballresearch.com (accessed April 7, 2003).

# Interview with Edd Roush

## Interview

**By:** Edd Roush

**Date:** 1966

**Source:** Roush, Edd. Interview by Lawrence Ritter. In Ritter, Lawrence. *The Glory of Their Times: The Story of the Early Days of Baseball Told by the Men Who Played It.* New York: Vintage, 1985, 218–222.

**About the Author:** Edd Roush (1893–1988) was a Hall of Fame centerfielder who played major league baseball for eighteen years, primarily for the Cincinnati Reds (1916–1926, 1931) and New York Giants (1916, 1927–1929). He also played for the Chicago White Sox and for Indianapolis and Newark of the Federal League. He compiled a .323 batting average during his career and won the National League batting title twice for the Reds (.341 in 1917 and .321 in 1919). Roush was one of the biggest stars of the 1919 Reds World Series–winning team. He ended his career with 268 stolen bases and was elected to the National Baseball Hall of Fame in 1962. ∎

## Introduction

In the early 1960s, baseball historian Lawrence Ritter conducted a series of oral-history interviews with some of the greats of the game of baseball. Seeking a more human side to the early days of the game, Ritter sought out ballplayers from the first part of the twentieth century who were a shade below the biggest stars of the day. One of the most notable was former Cincinnati Reds center fielder, Edd Roush, the only player interviewed to have participated in the infamous 1919 World Series between the Chicago White Sox and Cincinnati Reds.

The 1919 World Series between the American League champion White Sox and National League champion Reds featured one of the most notorious betting scandals in professional-sports history. The Reds won the Series, five games out of eight, over the heavily favored White Sox, winners of the 1917 World Series over the New York Giants. The Reds compiled a better record in the regular season, winning ninety-six games to the White Sox's eighty-eight, but the Sox's 1917 World Series experience made them heavy favorites with gamblers. While there was speculation during the Series that the games had been fixed, it was not the first upset in World Series history. In 1903, in the first World Series, the Boston Red Sox defeated the heavily-favored Pittsburgh Pirates; and in 1914 the Boston Braves upset the favored Philadelphia Athletics. But the speculation proved correct: eight Chicago White Sox players conspired to throw the Series to the Reds for payments promised them by gamblers, including noted gambler Arnold Rothstein. These players had complained bitterly about team owner

Cincinnati Reds' star outfielder Edd Roush warms up before a game.
© UNDERWOOD & UNDERWOOD/CORBIS. REPRODUCED BY
PERMISSION.

Charles Comiskey's treatment of his players and the mea-
ger salaries they received.

### Significance

Much of the historical focus on the 1919 World Series has been on how the Sox threw the Series. Of the
eight games played, the Sox controlled the outcome in
each of them. They lost games one and two behind deliberately poor pitching by Eddie Cicotte and Lefty
Williams, respectively. In game three, rookie pitcher
Dickie Kerr, not part of the fix, beat the Reds, 3–0. But
Chicago, again with subpar pitching by Cicotte and
Williams, lost games four and five. After Kerr won his
second game of the Series, the White Sox were down
4–2 in the Series. In game seven, to protest the lack of
payment for their part of the fix, the Sox won behind Cicotte. Game eight, and the Series, however, was lost by
Lefty Williams when he and his family were threatened
by gamblers.

The players involved in the scandal were pitcher Ed-
die Cicotte, first baseman Chick Gandil, center fielder
Oscar "Happy" Felsch, left fielder Joe Jackson, infielder
Fred McMullin, shortstop Swede Risberg, pitcher Claude
"Lefty" Williams, and third baseman Buck Weaver. His-
torians generally agree that, unlike the other players,

Weaver did play his hardest and did try to get his team
to win. However, he was still implicated, because he
knew of the fix and did not report it to the team. These
eight players became know as the "Black Sox," shortly
after news broke about the fix the following year. None
of them ever played organized baseball again, even
though they were acquitted in the 1921 trial. The scandal also led to the establishment of a baseball "commissioner" to oversee the sport. The first commissioner,
Judge Kenesaw Mountain Landis, ruled the game without question.

There has been relatively little written about the
Cincinnati Reds' role in the 1919 World Series, except
that they benefited from the White Sox's deliberate poor
play. This isn't surprising, given that the Sox seem to have
controlled the Series from the outset; they lost when they
meant to lose and won when they played to their fullest.
However, the Reds were an excellent team that year and
had every chance to win the Series, even if Chicago had
played to their full potential. But because of the widespread notion that Chicago lost the Series more than
Cincinnati actually *won* it, the Reds of 1919 are routinely
left off the list of best baseball teams of all-time.

### Primary Source

Interview with Edd Roush [excerpt]

> **SYNOPSIS:** In this excerpt from a 1966 interview con-
> ducted by writer Lawrence Ritter, former Cincinnati
> Red Edd Roush provides an oral account of the
> 1919 World Series. The interview is interesting for
> two reasons. First, it helps illustrate that the influ-
> ence of gambling was not isolated to the 1919 Black
> Sox, but was a rampant problem in baseball through-
> out the period. Second, it helps tell the story from
> the Reds' point of view. They played the games hard
> and assert, to a man, that they could have won the
> Series fair and square.

Yes, I knew at the time that some finagling was
going on. At least that's what I'd heard. Rumors were
flying all over the place that gamblers had got to the
Chicago White Sox, that they'd agreed to throw the
World Series. But nobody knew anything for sure until Eddie Cicotte spilled the beans a year later.

We beat them in the first two games, 9-1 and
4-2, and it was after the second game that I first
got wind of it. We played those first two games in
Cincinnati, and the next day we were to play in
Chicago. So the evening after the second game we
were all gathered at the hotel in Cincinnati, standing around waiting for cabs to take us to the train
station, when this fellow came over to me. I didn't
know who he was, but I'd seen him around before.

"Roush," he says, "I want to tell you something. Did you hear about the squabble the White Sox got into after the game this afternoon?" And he told me some story about Ray Schalk accusing Lefty Williams of throwing the game, and something about some of the White Sox beating up a gambler for not giving them the money he'd promised them.

"They didn't get the payoff," he said, "so from here on they're going to try to win."

I didn't know whether this guy made it all up or not. But it did start me thinking. Later on in the Series the same guy came over to me again.

"Roush," he says, "you remember what I told you about gamblers getting to the White Sox? Well, now they've also got to some of the players on your own ball club."

That's all he said. Wouldn't tell me any more. I didn't say anything to anybody until we were getting dressed in the clubhouse the next day. Then I got hold of the manager, Pat Moran, just before the pregame meeting.

"Before you start this meeting, Pat," I said, "there's something I want to talk to you about."

"OK," he says, "what is it?"

"I've been told that gamblers have got to some of the players on this club," I said. "Maybe it's true and maybe it isn't. I don't know. But you sure better do some finding out. I'll be damned if I'm going to knock myself out trying to win this Series if somebody else is trying to throw the game."

Pat got all excited and called Jake Daubert over, who was the team captain. It was all news to both of them. So at the meeting, after we'd gone over the White Sox lineup, Moran looked at Hod Eller, who was going to pitch for us that day.

"Hod," he said, "I've been hearing rumors about sellouts. Not about you, not about anybody in particular, just rumors. I want to ask you a straight question and I want a straight answer."

"Shoot," says Hod.

"Has anybody offered you anything to throw this game?"

"Yep," Hod said. Lord, you could have heard a pin drop.

"After breakfast this morning a guy got on the elevator with me, and got off at the same floor I did. He showed me five thousand-dollar bills, and said they were mine if I'd lose the game today."

"What did you say?" Moran asked him.

"I said if he didn't get damn far away from me real quick he wouldn't know what hit him. And the same went if I ever saw him again."

Moran looked at Eller a long time. Finally, he said, "OK, you're pitching. But one wrong move and you're out of the game."

Evidently there weren't any wrong moves. Because ol' Hod went out there and pitched a swell game. He won two of the games in that Series.

I don't know whether the whole truth of what went on there among the White Sox will ever come out. Even today nobody really knows exactly what took place. Whatever it was, though, it was a dirty rotten shame. One thing that's always overlooked in the whole mess is that we could have beat them no matter what the circumstances!

Sure, the 1919 White Sox were good. But the 1919 Cincinnati Reds were *better*. I'll believe that till my dying day. I don't care how good Chicago's Joe Jackson and Buck Weaver and Eddie Cicotte were. *We* had Heinie Groh, Jake Daubert, Greasy Neale, Rube Bressler, Larry Kopf, myself, and the best pitching staff in both leagues. We were a very underrated ball club.

I played center field for that Cincinnati club for 11 straight years, 1916 through 1926. I came to Cincinnati from the Giants in the middle of 1916, along with Christy Mathewson and Bill McKechnie.

Of course I started playing ball long before that, around 1909 or so, right here in Oakland City, Indiana. In those days every little town had an amateur club, and so did Oakland City. Never will forget it. I was only about sixteen at the time. Oakland City had a game scheduled with a neighboring town this day, and one of Oakland City's outfielders hadn't shown up. Everybody was standing around right on the main street of town—only a small town, you know—wondering what to do, when one of the town officials says, "Why not put that Roush kid in?"

I was kind of a shy kid, and I backed away. But the manager says, "Well, that's just what we'll do if he don't show up in five more minutes."

We waited for five minutes and the outfielder never did show, so they gave me a uniform and put me in right field. Turned out I got a couple of hits that day, and I became Oakland City's regular right fielder for the rest of the season.

The next year, of course, I was right in the middle of it. We reorganized the team—the Oakland City Walk-Overs, that's what we called ourselves—and had a pretty good club. In those days, you know, I used to throw with *either* hand. I'm a natural lefty, see, but when I was a kid I never could find a lefty's glove. So I just used a regular glove and learned to throw righty. Batted lefty, but got so I could throw with my right arm almost as well as with my left.

The year after that we got in quite a hassle. That would be 1911. Seems as though some of the Oakland City boys were getting $5 a game, and I wasn't one of them. So I started raising Cain about this under-the-table business and treating some different than others.

Wound up we had such an argument that I quit the home-town club and went over and played with the Princeton team. Princeton is the closest town to Oakland City, about 12 miles due west. And don't think that didn't cause quite a ruckus. Especially when Princeton came over to play Oakland City *at* Oakland City, with me in the Princeton outfield. A fair amount of hard feelings were stirred up, to say the least. I think there are still one or two around here never have forgiven me to this very day.

## Further Resources

**BOOKS**

Asinof, Eliot. *Eight Men Out: The Black Sox and the 1919 World Series.* 1963. Reprint, New York: Henry Holt, 1987.

Cook, William. *The 1919 World Series: What Really Happened?* Jefferson, N.C.: McFarland, 2001.

**PERIODICALS**

Goldman, David. "Shocking, Lurid, and True!" *Biography,* October 1997, 14–15.

**WEBSITES**

"The Black Sox." Chicago Historical Society. Available online at http://www.chicagohs.org/history/blacksox.html; website home page: http://www.chicagohs.org (accessed April 8, 2003).

"Famous American Trials: The Black Sox Trial, 1921." University of Missouri–Kansas City School of Law. Available online at http://www.law.umkc.edu/faculty/projects/ftrials /blacksox/blacksox.html; website home page: http://www .law.umkc.edu (accessed April 8, 2003).

**AUDIO AND VISUAL MEDIA**

*Eight Men Out.* Directed by John Sayles. Orion Pictures, 1988, VHS.

# GENERAL RESOURCES

## General

Craats, Rennay. *The 1910s*. Calgary: Weigl Educational Publishers, 2000.

Cross, Robin. *World War I in Photographs*. New York: Smithmark, 1996.

Empey, Arthur Guy. *Over the Top*. New York: G. P. Putnam's Sons, 1917.

*End of Innocence*. Alexandria, Va.: Time-Life Books, 2000.

Feinstein, Stephen. *The 1910s From World War I to Ragtime Music*. Berkeley Heights, N.J.: Enslow, 2001.

Hemmingway, Ernest. *Farewell to Arms*. New York: Scribner, 1957.

Jantzen, Steven. *Hooray For Peace, Hurrah for War; The United States During World War I*. New York: Knopf, 1971.

Katz, William Loren. *The New Freedom to the New Deal, 1913–1930*. Austin: Raintree Steck-Vaughn, 1993.

Lloyd, Alan. *The War in the Trenches*. New York: David McKay Company, 1976.

Opie, Robert. *The 1910s Scrapbook: The Decade of the Great War*. London: New Cavendish, 2000.

Sharman, Margaret. *1910s*. Austin: Raintree Steck-Vaughn, 1993.

Stewart, Gail. *1910s*. New York: Crestwood, 1989.

———. *World War I*. San Diego: Lucent, 1991.

Tielhard de Chardin, Pierre. *The Making of a Mind; Letters From a Soldier-Priest, 1914–1919*. New York: Harper and Row, 1965.

Trout, Steven. *Memorial Fictions: Willa Cather and the First World War*. Lincoln: University of Nebraska Press, 2002.

Tuchman, Barbara. *The Guns of August*. New York: MacMillan, 1962.

United States History Society. *1915 to 1920: Fighting for Democracy in World War I*. Skokie, IL: United States History Society, 1962–1968.

Werstein, Irving. *Over Here and Over There; The Era of the First World War*. New York: Norton, 1968.

## The Arts

Allen, Robert C. *Vaudeville and Film, 1895–1915: A Study in Media Interaction*. New York: Arno, 1980.

Atkinson, Brooks. *Broadway*. New York: Macmillan, 1970.

Bell, Bernard. *The Afro-American Novel and Its Tradition*. Amherst: University of Massachusetts Press, 1987.

Bernheim, Alfred L., and Sarah Harding. *The Business of the Theatre: An Economic History of the American Theatre, 1750–1932*. New York: Blom, 1932.

Berthoff, Warner. *The Ferment of Realism: American Literature, 1884–1919*. London: Cambridge University Press, 1965.

Bowser, Eileen. *The Transformation of Cinema*. New York: Scribners, 1990.

Brockett, Oscar G., and Robert R. Findlay. *Century of Innovation: A History of European and American Theatre and Drama Since 1870*. Englewood Cliffs, N.J.: Prentice-Hall, 1984.

Brown, Milton. *The Story of the Armory Show*. New York: Joseph H. Hirschorn Foundation, 1963.

Buerkle, Jack B., and Danny Barker. *Bourbon Street Black: The New Orleans Black Jazzman*. New York: Oxford University Press, 1973.

Butler, Ivan. *The War on Film.* New York: A. S. Barnes, 1974.

Chase, Gilbert. *America's Music From the Pilgrims to the Present,* 2nd rev. ed. New York: McGraw-Hill, 1966.

Cooperman, Stanley. *World War I and the American Novel.* Baltimore: Johns Hopkins University Press, 1967.

Cowart, Jack, and Juan Hamilton. *Georgis O'Keefe: Art and Letters.* Washington, D.C.: National Gallery of Art, 1987.

Craven, Wayne. *American Art: History and Culture.* New York: Harry N. Abrams, Inc., 1994.

Csida, Joseph, and June Bundy Csida. *American Entertainment: A Unique History of Show Business.* New York: Watson-Guptill, 1978.

Davis, Ronald L. *A History of Music in American Life, Volume II, The Gilded Years, 1865–1920.* Huntington, N.Y.: Krieger, 1980.

Duncan, Isadora. *The Art of the Dance,* edited by Sheldon Cheney. New York: Theatre Arts, 1928.

Elliott, Emory, ed. *Columbia Literary History of the United States.* New York: Columbia University Press, 1988.

Erenberg, Lewis. *Steppin' Out: New York Nightlife and the Transformation of American Culture, 1890–1930.* Westport, Conn.: Greenwood Press, 1981.

Everson, William K. *American Silent Film.* New York: Oxford University Press, 1978.

Ewen, David. *All the Years of American Popular Music.* Englewood Cliffs, N.J.: Prentice-Hall, 1977.

Ewen, David. *New Complete Book of the American Musical Theater.* New York: Holt Rinehart and Winston, 1970.

———. *The Story of America's Musical Theater.* Philadelphia: Chilton, 1961.

Farnsworth, Marjorie. *The Ziegfeld Follies.* New York: Bonanza, 1956.

Gerdts, William H. *American Impressionism.* New York: Abbeville Press, 1984.

Green, Martin. *New York: 1913.* New York: Macmillan, 1988.

Gregory, Horace, and Marza Zaturensha. *A History of American Poetry, 1900–1940.* New York: Harcourt, Brace, 1946.

Hazzard-Gordon, Katrina. *Jookin': The Rise of Social Dance Formations in African-American Culture.* Philadelphia: Temple University Press, 1990.

Heller, Adele, and Lois Rudnick. *1915: The Cultural Moment: The New Politics, The New Woman, The New Psychology, The New Art, and The New Theatre in America.* New Brunswick, N.J.: Rutgers University Press, 1991.

Hitchcock, H. Wiley, ed. *Music in the United States.* Englewood Cliffs, N.J.: Prentice-Hall, 1969.

Homer, William Innes. *Alfred Stieglitz and the American Avant-Garde.* Boston: New York Graphic Society/Little, Brown, 1977.

Homer. *Alfred Stieglitz and the Photo-Secession.* Boston: Little, Brown, 1983.

Hughes, Robert. *American Visions: The Epic History of Art in America.* New York: Alfred A. Knopf, 1997.

Humphrey, Robert E. *Children of Fantasy: The First Rebels of Greenwich Village.* New York: Wiley, 1978.

Isenberg, Michael T. *War on Film: The American Cinema and World War I, 1914–1941.* Rutherford, N.J.: Fairleigh Dickinson University Press, 1981.

Jasen, David A. *Tin Pan Alley: The Composers, the Songs, the Performers, and Their Times.* New York: Fine, 1988.

Jowett, Garth. *Film: The Democratic Art.* Boston: Little, Brown, 1976.

Kuritz, Paul. *The Making of Theatre History.* Englewood Cliffs, N.J.: Prentice Hall, 1988.

Lauter, Paul, ed. *The Heath Anthology of American Literature,* 2 vols. Lexington, Mass.: Heath, 1990.

Lingeman, Richard. *Theodore Dreiser: An American Journey,* 2 vols. New York: Putnam, 1986, 1990.

Lloyd, Ann. *The Illustrated History of the Cinema.* New York: Macmillan, 1986.

Loney, Glenn. *20th Century Theatre,* vol. 1. New York: Facts On File, 1983.

Magriel, Paul. *Chronicles of American Dance.* New York: Holt, 1948.

Mast, Gerald. *A Short History of the Movies,* rev. by Bruce F. Kawin. New York: Macmillan, 1992.

May, Henry F. *The End of American Innocence,* rev. ed. New York: Columbia University Press, 1992.

Mazo, Joseph H. *Prime Movers: The Makers of Modern Dance in America.* New York: Morrow, 1977.

Meserve, Walter. *An Outline History of American Drama.* New York: Feedback Theatre Books/Prospero Press, 1994.

Mordden, Ethan. *The American Theatre.* New York: Oxford University Press, 1981.

Morgan, Thomas L., and William Barlow. *From Cakewalks to Concert Halls: An Illustrated History of African-American Popular Music From 1895 to 1930.* Washington, D.C.: Elliott & Clark, 1992.

Musser, Charles. *Before the Nickelodeon: Edwin S. Porter and the Edison Manufacturing Company.* Berkeley: University of California Press, 1991.

———. *The Emergence of Cinema.* New York: Scribners, 1990.

Oliver, Paul. *The Story of the Blues.* Radnor, Pa.: Chilton, 1969.

Perkins, David. *A History of Modern Poetry: From the 1890s to the High Modernist Mode.* Cambridge, Mass.: Harvard University Press, 1976.

Peterson, Christina. *Alfred Stieglitz's Camera Notes.* New York: Norton, 1993.

Rose, Barbara. *American Art Since 1900.* New York: Praeger, 1968.

Ruyter, Nancy Lee Chalfa. *Reformers and Visionaries: The Americanization of the Art of Dance.* New York: Dance Horizons, 1979.

Seller, Maxine Schwartz, ed. *Ethnic Theatre in the United States.* Westport, Conn.: Greenwood Press, 1983.

Shipman, David. *The Great Movie Stars.* New York: Crown, 1970.

Sklar, Robert. *Movie-Made America: A Social History of American Movies.* New York: Random House, 1975.

Slide, Anthony. *The Encyclopedia of Vaudeville*. Westport, Conn.: Greenwood Press, 1994.

Tashijian, Dickran. *Skyscraper Primitives: Dada and the American Avant-Garde*. Middletown, Conn.: Wesleyan University Press, 1975.

Terry, Walter. *The Dance in America*, rev. ed. New York: Harper & Row, 1971.

Tirro, Frank. *Jazz: A History*. New York: Norton, 1977.

Toll, Robert C. *On With the Show: The First Century of Show Business in America*. New York: Oxford University Press, 1976.

Watson, Steven. *Strange Bedfellows: The First American Avant-Garde*. New York: Abbeville Press, 1991.

Wertheim, Arthur Frank. *The New York Little Renaissance: Iconoclasm, Modernism, and Nationalism in American Culture, 1908–1917*. New York: New York University Press, 1976.

Zeidman, Irving. *The American Burlesque Show*. New York: Hawthorn, 1967.

## Business and the Economy

Beasley, Norman. *Main Street Merchant: The Story of the J.C. Penney Company*. New York: Whittlesey House, 1948.

Benson, Susan P. *Counter Cultures: Saleswomen, Managers, and Customers in American Department Stores, 1890–1940*. Urbana: University of Illinois Press, 1988.

Bogart, Ernest L., and Donald L. Kemmerer. *Economic History of the American People*. New York: Longmans, Green, 1942.

Boyer, Richard O., and Herbert M. Morais. *Labor's Untold Story*. Pittsburgh: UERMWA, 1955.

Brooks, John. *The Autobiography of American Business*. Garden City, N.Y.: Doubleday, 1974.

Carnegie, Andrew. *Autobiography*. Boston: Houghton Mifflin, 1920.

Carosso, Vincent P. *The Morgans: Private International Bankers*. Cambridge, Mass.: Harvard University Press, 1988.

Copley, Frank Barkley. *Frederick W. Taylor: Father of Scientific Management*. vols. 1 and 2. New York: Kelley, 1969.

Dubofsky, Melvyn. *Industrialization and the American Worker, 1865–1920*. Arlington Heights, Ill.: H. Davidson, 1985.

———. *We Shall Be All: A History of the Industrial Workers of the World*. Chicago: Quadrangle, 1969.

Dulles, Foster Rhea. *Labor in America: A History*. New York: Crowell, 1949.

Ewen, Elizabeth. *Immigrant Women in the Land of Dollars: Life and Culture on the Lower East Side, 1890–1925*. New York: Monthly Review Press, 1985.

Foner, Philip S. *The AFL in the Progressive Era, 1910–1915*. New York: International Publishers, 1980.

Ford, Henry. *My Life and Work*. Garden City, N.Y.: Doubleday, Page, 1922.

Freeman, Joshua, et al. *Who Built America? Working People and the Nation's Economy, Politics, Culture, and Society*. vol. 2. New York: Pantheon, 1992.

*Great Stories of American Businessmen*. New York: American Heritage Publishing, 1972.

Green, James R. *The World of the Worker: Labor in Twentieth-Century America*. New York: Hill and Wang, 1980.

Greenwald, Maurice W. *Women, War, and Work: The Impact of World War I on Women Workers in the U.S.* Westport, Conn.: Greenwood Press, 1980.

Grubbs, Frank L. *Samuel Gompers and the Great War: Protecting Labor's Standards*. Wake Forest, N.C.: Meridional Publications, 1982.

Haywood, Big Bill. *Bill Haywood's Book: The Autobiography*. New York: International, 1929.

Hessen, Robert. *Steel Titan: The Life of Charles M. Schwab*. New York: Oxford University Press, 1975.

Kessler-Harris, Alice. *Out of Work: A History of Wage-Earning Women in the United States*. New York: Oxford University Press, 1982.

Lacy, Robert. *Ford: The Men and the Machine*. Boston: Little, Brown, 1986.

Mellon, Andrew. *Taxation: The People's Business*. New York: Macmillan, 1924.

Meyer, Stephen. *The Five-Dollar Day: Labor, Management and Social Control in the Ford Motor Company, 1908–1921*. Albany: State University of New York Press, 1981.

Montgomery, David. *The Fall of the House of Labor: The Workplace, the State, and American Labor Activism, 1865–1925*. Cambridge, Mass.: Cambridge University Press, 1987.

Morgan, Gareth. *Images of Organization*. Newbury Park, Calif.: Sage, 1986.

Myers, Margaret. *A Financial History of the United States*. New York: Columbia University Press, 1970.

Nevins, Allan. *Ford: The Times, The Man, The Company*. New York: Scribners, 1954.

O'Connor, Harvey. *Mellon's Millions: The Biography of a Fortune*. New York: Day, 1993.

Olney, Martha. *Buy Now, Pay Later*. Chapel Hill: University of North Carolina Press, 1991.

Patterson, James T. *America's Struggle Against Poverty, 1900–1980*. Cambridge, Mass.: Harvard University Press, 1986.

Penney, J. C. *Fifty Years With the Golden Rule*. New York: Harper, 1950.

———. *View From the Next Decade: Jottings From a Merchant's Daybook*. New York: Nelson, 1960.

Peterson, Joyce S. *American Automobile Workers, 1900–1933*. Albany: State University of New York Press, 1987.

Rosenweig, Roy. *Eight Hours for What We Will: Workers and Leisure in an Industrial City, 1870–1920*. New York: Cambridge University Press, 1985.

Rozwenc, Edwin C., ed. *Roosevelt, Wilson and the Trusts*. Boston: Heath, 1950.

Satterlee, Herbert. *J. Pierpont Morgan: An Intimate Portrait*. New York: Macmillan, 1939.

Taft, Philip. *Organized Labor in American History*. New York: Harper & Row, 1964.

Taylor, Frederick Winslow. *Principles of Scientific Management.* New York: Harper, 1911.

Wall, Joseph Frazier. *Andrew Carnegie.* New York: Oxford University Press, 1970.

### Websites

"Board of Governors of the Federal Reserve System." Available online at http://www.federalreserve.gov.

"The Clayton Antitrust Act (1914)." Available online at http://www.stolaf.edu/people/becker/antitrust/statutes/clayton.html.

"Federal Trade Commission." Available online at http://www.ftc.gov.

"The Five Dollar Day." Available online at http://www.hfmgv.org/education/smartfun/modelt/highlandpark/fivedollar/fivedollar.html.

"History Buff—The Triangle Shirtwaist Fire." Available online at http://www.historybuff.com/library/refshirtwaist.html.

"Images of the Woolworth Building." Available online at http://www.bluffton.edu/sullivanm/woolworth/woolworth.html.

"The Mann-Elkins Act." Available online at http://www.geocities.com/Colosseum/Field/1633/mann.html.

"Panama Canal History Museum." Available online at http://www.canalmuseum.com.

Schrag, Zachary Moses. "Nineteen Nineteen: The Boston Police Strike in the Context of American Labor." Available online at http://www.schrag.info/research/thesis.html.

"War Industries Board." Available online at http://www.lovesphere.org/h/history/Windust.html.

## Education

Anderson, James D. *The Education of Blacks in the South, 1860–1935.* Chapel Hill: University of North Carolina Press, 1988.

Beale, Howard K. *A History of Freedom of Teaching in American Schools.* Report of the Commission on the Social Studies, American Historical Association, part 16. New York: Scribners, 1941.

Beatty, Barbara. *Preschool Education in America: The Culture of Young Children From the Colonial Era to the Present.* New Haven, Conn.: Yale University Press, 1995.

Berrol, Selma Cantor. *Julia Richman: A Notable Woman.* Philadelphia: Balch Institute Press, 1993.

Berube, Maurice R. *American School Reform: Progressive, Equality, and Excellence Movements, 1883–1993.* Westport, Conn: Praeger, 1994.

Blum, Jeffrey M. *Pseudoscience and Mental Ability: The Origins and Fallacies of the IQ Controversy.* New York: Monthly Review Press, 1978.

Bourne, Randolph S. *The Gary Schools.* Cambridge, Mass.: MIT Press, 1970.

Button, H. Warren, and Eugene F. Provenzo Jr. *History of Education and Culture in America.* Englewood Cliffs, N.J.: Prentice-Hall, 1983.

Church, Robert L., and Michael W. Sedlak. *Education in the United States: An Interpretive History.* New York: Free Press, 1976.

Cremin, Lawrence A. *American Education: The Metropolitan Experience, 1876–1980.* New York: Harper & Row, 1988.

———. *The Transformation of the School: Progressivism in American Education, 1876–1957.* New York: Vintage, 1964.

Dabney, Charles William. *Universal Education in the South.* Chapel Hill: University of North Carolina Press, 1936.

Dawson Howard A., and M.C.S. Noble Jr. *Handbook on Rural Education: Factual Data on Rural Education, Its Social and Economic Backgrounds.* Washington, D.C.: National Education Association of the United States, Department of Rural Education, 1961.

Dworkin, Martin. *Dewey on Education.* New York: Columbia University Teachers College Press, 1959.

Dykhuizen, George. *The Life and Mind of John Dewey.* Carbondale: Southern Illinois University Press, 1973.

Eaton, William Edward. *The American Federation of Teachers, 1916–1961: A History of the Movement.* Carbondale: Southern Illinois University Press, 1975.

Eckberg, Douglas Lee. *Intelligence and Race: The Origins and Dimensions of the IQ Controversy.* New York: Praeger, 1979.

Evans, Brian, and Bernard Waites. *IQ and Mental Testing: An Unnatural Science and Its Social History.* Atlantic Highlands, New Jersey: Humanities Press, 1981.

Gould, Stephen J. *The Mismeasure of Man.* New York: Norton, 1981.

Graham, Patricia Albjerg. *S.O.S.: Sustain Our Schools.* New York: Hill & Wang, 1992.

Haley, Margaret A. *Battleground: The Autobiography of Margaret A. Haley.* Robert L. Reid, ed. Urbana: University of Illinois Press, 1982.

Harlan, Louis R. *Booker T. Washington: The Wizard of Tuskegee, 1901–1915.* New York: Oxford University Press, 1983.

———. *Separate and Unequal: Public School Campaigns and Racism in the Southern Seaboard States, 1901–1915.* Chapel Hill: University of North Carolina Press, 1958.

Hofstadter, Richard, and Wilson Smith. *American Higher Education: A Documentary History.* 2 vols. Chicago: University of Chicago Press, 1961.

Horowitz, Helen Lefkowitz. *Campus Life: Undergraduate Cultures From the End of the Eighteenth Century to the Present.* Chicago: University of Chicago Press, 1987.

———. *The Power and Passion of M. Carey Thomas.* New York: Knopf, 1994.

James, Thomas. *Public versus Nonpublic Education in Historical Perspective.* Stanford, Calif.: Institute for Research on Educational Finance and Governance, School of Education, Stanford University, 1982.

Jonich, Geraldine. *The Sane Positivist: A Biography of Edward L. Thorndike.* Middletown, Conn.: Wesleyan University Press, 1968.

Kamin, Leon. *The Science and Politics of IQ.* New York: Wiley, 1974.

Karier, Clarence J. *Roots of Crisis: American Education in the Twentieth Century.* Chicago: Rand, McNally, 1973.

———. *Shaping the American Education State, 1900 to the Present.* New York: Free Press, 1975.

Kliebard, Herbert M. *The Struggle for the American Curriculum, 1893–1958.* New York: Routledge & Kegan Paul, 1987.

Krug, Edward A. *The Shaping of the American High School.* New York: Harper & Row, 1964.

Lagemann, Ellen Condliffe. *The Politics of Knowledge: The Carnegie Corporation, Philanthropy, and Public Policy.* Chicago: University of Chicago Press, 1989.

———. *Private Power for the Public Good: A History of the Carnegie Foundation for the Advancement of Teaching.* Middletown, Conn.: Wesleyan University Press, 1983.

Lazerson, Marvin, ed. *American Education in the Twentieth Century: A Documentary History.* New York: Teachers College Press, Columbia University, 1987.

Lewis, David Levering. *W.E.B. Du Bois: Biography of a Race, 1868–1919.* New York: Holt, 1993.

Lucas, Christopher J. *American Higher Education: A History.* New York: St. Martin's Press, 1994.

Margo, Robert A. *Race and Schooling in the South, 1880–1950: An Economic History.* Chicago: University of Chicago Press, 1990.

Marks, Russell. *The Idea of IQ.* Washington, D.C.: University Press of America, 1981.

McLachlan, James. *American Boarding Schools: A Historical Study.* New York: Scribners, 1970.

McMillen, Neil R. *Dark Journey: Black Mississippians in the Age of Jim Crow.* Urbana: University of Illinois Press, 1989.

Morison, Samuel Eliot. *The Development of Harvard University Since the Inauguration of President Eliot, 1869–1929.* Cambridge, Mass.: Harvard University Press, 1930.

Murphy, Majorie. *Blackboard Unions: The AFT and the NEA, 1900–1980.* Ithaca, N.Y.: Cornell University Press, 1990.

Perlmann, Joel. *Ethnic Differences: Schooling and Social Structure Among the Irish, Italians, Jews and Blacks in an American City, 1880–1935.* New York: Cambridge University Press, 1988.

Pulliam, John D. *History of Education in America.* 3rd ed. Columbus, Ohio: Merrill, 1986.

Seagoe, May V. *Terman and the Gifted.* Los Altos, Calif.: Kaufmann, 1975.

Seller, Maxine Schwartz, ed. *Women Educators in the United States, 1820–1993: A Bio-Bibliographical Sourcebook.* Westport, Conn.: Greenwood Press, 1994.

Thayer, Vivian Trow. *Formative Ideas in American Education, From the Colonial Period to the Present.* New York: Dodd, Mead, 1965.

Torrance, Ridgely. *The Story of John Hope.* New York: Macmillan, 1948.

Tyack, David B. *The One Best System: A History of American Urban Education.* Cambridge, Mass.: Harvard University Press, 1974.

Tyack, David B., and Elizabeth Hansot. *Managers of Virtue: Public School Leadership in America, 1820–1980.* New York: Basic Books, 1982.

Vassar, Rena L. *Social History of American Education.* Chicago: Rand, McNally, 1965.

Veysey, Laurence R. *The Emergence of the American University.* Chicago: University of Chicago Press, 1965.

Walter, Robert L. *The Teacher and Collective Bargaining.* Lincoln, Nebr.: Professional Educators Publications, 1975.

Weaver, Warren. *U.S. Philanthropic Foundations: Their History, Structure, Management, and Record.* New York: Harper & Row, 1967.

Westbrook, Robert. *John Dewey and American Democracy.* Ithaca, N.Y.: Cornell University Press, 1991.

Zilversmit, Arthur. *Changing Schools: Progressive Education Theory and Practice, 1930–1960.* Chicago: University of Chicago Press, 1993.

**Websites**

"American Association of University Professors." Available online at http://www.aaup.org.

"American Federation of Teachers." Available online at http://www.aft.org.

"Dancing on the Highway." Available online at http://www.nsea.org/voice/EllenIreneLincoln.pdf.

Friedson, Reid. "Radical Eudcators in New York City, 1909–1915." Available online at http://www.socsci.kun.nl/ped/whp/histeduc/radicaled.html#P_4.

Hay, Jean. "The Personal Price of Free Speech, Scott Nearing: 1883–1983." Available online at http://www.jeanhay.com/OTHER/SCOTT.HTM.

"The New School for Social Research." Available online at http://cepa.newschool.edu/het/schools/newsch.htm.

Schugurensky, Daniel, ed. "1910: The Institutionalization of Industrial Education in Black Rural Schools." Available online at http://tcis.oise.utoronto.ca/daniel_schugurensky/assignment1/1910song-mi.html (accessed June 18, 2003).

"Smith Hughes Act of 1917." Available online at http://hcl.chass.ncsu.edu/garson/dye/docs/smith917.htm.

"Smith-Lever Act." Available online at http://www.reeusda.gov/1700/legis/s-l.htm.

"The Vexing Legacy of Lewis Terman." Available online at http://www.stanfordalumni.org/news/magazine/2000/julaug/articles/terman.html.

## Fashion and Design

Belasco, Warren James. *Americans on the Road: From Autocamp to Motel, 1910–1945.* Cambridge, Mass.: MIT Press, 1979.

Elting, John, and Michael McAfee, eds. *Military Uniforms in America,* vol. 4, *The Modern Era—From 1868.* Novato, Calif.: Presidio, 1988.

Freeman, John Crosby. *The Forgotten Rebel: Gustav Stickley and His Craftsman Mission Furniture.* Watkins Glen, N.Y.: Century House, 1966.

Hunt, William Dudley, Jr.. *Encyclopedia of American Architecture,* rev. by Robert T. Packard and Balthazar Korab. New York: McGraw-Hill, 1994.

Kaufmann, Edgar, and Ben Raeburn, eds. *Frank Lloyd Wright: Writings and Buildings.* New York: Horizon, 1973.

Kennett, Frances. *The Collector's Book of Fashion.* New York: Crown, 1983.

Ludwig, Coy L. *The Arts & Crafts Movement in New York State, 1890s–1920s.* Hamilton: Gallery Association of New York State, 1983.

Milbank, Caroline Rennolds. *New York Fashion: The Evolution of American Style.* New York: Abrams, 1989.

Murphy, Patricia Anne. *Cass Gilbert: Minnesota Master Architect.* Minneapolis: Minnesota University Gallery, 1980.

Nash, Eric Peter. *Frank Llyod Wright: Force of Nature.* New York: Smithmark Pulishers, 1996.

Peacock, John. *20th Century Fashion: The Complete Sourcebook.* New York: Thames & Hudson, 1993.

Pulos, Arthur J. *American Design Ethic: A History of Industrial Design to 1940.* Cambridge, Mass.: MIT Press, 1983.

Russell, Beverly. *Women of Design: Contemporary American Interiors.* New York: Rizzoli, 1992.

Schoeffler, O. E., and William Gale. *Esquire's Encyclopedia of 20th Century Men's Fashions.* New York: McGraw-Hill, 1973.

Sears, Stephen W. *The American Heritage History of the Automobile in America.* New York: American Heritage Publishing, 1977.

Shand-Tucci, Douglass. *Ralph Adams Cram: Life and Architecture.* Amherst: University of Massachusetts Press, 1995.

Smith, C. Ray. *Interior Design in 20th-Century America: A History.* New York: Harper & Row, 1987.

Via, Marie, and Margaret Searle, eds. *Head, Heart and Hand: Elbert Hubbard and the Roycrofters.* Rochester, N.Y.: University of Rochester Press, 1994.

Whiffen, Marcus, and Frederick Koeper. *American Architecture, 1607–1976.* Cambridge, Mass.: MIT Press, 1981.

## Government and Politics

Barbeau, Arthur D., and Henri Florette. *The Unknown Soldiers: Black American Troops in World War I.* Philadelphia: University of Pennsylvania Press, 1974.

Bass, Herbert J. *America's Entry into World War One.* Chicago: Holt, Rinehart and Winston, 1964.

Bordin, Ruth B. A. *Woman and Temperance.* New Brunswick, N.J.: Rutgers University Press, 1990.

Brandt, Allan. *No Magic Bullet: A Social History of Venereal Disease in the United States Since 1880.* New York: Oxford University Press, 1985.

Clemenden, Clarence C. *The United States and Pancho Villa; A Study in Unconventional Diplomacy.* Ithaca, N.Y.: Cornell University Press, 1961.

Coben, Stanley. *A. Mitchell Palmer: Politician.* New York: Columbia University Press, 1963.

Cooper, John Milton. *Pivotal Decades: The United States 1900–1920.* New York: Norton, 1990.

Eisenhower, John D. *Intervention! The United States and the Mexican Revolution, 1913–1917.* New York: W. W. Norton, 1993.

Ellis, John. *The Social History of the Machine Gun.* New York: Pantheon Books, 1975.

Ferrell, Robert H. *Woodrow Wilson and World War I, 1917–1921.* New York: Harper & Row, 1985.

Gilbert, Martin. *The First World War: A Complete History.* New York: Henry Holt, 1994.

Greenwald, Maurine. *Women, War, and Work; The Impact of World War I on Women Workers in the United States.* Westport, Conn.: Greenwood Press, 1980.

Grimshaw, Allen D., ed. *Racial Violence in the United States.* Chicago: Aldine, 1969.

Grossman, James R. *Land of Hope: Chicago, Black Southerners, and the Great Migration.* Chicago: University of Chicago Press, 1989.

Hawley, Ellis W. *The Great War and the Search for a Modern Order.* 2d ed. New York: St. Martin's Press, 1992.

Haynes, Robert V. *A Night of Violence: The Houston Riot of 1917.* Baton Rouge: Louisiana State University Press, 1976.

Higham, John. *Strangers in the Land: Patterns of American Nativism.* New Brunswick, N.J.: Rutgers University Press, 1955.

Johnson, John J. *A Hemisphere Apart: The Foundation of United States Policy Toward Latin America.* Baltimore: Johns Hopkins University Press, 1990.

Joughin, Louis, and Edmund Morgan. *The Legacy of Sacco and Vanzetti.* Chicago: Quadangle Press, 1964.

Keegan, John. *The First World War.* New York: Knopf, 1999.

Kennedy, David M. *Over Here: The First World War and American Society.* New York: Oxford University Press, 1980.

Leary, William M., Jr., and Arthur S. Link, eds. *The Progressive Era and the Great War, 1896–1920.* Arlington Heights, Ill.: AHM, 1978.

Link, Arthur S. *Woodrow Wilson and the Progressive Era, 1910–1917.* New York: Harper & Row, 1954.

Link, Arthur S., and Richard L. McCormick. *Progressivism.* Arlington Heights, Ill.: Harlan Davidson, 1983.

Lovell, S.D. *The Presidential Election of 1916.* Carbondale: Southern Illinois University Press, 1980.

Miller, William D. *Pretty Bubbles in the Air: America in 1919.* Urbana: University of Illinois Press, 1991.

Murphy, Paul L. *Red Scare: A Study of National Hysteria, 1919–1920.* Minneapolis: University of Minnesota Press, 1965.

Robertson, James Oliver. *No Third Choice: Progressives in Republican Politics, 1916–1921.* New York: Garland, 1983.

Shenton, James P. *Ethnicity and Immigration.* Washington, D.C.: American Historical Association, 1990.

Stallings, Lawrence. *The Doughboys, The Story of the AEF, 1917–1918.* New York: Harper and Row, 1963.

Steinson, Barbara J. *American Women's Activism in World War I.* New York: Garland, 1982.

Stone, Ralph A. *The Irreconcilables: The Fight Against the League of Nations.* Lexington: University of Kentucky, 1970.

———, ed. *Wilson and the League of Nations.* Huntington, N.Y.: Krieger, 1978.

Tuchman, Barbara. *The Zimmermann Telegram.* New York: Viking, 1958.

Vandiver, F.E. *Black Jack: The Life and Times of John J. Pershing.* College Station: Texas A&M University Press, 1977.

Vazquez, Josefina Zoraida, and Lorenzo Meyer. *The United States and Mexico.* Chicago: University of Chicago Press, 1985.

Widenor, William. *Henry Cabot Lodge and the Search for an American Foreign Policy.* Berekeley: University of California Press, 1980.

Womack, John, Jr. *Zapata and the Mexican Revolution.* New York: Knopf, 1969.

## Law and Justice

Abraham, Henry J. *Justices, Presidents, and Senators: A History of the U.S. Supreme Court Appointments From Washington to Clinton.* New York: Rowman & Littlefield, 1999.

Bickel, Alexander M., and Benno C. Schmidt Jr. *History of the Supreme Court of the United States: The Judiciary and Responsible Government, 1910–1921.* New York: Macmillan, 1985.

Franklin, John Hope, and Alfred A. Moss Jr. *From Slavery to Freedom: A History of African Americans.* New York: Knopf, 2000.

Hall, Kermit L., ed. *The Oxford Companion to the Supreme Court.* New York: Oxford University Press, 1992.

Harrison, Maureen, and Steve Gilbert, eds. *Landmark Decisions of the United States Supreme Court II.* Beverly Hills: Excellent Books, 1992.

Hindman, Hugh D., ed. *Child Labor: An American History (Issues in Work and Human Resources).* Armonk, N.Y.: M.E. Sharpe, 2002.

Katz, Esther, ed. *The Selected Papers of Margaret Sanger: The Woman Rebel, 1900–1928.* Chicago: University of Chicago Press, 2002.

Kelly, Alfred H., Winfred A. Harbison, and Herman Belz. *The American Constitution: Its Origins and Development—Vol. II.* 7th ed. New York: Norton, 1991.

Kohn, Stephen M. *American Political Prisoners: Prosecutions Under the Espionage and Sedition Acts.* Westport, Conn.: Praeger, 1994.

Mikula, Mark F., and L. Mpho Mabunda, eds. *Great American Court Cases.* Farmington Hills, Mich.: Gale Group, 2000.

Palmer, Kris E., ed. *Constitutional Amendments: 1789 to the Present.* Farmington Hills, Mich.: Gale Group, 2000.

Stevens, Doris. *Jailed for Freedom: American Women Win the Vote.* Troutdale, Oreg.: NewSage Press, 1995.

*West's Encyclopedia of American Law.* 2d ed. 12 vols. St. Paul, Minn.: West Publishing Co.

### Websites

"The Oyez Project of Northwestern University, a U.S. Supreme Court Multimedia Database." Available online at http://www.oyez.com (accessed April 20, 2003).

"The Presidents of the United States." Available online at http://www.whitehouse.gov/history/presidents/; website home page: http://www.whitehouse.gov (accessed April 20, 2003).

"The Triangle Shirtwaist Fire Trial." Available online at http://www.law.umkc.edu/faculty/projects/ftrials/triangle/trianglefire.html; website home page: http://www.law.umkc.edu/faculty/projects/ftrials/ftrials.htm (accessed April 20, 2003).

"U.S. Supreme Court Opinions." Available online at http://www.findlaw.com/casecode/supreme.html; website home page: http://www.findlaw.com (accessed March 16, 2003).

## Lifestyles and Social Trends

Blanke, David. *The 1910s.* Westport, Conn.: Greenwood Press, 2002.

Carson, Mina J. *Settlement Folk: Social Thought and the American Settlement Movement, 1885–1930.* Chicago: University of Chicago Press, 1990.

Cashman, Sean. *America in the Age of the Titans: The Progressive Era and World War I.* New York: New York University Press, 1988.

Chambers, John Whiteclay II. *The Tyranny of Change: America in the Progressive Era, 1890–1920.* New Brunswick, N.J.: Rutgers University Press, 2000.

Chudacoff, Howard P. *The Age of the Bachelor.* Princeton, N.J.: Princeton University Press, 2000.

Coffey, Frank, and Joseph Layden. *America on Wheels: The First 100 Years: 1896–1996.* Los Angeles: General Pub. Group, 1998.

Crunden, Robert M. *Ministers of Reform: The Progressives' Achievement in American Civilization, 1889–1920.* Champaign: University of Illinois Press, 1985.

Daniels, Roger. *Not Like Us: Immigrants and Minorities in America, 1890–1924.* Chicago: Ivan R. Dee, 1997.

Dubofsky, Melvin. *Industrialism and the American Worker, 1865–1920.* Arlington Heights, Ill.: Harlan Davidson, 1985.

Fairclough, Adam. *Better Day Coming: Blacks and Equality, 1890–2000.* New York: Viking, 2001.

Freeman, Joshua, et al. *Who Built America? Working People and the Nation's Economy, Politics, Culture, and Society.* vol. 2. New York: Pantheon, 1992.

Hale, Grace E. *Making Whiteness: The Culture of Segregation in the South, 1890–1940.* New York: Vintage Books, 1999.

Ichioka, Yuji. *The Issei: The World of the First Generation Japanese Immigrants, 1885–1924.* New York: The Free Press, 1990.

Jackson, Kenneth T. *Crabgrass Frontier: Suburbanization in the United States.* New York: Oxford University Press, 1985.

———. *The Ku Klux Klan in the City: 1915–1930.* Chicago: Ivan R. Dee, 1992.

Jacobson, Matthew F. *Whiteness of a Different Color: European Immigrants and the Alchemy of Race.* Cambridge, Mass.: Harvard University Press, 1999.

Jones, Jacqueline. *Labor of Love, Labor of Sorrow: Black Women, Work and the Family From Slavery to the Present.* New York: Basic Books, 1985.

Kennedy, David M. *Over Here: The First World War and American Society.* New York. Oxford University Press, 1980.

Kisseloff, Jeff. *You Must Remember This: An Oral History of Manhattan From the 1890s to World War II.* Baltimore: John Hopkins University Press, 2000.

Kraut, Alan. *The Huddled Masses: The Immigrant in American Society, 1880–1921.* Arlington Heights, Ill.: Harlan Davidson, 1982.

Leach, William. *Land of Desire: Merchants, Power, and the Rise of a New American Culture.* New York: Random House, 1993.

Lemann, Nicholas. *The Promised Land: The Great Black Migration and How It Changed America.* New York. A. A. Knopf, 1991.

Lender, Mark Edward, and James Kirby Martin. *Drinking in America.* New York: Free Press, 1987.

Leuchtenburg, William E. *The Perils of Prosperity 1914–1932.* 2d ed. Chicago: University of Chicago Press, 1993.

Lewis, David L. *W.E.B. Du Bois: Biography of a Race, 1868–1919.* New York: H. Holt, 1993.

Ling, Peter J. *America and the Automobile: Technology, Reform and Social Change.* Manchester, U.K.: Manchester University Press, 1990.

MacLean, Nancy K. *Behind the Mask of Chivalry: The Making of the Second Ku Klux Klan.* New York: Oxford University Press, 1995.

Marks, Carole. *Farewell, We're Good and Gone: The Great Black Migration.* Bloomington: Indiana University Press, 1989.

McCalley, Bruce W. *Model T Ford: The Car That Changed the World.* Iola, Wis.: Krause Publications, 1994.

Pegram, Thomas R. *Battling Demon Rum: The Struggle for a Dry America, 1800–1933.* Chicago: Ivan R. Dee, 1998.

Powers, Madelon. *Faces Along the Bar: Lore and Order in the Workingman's Saloon, 1870–1920.* Chicago: University of Chicago Press, 1998.

Robinson, David, and Martin Scorsese. *From Peepshow to Palace.* New York: Columbia University Press, 1995.

Rosenberg, Rosalind. *Divided Lives: American Women in the Twentieth Century.* New York: Hill & Wang, 1992.

Satter, Beryl. *Each Mind a Kingdom: American Women, Sexual Purity, and the New Thought Movement, 1875–1920.* Berkeley: University of California Press, 1999.

Scharff, Virginia. *Taking the Wheel: Women and the Coming of the Motor Age.* New York: Free Press, 1991.

Smith, Karen Manners. *New Paths to Power: American Women 1890–1920.* New York: Oxford University Press, 1994.

Strasser, Susan. *Never Done: A History of American Housework.* New York: Pantheon, 1982.

Van Slyck, Abigail A. *Free to All: Carnegie Libraries & American Culture, 1890–1920.* Chicago: University of Chicago Press, 1998.

Wiebe, Robert H. *The Search for Order 1877–1920.* New York: Hill & Wang, 1980.

Wukovits, John F., ed. *The 1910s.* San Diego: Greenhaven Press, 2000.

### Websites

"American Variety Stage: Vaudeville and Popular Entertainment, 1870–1920." Available online at http://memory.loc.gov/ammem/vshtml/vshome.html (accessed April 22, 2003).

"Bijou Dream." Available online at http://pages.zdnet.com/kinema/index.html (accessed April 22, 2003).

"By Popular Demand: Votes for Women's Suffrage: Pictures, 1850–1920." Available online at http://memory.loc.gov/ammem/vfwhtml/vfwhome.html (accessed April 22, 2003).

"Gateway to African American History, 1900–1940." Available online at http://charter.uchicago.edu/AAH/19001940.htm (accessed April 22, 2003).

"Snapshots: World War I." Available online at http://www.ibis-com.com/snpwwi.html (accessed April 22, 2003).

"Temperance & Prohibition." Available online at http://prohibition.history.ohio-state.edu/Contents.htm (accessed April 22, 2003).

## Media

Berger, Arthur Asa. *The Comic-Stripped American: What Dick Tracy, Blondie, Daddy Warbucks and Charlie Brown Tell Us About Ourselves.* New York: Walker, 1973.

Cornebise, Alfred A. *The Stars and Stripes: Doughboy Journalism in World War I.* Westport, Conn.: Greenwood Press, 1984.

Douglas, Susan. *Inventing American Broadcasting, 1899–1922.* Baltimore: Johns Hopkins University Press, 1987.

Edwards, Julia. *Women of the World: The Great Foreign Correspondents.* New York: Ivy Books, 1988.

Emery, Edwin, and Michael Emery. *The Press and America: An Interpretive History of the Mass Media.* Boston: Allyn and Bacon, 1996.

Forcey, Charles. *The Crossroads of Liberalism: Croly, Weyl, Lippmann, and the Progressive Era, 1900–1925.* New York: Oxford University Press, 1961.

Hohenberg, John. *Foreign Correspondence: The Great Reporters and Their Times.* 2d ed. Syracuse, N.Y.: Syracuse University Press, 1985.

Kessler, Lauren. *The Dissident Press: Alternative Journalism in American History.* Beverly Hills, Calif.: Sage, 1984.

Marschall, Richard. *America's Great Comic-Strip Artists.* New York: Abbeville Press, 1989.

Marzolf, Marion. *Civilizing Voices: American Press Criticism, 1880–1950.* New York: Longman, 1991.

Peterson, H. C., and Gilbert Fite. *Opponents of War, 1917–1918.* Seattle: University of Washington Press, 1968.

Peterson, Theodore. *Magazines in the Twentieth Century.* Urbana: University of Illinois Press, 1964.

Ponce De Leon, Charles L. *Self-Exposure: Human-Interest Journalism and the Emergence of Celebrity in America, 1890–1940.* Chapel Hill: University of North Carolina Press, 1992.

Schudson, Michael. *Discovering the News: A Social History of American Newspapers.* New York: Basic Books, 1978.

Swanberg, W.A. *Citizen Hearst.* New York: Scribners, 1961.

Tebbel, John. *Between Covers: The Rise and Transformation of Book Publishing in America.* New York: Oxford University Press, 1987.

Thomas, Dana Lee. *The Media Moguls: From Joseph Pulitzer to William S. Paley, the Wheelings and Dealings of America's News Merchants.* New York: Putnam, 1981.

Vaughn, Stephen. *Holding Fast the Inner Lines: Democracy, Nationalism, and the Committee on Public Information.* Chapel Hill: University of North Carolina Press, 1980.

### Websites

"America at Work, America at Leisure: Motion Pictures, 1894–1915." Available online at http://memory.loc.gov /ammem/awlhtml/awlhome.html (accessed April 22, 2003).

"Child Labor in America, 1908–1912: The Photographs of Louis W. Hine." Available online at http://historyplace.com /unitedstates/childlabor/index.html (accessed April 22, 2003).

"Conrad's Garage: Replaying the Earliest Days of Radio." Available online at http://www.npr.org/programs/atc/features /2001/nov/garage/011130.garage.html (accessed April 22, 2003).

"United States Early Radio History." Available online at http://EarlyRadioHistory.us/ (accessed April 22, 2003).

"Voices of the 20th Century: Sounds From the Past." Available online at http://www.ibiscom.com/vofrm.htm (accessed April 22, 2003).

## Medicine and Health

Abram, Ruth J., ed. *Send Us a Lady Physician: Women Doctors in America, 1835–1920.* New York: Norton, 1985.

Bates, Barbara. *Bargaining for Life: A Social History of Tuberculosis, 1876–1938.* Philadelphia: University of Pennsylvania Press, 1992.

Bean, William Bennett. *Walter Reed: A Biography.* Charlottesville: University Press of Virginia, 1982.

Bender, Arnold E. *A Dictionary of Food and Nutrition.* NewYork: Oxford University Press, 1995.

Bordley, James, and A. McGehee Harvey. *Two Centuries of American Medicine, 1776–1976.* Philadelphia: Saunders, 1976.

Brandt, Allan M. *No Magic Bullet: A Social History of Venereal Disease in the United States Since 1880.* New York: Oxford University Press, 1985.

Burrow, James G. *AMA: Voice of American Medicine.* Baltimore: Johns Hopkins University Press, 1963.

Caldwell, Mark. *The Last Crusade: The War on Consumption, 1862–1954.* NewYork: Antheneum, 1988.

Cangi, Ellen C. *Principles Before Practice: The Reform of Medical Education in Cincinnati Before and After the Flexner Report, 1870–1930.* Cincinnati, Ohio: University of Cincinnati Press, 1983.

Cassedy, James H. *Medicine in America: A Short History.* Baltimore: Johns Hopkins University Press, 1991.

Davies, Pete. *The Devil's Flu: The World's Deadliest Influenza Epidemic and the Scientific Hunt for the Virus that Caused It.* NewYork: Henry Holt, 2000.

Duffy, John. *The Healers: The Rise of the Medical Establishment.* New York: McGraw-Hill, 1976. Republished, *The Healers: A History of American Medicine.* Urbana: University of Illinois Press, 1979.

Etheridge, E.W. *The Butterfly Caste: A Social History of Pellagra in the South.* Westport, Conn.: Greenwood Press, 1972.

Ettling, John. *The Germ of Laziness: Rockefeller Philanthropy and Public Health in the New South.* Cambridge, Mass.: Harvard University Press, 1981.

Fishbein, Morris. *A History of the American Medical Association, 1847–1947.* Philadelphia: Saunders, 1947.

Flexner, Abraham. *Medical Education in the United States and Canada: A Report to the Carnegie Foundation for the Advancement of Teaching.* New York: Carnegie Foundation, 1910.

Gibson, John M. *Physician to the World: The Life of General William C. Gorgas.* Tuscaloosa: University of Alabama Press, 1989.

Lederer, Susan E. *Subjected to Science: Human Experimentation in America Before the Second World War.* Baltimore: Johns Hopkins University Press, 1995.

Nelson, Clark W. *Mayo Roots: Profiling the Origins of Mayo Clinic.* Rochester, Minn: Mayo Foundation for Medical and Educational Research, 1990.

Parascandola, John. *The Development of American Pharmacology: John J. Abel and the Shaping of a Discipline.* Baltimore: Johns Hopkins University Press, 1992.

*Professional Guide to Diseases,* 6th ed. Springhouse, Pa.: Springhouse, 1998.

Roe, D.A. *A Plague of Corn: The Social History of Pellagra.* Ithaca, N.Y.: Cornell University Press, 1973.

Ross, Walter S. *Crusade: The Official History of the American Cancer Society.* NewYork: Arbor House, 1987.

Teller, Michael E. *The Tuberculosis Movement: A Public Health Campaign in the Progressive Era.* Westport, Conn.: Greenwood Press, 1988.

Wheatleys, Steven Charles. *The Politics of Philanthropy: Abraham Flexner and Medical Education.* Madison: University of Wisconsin Press, 1988.

## Websites

"1918 Spanish Flu Pandemic." Available online at http://www.ninthday.com/spanish_flu.htm.

"Alexis Carrel—Biography." Available online at http://www.nobel.se/medicine/laureates/1912/carrel-bio.html.

"American Cancer Society." Available online at http://www.cancer.org.

"Brownsville Clinic." Available online at http://www.nyu.edu/projects/sanger/brownsville_clinic.htm.

"History of the Federal Children's Bureau." Available online at http://www.ssa.gov/history/childb1.html.

"Mayo Clinic." Available online at http://www.mayoclinic.org.

Medicine and Madison Avenue—Timeline." Available online at http://scriptorium.lib.duke.edu/mma/timeline.html.

"Reservation and Hospital Care Under the Office of Indian Affairs (c. 1890–1925)." Available online at http://www.nlm.nih.gov/exhibitions/if_you_knew/if_you_knew_06.html.

"Rockafellar, Nancy. The Flexner Report in Context.Available online at http://library.ucsf.edu/ucsfhistory/themes/themes_flexner.html.

"United States Cancer Mortality From 1900 to 1992." Available online at http://www.healthsentinel.com/Vaccines/DiseaseAndRelatedData_files/she.

## Religion

Abrams, Ray H. *Preachers Present Arms.* Scottsdale, Pa.: Herald Press, 1969.

Ahlstrom, Sydney H. *A Religious History of the American People.* New Haven, Conn.: Yale University Press, 1972.

Brown, Ira V. *Lyman Abbott: Christian Evolutionist.* Cambridge, Mass.: Harvard University Press, 1953.

Dolan, Jay P. *The American Catholic Experience: A History From Colonial Times to the Present.* Garden City, N.Y.: Doubleday, 1985.

Gaustad, Edwin S. *A Religious History of America.* New rev. ed. New York: HarperCollins, 1990.

Hennesey, James. *American Catholics: A History of the Roman Catholic Community in the United States.* New York: Oxford University Press, 1981.

Hertzberg, Arthur. *The Jews in America: Four Centuries of an Uneasy Encounter: A History.* New York: Simon & Schuster, 1989.

Hutchinson, William R. *The Modernist Impulse in American Protestantism.* Cambridge, Mass.: Harvard University Press, 1975.

Lippy, Charles H., ed. *Twentieth-Century Shapers of American Popular Religion.* New York: Greenwood Press, 1989.

Lippy, Charles H., and Peter Williams, eds. *Encyclopedia of the American Religious Experience.* New York: Scribners, 1988.

Marchand, C. Roland. *The American Peace Movement and Social Reform, 1898–1918.* Princeton: Princeton University Press, 1973.

Marsden, George M. *Fundamentalism and American Culture: The Shaping of Twentieth-Century Evangelicalism, 1870–1925.* New York: Oxford University Press, 1980.

Marty, Martin. *Pilgrims in Their Own Land: 500 Years of Religion in America.* Boston: Houghton Mifflin, 1984.

Meyer, Isidore S., ed. *Early History of Zionism in America.* New York: Arno, 1977.

Piper, John F., Jr. *The American Churches in World War I.* Athens: Ohio University Press, 1985.

Sandeen, Ernest R. *The Roots of Fundamentalism: British and American Millenarianism, 1800–1930.* Chicago: University of Chicago Press, 1970.

Weber, Timothy P. *Living in the Shadow of the Second Coming: American Premillennialism, 1875–1982,* rev. ed. Grand Rapids, Mich.: Academie Books, 1983.

## Science and Technology

Archer, Gleason L. *History of Radio to 1926.* New York: American Historical Society, 1938.

Benison, Saul, A. Clifford Barger, and Elin L. Wolfe. *Walter B. Cannon: The Life and Times of a Young Scientist.* Cambridge: Harvard University Press, 1987.

Bilstein, Roger E. *Flight in America: From the Wrights to the Astronauts.* Baltimore: Johns Hopkins University Press, 1984.

Blinderman, Charles. *The Piltdown Inquest.* New York: Prometheus Books, 1986.

Bowler, Peter J. *The Mendelian Revolution.* Baltimore: Johns Hopkins University Press, 1989.

Donovan, Frank. *Wheels for a Nation.* New York: Crowell, 1965.

Dreyer, Peter. *A Gardener Touched With Genius: The Life of Luther Burbank.* Berkeley: University of California Press, 1985.

Flink, James J. *America Adopts the Automobile, 1895–1910.* Cambridge, Mass.: MIT Press, 1970.

Ford, Henry. *My Life and Work.* Garden City, N.Y.: Doubleday, 1922.

Freidel, Robert, and Paul Israel. *Edison's Electric Light: Biography of an Invention.* New Brunswick, N.J.: Rutgers University Press, 1987.

Glick, Thomas F., ed. *The Comparative Reception of Relativity.* Dordrecht, Netherlands: D. Reidel, 1987.

Gould, Stephen J. *Hen's Teeth and Horse's Toes.* New York: Norton, 1983.

———. *The Mismeasure of Man.* New York: Norton, 1981.

Hale, Nathan G., Jr. *Freud and the Americans: The Beginnings of Psychoanalysis in the United States, 1876–1917.* New York: Oxford University Press, 1971.

Hayes, J. Gordon. *Robert Edwin Peary: A Record of his Explorations, 1886–1909.* London: Grant Richards, 1929.

Hobbs, William Herbert. *Peary.* New York: Macmillan, 1936.

Howard, Fred. *Wilbur and Orville: A Biography of the Wright Brothers.* New York: Knopf, 1987.

Josephson, Matthew. *Edison: A Biography.* New York: Mc-Graw-Hill, 1959.

Joslin, Rebecca R. *Chasing Eclipses: The Total Solar Eclipses of 1905, 1914, 1925.* Boston: Walton, 1925.

Kilmister, Charles W. *General Theory of Relativity.* New York: Pergamon, 1973.

Kline, Ronald R. *Steinmetz: Engineer and Socialist.* Baltimore: Johns Hopkins University Press, 1992.

Kohler, Robert E. *Lords of the Fly: Drosophila Genetics and the Experimental Life.* Chicago: University of Chicago Press, 1994.

———. *Partners in Science: Foundations and Natural Scientists, 1900–1945.* Chicago: University of Chicago, 1991.

Lacey, Robert. *Ford: The Men and the Machine.* Boston: Little, Brown, 1986.

Milliard, André. *Edison and the Business of Invention.* Baltimore: Johns Hopkins University Press, 1990.

Mitchell, Samuel Alfred. *Eclipses of the Sun.* New York: Columbia University Press, 1923.

Morgan, T. H. *The Genetics of Drosophila.* The Hague: M. Nijhoff, 1925.

Morris, Richard Knowles. *John P. Holland, Inventor of the Modern Submarine.* Annapolis, Md.: United States Naval Institute, 1966.

Pauly, Philip L. *Controlling Life: Jacques Loeb and the Engineering Idea in Biology.* Berkeley: University of California Press, 1990.

Reingold, Nathan, and Ida H. Reingold. *Science in America.* Chicago: University of Chicago Press, 1981.

Ross, Dorothy. *G. Stanley Hall: The Psychologist as Prophet.* Chicago: University of Chicago Press, 1972.

Silverman, Sydel, ed. *Totems and Teachers: Perspectives on the History of Anthropology.* New York: Columbia University Press, 1981.

Smith, Robert W. *The Expanding Universe: Astronomy's Great Debate, 1900–1931.* New York: Cambridge University Press, 1982.

Swenson, Loyd S., Jr. *The Ethereal Aether: A History of the Michelson-Morley-Miller Aether-Drift Experiments, 1880–1930.* Austin: University of Texas Press, 1972.

Wachhorst, Wynn. *Thomas Alva Edison: An American Myth.* Cambridge, Mass.: MIT Press, 1981.

Wohl, Robert. *A Passion for Wings: Aviation and the Western Imagination, 1908–1918.* New Haven, Conn.: Yale University Press, 1994.

Wright, Helen. *Explorer of the Universe: A Biography of George Ellery Hale,* 2d ed. Woodbury, N.Y.: American Institute of Physics, 1994.

### Websites

"The Bruce Medalists: Vesto Melvin Slipher." Available online at http://www.phys-astro.sonoma.edu/BruceMedalists/Slipher.

"Comet Halley." Available online at http://seds.lpl.arizona.edu/nineplanets/nineplanets/halley.html.

"General Relativity." Available online at http://archive.ncsa.uiuc.edu/Cyberia/NumRel/GenRelativity.html.

"Henry Fairfield Osborn Papers." Available online at http://www.clements.umich.edu/Webguides/A/AMOsborn.html.

"Images of the Woolworth Building." Available online at http://www.bluffton.edu/sullivanm/woolworth/woolworth.html.

"Piltdown: The Man That Never Was." Available online at http://unmuseum.mus.pa.us/piltdown.htm.

"Roosevelt Dam Brief History." Available online at http://www.apo.lc.usbr.gov/user/publicrl/rdhistory.html.

Ruby, Jay. "Franz Boas and Early Camera Study of Behavior." Available online at http://www.temple.edu/anthro/ruby/boas.html.

"Thomas H. Morgan—Biography." Available online at http://www.nobel.se/medicine/laureates/1933/morgan-bio.html.

"Welcome to the Los Angeles Aqueduct." Available online at http://web.ladwp.com/wsoweb/Aqueduct/default.htm.

## Sports

Armstrong, O.K. "The Funniest Football Game Ever Played." *Readers Digest,* October 1955, 53–57.

Asinof, Eliot. *Eight Men Out: The Black Sox and the 1919 World Series.* New York: Henry Holt, 1987.

Auker, Elden, *Sleeper Cars and Flannel Uniforms: A Lifetime of Memories From Striking Out the Babe to Teeing it Up With the President.* Chicago: Triumph Books, 2001.

Braathen, Sverre O. *Ty Cobb: The Idol of Baseball Fandom.* New York: Avondale, 1928.

Carroll, Bob, and Bob Gill. *Bulldogs on Sunday, 1919: Twilight of the Ohio League.* North Huntingdon, Pa.: PFRA, 1990.

Challmes, Joseph J. *The Preakness: A History.* Severna Park, Md.: Anaconda, 1975.

Creamer, Robert W. *Babe: The Legend Comes to Life.* New York: Simon and Schuster, 1974.

Durso, Joseph. *The Days of Mr. McGraw.* Englewood-Cliffs, N.J.: Prentice-Hall, 1969.

Farr, Finis. *Black Champion; The Life and Times of Jack Johnson.* New York: Scribner, 1964.

Halberstam, David. *The Teammates: A Portrait of Friendship.* New York: Hyperion, 2003.

Hawkins, Joel, and Terry Bertolino. *The House of David Baseball Team.* Chicago: Arcadia, 2000.

Heimer, Mel. *The Long Count.* New York: Atheneum, 1969.

Jordan, David M. *The Athletics of Philadelphia; Connie Mack's White Elephants, 1901–1954.* Jefferson, N.C.: McFarland, 1999.

Kaese, Harold. *The Boston Braves.* New York: Putnam, 1948.

Lester, Larry. *Black Baseball in Detroit.* Chicago: Arcadia, 2000.

Lowe, Stephen R. *Sir Walter and Mr. Jones: Walter Hagen, Bobby Jones, and the Rise of American Golf.* Chelsea, Mich.: Sleeping Bear Press, 2000.

Luisi, Vincent. *The New York Yankees: The First Twenty-five Years.* Charleston, S.C.: Arcadia, 2002.

Mallon, Bill, and Ture Widlund. *The 1912 Olympics, Results for All Competitors in All Events With Commentary.* Jefferson, N.C.: McFarland, 2002.

Michelson, Herb, and Dave Newhouse. *Rose Bowl Football since 1902.* New York: Stein and Day, 1977.

Names, Larry D. *The History of the Green Bay Packers: The Lambeau Years, Part 1.* Wautoma, Wisc.: Angel Press, 1987.

Nathan, Daniel A. *Saying It's So: A Cultural History of the Black Sox Scandal.* Urbana: University of Illinois Press, 2003.

Newcombe, Jack. *The Best of the Athletic Boys; The Whiteman's Impact on Jim Thorpe.* Garden City, N.Y.: Doubleday, 1975.

Nolan, William F. *Barney Oldfield; The Life and Times of America's Legendary Speed King.* New York: Putnam, 1961.

Okkonen, Marc. *The Federal League of 1914–1915: Baseball's Third Major League.* Garret Park, Md.: Society for American Baseball Research, 1989.

Poremba, David Lee. *The American League: The Early Years.* Chicago: Arcadia, 2000.

Roberts, Randy. *Jack Dempsey, the Manassa Mauler.* Baton Rouge: Louisiana State University Press, 1979.

Schoor, Gene. *The Jim Thorpe Story, America's Greatest Athlete.* New York: Messner, 1951.

Shaughnessy, Dan, and Stan Grossfield. *Fenway: A Biography of Words and Pictures.* Boston: Houghton Mufflin, 1999.

Sperber, Murray A. *Shake Down the Thunder: The Creation of Notre Dame Football.* New York: Henry Holt, 1993.

Stevens, Julia Ruth. *Major League Dad: A Daughter's Cherished Memories.* Chicago: Triumph Books, 2001.

Thomas, Henry W. *Walter Johnson: Baseball's Big Train.* Washington, D.C.: Phenom Press, 1985.

# PRIMARY SOURCE TYPE INDEX

*Primary source authors appear in parentheses. Page numbers in italics indicate images, and those followed by the letter t indicate tables.*

**Advertisements**

"A New Profession" (Thompson Company), *103*

"Packages That Speak Out" (Thompson Company), *104*

"Women in Advertising" (Thompson Company), *105*

**Autobiographies**

*All God's Dangers: The Life of Nate Shaw* (Shaw, Rosengarten), 115–117

*A Poet's Life: Seventy Years in a Changing World* (Monroe), 56–58

**Baseball cards**

"Chicago Cubs Baseball Card" (Liggett & Myers Co.; American Tobacco Company), *388*

"Cy Young Baseball Card" (Liggett & Myers Co.; American Tobacco Company), *390*

"Tris Speaker Baseball Card" (Liggett & Myers Co.; American Tobacco Company), *389*

**Booklets**

*The Cathedral of Commerce* (Cochran), 204, 206–207

**Broadsides**

"Votes for Women" (National American Woman Suffrage Association), *384*

"Why Women Want to Vote" (National American Woman Suffrage Association), *385*

"Women in the Home" (National American Woman Suffrage Association), *386*

**Catalogs**

"Craftsman Furniture Made by Gustav Stickley" (Stickley), *192*

**Clothing styles**

"Audacious Hats for Spineless Attitudes" *(Dress & Vanity Fair)*, *200*, *201*

"Flower Dresses for Lawn Fêtes" *(Ladies' Home Journal)*, *196*

"Shopping for the Well-Dressed Man" (Trevor), 213

"YWCA Overseas Uniform, 1918" (House of Worth), 218

**Congressional records**

"Henry Cabot Lodge: Corollary to the Monroe Doctrine" (Lodge), 237–238

**Court cases**

*"Dissent During World War I: The Kate O'Hare Trial: 1919"* (O'Hare, Wade), 306–309

**Crossword puzzles**

"Fun's Word Cross Puzzle" (Wynne), *391*

**Diaries**

*Leaves From the Notebook of a Tamed Cynic* (Niebuhr), 506–507

**Editorials**

"The Amateur" (Abbott, et al.), 583–585

"The Anniversary" *(New York Tribune)*, 396–399

"Capitalizing Race Hatred" *(New York Globe)*, 26–27

"For Freedom and Democracy" *(North American Review)*, 408–409

"The Negro Should Be a Party to the Commercial Conquest of the World" (Garvey), 373–374

"Votes for Women" (Du Bois), 240–241

**Essays**

"Are the Movies a Menace to the Drama?" (Matthews), 365–367

"Baseball and the National Life" (Bruce), 586–590

"On the Imitation of Man" (Tarbell), 346–347

"University Athletics" (Newcomb), 567–570

"What the Bible Contains for the Believer" (Pentecost), 490–491

**Eyewitness accounts**

"Eyewitness at the Triangle" (Shepherd), 64–66

**Fictional works**

*You Know Me Al: A Busher's Letters* (Lardner), 597–600

**Hair styles**

"Five Pretty Ways to Do the Hair" *(Ladies' Home Journal)*, 194

**Handbooks**

*The Churches of Christ in Time of War* (Federal Council of the Churches of Christ in America), 495, 497

*Girls and Athletics* (Morgan), 602–603

**Interviews**

Ford, Henry *(Detroit News)*, 101–102

Roush, Edd (Ritter), 620–622

"Wealthiest Negro Woman's Suburban Mansion" *(New York Times Magazine)*, 217

**Journal articles**

"The Atom and the Molecule" (Lewis), 538–541

"The Contribution of Psychology to Education" (Thorndike), 140–143

"A Direct Photoelectric Determination of Planck's 'h'," 531–534

"Globular Clusters and the Structure of the Galactic System" (Shapley), 542–546

"How Physical Training Affects the Welfare of the Nation" (Posse), 432–434

"Nursing as a Profession for College Women" (Foley), 429, 431

"On the Constitution of Atoms and Molecules" (Bohr), 526–527

"A Program for the Reconstruction of Judaism" (Kaplan), 501

"Progress in Pediatrics" (Van Ingen), 450–452

"The Project Method" (Kilpatrick), 184–186

"Psychology as the Behaviorist Views It" (Wilson), 529–530

"Why Should the Kindergarten Be Incorporated as an Integral Part of the Public School System?" (Claxton), 159–161

**Laws**

*New York Worker's Compensation Act* (New York State Legislature), 281–283

*Sedition Act of 1918* (Wilson), 411–412

*Smith-Hughes Act of 1917* (Smith, Hughes), 176–179

*Smith-Lever Act of 1914* (Smith, Lever), 162–164

*Volstead Act of 1919* (Volstead), 274

**Lectures**

*The Future of Electricity* (Steinmetz), 513–516

*A General Introduction to Psycho-Analysis* (Freud), 554–559

"The Imagining Ear" (Frost), 31–32

**Letters**

Cardinal Gibbons' Letter to the U.S. Archbishops (Gibbons), 498–500

to the Chicago *Defender*, 404–407

to Lindley Garrison (Bowen), 70–71

"Reply to the *New York Globe*" (Griffith), 27–29

**Magazine advertisements**

"Is There News in Shaving Soap?" (Thompson Company), 220

"Whether at Home or Away, Your Summer Equipment Should Include a Bottle of Listerine" (Lambert Pharmacal Company), *211*

"A Woman Can Always Look Younger Than She Really Is" (Arden), 215

**Magazine articles**

"Are Athletics Making Girls Masculine?" (Sargent), 578–581

"Audacious Hats for Spineless Attitudes" *(Dress & Vanity Fair)*, 200, 201

"The Church and the Labor Question" (Gladden), 477–478

"The Fight Against Venereal Disease" (Fosdick), 463–465

"The Flapper" (Mencken), 357–359

"How the Drug Dopers Fight" (Creel), 445–447

"How We Manage" (E. S. E.), 359–362

"Making Men of Them" (Burgess), 351–354

"The Next War" (Wiley), 466–468

"Popular Gullibility as Exhibited in the New White Slavery Hysteria" *(Current Opinion)*, 349–351

"Sex O'Clock in America" *(Current Opinion)*, 348–349

"What Is a Bungalow?" (Riley), 198–199

"The Woman Shopper: How to Make Her Buy" (Marcosson), 336–339

**Magazine covers**

*Boy With Baby Carriage* (Rockwell), *36*

**Manuals**

*The Measurement of Intelligence* (Terman), 172–174

*The Montessori Method* (Montessori), 156–158

**Maps**

*National Old Trails Road: Ocean to Ocean Highway* (Davis), *96*

**Memoirs**

"Last of the Vigilantes" (Tefft), 119–121

"Over the Top": By an American Soldier Who Went (Empey), 265–267

*Pioneer in Pro Football* (Cusack), 615–619

**Memos**

to Colonel Bruce Palmer (Brown), 604–607

Woodrow Wilson's Memorandum to His Secretary, Joseph Tumulty, 371

**Movie reviews**

"The Heart of the People" (Bourne), 447–449

**Movie stills**

Charlie Chaplin as the "Little Tramp," *33*

**Newsletters**

*The Woman Rebel* (Sanger), *394*

**Newspaper articles**

"Boxers Spend Last Night Under Guard" (Pulford), 612–614

"Burman Lowers Speedway Records" *(New York Times)*, 576–577

"Cabinet Discusses Prager's Lynching" *(New York Times)*, 314–315

"Chicagoans Cheer Tar Who Shot Man" *(Washington Post)*, 371–372

"A Crowd of Howling Negroes" *(Chicago Tribune)*, 414–416

"Find Influenza Germ" *(Washington Post)*, 462–463

"German is Lynched by an Illinois Mob" *(New York Times)*, 314

Primary source authors appear in parentheses. Page numbers in italics indicate images, and those followed by the letter *t* indicate tables.

"Germany Keen for Peace, but Expects and Is Ready to Battle for Years" (Swope), 399

"Ghastly Deeds of Race Rioters Told" (Chicago *Defender*), 416–419

"Johnson Wins in 15 Rounds; Jeffries Weak" (Sullivan), 571–573

"100 Sailors at Great Lakes Die of Influenza" *(Chicago Tribune)*, 460–462

"Ouimet World's Golf Champion" *(New York Times)*, 591–594

"Prager Asked Mob to Wrap Body in Flag" *(New York Times)*, 315–316

"The Prager Case" *(New York Times)*, 316

"Tried for Prager Murder" *(New York Times)*, 316

**Nonfiction works**

*The Brass Check* (Sinclair), 420–423

*The Conflict of Colour* (Weale), 334–335

*Democracy and Education* (Dewey), 171

*Drift and Mastery: An Attempt to Diagnose the Current Unrest* (Lippmann), 89–94

*Equal Pay for Equal Work* (Strachan), 135–138

*The Immigration Problem* (Jenks, Lauck), 342–345

*The Indian and His Problem* (Leupp), 132–134

*The Individual Delinquent* (Healy), 368–370

*A Living Wage: Its Ethical and Economic Aspects* (Ryan), 474–476

*The Mind of Primitive Man* (Boas), 517–520

*A New Conscience and an Ancient Evil* (Addams), 153–154

*Painless Childbirth* (Williams), 440–441

*The Passing of the Great Race* (Grant), 362–364

*The Physical Basis of Heredity* (Morgan), 551–553

*Psychology of the Unconscious* (Jung), 535–537

*Women Wanted* (Daggett), 107–108

*The Yosemite* (Muir), 243–246

**Novels**

*O Pioneers!* (Cather), 12–13

**Paintings**

*Evening Star, III,* 40

*The Masquerade Dress* (Henri), 10

**Pamphlets**

*Family Limitation* (Sanger), 253–254

*National Old Trails Road: Ocean to Ocean Highway* (Davis), 95

**Patent applications**

"Manufacture of Gasolene" (Burton), 521–523

**Photographs**

Child Labor Photographs by Lewis Hine, *380–382*

"Ford's Highland Park Plant" (Kahn), *191*

"Henry Ford in a Model T," *222*

"The Woolworth Building (Gilbert), *203*

**Plans**

*Preliminary Report of the Factory Investigating Commission:* Floor plan, *66*

**Poems**

"Chicago" (Sandburg), 38

"The Ideal Candidates" (Miller), 138

"September, 1918" (Lowell), 52

**Political cartoons**

"An Unequal Footing!" (Anonymous), *139*

**Political platforms**

Progressive Party (1912), 85–86

Socialist Party (1912), 86–87

**Posters**

"Warning: The Deadly Parallel" (Industrial Workers of the World), *401*

**Presentations**

"Orthopedic Surgery in War Time" (Osgood), 452–454

"Tobacco: A Race Poison" (Lichty), 438–439

"War and Mental Diseases" (Bailey), 455–457

**Reference works**

*Basket Ball: for Coach, Player and Spectator* (Angell), 608–610

*Modern Dancing* (Castle, Castle), 16–18

*The Principles of Scientific Management* (Taylor), 69–70

"Proper Dancing-Costumes for Women" (Castle), 208–209

**Reports**

*American Industry in War: A Report of the War Industries Board* (Baruch), 109–114

*Cardinal Principles of Secondary Education* (Commission on the Reorganization of Secondary Education), 180–183

*Changes in Bodily Form of Descendants of Immigrants* (Immigration Commission; Boas), 435–437

"Interchurch World Movement Report" (Interchurch World Movement), 503–505

*Medical Education in the United States and Canada: A Report to the Carnegie Foundation for the Advancement of Teaching* (Pritchett), 144–147

*Preliminary Report of the Factory Investigating Commission,* 66–67

*Relativity Theory of Gravitation* (Eddington), 548–550

*Report of the Committee on Academic Freedom and Tenure* (American Association of University Professors), 165–169

*The Social Evil in Chicago* (Vice Commission of Chicago), 340–341

**Scrapbooks**

Page from George Weiss's Scrapbook (Weiss), *596*

**Sculptures**

*Ethiopia Awakening* (Fuller), *15*

**Sermons**

"Cardinal's Golden Jubilee" (Gibbons), 480–481

*Prisoners of Hope and Other Sermons* (Brent), 487–489

**Short stories**

"Paper Pills" (Anderson), 53–55

**Songs**

"Mandy" (Berlin), 46–49

"Over There" (Cohan), 42–44

"St. Louis Blues" (Handy), 19–23

Primary source authors appear in parentheses. Page numbers in italics indicate images, and those followed by the letter *t* indicate tables.

**Speeches**

*Acres of Diamonds* (Conwell), 485–486

"An Address Delivered Before the National Colored Teachers' Association" (Washington), 149–151

Advocating "Dollar Diplomacy" (Taft), 73–74

"The College-bred Community" (Du Bois), 127–131

"The Endowment of Motherhood" (Moran), 442–443

"Henry Cabot Lodge Speaks Out Against the League of Nations, Washington, DC, August 12, 1919" (Lodge), 268–269

"The New Nationalism" (Roosevelt), 232–236

"Opposition to Wilson's War Message" (Norris), 262–264

Repudiating "Dollar Diplomacy" (Wilson), 74

"Some Considerations Affecting the Replacement of Men by Women Workers" (Goldmark), 458–460

"Woodrow Wilson: *The Tampico Affair*" (Wilson), 250–252

Woodrow Wilson's Declaration of War Message (Wilson), 258–260

**Statements**

"Emma Goldman at the Federal Hearing in Re Deportation" (Goldman), 270–273

"The Next and Final Step" (Baker), 354–357

**Supreme Court decisions**

*Abrams v. U.S.* (1919) (Holmes), 323–325

*Buchanan v. Warley* (1917) (Day), 302–304

*Bunting v. Oregon* (1917) (McKenna), 298–301

*Debs v. U.S.* (1919) (Holmes), 319–322

*Hoke v. U.S.* (1913) (McKenna), 288–291

*Houston, East & West Texas Railway Co. v. U.S.* (1914) (Hughes), 295–297

*Schenck v. U.S.* (1919) (Holmes), 317–318

*Selective Draft Law Cases* (1918) (White), 310–312

*Standard Oil Co. of New Jersey v. U.S.* (1910) (White, Harlan), 285–287

*Weeks v. U.S.* (1918) (Day), 292–294

**Tables**

"Composition and Characteristics of the Population for Wards of Cities of 50,000 or More: Lawrence" (Federal Bureau of the Census), 248*t*

**Telegrams**

from Arthur Zimmermann to Heinrich J. F. von Eckhardt, *256*

from U.S. Ambassador Walter Page to President Woodrow Wilson, *257*

**Testimonies**

*John F. and Horace E. Dodge v. Ford Motor Co., Henry Ford, et. al.* (1919) (Ford), 99–101

*Money Trust Investigation* (U.S. House of Representatives), 75–83

**Theological works**

*America in the Making* (Abbott), 482–484

*A Theology for the Social Gospel* (Rauschenbusch), 492–494

Primary source authors appear in parentheses. Page numbers in italics indicate images, and those followed by the letter *t* indicate tables.

# GENERAL INDEX

*Page numbers in bold indicate primary sources; page numbers in italic indicate images; page numbers in bold italic indicate primary source images; page numbers followed by the letter t indicate tables. Primary sources are indexed under the entry name with the author's name in parentheses. Primary sources are also indexed by title. All primary sources can be identified by bold page locators*

## A

AAUP (American Association of University Professors), 164–165
report, **165–169**

Abbott, Lyman, 481–482, *482*
editorial, **583–585**
theological work, **482–484**

Abegg, Richard, on atomic theory, 538

Abortion and midwives, 442
*See also* Birth Control

Abrams, Jacob, 323, *323*

*Abrams v. U.S.* (1919), 322–325, 411
Supreme Court decision (Holmes), **323–325**

Academic freedom, 164–169
*See also* Free speech

ACLU (American Civil Liberties Union) and the Sedition and Espionage Acts, 411

*Acres of Diamonds,* 484–486
speech (Conwell), **485–486**

Addams, Jane, 152, *153,* 379
nonfiction work, **153–154**

Addiction to patent medicines, 444

"An Address Delivered Before the National Colored Teachers' Association," 148–151
speech (Washington), **149–151**

Advertising
automobiles, 221–222
on baseball cards, 387–390

branding, 210 212
business of, 102–105
coupons, 389–390
dress patterns, *196,* 197
house ads, 102–105, 220–221
patent medicines, *444*
soaps, 219–221
to women, 221
women in, 104, *105*

AFL (American Federation of Labor).
*See* American Federation of Labor (AFL)

African Americans. *See* Blacks

Agricultural education, 161–164, *163,* 170, *175,* 175–179

"The Aim," editorial (Sanger), 393, 394

Alcohol. *See* Prohibition

*Alexander's Bridge* (Cather), 11

"Alexander's Ragtime Band" (Berlin), 50

"Alexandra" (Cather), 11

*All God's Dangers: The Life of Nate Shaw,* 114–117
autobiography (Shaw, Rosengarten), **115–117**

AMA (American Medical Association), 143

"The Amateur," 581–585
editorial (Abbott, et al), **583–585**

*America in the Making,* 481–484
theological work (Abbott), **482–484**

American Association of University Professors (AAUP), 164–165
report, **165–169**

American Birth Control League, 393

American Civil Liberties Union (ACLU) and the Sedition and Espionage Acts, 411

American Federation of Labor (AFL), 247, 400, 502–505

*American Industry in War: A Report of the War Industries Board,* 108–114
report (Baruch), **109–114**

American Judaism, 500–502

American Medical Association (AMA), 143

American Socialist Party. *See* Socialist Party

American Tobacco Company (ATC), 387–388
baseball cards, *388, 389, 390*

American Woman Suffrage Association (AWSA). *See* National American Woman Suffrage Association (NAWSA)

America's Sex Hysteria, 347–351
"Popular Gullibility as Exhibited in the New White Slavery Hysteria" *(Current Opinion),* **349–351**
"Sex O'Clock in America" *(Current Opinion),* **348–349**

Amputees, rehabilitation, 452, 453, *453*

"The Ancient Dress" (Henri), 9–11, *10*
Anderson, Sherwood, 53, *54*
     short story, **53–55**
Angell, E. D., 607–608
     reference work, **608–610**
"The Anniversary," 395–396
     editorial *(New York Tribune),*
     **396–399**
Anthropology, 434–437, 516–520
Anti-alcohol movement. *See* Prohibition
Anti-Saloon League, 354–357, *355*
Antismoking movement. *See* Tobacco
Antitrust legislation. *See* Trusts (business)
Apartheid and Jim Crow segregation, 373
Architecture
     Arts and Crafts movement, 193, 197–199
     bungalows, 197–199, *198*
     factories, 63, *66*, 190–191, *191*
     skyscrapers, 202, 204
     villas, 216–217
Arden, Elizabeth, 214–216
     magazine advertisement, *215*
"Are Athletics Making Girls Masculine?," 577–581, 601
     magazine article (Sargent), **578–581**
"Are the Movies a Menace to the Drama?," 364–367
     essay (Matthews), **365–367**
"The Aristocrats of Dance." *See* Castle, Irene; Castle, Vernon
Arts and Crafts Movement, 191–193, 197–198
Asch building (New York City), 63, *66*
Ashcan School (group of painters), 9
Asians, immigrant experience, *344*
Assembly lines, 98–99, *99*, 190, 222
Astronomy, galactic structure, 541–546, *543, 544*
ATC. *See* American Tobacco Company (ATC)
Athletics. *See* Sports
Atlanta University, fund-raising, 127–131
"The Atom and the Molecule," 537–541, *539*
     journal article (Lewis), **538–541**
Atomic structure
     chemical bonds, 537–541, *539*
     electrons, 525–527, *526*, 530–534

"Audacious Hats for Spineless Attitudes," 199–202
     clothing styles *(Dress & Vanity Fair), 200*
     magazine article *(Dress & Vanity Fair),* **201**
Auto-education, 156–158
Automobile business, 98–102
     assembly lines, *99*, 190, 222
     factories, 190, *191*, 222
     gasoline industry and, 524
Automobiles, Model T. *See* Model T automobiles
Automobiles, racing, 574–577, *575*
*The Awakening of Ethiopia. See Ethiopia Awakening*
AWSA. *See* National American Woman Suffrage Association (NAWSA)

**B**
"Baby Week," 450–452
Baden-Powell, Robert, founding of Boy Scouts, 351
Bailey, Pearce, 454
     presentation, **455–457**
Baker, Purley A., 354
     statement, **354–357**
Baline, Israel. *See* Berlin, Irving
Ballroom dance, 16–18, 207–209
Banking, 75–83, 79
Baruch, Bernard M., 108–109, *109*
     report, **109–114**
Baseball, 585–591, 595–596
     barnstorming, 595
     baseball cards, 387–390, *388, 389, 390, 587, 588, 589*
     "Black Sox" scandal, 619–622
     compared to other sports, 607
     fiction, 597–600
     players, 619–622, *620*
     satire, 597–600
     semi-pro, 582
"Baseball and the National Life," 585–591
     essay (Bruce), **586–590**
*Basket Ball: for Coach, Player and Spectator,* 607–611
     reference work (Angell), **608–610**
Basketball, *601*, 603, 604, 607–611, *609*
Battle of the Somme, *266*
Bayes, Nora (singer), *42, 45*
Beals, Jessie Tarbox (photographer), 379, 383

Behavioral psychology, 527–530, 554
Bergenson, Alexandra (character in *O Pioneers!),* 11, *13*
Berger, Victor, conviction, 305–306
Berkman, Alexander, 270, *272*
Berlin, Irving, 45–51, *50*
     song, **46–49**
BIA (Bureau of Indian Affairs), 132
Binet, Alfred, 172
Birth control, 252–254, 393–395
Birth Control Clinical Research Bureau, 393
*The Birth of a Nation* (Griffith), 24–30, *27, 28,* 364
Bisbee (AZ) deportation of miners, 117–121
Bishop's Plan of 1919, 474
Black Nationalist Movement, 372–373
"Black Sox" scandal, 619–622
Blacks
     caricatures, 333, *333*
     civil rights, 148, 150–151
     discrimination against, 333–335
     education, 127–131, *128,* 148–151
     housing rights, 301–304, *303*
     migration north, 116, 403–407
     Prohibition and, 437–438
     segregation, 148, 301, 333–334, 373
     sharecroppers, 114–117
     social standing, 216–217
     voting rights, 239–240, 301–304
     World War I work opportunities, 116, 403–407
Blues music, 18
Blythe, Vernon. *See* Castle, Vernon
Boas, Franz (anthropologist), 342, *435, 516–520, *517*
     nonfiction work, **517–520**
     report, **435–437**
Bohr, Niels, *525,* 525–527
     journal article, **526–527**
Bok, Edward (editor), 195
Bourne, Randolph, 447
     movie review, **447–449**
Bowen, Maurice W., 68
     letter, **70–71**
"Boxers Spend Last Night Under Guard," 611–614
     newspaper article (Pulford), **612–614**
Boxing, 570–574, *578,* 611–614, *613*
Boy Scouts, 351–354, *352*
*Boy With Baby Carriage,* 35–37
     magazine cover (Rockwell), *36*

Page numbers in bold indicate primary sources; page numbers in italic indicate images;
page numbers in bold italic indicate primary source images; page numbers followed by the letter *t* indicate tables.

Boys, development, 351–354, 367–370, *368*

Brandeis, Louis D., 79, 298, 317

*The Brass Check*, 419–423

nonfiction work (Sinclair), **420–423**

Breedlove, Sarah. *See* Walker, Madame C. J.

Brent, Charles Henry, 486–489, *487*

sermon, **487–489**

"The Brickyard." *See* Indianapolis 500

Brookings, Robert S., *109*

Brown, Elwood S., 603–604

memo, **604–607**

Browne, George, 31

Bruce, Henry Addington, 585–586

essay, **586–590**

*Buchanan v. Warley* (1917), 301–304

Supreme Court decision (Day), **302–304**

Budgeting, family. *See* Home economics

Bull Moose Party. *See* Progressive Party

Bungalows, 197–199, *198*

*Bunting v. Oregon* (1917), 298–301

Supreme Court decision (McKenna), **298–301**

Bureau of Education reports, **180–183**

Bureau of Indian Affairs (BIA), 132

Burgess, Thornton W., 351

magazine article, **351–354**

"Burman Lowers Speedway Records," 574–577

newspaper article *(New York Times)*, **576–577**

Burns, Tommy (boxer), 570

Burton, William, 520

patent application, **521–523**

Business education, 180

*See also* Vocational education

Byrne, Ethel, *253*


**C**

"Cabinet Discusses Prager's Lynching" *(New York Times)*, **314–315**

Calumet and Arizona (C&A) Mining Company, 117–121

"Capitalizing Race Hatred" *(New York Globe)*

editorial, 24, **26–27**

Cardinal Gibbons' Letter to the U.S. Archbishops, 498–500

letter (Gibbons), **498–500**


*Cardinal Principles of Secondary Education*, 179–183

report (Commission on the Reorganization of Secondary Education), **180–183**

"Cardinal's Golden Jubilee," 478–481

sermon (Gibbons), **480–481**

Caricatures, 333, *333*

Carlisle Indian School, *133*, 134

Carnegie Foundation for the Advancement of Teaching, medical schools evaluation, 143–147

Carroll, John (bishop), 498

Casa dei Bambini (Montessori), 155

Castle, Irene, 16–18, *17, 207*, 207–208, *209*

reference works, **16–17, 208–209**

Castle, Vernon, 16–18, *17, 207*

reference works, **16–17**

Catalogs containing building plans, 193, 198

*Catalogue of Craftsman Furniture Made by Gustav Stickley at The Craftsman Workshops*, 191–193

*The Cathedral of Commerce* (Cochran), 204, **206–207**

Cather, Willa, 11–13, *12*

novel, **12–13**

Catholic Church

church-state relations, 498

immigrants and, 478–480, 498

labor movement and, 474–476, 479–480

National Catholic Welfare Conference (NCWC), 474–475, 480

Censorship in movies, 346–347, 368

*Changes in Bodily Form of Descendants of Immigrants*, 434–437

report (Immigration Commission; Boas), **435–437**

Chaplin, Charlie, 32–34, *33, 34*, 288

Charlie Chaplin as the "Little Tramp," 32–34

movie still, *33*

Chemistry in atomic theory, 537–541

"Chicago," 37–39

poem (Sandburg), **38–39**

"Chicago Cubs Baseball Card" (Liggett & Myers Co.), *388*, 389–390

Chicago *Defender* (newspaper), 413–414

letters, **404–406**

newspaper article, **416–419**

*Chicago Poems* (Sandburg), 37–38


Chicago Race Riots, 413–419, *414, 417*

"A Crowd of Howling Negroes" *(Chicago Tribune)*, **414–416**

"Ghastly Deeds of Race Rioters Told" (Chicago *Defender)*, **416–419**

Chicago Renaissance, 53, 56

Chicago Teacher's Federation, 135

*Chicago Tribune* (newspaper), 413–414

newspaper articles, **414–416, 460–462**

Chicago Vice Commission, 340

report, **340–341**

"Chicagoans Cheer Tar Who Shot Man" *(Washington Post)*, **371–372**

Child labor, 379–383, *380, 381, 382*

Child Labor Act of 1916, 379

"Child Study" movement, 155

Childbirth, 439–443

Children

development theories, 351–354, 367–370, *368*

early education, 154–158, *155, 159–161, 160*

physical education, 429, 433–434

psychology, 528

*See also* Child labor; Pediatrics

Children's House (Montessori), 155

China, U.S. foreign policy, 72, 73–74

Christian Unity movement, 487, 494–497, 502–505

Chromosomes, 550–553

"The Church and the Labor Question," 476–478

magazine article (Gladden), **477–478**

Church-state relations, 480–484, 498

*The Churches of Christ in Time of War*, 494–497

handbook (Federal Council of the Churches of Christ in America), **495, 497**

Citizenship, responsibilities, 481–484

Civil rights

blacks, 148, 150–151

equal pay, 135–138

housing, 301–304, *303, 383*

*See also* Segregation; Voting Rights

Classrooms, *133, 140*

Claxton, Philander P., 159

journal article, **159–161**

Clayton Act of 1914, 284

Page numbers in bold indicate primary sources; page numbers in italic indicate images;
page numbers in bold italic indicate primary source images; page numbers followed by the letter *t* indicate tables.

"Clear and present danger" standard, 317

Cobb, Frank (journalist), 370

Cobb, Ned. *See* Shaw, Nate

Cocaine in Coca-Cola, 444

Cochran, Edwin A., 202
  booklet, **204, 206–207**

Cohan, George M., *41*, 41–45
  song, **42–44**

*College and the Future: Essays for the Undergraduate on Problems of Character and Intellect* (Rice), 566

"The College-bred Community," 127–131
  speech (Du Bois), **127–131**

Colleges and universities
  academic freedom, 164–169
  education role, 168–169, 570
  graduates, 127–131, 429–431
  scientific research role, 168
  sports, 566–570, *567*, 582, 584–585
  *See also* Land-grant colleges

*Collier's* magazine, *445*

Commercial education, 180
  *See also* Vocational education

Commercialized vice. *See* Prostitution

Commission on the Reorganization of Secondary Education
  report, **176–179**

Committee on Academic Freedom and Tenure, report, 165–169

Committee on Public Information (CPI), 410

Communists
  confiscation of printed materials, *412*
  deportation, 410–411
  *See also* Red Scare; *Sedition Act of 1918;* Socialist Party

"Composition and Characteristics of the Population for Wards of Cities of 50,000 or More: Lawrence," 246–249
  table (Federal Bureau of the Census), **248***t*

Comprehensive high schools, 180
  *See also* Secondary education

Comstock Act of 1873, 252–253, 288

*The Conflict of Colour,* 333–335
  nonfiction work (Weale), **334–335,** *372*

Congressional investigations, 75–83, 237–238, 435

Conservation Division, War Industries Board, 108–114

Consumer culture, 210–212, 336–339, 389–390

"The Contribution of Psychology to Education," 139–143
  journal article (Thorndike), **140–143**

Conwell, Russell H., 484–485
  speech, **485–486**

Cooperative Extension Service, 161–164

*Country Life in America,* 197

Coupons, advertising, 389–390

Court cases, 99–101, 281
  *See also* Supreme Court

Cozad, Robert. *See* Henri, Robert

CPI (Committee on Public Information), 410

"Craftsman Furniture Made by Gustav Stickley," 191–193
  catalog, *192*

*The Craftsman* magazine, 191, 193, 198

Creel, George, 443
  magazine article, **445–447**

Criminal warrants, 292–294

*The Crisis* (periodical), *239*

Crossword puzzles, 390–392, *391*

"A Crowd of Howling Negroes" *(Chicago Tribune),* **414–416**

Crystal Palace. *See* "Ford's Highland Park Plant"

Cultural assimilation, 131–134, *133,* 434–437

Culture and race, anthropology, 516–520

*Current Opinion* (magazine)
  articles, **348–349, 349–351**

Cusack, Jack, 614, 615
  memoir, **615–619**

"Cy Young Baseball Card" (Liggett & Myers Co.), *390*

**D**

Daggett, Mabel Potter, 106
  nonfiction work, **107–108**

Dancing, 16–18, 207–209

Dark Side of Wartime Patriotism, 370–372
  "Chicagoans Cheer Tar Who Shot Man" *(Washington Post),* **371–372**
  Woodrow Wilson's Memorandum to His Secretary, Joseph Tumulty, **371**

Davis, Charles Henry, 94
  map, *96*
  pamphlet, **95**

Day, William R., 292, 301
  Supreme Court decisions, **292–294, 302–304**

Debate Over *The Birth of a Nation,* 24–30
  editorial *(New York Globe),* **26–27**
  letter (Griffith), **27–29**

Debs, Eugene V., 84, *86*, 305, 319–322, *320*

*Debs v. U.S.* (1919), 319–322
  Supreme Court decision (Holmes), **319–322**

*Democracy and Education,* 169–171
  nonfiction work (Dewey), **171**

Democratic Party and Progressive Party, *234*

Dempsey, Jack (boxer), 611–614, *613*

Department of Agriculture Cooperative Extension Service, 161–164

Department stores, 336–339, *337, 338*

Deportations, 117–121, *118,* 270–273, 410–411
  *See also Sedition Act of 1918*

Design
  factories, 190, *191*
  furniture, 191–193
  houses, 197–199, *198,* 216–217
  skyscrapers, 202, 204
  *See also* Fashion

Dewey, John, 152, 169–171, *172,* 176, 183
  nonfiction work, **171**

Didactic system (Montessori), 156–158

"Digestit" advertising, *444*

Dillingham Immigration Commission, 434–435
  report, **435–437**

"A Direct Photoelectric Determination of Planck's 'h'," 530–534
  journal article (Millikan), **531–534**

Discrimination. *See specific populations*

"*Dissent During World War I: The Kate O'Hare Trial: 1919,*" 304–310
  court case (O'Hare, Wade), **306–309**

Doctors, 429, 441–443

Dodge Brothers Manufacturing Company, 98–99

*John F. and Horace E. Dodge v. Ford Motor Co., Henry Ford, et. al.* (1919) (Ford), **99–101**

Page numbers in bold indicate primary sources; page numbers in italic indicate images; page numbers in bold italic indicate primary source images; page numbers followed by the letter *t* indicate tables.

Dollar Diplomacy and Its Repudiation, 71–75
 Speech Advocating "Dollar Diplomacy" (Taft), **73–74**
 Speech Repudiating "Dollar Diplomacy" (Wilson), **74**
 USS *Dolphin* (Tampico Affair), 249–252
Douglass, Frederick, on women's rights, 239
Draft laws. *See Selective Draft Law Cases;* Selective Service Act of 1917
"Dreams in War Time" (Lowell), 51
Dreier, Mary (labor leader), 63
*Dress & Vanity Fair* magazine
 clothing styles, 199–201, **200,** 212–214, *213*
 *See also Vanity Fair* magazine
*Drift and Mastery: An Attempt to Diagnose the Current Unrest,* 88–94
 nonfiction work (Lippmann), **89–94**
Druggists, 429, 442
Du Bois, W. E. B., 14, 127–131, 148, *240*
 editorial, **240–241**
 speech, **127–131**
Du Picq, Charles Jean Jacques Joseph Ardant, 455
Duke, James Buchanan, 387–388

**E**
E., E. S., 359
 magazine article, **359–362**
Early Baseball Cards, 387–390
 "Chicago Cubs Baseball Card" (Liggett & Myers Co.), *388*
 "Cy Young Baseball Card" (Liggett & Myers Co.), *390*
 "Tris Speaker Baseball Card" (Liggett & Myers Co.), *389*
Economic policy, 84–85, 88, 108–114
Economides, Basil, 288
Ecumenical movement, 487, 494–497, 502–505
Eddington, Arthur, 546, *547,* 547–548
 report, **548–550**
Edison Company power plants, *514*
Education
 blacks, 127–131, *128,* 148–151, *170*
 classrooms, *133, 140*
 colleges and universities, 127–131, 168–169, 570
 federal government's role, 162–164

intelligence tests, 172–174
kindergarten, 155, 159–161, *160*
"Laws of Learning" (Thorndike), 139–140
medical, 143–147, 442
Native Americans, 131–134, *133*
philosophies, 169–171, 179–183, 183–186
scientific approach, 155
secondary schools, 175–179
self-education, 156–158
social hygiene, 152–154, 349
in social reform, 170–171
teachers' pay scales, 134–139
 *See also* Agricultural education; Progressive education movement; Vocational education
Educational psychology, 139–143
Effect, Law of (Thorndike), 139
The Eight (group of painters), 9
Einstein, Albert
 on photoelectric effect, 530, 531
 on relativity, 547–550
Electric power industry, 513–516, *514*
Electrons, atomic theory, *526,* 530, 537–541
Ellis, Harvey (architect), 193
Empey, Arthur Guy, 265–267
 memoir, **265–267**
"The Endowment of Motherhood," 441–443
 speech (Moran), **442–443**
Environmentalism (anthropology), 435
*Equal Pay for Equal Work* (Strachan), **135–138**
Equal Pay for Women Teachers, 134–139
 *Equal Pay for Equal Work* (Strachan), **135–138**
 "The Ideal Candidates" (Miller), **138**
 "An Unequal Footing!" (Anonymous), **139**
Espionage Act of 1917, 305, 306, 319, 410
 ACLU, 411
 arrests, 400
 *See also Sedition Act of 1918*
*Ethiopia Awakening,* 14–15
 sculpture (Fuller), *15*
Eugenics, 362
*Evening Star, III,* 39–41
 painting (O'Keeffe), *40*
Evidence. *See* Criminal warrants

Evolution and theology, 481–482
*The Evolution of Christianity* (Abbott), 482
Exclusionary rule, 292, 293
"Eyewitness at the Triangle" (Shepherd), **64–66**

**F**
Factories, *299, 503*
 assembly lines, 98–99, *99,* 190, 222
 changes, 492
 design, 190, *191*
 labor laws, 281–283
 scientific management, 68–71, *70,* 99
 women in the workforce, *459*
 worker safety, 63–68, *67,* 281, *282, 454*
 worker's compensation, 281–283
 *See also* Labor movement
*The Faith of Our Fathers* (Gibbons), 498
*Family Limitation,* 252–254
 pamphlet (Sanger), **253–254**
Farm workers, children, *380*
Farmers *See* Agricultural education
Fashion
 dancing, 207–209
 dresses, 195–197
 flappers, *358*
 golf attire, 212–214, *213*
 hair, 193–195, *194,* 216–217
 hats, 199–201, *200*
 men, 212–214, *213*
 skin care, 214–216
 uniforms, 217–219, *218*
"Father of the Blues." *See* Handy, W. C.
Fatima Turkish Blend Cigarettes, baseball cards, *388, 389*–390
FDA. *See* Food and Drug Administration (FDA)
Federal Bureau of the Census, 246–247
 table, **248t**
Federal Council of the Churches of Christ in America
 handbook, **495, 497**
Federal Reserve System, 75
Federal Trade Commission Act of 1914, 284
Feminist movement, 346–347, 359, 429, 442, 457–460
 *See also* Women

Page numbers in bold indicate primary sources; page numbers in italic indicate images;
page numbers in bold italic indicate primary source images; page numbers followed by the letter *t* indicate tables.

*Ferguson, Plessy v.* (1896), 301

"The Fight Against Venereal Disease," 463–465

    magazine article (Fosdick), **463–465**

"Find Influenza Germ" *(Washington Post),* **462–463**

The First Pulitzer Prizes, 395–400

    "The Anniversary" *(New York Tribune),* **396–399**

    "Germany Keen for Peace, but Expects and Is Ready to Battle for Years" (Swope), **399**

"Five Pretty Ways to Do the Hair," 193–195

    hair styles *(Ladies' Home Journal),* *194*

"The Flapper," 357–359

    magazine article (Mencken), **357–359**

Flappers, 357–359, *358*

Fletcher, F. F., *109*

Flexner, Abraham, 143–144

"Flower Dresses for Lawn Fêtes," 195–197

    clothing styles *(Ladies' Home Journal),* *196*

Foley, Edna L., 429

    journal article, **429–431**

Food and Drug Administration (FDA), 444, 465–466

Football, 566–567, *567, 582,* 614–619, *616*

"For Freedom and Democracy," 407–409

    editorial *(North American Review),* **408–409**

Ford, Henry, 98–102, 190, 221–223, *222*

    interview, **101–102**

    testimony, **99–101**

*Ford Motor Co., Henry Ford, et. al., John F. and Horace E. Dodge v.* (1919) (Ford), **99–101**

Ford Motor Company, 98–102, *99,* 190, *222*

"Ford's Highland Park Plant," *99,* 190–191, *222*

    photograph (Kahn), *191*

Foreign policy, 71–74, 236–238, *237,* 254–257, 407

    Mexico, 249–252, *251,* 410

Fosdick, Harry Emerson, 505

Fosdick, Raymond B.

    magazine article, **463–465**

Frayne, Hugh, *109*

Free speech, 316–319, 322, *411*

    *See also* Sedition Act of 1918

"Freedom of Contract" doctrine, 298

Freud, Sigmund, 535, 553–559

    lecture, **554–559**

Froebel, Friedrich (originator of kindergarten), 155, 159, 160

Frost, Robert, 30–32, *31*

    lecture, **31–32**

Fuller, Meta Vaux Warrick, 14–15

    sculpture, *15*

Fundamentalist movement, 490

*The Fundamentals: A Testimony to the Truth* (Pentecost), 489

"Fun's Word Cross Puzzle," 390–392

    crossword puzzle (Wynne), *391*

Furniture design, 191–193

*The Future of Electricity,* 513–516

    lecture (Steinmetz), **513–516**

**G**

Galactic structure, 541–546, *543, 544*

Gambling, "Black Sox" scandal, 619–622

Gardner, Howard, on intelligence testing, 172

Garrison, Lindley (Secretary of War), 70–71

Garvey, Marcus, *373*

    editorial, **373–374**

Gasoline refining, 520–525

*A General Introduction to Psycho-Analysis,* 553–559

    lecture (Freud), **554–559**

General relativity, 547–550

Genetics, 550–553

"German is Lynched by an Illinois Mob" *(New York Times),* **314**

Germany, 254–257, 265, 396, 399, 407

    *See also* World War I

"Germany Is Keen for Peace, but Expects and Is Ready to Battle for Years" (Swope), **399**

"Ghastly Deeds of Race Rioters Told" (Chicago *Defender),* **416–419**

Gibbons, James (Cardinal), 474, 478–480, *479,* 498–500, *499*

    letter, **498–500**

    sermon, **480–481**

Gifts, in Froebel's method, 159

Gilbert, Cass (architect), 202

    photograph, *203*

Girls. *See* Women

*Girls and Athletics,* 578, 600–603

    handbook (Morgan), **602–603**

Gish, Dorothy, *26*

Gish, Lillian, *26, 28*

Gladden, Washington, 476–477, *477*

    magazine article, **477–478**

"Globular Clusters and the Structure of the Galactic System," 541–546, *543, 544*

    journal article (Shapley), **542–546**

Goggin, Catherine, 135

Goldman, Emma, 253, 270–273, *272,* 306, 393

    statement, **270–273**

Goldmark, Josephine, 457

    speech, **458–460**

Golf, 212–214, *213,* 591–594

Gompers, Samuel (labor leader), 63

Gospel of Wealth, 476, 484–485, *485*

Government workers, 68–69, 70–71

"Grandfather clause," 301

Grant, Madison, 362

    nonfiction work, **362–364**

Gravitation, 547–550

Great Migration, 116, 403–407

"Great white hope," 570

Griffith, D. W., 24–30, *26*

    letter, **27–29**

*Guinn v. U.S.* (1915), 301

**H**

Hair care products, 216–217

Hair styles, 193–195

Handy, W. C., 18–24

    song, **19–23**

Harlan, John Marshall (Supreme Court justice), 284

    court decision, **286–287**

Harroun, Ray (race car driver), 574, *575*

Harvard Medical School, *144*

Harvard-Yale football game, 566, *567*

Hassan Cigarettes, baseball cards, 389

Hatch Experiment Station Act of 1887, 162, 175

Hats (fashion), 199–201, *200*

Haywood, "Big Bill" (IWW leader), 247, 249, 253, 305–306, 400

Healy, William, 367, 368

    nonfiction work, **368–370**

"The Heart of the People," 447–449

    movie review (Bourne), **447–449**

Henri, Marjorie, 9, *10,* 11

Henri, Robert, *9,* 9–11

    painting, *10*

Page numbers in bold indicate primary sources; page numbers in italic indicate images; page numbers in bold italic indicate primary source images; page numbers followed by the letter *t* indicate tables.

Henriksen, Olaf, baseball card, *589*

"Henry Cabot Lodge: Corollary to the Monroe Doctrine," 236–239

    congressional record (Lodge), **237–238**

"Henry Cabot Lodge Speaks Out Against the League of Nations, Washington, DC, August 12, 1919," 267–269

    speech (Lodge), **268–269**

"Henry Ford in a Model T," 221–223, *222*

Henry Ford's Business Philosophy, 98–102

    Interview with Henry Ford, **101–102**

    *John F. and Horace E. Dodge v. Ford Motor Co. Henry Ford, et. al.* (1919), **99–101**

Heredity, 550–553

Hetch Hetchy Valley, 241–246, *242*

High schools, comprehensive, 180

    *See also* Secondary education

Highland Park Ford Plant. *See* "Ford's Highland Park Plant"

Highways, 94–97

Hine, Lewis, 379–383

    photographs, *380–382*

Hoke, Effie, 288

*Hoke v. U.S.* (1913), 287–291

    Supreme Court decision (McKenna), **288–291**

Holmes, Oliver Wendell, Jr., 316, 319, 322, 411

    Supreme Court decisions, **317–319, 319–322, 323–325**

Home economics, 359–362, *360*

Hospitals, role in childbirth, 442–443

House of Worth (designer), 217–219

    clothing style, *218*

Household management. *See* Home economics

Houses

    design, 197–199, *198*, 216–217

    interiors, *360*

Housing rights, 301–304, *303*, 383

*Houston, East & West Texas Railway Co. v. U.S.,* 294–297

    Supreme Court decision (Hughes), **295–297**

"How Physical Training Affects the Welfare of the Nation," 432–434

    journal article (Posse), **432–434**

"How the Drug Dopers Fight," 443–447

    magazine article (Creel), **445–447**

*How the Other Half Lives* (Riis), 379

"How We Manage," 359–362

    magazine article (E. S. E.), **359–362**

Howard, Marion, articles, 393

Huerta, Victoriano (Mexican leader), 249–250

Hughes, Charles Evans, 294–295

    Supreme Court decision, **295–297**

Hughes, Dudley M., 175

    law, **176–179**

**I**

ICC. *See* Interstate Commerce Commission (ICC)

"The Ideal Candidates" (Miller), 138

ILGWU (International Ladies Garment Workers Union) strikes, 63

"The Imagining Ear," 30–32

    lecture (Frost), **31–32**

Imagism (school of poetry), 51–52

Immigrants, 12, 38, *436*

    anthropology, 434–437

    assimilation, 351

    attitudes toward, 333–335, 342–345, 362–364, 429

    Catholic Church and, 478–480, 498

    health examinations, *343*

    labor unions and, 247–249, 342

    Prohibition and, 354, 438

    public health, *343*, 448

    women, *344*

Immigration Commission (U.S.), 434–435

    report, **435–437**

*The Immigration Problem,* 342–345

    nonfiction work (Jenks, Lauck), **342–345**

Impressionism (painting style), 9

*In Prison* (O'Hare), 306

*The Indian and His Problem,* 131–134

    nonfiction work (Leupp), **132–134**

Indianapolis 500, 574–577, *575*

*The Individual Delinquent,* 367–370

    nonfiction work (Healy), **368–370**

Industrial education. *See* Agricultural education; Vocational education

Industrial organization

    assembly lines, *99*, 190, *222*

    scientific management, 68–71

Industrial Workers of the World (IWW), 393, *401*

    miners, 117–121

    textile workers, 247, 249

    union organizers lynched, 313

Influenza Epidemic, 460–463, *461*, 467–468

    "100 Sailors at Great Lakes Die of Influenza" *(Chicago Tribune),* **460–462**

    "Find Influenza Germ" *(Washington Post),* **462–463**

Ingels, J. P., *109*

Ingen, Philip Van, 449, 450

    journal article, **450–452**

*Inside the German Empire,* nonfiction work (Swope), 396, 399

Intelligence tests, 172–174

Inter-Allied Games, 603–607, *605*

Interchurch World Movement, 477, 502–505

    report, **503–505**

"Interchurch World Movement Report," 502–505

    report (Interchurch World Movement), **503–505**

International Ladies Garment Workers Union (ILGWU) strikes, 63

International Workers of the World (IWW). *See* Industrial Workers of the World (IWW)

Interstate commerce and state laws, 294–297, 298–301

Interstate Commerce Commission (ICC), railroad rates, 295

Interview with Edd Roush, 619–622

    interview (Ritter), **620–622**

IQ tests, 172–174

"Is There News in Shaving Soap?," 219–221

    magazine advertisement (Thompson), *220*

*Ives v. South Buffalo Railway Co.* (1911), 281

IWW. *See* Industrial Workers of the World (IWW)

**J**

J. Walter Thompson House Ads. *See* Thompson House Ads

James, William (psychologist), 139, 172

Japan-U.S. relations, 236–238, *237*

Jeffries, Jim (boxer), 570–574, *571*

Jewish Center (NYC), 500–501

Johnson, Jack (boxer), 570–574, *571*, 611

"Johnson Wins in 15 Rounds; Jeffries Weak," 570–574

    newspaper article (Sullivan), **571–573**

Page numbers in bold indicate primary sources; page numbers in italic indicate images;
page numbers in bold italic indicate primary source images; page numbers followed by the letter *t* indicate tables.

Journalism, 395, 419–423, 443, 445
*See also* Newspapers
Judaism, American, 500–502
Jung, Carl G., *536, 554*
nonfiction work, **535–537**
Juvenile delinquency, 351–354,
367–370, *368*

**K**

Kahn, Albert, 190
photograph, **191**
Kaplan, Mordecai M., 500–502
journal article, **501**
Keefe, Jack (fictional character),
597–600
Kerosene, 520
Kilpatrick, William Heard, 183–184
journal article, **184–186**
Kindergarten, 155, 159–161, *160*
Knights of Labor, 480
Knox, Philander C. (politician), 72–73

**L**

Labor law
child labor, 379–383
wages, 298, 474–476
women, 298, 457–460
work hours, 298
worker's compensation, 281–283
Labor movement
religion and, 474–476, 479–480,
492, 502–505
violence, 476
Labor unions, 281, 480
copper miners, 117–121
equal pay for women, 137
immigrants, 247–249, 342
textile workers, 247, 249
women in the workforce, 106–107
worker safety, 63
*See also* Strikes; *specific unions*
Lachowsky, Hyman, 323, *323*
*Ladies' Home Journal*
clothing styles, 195–197, *196*
hair styles, 193–195, *194*
Lambert Pharmacal Company
advertisements, 210–212
magazine advertisement, *211*
Land-grant colleges, 162–164, *163*
Lardner, Ring, 597, *598*
fictional work, **597–600**
"Last of the Vigilantes," 117–121
memoir (Tefft), **119–121**

Latin America and Monroe Doctrine,
249–252
Law of Effect (Thorndike), 139
Lawrence (MA)
population tables, 248*t*
textile workers, 247, *247, 249*
Laws
antitrust, 88, 284–288
building regulations, 63–64
commerce, 284
food and drug safety, 444, 465
interstate commerce *vs.* state law,
294–297, 298–301
obscenity, 252–253, 288
Prohibition, 273–275
prostitution, 288, 340, 348
segregation, 301–304
worker's compensation, 281–283
*See also* Espionage Act of 1917;
Labor law; *Sedition Act of
1918;* Selective Service Act
Laws of Learning (Thorndike),
139–140, 183
League of Nations, 267–269
League of Women Voters. *See* National American Woman Suffrage
Association (NAWSA)
Learning, Laws of (Thorndike),
139–140
*Leaves From the Notebook of a Tamed
Cynic,* 505–507
diary (Niebuhr), **506–507**
Leo XIII (Pope)
church-state relations, 480
labor movement, 474, 480
Letters to the Chicago *Defender,*
403–407
letters, **404–406**
Leupp, Francis E., 131–132
nonfiction work, **132–134**
Lever, Asbury Francis, 161
law, **162–164**
Lewis, Gilbert N., 537–538
journal article, **538–541**
Liberal theology, 490
*The Liberator* (periodical). *See The
Masses* (periodical)
Libido in psychology, 535, 553–554
Lichty, Daniel (doctor), 438
presentation, **438–439**
Liggett & Myers Co.
baseball cards, *388, 389, 390*
"Lights All Askew in the Heavens"
*(New York Times),* 549

Lipman, Samuel, 323, *323*
Lippmann, Walter, 88, *89*
nonfiction work, **89–94**
Liquor. *See* Prohibition
Listerine (product), 210–212, *211*
Little, Frank (union organizer), 313
The Little Tramp (character), 32–34,
*33, 34*
*A Living Wage: Its Ethical and Economic Aspects,* 474–476
nonfiction work (Ryan), **474–476**
Lodge, Henry Cabot, Sr., 236, 237,
267, 268, *268*
congressional record, **237–238**
speech, **268–269**
Lovett, Robert, *109*
Lowell, Amy, 51–52, *52*
poem, **52**
Loyalty oaths, 164–169
*Lusitania* sinking, U.S. entry into
World War I, 395–399, *396,* 407
The Lynching of Robert P. Prager,
313–316
"Cabinet Discusses Prager's Lynching" *(New York Times),*
**314–315**
"German is Lynched by an Illinois
Mob" *(New York Times),* **314**
"Prager Asked Mob to Wrap Body
in Flag" *(New York Times),*
**315–316**
"The Prager Case" *(New York
Times),* **316**
"Tried for Prager Murder" *(New
York Times),* **316**
Lynchings, 313–316, *334*

**M**

Mabie, Hamilton W.
editorial, **583–585**
Macy's department store, *337*
Magazines. *See specific titles*
"Making Men of Them," 351–354
magazine article (Burgess),
**351–354**
"Mandy," 45–51, *46*
song (Berlin), **46–49**
Mann Act of 1910, 288, 340, 348
Manual education. *See* Vocational education
"Manufacture of Gasolene," 520–525
patent application (Burton),
**521–523**
Marcosson, Isaac F., 336
magazine article, **336–339**

Page numbers in bold indicate primary sources; page numbers in italic indicate images;
page numbers in bold italic indicate primary source images; page numbers followed by the letter *t* indicate tables.

Marines, *251*

Marketing, 336–339

*See also* Advertising

*The Masquerade Dress,* 9–11

painting (Henri), **10**

*The Masses* (periodical), 400, *402*

Matthews, Brander, 364

essay, **365–367**

McKenna, Joseph (Supreme Court justice), 288, 298

Supreme Court decisions, **288–291, 298–301**

*The Measurement of Intelligence,* 172–175

manual (Terman), **172–174**

*Medical Education in the United States and Canada: A Report to the Carnegie Foundation for the Advancement of Teaching,* 143–147

report (Pritchett), **144–147**

Medical profession

education, 143–147, *144,* 442

professional standards, 429

Medicine

anesthesia, 439–441

influenza epidemic, 460–463

nursing careers, 429–432

*See also* Childbirth; Pediatrics; Public health

Medicines, patent. *See* Patent medicines

Memorandum to Colonel Bruce Palmer, 603–607

memo (Brown), **604–607**

"Memphis Blues" (Handy), 18

Mencken, Henry L., 357

magazine article, **357–359**

Mendelian genetics, 550

"Mending Wall" (Frost), 30–31

Mental hygiene. *See* Psychology

Mexico, relations with United States, 236–238, *237,* 249–252, *251,* 255

Midwives *vs.* obstetricians, 441–443

Military draft. *See* Selective Service Act

"Military Olympics," 603–607, *605*

Milky Way, structure, 541–546

Miller, Alice Duer, 135

poem, **138**

Millikan, Robert A., 530–531, *532*

journal article, **531–534**

*The Mind of Primitive Man,* 516–520

nonfiction work (Boas), **517–520**

Mine workers, 117–121, *118, 381*

Minor, Robert (artist), 400, 402

Mission style furniture, *192,* 193

Model T automobiles, 98–102, *99,* 221–222, *222*

Ford's Highland Park Plant, 190, 222

gasoline industry and, 524

*Modern Dancing,* 16–18

reference work (Castle, Castle), **16–17, 207–209**

*Money Trust Investigation,* 75–83

testimony (Morgan), **75–77, 79–83**

Monopolies. *See* Trusts

Monroe, Harriet, 55–58

autobiography, **56–58**

Monroe Doctrine, 236–237, 249–252

Montessori, Maria, 154–156, *155*

manual, **156–158**

*The Montessori Method,* 154–158

manual (Montessori), **156–158**

Moran, John F., 441–442

speech, **442–443**

Morgan, J. Pierpont, 75, *76, 78,* 232

testimony, **75–77, 79–83**

Morgan, Mary C., 600–601

handbooks, **602–603**

Morgan, Thomas Hunt, 550–553

nonfiction work, **551–553**

Morrill Acts of 1862 and 1890, 162, 175

*Mother Earth* (magazine), 270

Movie posters, *27, 34*

Movie stills, *28, 33, 365*

Movie theaters, *366*

Movies

censorship, 346–347, 368

compared to theater, 364–367

development of styles, 25–30, 364

juvenile delinquency and, 367–370

public health documentaries, 447–449

Muir, John, 241–243

nonfiction work, **243–246**

*Muller v. Oregon* (1908), 298

"My First Novels (There Were Two)" (Cather), 11

"Mystery of the Phantom Policeman," 615

## N

NAACP (National Association for the Advancement of Colored People), 24–25, 29, *240*

Du Bois, W. E. B., 127

Supreme Court arguments, 301–302

Narcotics, 439–441, 443–444

National American Woman Suffrage Association (NAWSA), 239–240, 383–387, *387*

National American Woman Suffrage Association (NAWSA) Broadsides, 383–387

"Votes for Women," **384**

"Why Women Want to Vote," **385**

"Women in the Home," **386**

National Association for the Advancement of Colored People. *See* NAACP (National Association for the Advancement of Colored People)

National Catholic Welfare Conference (NCWC), 474–475, 480

National Child Labor Committee (NCLC), 379–383

National Council of Churches. *See* Federal Council of the Churches of Christ in America

National Education Association, Commission on the Reorganization of Secondary Education

report, **180–183**

National Highways Association, 94, *95*

map, *96*

*National Old Trails Road: Ocean to Ocean Highway,* 94–97

map (Davis), *96*

pamphlet (Davis), **95**

National Training School for Women and Girls (Washington, DC), *128*

National Woman Suffrage Association (NWSA). *See* National American Woman Suffrage Association (NAWSA)

Native Americans, 131–134, *133,* 582–585

NAWSA. *See* National American Woman Suffrage Association (NAWSA)

NCLC. *See* National Child Labor Committee (NCLC)

NCWC. *See* National Catholic Welfare Conference (NCWC)

"The Negro Should Be a Party to the Commercial Conquest of the World," 372–374

editorial (Garvey), **373–374**

*A New Conscience and an Ancient Evil,* 152–154

nonfiction work (Addams), **153–154**

Page numbers in bold indicate primary sources; page numbers in italic indicate images;
page numbers in bold italic indicate primary source images; page numbers followed by the letter *t* indicate tables.

"New Freedom" program, 79, 84–85, 88
"The New Nationalism," 232–236
    speech (Roosevelt), **232–236**
New Parties Challenge the Economic System, 83–88
    Progressive Party Platform of 1912, **85–86**
    Socialist Party Platform of 1912, **86–87**
"A New Profession" (Thompson Company), *103*
New Theology, 476, 490
New York City
    "Baby Week," 450–452
    building regulations, 63–64
    skyline, 204
    teacher pay scales, 135–138
*New York Globe* (newspaper), 26–29
    editorial, **26–27**
New York (state) Factory Investigating Commission, 63–64
    floor plan, *66*
    report, **66–67**
New York (state) Legislature
    law, **281–283**
*New York Times* (newspaper)
    newspaper articles, **313–316, 576–577, 591–594**
*New York Tribune* (newspaper)
    newspaper article, **396–399**
*New York Worker's Compensation Act 1910,* 281–283
    law (New York Legislature), **281–283**
*New York World* (newspaper) puzzles, 392
Newcomb, Simon, 566
    essay, **567–570**
Newspapers, 390–392, *391,* 395, 419–423
    *See also* Journalism; *specific titles*
Newtonian physics. *See* Gravitation
"The Next and Final Step," 354–357
    statement (Baker), **354–357**
"The Next War," 465–468
    magazine article (Wiley), **466–468**
Nicaragua-U.S. foreign policy, 72–74
Niebuhr, Reinhold, 505–507
    diary, **506–507**
No-Man's-Land (World War I), 265
Norris, George W. (Senator), *261,* 261–264
    speech, **262–264**

*North American Review* (journal), 407–409
    editorial, **408–409**
*North of Boston* (Frost), 30–31
Northern Securities Company, antitrust action against, 284
Nurses, 429–431, *430, 451, 456, 467*
"Nursing as a Profession for College Women," 429–432
    journal article (Foley), **429–431**
NWSA. *See* National American Woman Suffrage Association (NAWSA)

**O**

*O Pioneers!,* 11–13, *13*
    illustrations, *13*
    novel (Cather), **12–13**
Obscenity laws, 252–253, 288
Obstetricians v. midwives, 441–443
Occupations, in Froebel's method, 159
Office of Indian Affairs, 132
O'Hare, Kate Richards, 304–310, *305*
    court case, **306–309**
O'Keeffe, Georgia, *39,* 39–41
    painting, *40*
"Old-Stock" Americans. *See* Immigrants
Olympics competitions, 582
    "Military Olympics," 603–607, *605*
"On the Constitution of Atoms and Molecules," 525–527
    journal article (Bohr), **526–527**
"On the Imitation of Man," 345–347
    essay (Tarbell), **346–347**
"100 Sailors at Great Lakes Die of Influenza" *(Chicago Tribune),* **460–462**
"Opposition to Wilson's War Message," 261–264
    speech (Norris), **262–264**
*Oregon, Bunting v.* (1917)
    Supreme Court decision (McKenna), **298–301**
*Oregon, Muller v.* (1908), 298
"Orthopedic Surgery in War Time," 452–454
    presentation (Osgood), **452–454**
Osgood, Robert B., 452
    presentation, **452–454**
*Other People's Money and How the Bankers Use It* (Brandeis), 79
Ouimet, Francis, 591–594, *593*
"Ouimet World's Golf Champion," 591–594

newspaper article *(New York Times),* **591–594**
"Over the Top": By an American Soldier Who Went, 265–267
    memoir (Empey), **265–267**
"Over There," 41–45, *42*
    song (Cohan), **42–44**

**P**

"Packages That Speak Out" (Thompson Company), *104*
Page, Walter (diplomat), 255
    telegram, *257*
Page from George Weiss's Scrapbook, 595
    scrapbook (Weiss), **596**
Paine, Billy, 35
*Painless Childbirth,* 439–441
    nonfiction work (Williams), **440–441**
Palmer, A. Mitchell (U.S. Attorney General), 270, 319, 410
Palmer Raids, 270
Panama Canal, U.S. foreign policy, 236–238
"Paper Pills," 52–55
    short story (Anderson), **53–55**
*The Passing of the Great Race,* 362–364
    nonfiction work (Grant), **362–364**
"The Pasture" (Frost), 30–31, *32*
Patent medicines, 443–447, *444, 445,* 520
PD (Phelps, Dodge and Company), 117–121
Pediatrics, 449–452, *450*
Pentecost, George F., 489–491
    essay, **490–491**
Pestalozzi, Johann (educator), 159
Petherbridge, Margaret, crossword puzzle editor, 392
Petroleum industry, 520–525, *524*
"Phantom Policeman Mystery," 615
Pharmacists, 429, 442
Phelps, Dodge and Company (PD), 117–121
"The Philosopher" (Anderson). *See* "Paper Pills"
Photoelectric effect, 530–531
Photographs by Lewis Hine, 379–383
    photographs (Hine), **380–382**
*The Physical Basis of Heredity,* 550–553
    nonfiction work (Morgan), **551–553**

Page numbers in bold indicate primary sources; page numbers in italic indicate images;
page numbers in bold italic indicate primary source images; page numbers followed by the letter *t* indicate tables.

Physical education, 432–434, *433*
    diet and food, 608, 609–610
    morality and, 603–607
    university and college sports,
        566–570
    women, 577–581, *578,* 600–603
Physicians, 429, 441–443
Physics, 547–550
    *See also* Atomic structure
"Picture brides," *344*
*Pictures of the Floating World* (Lowell), 51–52
Pierce, Palmer E., *109*
Pinchot, Gifford, 242–243
*Pioneer in Pro Football,* 614–619
    memoir (Cusack), **615–619**
Planck's constant, 525–527, 530–534, *531*
Planned Parenthood (organization), 393
*Plessy v. Ferguson* (1896), 301
Poetry
    poetic forms, 37, 51, 56
    spoken language, 30–32
*Poetry: A Magazine of Verse,* 37, 56–58
*A Poet's Life: Seventy Years in a Changing World,* 55–58
    autobiography (Monroe), **56–58**
Populist Party and railroad regulation, 295
Posse, Rose (Baroness), 432
    journal article, **432–434**
Post-traumatic stress disorder, 455–457, *456*
Power industry, 513–516
Prager, Robert P., 313–316
"Prager Asked Mob to Wrap Body in Flag" *(New York Times),* **315–316**
"The Prager Case" *(New York Times),* **316**
*Preliminary Report of the Factory Investigating Commission,* 63–64
    floor plan, *66*
    report, **66–67**
*The Principles of Scientific Management* (Taylor), **69–70**
*Prisoners of Hope and Other Sermons,* 486–489
    sermon (Brent), **487–489**
Pritchett, Henry S., 143
    report, **144–147**
"A Program for the Reconstruction of Judaism," 500–502
    journal article (Kaplan), **501**

"Progress in Pediatrics," 449–452
    journal article (Van Ingen), **450–452**
Progressive education movement, 152–154, 169–170, 183–186
Progressive Party, 83–85, *85,* 232–236, *233, 234,* 482
Progressive Party Platform of 1912, **85–86**
Prohibition, 273–275, 354–357, *356*
    Anti-Saloon League, 354–357, *355*
    anti-tobacco campaigns, 437–438
    destruction of alcohol, *275*
    immigrants and, 354, 438
    World War I and, 275, 354, 437–438
"The Project Method," 183–186
    journal article (Kilpatrick), **184–186**
Propaganda, World War I, *407,* 410
"Proper Dancing-Costumes for Women," 207–210
    reference work (Castle), **208–209**
Property rights of blacks, 301–304
Prosthetics, 452, 453–454, *454*
Prostitution, 152–154, 288–291, 340–341, 463
    *See also* Mann Act of 1910; White slavery
Protestant positions, 476–478, 481–482, 487, 502–505
Psychoanalysis, 553–559
Psychology
    behaviorist school, 527–530, 554
    Jung's theories *vs.* Freud's, 535
    "New Psychology," 172
    World War I, 454–457
Psychology, educational, 139–143
"Psychology as the Behaviorist Views It," 527–530
    journal article (Watson), **529–530**
*Psychology of the Unconscious,* 534–537
    nonfiction work (Jung), **535–537**
Public health, *451,* 465–468, *467*
    immigrants, *343, 448*
    influenza epidemic, 460–463, *461*
    pediatrics, 449–452
    prostitution, 288, 340–341
    tobacco, 437–439
    tuberculosis, 447–449, *448*
    venereal disease, 463–465, *464*
Pujo, Arsene, 75, *76*

Pulford, George R., 611, 612
    newspaper article, **612–614**
Pulitzer, Joseph (journalist), 395, *398*
Pulitzer Prizes, 395
Pullman Strike, 319
Pure Food and Drug Act 1906, 444, 465
Puzzles, newspaper, 390–392, *391*

**Q**

Quantum mechanics, 526, 531

**R**

Race and culture, anthropology, 516–520
Race riots, 413–419, *414, 417*
Racing automobiles. *See* Automobiles, racing
Racism
    academic arguments for, 333–335, 516–520
    lynchings, *334*
    sports, 570–574, 582–585, 611, 615
    women's suffrage and, 239–240
    *See also* Blacks; Immigrants; Segregation
Railroads, 295, *296,* 319
Rauschenbusch, Walter, 477, *493,* 495
    theological work, **492–494**
Ray, Ted (golfer), 591–594
Recombination, genetic, 550–553
Reconstructionist movement in Judaism, 500–502
Red Scare, 270, 322–323, 370–371
Relativity, general theory, 547–550
Religion
    Judaism, 500–502
    labor movement and, 474–476, 479–480, 492, 502–505
    *See also* Christian unity movement; Ecumenical movement; Fundamentalist movement; Gospel of Wealth; Liberal theology; Social Gospel movement
"Reply to the *New York Globe*" (Griffith), **27–29**
*Report of the Committee on Academic Freedom and Tenure,* 164–169
    report (American Association of University Professors), **165–169**
*Report on the Relativity Theory of Gravitation,* 546–550
    report (Eddington), **548–550**
Republican Party, 232, *234*
Riis, Jacob, *How the Other Half Lives,* 379

Page numbers in bold indicate primary sources; page numbers in italic indicate images;
page numbers in bold italic indicate primary source images; page numbers followed by the letter *t* indicate tables.

Riley, Phil M., 197
    magazine article, **198–199**
*The Rising Tide of Color Against
    White World-Supremacy* (Stod-
    dard), 333
Ritter, Lawrence, 619
    interview, **620–622**
Riveters, *110*
Roads and highways, 94–97
Rockefeller, John D., 270, 284, *284,
    285,* 345
Rockwell, Norman, *35,* 35–37
    magazine cover, *36*
Roosevelt, Theodore, *233, 499*
    economic policy, 84–85, 88,
        232–236, 284
    editorial, **583–585**
    Hetch Hetchy Valley reservoir, 242
    Monroe Doctrine corollary, 237
    Progressive Party, 84–85, 232, *233,
        234*
    speech, **232–236**
    split with William Howard Taft,
        84–85, 232
Rosengarten, Theodore, 114–115
Roush, Edd, 619–622, *620*
    interview, **620–622**
Rubenstein, Helena, 214
Russian revolution, 322–323
Rutherford, Ernst, on atomic structure,
    525–527
Ryan, John A., 474–475
    nonfiction work, **474–476**

**S**

Sandburg, Carl, 37–39, *38*
    poem, **38–39**
Sanger, Margaret, 252–253, *253,*
    392–395, *393*
    newsletter, **394**
    pamphlet, **253–254**
Sargent, Dudley A., 577–578
    magazine article, **578–581**
*Saturday Evening Post* (magazine),
    35–37, *36,* 597
Schenck, Charles T., 317
*Schenck v. U.S.* (1919), 316–319, 322,
    411
    Supreme Court decision (Holmes),
        **317–319**
Schwartz, Jacob, 323
Scientific Management, 68–71, *70*
    Letter to Lindley Garrison
        (Bowen), **70–71**

*The Principles of Scientific Man-
    agement* (Taylor), **69–70**
Scientific racism, 517
    *See also* Racism
Search warrants, 292, 293
Secondary education, 175–179,
    179–183
*Sedition Act of 1918,* 305, 306, 313,
    319, 322–323, 410–413
    ACLU, 411
    arrests, 400
    law (Wilson), **411–412**
    *See also* Espionage Act of 1917
Segregation, 148, 301, 333–334, 373
    *See also* Racism
Seidel, Emil, *86*
*Selective Draft Law Cases,* 310–313
    Supreme Court decision (White),
        **310–312**
Selective Service Act of 1917,
    310–312, *311,* 317, 322, 404, 410
Self-education, 156–158
Senate, foreign policy, 237, 261–262,
    267–269
"Separate but equal" doctrine, 301
"September, 1918," 51–52
    poem (Lowell), **52**
Sex
    attitudes toward, 347–351, *349*
    psychology, 535, 553–554
    women, 393–395
    *See also* Prostitution
Sex education, 152–154, 349
Shapley, Harlow, 541–542, *542*
    journal article, **542–546**
Sharecroppers, 114–117
Shaw, Nate, *114,* 114–117
    autobiography, **115–117**
Shell shock, 455–457, *456*
Shepherd, William Gunn (reporter),
    63, 64
    eyewitness account, **64–66**
Sherman Antitrust Act of 1890, 88,
    284–288
"Shopping for the Well-Dressed Man,"
    212–214
    clothing styles (Trevor), **213**
Shreveport (LA) case, 294–397
Sierra Club, 241
Silent movies. *See* Movies
Sinclair, Upton, 419–423, *421*
    nonfiction work, **420–423**
Skyscrapers, 202, 204

Smith, Alfred E. (politician), 63
Smith, Charlie (football player), 615
Smith, Hoke, 162, 175
    laws, **162–164, 176–179**
*Smith-Hughes Act of 1917,* 162, 170,
    175–179
    law (Smith, Hughes), **176–179**
*Smith-Lever Act of 1914,* 161–164,
    175
    law (Smith, Lever), **162–164**
Snodgrass, Frederick C., baseball card,
    *587*
Soap advertisements, 219–221
Social education, 170–171
*The Social Evil in Chicago,* 340–342
    report (Vice Commission of
        Chicago), **340–341**
Social Gospel movement, 476, 485,
    492–494
Social hygiene, 152–154, 349
"Social Reconstruction: A General Re-
    view of the Problems and Survey
    of Remedies" (Ryan), 474
Socialist Party, 84–85, *86,* 304–306,
    319
Socialist Party Platform of 1912,
    **86–87**
Soldiers, World War I, 265–267, *266,
    506*
    athletic activities, 603–607, *605*
    shell shock, 455–457, *456*
"Some Considerations Affecting the
    Replacement of Men by Women
    Workers," 457–460
    speech (Goldmark), **458–460**
"Some Instances of Subconscious Cre-
    ative Imagination" (Jung), 535
*South Buffalo Railway Co., Ives v.*
    (1911), 281
Spanish influenza. *See* Influenza Epi-
    demic
Speaker, Tris (baseball player), 388,
    *389*
Speed records, auto racing, 574–577
Spencer, Herbert (philosopher), 179,
    *180*
Sports
    auto racing, 574–577
    Olympics, 581–585
    promotion, 611
    soldiers, 603–607
    universities, 566–570
    volleyball, 603, 607
    women, 577–581, *578,* 600–603,
        *601*

Page numbers in bold indicate primary sources; page numbers in italic indicate images;
page numbers in bold italic indicate primary source images; page numbers followed by the letter *t* indicate tables.

Sports, *continued*

*See also* Baseball; Basketball; Boxing; Football; Golf

"St. Louis Blues," *18,* 18–24, *19*

song (Handy), **19–23**

Stahl, Jacob G., baseball card, *588*

*Standard Oil Co. of New Jersey v. U.S.* (1910), 283–287

Supreme Court decision (White, Harlan), **285–287**

Standard Oil Company, 284–287, *285,* 345, 520

Standardization, War Industries Board (United States), 108–114

*Stanford-Binet* intelligence test, 172–174

Stanton, Elizabeth Cady, 239–240

State-church relations, 480–484, 498

"Statement by Emma Goldman at the Federal Hearing in Re Deportation," 270–273

statement (Goldman), **270–273**

Steel workers, 502–505, *503*

Steimer, Mollie, 306, 323, *323*

Steinmetz, Charles Proteus, 513–516, *516*

lecture, **513–516**

Sterilization, forced, 362

"The Sterling Silver Moon" (Berlin). *See* "Mandy"

Stevenson, Elliott G. (lawyer), 99–101

Stewart, Lyman, 490

Stickley, Gustav, 191–193

catalog, **192**

Stieglitz, Alfred (art gallery owner), 41

Stoddard, *The Rising Tide of Color Against White World-Supremacy,* 333, 372

Stokowski, Leopold, on patriotism, 370, 371

Stopwatch observation, 68–69, 70–71

Stores, department. *See* Department stores

Strachan, Grace C., 134–135

nonfiction work, **135–138**

Strikes

copper mining, 118

garment workers, 63

railroad, 319

steel industry, 502–505

textile workers, 247, 249

Watertown Arsenal, 68

Sullivan, John L., 570

newspaper article, **571–573**

Supreme Court

*Abrams v. U.S.* (1919), 322–325, 411

*Buchanan v. Warley* (1917), 302–304

*Bunting v. Oregon* (1917), 298–301

"clear and present danger" standard, 317

free speech, 317–319

"Freedom of Contract" doctrine, 298

*Guinn v. U.S.* (1915), 301

*Hoke v. U.S.* (1913), 287–291

*Muller v. Oregon* (1908), 298

NAACP, 301–302

*Schenck v. U.S.* (1919), 316–319, 322, 411

Sedition and Espionage Acts, 305–306, 411

"Separate but equal" doctrine, 301

*Standard Oil Co. of New Jersey v. U.S.* (1910), 283–287

Surgery in World War I, 452–454

Swope, Herbert Bayard, 395

newspaper article, **399**

Syphilis, public health campaigns, 463–465, *464*

**T**

Taft, William Howard, *72*

antitrust actions, 232, 284

"Dollar Diplomacy," 71–74

economic policy, 84–85

speech, **73–74**

split with Theodore Roosevelt, 84–85, 232

Tampico Affair (Mexican-U.S. relations), 249–252, *251*

Tandy, Vertner Woodson (architect), 217

Tarbell, Ida (journalist), 284, 345, *346*

essay, **346–347**

Taylor, Frederick W., 68, *69*

reference work, **69–70**

Teachers, 156–158, 160–161

pay scales, 134–139, *136*

Tefft or Teft, Miriam E., 117–121

memoir, **119–121**

Tenant farmers, 114–117

Tenements, 67, 379, *383*

Terman, Lewis M., 172

manual, **172–174**

*Testem Benevolentiae* (Leo XIII), 480

Textile workers, 247, *247,* 249

Theater, compared to movies, 364–367

Theology and evolution, 481–482

*A Theology for the Social Gospel,* 492–494

theological work (Rauschenbusch), **492–494**

Thermal cracking (petroleum refining), 521–523

Third World, American attitudes, 333–335, 372–373

Thompson, James Walter, 102

J. Walter Thompson Company ads, 219–221

J. Walter Thompson House Ads, 102–105, 220–221

"Is There News in Shaving Soap?" (advertisement), *220*

"A New Profession" (advertisement), *103*

"Packages That Speak Out" (advertisement), *104*

"Women in Advertising" (advertisement), *105*

Thorndike, Edward L., 139–140, 172, 183

journal article, **140–143**

Thorpe, Jim, *582,* 582–585, *583,* 615, *616*

"Tin Lizzie." *See* Model T automobiles

Tobacco

baseball cards, 387–390

public health concerns, 437–439

"Tobacco: A Race Poison," 437–439

presentation (Lichty), **438–439**

*Toledo Blade* (newspaper), 611

Trade unions. *See* Labor unions

Trades education. *See* Vocational education

Trains. *See* Railroads

*The Tramp* (movie), *33*

Traub Brothers department store, *338*

Trench warfare, 265–267, *266,* 400, 455

Trevor, Robert Lloyd, 212

clothing styles, **213**

Triangle Shirtwaist Factory Fire, 63–68, *64, 282, 283*

"Eyewitness at the Triangle" (Shepherd), **64–66**

*Preliminary Report of the Factory Investigating Commission, 66,* **66–67**

"Tried for Prager Murder" (*New York Times*), **316**

Page numbers in bold indicate primary sources; page numbers in italic indicate images;
page numbers in bold italic indicate primary source images; page numbers followed by the letter *t* indicate tables.

"Tris Speaker Baseball Card" (Liggett & Myers Co.), *389*

Trusts (business)
antitrust attitudes, 88–94
antitrust legislation, 88, 232, 284–288
Money Trust, 75–83
tobacco companies, 387–389

Tuberculosis prevention, 447–449, *448*

Tumulty, Joseph (presidential secretary), 371

Tuskegee Institute, 127, 148, *170*

"Twilight Sleep" (anesthesia), 439–441

Typhoid fever inoculation, 467, *467*

**U**

"An Unequal Footing!" (Anonymous), **139**

Uniforms for women, 217–219, *218*

United Negro Improvement Association (UNIA), 372

*U.S., Abrams v. See Abrams v. U.S.*

*U.S., Debs v. See Debs v. U.S.*

*U.S., Guinn v.* (1915), 301

*U.S., Hoke v. See Hoke v. U.S.*

*U.S., Houston, East & West Texas Railway Co. v. See Houston, East & West Texas Railway Co. v. U.S.*

*U.S., Schenck v. See Schenck v. U.S.*

*U.S., Standard Oil Co. of New Jersey v. See Standard Oil Co. of New Jersey v. U.S.*

*U.S., Weeks v. See Weeks v. U.S.*

United States Bureau of Education reports, **180–183**

United States Department of Agriculture Cooperative Extension Service, 161–164

United States Federal Bureau of the Census, 246–247
table, **248**t

United States Federal Reserve System, 75

United States Federal Trade Commission, 284

United States Food and Drug Administration (FDA), 465–466

United States Steel, antitrust action against, 232, 284

United War Work Campaign, 502

Universities. *See* Colleges and universities

"University Athletics," 566–570
essay (Newcomb), **567–570**

Untermyer, Samuel (lawyer), 75–83

Urban realism (painting style), 9

**V**

*The Vagabond* (movie), *34*

Vallée, Rudy, *19*

Van Ingen, Philip, 449
journal article, **450–452**

*Vanity Fair* magazine, 212–214, *213, 215*
*See also Dress & Vanity Fair* magazine

Vardon, Harry (golfer), 591–594

Venereal disease, public health campaigns, 463–465, *464*

Vice Commission of Chicago, 340
report, **340–341**

Victory Loan Day fair, *371*

Vigilante violence
labor movement, 476
racism, *334*
World War I, 313–316, *315, 370–372*

Villa Lewaro, 216–217

Vocational education, 148–151, 169–171, *170*
amputees, 452, *453*, 454
commercial, 180
*See also* Education, blacks

Vocational Education Act. *See Smith-Hughes Act of 1917*

Volleyball, 603, 607

Volstead, Andrew, 273
law, **274**

*Volstead Act of 1919*, 273–275
law (Volstead), **274**

von Eckhardt, Heinrich J. F. (German diplomat), 255, 256

"Votes for Women," 239–241
broadside (NAWSA), **384**
editorial (Du Bois), **240–241**

Voting rights
blacks, 239–240, 301–304
women, 239–241, 345–346, 383–387, 392–393

**W**

Wade, Martin J., 304
court case, **306–309**

Wage regulations, 298, 459, 474–476

Wagner, Robert F. (politician), 63

Walker, Madame C. J., *216*, 216–217
interview, **217**

"War and Mental Diseases," 454–457
presentation (Bailey), **455–457**

War Industries Board (United States), *109*
report, **109–114**
standardization, 108–109

Warde, Frederick (actor), *365*

*Warley, Buchanan v. See Buchanan v. Warley*

"Warning: The Deadly Parallel," 400–403
poster (Industrial Workers of the World), *401*

Warrants, criminal, 292–294

Washington, Booker T., 127, 148, *149*
speech, **149–151**

Washington, Jesse (lynching victim), *334*

*Washington Post* (newspaper)
newspaper article, **462–463**

Watertown Arsenal, 68–69, 70–71

Watson, Bertha. *See* Sanger, Margaret

Watson, John B., *528*, 528–529
journal article, **529–530**

WCC (World Council of Churches), 487

Weale, B. L. Putnam, 333, 372
nonfiction work, **334–335**, 372

"Wealthiest Negro Woman's Suburban Mansion," 216–217
interview (Walker), **217**

Weaver, Buck (baseball player), 620

*Weeks v. U.S.* (1918), 292–294
Supreme Court decision (Day), **292–294**

Weiss, George, 595
scrapbook, **596**

"What Every Girl Should Know" (Sanger), 253

"What Is a Bungalow?," 197–199
magazine article (Riley), **198–199**

"What the Bible Contains for the Believer," 489–491
essay (Pentecost), **490–491**

"Whether at Home or Away, Your Summer Equipment Should Include a Bottle of Listerine," 210–212
magazine advertisement (Lambert Pharmacal Company), *211*

White, Edward D., 284, 310
Supreme Court decisions, **285–286, 310–312**

"White Death" (tuberculosis), 447–449, *448*

Page numbers in bold indicate primary sources; page numbers in italic indicate images;
page numbers in bold italic indicate primary source images; page numbers followed by the letter *t* indicate tables.

"The White Mulberry Tree" (Cather), 11

White Slave Traffic Act of 1910. *See* Mann Act of 1910

White slavery, 287–291, 348, 349–351

*The White Terror* (movie), review, 447–449

"Whole Man for Whole God" (Brent), 487–489

"Why Should Kindergarten Be Incorporated as an Integral Part of the Public School System?," 159–161

journal article (Claxton), **159–161**

"Why Wait?" article (Howard), 393

"Why Women Want to Vote," broadside (NAWSA), **385**

Wiley, Harvey Washington, 465, 466, *466*

magazine article, **466–468**

Willard, Daniel, *109*

Willard, Jess (boxer), 571, 611–614, *613*

Williams, Henry Smith, 439

nonfiction work, **440–441**

Wilson, Woodrow, *72, 260*

Debs conviction, 319

"Dollar Diplomacy," 72–74

economic policy, 88, 109

essays, 566

Fourteen Points, 258, 267–268

Hetch Hetchy Valley reservoir, 242

League of Nations, 267–268

memo, **371**

"New Freedom" program, 79, 84–85

speeches, **74, 250–252, 258–260**

World War I, 255–262, *260*, 370–371, 395–396, 400

*Winesburg, Ohio* (Anderson), 53

WMC (World Missionary Conference), 487

Wobblies. *See* Industrial Workers of the World (IWW)

"A Woman Can Always Look Younger Than She Really Is," 214–216

magazine advertisement (Arden), **215**

*The Woman Rebel*, 253, 392–395

newsletter (Sanger), **394**

"The Woman Shopper: How to Make Her Buy," 335–339

magazine article (Marcosson), **336–339**

Women

advertisements aimed at, 221, 335–339

advertising professionals, 104, *105*

consumer culture, 336–339

fashions, 193–197, *194, 196, 199–201, 200*

flappers, 357–359, *358*

immigrants, *344*

medical schools teaching, 144

nursing careers, 429–431, *430*

pay scales for teachers, 134–139, *136*

physical education, 432–434, *433, 577–581*

roles, 195, 345–347

sexual freedom, 393–395

sports, *578*, 580–581, 600–603, *601*

uniforms, 217–219

voting rights, 239–241, 345–346, 383–387, 392–393

work hours regulations, 298

workforce, *106*, 106–108, *299, 336, 461*

workforce, World War I, 219, 457–460, *458, 459*

working class, *393*

"Women in Advertising" (advertisement), **105**

"Women in the Home," broadside (NAWSA), **386**

*Women Wanted*, 106–108

nonfiction work (Daggett), **107–108**

Women's magazines. *See specific titles*

Women's Trade Union League, 63

"Woodrow Wilson: The Tampico Affair," 249–252

speech (Wilson), **250–252**

Woodrow Wilson's Declaration of War Message, 258–261

speech (Wilson), **258–260**

Woolworth, Frank W., *202*

The Woolworth Building, 202–207, *205*

*The Cathedral of Commerce* (Cochran), **204, 206–207**

"The Woolworth Building" (Gilbert), *203*

Word cross. *See* Crossword puzzles

Work hour regulations, 298

Worker safety, 63–68, 281, *282*, 457–460

Worker's compensation laws, 281–283

World Council of Churches, 487

World Missionary Conference, 487

World Series, "Black Sox" scandal, 619–622

World War I, 322–323, 370–371

advocacy, 407–409

agricultural production in war effort, *175*

American involvement, 255–264, *260*, 407–409

blacks in workforce, 116, 403–407

deportations, 117–121, *118*, 270–273, 410–411

dissent, 322–323, 400–403, *401, 402, 412, 420*

draft laws, 270, 310–312, *311*

German positions, 265, 396, 399

Great Migration, 116, 403–407

influenza epidemic, 460–463, 467–468

Inter-Allied Games, 603–607

labor unions, 117–121

*Lusitania* sinking, 395–399, 407

patriotism, 370–372, *371*

posters, *218, 259, 408, 450, 458*

Prohibition and, 275, 354, 437–438

propaganda, *407*, 410

protests, 270, 319–322, *320, 322–325*

religious positions, 482, 494–497, *496*, 502–507

riveters, *110*

shell shock victims, 454–457, *456*

Social Gospel movement, 492–494

Socialist Party position, 304–306, 319

soldiers, 265–267, *266, 506*, 603–607, *605*

songs, 45

sports, 603–607

surgery improvements, 452–454

uniforms (YWCA), 217–219, *218*

United War Work Campaign, 502

venereal disease prevention, 463–465, *464*

veterans, disabled, 452–454, *453*

vigilante violence, 313–316, *315*, 370–372

women in the workforce, 106–108, *218, 219*, 457–460, *458, 459*

workforce after war, 413–419, 454

YMCA, 603–607

YWCA, 217–219, *458*

*See also* Espionage Act of 1917; Red Scare; *Sedition Act of 1918;* Trench warfare

Page numbers in bold indicate primary sources; page numbers in italic indicate images; page numbers in bold italic indicate primary source images; page numbers followed by the letter *t* indicate tables.

Worth, Charles (fashion designer), 219

Wynne, Arthur, 390–392

    crossword puzzle, *391*

## Y

Yale-Harvard football game, 566, *567*

Yellow journalism, 395

*Yip! Yip! Yaphank* (Berlin), 50–51

YMCA, occupation troops in Europe, 603–607

*The Yosemite,* 241–246

    nonfiction work (Muir), **243–246**

Yosemite National Park, 241–246

*You Know Me Al: A Busher's Letters,* 597–600

    fictional work (Lardner), **597–600**

Young, Cy (baseball player), 388, *390*

Young, Ella Flagg (social activist), 152

"YWCA Overseas Uniform, 1918," 217–219

    clothing style (House of Worth), *218*

YWCA posters, *218, 458*

## Z

Ziegfield Follies, 45, 50, 51

Zimmermann, Arthur (German diplomat), 254, 255

    telegram, *256*

The Zimmermann Telegram, 254–258, 407, 410

    Telegram from Arthur Zimmermann to Heinrich J. F. von Eckhardt, *256*

    Telegram from U.S. Ambassador Walter Page to President Woodrow Wilson, *257*

Page numbers in bold indicate primary sources; page numbers in italic indicate images;
page numbers in bold italic indicate primary source images; page numbers followed by the letter *t* indicate tables.